DATE DUE

THE OXFORD HANDBOOK OF

CULTURAL SOCIOLOGY

THE OXFORD HANDBOOK OF

CULTURAL

SOCIOLOGY

Edited by

JEFFREY C. ALEXANDER

RONALD N. JACOBS

PHILIP SMITH

OXFORD

UNIVERSITY PRESS

OXFORD
UNIVERSITY PRESS

Oxford University Press, Inc., publishes works that further
Oxford University's objective of excellence
in research, scholarship, and education.

Oxford   New York
Auckland   Cape Town   Dar es Salaam   Hong Kong   Karachi
Kuala Lumpur   Madrid   Melbourne   Mexico City   Nairobi
New Delhi   Shanghai   Taipei   Toronto

With offices in
Argentina   Austria   Brazil   Chile   Czech Republic   France   Greece
Guatemala   Hungary   Italy   Japan   Poland   Portugal   Singapore
South Korea   Switzerland   Thailand   Turkey   Ukraine   Vietnam

Published by Oxford University Press, Inc.
198 Madison Avenue, New York, New York 10016

www.oup.com

Oxford is a registered trademark of Oxford University Press

Library of Congress Cataloging-in-Publication Data
The Oxford handbook of cultural sociology /
edited by Jeffrey C. Alexander, Ron Jacobs, Philip Smith.
p.   cm.
Includes bibliographical references and index.
ISBN 978-0-19-537776-7 (cloth : alk. paper)
1. Culture.   I. Alexander, Jeffrey C., 1947–
II. Jacobs, Ronald N.   III. Smith, Philip.
HM621.O94 2011
306—dc22
2010049244

To the Memory of Clifford Geertz

CONTENTS

Acknowledgements   xi
List of Contributors   xiii

1. Introduction: Cultural Sociology Today   3
   Jeffrey C. Alexander, Ronald N. Jacobs, and Philip Smith

PART I   THE CULTURAL METHOD IN SOCIOLOGY

2. Cultural Sociology as Research Program: Post-Positivism,
   Meaning, and Causality   27
   Isaac Ariail Reed

3. Rationalization Processes inside Cultural Sociology   46
   Richard Biernacki

4. Four Ways to Measure Culture: Social Science, Hermeneutics,
   and the Cultural Turn   70
   John W. Mohr and Craig Rawlings

PART II   THE ECONOMIC AS CULTURE

5. Culture and the Economy   117
   Carlo Tognato

6. Culture and Economic Life   157
   Lyn Spillman

PART III   THE POLITICAL AS CULTURE

7. From Moral Sentiments to Civic Engagement: Sociological
   Analysis as Responsible Spectatorship   193
   Robin Wagner-Pacifici

8. Reinventing the Concept of Civic Culture   207
   Paul Lichterman

9. Cultural Sociology and Civil Society in a World of Flows: Recapturing Ambiguity, Hybridity, and the Political   232
   Gianpaolo Baiocchi

PART IV THE MEDIA AS CULTURE

10. Mediatized Disasters in the Global Age: On the Ritualization of Catastrophe   259
    Simon Cottle

11. Media, Intellectuals, the Public Sphere, and the Story of Barack Obama in 2008   284
    Eleanor Townsley

12. Entertainment Media and the Aesthetic Public Sphere   318
    Ronald N. Jacobs

PART V RACE AND IMMIGRATION AS CULTURE

13. Rethinking the Relationship of African American Men to the Street   343
    Alford A. Young, Jr.

14. Ethnicity, Race, Nationhood, Foreignness, and Many Other Things: Prolegomena to a Cultural Sociology of Difference-Based Interactions   365
    Giuseppe Sciortino

15. Burning Schools/ Building Bridges: Ethnographical Touchdowns in the Civil Sphere   390
    Mats Trondman

PART VI RELIGION AS CULTURE

16. The Constitution of Religious Political Violence: Institution, Culture, and Power   429
    Roger Friedland

17. Globalization and Religion   471
    Kenneth Thompson

PART VII SOCIAL MOVEMENTS AS CULTURE

18. Narrative and Social Movements   487
    Francesca Polletta and Pang Ching Bobby Chen

19. The Politics of Authenticity: Civic Individualism and the
    Cultural Roots of Gay Normalization   507
    Steven Seidman, Chet Meeks, and James Joseph Dean

PART VIII TRAUMA AS CULTURE

20. Rethinking Conflict and Collective Memory: The Case of Nanking   529
    Barry Schwartz

21. Cultural Trauma: Emotion and Narration   564
    Ron Eyerman

22. Remembrance of Things Past: Cultural Trauma,
    the "Nanking Massacre," and Chinese Identity   583
    Jeffrey C. Alexander and Rui Gao

PART IX EVENTS AS CULTURE

23. Events as Templates of Possibility: An Analytic Typology
    of Political Facts   613
    Mabel Berezin

24. Cultural Pragmatics and the Structure and Flow of
    Democratic Politics   636
    Jason L. Mast

PART X MATERIALITY AS CULTURE

25. Consumption as Cultural Interpretation: Taste,
    Performativity, and Navigating the Forest of Objects   671
    Ian Woodward

26. The Force of Embodiment: Violence and Altruism in
    Cultures of Practice   698
    Arthur W. Frank

27. Music Sociology in a New Key   722
    Lisa McCormick

PART XI KNOWLEDGE AS CULTURE

28. Narrating Global Warming   745
    Philip Smith

Part XII Classification and Ambiguity
as Culture

29. Broadening Cultural Sociology's Scope: Meaning-Making
    in Mundane Organizational Life   763
    Nina Eliasoph and Jade Lo

30. Inbetweenness and Ambivalence   788
    Bernhard Giesen

Index   805

ACKNOWLEDGEMENTS

....

Putting together a Handbook with thirty-five busy contributors is a rather daunting administrative project. We are grateful to James Cook, our editor at Oxford University Press, for suggesting we first take it up, and to Nadine Amalfi, Senior Administrator at Yale's Center for Cultural Sociology, for her perseverance and perspicacity in overseeing its coordination from gestation to publication. We also note with gratitude Bernadette Jaworsky for the admirable index she constructed at project's end. Finally, we thank G. Hari Kumar at SPi Global for working efficiently and patiently to oversee the transformation from typescript to book.

Contributors

Jeffrey C. Alexander, Lillian Chavenson Saden Professor of Sociology at Yale University, works in the areas of theory, culture and politics, developing a meaning-centered approach to the tensions and possibilities of modern social life. He is a Director of the Center for Cultural Sociology, also at Yale. His recent publications include: *Understanding the Holocaust: A Debate* 2009; *A Contemporary Introduction to Sociology: Culture and Society in Transition* (with Kenneth Thompson 2008); *Social Performances: Symbolic Action, Cultural Pragmatics, and Ritual* (with Bernhard Giesen and Jason Mast 2006); *Cultural Trauma and Collective Identity* (with Eyerman, Giesen, Sztompka, and Smelser 2004); and *The Meanings of Social Life: A Cultural Sociology*, 2003. In his major work *The Civil Sphere* (2006), Alexander developed a new cultural-sociological theory of democracy, a perspective that provides the foundation *The Performance of Politics: Obama's Victory and the Democratic Struggle for Power* (2010) and his newest volume, *Performative Revolution in Egypt: An Essay in Cultural Power* (2011).

Gianpaolo Baiocchi is Associate Professor of Sociology and International Studies at Brown University. He is the author of *Militants and Citizens* (Stanford UP 2005), and co-author of *Bootstrapping Democracy* (Stanford UP 2011), with Patrick Heller and Marcelo K. Silva. His most recent work is on the travel and translation of ideas about democracy and empowerment from social movements in Brazil to other parts of the world.

Mabel Berezin, Associate Professor of Sociology at Cornell University, is a comparative historical sociologist whose work explores the intersection of political and cultural institutions, with an emphasis on modern and contemporary Europe. She is the author of *Illiberal Politics in Neoliberal Times: Culture, Security, and Populism in the New Europe* (Cambridge University Press 2009) and *Making the Fascist Self: the Political Culture of Inter-war Italy* (Cornell 1997). Most recently, she is the editor of a special issue of *Theory and Society* (38 (4) 2009), entitled "Emotion and Rationality in Economic Life."

Richard Biernacki teaches sociology and history at the University of California, San Diego.

Pang Ching Bobby Chen is a PhD student in Sociology at the University of California, Irvine. His interests include cultural sociology, social movements, historical sociology of emotions, mass media and deliberative democracy. He is currently working on two projects: one, on understanding the construction of social movement actors' emotions in the public sphere; the other on gender dynamics in public deliberation.

Simon Cottle is Professor of Media and Communications and Deputy Head of the School of Journalism, Media and Cultural Studies at Cardiff University. His latest books are *Mediatized Conflict* (2006), *Global Crisis Reporting* (2009) and *Transnational Protests and the Media* (with Libby Lester) (2010) and he is currently writing *Disasters and the Media* (with Mervi Pantti and Karin Wahl-Jorgensen). He is the Series Editor of the Global Crises and the Media Series for Peter Lang publishing.

James Joseph Dean is Assistant Professor of Sociology at Sonoma State University. His research focuses on the sociology of sexualities, particularly the sociology of heterosexualities. Recent publications include an article analyzing cultural shifts in gay, lesbian, and queer films in *Sexualities* (2007, Vol. 10, No. 3) and a book chapter on intersectionality, sexualities, and the politics of multiple identities in *Theorising Intersections: Sexual Advances*, edited Yvette Taylor, Sally Hines, and Mark Casey (Palgrave 2010). Currently, he is completing a book manuscript that explores the gendered and racial character of heterosexual identities in the context of lesbian and gay visibility.

Nina Eliasoph is an Associate Professor of Sociology at the University of Southern California. She is the author of *Avoiding Politics: How Americans Produce Apathy in Everyday Life* (Cambridge University Press 1998) and *Making Volunteers: Civic Life After Welfare's End* (Princeton University Press 2011).

Ron Eyerman is Professor of Sociology and a Director of the Center for Cultural Sociology at Yale University. His areas of research include social theory, trauma and memory and he has taught undergraduate and graduate classes and seminars on these topics. Recent books include *The Assassination of Theo van Gogh* and *The Trauma of Political Assassination*.

Arthur W. Frank is Professor of Sociology at the University of Calgary. He is the author of *At the Will of the Body, The Wounded Storyteller, The Renewal of Generosity*, and most recently, *Letting Stories Breathe: A Socionarratology*. He is on the editorial board of several journals, including *Body & Society*, and is a contributing editor to *Literature and Medicine*. He has been visiting professor at the University of Sydney, University of Toronto, Ritsumeikan University in Kyoto, Japan, and University of Central Lancashire in Preston, England.

Roger Friedland is Professor of Religious Studies and Sociology at the University of California, Santa Barbara. Friedland works on the question of institution as a religious phenomenon, and on politicized religions a case through which to explore this approach. He is also working with Paolo Gardinali and John Mohr on the relation between eroticism, love and religiosity among American university students. He is author of "Institution, Practice and Ontology: Towards A Religious Sociology," in *Ideology and Organizational Institutionalism, Research in the Sociology of Organizations*, ed. by Renate Meyer, Kerstin Sahlin-Andersson, Marc Ventresca and Peter Walgenbach (2009).

Rui Gao completed her PhD in Sociology at Yale University in 2011. She got her M.A and M.Phil degree in sociology from Yale University, her B.A. degree in English and English Literature from Beijing Foreign Studies University and she has also been studying and doing research at the University of Tokyo. Her fields of interests include cultural sociology, sociological theories, media studies, critical communication studies, gender studies, feminist studies, China studies, etc. Her latest publications include a forthcoming article titled "Revolutionary Trauma and Representation of the War: the Case of China in Mao's Era,"(in *Narrating Trauma* edited by Ron Eyerman, Jeffrey Alexander, and Elizabeth Breese, Paradigm Publishers) and translation works that focus on fields of journalism and mass communication.

Bernhard Giesen holds the Chair for Macro-sociology in the Department of History and Sociology at the University of Konstanz (Germany) and is a member of the executive board of the Center of Excellence 16 "Cultural Foundations of Social Integration" at the University of Konstanz. He has held visiting positions at the Department of Sociology at Yale University, the Department of Sociology at the University of California, Los Angeles, the Committee for Social Thought (Chicago), the Department of Sociology at New York University, and the Center for Advanced Studies at Stanford University. Bernhard Giesen works in the areas of cultural and historical sociology and sociological theory and has extensively published on collective memory, trauma, intergenerational conflict and collective rituals. Among his latest book publications are *Social Performance. Symbolic Action, Cultural Pragmatics and Ritu*al (ed. with J.C. Alexander and J.L. Mast, Cambridge 2006); *Religion and Politics. Cultural Perspectives* (ed. With D. Suber, Leiden 2005); *Cultural trauma and collective identity* (ed. with J.C. Alexander et al., Berkeley 2004); *Triumph and Trauma* (Boulder 2004); *Intellectuals and the Nation. Collective Identity in a German Axial Age* (Cambridge 1998).

Ronald N. Jacobs is Associate Professor of Sociology at the University at Albany, State University of New York. His research focuses on culture, media, and the public sphere. His current work is concentrated in two areas: (1) a study of media intellectuals and the social space of opinion, and (2) a study of entertainment media and the aesthetic public sphere.

Paul Lichterman is Professor of Sociology and Religion at the University of Southern California. He is author of *Elusive Togetherness* (Princeton 2005), *The Search for Political Community* (1996), and a variety of articles on social movement groups, community service organizations, cultural and social theory.

Jade Lo is a Visiting Assistant Professor of Sociology at the University of California, Los Angeles. She got her Ph.D. from the Department of Management and Organization at at the University of Southern California.

Jason L. Mast is a postdoctoral fellow with the Karl Mannheim Chair of Cultural Studies at Zeppelin University in Germany. He co-edited a volume on Social Performance (2006) with Jeff Alexander and Bernhard Giesen, which features his chapter on the "Cultural Pragmatics of Event-ness." His forthcoming book analyzes the performative dimensions of power and legitimacy during the Clinton presidency.

Lisa McCormick is an Assistant Professor in the Department of Sociology at Haverford College. She earned her PhD in Sociology from Yale University. With Ron Eyerman, she is co-editor of *Myth, Meaning, and Performance: Toward a Cultural Sociology of the Arts* (Paradigm 2006). Her article "Higher, Faster, Louder: Representations of the International Music Competition" won the SAGE Prize for Excellence and Innovation for the best paper published in *Cultural Sociology* in 2009.

Chet Meeks was Assistant Professor of Sociology at Georgia State University before his untimely death in 2008. His research and teaching interests included contemporary social theory, sexuality studies, and cultural sociology. His publications included co-authoring (with Steven Seidman and Francie Traschen) the article "Beyond the Closet? The Changing Social Meaning of Homosexuality in the United States" in *Sexualities* (1999, Vol. 2 , No. 1), the article "Civil Society and the Sexual Politics of Difference" in *Sociological Theory* (2001, Vol. 19, No. 3), and co-editing *Introducing the New Sexuality Studies: Original Essays and Interviews* (Routledge, 2006).

John Mohr is Professor of Sociology at the University of California, Santa Barbara where he also serves as Director of the Social Sciences Survey Research Center. He received his Ph.D. in sociology from Yale University. Along with Roger Friedland he is co-editor of *Matters of Culture* (Cambridge University Press 2004) and author of a number of articles concerned with the use of formal models in cultural analysis, the history of the welfare state, and the racial politics of affirmative action (www. soc.ucsb.edu/ct). He is currently writing about the institutional foundations of nanotechnology.

Francesca Polletta is a Professor of Sociology at the University of California, Irvine. She studies social movements, experiments in radical democracy, and culture in politics. She is the author of *It Was Like a Fever: Storytelling in Protest and Politics* (Chicago 2006), *Freedom Is an Endless Meeting: Democracy in American Social Movements* (Chicago 2002) and editor, with Jeff Goodwin and James M. Jasper, of *Passionate Politics: Emotions and Social Movements* (Chicago 2001). She is currently studying how plot shapes audiences' responses to accounts of sexual assault and, in another project, how gender affects public deliberation.

Craig Rawlings is an Institute for Education Science (IES) Postdoctoral Fellow at Stanford University's Institute for Research in Education Policy and Practice (IREPP). He completed his B.A. in International Studies at the University of Oregon, his M.A. in Sociology from Rutgers University, and Ph.D. in Sociology from the University of California, Santa Barbara. His dissertation research was funded by the Social Science Research Council-Sloan Foundation and the National Science Foundation, and focused on organizational change and gender segregation in American higher education since the early 1970s. His work seeks to bridge structural and cultural explanations of how social actors (individuals, colleges, academic departments) influence one another. He is particularly interested in the ways that social networks and status inequalities help shape influence processes. With Dan McFarland, he is currently working on a number of projects concerning peer influences on faculty productivity, as well as the social and structural bases that facilitate the spread of knowledge between academic departments.

Isaac Ariail Reed is Assistant Professor of Sociology at the University of Colorado at Boulder, where he is also the Director of the Sociology Honors Program. He is the author of *Interpretation and Social Knowledge* (University of Chicago Press 2011), and of several articles in social theory, cultural sociology, and historical sociology, including "Why Salem Made Sense: Culture, Gender, and the Puritan Persecution of Witchcraft" (2008). One of his current projects addresses power and performance in conflicts over science and religion in American history.

Barry Schwartz, Professor Emeritus of Sociology, University of Georgia, is author of numerous articles and seven books, including *Abraham Lincoln and the Forge of National Memory*, which traces popular views of Lincoln from 1865 to the 1920s. His second volume, *Abraham Lincoln in the Post-Heroic Era: History and Memory in the Late Twentieth Century*, tracks Lincoln perceptions from the Depression decade to the turn of the twenty-first century. He is now working on *The Gettysburg Address in American Memory*, a book-length treatment of the original and drastically changing meanings of Lincoln's famous eulogy. Schwartz's research on collective memory addresses many issues in many national cultures, including memories of shameful and exemplary events in the United States, Europe, the Middle East, and Asia. His most recent book with Mikyoung Kim deals with *Northeast Asia's Difficult Past*. Barry Schwartz's recent work also addresses the problem of the historical Jesus through the lens of collective memory theory and method. These works develop common themes: the resistance of historical reality to social construction, the functions of forgetting, memory as a source of national unity and disunity, the tension between mnemonic continuity and social change, and the enduring need of individuals to find orientation and meaning for their lives by invoking, assessing, embracing, rejecting, revising, and judging the past.

Giuseppe Sciortino teaches sociology at the Università di Trento, Italy. His main interests are social theory, migration studies and cultural sociology.

Steven Seidman is Professor of Sociology at the State University of New York at Albany. He is the author of, among other books, *Romantic Longings: Love in America, 1830–1980* (Routledge, 1991), *Embattled Eros: Sexual Politics and Ethics in America* (Routledge, 1992), *Difference Troubles: Queering Social Theory and Sexual Politics* (Cambridge University Press, 1997), *Beyond the Closet: The Transformation of Gay and Lesbian Life* (Routledge, 2002), and *The Social Construction of Sexuality*, Second Edition (W.W. Norton, 2010). He is co-editor of *Social Postmodernism: Beyond Identity Politics* (Cambridge University Press, 1995), editor of *Queer Theory/Sociology* (Blackwell, 1996), co-editor of *Handbook of Lesbian & Gay Studies* (Sage, 2002), and co-editor of *Introducing the New Sexuality Studies: Original Essays and Interviews* (Routledge, 2006).

Philip Smith is Professor of Sociology and a Director of the Yale Center for Cultural Sociology. He has written widely in the field of cultural sociology and cultural theory. Recent books include *Why War?* (Chicago 2005); *Punishment and Culture* (Chicago 2008) and *Incivility: The Rude Stranger in Public* (Cambridge 2010, with R. King and T. Phillips).

Lyn Spillman's research interests are grounded in cultural, historical, and economic sociology. Her works include *Solidarity in Strategy: Making Business Meaningful in American Trade Associations* (University of Chicago Press, forthcoming); *Nation and Commemoration: Creating National Identities in the United States and Australia* (Cambridge University Press, 1997); the anthology *Cultural Sociology* (Blackwell, 2002); as well as articles and chapters on cultural theory, collective memory, nationalism, and business culture. A recipient of a Guggenheim Fellowship and the A.S.A's Fund for the Advancement of the Discipline Award, she received her Ph.D. from the University of California at Berkeley and teaches in the Sociology Department, University of Notre Dame.

Kenneth Thompson is Professor Emeritus of Sociology at the Open University, UK, and has also taught at Yale, UCLA, Rutgers, Smith College and Bergen University (Norway). He is a former member of the Executive Committee of the International Sociological Association and was Co-president of its Research Committee 16, 'Sociological Theory'; he was a member of the Executive Committee of the British Sociological Association and was President of its Sociology of Religion section. In addition to sociological theory, his research interests include issues of cultural identity and moral regulation in relation to media and everyday life practices. His publications include: *Moral Panics; Media and Cultural Regulation; Beliefs and Ideology; Emile Durkheim; Auguste Comte; Sartre; Bureaucracy and Church Reform;* and *A Contemporary Introduction to Sociology* (with Jeffrey Alexander).

Carlo Tognato is currently Visiting Research Fellow at the School of History and Politics and at the Indo-Pacific Governance Research Centre of the University of Adelaide. He is also Faculty Fellow at the Center for Cultural Sociology at Yale University. He has been Director of the Center for Social Studies and Associate Professor of Sociology at the National University of Colombia in Bogotá. His research focuses on symbolic communication in the economic arena and on the working of the public sphere in deeply divided societies.

Eleanor Townsley is Professor and Chair of Sociology and Anthropology at Mount Holyoke College. She is interested in the role of intellectuals and ideas in social change.

Mats Trondman is Professor of Cultural Sociology at the Center for Cultural Sociology, Linnaeus University in Sweden. He was the founding editor of the Sage journal *Ethnography* together with Paul Willis, with whom he also wrote the "Manifesto for Ethnography" in 2000. Over the years Trondman has covered a large number of theoretically informed empirical research topics such as: musical taste and lifestyle; social and cultural mobility; counter cultures; the transformation of the Swedish Welfare Society during 1990s; sports; the Arts; social and cultural policy;

childhood studies, issues of multiculturalism, education, and schooling. His main focus is youth culture research and social and cultural theory which often combines with aspects of political philosophy. He has published eight books in Swedish. The most well known is on class travelling, that is, working class kids becoming academics. He has also published more than one hundred articles and reports, as well as being a public speaker, columnist and occasional writer for the Art pages in the Swedish press. Trondman is currently working on a large research project in Malmö, Sweden – An Educational Dilemma: School Achievement and Multicultural Incorporation – financed by the Swedish Research Council. The project is informed by Jeffrey C. Alexander's cultural sociology. He is also collaborating with Paul Willis and John Hughes on a book on socio-symbolic homologies.

Robin Wagner-Pacifici Professor of Sociology at the New School for Social Research at Swarthmore College. She is the author of *The Art of Surrender: Decomposing Sovereignty at Conflict's End* and *Theorizing the Standoff: Contingency in Action*, winner of the 2001 American Sociological Association's Culture Section Best Book Award. Her work analyzes violent events and their mediations. An article on the "restlessness" of historical events was recently published (March, 2010) in *The American Journal of Sociology*.

Ian Woodward is Senior Lecturer in cultural sociology at the School of Humanities and Deputy Director, Griffith Centre for Cultural Research, at Griffith University, Brisbane, Australia. He has research interests in the sociology of consumption, aesthetics and material culture, and in the cultural dimensions of cosmopolitanism. He has published research papers in leading journals such as *Theory, Culture and Society; The British Journal of Sociology; The Sociological Review; Journal of Material Culture; Journal of Contemporary Ethnography* and *Poetics*. His critical survey of the field of material culture studies, *Understanding Material Culture*, was published by Sage in 2007. With Gavin Kendall and Zlatko Skrbis, he is co-author of *Sociology of Cosmopolitanism* (Palgrave 2009). He is an Editor of the *Journal of Sociology* and in 2010–2011 he was a Fellow of the Kulturwissenschaftliches Kolleg, University of Konstanz, Germany.

Alford A. Young, Jr. is Arthur F. Thurnau Professor and Chair of the Department of Sociology at the University of Michigan. He also holds an appointment in the Center for Afroamerican and African Studies. He has published *The Minds of Marginalized Black Men: Making Sense of Mobility, Opportunity, and Future Life Chances* (Princeton University Press 2004) and co-authored *The Souls of WEB Du Bois* (Paradigm Publishers 2006). He has published articles in *Sociological Theory; The Annual Review of Sociology; Symbolic Interaction; Ethnic and Racial Studies*, and other journals. Young is completing a manuscript entitled, "From the Edge of the Ghetto: African Americans and the World of Work," and is also working on a follow-up manuscript to the *The Minds of Marginalized Black Men*, that examines how African American men who were reared in poverty but who have engaged extreme upward mobility as young adults discuss learning to navigate of race and class-based constraints over the course of their lives.

THE OXFORD HANDBOOK OF

CULTURAL
SOCIOLOGY

CHAPTER 1

INTRODUCTION: CULTURAL SOCIOLOGY TODAY

JEFFREY C. ALEXANDER, RONALD N. JACOBS, AND PHILIP SMITH

THE "handbook" became a popular format for sociology publication in the early 1990s. We find influential titles from that era, such as the *Handbook of Qualitative Research* or *Handbook of Economic Sociology*. These reflected the confidence of publishers that a substantial field existed and, along with it, a ready market for a somewhat bulky and expensive product. The "handbook" serves, therefore, as an oblique indicator of the balance of power and interest in a discipline.

Over recent decades, cultural sociology has been represented for the most part in lesser, sub-handbook ways. During the time other fields were acquiring their handbooks, cultural sociology had to make do with edited collections of previously published papers, initially scavenging component essays from philosophy, cultural history, literature, gender and media studies, and anthropology. Pioneering in this regard was the volume of Jeffrey Alexander and Steven Seidman, with its assemblage of empirical studies influenced by both structuralism and poststructuralism, classical and contemporary theory (1990). Seven years later, Elizabeth Long (1997) still had to bring together sociologists, anthropologists, historians, and cultural studies scholars in order to reflect on the possibilities for cultural sociology. True enough, specialist collections from within sociology popped up early on, these dealing with particular theoretical matters such as symbolic boundaries (Lamont and Fournier 1993) or the uses of Durkheim's later, cultural theory (Alexander 1988). Yet, most volumes in the 1990s claiming to offer a synthetic overview tried to constitute the still emerging field through an act of interdisciplinary bricolage. Only around the turn of the century do we find the first panoramic collections of representative, influential, or at least highly cited items culled more or less exclusively from the major sociological journals (Smith 1998b, Spillman 2001). The support of ancillary disciplines was no longer needed to flesh out a volume. The introductory chapters to these works (e.g., Smith 1998a) also provided some of the first genealogies, explanations, and retrospectives on the rise of "cultural sociology," a familiar academic genre we are replicating here. The inwardly turned and self-reliant style of these circa-millennial collections is not insignificant; it indicates how far the enterprise had already proceeded, that it was seen to exist, and that accounts were needed. Reflexivity had begun.

In the first decade of the twenty-first century, the process of distinguishing a "meaning-aware" kind of sociology from its competitors in adjacent fields continued. The collection by Roger Friedland and John Mohr explored the convergence between "the cultural turn in sociology and the sociological turn by humanists" (Friedland and Mohr 2004: 3). The contributors to that volume—mostly sociologists, but supplemented by political theorists, cultural studies practitioners, and professors of religious studies—explored how to make meaning more central to sociology, and how the discipline might (or might not) use methods developed in the humanities in order to overcome the overly rigid duality between meaning and materiality. Around the same time, Mark Jacobs and Nancy Weiss Hanrahan (2005) brought together more than thirty sociologists who had made the "cultural turn." While there was a diverse array of approaches to meaning and society represented in this volume, Jacobs and Hanrahan suggested what held everything together was an "aesthetic conception of culture" that promised "to move beyond the cultural turn, by unifying on a more general level the variety of contemporary usages" (Jacobs and Hanrahan 2005: 10). In the Routledge *Handbook of Cultural Sociology* that aims to globalize "cultural sociology," editors John Hall, Laura Grindstaff, and Ming-Cheng Lo (2010: 5) point to a "broad program" that includes a range of disciplines outside sociology and a wide diversity of approaches within it.

What is missing from all these important contributions is the attempt to define, name, or stake out a specific mode of inquiry called "cultural sociology," and to demonstrate the centrality of this theoretical orientation in the contemporary sociological field. Instead, the goal seems to have been to make generic sociology more aware of the cultural turn. To be sure, this was an important move to make, and it has been largely successful. Culture is now a legitimate, well-established object of sociological inquiry, in a way that it was not twenty years ago. For a cultural sociology to continue to flourish, however, it must focus on more than disciplinary infiltration and legitimation. Our concern is that growth and innovation in cultural sociology will be constrained if the best we can do is to mount a broad petition to the wider discipline for a place at the table. A more ambitious agenda is required, one that reflects how an emerging cultural sociology provides a new way of seeing and modeling social facts. It requires commitment to particular theoretical logics when it comes to explaining social action and social order.

The collections were also curiously pitched. The project of disciplinary legitimation opened a gap between their broad appeals for inclusion and the concerns that actually animate the work of practicing cultural sociologists. With the benefit of hindsight, it is now clear that the frameworks and the issues organizing these volumes do not, in fact, thematize the most pressing concerns that energize the now crystallized field of cultural sociology. On one side, defining culture as a "myriad [of] socially produced, arranged, and employed symbolic and material aspects of the world," as Hall et al. do (2010: 5), creates a tent so big that it covers virtually all the sins of the cultural-intellectual world. On the other side, while Jacobs and Hanrahan attempt to identify a single unifying framework, most sociologists studying culture do not, in fact, endorse an aesthetic conception of culture, at least not explicitly. Contrary to Long's (1997) suggestion, which echoed Seidman's, most sociologists who studied culture in the 1990s did not take their inspiration from cultural studies, though a decade earlier they might have; nor did they not spend much time playing cultural studies off against sociology as a way of relativizing the latter. Indeed, the proclivities of practicing cultural sociologists mostly ran in exactly the opposite direction. Cultural studies was understood to be in need of a sociological fix. It was often taken by sociologists to be impressionistic and even tendentious in contrast with their own efforts to study culture in less political, more systematic, and more disciplinary ways (e.g., Sherwood, Smith, and Alexander 1993). That said, most cultural sociology published in journal articles and books does not address itself to "sociology as a discipline," nor does it devote its primary energies to documenting the distinctive contributions that sociology offers to the study of culture. Rather, it gets on with explaining stuff, or with developing tools to do this explaining. This is as it should be, and no different from the manner other well-established subdisciplines have advanced research and theory. What we are suggesting is that broad calls for legitimation do not reflect routine practice but rather are appeals to an imagined audience of outsiders.

There is a pressing need, then, for a different kind of edited collection, for an intervention that is responsive to the real developments and disagreements that are taking place within the field itself rather than a sales pitch to onlookers and potential converts. We see our volume as answering this call. While we are confident this book will contribute to the larger discipline of sociology, and also to the cultural sciences more generally, our starting point is with cultural sociology itself. We wish to document and reflect on the independent debates and modes of thought that have developed therein.

In order to provide the rationale for this approach, we offer an account of the origins of cultural sociology and how it has grown into the maturity it enjoys today. Our story weaves two different narrative strands. First, there is an interdisciplinary epic that can be summed up with the words "cultural turn." This concerns an epochal transformation in the human sciences. Second, and closer to home, there is an intra-disciplinary family drama. This charts the rejection of Parsonian functionalism and its consequences, the rediscovery of culture in sociology in the 1990s, and the need to reflect on what could be learned from adjacent disciplines about cultural analysis. This incestuous tale ends with the identification of key differences and disagreements between a "cultural sociology" and a "sociology of culture"—a major distinction that emerged in the late 1990s and, in retrospect, can be seen as marking a turning point in the developing field. These intra-disciplinary developments have sharpened boundaries among sociologists, yet they have also enabled a productive dialogue to develop about the different ways to do cultural sociology. Once this saga is told, we will be at the plot point where the contributors to the *Oxford Handbook of Cultural Sociology* can enter the stage.

THE EMERGENCE OF CULTURAL SOCIOLOGY

As we have written elsewhere (Alexander 1987; Alexander and Smith 2001, 2010; Smith 1998a), the pre-history of cultural sociology has its origins in the demise of Parsonian functionalism from the mid-1960s onward. Seemingly unable to account for violent conflict and apparently blind to the existence of power, the functionalist paradigm was rejected in the wider sociological community. Fatally, it had given too much emphasis to value integration and the normative steering of social action. It is hardly surprising that this rebellion against Parsons led, in turn, to a wider move against cultural explanation. Rather than looking for better ways to theorize culture, scholars lost interest and switched out to rational choice, or to structural and institutional explanations of social life.

The turn against overly abstract notions of values and norms did not, in fact, have to be paired with a rejection of cultural explanation, despite the fact this was the choice that most sociologists made or the only path they could see. Outside of sociology, important conceptual advances had already been made that offered new resources for thinking about meaning-centered social analysis in a non-Parsonian idiom. From Wittgenstein's linguistic philosophy, cultural scholars were encouraged to stop looking "inside the mind" to discover meaning, but rather to discover the rules and conventions that organized different contextual language games or "forms of life." From the structuralism and the semiotics of Lévi-Strauss and Barthes, thinkers were encouraged to imagine culture and meaning as if they were part of an autonomous language system of systematically linked and opposed elements. From the cultural anthropology of Douglas, Turner, and especially Geertz came the argument that the cultural analyst could not effectively understand the social role of meaning unless he or she took the time to describe its logics and gestures in painstaking detail. "Believing, with Max Weber, that man is an animal suspended in webs of significance he himself has spun," wrote Geertz (1973: 5) in what was surely his most often quoted passage, "I take culture to be those webs, and the analysis of it to be therefore not an experimental science in search of law but an interpretive one in search of meaning." The tools for conversion were there: Now Saul could become Paul. Only in sociology he didn't.

Outside of sociology, the cultural tide to which these scholars contributed was running at full flood by the early 1980s. For example, in history, figures like Lyn Hunt and William Sewell Jr. wrote deeply influential books about the French Revolution, highlighting the importance of cultural practices, rituals, and discourses. These works, which followed a more general cultural turn in European historiography, floated up the river to herald the arrival of a "new cultural history," a broad movement that rejected master narratives and material reductionism in favor of close readings of texts, pictures, actions, and other cultural artifacts. There were also evolutions of the cultural turn unfolding in the next generation of anthropology, such as the "writing culture" movement of Clifford and Marcus and the radically antimaterialist yet historically sensitive semiotics of Marshall Sahlins. And all the while, the interdisciplinary project of cultural studies had been spreading like wildfire throughout the Anglo-American world, reaching its high point with the 1992 volume edited by Grossberg, Nelson, and Treichler. All of these movements in cultural analysis were deeply interdisciplinary, with the same key influences coming up again and again: Barthes, Derrida, Gramsci, Geertz, E. P. Thompson, Frye, and Foucault.

The intellectual developments of this cultural turn have offered, indeed as early as the 1960s and 1970s, the possibility for developing complex sociological accounts that could take and use meaning seriously. There were no takers. By the mid-1980s, there was a tentative uptake in the discipline, with a focus given to institutional and pragmatic uses of meaning. The interest here was seeing meaning as a resource, as a "tool" (Swidler 1986), as a routine, or as a ploy with which to shape claims for legitimacy, cement power, or simply get through life. It could also be seen as the "product" of industries and markets, as we find in the influential "production of culture" paradigm advocated by Wendy Griswold, Paul DiMaggio, Richard Peterson, Diana Crane, and others. In general, then, the cultural turn in sociology through the 1980s can be seen as a series of accommodations to the still disenchanted world of post-Parsonian sociology rather than an opening up to the possibilities for a truly cultural sociology.

This is not to deny cultural sociology's Johnny Appleseeds. In the era from 1985 to 1995, a number of important scholars were, in fact, pioneering quite a different kind of approach. Viviana Zelizer wrote influential books on the cultural dimensions of economic life, in a way that seemed to combine the *Annales* focus on *mentalité* with earlier Weberian and Durkheimian theories about the limits of economic reductionism. William Sewell Jr., already an important figure in the new cultural history, entered specifically sociological debates to advocate rethinking the relationship of culture and agency. Steven Seidman, drawing on the work of Foucault and cultural studies, leveraged the insights of postmodernism to challenge the sociological project of abstract, general theory, encouraging a new generation of theorists to move toward the more concretized forms of social theory so prominent in history, anthropology, and gender studies. Jeffrey Alexander, a co-editor of this volume, combined Weber's hermeneutic methods with semiotic and late-Durkheimian theory, arguing that sociology already had good resources for developing a meaning-centered sociology, if only it looked in the right places. These interventions challenged the received wisdom that a social explanation should always privilege structural or material factors. Also in these early years, Robin Wagner-Pacifici (1986) began her cultural explorations into the meaning contours of violence and confrontation; Michele Lamont (1993) initiated studies of moral boundaries and social stratification; and Eviatar Zerubavel (1993) combined cognitive science with cultural analysis to probe social fears and divisions. The early work of these and other authors (e.g., Edles 1998) laid the foundation for the remarkable rise to centrality of cultural sociology after the mid-1990s.

This process of decline and rise was not only a matter of the spirit or the life of the mind. It was accompanied by generational transition. Because culture was abandoned by the anti-Parsonians of the 1960s and 1970s, it paradoxically came to offer a space for reputation building or simply for developing alternative explanations to the now dominant neo-Marxian, neo-Weberian, and neo-institutional ways of thinking. By adopting a risky career strategy, the younger scholars of the 1980s and early 1990s could stand out from the crowd. The process was not, of course, purely instrumental. Risk-taking itself indicates a genuine commitment: There began to be a widespread feeling that the move against culture had gone too far. In the push for a hard-headed realism, sociological analysis had, in truth, become unrealistic. Surely, life was more than a collection of strategies, ideologies, institutions, and coercions? With the cultural turn having thoroughly infiltrated much of the rest of the campus, this new generation of qualitative sociologists recognized that structuralism, poststructuralism, cultural anthropology, cultural history, and literary criticism offered real alternatives, to not only conventional explanation but also other kinds of challenges to mainstream sociology. The humanism of symbolic interactionism foundered on its proximity to common sense and its propensity to replace analysis with descriptions of settings. Ethnomethodology, by contrast, became an increasingly Machu Picchu-like refuge from normal social science: remote, inaccessible, and eventually forgotten.

Changing institutional factors supported the work of this new generation of emerging cultural sociologists. The creation of the American Sociological Association's Culture Section allowed a collective identity to be formed and gave legitimacy to a particular way of doing sociology. Promotion committees would no longer be quite so wary of people describing themselves as cultural sociologists once there was this ASA imprimatur. The highest-status generalist journals remained rigidly in the anti-Parsonian mold and were, for the most part, suspicious of the cultural turn. But several refereed locations were open to cultural arguments, particularly British journals and the more theory-oriented journals in the United States. University presses were generally more receptive to cultural sociology than the journals, with important series emerging at Cambridge, Chicago, California, Duke, Minnesota, and Princeton. As a result, many cultural sociologists who received their PhDs in the 1990s were able to publish high-visibility books. This was obviously important for establishing the careers of these new scholars. More significant, perhaps, was the way this onslaught of new books made it harder to ignore cultural explanation as a legitimate perspective for sociology.

As a result of these intellectual and institutional developments, the contemporary landscape looks decidedly different from the one of the mid-1980s. Sociologists who used to be hostile to meaning have now had to accept that culture is a core object of sociological investigation, or an explanation that at least obligates mainstream scholars to engage in efforts at refutation. This growing legitimacy has allowed for more nuanced distinctions to develop within the field. Identified and named for the first time in 1996 (Alexander 1996), "cultural sociology" and the "sociology of culture" have increasingly come to be seen as two distinct paths of inquiry. For a long time, a sociology of culture was the default position for sociologists interested in meaning. Finding its purest expression in the Bourdieu- and Becker-inspired world of the "production of culture" paradigm, the focus was on culture industries and cultural consumption. Such a sociology of culture was more easily incorporated into mainstream sociology. It did not encroach on the empirical domain of other research specialities: Who else was investigating publishing houses, symphony orchestras, or country music? More importantly, it made use of familiar tropes of "social" explanation in order to account for empirical outcomes. Editors' gate-keeping decisions, audience status aspirations, entrepreneurs' organizational capacities were conceived as determining which books sold, records got played, or concerts were performed—not the seemingly ineffable meanings contained within these expressive art forms themselves. It is no surprise that this paradigm had some early success getting attention in the mainstream journals, or that it had sufficient momentum to develop its own house journal, the somewhat misleadingly named *Poetics*.

Yet, by the early 2000s, it was clear that an increasingly confident cultural sociology had emerged as an alternative paradigm to the once dominant sociology of culture. Hooked far more deeply by the cultural turn, cultural sociology sought to broadly reconfigure sociology as an interpretive-cum-explanatory enterprise rather than to explain narrow empirical outcomes related to "cultural things." For the cultural sociologist, meaning drives the entirety of social life. Cultural sociologists did not restrict their attention to the cultural industries, but instead, they studied politics, religion, social movements, race, civic engagement, and a variety of other social processes—from a cultural perspective. Later in this volume, John Mohr and Craig Rawlings suggest that what is "most distinctive" about "post-cultural turn scholarship" is the "far more nuanced appreciation of how the meaningfulness of social life creates the foundation for that which is the material, the practical, the structural, the social, even perhaps, the biological sides of social life," and conclude that it's "the sense of how culture constitutes the social world of things (rather than how a logic of things defines the rules of culture) that most precisely delineates post- from pre-cultural turn scholarship." Initially an eccentric outlier, cultural sociology has come to be increasingly well represented in the theory journals and in the university press catalogues, with institutional recognition and autonomy cemented by the emergence in 2007 of the British Sociological Association's journal *Cultural Sociology*. As Hall and colleagues introduce the Routledge handbook, "The big surprise was not that the sociology of culture, like other specialties, became a recognizable and increasingly coherent subfield, but that cultural issues began to permeate virtually all subfields of sociology, such that today people conventionally talk about a 'cultural sociology'—that is a general sociology that is cultural on every front, in every subdiscipline." The result is "a cultural sociology that permeates every topic and issue of sociological analysis" (Hall, Grindstaff, and Lo 2010: 3, 5). We agree.

THE IMPACT OF CULTURAL SOCIOLOGY

If culture is now a big player in sociology, what substantive difference has this made? As we see it, cultural sociology has transformed, brought back, and created academic fields of inquiry. Each of these is reflected in this handbook. We turn first to the issue of transformation. The emergence of cultural sociology has allowed well-established research areas to be challenged and invigorated. Economic sociology is perhaps the least likely and the most striking of these and can serve as a representative case. From the time of Marx onward, it was assumed that economic life shaped culture as a domain of pure objectivity. If one did not subscribe to his materialist worldview, then one believed in the liberal proposition that price reflected the logic of supply and demand, that rational actors made economic decisions, that economic indicators were statistical tools with narrow technical significance, and that economic institutions were primarily of sociological impact because of their technical function in regulating the economy. Today, each of these propositions has been challenged by cultural sociology (cf. Alexander 2011). The work of Viviana Zelizer, in particular, has inspired a generation of economic sociologists to show how pricing often reflects the cultural attribution of value rather than market forces, or any intrinsic worth based on the labor theory of value. Rene Almeling (2009), for example, shows how the dollar valuation of sperm and egg donation reflects gendered discourses and understandings. Frederick Wherry's (2008) study of the international craft market illustrates that the price of artifacts and artworks is influenced by the attribution of authenticity or the qualities of the social interactions between buyers and artisans. In his study of the Argentinian inflationary crisis, Martin de Santos has shown how statistical indicators of market exchange culturally outstrip narrow technical responsibilities, how they are constructed by and interpreted by broad discourses such as those about national decline (de Santos 2009). In this volume, Carlo Tognato suggests that modern economic institutions such as Germany's Central Bank are connected to sacred centers of the collective imagination. They can be symbols of national identity and become propagators of myths about sovereignty, stability, or progress. Such discursive and iconic meanings can have profound implications for economic life, for example, by promoting the confidence that allows long-term investments to be made. Also in this volume, Ian Woodward argues that "what we call 'the economy' is fundamentally a networked system of symbolic exchange," in which powerful cultural meanings imbed themselves in material things that exercise magnetic iconic power over consumers' imaginations. Woodward suggests, indeed, that only a strongly cultural sociology can illuminate the economic currents that sustain modern consumer life.

Cultural sociology has managed to bring other fields back in. The study of collective memory, for example, has become far more important than at any time in its hundred-year history. It is now core business for cultural sociology (e.g., Olick, Vinitzky-Seroussi, and Levy 2011) and represented strongly in this collection (see Schwartz; Alexander and Gao). The sociology of the mass media, which peaked in the 1970s and early 1980s in the United States with newsroom ethnographies, is now experiencing a revival, with a renewed focus on the relationship between media, culture, and the public sphere (Jacobs 2009; Townsley, this volume). The influence of cultural sociology is obvious here, as media sociologists emphasize the importance of festive viewing, scandal, crisis, and social drama, and a view of the media as communicative and expressive rather than solely instrumental or ideological. The result is an empirical model of communicative actions that corrects the cultural deficits of elite theories of media brain washing and Habermasian theories of rational deliberation.

Finally, there have been new fields created. Research on cultural trauma and collective identity stands out as a case in point. Constructed over the past few years from a number of resources, including those of collective memory, this new mid-level theory explores the ways in which nations and social groups respond to experiences of collective suffering that challenge core meaning structures. The cultural trauma model has inspired scholars around the globe to explore events as diverse as war, assassination, genocide, revolution, civil war, and natural disasters in a new way (Alexander et al. 2004; Eyerman 2008; Eyerman, Alexander, and Butler Breese 2011). In this volume, Eyerman presents a synthetic overview of this developing body of theory and case studies, and shows how it can explain public reactions to, and the long term effects of, political assassinations. Arguing that a cultural-sociological approach distinguishes naturalistic traumatic occurrences from culturally constructed social events, Eyerman asserts that "cultural traumas are not things, but processes of meaning making and attribution, contentious contests in which various individuals and groups struggle to define a situation and to manage and control it" (see also Alexander and Gao, this volume).

TENSIONS AND COMMONALITY

Despite its shared focus on meaning-making as a powerful and relatively autonomous dimension of social life, cultural sociology is a church, not a sect. This volume testifies to cultural sociology's rise to authority, but it aims also to capture the tensions within this now well-established but scarcely unified field. In the doing of cultural sociology, our authors confront choices about analytic priorities, methods, topics, epistemologies, ideologies, and even modes of writing. We have suggested some of these tensions and presuppositional choices already. Many can be traced back through the history of inquiry in the social sciences and humanities and have long generated famous polemics. Although the editors of this volume are associated with the Strong Program in cultural sociology that emerged at UCLA and finds its present home at Yale (see Alexander and Smith 2001, 2010), in this handbook we present the new cultural sociology in an ecumenical rather than dogmatic manner, displaying its plurality and tensions in what we hope will be a productive way. For, it is not only their commonalities but also their differences that provide the intellectual reference points for cultural sociologists to practice their trade. They are the points on the compass within which cultural sociologists make conceptual decisions, interpret empirical data, and aim their interventions into field-specific debates. We turn now to some of the key analytical distinctions that animate the chapters that follow.

Pattern/Ambiguity, Structure/Event

While all cultural sociologists are committed to meaning-centered analysis, there are different levels of commitment to the idea that culture should be studied as if it is a language with a set of meaning structures or, instead, as a series of relatively nonstructured poetic gestures. Advocates of the latter approach see cultural sociology as providing a sensitizing and illuminating hermeneutic; proponents of the former point to generality beyond the case, yearning for more formal and systemic, and sometimes even quantitative, models of meaning. One way of framing this contrast is to talk about pattern as compared with ambiguity; another is to juxtapose structure with event.

Many cultural sociologists map out cultural structures and engage in a kind of hermeneutical and interpretive model building. The idea here is to understand the robust forms that repeat over instances and offer steering mechanisms for social life that have predictable contours. Scholars taking this path argue that meanings are widely distributed, notwithstanding locality, contingency, and historically bounded nuance. In his contribution, for example, Barry Schwartz shows that representations of the Nanking Massacre fall out into discrete types, that various narrations of the tragic event can be compared to one another as representative "types." The subtleties of this or that history text are of relevance primarily as clues that permit classification. Likewise, in Philip Smith's chapter, the broad public narratives of global warming are to be understood as moving through a range of genre types, each of which has defined features that allocate risk perceptions; and Smith suggests, in fact, that similar genre logics can be found in other, seemingly very different risk contexts, such as national buildups to war. Lyn Spillman, while pointing to vibrant scholarship about local processes of economic meaning-making, calls for studies that identify the larger and more enduring cultural frameworks that make local practices intelligible.

In his famous essay on the Balinese cockfight, Geertz took his distance from such an approach, which he identified with Lévi-Strauss's effort to eliminate the confusion and contradictions of myth. Geertz insisted that it is the event itself that makes meaning, that events express many things at once, that meanings can be captured only obliquely by evocations and analogies. In this volume, Robin Wagner-Pacifici makes a similar case for a more lyrical approach to cultural sociology. Her aim is to capture the nuance and subtlety of social life. Rather than seeing culture as codes and narratives, the focus is on silences, ambiguities, and textures.

If the ambiguity theorist tells us things are always more subtle than they appear, the pattern theorist insists that culture is more straightforward than we might imagine. For example, in their overview of the gay and lesbian movement's forty-year history, Steven Seidman, Chet Meeks, and James Dean readily acknowledge the continuous "symbolic contestation over the meaning and regulation of the body and desire" and its constantly shifting "narrative struggles over the sequencing and main plot lines of history." They argue, nonetheless, that a single cultural code, "civic individualism," has created "an intelligible and coherent sense of order by classifying, arranging and assigning moral value" as this movement has moved from its early radical beginnings to the normalization of gay and lesbian identities today. Declaring that "this code formed the cultural context that structured the development of American sexual politics," they explain how "civic individualism has shaped a friendly cultural environment for a politics of normalization, while forming an inhospitable cultural context for a liberationist or transformative politic":

> A code structures the practice of representation, narration, and discourse.... Once a code is formed and socially embedded, it is not easily dislodged or undermined.... Whether a political agenda is received as reasonable or compelling will depend in part on whether it articulates the codes that organize the lifeworld in a language that feels "right" or "appropriate."

Giuseppe Sciortino makes the case for rethinking the relation between social boundaries and cultural otherness on a similar point. Sciortino acknowledges the "variety of fine-grained ethnic, racial and nationalistic representations" upon which groups draw in struggles over difference and power, but he insists that "difference-based idioms and narratives" are conceived by social actors "as existing within a much larger set of symbolic resources available to participants in the civil sphere." He argues, indeed, that "in order to be heard, specific claims *must* be formulated in reference to [this] set," and labels reductionist the claim that these symbolic boundaries are "homologous" with more contingent and "social" divisions (italics added). Indeed, it is precisely "the absence of any neat alignment between social and cultural boundaries," Sciortino explains, that "energizes difference-based claims in the public sphere." To be sure, boundary-making is affected by "asymmetric power relations," but "it is also a cultural activity linked to a *vision* of the world, triggered and regulated by overarching semiotic structures that classify events and possibilities in structured patters of codes and narratives" (italics added).

Mats Trondman's ethnographic investigation into immigrant struggles for multicultural incorporation in Sweden, and native Swedish resistance to it, argues in the same way. "How is it and what can it look like," Trondman asks, "when people in their everyday lives—despite unequal distribution of material, social, and symbolic resources—reconnect with strong commitments to values of solidarity and feelings for others whom they do not know in support of social integration and multicultural incorporation?" The simple positing of this as a "question," Trondman points out, suggests the pivotal position of "cultural autonomy" in what less culturally musical sociologists take to be merely divisive material conflicts over boundary position. Trondman's probing, Geertz-like ethnographic queries reveal that many Muslim immigrants, despite their anger and resentment, still yearn for recognition and for the success of Sweden's social democratic ideals. "I am allowed to live here," explains his informant Mohammad, "and you try to help me...but you, man, you live in Sweden. Do you feel me? I also want to fight for your good society." On the other side of the conflict, Trondman shows that Swedish parents who put up ferocious resistance to a school principal's proposal to incorporate immigrant children became acutely embarrassed when media reports depict the confrontation as "rancorous": "They did not like to read about themselves as aggressive and prejudiced citizens rejecting the integration of less privileged children. It did not really sit well with the self-image that most of the middle class parents had about themselves, and how they wanted to be represented in public." Responding to being stigmatized vis-à-vis democratic codes, parents reacted in contingent ways. For some, "the chronicle stilled the loud debate and opened up the floor for a democratic process in search of a public civility." For others, "the most outspoken, angry, and oppositional parents," the response was to become silent and remove their children from the school. In Trondman's view, it is the relative autonomy of culture structures that allows these two contingent and opposing reactions to be properly understood: "They tell stories from the opposite sides of a city that despite all differences, twists and mutilations reverberate the same beliefs in and social hope for social integration and multicultural incorporation."

Sometimes cultural sociologists suggest that pattern and ambiguity are interconnected, that one inevitably gives rise to the other. Bernhard Giesen's paper shows that classifications themselves generate the ambiguities of "inbetween"—betwixt and between—things and experiences, which are often seen as monstrous, as garbage, as temptations, or as symbolically dangerous. The picture he gives is of social life as a creative tension between the routine and knowable and the extraordinary, forbidden, and mysterious. Other scholars analyze the struggles that societies undergo to fix the ambiguous. Thompson argues that the recent growth in Pentecostalism is due to its cultural ambiguities, which allow its practitioners to adapt the meanings of the religious practices to the exigencies of the local culture. Against the idea that there is an inevitable cultural movement toward secularization, Thompson suggests that discourses of religion and globalization are intersecting in new and interesting ways. The result is a variety of new and hybrid forms, which recombine cultural patterns, even as they maintain the deep binary cultural relationship between the religious and the secular.

Sometimes the tension between pattern and ambiguity presents itself as a conflict between institution and movement, or event and routine. We can see cultural patterns as relatively enduring and even as permanent, causing social life to engage in repeated and familiar iterations. Or, we might see them as enabling innovation, change, and flexibility. Writing on the body, Arthur Frank notes that systems of meaning are deeply internalized in the self and its material carriers. The body is wired with a "habitus" that refuses some possibilities for action—or at least makes these more difficult to imagine and enact. Frank himself was a good sharpshooter and athlete, but his body did not feel right as a soldier's body. He writes that "the body is comfortable [when] what it is doing is somehow right, necessary, and unavoidable.... Bodies are trained by cultures to feel this way."

This story of reproduction finds clear echoes in Roger Friedland's insistence, against more purely voluntaristic approaches to culture, on the importance of institutionalization. Opposing instrumental understandings of politicized religious movement, Friedland suggests that they cannot be understood merely as the struggles of different groups to control material resources and/or to exercise state power. "Nations do not exist [only] on the ground," he insists, but also "must be constructed in the mind." Yet, while this ideational domain does open possibilities for cultural creativity, institutional cultures enclose agency by channeling it in predictable ways. Friedland points to the patterned restrictions that institutionalization places on efforts at cultural reconstruction, observing that social life unfolds according to powerful symbolic "logics" which demand iteration and routine reproduction.

By contrast, Mabel Berezin insists that social life—at least in the political sphere—consists of events. These are moments of crisis and contingency where the flow of history pushes up against the social. This history is less about determinism and routine than a succession of meaningful, interpreted, and consequential events playing out one after another. "In contrast to historical institutionalism," she argues, "events are important for what they force us to imagine—and these imaginings may generate hope as well as fear, comfort as well as threat—rather than how they determine choice." Against Friedland's institutional logic of iteration, the message here is one of transformation. Lisa McCormick's investigation of the field of music sociology reaches a similar conclusion. Where most existing studies in the music sociology field focus too strongly on institutional factors, such as the organizational capacities that enable large-scale musical works to be performed, recorded, and distributed, McCormick turns music sociology to the contingencies of performance and the deeply subjective meanings on which successful performances depend. Consequently, she insists that we must "develop virtuosity in interpreting musical and social texts equal to that already demonstrated in analyzing social structures and institutional settings."

In his account of the travails that marked Bill Clinton's presidency, Jason Mast finds that sharply etched tropes about moral character provided the cultural background to the social dramas that roiled the Democrat's two scandal-scarred terms. At the same time, Mast insists that "the meanings of power, authority, legitimacy, and democracy are relational and processual," and that "while their meanings are rooted in cultural structures, they are also dynamically negotiated through performative struggles." In "classical and modern forms of cultural sociology," Mast writes, "the understanding of cultural structures and meaningful action focused on ritual behavior"—"highly stylized moments that created parallels with actions in primitive societies." As an alternative, he points to "a radically new form of cultural sociology that promises to maintain the emphasis on meaning while avoiding the drawbacks of ritual theory," and he presents the theory of "cultural pragmatics" as having "initiated the performative turn in sociology."

> Performance theory pays attention to background structures of meaning, but takes a pragmatic understanding of whether actors can effectively embody them.... Scripts have to be forged out of these background representations, and this requires creativity.... Actors need a place to stand, a stage, and access to means of symbolic production.... Politics flows in episodes, and actors work within and between episodes to control micro-events so that they are well positioned when large-scale events, which compel broad public attention, form and appear to take on a life of their own.

In her study of Barack Obama's rise to power, Eleanor Townsley also gives emphasis to the transformative potentials inherent in a cultural understanding of the public sphere—in this case, to the powerful critical space of open public commentary. Obama's election depended not only on entrenched structures of field-specific autonomy (Bourdieu), and the application of critical rationality (Habermas), but also on the evanescent vagaries of interpretation and performance. Townsley suggests a relational theory of field-specific cultural autonomy. A successful or "fused" performance requires more than the skilled alignment of background representations, foregrounded scripts, actor, role, and scene. For real transformation to occur, audiences in different cultural fields must come to believe not only that a performer is authentic, but also that his or her presence holds out the promise that their particular cultural field can increase its autonomy and its influence.

Hierarchy and Solidarity

Cultural analysis can study hierarchy or solidarity. Although talk of ideology is now outré, cultural sociologists still believe that meanings can drive domination and exclusion. They can provide a basis for stigma and hegemony, for status rankings, and for the standards of evaluation that judge effective performance and hence the attainment of legitimate power. Yet, culture can also indicate the existence of horizontal ties of belonging. Culture makes it easier to form networks, to generate shared collective projects, and to reproduce social capital, as Friedland's earlier discussion of institutions makes clear. At issue are the motivations of social actors. Are individuals driven by the desire to distinguish themselves, to attain or to reproduce a certain amount of social privilege, to justify (or challenge) existing social conditions? Or, alternatively, are they motivated by the desire to belong to something larger than themselves, to experience a sense of social communion, to develop a shared understanding of their existential condition? To a certain extent, these questions represent fundamentally different presuppositions about the nature of social action and social order. The contributors to this handbook represent a wide range of decisions regarding these different presuppositional options. What they share, however, is an effort to avoid rigid dualisms, often conceptualizing hierarchy and solidarity as parts of a shared cultural environment.

Jacobs's chapter on the aesthetic public sphere is a good example of a cultural sociological approach to power and solidarity. Entertainment media encourage the formation of aesthetic publics, in which public commentary about cultural programming and cultural policy is linked to a broader discussion of society, politics, and public life, commentary that expands the boundaries of public attention and participation (solidarity). At the same time, the aesthetic public sphere is also shaped by existing cultural hierarchies that privilege "the serious" over "the entertaining." This places clear limits on the aesthetic public sphere, by maintaining the always-present possibility that participants in aesthetic publics will be called on to justify their interests against an elitist seriousness that blocks a more popular, and wider, solidarity. Examining the global expansion of American entertainment television, Jacobs notes its contradictory effects. American popular "entertainment" is anti-elitist at home, but it is often regarded as hegemonic and elitist abroad. Yet, resistance to America's globalizing media often triggers local television production, a development that expands cultural equality and international solidarity.

Gianpaolo Baiocchi's chapter provides a critical interrogation of the cultural sociology of civil society, viewed from the perspective of the Global South. At issue is the way that the colonial history of the Global South transforms the meanings and the experiences of civil society and democracy. For example, the discourse of liberty and freedom has often been seen as part of an exogenous imperial statecraft, such that the discourse of civil society becomes part of a "civilizing mission" imposed from the outside (hierarchy). One should not, in other words, assume the emancipatory quality of civil society discourse in the Global South: The continuing vitality of populist movements demonstrates how this discourse has been characterized to the contrary, as a force of cultural domination. While there is indeed a relatively stable and autonomous meaning structure that organizes the civic code, Baiocchi acknowledges, he also demonstrates that "there is an element of ambiguity and hybridity at the core of that culture in much of the world." Encouraging us to "provincialize" our social theory from the perspective of the postcolonial world, Baiocchi suggests that the boundaries of the civil sphere are more uncertain, more in flux, and more politically loaded than we might have imagined.

Alford Young's article about race, gender, and the city takes a more conceptual and metatheoretical approach to cultures of hierarchy and solidarity. Young argues that "the street" has become a powerful signifier representing the experiential world of urban African American men. On the one hand, "the street" represents the heroic attempts by disadvantaged black men to carve out a space of mutual belonging and respect within a spatial environment of extreme structural disadvantage. On the other hand, "the street" is part of a public culture that encourages a fear of black men in public places—a fear that dovetails effectively with policies of social control. In this sense, the semiotics of "the street" provides a central mechanism for social marginalization (hierarchy) at the same time as it highlights the terrain of agency, respect, and belonging (solidarity). But this is not the end of

Young's analysis. Provocatively, he argues that social scientists have reproduced the semiotic of "the street" in their research on urban black men, painting a partial and incomplete portrait of African American selfhood that blocks a more balanced social awareness of alternative sources (and locales) for creating urban African American male identities.

The contribution by Francesca Polletta and Bobby Chen contributes to this debate by reflecting on the conditions that make stories effective as cultural tools for challenging power. Narrative is consistently effective for building solidarity and enlisting support, but its political effectiveness depends on a number of cultural and institutional factors. Culturally, effective stories must avoid two dangers; if they are too explicit, or if they stray too far from familiar plotlines, they are likely to be ineffective. Institutionally, effective narratives must confront a basic ambivalence about the status of stories, as compared to other kinds of claims-making. There is a tendency to see stories as "normatively powerful but politically unserious," a fact that places extra cultural burdens on social movement, and particularly on those speakers coming from lower-status groups. The skilled narrator can overcome these challenges through his or her exceptional literary skills and cultural performances. Polletta and Chen remind us that the conditions of reception for these narratives are unevenly distributed, and that studying the structure of this unevenness needs to be a part of cultural sociology.

Discourse and Materiality

There is a long-standing complaint that cultural sociology is prone to idealism. Although this criticism can take many forms, a common argument is that it captures the world of ideas but not the hard materiality of social life. Today, cultural sociologists are acutely aware of this tension between discourse and materiality, and of the need to do something about it. One strategy is to turn the tables and insist that material things and their uses are shaped by meanings, whether semiotic codes or simply aesthetic reactions to visual or tactile surfaces. In her chapter on culture and economic sociology, Spillman argues that something as hard-headed and materialist as "economic interest" is best understood as a collective representation of social values and collective identity. Another strategy, however, is to show that meaning gets special power when embodied in materiality. Woodward shows that it is not so much the abstract discourse of wine but its sensuous taste, smell, and visual experience that drinkers imbibe (cf. Woodward and Ellison 2011). Calling for the "integration of materiality with narrative," Woodward describes "a cultural sociological model that fuses performative understandings of the materiality and sensuality of consumption with consideration of the power of myth."

Public Ritual and the Everyday

For too long, sociologists approached their subject matter as if they had to choose between a Durkheimian focus on public rituals and a Goffmanian emphasis on the everyday. This was unfortunate for cultural sociology, because it contributed to an unnecessary dualism between structure and contingency that seemed to separate the public sphere and the private lifeworld. Ritual theory emphasized public events, and adopted a Durkheimian program of mapping out the structure of the ritual process. Contingency was either avoided or else bracketed within a model that led step-by-step from liminality to reaggregation (Turner 1969). Set against such public ritual analysis were ethnomethodological and interactionist studies of everyday life, which concentrated on the abilities of creative actors to improvise, transpose, and "ad-hoc" meanings in what were taken to be completely contingent ways. Even when meaning structures were acknowledged, they were subordinated to the seemingly limitless ability of actors to bend these structures to their own needs, to use culture as a tool, at least during "settled times" (Swidler 1986).

In recent years, cultural sociologists have broken down this dualism, trying to account for the interplay of structure and contingency that informs cultural environments in the lifeworld as well as the public sphere. In the study of public events, some cultural sociologists have moved away from the older ritual theories of Turner and Durkheim to embrace Alexander's cultural performance model (Alexander 2004) that explains emotional fusion as the contingent outcome of a complex of interactions and structures. In his contribution on media and crisis, for example, Simon Cottle argues that today's mediatized rituals are more unpredictable, contested, and disruptive than either functionalist or Marxian theories of media events would suggest. This is due to a variety of factors, including the autonomous logics of journalism, the competitive dynamics of multiple public spheres, as well as the contingent challenges of creating re-fusion through effective cultural performances. The intersection of these different cultural dynamics results in a situation where the performative production of mediatized crises can have vastly different cultural and political consequences, as Cottle demonstrates for empirical cases such as Hurricane Katrina, the South Asian tsunami of 2004, and the Sichuan earthquake of 2008.

In the study of everyday life, cultural sociologists have turned away from the extreme situationalism of Goffman and Garfinkel in order to develop a more balanced account of cultural structure and contingency in the lifeworld. For Paul Lichterman, this involves a pragmatic understanding of collective action and civic culture, in which the meaning of "civic" is enmeshed within social spaces of collective problem solving. "To ask about civic culture," Lichterman argues, "we focus most sharply on the cultural conditions for citizens to work together and solve problems." By defining civic culture as a type of activity rather than a specific institutional space, Lichterman proposes a more flexible definition that refuses to define what counts as civic, and that refuses the a priori binary separating civil society and the state. At the same time, these collective problem-solving activities are contained within a broader cultural environment of public vocabularies, codes, and dramas about what makes a good citizen or a virtuous society. These broader meaning structures, placed in such bold relief during public rituals, must be enacted in everyday interactions over collective goods. Here, they are intersected by more local civic customs and group styles, as Lichterman demonstrates in his own empirical research on religions organizations and ethically motivated social movements.

The contribution by Nina Eliasoph and Jade Lo likewise applies a cultural pragmatism to meaning-making in organizations. They are critical of the influence that Garfinkel's ethnomethodology has had on the study of everyday life, suggesting that its focus on social life as a purely in situ practical accomplishment fails to explore how there can be stability across local sites. Relying instead on Cicourel's theory of typification, they explore how people identify patterns of coordination when they enter an organization, how they transfer social practices from one local site to another, and how organizations "tinker" with the meanings of their everyday practices in order to make them understandable and meaningful to a variety of different constituencies and publics. Taken together, these local typifications produce an "accumulation of small differences" that offer individuals important clues about the kind of organization they are facing and about the organizational style it imposes on everyday interactions. These organizationally specific typifications exemplify the relative autonomy of culture, but they are more local and flexible, and interaction with them tends to be "de-fused," nonritualized, and outside of the big public view.

Interpretation, Explanation, and Validity

At the end of this discussion of the tensions marking "best practices" in contemporary cultural sociology, we turn to the questions of method and epistemology to which the opening pages of our *Handbook* are devoted. In the late nineteenth century, Windelband's neo-Kantian distinction between idiographic and nomothetic crystallized the sense that, because efforts to understand cultural meanings pay close attention to detail, nuance, and creativity, they cannot begin to approach the generality and systematicity of the covering laws that characterize scientific explanation. Though challenged and tweaked in all sorts of different ways—most notably by Dilthey's insistence that the sciences of the spirit (*Geisteswissenschaften*) can discover forms of supra-historical cultural generality—the sense that the interpretive analysis of meaning demands the surrender, not merely of the scientific method but of rationality itself, has continued to be an influential shibboleth right up to the present day. What has changed, perhaps, is that with the growing disciplinary and real-worldly ambitions of the social sciences, ambitions that intensified in the second half of the last century, Windelband's primordial distinction has become less an argument about social versus natural science than one that expresses deep tensions within modern social science itself.

Small wonder that this tension has reproduced itself with a vengeance inside the cultural sociological field. There is a clash between those who place a priority on producing fine-grained interpretations that do justice to the complexity of their subjects' worldviews, on the one hand, and analysts more concerned with assessing how representative and typical are these beliefs, on the other. Scholars in the latter camp are more interested in sampling and frequency, and in measuring correlations between beliefs and noncultural variables. Those in the former concentrate more on interpreting the internal structure and patterning of cultural meanings, on mapping out and understanding the relations between symbolic parts and ideational wholes. Of course, in an ideal world, we would have a cultural sociology of infinite interpretative sensitivity specifying precisely to what degree these cultural structures were shared, by how many social actors, in which demographics, and for how long a time. The reality is that these criteria are rarely if ever met at the same time. The push to measure how widely accepted values are often leads to banality or to a coarse insensitivity to nuance. Witness the failure of formal content analysis—counting the number of times words are mentioned—to have any significant leverage in contemporary cultural sociology. By contrast, while thick descriptions of meaning have often produced virtuoso interpretations, such deep readings tend to finesse the issue of breadth. How representative are these beliefs? Which groups and individuals subscribe to them? Have the best interpreters been selective in their reading of the evidence? Are the authors of spectacular accounts actually making sense of empirical meanings, or are they merely good writers who are skilled at packaging highly idiosyncratic and subjective views?

Richard Biernacki and John Mohr articulate these alternative positions, even as they modify them in subtle but significant ways. Defending the Weberian emphasis on hermeneutic case studies—a tradition whose philosophical roots go back to not only Windelband but also Rickert and Dilthey—Biernacki mounts a powerful attack on methodological formalism. He regards as deeply corrosive the earnest efforts of many contemporary cultural sociologists to correlate cultural meanings with some other, formally constructed model of something noncultural, a substance that gets turned into an independent variable determining the internal structure of meaning itself. Such modeling efforts are actually "rationalization processes" that mimic mechanical modernization more broadly, in Biernacki's view. Reified and abstract models provide "spatial scaling," maximally for the purpose of measurement, minimally for less quantitative estimations of more and less. Privileging form over meaning, spatial scaling ranks culture on purely imagined dimensions—high and low, near and far—that, while suggestive, do not actually exist inside meanings themselves. Thus, modeling pre-shapes interpretive understanding and takes cultural analysts outside the subjective world of actors' meanings; it creates a "realism effect" that decontextualizes and flattens the rich multidimensionality of cultural life (cf. the debate between Biernacki 2009 and Evans 2009).

Mohr confronts such criticism head on, arguing for the "advantages of formalism." Models that simplify, measure, and scale are essential to think with, for they provide objects that can "stand in" for the infinitely complex patterning of cultural imaginations. Mohr denies Biernacki's claim that formal models take analysis outside of culture. As Mohr sees it, there is formal modeling before and after the cultural turn. Before-modeling emphasized "exogeneity," but after-modeling provides cultural models that can map the contours of meaningful form itself. Such eminent sociologists *of* culture as Bourdieu, Collins, and Dimaggio have not made this shift. By contrast, in the later writings of Harrison White, we find an extraordinary 180 degree turn against such materialist network models. It is to this new way of mathematically modeling meaning and narration that Mohr invites us to turn. Such formal models can teach us how to be more careful readers of social texts, providing "structure-preserving transformations" of symbolic discourse rather than ways to stand outside it. The question today, as Mohr sees it, is not whether to "move from quality to quantity," but how and when to do so.

Isaac Reed holds that it is not only unnecessary but also unwise to take sides in this self-lacerating, if historic, debate. Yes, cultural sociology is interpretive and meaning-focused. The reason, however, has not to do with the peculiarities of this subfield but with the nature of social explanation itself. If, as Reed argues, "social reality doesn't exist as such, but rather emerges from historically specific meaning-structures," then surely it follows that "sociological knowledge itself is hermeneutic" and, if this is so, that cultural sociology should see itself not as an entirely different method but rather "as a particularly strong version of the project of sociological interpretation" itself. Reed sketches two kinds of broad interpretive constructs, which cover the range of sociological analysis, whatever the special topic or method. "Minimal interpretations" provide social observers with the lower case "facts" that, taken together, generate the sum total of positive empirical knowledge at a particular place and time. "Maximal interpretations" build on these interpreted facts but leap to broader narratives about social patterning and causation. In the kinds of maximal interpretations associated with strong programs of cultural sociology—those that aim "to understand the meanings that surround action"—such causal forces are described as binary codes, narratives, and metaphors. Cultural sociologists provide evidence for large causal claims by pointing to a distinctive set of minimally inter-preted social facts: the subjective "reasons" that actors themselves offer for their actions. If cultural sociology is, indeed, "a program for the explanation of social action," as Reed contends, and not merely an idiographic act of relativistic virtuoso interpretation, then practitioners must accept the philosopher Donald Davidson's claim that, in the human as compared to the natural world, "reasons are causes."

In the pages that follow, readers will enter the newly crystallized world of cultural sociology, a world in which action is symbolic and order cultural, if not wholly then at least in significant part. Beyond these cultural-sociological precepts, however, readers will find a remarkable variety of pathways for engaging in cultural sociology. Some essays illustrate an approach in a performative way. Others take the shape of programmatic injunctions. All offer a template for pushing forward our inquiry into the ways that meaning shapes social life. At the end of the day, this is what cultural sociology is all about.

REFERENCES

Alexander, Jeffrey C. 1987. *Twenty Lectures: Sociological Theory Since World War Two.* New York: Columbia University Press.

———. 1988. ed. *Durkheimian Sociology: Cultural Studies.* Cambridge, UK: Cambridge University Press.

————. 1996. "Cultural Sociology or Sociology of Culture?" ASA Culture Newsletter. *Culture* 10, (3–4): 1–5.

————. 2004. "Cultural Pragmatics: Social Performance Between Ritual and Strategy." *Sociological Theory* 22: 527–73.

————. Forthcoming. "Market as Narrative and Character: For a Cultural Sociology of Economic Life." *Journal of Cultural Economy*.

Alexander, J., and Philip Smith. 2001. "The Strong Program in Cultural Theory: Elements of a Structural Hermeneutics." In J. Turner, ed., *Handbook of Social Theory*, pp. 135–50. New York. Kluwer Academic.

————. 2010. "The Strong Program: Origins, Achievements, Prospects." In John R. Hall, Laura Grindstaff, and Ming-Cheng Lo, eds., pp. 13–24. *Handbook of Cultural Sociology*. London: Routledge.

Alexander, Jeffrey C., and Steven Seidman, eds. 1990. *Culture and Society: Contemporary Debates*. Cambridge, UK: Cambridge University Press.

Alexander, Jeffrey C., Bernhard Giesen, and Jason Mast, eds. 2004. *Social Performance: Symbolic Action, Cultural Pragmatics, and Ritual*. Cambridge, UK: Cambridge University Press.

Almeling, Rene. 2009. "Gender and the Value of Bodily Goods: Commodification in Egg and Sperm Donation." *Law and Contemporary Problems* 72 (3): 37–58.

Biernacki, Richard. 2009. "After Quantitative Cultural Sociology: Interpretive Science as a Calling." In Isaac Reed and J. Alexander, eds., *Meaning and Method: The Cultural Approach in Sociology*, pp. 119–208. Boulder, CO: Paradigm.

de Santos, Martin. 2009. "Fact-Totems and the Statistical Imagination: The Public Life of a Statistic in Argentina 2001." *Sociological Theory* 27 (4): 466–89.

Edles, Laura. 1998. *Myth and Symbol in the New Spain*. New York: Cambridge University Press.

Evans, John. 2009. "Two Worlds in Cultural Sociology." In Isaac Reed and J. Alexander, eds., *Meaning and Method: The Cultural Approach in Sociology*, pp. 208–52. Boulder, CO: Paradigm.

Eyerman, Ron. 2008. *The Assassination of Theo van Gogh: From Social Drama to Cultural Trauma*. Durham, NC: Duke University Press.

Eyerman, Ron, Jeffrey C. Alexander, and Elizabeth Butler Breese, eds. 2011. *Narrating Trauma: On the Cultural Construction of Social Suffering*. Boulder, CO: Paradigm.

Friedland, Roger, and John Mohr. 2004. eds. *Matters of Culture: Cultural Sociology in Practice*. Cambridge, UK: Cambridge University Press.

Geertz, Clifford. 1973. *The Interpretation of Cultures*. London: Hutchinson.

Hall, J., L. Grindstaff, and L. Ming-Leung, eds. 2010. *Handbook of Cultural Sociology*. London: Routledge.

Jacobs, Mark, and Nancy Weiss Hanrahan. 2005. eds. *The Blackwell Companion to the Sociology of Culture*. Boston: Wiley.

Jacobs, Ronald N. 2009. "Culture, The Public Sphere, and Media Sociology: A Search for a Classical Founder in the Work of Robert Park." *The American Sociologist* 40: 149–66.

Lamont, Michele. 1993. *Money, Manners, and Morals*. Princeton, NJ: Princeton University Press.

Lamont, Michele, and Marcel Fournier, eds. 1993. *Cultivating Differences: Symbolic Boundaries and the Making of Inequality*. Chicago: University of Chicago Press.

Long, Elizabeth. ed. 1997. *From Sociology to Cultural Studies: New Perspectives*. New York: Wiley.

Olick, Jeffrey, Vered Vinitsky-Seroussi, and Daniel Levy, eds. 2011. *The Collective Memory Reader*. New York: Oxford University Press.

Sherwood, Steven, P. Smith, and J. Alexander. 1993. "The British Are Coming…Again! The Hidden Agenda of 'Cultural Studies.'" *Contemporary Sociology* 22 (2): 370–75.

Smith, Philip. 1998a. "The New American Cultural Sociology." In Philip Smith, ed., *The New American Cultural Sociology*, pp. 1–14. Cambridge, UK: Cambridge University Press.

Smith, Philip, ed. 1998b. *The New American Cultural Sociology*. Cambridge, UK: Cambridge University Press.

Spillman, Lyn, ed. 2001. *Cultural Sociology: Blackwell Readers in Sociology*. Oxford: Wiley-Blackwell.

Swidler, Ann. 1986. "Culture in Action: Symbols and Strategies." *American Sociological Review* 51: 273–86.

Turner, Victor. 1967. *The Ritual Process*. Chicago: Aldine.

Wagner-Pacific, Robin. 1986. *The Moro Morality Play: Terrorism as Social Drama*. Chicago: University of Chicago Press.

Wherry, Frederick F. 2008. *Global Markets and Local Crafts*. Baltimore: Johns Hopkins University Press.

Woodward, Ian, and David Ellison. Forthcoming. "How to Make an Iconic Commodity: The Case of 'Penfold' Grange Wine." In J. C. Alexander, Dominik Bartmanski, and Bernhard Giesen, eds., *Iconic Power: Materiality and Meaning in Social Life*. New York and London: Palgrave Macmillan.

Zerubavel, Eviatar. 1993. *The Fine Line*. Chicago: University of Chicago Press.

PART I

THE CULTURAL METHOD IN SOCIOLOGY

CULTURAL SOCIOLOGY AS RESEARCH PROGRAM: POST-POSITIVISM, MEANING, AND CAUSALITY

ISAAC ARIAIL REED

THE PROBLEMATIC STATUS OF CULTURAL INTERPRETATIONS

What is the development of an interpretive understanding of culture if not a contribution to the causal explanation of social action? Consider some possibilities. One could propose an interpretation of Calvinist attitude toward work that was a judgment of its relationship to the true doctrine of Christianity. One could develop a queer reading of *Twelfth Night* that is specifically designed to (help to) subvert, and eventually change, the understandings of gender and sexual desire currently dominant in the West. One could propose an understanding of the Balinese cock-fight that grasps the aesthetic brilliance with which that cultural practice thematizes the existential and social problems that trouble the Balinese, and thus recognizes in the cockfight what literary critics have long recognized in *King Lear* or *The Brothers Karamazov*. One could examine the coffee-shop discussions of elites in Western Europe in the seventeenth and eighteenth centures so as to recover the kernel of reason essential to any democracy—even to those democracies that attempt to include more than propertied white men. All of these would be *interpretations of meaning*. And they all, in one way or another, distance themselves from the supposed scientism of explanation and cause. One might be tempted to assert, once and for all, that the interpretation of cultures is "not an experimental science in search of law but an interpretive one in search of meaning"—with the implication that causality is on the side of scientific laws (Geertz 2000b, 5). Unfortunately, this is too often how interpretation is interpreted.

First, all of the above interpretations depend—if only partially, parasitically, or implicitly—on a claim about the reality of meaning and its significance for humans doing what they do. Max Weber, quite properly, did not care much for what "true" Chirstian doctrine was, but the fact that the Calvinists did care was immensely consequential. If there is not something *in* Shakespeare's comic masterpeice which suggests that sex, gender, and desire are a bit less stable than we tend to assume, then we would not use it to make that precise point. Cockfighting may be an aesthetic phenomenon with which the Balinese read themselves to themselves, but what they are "reading" is real social meaning. And as for those coffee shops—they may not have, by themselves, brought down the Bastille, but they did, in some small way, help.

Or did they? Maybe meaning is real, but it does not matter. It exists, but not as a causal motor of action, history, etc. This would tell us why social scientists explain, while cultural critics interpret. Perhaps the meaningful effluvia of human life are awfully nice to have around—maybe even necessary in some sense of the term—but should not be mistaken for the motors of history. But cultural sociology, as is well known by now, has no patience for Marxist catechism—indeed it has spilled a great deal of ink attempting to refute it. Cultural sociology, then, needs the negation of the negation—an understanding of itself as not just against reductionism, but as a positive program for the construction of sociological knowledge. In this short essay, I want to situate cultural sociology epistemologically, as a step towards its self-understanding as a research program. To do this, one must comprehend the larger context of "post-positivist" social science. For this purpose, it will be useful to outline an understanding of what sociological knowledge is and does, that is, in a broad and weak sense, hermeneutic. Cultural sociology itself will then emerge as a particularly strong or meaning-centered version of a broader project of sociological interpretation.

MINIMAL AND MAXIMAL INTERPRETATIONS

A *minimal interpretation* is a report upon some social actions that happened. Minimal interpretations tend to be unironic (and to lack a distinctive style or genre more generally), and they can often serve as the consensus upon which further scholarly conflict is based. Minimal interpretations tend to string together various pieces of evidence (sometimes both qualitative and quantitative) to create a *case.*

A *maximal interpretation* is a synthesis of abstract theoretical terms with one or more minimal interpretations. This synthesis is the means to the end of making the knowledge of the social actions under study deeper, more general or generalizable, or more effective and useful for the execution of future social actions. Maximal interpretations in the human sciences tend to be controversial. They are structured by certain discursive genres or tropes, and they involve theoretical presuppositions.

When human scientists insist upon "the facts of the matter," demand empirical responsibility, and dispute the evidential support for a certain explanation or theory, they use minimal interpretations. In doing so, they rely on meaning and subjectivity, but they rely on *just enough* meaning and subjectivity to report what happened. Durkheim noted that social facts inevitably have a certain element of subjectivity, but insisted that we treat them "as things" (Durkheim 1982). The ultimate implication of this is that there are aspects of social life that scholars, following some basic rules of evidence-gathering and non-contradiction, can agree upon. It is true that in 1789 feudal privileges were abolished in France; that presently the educational outcomes of those Americans that self-identify as black are less good than the educational outcomes of those that self-identify as white; and that the number of American troops in Iraq increased in specifiable amounts between 2003 and 2008. All of these facts are indeed interpretations—they require knowledge of what it means to be an American soldier and how nation-states are understood in the post-1945 era, or knowledge of racial categorization as a continuing and impactful element of American social life, or knowledge of what feudalism and the ancien regime were. And yet, somehow, scholars—and more generally human beings possessed of a willingness to consider evidence and argument as autonomous from the character or status of the person using the evidence or making the argument—can come to a certain amount of agreement here. It is not a coincidence that the statements that such people can agree on have been massively stripped of theoretical language, and that they rely ultimately on meanings understood easily by scholars, journalists, and statisticians.

And yet, the problem with minimal interpretations is precisely their minimality. They do not answer questions like: *why* did the presence of American troops increase in Iraq; *what is to be done* to make educational outcomes more equal in the United States; or *whether* the French Revolution was a political revolution with social consequences or a social revolution with political consequences (and, in either case, whether something called "ideology" played a role in bringing it about). To answer these sorts of questions, human scientists reach for their theories. In doing so, they bring to bear upon the social facts under study a massively overgrown, wildly dispersed, notoriously unwieldy, and problematically hermetic discursive formation—the meaningful world of social, political, and cultural theory.

This world of theory is full of models for social reality, judgments about justice and democracy, and heuristics for understanding difference. In the course of analysis, researchers in the human sciences bring together these abstractions with minimal interpretations. How they do so says a lot about their epistemological commitments and the ultimate goals of their work. But one thing is certain: with maximal interpretation comes disputation; with in-depth knowledge comes skepticism about the sources of that knowledge; with causal argumentation comes presuppositions about the nature of human motivation; with normative judgment comes the interrogation of political assumptions.

An Example: The Protestant Ethic and the Spirit of Capitalism

Max Weber's best-known monograph begins with a minimal interpretation: "the fact that business leaders and owners of capital, as well as the higher grades of skilled labour, and even more, the higher technically and commercially trained personnel of modern enterprises, are overwhelmingly Protestant"(Weber 2003: 35). This minimal interpretation is discussed in the opening pages of the first chapter: possible objections are considered, the scope of the trend's reach is clarified, some causes for it are speculated upon, and some tentative propositions made in terms of its larger significance. But as a minimal interpretation, it stands and falls with evidence. One does not have to believe Weber's explanation of the origins of Occidental capitalism to believe this fact.

Weber produces more minimal interpretations throughout his text, including some that are more "subjective." For example, Benjamin Franklin saw honesty and frugality as useful, but did not reduce honesty and frugality to their usefulness (Weber 2003: 52–53). Luther was not interested in the pursuit of worldly goods as an end in and of itself (Weber 2003: 42), and his understanding of the calling led him to suggest people stay in the professions handed to them by tradition (Weber 2003: 44). And so on. But Weber's book is not merely the sum of these minimal interpretations. Rather, these minimal interpretations become part of a maximal interpretation when they are worked over by social theory and the logic of comparison set out in the preface, with the result—the maximal interpretation—being the "Weber thesis" in its unity and power. A variety of key passages could be quoted, but for one:

> One of the fundamental elements of the spirit of modern capitalism, and not only of that but of all modern culture: rational conduct on the basis of the idea of the calling, was born—that is what this discussion has sought to demonstrate— from the spirit of Christian asceticism. One has only to reread the passage from Franklin, quoted at the beginning of this essay, in order to see that the essential elements of the attitude which was there called the spirit of capitalism are the same as what we have just shown to be the content of the Puritan worldly asceticism, only without the religious basis, which by Franklin's time had died away. (Weber 2003: 180)

This is not to mention, of course, the variety of normative judgments that Weber, despite himself, allows into the study, and which have been the subject of much debate in social theory. But at its core Weber's book is the development of a deep causal claim, which comparatively differentiates the West from other regions of the globe and explains the takeoff of modern capitalism in the West as, at least in part, a result of the "elective affinity" between the Protestant ethic and the spirit of capitalism.

As a maximal interpretation, this claim cannot be arrived at by stringing together historical chronologies, qualitative descriptions of authors, and quantitative correlations. The facts are not enough. It is rather that the facts have to become *evidence for* some deeper claim—in this case a causal one. In the passage quoted above, Weber's call to the reader to "reread the passage from Franklin" reveals this logic of maximal interpretation. The first-time reader, presumably, will not understand the full import of Franklin's words upon initial reading. By the end of the monograph, however, Weber has slowly built up more and more maximal interpretations—first, that there was such an ideational formation as the "spirit of capitalism"; second, that there was such an ideational formation as the "protestant ethic"; and finally, that the two have an elective affinity for each other. In the context of these maximal interpretations, Franklin's words become part of a broader whole—a whole influenced and inflected by theory, and with a claim upon history that attempts to tell a causal, comparative story and not merely report what happened.

Post-Positivism and Dispute over Maximal Interpretations

We can use this distinction between minimal and maximal interpretations to better understand what "post-positivist" sociology is and the relationship of cultural sociology to other post-positivist epistemic stances. What was really at stake in the "interpretive," "historical," "political," or "Kuhnian" critiques of positivism?

Positivism was—and is—at its heart an attempt to (1) ground minimal interpretations in observable, measurable evidence, and (2) ground a certain sort of maximal interpretations (explanations/predictions) in inductive generalization from many minimal interpretations. Covering laws are maximal interpretations in positivism, and they can be used to "subsume" any number of minimal interpretations.

The critiques of positivism were fivefold. Together they make up "post-positivism." They were:

(1) *The evidence critique.* True minimal interpretations may not always be expressible in quantitative terms, and may require certain sorts of inference that are not reducible to observation (e.g., Denzin 1997, Denzin 1989).

(2) *The normative critique.* There are justifiable maximal interpretations that are not predictive or retrodictive explanations—for example, overarching interpretations of the character of certain societies and critiques of certain social relations as unjust (e.g., Bernstein 1978: 171–236).

(3) *The theory-relevance critique.* Maximal interpretations are not *only* grounded in minimal interpretations—they also rely upon theoretical, metatheoretical, or metahistorical "presuppositions." These presuppositions cannot be pared down to theories of the middle range (e.g., Alexander 1982, White 1973).

(4) *Dominance of theory critique.* Minimal interpretations are largely formed or determined by the maximal interpretations that they supposedly support—and perhaps they should be (Seidman 1994).

(5) *Sociology of science critique.* The theories an investigator "chooses" to help create maximal interpretations actually derive from social structural forces that act upon her—and thus a "sociology of sociology" is needed (Friedrichs 1970, Gouldner 1970).

It is the combination of (4) and (5) that leads to relativism, for if theories determine facts, and theory choice is determined by structural position and/or politico-economic interest, then, indeed, there is no such thing as the rational pursuit of true knowledge as it has been imagined in the Western philosophical tradition since Plato. Post-positivism should not be reduced to the combination of critiques (4) and (5), however. I will return to the sorts of epistemological positions often termed "postmodern" or "post-structural" later. For now, let us notice that these five post-positivist critiques open up a space wherein new intellectual formations for understanding and producing social knowledge can emerge, and ask what some of these intellectual formations are.

Interpretive Empiricism

One position that emerged into this space drew upon longstanding traditions of urban ethnography in sociology. It takes the evidential critique of positivism as central, and argues for qualitative evidence—and particularly ethnographic evidence of social actors in their "natural" settings—to be the basis of a new regime of sociological truth. Such a position can be highly "constructionist" in the sense of Blumer—objects enter social life in so far as they have meaning assigned to them by individuals engaged in interaction with other individuals (Blumer 1969).

This approach to social knowledge, articulated famously in *The Discovery of Grounded Theory* by Glaser and Strauss (1967), and carried forward by a variety of methodological positions concerning qualitative sociology and especially ethnography, is deeply suspicious of theory and highly attentive to locality. Originally positioned against the deductive armature of the Parsonian apparatus, it now resists both positivism and realism for the explicit reason that both fail to recognize the specificity of social context and the "persistence of the particular" (Wrong 2005).

This position has also integrated the sociology of science critique of positivism by interrogating repeatedly the investigator's role in the construction of knowledge with particular attention to possible dynamics of social power between the investigator and the investigated (Denzin 2003, Denzin and Giardina 2007). Nonetheless, the goal is still to have the case emerge from engagement with social reality as it is lived in this or that corner of the world.

Interpretive empiricism emphasizes the way in which minimal interpretations need to be constructed with actors' categories, and the way in which interaction must be attended to closely so as to grasp the construction of various social realities. What is less clear in such a position is how maximal interpretations are to be constructed, and what, exactly, they claim. One strand of epistemological thought on ethnography eschews both the generalization of findings *and* the claim to causally *explain* the case at hand. It is just this kind of devolution from strong knowledge claims that makes realism an appealing post-positivist alternative.

Realism

In 1962 Grover Maxwell published an article titled "The Ontological Status of Theoretical Entities," in which he argued fiercely, and with significant humor, against both instrumentalist and strictly empiricist or logical positivist philosophies of natural science. And, as his title indicated, he argued for a scientific realism based upon the idea that the theoretical terms used in natural scientific explanation (the very terms that empiricists wanted to eliminate or "reduce" to observation statements) were, in fact, real. The way in which he meant "real" was startlingly simple and, for many, immensely clarifying. Accepting that the sentences that make up scientific laws are where theoretical terms tend to be found, he argued that lawlike sentences

> tell us, for example, how theoretical entities of a given kind resemble, on the one hand, and differ from, on the other, the entities with which we happen to be more familiar. And the fact that many theoretical entities, for example those of quantum theory, differ a great deal from our ordinary everyday physical objects is no reason whatever to ascribe a questionable ontological status to them or to contend that they are merely "calculating devices." After all, the very air we breathe as well as shadows and mirror images are entities of quite different kinds from chairs and tables, but this provides no grounds for impugning their ontological status. (Maxwell 1962: 24)

Since the early sixties, the movement of scientific realism has taken off in philosophy, particularly via the work of Rom Harre (1963, 1993, Harre and Madden [1975]), Harre's student Roy Bhaskar (1993, 1979, 1997, 1989), Hilary Putnam (1987, 1975, 1983, 1988), and Mario Bunge (1959, 2006, 1996, 1977, 1998). It has also become an influential source of ideas for the philosophy of social science (Steinmetz 1998, Reed 2008).

Even within just this paragraph from Maxwell, however, we can find some highly suggestive ideas for how to think about social scientific knowledge in a post-positivist way. In particular, it might be that "society," "collective behaviors," "social structures," "opportunity structures," "the capitalist mode of production," or a myriad of other theoretical terms in sociology refer to entities that "differ a great deal from our ordinary everyday physical objects" but which are nonetheless still deserving of ontological status. Sociology might be the science of entities that are of a "quite different" kind.

The critique of positivism implied that theory mattered for building maximal interpretations, but it did not specify how it mattered. Realism fills this void. Realists argue for an ontological role for theoretical concepts and models. Thus, formally speaking, the post-positivist proposal of realism is:

(3') *Necessity of ontological theories.* Maximal interpretations are produced when social ontologies are used to explain minimal interpretations. Rational judgment enables minimal interpretations to "test" different theories—with different ontological commitments—and thus to produce the most true maximal interpretations.

This is the core idea of any realism. But there are different realisms, and their differences depend on how the evidential critique and the normative critique of positivism are handled. If, for example, quantitative data techniques are still generally valued as the most reliable and valid way to produce minimal interpretations, and normative critique is set aside as separate from the project of value-free inquiry, then the result is a sort of "realism-positivism" alliance such as that advocated by John Goldthorpe (2007) between Rational Action Theory and the Quantitative Analysis of Data. If, on the other hand, the evidential critique of positivism is taken on board *and* the normative critique of positivism is taken on board, then the result is Roy Bhaskar's critical realism, which accepts hermeneutics as a source of minimal interpretations and articulates a connection between social ontology and human emancipation (Bhaskar 1986).

The general move, in sociology, toward the identification of "mechanisms" as the main purpose of theory and as the driving, organizing force in empirical investigations, is commensurate with realism as a post-positivist epistemology. This is perhaps nowhere clearer than in Hedström's and Swedberg's differentiation of mechanism-based explanations from the avatar of positivist philosophy of science, the covering-law model. They object that positivism left the "black box" of causality unopened:

> The covering-law model provides justification for the use of "black-box" explanations in the social sciences because it does not stipulate that the mechanism linking *explanans* and *explanandum* must be specified in order for an acceptable explanation to be at hand. This omission has given leeway for sloppy scholarship, and a major advantage of the mechanism-based approach is that it provides (or encourages) deeper, more direct, and more fine-grained explanations. The search for generative mechanisms consequently helps us distinguish between genuine causality and coincidental association, and it increases the understanding of why we observe what we observe. (Hedström and Swedberg 1998: 8–9)

In the last instance, all varieties of social scientific realism are premised on the feasibility of social ontology. Several detailed objections to the reliance of various social scientific realisms on ontology have emerged in the theoretical literature recently (Kemp 2005, King 2004, Reed and Alexander 2009a). In a less precise way, however, the return to rationality claimed by realism has always had a post-positivist counterpoint in the skepticism of so-called postmodern epistemologies.

(Epistemological) Postmodernism

Doubts about realism can throw one into the arms of its avowed enemy: "postmodernism." *If* theory does not have a stable referent *and* we accept, to some degree, the critiques of positivism, then perhaps the correct answer is that maximal interpretations are impossible—or that maximal interpretations do not do what they claim to do, and are, as a result, not a reasonable or ethical goal for the human sciences. Despite the ease with which postmodernism and post-structuralism are often summarized, conflated, and dismissed, there are in fact a variety of issues that can be grouped under the moniker (specter?) of postmodern doubt. Three of them seem of particular importance to social science epistemology:

> Postmodern thesis 1: *Maximal interpretations are exercises in social power and domination.* To paraphrase Foucault, deep knowledge is made for cutting deeply.
>
> Postmodern thesis 2: *The primary source of maximal interpretations is either the "political" concerns or the "discursive" frame of the investigator.* That is, you can have maximal interpretations, but do not expect them to give you deeper knowledge of the case. Rather, maximal interpretations *use* the case to develop a politics of the present, or they mobilize the case in the service of an overarching vision of history, culture and/or society.
>
> Postmodern thesis 3: *Minimal interpretations are dependent to a high degree on the maximal interpretations they supposedly support, and maximal interpretations are as described in thesis 1 or thesis 2.* This is the thesis that strikes most directly at the regulating scholarly ideals of objectivity, the marshalling of evidence, and the possibility of supposedly un-interpreted "facts" or "truth." In the casual and pejorative references to postmodernism, this is probably what the term is used to indicate.

But there is no reason to think that because there is a politics to knowledge, there is *only* a politics to knowledge. Nor is there reason to think that all knowledge is implicated in the reproduction of social power to the same degree or in the same way. Epistemological postmodernism, then, is an extreme version of the critique of positivism. It is a position that closes down, rather than opening up, the possibility for a constructive post-positivist knowledge program which retains the social scientific imperative to investigate the empirical.

Cultural Sociology

The problem, then, for cultural sociology is that it does not "fit" any of these post-positivist epistemologies.[1] Its knowledge products are consistently theory-laden, and, thus, it is not a version of interpretive empiricism. It consistently relativizes, historicizes, or culturalizes claims about the direct causal effects of "social structure," which puts it at odds with the ontological program of realism and with general theories of society and social mechanisms. Finally, it is quite obviously engaged in making stable and strong knowledge claims, which belie any association between cultural sociology and postmodernism. So how does cultural sociology mold the critique of positivism into a new shape?

First, we might notice that cultural sociology embraces the evidential critique of positivism, but, rather than fetishising any particular method (such as participant observation), it adopts a methodological agnosticism. Cultural-sociological knowledge claims have been made on the basis of archival work, structured or unstructured interviews, survey data and linear regression, etc. While it tends to lean toward qualitative work, cultural sociology is not *in principle* opposed to quantification per se, *if* these methods can be used in a way that aids the interpretation and reconstruction of meaning rather than claiming to eliminate the problem of interpretation. In particular, there is contentious dispute *within* cultural sociology concerning whether abstract coding schemes enable an investigator to verify the existence of a meaning schema across a wide swath of texts or persons, or whether they disable the kind of contextually sensitive interpretation that form the basis for cultural sociology's ability to explain social action in the first place (Reed and Alexander 2009b). Thus, cultural sociology is not a method in the sense of insisting upon a single practical technique of gathering evidence, and it is not a methodology in the sense of curbing epistemic uncertainty via reliance on a certain method. For cultural sociology, the successful production of sociological truth requires the adept mobilization of theory.

Second, while the theory mobilized in cultural sociology can (and usually does) have a normative component, this is subordinated to the hermeneutic imperative to understand the meanings that surround action. To follow an argument of Bauman's (1987), cultural sociology is never willing to subsume the role of the interpreter to the role of the legislator. It thus shares a particular attitude towards immanent critique with the hermeneutics of Michael Walzer: a deep suspicion of the full-scale importation of utopian visions from elsewhere—and in particular from the theorist's head. Rather, cultural sociology follows Walzer's insight that "the moral world and the social world are more or less coherent, but they are never more than more or less coherent" (Walzer 1987: 22). Certainly, it could be said that meanings-in-society are never more than more or less coherent. Criticism, then, comes from the development of reinterpretations that exploit this state of affairs, bending and rebending the narratives of the public sphere, pushing on the contradictions between different sorts of democratic impulses, etc.

Thus, in cultural sociology, theory is mobilized to understand social reality. However, both this reality and the theories used to understand it are understood pluralistically. One of the implications of critical realism's call for social ontology is that general theories must be ontologically consistent with each other, since what they do is directly reference social reality *as such*. Cultural sociology, in contrast, questions whether the formalisms of general theory can ever give enough of an account of social reality to produce compelling explanations of action. Rather, it is the purpose of theory to bring out, in this or that case, deep meanings that are not immediately obvious to the investigator or to the investigator's subjects. These meanings, recovered and reconstructed, provide the real intellectual torque to social analysis. These theories can be quite varied: They need only to provide *case-centered insight* to be useful in the production of sociological truth. For cultural sociology, social reality does not exist *as such*, but rather emerges from historically specific meaning-structures (though these structures can be structures of the *longue durée*).

If cultural sociology is not politico-normative, ontological-realist, interpretive-empiricist, and relativist, what is it? I will argue that it is a program for the explanation of social action. Cultural sociology shares the goals of sociological research programs that are empiricist and realist, but is based on radically different presuppositions about how these goals are to be achieved.

The Presuppositions of Cultural Sociology as a Research Program in Social Science

The core activity of the cultural sociologist is to correctly interpret symbolic structures—to grasp the deep meanings that surround a certain set of social actions. But, if this activity is to be understood as leading the investigator to explanations of social action, what does it presuppose? In my view, symbolic interpretation presupposes the following: (1) reasons are causes, (2) cultural theory is nominalist, and (3) the sociohistorical world is metaphysically pluralist. Together, these presuppositions describe how the cultural sociologist is able to make explanatory knowledge claims about social life.

Reasons Are Causes

For most of the twentieth century—despite the articulate objections of the philosophy of history (e.g., Collingwood 1965, Collingwood 1946)—"explanation" was associated, in philosophy and in the social sciences, with the positivist search for covering laws, and explanation and interpretation were radically separated. In delving into the "black box" left unopened by positivism, realism has brought explicitly causal language out of the closet, but in so doing, it has maintained its distance from "interpretation."

The more ambiguous legacy of neo-pragmatism, and in particular the work of Donald Davidson, however, is suggestive of a quite different possibility. There are reasons to think, on the basis of Davidson's work, that one can identify causes in a more singular or "individualized" way that dovetails with the way cultural sociology uses theory to "ferret out hidden meanings" or, following Weber, uses theory to analyze "historical individuals," such as the spirit of capitalism.[2]

Davidson's iconic work in the philosophy of action and interpretation emerged at a time when the covering law model of scientific explanation was finally losing hold in analytical philosophy. His teacher, W.V.O. Quine, was instrumental in the general demise of logical positivism. Davidson took on one of the oldest divides in Western philosophy—the separation of mind and body. In particular, he challenged the longstanding empiricist notion that while the physical world was subject to causal relations, the mind was different: The relationship of reasons to actions was logical, not causal. Simultaneously, he refused to reduce the mental to the physical. He thus set out to show that, in terms of how we give explanations, there is no linguistic difference between pointing to a physical cause in an explanation and pointing to a reason. "He moved his hand off the stove because the stove was hot" provides a causal story about a certain action. So does the sentence, "He turned left because he wanted to get to Boulder, Colorado."

Davidson proceeded to explore the implications of this argument in many ways throughout his career and to buffer it with a variety of distinctions.[3] Importantly, Davidson argued that reasons may be causes even if their relationship to any sort of causal law is obscure. If an agent has certain pro-attitudes and beliefs, and if, in retrospect, we can see that these pro-attitudes and beliefs provide the reason why that agent acted in a certain way, then those pro-attitudes and beliefs are the cause of that action, *regardless of whether a more generalized regularity can be established between those "kinds" of pro-attitudes and beliefs and that "kind" of action.*

Furthermore, Davidson's definition of "pro-attitudes"—those states of mind that can combine with the beliefs of the actor to bring about an action—includes "desires, wanting, urges, promptings, and a great variety of moral views, aesthetic principles, economic prejudices, social conventions, and public and private goals and values in so far as these can be interpreted as attitudes of an agent directed toward actions of a certain kind" (Davidson 2006: 23). And, later on in the same, path-breaking essay, he insists explicitly that, concerning pro-attitudes, "Fortunately, it is not necessary to classify and analyze the many varieties of emotions, sentiments, moods, motives passions, and hungers whose mention may answer the question, 'why did you do it?'" (Davidson 2006: 26).

It is perhaps rather redundant to point out that, for the cultural sociologist, it is *absolutely necessary* for the researcher to classify and analyze the subjective origins of social action. What Davidson and the post-Davidsonian philosophy of action have developed, then, is an account of a human actor that works in tandem with cultural sociology's focus on collective representations. Agents act upon reasons. These reasons can be given as part of a causal explanation of an agent's action. But reasons can come from almost any sort of meaning-formation: aesthetics, morality, economic prejudices…the list goes on. Thus the upshot of the philosophy of action seems to be: to look for singular causes of actions in "reasons." But in order to discover the source of reasons, one must analyze social meaning.

This intellectual division of labor makes sense, since the philosophy of action, in principle at least, develops universal accounts of action that apply to all humans. The purpose of cultural sociological research, on the other hand, is to develop deeper understandings of certain historically located social actions. What the philosophy of action provides, then, is a sort of ontological substrate upon which more substantive and specific accounts of history and social action can be developed.

Davidson, then, gives us the broad, philosophical account of what must be true about actors if, as cultural sociologists intuit, the meanings they share in a certain time and space are what cause their action. The problem, then, for cultural sociology, comes down to this: What are the symbolic inputs to subjectively-guided social action? It is only in so far as cultural sociologists can marshal empirical evidence and theoretical understanding of this link that they will be able to claim that they are building sociological explanations.

Cultural Theory is Nominalist

In trying to figure out how this would work, it is all too easy to let go of the uniqueness of the cultural-sociological program for social knowledge. One could simply propose culture as the basis for the new realism: Create a universal model of culture, apply it widely, and claim that its explanatory scope is connected to its ability to theorize social life as such. This was the Parsonian project, to be sure, but it is also evident in Lévi-Strauss and in certain contemporary forms of neo-Durkheimianism. The pressure to move in this direction is immense, for in going this route, the investigator plays on the turf of the realists and claims the authority of science. The problem, however, is that cultural difference tends to foil these explanations, and their generality can be a tremendous weakness—particularly since the very premise of the cultural-sociological project is that we have to *understand* the subjects under study. However, in efforts to recognize the particular, it is all too easy to relinquish the structural imagination and the theory that goes with it. One *could* just tell a story via a string of immediate causes or stick only to actors' categories. But even if one finds this a satisfactory way to do investigation (and I do not), there remains the problem that the philosophers of history have made clear: Tropes and theoretical presuppositions sneak into such empiricist explanations anyway (White 1973).

It is to the credit of John R. Hall that he has confronted this dilemma directly in a paper, whose significance for social science epistemology cannot be underestimated, entitled "Cultural Meanings and Cultural Structures in Historical Explanation" (2000). Hall proposes that the generalized theories of cultural sociology only do half the work of explanation because the "abstracted generic cultural structures" (Hall 2000: 341) they articulate do not have concrete efficacy. The analyst can use theory to recognize these structures in her data, but in doing so she will not have arrived, yet, at an explanation. To the cultural structures, she must add the cultural meanings that intersect with them and fill them out. These "cultural meanings" are "invented, received, synthesized, reworked, and otherwise improvised idea-patterns" (Hall 2000: 341)—they are meaningful content with a *singular* history. Hall's argument is that it is only in the intersection of these two that culture can be said to have causal efficacy.

Hall's terminology is a little bit confusing, since the formal "structures" that repeat themselves across cultures (binary divisions, narratives, etc.) are routinely thought of as part of meaning as well, but his argument is right on the mark. Hall makes the distinction because he wants to be clear that the theoretical identification of "structures" never has direct, concrete grasp of the social actions under analysis. Rather, elucidating these structures prepares the ground for a deep understanding of the workings of particular symbol sets, at particular times, for particular people. The shared meanings that actually drive action thus combine structural "form" and historical "content," and only when the investigator has elucidated both, can she claim to have arrived at a cultural explanation of social action.

Hall thus makes clear a fundamental difference between cultural sociology and realism: *Cultural sociology does not ascribe ontological status to the formal structures that its theories articulate.* For this reason, its structural theories can function pluralistically—they do not have to, and indeed should not, combine into a single, coherent, Theory of Culture.[4] But the lack of a single coherent theory of culture does not mean that one cannot build cultural explanations. That is because the world of culture-in-social-action is itself pluralist; it is a "dappled world."

Metaphysical Pluralism

There is a clear implication of this approach towards theories of culture—the social world is constituted and re-constituted by meaning, and is thus pluralistic, as opposed to conforming to one ontological scheme.[5] Thus the world comes to its interpreters in socio-historical patches of structured meaning. A sociological realist would insist that the theoretical terms, such as "narrative" or "binary structure" so common to cultural-sociological analysis, must have a real referent if the explanations that cultural sociology builds with them are to make a claim to truth. This is the conceptual blackmail of realist post-positivism: *Either* cultural sociology is a covert realism of culture *or* it is postmodern, relativist, or "subjective." But in fact, cultural sociology is neither: Its theoretical terms are abstract and only describe the efficacy of culture when "fitted out" by certain concretely efficacious meanings (e.g., the specific binaries of contemporary civil society, the narrative structure of the American dream).

To take a well-known example, consider Geertz's nominalist use of Bentham's concept of "deep play"(2000a). For Geertz, "deep play" as an abstract object, it does not exist on its own. Rather, it only exists in so far as it is fitted out by certain concrete meanings, performed on the ground at certain times and in certain places. These are the pluralistic cultural worlds that the investigator confronts with her abstract theoretical terms. There *is* deep play at both a Balinese cockfight and an American dog track, but it is precisely the differences between these concrete instantiations of deep play that make the difference for explanation.

This turns cultural sociology towards a more historically sensitive, Weberian position, and away from the version of Saussure that Lévi-Strauss (1963) adopted and promulgated. When Saussure (1966) differentiated *langue* and *parole*, his mistake was not the distinction itself, but the radical way in which it was made, and the ensuing focus upon *langue* as the ontological reality of language—and later, for Lévi-Strauss, the ontological structure of kinship and culture. Saussure failed to recognize that, in their concrete and diachronic efficacy, *langue* and *parole* come together dialectically in something that Bahktin (1986) would later call speech genres and which we could analogize to Wittgenstein's forms of life. Something similar needs to be recognized by cultural sociology if it is going to carry the Saussurean legacy forward.[6]

For, it is the concrete forms of life that deliver the symbolic inputs into actors' acting intentionally. If reasons are causes, then it is not the formal structures of the symbolic environment for action that *alone* form the pro-attitudes and beliefs that make up reasons, but rather the speech genres and meaningful performances of social life that mold the reasons that motivate actors.

If we take this viewpoint, we can say that the following happens in cultural sociological explanation. The investigator's knowledge of abstract theory allows her to merge empirical knowledge of a case with a recognition of "cultural structures" and thus to grasp the deep meanings that give "structure to the conjuncture." Concretely, then, cultural sociology participates in the classic sociological mode of "structural" explanation. But the way in which it does this is historically sensitive, and, for this reason, theoretically pluralistic. Cultural sociology, to help generate explanations, theorizes the synchronic structures of culture; but these never explain social action by themselves. Rather, these abstract structures must be "fitted out" by specific, diachronic meanings—of coffee shops and cockfights, for example—to become the basis for explanatory knowledge claims. Cultural structures *as such* exist primarily in the heads of the theorists who theorize them. But when these structures are recognized in empirical evidence, and it becomes clear how they are fitted out by certain meanings at a certain place and time, the structures take on the power of the real, becoming part of the symbolic inputs into social action. This is the basis for a causal hermeneutics and a cultural sociology that is also a historical sociology.

Conclusion: Interpretation and Explanation

When, in the 1960s and 1970s, social theorists in the United States and Western Europe revolted against their teachers, they inaugurated, among other things, the cultural turn. In this context—where Clifford Geertz had to break from Talcott Parsons, Charles Taylor had to reject behaviorist political science, and an entire generation of French thinkers had (to try) to leave Jean-Paul Sartre and Claude Lévi-Strauss behind—the antagonism between "interpretive" perspectives and "scientism" may have been useful in a variety of ways. As a signifier for "anti-science" or "anti-positivism," however, the term risks, at this point in time, becoming an impediment to the development of interpretive thought itself. For, "interpretation" needs to show that the core task of sociological research—the explanation of social action—has been misconstrued. Cultural sociology, indeed, stands against a model of sociological research wherein explanations are constructed only in the terms of something called "external" causes, which are then shoehorned into an analogy with Aristotle's efficient causes or Hume's constant conjunctions. But it does not stand against the *goal* of social explanation, but rather the *means* currently hegemonic for getting there. Can we not develop a new set of causal imageries from our myriad investigations into the effect of symbols on human subjects? To do this while retaining interpretive sensitivity to the textuality and complex meanings of social life is the real challenge for cultural sociology. If it can meet this challenge, cultural sociology will have contributed to the sort of multidimensional, historical sociology envisioned by Max Weber, who took the position that "a correct causal interpretation of a concrete course of action is arrived at when the overt action and the motives have both been correctly apprehended and at the same time their relation has become meaningfully comprehensible" (1978: 12).

NOTES

1. Nor does cultural sociology have an external, political, or movement-based purpose to give it unity and thus allow a radical and productive epistemic pluralism—as do, for example, feminist studies or post-colonial studies.

2. It is important to emphasize that what follows is an honest attempt to read Davidson's intended meanings with the tremendous benefit of hindsight. Davidson backed away from a full condemnation of the covering law model, offering a "compromise view" in his article "Causal Relations" (1967). For further discussion of this compromise, see Heathcote and Armstrong (1991).

3. Some of these—such as the difference between beliefs and pro-attitudes—have been severely criticized in the philosophical literature. Davidson's other major contribution to philosophy was his work on "radical interpretation" and the principle of hermeneutic charity. He suggested that the interpretation of others necessarily invoked a certain commitment to seeing them as rational beings, most of whose beliefs are true—or, at least, we have to accept them as true if we are to learn how to communicate with these other people, and, possibly, to criticize some of their beliefs as false. These arguments are very close to those of Richard Rorty's anti-essentialist arguments concerning the pragmatics of interpretation and, as Charles Taylor has made exceedingly clear, run directly counter to the insights generated by meaning-centered social research (Taylor 1995, Taylor 2002). But we need not accept Davidson's ideas concerning the interpretation of others to consider the implications of the reasons-as-causes argument for cultural sociology.

4. This is a tension within cultural approaches in sociology that is perhaps most evident in the difference between Geertz, the pluralist and localist, and certain followers of Parsons, notably Richard Munch. See Geertz (2000b) and Munch and Smelser (1992).

5. Many of these arguments were inspired by, though ultimately they are different from, those of Nancy Cartwright in *The Dappled World* (1999). There, she also develops a nominalist attitude towards theoretical terms (she compares the relationship between theory in physics and the causal sequences it can actually model to the relationship between a moral and the fable that exemplifies it), and she connects this nominalism to a "metaphysical nomological pluralism." This she conceives on the order of Aristotelian

searches for "natures." I share a good deal of Cartwright's attitude toward the relationship between the abstract and the concrete in theory and research. However, I would maintain that the historical "dappledness" or pluralism of the human world is itself constituted, in part, by the role of concepts and worldviews—something, of course, which one does not have to grapple with in physics, no matter what other difficulties and uncertainties attend to scientific study.

    6. This amounts to a more hermeneutic reading of Saussure, the ultimate philosophical reference being Dilthey (1976, 1996). See also Simmel (1980).

REFERENCES

Alexander, Jeffrey C. 1982. *Theoretical logic in sociology.* Berkeley: University of California Press.

Bakhtin, M. M. 1986. *Speech genres and other late essays.* Austin: University of Texas Press.

Bauman, Zygmunt. 1987. *Legislators and interpreters: on modernity, post-modernity, and intellectuals.* Ithaca, NY: Cornell University Press.

Bernstein, Richard J. 1978. *The restructuring of social and political theory.* Philadelphia: University of Pennsylvania

Bhaskar, Roy. 1979. *The possibility of naturalism: a philosophical critique of the contemporary human sciences.* Atlantic Highlands, NJ: Humanities Press.

———. 1986. *Scientific realism and human emancipation.* London: Verso.

———. 1989. *Reclaiming reality: a critical introduction to contemporary philosophy.* London; New York: Verso.

———. 1993. *Dialectic: the pulse of freedom.* London; New York: Verso.

———. 1997. *A realist theory of science.* London; New York: Verso.

Blumer, Herbert. 1969. *Symbolic interactionism: perspective and method.* Englewood Cliffs, NJ: Prentice-Hall.

Bunge, Mario Augusto. 1959. *Causality: the place of the causal principle in modern science.* Cambridge, MA: Harvard University Press.

———. 1977. *Ontology.* Dordrecht, The Netherlands; Boston: Reidel.

———. 1996. *Finding philosophy in social science.* New Haven, CT: Yale University Press.

———. 1998. *Social science under debate: a philosophical perspective.* Toronto; Buffalo: University of Toronto Press.

———. 2006. *Chasing reality: strife over realism.* Toronto: University of Toronto Press.

Cartwright, Nancy. 1999. *The dappled world: essays on the perimeter of science.* Cambridge, UK; New York: Cambridge University Press.

Collingwood, R. G. 1946. *The idea of history.* Oxford: Clarendon Press.

———. 1965. *Essays in the philosophy of history.* Austin: University of Texas Press.

Davidson, Donald. 1967. "Causal relations." *Journal of Philosophy* 64: 691–703.

———. 2006. "Actions, reasons, and causes." In *The essential Davidson.* New York: Oxford University Press.

Denzin, Norman K. 1989. *Interpretive interactionism.* Newbury Park, CA: Sage Publications.

———. 1997. *Interpretive ethnography: ethnographic practices for the 21st century.* Thousand Oaks, CA: Sage Publications.

———. 2003. *Performance ethnography: critical pedagogy and the politics of culture.* Thousand Oaks, CA: Sage Publications.

Denzin, Norman K. and Michael D. Giardina. 2007. *Ethical futures in qualitative research: decolonizing the politics of knowledge*. Walnut Creek, CA: Left Coast Press.

Dilthey, Wilhelm. 1976. "The construction of the historical world in the human studies." In H. P. Rickman, ed. *Dilthey: selected writings*. New York: Cambridge University Press.

———. 1996. *Selected works, Volume IV: hermeneutics and the study of history*. Princeton, NJ: Princeton University Press.

Durkheim, Emile. 1982. *The rules of sociological method*. New York: Free Press.

Friedrichs, Robert Winslow. 1970. *A sociology of sociology*. New York: Free Press.

Geertz, Clifford. 2000a. "Deep play: notes on the Balinese cockfight." In *The interpretation of cultures*. New York: Basic Books.

———. 2000b. "Thick description: toward an interpretive theory of culture. In *The interpretation of cultures*. New York: Basic Books.

Glaser, Barney G. and Anselm L. Strauss. 1967. *The discovery of grounded theory: strategies for qualitative research*. Chicago: Aldine Publishing Company.

Goldthorpe, John H. 2007. *On sociology*. Stanford, CA: Stanford University Press.

Gouldner, Alvin Ward. 1970. *The coming crisis of Western sociology*. New York: Basic Books.

Hall, John R. 2000. "Cultural meanings and cultural structures in historical explanation." *History and Theory* 39: 331–347.

Harré, Rom. 1963. *An introduction to the logic of the sciences*. London, New York: Macmillan; St. Martin's Press.

———. 1993. *Laws of nature*. London; Newburyport, MA: Duckworth; distributed in United States by Focus Information Group.

Harre, Rom and E. H. Madden. 1975. *Casual powers: a theory of natural necessity*. Oxford: B. Blackwell.

Heathcote, Adrian and D. M. Armstrong. 1991. "Causes and laws." *Nous* 25(1): 63–73.

Hedström, Peter and Richard Swedberg, Eds. 1998. *Social mechanisms: an analytical approach to social theory*. Cambridge, UK; New York: Cambridge University Press.

Kemp, Stephen. 2005. "Critical realism and the limits of philosophy." *European Journal of Social Theory* 8(2): 171–191.

King, Anthony. 2004. *The structure of social theory*. London; New York: Routledge.

Lévi-Strauss, Claude. 1963. *Structural anthropology*. New York: Basic Books.

Maxwell, G. 1962. "The ontological status of theoretical entities." *Minnesota Studies in the Philosophy of Science* 3: 3–27.

Munch, Richard and Neil J. Smelser, Eds. 1992. *Theory of culture*. Berkeley, CA, University of California Press.

Putnam, Hilary. 1975. *Mind, language, and reality*. Cambridge, UK; New York: Cambridge University Press.

———. 1983. *Realism and reason*. Cambridge, UK; New York: Cambridge University Press.

———. 1987. *The many faces of realism*. La Salle, IL: Open Court.

———. 1988. *Representation and reality*. Cambridge, MA: MIT Press.

Reed, Isaac. 2008. "Justifying sociological knowledge: from realism to interpretation." *Sociological Theory* 26(2): 101–129.

Reed, Isaac and Jeffrey Alexander. 2009a. "Social science as reading and performance: a cultural-sociological understanding of epistemology." *European Journal of Social Theory* 12(1): 21–41.

Reed, Isaac and Jeffrey C. Alexander. 2009b. *Meaning and method: the cultural approach to sociology*. Boulder, CO: Paradigm Publishers.

Saussure, Ferdinand de. 1966. *Course in general linguistics*. New York: McGraw-Hill.

Seidman, Steven. 1994. *The Postmodern turn: new perspectives on social theory*. New York: Cambridge University Press.

Simmel, Georg. 1980. *Essays on interpretation in social science.* Totowa, NJ: Rowman & Littlefield.

Steinmetz, G. 1998. "Critical realism and historical sociology. A review article." *Comparative Studies in Society and History* 40(1): 170–186.

Taylor, Charles. 1995. "Overcoming epistemology." In *Philosophical arguments.* Cambridge, MA: Harvard University Press.

———. 2002. "Foundationalism and the inner-outer distinction." In Nicholas H. Smith, ed. *Reading McDowell: On Mind and World.* London: Routledge.

Walzer, Michael. 1987. *Interpretation and social criticism.* Cambridge, MA: Harvard University Press.

Weber, Max. 1978. *Economy and society: an outline of interpretive sociology.* Berkeley: University of California Press.

———. 2003. *The Protestant ethic and the spirit of capitalism.* Mineola, NY: Dover Publications.

White, Hayden V. 1973. *Metahistory: the historical imagination in nineteenth-century Europe.* Baltimore: Johns Hopkins University Press.

Wrong, Dennis Hume. 2005. *The persistence of the particular.* New Brunswick, NJ: Transaction Publishers.

CHAPTER 3

....

RATIONALIZATION PROCESSES INSIDE CULTURAL SOCIOLOGY

....

RICHARD BIERNACKI

EVERY sociologist may recall from Max Weber how rationalization processes across the arts call on spatial metaphors to create methods of representation. Western Europe distinguished itself, Weber said, by "that type of classic rationalization of all art—in painting by the rational utilization of lines and spatial perspective—which the Renaissance created for us" (Weber 2001, xxx). Rationalization, in this instance, means that representation no longer clings to bodily sense experience of objects, but relies on the emptied formalism of extensional lines. Correlatively for European music, form triumphed over meaningful reception. Weber said that late-medieval church composers abstracted sound into a new analytic dimension—tonality—apart from the original physical dimensions of stringed or wind instruments. This pure continuum of tonality, with its quasi-spatial distances between notes, established an aesthetic iron cage: It threw Western music, Weber said, "repeatedly into long dragging chains" (Weber 2004, 253).

My purpose is to explore the habits by which cultural sociologists, as rationalizing artists with regard to social meaning rather than of just sound or sight, rely on analytic continua with spatial scaling and with potentially similar reifying effects. By "spatial scaling" I refer only to investigation and explanation that relationally *ranks* cases on an imagined "dimension" as, for example, "near" versus "far" from an endpoint or as "high" versus "low." A familiar instance is Pierre Bourdieu's model for interpreting every kind of aesthetic, social, or corporeal action by its scalable symbolic "distances" from economic necessity and by the agents' relational locations in a shared social "space." Thus, "the literary field is a space of objective relations

between positions" (Bourdieu 1993, 179). Bourdieu is a convenient point of reference, but my intent is not to target a particular substantive theory. Instead my purpose is to use the figure of spatial scaling as a point of entry to uncover the basic
logic by which many sociologists have come to conceive the relation between what
is culturally meaningful and what lies "outside" culture (or our concept of culture).
How sociologists invoke what lies "outside" culture shapes their use of evidence and
their ability to grasp meanings from the ground up. It constitutes their evidentiary
practices when they imagine that the terms they adopt *or* dispute—such as class or
technology, like mass printing—have obviously given referents in human history. It
also enables them to mistake their own constructs as purely "analytic" when these
constructs actually pre-shape the form in which we recognize the contexts, thus the
meanings, of human practice. "Analytic" or hypothetical continua thereby *operate*
as if they were objective extra-linguistic pigeonholes enframing the culture under
examination. What is "outside" culture also constitutes inquiry when sociologists
distinguish what is conventionally recognized within a culture by contrasting it to a
naturally shared "world"—whatever that supposedly shared thing is that different
cultures divide up in different ways. To show that these self-mystifying operations
are typically effected by applying a theory with an implicit "spatial" structure, I will
dissect four extremely disparate and widely telling exemplars of cultural research.
Each of them correlates rankings across two or more spatial scales, and in so doing,
I think, each mistakes their own abstractions for how the meanings work that they
aspire to excavate and explain. These four exemplars suggest that cultural sociology
would benefit from dialogue with skeptical counter-principles for establishing—
and questioning—our objects of explanation. I will introduce three such counter-
principles that ring superficially like anti-realistic or even "postmodern" principles
but are required to read cultural and historical sources with greater restraint and
rigor. A positive case model, Gareth Stedman Jones's *Languages of Class*, shows how
these propaedeutics can work and how they awaken critical reassessment of accumulated findings.

Cultural sociologists implicitly position practices and cultural artifacts in spatial frames when they isolate a new "dimension" of meaning in social life, envisioned
as an analytic continuum. In cultural sociology, we encounter not just Pierre
Bourdieu's high versus low cultural expertise, but automatic versus deliberative
cognition diagrammed in a "space of orientations to action" (DiMaggio 2002, 277);
high versus low accumulations of "symbolic capital" by states as they organize social
relations (Loveman 2005); substantive versus formal rationality charted by gradually shifting degrees (Evans 2009, 219); or a cultural "median point" between the
human and the nonhuman orders (Latour 1993, 86, 96). Used self-critically, extensional dimensions are inspiring tools. When we treat them as norms in searching for
meanings and for organizing findings, however, we turn them into an obscure formalism as Weber diagnosed.

My hypothesis is that spatial imagery and its affiliated habits of "seeing as" are
distorting as models "for" reality when sociologists base their explanations on a set
of practices that I call "parallel scaling." This transpires when investigators explain

cultural outcomes by correlating positions across two or more quasi-spatial scales, as Bourdieu correlates high/middle/low cultural positions with allegedly underlying high/middle/low social locations. Let me identify the reifying effects of this reliance on spatial dimensions by introducing a rich parable from which I can extract a model for sociology.

The Domain of Color as a Paradigm for Cultural Analysis

Perhaps the preeminent textbook example of how cultural practices generate meanings and reference in social life is the creation of distinct color categories from the spectrum of hues in the rainbow (Brown 1965, pp. 315–316). Most everyone recognizes infinitely graduated hues as a pre-given dimension without naturally given breaks or units. Cultures seem to sponsor color categories by conventionally segmenting this spectrum and not by naming pregiven discrete essences. By slicing into the spectrum at different points, communities may combine hues that English speakers separate or create finer distinctions we fail to recognize. Imposing arbitrary divisions on a shared universal is a paradigm for culture among many sociologists. As Evitar Zerubavel has written, "Cultures carve different archipelagos of meaning out of *the same* reality" (Zerubavel 1997, my emphasis).

Notice how the "arbitrariness" of culture from this point of view requires that we take for granted an extra-linguistic referent "outside" culture. In the domain of color, the referent is an extensional continuum because the spectrum of hues either sets up distances between the colors or positions them as spatial "opposites" on the color wheels many of us have absorbed from school. The explanatory issue posed by such purified spatial arranging is of the kind that Karl Marx took up in his own version of cultural analysis. Marx sought to explain the creation of reified universals, as he did most famously for the commercial abstractions of bourgeois society. In his analysis of exchange value as such, not just of variation in commodity values, Marx pursued an analogue to our question here. That question is how *did* historical agents come to posit the color spectrum itself as natural and universal? We seem ready to acknowledge that this linear dimension's subcategories, the color distinctions, are contingent and human-made. But this absurdly begs the question of how people cognized and created the linear dimension of a spectrum of hues in the first place. (Marx parodied a perfectly analogous inversion when he ridiculed how the linear dimension of exchange value appears natural whereas the specific use-values of commodities appear arbitrary in bourgeois society (Marx 1990, 177).) Spatial dimensions in cultural sociology often work similarly as "natural" preexistent containers for sub-distinctions.

From historical and ethnographic records, it appears that the whole arena of colors, as an isolable dimension of reality, is scarcely a given. Many cultures do not recognize it as a lexical domain (Lucy 1997, 330). This is spectacularly apparent in places like Bellona Island in Polynesia, where speakers make seemingly color-like analogies between objects based on whether the objects are vertical, expansive, or impress sharp emotional experiences. For example, the Bellonese employed a term for "large, light-colored surfaces often standing in a vertical position," which included bleached walls of a house, piled objects, and hanging mats (Kuschel and Monberg 1974, 221, 228–229). Closer to our own language, Old English lacked a word for color, but used several for the domain of "appearance," including brightness and texture (Barley 1974, 21).

This multifariousness should not astound. Colorific appearances reach us bundled with the shapes and configurations of moving objects that shift by illumination. Accordingly, we may have learned to think of color as an atemporal state, but in many cultures it seems more like an event or a process (Dixon 1982). The ancient Greeks and medieval Europeans, for example, had adjectives for indicating how dark surfaces actively gleamed (Irwin 1974, 202; Saunders and van Brakel 1997, 176). Something like "green" in ancient Greek was linguistically a becoming, a term applicable to liquids that flowed, such as tears or honey, or to substances that displayed moistening (Irwin 1974, 29, 201). The indubitable reality of color experience does not instruct cultural analysts how to take it apart.

We engage a tantalizing question when we ask, how did Europeans come to institutionalize color as an independent "dimension" of experience with its own valences and orderings by hue? Social scientific accounts that take color based on hue as a natural dimension "outside" culture seem always to end up with a story in which the historical endpoint for foreign cultures is recognizing color as modern Europeans do. The instigating exemplar of such accounts was that of Brent Berlin and Paul Kay, who concluded in 1969 that "there exist universally for humans eleven *basic* perceptual color categories, which serve as the psychophysical referents of the eleven or fewer *basic* color terms in any language" (Brent and Kay 1969, 104, my emphasis). In this research tradition, history actualizes a dimension that was bound to exert its influence, a trope, which, we shall see, almost always follows from scaling cultural outlooks to natural referents (MacLaury, 1992).

To sketch an alternative approach, let me suggest how color was constructed out of what sociologists of science call nomological practices: standardized ways of manipulating materials and describing them in a manner that causes stable phenomena to emerge (Cartwright, 2002). In Middle English what we look back on as hue, brightness, and luminosity all contributed together as to how people applied color-like terms (Burnley 1976, 44; Ostheeren 1971, 47). The contingent, peculiar practice that isolated and stabilized hue and its description as a fixed entity was in all likelihood the growth of commerce in dyed fabrics. Change in the semantic field for color in English, for example, was driven by the importation of bright fabric and dye ingredients from the Levant and then from Renaissance Italy. The dyes sponsored a cognitive refocusing on color as a discrete state of an object. Business institutions in dyed fabrics created an independent realm of equivalencies and contrasts. In Chaucer's English, words such as "hue" occurred more frequently in reference to dyes, clothing, and textiles than in reference to animals or foliage (Biggam 1993, 53). By 1600, therefore, English speakers separated "color" from other adjectives for appearances. Merchant regulations and guild statutes standardized dyes to guarantee consistency for far-flung customers, who treated color as the literal substance of a transaction. Dye processes were standardized by allotting workshops (or whole guilds) to use just one type of textile fiber and/or color (Nieto-Galan 1996, 27; Greenfield 2005, 16–17). Hue became a model "for" color by replicable craft techniques. When Newton in the eighteenth century showed how hues could be calibrated as constituents of colorless sunlight, colors received their particular positions along an experimentally purified spatial dimension, be it a linear gradation or a circular wheel of hues (Kuehni and Schwarz 2008, 124, 341–343). Yet to this day skeptical cognitive scientists fail to confirm that hue is a genuinely separable entity either in human perception or along our neural channels (Saunders and van Brakel 1997).

From this paradigmatic case, let me preview the misleading effects of parallel scaling in cultural sociology.

(1) A "decontextualizing effect": Because it posits degrees of a generalizable quality or substance behind a community's historically peculiar signifying practices, an extensional continuum would have us imagine there is an essence behind our linguistic representations as well, be it "intellectual energy," symbolic capital, social discipline, or what have you. Hue is ready at hand. We can point to it in experience; but what makes it a natural kind that precedes the invention of a culture's color categories? The extensional scale unjustifiably posits a neutral meta-language for comparing color lexicons across histories and regions (Forster 1998, 412).

(2) A "flattening effect": Applying a spatial dimension is apt to suppress potential anomalies by positioning odd cases somewhere between poles, "in the middle," or, given the abstractness of the dimension, as "tending" one way without further analysis of what such a claim entails. This is apparent when research requires linguistic translation. No matter what, the sociologist is authorized to translate artifacts into the natural terms of the continuum to see what the artifacts "really" mean. For three decades, Kay and Berlin tinkered with their conversion of color distinctions in foreign cultures onto our own scaling of hue. Important anomalies remained indigestible. Some cultural communities used two terms for yellow, one which applied to black as well; others used the same term for both white and red (Saunders 2007, 472; van Brakel 1993; Saunders and van Brakel 2001, 542). These interpretive challenges are secondary only if we "know" the dimension of hue is a self-standing core referent (Forster 1998, 410; Saunders 2000).

The practical lesson for cultural analysts is to appreciate the epistemological gains of bracketing any assumption of a shared referent for what we call color or hue, as well as for other rubrics, as we shall see. In Middle English, for example, color-like distinctions were embedded in evaluative and explanatory models as much as in a descriptive lexicon. When a male poet portrayed his beloved as having "grei" eyes and compared them to grey swords, he invoked the causal power of brightness over

	Starting Point (underlying dimension that ranks values of a variable)	Intermediary Bridge (operant that translates the starting point to the end point)	End point (reemergence of the original rankings on a parallel dimension)
Segmenting the spectrum into color categories	Differing wave-lengths of light, spectrum of hues	Individuals' and groups' color perceptions	Positioning of colors on dimension of hue
Bourdieu: Distinction or work on "The Literary Field"	High versus low capital resources in a complex space of positions	Habitus	High versus low status cultural consumption and cultural creation
Randall Collins: Sociology of Intellectuals	Relative density and centrality of a philosopher's network ties	High versus low creative energy, strategic network insight	Individual philosopher's accomplishments
Philip Gorski: Disciplinary Revolution	Theological and institutional resources for surveillance	Social discipline, high versus low	Collectively efficacious order, state efficiency
	"Isolates" independent variables and provides materials of continuity that underpin the translation of inputs into outputs	All-purpose but theoretically ambiguous operant. Merges objective conditions and subjectivity; mediates individual and collective levels of analysis; mixes utilitarian adaptation and semiotic logic	Dependent variable explicitly operationalized; "observed" parallels across dimensions substitutes for inquiry into qualitative mechanisms by which the bridge variable produces the outcome

Figure 3.1 The Logic of Parallel Scaling

people (Burnley 1976, 44; Ostheeren 1971, 47; Biggam 1993, 51). The Middle English equivalents of our "black" and "brown," dark as they seem to us, could mark a type of glow and thereby indicate what we take as an opposite, the holy clarity of light. We escape our native pigeon holes only by suspending the "natural" referents of color.

PARALLEL SCALING

Parallel scaling in cultural sociology, as in the domain of color, proceeds in three stages. As in Figure 3.1, it starts with a "spatial dimension" that establishes the infra-structure for imagining substantial continuity in the social process that translates an introductory scale into a final cultural scale (for color, this natural infrastructure is wave lengths of light). Then the scaling interposes a kind of "bridge variable" that enables the social agents under examination to effect the correlations among positions on the scales (for the domain of color, "perception"). Parallel scaling concludes by portraying the final outcome on a new scale as a re-expression of positions on the inaugural one (for color, distinctions of hue). To expose the conceptual limits of Figure 3.1, the final exemplar from cultural sociology (Gorski 2003) is partially resistant to my typification, making evident this table's potential ambiguities.

As diagrammed, the "bridge variable" is always a human action with the status of a metaphysical hybrid. This variable mediates between objective conditions and subjective experience, between collective constraints and individual action, and ultimately, between the order of pragmatic adaptation versus that of semiotic logic. Few if any theories surpass these aporia. All I wish to indicate is that the theoretical tensions concentrate in the bridge variable, as with Bourdieu's protean habitus, for example. The habitus is both constraining and improvisational, a passive register of social space and still agentic, indeed, a combination of so many opposites it has led many a critic to despair (Alexander 1995, 128–216).

Second Case Study: Bourdieu's Parallel Scaling

As Figure 3.1 recalls for us, Bourdieu conceives the economy, and its nested "fields" of social positions, through metaphors of spatial dimensions and locations. It functions similarly to physical space in physics as that which lies behind socio-cultural phenomena—in this instance, practice—as a naturally pre-given grid or frame. "The principle of division into logical classes which organizes the perception of the social world is itself the product of the internalization of the division into social classes" (Bourdieu, 2007, 170). Exactly as the imputed variable of color perception bridges two universes—the positions in the spectrum of light versus the appropriation of those positions in distinctive forms of cultural expression—so Bourdieu's concept of habitus translates the ranked "spectrum" of socio-economic positions into symbolic production and expression. "The habitus is a metaphor of the world of objects" (Bourdieu 1990, 76–77). Let me focus on how Bourdieu's dimensions come to life as "real" through rigidified evidentiary practices.

"Decontextualizing Effect": The habitus is above all an essence that each person mobilizes whatever the context of action. Habitus as an accustomed mode of consumption "is the generative formula of a life-style, a unitary set of distinctive preferences which express the same expressive intention in the specific logic of each of the symbolic sub-spaces, furniture, clothing, language or body hexis" (Bourdieu 2007, 173.) By attending to how data artifacts can be inserted into positions on spatial scales in Bourdieu's *Distinction*, we overlook more basic questions about culture in action. Why does Bourdieu, in his celebrated test situations in *Distinction*, forego the study of the agents' actual engagement in practices of art or music? Bourdieu instead elicits statements from the agents *about* art and music in a setting saturated with social judgment, tapping into the agents' test-taking savvy and knowledge of what counts as high-status answers (Rancière 2003, 187). If Bourdieu had examined the agents' in situ appreciations of music and their immediate lived relation to it, he might have discovered how the corporeally embedded habitus takes shape in the individual and genuinely unfolds before us. But inquiry outside a setting of overt social judgment could uncover a plethora of qualitatively distinct modes of engagement with music, independent of status concerns. Instead, Bourdieu's response-situations and test instruments represent controls that create data capable of registering only the priority of Bourdieu's own dimensions of social location.

After he elicited second-order commentaries *about* culture, Bourdieu ranked these artifacts of "taste" on a class scale by cultivating a peculiar way of looking at tables. We learn to see and "know" that *overlaps* in tastes across classes are "noise," whereas slight *differences* in distributions are "essential." For instance, in Bourdieu's data, a *majority* of respondents from every combination of class and educational backgrounds believes that a sunset over the sea can make a beautiful photograph (Bourdieu 2007, 38). Despite this relative consensus, Bourdieu contends there is a powerful link between the sunset theme and lower-class taste because he has primed us to assume a priori there is an intrinsic tether between the pregiven dimension of classes and the correlative metric of tastes. Football "combines all features that repel the dominant class," including "submission to collective discipline" and "the exaltation of competition." Yet the upper-most class, the senior executives and professionals, regularly practice football at about the average rate as others. The portion of male respondents who regularly play football varies from 2.5 to 6 percent across class fractions, with 4 percent of the senior executives and professionals playing. The majority of respondents in each class practiced no sport (Bourdieu 2007, 214, 216). It is enough to map the taste overlaps *at the level of the individual* across spatially distant social classes, Tony Bennett has shown, to discredit the assumption that "classes constitute—in their relation to each other—the bases for unified habitus" (Bennett 2008, 62, 70; Lahire 2004, 164).

"Flattening Effect": Jacques Rancière held the flattening effect up for examination when he satirized Bourdieu's use of evidence in "The Sociologist King" (Rancière 2003, 165–202). Bourdieu in *Distinction* elicited the operation of the habitus by having test subjects comment upon a photograph of an old woman's hands. The aesthetic disposition toward such an image from Bourdieu's perspective is "a generalized capacity to neutralize ordinary urgencies and to bracket ends," a disposition that requires a remoteness from the practical exigencies of the social world that only economic privilege can sustain (Bourdieu 2007, 54). But as Rancière indicates, Bourdieu's universal spectrum of classes and of correspondingly stratified tastes suppresses in advance the significance of non-confirming evidence. Bourdieu located responses' "distance from the world" by ad hoc reframing. The low-standing clerical worker who remarks, "It's as if it was a painting that had been photographed," on the face of it seems more aesthetically engrossing than the high-standing teacher who says, "These two hands unquestionably evoke a poor and unhappy old age" (Bourdieu 2007, 44–45). More basically, Bourdieu assumes that his scale of aesthetic distance, the underlying dimension of all comments on art, *always* is in evidence in a phenomenon. So he assumes without ado that an unwillingness to engage one's aesthetic disposition with a particular stimulus—photography—is a token of the general absence of such a formal disposition overall.

For cultural sociology, the issue is how parallel scaling authorizes the controls that make Bourdieu's linear dimensions of ranking emerge as natural. In *Distinction*, for example, they require that we take a respondent's choice out of fixed-answer options, *not* as portraying an agent engaged in an interview situation, but as the signature of the unitary entity of the habitus outside the particular social involvement (Danziger 1990, 192). For football, for instance, Bourdieu legislates what the sport "is" as a meaningful referent across class cultures: Football "repels" the dominant class because of the experience it imparts to its players of subordination to a team. To make the data fit the parallel scaling of class and cultural taste, we have to accustom ourselves to seeing this feature of football as intrinsic and salient, independent of experiential evidence. And we have to imagine that there such a general cross-cultural revulsion by elites against collective discipline (forgetting, say, the Oxford/Cambridge rowing clubs). In sum, to make the linear scaling work, we have to induct ourselves into a scientific culture in which there are essential correlating linear dimensions already "there," and our job is to naturalize translation into them—just, as, in the domain of color, we "should" be able to translate color practices into the purified dimension of hue.

THIRD CASE STUDY: FROM NETWORKS TO IDEAS

There is no exemplar of parallel scaling more ambitious than that of Randall Collins's sprawling volume, *The Sociology of Philosophies*. Collins's bridge variable for explaining the invention of philosophical work is creative, intellectual enthusiasm, a variable that functions for parallel scaling, at least, in much the same way as does the habitus. It bridges the objective network of intellectual positions, the initial cause, to the final output, the composition of enduringly creative, philosophical work throughout world history. Collins converts the intellectuals' relative accomplishments into a spatial dimension by measuring the page space dedicated to each of their life works in reference histories and handbooks of philosophy (Collins 1998, 58). Likewise, Collins scales each philosopher's network centrality by ties to other highly influential thinkers. Then, Collins describes how network resources translate into high accomplishment: "Creative enthusiasm is nothing but the emotional energy specific to intellectuals who are in those crucial network positions....To say that the community of creative intellectuals is small is really to say that the networks are focused at a few peaks" (Collins 1998, 52, 78). Network centrality lends a thinker the most up-to-date cultural capital, emotional support, and sense of where the action is. These drivers make networks, not people, the genuine causes, necessary and sufficient, of new ideas (Collins 1998, 77). How does this powerful sociological argument predetermine the appraisal of social meanings on the ground?

"Decontextualizing effect": By locating works on an extensional continuum of relative creativity, Collins reifies philosophy as a ghostly dimension that stands *behind* its exemplifying practices. As Collins explains it, philosophy's content is to formulate ideas with great generality. This transpires whenever a community of intellectual specialists appears. If Plato and Socrates had never inaugurated the demands for separating knowledge from word games, the unending chatter of the Sophists would still count for Collins as the unfolding of philosophy. Just as "color" was turned into a fact that preexisted any culture's recognition of it, so philosophy is converted into a natural fact that exists outside particular traditions of reasoning. That is how Collins compares versions of science, religion, mathematics, and ethics across civilizations as *necessarily* indexing "the same" compacted, cross-cultural referent. What if the pages of coverage in history reviews, by which Collins measures a philosopher's creativity, were an artifact of post hoc, formulaic canons? No problem, because the universal object of study—"general" ideas—stands above any particular meanings or object-instances. To be sure, Collins can present a chronicle which illustrates his circular assumption that the spread of ideas in a network reflects the ability of savvy intellectual producers to satisfy market demands. For a cultural sociology that was not hijacked by this a priori scaling of network ranking to creativity ranking, the interpretive challenges would include understanding *how* a philosophical question was formulated; *why* it seemed to hold people in its grip; and *what* made an answer seem less puzzling than the question—cultural "mechanisms," if you will (Forster 1998, 427).

The a priori scaling of networks into parallel levels of creativity obviates demonstration of their correlation. Genuine inquiry would gauge the distribution of the independent variable, network position, across the population of philosophers in the field. Instead, Collins samples on the dependent variable to exclude from view anyone who enjoyed high network centrality but who might have demonstrated minimal accomplishments. Consider Collins' map of ties in the German Network, 1735–1835 (Collins 1998, 624). No one had more interlocutors and personal intellectual ties with the greats featured in Collins' diagram—which includes Fichte, Schelling, and Hegel—than did Prof. Dr. Friedrich Immanuel Niethammer, co-editor after 1797 of Germany's philosophical clearing house in Jena. For example, much of what we know about Hegel's personal thinking comes from Niethammer, one of Hegel's closest friends after 1800 (Hegel 1961, 4: 273). Despite exceptionally favorable network resources, Niethammer does not appear in the diagram because he had no memorable accomplishments (Wenz 2008; Schelling 1962, 1:61; Fichte December 6, 1968, 1793). Worthy intellectual nobodies like Niethammer were networked everywhere. By circularly self-fulfilling logic, however, Collins effaces from his diagram all evidence of such persons who could challenge his parallel scaling of network ties to accomplishment.

The phenomenon of network centrality is a transhistorical variable whose form and function can be represented in the same network diagrams no matter what the venues of communication, sociality, technologies of publication, or institution supports. Any scrap of philosophical communication can "stand for" a pre-existing network. For example, Collin constructs a secure incubating position for David Hume, esteemed by some as the greatest philosopher in modern times. Hume presented his complete philosophical system as a young man in his staggering work, the *Treatise of Human Nature*. But Hume left school at age 14 with no record of distinction. Hume disparaged formal education, wrote the *Treatise* in extraordinary isolation abroad, and so far as the record reveals, deliberately did not discuss a single idea of the *Treatise* with anyone in Collins' network diagram until the whole was a system and on its way to a printer (Mossner 1958, 32; Mossner 1954, 118; Stewart 2005, 25; Greig 1932, 1:24, 43). What is temporally *cause* and what is *effect* in the network diagrams? If Hume's intellectual power is attributable to network centrality, the scaling of network resources to accomplishments is circularly formalistic.

"Flattening effect": To portray philosophies as products competing for attention in the market, Collins has to create salient dimensions for them that make them easily distinguishable. For example, Collins writes that "the Epicureans represented the 'far left' of materialism, with the Stoics in the compromise position at the center" (Collins 1998, 107). On what foundation does this spatial metaphor stand? Materialism did not crystallize as an easily summonable term until the modern rise of physics and mechanistic explanation (Rée 1978, 23–25). Could it nonetheless have been *approximately* salient as a "dimension" to ancient Greek consumers who chose philosophical products? None other than Karl Marx, who knew a bit about materialism, wrote on Epicurus' concept of material atoms. As Marx accurately noted in his PhD thesis, Epicurus insisted that atoms swerved through space based on their inward self-direction. Epicurus ruled out therefore the possibility of structured relations among mutually reacting materials. To label Epicurus a materialist by Marx's own perspective was anachronistic vocabulary without sense: In Epicurus "one sees there is no interest present in investigating the actual ground of objects," only in achieving a secure tranquility of self-consciousness (Marx 1983, 61). If one insists a priori that Epicurus must be ranked somewhere on the dimensional scale of relative materialism versus idealism, one can defend probably any positioning. But the endeavor nullifies inquiry by perversely *assuming* intellectuals of the era reached their commitments based on this material versus ideal dimension—a linear dimension of contemporary theory that Collins reifies as universally applicable. Most evidence discloses instead that intellectuals of the ancient world, and many in more recent eras, adopted their stances based on atheoretical, personal spirituality or historically embedded life ethics (Hadot 1995; Foucault 2001, 29; Hadot 2002).

Taking Apart the Model of Parallel
Scaling: *The Disciplinary Revolution*

What happens when an investigator problematizes the rank of a case on the initial "starting" dimension in Figure 3.1 to avoid the self-confirming logic we have diagnosed thus far? Philip Gorski illustrates this nuanced use of parallel scaling in *The Disciplinary Revolution: Calvinism and the Rise of the State in Early Modern Europe*. Gorski undertakes to explain the construction of resource-efficient states in Reformation-era Europe (Gorski 2003). With judicious concern for scholarship, he identifies contributory rather than sufficient causes (Gorski 2003, 118–119). Gorski's central variable, social discipline, is the bridge variable that connects religiously influenced institutions of surveillance to his social output—strongly effective states. In comparative perspective, Gorksi suggests, Calvinist theology comprises the most extreme religious input because it makes each individual responsible for watching over others (Gorski 2003, 21, 124). When Gorski correlates social discipline with state building, he certifies only Calvinism as "high" on both variables, and he leaves other cases relatively ungraded but certainly lower (Gorski 2003, 155). The book's three-stage passage—from confession, to discipline, to state efficiency—amplifies cultural sociologists' longstanding arguments about the peculiar contributions of Protestantism to state building (Corrigan and Sayer, 1985, 46–47).

If we try to peg societies as to how they fit onto a yardstick of discipline, we imagine that diverse kinds of admonishing activities are tokens of a totalizing project. "Insofar as possible, one should consider all aspects of the disciplining process (e.g., religious, social, and political) across the entire period (ca. 1500–1750)," Gorski writes (Gorski 2003, 118). Following the logic of spatial scaling, we are supposed to imagine that it is possible to sum categorically dissimilar activities across populations into greater or lesser degrees of summonable obedience and orderliness: "[W]e should not focus only on religious discipline or social discipline, but examine as many different dimensions of the disciplining process as possible." By this aggregative method, then, "polities dominated by Calvinists and other ascetic Protestants were more orderly, more regulated, and more fully rationalized than polities dominated by orthodox Lutheranism or reformed Catholicism" (Gorski 2003, 155).

Once Gorski has us assume that discipline is a universal dimension standing behind culturally varying types of conduct, he may short circuit the genuine challenges of interpreting evidence. Gorski adduces important evidence of lower rates of murder, premarital sex, and/or postconceptual nuptiality in Calvinist-dominated societies (Gorski 2003, 124). In my view, the question for cultural sociology is why we should rhetorically count any such kinds of life events as a "measure of social order" (Gorski 2003, 54). What turns discrete object instances into representatives of this ideal dimension—social discipline and order? Consider an interpretive dilemma: In keeping with Gorski's hypothesis, murder declined with the triumph of Calvinism in seventeenth-century Zurich. Yet Calvinism may have carried an ominous complement, a dramatic acceleration in suicides. If we lend credence to the statistics, one form of violent death was neatly replaced by another in Zurich, each the quantitative mirror image of the other portrayal of casualties (Hsia 1989, 163). Suicide could indicate a culturally more serious breach of order for Calvinism because in some circumstances it supposedly extinguished not just the body but the soul.

The lesson, perhaps, is that there is no naturally evident statistic to be read as a token for a larger whole. If some Calvinist-dominated communities were obsessed with profiling extra-marital sex as *the* chief sin, it is difficult to know whether hysterical public campaigns targeting this specific behavior makes that behavior a less valid measure of state-relevant social order overall (Graham 1994, 157; Benedict, 2002, 470). Much comparative evidence suggests that sexual misdemeanors were not predictive of other features of social disposition in Reformation towns (Benedict 2002, 487). How cultures differ from each other overall may not necessarily be generalizable from narrowly chosen sites of action, such as premarital sex.

The more specific question of meaning is whether premarital sex resulted from culturally similar kinds of actions in similar contexts such that it is sensible to scale a region's relative lack of discipline or order by its relative rates of reported illegitimate births. Since many such births seem to have come from single women subordinated as domestic servants, it may not make sense to interpret their situated behavior leading to illegitimacy as a breach of societal-level discipline (Gowing 2001, 45–46). The model for the relation of wife to husband, after all, was that of servant to master. Some widowers considered themselves effectively consensually "married" to their maids (Harrington 1995, 241). In Italy, the context of action seems stranger, for some in peasant communities believed that premarital sex evaded the witches who cast spells of infertility on those officially coupled. There, sexual activity among the unmarried, who intended to wed, struck many as conventionally pro-family (Black 2004, 102). Indeed, church, folk community, and state definitions of marriage or illegitimacy in early modern Europe were frequently in conflict. For example, many children of unwed mothers on the fringes of urban society in the Netherlands likely did not surface in statistics of illegitimate births, as Simon Schama observed: "These figures do not, of course, give much idea of overall illegitimacy rates, *expressed as they are, as a percentage of the baptized*" (Schama 1987, 438, my emphasis). When cases of disputed marriage agreements came before the courts, Protestant magistrates in one survey were more likely than their Catholic counterparts to read premarital sex as evidence of a legal obligation to marry (Safley 1984, 186). Illicit behavior might not exist outside the official acts that registered it.

Comparativists sometimes establish "conceptual equivalence" of actions across contexts by showing that the conduct has similarly relevant consequences (Sears 1961, 453–454). But there seems little reason to suppose that engaging in extramarital sexuality discreetly has implications for public order or for a person's contribution to state-building. We might, to the contrary, figure private hedonism as an outlet for letting off steam in the face of successful disciplinary mobilization in public life (Marcuse 1964, 73–75).

Uncertainty about what can serve as a token of "discipline" can make a positive contribution if it stimulates more illuminating questions about interpreting the evidence. As Gorski underscores, the cleanliness of Dutch streets and interior rooms was legendary. Why did tidiness symbolically *matter* to individual experience? Dutch society was the birthplace of the capitalist world's mass culture of material consumption. Jan de Vries speculated that the extraordinary output and display of consumer goods might have been "particularly well suited to the temper and purpose of the Confessional era" (de Vries 2008, 57). How? In part, historians suggest, when people sought contact with sanctity through their everyday poise, they became dependent on experiencing orderly, careful use of their newly enriched material world (Peterson 2001). Neatness and gentility seem to have served, therefore, as a metaphor of interchange between the transcendental sacred and human life in the present. If it was a way of symbolically figuring experience, cleanliness may be explained as a self-patterned expression of feeling, analogous perhaps to what goes on in American suburbia, rather than as normative discipline (Schama 1987, 375–386).

The challenge of identifying the source of self-regulation is especially engaging for Holland because it was home to partially competing templates for manners and morals: Erasmian ethics, bourgeois codes of sophistication, neo-stoicism from the academies, newly professionalized controls over the soldiery, and, finally, plebian concern for voluntary piety unencumbered by church dictates. "The most striking and significant fact for the early religious history of the Dutch Republic is the number of people who belonged to no church at all," the historian Benjamin Kaplan concluded from a survey of Calvinists' minority status. "This was a phenomenon without precedent or parallel in Europe" (Kaplan 1994, 655).[1] Whether Dutch ordering of the person should be read as most essentially the work of Calvinist regulation is a tantalizing question, an invitation to intensive micro-level interpretation of life practices (Pollmann 2002, 423–438). Once we appreciate how the Calvinist consistories had to negotiate their influence with the "little people," it is useful to invoke a "disciplining process" if it leads us to ask more carefully *how* transactions of power between the churches and the populace actually functioned (Benedict 2002, 523, 531; Kaplan 1994, 668).[2]

Gorski obviously departs from parallel scaling somewhat because he does not *define* the religious starting points of Protestant confession or Catholic faith by their summable rankings relative to each other in intrinsic resources for social discipline. In asking how confession may translate into discipline, therefore, his study offers a rich if potentially destabilizing agenda. We might use it to pose the very difficult comparative question, for example, whether there *is* a sensible counterfactual baseline or null hypothesis for assessing the *effect* of disciplinary campaigns in a region. Once we consider alternative conduits for shaping conduct and variation induced by situational context, we may subscribe instead to the most recent scholarship according to which, "It seems no longer likely that church discipline contributed to a successful process of social disciplining, as was held by an older historiography" (Lotz-Heumann 2007, 6:260). But whether there are reasonable cross-cultural indicators of discipline in the first place should be treated as an open question as well. We cannot assume in advance that statistics from different cultures refer to "the same," underlying dimension of practice. The concept of discipline can illuminate evidence if we use it to debate the respects in which it is applicable.

Broader Extensions to Cultural Sociology

These four exemplary studies sensitize us to the hypothesis that there is a deleterious tie between spatial metaphors and models that obscure social meanings as much as they access it. To appraise this tie at work more generally, consider how sociologists are apt to scale cultural differences between cases as "large" or "small" and then extrapolate as a corollary how much of the variation between the cases the cultural differences can be expected to explain. "Culture's constitutive effect tends to operate over broad, temporal, and spatial dimensions," Paul DiMaggio wrote in his classic essay "Culture and Economy." The further apart in time or space the settings are that we compare, the more the settings reveal how culture sets up the preconditional categories or understandings for the agents' universe of action. Conversely, DiMaggio reasoned, "The shorter the duration and the more similar the units being compared, the more likely it is safe to ignore culture and rely instead on structural explanations, including ones based on self interest, of observed variation" (DiMaggio 1994, 47). This conclusion does not lack rationales, yet the yardstick for "large" versus "small" distances between cases also rules out what cultural sociology urgently needs as a supplement: self-critical *discovery*. Should we not examine how "small" nonobvious differences in meaning between affiliated cases may carry "large" consequences? Cannot "closely" spaced cases nonetheless constitute crucially different universes of action once we appreciate how qualitative difference in meaning has preconditioned action in "incidentally" decisive ways? Europe's closely intertwined but linguistically and governmentally divided regions offers a laboratory for such exploration. For example, the history of literary property in Western Europe in the eighteenth and nineteenth centuries suggests that slight variation across lands in the understandings of originality and ownership of texts had ramifying effects on law, publication markets, and authorial creativity (Hesse 1991, 224–245; Biernacki 2000). In nineteenth-century European industrial development, Germany and Britain were closely intertwined, yet the subtle difference between their practices for quantifying labor as a commodity could yield secular differences in their patterns of capital investment and in union ideologies (Biernacki 2001). For qualitatively irreducible phenomena of cultural meaning and for aesthetic or political revolutions, we disable inquiry if we suppose there is a pre-given correspondence between the apparent "size" of cultural differences and the "size" of historically consequential effects.

Three Alternative Working Rules

To manage the distortions of spatial metaphors, let me offer three cautionary principles for research on culture.

First Corrective: How do we grasp a cultural context without letting our instruments mislead us as to how meanings are organized on the ground? Our ordinary language and thought are always tied to spatial analogies. But we can avoid their reifying effects if we consistently question whether we know what a culture's own practices "refer to" or are "based on." Suspending our assumptions about reference is an epistemological proviso for tying inquiry to primary evidence, not for a flight to postmodernism. For example, Stedman Jones, in his brilliant *Languages of Class*, took as his puzzle the status of "class" inside early industrial Britain's largest movement of radical protest, that of Chartism (Stedman Jones 1983). He illustrated a popular Chartist vocabulary of class (Stedman Jones 1983, 156–157). But the social scientific assumption that class "refers to" the economy or social relations is exactly what derailed a train of earlier research into Chartism. Investigators had created their own problems by viewing the social relations of production as the primary rubric and the Chartists' political phrasing as an incidental parsing of this dimension. Yet Stedman Jones finds evidence that the Chartists' diagnosis did not originate in relations of production in civil society. Nor did the radical Chartists grasp the form of production as a problem to be solved (Stedman Jones 1983, 128). Instead, the unionists, utopians, and radical reformers believed that the cause of distress was the state's usurpation of rights of fair exchange, which they called "class legislation" (Stedman Jones 1983, 163). By appreciating the Chartists' limits, their concern for political corruption and monopoly, Steadman Jones successfully simplifies explanation. The Chartists's critique of the state's violation of natural "rights in labor" united diverse occupational groups in strikes and petitioning (Stedman Jones 1983, 158, 171). But the movement's root diagnosis seemed inapposite once the most discriminatory abuses of state power were removed from public view. In sum, we can explain why discontent took the form of Chartism and why Chartism sealed its own defeat (Stedman Jones 1983, 177).

One of the best known advocates of deconstruction in historical analysis, Joan Scott, reasoned that the take-home lesson from Stedman Jones' evidence is that the referential meaning of "class" was incidental or null (Scott 1999, 53–67). To insist reference was secondary or inoperable, however, presumes an investigator can legislate what real, sensible reference would have comprised. All I propose, and all Stedman Jones illustrates, is that in analysis, we let the cultural agents themselves manage the business of how their symbolic devices "refer" in their lives. Cultural sociologists would benefit from considering how literary investigators have historicized the relation between representation and reference as an examinable problem that cultural agents endeavor to "solve" by assorted methods (Poovey 2008, 89; Assmann, 1980, 141).

This productive skepticism about the workings of reference forces us to reconsider our own comparative logic as well. To cite a laboratory example, reader reception experimenters gave an intricate poem to different social groups to study the effect of group differences in culture on readers' understanding (Holub 1984). What is the object to which the responses "refer"? The same poem or the same printed lettering? In her canonical article, "The Fabrication of Meaning," Wendy Griswold employed a similar comparative designed to identify international differences in the reception of "the same" novels of George Lamming. These set-ups control whether readers are receiving the same black ink on the same white pages. Yet the standard interpretation assumes there is "the same" shared and meaningful referent in place across the cultures before the literati figure it more complexly. How do we know readers are dealing in different ways with "the same" semantically meaningful work, what we signify by "the poem" or "the novel," as contrasted to "the black ink on the page"? The intended purpose of comparison can be achieved only *after* we ascertain that, across cultures, the reviewers did have a meaningfully shared referent in experience before they rhetorically figured and evaluated it in their writings. For example, did Griswold's literary reviewers recognize and summarize the basic plots of the novels in similar ways? We have to find semantic criteria (not extra-linguistic physical criteria) to decide whether reviewers across communities are talking about "the same" thing (Culler, 1975).

Second Working Corrective: As a practical corollary, we should dispense with expectancies of primary rubrics versus their secondary elaborations. We saw how misleading it was to assume that color terms are variants of hue, or, more broadly, that there is a natural domain of color.[3] By analogy, then, as Michèle Lamont has suggested, we cannot presume that there is an underlying, primary rubric of social "status" that middle-class and working-class cultures both reference but interpret in different ways (Lamont 2000). Nor, for example, that there is in capitalism a naturally denoted economic factor of "labor" upon which cultures happen to elaborate differing, second-order connotations (Biernacki 1995). Even the concept of "number"—the supposed paragon of a context-free entity underlying mathematical systems—turns out to be misleading. Ancient cultures, for example, made anomalous use of counting and had such distinctive methods for mathematical proof that it appears they had various senses of number other than of empty equivalent units (Feyerabend 1999, 88).

Skepticism about standardized reference is a stock in trade among micro-historians who can show sociologists how it leads to evidentiary rigor. For instance, if we ask what "printing" indexed for literary readers after Gutenberg invented his new kind of press, it is misleading to presume printing was a technological entity with mechanically basic characteristics. The rubric of print dissemination—mass production of identical texts from an author's manuscript—is our retrospective projection, as Adrian Johns showed in *The Nature of the Book*. As Johns documents, compositors into the eighteenth century fiddled with correcting the typeset of each printed sheet such that the model of a "standardized impression," or even of a typical version of a book edition, was inapplicable. Printers did not copy authors' words but edited pieces on the spot with each small press run (Johns 1998, 91, 101, 637). The authorial fixity and mass uniformity of printing, Johns discovered, were delicate social accomplishments. Michael Warner argued more fundamentally that we cannot identify printing except by contextual definition within the culture of the time. "The assumption that technology is prior to culture results in a kind of retro-determination whereby the political history of a technology is converted into the unfolding nature of that technology," Warner wrote in *Letters of the Republic*. "Early printers in no way distinguished their work from hand-produced documents." For cultural sociology it is significant that printing as a category of action for producers or readers came into existence only with development of ideologies for using print in novel ways (Warner 1990, 8–9).

Third Working Corrective: The most basic way in which cultural sociologists may suspend pre-given rubrics is in their own packaging of meanings. Perhaps to follow the logic of variable analysis, cultural sociologists sometimes report on constellations of meanings in terms of magnitudes on dimensions, such as greater or lesser degrees of cultural coherence or dissension. As Neil Smelser once wrote on the issue of coherence, however, "The salient question is *not* how coherent or incoherent is a culture." That question lacks pertinence, because the degrees of coherence we discern "is in large part a construct about the society or group under study rather than a simple empirical attribute to be apprehended, recorded, and described" (Smelser 1992, 23). The same artifactual quality arises when we report that, for example, Japanese organizational culture can be ranked as "higher" on "collectivity orientation" based on a battery of indices (DiMaggio 1994, 34). If we imagine further that such a report corresponds to meanings on the ground, it comprises a categorical mistake that is apt to generate nonsense. A statistic or an ocean tide can be relatively "high," each in its own way. But meaning in most historical processes on the ground comes in exemplary constellations, in figures of practice, not in quasi-mechanical "emphases" or in rankings along a dimension.

The purpose of cultural analysis then is not to reach population summaries or ordinal estimates of what we find in cultures, only to discover the semiotic mechanisms of historical action. Following Max Weber, we can rethink the task of generalization as that of discovering characteristic constellations or iconic exemplars of how actions unfold. It is a permanent challenge to method in cultural sociology that meanings in operation remain tied to specific prototypes. We are familiar with this from Weber's vignette of the "ascetic Protestant" or from Wendy Griswold's genre of "city comedy" in her *Renaissance Revivals* (Griswold 1986, 15–19). As we know, Weber marshals Richard Baxter in *The Protestant Ethic* as a prototype that compacts the semiotic predicaments of Puritans' everyday life. Somewhat similarly, Griswold calls on the playwright Ben Jonson to typify dramas of urban guile. To suggest why such crystallized exemplars are indispensable, consider our everyday cognitive processes (Kövecses 2000, 176). As the psychologist Eleanor Rosch put the question, consider what happens when we try to converge upon the characteristic significance of birds in our culture. We usually select prototypes, such as sparrows or robins, rather than offer a list of necessary and sufficient attributes. A penguin or a clucking hen logically might satisfy the ascertainable definitional criteria of "birdness" but remains somehow inept for excavating focal meanings (Rosch 1973, 138, 142). This reliance on salient priming features and perceptual resemblance to the core members of a family is partly what Max Weber was getting at when he insisted that significance in historical evidence is not retrievable from "simple class" concepts. A "class concept," Weber explained, defines the meaning of belonging to a category by criterial attributes, checking off genus and differentia (Weber 1949, 100–104). "[N]o class or generic concept," that is, a concept that positions cases in a grid, "has a 'typical' character," he concluded (Weber 1949, 101).

Before our time Weber was right that efforts to excavate meaningful action by such simple "class" concepts miss the mark. But Weber falsely stereotyped practices of natural science when he imagined as well that "the coming of age of science in fact always implies the transcendence of the ideal-type" (Weber 1949, 101). Reliance on complex prototypes for producing and reading evidence remains integral to many natural sciences, as historians such as Thomas Kuhn showed by painstakingly reconstructing knowledge-making in action (Kuhn 1996, 44, 192). Natural scientists generalize by building creative analogies to benchmark cases, much as Weber recommended via ideal-typical characterizations (Andersen, et al, 2006). For cultural sociologists, vigilant skepticism about the handling of abstract extensional variables is faithful to this search for typical explanatory mechanisms, not a subscription to anti-scientific particularism.

The concepts we use to read the meanings of the evidence have to be potentially disqualifiable all the way down, however basic they are—including "religion" and "the person" as modern invented concepts, for example (Bossy 1982; Shweder and Bourne 1991, 122–124; Smith 1997). There is no ground for assuming that our analytic categories convey messages that are more fundamental than those we subject to our interpretation. Unless basic rubrics can be disqualified by the evidence, all that cultural analysis can accomplish is to break a cultural whole into pieces whose shapes miraculously conform to sociologists' pre-given categories. The example of color also shows how misleading conforming facts of "reference" can be for establishing the validity of analytic categories or equivalencies across cultures. For example, having respondents point to bits of our own culture's industrially perfect color samples to approximate the referent of their native vocabulary does nothing more than elicit responses by our own, preferred divisions and sort them by our own customs. Inducing respondents to pick a "color" through our own classificatory system deprives the act of referring of evidentiary weight. For an analogy, the linguist John Lucy considers our "referring" to lost luggage through the pictorial charts of a foreign airline—it reveals nothing about our native linguistic practices for classifying luggage (Lucy 1997, 321, 331). Through relentless detail, I have endeavored to show how returning to the context of evidence converts basic terms such as "hue" or "discipline" into essentially contested concepts, not descriptors.

The German critical tradition in classical social theory, extending from Marx to Weber and beyond, emerged to puncture and take apart the reifying effects of our own models and of spatialized dimensions in particular. In Weber's ideal type method, the active role our constructs play in artifactually apprehending a culture should be made explicit in our appreciation of the culture's makeup. As everyone knows, an "ideal type" in Weber's research program is an extreme distillation of traits in iconic form that can be compared to historical evidence. To be sure, documentary sources are readable only through some kind of selective lens. For the evidence to rub against the ideal type, however, all that is required is that we consider documents through a multiplicity of theoretic perspectives, some of which are independent of the ideal type or some of which mimic perspectives from inside the primary evidence. This use of ideal types differs in three ways from the contemporary practice of proposing "analytic" continua: (1) There is no warrant for the imaginative shape that an ideal type assumes. It is not legitimated by a classificatory grid, and it is not a "class concept," one based on "simple classification" of genus and species (Weber 1949, 100–101). A case is not summed analytically by the values of variables. (2) The ideal type, as a figural prototype, dramatically heightens and exaggerates the relations among meanings in historical constellations rather than getting at what "underlies" them. (3) The knowledge one gains from an ideal type is based on contrast against (not fit with) the interpreted evidence. It creates a stance for appreciating the distance between prototype constellations and discrepant meanings, not for explanation through correlations of scaled variables. In particular, Weber rejected as misleading reification the attempt to explain historical patterns as outcomes of countervailing or mutually clashing forces on dimensions, "a spatial and physical image" (Weber 1949, 187).

SIGNING OFF

More than four decades ago, Aaron Cicourel remarked in *Method and Measurement in Sociology* that "the very features of secularized society, the rationalization of everyday life, have become an object of study for the sociologist, but also a prison for him" (Cicourel 1964, 37). Cicourel had in mind the sociologist's reliance on ready-to-hand data whose formatting by bureaucratic agencies into abstract dimensions already cut across the operative meanings of actions the data allegedly measured. The maxim was that the task of sociology, preparatory to explanation, is to seek meaning afresh. What an irony if cultural sociologists, by imposing their own parallel scalings on rich qualitative sources, were to build a new kind of prison for themselves from scratch.

NOTES

1. For trends in church membership during the seventeenth century, see Benedict 2002, 199–200 and Duke 1990, 270–271, 293.

2. For anecdotal evidence of countryside "popular opposition" to Calvinist norms for marriage, see Schilling 1994, 27.

3. On the absence of natural criteria for distinguishing between basic versus secondary color terms, see Maffi and Hardin 1997, 351.

REFERENCES

Alexander, Jeffrey. 1995. *Fin de Siècle Social Theory*. London: Verso, 1995.

Andersen, Hanne, Barker, Peter, and Chen, Xiang. 2006. *The Cognitive Structure of Scientific Revolutions*. Cambridge, UK: Cambridge University Press.

Assmann, Aleida. 1980. *Die Legitimität der Fiktion*. Munich: Wilhelm Fink.

Barley, Nigel. 1974. "Old English Color Classification: Where Do Matters Stand?" In *Anglo-Saxon England 3*, Peter Clemoes (ed.), pp. 15–28. Cambridge, UK: Cambridge University Press.

Benedict, Philip. 2002. *Christ's Churches Purely Reformed*. New Haven, CT: Yale University Press.

Bennett, Tony. 2008. "Habitus Clivé: Aesthetics and Politics in the Work of Pierre Bourdieu." In *New Directions in American Reception Study*, Philip Goldstein and Jaes Machor (eds.), pp. 57–86. Oxford: Oxford University Press.

Berlin, Brent, and Kay, Paul. 1969. *Basic Color Terms. Their Universality and Evolution*. Berkeley: University of California Press.

Biernacki, Richard. 1995. *The Fabrication of Labor. Germany and Britain, 1640–1914*. Berkeley: University of California Press.

———. 2000. "The Social Manufacture of Private Ideas in Germany and Britain, 1750–1830." *Jahrbuch Wissenschaftskolleg zu Berlin* Jahrbuch 1998–1999: 221–246.

———. 2001. "Labor as an Imagined Commodity." *Politics and Society* 29: 173–206.

Biggam, C. P. 1993. "Aspects of Chaucer's Adjectives of Hue." *The Chaucer Review* 28: 41–53.

Black, Christopher. 2004. *Church, Religion and Society in Early Modern Italy*. London: Palgrave Macmillan.

Bossy, John. 1982. "Some Elementary Forms of Durkheim." *Past and Present* 95: 3–18.

Bourdieu, Pierre. 1990. *The Logic of Practice*. Cambridge, UK: Polity Press.

———. 1993. "Principles of a Sociology of Cultural Works." In *Explanation and Value in the Arts*, Salim Kemal and Ivan Gaskell (eds.), pp. 173–189. Cambridge, UK: Cambridge University Press.

———. 2007. *Distinction. A Social Critique of the Judgement of Taste*. Cambridge, MA: Harvard University Press.

Brown, Roger. 1965. *Social Psychology*. New York: Free Press.

Burnley, J. D. 1976. "Middle English Colour Terminology and Lexical Structure." *Linguistische Berichte* 44: 39–49.

Cartwright, Nancy. 2002. "The Limits of Causal Order: From Economics to Physics." In *Fact and Fiction in Economics*. Uskali Mäki (ed.), pp. 137–151. Cambridge, UK: Cambridge University Press.

Cicourel, Aaron. 1964. *Method and Measurement in Sociology*. Glencoe, IL: Free Press.

Collins, Randall. 1998. *The Sociology of Philosophies. A Global Theory of Intellectual Change*. Cambridge, MA: Belknap of Harvard University Press.

Corrigan Philip, and Sayer, Derek. 1985. *The Great Arch. English State Formation as Cultural Revolution*. Oxford: Basil Blackwell.

Culler, Jonathan. 1975. "Defining Narrative Units." In *Style and Structure in Literature*, Roger Fowler (ed.), pp. 123–142. Oxford: Basic Blackwell.

Danziger, Kurt. 1990. *Constructing the Subject. Historical Origins of Psychological Research*. Cambridge, UK: Cambridge University Press.

De Vries, Jan. 2008. *The Industrious Revolution*. Cambridge, UK: Cambridge University Press.

DiMaggio, Paul. 1994. "Culture and Economy." In *The Handbook of Economic Sociology,* Neil Smelser and Richard Swedberg (eds.), pp. 27–57. Princeton, NJ: Princeton University Press.

———. 2002. "Why Cognitive (and Cultural) Sociology Needs Cognitive Psychology." In *Culture in Mind. Toward a Sociology of Culture and Cognition,* Karen Cerulo (ed.), pp. 274–281. New York: Routledge, 2002.

Dixon, R. 1982. "Where Have All the Adjectives Gone?" In *Where Have All the Adjectives Gone and Other Essays in Semantics and Syntax,* R. Dixon (ed.), pp. 1–62. Berlin: Walter de Gruyter.

Duke, Alastair. 1990. *Reformation and Revolt in the Low Countries.* London: Hambledon Press.

Evans, John. 2009. "Two Worlds in Cultural Sociology." In *Meaning and Method: The Cultural Approach to Sociology,* Isaac Reed and Jeffrey Alexander (eds.), pp. 208–252. Boulder, CO: Paradigm Publishers, 2009.

Feyerabend, Paul. 1999. *Conquest of Abundance.* Chicago: University of Chicago Press.

Fichte, Johann Gottlieb. 1968. Vol. 2. *Fichte Briefwechsel.* Suttgart-Bad Cannstadt: F. Frommann Verlag.

Forster, Michael N. 1998. *Hegel's Idea of a Phenomenology of Spirit.* Chicago: University of Chicago Press.

Foucault, Michel. 2001. *L'herméneutique du sujet.* Paris: Gallimard Le Seuil.

Gorski, Philip. 2003. *The Disciplinary Revolution: Calvinism and the Rise of the State in Early Modern Europe.* Chicago: University of Chicago Press.

Gowing, Laura. 2001. "Ordering the Body: Illegitimacy and Female Authority in Seventeenth-Century England." In *Negotiating Power in Early Modern Society,* Michael Braddick and John Walter (eds.), pp. 43–62. Cambridge, UK: Cambridge University Press.

Graham, Michael. 1994. "Social Discipline in Scotland, 1560–1610." *Sixteenth Century Essays and Studies, Sin and the Calvinists* 32: 129–151.

Greenfield, Amy. 2005. *A Perfect Red.* New York: HarperCollins.

Greig, J. Y. T. 1932. *The Letters of David Hume* Vol. 1. Oxford: Clarendon Press.

Griswold, Wendy. 1986. *Renaissance Revivals.* Chicago: University of Chicago.

Hadot, Pierre. 1995. *Philosophy as a Way of Life: Spiritual Exercises from Socrates to Foucault.* Oxford: Blackwell.

———. 2002. *What Is Ancient Philosophy?* Cambridge, MA: Harvard University Press.

Harrington, Joel. 1995. *Reordering Marriage and Society in Reformation Germany.* Cambridge, UK: Cambridge University Press.

Hegel, Georg Wilhelm Friedrich. 1961. Vol. 4. *Briefe von und an Hegel.* Johannes Hoffmeister, ed. Hamburg: Felix Meiner.

Hesse, Carla. 1991. *Publishing and Cultural Politics in Revolutionary Paris, 1789–1810.* Berkeley: University of California Press.

Holub, Robert. 1984. *Reception Theory. A Critical Introduction.* London: Methuen.

Hsia, R. Po-chia. 1989. *Social Discipline in the Reformation: Central Europe 1550–1750.* London: Routledge.

Irwin, Eleanor. 1974. *Colour Terms in Greek Poetry.* Toronto: Hakkert.

Johns, Adrian. 1998. *The Nature of the Book. Print and Knowledge in the Making.* Chicago: University of Chicago Press.

Kaplan, Benjamin. 1994. "Remants of the Papal Yoke": Apathy and Opposition in the Dutch Reformation." *The Sixteenth Century Journal* 25: 653–669.

Kövecses, Zoltan. 2000. *Metaphor and Emotion.* Cambridge, UK: Cambridge University Press.

Kuehni, Rolf, and Schwarz, Andreas. 2008. *Color Ordered. A Survey of Color Order Systems from Antiquity to the Present.* Oxford: Oxford University Press.

Kuhn, Thomas. 1996. *The Structure of Scientific Revolutions.* Chicago: University of Chicago Press.

Kuschel, Rolf, and Monberg, Torben. 1974. "'We Don't Talk Much about Colour Here': A Study of Colour Semantics on Bellona Island." *Man* 9: 213–242.

Lahire, Bernard. *La culture des individus. Dissonances culturelle et distinction de soi.* Paris: Éditions la découverte, 2004.

Lamont, Michèle. 2000. *The Dignity of Working Men.* Cambridge, MA: Harvard University Press.

Latour, Bruno. 1993. *We Have Never Been Modern.* Cambridge, MA: Harvard University Press.

Lotz-Heumann, Ute. 2007. "Imposing Church and Social Discipline." In *The Cambridge History of Christianity. Reform and Expansion 1500–1660*, Vol. 6, R. Po-chia Hsia (ed.), pp. 244–260. Cambridge, UK: Cambridge University Press.

Loveman, Mara. 2005. "The Modern State and the Primitive Accumulation of Symbolic Power." *American Journal of Sociology* 110: 1651–1683.

Lucy, John A. 1997. "The Linguistics of 'Color.'" In *Color Categories in Thought and Language*, C. L. Hardin and Luisa Maffi (eds.), pp. 320–346. Cambridge, UK: Cambridge University Press.

MacLaury, Robert. 1992. "From Brightness to Hue: An Explanatory Model of Color-Category Evolution." *Current Anthropology* 33: 137–186.

Maffi, Luisa, and Hardin, C. L. 1997. "Closing Thoughts." In *Color Categories in Thought and Language*, Luisa Maffi and C. L. Hardin (eds.), pp. 347–372. Cambridge, UK: Cambridge University Press, 1997.

Marcuse, Herbert. 1964. *One-Dimensional Man. Studies in the Ideology of Advanced Industrial Society.* Boston: Beacon Press.

Marx, Karl. 1983. *Die Promotion von Karl Marx, Jena, 1841.* Berlin: Dietz Verlag.

———. 1990. *Capital. Volume One.* London: Penguin Classics.

Midelfort, H. C. Erik. 1995. "Selbstmord im Urteil von Reformation und Gegenreformation." In *Die katholische Konfessionalisierung*, Wolfgang Reinhard and Heinz Schilling (eds.), pp. 296–310. Gütersloh: Gütersloher Verlagshaus.

Mossner, Ernest Campbell. 1954. *The Life of David Hume.* Austin: University of Texas Press.

———. 1958. "Hume at La Flèche, 1735: An Unpublished Letter." *University of Texas Studies in English* 37: 30–33.

Nieto-Galan, Agusti. 1996. "The Use of Natural Dyestuffs in Eighteenth-Century Europe." *Archives internationales d'histoire des sciences* 46: 23–38.

Ostheeren, Klaus. 1971. "Toposforschung und Bedeutungslehre." *Anglia* 89: 1–47.

Peterson, Mark A. 2001 "Puritanism and Refinement in Early New England: Reflections on Communion Silver." *William and Mary Quarterly* 58: 307–346.

Pollmann, Judith. 2002. "Off the Record: Problems in the Quantification of Calvinist Church Discipline." *The Sixteenth Century Journal* 33: 423–438.

Poovey, Mary. 2008. *Genres of the Credit Economy.* Chicago: University of Chicago Press.

Rancière, Jacques. 2003. *The Philosopher and His Poor.* Durham, North NC: Duke University Press.

Rée, Jonathan. 1978. "Philosophy and the History of Philosophy." In *Philosophy and Its Past*, Jonathan Rée et al. (eds.), pp. 3–39. Atlantic Highlands, NJ: Humanities Press.

Rosch, Eleanor H. 1973. "On the Internal Structure of Perceptual and Semantic Categories." In *Cognitive Development and the Acquisition of Language*, Timothy Moore (ed.), pp. 111–144. New York: Academic Press.

Safley, Thomas Max. 1984. *Let No Man Put Asunder. The Control of Marriage in the German Southwest: A Comparative Study, 1559–1600*. Kirksville: Northeast Missouri State University.

Saunders, Barbara. 2000. "Revisiting Basic Color Terms." *Journal of the Royal Anthropological Institute* 6: 81–99.

———. 2007. "Towards a New Topology of Colour." In *Anthropology of Color*, Robert MacLaury, et al. (eds.), pp. 467–479. Amsterdam: J. Benjamins.

Saunders, Barbara, and van Brakel, J. 1997. "Are There Non-Trivial Constraints on Colour Categorization? " *Behavioral and Brain Sciences* 20: 167–228.

———. 2001. "Rewriting Color." *Philosophy of the Social Sciences* 31: 538–556.

Schama, Simon. 1987. *The Embarrassment of Riches*. New York: Vintage Books.

Schelling, Friedrich Wilhelm Joseph. 1962. Vol. 1. *Schelling Briefe und Dokumente*. Horst Fuhrmans (ed.). Bonn: H. Bouvier.

Schilling, Heinz. 1994. "Reform and Supervision of Family Life in Germany and the Netherlands." In *Sin and the Calvinists: Morals Control and the Consistory in the Reformed Tradition*, Raymond Mentzer (ed.), pp. 15–61. Kirksville: Northeast Missouri State University.

Scott, Joan Wallach. 1999. *Gender and the Politics of History*. Rev. ed. New York: Columbia University Press.

Sears, Robert. 1961. "Transcultural Variables and Conceptual Equivalence." In *Studying Personality Cross-Culturally*, Bert Kaplan (ed.), pp. 445–455. New York: Harper & Row.

Shweder, Richard, and Bourne, Edmund. 1991. "Does the Concept of the Person Vary Cross-Culturally?" In *Thinking Through Culture*, Richard Shweder (ed.), pp. 113–155. Cambridge, MA: Harvard University Press.

Smelser, Neil. 1992. "Culture: Coherent or Incoherent." In *Theory of Culture*, Richard Münch and Neil Smelser (eds.), pp. 3–28. Berkeley: University of California Press.

Smith, Roger. 1997. "Self and Selfhood in the Seventeenth Century." In *Rewriting the Self. Histories from the Renaissance to the Present*, Roy Porter (ed.), pp. 29–48. London: Routledge.

Stedman Jones, Gareth. 1983. *Languages of Class. Studies in English Working-Class History 1832–1982*. Cambridge, UK: Cambridge University Press.

Stewart, M.A. 2005. "Hume's Intellectual Development, 1711–1752." In *Impressions of Hume*, M. Frasca-Spada and P. J. E. Kail (eds.), pp. 1–58. Oxford: Clarendon Press.

Van Brakel, J. 1993. "The Plasticity of Categories: The Case of Colour." *British Journal for the Philosophy of Science* 44: 103–135.

Warner, Michael. 1990. *Letters of the Republic*. Cambridge, MA; Harvard University Press.

Weber, Max. 1949. *On the Methodology of the Social Sciences*. Glencoe, IL: Free Press.

———. 2001. *The Protestant Ethic and the Spirit of Capitalism*. London: Routledge.

———. 2004. *Max Weber Zur Musikzosiologie. Nachlaß 1921*. Tübingen: J.C.B. Mohr.

Wenz, Gunther. 2008. *Hegels Freund und Schillers Beistand: Friedrich Immanuel Niethammer (1766–1848)*. Göttingen: Vandenhoeck & Ruprecht.

Zerubavel, Evitar. 1997. *Social Mindscapes. An Invitation to Cognitive Sociology*. Cambridge, MA: Harvard University Press.

CHAPTER 4

FOUR WAYS TO MEASURE CULTURE: SOCIAL SCIENCE, HERMENEUTICS, AND THE CULTURAL TURN

JOHN W. MOHR[1] AND CRAIG RAWLINGS[2]

INTRODUCTION

"The business of pinning numbers on things—which is what we mean by measurement—has become a pandemic activity in modern science and human affairs. The attitude seems to be: if it exists, measure it. Impelled by this spirit, we have taken the measure of many things formally considered to lie beyond the bounds of quantification. In the process we have scandalized the conservatives, created occasional chaos, and stirred a ferment that holds rich promise for the better ordering of knowledge" (Stevens 1959).[3]

In this essay, we review some of the ways in which measurement practices have been applied to create formal models of culture in the social sciences. We make use of two distinctions. We talk about the kinds of modeling projects that happened before as compared to those that happened after the sweep of cultural turns that have moved through the social sciences over the last few decades. Second, we talk about types of formal modeling projects that have explicitly hermeneutic goals in comparison to those that do not. Practitioners of the former sort want to use measurement tools to make interpretations to unlock useful readings of texts. Those of the latter persuasion seek robust measures of cultural forms that can be fitted onto other explanatory frames.

We use the term model in a highly restricted sense. For us, a model must include the study of empirical (collected) data, analyzed with quantitative or other formal pattern analysis procedures so as to obtain a structure-preserving reduction into a simpler, more easily describable set of features or characteristics.[4] We use culture, on the other hand, in an unrestricted way. For the purpose of this essay, we include as cultural forms whatever the modeler presumes them to be.[5] We begin with a discussion of the nature of formal measurement models in the social sciences. We describe these as the products of a dually ordered system of practice that are articulated into discursive formations that constitute distinctive styles of gathering, conceptualizing, and analyzing data. We compare this mode of scholarship to more hermeneutic styles of research, which leads us to comment briefly on recent debates over method in the social sciences. The chapter then shifts focus as we turn to a detailed discussion of four different types of formal (measurement) models that have been especially important to the cultural sciences over the last century.[6] We conclude by revisiting the problem of how to conceptualize a scientific hermeneutics by comparing our theorization of the practice of data analysis to Ricoeur's theorization of the practice of text analysis.

FORMAL MODELS OF CULTURE—A DEFINITION AND FOUR FUNCTIONS

What is a formal model? In our usage, a formal model is the product of a *data analysis*. The first term here, *data*, refers to a social object that we (as practitioners) construct to stand in for the object of our investigation; in this case, for some aspect of the social world. To gather data, we invoke measurement conventions about features of the social world or situation, conventions about what ought to be noticed and recorded. Data collection itself is an institutionalized social technology, organized through professional projects, made up of ensembles of activities that are defined, enacted, differentiated in function, ordered in series, elaborated, and extended, even as they are also dually articulated into corresponding theoretical discourse systems concerning the nature of the social—its character and its secrets. What results is a socially produced ensemble of craft skills that can be more or less stable over time.[7] The act of data gathering relies on conventions regarding the recording of: (1) a counting of things in the world (which implies the Kantian problem of noticing things in the world); (2) a distinguishing of definable features of things in the world; (3) a mapping of relations linking things (or features of things) in the world to one another; and so on.[8] Data, then, are the organized collection of this information, derived from a series of acts of measurement, stored in a retrievable fashion. Data collection is thus dependent on both particular theories of measurement and select repertoires of measuring practices.

Much the same could be said about the *analysis of data*.[9] One engages in specific acts (or sets of acts) of formal analysis (drawn from collectively shared repertoires of statistical, mathematical, or logical data reduction practices) in order to produce a formal model (which we define now more specifically as a reduced form representation of a larger, more complexly ordered system of information organized as a "dataset"). An *analysis* depends on some specifiable process for reducing this larger complexity (contained in the data) by a structure preserving mapping (a homomorphism) achieved by an agreed on set of analytic practices (hence, a transformation toward greater simplicity based on an elaborated theory of pattern reduction that may or may not be already absent from the mind as background consciousness).[10] To make a model, one first takes the data as measured (and thus always already pre-interpreted), stakes a claim on a conventionally acceptable structure preserving transformation of the dataset, and offers a narrative account of why this is a valuable simplification (what it helps us to understand, why understanding this is interesting, etc.). All this must be presented in an effective rhetorical form (e.g., McCloskey 1986; Bazerman 1988; Dear 1991). Thus, a data analysis involves claims and interpretations (some of which are explicit, most of which are not) about how and why the designated model maps onto a theory about the social world as represented by the specific (as available) set of data (Breiger 2000, 2002). In a given social field, the stronger the linkages and the deeper the resonances, the more analytically elegant, intellectually "sound," aesthetically pleasing, technologically advanced, helpful to a valued theory, inspiring to others, aligned with vested interests, etc., the greater the "value" of the analysis (and the model).[11]

In other words, science is a human institution like any other, defined by its own peculiar rules, moralities, systems of social organization, styles of practice, forms of knowing, types of religiosities, and all the rest.[12] As is true of other academic knowledge production programs (e.g., analytic philosophy, critical theory, literary criticism, and so on), formalist social science has its own distinctive institutional characteristics as well as its own unique advantages and disadvantages. In this essay, we focus on what we see as the advantages of formalism as they apply to the study of culture. In this respect, we feel, like Bourdieu, that scientific work has tangible benefits. Bourdieu writes, "The 'art' of the scientist is indeed separated from the 'art' of the artist by two major differences: on the one hand, the importance of the formalized knowledge which is mastered in the practical state, owing in particular to formalization and formularization, and, on the other hand, the role of the instruments, which, as Bachelard put it, is formalized knowledge turned into things. In other words, a twenty-year-old mathematician can have twenty centuries of mathematics in his mind because formalization makes it possible to acquire accumulated products of non-automatic inventions, in the form of logical automatisms that have become practical automatisms" (Bourdieu 2004, p. 40).[13]

We begin by proposing four kinds of intellectual (knowledge) functions that formal modeling can contribute to an analysis of culture. These move upward from less to more highly ordered types of knowledge interventions:

(1) **Representation Function**: Much of human perception and cognition occurs through informational systems that are geared toward condensing complexity to simplicity and for providing ordered representations of more complex wholes. Data analysis performs a similar type of condensing function: it compresses the vast complexity of a social situation into a measurable simplicity of specified variables. On the downside, the process demands a necessary brutalization of reality since most available information must be discarded. Indeed there is actually a *double distortion* taking place here since both the *data process* and the *analysis process* take us (by design) from complexity to simplicity, from more to less information. On the upside, one has the ability (within certain bracketed ranges of convention) to forcefully influence how these representational processes occur and thus to influence the logic of the discovery process.[14]

(2) **Heuristic Function**: Formal models perform a heuristic function in the sense that they gather our thoughts for us and ground them in an understanding. They collapse disparate things and relations into meaningful bundles; they gather bits of information into larger aggregate formations—narrative forms, action sequences, classificatory systems, and the like. They hold complicated relational systems steady and still in our mind, and, thus, they anchor our cognitions about things in the world, providing unifying gestalts that are often iconic or narrative in form.[15]

(3) **Power Function**: Data analysis (as we have defined it here) also has a power function in the sense that formal models operate as representational embodiments, extensions of our thoughts into material space. In this sense, data analysis extends our cognitive capacities in much the same way as any tool (or technology) allows us to achieve greater material impact by amplifying our natural physical capacities.[16] To borrow a concept from Paul Ricoeur, one can say that the objectification of data analysis is in some ways parallel to the process that occurs when discourse is objectified as a text. Specifically, data analysis creates what, following Ricoeur (1971), we think of as a second order externalization (and thus, as with Ricouer, we see this as a kind of materialization function) by taking our theories about the world, giving them material form (as data, however hobbled), interacting with them, (however roughly, through analysis), and, then interpreting them, (however heroically through a reading of signs within a field of meanings and actions, as a part of the lived habitus of model building). Data analysis filters our thoughts through the material world. By watching how those waves come back to us again, in what ways they are bent or changed, we learn.[17]

(4) **Sociality Function**: Finally, data analysis both facilitates and is critically dependent upon the social organization of knowledge production. Data projects derive from (and are produced by) social technologies that are built by craft communities of professional academics located in scientific fields. Data analysis allows for a particular style of collaboration because externalized data (and the methods that produce them) facilitates a distribution of work across many researchers and research sites.[18] In the natural and physical sciences (especially) these linkage systems (articulation structures connecting material objects, styles of action,

systems of discourse, and deeper institutional logics together) have enabled the production of especially fine-grained divisions of labor, allowing for large multiplier effects and the concomitant production of highly complex (industrial scale) systems of knowledge production that can generate powerful bursts of technological (and intellectual) innovation.

METHODS DEBATES—BEFORE
AND AFTER THE CULTURAL TURN

But what if these knowledge functions are of no use when it comes to studying human institutions because the basic methods of scientific investigation are poorly suited to the kinds of knowledge-gathering activities necessary for an adequate study of the social? This issue has been the source of multiple, long-standing philosophical disagreements in the humanities and social sciences. Our only comment on this complex matter is to point out that in recent years this debate has fundamentally shifted ground. What used to be an argument (in the 1970s) about the nature of human culture and its implications for knowledge practices in the social sciences has now moved (and has been moving for a while) to a series of new debates concerning the proper way to interpret the meaning of cultural texts. In other words, the discussion has jumped from the *theory* of cultural analysis to the *method* of cultural analysis. Like the last debate, the current argument is often played out across divides of methodological practice (e.g., the tensions are often at their highest between quantitative and qualitative scholars, and these divides serve as frequent fault-lines in departmental, disciplinary, and interdisciplinary politics), but the issues are very different today than they were thirty years ago.[19]

A key issue back then was whether human actions and institutions are fundamentally different from other kinds of phenomena (of the sort studied by natural scientists) because humans are critically oriented toward meaning. What goes on in human life is broadly oriented towards the ways that humans understand their lifeworlds. Scholars of the social world need to understand what is being understood. But the regularities governing human meanings are fundamentally different than the kinds of laws that are the objects of traditional (natural) scientific modes of explanation. Trial and error, hypothesis testing, all of this may be well and good for explaining the natural world, but these procedures will not carry us through the work that we must do if we are to interpret human action that is fluid, malleable, self-produced, and not anchored in invariant principles or rules.

An edited volume by Rabinow and Sullivan (1979), published thirty years ago as a self-proclaimed manifesto of "the hermeneutic turn," made this argument. The volume's introductory essay explains what was at stake. "(A)s long as there has been a social science, the expectation has been that it would turn from its humanistic infancy to the maturity of hard science, thereby leaving behind its dependence on value, judgment, and individual insight" (p. 1). Citing Kuhn's description of what must happen for a field of science to move from a chaotic "pre-paradigm" state into a fully developed scientific system, Rabinow and Sullivan confidently proclaim, "Now the time seems ripe, even overdue, to announce that there is not going to be an age of paradigm in the social sciences. We contend that the failure to achieve paradigm takeoff is not merely the result of methodological immaturity, but reflects something fundamental about the human world" (p. 4). The volume reprinted classic essays by Thomas Kuhn, Clifford Geertz, Charles Taylor, Paul Ricouer, and H. G. Gadamer (among others), all of them "exemplary of the interpretive or hermeneutic approach to the study of human society" (p. 1).[20]

Many of these essays continue to serve as powerful foundational statements for the human and social sciences, but the debate that had so inflamed the passions of the day and framed the logic of the book is now largely moot. The key difference is the cultural turn itself. Thirty years ago the question of culture was still in dispute; today it is not. Somewhere between then and now nearly all practicing social scientists, even the most quantitatively inclined, experienced some version of a "cultural turn." Thus it is now a veritable tenet of modern social sciences that the world *is* socially constructed, which is to say that knowledge of this state of affairs is now included as part of the collectively shared intellectual background, or, to use Holton's (1988) imagery, the underlying thematic of this set of interlocking intellectual fields.[21]

But just what this means is complex. For us, a key difference is the shift from assuming that culture is constituted by a logic deriving from other kinds of things—the economic base, the material infrastructure, the tyranny of numbers, the demands of biology, the mandates of function, the transformations of structure, the rhythms of the super-organic—or whether culture is instead seen as being the ever-present and inseparable other side of the material, the meaningful complement to embodied practices, and thus treated as something which in fact makes up (constitutes) other kinds of things. This further presumes, or so we would argue, a mutual constitution of the cultural and the non-cultural, a duality of meanings and things, as culture is in turn shaped by what it constitutes (e.g., Giddens 1979; 1984; Friedland and Alford 1991; Sewell 1992; Orlikowski 1992; Breiger 2000; Friedland 2009).

Although this division is quite similar to Kauffman's (2004) distinction between the kind of cultural research that emphasizes a connection to *exogenous* factors (hence the goal is to make linkages between cultural and social processes) and more recent styles of cultural analysis concerned instead with *endogenous* cultural processes (in which the goal is to see how culture itself operates according to a more specific internal logic), in fact, we mean something different. Both before and after the cultural turn, there have been some cultural scholars who emphasized the linking of cultural and social processes together in exogenous analyses and others who focused on the identification and explication of internal mechanisms defined (endogenously) within the cultural system itself. In other words, the tension between endogenous and exogenous approaches to cultural analysis that Kauffman has identified cycle through the discipline (in fractal style, as Abbott 2001 might say). What is different for us and what is designated by our use of the notion of a cultural turn (which suggests a movement from one gestalt system to another) is the sense of the social world as being broadly constituted through systems of shared meanings (in a Wittgenstein language-game sense of the term). And so, what is perhaps most distinctive about post-cultural turn scholarship is the far more nuanced appreciation of how the meaningfulness of social life creates the foundation for that which is the material, the practical, the structural, the social, and even the biological sides of social life. It is thus the sense of how culture constitutes the social world of things (rather than how a logic of things defines the rules of culture) that most precisely delineates a post- from a pre-cultural turn orientation.

Of course the particular way in which the cultural turn has been experienced, understood, internalized, theorized, or resisted varies broadly. For many American social scientists, the "social construction" of the social world exists just as Berger and Luckman (1967) explained it (or perhaps it was Kuhn 1962), and they do not worry much about the matter or reflect on what it means for what they do when they go to work everyday. For others, the analysis of how culture constitutes the social is the very focus of their work. The theoretical basis for understanding culture is, of course, quite complex, Culture is seen as part of a whole, as elements of a dialectic, as a dually structured order linking, for example, material and cultural domains.[22] Others, see it as fragmented, idiosyncratic, de-centered. But, in general it is, we think, true enough, that the accepted theoretical foundations of most social scientific fields today (at least in the American case) include some version of social constructionism as a core element defining the theoretical background.[23]

To give just a few quick examples, consider the sociology of organizations (the field we know best). The new institutionalists, who have been strongly constructionist from their beginnings in the late 1970s, have arguably emerged as the dominant perspective in the field today. More tellingly, even the organizational ecologists (the other huge success story in this arena) have made their own cultural turn over the years. In the 1970s, their theories were based on the logic of biological ecosystems. By the 1990s, their work was grounded in arguments about legitimation and the socially constructed character of value. In the last decade, the core of the program has turned to emphasize the study of the communication of cultural codes as a new method for analyzing the ecological space of organizations.[24] This framework is made explicit in the latest book by Michael Hannan and his colleagues:

> We attempt to develop a fresh perspective on forms and populations. This approach…emphasizes the social construction of categories, forms, and populations. In this respect, it follows the institutionalist tradition started by Max Weber and reinvigorated by Philip Selznick, which strongly suggested that normative matters needed to be incorporated in any attempt to understand organizations. That is, organizations should not just be analyzed objectively in terms of their patterned activities, functions, and external ties—they must also be considered in terms of their social meanings and interpretation given to them by contemporaneous actors (Hannan, Pólos, and Carroll 2007, p. 31).

Table 4.1 Debates over Method: Up to, Including, and
Beyond the Cultural Turn

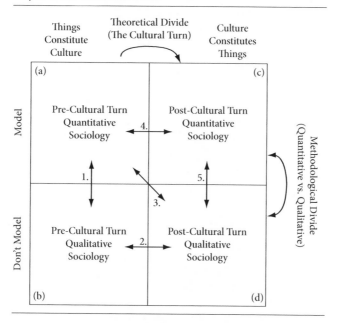

Another example is social network analysis. Thirty years ago, many within this intellectual community were self-consciously anti-cultural positivists. During the 1990s (as we will explain presently), a number of the leading figures in this community began their own version of a cultural turn, and since that time many others have followed.

This is not to say that the debate over method has come to an end. On the contrary, in some ways, it has intensified as it has shifted shape. Table 4.1 can help to visualize this transformation. Here, we follow John Hall's (2004) procedure for differentiating culture scholars along two binary dimensions. Hall distinguished individuals according to "whether they conceptualize phenomena in *meaningful* versus *non-meaningful* terms" (Hall 2004, p. 117). We operationalize this idea differently, however, by placing culture scholars, who have what we call a pre-cultural turn sensibility in the left column, and post-cultural turn intellectual projects on the right. As our column headers suggest, what matters for us in this distinction is not just meaningfulness per se (because cultural modelers have long had an interest in analyzing meaning), but also the way in which meaning operates within an explanatory narrative. As we noted earlier, pre-cultural turn scholarship tended to emphasize how various kinds of things (that exist outside of culture) drive, organize, or constitute the logic of cultural forms. In contrast, post-cultural turn scholarship tends to highlight the ways in which culture (and meaning) is itself constitutive of the other things that make up the social world.[25] Pre-cultural turn theorizing tends to isolate culture from other aspects of the social. Post-cultural turn scholarship seeks to systematically unpack the co-constitution of the cultural and the noncultural.

As the table suggests, the central dispute of the cultural turn era (as reflected, for example, in the Rabinow and Sullivan text) was an argument that stretched across both a theoretical and methodological divide, separating post-cultural turn qualitative sociologists and pre-cultural turn quantitative sociologists (arrow #3 in Table 4.1). The crossing of two dimensions of differentiation results from the uneven development of the field, with qualitative and interpretivist scholars making an earlier and in some ways more forceful cultural turn than their formalist colleagues who often came along later and with less enthusiasm. Today, the argument is more likely to erupt between post-cultural qualitative scholars and post-cultural turn quantitative analysts (hence, arrow #5).[26] But to understand the character of those arguments, we need to more fully distinguish between the different approaches to modeling culture, especially the differences between what we will call hermeneutic and non-hermeneutic styles of formal analysis.

FOUR TYPES OF CULTURE MODELS

The divide between quantitative and qualitative methodologies may be less of a binary distinction than a disjoint gradient. At least when we reflect on the variety of formal approaches that have been used for modeling culture, it is clear that some are far more interpretively intentioned than are others. In this section of the chapter, we will highlight that distinction as we describe four types of modeling strategies that have (classically) been used to analyze culture. To be clear, we are now focusing on just the top row of Table 4.1 (analyses using quantitative measurement models), but we are going to split this group again horizontally along a new fissure, distinguishing between those modeling projects that are hermeneutic and those that are not (see Table 4.2).

Here, we must clarify from the start that we use the term "hermeneutic" in a particular sense. We focus on the definition of hermeneutic that has been suggested by Paul Ricoeur who we cited earlier and whose work has been central to the field. According to Ricoeur (1971), "The word 'hermeneutics' concerns the rules required for the interpretation of the written documents of our culture" (1971, p. 197). Although, it is true that Ricoeur sees the model of the text as an exemplar for other types of interpretation, as Ricoeur's own work makes clear, spoken language differs from written language in a number of important ways (and, as we will explain later, one must carefully distinguish the two when considering the problem of interpretation). Recognizing that this solution leaves open a whole variety of other theoretical and methodological conundrums (about agency, subjectivity, speech activity, intersubjectivity, and the like), we nonetheless will follow Ricoeur's conception of hermeneutics as a way to begin this discussion. In each cell, we have named one scholar (whose work we will describe in some detail) because they provide ideal typical illustrations of the four types of cultural modeling styles of interest to us here.

Table 4.2 Four Types of Culture Models: Interpretive vs. Non-Interpretive, and Pre- vs. Post-Cultural Turn

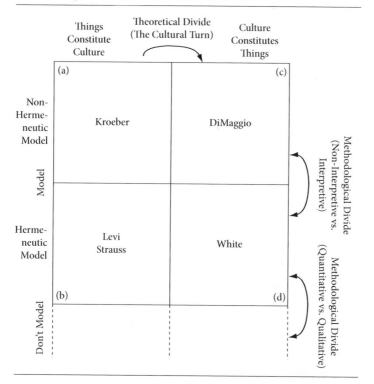

Cell A. Pre-Cultural Turn/Non-Hermeneutic: Alfred Kroeber

Probably because their work was inherently comparative, anthropologists were the original masters of the culture concept. So it is no surprise that Alfred Kroeber, a leading anthropologist, was one of the first American social scientists to develop a modern approach to modeling culture. Kroeber's interest was similar to Durkheim's in that Kroeber wanted to demonstrate that culture existed, that it had its own character or logic to it, and that it operated at some remove, outside of, and above the heads of particular individuals who otherwise participate in it. He wanted to prove this with scientific rigor, and so he took up the study of women's evening dresses as a way to address the problem (Kroeber 1919).

Kroeber begins his paper by describing the rising and falling of various cultural trends, trends that have a kind of sweep and force that reflect something bigger and broader than any particular individual experience. Even a genius like Shakespeare must be seen in historical context because, as Kroeber explains, there is a clear pattern that underlies "the story of the Elizabethan drama from its stiffly archaic inceptions through the awakening in Greene and Marlowe, the Shakespearian glory, the slackening to the level of Fletcher...to the close of playhouses by the civil war, the picture of an even-sided curve rises in the mind." The curve might strike us as tracing something like the ebb and flow of a specific literary genre within an institutional field, but Kroeber sees something different. His culture concept is framed by his location within the emerging intellectual field of American anthropology as it existed a century ago. He thus leans more toward a functional aesthetics where the quality of cultural forms vary absolutely, not just as cultural traits defined by the presence or absence of specific practices and conventions, but rather, also, as expressions of cultural excellence.[27] Arrayed on a timeline, Shakespeare's "masterpieces…fall in the first decade of the seventeenth century. His more prolix and less intense tragedies and comedies, and the plays of contemporaries nearest him in achievement, precede and follow by a few years. Each quinquennium more distant from the culmination is marked by greater crudity in recession, more extended laxity in progression of time…" (p. 235). Thus for Kroeber, the quality of cultural expression goes from low to high and then back down again in a pulse of authentic creativity that quickly burns itself out. And this pulse, it turns out, is not that of any person or individual. It is the rhythm of culture itself that Kroeber is following.

Kroeber explains, "If such a surge stood unique, it would be meaningless. But it is so often repeated in the history of aesthetics that something of a generic principle must be involved. The classic French drama…the Dutch and Flemish schools of painting…and, we might add, philosophy—each of these isolable movements has been traced through similar course of origin, growth, climax, decline, and either death or petrification, analogous to the life stories of organisms" (p. 236). Here then is a second expression of Kroeber's historicity. When he thinks about patterns in cultural forms, he sees them as expressions of a larger force of nature that is operating on social processes, perhaps some deep underlying logic that governs all of human culture, and, according to which, every cultural form must respond.[28] This suggests a force of culture that is more than just what humans experience (or, at least, more than what they are knowledgeable of). This culture is driven by abstract causal forces, factors lying outside the parameters of individual human experience, and in that sense, although this would clearly count as a kind of endogenous approach to culture (Kauffman 2004), it shows how culture that is decoupled from an adequate sense of the social leads to a different kind of exogenity, to a logic that is both immanent to and also outside of culture itself. This is why we classify Kroeber as an example of what we are calling a pre-cultural turn analytic sensibility. For although he was completely focused on analyzing culture, and in spite of his other impressive contributions to the field, Kroeber was weighed down by theoretical tools that were thoroughly marked by his historical, situational, and professional period, such that, ultimately, for Kroeber, things (which, in this case, are largely abstractions) constitute the logic of culture (rather than the other way around).

We have placed Kroeber in the top row of Table 4.2 because he employed a non-hermeneutic style of the formal model. In this regard, Kroeber stands at the beginning of a long line of formal modelers in the social sciences. The problem, at least as Kroeber saw the matter, is that "the variability of the phenomena is qualitative whereas a workable law or deterministic principle must be quantitative in nature." And thus he confronted the classic question, how does one move from quality to quantity?[29] He considers, for example, the possibility of using a set of informants to make numerical judgments about the qualities of particular cultural objects, but he rejects this strategy because "it would rest on a series of composite photographs of verdicts as to qualities, and not on verifiable measurements" (p. 236). However, Kroeber was also involved in archeological research so he had an expectation that material artifacts could be used to deduce the properties of cultural forms and, indeed, "manufactured objects offer an approach which no other class of civilizational data present: they can be accurately and easily measured." Still the quantity of found artifacts are "often insufficiently large, or from interrupted periods, or of uncertain date" (p. 238). And, more than this, many objects (especially if they are more utilitarian in nature) are less responsive to cultural trends.

This explains why Kroeber turns to the study of women's evening dresses. On the one hand, dresses are good to model with because they are especially cultural in nature. They are "material objects whose chief end is ornament." They are impractical, specialized, highly aestheticized, and, as Kroeber's explains, "the variations are therefore purely stylistic" (p. 239) and thus more likely to exhibit long term cultural trends undistorted by the periodic shifts of utilitarian demands and inventions. Moreover, in contrast to the vagaries accompanying the analysis of archeological artifacts, Kroeber turns to study women's evening wear precisely because the data can be gathered. The styles were preserved in texts, as images published in fashion magazines. "Such journals have existed for over a century; they are exactly dated; and they bring together in each volume a considerable number of examples to which rule or calipers can be applied without hindrance" (p. 238). Kroeber sampled annually starting from the year he was doing this research, 1918, to as back as far as 1844.[30]

Kroeber looked for a set of simple metrics that he could use to gauge stylistic changes over time. He describes how, as a graduate student at Columbia (around 1900) he had first tried to tackle the problem by measuring all relevant features of the dresses, but he was frustrated by his efforts. "One might measure collars or sleeves or ruffles for some years, and then collars and sleeves and ruffles disappeared....If one took as a base the total length of the figure, coiffures fell and rose by inches from time to time, or were entirely concealed by hats or nets. I abandoned the plan as infeasible" (p. 239). But he returned to the project nearly twenty years later with a new set of intuitions. The second time around he limited himself to eight simple measurements (four lengths and four widths) that could be applied across the entire range of his data. He began by measuring: "1. Total length of figure from the center of the mouth to the tip of the toe. If the shoe was covered, the lowest point of the skirt edge was chosen. The selection of the mouth obviated all difficulties arising from alteration of hairdress" (1919, p. 239). Thus, Kroeber starts with a very practical concern, how to measure features of cultural forms that would apply across the range of variation of all objects within the field. He then proceeds to record the length of skirt (calculated by measuring from the floor to the bottom of the skirt and subtracting from the first measurement), the waist (minimum width), the "length of décolletage...[d]iameter of the skirt at its hem..." as well as the width of the shoulders "or more accurately, the width of the décolletage across the

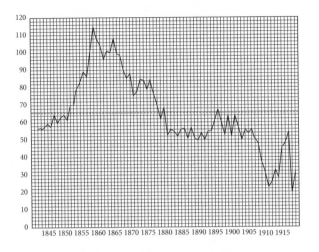

Figure 4.1 Kroeber's Model of Cyclic Patterns in Women's Dress Fashions
Source: Copied from Kroeber 1919, p. 247.

shoulder" (p. 240). He measured ten dress images for each year, "the first ten suitable for measurement being taken from each volume so as to insure random instead of subjective selection…" (p. 240). He calculated ratios for all of the measures and plotted the values on a set of three graphs with a horizontal axis marking off each year in his study, and a vertical axis marking off the ratio values on a percentage scale (see Figure 4.1).[31]

Figure 4.1 illustrates Kroeber's model of stylistic trends in the widths of women's skirts. It is a simple graph. It tracks what might appear to be a relatively unexciting wave or trend line, rising up, falling down again (although the down slope seems to have some interruptions on its way to the bottom). Presumably, it will rise up again and fall down again, or, at least, so Kroeber wants us to believe. Kroeber's interest in this work is to illustrate, with scientific formality and repeatable results that a logic of culture exists, that it is bigger than, and thus external from, any individual self. As he surveys his results, he matches the data analysis step by step to things that he knows about the cultural forms he is investigating. He also gently works in a set of theoretical assumptions about what may be going on in the graph. In the process, he narrates his model into life. Here is how he describes this graph:

> When our record opens in 1844, it finds evening toilettes of moderate skirt width, 57 per cent. of the body length. (*) For several years the proportion fluctuates mildly, gradually rising.
>
> In 1851, having attained a percentage of 61, the width of skirt suddenly begins to mount rapidly and continuously, until the plotted curve skyrockets to the extreme maximum of 116 in 1859. This is the apex of the crinoline hoop skirt fashion, when the flare of the skirt exceeds the height of the person. In eight years the skirt diameter has nearly doubled.
>
> From 1859 on, the history of the skirt may be summarily described as a fifty years' progressive constriction.

> The narrowing after 1859 is not as rapid as the widening immediately preceding; but within three years the proportion has fallen from 116 to 96. At this point a new sub-factor enters: the train. The skirt as a whole continues to lose fulness (sic), but the attached train more than compensates for the shrinkage of diameter at its base. The plot therefore shows a checking of the descent, a new rise, and a secondary maximum of 108 in 1865. {* Mouth to toe, or to lowest point of skirt if the toe is covered} (pp. 247–248)

His narration follows the graph from its beginning to its end, and he repeats the process with each of the other graphs (which track the other measured qualities of the dress). What he finds are some surprisingly coherent wave trends reflecting the character of stylistic changes. In Kroeber's terms,

> We have, I think, now found reasonable evidence of an underlying pulsation in the width of civilized women's skirts, which is symmetrical and extends in its up-and-down beat over a full century; of an analogous rhythm in skirt length, but with a period of only about a third the duration; some indication that the position of the waist line may completely alter, also following a "normal" curve, in a seventy-year period; and a possibility that the width of shoulder exposure varies in the same manner, but with the longest rhythm of all, since the continuity of tendency in one direction for seventy years establishes a periodicity of about a century and a half, if the change in this feature of dress follows a symmetrically recurrent plan (pp. 257–258).

And so, with a simple measurement protocol, one that is easy to understand, and replicate Kroeber provides a model of what appears to be systemic cycles (he calls them waves) of incremental change in the styles of women's dress fashions.[32] Kroeber's piece is a classic in the history of formal models of culture, not only because of what he was able to show, but also because the work provides an excellent example of a very particular approach to modeling culture.

In this work, Kroeber illustrates a style of cultural modeling that reflects a pre-cultural turn analytic sensibility because for Kroeber culture is ultimately an artifact decoupled from the broader institutional systems that make up the social order as well as from the set of cultural understandings that constitute these systems. Culture has its own logic (and the study looks to unpack an endogenous quality of the cultural forms), but the motor for that logic is outside of the lived experiences and meanings of individuals in that world and even in a sense (perhaps) outside of the social itself. Kroeber is imprecise about this. At one point he notes, "There is something in these phenomena, for all their reputed arbitrariness, that resembles what we call law: a scheme, an order on a scale not without a certain grandeur. Not that fashion of a future date can be written now. Every style is a component of far too many elements, and in part uniquely entering elements, to make true prediction possible" (p. 258). But, in the end, there is something, ineffable, perhaps, that explains these cultural forms. "The super-organic or superpsychic or super-individual that we call civilization appears to have an existence, an order, and a causality as objective and as determinable as those of the subpsychic or inorganic" (p. 263).[33]

Kroeber's project also reflects a non-hermeneutic style of cultural modeling because the data are *not* used to gain understanding about what people think about; what they think that they are doing; or even what the underlying parameters of the cultural meaning systems are that enable certain types of thinking to occur. Instead, culture, for Kroeber, is a particular kind of social object. It is embodied in material artifacts that have variable qualities and manifestations whose shape and character can be modeled. In Kroeber's essay, culture is everywhere and nowhere. The subject of research is style, and yet there are no stylish people in this paper. There are no knowing agents or reference to talk about the meanings or experiences of fashion. What is being studied instead are the after-effects of the actions of culturally knowledgeable people. We are left with material artifacts, things that were made, and our task is to carefully examine and compare these objects, one to the other, as a way to begin to understand them. It is truly as if we are archaeologists trying to learn something about the culture of an ancient people, and all we have available to observe are the potsherds left behind in the dirt. As an archeologist, one has limited access to the lived experience of the people one wishes to understand, and so one must do what one can, gather up whatever evidence can be gathered, study it very carefully, pay attention to features of design, construction, style, and then one can infer what it was that may have been going on. But, of course, Kroeber did not need to study women's evening dresses in this manner. He was, after all, an accomplished ethnographer, renowned for his fieldwork among native American tribes (it was, Kroeber who worked with, and famously wrote about, the Ishi, the last of the Yahi Indians). Thus, he could have chosen to do a study in which he talked with women who purchased dresses. He could have interviewed magazine editors, seamstresses, and the men who escorted these women to their evening events. But in this stream of research, he made a different choice. He chose, first of all, to study texts, not people, and to use a data analysis technique that led to him to gather very small bits of information across a large expanse of time, a strategy with which he hoped to identify characteristics of stylistic change that would not be otherwise observable using the methodology of conventional ethnography.

Cell B. Pre-Cultural Turn/Hermeneutic: Lévi-Strauss

This then raises the question of what would a hermeneutically focused formal model of culture look like? The key distinction, by our accounting, is whether the researcher has the goal of developing a formal measurement model which is intended to help explicate, summarize, or to otherwise cast light *directly on the meanings* inscribed in a cultural text. Claude Lévi-Strauss, another leading anthropologist of his day, can help illustrate this type of modeling project. A key figure in the history of structuralism, Lévi-Strauss made significant contributions both to the theory of kinship and also to the analysis of cultural myths. He did this, most especially, by developing ways of applying the lessons he had learned from structuralist linguistics to the study of other types of human institutions. It is particularly

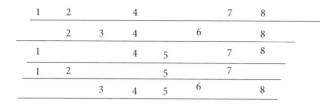

Figure 4.2 Lévi-Strauss's Model of the Structural Logic of a Myth

Source: Copied from Lévi-Strauss 1963, p. 213.

with respect to the study of myths that Lévi-Strauss pioneered the use of formal models of culture that advanced an explicitly hermeneutic goal. Although he did not (generally speaking) use statistical forms of data analysis, he nonetheless measured features of the meanings within the myths and employed a form of Boolean logic to collapse complex structures into simpler forms.[34] He did this to produce formal models (structure preserving homomorphic reductions) of mythical stories. In generating these models, his goal was very consciously interpretive; he sought to make their meanings clear and to reveal the deeper underlying pattern of relations that would capture the symbolic code. In this sense Lévi-Strauss was very much a pioneer in the development of hermeneutically oriented formal measurement models of culture.

One of the earliest and still most recognizable examples of Lévi-Strauss' efforts can be found in his essay on "The Structural Study of Myth." Figure 4.2 reproduces his model of the structures of meaning in a mythical narrative, the kind of model that Lévi-Strauss applies to provide a reading of the Oedipus myth. In this essay, he argues that the goal of an interpretation is different when one works at the level of myth than when one works at the level of a linguistic statement. Although myths are a part of language and must (in general) be modeled in an analogous fashion (in terms of the relations that link them together as a system), Lévi-Strauss also makes clear that myths operate in a different discursive register. Rather than looking to find the patterns of relations that link particular phonemes, morphemes or sememes together into coherent sounds, concepts, and sentences, Lévi-Strauss argues that it is necessary to look for the relevant "mythemes" that make up the "gross constituent units" of the myth. This involves the task of linking sentences together in patterns of relations and, more than this, an investigation of the various "bundles of relations" that constitute the core elements of the myth.

Lévi-Strauss' technique depends on breaking the myth into simple sentences (or "*statements*") and then looking for commonalities in the semantic functions that each sentence performs. In the case of the Oedipus myth, the statements are semantically (and thus structurally) divided into common bundles of relations. Figure 4.2 shows the layout of such an analysis with the sentences arrayed across each row in the order of their telling, but they are also grouped into columns and assigned numbers (1–8) that correspond to the bundle of relations that each mytheme belongs to. "All the relations belonging to the same column exhibit one common feature which it is our task to discover" (p. 215). The first such bundle from the Oedipus myth includes a series of statements in which blood relations are overemphasized, "Cadmos seeks his sister Europa, ravished by Zeus," "Oedipus marries his mother, Jocasta," "Antigone buries her brother, Polynices, despite prohibition." The second bundle of relations have to do with the underrating of blood relations—"The Spartoi kill one another," "Oedipus kills his father, Laios," "Eteocles kills his brother, Polynices." The third bundle has to do with monsters that are being slain, while the fourth bundle has to do with difficulties in walking straight and standing upright.

Lévi-Strauss explains that if the goal is "to *tell* the myth, we would disregard the columns and read the rows from left to right and from top to bottom. But if we want to *understand* the myth, then we will have to disregard one half of the diachronic dimension (top to bottom) and read from left to right, column after column, each one being considered as a unit" (p. 214). In the process, Lévi-Strauss provides a simplified understanding of the deeper system of relations that ties the myth together as a set of complementary relational systems. His vision is very structuralist at this level—he writes, "It follows that column four is to column three as column one is to column two. The inability to connect two kinds of relationships is overcome (or rather replaced by) the assertion that contradictory relationships are identical inasmuch as they are both self-contradictory in a similar way" (p. 216).

By applying these methods, Lévi-Strauss strips the myth down to its bare elemental form, thereby revealing a kind of structural map with which the *meaning* of the myth can then be more easily understood. Thus Lévi-Strauss's interpretation of Oedipus: "The myth has to do with the inability, for a culture which holds the belief that mankind is autochthonous [born from the earth], to find a satisfactory transition between this theory and the knowledge that human beings are actually born from the union of man and woman. Although the problem cannot be solved, the Oedipus myth provides a kind of logical tool which relates the original problem—born from one or born from two?—to the derivative problem: born from different or born from the same? By a correlation of this type, the overrating of blood relations is to the underrating of blood relations as the attempt to escape autochthony is to the impossibility to succeed in it" (p. 216).[35]

In spite of his commitment to developing hermeneutically grounded formal models, Lévi-Strauss was nonetheless locked into a pre-cultural turn theoretical sensibility. Like Kroeber, Lévi-Strauss was very much focused on what Kauffman might describe as an endogenous analysis of culture, and yet, also like Kroeber, there was a strong sense of something else outside of the cultural artifacts themselves, some other more fundamental logic that constituted culture's dynamic essence. For Lévi-Strauss, the essential force behind the logic of culture (and this includes other social institutions which were also understood to be structured like a language) derived from "the universal laws which make up the unconscious activity of the mind" (1963, p. 65). Here Lévi-Strauss talks of constructing "a sort of periodic table of linguistic structures that would be comparable to the table of elements which Mendeleieff introduced into modern chemistry" (1963, p. 58), and he praises Kroeber's work on women's fashion noting, "a remarkable analogy between these researches and those of a contemporary biologist, G. Teissier, on the growth of the organs of certain crustaceans" (1963, p. 59). In other words, for Lévi-Strauss, much like Kroeber, the analysis of culture was driven by the pursuit of an essential core that served as an anchor and an origin (an arché in Foucault's sense) for cultural expression.[36] This meant that the goal of Lévi-Strauss's analysis was not ultimately interested in analyzing the ways that material practices, social structures, and other *objective* social processes might be understood as culturally constituted and (dually) constituting activities, rather, Lévi-Strauss hoped to understand how some things (exogenous factors, outside and beyond the lived experience of culture) ultimately explain the logic of cultural forms.

Cell C. Post-Cultural Turn/Non-Hermeneutic: DiMaggio

During the 1960s, with the exception of qualitative researchers who were mostly working at a more micro-level focus, the study of culture largely went out of fashion in American sociology.[37] The concept had been devalued, thanks in part to its close association with Talcott Parsons' theories, but also, in this period of middle-range sociology, research concerns had shifted toward more micro- and meso- levels of social life whereas culture had conventionally been treated as something describing society as a whole. In practice, a new appreciation for the interpretation of culture was being developed by emerging communities of qualitative sociologists during this era, but that work was not getting picked up by quantitative scholars who were focused on their own middle-ranged theoretical projects. Also during this period the use of attitude measures (and other types of interpretive measurement techniques) were coming to be used less frequently as many sociological subfields embraced more "objectivist" approaches to data modeling. This means that qualitative and quantitative scholars were tending to go their separate ways, and culture (with a few notable exceptions such as political sociology which was still focused on the role of opinions in generating outcomes) largely ceased to be an object for quantitative analysis.[38]

Richard Peterson was one of the first American sociologists to put culture, understood in a more meso-level (and hence in a more modern institutional sense), back on the agenda for those who used measurement models to study the social world. Peterson had been trained as an organizational sociologist, had worked with Alvin Gouldner, and also had a deep and abiding interest in music. He brought the two interests together in his work on cycles in symbol production (Peterson and Berger 1975). Like Kroeber, Peterson's efforts were non-hermeneutic: they were not concerned with the interpretation of the meanings of cultural forms. Rather his goal was to find a solid and defensible metric for measuring variability in cultural forms which could then be explained with respect to the conditions within a particular social domain, in this case, in an industry—the popular song industry. But Peterson went considerably further than Kroeber in that he also grounded his model for explaining the variation in cultural forms not in abstract notions (of the super-organic) but instead, in a sophisticated and elaborate theory and analysis of the social organization of the culture industry.

An important next step was taken by Paul DiMaggio who followed Peterson's lead in grounding his study of culture in a detailed analysis of the social structural terrain in which the cultural forms were embedded. Borrowing from the most advanced methodological traditions of American stratification research, DiMaggio developed a sophisticated and nuanced way of measuring variations in the cultural form itself. In his work on cultural capital, for example, he used a factor analysis to find patterns in the ways in which high school students are oriented with respect to their understanding of, appreciation of, and practical experience with elite cultural forms. Following Bourdieu, DiMaggio theorized that students would have acquired cultural sensibilities and orientations from the lived experiences and cultural milieu (e.g., the habitus) of their household of origin, and that those students who had mastered the skills and knowledge associated with elite forms of culture would be in possession of a high volume of what Bourdieu called cultural capital.

DiMaggio's (1982) studies showed that one could use technical methodologies (from the American social stratification tradition) to analyze data about an individual's relationship to culture and then use that metric as an effective predictor of students' success (as measured by grades achieved in high school). Figure 4.3 shows an example of one of DiMaggio's models of culture. The table summarizes the results from a large number of regression models. The first row shows results from trying to predict the grades of the daughters of men who did not complete high school. The first column has the contribution to explained variance of the students' scores on measures of intelligence. The beta coefficient (0.2930***) shows that effect in a standardized metric that can be easily compared to the contributions of variance from other predictor variables (such as column three which has the measured effect of cultural capital (0.1636***). DiMaggio also reports the overall variance explained ($R^2 = 0.1453$) and the amount of extra variation explained once the cultural measures are included in the models (0.0310). The largest effects for high levels of cultural capital occur among the daughters of college educated men, where the overall contributions to explained variance in grades are quite high. In models such as this, DiMaggio helped bring culture back to the statistical mainstream as a measured quality of social life shown to be on par with other, more presumably objective features of social organization.[39]

DiMaggio's models are non-hermeneutic. Without interpreting anyone's understandings, (e.g., using measures of more subjective phenomena) as in the more traditional survey approaches to culture (conceptualized as clusters of attitudes, values, norms, and beliefs), DiMaggio showed that survey technology could usefully be employed to measure significant cultural phenomena. With this he was able to demonstrate the importance of culture as a causal variable while still relying on more "objective" types of measures—visits to museums, piano lessons, familiarity with high culture, iconic figures, that were easy for mainstream quantitative sociologists to accept as having reasonable face validity.[40]

Dependent Variable		1	2	3	4	R^2	Increase in R^2 with Vars. 2–4
		Females with Non-High School Graduate Fathers				N = 342	
Grades in All Subjects	B	.5006	.3136	2.2030	.7400	.1453	.0310
	s.e.	.0660	.3966	.5010	.4966		
	beta	.2930***	.0331	.1636***	.0614		
Grades in English	B	.0440	.0906	.3312	−.0195	.1148	.0452
	s.e.	.0086	.0504	.0651	.0633		
	beta	.2093***	.0788	.2036***	−.0133		
Grades in History	B	.0654	.0958	.2638	.0213	.1358	.0272
	s.e.	.0093	.0546	.0705	.0685		
	beta	.2840	.0761	.1479***	.0145		
Grades in Manthematics	B	.0450	.0693	−.0005	.1535	.0442	.0075
	s.e.	.0098	.0577	.0745	.0724		
	beta	.1943***	.0548	−.0003	.0951*		
		Females with High School Graduate Fathers				N = 342	
Grades in All Subjects	B	.6216	−.8526	2.7058	.3466	.1776	0.494
	s.e.	.0980	.5542	.6034	.6064		
	beta	.3266***	−.0844	.2238***	.0301		
Grades in English	B	.0629	.0831	.3641	−.0114	.1755	.0659
	s.e.	.0115	.0657	.0715	.0722		
	beta	.2906***	−.0720	.2608***	.0086		
Grades in History	B	.0634	−.0008	.4029	.0278	.1640	.0611
	s.e.	.0132	.0749	.0816	.0824		
	beta	.2585***	−.0006	.2546***	.0185		
Grades in Mathematics	B	.0870	−.1431	.2245	.0647	.1384	.0230
	s.e.	.0141	.0804	.0875	.0884		
	beta	.3356***	−.1034	.1343*	.0406		
		Females withcollege Graduate Fathers				N = 113	
Grades in All Subjects	B	.7317	−.6325	4.1952	−.2707	.2034	.0910
	s.e.	.1738	1.0617	1.1567	1.2902		
	beta	.3714***	−.0530	.2968***	−.0174		
Grades in English	B	.0913	−.0148	.4244	−.0566	.2093	.0729
	s.e.	.0214	.1264	.1386	.1561		
	beta	.3894***	−.0108	.2649**	−.0317		
Grades in History	B	.0673	−.0764	.6174	.0944	.1644	.1160
	s.e.	.0247	.1459	.1600	.1801		
	beta	.2557**	−.0496	.23431***	.0470		
Grades in Mathematics	B	.0702	−.0924	.3971	.0661	.1216	.0578
	s.e.	.0235	.1387	.1521	.1713		
	beta	.2877**	−.0647	.2380*	.0355		

  * p ≤ .05, two-tailed.
  ** p ≤ .01, two-tailed.
  *** p ≤ .001, two-tailed.

Figure 4.3 DiMaggio's Model of the Predictive Power of Cultural Capital

Source: Table 5, DiMaggio 1982, p. 197.

DiMaggio's models are, on the other hand, very much a reflection of a post-cultural turn sensibility. The main innovation here was borrowed from Pierre Bourdieu, the notion of treating culture as a resource that was concrete, fungible, measurable, that operated in tangible ways, and could be used in models to explain respectable amounts of variance in data sets just like other types of status attainment factors studied in the Wisconsin tradition of data analysis. By featuring cultural capital prominently as an independent variable, highlighting a case where culture clearly explains things, this essay was marked as one of the early successes of the new (American) cultural sociology project, an early expression of what we now call "the cultural turn."[41] But, all of this work is still in a sense very much within the frame of Kroeber's approach to modeling culture in the sense that the core meanings of these cultural phenomena are not the object of investigation. Not meanings, understandings, the content of talk, nor the way of knowing what is known are being modeled in these projects. Instead, culture is modeled as objects that are thought to be reflections, effects, or markers of that which is known, understood, or experienced. Thus the explanatory project is concerned with the effects of culture, not its meaning. In the sense we have outlined here, these are non-hermeneutic styles of modeling culture. This does not mean, by the way, that DiMaggio is unconcerned or uninterested in these matters. On the contrary, his work has always highlighted the power of culture (understood as systems of meanings) to influence the social. The question instead has to do with a strategy for analysis—what is the best way to model culture and its effects?[42]

Cell D. Post-Cultural Turn/Hermeneutic: White

More recently a different group of formal modelers have come on the scene who also begin from a post-cultural turn theoretical sensibility but who differ in that they focus very specifically on modeling meaning, which is to say, they are working to develop tools (e.g., styles of formal data analysis) that can gain a better purchase on the interpretative qualities of discourse systems. Their goal, at some level and in some fashion, is to use data analysis to offer a kind of reading of a cultural text or, if not that, than at least to devise models that can serve as effective tools to reveal hitherto unseen features of discourse systems that can usefully contribute to a more effective reading of a cultural text. In other words, like Lévi-Strauss, these scholars focus on using formal models to enhance their capacity to read and interpret systems of cultural meanings. Also like Lévi-Strauss, many of the scholars in this group are interested in the development of formalist styles of relational structuralism as a way into the problem of measuring and interpreting culture. They are, to borrow a phrase from Alexander and Smith (2001), *structural hermeneuticists* because they apply structuralist methodologies in the pursuit of hermeneutic goals. In contrast to Lévi-Strauss, however, this new generation is not bound to the same kind of pre-cultural turn sensibilities (such as the emphasis on functional theories of cognition) that had plagued Lévi-Strauss. A more salient precursor here might be another anthropologist, Clifford Geertz (1973), who called for a semiotic theory of culture, by which he meant an approach to cultural analysis where meanings are foundational to experiences, are themselves structured like a language, and are articulated into systems of lived experience and practice.[43]

Harrison White is our exemplar figure for this cell. In the main this is because White's current intellectual project, starting most clearly with the publication of the first edition of *Identity and Control* (1992), has been dedicated to a systematic rethinking of the sociology of agency, culture, and institutional analysis from a perspective that highlights the use of social network theories, methodologies, and sensibilities. To this task, White brings a long and distinguished career of scholarly work concerned with the development of different variants of structuralist theorizing. Indeed, by the time the first edition of *Identity and Control* was published, White had already been (for several decades) one of the leading figures in the social scientific program of social network analysis.[44]

In the early 1960s, after reading Lévi-Strauss and becoming fascinated by the social and mathematical problems raised in structuralist analysis, White began developing and extending the theory and method for applying relational mathematics to the study of the social organization of groups. This was a style of formal analysis that emphasized not persons (or objects) but relations (or ties); not the essential features of things, but the configurational patterns of relations that constitute the core logic of social structures. And while DiMaggio (forthcoming) argues that network analysis is, in many ways, the perfect style of data analysis for the formal study of culture, in point of fact, most network analysts were, at least at the beginning, largely disinclined to pursue questions of culture, especially a hermeneutically oriented analysis of culture.

Traditionally known as one of the most "geeky" specialties in sociology (because it was one of the places where mathematical theory and sociology melded in productive ways), network analysis was also, for many years, a bastion for a certain kind of materialist fundamentalism. This perspective treated the measurement of objective relations (network ties) as a more effective analytic strategy than anything that could be gleaned from listening to what was said in subjective accounts of individuals who were living inside highly constraining social network structures. Such data was regarded with suspicion because, when asked, it was presumed that these individuals would willingly offer, *retrospectively*, rational accounts of actions that may well have been undertaken for largely tacit, implicit, or otherwise unknown reasons (or so went one account). In other words, up until the time that White himself led what can be described as a cultural turn in the social scientific subfield of network analysis, the tradition had long been associated with an attitude that saw cultural analysis as being more or less antithetical to the development of useful models of social life.[45] White broke with his more objectivist colleagues when he began to develop his broader theory of action and control (1992, 2008). The epistemic character of this break shows all the more reason why White's own turn toward culture was significant (and why we see him as the exemplar figure for this cell). Not only did White put matters of interpretation on the agenda for social network analysis more broadly, he also, over the years, encouraged his students (who have themselves gone on to be leaders in both of these sub-fields) to pursue projects that grappled in fundamental ways with theoretical questions that focused on matters of culture.[46]

In his new project, White has been working to develop something like a generalized phenomenology of network life that emphasizes how the experience of being an agent seeking forms of control in a network world is constituted through a series of other types of relational systems, systems of talk organized into conversations, groups of regularly interacting others who share common systems of discourse, common discourses that materialize into institutional systems of rhetoric, and so on.[47] Moreover, White has made his intentions in this regard quite clear. Culture and the localized sense of meaningfulness (and within that, the relational systems of meanings that make culture and meanings operate) are profoundly foundational (indeed constitutive) of the lived experience of social agents as they maneuver their way across interlocking network spaces. Thus the more subjective side of network life—the meanings, narratives, conversations, styles of talk, genres of understanding, and logics of cultural fields more broadly—are themselves the proper object of formal modeling, or, as White puts it, "Interpretative approaches are central to achieving a next level of adequacy in social data…" (White 1997, pp. 57–58).

Following White's lead, a number of social network scholars took up the interpretative study of culture and started modeling meanings. This group of "hermeneutic structuralists" have deployed two key principles. First, following in the path of semiotics and discourse theory, cultural meanings are understood to consist of relational systems within which sign elements are linked together in networks of similarity and difference (Mohr 1998). So, for example, Gibson (2003) models conversations as social networks; Bearman and Stovell (2000) use network models to analyze the narrative structures buried in the life stories of Germans living inside Nazi Germany; while Smith (2007) uses similar procedures to compare and contrast models of the same historical narratives seen from two different perspectives, two ethnic communities living alongside the Yugoslovian/Italian border. Ruef (1999) used text data to map the discursive logic of the health care industry, and Rawlings and Bourgeois (2004) do the same for higher education (to name but a few examples).

The second principle describes the notion of an ordered duality, according to which two discrete institutional subdomains are shown to be connected in such a way that they can be modeled as uniquely ordered structural logics that are linked through an articulation of co-constitution. Mohr and Duquenne (1997) use Galois' lattices to interpret the dual institutional logic of Progressive Era poverty categories and their corresponding relief practices. Mische and Pattison (2000; Mische 2007) use lattices to model the dualities that link political ideologies with the organizational histories of Brazilian youth activists. Reviews of popular music are analyzed by van Venrooij (2009a, 2009b) who uses correspondence analysis to model the co-constitution of musical genre categories (defined with reference to the embeddedness of each album within the field of aesthetic discourse) with the social organizational logic of the music industry itself (major or independent producers, white or black artists, men or women). Breiger (2000) generalizes about these types of projects, fashioning what he calls a methodological toolkit for practice theory, which he then applies to data in order to model the dually ordered logic of power and precedent within U.S. Supreme Court decisions. Mohr and White (2008) theorize these types of dually ordered relations in the context of a general logic of institutions that seeks to link "together different orders and realms of social life, notably the agentic with the structural, the symbolic with the material, and the micro with the meso and the macro structures of social organization" (p. 485).

To give an example of the kind of culture model that is being developed under this analytic framework, we have reproduced a figure from one of our own articles, "Modeling Foucault: Dualities of Power in Institutional Fields" by Mohr and Neely (2009) (see Figure 4.4.). This image was created from a block model analysis

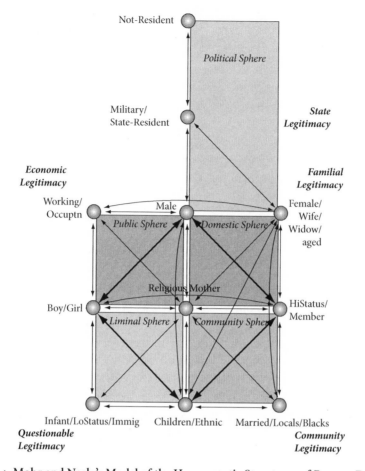

Figure 4.4 Mohr and Neely's Model of the Hermeneutic Structures of Poverty Discourse

Source: Copied from Figure 4, Mohr and Neely 2009, p. 229.

of relational ties within a textual database collected from the 1888 edition of the New York City Charity Directory.[48] Information was recorded from the 168 identifiably custodial institutions listed in that year's directory (this included all the orphanages, lunatic asylums, men's and women's prisons, reform colonies, poor houses, industrial schools, homes for fallen girls, and so on, that were located geographically within the Borough of Manhattan in New York City). We collected the full texts of all statements that were made regarding the identities of people that were (or at least were claimed to be) included for treatment (as was reported by each custodial institution in its self-description for the Directory). In the paper, models are used to identify four different types of classification systems, each grounded in a different logic of power as suggested by Foucault's writings. In Figure 4.4 our focus was on systems of power as subjection that were deployed in the meta-institutional domain of discourse (in contrast to systems of power that involve practices and technologies and those that operate at the level of the institutional field).[49]

Block models were originally developed by Harrison White and his students in the 1970s as a data reduction technique that was intended to identify and map role structures in social networks. The procedure collects together those individuals in a network that are "structurally equivalent" to one another by virtue of their standing in similar patterns of relations to all others in the network (White, Boorman, and Breiger 1976; Boorman and White 1976). In Figure 4.4, this method of analysis was applied to a dataset consisting of texts—statements taken from the discourse system regarding identity classifications that were in use (and intelligible) in this institutional field. Specifically we looked to discover which identity terms were structurally equivalent to which others with respect to their patterns of use. So, for example, the category of being *female*, a *wife*, *widowed*, and *elderly* are structurally equivalent to one another, which is to say, they occupy the same role position with respect to the deeper system of institutional (discursive) meanings operating in this segment of the field. Said differently, according to the assumptions of this model, we can say that these identity terms are (institutionally speaking) synonymous—they *mean* the same thing.

The second virtue of a blockmodel analysis is that it provides a mapping of the overall relational logic of the identity categories because the models show which terms overlap with which others with respect to their usage profiles (in Figure 4.4 this is represented by the links connecting points). Following on the basic assumptions of semiotic theory, we presume that the meaning (at the level of discourse) of any term (any role cluster of terms in this case) is defined relationally by its location vis-à-vis the other significant terms in the relevant code system. Thus, from this higher-order structural mapping we can perhaps obtain some understanding of the "sense" of the system and of how ideas and meanings within the field of custodial organizations go together in a culturally (or institutionally) intuitive way.[50] From Figure 4.4 we find the traces of a fairly coherent interlocking structure of discursive spheres, a core structure made up of four sets of complementary systems of legitimacy—economic, familial, community, and a sphere that we label as questionable (or liminal) legitimacy. Above this is a fifth sphere of state-level legitimation. Each of these spheres captures a specific region of institutional meaning that provides sets of common understandings about the kinds of categories of people who are appropriate for the very different forms and styles of incarceration that were in operation in New York City at that time.

To complicate matters further, we find superimposed on this structure what looks to be the vestiges of another more traditional cultural logic. This subgraph is defined by four vertices—Male, Children, Boy/Girl, and HiStatus/Member (which is marked in Figure 4.4 with **bold** lines). In the paper, we argued that this discursive substructure closely resembles the kinds of structural patterns that characterize the logic of kinship systems (concerned with the exchange of marriage partners) that Lévi-Strauss (1949) and other anthropologists have described. This structure revolves around the mother (at the hub), and involves a linking of males to high-status others (who nonetheless share membership in an identity community), which is in turn linked to children, and then, to boys and girls, who are again linked back to the masculine head of household. Perhaps, at the meta-institutional level at least, the institutional logic (or discursive formation) that anchors the identity system within the custodial field is defined by a combination of different rhetorics of legitimation (and illegitimation) that are wound round one another in historically specific tangles.

Our claim for a model such as this is that it helps make sense of what is going on in the text because it provides a vision of a deeper structural logic underlying and giving meaning to the collection of individual statements. This parallels what Foucault (1972) claimed to be the function of a discursive formation, which he defined as the "historically produced, loosely structured combinations of concerns, concepts, themes, and types of statements" which serve to give meaning to the basic units or elements of discourse (which were the statements or "énoncé"). Any given statement, according to Foucault, necessarily presumes a great deal that is above and beyond any purely linguistic meanings, and, thus, it is only through the grounding of a particular discursive formation that a bundle of statements can be made intelligible. In Figure 4.4, the statements (in Foucault's sense) are the various organizational claims about the identities of people that are institutionalized within each organization. These linguistic meanings themselves are never completely lost to the analysis. Rather, the blockmodel works by reducing the complexity of the relational system within the text to something that is easier to read in two specific ways. First, the terms are distributed (through the analysis) into discrete groups of structurally equivalent terms. These groupings can thus provide a sense of what part of the meaning of a given concept (understood now in the discursive sense) is possibly most salient for proper reading of the institutional system. Second, the graph itself helps to provide an interpretation of the discursive formation by showing the arrangement of parts, and, thus, which segments of the discourse structure align with which other segments, thereby providing clues as to what kinds of factors could be in play or what dimensions would be most salient if we are now faced with the task of making sense of the text represented as a formal model.

Thus, in this last style of work, formal models of culture are used to highlight the ways in which cultural systems are organized as patterns that interlink alternative relational bundles of meaning. These models are intended to aid our ability to interpret the meaningful character of cultural systems and to assist in what Ricoeur calls "the genius of guessing" (1971, p. 212). But, unlike Lévi-Strauss, these investigations are not geared toward the ultimate identification of essential properties of things (or generalized universal rules) that constitute (by an arché or a telos) the essential nature of cultural forms. Instead these models are focused on understanding some of the various ways in which cultural forms co-constitute domains of the social (and material) world in an ongoing and complex process of social construction, destruction, and re-construction.

THE FORMAL MODEL OF A TEXT: MEANINGFUL
ACTION CONSIDERED AS A DATASET

Earlier we invoked the work of Paul Ricoeur as a way to define the concept of herme-neutic interpretation—"the rules required for the interpretation of the written documents of our culture" (1971, p. 197). In this last section of the chapter, we want to look more closely at the connection between Ricoeur's (1971) ideas about the use of hermeneutic methodologies in the social sciences and our own ideas about the use of formal measurement models for analyzing culture.

First, for Ricouer it is important to distinguish the study of discourse from the study of language. Discourse, that which is said, is an action in the world. Language, in contrast, is an abstraction. "(I)t is as discourse that language is either spoken or written" (p. 197). Ricoeur proceeds to identify four critical distinctions that flow from this. (1) Temporality: "Discourse is always realized temporally and in the pres-ent whereas the language system is virtual and outside of time"; (2) Subjectivity: "Whereas language lacks a subject in the sense that the question 'who is speaking?' does not apply at its level, discourse refers back to its speaker by means of a complex set of indicators such as personal pronouns"; (3) Symbolisation: "Whereas the signs in language only refer to other signs within the same system, and whereas language therefore lacks a world just as it lacks temporality and subjectivity, discourse is always about something. It refers to a world which it claims to describe, to express, or to represent. It is in discourse that the symbolic function of language is actual-ized"; and (4) Otherness: "Whereas language is only the condition for communica-tion for which it provides the codes, it is in discourse that all messages are exchanged. In this sense, discourse alone has not only a world but another, another person, an interlocutor to whom it is addressed" (p. 202).

But it is not only a focus on discourse that is important. In particular Ricoeur wants to pay attention to discourse that is written, that is, to texts themselves. There are several reasons for this. As Ricoeur explains, texts contain a complex layering of meanings that spoken discourse lacks. To highlight this, Ricoeur compares written text to spoken speech in the same way that he contrasts language and discourse. (1) Temporally, speech is "a fleeting event" (p. 198). A written text, on the other hand, *fixes* the event by inscribing it in material form.[51] In the process, the meaning of the speech event expands beyond its original intent, or, as Ricoeur puts it, "What we inscribe is the *noema* of the speaking. It is the meaning of the speech event not the event as event" (p. 199). (2) Regarding subjectivity, with spoken language "the subjective intention of the speaking subject and the meaning of the discourse over-lap each other in such a way that it is the same thing to understand what the speaker means and what his discourse means.... With written discourse, the author's inten-tion and the meaning of the text cease to coincide" (p. 200). And thus, "...the text's career escapes the finite horizon lived by the author. What the text says now mat-ters more than what the author meant to say, and every exegesis unfolds its proce-dures within the circumference of a meaning that has broken its moorings to the

psychology of its author" (p. 201).[52] Similarly with respect to (3), the symbolic function of speech, "in spoken discourse this means that what the dialogue ultimately
refers to is the situation and to the interlocutors. This situation in a way surrounds
the dialogue, and its landmarks can all be shown by a gesture, or by pointing a
finger, or designated in an ostensive manner by the discourse itself through the
oblique reference of those other indicators which are the demonstratives, the
adverbs of time and place, and the tense of the verb." This is in contrast to the written text that is freed from the ostensive limits of any particular situation and in fact
opens up for us symbolic worlds that transcend the immediacy of the present. It is
writing "which frees us from the visibility and limitation of situations by opening
up the world for us, that is, new dimensions of our being-in-the-world...only
writing, in freeing itself, not only from its author, but from the narrowness of the
dialogical situation, reveals this destination of discourse as projecting a world"
(p. 202).[53] And finally, as Ricoeur says, (4), "It is perhaps with the fourth trait that
the accomplishment of discourse and writing is most exemplary. Only discourse,
not language, is addressed to someone. This is the foundation of communication.
But it is one thing for discourse to be addressed to an interlocutor equally present
to the discourse situation, and another to be addressed, as is the case in virtually
every piece of writing, to whoever knows how to read. The narrowness of the dialogical relation explodes" (p. 202).[54]

Pointing to these differences Ricoeur explains that these qualities make the text
(and the reading of texts) an especially appropriate model for the social sciences
more generally. Indeed, he proposes to replace Weber's description of the object of
the human sciences as the study of "meaningfully oriented behavior" with the study
instead of the "readability-characters" that define behavior. "My claim is that action
itself, action as meaningful, may become an object of science without losing its
character of meaningfulness, through a kind of objectification similar to the fixation which occurs in writing" (p. 203). Thus, Ricoeur suggests that this fixation of
meaning that characterizes written texts (the escape from the immediacy of the
moment, the de-coupling from the mental intention of the author, the movement
beyond the ostensive situation, and the change to a universal form of address) leads
to a kind of shift in levels. The text defines an essential externalization of the speech
act, a transformation into a form of discourse that depends upon an objectified
embodiment of meaning in the material world. "This objectification is made possible by some inner traits of the action which are similar to the structure of the
speech-act and which make doing a kind of utterance" (p. 204).

Ricoeur proceeds to explain how speech acts provide a model for human action
more generally, and he finishes by showing how the methodologies that are appropriate for analyzing texts would be equally appropriate to the task of analyzing other
forms of social action. This implies a specifically hermeneutic method where the
goal is not to know an essence or an originary, but rather to gain an understanding
of the text in its various shared embodiments and intentionalities and to recognize
how it is that this very layering of understandings in fact constitutes the text as a
meaningful entity.

According to Ricoeur, one important reason to use the model of hemerneutic interpretation is that it "provides a solution for the methodological paradox of the human sciences"(p. 209) by highlighting "the dialectical character of the relation between *erklären* and *verstehen* as it is displayed in reading." In other words, precisely because the text is caught somewhere between the author and the reader— "(t)o understand a text is not to rejoin the author"(p. 210)—that an interpretation of a text demands both forms of understanding be brought to bear, both explanation and comprehension. "There is a problem of interpretation not so much because of the incommunicability of the psychic experience of the author but because of the very nature of the verbal intention of the text. This intention is something other than the sum of the individual meanings of the individual sentences....This plurivocity is typical of the text considered as a whole, open to several readings and to several constructions" (p. 212). And yet in spite of this plurivocity (and indeed, precisely because of it), texts are amenable to a style of formal analysis, "and the validation of an interpretation applied to it may be said, with complete legitimacy, to give a scientific knowledge of the text" (p. 212). Moreover, when considering Lévi-Strauss' contribution to the modeling of myths, Ricoeur asks whether it is not after all that the "function of structural analysis is to lead from a surface semantics, that of the narrated myth, to a depth semantics, that of the boundary situations which constitute the ultimate 'referent' of the myth?" (p. 217). Thus, Ricoeur concludes that structural analysis (of the sort described in the examples provided here) is "a stage—and a necessary one—between a naïve interpretation and a depth interpretation...then it would be possible to locate explanation and understanding at two different stages of a unique *hermeneutical arc*" (p. 218). For Ricoeur, the two modes of knowing in the social sciences are necessarily linked. "Guess and validation are in a sense circularly related as subjective and objective approaches to the text" (pp. 212–213).

This argument by Ricoeur for substituting the model of the text for more traditional theories of social science,inspired us to wonder if we could extend Ricoeur's arguments to also address the questions we have raised here regarding the use of formal models for interpreting texts. Just as the text, in contrast to spoken speech, produces a discursive action that operates at a different level of temporality, subjectivity, symbolization, and otherness, so too we think that an analysis of formal measurements of the text, in contrast to the the text itself, produces a style of knowing that operates at a different level of temporality, subjectivity, symbolization, and otherness and that understanding this difference may help us to better appreciate the problems associated with using formal measurement models to analyze culture.[55] Thus, with respect to (1) temporalization, a formal model of a text allows for the focused deconstruction and reconstruction of temporal ordering in a manner that is fundamentally different than a traditional textual analysis because textuality (in both the telling and the hearing) is invariably linked to specific genres of narrativity (think again of Lévi-Strauss's distinction between the reading and understanding of a myth). In contrast, data analysis may operate with equal facility both synchronically and diachronically (Bearman and Stovell 2000), both forward and backward, across very small or extremely large expanses of time (Moretti 2005). Thus when viewed through the lens of a dataset, the temporality of a text can itself can be incorporated into the analysis in such a way that it is theorizable, measurable, and, subject to a kind of material externalization that gives us access to other ways of understanding.

In the case of (2) subjectivity, if the written text is distinctive from spoken discourse because it breaks the link between the author's intent and the meaning of the text, a similar sort of rupture occurs in the analysis of the text as data, a break opens up between the intention of the modeler and the meaning of the data.[56] Like textual discourse that goes out from the mind of the speaker and assumes material form, so too, a dataset, once it has been collected, has its own embodiment, its own dead letter of information, and the modeler is forever committed to living with its otherness.[57] This is not to say that a modeler has to take the first attempt of an analysis as final, or, for that matter, that one need hold on to one's original plans, hypotheses, or presumptions. But, once one commits oneself to a measurement and a dataset, then one can contextualize one's findings, enhance the imagery, and locate the findings with respect to a literature, but one cannot change the information contained in the data to suit one's preferences or expectations. Thus in a fashion that is in some ways analogous to the externalization (indeed, the alienation) experienced by the author of a text, a text modeler is both the master of and mastered by one's data.[58]

Another parallel occurs at the level of (3) symbolization, which in the case of the written text claims a freedom from the "ostensive limits of any particular situation" or a particular speech act and thus becomes capable of expressing a broader symbolic world. Data analysis implies a similar sort of leveling-up to a broader social world in that it at least potentially contains information from a higher level of sociality, a sample of texts, a distribution of authors, and a collection of writings from across a field. Thus it allows for a kind of aggregation of acts of meaning in the same way that institutionalists from Durkheim forward have been seeking to understand social order. Said differently, a formal model of culture has the capacity to open up a world that is institutional in character: It can take in data from across a broad social space as information.[59] This is not to say that unless you use a formal model you cannot make comparisons between texts, for what else is a hermeneutic analysis if it is not about an opening up to a multiplicity of texts? Rather our point is that perhaps in this moment, the level that separates the reading of the text from the reading of the text as a dataset begin to approach one another at a kind of articulation point whose structure we are seeking to explicate.

Finally, at the level of (4) otherness, recall that the written text is distinct from spoken speech because only in the text is the audience made general, as a product of the text itself. The same could be said of a data analysis which is not only about an opening up to a generalized discursive other. It is also about making the project of knowing that what is shared by and co-constructed by a community of guild members, craftspeople, and professional scholars, who, in the case of a data analysis, share not only in a conversation but also in an awareness, and critical appreciation, of all the other materialities (as described above) that characterize the analysis of the text as a dataset. In short, we agree with Ricoeur's contenton that the model of the text is a good way conceptualize the dilemmas of the human sciences more generally, and, as we have suggested here, it is also a good framework for thinking about the problem of how to formally model a text.

CONCLUSION

In this essay, we have discussed some ways that formal measurement models have been used to study culture. We began by defining these models as the product of data analysis, which we described as a social technology, hence a set of theories and practices, methods of knowing and observing, that are enacted by communities of practitioners who construct regimes of analytic practice through their participation in them. We suggested four knowledge functions that formal models can usefully perform, and we argued that the old debates over method had grown stale at least in part because the terrain had shifted, as both quantitative and qualitative practitioners have increasingly found themselves working the same space, looking for meanings that are locked into texts. This has led to a series of new debates about the nature of the hermeneutic method itself.[60] We then described four types of formal modeling strategies that have been applied in the study of culture, before and after the cultural turn, with hermeneutic goals or not. This gave us the four cells in which to locate the work of Kroeber, Lévi-Strauss, DiMaggio, and White as exemplars of different styles of culture modeling. We finished with a comparison of Ricoeur's ideas about written (as opposed to spoken) discourse to our own ideas about the use of formal (as opposed to qualitative) styles of understanding cultural texts.

There are certain obvious limitations to what we have proposed. Probably the most important of these is that by confining ourselves to the study of written texts as both a practice and an exemplar for exegesis, we have foreclosed on the possibility of learning about the process by which meaning is actively produced, the way that speaking is located in a lived, dialogic process of agents and interactions and ways of making sense. We are thus responsible for promoting what Calhoun and Sennett (2007, p. 5) would describe as "a study of paintings not painting, of values not valuing." In response, we would argue that an overvaluing of the text (a transgression of which we are surely guilty) ultimately says more about the incompleteness of the present project than it does about the fundamental nature of the problem itself (e.g., the relation between formal measurement and interpretation). There are any number of formal modelers studying culture who are more concerned with analyzing the agentic moment than we have given voice to here. Indeed, Harrison White himself is currently much more interested in agency and action and far less focused on textuality and institution than our account might suggest (e.g., White 2008; Godart and White 2010). For that matter, our own focus on the institutional moment (here and elsewhere) has always reflected more of a strategy for developing a useful approach to data analysis than it is a commitment to a static vision of the social. This then is precisely the type of disadvantage one incurs in this style of work—an example of the type of reductionism that one must sometimes embrace— but one does so in the hope that the costs are outweighed by the benefits (and that one's analytic advance will lead to further improvements and less reductionism).

The problem is not just under-development, however. There are good strategic reasons to study structure. If, we see the social world as fundamentally ordered along the duality of agency and structure, then this will tend to produce a corresponding duality of methods in the human sciences. Giddens (1979) theorizes this quite usefully; he suggests that we distinguish the sociology of "strategic conduct" (painting) from the sociology of "institutional analysis" (paintings), and he proposes that each of these projects necessarily depends on a kind of a bracketing (he says a methodological epoché) of the other. While it is true enough that it would be wrong to understand culture only from the perspective of written text (rather than spoken speech), it would be equally wrong to do the reverse. This is not only because the dialectic between speech and language is an important part of the whole that is lived experience, but, in equal measure, we would say (along with Ricoeur) that a scientific approach is as an important part of the whole that makes up the methodology of the human sciences.

We do not, however, mean to suggest, that a formalized mode of text analysis can or should displace traditional hermeneutics. Though it has not been the focus of our chapter, we think that the various modes of knowing each have their own unique costs and benefits.[61] Nor do we presume that hermeneutic scholars are not themselves similarly beholden to their own styles of obligatory practices, their own sets of craft skills, guild knowledge, caches of collective wisdom, and so on. But we do think that what is perhaps most distinctive about interpretively intentioned measurement models of culture is how a particular kind of social technology can be built, shaped, and wielded to good effect. When this happens, the nature of the text (its discursive register) and the style of interpretative practice that can help us read the meaning of that text is transformed in a fashion that (as we have argued here) is in some ways rather like the difference between spoken and written discourse that Ricouer has described. Recall that ultimately Ricoeur's ambition was to offer "a fresh approach to the question of the relation between *erklären* (explanation) and *verstehen* (understanding, comprehension) in the human sciences" (Ricouer 1971, p. 209). This has been our goal as well.

NOTES

We thank Jeff Alexander for encouraging us to "do something daring and original" and for working supportively with us throughout the various stages of this process. Thanks also to Ron Breiger, Clayton Childress, Paul DiMaggio, Elvin Hatch and Corinne Kirchner for giving one of our (several) drafts a close reading and for offering valuable and substantive suggestions (not all of which we have been able to incorporate or address). Special thanks also to John Hall whose advice and thoughtful commentary on early versions of the paper were critical to the development of our argument. We also thank (especially) Roger Friedland, Josep A. Rodriguez, Kess van Rees, and Marc Ventresca for many enlightening conversations on the topics covered in this essay.

1. Dept. of Sociology, University of California, Santa Barbara. Email: mohr@soc.ucsb.edu.

2. Institute for Research on Education Policy and Practice, Stanford University. Email: craigr@stanford.edu.

3. From an essay that Stevens contributed to a volume of papers initially presented at a 1956 symposium on "Measurement" sponsored by the American Association for the Advancement of Science (1959, p. 18). Stevens was the Harvard psychologist who invented the canonical measurement scales (nominal, ordinal, interval, ratio). He was one of a cohort of practitioner/theorists who developed many of the conventions for formal analysis in the modern social sciences. He was also, like many in this cohort, very reflexive about the process. As he wrote some years earlier, "The stature of a science is commonly measured by the degree to which it makes use of mathematics. Yet mathematics is not itself a science, in any empirical sense, but a formal, logical, symbolic system—a game of signs and rules" (Stevens, 1951, p. 1). We say more about these issues below.

4. This definition actually allows for a broad range of methodological endeavors, but it does restrict us to talking about projects where a set of data is analyzed for patterns and reduced by some formal means. This would include some more formalist styles of what has traditionally been called qualitative work and it would also exclude some types of quantitative scholarship that is more purely metaphoric or imaginary in style (see, e.g., Macy and Willer, 2002). This is an admittedly unusual specification since we are insisting on the practice of data collection as a criterion for inclusion (whereas, even among quantitative scholars, common usage would, on the contrary, think of models as abstractions from the real). Indeed, as Elvin Hatch (personal communication) reminds us, there are many formal modeling traditions in the social sciences that do not rely at all on the kinds of quantitative measurement practices that we are emphasizing here. But we employ this definition advisedly, as a way to delimit the range of claims we want to specify in the more philosophical sections of this essay.

5. This does not mean we think the matter is simple or unproblematic. On the contrary, we see a theory of culture as engaging a far more complex debate than what we are prepared to deal with here. Our interest is more limited, by focusing our taxonomy on variations in method, we are in fact hoping to learn something new about the way that culture has come to take on theoretical meaning in the social sciences.

6. Let us be clear, our goal is not to review the literature on measuring cultural meaning (which would be a very large task indeed) but rather to set out in an admittedly idiosyncratic fashion a set of ideal-types which are intended to illustrate some of the broader processes that are in play.

7. Science studies scholars have helped us see scientific worlds (including social scientific worlds) as normal places where people interact in normal ways, even as they work at constructing extraordinary communities, technologies, and insights. These studies have also sensitized us to the ways that science is also a distinctive endeavor located in a specific social space; it is constituted in structures of articulation connecting things, actions, and logics (e.g., Latour and Woolgar 1979; Latour 1987; Knorr-Cetina 1999).

8. There are, of course, different ways to count. There has been a flood of important work on the institutional construction of data and statistics over the last few decades, works like Hacking (1975), Porter (1986), Ventresca (1995), and Platt (1996).

9. We draw here on the work of a number of scholars who have eloquently helped to theorize the character of data analysis in the social sciences as a particular kind of socially constructed collective endeavor. See, for example, Cicourel (1964), Duncan (1984), Breiger (2000), and Bourdieu (2004). These should be compared to the writing on these topics that occurred in the decades immediately following the Second World War. This was the time when, as a result of a number of technological developments (some the result of increased hybridization of scientific practices that occurred around the war effort), new conventions and techniques for collecting data and formalizing its analysis were being tinkered with and tried out by a cohort of theorist/practitioners from across the social sciences. Over the course of a decade or so, these scholars virtually invented much of what is now taken for granted (background assumptions) for the modeling practices of the modern social sciences. Paul Lazarsfeld, for example, was central to the process of constructing a social scientific theory of data analysis (including grappling with key constructs such as "the variable") that still undergirds much of mainstream American sociology. Kurt Lewin is another who helped provide the foundations for the development of modern social network analysis. The psychologist S. S. Stevens (whose quote we use to begin the chapter) is a third example.

10. Most obviously in American social sciences, pattern reduction practices have largely relied on the corpus of traditional statistical models, especially those associated with linear modeling traditions that emerged in American social science departments most forcefully after the Second World War as the dominant measurement paradigm. See Abbott (1988) for a classic assessment and critique.

11. Bourdieu describes the nature of scientific fields thus, "The structure of the power relation that constitutes the field is defined by the structure of the distribution of the two kinds of capital...scientific capital: a capital of strictly scientific authority, and a capital of power over the scientific world which can be accumulated through channels that are not purely scientific (in particular, through the institutions it contains) and which is the bureaucratic principal of temporal powers over the scientific field such as those of ministers and ministries, deans and vice-chancellors or scientific administrators..." (2004, p. 57).

12. Friedland (2009), who argues for taking religion as the model for institutional analysis, provides a powerful theoretical grounding for such a conception.

13. Ernst Cassirer provides some of the earliest and most effective arguments concerning the virtues of formal analysis in the natural and social sciences (Mohr 2010). Cassirer writes, with formalization "the world of sensible things...is not so much reproduced as transformed and supplanted by an order of another sort" (1953, p. 14).

14. Qualitative methods do this same thing in different but similar ways. Our point is that these are modes of practice.

15. Hesse (2000) describes how models work in science more generally. Tufte (1983) is a classic example of how visualization of data allows the researcher to see and theorize differently.

16. Technology is a species of power and we can ask questions about how and on what object any power is exercised" (Jonas 2004, p. 24). Bourdieu has a useful description of what we think of as the material benefits of a formal analysis. He says, "The specificity of the scientific field is partly due to the fact that the quantity of accumulated history is especially great, owing in particular to the 'conservation' of its achievements in a particularly economical form, with for example organization into principles and formulae or in the form of a slowly accumulated stock of calibrated actions and routinized skills" (Bourdieu 2004, p. 35).

17. We develop this argument in more depth at the end of the chapter.

18. Once again, knowledge production is also distributed in other nonscientific academic fields but again the distribution mechanisms there are different. So what we are describing here is something like a mode of knowledge production.

19. Abbott's (2001) theory of binary splitting (he describes in terms of fractals) may apply here.

20. The volume actually grew out of a NEH seminar directed by Robert Bellah held at the University of California Berkeley in 1976–1977.

21. Here again, we have touched on a huge topic. Elsewhere, we have written on developments in the case of American sociology, see Friedland and Mohr (2004).

22. On the distinction between structural and systemic styles of theorizing culture, see John Hall (2004, p. 117).

23. Naturally, there are also exceptions—scholars who still carry a torch for an older intellectual paradigm (though in truth, much of this is generational, and, change happens as older cohorts pass from the scene). On the other hand, the rise of new types of biologically determinant explanations (as in some contemporary versions of evolutionary psychology for example) might count as counter-examples to this broader trend; they are anomalies from this perspective, or in the spirit of Abbott (2001) and Collins (1998), they are the (inevitable?) counterbalancing contenders for the intellectual attention space.

24. The work of scholars such as Podolny (1993) and Zuckerman (1999) were also critical here. Mohr and Guerra-Pearson (2010) provide a more detailed commentary on these developments.

25. Of course, there were also strong culturalist projects (emphasizing endogenous studies of culture) before the modern cultural turn. Most obviously, in anthropology, Boas and his students (e.g., Margaret Mead, Ruth Benedict, Edward Sapir, and Alfred Kroeber, who we discuss below) held cultural-centric perspectives. So did Lévi-Strauss (who we also discuss below). But, these were often exceptions to the larger intellectual trends of the time and, as we show in the case of Kroeber and Lévi-Strauss, there was still a tendency to link culture back to exogenous forces of one sort or another (see Hatch 1973). What is missing here is the deeper sense of how culture constitutes the social (and vice versa).

26. See, for example, the debates published in Reed and Alexander (2009).

27. This is reminiscent of the cultural idealism of Matthew Arnold; see Williams (1983).

28. In 1919 Kroeber was pushing back against Spencerian theories of the "superorganic," but just what would take its place was still quite unclear. As he says in the introduction to his career summarizing text, *The Nature of Culture* (1952), "The risk in a high degree of consciousness of a separate order is that of going on to reify its organization and phenomena into an autonomous sort of substance with its own inner forces—life, mind, society, or culture. I have probably at times in the past skirted such lapsing and have at any rate been charged with mysticism. However, mysticism is by no means a necessary ingredient of level recognition. The value of the recognition is largely methodological. It is only by a *de facto* cultural approach to cultural phenomena that some of their most fundamental properties can be ascertained....However, if one is going to be broadly theoretical or philosophic about culture, it seems to me that its acceptance as a distinctive order of phenomena in nature cannot be evaded" (p. 4).

29. Espeland and Stevens (1998) provide the classic discussion of the problem.

30. He first uses *Petit Courrier des Dames*, beginning in 1844 "for the reason that that was the first volume of a fashion journal which I happened to know to be accessible in

New York City" (p. 243). Because of a break in the availability of the data series, Kroeber switches to *Harper's Bazar* as of 1868.

31. In spite of these efforts, Kroeber still has a very hard time collecting his data. "Insufficiency of material or oversight has resulted in a few years being represented by only nine sets of measurements. Unfortunately also, there is a scarcely a year for which ten illustrations could be found in each of which all eight measurements were recordable. A gown may be shown very completely in full face except for one corner of the skirt, which is hidden behind the chair of a seated companion. The basal skirt width can often be pretty well guessed in such cases, and an estimate was generally made; but only actual measurements have been included in the averages discussed.... The consequence of all these little circumstances is that the majority of the eight features observed are represented, year by year, by less than 10 measurements, sometimes only by four or five" (p. 241).

32. Kroeber returns to this project 20 years later and publishes a second paper with Jane Richardson as the first author. They have added data, extending the series from 1787 to 1936 and significantly increased the mathematical sophistication.

33. At other moments, Kroeber is far less metaphysical about all of this and he leans toward explanations that emphasize mechanisms of social attention, suggesting that to be noticed as different in matters of style, you can't go back (in dress length, e,g.), you have to go forward. This "ratchet effect" in the sequencing of style behavior is picked up and developed more fully in Lieberson's (2000) efforts to model cultural forms by studying changes in first names. Lieberson moves the explanation away from culture as an abstraction and anchors it in an understanding about social cognitions.

34. Some sociologists have been especially keen to develop new kinds of Boolean methods of data analysis that are extensions of this style of thinking (see Ragin 1987, 2000; Abbott 2004; Hannan, Pólos, and Carroll 2007).

35. Ricoeur argues that there is, in fact, a dialectical relation linking the two forms of understanding in the social sciences, explanation (*erklären*) is dialectically tied to interpretation (*verstehen*). To illustrate his contention, he points to this same analysis by Lévi-Strauss in order to make the argument that scientific understanding always demands interpretation as its precondition. "First, even in the most formalised presentation of myths by Lévi-Strauss, the units which he calls 'mythemes' are still expressed as sentences which bear meaning and reference. Can anyone say that their meaning as such is neutralised when they enter into the 'bundle of relations' which alone is taken into account by the 'logic' of the myth? Even this bundle of relations, in its turn, must be written in the form of a sentence. Finally, the kind of language-game which the whole system of oppositions and combinations embodies, would lack any kind of significance if the oppositions themselves, which, according to Lévi-Strauss, the myth tends to mediate, were not meaningful oppositions concerning birth and death, blindness and lucidity, sexuality and truth. Besides these existential conflicts there would be no contradictions to overcome, no logical function of the myth as an attempt to solve these contradictions" (1971, p. 217).

36. In his writing on Nietzsche, Foucault describes this as "an attempt to capture the exact essence of things, their purest possibilities, and their carefully protected identities, because this search assumes the existence of immobile forms that precede the external world of accident and succession" (1977, p. 142).

37. In the following sections we focus exclusively on the American field of sociology. During this era other (national) intellectual communities worked through parallel disputes but a commentary on those histories is beyond the scope of this essay.

38. This is a very incomplete treatment of a very complex topic. Mohr and Rawlings (2010) provide a more detailed history of these developments. It must also be said that subjective measurement strategies (for example, those using survey data or the various types of socio-cognitive modeling projects that measure meaning in quasi-laboratory conditions) certainly never died out and, in fact, have only grown more refined and powerful over time. Our (admittedly narrow) focus in this essay has emphasized a totally different, though in many ways parallel, theory of meaning and measurement.

39. In later work, DiMaggio and Mohr (1985) extend this work to show that this measure of cultural capital can also be used in models to predict students' overall educational attainment as well as the educational attainment of their spouse. Mohr and DiMaggio (1995) apply models to consider inter-generational transfers of cultural capital.

40. DiMaggio used the Project Talent dataset (from the early 1960s) that had a broad array of culture measures.

41. DiMaggio is also an important figure in the new institutional approach to organizational analysis that we described earlier. There are close parallels to the theorization and analyses of culture in both projects (not so surprising since he was a key theorist in both projects). In the new institutional school, the meaningfulness of cultural understandings is seen as primary. As in Peterson's work, institutionalists developed sophisticated models to study the social organization of industries and organizational fields. And like DiMaggio's cultural capital studies, institutionalists from the beginning employed formal modeling techniques to take the measure of cultural forms. It is another post-cultural turn project because new institutionalists conceive of their task as the mapping out of the causal effects of cultural processes in organizational fields. Originally, their approach to modeling was to use non-interpretative (explanatory) models of culture to illustrate, for example, the increasing homogenization of organizational forms within an organizational field. More recent work has shifted toward more hermeneutic styles of modeling meaning (see essays and commentary collected in Powell and DiMaggio 1991 and, for more recent work, Greenwood et al. 2008). Ventresca and Mohr (2004) provide a more full account.

42. Although originally a pioneer of non-hermeneutic cultural modeling, DiMaggio has always pushed the field forward and he has since gone on (especially in some more recent work) to develop new approaches to modeling hermeneutic processes (thus moving down to cell D). See, for example, DiMaggio, Goldberg, and Shepherd (2008).

43. Of course, Geertz (1973) was highly critical of Lévi-Strauss whose work comes in for specific critique in several chapters of this text. But notice that the critique does not address or even consider Lévi-Strauss's hermeneutic project, Geertz's rebuke focuses on Lévi-Strauss's insistence on a pre-cultural turn construct of culture as something that takes shape and form from something that is outside of it, and thus ontologically prior to discourse, which (again) in Lévi-Strauss's case was the primacy of a certain style of cognitive determinism.

44. Mullins (1973) identifies White as the leader of the social network analysis tradition and it is useful to know that White had personally mentored a large proportion of the leading figures in that field.

45. This is an overstatement when one considers the long tradition of using formal models by anthropologists (D'Andrade, etc.) and others (psychologists such as Osgood, e.g.) to develop interpretative approaches to culture. There were also a number of important hermeneutically inclined precursors in the field of social network analysis itself. See Mohr (1998) for a more extensive review.

46. See Mullins (1973), Aazrian (2005), Fuhse (2009), Kirchner and Mohr (2010), and Mische (forthcoming) for more detailed histories.

47. The key source is still the first and now (in some ways, very different) second edition of *Identity and Control* (1991, 2008).

48. The original database includes information on all the organizations in the directory at different intervals of time. In this model, we only included information from one small part of that larger dataset.

49. Figure 4.4 only considers the subset of identity terms that are derived from a meta-institutional level, but in the paper, another set of institutional level identity terms is also modeled. So, for example, in this analysis it is general status designations (gender, race, class, age, etc. that are being modeled), whereas the institutional level identity categories include categories that are owned by professional communities within a given institutional field, in this case it includes categories such as the homeless, the neglected, the nervous, the unruly, the drunk, the fallen, and so on. In the paper, both identity matrices are analyzed separately and then again together.

50. It is important to emphasize that a fully informed understanding of the history and context of these events is a necessary prerequisite to effectively conducting this style of research. Both for generating the dataset and for analyzing the dataset, the methods described here will not automatically produce new knowledge so much as they will help one to build on one's knowledgable understandings by allowing one to see and interpret a broader, more fully detailed mapping of these social institutions.

51. Ricoeur links this to Plato's Phaedo, "Writing was given to men to 'come to the rescue' of the 'weakness of discourse', a weakness which was that of the event. The gift of the *grammata*—of that 'external' thing, of those 'external marks', of that materialising alienation—was just that of a 'remedy' brought to our memory....It replaced true reminiscence by material conservation, and real wisdom by the semblance of knowing" (1971, p. 199).

52. "Henceforth, only the meaning 'rescues' the meaning, without the contribution of the physical and psychological presence of the author. But to say that the meaning rescues the meaning is to say that only interpretation is the 'remedy' for the weakness of discourse which its author can no longer 'save'" (p. 201).

53. "For us, the world is the ensemble of references opened up by the texts" (p. 202).

54. "Instead of being addressed just to you, the second person, what is written is addressed to the audience that it creates itself. This, again, marks the spirituality of writing, the counterpart of its materiality and of the alienation which it imposes upon discourse" (p. 203).

55. Here again, Ricouer's ideas apply, "The hierarchy of the levels of language includes something more than a series of articulated systems: phonological, lexical, and syntactic. We actually change levels when we pass from the units of a language to the new unit constituted by the sentence or the utterance. This is no longer the unit of a language, but of speech or discourse. By changing the unit, one also changes the function, or rather, one passes from structure to function" (Ricoeur 1974, p. 86).

56. Breiger (2002) provides a number of compelling examples of this point.

57. Unless, of course, one concludes that the data are so problematic that they need to be modified in some allowably legitimized corrective fashion—removing outliers, weighting the sample, going back for supplementary data, etc. We are, after all, resilient in our acts as agents in a field.

58. Of course, news about ethical violations and the occasional outright fraud does occur in science, but it is nonetheless really more the exception that defines the rule. Scientific practitioners, as a lot, are deeply committed to the rule of data, to a genuine system of externalization, and thus to a style of life that is organized around a sense of professional ethics and craft skills.

59. Of course, there are other uses for data analysis beyond the study of the institution, but the analogy we think still holds because what is at issue is how a data analysis can be used to symbolize a broader logic that embodies a theory of the social world.

60. Mohr and Rawlings (2010) develop this argument in greater detail.

61. As Ricoeur says with respect to the dialectic between language and speech, "The triumph of the structural point of view is at the same time a triumph of the scientific enterprise. By constituting the linguistic object as an autonomous object, linguistics constitutes itself as a science. But at what cost? Each of the axioms we have listed is both a gain and a loss" (Ricoeur 1974, p. 83).

REFERENCES

Abbott, Andrew. 1988. "Transcending General Linear Reality." *Sociological Theory*, 6: 169–186.

———. 2001. *Chaos of Disciplines*. Chicago: University of Chicago Press.

———. 2004. *Methods of Discovery: Heuristics for the Social Sciences*. New York: Norton.

Abbott, Andrew, and Alexandra Hrycak. 1990. "Measuring Resemblance in Sequence Data: An Optimal Matching Analysis of Musicians' Careers." *American Journal of Sociology*, 96: 144–185.

Alexander, Jeffrey C., and Philip Smith. 2001. "The Strong Program in Cultural Sociology." Pp. 135–150 in *The Handbook of Sociological Theory*, edited by Jonathan Turner. New York: Kluwer.

Azarian, G. Reza. 2005. *The General Sociology of Harrison C. White: Chaos and Order in Networks*. New York: Palgrave.

Bazerman, Charles. 1988. *Shaping Written Knowledge: The Genre and Activity of the Experimental Article in Science*. Madison: University of Wisconsin Press.

Bearman, Peter S., and Katherine Stovel. 2000. "Becoming a Nazi: A Model for Narrative Networks." *Poetics*, 27: 69–90.

Berger, Peter, and Thomas Luckmann. 1984. *The Social Construction of Reality*. London: Penguin.

Billisoly, Roger. 2008. *Practical Text Mining with PERL*. New York: Wiley.

Bourdieu, Pierre. 1984. *Distinction: A Social Critique of the Judgment of Taste*. Translated by Richard Nice. Cambridge, MA: Harvard University Press.

———. 2004. *Science of Science and Reflexivity*. Chicago: University of Chicago Press.

Boorman, Scott A., and Harrison C. White. 1976. "Social Structures from Multiple Networks: II. Role Structures." *American Journal of Sociology*, 81: 1384–1446.

Breiger, Ronald L. 1974. "The Duality of Persons and Groups." *Social Forces*, 53: 181–190.

———. 2000. "A Tool Kit for Practice Theory." *Poetics*, 27: 91–115.

———. 2002. "Writing and Quantifying Sociology." In *Writing and Revising the Disciplines*, edited by Jonathan Monroe. Ithaca, NY, and London: Cornell University Press.

Calhoun, Craig, and Richard Sennett. 2007. *Practicing Culture: Taking Culture Seriously*. London. Routledge.

Cassirer, Ernst. 1953 [1910]. *Substance and Function (Substanzbegriff und Funktionsbegriff)* Translated by William Curtis Swabey and Marie Collins Swabey. New York: Dover.

Churchman, C. West. 1959. "Why Measure?" Pp. 83–94 in *Measurement: Definitions and Theories*, edited by C. W. Churchmen and Philburn Ratoosh, New York: Wiley.

Cicourel, Aaron V. 1964. *Method and Measurement in Sociology*. New York: Free Press.

Collins, Randall. 1998. *The Sociology of Philosophies: A Global Theory of Intellectual Change.* Cambridge, MA: Harvard University Press.

Converse, Jean M. 2009. *Survey Research in the United States: Roots and Emergence 1890–1960*. New Brunswick, NJ: Transaction Press.

Coombs, C. H., Howard Raiffa, and R. M. Thrall. 1954. "Mathematical Models and Measurement Theory." Pp. 19–37 in *Decision Processes*, edited by R.M. Thrall, C.H. Coombs, and R.L. Davis. New York: Wiley.

Dear, Peter, ed. 1991. *The Literary Structure of Scientific Argument: Historical Studies.* Philadelphia: University of Pennsylvania Press.

DiMaggio, Paul J. 1982. "Cultural Capital and School Success: The Impact of Status-Culture Participation on the Grades of U.S. High School Students." *American Sociological Review*, 47: 189–201.

———. 1987. "Classification in Art." *American Sociological Review*, 52: 440–455.

———. Forthcoming. "Cultural Networks." In *The Sage Handbook of Social Network Analysis*, edited by John Scott and Peter J. Carrington. London: Sage Publications.

DiMaggio, Paul J., and John W. Mohr. 1985. "Cultural Capital, Educational Attainment and Marital Selection." *American Journal of Sociology*, 90(6): 1231–1261.

DiMaggio, Paul J., Amir Goldberg, and Hana Shepherd. 2008. "Science vs. Religion?: A New Look at an Old Opposition Using Data on Public Attitudes in the U.S." Paper presented at the American Sociological Association meetings, Boston, MA.

Douglas, Mary. 1996. *Natural Symbols: Explorations in Cosmology*. London: Routledge.

Duncan, Otis Dudley. 1984. *Notes on Social Measurement*. New York: Russell Sage Foundation.

Dreyfus, Hubert. 1972. *What Computers Can't Do: The Limits of Artificial Intelligence.* New York: Harper Colophon.

———. 2009. *On the Internet*. London: Routledge.

Espeland, Wendy Nelson, and Mitchell L. Stevens. 1998. "Commensuration as a Social Process." *Annual Review of Sociology*, 24: 313–343.

Foucault, Michel. 1970. *The Order of Things: An Archaeology of the Human Sciences.* New York: Pantheon Books.

———. 1972. *The Archaeology of Knowledge*. New York: Harper and Row.

———. 1977. *Language, Counter-Memory, Practice: Selected Essays and Interviews*. Ithaca, NY: Cornell University Press.

Friedland, Roger. 2009. "Institution, Practice, and Ontology: Towards a Religious Sociology." Pp. 45–83 in *Ideology and Organizational Institutionalism, Research in the Sociology of Organizations 27*, edited by Renate Meyer, Kerstin Sahlin-Andersson, Marc Ventresca, and Peter Walgenbach. Bingley, UK: Emerald Group Publishing.

Friedland Roger, and Robert Alford. 1991. "Bringing Society Back In: Symbols, Practices and Institutional Contradictions." Pp. 232–263 in *The New Institutionalism in Organizational Analysis*, edited by W. W. Powell and P. DiMaggio. Chicago: University of Chicago Press.

Friedland, Roger, and John Mohr. 2004. "The Cultural Turn in American Sociology." Pp. 1–68 in *Matters of Culture: Cultural Sociology in Practice*. Cambridge, UK: Cambridge University Press.

Fuhse, J. A., 2009. "The Meaning Structure of Social Networks." *Sociological Theory*, 27: 51–72.

Geertz, Clifford. 1973. *The Interpretation of Cultures*. New York: Basic Books.

Gibson, D. R. 2003. "Participation Shifts: Order and Differentiation in Group Conversation." *Social Forces*, 81: 1135–1181.

Giddens, Anthony. 1979. *Central Problems in Social Theory: Action, Structure and Contradiction in Social Theory.* Berkeley: University of California Press.

———. 1984. *The Constitution of Society. Outline of the Theory of Structuration.* Cambridge, UK: Polity.

Godart, Frederic C., and Harrison C. White. 2010. "Switchings under Uncertainty: The Coming and Becoming of Meanings." Poetics, 38:567–586.

Greenwald, Maurine W., and Margo Anderson. 1996. *Pittsburgh Surveyed: Social Science and Social Reform in the Early Twentieth Century.* Pittsburgh: University of Pittsburgh Press.

Greenwood, Royston, Christine Oliver, Kerstin Sahlin, and Roy Suddaby, eds. 2008. *The Sage Handbook of Organizational Institutionalism.* Thousand Oaks, CA: Sage Publications.

Gubrium, Jaber, and James Holstein. 1997. *The New Language of Qualitative Method.* Oxford: Oxford University Press.

Hacking, Ian. 1975. *The Emergence of Probability: A Philosophical Study of Eraly Ideas About Probability Induction and Statistical Inference.* Cambridge, UK: Cambridge University Press.

Hall, John. 2004. "Theorizing Hermeneutic Cultural History." Pp. 110–139 in *Matters of Culture: Cultural Sociology in Practice.* Cambridge, UK: Cambridge University Press.

Hannan, Michael T., László Pólos, and Glenn R. Carroll. 2007. *Logics of Organization Theory: Audiences, Codes, and Ecologies.* Princeton, NJ: Princeton University Press.

Hatch, Elvin. 1973. *Theories of Man and Culture.* New York: Columbia University Press.

Heidegger, Martin. 2004. "Question Concerning Technology." Pp. 35–51 in *Readings in the Philosophy of Technology*, edited by David M. Kaplan. Lanham, MD: Rowman & Littlefield.

Hesse, Mary. 2000. "Models and Analogies." Pp. 299–307 in *A Companion to the Philosophy of Science*, edited by W. H. Newton-Smith. Oxford: Blackwell.

Holton, Gerald. 1988 [1973]. *Thematic Origins of Scientific Thought: Kepler to Einstein.* Cambridge, MA: Harvard University Press.

Hutchins, Edward. 1995. *Cognition in the Wild.* Cambridge, MA: MIT Press.

Ingram, David. 1994. "Foucault and Habermas on the Subject of Reason." Pp. 215–261 in *The Cambridge Companion to Foucault*, edited by Gary Gutting. Cambridge, UK: Cambridge University Press.

Jonas, Hans. 2004. "Towards a Philosophy of Technology." Pp. 17–33 in *Readings in the Philosophy of Technology*, edited by David M. Kaplan. Lanham, MD: Rowman & Littlefield.

Kaufman, Jason 2004. "Endogenous Explanations in the Sociology of Culture." *Annual Review of Sociology*, 30: 335–357.

Kirchner, Corinne, and John W. Mohr. 2010. "Meanings and Relations: An Introduction to the Study of Language, Discourse, and Networks." *Poetics*, 38: 555–566.

Kittler, Frederich A., and Michael Metteer. 1992. *Discourse Networks, 1800/1900.* Palo Alto, CA: Stanford University Press.

Knorr-Cetina, Karin. 1999. *Epistemic Cultures: How the Sciences Make Knowledge.* Cambridge, MA: Harvard University Press.

Kroeber, Alfred L. 1919. "On the Principle of Order in Civilization as Exemplified by Changes of Fashion." *American Anthropologist*, 21(3): 235–263.

———. 1952. *The Nature of Culture.* Chicago: University of Chicago Press.

Kuhn, Thomas. 1962. *The Structure of Scientific Revolutions.* Chicago: University of Chicago Press.

Latour, Bruno. 1987. *Science in Action*. Cambridge, MA: Harvard University Press.

Latour, Bruno, and Steve Woolgar. 1979. *Laboratory Life: The Social Construction of Scientific Facts*. Beverly Hills, CA, and London: Sage Publications.

Lazarsfeld, Paul F. 1961. "Notes on the History of Quantification in Sociology—Trends, Sources and Problems." Pp. 147–203 in *Quantification: A History of the Meaning of Measurement in the Natural and Social Sciences*, edited by Harry Woolf. New York: Bobbs-Merrill.

———. 1968. "Foreword." Pp. vii–x in *The Logic of Survey Analysis*, edited by Morris Rosenberg. New York: Basic Books.

Lazarsfeld, Paul F., and Alan H. Barton. 1982 [1955]. "Some Functions of Qualitative Analysis in Social Research." Pp. 239–285 in *The Varied Sociology of Paul Lazarsfeld*, edited by Patricia Kendall. New York: Columbia University Press.

Lévi-Strauss, Claude. 1963. *Structural Anthropology*. New York: Basic Books.

———. [1949] 1969. *The Elementary Structures of Kinship*. Boston: Beacon Press.

Lieberson, Stanley. 2000. *A Matter of Taste: How Names, Fashions, and Culture Change*. New Haven, CT: Yale University Press.

Macy, Michael W., and Robert Willer. 2002. "From Factors to Actors: Computational Sociology and Agent-Based Modeling." *Annual Review of Sociology*, 28: 143–166.

McCloskey, Donald N. 1986. *The Rhetorics of Economics*. Madison: University of Wisconsin Press.

Merton, Robert K. 1973. "The Normative Structure of Science." In *The Sociology of Science: Theoretical and Empirical Investigations*. Chicago: University of Chicago Press.

Mische, Ann. 2007. *Partisan Publics: Contention and Mediation across Brazilian Youth Activist Networks*. Princeton, NJ: Princeton University Press.

———. Forthcoming. "Relational Sociology, Culture, and Agency." In *The Sage Handbook of Social Network Analysis*, edited by John Scott and Peter J. Carrington. London: Sage Publications.

Mische, Ann, and Philippa Pattison. 2000. "Composing a Civic Arena: Publics, Projects, and Social Settings." *Poetics*, 27: 163–194.

Mohr, John W. 1998. "Measuring Meaning Structures." *Annual Review of Sociology*, 24: 345–370.

———. 2010. "Ernst Cassirer: Science, Symbols and Logic." Pp. 113–122 in *Sociological Insights of Great Thinkers: From Aristotle to Zola*, edited by Christofer Edling and Jens Rydgren. New York: Praeger.

Mohr, John W., and Brooke Neely. 2009. "Modeling Foucault: Dualities of Power in Institutional Fields." Pp. 203–256 in *Ideology and Organizational Institutionalism, Research in the Sociology of Organizations 27*, edited by Renate Meyer, Kerstin Sahlin-Andersson, Marc Ventresca, and Peter Walgenbach. Bingley, UK: Emerald Group Publishing.

Mohr, John W., and Craig Rawlings. 2010. "Formal Models of Culture." Pp. 118–128 in *A Handbook of Cultural Sociology*, edited by John Hall, Laura Grindstaff, and Ming-cheng Lo. London: Routledge.

Mohr, John W., and Francesca Guerra-Pearson. 2010. "The Duality of Niche and Form: The Differentiation of Institutional Space in New York City, 1888–1917." Pp. 321–368 in *Categories in Markets: Origins and Evolution*, Vol. 31, *Research in the Sociology of Organizations*, edited by Greta Hsu, Ozgecan Kocak, and Giacomo Negro. Bingley, UK: Emerald Group Publishing.

Mohr, John W., and Harrison C. White. 2008. "How to Model an Institution." *Theory and Society*, 37: 485–512.

Mohr, John W., and Paul DiMaggio. 1995. "The Intergenerational Transmission of Cultural Capital." *Research in Social Stratification and Mobility*, 14: 169–200.

Mohr, John W., and Vincent Duquenne. 1997. "The Duality of Culture and Practice: Poverty Relief in New York City, 1888–1917." *Theory and Society*, 26: 305–356.

Moretti, Franco. 1998. *Atlas of the European Novel, 1800–1900*. New York: Verso.

———. 2005. *Graphs, Maps, Trees*. New York: Verso.

Mullins, N. 1973. *Theories and Theory Groups in Contemporary American Sociology*. New York: Harper & Row.

Orlikowski, W. J. 1992. "The Duality of Technology: Rethinking the Concept of Technology in Organizations." *Organization Science*, 3: 398–427

Pattison, Philippa E., andRonald L. Breiger. 2002. "Lattices and Dimensional Representations: Matrix Decompositions and Ordering Structures." *Social Networks*, 24: 423–444.

Peterson, Richard A., and D. G. Berger. 1975. "Cycles in Symbol Production: The Case of Popular Music." *American Sociological Review*, 40: 158–173.

Platt, Jennifer. 1996. *A History of Sociological Research Methods in America: 1920–1960*. Cambridge, UK: Cambridge University Press.

Podolny, Joel M. 1993. "A Status-Based Model of Market Competition." *American Journal of Sociology*, 98: 829–872.

Porter, Theodore M. 1986. *The Rise of Statistical Thinking 1820–1900*. Princeton, NJ: Princeton University Press.

Powell, Walter W., and Paul J. DiMaggio. 1991. *The New Institutionalism in Organizational Analysis*. Chicago: University of Chicago Press.

Rabinow, Paul, and William Sullivan. 1979. *Interpretive Social Science: A Reader*. Berkeley: University of California Press.

Ragin, Charles. 1987. *The Comparative Method: Moving Beyond Qualitative and Quantitative Strategies*. Berkeley: University of California Press.

———. 2000. *Fuzzy-Set Social Science*. Chicago: University of Chicago Press.

Rawlings, Craig M., and Michael D. Bourgeois. 2004. "The Complexity of Institutional Niches: Credentials and Organizational Differentiation in a Field of U.S. Higher Education." *Poetics*, 32: 411–437.

Reed, Isaac, and Jeffrey C. Alexander. 2009. *Meaning and Method: The Cultural Approach to Sociology*. Boulder, CO: Paradigm Publishers.

Richardson, Jane, and Alfred L. Kroeber. 1940. "Three Centuries of Women's Dress Fashions: A Quantitative Analysis." *University of California Anthropological Records*, 5(2): 111–154.

Ricoeur, Paul. 1971. "The Model of a Text: Meaningful Action Considered as a Text." Reprinted as Chapter 8 in *Hermeneutics & the Human Sciences*, edited and translated by John B. Thompson. Cambridge, UK: Cambridge University Press.

———. 1974. "Structure, Word, Event." Pp. 79–96 in *The Conflict of Interpretations: Essays in Hermeneutics*, edited by Don Ihde. Evanston, IL: Northwestern University Press.

Rossi, Ino. 1983. *From the Sociology of Symbols to the Sociology of Signs*. New York: Columbia University Press.

Ruef, Martin. 1999. "Social Ontology and the Dynamics of Organizational Forms: Creating Market Actors in the Healthcare Field, 1966–1994." *Social Forces*, 77: 1403–1432.

Sewell, William H., Jr. 1992. "A Theory of Structure: Duality, Agency, and Transformation." *The American Journal of Sociology*, 98(1): 1–29.

Smith, T. 2007. "Narrative Boundaries and the Dynamics of Ethnic Conflict and Conciliation." *Poetics*, 35: 22–46.

Sorokin, Pitirim. 1956. *Fads and Foibles in Modern Sociology*. Chicago: Henry Regnery.

Stern, David. 2000. "Practices, Practical Holism, and Background Practices." Pp. 53–69 in *Heidegger, Coping, and Cognitive Science: Essays in Honor of Hubert L. Dreyfus*, Vol. 2, edited by Mark A. Wrathall and Jeff Malpas. Cambridge, MA: MIT Press.

Stevens, S. S. 1951. "Mathematics, Measurement, and Psychophysics." Pp. 1–49 in *Handbook of Experimental Psychology*, edited by S. S. Stevens. New York: Wiley.

———. 1959. "Measurement, Psychophysics, and Utility." Pp. 18–63 in *Measurement: Definitions and Theories*, editedby C. W. Churchmen and Philburn Ratoosh. New York: Wiley.

Turner, Charles F., and Elizabeth Martin. 1984. "Introduction." Pp. 3–21 in *Surveying Subjective Phenomena*, Vol. 1, edited by by Charles F. Turner and Elizabeth Martin. New York: Russell Sage Foundation.

Ventresca, Marc. 1995. "When States Count: Institutional and Political Dynamics in Modern Census Establishment, 1800–1993." Ph.D. diss., Department of Sociology, Stanford University.

Ventresca, Marc, and John W. Mohr. 2002. "Archival Research Methods." Pp. 805–828 in *The Blackwell Companion to Organizations*, edited by Joel Baum. Oxford: Blackwell Publishers.

Van Venrooij, Alex. 2009a. "The Aesthetic Discourse Space of Popular Music: 1985–86 and 2004–05." *Poetics*, 37: 315–332.

———. 2009b. *Classifications in Popular Music: Discourses and Meaning Structures in American, Dutch and German Popular Music Reviews*. Rotterdam, The Netherlands: Erasmus Research Centre for Media, Communication and Culture.

White, Harrison C. 1963. *An Anatomy of Kinship: Mathematical Models for Structures of Cumulated Roles*. Englewood Cliff, NJ: Prentice Hall.

———. 1992. *Identity and Control: A Structural Theory of Social Action*. Princeton, NJ: Princeton University Press.

———. 1997. "Can Mathematics be Social? Flexible Representations for Interaction Process and Its Socio-Cultural Constructions." *Sociological Forum*, 12: 53–71.

———. 2008. *Identity and Control: How Social Formations Emerge*. Princeton, NJ: Princeton University Press.

White, Harrison C., Scott A. Boorman, and Ronald L. Breiger. 1976. "Social Structure from Multiple Networks I: Blockmodels of Roles and Positions." *American Journal of Sociology*, 81: 730–780.

Williams, Raymond. 1983. *Culture and Society 1780–1950*. New York: Columbia University Press.

Zerubavel, Eviatar. 1997. *Social Mindscapes: An Invitation to Cognitive Sociology*. Cambridge MA: Harvard University Press.

Zuckerman, Ezra W. 1999. "The Categorical Imperative: Securities Analysts and the Illegitimacy Discount." *American Journal of Sociology* 104: 1398–1438.

PART II

THE ECONOMIC AS CULTURE

CHAPTER 5

CULTURE AND
THE ECONOMY

CARLO TOGNATO

INTRODUCTION

A great variety of social theorists have repeatedly denounced the almost inexorable process of disenchantment within modern societies that allegedly leads technical rationality to progressively displace any non-instrumental cultural logic from social life[1]. Such a pessimistic understanding of modernity adds to a particularly grim picture of the economy. Supporters of this view, after all, consider that rational disenchantment has pushed furthest in the economic arena. The recent birth of the euro, they argue, provides a typical example of this. The euro, in the end, is a purely functional artifact—just money without identity: "No one loves it, all accept it" (Hörisch 2004, p. 122).

If such a reading of the economy were correct, then romantics that entered the economic sphere after the spur of cultural reenchantment would be warned: "Abandon all your hope those who enter." The reality of economic life, however, seems to point to a different direction. During the transition to the European Monetary Union, for example, a reader of the *Financial Times* summarized the reading as European governments made of the Maastricht criteria: "The difference between happiness and misery is a 0.2 per cent deficit of the gross domestic product! A 2.9 per cent deficit is fine and enables one to live in happiness and bliss, while a 3.1 per cent deficit condemns a country to chaos, misery, and eternal damnation."[2] On the occasion of the European Council meeting that launched the euro, in turn, the Portuguese Prime Minister saluted the new currency: "As Jesus Christ decided to found a church, he told Peter: 'You are Peter and upon this rock I will build my church.' Today we can say: 'You are Euro, and upon this new currency, we will build our Europe.'"[3] Then, during the celebration of the appointment of the President and Vice-President of the European Central Bank, Hans Tietmeyer, then President of the Deutsche Bundesbank, one of the purest institutional distillates of modern technical rationality, addressed an audience of bankers and public officials with a prayer of Sarastos, high priest of Ancient Egypt.[4] Finally, in a scientific colloquium, Otmar Issing, then Chief Economist of the Deutsche Bundesbank, confessed that any appointee to the Board of the Bundesbank experiences a transformation of his own identity that is comparable to the one Thomas Beckett underwent when Henry II appointed him Archibishop of Canterbury. Beckett turned into a strenuous defender of the Church's interests, dared contradict the Crown of which he had been till then a faithful servant, and took up his new responsibilities to the point of accepting martyrdom (Issing 1991, pp. 7–8). These examples seem to suggest that cultural codes, metaphors, rituals, and identities still matter in the modern economy. Rational disenchantment, as a consequence, might be less pervasive than many social theorists would have us believe.

Economists have traditionally underplayed the role of culture in the economy, fearing that cultural explanations would sacrifice the profession's commitment to testable hypotheses (Guiso, Sapienza, and Zingales 2006). In the past two decades, however, the establishment of a neo-institutionalist tradition within economics has marked a clear departure in this respect (North 1990, 1994). By drawing on the work of Banfield (1958), Putman (1993), and Fukuyama (1995), economists have started to systematically recognize the influence of culture on trust and hence on economic performance (Landes 1993; Knack and Keefer 1996; La Porta, et al. 1997).

Economic sociology, in turn, has experienced in the past three decades a vibrant revival. During this period, a culturalist strand of scholarship has persistently claimed that culture has not at all been squeezed out of the market. On the contrary, it actively participates to shape economic action and even makes it viable. Still, its contributors could have pushed their cultural analysis even further. In this chapter, I will discuss how far they went and what they possibly missed. Doing so will provide a clearer picture of the intellectual mission of a cultural sociology of the economy, its theoretical horizon, and its pragmatic relevance in times of economic crisis.

With particular reference to this latest point, I will suggest, people today are starting to doubt whether an economic profession that could not anticipate or prevent the current crisis will be able to repair it. Corporations across all industrial sectors are involved in scandals that are dangerously undermining the confidence of the public. And central banks are being forced to bring down interest rates to a level at which monetary policy simply becomes powerless before deflationary pressures. Soon enough, as deflation deepens and unemployment lines get longer and longer, the general public will start to wonder whether it is time to do away with independent central banks whose single-minded institutional task—the control of inflation—has suddenly passed out of fashion. At this historical juncture, economists and economic institutions may undergo a crisis of confidence with unpredictable consequences on the economic system. Scholars have a moral obligation to offer fresh insights into the mechanisms that sustain public confidence or help to repair it. I will argue that a cultural sociology of the economy is specifically equipped to contribute in this respect.

Over the past three decades, the culturalist strand of scholarship within economic sociology has tended to restrict its horizon of observation on single institutional settings. By putting the question of confidence and legitimacy at its analytical core, and by taking scandals as its primary empirical focus, a cultural sociology of the economy, instead, attempts to overcome the "middle range malaise" of such scholarship by concentrating on the connections between institutional settings on the one hand and the central myths that underpin the functioning of the economy on the other. Functionalists did try to push in this direction, but the analytical horizon of their value sociology fell short of letting them appreciate the full role of myth and ritual in economic life. A cultural sociology of the economy, on the contrary, capitalizes on the richer understanding of cultural structures and practices sociologists have gained since the demise of Parsonsian sociology.

Before proceeding, I will lay out the structure of this chapter. I will start by briefly tracking the precursors of a cultural analysis of economic life within classical sociological theory. Then, I will do the same with reference to contemporary economic sociology. This will allow me to show in what way a cultural sociology of the economy builds on both sociologies, while at the same time distancing itself from them in important ways. After pinning down the intellectual vocation and the theoretical horizon of a cultural sociology of the economy, I will devote the second part of this chapter toward grounding its pragmatic relevance. A cultural sociology of the economy, I will suggest, promises to contribute to the advancement of three fields of inquiry that have experienced an exciting development in the past three decades— the literature on organizational legitimacy, on the sociology of financial markets, and on the sociology of money. Pushing the research frontier of these three literatures ahead into a more decisively culturalist direction will enable sociologists to tackle three of the most pressing problems that loom on the horizon of the current world economic crisis: the loss of confidence on the part of the general public for private corporations, the economic profession, and independent central banks.

CLASSICAL SOURCES OF A CULTURAL SOCIOLOGY OF THE ECONOMY

Different classical sources provide a fertile ground from which a cultural sociology of the economy can draw for the purpose of nurturing its intellectual project. Economic sociologists have traditionally included Durkheim, Weber, Parsons, and Polanyi among their classics. These are important referents also for a cultural sociology of the economy, as well, although the later Durkheim of *The Elementary Forms of Religious Life* tends to be far more important for cultural sociologists than for economic sociologists. Recently, Swedberg (2004) has recognized Alexandre de

Tocqueville as an important classic in economic sociology. I will here suggest that Tocqueville also deserves equal recognition within a cultural sociology of the economy. By directly addressing the cultural linkages between democracy and capitalism, after all, the French thinker touched on one of the core research interests of this field of inquiry that, I will argue, makes it most useful under the current historical circumstances. At a time when economists and major economic institutions run the risk of losing the confidence of the public as a result of the ongoing world economic crisis, shedding light over such linkages may help understand how to maintain and, if necessary, how to repair such confidence.

Bearing this in mind, I will only briefly touch on the contributions of Durkheim, Weber, Parsons, and Polanyi that are most relevant for the construction of a cultural sociology of the economy and dwell instead a little bit longer on Tocqueville's *Democracy in America*, which has traditionally received lesser attention in economic sociology.

Economic sociologists generally tend to emphasize the early Durkheim of *The Division of Labour in Society, Professional Ethics and Civic Morals*, and *Suicide*. A cultural sociology of the economy definitely values the early Durkheim's references to the autonomous role collective beliefs and morality respectively play in the emergence of private property and in the maintenance of contractual obligations. The later Durkheim of *The Elementary Forms of Religious Life*, however, is a much more crucial reference for a cultural sociology of the economy. Recently, Smelser and Swedberg (2005, pp. 10–11) have referred to it while stressing the central role morality plays in Durkheim's economic sociology. Still, they do so in a rather tangential way. A cultural sociology of the economy, instead, places *The Elementary Forms* at its core. After all, people invest economic life with sentiment and meaning, and their understanding of economic reality is mediated by the collective representations of that reality. As a result, Durkheim's analysis of the ritual mechanisms by which people establish shared meaning becomes especially critical.

Max Weber constitutes another central referent for any cultural sociologist committed to recover the autonomous influence of culture on economic life. His conception of economic action as inherently meaningful and his extensive work on the economic ethics of Protestantism, Confucianism, Hinduism, and Judaism constitute an important resource on which cultural sociologists can build (Weber [1922] 1978, [1904] 1998, [1915] 1946a, [1920] 1946b, [1946] 1971). A cultural sociology of the economy, though, will distance itself from Weber's tragic thesis on the disenchantment of modernity and will instead strive to systematically recognize the instances of cultural reenchantment in modern economic life.

Talcott Parsons, together with Neil Smelser, are other important referents for a cultural sociology of the economy. Their exploration of the boundary exchanges between the economy and the cultural-motivational subsystem spurs cultural sociologists to think of the role of culture in economic life in more systemic terms. Parson and Smelser's *Economy and Society* (1956) as well as Smelser's (1963, 1976) subsequent work in economic sociology, however, did not manage to relevantly impact the subfield. For a cultural sociology of the economy, their attention to the role of norms and values in economic life is surely important but falls short of being sufficient. After all, symbols, cultural codes, narratives, genres, and cultural practices as well deserve to be considered.

Karl Polanyi, in turn, has become particularly fashionable among economic sociologists since the birth of the new economic sociology, which has borrowed from him the concept of "embeddedness" (Polanyi [1944] 1957, [1957] 1971; Polanyi, Arensberg, and Pearson [1957] 1971). Polanyi attacks neoclassical economics for its formalism and for conceiving the economy as a process that is totally disembedded from institutional and cultural contexts. Instead, he points out, economic activities and institutions are embedded in noneconomic motives and institutions, and, therefore, social and institutional contexts in the end permeate the logic of means-ends (Polanyi, Arensberg, and Pearson [1957] 1971). Polanyi further develops this thesis as he discusses his typology of exchange relations—reciprocity, redistribution, and market exchange. The first two, he suggests, are embedded in social relations (Polanyi [1944] 1957, p. 46). In particular, reciprocity builds on friendship, kinship, among other different social ties, whereas redistribution relies on other political and religious underpinnings. On the other hand, the other pattern of integration—market exchange—is guided according to Polanyi only by the pursuit of gain: "A market economy is an economic system controlled, regulated, and directed by markets alone; order in the production and distribution of goods is entrusted to this self-regulating mechanism" (Polanyi [1944] 1957, p. 68). Economic sociologists have recently criticized such a conclusion and have shown, instead, that market exchange as well is embedded into noneconomic norms and institutions (Lie 1991). A cultural sociology of the economy surely coincides with such a reading of this important classic.

Swedberg (2004, p. 3) has recently argued that Tocqueville's *Democracy in America* deserves a place among the classics in economic sociology. His book, after all, provides an important complement to Weber's *Protestant Ethics*. On the one hand, Tocqueville shows that consumerism, rather than asceticism, was an important building block of the American religious practices and that the endless drive among Americans to consume more and more without ever being fully satisfied[5] crucially contributed to keep the American economy dynamic. On the other hand, Tocqueville reminds us that the American Christian tradition managed to exercise some control over consumerism, thereby avoiding the anomie and the anxiety that an endless pursuit of unsatisfiable desires would otherwise trigger within the population (Swedberg 2004, p. 18). In short, the spirit of American capitalism according to Tocqueville could build both on the spirit of American traditional religion and on the spirit of freedom that characterizes American civilization (Tocqueville 1956, p. 43; in Swedberg 2004, p. 27).

These elements in Tocqueville's analysis are clearly relevant for a cultural sociology of the economy, as well. I would argue, though, that *Democracy in America* deserves its inclusion among the classics of this field even more because of Tocqueville's analysis of the linkages between American democracy and American capitalism. According to Tocqueville, a free democratic society leads to a vibrant economy. Democracies cultivate an ideal of the individual—rational and calm—that is particularly suitable to the market arena. They stimulate the creation of voluntary organizations, thereby developing those organizational skills that are so valuable in the economy. They make people comfortable with chance and uncertainty, a necessary disposition to survive in the market arena. And they orient their citizens toward the present rather than the past as in aristocratic societies or than the future as among the followers of religion. Such orientation, in turn, positively contributes to sustain market activities. Teasing out, as Tocqueville does, the values and cultural practices that democracy and capitalism have in common is one first step toward a comprehensive understanding of the cultural linkages between democracy and the capitalist economy. What is missing, though, is an acknowledgment that democracy occupies a central position in modern societies that turns it into a pillar of collective identity. As a result, linkages between democracy and the economy are not only conducive to enhance functional performance in the economic arena, but also help to shift the economy and its institutions to the center, root them into collective identity, and make them more robust as a consequence of their cultural reenchantment.

After referring to the five classics, a cultural sociology of the economy would be well advised to refer to for inspiration. I will now consider the body of scholarship within contemporary economic sociology that has systematically pursued a cultural analysis of economic life. This literature, after all, provides the launching pad from which a cultural sociology of the economy can take off.

Cultural Analysis in Contemporary Economic Sociology

In the course of the 1980s, a new economic sociology, built on Polanyi's notion of embeddedness (Polanyi [1944] 1971, 1957), took shape. This new research program set out to recover the role of social relations in market processes. The works of White (1981) on production markets as role structures; Burt (1983) on networks and market competition; Baker (1984) on the social structure of securities markets; and Granovetter (1974, 1985) on social ties in labor markets set the beginning of this research tradition. Later, its contributors made an effort to complement the early structural orientation of the field. Baker, for example, added interactionism to White's network perspective (Baker and Faulkner 1991). Podolny (1993) focused on status order and positions rather than roles in the analysis of production markets. Fligstein (1996) complemented the embeddedness approach with the cultural frame perspective. And Granovetter (1990a, pp. 108–110; 1990b, pp. 95–106) made an effort to bring Berger and Luckmann's (1966) constructivism into the network approach (Swedberg 1997, p. 165). More recently, Carruthers and Babb (2000) have accepted that "modern markets are filled with meaning." Therefore, to understand production and consumption, it is necessary to take stock of the systems of cultural meaning in which they are embedded.

This later turn on the part of Carruthers and Babb (2000) appears to make an effort to respond to those critics who have complained that previous efforts to bring culture into the horizon of the new economic sociology have not gone far enough (Lie 1997; Zukin and DiMaggio 1990; Nee and Ingram 1998; Krippner 2001). In particular, according to Krippner (2001), the social embeddedness approach that sprung out of Granovetter's seminal work did away with the very social relations it meant to recover and focused exclusively on the structure of the ties. As a result, neither their social content nor their different meanings played any role. On such ground, Krippner concludes, the new economic sociology has not met its promise of recognizing, along with Polanyi, that the study of economic life calls for the analysis of the concrete institutions that shape economic practice and that "markets, even in ideal form, are not the expression of primal, timeless instincts; they are rather fully social institutions, reflecting a complex alchemy of politics, culture, and ideology" (Krippner 2001, p. 782).

While new economic sociologists have apparently run into such difficulties, a culturalist strand of scholarship within economic sociology has instead managed to strike a more effective balance between social-structural and cultural analysis. Different contemporary anthropologists, cultural historians and cultural studies specialists, mostly working on consumption and money, have served as a source of inspiration for this literature (Douglas 1967; Geertz 1973; Sahlins 1976; Douglas and Isherwood 1979; Crump 1981; Agnew 1986; Appadurai 1986; Reddy 1984; Taussig 1986; Miller 1987). Karin Knorr Cetina, Mitchel Abolafia, Nicole Biggart, and Viviana Zelizer are possibly the four most accomplished contributors to this line of research.

Karin Knorr Cetina is one of the leading figures of a new field of inquiry—the sociology of finance—that has emerged over the past decade out of a fruitful convergence between economic sociology and the social studies of science. Unlike the other three major contributors to the culturalist strand within economic sociology, her work has a markedly phenomenological character. Global currency markets, she observes, are "collective disembodied systems generated entirely in a symbolic space" (Knorr 2005, p. 38). The global world they contribute to bring about is delivered to its participants by a "constellation of technical, visual, and behavioral components packaged together on financial screens." Such screens, she insists, are not windows on physically different realities. They *are* the reality of financial markets. They are the core of the market and most of its context (Knorr 2005, p. 45). Through the screens the market "brings out its life-like depth....As an omnipresent complex 'Other', the market on screen takes on a presence and a profile in its own right with its own self-assembling and self-integrating features" (Knorr 2005, p. 48).

By focusing on the interaction between human and nonhuman actants, Knorr Cetina opens up a fascinating window into the lifeworld of financial markets. One gets the impression, though, that the horizon of meaning she adopts for the purpose of capturing such a lifeworld is too narrow to account for the semantic richness of some of her ethnographic material. For example, in one occasion she observes that "when traders arrive in the morning, they strap themselves to their seats, figuratively speaking" (Knorr 2005, p. 44). Abolafia finds in his ethnography of Wall Street that traders compare themselves with fighter-jet pilots. If this is the case, then their strapping to their seats is a bit more than just figurative. Rather, it echoes a dimension of their lifeworld that apparently escapes Knorr Cetina's horizon of interpretation. In her study with Urs Bruegger on the foreign exchange market in Zurich, in turn, she remarks that sex and violence permeate the vocabulary by which traders describe their relation to the market (Knorr and Bruegger 2000, p. 154). References to sex and violence have traditionally characterized military talk and therefore appear to be consistent with the finding that traders see themselves as fighter-jet pilots. If this is the case, one may start to wonder whether the morning after a particularly "bloody" day of trading, traders will get back to their computers and feel they "love the smell of napalm in the morning." Or alternatively, whether in the course of a coordinated attack against a currency, they will hear the trumpets of Wagner's *Walkiries*. If one believes that meaning is not just the endogenous product of a given setting of interaction but rather has a citational character, then one will be bound to expand the horizon of interpretation in order to correctly pin down the lifeworld of a given object of analysis. For the case at hand, this implies that scholars will have to push the analysis much further in order to capture the cultural embeddedness of trading. Doing so will enable them to track the spurs of those intertextual references that might pin down the "global" lifeworld of financial markets to specific cultural contexts. And this could ultimately give away the fact that what appears to be global might be in the end just a prolongation of some cultural specificity.

Like Knorr Cetina, Mitchel Abolafia has worked on financial markets. In his 1996 ethnography, *Making Markets* (1996), the author shows in what ways the exercise of self-interest within three different trading floors reflects a panoply of local institutional and cultural mechanisms—the "elaborate occupational cultures that prescribe manners, attitudes, and styles of play," the "scripts defining who can play and how the game should be played," and the broader cultural horizon within which such scripts are embedded (Abolafia 1996, p. 231).

While recognizing that trading is a deep play in which there is much more at stake than just money (Abolafia 1996, p. 17), Abolafia clearly draws from Geertz (1973). Still, this is not the only inspiration the author draws from anthropology. Victor Turner's notion of social drama, as well, helps him pin down the cultural structure that underpins the unfolding of Michael Milken's scandal, which he discusses at the end of his book. His analysis of the dramatic dimensions of such a scandal, however, never gets him as far as taking a performative turn in his study.

His discussion of the scandal also sheds light over the limits of his approach to the analysis of cultural embeddedness. For example, when Milken justifies financial innovation as a means to overcome discrimination among entrepreneurs with regard to access to funding, Abolafia does not seem to hear the echo in Milken's argument of that discourse of the American civil society within which the principle of equality among citizens is inscribed, and which constitutes the cultural horizon within which Milken may have possibly articulated his argumentative strategy. Surely, Abolafia accounts to some important extent for the cultural embeddedness of trading and pushes it far enough to capture the linkages between trading and other fields of action like gambling and combat, which in turn lead traders to compare themselves with fighter pilots and professional athletes—disciplined, coolheaded, focused, and emotionally distant (Abolafia 1996, p. 18). Yet, he does not seem to count on a clear analytical criterion that enables him to decide how far one should push the analysis in order to adequately account for the cultural embeddedness of the object under inquiry.

Finally, Abolafia draws from Swidler's (1986, p. 284) understanding of culture as "a repertoire of capacities from which varying strategies of action may be constructed." However, since Abolafia shows that identities and emotions also play an important role in the way traders carry out their job, one wonders whether a deeply instrumental and totally malleable understanding of culture can actually reflect their experience. After all, one would expect that the internal logic of culture and the emotional investments traders make on particular cultural scripts would increase their rigidity and therefore their autonomous effects on traders' actions.

Together with Knorr Cetina and Abolafia, Nicole Biggart is one of the most accomplished contributors to the culuralist strand within economic sociology. In her *Charismatic Capitalism* (1989), Biggart uses a Weberian framework to show that modern capitalism has allowed the survival of organizational forms such as direct-selling organizations that seem to have escaped the iron-cage logic of rational disenchantment. Such organizations, she points out, are charisma-based rather than legal-rational. They allow and foster cooperative rather competitive relations within their staff. They encourage rather than repress emotions on the part of their members. And they use social networks to reach their business goals rather than cutting them off.

In her analysis of direct-selling organizations, Biggart devotes her attention to the role values, collective representations and beliefs, narratives, and rituals play in their operation. Echoing Tocqueville's insights on the spirit of American capitalism, she observes that in the nineteenth century Protestant ethics in America got twisted, and wealth was no longer seen as a sign of God but rather as a result of individual accomplishment and character. On such ground, meritocracy, initiative, and perseverance were positively valued and ended up by constituting the core set of values that still inspires direct-selling organizations. After pinpointing the ethics that underpin the operations of such organizations, Biggart could have addressed the cultural codes that most directly inspire such values. Alexander and Smith (1993), and Alexander (2006) would provide a neat basis to start from. Instead, she pursues, in a different direction, the analysis of collective representations and beliefs as well as the narratives that set them in motion. For example, the author shows that the idea of family structures both identities and actions within direct-selling organizations (Biggart 1989, p. 14) Kinship terms, as a result, describe work relations as between daughter-dealers and mother-managers. Meetings are represented as family reunions. And home parties, where the selling is conducted, are referred to as dates. Apart from family, religion also provides a constellation of metaphors that contribute to structure the experience of direct-selling organizations. For example, their members attribute a transformational power to the products they sell to the point that they "obscure the financial transaction that in fact is taking place: they present themselves as direct-selling companies that paradoxically do not sell" (Biggart 1989, p. 116). Quite interestingly, while Biggart refers to Douglas and Isherwood's work on the anthropology of consumption to discuss the transformation in meaning that products undergo in direct-selling organizations, she does not push her analysis to the point of systematically discussing the performative dimensions of such a process and therefore the elements that influence its authenticity. Despite that, Biggart's analysis goes as far as hinting at performance when she addresses the ritual dimensions of direct-selling organizations. For example, she points out, public confessional rituals set the stage for witnessing the transformation of the self members of direct-selling organizations undergo as they grow within such organizations. Also, public celebrations serve as rituals in which the miraculous powers of leaders get reaffirmed.

Together with Knorr Cetina, Biggart, and Abolafia, Viviana Zelizer is another outstanding contributor to the culturalist strand within economic sociology. Surely, she is the scholar who has carried out such an approach with the greatest coherence over the longest period of time (Zelizer 1979, 1985, 1994, 2005). Zelizer's analysis successfully integrates cultural with structural analysis. To explain the emergence of the American insurance industry; or the social construction of the economically useless and yet emotionally priceless child between 1870 and 1930 in America; or the changing social meanings of money, Zelizer takes stock both with the effects of cultural frames as well as of class and family structures. All along in her career, Zelizer has stressed the importance of overcoming the "mythology" within economic sociology that conceives two hostile worlds—one of rationality, efficiency, and impersonality, on the one side, and one of self-expression, cultural richness, and intimacy, on the other—which are crucial to keep separate in order to avoid mutual corruption. At the same time, her work must be commended for resisting the temptation to reduce economic phenomena to economic calculation culture, or power and for insisting that "we have no choice but to pave crossroads connecting continuously negotiated, meaning-drenched social relations with the whole range of economic processes" (Zelizer 2005a, p. 349).[6] Finally, it is important to remember Zelizer's insistence, particularly in her later works, on one pragmatic point. By vindicating the salience of culture in modern economic life, a culture-sensitive economic sociology will not be doomed to marginality. Instead, it will be able to add value to the analysis of important macroeconomic phenomena that economists have not quite fully grasped. Although Zelizer is particularly vocal on this point, immediate pragmatic relevance is apparently also one of the characterizing features of the contributions by Biggart and Abolafia to the culturalist strand of economic sociology that distinguishes their work from the culture-sensitive work of other sociologists.

Zelizer's work has systematically shed light over the pervasive intrusion of different cultural logics into the market sphere. In this sense, she has contributed to the line of research within sociology that has been vindicating for the margin for cultural reenchantment in modern life. Also, she has paid constant attention to the cultural embeddedness of economic action. Like Abolafia, however, it is unclear whether she relies on a clear analytical criterion that helps her decide whether her analysis of cultural embeddedness has gone sufficiently far and how far ahead it could possibly push. Without making such a criterion explicit, the reader cannot decide whether her treatment of cultural embeddedness is sufficiently encompassing. Finally, Zelizer acknowledges that economic phenomena can undergo a process of cultural transformation that is mediated both by culture and social structure. Still, she does not directly address the contingency and the instability of such a process nor does she explicitly tackle it as a matter of cultural performance.

The need for a performative turn in her analysis cannot but be all the more urgent as her research moves into the field of economic ethics. Zelizer (2007, p. 9) has recently stressed the importance for sociology to understand how ethical questions arise in economic life, what their distinctive properties are, how economic actors respond to them, what produces violations, and what effects such responses have on economic performance. To answer such questions, she continues, it is not sufficient to look at the work moral philosophers, feminist thinkers, economists, and economic sociologists have produced in their studies of professions, crime, inheritance, consumption, care, and corruption. Rather, it is necessary to examine the relationship between general ethical contexts and the specific forms of code organizations adopt. "National ethical traditions," after all, "shape contrasting approaches to both the construction and the contents of formal ethical codes" (Zelizer 2007, p. 20). Still, the scripts people resort to in order to come across as economically ethical are only part of the story. Discursive competence is not sufficient to come across as authentically committed to ethical behavior in the economic arena. Actors, instead, need to be performatively competent in this respect. This is why a performative turn in Zelizer's most recent research agenda is all the more urgent.

Outline of a Cultural Sociology of the Economy

The debate among economic sociologists over the opportunity to introduce cultural analysis within their horizon of inquiry has traditionally focused on the question of whether cultural analysis should replace social-structural analysis or whether it should complement it. Zelizer, for example, has advocated for the latter. Similarly, DiMaggio distanced himself from a full-scale cultural analysis of the economy and has suggested instead that economic sociology "should include a 'cultural' component—but not more" (DiMaggio 1994, p. 27).

The narrow focus of such a debate has prevented the profession from systematically discussing how scholars should go about accounting for the cultural dimension of economic life. Should they take a cultural-structural approach? Or should they rather adopt a pragmatic focus? Or, alternatively, should they resort to a framework that integrates both perspectives? Furthermore, taking stock with the role of culture in the economy implies addressing the phenomenon of cultural embeddedness of economic action. So, how far should scholars push the analysis of such a phenomenon? And where should they draw the line? These are the basic theoretical questions that structure the core of a cultural sociology of the economy. In this section, I will argue that the emerging field of neo-Durkheimian sociology, which in the past two decades has systematically addressed the phenomenon of cultural reenchantment in modern societies, can provide one possible set of answers to such questions. Answering them, I will suggest, will help distinguish the inner theoretical makeup of a cultural sociology of the economy from the culturalist strand of scholarship within economic sociology.

To make my point, I will proceed by steps. I will start by showing how the later Durkheim of *The Elementary Forms of Religious Life* can help make sense of cultural reenchantment in modern societies, and what the limits of Durkheim's analytical framework are in this respect. This will allow me to introduce the neo-Durkheimian extension of his framework. Then, after teasing out the main analytical features of neo-Durkheimian analysis, I will be able to draw its implications with respect to the two questions I have introduced at the beginning of this section: how to study the cultural dimension of economic life, and how to go about the study of cultural embeddedness.

Traditional communities constituted the main focus of Durkheim's *Elementary Forms of Religious Life*. Still, the author explicitly envisaged the possibility of applying his framework to the analysis of social life in modern societies. After all, as Smith and Alexander (2005, p. 26) have recently acknowledged, Durkheim considered that the internal patterning of religious life and social organization in modern societies are homologous. He stressed the power and compulsion that characterizes both religious and social symbols. He showed that value-conflicts in modern societies get transfigured into an agonic struggle between the sacred and the profane. He recognized that actors still move to avoid pollution and to restore purity. And finally, he acknowledged the lasting power of the ritual in modern societies for the purpose of establishing solidarities. In other words, to put it with Alexander (1988, p. 177), Durkheim did not merely lay out a sociology of religion but rather put forward a religious sociology that used religion as a metaphor to understand society.

Since the 1980s, a neo-Durkheimian tradition has emerged within sociological theory that has systematically applied Durkheim's "religious sociology" to the study of different spheres of social life in modern societies (Smith and Alexander 2005, p. 14). As the research tradition consolidated, though, the limits of Durkheim's framework have become increasingly apparent. Scholars have recognized that, as a result of structural differentiation, and due to conflict, competition, and reflexivity, social integration in modern societies is much more fragile and contingent than

Durkheim envisaged. The experience of meaning is much less immediate as a result of its being mediated by drama and contrivance. These differences have led Smith and Alexander (2005, p. 26) to suggest that drawing a straightforward homology from Durkheim between traditional and modern societies is "not enough and too much." As a consequence, neo-Durkheimians have had to resort to a more general analytical framework that enables them to approach modern social life as a cultural accomplishment without reducing its contingency and its instability. Alexander's latest macrosociological theory of social action as performance has provided a powerful tool in this respect (Alexander 2006).

On such a ground neo-Durkheimians have been able to argue that modern societies—to put it with Shils (1975)—still have a sacred center that works as their "ultimate and irreducible" transcendent core. They have been able to acknowledge that at the symbolic level all spheres of social life are still latently linked to the center and that whenever social action moves to the center, it can rise above the profane realm of routine function and partake in the sacredness of collective identity. This is what according to neo-Durkheimians makes cultural reenchantment possible in modern societies. On the other hand, they have recognized that for social action to move to the center, cultural linkages must be turned on effectively, and this constitutes a highly unstable performative accomplishment.

These considerations bear two important analytical implications. First, taking stock of the cultural embeddedness of social action implies accounting for the rich web of cultural linkages that latently anchor it to the center.[7] To adequately deal with cultural embeddedness, as a result, analysts must consider the center as their relevant horizon of interpretation. Second, since cultural reenchantment crucially depends on the effectiveness of the linkages—and since this is a matter of cultural performance—neither a purely cultural-structuralist nor a purely action-oriented framework is suitable to capture that. Rather, one must resort to one framework that integrates both perspectives. Alexander's cultural pragmatics satisfies such a requirement.

These conclusions surely provide an answer to the two basic theoretical questions that stand at the core of a cultural sociology of the economy. At the same time, though, it raises a new question that falls beyond the analytical horizon of the culturalist strand of scholarship within economic sociology. What stands at the sacred center of modern societies, after all?

According to Alexander, democracy constitutes an important building block of the center and therefore contributes to define the identity of modern societies. Democracy, he maintains, is not just a set of technical rules. Rather, it is "a world of great and idealizing expectations, but also overwhelming feelings of disgust and condemnation." This world, he insists, is articulated through "a transcendental language of sacred values of the good and profane symbols of evil" (Alexander 2006, p. 4), "a historically contingent final vocabulary," to put it with Rorty (1989, pp. 190–192), by means of which people express what brings them together and what sets them apart (Alexander 2006, p. 56). Such a language consists of "a highly generalized symbolic system that divides civic virtue from civic vice in a remarkably stable and consistent way." Its general structure can be isolated and approached as "a relatively autonomous symbolic form" (p. 56). Alexander and Smith (1993) and subsequently Alexander (2006) show that such structure can be represented as a system of binary attributes that define legitimate and illegitimate motivations, social relations and institutions in democratic societies. Such cultural codes, in the end, are a core building block of the sacred center of modern societies.

Baiocchi (2006) has recently shown that alternative discourses may compete against that of civil society in the makeup of the symbolic center of democratic societies. For example, in the specific case of Brazil, he shows that the codes of liberty and repression, based on the liberal tradition, must compete against a corporatist code that draws from a nonliberal political culture in which the collective primes over the individual.

If the analysis of the above-mentioned authors is correct, then it is possible to conclude that in modern secular societies, different spheres of social life, for example, the economy, are latently linked to a sacred symbolic center. Such a center is structured by the discourses of political legitimation citizens resort to in order to determine who is in and deserves the solidarity of the other fellow citizens and who is out and can therefore be neglected. Alexander's codes of liberty and repression or Baiocchi's corporatist code are the cultural structures that can makeup the center of democratic societies at different stages of modernization. Understanding the meaning of economic action will therefore require that the analyst takes stock with the immediate cultural context within which economic action is embedded; but also on the one hand with the rich network of symbolic linkages that latently connect economic action to the cultural codes at the center and on the other with the performative conditions that turn such linkages effective.

Such considerations help better qualify the topography that underpins Spillman's (1999) map of a cultural sociology of the economy. According to Spillman (1999, p. 1047), such a field should concentrate on the analysis of three phenomena: the cultural construction of the objects of market exchange, the cultural construction of parties to market exchange, and finally the cultural construction of the norms of exchange. The literature on consumer culture (Tomlison 1990, Biernacki 1995) and the sociology of the state literature (Pusey 1991), as Spillman (1999, p. 1054) points out, have addressed the first phenomenon, that is, the commodification of previously uncommodified spheres. Still, Spillman continues, it is necessary to systematically account for such a process as one of contested reframing, as Zelizer (1985) did with reference to life insurance and Frenzen, Hirsch, and Zerillo (1994) did with regard to the transformation of debt into the socially more acceptable consumer credit. The cultural construction of the parties to market exchange, in turn, she adds, needs to be approached in terms of construction of a peculiar kind of imagined community (Anderson 1991). Cultural sociologists can help in this respect by shedding light over the relevant cultural boundaries: how they change and how they get redesigned. "The idea of imagined community," she insists, "should be used to extend the notion of embeddedness typically understood in terms of structural dimensions of network" (Spillman 1999, p. 1058). Finally, she concludes, a cultural sociology of the economy must take stock with the plurality of logics of action and of vocabularies of motive that permeate market exchange.[8] This implies tracking the norms, the narratives, and the rituals that underpin and help legitimize it (Spillman 1999, pp. 1061–1062). According to Spillman, three literatures have contributed to this respect: that of state/market relations (Carruthers 1996; Dobbin 1994; Fligstein 1996; Pusey 1991); consumer society and on advertising (Frenzen, Hirsch, and Zerillo 1994; Tomlison 1990) and the meaning of money (Zelizer 1994; Carruthers and Espeland 1997).

Now, looking at Spillman's map with neo-Durkheimian lenses will help realize that the three lines of inquiry she identifies are no isolated basins. Rather, their waters flow from the very same source—the sacred center of society. Distance from, and connection with, the center are in the end the topographic principles that organize such a map.

After briefly laying out the central features of a cultural sociology of the economy, it is now possible to refer back to the authors I presented in the previous two sections and identify the main points of difference and contact between them.

I will start with the classics. A cultural sociology of the economy builds on the late Durkheim of *The Elementary Forms of Religious Life* but does not stop there. Rather, it follows the interpretative stream from Durkheim through Parsons, Shils, and Douglas to the neo-Durkheimian tradition that emerged in the 1980s and extended Durkheim's analytical framework to better fit modern complex differentiated societies.

Also, a cultural sociology of the economy is sympathetic with a systemic perspective that is keen to systematically track the boundary exchanges between the economy and the other spheres of social life. After all, if this were not the case, the field would not be interested in taking into consideration the rich network of symbolic linkages that connects the economy with the sacred center of society. This constitutes a point of contact with the *Economy and Society* perspective Parsons and Smelser advocated. On the other hand, the focus on the symbolic and the performative marks a clear departure from the value sociology that underpins Parsons and Smelser's economic sociology.

With reference to Weber, in turn, a cultural sociology of the economy shows that economic life in modern societies is still linked to powerful sources of charisma that occasionally get turned on. Under such circumstances, economic interaction is transformed into a matter of collective identity and acquires the features that flow from the sacred.

A cultural sociology of the economy relies on an analytical criterion that makes it possible to determine how far the analysis of cultural embeddedness of economic action should push. This enables cultural sociologists to meet Polanyi's invitation to adequately address the embeddedness of economic action and economic institutions. On the other hand, unlike Polanyi, the field does not consider that the deepening of a capitalist economy necessarily implies a disembedding effect from social life. Market exchange, instead, is firmly embedded into culture. Only, this time, as capitalism deepens, one witnesses a relative strengthening of the latent symbolic linkages between the economic sphere and the sacred center of society with respect to the linkages between the other spheres of social life and the center.

Finally, a cultural sociology of the economy understands the relationship between capitalism and democracy in modern society in terms of the symbolic linkage of the economic sphere to the sacred center of society whereby the identity of society is coded. The field therefore reads Tocqueville more from a Durkheimian perspective than from a Weberian one.

With the culturalist strand within economic sociology, in turn, a cultural sociology of the economy shares the belief that the economic sphere in capitalist societies is still permeated by culture and cultural practices. Unlike such tradition, however, it explicitly acknowledges that the economic sphere is linked to the sacred center of society where the very identity of society is defined, and, therefore, whenever such linkages are effectively turned on, economic action turns into a matter of identity. This provides an analytical criterion to establish how far the analysis of cultural embeddedness should push, what it would call for, and why analysts should address the performative dimension of the cultural transformation of economic action into a matter of collective identity.

In this section, I have suggested that a cultural sociology of the economy is characterized by a number of analytical questions and operational concerns that differentiate it from other culture-sensitive analyses of the economy within sociology. For the next question, on the other hand, following Zelizer's recommendation, I will suggest that such a field is also immediately relevant at the pragmatic level. More precisely, it promises to contribute to push ahead into a more decisively culturalist direction the research frontier of three literatures—on organizational legitimacy, the sociology of financial markets, and the sociology of money—and enable, as a result, sociologists to tackle three of the most pressing problems that loom at the horizon of the current world economic crisis: The loss of confidence within the general public for private corporations, the economic profession, and independent central banks.

The Use of a Cultural Sociology
of the Economy

As the world moves toward an economic crisis of historic proportions, the legitimacy of private corporations, economic professions, and independent central banks starts to shake. Around the world, private corporations have been hit by a long stream of scandals that has contributed to undermine their institutional credibility. Economists have not been able to anticipate or warn against the crisis, and people are now wondering whether they will be up to the task of steering the boat out of the current fog. Central banks, in turn, have responded to the deepening deflation by cutting interest rates to unprecedented levels. As monetary policy becomes increasingly powerless concerning the recession, people will start to wonder what the use of independent central banks is if their only institutional task—the control of inflation—has suddenly passed out of fashion as a result of the crisis. As private corporations, economists, and independent central banks run the risk of losing people's confidence, it is imperative to understand the mechanisms that underpin its creation, maintenance, and repair. A cultural sociology of the economy can contribute in this respect by helping understand the deep sources of legitimacy of economic institutions in modern societies.

To understand how private corporations can defend their legitimacy in times of crisis, I will first draw from the literature on organizational legitimacy that has been consolidating in the past three decades. Such a literature, I will suggest, misses the important dimensions of the defense of legitimacy a cultural sociology of the economy can instead help recover, thereby opening up a whole field of inquiry sociologists have not systematically yet explored.

Different definitions of organizational legitimacy are currently available in the literature. According to Maurer (1971, p. 361), for example, legitimacy has to do with the process by which an organization justifies its right to exist. Suchman (1995, p. 574), in turn, suggests that organizational legitimacy is a "generalized perception or assumption that the actions of an entity are desirable, proper, or appropriate within some socially constructed system of norms, values, beliefs, and definitions."[9]

For the study of organizational legitimacy, Weber constitutes one important classical referent. Administrative systems, he suggests, draw legitimacy from either charisma, tradition, or law. In 1960, Parsons proposed a cultural institutional perspective and stressed the importance for organizational goals to link to wider societal values and functions.

In the past three decades, two main approaches have contended the field of organizational analysis. On the one hand, the ecological perspective has treated legitimacy just as a parameter that influences the emergence and decline of organizational populations over time (Carroll and Hannan 2000; Hannan and Freeman 1992). As a result, it has not dwelt on the mechanisms that construct it. The institutionalist perspective, on the other hand, has done so by showing that organizations achieve legitimacy by adjusting their structures, procedures, policies, and goals with legal norms and regulations, field-level norms, or taken-for-granted cultural constructs.

Within the institutionalist camp, then, some have emphasized passive adherence on the part of organizations to the structuration dynamics that unfold at the field level and have therefore downplayed managerial agency and manager-stakeholder conflict (Barron, et al. 1986; Baum and Powell 1995; DiMaggio and Powell 1983; Meyer and Rowan 1977; Scott 2001; DiMaggio and Powell 1983; Meyer and Scott 1983; Powell and DiMaggio 1991; Zucker 1987). Others, on the contrary, have stressed active adherence, thereby pointing out that organizations instrumentally use and manipulate evocative symbols of conformity with widely held social values to obtain public support. Such a strand, to put it with Suchman, presupposes a high degree of management control over the legitimation process, an "almost limitless malleability of symbols and rituals against the exogenously constrained recalcitrance of tangible, real outcomes" (Pfeffer and Salancik 1978; Ashforth and Gibbs 1990; Dowling and Pfeffer 1975; Pfeffer 1981).

Organizational crises—accidents, scandals, and product safety incidents— constitute a privileged field to observe what the foundations of legitimacy are, how legitimacy gets maintained, and how it can be possibly repaired (Marcus and Goodman 1991; Bucholz, Evans, and Wagley 1985; Godson 1975; Keirmann, and Olsen 1972; Kemeny 1979; Perrow 1984; Sethi 1977; Sharplin 1985; Shrivastava 1987; Starling and Baskin 1984; Sturdivant 1985; Davidson, Chandy and Cross 1987; Fields and Janjigian 1989; Marcus and Goodman 1989; Boulton 1978; Fisse and Braithwaite 1983; Franklin 1986; Post 1978; Sampson 1973; Litschert and Nicholson 1977; Davidson and Worrell 1988; Goodpaster 1984; Sapolsky 1986; Starling and Baskin 1985; Whiteside 1972; Bromiley and Marcus 1989). On such terrain, institutional analysis has been fruitfully complemented by impression management studies. Institutionalists, on the one hand, have shown that organizations introduce structural reforms and changes in their procedures or staff in order to meet field-level norms. In other words, analysts working along this tradition focus on the content of the measures that help maintain, repair, or recover organizational legitimacy. Impression management scholars, on the other hand, have focused instead on the communicative techniques that organizations, and particularly their spokespersons, resort to for the purpose of defending themselves (Goffman 1973, 1974, 1981; Schenkler 1980; Tedeschi and Reiss 1981; Tedeschi 1981). Contributors to this approach have therefore been interested in tracking the verbal accounts by which organizations deny or admit their responsibility, blame others, offer excuses, explain or justify their deeds, and apologize (Elsbach 1994; Elsbach and Sutton 1992; Elsbach and Sutton 1998; Marcus and Goodman 1991; Sutton and Callahan 1987; Sutton and Kramer 1990; Suchman 1995; Leary and Kowalski 1990; Giacalone and Rosenfeld 1989, 1991; Staw, Mckechnie, and Puffer 1983; Bettman and Weitz 1983; Salancik and Meindl 1984; Metzler 2001; Fisse and Braithwaite 1983). Impression management scholars have also occasionally resorted to stigma theory while addressing the communicative tactics organizations adopt to eschew or deal with stigma (Sutton and Callahan 1987; Goffman 1963; Page 1984; Jones et al. 1984).

Both institutionalists and impression management scholars, however, have missed out on a number of important issues crucial to the management of an organizational crisis and therefore to the recovery or repair of legitimacy. Focusing on the mere scripts organizations follow in their verbal accounts completely neglects all the other dimensions that make up the cultural pragmatics of apologies, denials, explanations, and justifications, and that ultimately determines whether they will be received by the public as authentic and therefore satisfactory. A script must distill a whole set of background collective representations—symbols, codes, narratives, and genres—that the public considers to be consistent with the meaning the script seeks to project on its audiences. Also, the actors must match the script they are uttering and the collective representations they are seeking to evoke through their performance. Similarly, the staging of the apologies, denials, explanations, and justifications, the means that are brought together to produce the performance, the way social power is perceived to be influencing it, and the composition of the audiences will crucially impact on the reception that organizations will get. In other words, it may well happen that the very same script will be received satisfactorily by some specific audience in a particular performative setting and will instead be rejected in an alternative one.

Bringing in the performative horizon within which legitimacy can be maintained, challenged, repaired, and recovered yields two corollaries that help clarify two further elements both the institutionalist and the impression management perspectives miss and a cultural sociology of the economy, instead, helps capture. The logic of technical reason generally structures the profane realm of routine organizational life. When the legitimacy of an organization, and therefore its right to exist as such, are challenged, and when, as a result, the stakes of both the organization and its challengers soar, either party may consider escalating conflict by shifting the game by symbolic linkage onto some alternative arena in which each party can mobilize new allies in its favor, reverse the distribution of forces on the field, and possibly win the battle over the organization's legitimacy. As a result of the process of competitive symbolic linkage among the players, the struggle will in the end land onto some arena that works as a focal point for the general public. This is what some sociologists would refer to as the symbolic center of society. When the crisis gets to the center, it is no longer something that has to do with the profane realm of routine institutional life in which technical arguments are enough to win an argumentative battle. Rather, it becomes something that pertains, and possibly shakes the values, beliefs, and symbols that identify society as such. It will have entered the absolute sacred space of identity.

As Alexander has shown, the language and the structures of feelings that underpin democracy are one crucial building block of the center of modern societies. In the course of a crisis, as a consequence, both the organization and its challengers will have an incentive to recast the vocabulary of technical reason within the structures of meaning making up the codes of liberty and repression that constitute the center. Since in some societies, however, other discourses of political legitimation, based on alternative structures of meaning, contend the definition of the center, it is possible that, in the battle for legitimacy, the organization and its opponents will adopt different vocabularies. In this case, their confrontation may occasionally lead to a tragicomedy of errors.

If the center of society is the relevant horizon within which the struggle for organizational legitimacy is embedded, then the codes that constitute the center will need to be considered in order to account for the full meaning of the organization's announcements. This pushes the analysis further with respect to the reach of impression-management studies, but it also does so with respect to the cultural institutionalism Parsons supported, which in turn focused exclusively on norms and values and left out other important elements that make up the cultural environment of action (Alexander 1988a).

Such a conclusion may also contribute to sharpen up the neo-institutionalist argument on rationality as a legitimizing myth (Meyers and Rowan 1977). When organizations appeal to the rationality of their procedures as a legitimacy title, the meaning of such a rationality crucially depends on the horizon of interpretation within which one reads it and on the resolution of the lenses with which one looks at it. It can be pure and simple technical rationality. Or it can alternatively be technical rationality turned into a transcendent cultural logic that contributes to the composition of the sacred center of society. In this case, it may work as a myth. At the center, though, rationality turned into a transcendent cultural logic may be embedded within the different structures of meanings that can make up the center. For example, it may be part of the codes of liberty and repression that concurs to constitute the symbolic core of modern democratic societies. For this reason, the horizon of analysis a cultural sociology of the economy takes as reference can help sharpen up the neoinstitutionalist understanding of rationality as a legitimizing myth.

In conclusion, nowadays private corporations have been hit by scandals of corruption, political irresponsibility, and greed. As they come under attack, public debate over their misbehavior will increasingly follow the cultural logic of the discourse of civil society that contributes to makeup the symbolic core of modern democratic societies and, occasionally, the logic of alternative discourses of political legitimation that may contend the control of the symbolic center of such societies. The battle over organizational legitimacy, in other words, will no longer be fought in terms of technical rationality but rather in terms of civic virtues and civic vices. Also, the battle may well stretch across multiple institutional arenas—mass media, legal, scientific, political-bureaucratic, aesthetic, and religious. Cultural sociologists are well equipped to show in what way, along the battle over their own legitimacy, private corporations may strive to translate their interests by resorting to the cultural codes that structure the symbolic center of their own societies in an effort to maintain, recover, or repair their own legitimacy.

After hinting at the way a cultural sociology of the economy may contribute to address one pragmatic problem that is looming at the horizon of the current world economic crisis—the loss of public confidence into private corporations—I will now discuss how cultural sociologists may help shed light over the mechanisms that influence public confidence into the community of economists. To do so, I will first draw from the sociology of finance literature that has emerged over the last decade and show in what way a cultural sociology of the economy can complement it.

During the last decade, a new literature has emerged—the sociology of financial markets—that has built on economic sociology and anthropology on the one hand and the social studies of science on the other. As Beunza, Hardie, and Mackenzie (2006) have recently pointed out, the new field does with trading floors what the social studies of science has previously done with laboratories. In other words, it approaches financial markets as "heterogeneous assemblages of human beings and technical devices, devoted to the production of workable knowledge" (p. 39) and seeks to recover their materiality, which, following Mackenzie (2007, p. 357), is not just about physicality but rather about physical objects, technological systems, human bodies, legal systems, cultures, procedures, beliefs, and social relations expressed by objects and bodies.

With particular reference to culture, the sociology of financial markets has pushed the analysis far enough to take stock with different forms of it: cultural scripts, cultural styles, discourses, frames, the influences by fiction literature on economic reality, collective identities, and even the more performative dimensions of culture that involve emotions and the bodies. More concretely, Mackenzie (2007) has followed Thrift (2000) and Maurer (2001, 2005) in taking stock with the cultural geographies of derivatives and has shown that financial markets have their own internal cultures, follow different cultural scripts, and are characterized by different styles. For example, he contrasts Chicago's rough and tumble style with London's gentlemanly capitalism and observes how the cultural script that has traditionally related investment to gambling structures the market of derivatives (Goede 2005). MacKenzie (2007, p. 368) has also been keen on tracking down the concrete channels through which culture actually impacts economic reality. "'Culture,'" he says, "is…not simply 'the context' within which derivative trading takes place. Via matters, such as the law of gambling, it shapes and is enmeshed with the detailed mechanics of this trading." Yenkey (2007), on his part, has shown how the meaning of information and transparency in the U.S. securities markets has changed over time during the twentieth century. Information disclosure, he argues, was earlier justified as a measure to prevent a corporation from carrying out actions that would damage the interests of individuals. Later, however, it got grounded by quite a different discourse, that is, the right of investors to gain equal access to profit opportunities. Czarniawska (2005), in turn, has shown how fictional representations of women in finance may influence the way they are actually perceived in real life and has referred to Abolafia (1996) for the purpose of acknowledging that social processes can indeed get structured by cultural genres. Hardie and Mackenzie (2006) have introduced along with Callon (2005) and Callon and Caliskan (2005) the notion of *agencement* to capture the idea that agency is not only made up by human beings "embedded in institutions, conventions, personal relationships" but rather by human bodies as well as "prostheses, tools, equipment, technical devices, algorithms, etc." Frames, the authors add, influence such *agencement*. Preda (2005), on his part, has drawn from Pollner (2002, p. 231) to conceive investors as an "imagined community" and has set out to establish what such an imagined community is about and how it comes about. His analysis of investors has also gone as far as acknowledging the influence of the literary field on the configuration of the investor. Moral pamphlets, comedies, satire, and visual allegories, for example, played a role in shaping the figure of the investor during the eighteenth century. Preda's analysis has also taken into consideration some of the more performative dimensions of culture such as the *mis-en-scene* during the eighteenth century of the figure of the investor in a closed world of alleys and pubs. Hassoun (2005) has further contributed to address the performative side of culture by tackling the expression of various types of emotions—sympathy, aggressiveness, admiration, anger, rivalry, shame, and humiliation—on the trading floors and by shedding light over the categories of indigenous thought, to put it with Mauss ([1906] 1968), that signify such emotions. Finally, Zaloom (2003, 2004, 2006) has explicitly taken stock with the role of the body in financial markets. For example, in her participative ethnography, Zaloom has reported that training had also to do with training "our bodies to operate as uninterrupted conduits between the dealing room and the online world, allowing our fingers to become seamless extensions of our economic intentions" (Caitlin Zaloom in Beunza, Hardie, and Mackenzie 2006, p. 731).

Such an extensive engagement on the part of the sociology of financial markets with a broad spectrum of cultural phenomena, however, does not make a cultural sociology of the economy redundant within such a field of inquiry. To see why, it is useful to address the way the sociology of financial markets deals with the question of the performativity of economics. Callon's thesis on the performativity of economics has been one of the shaping forces of the sociology of financial markets. According to Callon (1998, p. 30) "the economy is embedded not in society but in economics." While showing the performative effects economics has on the economic reality of financial markets, sociologists working within this emerging field of inquiry have been careful to acknowledge that performativity becomes possible not in a social vacuum but rather as a result of the social embeddedness of economics. Mackenzie and Millo (2003), for example, explicitly show that the performative effects of economics are not brought about by *homines oeconomici* but rather by social agents who are influenced by cultures, moral communities, and places of political action. The cultural and legal barriers to the creation of financial derivative markets in the United States in the late 1960s and early 1970s were overcome by economics. Still, the peculiar culture and social structures of the Chicago markets influenced the chances that certain economic ideas had to become popular among traders and shape their activities as a consequence. For this reasons, the performativity of the classic option pricing theory was not "a matter of simple self-fulfilling prophecy (Merton 1949) or of the discovery of the correct way to price options. It was a contested, historically contingent outcome" (Mackenzie and Millo 2003, p. 138). "Economics indeed facilitated the emergence of derivative markets by disembedding derivatives from the pervasive moral framework in which they were dangerously close to wagers. However, neither economists on their own nor the unaided persuasive power of economic theory created" the institutions that would later preside over the organization of the derivative markets in Chicago (Mackenzie and Millo 2003, p. 139). Mackenzie and Millo (2003) plausibly argue that the justification of derivatives in terms of public interest that a number of prestigious Princeton economists put forward played an important role to overcome the suspicion the public had felt about derivatives since the 1929 crash. While the authors seem to take for granted that the general public would believe the opinion of such economists in that specific case, one cannot do so and expect that the public will always automatically believe economists and economics in any society and under any historical circumstances, which is in turn quite crucial to support Callon's performativity thesis. The growing literature on the public understanding of science can serve as a platform to reflect on the mechanisms that help ground such belief (Farr 1993; Gross 1994; Nelkin 1994; Bud 1995; Baurer 1995; Michael 1998; Irwin 2001; Leggett and Finlay 2001; Valenti 2002; Bates 2005; Cretaz 2006; Wagner 2007).[10] Still, such literature has not pushed far enough in the analysis of the cultural mediations that ultimately produce it. A cultural sociology of the economy may therefore come in to do the job by contributing, with its special sensibility, to the construction of legitimacy in the public sphere.

Following my argument with reference to private corporations, one might conjecture that linking economics to the codes of liberty and repression at the symbolic center of democratic societies might work toward legitimizing it before the general public. Quite interestingly, though, the symbolic transformation that appears to have legitimized economics so far has pointed to a radically different direction. In modern western societies, in other words, economics has taken, in the eyes of the public, the position theology used to occupy before modernity. The theologian of secularization, Harvey Cox, for example, has drawn the attention to the covert operation in public discourse over the economy of myths of origin, legends of the fall, and doctrines of sin and redemption. "The lexicon of *The Wall Street Journal* and the business sections of *Time* and *Newsweek*," says Cox (1999, p. 19), "bear a striking resemblance to Genesis, the Epistle to the Romans, and Saint's Augustine's City of God." Behind descriptions of market reform, monetary policy, and the convolution of the Dow, he adds, it is possible to make out "pieces of a grand narrative about the inner meaning of human history, why things had gone wrong, and how to put them right." Within the community of economists, McCloskey has denounced economics as "modernist faith" with its own "Ten Commandments and Golden Rule," its "nuns, bishops, and cathedrals," its "trinity of fact, definition, and holy value," its starting as a "crusading faith" and its later hardening "into ceremony" (in Nelson 2001, p. xx). Heyne (1996, p. 1) has suggested that "any economist seeking to understand the world of human interactions with the hope to make them more effective operates within a theological framework." Along a similar line, Cramp (1994, p. 187) has argued that, to understand the economy, one needs the "knowledge of who we are and why we are here," which is a fundamentally theological question. And Nelson (1991, 2001) has suggested that economics embodies a hidden metaphysics that provides a way of ordering, interpreting, and giving meaning to events, as well as a source of ultimate meaning and purpose for human beings. At the core of such metaphysics, Nelson continues, there is the belief that scarcity is the primary cause of pain, suffering, and death, and that by virtue of its inspirational power, economics can save us from the consequences of scarcity. As Sahlins (2000, p. 531) puts it, humanity received pain and death as a punishment for Adam's sin. "Still, God was merciful. He gave us Economics." And it is out of such inspirational power that economists have come to claim their moral ground to exercise today the authority theologians used to exercise in the past (Nelson 1991, p. 8). And this is responsible for the ever-expanding role economics and economists have taken up in modern societies:

> An economics devoid of theological significance would be cautious, hesitant,
> retiring—a pale imitation as compared with the central role of economic
> thinking in the events of the past three centuries. Only a religion, and not a mere
> system of ordering practical affairs, could have had such vast power to shape the

modern era. Even when they intend otherwise, economists who join the
economics profession may become part of the life and ritual of a community
grounded in a powerful secular theology. (Nelson 1994, p. 236)

Mackenzie and Millo (2003) have recently observed that in Malaysia in the late 1990s
and early 2000s the legitimation of derivatives passed by enrolling Islamic jurists rather
than neoclassical economists (Kamali 1997, Maurer 2001). The above-mentioned
cultural horizon within which economics may have become legitimate in Western
societies may suggest that the logic of the two situations is probably not that radically distant from a cultural standpoint.

The logic of the cultural mediations that would appear to legitimize economics
and the community of economists in modern societies would therefore seem to run
counter to the logic supporting the legitimacy of private corporations. The latter,
after all, appear to draw their legitimacy by linking themselves to the codes of liberty
and repression that make up the symbolic center of modern democratic societies,
while the former seem to have done so by undergoing a process of cultural transformation in the public sphere that has established them respectively as a secular theology and as a priesthood. Such a contrast is quite puzzling. Possibly, as a result of the
current world economic crisis and of the possible crisis of confidence the economic
profession may undergo, the discipline may be drawn to gradually tap into an alternative source of legitimacy by appearing less priestly and more democratic. A cultural sociology of the economy can help tackle the differences in legitimation
between private corporations and the community of economists and can shed light
over the possible shifts in the sources of legitimation the community of economists
may experience in the near future.

After hinting at the way a cultural sociology of the economy may contribute to
address another pragmatic problem that is looming at the horizon of the current
world economic crisis—the loss of public confidence into the community of economists—I will now discuss how cultural sociologists may help shed light over the
mechanisms that influence public confidence for independent central banks. To do
so, I will first draw from the sociology of money literature and show in what way a
cultural sociology of the economy can complement it.

Most of the nineteenth- and twentieth-century social theory has stigmatized
the amoral, or even the immoral, dimensions of modern money. Utilitarians, for
example, considered money to be indifferent to nonpecuniary values. Marx, on his
part, regarded money to constitute a reality without any intrinsic meaning (Marx
[1844] 1964, p. 169; [1858–1859] 1973, p. 222; [1867] 1984, p. 96; [1858] 1972, p. 49).[11]
Weber and Simmel, in turn, saw it as a vehicle of the process of rationalization of
modern social life (Weber [1946] 1971, p. 331; [1922] 1978, p. 86; Simmel [1908] 1950,
p. 412).[12] Collins (1979, p. 190) remarks that sociologists have traditionally regarded
money as if it were not a social reality and have dismissed its ritual use as an example of "residual atavism" (Simmel [1900] 1978, p. 441; in Zelizer 1989, p. 345).

In the course of the past two decades, though, a new body of literature—to put
it with Maurer (2006, p. 19)—has turned "away from Western folk theories of
monetary transformation (the root of all evil, the camel through the eye of the

needle...) embodied in influential accounts from Aristotle to Marx, Weber, and Simmel." This literature has built on a number of contributions that, within anthropology, psychology, and sociology, have resisted the above-mentioned stereotyped representations of money. Anthropologists have documented how money is morally or ritually ranked within primitive societies and have been, as a result, far more sensitive to the fact that money can exist outside the market and can become a nonmarket medium (Polanyi 1957, pp. 264–266; Bohannan 1959; Dalton 1965; Einzig 1966; Thomas and Znaniecki [1918–1920] 1958, pp. 164–165; Akin and Robbins 1999; Guyer 1995b; Parry and Bloch 1989; Gamburd 2004; Znoj 1998; Crump 1981, pp. 125–130; Melitz 1970). Douglas (1967), for example, stressed that money can acquire a social or sacred character when it is used ritually or to amend status. Economic psychologists, in turn, have challenged the idea of fungibility of money (Lea, Tarpy, and Webley 1987, pp. 319–342). And within the sociological profession, Simiand (1934) provided a very rare statement about the extra-economic social basis of money and the symbolic, sacred, and magical significance it can manifest.

More recently, Belk and Wallendorf (1990, pp. 35–36) have pointed out that the economic view misses "the more emotional, qualitative meanings of money" and the way in which affect, norms and values mediate the dealings with it. Following the psychoanalytic perspective, Belk and Wallendorf (1990, p. 46) agree with Krueger (1986, p. 3) that "money is probably the most emotionally meaningful object in contemporary life; only food and sex are its close competitors as common carriers of such strong and diverse feelings, significances, and strivings." At the same time, Belk and Wallendorf (1990, p. 35) have remarked that "contemporary money retains sacred meanings" and that the crossing by money of the boundary between the sacred and the profane is regulated even within modern societies through ritual processes. "Contemporary consumer society," Belk and Wallendorf (1990, p. 36) add, "has been characterized as one that often venerates money and imbues it with meaning. Money is revered, feared, worshipped, and treated with the highest respect. Money is, in sociological parlance, considered sacred" (Durkheim 1915). These authors find evidence of the sacredness of money in the sacrifices that are made for money, in its contaminating character, and in the myth, mystery, and ritual that are involved in the acquisition and use of it. Their reading echoes a similar reflection by Desmonde about the sacred dimension of money:

> To many of us, money is a mystery, a symbol handled mainly by the priests of
> high finance and regarded by us with much of the same reverence and awe as the
> primitive feels toward the sacred relics providing magical potency in a tribal
> ritual. As if in a higher plane of reality, the symbol seems to operate in an
> incomprehensible, mystical way, understood and controllable only by the magic
> of brokers, accountants, lawyers, and financiers.... Like spellbound savages in the
> presence of the holy, we watch in wonder the solemn proceedings, feeling in a
> vague, somewhat fearful way that our lives and the happiness of our children are
> at the mercy of mysterious forces beyond our control....Apart from the esoteric
> rites of high finance, money seems to function in everyday life much like a
> miraculous talisman, bringing to us the gratification of almost every conceivable
> desire. Wherever we go, if we have money, people hasten to do our bidding, as if

placed under a magical charm by the presence of these worn-down coins and
soiled pieces of green paper.... Like a magical charm, money brings power, which
can be used either for good or bad purposes. (Desmonde 1962, pp. 3–5)[13]

It is, however, Viviana Zelizer who, in the past two decades, has spearheaded a whole
research program on money that has successfully countered the received wisdom
within sociology about its nature and its functioning in modern societies. Zelizer's
work (1989, 1994, 1996, 2000, 2005) on the social meaning of money constitutes the
culmination of a decade of research on the relations between market and morals.

Along with Zelizer's micro-cultural approach to the study of money, though,
particularly in the past decade, a macro-cultural line of research has emerged that
has recognized the role played by money in the consolidation of national space and
in the production and reproduction of citizens within it (Carruthers and Babb 1996,
Gilbert 1999, 2005; Gilbert and Helleiner 1999; Helleiner 1997, 1998, 1999; Hewitt
1994, 1999; Pointon 1998; Foster 1999; Zelizer 1999). Occasionally, this literature has
stressed the transformation of national currencies into national symbols and has
emphasized the highly emotional charge that is attached to them as a result of such
transformation.

A cultural sociology of the economy can build on it and help systematically
account for the consequences that the linkage of a national currency to the symbolic
center of society can have on the legitimation of the independent central bank.
Tognato (2008) provides a clear example in this respect with reference to the Deutsche
Bundesbank. Since World War II, he suggests, two different self-understandings of
the German society have contended the symbolic center of the Federal Republic: the
so-called Holocaust identity and the *Wirtschaftswunder* identity (Giesen 1998).
The latter appealed to the economic miracle that the Federal Republic experienced
in the 1950s and 1960s both as a medium to expunge the *Angst* for the recent past
from the conscience of the average German citizen and as a pretext for reclaiming
full sovereignty for the Federal Republic, thereby liberating it from the state of
political submissiveness into which it had been boxed since World War II. Tognato
observes that the experience of the hyperinflation in the early 1920s, the destabilizing effects that monetary chaos had on the Weimar Republic, the subsequent rise to
power of Hitler and the establishment of the Nazi dictatorship, the experience of
World War II, the destruction and humiliation that came with it, and the horrors
that were perpetrated in the concentration camps set the stage for a linkage of the
D-Mark to the *Wirtschaftwunder* identity. The D-Mark, as a result, turned into "*the*
national symbol",[14] the only one which Germans could be proud of,[15] something
that gave them back their self-esteem after the atrocities of the Nazi regime,[16] that
rescued them "from the political, economic, and moral ruins of the war,"[17] and
helped "the German Phoenix rise from the ashes of World War II."[18] The D-Mark,
in a way, gave Germans "a piece of identity, even before that the national anthem
and the national flag came."[19] As the D-Mark turned into a national symbol, the
Deutsche Bundesbank became its custodian. And as the D-Mark acquired in
Germany a profound existential value for the person in the street, the Bundesbank
got transformed into an institutional solution to the *Angst* that the German past

still produced. The Bundesbank was founded as an economic institution, but in the course of its history it took up the latent function of an existential device. A a result, it became absolute (Tognato 2008). Such transformations in meaning reflected the ongoing anchoring of German monetary affairs to the existential dimension of the *Wirtschaftwunder* identity. At the same time, symbolic linkage also applied to the political dimension of the *Wirtschaftswunder* identity. In other words, the Bundesbank turned into the instrument that enabled Germany to exercise its full sovereignty, at least within the monetary sphere, thereby breaking free from the regime of semi-sovereignty into which the Federal Republic had been embedded since World War II. As the *Financial Times*, for example, put it, the Bundesbank constituted a formidable "Bundesbunker," which was impossible to penetrate.[20] The reconstitution of German monetary affairs at the symbolic center of German society triggered a latent moralization of the German monetary arena. Inflation would take up a moral connotation, and central bankers would therefore be legitimized to ask the public for sacrifices in order to keep it under check. As money and monetary policy acquired moral meaning, then the central bank would also undergo a transformation and turn into the moral compass of a society, as David Horowitz, former President of the Bank of Israel, once put it. Its authority would no longer be strictly technical. As some observers have remarked with reference to the Bundesbank, its authority "stems from moral prowess as well as economic muscle."[21] Tognato (2008) shows that once the German monetary game got to the symbolic center of society and underwent a process of moralization, narrative frames drawn from the Christian tradition come into play and prevented it from losing its moral dimension. For example, the conquest of the moral ground that monetary stability can secure became framed as a perpetual challenge that never ends and that calls for a continuous struggle (Tietmeyer 1997).

Following Tognato (2008), it would appear that the legitimacy of the most beloved independent central bank in the world did not stem from a symbolic linkage to the codes of liberty and repression that make up the symbolic center of modern societies, but rather correlated to a different set of cultural elements that make up German political culture and appear to constitute an important dimension of the German symbolic center. Kennedy (1991, p. 4) has observed that "in many respects the Bundesbank incorporates the ideals of an earlier age of political development. Largely immune to the pressures of pluralistic politics, it sees itself as the representative of a good higher than particular interests." Such an ethos, she continues, is not just a technique or a policy style. Rather, it is rooted to the ideal of *Rechtstaat* and the German political theory that has traditionally attributed special dignity to the instruments of the state that are supposed to enhance the public good over particularistic interests (Kennedy 1991, pp. 2–3, 10–12). Furthermore, it rests on a civil service tradition that, since Hegel, has elevated German civil servants to the rank of a "universal class" that stands for the ethical interest of the whole. In May 1945, she continues, the Constitutional Court ruled for the so-called *Traditionsbruch*, according to which public officials would no longer serve the state as a living and permanent continuity but would rather serve the constitutional order" (Smith 1979, p. 68–69; in Kennedy 1991, p. 12). Despite such a break, however, the Bundesbank and the Constitutional Court have probably continued to constitute the only two institutional spheres in which the old tradition of German civil service has survived (Kennedy 1991, p. 28).

As the world economic crisis deepens, one must therefore wonder what deep sources of legitimacy independent central banks around the world will be able to draw on in order to resist the consequences of an increasing skepticism on the part of the public about the maintenance of an institutional task—the control of inflation—that will appear as going out of fashion. A cultural sociology of the economy may help shed light in this respect.

I have begun this section by indicating three possible fields of application of a cultural sociology of the economy. I have suggested that, as the ongoing world economic crisis deepens, private corporations, economists, and independent central banks may run the risk of losing people's confidence. As a result, it becomes imperative to understand the mechanisms that underpin its creation, maintenance, and repair. A cultural sociology of the economy can contribute in this respect by enhancing our understanding of the deep sources of legitimacy of economic institutions in modern societies. To make my point, I have built on three different literatures—that on organizational legitimacy, the emerging sociology of financial markets, and the sociology of money.

CONCLUSION

Many believe that the economy constitutes one of the most disenchanted spheres of modern social life. Norms and values but also cultural codes, metaphors, rituals, and identities, however, still shape economic experience in our days. A cultural sociology of the economy is there to remind us of this.

Different classics provide a fertile ground from which such sociology can draw for the purpose of nurturing its intellectual project. The later Durkheim of *The Elementary Forms of Religious Life*, Weber, Parsons, Polanyi, and Alexandre de Tocqueville constitute important referents in this respect.

While economists have just recently started to take stock of culture, during the past three decades, a culturalist strand of scholarship within economic sociology has insisted on the persisting role of culture in modern economic life. Karin Knorr Cetina, Mitchel Abolafia, Nicole Biggart, and Viviana Zelizer are the four most accomplished contributors to this line of research.

The debate among economic sociologists over the opportunity to introduce cultural analysis within their horizon of inquiry has traditionally focused on the question of whether cultural analysis should replace social-structural analysis or whether it should complement it. The narrow focus of such a debate has prevented the profession from systematically discussing how scholars should go about accounting for the cultural dimension of economic life. Should they take a cultural-structural approach? Or should they rather adopt a pragmatic focus? Or should they instead resort to a framework that integrates both perspectives? Furthermore, taking stock with the role of culture in the economy implies addressing the phenomenon of cultural embeddedness of economic action. So, how far should scholars push the analysis of such a phenomenon? And where should they draw the line? These are the basic theoretical questions that structure the core of a cultural sociology of the economy. I have argued that the emerging field of neo-Durkheimian sociology, which in the past two decades has systematically addressed the phenomenon of cultural reenchantment in modern societies, can provide one possible set of answers to such questions. Answering them, I have suggested, helps distinguish the inner theoretical makeup of a cultural sociology of the economy from the culturalist strand of scholarship within economic sociology.

I have then concluded that, from a pragmatic standpoint, a cultural sociology of the economy can help tackle three of the most pressing problems that loom on the horizon of the current world economic crisis: the loss of confidence within the general public for private corporations, the economic profession, and independent central banks. And more precisely, it can do so by shedding light over the mechanisms by which such confidence can be maintained, recovered, or repaired. To make this point, I have shown how cultural sociologists can help advance the analysis in this respect further beyond the frontier of three relevant literatures—that on organizational legitimacy, the sociology of financial markets, and the sociology of money.

NOTES

1. See for example Marx ([1844] 1964), Maine (1875), Tönnies ([1887] 1955), Durkheim ([1893] 1947), Weber ([1904] 1998), Simmel ([1900] 1978), Habermas (1984).

2. "No sense in strict 3% deficit as the magic figure for Emu. Letters to the Editor," *The Financial Times*, June 3, 1997, USA Edition, p. 12.

3. Otmar Issing, "Wider die Papiergaunerreien," *Frankfurter Allgemeine Zeitung*, April 6, 1996, p. 17.

4. "O Isis and Osiris, give/the spirit of Wisdom to the new pair./Guide the steps of the wanderers./Strengthen them with patience in danger" (Tietmeyer 1997b, p. 11).

5. Tocqueville ([1835–40] 2000, p. 511) stresses that people "dream constantly of the goods they do not have." In Swedberg (2004, p. 8).

6. See also Zelizer (2007, p. 1060).

7. The analysis of such cultural linkages may entail tracking the metaphoric transformations of economic phenomena that help catapult them onto the center, the narrative strategies actors resort to, the specific genres they tap into, and even the visual representations they draw from. With particular reference to the latter, Emmison (1986) offers an interesting example.

8. See DiMaggio (1994, p. 39; 1990, pp. 117–119) and Davis (1996, pp. 213–226) in Spillman (1999, p. 1061).

9. See also Scott (2001) and Aldrich (2001).

10. See also the entire first volume of *Public Understanding of Science* (1992).

11. In Zelizer (1989, pp. 345–346).

12. In Zelizer (1989, pp. 344–346).

13. See also Crump (1992, pp. 669–677).

14. Jordan Bonfante, "A German Requiem," *Time Magazine*, July 6, 1998, p. 21.

15. Ibidem.

16. Susanne Nicolette Strass, "Abschied vom einem stark Stück Deutschland," *Frankfurter Neue Press*, June 20, 1998.

17. Jan Fleischhauer, "Der Erzbischof aus Frankfurt," *Der Spiegel*, Nr. 23, 1997.

18. Bonfante, "A German Requiem."

19. "Die DM hat den Deutschen ein Stück Identität gegeben," *Süddeutsche Zeitung*, June 22, 1998; Kohl Helmut Kohl, "50 Jahre Deutsche Mark," *Presse- und Informationsamt der Bundesregierung*, July 7, 1998, Nr. 49, p. 632.

20. "In the Bundesbunker," *Financial Times*, July 17, 1992, p. 18.

21. D. Marsh, P. Norman, Q. Peel, and C. Parkes, "Tietmeyer: high-priest of hard money doctrine," *The Financial Times*, October 1, 1993.

REFERENCES

Abolafia, Mitchel. 1996. *Making Markets: Opportunism and Restraint on Wall Street.* Cambridge, UK: Cambridge University Press.

Agnew, Jean-Christophe. 1986. *Worlds Apart in Anglo-American Thought, 1550–1750.* Cambridge, UK: Cambridge University Press.

Akin, David, and Joel Robbins. 1999. *Money and Modernity. State and Local Currencies in Melanesia.* Pittsburgh: University of Pittsburgh Press.

Aldrich, Howard. 2001. *Organizations Evolving.* Thousand Oaks, CA: Sage Publications.

Alexander, Jeffrey. 1988a. *Action and Its Environments.* New York: Columbia University Press.

———. 1988b. "Religious Sociology and Cultural Sociology." Pp. 1–21 in *Durkheimian Sociology: Cultural Studies*, edited by Jeffrey Alexander. New York: Cambridge University Press.

———. 2006. *The Civil Sphere.* Oxford: Oxford University Press.

Alexander, Jeffrey, and Philip Smith. 1993. "The Discourse of American Civil Society: A New Proposal for Cultural Studies." *Theory and Society* 22(2): 151–207.

Anderson, Benedict. 1991. *Imagined Communities: Reflections on the Origin and Spread of Nationalism.* Rev. ed. London and New York: Verso.

Appadurai, Arjun. 1986. "Introduction: Commodities and the Politics of Value." Pp. 3–63 in *The Social Life of Things: Commodities in Cultural Perspective*, edited by Arjun Appadurai. Cambridge, UK: Cambridge University Press.

Ashforth, Blake, and Barrie Gibbs. 1990. "The Double-Edge of Organizational Legitimation." *Organization Science* 1: 177–194.

Baiocchi, Gianpaolo. 2006. "The Civilizing Forces of Social Movements: Corporate and Liberal Codes in Brazil's Public Sphere." *Sociological Theory* 24(4): 285–311.

Baker, Wayne. 1984. "The Social Structure of a National Securities Market." *American Journal of Sociology* 89: 775–811.

Baker, Wayne, and Robert Faulkner. 1991. "Role as Resource in the Hollywood Film Industry." *American Journal of Sociology* 97: 279–309.

Banfield, Edward. 1958. *The Moral Basis of a Backward Society*. New York: Free Press.

Barron, James, Frank Dobbin, and P. Devreaux Jennings. 1986. "War and Peace: The Evolution of Modern Personnel Administration in US Industry." *American Journal of Sociology* 92: 350–383.

Bates, Benjamin. 2005. "Public Culture and Public Understanding of Genetics: A Focus Group Study." *Public Understanding of Science* 14: 47–65.

Baum, Joel, and Walter Powell. 1995. "Cultivating an Institutional Ecology of Organizations." *American Sociological Review* 60: 529–538.

Baurer, Martin. 1995. "Familiarizing the Unfamiliar." *Public Understanding of Science* 4: 205–210.

Belk, Russell, and Melanie Wallendorf. 1990. "The Sacred Meaning of Money." *Journal of Economic Psychology* 11: 35–67.

Berger, Peter and Thomas Luckmann. 1966. *The Social Construction of Reality: A Treatise in the Sociology of Knowledge*. London: Penguin.

Bettman, James, and Barton Weitz. 1983. "Attributions in the Board Room: Causal Reasoning in Corporate Annual Reports." *Administrative Science Quarterly* 28: 165–183.

Beunza, Daniel, Iain Hardie, and Donald Mackenzie. 2006. "A Price Is a Social Thing: Towards a Material Sociology of Arbitrage." *Organization Studies* 27: 721–734.

Biernacki, Richard. 1995. *The Fabrication of Labor: Germany and Britain, 1640–1914*. Berkeley and Los Angeles: University of California Press.

Biggart, Nicole Woolsey. 1989. *Charismatic Capitalism. Direct Selling Organizations in America*. Chicago and London: University of Chicago Press.

Bohannan, Paul. 1959. "The Impact of Money on an African Subsistence Economy." *Journal of Economic History* 19: 491–503.

Boulton, David. 1978. *The Grease Machine*. New York: Harper & Row.

Bromiley, Philip, and Alfred Marcus. 1989. "The Deterrent to Dubious Corporate Behavior: Profitability, Probability and Safety Recalls." *Strategic Management Journal* 10: 233–250.

Buchholz, Rogene, William Evans, and Robert Wagley. 1985. *Management Responses to Public Issues: Concept and Cases in Strategy Formulation*. Englewood Cliffs, NJ: Prentice-Hall.

Bud, Robert. 1995. "Science, Meaning and Myth in the Museum." *Public Understanding of Science* 4: 1–16.

Burt, Ronald. 1983. *Corporate Profits and Cooptation*. New York: Academic Press.

Callon, Michel, and Koray Caliskan. 2005. "New and Old Directions in the Anthropology of Markets." Paper presented to the Wenner-Grenn Foundation for Anthropological Research, New York, April 9.

Callon, Michel, ed. 1998. *The Laws of the Markets*. Oxford: Blackwell.

Callon, Michel. 2005. "Why Virtualism Paves the Way to Political Impotence: A Reply to Daniel Miller's Critique of *The Law of the Markets*." *Economic Sociology: European Electronic Newsletter* 6(2): 3–20.

———. 2007. "What Does It Mean to Say That Economics Is Performative?" Pp. 311–357 in *Do Economists Make Markets? On the Performativity of Economics*, edited by Donald MacKenzie, Fabian Munesa, and Lucia Siu. Princeton, NJ: Princeton University Press.

Carroll, Glenn, and Michael Hannan. 2000. *The Demography of Corporations and Industries*. Princeton, NJ: Princeton University Press.

Carruthers, Bruce. 1996. *City of Capital: Politics and Markets in the English Financial Revolution*. Princeton, NJ: Princeton University Press.

Carruthers, Bruce, and Sarah Babb. 1996. "The Color of Money and the Nature of Value: Greenbacks and Gold in Postbellum America." *American Journal of Sociology* 101(6): 1556–1591.

———. 2000. *Economy/Society. Markets, Meanings, and Social Structure.* Thousand Oaks, CA: Pine Forge Press.

Carruthers, Bruce, and Wendy Espeland. 1997. "The Price is Right: On Money and Morality." Paper presented at the Annual Meeting of the American Sociological Association, Toronto.

Collins, Randall. 1979. "Review of *The Bankers*, by Martin Mayer." *American Journal of Sociology* 85: 190–194.

Cox, Harvey. 1999. "The Market as God: Living with the New Dispensation." *Atlantic Monthly* 283(3): 18–23.

Cramp, A. B., 1994. "Mapping of (Economic) Meaning: Here Be Monsters." In *Economics and Religion*, edited by H. Geoffrey Brennan and A. M. C. Waterman. Boston: Kluwer.

Cretaz, Fabienne von Roten. 2006. "Do We Need a Public Understanding of Statistics?" *Public Understanding of Science* 15: 243–249.

Crump, Thomas. 1981. *The Phenomenon of Money.* London: Routledge & Kegan Paul.

———. 1992. "Money as a Ritual System." *American Bahavioral Scientist* 35 (6): 669–677.

Czarniawska, Barbara. 2005. "Women in Financial Services: Fiction and More Fiction" Pp. 121–137 in *The Sociology of Financial Markets*, edited by Karin Knorr Cetina and Alex Preda. Oxford: Oxford University Press.

Dalton, George. 1965. "Primitive Money." *American Anthropologist* 61(1): 44–65.

Davidson, Wallace, and Dan Worrell. 1988. "The Impact of Announcements of Corporate Illegalities on Shareholders Returns." *Academy of Management Journal* 31: 195–200.

Davidson, Wallace, P. Chandy, and Mark Cross. 1987. "Large Losses, Risk Management and Stock Returns in the Airline Industry." *Journal of Risk and Insurance* 57: 162–172.

Davis, John. 1996. "An Anthropologist's View of Exchange." *Social Anthropology* 4: 213–226.

Desmonde, William. 1962. *Magic, Myth, and Money.* New York: Free Press of Glencoe.

DiMaggio, Paul. 1990. "Cultural Aspects of Economic Action and Organization." Pp. 113–136 in *Beyond the Marketplace: Rethinking Economy and Society*, edited by Roger Friedland and A. F. Robertson. New York: Aldine de Gruyter.

———. 1994. "Culture and the Economy." Pp. 22–57 in *The Handbook of Economic Sociology*, edited by Neil Smelser and Richard Swedberg. Princeton, NJ: Princeton University Press.

DiMaggio, Paul, and Walter Powell. 1983. "The Iron Cage Revisited: Institutional Isomorphism and Collective Rationality in Organization Fields." *American Sociological Review* 48: 147–160.

Dobbin, Frank. 1994. *Forging Industrial Policy: The United States, Britain and France in the Railway Age.* Cambridge, UK, and New York: Cambridge University Press.

Douglas, Mary. 1967. "Primitive Rationing." Pp. 119–145 in *Themes in Economic Anthropology*, edited by Raymond Firth. London: Tavistock.

Douglas, Mary, and Baron Isherwood. 1979. *The World of Goods. Towards an Anthropology of Consumption.* New York: Basic Books.

Dowling, John, and Jeffrey Pfeffer. 1975. "Organizational Legitimacy: Social Values and Organizational Behavior." *Pacific Sociological Review* 18: 122–136.

Durkheim, Emile. [1893] 1947. *The Division of Labour in Society.* Trans. by George Simpson. Glencoe, IL: Free Press.

———. 1951. *Suicide.* New York: Free Press.

———. 1957. *Professional Ethics and Civic Morals.* London: Routledge.

———. [1915] 1995. *The Elementary Forms of Religious Life.* Trans. by Karen Fields. New York: Free Press.

Einzig, Paul. 1966. *Primitive Money.* Oxford: Pergamon.

Elsbach, Kimberly. 1994. "Managing Organizational Legitimacy in the California Cattle Industry. The Construction and Effectiveness of Verbal Accounts." *Administrative Science Quarterly* 39(1): 57–88.

Elsbach, Kimberly, and Robert Sutton. 1992. "Acquiring Organizational Legitimacy through Illegitimate Actions: A Marriage of Institutional and Impression Management Theories." *Academy of Management Journal* 35(4): 699–738.

———. 1998. "Averting Expected Challenges through Anticipatory Impression Management: A Study of Hospital Billing." *Organization Science* 9: 68–86.

Emmison, Michael. 1986. "Visualizing the Economy: Fetishism and the Legitimation of Economic Life." *Theory, Culture & Society* 3: 81–96.

Farr, Robert. 1993. "Common Sense, Science and Social Representations." *Public Understanding of Science* 2: 189–204.

Fields, Andrew, and Vahan Janjigian. 1989. "The Effect of Chernobyl on Electric-Utility Stock Prices." *Journal of Business Research* 18: 81–88.

Fisse, Brent, and John Braithwaite. 1983. *The Impact of Publicity on Corporate Offenders.* Albany: State University of New York Press.

Fligstein, Neil. 1996. "Markets as Politics: A Political-Cultural Approach to Market Institutions." *American Sociological Review* 61: 656–673.

Foster, Robert. 1999. "In God We Trust. The Legitimacy of Melanesian Currencies." Pp. 214–231 in *Money and Modernity: State and Local Currencies in Melanesia*, edited by David Atkins and Joel Robbins. Pittsburgh: University of Pittsburgh Press.

Franklin, Roger. 1986. *The Defender: The Story of General Dynamics.* New York: Harper & Row.

Frenzen, Jonathan, Paul Hirsch, and Philip Zerillo. 1994. "Consumption, Preferences, and Changing Lifestyles." Pp. 403–425 in *The Handbook of Economic Sociology*, edited by Neil Smelser and Richard Swedberg. Princeton, NJ: Princeton University Press.

Fukuyama, Francis. 1995. *Trust: The Social Virtues and the Creation of Prosperity.* New York: Free Press.

———. 2003. "Still Disenchanted? The Modernity of Postindustrial Capitalism." CSES Working Paper Series #3, Department of Sociology, Cornell University, Ithaca, NY.

Gamburd, Michelle. 2004. "Money That Burns Like Oil: A Sri Lankan Cultural Logic of Morality and Agency." *Ethnology* 43(2): 167–184.

Geertz, Clifford. 1973. *The Interpretation of Cultures.* New York: Basic Books.

Giacalone, Robert, and Paul Rosenfeld, eds. 1989. *Impression Management in the Organization.* Hillsdale, NJ.: Erlbaum.

———. 1991. *Applied Impression Management.* Newbury Park, CA: Sage Publications.

Giesen, Bernhard. 1998. *Intellectuals and the Nation: Collective identity in a German Axial age.* Cambridge, UK: Cambridge University Press.

Gilbert, Emily. 1999. "Forging a National Currency: Money, State-Making and Nation-Building in Canada." Pp. 25–46 in *Nation-States and Money: The Past,* the Present and the Future of National Currencies, edited by Emily Gilbert and Eric Helleiner. London: Routledge.

———. 2005. "Common Cents: Situating Money in Time and Space." *Economy and Society* 34(3): 357–388.

Gilbert, Emily, and Eric Helleiner, eds. 1999. *Nation-States and Money: The Past, the Present and the Future of National Currencies.* London: Routledge.

Godson, John. 1975. *The Rise and Fall of the DC-10.* New York: David Mckay.

Goede, Marieke de. 2005. *Virtue, Fortune and Faith: A Genealogy of Finance.* Minneapolis: University of Minnesota Press.

Goffman, Ervin. 1961. *Encounters.* Indianapolis, IN: Bobbs Merrill.

————. 1963. *Stigma: Notes on the Management of Spoiled Identity.* Englewood Cliffs, NJ: Prentice-Hall.

————. 1967. *Interaction Ritual: Essays on Face-to-Face Behavior.* Garden City, NY: Doubleday/Anchor.

————. 1969. *Strategic Interaction.* Philadelphia: University of Pennsylvania Press.

————. 1973. *The Presentation of Self in Everyday Life.* Woodstock, NY: Overlook Press.

————. 1974. *Frame Analysis.* New York: Harper Colophon.

————. 1981. *Forms of Talk.* Philadelphia: University of Pennsylvania Press.

Goodpaster, Kenneth. 1984. *Ethics in Management.* Cambridge, MA: Harvard Business School.

Granovetter, Mark. 1974. *Getting a Job: A Study of Contacts and Careers.* Cambridge, MA: Harvard University Press.

Granovetter, Mark. 1985. "Economic Action and Social Structure: The Problem of Embeddedness." *American Journal of Sociology* 91(3): 481–510.

————. 1990a. "Interview." Pp. 96–114 in *Economies and Sociology: Redefining Their Boundaries,* edited by Richard Swedberg. Princeton, NJ: Princeton University Press.

————. 1990b. "The Old and the New Economic Sociology: A History and an Agenda." Pp. 89–112 in *Beyond the Market Place: Rethinking Economy and Society,* edited by Roger Friedland and A. F. Robertson, New York: Aldine de Gruyter.

Gross, Alan. 1994. "The Roles of Rhetoric in the Public Understanding of Science." *Public Understanding of Science* 3: 3–23.

Guiso, Luigi, Paola Sapienza, and Luigi Zingales. 2006. "Does Culture Affect Economic Outcomes?" *Journal of Economic Perspectives* 20(2): 23–48.

Guyer, Jane, ed. 1995. *Money Matters: Instability, Values and Social Payments in the Modern History of West African Communities.* Portsmouth, NH: Heinemann.

Habermas, Jürgen, 1984. *The Theory of Communicative Action, Vol. 1—Reason and the Rationalization of Society.* Boston: Beacon.

Hannan, Michael, and John Freeman. 1992. *The Dynamics of Organizational Populations.* New York: Oxford University Press.

Hardie, Iain, and Donald Mackenzie. 2006. "Assembling an Economic Actor: The Agencement of a Hedge Fund." Paper presented at the New Aspects in a Financialized Economy and Implications for Varieties of Capitalism Workshop, Institute of Commonwealth Studies, London, May 11–12.

Hassoun, Jean-Pierre. 2005. "Emotions on the Trading Floor: Social and Symbolic Expressions." Pp. 102–120 in *The Sociology of Financial Markets,* edited by Karin Knorr Cetina and Alex Preda. Oxford: Oxford University Press.

Helleiner, Eric. 1997. "One Nation, One Money. Territorial Currencies and the Nation-State." Working Paper 17. Oslo, Norway: Arena.

————. 1998. "National Currencies and National Identities." *American Behavioral Scientist* 41: 1409–1436.

————. 1999. "Historicizing Territorial Currencies: Monetary Space and the Nation-State in North America." *Political Geography* 18: 309–339.

————. 2002. "One Money, One People. Political Identity and the Euro." Pp. 183–202 in *Before and Beyond EMU,* edited by Patrick Crowley. London: Routledge.

Hewitt, Virginia. 1994. *Beauty and the Banknote: Images of Women on Paper Money.* London: British Museum Press.

————. 1999. "A Distant View. Imagery and Imagination in the Paper Currency of the British Empire, 1800–1960." Pp. 97–116 in *Nation-States and Money: The Past, the Present and the Future of National Currencies,* edited by Emily Gilbert and Eric Helleiner. London: Routledge.

Heyne, Paul. 1996. "Theological Visions in Economics and Religion." *Forum for Social Economics* 25(2): 1–7.

Hörisch, Jochem. 2004. *Gott, Geld, Medien*. Frankfurt am main: Suhrkamp Verlag.

Irwin, Alan. 2001. "Constructing the Scientific Citizen: Science and Democracy in the Biosciences." *Public Understanding of Science* 10: 1–18.

Issing, Otmar. 1991. "*Geldpolitik im Spannungsfeld von Politik und Wissenschaft.*" Speech delivered at the Scientific Colloquium in occasion of the 65th Birthday of Prof. Dr. Dr. h.c. Norbert Kloten, Stuttgart, March 15.

Jones, Edvard, et al. 1984. *Social Stigma: The Psychology of Marked Relationships*. New York: WHO.

Kamali, Mohammed. 1997. "Islamic Commercial Law: An Analysis of Options." *American Journal of Islamic Social Science* 14: 17–37.

Kemeny, John. 1979. *The Need for Change: The Legacy of TMI*. Washington, DC: U.S. Government Printing Office.

Kennedy, Ellen. 1991. *The Bundesbank: Germany's* Central Bank in the International Monetary System. London: Pinter.

Knack, Stephen, and Philip Keefer. 1996. "Does Social Capital Have an Economic Payoff? A Cross-Country Investigation." *Quarterly Journal of Economics* 112(4): 1251–1288.

Knorr Cetina, Karin. 2005. "How Are Global Markets Global? The Architecture of a Flow World." Pp. 38–61 in *The Sociology of Financial Markets*, edited by Karin Knorr Cetina and Alex Preda. Oxford: Oxford University Press.

Knorr Cetina, Karin, and Urs Bruegger. 2000. "The Market as an Object of Attachment: Exploring Postsocial Relations in Financial Markets." *Canadian Journal of Sociology* 25(2): 141–168.

———. 2002. "Global Microstructures: The Virtual Societies of Financial Markets." *American Journal of Sociology* 107(4): 905–950.

Kohl, Helmut. "50 Jahre Deutsche Mark." Speech by the Federal Chancellor. Presse- und Informationsamt der Bundesregierung, 07/07/1998, Nr. 49.

Krippner, Greta. 2001. "The Elusive Market: Embeddedness and the Paradigm of Economic Sociology." *American Journal of Sociology* 30(6): 775–810.

Krueger, David. 1986. "Money, Success, and Success Phobia." Pp. 3–16 in *The Last* Taboo: Money as a Symbol and Reality in Psychotherapy and Psychoanalysis, edited by David Krueger. New York: Brunner & Masel.

Landes, David. 1993. *The Wealth and Poverty of Nations*. New York: Norton.

La Porta, Rafael, Florencio Lopez de Silanes, Andrei Shleifer, and Robert Vishny. 1997. "Trust in Large Organizations." *American Economic Review* 87(2): 222–279.

Lea, Stephen, Roger Tarpy, and Paul Webley. 1987. *The Individual in the Economy: A Survey of Economic Psychology*. Cambridge, UK: Cambridge University Press.

Leary, Mark, and Robin Kowalski. 1990. "Impression Management: A Literature Review and Two Component Model." *Psychological Bulletin* 107: 34–47.

Leggett, Monica, and Marie Finlay. 2001. "Science, Story, and Image: A New Approach to Crossing the Communication Barrier Posed by Scientific Jargon." *Public Understanding of Science* 10: 157–171.

Lie, John. 1991. "Embedding Polanyi's Market Society." *Sociological Perspectives* 34(2): 219–235.

———. 1997. "Sociology of Markets." *Annual Review of Sociology* 23: 341–360.

Litschert, Robert, and Edward Nicholson. 1977. *The Corporate Role and Ethical Behavior*. New York: Petrocelli/Charter.

MacKenzie, Donald. 2003. "An Equation and Its World: Bricolage, Exemplars, Disunity and Performativity in Financial Economics." *Social Studies of Science* 33: 831–868.

————. 2007. "The Material Production of Virtuality: Innovation, Cultural Geography, and Facticity in Derivative Markets." *Economy and Society* 36(3): 355–376.

MacKenzie, Donald, and Yuval Millo. 2003. "Constructing a Market, Performing Theory: The Historical Sociology of a Financial Derivatives Exchange." *American Journal of Sociology* 109(1): 107–145.

Maine, Henry. 1875. *Lectures on the Early History of Institutions*. London: J. Murray.

Marcus, Alfred, and Robert Goodman. 1991. "Victims and Shareholders: The Dilemmas of Presenting Corporate Policy During a Crisis." *Academy of Management Journal* 31(29): 281–305.

Martin, Christine. 2004. "Vernichtetes Geld und vernichtendes Geld: Das Geldmotiv in den zwei zeitgenoessischen Romanen 'Die Nacht der Haendler' von Gert Heidenreich und 'MOI' von Heiko Michael Hartmann." Master Thesis, Department of German and Slavic Studies, University of Waterloo.

Marx, Karl. [1844] 1964. "The Power of Money in Bourgeois Society." In *The Economic and Philosophic Manuscripts of 1844*. New York: International.

————. [1858] 1972. *A Contribution to the Critique of Political Economy*, edited by Maurice Dobb. New York: International.

————. [1858–1859] 1973. *Grundrisse*. New York: Vintage.

————. [1867] 1984. *Capital*. Vol. 1, edited by Friedrich Engels. New York: International.

Maurer, Bill. 2001. "Engineering an Islamic Future: Speculations on Islamic Financial Alternatives." *Anthropology Today* 17(1): 8–11.

————. 2005. *Mutual Life, Limited: Islamic Banking, Alternative Currencies, Lateral Reason*. Princeton, NJ: Princeton University Press.

————. 2006. "The Anthropology of Money." *Annual Review of Anthropology* 35: 15–36.

Maurer, John. 1971. *Readings in Organizational Theory: Open System Approaches*. New York: Random House.

Mauss, Marcel. [1906] 1968. "Introducción a la Analyse de Quelques Phénomène Religieux." In *Oevres*, edited by V. Karady and M. Mauss. Paris: Minuit.

McCloskey, Deirdre. 1985. *The Rhetoric of Economics*. Madison: University of Wisconsin Press.

Melitz, Jacques. 1970. "The Polanyi School of Anthropology on Money: An Economist's View." *American Anthropologist* 72: 1020–1040.

Merton, Robert. 1949. "The Self-Fulfilling Prophecy." Pp. 179–195 in *Social Theory and Social Structure*, by Robert Merton. New York: Free Press.

Metzler, Maribeth. 2001. "Responding to the Legitimacy Problem of Big Tobacco: An Analysis of the 'People of Philip Morris' Image Advertising Campaign." *Communication Quarterly* 49: 366–381.

Meyer, John, and Brian Rowan. 1977. "Institutionalized Organizations: Formal Structure as Myth and Ceremony." *American Journal of Sociology* 83: 340–362.

Meyer, John, and Richard Scott. 1983. *Organizational Environments: Rituals and Rationality*. Beverly Hills, CA: Sage Publications.

Michael, Mike. 1998. "Between Citizen and Consumer: Multiplying the Meanings of the 'Public Understanding of Science.'" *Public Understanding of Science* 7: 313–327.

Miller, Daniel. 1987. *Material Culture and Mass Consumption*. Oxford: Blackwell.

Nash, Keir, Dean Mann, and Phil Olsen. 1972. *Oil Pollution and the Public Interest: A Study of the Santa Barbara Oil Spill*. Berkeley: Institute of Government Studies, University of California.

Nee, Victor, and Paul Ingram. 1998. "Embeddedness and Beyond: Institutions, Exchange and Social Structure." Pp. 19–45 in *The New Institutionalism in Sociology*, edited by Mary Brinton and Victor Nee. New York: Russell Sage Foundation.

Nelkin, Dorothy. 1994. "Promotional Metaphors and Their Popular Appeal." *Public Understanding of Science* 3: 25–31.

Nelson, Robert H. 1991. *Reaching for Heaven on Earth; The Theological Meaning of Economics.* Lanham, MD.: Rowan & Littlefield.

———. 1994. "Economics as Religion." In *Economics and Religion,* edited by H. Geoffrey Brennan and A. M. C. Waterman. Boston: Kluwer.

———. 2001. *Economics as Religion: From Samuelson to Chicago and Beyond.* University Park: Pennsylvania State University Press.

———. 1990. *Institutions, Institutional Change and Economic Performance.* Cambridge, UK, and New York: Cambridge University Press.

North, Douglass. 1994. "Economic Performance through Time." *American Economic Review* 84: 359–367.

Page, Robert. 1984. *Stigma.* London: Routledge & Kegan Paul.

Parry, Jonathan, and Maurice Bloch, eds. 1989. *Money and the Morality of Exchange.* Cambridge, UK: Cambridge University Press.

Parsons, Talcott, and Neil J. Smelser. 1956. *Economy and Society.* New York: Free Press.

Perrow, Charles. 1984. *Normal Accidents: Living with High-Risk Technologies.* New York: Basic Books.

Pfeffer, Jeffrey. 1981. "Management as Symbolic Action: The Creation and Maintenance of Organizational Paradigms." Pp. 1–52 in *Research in Organizational Behavior,* edited by Larry Cummings and Barry Staw. Greenwich, CT: JAI Press.

Pfeffer, Jeffrey, and Gerald Salancik. 1978. *The External Control of Organizations.* Stanford, CA: Stanford Business Books.

Podolny, Joel. 1993. "A Status-Based Model of Market Competition." *American Journal of Sociology* 98: 829–872.

Pointon, Marcia. 1998. "Money and Nationalism." Pp. 229–254 in *Imagining Nations,* edited by Geoffrey Cubitt. Manchester, UK: Manchester University Press.

Polanyi, Karl. [1944] 1957. *The Great Transformation: The Political and Economic Origin of Our Times.* Boston: Beacon Press.

———. [1957] 1971. "The Economy as Instituted Process." Pp. 139–174 in *Primitive, Archaic and Modern Economies,* edited by George Dalton. Boston: Beacon Press.

Polanyi, Karl, Conrad Arensberg, and Harry Pearson. [1957] 1971. "The Place of Economies in Society." Pp. 239–242 in *Trade and Market in the Early Empires,* edited by Karl Polanyi, Conrad Arensberg, and Harry Pearson. Chicago: Henry Regnery.

Pollner, Melvin. 2002. "Inside the Bubble: Communion, Cognition and Deep Play at the Intersection of Wall Street and Cyberspace." Pp. 230–246 in *Virtual Society? Technology, Cyberbole, Reality,* edited by Steve Woolgar. Oxford: Oxford University Press.

Post, James. 1978. *Corporate Behavior and Social Change.* Reston, VA: Reston Publishing.

Powell, Walter, and Paul DiMaggio, eds. 1991. *The New Institutionalism in Organizational Analysis.* Chicago: University of Chicago Press.

Preda, Alex. 2005. "The Investor as a Cultural Figure of Global Capitalism" Pp. 141–162 in *The Sociology of Financial Markets,* edited by Karin Knorr Cetina and Alex Preda. Oxford: Oxford University Press.

Pusey, Michael. 1991. *Economic Rationalism in Canberra: A Nation-Building State Changes its Mind.* Cambridge, UK: Cambridge University Press.

Putnam, Robert, Robert Leonardi, and Raffaella Nannetti. 1993. *Making Democracy Work: Civic Traditions in Modern Italy.* Princeton, NJ: Princeton University Press.

Rambo, Eric. 1994. "A Culturalist Perspective on Economic Welfare." *Culture* 8(3–4): 1, 4–7

Reddy, William M. 1984. *The Rise of Market Culture: The Textile Trade and French Society, 1750–1900.* Cambridge, UK: Cambridge University Press.

Rorty, Richard. 1989. *Contingency, Irony and Solidarity*. New York: Cambridge University Press.

Sahlins, Marshall. 1976. *Culture and Practical Reason*. Chicago: University of Chicago Press.

——. 2000. "The Sadness of Sweetness; or, the Native Anthropology of Western Cosmology." Pp. 537–583 in *Culture in Practice. Selected Essays*, edited by Marshall Sahlins. New York: Zone Books.

Salancik, Gerald, and James Meindl. 1984. "Corporate Attributions as Strategic Illusions of Management Control." *Administrative Science Quarterly* 29: 238–254.

Sampson, Anthony. 1973. *The Sovereign State of ITT*. New York: Stein & Day.

Sapolsky, Harvey. 1986. *Consuming Fears*. New York: Basic Books.

Schenkler, Barry. 1980. *Impression Management*. Monterrey, CA: Brooks Cole.

Scott, Richard. 2001. *Institutions and Organizations*. Thousand Oaks, CA: Sage Publications.

Sethi, S. Prakash 1977. *Up Against the Corporate Wall*. 3rd ed. Englewoods Cliffs, NJ: Prentice-Hall.

Sharplin, Arthur. 1985. "Union Carbide of India Ltd.: The Bhopal Tragedy." *Case Research Journal* 23: 229–248.

Shils, Edward. 1975. *Center and Periphery. Essays in Macrosociology*. Chicago: University of Chicago Press.

Shrivastava, Paul. 1987. *Bhopal: Anatomy of a Crisis*. Cambridge, MA: Ballinger.

Simiand, Francois. 1934. "La Monnaie, Réalité Sociale." *Annales Sociologiques*, ser. D: 1–86.

Simmel, Georg. [1908] 1950. *The Sociology of Georg Simmel*, edited by Kurt Wolf. Glencoe, IL: Free Press.

——. [1900] 1978. *The Philosophy of Money*. London: Routledge & Kegan Paul.

Smelser, Neil. 1963. *The Sociology of Economic Life*. Englewood Cliffs, NJ: Prentice-Hall.

——. 1976. *Comparative Methods in the Social Sciences*. Englewood Cliffs, NJ: Prentice-Hall.

Smelser, Neil, and Richard Swedberg. 2005. *The Handbook of Economic Sociology*, 2nd ed. Princeton, NJ: Princeton University Press

Smith, Gordon. 1979. *Democracy in Western Germany: Parties and Politics in the Federal Republic*. London: Heineman.

Smith, Philip, and Jeffrey Alexander. 2005. "Introduction: the New Durkheim." Pp. 1–37 in *The Cambridge Companion to Durkheim*, edited by Jeffrey C. Alexander and Philip Smith. Cambridge, UK: Cambridge University Press.

Spillman, Lyn. 1999. "Enriching Exchange: Cultural Dimensions of Markets." *American Journal of Economics and Sociology* 58(4): 1047–1071.

Starling, Grover, and Otis Baskin. 1985. *Issues in Business and Society: Capitalism and Public Response*. Boston: Kent Publishing.

Staw, Barry, Pamela McKechnie, and Sheila Puffer. 1983. "The Justification of Organizational Performance." *Administrative Science Quarterly* 26: 501–524.

Sturdivant, Frederick. 1985. *The Corporate Social Challenge: Case and Commentaries*. Homewood, IL: Richard D. Irwin.

Suchman, Mark. 1995. "Managing Legitimacy: Strategic and Institutional Approaches." *Academy of Management Review* 20(3): 571–610.

Sutton, Robert, and Anita Callahan. 1987. "The Stigma of Bankruptcy: Spoiled Organizational Image and its Management." *Academy of Management Journal* 30(3): 405–436.

Sutton, Robert, and Roderick Kramer. 1990. "Transforming Failure into Success: Impression Management, the Reagan Administration, and the Iceland Arms Control Talks." Pp. 221–245 in *International Cooperation and Conflict: Perspectives from Organizational Theory*, edited by Robert Kahn and Mayer Zald. San Francisco: Jossey-Bass.

Swedberg, Richard. 1987. "Economic Sociology: Past and Present." *Current Sociology* 35: 1–221.

———. 1997. "New Economic Sociology: What Has Been Accomplished? What Is Ahead?" *Acta Sociologica* 40: 161–182.

———. 2004. "Toqueville and the Spirit of American Capitalism." Paper presented at the Norms, Beliefs, and Institutions of 21stCentury Capitalism: Celebrating Max Weber's *The Protestant Ethic and the Spirit of Capitalism* Conference, October 8–9, 2004, Cornell University, Ithaca, NY.

Swidler, Ann. 1986. "Culture in Action: Symbols and Strategies." *American Sociological Review* 20: 273–286.

Taussig, Michael. 1986. *The Evil and Commodity Fetishism in South America*. Chapel Hill: University of North Carolina Press.

Tedeschi, James. 1981. *Impression Management Theory and Social Psychological Research*. New York: Academic Press.

Tedeschi, James, and Marc Reiss. 1981. "Identities, the Phenomenal Self, and Laboratory Research." Pp. 3–22 in *Impression Management Theory and Social Psychological Research*, edited by J. Tedeschi. New York: Academic Press.

Thomas, William, and Florian Znaniecki. [1918–1920] 1958. *The Polish Peasant in Europe and America*. New York: Dover Publications.

Thrift, Nigel. 2000. "Pandora's Box? Cultural Geography of Economics." Pp. 689–704 in *Oxford Handbook of Economic Geography*, edited by Gordon Clark, Meric Gertler, and Maryann Feldman. Oxford: Oxford University Press.

Tietmeyer, Hans. 1997a. "Monetary Stability—A Perpetual Challenge." Speech delivered by the President of the Deutsche Bundesbank, First European Equity Traders Convention of the Federation of European Stock Exchanges, Frankfurt am Main, June 19.

———. 1997b. "Der Euro: ein entnationalisiertes Geld." Speech delivered by the President of the Deutsche Bundesbank, Österreichisch-Deutschen Kulturgesellschaft, Wien, November 27.

Tocqueville, Alexis de. 1959. *Journey to America*. Translated by George Lawrence, edited by J. P. Mayer. New Haven, CT: Yale University Press.

———. [1835–1840] 2000. *Democracy in America*. Translated and edited by Harvey Mansfield and Delba Winthrop. Chicago: University of Chicago Press.

Tognato, Carlo 2008. "Bringing Culture Back In: A Neo-Durkheimian Perspective on Central Banking." *Innovar* 18(31): 93–116.

Tomlison, Alan, ed. 1990. *Consumption, Identity and Style: Marketing, Meanings, and the Packaging of Pleasure*. London and New York: Routledge.

Tönnies, Ferdinand. [1887] 1955. *Community and Association*. London: Routledge and Kegan Paul.

Valenti, JoAnn. 2002. "Communication Challenges for Science and Religion." *Public Understanding of Science* 11: 57–63.

Wagner, Wolfgang. 2007. "Vernacular Science Knowledge: Its Role in Everyday Life Communication." *Public Understanding of Science* 16: 7–22.

Weber, Max. [1915] 1946a. "The Social Psychology of the World Religions." Pp. 267–301 in *From Max Weber*, edited by Hans Gerth and C. Wright Mills. Oxford and New York: Oxford University Press.

———. [1920] 1946b. "The Protestant Sects and the Spirit of Capitalism." Pp. 302–322 in *From Max Weber*, edited by Hans Gerth and C. Wright Mills. Oxford and New York: Oxford University Press.

———. [1946] 1971. "Religious Rejections of the World and Their Directions." Pp. 323–359 in *From Max Weber: Essays in Sociology*, edited by H. Gerth and C. Wright Mills. Oxford and New York: Oxford University Press.

————. [1922] 1978. *Economy and Society: An Outline of Interpretative Sociology*, Vol. 1, edited by Guenther Roth and Claus Wittich. Berkeley and Los Angeles: University of California Press.

Weber, Max. [1904] 1998. *The Protestant Ethic and the Spirit of Capitalism*, 2nd ed. Los Angeles: Roxbury.

White, Harrison. 1981. "Where Do Markets Come From?" *American Journal of Sociology* 87: 517–547.

Whiteside, Thomas. 1972. *The Investigation of Ralph Nader*. New York: Arbor House.

Yenkey, Christopher. 2007. "Morality, Rationality, and the Social Meaning of Information: The Institutionalization of Transparency in the U.S. Securities Markets." CSES Working Paper Series #40, May.

Zaloom, Caitlin. 2003. "Ambiguous Numbers: Trading Technologies and Interpretation in Financial Markets." *American Ethnologist* 30: 258–272.

————. 2004. "The Productive Life of Risk." *Current Anthropology* 19: 365–391.

————. 2006. *Out of the Pits: Trading and Technology from Chicago to London*. Chicago: University of Chicago Press.

Zelizer, Viviana. 1979. *Morals and Markets: The Development of Life Insurance in the United States*. New York: Columbia University Press.

————. 1985. *Pricing the Priceless Child: The Changing Social Value of Children*. New York: Basic Books.

————. 1988. "Beyond the Polemics on the Market: Establishing a Theoretical and Empirical Agenda." *Sociological Forum* 3: 614–634.

————. 1989. "The Social Meaning of Money: 'Special Monies.'" *American Journal of Sociology* 95(2): 342–377.

————. 1992. "Repenser le Marché." *Actes de la Recherche en sciences sociales* 94: 3–26.

————. 1994. *The Social Meaning of Money*. New York: Basic Books.

————. 1996. "Payments and Social Ties." *Sociological Forum* 11: 481–495.

————. 1999. "Official Standardization vs. Social Differentiation in Americans' Uses of Money." Pp. 82–96 in *Nation-States and Money: The Past, the Present and the Future of National Currencies*, edited by Emily Gilbert and Eric Helleiner. London: Routledge.

————. 2000. "The Purchase of Intimacy." *Law & Social Inquiry* 25(3): 817–848.

————. 2005a. "Culture and Consumption." Pp. 331–354 in *The Handbook of Cultural Sociology*, 2nd ed., edited by Neil Smelser and Richard Swedberg. Princeton, NJ: Princeton University Press.

————. 2005b. *The Purchase of Intimacy*. Princeton, NJ: Princeton University Press.

————. 2007. "Ethics in the Economy." *Journal for Business, Economics, and Ethics* (ZfWU) 1: 8–23.

Znoj, Heinzpeter. 1998. "Hot Money and War Debts: Transactional Regimes in Southwestern Sumatra." *Comparative Studies in Society and History* 40: 193–222.

Zucker, Lynne. 1987. "Institutional Theories of Organizations." *Annual Review of Sociology* 13: 443–644.

Zukin, Sharon, and Paul DiMaggio, eds. 1990. *Structures of Capital: The Social Organization of the Economy*. Cambridge, UK: Cambridge University Press.

CHAPTER 6

....

CULTURE AND ECONOMIC LIFE[1]

....

LYN SPILLMAN

MANY economic sociologists now assume that culture matters in economic life. Research about economic meaning-making proliferates, despite earlier hesitations about the supposedly "primordial" or "diffuse" nature of cultural explanation. This research challenges economists' universalistic assumptions about the micro-interactional and motivational meaning of economic action. It also improves on vague sociological stereotypes of "market society," especially by attending closely to meaningful market action in firms and industries.[2]

Yet so many different conceptual languages and lines of inquiry now address "economic culture" that their proliferation threatens to dissipate the promise of cultural explanation of economic life (Jacobs and Spillman 2005). How exactly does culture matter? A chorus of dissonant voices would now articulate different sorts of answers to this question. Some would emphasize the wider "constitutive" role of culture in economic institutions, whereas others would focus on the more immediate "regulative" importance of categories, norms, and values for economic action (DiMaggio 1994; Campbell 1998). Some scholars would locate the influence of culture in national governance patterns, some in meso-level institutional fields, and some in organizational interactions. Some would emphasize the cognitive dimensions of culture; others the normative. Many see meaning-making in all economic action, including in supposedly abstract and rational markets: Others preserve the distinction between pure, rational, utilitarian market action and a much larger class of actions with mixed and variable meanings (along the lines of Weber's distinction between economic action and economically oriented action [1978, 1: 63–64]).[3] Taken together, overviews of culture in economic life treat a disparate laundry list of empirical topics—ranging from consumption to organizational culture to policy regimes. As a result, "culture" is becoming, once again, a residual category of analysis. So, whereas the first edition of the important *Handbook of Economic Sociology* provided a valuable overview of culture and economy (DiMaggio 1994), the second edition, a decade later, treated culture explicitly only with respect to consumption (Zelizer 2005a). This was a relatively peripheral recognition considering economic sociology's bias toward the social organization of production, distribution, and finance in industries, organizations and networks, especially considering all the investigation of economic culture in the intervening decade.[4]

In this chapter, I challenge and resolve this analytic eclecticism. Proliferation and eclecticism are not due to vagueness in the general idea of culture, as is sometimes assumed—such vagueness characterizes popular understanding of any social science concept. Rather, it is a sign of the need for a more comprehensive and explicit engagement with cultural theory.

Theoretically, we can distinguish three different types of cultural processes—production, action, and discourse (Spillman 1995, 2007a), and these processes are also evident in economic life. First, cultural production forms and sustains fields of economic action. Neo-institutionalist studies illustrate this, but so too do other lines of inquiry, such as cross-national studies of industry governance. Second, examining fluid symbolic repertoires helps understand variable economic practice. Zelizer (e.g., 2005b) is the leading scholar of cultural embeddedness of this sort: Other important lines of inquiry are being developed by scholars of organizational culture, and in Biggart and Beamish's (2003) call for more attention to local conventions. Third, some scholars analyze the underlying discourses that *orient* cultural production and *structure* cultural repertoires. Several prominent economic sociologists recognize the constitution of markets and industries in "common discourses" (White 2002a, 299) or "conceptions of control" (Fligstein 2001a, 18), and scholars such as Boltanski and Thévenot (2006) are proposing new analyses of discourses constituting such widely understood economic categories such as management, price, and rationality.

I first argue that there are three different ways to investigate the role of culture in economic life. Distinguishing these three different dimensions of meaning-making reduces potentially crippling confusion about cultural processes, shows how different sorts of work might speak to each other, and provides a platform for formulating new research questions, building more systematically on existing work [5]

On this basis, I go on to argue that more should be done to analyze economic discourse. Of the three types of meaning-making, this third dimension remains the least well understood and the most neglected, particularly in American economic sociology. Systematic and closely interpretive thick description of generalized meaning structures—which orient the production of economic culture in different domains and are instantiated in variant practice—will strengthen the foundations of economic sociology by reinvigorating and updating the classic insights of scholars like Sahlins (1976), Douglas and Isherwood (1979), and Polanyi (1957a,b) into the cultural construction of fundamental principles of economic life.

THE PRODUCTION OF ECONOMIC MEANING

The majority of economic sociologists interested in culture pursue some variant of the cultural production perspective, which examines: "How the symbolic elements of culture are shaped by the systems within which they are created, distributed, evaluated, taught, and preserved" (Peterson and Anand 2004, 311; Crane 1992; Peterson 1979). Historically specific contexts of cultural production influence the legitimate form and status of *participants* in production, exchange, and consumption: They influence explicit and implicit *norms* in economic processes, and they influence the form and legitimacy of *objects* of exchange (Spillman 1999).

For example, theories of economic governance develop a Weberian line of argument and show how rational self-interested economic action is shaped by the historically and comparatively variable political-institutional contexts within which it is undertaken. For governance theorists, as for Weber, rational, self-interested economic action is itself contingently bounded by institution-level "norms, rules, conventions, habits, and values": "Individual action is influenced by the hold that institutions have on individual decision making" (Hollingsworth 2000, 601; Hollingsworth and Boyer 1997, 3; Campbell, Hollingsworth, and Lindberg 1991). They identify ways in which the basic coordination of economic action might be accomplished and how it might vary, following the principle that "institutions exert patterned higher-order effects on the actions, indeed the constitution, of individuals and organizations without requiring repeated collective mobilization or authoritative intervention to achieve these regularities…" (Jepperson, cited in Clemens and Cook 1999, 444–445).[6]

So governance theorists develop the now well-accepted argument that capitalism is not a generic, globally uniform institution, but varies according to the ways in which it is socially embedded.[7] The transactions of economic actors—especially firms—in different countries, sectors, and industries require frameworks of coordination, which vary. A "governance system" is "the totality of institutional arrangements—including rules and rule-making agents—that regulate transactions inside and across the boundaries of an economic system" (Hollingsworth, Schmitter, and Streeck 1994, 5):

> …Our concept of governance refers broadly to the full range of institutional possibilities for deriving collective decisions in an economy. The objectives of economic governance are efficiently and adaptively to co-ordinate the activities of firms and their 'relevant environments', that is, customers, suppliers, competitors, labour, technology generators, government agencies, etc.… (Hollingsworth and Lindberg 1985, 221)

Governance theorists focus on the various social relationships and norms with which major economic actors in a given context organize such tasks as coordinating supply, production, and distribution, setting prices and standards, managing labor and competition, allocating capital, disseminating information, and innovating. Important governance forms for accomplishing such tasks are corporate hierarchy, networks, associations, and markets: Some scholars also treat state and community as alternate forms of economic governance. One important determinant of significant variation in economic governance is the role of the state in creating the conditions under which different forms of economic governance and action are favored with sanctions and regulation. Along Weberian lines, many governance scholars also stress that ideal-typical markets, corporate hierarchies, networks, and associations are usually mixed in reality, so sectors and industries within different countries may have different governance principles, though "one particular arrangement is more dominant in a particular configuration…" (Hollingsworth 2000, 613).

Supporting this position are many cross-national and case studies of the social organization and change of industry sectors. To take one among many examples, O'Brien (1994) contrasts governance arrangements in American and Japanese steel industries in terms of how they influence cultural understandings of legitimate partners in exchange (e.g., independent firms vs. networks of formally independent producers) and norms of exchange (e.g., arms-length market vs. extended informal reciprocity), and, in turn, how this meaning-making affects economic strategy and performance. The cultural production processes in governance arrangements also explain within-country sectoral change: For instance, Arnold (1991) shows how cultural understandings of exchange partners and norms of exchange changed within the American hospital industry, from multilateral networks and associations to markets and corporate hierarchies, after the introduction of Medicare health insurance in 1965.

Governance theory is an important specification and development of a classically sociological form of argument—that social context generates meaning—which is also more widely evident in the work of many other economic sociologists. Dobbin, for example, shows how the efficient organization of railways came to mean very different things in the United States, England, and France (1994b; see also Dobbin 1993). Bandelj (2008, ch. 3) shows how post-socialist foreign investment in Eastern Europe (involving changing market actors and new norms of exchange) was affected by different institutionalization and legitimation processes in different countries. Fourcade (2009) shows how the discipline and influence of economics itself was institutionalized differently in France, Britain, and the United States. Roy develops an historically grounded political account—challenging economists' abstract functional accounts—of the rise of the large industrial corporation as a key market actor in the American economy in the late nineteenth century, noting, for instance, that "institutions shape the taken-for-granted categories that reify frequently repeated social practices into 'things' like money, markets, corporations, and institutions themselves" (1997, 140).

It is possible that, on first encounter, some cultural sociologists unacquainted with economic sociology may not recognize that governance theory makes important claims about economic culture. Nevertheless, it is important to any understanding of culture and economic action for its theoretically well-developed and empirically well-supported account of cultural variation in economic action at the meso- and macro-social levels. Elaborating an essentially Weberian approach to economic culture, it makes an important counterweight to the power of the universalizing tendencies of neoclassical macro-economics.

But perhaps the most influential variant of "cultural production" arguments in economic sociology is neo-institutionalism, which, like governance theory, examines how fields of economic action are created, sustained, and changed. Unlike governance theory, neo-institutionalism generally attends more to meso-level interorganizational relations than to a broader comparative and historically sensitive typology of field processes (DiMaggio and Powell 1991a, b; Hollingsworth 2000, Campbell and Pederson 2001). From a neo-institutionalist perspective, most economic action takes place within intrinsically relational, supra-organizational institutional fields, which "take on an independent status that has a powerful normative effect on subsequent interaction. Once socially defined institutional environments are in place, changes in organizational form are often driven more by considerations of legitimacy than by concern for rational adaptation or efficiency" (Fligstein and Freeland 1995, 32). These neo-institutionalist views of economic action are essentially cultural because "institutions are rules and shared meanings that define social relations, help define who occupies what position in those relations, and guide interaction by giving actors cognitive frames or sets of meanings to interpret the behavior of others…" (Fligstein 2001b, 108; cf. DiMaggio and Powell 1991a, 9, 64–65; DiMaggio 1993; Meyer and Rowan 1977; Campbell and Pederson 2001).

Cultural production and diffusion help explain both continuity and change in organizational fields of economic action. Cognitive homogeneity and normative legitimacy imperatives are sources of continuity (DiMaggio and Powell 1991b, 69–71; Meyer and Rowan 1977). Attention to cognition, its constraints, and its categorical resolution of ambiguities informs the work of organizational scholars who examine how institutional logics provide cognitive support for "focusing the attention of organizational actors on a limited set of issues and solutions…" (Thornton 2002, 83; Ocasio 1997, 193). Similarly, White suggests that a "socially constructed set of cognitive habits"—comparability signals and cost schedules—structure production markets (2002b, 103; Vaughn 2002).

Cultural Production and Exchange Partners Institutionalist processes of cultural production influence the *constitution of legitimate actors* in a field of exchange, and their status within that field. Davis discusses a number of studies that show diffusion of legitimate models of firm organization within fields of production and exchange, and ways that assessment of firm performance in relation to rivals and peers depends on "cognitive models of industry participants" (2005, 485, 489). For example, Lounsbury, Ventresca, and Hirsch show how field "frames," originally produced by recycling activists, generated, in the heat of policy and industry battles of the 1980s, a new for-profit recycling industry from solid waste management firms that were earlier organized to conduct waste-to-energy incineration. Two aspects of this account should be highlighted here. First, their perspective emphasizes institutions as "cultural rules," "generative of interests, identities, and appropriate practice models that take shape at the interface of wider socio-cultural contexts" (2003, 75). Second, they emphasize the politics of cultural production—and in this case, as in a flurry of other recent studies, the links between social movements, policy, and industry formation and transformation (Schneiberg, King and Smith 2008; Rao 1998; King and Soule 2007; Weber, Heinze, and DeSoucey 2008). In another example of field formation and change, Anand and Peterson show how actors in the commercial music industry are constituted by, and oriented to, market information that provides a common focus of attention—*Billboard* charts—and how change in the nature of that market information "creates a cognate change in participants' understanding of the field itself"—in this case, improving the position of multilabel conglomerates compared to independents (2000, 281; for a change in the opposite direction, see Peterson 1990).

Much of the extensive research and theoretical development along these lines focuses on fields and organizations involved in production, distribution, and exchange, but analogous arguments about the cultural production of economic actors are made by some students of consumption.

Broadly speaking, consumers are themselves shaped *as consumers* by their exchange partners, especially retailers. For instance DuGay (1993, 366) analyzes how "market dependent consumption is playing a greater constitutive role in the formation of subjectivity and identity" and retailing techniques "actively 'make up' the consumer." Cook (2004) shows how children were actively constructed as consumers by American retailers from the early twentieth century. Miller (2006) explores how competing meanings of consumption are developed and mobilized in conflicts over different models of book retailing. Rao (1998) examines the emergence of a rationalized organizational model of consumer watchdog organizations as independent scientific testing agencies, rather than crusaders for workers' improved living standards.

Cultural Production and Objects of Exchange Processes of cultural production influence *objects of exchange*, as well as participants in exchange processes. Social processes of categorization, standardization, and commensuration are important ways objects of exchange are constituted and assessed (Espeland and Stevens 1998; Espeland and Sauder 2007). So, for instance, when new market information on the commercial music industry was introduced, new market niches, like Latin music, were also formed (Anand and Peterson 2000, 281). Lounsbury and Rao (2004) investigate how trade and industry media in finance create and change product categorizations, and the industry politics of category change, as, for instance, when growth funds were distinguished from less risky mutual funds in the 1960s. Similarly, Bryan and Rafferty (2007, 140) provide sociological insight on the rise of apparently opaque trades in financial derivatives, arguing that they "establish pricing relationships that readily convert between ('commensurate') different forms of asset." And more generally, Carruthers and Stinchcombe theorize market liquidity as crucially dependant on generalized knowledge of an object of exchange, and

> various strategies help to create generalized knowledge, including standardization and simplification of the asset (e.g., rendering it physically homogenous, as in the case of grading wheat; legally homogenizing it, as in the case of company shares; stratifying, classifying, and grouping it by types of risk, as in the securitization of

home mortgages; or providing third party guarantees of value). The promulga-
tion of classification schemes orients expectations, creates a framework for shared
understandings, and so renders things cognizable. These schemes help to
constitute public knowledge, and hence market liquidity.... (1999, 356)

The process of cultural production involved in forming marketable objects of
exchange is usually understood as a "top down" process, in the sense that industry
producers are viewed as the key cultural producers as well. However, in some circumstances, perhaps especially in newly forming markets, potential or actual consumers may co-construct objects of exchange. So, for instance, Burr emphasizes
that the emergence of a market for bicycles in the United States in the late nineteenth century was heavily dependant on often pro-active consumer organizations:
"Legitimating use (not merely purchase) of the product and building an organizational community were two important activities in creating the U.S. bicycle market,
and consumers participated in these activities as much as producers did" (2006,
418; see also Thrift 2006, 287–290).

Cultural Production and Norms of Exchange Expectations and judgments about
how exchange should be conducted also vary widely according to industry field,
national context, and so on (Spillman 1999, 1060–1061). The ideal-typical norm of
anonymous, arms-length, profit-seeking exchange is often, perhaps mostly, qualified to some degree by norms of reciprocity grounded in multifaceted, extended
social relations (e.g., Uzzi 1996, 1997; Granovetter 1985; DiMaggio and Louch 1998;
Dore 1992; Zelizer 1994), although some social contexts will promote *homo economicus* exchange (Abolafia 1996). Cultural production of norms of exchange has
been demonstrated even in finance industries often considered by outsiders to be
relatively disembedded: For instance, Lounsbury shows for the mutual funds industry that historical, geographical, and professional influences generated firms with
different models of what makes a good investment, so, ultimately, "inefficiency and
poor performance were not the universal decision-making triggers that they are
conventionally argued to be, but were contingent upon trustee and performance
logics" (2007, 302). Greenwood, Suddaby, and Hinings (2002) analyze how professional associations influenced a change in the normative understanding of what
good accounting service should be, and Ahmed and Scapens (2003) also illustrate
institutional influences on changes in accounting rules.

Cultural production influencing normative models of transactions can be seen,
too, in a growing sociological literature on prices and pricing. For instance,
Zuckerman (2004) finds that publicly traded corporations' stock performance is
influenced by the "industry based category structure" produced by industry analysts. According to Uzzi and Lancaster, in their study of corporate law firms, social
embeddedness—including status as well as ties—"affects prices by adding unique
value to exchanges...lower transaction costs, more efficient production, better
product differentiation, or conspicuous consumption" (2004, 339–340; cf. Uzzi
1999; Podolny 1993). For Yakubovich, Granovetter, and McGuire (2005), cultural
politics at the founding of the U.S. electrical industry drove the adoption of a system for pricing electricity which favored large central stations. King and Soule

(2007) found that stock prices are influenced by targeted protests, with media coverage conditioning this effect.[8]

So governance theory and neo-institutionalism examine processes of cultural production for economic action, and more generic social-constructionist arguments about the constitution of economic actors, objects of exchange, and exchange norms are now so widespread that the fundamental influence of the cultural turn in this line of economic sociology is taken for granted, to the extent that some authors mentioned above would likely disavow the categorization of their arguments as "cultural." In some instances above, the cultural argument is "endogenous" (Kaufman 2004): Cultural circumstances generate cultural outcomes, as when new categorizations create new financial instruments for exchange. In others, the argument is exogenous, in the sense that different structural arrangements influence economic culture differently, as when market and network governance structures lead to different norms of exchange in American and Japanese steel industries. But regardless of the precise form of the argument, or conceptual language, all these authors and many more are showing that, contrary to popular and scholarly stereotype, economy and culture are not contrasting social arenas with differing logics and principles. While this line of argument is not as fully interpretive as many cultural sociologists may prefer—and often stresses social dynamics beyond the cultural—it makes important contributions to bridging cultural, structural, and economistic explanations of economic action. Three further accounts of the production of economic meaning show the richness of this line of inquiry in more depth.

In *Markets from Culture: Institutional Logics and Organizational Decisions in Higher Education Publishing* (2004; cf. 2002, 2001; Thornton and Ocasio 1999), Patricia Thornton makes a strong argument for the impact of cultural models of industries on firm leadership, strategy, and structure. Using longitudinal information on individuals, organizations, and their market environments, along with open-ended interviews, she examines the consequences of "editorial" and "market" institutional logics in higher-education publishing and the increasing dominance of the latter from the 1970s. She argues that shifts in the prevailing industry logic cause changes in the sources of power that affect leadership succession, changes in the formal organization structure and changes in corporate strategies such as acquisitions. Cultural logics are influential because they "focus the attention of decision makers in organizations on issues and solutions that are consistent with the prevailing institutional logic...," and Thornton elaborates a theory of organizational attention to support this mechanism. Her overall finding of "higher order institutional logics moderating the meaning of social and economic forces" is supported in each of the three arenas she studies—leadership, structure, and strategy—and is further reinforced because the influence of competing explanations changes according to cultural context: "The effects of both relational networks and market competition on organizational decisions are robustly and consistently particular, that is, culturally contingent..." (2004, 12, 139, 140). Thus, processes of cultural production influence actors in these exchange processes.

Kieran Healy (2006; see also Espeland 1984) advances sociological understanding of the organized cultural production of norms of exchange by examining contentious objects of exchange—human blood and organs. In *Last Best Gifts: Altruism and the Market for Human Blood and Organs*, he finds that procurement organizations actively produce cultural understandings of donation, mostly, but not always, as an altruistic gift, and their cultural accounts influenced what Thornton would call their own "focus of attention" in the initial uncertainty of HIV threats to the blood supply. Moreover, different ways of organizing procurement significantly affect rates of donation, both the regional rates of organ donation in the United States and cross-national rates of blood collection. Simply pitting altruistic against commodified norms of exchange, even for these hotly debated objects of exchange, misses the greater significance of the rationalized organization of exchange, whether gift or sale, or, more likely, some complex symbolic mix of the two forms. "Modern systems of procurement and exchange of human goods depend on complex organizations, which set the context for the exchange and establish the relationship with their suppliers....Whether exchange is commodified may matter less than whether it is *industrialized*....Rationalizing tendencies of formal organizations do just as good a job of taking distinct, particular, incommensurable gifts and processing them into general, homogeneous, comparable items" (132–133). In this study, organizations affect norms of exchange.

Finally, Fligstein (1996, 2001a) presents an important general theory of markets that encompasses many ideas about the analysis of cultural production in economic life that we have seen so far. Drawing together themes from several different threads of economic sociology in *The Architecture of Markets: An Economic Sociology of Twenty-First-Century Capitalist Societies*, Fligstein argues that stable markets are fields of structured, institutionalized exchange in which "the product has legitimacy with customers, and the suppliers of the good or service are able to produce a status hierarchy in which the largest suppliers dominate the market and are able to reproduce themselves on a period-to-period basis" (2001a, 30–31). Markets vary according to participating actors' shared understandings about property rights, governance structures, rules of exchange, and conceptions of control. Given such a set of shared understandings of participants, objects, and norms involved in exchange, firms orient their actions to avoid threats, to "cope with competition and stabilize their various relationships" (2001a, 17). Variation in markets may be examined along these lines cross-nationally, between industries within one state or over time within markets. Market emergence and change are generated in cultural politics that "resemble social movements" (2001a, 76) at the levels of the state, the market, and the firm. So, in Fligstein's "political-cultural" theory of markets:

> The production of market institutions is a cultural project in two ways. Property
> rights, governance structures, conceptions of control, and rules of exchange
> define the social institutions necessary to make markets. These organizing
> technologies provide actors with tools to engage in market activity. Market worlds
> are social worlds; therefore, they operate according to principles like other social

worlds. Actors engage in political actions vis-à-vis one another that reflect local
cultures that and define social relations, who is an actor, and how actors can
interpret one another's behavior.... [sic] (2001a, 70)

So attention to processes of organized meaning-making, or cultural production,
has been an important conceptual resource for economic sociologists challenging
universalistic, individualistic, and essentially a-cultural accounts of economic institutions and economic action. Although many economic sociologists may focus
more on network structures, organizational processes, or comparative, macro-
political influences on economic action, "culture" and "economy" are no longer
counterpoised. Scholars examining cultural production of economic meaning make
crucial links across the culture/economy divide.

Economic Meaning in Action

The various "cultural production" accounts of meaning in economic action discussed above are more frequently challenged by scholars who suggest, in one way or
another, that they miss fluid and variant meaning-making agency on the ground, at
the level of the actor, rather than the institution, making actors "cultural dopes" following institutional scripts. Such challenges treat culture as practice, rather than as
a production process, and often highlight variation, change, agency, and multivo-
cality in cultural repertoires. These challenges are sometimes treated as competing
accounts of culture in economic life, but in fact, they should be understood as
complementary.

Neo-institutionalist accounts of economic institutions and economic action
have faced sustained challenges along these lines (to the extent that much of the
research now conducted under the label of neo-institutionalism examines change
rather than stability). Critics have argued that neo-institutionalism's theorization of
field-level continuity in economic action has overstated isomorphism and homogeneity among actors. For instance, Kraatz and Zajac (1996) found that different sorts
of demands on organizations can inhibit conformity to legitimate models and
increase organizational diversity within a field. In response, a large body of work
now extends neo-institutionalist principles to accounts of change and innovation.
Endogenous change in fields may emerge from the transposition of different institutional logics, multiple inconsistent meanings within institutions, and unintended
consequences (Friedland and Alford 1991; Schneiberg and Clemens 2006; Schneiberg
2007; Clemens and Cook 1999; Meyer and Rowan 1977; Leblebici et al. 1991). Of
course, change also relies on meaning-making for its diffusion (Strang and Meyer
1993, 506; Hirsch 1986; Davis 2005, 490–491). And new fields of economic action
may form when "templates for organized action" are transposed from other domains,
usually in the face of economic and political changes in the broader environment
(Davis 2005, 487; cf. Strang and Meyer 1993, 506; Hirsch 1986).

These processes highlight variation among and within organizations and across different markets, agentic economic actors facing uncertainty and multivocal cultural repertoires.

First, as Pederson and Dobbin (2006) point out, research on organizational culture emphasizes discrete, unique meaning-making processes characteristic of organizations as subcultures, in ways which seem to contradict neo-institutionalist claims about shared organizational effects. For Ocasio, for example, firms vary in their response to external environments according to distributed patterns of organizational attention, that is "how the organization distributes and controls the allocation of issues, answers and decision-makers within specific firm activities, communications, and procedures." External environments provide "repertoires of issues and answers" but subcultural cognitive processes determine particular actions (1997, 191, 193). Goodstein, Blair-Loy, and Wharton also stress, against neo-institutionalism, distinctive, internal organizational responses to "external institutional and strategic environments" (2009, 44), although, compared to Ocasio, they base their argument more on core moral ideologies that underpin internal organizational legitimacy than on distributed cognition (for related examples, see Kunda 1992; Simons and Ingram 1997; Morrill 1995; Jackall 1988). Whether cognitive or normative, an emphasis on organizational culture or subculture focuses on variable meaning-making in action, rather than the institutionalized production of meaning. However, as Pederson and Dobbin argue, research on cultural production in institutional fields and research on distinctive organizational subcultures, on organizational convergence and organizational divergence, essentially treat different sides of the same coin (2006: cf. Abrahamson and Formbrun 1994).[9]

Other research in this vein emphasizes cultural differentiation within, rather than between, organizations. For Hallett (2003; Hallett and Ventresca 2006), for instance, organizations are "negotiated orders" in which symbolic power influences the emergence of dominant but by no means universally shared organizational meanings. For Van Maanen and Barley, complex organizations are often permeated with multiple groups—"tribal federations or fiefdoms"—which generate cultural fragmentation and loose coupling (1984, 335; cf. Martin 2002, ch. 4). And Binder, developing Hallett and Ventresca's (2006) notion of "inhabited institutions," argues directly against neo-institutionalist theory that

> ...organizations are not merely the instantiation of the environment, institutional logics "out there"...where workers seamlessly enact preconscious scripts valorized in the institutional environment. Instead, they are places where people and groups (agentic actors, not "institutional dopes") make sense of, and interpret, institutional 'vocabularies of motive', and act on those interpretations—the central premise of symbolic interactionism. (2007, 551)

Her ethnographic case study shows diverse understandings and practices or "local meaning systems" in different parts of the same organization.

The particularities of meaning-making in practice are also emphasized by scholars who explore how institutional orders actually operate in markets, industries, and fields, as well as by those interested in organizations. For instance, Biggart and Beamish, like the organizational scholars above, argue that institutional theories lack a robust account of "economic patterning through action" and, combining cues from symbolic interactionism and the French "Economics of Convention" school, suggest that explicit and implicit conventions—like standards, categories, customs, and habits—are "institutional theory writ small" (2003, 450, 457). In research on the commercial building industry, they explore how a complex and uncertain market field is sustained with

> ...shared cognitive categories and decision making strategies [which] reflect an intersubjectively meaningful system of norms and conscious beliefs concerning accepted standards, justifications for action, and from this, social accountability. These are embodied in and acted on through tacit assumptions, situated performances, decision-making preferences, and ethical standards. Conventional practices play a strong part in organizing participation in the production of complex multi-million dollar projects. Market actors both rely on industry conventions...and interpretive frameworks...to repeatedly make economic judgments in dynamic social contexts, without complete information, and with the aspiration of assuring opportunities in the future....(Beamish and Biggart 2005, 7)

They demonstrate the importance of essentially local conceptions and assessments of the product, and norms for successful market activity over time, arguing that Fligstein's broad notion of "conceptions of control" in markets needs to be complemented with an analysis of more localized intersubjective meaning construction.

Attention to "localized" intersubjective meaning-construction in practice also characterizes close studies of a wide variety of other markets. In the course of Uzzi's (1997) analysis of network embeddedness in a New York apparel industry, he also provides solid evidence of participants' construction and reconstruction of the meaning of their social ties, differentiating different sorts of partners in exchange, various ways of understanding information about objects of exchange, and different norms of market engagement. Wherry (2008a, ch.5) closely analyzes the interactional processes through which handicrafts in artisans' markets are labeled authentic, or not. Harrington (2008) investigates small group interactions shaping popular investment decisions. Smith (1989) shows how types of auction practices—for objects ranging from art works to used cars to livestock—vary according to varying demands for price legitimacy from different participating and nonparticipating groups. Abolafia's (1996; cf. Zaloom 2006) well-known comparison of bond, stock, and futures markets richly demonstrates how, over time, different subcultural norms of exchange are created and recreated. Bruegger and Knorr-Cetina (2002) analyze global foreign exchange markets in terms of their "local"—micro-interactional—order, which sustains reciprocity and solidarity in norms and rituals (implicit conventions) that establish relationships and transfer information. Pryke and Du Gay discuss a rich vein of research that draws on the work of Latour, Callon, and MacKenzie to explore supposedly abstract, rational financial markets' creation and recreation in "systematic forms of knowledge" based on "material practices, orderings, and discourses" (2007, 340, 341; cf. Callon 1998; MacKenzie 2004, 2006, 2007; MacKenzie and Millo 2003).

These studies and many other investigations of specific markets, industries, and fields provide rich evidence of economic meaning-making in practice, even when the authors frame their investigations in somewhat different theoretical terms, as is often the case. Very evident here is the analytical eclecticism that, I noted above, threatens to dissipate awareness of the significance of cultural analysis of economic life, and that suggests the need for more strenuous engagement by sociologists well-grounded in cultural theory.

Nevertheless, research on the construction and reconstruction of "subcultural" meaning systems in practice—across different organizations, industries, and markets—provides a theoretical and empirical complement to research which focuses on more remote, often more systematic, processes of cultural production. Readers are often led into worlds as unfamiliar and intriguing as the supposedly deviant and marginalized subcultures that preoccupied earlier interactionist ethnographers. Like those earlier ethnographers, and in contrast with "cultural production" approaches like neo-institutionalism, this research often makes subcultural actors' agency in their worlds an explicit concern, as in Binder's comment above.

Indeed, culturally oriented economic sociologists' engagement with the problem of understanding agency in economic action offers a number of ideas more broadly valuable for cultural sociologists. For instance, arguing that "actors...are not just captured by shared meanings in their fields...." Fligstein theorizes a new "microfoundation" for agency in institutional fields by developing a concept of social skill grounded in symbolic interactionism—"the ability to induce cooperation among others" with meaning-producing practices (2001b, 111, 112). Field innovation and field reproduction, as well as the power relations these processes entail, both rely to different degrees on actors' meaning-making agency.

Bandelj (2008, ch. 6) also offers useful contributions to our understanding of agency in her ambitious multilevel account of how states, networks, and culture influence even an apparently rather abstract and aggregate macroeconomic process, foreign direct investment (FDI). She pursues her case against economistic explanation of FDI from cross-national comparisons of economic and political-institutional determinants, to an examination of embedded firm-level processes, to a micro-level consideration of investors' action—usually considered the ideal type of instrumental rational action. Taking conditions of situational uncertainty neglected in instrumentally rationalist accounts seriously, she gives equal place to action based on commitment (when means take precedence over ends), "muddling through" (when means change in the course of goal-oriented action), and improvisation (when both means and ends evolve). Her argument here develops the distinction, increasingly common if often implicit in the work of cultural sociologists interested in meaning-making at the level of practice, between culture as ends and culture as means (cf. Beckert 1996; Dobbin 1994a; see also Baez and Abolafia 2002).

As well as offering contributions to understandings of agency in meaning-making, scholars who focus on economic culture in practice also attend to the existence of multivocal, often diffuse, cultural repertoires that allow various meanings to be attributed to the same economic actions and objects. For instance, Hirsch (1986) provides a vivid discourse analysis of the melodramatic metaphorical language in which hostile takeovers were understood over a twenty-five year period, tracing a shift from strong stigmatization to normalization. Such a focus on cultural repertoires for understanding situated economic action can be particularly valuable in this context because the dominance of economic theories is such a powerful "null hypothesis" for almost all inquiries in economic sociology. Since economistic perspectives, constantly under challenge from economic sociologists, so often presume that the meanings of market exchange—that is, of the relevant actors, objects, and exchange norms involved—are self-evident and transparent, the idea captured in the metaphors of "repertoire" or "toolkit," that actors may understand the same thing differently according to situation, and may mobilize meanings strategically, makes a useful theoretical counterweight that allows empirical questions putting interpretation at the center of analysis.

Viviana Zelizer's influential examination of economic culture draws much of its force from her sustained attention to precisely this line of argument. Her extensive empirical studies of economic meaning-making in practice provide close interpretation of variable meanings in cultural repertoires and, in so doing, drive home the point that the meaning of economic action is never simple, nor simply "economic." So, for instance, in *The Social Meaning of Money* (1994; cf. Carruthers and Espeland 1998; Lamont 1992), she shows how this supposedly transparent, unmarked medium of exchange is, in fact, densely configured with variant meanings in everyday life practice. In *The Purchase of Intimacy* (2005b), she explores the many, varied ways in which economic exchange is intrinsic to intimate relations. Her exploration of variant meanings always shows rich, neglected cultural repertoires in practice. Beyond that, the cumulative force of her work sustains and develops the argument that no serious case can be made for broad distinctions between economic and other forms of action (whether these realms are viewed as "separate spheres," or more critically as "hostile worlds"). However, neither are they simply reducible (a "nothing but" approach). As she summarizes:

> *Neither Hostile Worlds nor Nothing But accounts adequately describe, much less explain, the interplay of monetary transfers and social ties, whether relatively impersonal or very intimate.
>
> *Both intimate and impersonal transactions work through Differentiated Ties, which participants mark off from each other through well-established practices, understandings, and representations.
>
> *Such differentiated ties often compound into distinctive circuits, each incorporating somewhat different understandings, practices, information, obligations, rights, symbols, idioms, and media of exchange.
>
> *Far from determining the nature of interpersonal relationships, media of exchange (including legal tenders) incorporated into such circuits take on particular connections with the understandings, practices, information, obligations, rights, symbols, and idioms embedded in those circuits.
>
> *Indeed, participants in such circuits characteristically reshape exchange media to mark distinctions among different kinds of social relationships.
> (2004, 140)[10]

In its focus on the active construction and reconstruction of multiple, differentiated meanings, Zelizer's work exemplifies the approach of all those who prioritize the close, particular examination of economic meaning-making in practice.

More than many of the authors mentioned above, she shifts the empirical terrain for examining economic meaning-making from "economic" sites strictly considered—usually, organizations and markets—to economic action in everyday life. Obviously, she is challenging reified distinctions between arenas of production, exchange, and consumption. For example, she frequently emphasizes that the household is as much an arena of production as of consumption. But her arguments do resonate in many important ways with the extensive research on consumers and consumption which is sometimes considered the central topic of "culture and economy" studies. We saw earlier a number of studies examining how institutions and fields produce models of consumers and consumer action: A vast literature also investigates consumer action in practice, generally showing ways in which particular meanings of consumption are not individualistic but deeply embedded in what Zelizer would call circuits of differentiated ties (for an overview, see Zelizer 2005a; for a classic statement of this argument, see Douglas and Isherwood 1979; and for a recent example, Brown 2009). To take just two examples, Stillerman shows that for working class couples in Chile, "personal ties influence consumption choices; consumption may be a means to cement personal ties; and consumption is one way that social classes police their boundaries with other groups..."(2004, 74). And in a contrasting but not contradictory case study, Prasad (1999) shows how customers of prostitutes understand their market exchange in positive moral terms as formally free and honest because of the absence of intimate ties.

Economic Discourse

We have seen so far all the proliferating investigation into "culture and economy" which places one of two different cultural processes at the center of analysis, cultural production, or interactional practice. If we were to take at face value investigators' many self-proclaimed cultural influences and contributions, or treat distinctions between different empirical sites as analytic differences (culture in organizations, consumption, etc.), claims about the importance of culture in economic life would begin to sound like empty pieties. But using cultural sociology to understand research in culture and economy in this way helps bring disparate studies into dialog with each other, show unacknowledged connections and complementarities, and create the potential for more accumulation of knowledge and theoretical synthesis (Spillman 2007a).

But clarifying the theoretical grounding of existing research on economic culture in this way also highlights an important gap. Analysis of cultural production and analysis of cultural practice both ultimately limit our understanding of economic culture. These analyses seriously restrict the scope of cultural generalization, by shifting the analytic focus away from meaning to its external conditions and its variable performance (Alexander, 2011 Volume 4, Issue 4, pp. 477–488). Many scholars who focus on processes of cultural production discuss how promoting different models of investing or different notions of a product affect a firm's economic action without close interpretive attention to the meanings themselves. Similarly, many scholars examining contingent, local processes of meaning-making in practice show us how people or organizations use various interpretations of industry status, money, organizational position, exchange norms, and so on according to context, but their analysis of the cultural repertoires involved is ancillary to the central focus on action. These approaches, focusing on institutional production or interactional practice, leave an empty center, that is, economic culture itself. Both these sorts of studies lead to a proliferating array of particular and local insights about contemporary economic meanings, but not to generalization about the larger cultural frameworks or patterns of meaning which constrain and enable particular instances of meaning-making.

The project of coming to a new understanding of economic meaning-making at this more generalized cultural level offers an important and potentially very fruitful direction for further inquiry for cultural sociologists.

There have been several important calls for such cultural generalization. For example, Mohr argues that

> …in spite of the theoretical emphasis on institutionally shared meanings, empirical research by institutionalists has been surprisingly shy about engaging in an interpretative analysis of these meanings.…Similarities and differences in the structure of organizations, their goal statements, their ideologies, and the practices that they employ are measured and compared, but the ideas themselves, the meanings which are embodied in these institutional rules and are expressed by all these homogeneous organizational structures, are absent from view.…(2009, 21–22; see also Mohr and Duquenne 1997; Mohr and Neely 2009; Alexander, 2011 Volume 4, Issue 4, pp. 477–488)

Along similar lines, White asserts the centrality of discourse in constituting actor networks of firms and emergent production markets because "business activities are sustained…only as common discourses are generated and shared…" (2002a, 299).[11] And from a different angle, challenging an overemphasis on culture in practice, Thévenot argues that "some sociological reductions to practices and local situations miss the relevance of…forms of generalization, and the kind of transformation which is needed to build them out of more localized and personalized relations…" (2001, 407).

What would such inquiries into economic culture look like? They should simultaneously fulfill two conditions: First, they should provide closely interpretive, thick description of extended evidence of economic discourse; and second, they should analyze the underlying structure of that discourse in terms that allow generalization across different empirical sites.[12] Ideally, they will also specify historical, institutional, and political conditions of the focal discourse and its variants, without diluting or marginalizing attention to meaning-making itself. There is not yet an extensive or coherent body of studies fulfilling these conditions well, but some leads and illustrations demonstrate a basis for proceeding.

For example, the issue of how relations between market actors are created and sustained in industry fields is a core concern in the work of Fligstein, White, Granovetter, and many other leading economic sociologists, as well as the underlying question of the neo-institutional analysis discussed above. The cultural constitution of such relations is widely recognized, and elements of what that might involve are widely discussed in institutional studies of cognitive isomorphism; in Fligstein's notion of "conceptions of control"; in White's analysis of topics like accounting, signaling mechanisms, and cost schedules; and in other ways too numerous to canvass here. Porac, Ventresca, and Mishina advance this line of work because they develop a useful and well-informed framework for integrating many of these otherwise theoretically dispersed elements in an overview of "interorganizational collective cognitive structures," or in other words, collective representations. More than many other economic sociologists, they are interested in "an explicit focus on conceptualizing and describing the collective cognitive structures underlying interorganizational relations" (2002, 3), and they emphasize that stories are crucial in shaping an ongoing understanding of industry fields. In their analysis, these are composed of four interrelated types of industry beliefs: product ontologies, definitions of market structure and boundaries, industry "recipes" or strategies of action, and organizational reputation and status rankings. They are careful to distinguish discourse from variant practice, avoiding implications of necessary consensus but still allowing the possibility of cultural generalization. And while they are not concerned in this theoretical synthesis to develop closely interpretive thick description themselves, they do build on many studies that provide elements of such empirical backing, and they provide a promising foundation for further cultural research.

Two illustrations can give some indication of what this model for generalizing about collective representations in markets might look like. Weber, Heinze, and DeSoucey (2008) analyze the formation of a new niche market for grass-fed meat and dairy in a movement that mobilized coalitions of producer-activists in the process of market creation—to use the formulation above—creating product ontologies, market boundaries, and industry recipes. Central to their analysis are "the semiotic codes that organized the movement's emergent cultural system," codes contrasting "sustainable vs. exploitative," "authentic vs. manipulated," and "natural vs. artificial." (2008, 531, 538–542), and they show carefully how these codes are used by actors in the nascent industry. This semiotic analysis clearly offers the potential for cultural generalization beyond their case study. In another example, Ghaziani and Ventresca (2005) adopt a wider focus when they analyze the emergence and multiple interpretations of a widespread collective representation for industry recipes—the spread of the idea of a "business model" from the nineties—by examining the interactions between global and local meanings and usages in the business press. While both these studies build on and address issues also treated in other studies discussed earlier—institutional production of industry norms and variant meaning-making practices—they focus more directly and extensively on the close interpretation and generalization about meanings available for mobilization in the cultural production and practical action.

Some other promising studies of economic discourse explore broadly generalizable, cultural understandings evident in many different arenas of economic action, such as ideas about price, rationality, management, and consumption. This work is important for its explicit and extended attention to generalized discursive structures. However, it often remains limited because it remains somewhat hypothetical and disconnected from the systematic, close empirical examination also necessary for strong cultural generalization. Developing better connections between proposals about economic discourse and more systematic, empirical interpretive investigation exploring those proposals is crucial for future understanding of culture and economy.

For instance, Wherry (2008b) theorizes the cultural construction of price and the way it signals assessments of market actors. Binary oppositions between calculating/noncalculating and near to/far from normative behavior generate different sorts of assessments, distinguishing, for instance, between foolishness and frivolity according to the purchaser's status. This analysis focuses on consumption, connecting cultural constructions of price with processes of status distinction like those analyzed by Bourdieu; but since both price and status are important in other sorts of markets, Wherry's theorization should also have even more consequential implications for interaction in less anonymous exchanges characteristic of other markets studied by economic sociologists, as in White's (2002b) discussion of the signaling significance of price in production markets, Zuckerman's (1999) analysis of the influence of cultural categorization on stock market prices, and other studies mentioned earlier.

Illouz (2008, ch. 3) and Gill (2008) both analyze discourse about rationality and rationalization in organizations and work processes. Challenging conventional assumptions about increasing rationalization in economic life, Illouz examines the influence of psychological discourse in American management in the twentieth century and argues that rationalizing management went hand in hand with increasing attention to emotion: "By linking professional competence with emotions, they have constructed a managerial identity around the idea that 'personality attributes' and emotional style are a legitimate basis for managerial authority, with the ultimate economic justification that they are conducive to cooperation and productivity" (2008, 82). Gill finds, on the other hand, that accounting—which White, Callon, and many others see as one of the core cultural constructs of business—is indeed characterized by a systematic process of heightened formal rationalization. However, he also shows that this heightened rationalization systematically generates substantive disillusionment among the accountants he interviews. In both these studies, the discourse of rationality is intrinsically tied to, rather than exclusive of, emotion and morality, but in different ways.

Boltanski and Thévenot develop a broader framework for understanding this sort of meaning-making, by analyzing the basis of rationales for agreement and dispute, the ontological and evaluative categories expressing claims about "higher common principles" making management action meaningful. Deriving models from political philosophies of the common good, they then examine how these models "take shape today, in situations realized within a single space (that of a business firm) and among a single set of persons (the firm's employees)" (2006, 153) with illustrations from a small purposive selection of business handbooks. They include among these models not only "market" and "industrial" principles but also "inspired," "domestic," "fame," and "civic" understandings of categories and principles of evaluation relevant to economic action. This approach, Thévenot suggests, "...offers an analytical tool to operate comparative research on firms, markets and other organizational arrangements" and also "a way to escape the use of extremely general categories (rationalization, modernity), or tautological national characters, or purely contextual stories" (2001, 405, 419; see also Boltanski and Chiapello 2005; Jagd 2004). That is, investigation of economic discourse offers more potential for generalization about economic culture itself than simply examining its external determinants or performative instantiation.

This framework could also help clarify and compare other, more particular and less well substantiated, proposals about broad changes in economic culture. For instance, Thrift (2001) argues that a new model of capitalist economic action emerged in the 1990s that promoted rapid, adaptable, participatory action which was "passionate," perhaps along the lines of Boltanski and Thévenot's "inspired polity." In a different direction, Shamir argues that shifting conceptual distinctions between "market" and "society," originating with neoliberalism, facilitate "the responsibilization of market entities to assume the caring and welfare moral duties that were once assigned to civil society and government entities" (2008, 10)—in Boltanski and Thévenot's terms, a "civic" model (although according to Shamir, these duties are then also understood in utilitarian and instrumental terms). The proposals of Boltanski and Thévenot, Thrift, Shamir, and others about variation and change in widely available understandings of capitalist economic action should be explored further in systematically designed, comparative, thick description that builds on what economic sociology can already tell us about governance theory, institutions, organizational cultures, and what Porac, Ventresca, and Mishina, above, call "interorganizational collective cognition." Cultural sociologists are well positioned to pursue this agenda.

Topics like business models, product ontologies, price, rationality, and management principles provide rich material for generalized discourse analysis that places meaning at the center of economic action.[13] Indeed, a more systematic understanding of this sort of collective representation seems necessary to provide a better foundation for generalizing about economic culture across particular analyses of cultural production and practice. Another general collective representation even more fundamental to modern economic action is the idea of economic interests. While governance scholars and neo-institutionalists have shown many particular ways in which economic interests are constructed in institutional fields, and those who examine local meaning systems in practice show even greater variance in the ways economic actors understand interests, the general idea that economic action involves the pursuit of interests remains as unexamined as it has been in economics itself. Yet a fully cultural approach to economic action should resist this naturalization and examine the very idea of "economic interests" as a collective representation (Spillman 2007b, 2009; Spillman and Strand forthcoming). For instance, Spillman (forthcoming) shows that even business associations rely on generalized solidarity as much as interests in their claimsmaking.

Analysis of discourse about consumption has a longer intellectual tradition than these attempts to examine the ways in which culture constitutes what was formerly understood simply as the rational pursuit of business interests in production and exchange (see Zelizer 2005a and other studies mentioned above, which typically include thick descriptions of cultural categories and evaluations associated with consumption, in addition to analysis of institutions and practices). Johnston provides a useful contemporary model in her case study of "ethical consumer discourse" created by Whole Foods Market. She notes that attention to discourse captures the "constitutive effects of language on social life" and especially how "discursive activities create, sustain, and legitimate relationships of power and privilege" while also helping to understand nuance in meaning-making (2008, 233–234). She examines in detail how different elements of the "citizen-consumer hybrid" are articulated and how tensions between different normative understandings of exchange emerge from this discourse. Thus, discourse analysis here can provide a richer understanding of meaning-making, which bridges insights one might derive from a more institutional analysis of the development of the "business model," and insights one might draw from examination of how Whole Foods' marketing strategy is understood in practice. She addresses both these elements of the story too.

As is evident in many of these examples, an emerging theme in analysis of economic discourse across different empirical sites is the extent to which ethical and normative meaning is an intrinsic part of economic action, not only for consumers (cf. Zelizer 2005a and Prasad 1999, above), but even where conventional views have long made strict distinctions between hard-nosed business pursuits of rational interest and other realms of action (cf. Fourcade and Healy 2007; Alexander, 2011 Volume 4, Issue 4, pp. 477–488). Discourse analysis often provides grounds for ideology critique and remains useful for that purpose, as in Johnston's discussion of inherent limits to citizen-consumer discourse.[14] But as Chiappello (2003) argues, discourses may be simultaneously integrating, mystifying, and critical. Perhaps more importantly, they become social facts in themselves, with potentially performative consequences, just as scholars like Callon (1998) and MacKenzie and Millo (2003; cf. MacKenzie 2004, 2006, 2007) argue, has been true of economics as a discipline (see also Reddy 1984 for a historically grounded argument along these lines.)

In my view, economic sociologists need no longer hesitate to analyze broad cultural patterns in economic action, as well as particular cultural processes in particular arenas. Exploring the fundamental cultural grounding of economic action is ultimately essential for better understanding of what is often taken for granted in explaining variation, conflict, and change in particular contexts. Such particular contexts are always framed by broader discursive fields: If those discursive fields are unchallenged, they go unnoticed; but any comparison, conflict, or change will show how essential they are for routine action even when taken for granted.

CONCLUSION

Sociology is now following those anthropologists who

> …assert that economic activity is part of culture and a product of social organisation. It is not the result of an autonomous force, analogous say to gravity, but is the product of social creativity, of human ingenuity and inventiveness. We speak of economic activities rather than of economic behaviour because we deny that the economic things people do are the working-out of necessity, and because we assert in contestation that they are the product of will and intention and agreement. They are in this sense no different from kinship, religion, and art.…(Davis 1996, 219)

In this chapter, I have mapped a heavily populated field of inquiry which is both illustrative of, and central to, the significance and power of the cultural turn. We have seen first how economic life is shaped in processes of cultural production explored in governance theory, neo-institutionalism, and in the work of other scholars who conduct comparative and historical inquiry into different ways production, distribution, exchange, and consumption are organized. Second, we have seen how actors create and respond to their institutional, organizational, and relational contexts actively, mobilizing fluid and various cultural repertoires. Third, we have explored some proposals and models for putting economic discourse at the center of analysis, an approach which remains empirically underdeveloped but has the potential to demonstrate in new ways how culture is constitutive of economic action. Cultural sociologists have good reason to take the economy very seriously as one of the most widely significant topics on which renewed attention to meaning-making processes has already produced important advances and promises many more.

NOTES

1. Thanks to Elizabeth Blakey Martinez and Michael Strand for research assistance, and to Wendy Griswold, Rachel Harvey, Ron Jacobs, Elizabeth Blakey Martinez, Mike Strand, Richard Swedberg, and Fred Wherry for their helpful readings.

2. The strength of cultural approaches was not to be expected when the foundations of contemporary economic sociology were laid in the mid-1980s. At first, many influential economic sociologists considered "culture" too diffuse and inchoate an analytic category to

be useful (Granovetter 1985; Hamilton and Biggart 1988; see also DiMaggio and Louch 1998; Spillman 1999, 1051; Swedberg 2003, 245).

Despite these hesitations, cultural analysis in economic sociology became one among several important lines of inquiry, which also include network, organizational, and comparative-historical perspectives (Swedberg 2003). Contemporary economic sociologists provide extensive evidence of different ways the systematic pursuit of profitable production and exchange is shaped by social context. Broadly, they show how production, distribution, and exchange are shaped by differing national institutions, changing industry arrangements, diverse organizational forms, particular network patterns, and various cultural categories and norms. Diffuse usages of cultural analysis turned out to be productive: However, as I argue here, scholarship on economic culture became inchoate because most economic sociologists failed to attend more than opportunistically to cultural theory.

The subfield is well supplied with a number of key works that trace its contours and review its issues and history (Smelser and Swedberg 1994, 2005; Swedberg 1998, 2003, 2004; Dobbin 2004; Guillén et al. 2002; Granovetter and Swedberg 2001; Biggart 2007, 2002; Carruthers and Babb 2000; Carruthers 2005; Lie 1997; Knorr-Cetina 2005). Parsons and Smelser (1964; see also Smelser 1991) and Stinchcombe (1983) remain somewhat neglected as precursors of the late-twentieth-century revitalization of economic sociology. Trigilia (2002) and Beckert (2002) provide extended theoretical histories grounding new arguments focusing, respectively, on more macro and more micro theoretical foundations. Smelser (1976; 1959) provides an early overview, and Geertz (1978), Friedland and Robertson (1990b), Martinelli and Smelser (1990), and Zelizer (1988) make agenda-setting statements that remain useful. For sympathetically critical views of the field, see Barber (1995), Krier (1999), and Krippner (2001). Abell (2003) challenges economic sociology for lacking rigor and parsimony compared to the modified rational choice models of economics.

3. Of course, Weber made both economic action and interpretation central to his sociology, and underlying this distinction is a more profound "interpretive economic sociology," which remains the most systematic theorization of culture and economic action. Thanks to Richard Swedberg for emphasizing this point. See Weber (1978, Vol. 1; 1998) and Swedberg (1998). The systematic theory Weber elaborated only highlights all the more the opportunistic and diffuse ways culture has been understood in contemporary economic sociology.

4. DiMaggio (1994) provides a balanced synthesis and assessment of disparate bodies of mostly meso-level sociological work on culture in production, exchange, and consumption through the 1990s, as does Hamilton (1994) for macro-cultural studies. Campbell (1998) develops a useful framework for understanding the different ways ideas may affect economic policy. Dobbin (1994a) develops an overview of cultural challenges to explanation in terms of rationality, efficiency, and interests. Spillman (1999) extends those overviews by reviewing studies of meaning-making about objects, communities, and norms of exchange. Anthropological approaches to economic life emphasizing substantive historical and comparative variety in the meaning of everyday economic action are discussed in Marcus (1990), Davis (1996), and Barth (1997). Biggart and Beamish (2003) synthesize research on cultural categories and practices and argue for the significance of conventions for theories of market order. Zelizer (2002), Fourcade and Healy (2007), Fourcade (2007), and Levin (2008) discuss different views of the relationship between economy and culture and argue for approaches that conflate earlier distinctions. While valuable, these overviews and the rich range of empirical studies they survey differ so much in their conceptual vocabularies and levels of analysis that no clear consensus about what we know and what we should learn about the ways meaning-making relates to economic action emerges, except for the shared point that strong analytic distinctions between culture and economy should be rejected.

Perhaps surprisingly, one of the most widely known contemporary theories of culture, that of Bourdieu, has so far found little purchase in economic sociology. As Swedberg summarizes, his work on habitus, cultural capital, and fields may be applied to economic as much as to other forms of action (1998, 241–245). Bourdieu (2005) develops an argument for economic embeddedness in terms of his field theory, with the empirical case of the French single-family housing market, criticizing economic sociologists for ignoring too often relational dynamics in fields (e.g., 39, 233). However, many of his most direct reflections on economic processes (e.g., 1998) implicitly tend to replicate the oppositions between economy and society that economic sociology challenges (because it mostly focuses on more middle-range phenomena like institutions, organizations, networks, conventions, practices, and discourses).

5. Because my argument here is based on contemporary theories of culture, rather than extant empirical variation in the wide range of topics examined by economic sociologists, it cross-cuts standard macro/meso/micro distinctions, applying to all three levels. Moreover, production approaches, repertoire approaches, and discourse approaches may each be either constitutive of economic institutions—thus involving long-term but relatively immutable consequences—or regulative of economic action—in ways that are more consequential in the short term. These standard analytic distinctions are, of course, important in the formulation of particular research problems, but they do not provide a theoretical basis for a general understanding of how culture matters in economic life.

6. For a broad overview of governance theories, including institutionalist perspectives, see Fligstein and Freeland (1995).

7. Hollingsworth, Schmitter, and Streeck (1994); Hollingsworth and Boyer (1997); Biggart and Guillén (1999). For other arguments about comparative capitalisms, see, for example, Fligstein and Freeland (1995); O'Sullivan et al. (2005); Bandelj (2008); Dobbin (1994b).

8. For a discussion of the theoretical pros and cons of analyzing the social construction of price in the stock market, see also Zajac and Westphal (2004a, 2004b) and Zuckerman (2004). Smith (1989) and Wherry (2008b), discussed below, also contribute to sociological understandings of pricing.

9. This combined influence of external models and internal differentiation is better understood and more accepted in political sociology: organizations operate in institutional fields in much the same way that nation-states follow global models but develop claims about distinctive identity (Spillman and Faeges 2004; Spillman 1997).

10. See also Zelizer (1983, 1999, 2005b) and, for a useful early overview of these works and of economic sociology's founding problematic, Zelizer (1988).

11. White suggests that different sorts of markets operate through different "registers" or subcultural commonalities within this broader discursive constitution. He sees discourse analysis as fundamental to his theory of markets and calls for "developing explicit measures and models of discourse, and of culture more generally, for operationalization of these mechanisms [of market functioning]" (2002a, 326). However, he has in mind sociolinguistic analysis of discourse, which theorizes relations and higher-order emergence in terms of indexicality. In my view, this would result in overly formal analysis at the expense of substantive, historically grounded understanding more characteristic of the analysis of discourse in cultural sociology. For a brief overview of some of the specific ways he understands culture as crucial in markets, see White (2000, 2002b), and for an early statement White (1981).

12. Sahlins's (1976, chs. 4–6) classic study of the cultural construction of "utility" might be considered a precursor in this regard.

13. Macro-economic indicators, and financial crises, are also fruitful topics for this line of research (De Santos 2003, 2009; Alexander, 2011 Volume 4, Issue 4, pp. 477–488).

14. Interestingly, Martin (1999) argues that elaborate discursive critiques of a shift to consumerism in the twentieth century are themselves based on assumptions about economic changes that did not, in fact, happen. In a similar sort of finding, Guillén (2001) and Fiss and Hirsch (2005) show that in the last decades of the twentieth century, talk about globalization rapidly outpaced economic globalization itself.

REFERENCES

Abell, Peter. 2003. "On the Prospects for a Unified Social Science: Economics and Sociology." *Socioeconomic Review* 1: 1–26.

Abolafia, Mitchell. 1996. *Making Markets: Opportunism and Restraint on Wall Street.* Cambridge, MA: Harvard University Press.

Abrahamson, Eric, and Charles J. Formbrun. 1994. "Macrocultures: Determinants and Consequences." *Academy of Management Review* 19(4): 728–755.

Ahmed, Mirghani N., and Robert F. Scapens. 2003. "The Evolution of Cost-based Pricing Rules in Britain: an Institutionalist Perspective." *Review of Political Economy* 15(2): 173–191.

Alexander, Jeffrey C. Forthcoming. "Market as Narrative and Character: For a Cultural Sociology of Economic Life." *Journal of Cultural Economy.*

Anand, N., and Richard A. Peterson. 2000. "When Market Information Constitutes Fields: Sensemaking of Markets in the Commercial Music Industry." *Organization Science* 11(3): 270–284.

Arnold, Patricia J. 1991. "The Invisible Hand in Healthcare: The Rise of Financial Markets in the U.S. Hospital Industry." Pp. 293–316 in John L. Campbell, J. Rogers Hollingsworth, and Leon N. Lindberg, eds. *Governance of the American Economy.* Cambridge, UK, and New York: Cambridge University Press.

Baez, Bien, and Mitchell Y. Abolafia. 2002. "Bureaucratic Entrepreneurship and Institutional Change: A Sense-Making Approach." *Journal of Public Administration Research and Theory* 12: 525–552.

Bandelj, Nina. 2008. *From Communists to Foreign Capitalists: The Social Foundations of Foreign Direct Investment in Postsocialist Europe.* Princeton, NJ, and Oxford: Princeton University Press.

Barber, Bernard. 1995. "All Economies are 'Embedded': The Career of a Concept, and Beyond." *Social Research* 62: 387–413.

Barth, Fredrik. 1997. "Economy, Agency and Ordinary Lives." *Social Anthropology* 5: 233–242.

Beamish, Thomas D., and Nicole W. Biggart. 2005. "Market Construction: Sensemaking in the Commercial Building Industry." Unpublished paper, Department of Sociology, University of California, Davis.

Beckert, Jens. 1996. "What Is Sociological About Economic Sociology? Uncertainty and the Embeddedness of Economic Action." *Theory and Society* 25: 803–840.

———. 2002. *Beyond the Market: The Social Foundations of Economic Efficiency.* Trans. Barbara Harshav. Princeton, NJ, and Oxford: Princeton University Press.

Biggart, Nicole W., ed. 2002. *Readings in Economic Sociology.* Malden, MA, and Oxford: Blackwell.

————. 2007. "Coming and Going in Economic Sociology." *American Behavioral Scientist* 50(8): 991–992.

Biggart, Nicole W., and Mauro F. Guillén. 1999. "Developing Difference: Social Organization and the Rise of the Auto Industries of South Korea, Taiwan, Spain, and Argentina." *American Sociological Review* 64: 722–747.

Biggart, Nicole W., and Thomas D. Beamish. 2003. "The Economic Sociology of Convention: Habit, Custom, Practice, and Routine in Market Order." *Annual Review of Sociology* 29: 443–464.

Binder, Amy. 2007. "For Love and Money: Organizations' Creative Responses to Multiple Environmental Logics." *Theory and Society* 36: 547–571.

Boltanski, Luc, and Eve Chiapello. 2005 [1999]. *The New Spirit of Capitalism.* Trans. Gregory Elliott. London and New York: Verso.

Boltanski, Luc, and Laurent Thévenot. 2006 [1991]. *On Justification: Economies of Worth.* Trans. Catherine Porter. Princeton, NJ, and Oxford: Princeton University Press.

Bourdieu, Pierre. 1998. *Acts of Resistance: Against the Tyranny of the Market.* Trans. Richard Nice. New York: New Press.

————. 2005. *The Social Structure of the Economy.* Trans. Chris Turner. Cambridge, UK: Polity Press.

Brown, Keith. 2009. "The Social Dynamics and Durability of Moral Boundaries." *Sociological Forum.* 24: 854–876.

Bruegger, Urs, and Karin Knorr-Cetina. 2002. "Global Microstructures: The Virtual Societies of Financial Markets." *American Journal of Sociology* 107: 905–995.

Bryan, Dick, and Michael Rafferty. 2007. "Financial Derivatives and the Theory of Money," *Economy and Society* 36: 134–158.

Burr, Thomas. 2006. "Building Community, Legitimating Consumption: Creating the U.S. Bicycle Market, 1876–1884." *Socioeconomic Review* 4: 417–446.

Callon, Michel, ed. 1998. *The Laws of the Markets.* Oxford and Malden, MA: Blackwell Publishers/The Sociological Review.

Campbell, John L. 1998. "Institutional Analysis and the Role of Ideas in Political Economy." *Theory and Society* 27: 377–409.

Campbell, John L., J. Rogers Hollingsworth, and Leon N. Lindberg, eds. 1991. *Governance of the American Economy.* Cambridge, UK, and New York: Cambridge University Press.

Campbell, John. L., and Ove K. Pedersen, eds. 2001. *The Rise of Neoliberalism and Institutional Analysis.* Princeton, NJ: Princeton University Press.

Carruthers, Bruce G. 2005. "Historical Sociology and the Economy: Actors, Networks, and Context." Pp. 333–354 in Julia Adams, Elisabeth Clemens, and Ann Orloff, eds. *Remaking Modernity: Politics, History, and Sociology.* Durham, NC, and London: Duke University Press.

Carruthers, Bruce G., and Arthur Stinchcombe. 1999. "The Social Structure of Liquidity: Flexibility in Markets, States, and Organizations." *Theory and Society* 28: 353–382.

Carruthers, Bruce G., and Sarah L. Babb. 2000. *Economy/Society: Markets, Meanings, and Social Structure.* Thousand Oaks, CA, and London: Pine Forge Press.

Carruthers, Bruce G., and Wendy Nelson Espeland. 1998. "Money, Meaning and Morality." *American Behavioral Scientist* 41: 1384–1408.

Chiappello, Eve. 2003. "Reconciling the Two Principle Meanings of the Notion of Ideology: The Example of the 'Spirit of Capitalism.'" *European Journal of Social Theory* 6: 155–171.

Clemens, Elisabeth S., and James M. Cook. 1999. "Politics and Institutionalism: Explaining Durability and Change." *Annual Review of Sociology* 25: 441–466.

Cook, Daniel Thomas. 2004. *The Commodification of Childhood: The Children's Clothing Industry and the Rise of the Child Consumer*. Durham, NC: Duke University Press.

Crane, Diana. 1992. *The Production of Culture: Media and the Urban Arts*. Newbury Park, CA: Sage.

Davis, Gerald F. 2005. "Firms and Environments." Pp. 478–502 in Neil J. Smelser and Richard Swedberg, eds. *Handbook of Economic Sociology*, 2nd ed. Princeton, NJ: Princeton University Press and New York: Russell Sage Foundation.

Davis, John. 1996. "An Anthropologist's View of Exchange." *Social Anthropology* 4: 213–226.

De Santos, Martin. 2003. "Performances in Search of an Author: The Symbolic Life of an Economic Indicator." *Yale Journal of Sociology* 3: 63–75.

———. 2009. "Fact-Totems and the Statistical Imagination: The Public Life of a Statistic in Argentina 2001." *Sociological Theory* 27(4): 466–489.

DiMaggio, Paul. 1993. "Nadel's Paradox Revisited: Relational and Cultural Aspects of Organizational Structure." Pp. 118–142 in Nitin Noria and Robert G. Eccles, eds. *Networks and Organizations: Structure, Form, and Action*. Boston: Harvard Business School Press.

———. 1994. "Culture and Economy." Pp. 27–57 in Neil J. Smelser and Richard Swedberg, eds. *Handbook of Economic Sociology*, 1st ed. Princeton NJ: Princeton University Press and New York: Russell Sage Foundation.

DiMaggio, Paul, and Hugh Louch. 1998. "Socially Embedded Consumer Transactions: For What Kinds of Purchases Do People Most Often Use Networks?" *American Sociological Review* 63: 619–637.

DiMaggio, Paul, and W. W. Powell. 1991a. "Introduction." Pp. 1–38 in W. W. Powell and Paul DiMaggio, eds. *The New Institutionalism in Organizational Analysis*. Chicago: University of Chicago Press.

———. 1991b [1983]. "The Iron Cage Revisited: Institutional Isomorphism and Collective Rationality in Organizational Fields." Pp. 63–82 in W.W. Powell and Paul DiMaggio, eds. *The New Institutionalism in Organizational Analysis*. Chicago: University of Chicago Press.

Dobbin, Frank. 1993. "The Social Construction of the Great Depression: Industrial Policy During the 1930s in the United States, Britain, and France." *Theory and Society* 22: 1–56.

———. 1994a. "Cultural Models of Organization: The Social Construction of Rational Organizing Principles." Pp. 117–141 in Diana Crane, ed. *The Sociology of Culture*. Oxford: Blackwell.

———. 1994b. *Forging Industrial Policy: The United States, Britain and France in the Railway Age*. Cambridge, UK, and New York: Cambridge University Press.

———, ed. 2004. *The New Economic Sociology: A Reader*. Princeton, NJ, and Oxford: Princeton University Press.

Dore, Ronald. 1992. "Goodwill and the Spirit of Market Capitalism." *British Journal of Sociology* 34: 459–482.

Douglas, Mary, and Baron Isherwood. 1979. *The World of Goods*. New York: Basic Books.

DuGay, Paul. 1993. "Numbers and Souls: Retailing and the De-Differentiation of Economy and Culture." *British Journal of Sociology* 44: 563–587.

Espeland, Wendy. 1984. "Blood and Money: Exploiting the Embodied Self." Pp. 131–155 in Joseph A. Kotarba and Andrea Fontana, eds. The *Existential Self in Society*. Chicago: University of Chicago Press.

Espeland, Wendy, and Michael Sauder. 2007. "Rankings and Reactivity: How Public Measures Recreate Social Worlds." *American Journal of Sociology* 113: 1–40.

Espeland, Wendy, and Mitchell Stevens. 1998. "Commensuration as a Social Process." *Annual Review of Sociology* 24: 313–343

Fiss, Peer C., and Paul M. Hirsch. 2005. "The Discourse of Globalization: Framing and Sensemaking of an Emerging Concept." *American Sociological Review* 70: 29–52.

Fligstein, Neil. 1996. "Markets as Politics: A Political-Cultural Approach to Market Institutions." *American Sociological Review* 61: 656–673.

———. 2001a. *The Architecture of Markets: An Economic Sociology of Twenty-First Century Capitalist Societies.* Princeton, NJ, and Oxford: Princeton University Press.

———. 2001b. "Social Skill and the Theory of Fields." *Sociological Theory* 19: 105–125

Fligstein, Neil, and Robert Freeland. 1995. "Theoretical and Comparative Perspectives on Corporate Organization." *Annual Review of Sociology* 21: 21–43.

Fourcade, Marion. 2009. *Economists and Societies: Discipline and Profession in the United States, Britain and France, 1890s–1990s.* Princeton, NJ: Princeton University Press.

Fourcade, Marion, and Kieran Healy. 2007. "Moral Views of Market Society." *Annual Review of Sociology* 33: 285–311.

Fourcade-Gourinchas, Marion. 2007. "Culture and Economy." Pp. 933–936 in George Ritzer, ed. *Blackwell Encyclopedia of Sociology*, Vol. 2. Malden, MA, and Oxford: Blackwell.

Friedland, Roger, and A. F. Robertson, eds. 1990a. *Beyond the Marketplace: Rethinking Economy and Society.* New York: Aldine de Gruyter.

Friedland, Roger, and A. F. Robertson. 1990b. "Beyond the Marketplace." Pp. 3–49 in *Beyond the Marketplace.* New York: Aldine de Gruyter.

Friedland, Roger, and Robert Alford. 1991. "Bringing Society Back In: Symbols, Practices, and Institutional Contradictions." Pp. 232–263 in Walter W. Powell and Paul J. DiMaggio, eds. *The New Institutionalism in Organizational Analysis.* Chicago: University of Chicago Press.

Geertz, Clifford. 1978. "The Bazaar Economy: Information and Search in Peasant Marketing." *American Economic Review* 68: 28–32.

Ghaziani, Amin, and Marc J. Ventresca. 2005. "Keywords and Cultural Change: Frame Analysis of 'Business Model' Public Talk, 1975–2000." *Sociological Forum* 20: 523–559.

Gill, Matthew. 2008. "Rationalization Defeats Itself: The Limits to Accounting's Framing of Economic Life." *Socio-Economic Review* 6: 587–609.

Goodstein, Jerry, Mary Blair-Loy, and Amy S. Wharton. 2009. "Organization-Based Legitimacy: Core Ideologies and Moral Action." Pp. 44–62 in Isaac Reed and Jeffrey C. Alexander, eds. *Meaning and Method: The Cultural Approach to Sociology.* Boulder, CO, and London: Paradigm Publishers.

Granovetter, Mark. 1985. "Economic Action and Social Structure: The Problem of Embeddedness." *American Journal of Sociology* 91: 481–510.

Granovetter, Mark, and Richard Swedberg, eds. 2001. *The Sociology of Economic Life*, 2nd ed. Boulder, CO: Westview Press.

Greenwood, R., R. Suddaby, and C. R. Hinings. 2002. "Theorizing Change: The Role of Professional Associations in the Transformation of Institutionalized Fields." *Academy of Management Journal* 45: 58–80.

Guillén, Mauro F. 2001. "Is Globalization Civilizing, Destructive, or Feeble? A Critique of Five Key Debates in the Social Science Literature." *Annual Review of Sociology* 27: 235–260.

Guillén, Mauro F., Randall Collins, Paula England, and Marshall Meyer, eds. 2002. *The New Economic Sociology: Developments in an Emerging Field.* New York: Russell Sage Foundation.

Hallett, Tim. 2003. "Symbolic Power and Organizational Culture." *Sociological Theory* 21: 128–149.

Hallett, Tim, and Marc Ventresca. 2006. "Inhabited Institutions: Social Interaction and Organizational Forms in Gouldner's Patterns of Industrial Bureaucracy." *Theory and Society* 35: 213–236.

Hamilton, Gary G. 1994. "Civilizations and the Organization of Economies." Pp. 183–205 in Neil J. Smelser and Richard Swedberg, eds. *Handbook of Economic Sociology*, 1st ed. Princeton, NJ: Princeton University Press and New York: Russell Sage Foundation.

Hamilton, Gary G., and Nicole W. Biggart. 1988. "Market, Culture, and Authority: A Comparative Analysis of Management and Organization in the Far East." *American Journal of Sociology* 94: S52–S94.

Harrington, Brooke, 2008. *Pop Finance: Popular Finance and the New Investor Populism*. Princeton, NJ: Princeton University Press.

Healy, Kieran. 2006. *Last Best Gifts: Altruism and the Market for Human Blood and Organs*. Chicago: University of Chicago Press.

Hirsch, Paul M. 1986. "From Ambushes to Golden Parachutes: Corporate Takeovers as an Instance of Cultural Framing and Institutional Integration." *American Journal of Sociology* 91: 800–837.

Hollingsworth, J. Rogers. 2000. "Doing Institutional Analysis: Implications for the Study of Innovations." *Review of International Political Economy* 7: 595–644.

Hollingsworth, J. Rogers, and Leon Lindberg. 1985. "The Governance of the American Economy: The Role of Markets, Clans, Hierarchies, and Associative Behaviors." Pp. 221–254 in Wolfgang Streeck and Philippe. C. Schmitter, eds. *Private Interest Government: Beyond Market and State*. Beverly Hills, CA: Sage.

Hollingsworth, J. Rogers, and Robert Boyer, eds. 1997. *Contemporary Capitalism: The Embeddedness of Institutions*. Cambridge, UK, and New York: Cambridge University Press.

Hollingsworth, J. Rogers, Philippe C. Schmitter, and Wolfgang Streeck, eds. 1994. *Governing Capitalist Economies: Performance and Control of Economic Sectors*. New York and Oxford: Oxford University Press.

Illouz, Eva. 2008. "From *Homo economicus* to *Homo communicans*." Pp. 58–104 in *Saving the Modern Soul: Therapy, Emotions, and the Culture of Self-Help*. Berkeley and Los Angeles: University of California Press.

Jackall, Robert. 1988. *Moral Mazes: The World of Corporate Managers*. New York: Oxford University Press.

Jacobs, Mark, and Lyn Spillman. 2005. "Cultural Sociology at the Crossroads of the Discipline." *Poetics* 33: 1–14.

Jagd, Soren. 2004. "Laurent Thévenot and the French Convention School: A Short Introduction." *Economic Sociology: European Electronic Newsletter* 5(3): 2–9.

Johnston, Josée. 2008. "The Citizen-Consumer Hybrid: Ideological Tensions and the Case of Whole Foods Market." *Theory and Society* 37: 229–270.

Kaufman, Jason, 2004. "Endogenous Explanation in the Sociology of Culture." *Annual Review of Sociology* 30: 335–357.

King, Brayden G., and Sarah A. Soule. 2007. "Social Movements as Extra-Institutional Entrepreneurs: The Effect of Protests on Stock Price Returns." *Administrative Science Quarterly* 52: 413–442.

Knorr Cetina, Karin. 2005. "The Market." *Theory, Culture and Society* 23: 552–556.

Kraatz, Matthew S., and Edward J. Zajac. 1996. "Exploring the Limits of New Institutionalism: The Causes and Consequences of Illegitimate Organizational Change." *American Sociological Review* 61: 812–836.

Krier, Dan. 1999. "Assessing the New Synthesis of Economics and Sociology: Promising Themes for Contemporary Analysis of Economic Life." *American Journal of Economics and Sociology* 58: 669–696.

Krippner, Greta R. 2001. "The Elusive Market: Embeddedness and the Paradigm of Economic Sociology." *Theory and Society* 30: 775–810.

Kunda, Gideon. 1992. *Engineering Culture: Control and Commitment in a High-Tech Corporation.* Philadelphia: Temple University Press.

Lamont, Michele. 1992. *Money, Morals, and Manners: The Culture of the French and the American Upper-Middle Class.* Chicago and London: University of Chicago Press.

Leblebici, Huseyin, Gerald R. Salancik, Anne Copay, and Tom King. 1991. "Institutional Change and the Transformation of Interorganizational Fields: An Organizational History of the U.S. Radio Broadcasting Industry." *Administrative Science Quarterly* 36: 333–363.

Levin, Peter. 2008. "Culture and Markets: How Economic Sociology Conceptualizes Culture." In Amy Binder, Mary Blair-Loy, John Evans, Kwai Ng, and Michael Schudson, eds. "Cultural Sociology and Its Diversity." *Annals of the American Academy of Political and Social Science* 619: 114–129.

Lie, John. 1997. "Sociology of Markets." *Annual Review of Sociology* 23: 341–360.

Lounsbury, Michael. 2007. "A Tale of Two Cities: Competing Logics and Practice Variation in the Professionalization of Mutual Funds." *Academy of Management Journal* 50: 289–302.

Lounsbury, Michael, and H. Rao. 2004. "Sources of Durability and Change in Market Classifications: A Study of the Reconstitution of Product Categories in the American Mutual Fund Industry, 1944–1985." *Social Forces* 82: 969–999.

Lounsbury, Michael, Marc Ventresca, and Paul Hirsch. 2003. "Social Movements, Field Frames and Industry Emergence: A Cultural-Political Perspective on U.S. Recycling." *Socio-Economic Review* 1: 71–104.

MacKenzie, Donald. 2004. "The Big, Bad Wolf and the Rational Market: Portfolio Insurance, the 1987 Crash and the Performativity of Economics." *Economy and Society* 33: 303–334.

———. 2006. *An Engine, Not a Camera: How Financial Models Shape Markets.* Cambridge, MA, and London: MIT Press.

———. 2007. "The Material Production of Virtuality: Innovation, Cultural Geography and Facticity in Derivatives Markets." *Economy and Society* 30: 355–376.

MacKenzie, Donald, and Yuval Millo. 2003. "Constructing a Market, Performing Theory: The Historical Sociology of a Financial Derivatives Exchange." *American Journal of Sociology* 109: 107–145.

Marcus, George E. 1990. "Once More into the Breach between Economic and Cultural Analysis." Pp. 331–352 in Roger Friedland and A. F. Robertson, eds. *Beyond the Marketplace: Rethinking Economy and Society.* New York: Aldine de Gruyter.

Martin, Joanne. 2002. *Organizational Culture: Mapping the Terrain.* Thousand Oaks, CA, and London: Sage.

Martin, John Levi. 1999. "The Myth of the Consumption-Oriented Economy and the Rise of the Desiring Subject." *Theory and Society* 28: 425–453.

Martinelli, Alberto, and Neil J. Smelser, eds. 1990. *Economy and Society: Overviews in Economic Sociology.* London: Sage.

Meyer, John W., and Brian Rowan. 1977. "Institutionalized Myths: Formal Structure as Myth and Ceremony." *American Journal of Sociology* 83: 340–363.

Miller, Laura J. 2006. *Reluctant Capitalists: Bookselling and the Culture of Consumption.* Chicago and London: University of Chicago Press.

Mohr, John W. 2009. "Implicit Terrains: Meaning, Measurement and Spatial Metaphors in Organizational Theory." Unpublished paper, Department of Sociology, University of California, Santa Barbara.

Mohr, John W., and Brooke Neely. 2009. "Modeling Foucault: Dualities of Power in Institutional Fields." Pp. 203–255 in Renata Meyer, Kerstin Sahlin-Andersson, Marc Ventresca and Peter Walgenbach, eds. *Instituions and Ideology*, Vol. 27, *Research in the Sociology of Organizations*. Bingley, UK: Emerald.

Mohr, John W., and Vincent Duquenne. 1997. "The Duality of Culture and Practice: Poverty Relief in New York City, 1888–1917." *Theory and Society* 26: 305–356.

Morrill, Calvin. 1995. *The Executive Way: Conflict Management in Corporations*. Chicago and London: University of Chicago Press.

O'Brien, Patricia. 1994. "Governance Systems in Steel: The American and Japanese Experience." Pp. 43–71 in J. Rogers Hollingsworth, Philippe C. Schmitter, and Wolfgang Streeck, eds. *Governing Capitalist Economies: Performance and Control of Economic Sectors*. New York and Oxford: Oxford University Press.

Ocasio, William. 1997. "Towards an Attention-Based View of the Firm." *Strategic Management Journal* 18: 187–206.

O'Sullivan, Mary, Gary Herrigel, T. J. Pempel, and Wolfgang Streeck. 2005. "Symposium on the 'Origins of Non-liberal Capitalism.'" *Socio-Economic Review* 3: 545–587.

Parsons, Talcott, and Neil J. Smelser. 1964. *Economy and Society: A Study of the Integration of Economic and Social Theory*. New York: Free Press.

Pederson, Jesper S., and Frank Dobbin. 2006. "In Search of Identity and Legitimation: Bridging Organizational Culture and Neoinstitutionalism." *American Behavioral Scientist* 49: 897–907.

Peterson, Richard A. 1979. "Revitalizing the Culture Concept." *Annual Review of Sociology* 5: 137–166.

———. 1990. "Why 1955? Explaining the Advent of Rock Music." *Popular Music* 9: 97–116.

Peterson, Richard A., and N. Anand. 2004. "The Production of Culture Perspective." *Annual Review of Sociology* 30: 311–334.

Podolny, Joel M. 1993. "A Status-Based Model of Market Competition." *American Journal of Sociology* 98: 829–872.

Polanyi, Karl. 1957a [1944]. *The Great Transformation*. Boston: Beacon Press.

———. 1957b. "The Economy as Instituted Process." Pp. 243–270 in Karl Polanyi, Conrad M. Arensberg, and Harry W. Pearson, eds. *Trade and Market in the Early Empires*. Glencoe, IL: Free Press.

Porac, Joseph, Marc Ventresca, and Yuri Mishina, 2002. "Interorganizational Cognition and Interpretation." Pp. 579–598 in J. A. C. Baum, ed. *Blackwell Companion to Organizations*. New York: Blackwell.

Powell, Walter W., and Paul DiMaggio, eds. 1991 [1983]. *The New Institutionalism in Organizational Analysis*. Chicago: University of Chicago Press.

Prasad, Monica. 1999. "The Morality of Market Exchange: Love, Money, and Contractual Justice." *Sociological Perspectives* 42: 181–214.

Pryke, Michael, and Paul DuGay. 2007. "Take an Issue: Cultural Economy and Finance." *Economy and Society* 36: 229–254.

Rao, H. 1998. "Caveat Emptor: The Construction of Nonprofit Consumer Watchdog Organizations." *American Journal of Sociology* 103: 912–961.

Reddy, William M. 1984. *The Rise of Market Culture: The Textile Trade and French Society, 1750–1900*. Cambridge, UK: Cambridge University Press.

Roy, William G. 1997. *Socializing Capital: The Rise of the Large Industrial Corporation in America*. Princeton, NJ: Princeton University Press.

Sahlins, Marshall. 1976. *Culture and Practical Reason*. Chicago and London: University of Chicago Press.

Schneiberg, Marc. 2007. "What's on the Path? Path Dependence, Organizational Diversity and the Problem of Institutional Change in the US Economy, 1900–1950." *Socio-Economic Review* 5: 47–80.

Schneiberg, Marc, and Elisabeth S. Clemens. 2006. "The Typical Tools for the Job: Research Strategies in Institutional Analysis." *Sociological Theory* 24: 195–227.

Schneiberg, Marc, Marissa King, and Thomas Smith. 2008. "Social Movements and Organizational Form: Cooperative Alternatives to Corporations in the American Insurance, Dairy, and Grain Industries." *American Sociological Review* 73: 635–667.

Shamir, Ronen. 2008. "The Age of Responsibilization: On Market-Embedded Morality." *Economy and Society* 37: 1–19.

Simons, Tal, and Paul Ingram. 1997. "Organizations and Ideology: Kibbutzim and Hired Labor, 1951–1965." *Administrative Science Quarterly* 42: 783–813.

Smelser, Neil J. 1959. "A Comparative View of Exchange Systems." *Economic Development and Cultural Change* 7: 173–182.

———. 1976. *The Sociology of Economic Life*. 2nd ed. Englewood Cliffs, NJ: Prentice Hall.

———. 1991. "The Marshall Lectures and *Economy and Society*." *Sociological Inquiry* 61: 60–67.

Smelser, Neil J., and Richard Swedberg, 1994a. "The Sociological Perspective on the Economy." Pp. 3–26 in Neil J. Smelser and Richard Swedberg, eds. *Handbook of Economic Sociology*, 1st ed. Princeton, NJ: Princeton University Press and New York: Russell Sage Foundation.

———, eds. 1994b. *The Handbook of Economic Sociology*. Princeton, NJ: Princeton University Press and New York: Russell Sage Foundation.

———, eds. 2005. *The Handbook of Economic Sociology*, 2nd ed. Princeton, NJ: Princeton University Press and New York: Russell Sage Foundation.

Smith, Charles W. 1989. *Auctions: The Social Construction of Value* New York: Free Press.

Spillman, Lyn. 1995. "Culture, Social Structure, and Discursive Fields." *Current Perspectives in Social Theory* 15: 129–154.

———. 1997. *Nation and Commemoration: Creating National Identities in the United States and Australia*. Cambridge, UK, and New York: Cambridge University Press.

———. 1999. "Enriching Exchange: Cultural Dimensions of Markets." *American Journal of Economics and Sociology* 58: 1041–1071.

———. 2007a. "Culture." Pp. 922–928 in George Ritzer, ed. *The Blackwell Encyclopedia of Sociology*, Vol. 2. Oxford: Blackwell.

———. 2007b. "'As we look ahead to the new year . . ,': Culture and Interests." *Culture* 22(1): 1–5.

———. 2008. "Cultural Sociology and Its Others." *Culture* 22(2): 1–4

———. 2009. "A Special Camaraderie with Colleagues: Business Associations and Cultural Production for Economic Action." Pp. 17–43 in Isaac Reed and Jeffrey Alexander, eds. *Meaning and Method: The Cultural Approach to Sociology*. Yale Series in Cultural Sociology. Boulder, CO: Paradigm Publishers.

———. Forthcoming. *Solidarity in Strategy: Making Business Meaningful in American Trade Associations*. Chicago: University of Chicago Press.

Spillman, Lyn, and Russell Faeges. 2004. "Nations." Pp. 409–437 in Julia Adams, Elisabeth S. Clemens, and Ann Shola Orloff, eds. *Remaking Modernity: Politics and Processes in Historical Sociology*. Durham, NC: Duke University Press.

Spillman, Lyn, and Michael Strand. Forthcoming. "Interest-Oriented Action." *Annual Review of Sociology*.

Stillerman, Joel. 2004. "Gender, Class and Generational Contexts for Consumption in Contemporary Chile." *Journal of Consumer Culture* 4: 51–78.

Stinchcombe, Arthur. 1983. *Economic Sociology*. New York: Academic Press.

Strang, David, and John W. Meyer. 1993. "Institutional Conditions for Diffusion." *Theory and Society* 22: 487–511.

Swedberg, Richard. 1994. "Markets as Social Structures." Pp. 255–282 in Neil J. Smelser and Richard Swedberg, eds. *The Handbook of Economic Sociology*, 1st ed. Princeton, NJ: Princeton University Press and New York: Russell Sage Foundation.

———. 1998. *Max Weber and the Idea of Economic Sociology*. Princeton, NJ: Princeton University Press.

———. 2003. *Principles of Economic Sociology*. Princeton, NJ, and Oxford: Princeton University Press.

———. 2004. "What Has Been Accomplished in New Economic Sociology and Where Is It Heading?" *European Journal of Sociology* 45: 317–330.

Thévenot, Laurent. 2001. "Organized Complexity: Conventions of Coordination and the Composition of Economic Arrangements." *European Journal of Social Theory* 4: 405–425.

Thornton, Patricia H. 2001. "Personal Versus Market Logics of Control: A Historically Contingent Theory of the Risk of Acquisition." *Organization Science* 12: 294–311.

———. 2002. "The Rise of the Corporation in a Craft Industry: Conflict and Conformity in Institutional Logics." *Academy of Management Journal* 45: 81–101.

———. 2004. *Markets from Culture: Institutional Logics and Organizational Decisions in Higher Education Publishing*. Stanford, CA: Stanford University Press.

Thornton Patricia H., and William Ocasio. 1999. "Institutional Logics and the Historical Contingency of Power in Organizations: Succession in the Higher Education Publishing Industry, 1958–1990." *American Journal of Sociology* 105: 801–843.

Thrift, Nigel. 2001. "'It's the Romance, not the Finance That Makes Business Worth Pursuing': Disclosing New Market Culture." *Economy and Society* 30: 412–432.

———. 2006. "Re-Inventing Invention: New Tendencies in Capitalist Commodification." *Economy and Society* 35: 279–306.

Trigilia, Carlo. 2002. *Economic Sociology: State, Market, and Society in Modern Capitalism*. Trans. Nicola Owtram. Oxford and Malden, MA: Blackwell.

Uzzi, Brian. 1996. "The Sources and Consequences of Embeddedness for the Economic Performance of Organizations: The Network Effect." *American Sociological Review* 61: 674–698.

———. 1997. "Social Structure and Competition in Interfirm Networks: The Paradox of Embeddedness." *Administrative Science Quarterly* 42: 35–67.

———. 1999. "Embeddedness in the Making of Financial Capital: How Social Relations and Networks Benefit Firms Seeking Finance." *American Sociological Review* 64: 481–505.

Uzzi, Brian, and Ryon Lancaster. 2004. "Embeddedness and Price Formation in the Corporate Law Market." *American Sociological Review* 69: 319–344.

Van Maanen, John, and Stephen R. Barley. 1984. "Occupational Communities: Culture and Control in Organizations." *Research in Organizational Behavior* 6: 287–365.

Vaughn, Diane. 2002. "Signals and Interpretive Work: The Role of Culture in a Theory of Practical Action." Pp. 21–54 in Karen Cerulo, ed. *Culture in Mind: Toward a Sociology of Culture and Cognition*. New York: Routledge.

Weber Klaus, Kathryn L. Heinze, and Michaela DeSoucey. 2008. "Forage for Thought: Mobilizing Codes in the Movement for Grass-fed Meat and Dairy Products." *Administrative Science Quarterly* 53: 529–567.

Weber, Max. 1978 [1922]. *Economy and Society: An Outline of Interpretive Sociology*, 2 vols. Eds. Guenther Roth and Claus Wittich. Berkeley and Los Angeles: University of California Press.

———. 1998 [1904]. *The Protestant Ethic and the Spirit of Capitalism*, 2nd ed. Los Angeles: Roxbury.

Wherry, Fred. 2008a. *Global Markets and Local Crafts: Thailand and Costa Rica Compared.* Baltimore: Johns Hopkins University Press.

———. 2008b. "The Social Characterization of Price: The Fool, the Faithful, the Frivolous, and the Frugal." *Sociological Theory* 26: 363–379.

White, Harrison C. 1981. "Where Do Markets Come From?" *American Journal of Sociology* 87: 517–547.

———. 2000. "Modeling Discourse In and Around Markets." *Poetics* 27: 117–133.

———. 2002a. *Markets from Networks: Socioeconomic Models of Production.* Princeton, NJ: Princeton University Press.

———. 2002b. "Cognition in Social Constructions: Market Rivalry Profile Versus Cost Schedule." Pp. 101–121 in Karen C. Cerulo, ed. *Culture in Mind: Toward a Sociology of Culture and Cognition.* New York and London: Routledge.

Yakubovich, Valery, Mark Granovetter, and Patrick McGuire. 2005. "Electric Charges: The Social Construction of Rate Systems." *Theory and Society* 34: 578–612.

Zajac, Edward J., and James D. Westphal. 2004a. "The Social Construction of Market Value: Institutionalization and Learning Perspectives on Stock Market Reactions." *American Sociological Review* 69: 433–457.

———. 2004b. "Should Sociological Theories Venture into 'Economic Territory?' Yes!" *American Sociological Review* 60: 466–471.

Zaloom, Caitlin M. 2006. *Out of the Pits: Traders and Technology from Chicago to London.* Chicago: University of Chicago Press.

Zelizer, Viviana A. 1983. *Morals and Markets: The Development of Life Insurance in the United States.* New Brunswick, NJ: Transaction.

———. 1988. "Beyond the Polemics on the Market: Establishing a Theoretical and Empirical Agenda." *Sociological Forum* 3: 614–634.

———. 1994. *The Social Meaning of Money.* New York: Basic Books.

———. 1999. "Multiple Markets: Multiple Cultures." Pp. 193–212 in Neil J. Smelser and Jeffrey C. Alexander, eds. *Diversity and Its Discontents: Cultural Conflict and Common Ground in Contemporary American Society.* Princeton, NJ: Princeton University Press.

———. 2002. "Enter Culture." Pp. 101–125 in Mauro F. Guillén, Randall Collins, Paula England, and Marshall Meyer, eds. *The New Economic Sociology: Developments in an Emerging Field.* New York: Russell Sage Foundation.

———. 2004. "Circuits of Commerce." Pp. 122–144 in Jeffrey C. Alexander, Gary T. Marx, and Christine L. Williams, eds. *Self, Social Structure, and Beliefs: Explorations in Sociology.* Berkeley and Los Angeles: University of California Press.

———. 2005a. "Culture and Consumption." Pp. 331–354 in Neil J. Smelser and Richard Swedberg, eds. *The Handbook of Economic Sociology*, 2nd ed. New York: Russell Sage Foundation and Princeton, NJ, and Oxford: Princeton University Press.

———. 2005b. *The Purchase of Intimacy.* Princeton, NJ, and Oxford: Princeton University Press.

Zuckerman, Ezra W. 1999. "The Categorical Imperative: Securities Analysts and the Illegitimacy Discount." *American Journal of Sociology* 104: 1398–1438.

———. 2004. "Structural Incoherence and Stock Market Activity." *American Sociological Review* 69: 405–432.

PART III

THE POLITICAL AS CULTURE

FROM MORAL SENTIMENTS TO CIVIC ENGAGEMENT: SOCIOLOGICAL ANALYSIS AS RESPONSIBLE SPECTATORSHIP

ROBIN WAGNER-PACIFICI

SOCIOLOGY as a discipline has always been situated in the epistemological borderland between the sciences and humanities. Over the decades, arguments have gone back and forth. There are those who claim the goal of the discipline is to discover "laws," make predictions, quantify reality, and develop formal models. Surveys of the field highlight the dominance of this scientific model for sociology. The rise of cultural sociology since the 1980s can be understood, in part, as a way for those concerned with *meaning* to produce intellectual work aligned with that model. In these studies, meaning is linked to cognition and to processes of institutionalization, and it is measured. The rise of the comparative method and the push for an explanation (as opposed to an interpretation), even in case study research, is also emblematic of this movement.

What I want to argue in this chapter is for an entirely different understanding of the goals of cultural sociology. The accommodation with science and with accounting for outcomes has come at the expense of hermeneutic sensitivity. The time has come to place interpretative sensibility higher on our list of priorities. So my call will be for a different subject position, that of the "spectator," to replace that of the "social scientist." The role of the spectator has definite political and aesthetic roots and resonances that require elaboration. I will further argue that greater attention needs to be given to the act of writing and to the textual reconstruction of situations and settings. The dream of cultural sociology should be of fidelity: to moods and experiences; to locations and dramas; and to the truth of experience, however fleeting or ineffable. This fidelity can come through the careful act of witnessing.

My argument here is not entirely original. I show that it can be situated in a venerable tradition. I track back to the works of Adam Smith and follow the threads leading from his writings to build the case for a new kind of cultural sociology. Although I do not claim this is the only thing cultural sociologists should be doing; I do suggest some important lessons need to be taken on board if cultural sociology is to continue to flourish.

The specter of the "invisible hand" appears in both major philosophical works of the Scottish Enlightenment intellectual, Adam Smith. It appears first in Smith's *The Theory of Moral Sentiments* and then, more consequentially, in his later work, *The Wealth of Nations*. In both (dis)appearances, this invisible hand alchemically transforms the actions of self-interested individuals into mutually beneficial social arrangements—literally behind their backs. Society as a whole benefits from each individual following his or her self-interest. The image of an invisible hand with transcendent overtones is a powerful one. But it also suggests a world in which the very states of visibility and invisibility are worthy of consideration. While Adam Smith is perhaps better known for *The Wealth of Nations*, with its paeans to the free market, this essay will draw from his careful construction of the very concept of the "visible" and the "invisible" in his more explicitly moral-philosophical study, *The Theory of Moral Sentiments*. In that study, Smith works to understand the important role of spectatorship in the development of morality. And spectatorship is fundamentally concerned with relationships between visibility and invisibility, with those who are seen and those who see.

In my own study of the endings of military conflicts, *The Art of Surrender: Decomposing Sovereignty at Conflict's End*, I discovered how important a role spectators play, both official and unofficial. The official witnesses to the ending of war, for example, "are held to observe the actions of other, more central, actors who are the protagonists of social and historical progress and transformation.... These figures do not simply watch. They ratify and notarize. They escort the principals to sites of exchange and transition. They comment on events, evoking and interpreting them for those not present.... Thus [I came to understand] we must also read history through the eyes of those who bear witness to it."[1]

My commitment to the idea of the centrality of witnesses is neither unique nor original. It was indeed Smith who, in *The Theory of Moral Sentiments*, built a theory of social morality around the figure of the "impartial spectator." Here I want to think anew about the paradoxical centrality of the spectator. And I want to propose that we think anew about the figure of the sociologist as, precisely, a spectator. It may actually be the case that we sociologists do not yet have a sufficient understanding of what spectatorship consists of, and, thus, we cannot do full justice either to our roles as spectators or to the people, institutions, and events that we observe.

What did Smith have in mind with his idea of the "impartial spectator"? Preoccupied, as were other philosophers of the time, with the possibilities of sympathy between individuals, Smith developed the figure of the spectator as one who is able to put him or herself in the position of another. He or she regards the actions, reactions, and emotions of others—with sympathy for those who suffer, approbation and gratefulness for those who alleviate the suffering of others, and resentment for those who cause the suffering of others. Most of all, the spectator *judges* others and, in a symmetrical manner, casting an eye on his or her own actions, judges him or herself: "When I endeavour to pass sentence upon [this action of mine], and either to approve or condemn it, it is evident that in all such cases, I divide myself, as it were, into two persons; and that I, the examiner and judge, represent a different character from that other I, the person whose conduct is examined into and judged of."[2] The individual becomes witness to him or herself.

This internal split—the actor who carries within his or her own internal spectator—has come down to us through the centuries since Adam Smith theorized it in his understanding of moral sentiments. It has made appearances in various disciplinary idioms; now as the Freudian tri-partite id, superego, and ego and George Herbert Mead's I and Me. In all cases, the split suggests the possibility of alternating perspectives and of dialogue (dialogue even at the core of the individual self). In this essay, the preoccupation is less with the fact of the internal split itself than with what the foregrounding of the spectatorial role in Smith's theorem suggests about the immanent possibilities of sociological spectatorship. In other words I want to build on Smith's concept of the "impartial spectator," and I want to transpose it into a sociological idiom rather than one of moral philosophy. In examining these possibilities, four initial problems present themselves, and I will take on these problems in turn. They include: (1) the problem of the alleged distinction between action and observation; (2) the problem of identifying appropriate objects of observation or, in other words, of identifying the appropriate "spectacle"; (3) the problems of perspective, proximity, and recognizability; and finally, (4) the problem of the modes of transmission of the observations and reflections of the spectator. In conclusion, I will attempt to connect these issues regarding the spectator to the logical impossibility of sociology understood as the discipline responsible to the present. Notwithstanding this logical impossibility, we nevertheless push on asymptotically toward this goal, and I'll try to indicate how.

PROBLEM 1: THE ALLEGED DISTINCTION BETWEEN ACTION AND SPECTATORSHIP

Traditional thinking about the contrast between active and contemplative stances toward the world might incline one to pit social spectatorship against social action. Just track the verbs in Michael Burawoy's mobilizing "Public Sociology," his personal statement for candidacy for the presidency of the American Sociological Association in 2002: "As mirror and conscience of society, sociology must *define, promote* and *inform* public debate about deepening class and racial inequalities, new gender regimes, environmental degradation, market fundamentalism, state and non-state violence. I believe that the world needs public sociology—a sociology that transcends the academy—more than ever. Our potential publics are multiple, ranging from media audiences to policy makers, from silenced minorities to social movements. They are local, global, and national. As public sociology *stimulates* debate in all these contexts, it *inspires* and *revitalizes* our discipline. In return, theory and research give legitimacy, direction, and substance to public sociology. Teaching is equally central to public sociology: students are our first public for they carry sociology into all walks of life. Finally, the critical imagination, *exposing* the gap between what is and what could be, *infuses* values into public sociology to remind us that the *world could be different.*"[3] These verbs are active, to be sure, but unspecific. The material on which they work, and the ways in which they do it, are generic to a fault—the academy, media audiences, silenced minorities, and students on the one hand; stimulation, inspiration, and promotion on the other. While the initial image of a mirror indicates a definitive role for reflection, the subsequent verbs of action leap into the fray. Alternatively, in reinvigorating the concept of the sociologist as spectator, and of spectatorship, or witnessing, *as* action, we might just redirect attention away from these verbs of action and their anticipated publics. We might examine the specific mechanisms and modalities of sociological perceptions and mediations themselves. In doing so, we need to take very seriously the reality that all perception is always mediated or, in a more Smithian type of idiom (as will be examined shortly), always indirect. Perceptions materialize through the mediations of language and images, the mediations of inherited forms of aesthetic composition, the mediations of extant models of social interaction and organization, and through what Frederic Jameson called "the political unconscious." And perceptions are inflected by emotions (something Smith was keenly interested in). So there is no unmediated perception. In this sense, Adam Smith didn't need Foucault to tell him that the *spectacle is already inside the spectator.*

Problem 2: Identifying the Appropriate Objects of Observation, Identifying the Appropriate "Spectacle"

If we continue to transpose Smith's *moral spectator* onto the image of the *sociological spectator*, what is it that this spectator should attend to? What or whom should be the objects of observation? British sociologist John Holmwood agrees with Burawoy that "civil society is the distinctive object domain of sociology" (in contrast to the market or the state), but wants sociology to constitute a contested "field" in its interpretations of that domain.[4] Jeffrey Alexander takes this mandate to examine civil society seriously in his magisterial book, *The Civil Sphere*. It is particularly in this book's idea/ideal of the civil sphere in democratic societies, with its ambition toward universality, that the link to Smith is highlighted: "[A] collectivity so constituted supports a civil sphere only to the degree that collective self-consciousness can extend so widely and deeply that it can, in principle, include as full members every grouping and individual composing it."[5] Such universal inclusion (even if only every theoretical) requires the contingent possibility that all members could, in theory, change places with all others.

Thus, the division of individuals into spectators and actors is always provisional and never existential. The French sociologist, Luc Boltanski, described Adam Smith's system of subject positions in the following way: "a model, or a structure, that is a system of places comprising positions whose occupants are not specified....Each anticipates how he will be imagined by the other and the compositions of these anticipations generate an equilibrium...."[6] Thus, it is this *system* of positions, with its theoretical interchangeability, or reversibility, that makes the spectator possible. Further, the observed actors and reactors know they are being watched—both by themselves in terms of their own internal "impartial spectators" and in terms of those others who are temporarily in the position of spectator. In the context of recent historical experiences of oscillation between governmental hypersurveillance on the one side and extreme secrecy on the other, at least in the United States, we sociologists should take solace from studies revealing stolid and persistent government transparency in certain administrative agencies. Here the connection that merits consideration is that between spectatorship and oversight. One such study is concerned with the steadily disclosure-oriented work of bureaucrats such as the U.S. government's Inspector General currently being carried out by Michael Schudson. Schudson argues that in spite of scandals, secrecy, and surveillance, the United States' political culture has tended toward an ever-more convinced transparency.[7] In a similar manner, Alexander highlights the usually overlooked role of the political "office" when questions of civil society are raised: "When solidarity is more expansive, and the pressures of 'society' become more explicit and powerful, office becomes an outpost of civil society directly inside the state....The moral obligation is to wield power on behalf of others."[8] These studies demonstrate the obdurate effectiveness of officially allocated and licensed spectators, even in a less than transparent historical moment.

So the impartial spectator must be outside the spectacle in order to bear witness to it (officials charged with oversight are paradoxically obliged to be outside the spectacle while embedded within it). But such a positioning must be reversible and provisional. The spectator's sympathy derives from his or her ability to enter the body and mind of those observed, the ability to exchange places.

PROBLEM 3: PERSPECTIVE, PROXIMITY, AND RECOGNIZABILITY

These qualifications raise important problems of location, perspective, and identification. If Burawoy has focused on the why and what of sociology, I am concerned more with the where, when, and how of it. If spectatorship is understood as a very specific kind of action, one that is implicated by design in the social spectacle under observation, we cannot understand the relationship between the spectator and the observed as essentially dyadic in nature. Rather these actors, or subject positions, exist in a web of relations, one that I designate a web of cross-witnessing.[9] Thus, the spectator observes agents acting and acted upon. The spectator recounts and reimagines the agents and their fates to others, thereby drawing in new witnesses, new third parties. The spectator thus remains in the transmission business. All of this action of observation, identification, and transmission is understood by Smith as establishing a dynamic system of direct and indirect sympathies. Smith writes: "As our sense, therefore, of the propriety of conduct arises from what I shall call a *direct sympathy* with the affections and motives of the person who acts, so our sense of its merit arises from what I shall call an *indirect sympathy* with the gratitude of the person who is, if I may say so, acted upon."[10]

Recognitions and loci of identification thus keep shifting, and they are only able to do so because an idea of *distance* inserts itself into the schema. This distance is critical, not incidental, for judgments and comparisons. It may be material distance that provides an angle of vision onto the observed; and it may be conceptual or psychological distance that provides the space of separation between the different selves and between self as actor and the self as impartial spectator. At its most geometric, the system described keeps generating third parties, whose vision is always imagined to be recalibrating the distances and observations we make toward a goal of just judgments: "We must view [the interests of others] neither from our own place nor yet from his, neither with our own eyes nor yet with his, but from the place and with the eyes of a third person, who has no particular connexion with either, and who judges with impartiality between us. This is the only station from which both can be seen at equal distances, or from which any proper comparison can be made between them."[11] The eyes of a third person, a perhaps yet unencountered witness or interlocutor, are always to be taken into consideration in this system of positions.

I quote at length from Smith here to give an idea of how careful he was to establish this system of direct and indirect sympathies and judgments as he developed his theory of moral sentiments. Sociology has a structurally analogous set of problems with its own observational perspectives, claims, and evaluations. Where is the locus of sociology? The conundrums associated with this question derive first from sociology's institutional and organizational embeddedness in academia and academic roles (suggesting some kind of interested implication in the institution of academia itself); second, from sociology's spatial distance from its subjects of observation and analysis; and third, from sociology's temporal distance from them as even a discipline impossibly focused on the social formations and interactions of the present seeks to grasp interactions and relationships that are quickly receding into the past.

Adam Smith's preoccupations with the human capacities for sympathy, spectatorship, and reversibility pushed him to consider the limit case—moral sentiments at the greatest imaginable distance. He wrote: "All men, even those at the greatest DISTANCE, are no doubt entitled to our good wishes, and our good wishes we naturally give them. But if, notwithstanding, they should be unfortunate, to give ourselves any anxiety upon that account, seems to be no part of our duty. That we should be but little interested, therefore, in the fortune of those whom we can neither serve nor hurt, and who are in every respect so very remote from us, seems wisely ordered by Nature...."[12] As will be noted below, technologies of communication and transportation and political epistemes of universal civil societies, have expanded the zones of possible spectatorial interest beyond Smith's moral and material imaginings.

Sociological spectators differentially make the case for choosing a particular institutional, spatial, and temporal distance from their subjects largely by adopting diverse methodologies of participant observation, ethnography, large-scale surveys, archival analysis, and mathematical modeling of society. Ongoing debates about the values and effectiveness of these differential positionings raise important questions about what actually happens when these chosen distances are achieved. Don't these delineated distances create as many problems as they resolve? For example, they reveal the problem of the appropriateness of perspective—how close up, how distant a vantage point? How many things should be included in the view; what should be the extent of the frame? How many things should be excluded as irrelevant? What kind of attention should be given to the surface, to impressions or even "impression management" (in Goffman's famous phrase); what kind of an attempt should be made to get beneath this surface? These potential perspectival peregrinations reveal some of the costs and benefits of familiarity, among other things. An ability to switch places with the subjects of sociological spectatorship might seem to derive from experiential familiarity. But the sympathy of the spectator that benefits from this ability to "switch places" with the observed seems less threatened by a literal inability to be familiar with those far away than by the contradictory demand of *defamiliarization* (both theoretical and methodological) required to make theoretically sophisticated sociological sense.

The great Italian historian Carlo Ginzburg has examined questions of the relationship between spectatorship, distance, and perspective in his recent book, *Wooden Eyes: Nine Reflections on Distance.* He reflects on the way in which writers such as Tolstoy sought to overcome assumptions about reality and sought to look at things as if they had no meaning, "as if they were a riddle." Reality's availability is elusive, and defamiliarization aids the observer by revealing assumptions about reality to be obstacles to truth. Focus comes after being stopped in one's tracks by incomprehension. Different writers take different paths toward this "truth," however, and style matters quite a bit. For example, Ginzburg contrasts Tolstoy's penetrations with Proust's impressionism: "Proust seems in some ways to have the opposite end in view—to be trying to preserve the freshness of appearances against the intrusion of ideas, by presenting things 'in the order of perception' and still uncontaminated by causal explanations....The results however are quite different: in [Tolstoy's] case, social and moral critique, and in [Proust's] an impressionistic immediacy."[13] Sociologists need to be aware of the different stakes and claims accompanying such choices, the powers of moral critique, and the powers of transmitting an impression.

PROBLEM 4: MODES OF TRANSMISSION

Identifying authorial stylistic differences forces us to attend to style in sociological spectatorship and transmission. The modes of observation and the modes of transmission are every bit as crucial as the dualistic abilities to sympathize and defamiliarize. So we need to be self-conscious about our modes of transmission. Decisions we make about style will depend on goals of transmission (provocation, contemplation, mobilization). It will also depend on whether we believe that truth lives on surfaces and impressions, like Proust, or if it lives underneath the surface, like Tolstoy. And then there is the critical question of genre: What are our instruments of sociological conveyance? Do we write essays, scientific reports, articles, books, or dossiers? Do we draft tables or charts or generate other kinds of images? Do we participate in hybrid projects, part academic, part judicial, or part criminological, for example, by writing legal briefs or police reports. We sociological spectators must understand these different mediations in terms of their different capacities—what they can and cannot conjure and how they do it. Can they conjure temporality, for example? And to be more precise, is the temporality they can conjure that of sequence, that of duration, that of causality, or that of simultaneity? Each of these temporalities reveals different angles of vision on social life. And each thus conjures a different social order, or different aspects of a social order.

Pressing further here, eloquence is itself something to be taken seriously, not to be dismissed as unscientific or disarming. Sociologists, such as Luc Boltanski and Andrew Abbott, have reflected on the functions and resonances of eloquence in ways that I think actually take the spectatorial vision of sociology quite seriously. Boltanski writes about the perception of suffering "at a distance," that is, suffering perceived via mass mediations like the newspaper and the television, and he examines the theoretical and political consequences of a politics of pity in his book *Distant Suffering*. Working through the complex relations of the spectator and sufferer, considering the pull of an identifiable single sufferer and the necessity of generalization for all politics, including a politics of pity, he refuses to minimize the effect of style. "Pity," he writes, "generalizes in order to deal with distance, and, in order to generalize, becomes eloquent, recognizing and discovering itself as emotion and feeling."[14] Boltanski effectively recuperates *eloquence* as a sociological desideratum, even (perhaps especially) for sociology at a distance. In a recent article, Andrew Abbott makes a similar move with his prolegomenon for a "lyrical sociology." Abbott seeks to shift attention away from narrative, with its intrinsic investment in linear causality and diachrony. He claims a role, instead, for a lyrical stance in sociological writing, one that is engaged, and rooted (or located), in a particular place and at a particular time. He writes that the lyrical is "momentary.... It is not about an outcome. It is not about something happening. It is about something that *is*, a state of being."[15] He includes in this category of writing such works as historian E. P. Thompson's *The Making of the English Working Class*, anthropologist Malinoski's *Argonauts of the Western Pacific*, and sociologist Michael Bell's

Childerley, all of which are, in spite of their differing subjects, vivid and engaged attempts to image up particular moments of time and the actors found there. Abbott highlights a paradox at the heart of this conjuring of the present that is part of sociology's mandate to represent the present: "Paradoxically, the best representations of historical passage as a phenomenon are not plots, not sequences of events, but rather the momentary Bergsonian durations of tensed time, which are always centered on a particular, indexical present."[16] In other words, there are more or less effective ways to transmit this witnessing of the passing present.

Abbott and Ginzburg, and Boltanski make us pay attention to the varying relations between stylistic choices and spectatorial purview. Does one aim to reveal something, to bring it to life, to make connections apparent that were not previously clear, or, alternatively, primarily to identify causes? Abbott claims that the aim of identifying causes drives the forms of sociological *narratives*, but that not all sociology can or should traffic in causality. The differences among aims do matter and ultimately demonstrate the significance of what might be called the aesthetic aspect of the sociological imagination. If the sociological spectator is a mirror for society (Burawoy's term), sociologists need to take seriously the theories of mimesis. In other words, there is no way to understand the sociologist as spectator without understanding how perception and transmission are bound up with representation.

So to recap the argument: Responsible sociological spectatorship draws from the same moral philosophical grounding as Smith's theory of the "impartial spectator" in its claims of sympathy and subject position reversibility. It must also become representationally responsible, in other words responsible to understanding the reality shaping consequences of modes of perception, mediation, and transmission of sociological ideas. Can these two kinds of responsibility simply piggy-back on each other? Do they not, rather, highlight a contradiction identified earlier, between the sympathetic knowing of the "other" in Smith's world and the adamant "unknowing" of the other in the defamiliarized sociological world? In slightly different words, how do disinterestedness, judgment, engagement, and intervention interact in the sociological project?

In this final section of the essay, I will try to undertake these apparent counter-indications in the idea of sociology as responsible spectatorship. I will do so by offering a few novel ideas about legitimate spectatorial opportunities for sociologists. And I do so, precisely, by examining the specificities of the scenes chosen for sociological analysis and by identifying the capacities of the modes of representation chosen to transmit these scenes to other spectators.

I'll start by stating the obvious. It is hard to capture states of being, and it is equally hard to capture movement from one state of being to another. So, one way to be theoretically and methodologically honest about these difficulties is to take them on directly. Just as Boltanski and Abbott have parsed the differences among genre choices for their individual capacities, I too want to focus on genre choices. I will propose some unusual genre choices as particularly effective for revealing and resolving the difficulties in capturing states of being and movement between them. Another way to think about these genre choices is that they help get us closer to that impossible idea that sociology as a discipline makes its intervention in the present. The social ambit and significance of the scenes conjured up range from the everyday to the momentous. But none of the scenes are banal, most certainly not those of the everyday. Diverging from normal sociological approaches, the focus has to shift in two ways: first, from discourse and discursive argumentation to *images and scenes*, and second, from an interest in action and interaction to a focus on *inaction*.

With all of its "great blooming, buzzing confusion," in William James' famous phrase, society often appears obdurate and unmovable. Such congealings can take the form of boring repetition in which nothing ever seems to change, of ritual in which the past is evoked in order to make it live again, or of startled pauses in which a transformation seems imminent and time is needed in order to absorb the revelation. Getting a handle on pauses, frozen moments, and temporary congealments presents its own challenges. While sociologists have developed tools for analyzing the dynamism of action and interaction, they have not, with few exceptions, been sufficiently concerned to understand the embodiments and informings of stillness, tedium, or revealed moments (or what I'm calling here inaction) that may have their own power.

Here, theories of representation that focus on pictorial images can be usefully interrogated. Images, unlike discursive texts, can present a scene "all at once." In his famous treatise on the difference between poetry and painting, Gotthold Lessing wrote that "painting, with regard to compositions in which the objects are co-existent, can only avail itself of one moment of action, and must therefore choose that which is the most pregnant, and by which what has gone before and what is to follow will be most intelligible."[17] The co-existence of objects involves both temporal and spatial simultaneity, and only those spectators positioned correctly can take in an artistic image in a moment. Unlike texts, which are fatally dependent on language's linearity and thus the kind of implicit transformational syntax of cause and effect that Abbott critiques when he takes on narrative, images can thus appear outside of time or capture one moment of time.

A few scholars have pushed further to theorize the relationship between developments in the visual arts and developments in social and political organization, cognition, and space. For example, from the field of International Relations, John Gerard Ruggie has linked the invention of single-point perspective to the possibilities and imperatives of single-fixed viewpoints—thus to the development of the modern state: "What was true in the visual arts was equally true in politics: political space came to be defined as it appeared from a single fixed viewpoint. The concept of sovereignty, then, was merely the doctrinal counterpart of the application of single-point perspectival forms to the spatial organization of politics."[18] The phrase "the spatial organization of politics" should not be taken lightly or only metaphorically. The exploration of the possibilities of sociological spectatorship being developed here has everything to do with specificities of space and spatial relationships. Distance and proximity, visibility and invisibility, depth analysis and impression management, all are fundamentally a function of spatial relationships.

There are a number of new theories of iconology being developed to rethink the work of images, and the spectator is always an important figure in them. And, not surprisingly, we find questions of spectatorial proximity and involvement to be key. Art historian Michael Fried has highlighted the critical moment of realist painting, what he calls the moment of the "magic of absorption" at the end of the sixteenth century, when painters represented figures literally absorbed in their own activities. Such paintings actually worked to *deny* the presence of any beholder outside the composed scene, including the spectator of the painting. The absorption of the represented actors in their everyday lives of family and work guaranteed a nontheatrical vision of reality, a reality that proceeds with or without a spectator. In his analyses, Fried alludes to a deep ambivalence about spectatorship in society. We need spectators and the knowledge of them to engage in the reflections and reversals that Smith imagines as the core of a system of moral sentiments. Yet we sociological spectators also imagine a social world that proceeds on its own in order for us to capture its reality. It is only by way of such imagining that the spectator can be certain that the subjects are not "acting" for his or her benefit. Fried quotes Wittgenstein: "Nothing could be more remarkable than seeing someone who thinks himself unobserved engaged in some quite simple everyday activity....We should be seeing life itself."[19] Such a scene caught up in its own autonomy functions as what Fried calls the "near-documentary mode," as true of contemporary photographs as of sixteenth- century genre paintings. Issues of proximity and involvement remain key—how close up should we get to examine a scene and what distance brings most of a scene's elements and relationships to light? Are we as equipped to capture its stillness as we are to capture its dynamism (its causal history, extended meaning, and trajectory)? Can we recognize the structure of relations that take shape? Can we illustrate for others that "moment" of stillness, inaction, or revelation? Of course, we do not anticipate a sociological painting in a concrete sense, but some of the works Abbott calls lyrical float resonant images in their discursive rivers. While less felicitous than the lyrical harmonics in the works described by Abbott, the "maps" of network analysis (the dark blobs of intersecting circuits), may serve as rudimentary snapshots of webs of relations at particular moments of time or, we could say, *hypostasized* moments of time. Most important here, it is possible to imagine a sociological version of Adam Smith's system of interchangeable positions and direct and indirect vectors of sympathy.

On the other end of the continuum from the everyday are scenes that are poised on the edge of dramatic transformation. These are scenes of liminality in which there is anticipation of imminent movement from one state of being to another. But the movement can only be implied and never grasped. Communications scholar Barbie Zelizer has developed a study of a series of these kinds of scenes that appear with remarkable frequency in news reports—what she calls "about to die" images. The most famous, perhaps, is that taken by photographer Eddie Adams of the impending shooting of a suspected Viet Cong soldier by a South Vietnamese colonel during the Vietnam War. This photo is transfixing because it bears witness to the impossibility of capturing the moment of death or the moment of any action indeed. It's a photo that grabs our attention and simultaneously shuts us out. The photo takes us to the brink of transformation but reminds us of the elusiveness of the present. As Zelizer writes: "The about-to-die image differs [from images of death] in that it centers not on the finality of death but on its possibility and, conversely, its impossibility."[20] Such images also reminds us of the dualism of all representation, where some things can be communicated by some mediations, and other things will necessarily remain out of sight or out of reach. Thus, we experience the impossibility of complete "sympathy" to use Smith's terms.

Nevertheless, the network of sympathy evoked by a system of spectatorially derived moral sentiments, provides a surprising range of emotional experiences. Smith allows that sympathy so developed can even extend to the dead; those who are, in fact, themselves now beyond the realm of the experiential: "If the injured should perish in the quarrel, we not only sympathize with the real resentment of his friends and relations, but with the imaginary resentment which in fancy we lend to the dead, who is no longer capable of feeling that or any other human sentiment. But as we put ourselves in his situation, as we enter, as it were, into his body, and in our imaginations, in some measure, animate anew the deformed and mangled carcass of the slain, when we bring home in this manner his case to our own bosoms, we feel upon this, as upon many other occasions, an emotion which the person principally concerned is incapable of feeling, and which yet we feel by an illusive sympathy with him."[21] Here, as in the entire discussion of his developing theory of moral sentiments, the sympathy of the spectator consists of a combination of judgment and emotion. Such a focus returns us to sociological spectatorship—its possibilities and its limitations.

So far, I've staked out a certain territory for sociological analysis as responsible spectatorship in the epistemological sense—what vantage points, perspectives, and representations do and how they do it. What about in the moral, or normative, sense? How does our spectatorship participate in making normative judgments in the ways that the concept of "public sociology" proposes? Judgment must occur in order for the sociological critical imagination to, in Burawoy's words, "remind us that the *world could be different*."

But theorists, such as Boltanski and Abbott, explicitly exclude judgment from their chosen projects (a politics of pity for the former, a lyrical sociology for the latter). They make a claim that in order to apprehend or engage the moment, or the present, there needs to be a suspension of judgment. Judgment requires a past and demands a future (even one that is utopian). Interestingly and surprisingly, Adam Smith would seem to agree. The judgments of the impartial spectator occur before and after actions. He writes: "There are two different occasions upon which we examine our own conduct, and endeavour to view it in the light in which the impartial spectator would view it: first, *when we are about to act;* and secondly, after we have acted."[22] Of course, my "about to act" moment may be your moment of action. My past may have been your "about to act" moment—and so on and so forth. Thus, we are all spectators of ourselves and of each other, living in intersecting time frames and action frameworks.

Some sociologists might object to the focus on disciplinary spectatorship, distance, vision, and transmission proposed in this essay. They might criticize the interpretive modality and the emphasis on writing as singular rather than generalizable forms of knowledge. As well, certain methodologies, such as ethnography or case studies, seem to be privileged over surveys or comparative analyses in this focus. Further, an implicit preference for "lyrical" writing to capture and transmit the moments of vision, sympathy, and revelation might be criticized as requiring skills of a different order than those best serving the social scientific enterprise. And finally, the activist orientation of the public sociologist might seem to be deactivated by the suspension of judgment in the apprehension of the cross-witnessed system of positions.

In response to such objections, I would argue for the fundamental necessity of a sociological understanding of the roles and tasks of spectators or witnesses. These roles and practices cannot simply be assumed, taken for granted, or reduced to the elimination of methodological flaws. The tensions between familiarity and de-familiarization, proximity and distance, and observation and action can be productive ones for sociologists. They provide what Hannah Arendt called the "interspace" that both separates and brings together individuals engaged in a common political project. The point is that a responsible sociological spectatorship should find ways of analytically grasping diverse social states of being, different perspectives, direct and indirect sympathies, and mediating representations—if for no other reason than to make even more complex and rich our own representations and our own judgments. This is civic engagement of a different order, but one that takes the work of culture seriously.

NOTES

1. Robin Wagner-Pacifici, *The Art of Surrender*, page 29.
2. Adam Smith, *The Theory of Moral Sentiments*, p. 113.
3. Michael Burawoy, "Personal Statement," American Sociological Association *Footnotes*, March 2002. http://www.asanet.org/footnotes/mar02/fn11.html.
4. John Holmwood, "Sociology as Public Discourse and Professional Practice," p. 47.
5. Jeffrey C. Alexander, *The Civil Sphere*, p. 43.
6. Luc Boltanski, *Distant Suffering*, p. 39.
7. Michael Schudson, paper delivered at the University of Pennsylvania, March, 2007: "Civility, Democracy, and the Culture of Frankness."
8. Jeffrey C. Alexander, *The Civil Sphere*, p. 134.
9. Robin Wagner-Pacifici, *The Art of Surrender*, p. 41.
10. Adam Smith, *The Theory of Moral Sentiments*, p. 74.
11. Ibid, p. 135.
12. Adam Smith, *The Theory of Moral Sentiments*, p. 140.
13. Carlo Ginzburg, *Wooden Eyes*, p. 18.
14. Luc Boltanski, op cit., p. 5.

15. Andrew Abbott, "Against Narrative," p. 75.

16. Ibid, p. 86.

17. Gotthold Lessing, *Laocoon*, p. 150.

18. John Gerard Ruggie, "Territoriality and Beyond," p. 159.

19. Michael Fried, "Jeff Wall, Wittgenstein, and the Everyday," p. 517.

20. Barbie Zelizer, *About to Die*, p. 24 (manuscript).

21. Adam Smith, *The Theory of Moral Sentiments*, p. 71.

22. Ibid, p. 57.

REFERENCES

Andrew Abbott. 2007. "Against Narrative: A Preface to Lyrical Sociology." *Sociological Theory* 25(1): 67–99.

Alexander, Jeffrey C. 2006. *The Civil Sphere*. New York: Oxford University Press.

Boltanski, Luc. 1999. *Distant Suffering: Morality, Media and Politics*. Cambridge, UK: Cambridge University Press.

Burawoy, Michael. 2002. "Personal Statement." American Sociological Association *Footnotes*, March. http://www.asanet.org/footnotes/mar02/fn11.html.

Fried, Michael. 2007. "Jeff Wall, Wittgenstein, and the Everyday." *Critical Inquiry* 33(3): 495–526.

Ginzburg, Carlo. 2001. *Wooden Eyes: Nine Reflections on Distance*. Translated by Martin H. Ryle and Kate Soper. New York: Columbia University Press.

Holmwood, John. 2007. "Sociology as Public Discourse and Professional Practice: A Critique of Michael Burawoy." *Sociological Theory* 25(1): 46–66.

Lessing, Gotthold Ephraim. 1874. *Laocoon: An Essay Upon the Limits of Painting and Poetry*. Preface by Robert Phillimore, translated by Ellen Frothingham. Oxford: Oxford University Press.

Ruggie, John Gerard. 1993. "Territoriality and Beyond: Problematizing Modernity in International Relations." *International Organization* 47(1): 139–174.

Smith, Adam. 1976. *The Theory of Moral Sentiments*. Edited by D. D. Raphael and A. L. Macfie. Oxford: Clarendon Press.

Wagner-Pacifici, Robin. 2005. *The Art of Surrender: Decomposing Sovereignty at Conflict's End*. Chicago: University of Chicago Press.

Zelizer, Barbie. 2011. *About to Die: How News Images Move the Public*. Oxford: Oxford University Press.

CHAPTER 8

REINVENTING THE CONCEPT OF CIVIC CULTURE

PAUL LICHTERMAN

THE concept of civic culture has a troubled history. Popularized in academic study by political scientists in the 1960s, the concept confused empirical realities with the normative understandings of "civic" that mainstream American social science tended to take for granted. It equated individual survey responses with national, cultural patterns, showing us relatively little about culture, as many sociologists now understand the term. It suffered wounding critiques and faded to relative obscurity in the 1970s and 1980s. Concerns about declining civic engagement in the United States and curiosity about a tremendous growth of nongovernmental organizations (NGOs) around the globe have brought the notion of "civic" life back into the sociological research agenda.

Prominent lines of research now investigate civic action without doing enough conceptual work to rescue "civic" and "culture" from earlier dead-ends. This essay offers a stronger conceptual footing for the concept of civic culture and shows what sociology can gain from it. A better concept of civic culture gives us a stronger, comparative, and contextual perspective on voluntary associations—the conventional American empirical referent for "civic"—and also improves our sociologies of religion and social movements, two areas of research that touch frequently on civic culture as defined here.

To make these arguments, it is best to start with the classic perspective on civic culture and its current incarnations, and see why we need better conceptual groundwork than they have offered. The alternative approach I present here is rooted in a pragmatist understanding of collective action. "Civic" will mean a social space for collective problem solving by actors who pursue a good they define as relevant to some larger collectivity. My approach to civic culture both builds on and departs in some ways from newly prominent understandings of culture in sociology. Ethnographic illustrations from a variety of volunteer groups, social movement organizations, and religious associations will demonstrate this approach's virtues.

Civic culture does not sound so different from political culture—also an increasingly popular topic of research. As with political culture, we would not want to say that some symbolic forms always or never "count" as civic culture. Both concepts are ways of seeing; it is best to treat them as somewhat different lenses, coming from overlapping but not identical conceptual traditions often used for understanding similar activities. Elsewhere I define political culture as culture that supports claims-making about resources, identities, or visions of society (Lichterman and Cefaï 2006). To make some simple distinctions quickly, we can think of "civic culture," then, as encompassing a broader circle of public activity: It is the cultural context for problem-solving activity, whether we (or they) consider that activity "political" or not. Often, of course, that problem solving will include claims-making. Investigating civic action or civic culture, we ask about how people create and maintain problem-solving spaces, apart from questions about the claims people make in those spaces. To ask about civic culture we focus most sharply on the cultural conditions for citizens to work together and solve problems. To investigate political culture, we focus most sharply on claims-making processes, keeping our eyes out for when claims conflict, when claims or claimants appear or disappear.

THE CLASSIC APPROACH TO CIVIC CULTURE

Tocquevillian Roots

Many scholars of civic culture have been influenced by Alexis de Tocqueville's observations (1969) on Americans' civic voluntarism. It helps to recall that his observations were more complicated and ambivalent than those of contemporary American readings which suppose that Tocqueville celebrated civic groups as generators of virtue and worth copying anywhere around the world. The nineteenth-century French writer and traveler understood American civic relationships to be somewhat precarious and part of a difficult, peculiarly American balance of competing tendencies. *Democracy in America* pictured two sets of American public "mores" in tension with each other. One of these does not even sound very civic-minded: It was the Americans' penchant for withdrawing into their small private circles. Political liberty and relatively equal material conditions, in Tocqueville's view, freed individuals to withdraw from public affairs and carve out private lives with a few, close, similarly minded others. "Each citizen isolate[s] himself from the mass of his fellows and withdraw[s] into the circle of family and friends.... [H]e gladly leaves the greater society to look after itself." As Tocqueville saw it, Americans had the custom of "forever forming associations"[1] mainly because they figured that groups could advance private interests more effectively than individuals alone. Egalitarian group effort made sense in a society of individuals willing to accept each other as relative equals.[2]

Through interaction in civic groups, Tocqueville imagined, people's imaginations and "hearts" would grow bigger for their fellow citizens. The mores of narrowly self-interested action would expand into "self-interest properly understood," and Americans would develop a second set of mores, particularly the habit of serving others outside their own small circles.[3] That does not mean Americans would cease to have particular interests. But by engaging in civil associations, Americans would stretch their social horizons, seeing a good beyond their immediate, private good. Civic associations would counterbalance the inclination to private pursuits with like-minded friends. Americans perpetually would feel tugged in two directions, but civic groups, Tocqueville hoped, would stretch the narrow social horizons that a commerce-driven society otherwise would cultivate. They would help people develop new shared meanings: "self-interest properly *understood*" (emphasis mine), Tocqueville wrote. Tocqueville was implying that working together could *mean* different things. He distinguished collective action based on calculating self-interest or group-interest with collective action driven by a taste for serving others. His had, in sum, partly a *cultural* understanding of civic life, and it is fitting to begin an investigation of civic culture with his enduring if fragmentary insights.

A Modern Classic and Its Enduring Influence

Tocqueville's account influenced other writers who focused more narrowly on particular aspects of civic culture, whether or not they used the phrase. At mid-century, social scientists read Louis Hartz' thesis (1955) on political liberalism in America, which highlighted one of the cultural strands woven into Tocqueville's more complicated picture. Edward Banfield's case study of a southern Italian village (1958) affirmed Tocqueville's argument with a negative case. The villagers failed to act together for the common good because their "amoral familism" cultivated the pursuit of short-term, individual or familial interest, and the distrust of anyone claiming to do otherwise. But we find the widest-ranging and most systematic study in the Tocquevillian tradition with Gabriel Almond's and Sidney Verba's *The Civic Culture* (1963).

A defining statement in the 1960s, Almond and Verba's study remains the classic account of civic culture, a large if ambivalent reference point for current discussions. It compared survey data on values, attitudes, opinions, and beliefs from the United States, England, Germany, Italy, and Mexico. The authors treated civic culture not in terms of Tocqueville's vague "mores" but as *psychological* orientations toward the political system. They developed a typology of civic cultures; they found "parochial," "subject," and "participation" types. In their fusion of descriptive and normative assessments, a society with a truly "civic culture" included some mix of all three types, a mix that would maintain a political system's stability, keeping citizens reasonable and trusting of their polity's functioning. It is easy to hear the concerns of Talcott Parsons' social system theory (Parsons and Shils 1951) in Almond and Verba's work with its emphasis on internalized values and its allegiance to the paradigm of political modernization. As did its theoretical forebears, *The Civic Culture* defined healthy relationships between civic culture and political and social structure as close-fitting and stable ones.

The study's conceptual and normative assumptions attracted powerful criticisms. The study affirmed political quiescence as the normal state of affairs (Pateman 1980). It took as universal the particular, liberal democratic, dominant self-understandings of the postwar United States and United Kingdom, while "traditionalism" and "familism" characterized the less developed political cultures of Mexico or Italy. The survey findings seemed to ratify Banfield's account in the case of Italy, but the study raised questions about the limits of survey data for comparing politics cross-nationally: Could we really say that Italians had less "pride" in their government than did Germans on the basis of survey responses, or did answering the question itself entail different cultural assumptions in each case (MacIntyre 1972)? How could we generalize cross-nationally about political parties if parties occupy vastly different institutional positions in different nations? Recent moves to reconceptualize culture brought *The Civic Culture* under additional scrutiny. By the 1990s, far fewer sociologists would treat "culture" as the sum of individual, private attitudes elicited in survey research as Almond and Verba and many others had done.

Almond and Verba's abstract holism and methodological individualism sit uncomfortably with the contemporary tendency to highlight multiplicity and variability in culture. Most scholars now view culture as collectively held, not a sum of individually nurtured beliefs and attitudes. Still, some of the most prominent contemporary works on civic culture continue to focus on individual orientations and practices. They also exhibit Almond and Verba's inventorying spirit. Verba, Schlozman, and Brady (1995) produced an exhaustive survey of Americans' civic skills and practices. Political scientist Ronald Inglehart organized a series of national surveys (1977, 1981, 1990) which suggested that citizens of Western industrial democracies, and especially the highly schooled citizens, increasingly have valorized lifestyle, self-actualization, and a clean environment over material wealth. Cross-national surveys of values and opinions pose some of the same problems of context and interpretation that MacIntyre scored in Almond and Verba's work. If we take civic "culture" loosely as the public behaviors and norms of mutual trust in a society, then Robert Putnam's much-discussed work on civic engagement and social capital in the United States (1996, 2000) and abroad (Putnam and Goss 2002) represents another effort to measure a society's civic propensities in a way that recalls Tocquevillian themes.

We have, in short, a classic perspective on civic culture that understands "civic" in normative terms and defines culture as the sum of individual attitudes and habits across a whole society. In important ways, Tocqueville's treatment of civic relationships was more cultural than the dominant, classical perspective his work empowered. As Somers and others have argued (Somers 1995), it is a curiously a-cultural perspective on civic culture. The complex of assumptions in *The Civic Culture* play out in current researchers' tendency to distinguish civic practices quantitatively (more or fewer group memberships or trust behaviors) without distinguishing different *meanings* of what would be the same practice "on paper" (Lichterman 2006). This line of inquiry invites large problems of interpretation in cross-national research. And it requires that we agree ahead of time on what counts as virtuously democratic discourse and practice. Enduring troubles with the classic concept of civic and accumulating insights in cultural sociology bid us reinvent the concept of civic culture for new research.

Toward a Better Definition

"Civic"

As I have argued elsewhere (Lichterman 2005, 2006), the pragmatic tradition in the United States offers starting points for a treatment of civic relationships that complements Tocqueville's in some ways but avoids troublesome assumptions. Civic, in this pragmatic approach, refers to people participating in voluntary, collective problem-defining and problem-solving action that participants imagine to be significant to some collective identity, not necessarily their own, whether local, national, or global. Not just philosophical pragmatists, such as John Dewey (for instance, 1927) or Jane Addams (2002 [1902]), but a larger pragmatic sociology of "social control" in the earlier twentieth century wanted to understand how American society could steer itself and control itself democratically, rather than rely solely on market or administrative solutions to social problems (see Janowitz 1975). A wide range of theory on civil society or the civic focuses on collective problem solving and its significance for larger collectivities, from Tocqueville (1969 [1835]) and Addams (2002 [1902]), to Durkheim (1957), and Etzioni (1968).

Unlike substantial parts of this varied theoretical discussion, I do not take civic relationships to be necessarily inclusive or virtuous. Different kinds of civic groups include or exclude to varying degrees. For example, as Jason Kaufman argues (2002) in his historical study of nineteenth-century American civic organizations, fraternalism taught Americans that "self-segregation [is] acceptable, if not preferable to cooperation and collectivization." Civic groups address problems of the collectivities they represent or identify with, but they do not necessarily practice broadminded "civic virtue." Breaking with commonsense usage, civic is a descriptive rather than an evaluative term in my approach.

This approach to civic departs as well from some other uses in sociology. In recent work, for instance, Jeffrey Alexander (2006) addresses "the civil sphere" as a set of institutions that over many decades tended to broaden the bounds of societal community, embracing more and more kinds of citizens in an increasingly universalistic solidarity. "Civic" in this view is an historical project more than a finished accomplishment, and, in that sense, this view shares with mine a cautious regard for actually existing forms of citizenship, eschewing easy celebrations of civic actors. My approach starts from a focus on action rather than institutions. It recognizes as well that a lot of collective problem solving happens inside institutions in the conventional sense of the term, and that some forms of collective problem solving are institutionalized in the neo-institutionalist sense of action that is both patterned and largely routine (see DiMaggio and Powell 1991). The framework introduced here helps us study these kinds of civic action. It does not look for civic culture only in the small face-to-face groups lauded in neo-Tocquevillian accounts of civic life (for instance, Putnam 2000; Berger and Neuhaus 1977). The focus on action is important partly because so much of the scholarly rediscovery of things "civic" also has attended to group action but in a partial and ahistorical way. The action-centered approach here hopes, among other goals, to counteract this popular but less helpful focus on group action.

Typically, when scholars speak of civic groups, they have in mind voluntary associations or voluntary institutions that function largely outside of market relations or governmental control. They picture community centers, service clubs, citizen advocacy groups, social movement organizations, nonprofit service providers, town hall forums, volunteer associations, e-mail discussion groups, and religious congregations or faith-based alliances. So these may be the places we look first for civic culture, and they are the places where much previous scholarship assumes we would find civic virtues. But since the definition of civic here depends on a kind of activity, not a single institutional sector of society or a kind of virtue, we may find civic culture as well inside governmental agencies or commercial enterprises, wherever people define themselves as working voluntarily on a cause, solving problems together on behalf of some collective identity. We need not limit civic culture to face-to-face groups or noninstitutional action.

"Culture"

What should we mean by culture? As many sociologists of culture now would put it, culture is a set of publicly shared, symbolic patterns that enable and constrain what people can say and do together. Sociologists have named these patterns discourses, vocabularies, codes, practices, styles, and other terms partly because different theoretical schools animate the study of culture today and partly because "culture" is no single thing. There are different elements of culture, just as networks, status hierarchies, or role sets all can be thought of as kinds of "social structure," a term that we rarely try to reduce to one conceptualization or one "variable." Culture *structures* people's ability to communicate. Culture exists beyond any single interaction, but we find culture *in* interaction in specific settings, not in abstract society-wide "values" or "character."

Using the cultural level of analysis, we see and hear how culture shapes the possibilities in any one interaction, textual communication, or virtual site.[4] Culture gives us the vocabularies, images, codes, or styles of interaction that organize ideas and experience into communicable form. People do not develop ideas and then put them into words that reflect the ideas transparently. Rather, communication is structured from the start—which is not to say completely determined, much less programmed—by different kinds of cultural forms. It is for that reason, to note just one striking illustration, that while millions of Americans do volunteer work every year, researchers hear but a relatively few ways that volunteers talk about why it is good to be a volunteer (Wuthnow 1991). Millions of volunteers and a few ways to talk about volunteering—that is shared culture at work.

We can name *civic culture* as the cultural patterns that shape the means or ends of civic action. When citizens solve problems together, some of what they say and do together is structured by widespread ways of speaking and ways of coordinating action—civic culture—that they are not making up from scratch. There is no culture that is fundamentally, absolutely, or necessarily "civic" or "not civic." Civic culture refers to cultural forms that people are using in particular sites—whether real, textual, or virtual—to solve problems together. In different regions, societies, or time periods, different kinds of culture may become civic culture, more or less frequently among wider or more specific populations. "Civic culture" in the abstract does not exist, but people use, enact, or rely on cultural forms to solve problems together publicly so the forms they are using together in those instances are civic. As sociologists Boltanski and Thévenot (1991) would point out, people have a rationale of "civic virtue" available when they justify their acts, but people may also use other rationales, too—economic expediency or the authority of expertise, for example—when they are solving problems together in some settings at some times. In those settings and times, these other "noncivic" rationales would be part of civic culture.

If civic culture like other kinds of culture is relatively autonomous from other social-structural relations, then the Tocquevillian approach with its emphasis on mores, attitudes, habits, and practices, problematic though it is, has advantages over a competing, Marxian approach inspired by Antonio Gramsci (1971; see Alexander 2006). Gramscians would not often use the phrase "civic culture," but Gramsci's focus on the role of civic organizations beyond the market in Western capitalist societies has, in effect, made civic culture a subject for some contemporary Gramsci-inspired research (Lancaster 1988, Kertzer 1990). For Gramsci, more than Tocqueville, public language and public group practices ultimately complemented or at least rarely challenged the interests of a dominant social class. Gramscian treatments usually have emphasized the structuring power of class relations, not culture, when analyzing public communication (for instance, Hall 1977).

In my approach, in contrast, the important influence of social-structural inequality and domination on forms of civic culture and their distribution is an analytically separate question (Lichterman 1995b), much as cultural and social relations interpenetrate in everyday life. In earlier research, I showed, for instance, that different kinds of environmental activists prefer different ways of defining and organizing action around environmental problems (Lichterman 1996). In the 1990s, activists in the American Green movement talked big, advocating fundamental transformations of environmental policy and radical cultural change and presumed that good activists were people who carried their politics as a 24-hour-a-day calling. Contrast this personalized politics with a more specifically policy-centered and locale-centered environmentalism that fights toxic waste in the name of environmental justice and views local communities more as political actors than individuals. We could say each carries different bundles of civic culture. Activists in each have tended to have different educational and occupational backgrounds. The less-schooled anti-toxics activists may sometimes have wondered what exactly the Greens were talking about, and why Greens' emphasis on verbosity and individuality may have been frustrating. In return, Green activists chafed at the other activists' collectivism and lack of enthusiasm for talk about "the bigger picture." But it would do little for the empirical record to say, "The Greens used their culture to dominate the grassroots environmental movement." The tensions between their taste for individually nuanced, ideological argument and their genuine desire to make common cause with anti-toxic activists was an important sociological—as well as practical—problem that we only avoid rather than illuminate if we insist that class differences in cultural practices must translate into social-structural domination. Given the U.S. Green movement's relative marginality during the study, it would have been almost laughable to criticize them for cultural domination. Rather than simply reflecting social domination, civic culture wields its own kind of power over the people who practice it if no one else, and so it is worthwhile to look more closely at different elements of civic culture pictured in recent research.

ELEMENTS OF CIVIC CULTURE

Public Vocabularies, Codes, and Dramas

The "late-Durkheimian" approach to public culture (Alexander 1988) treats civic culture as a set of publicly shared representations of what makes a good citizen or a good society. These studies share the fundamental insight that words do not reflect underlying ideas or interests transparently. Rather, communication is structured from the start by cultural forms that exist somewhat independently of group interests. Important earlier examples of such an approach include William Sewell's (1980) study of changes in nineteenth-century French discourse, which showed that industrial workers had to invent new "political idioms" to leave the universe of the old regime corporations. A recent outpouring of U.S. work conceives shared representations in several different ways. One is the concept of "cultural vocabulary," another is "cultural code," and a third is "drama."

Studies of moral vocabularies belong to a larger trend in sociology, a growing focus on public language. Different schools of research on public language all pay attention to language itself rather than taking language as a proxy for abstract, motivating "values."[5] Sociologists have given a lot of attention to the vocabularies people use in public life to talk about what makes a good person, a good act, or a good society.[6] These vocabularies are part of the means for public problem solving in that they inform notions of what constitutes worthwhile problems and good solutions, and what kind of person should be a problem solver. In my research on religious community service groups (2005), I heard people speak from biblically inspired vocabularies of social justice and compassion when they talked about how churchgoers should respond to the 1996 welfare policy reforms, and use secular vocabularies when speaking of citizenly duty. I was hearing elements of civic culture when they spoke. The words and phrases—literally, the vocabularies—were elements of shared, public culture and not just made up on the spot. Even the most cursory knowledge of the Bible, or American culture for that matter, would tell the listener that these were not particular to the groups I studied. Idioms of social justice and compassion have long histories in the Judeo-Christian traditions. They influence—not strictly determine, but influence—what adherents of those traditions can say meaningfully at least some of the time.

One widely read application of this approach to civic culture in the United States is Robert Bellah and co-authors' *Habits of the Heart*, an interview study of middle-class Americans' moral and political reasoning. Most often, Bellah and his team heard languages of individualism, such as when many of their interviewees said that their public commitments depended on "what I can get out of it" or "what feels good to me right now." Americans articulated their commitments in civic-republican or Biblical language less often and more haltingly. The authors proposed that an active, democratic citizenry would be hard to sustain over time if Americans' primary cultural vocabulary was so self-oriented. While their preface to a second edition (1996) took Robert Putnam's (2000) much-discussed figures on declining American civic group memberships as confirmation of their fears, other research pointed out that self-expressiveness led some American activists to create broad-minded civic projects (Lichterman 1996; see also Faucher-King 2005).

A complex society's cultural mainstream holds more than one set of moral vocabularies. Rhys Williams (1995) illustrated that social movements draw on different rhetorics of the public good—the good of individual rights or environmental stewardship, for instance. Some representations are politically subordinate or subcultural. Mark Warren (2001), Richard Wood (1994, 1999, 2002) and Stephen Hart (2001) showed that shared religious vocabularies such as those available in Catholic social teachings could work as civic culture, by helping urban social movements convince residents of low-income, minority communities to join struggles against corporations and local bureaucrats. Wood found that the most effective religious vocabularies were the ones that helped activists grasp the problem of ambiguity in their political environments instead of ignoring or trying to transcend it. All of these studies have discerned vocabularies from qualitative analysis of interviews, ethnographic field notes, or texts. They depend on the analyst's familiarity with a larger cultural or the intellectual history behind the groups under study, and so their claims are interpretive as well as causal; they travel far but do not leave the hermeneutic circle. The Bellah team chose historical, cultural exemplars such as Benjamin Franklin and Walt Whitman to represent strands of American individualism alive in the late twentieth century. French sociologists Boltanski and Thévenot (1991) have pursued a somewhat similar strategy, identifying public vocabularies of moral or political justification from great Western philosophical texts.

Other researchers have conceived civic culture in terms of codes that organize public discourse. Sociologists Jeffrey Alexander (2006) and Philip Smith (Alexander and Smith 1993) identified a set of binary codes in public life that have organized U.S. political debate over the past two centuries. Socialized to these implicit codes, citizens divide actors, relationships, and institutions into binary categories of evaluation, casting "good" political actors as "active, not passive" or good political relations as "open and trusting" rather than "closed and secretive" (Alexander and Smith 1993, pp. 162–163). During the Watergate hearings, for instance, both the adversaries and defenders of President Nixon called their own side reasonable and cast the opposing side as irrational or secretive. Parallel to students of cultural vocabularies, scholars of binary codes search for subordinate or subcultural codes that are patterned and enduring: Ronald Jacobs' study (2000) of media discourse surrounding the Rodney King beating found codes in the African American press somewhat different from those organizing depictions of the beating and subsequent riots in mainstream forums. Different sets of codes may organize political debate in other societies; "authoritarian" and "collectivist" as well as democratic codes may have propelled the terms of national debate in Brazil since the 1990s (Baiocchi 2006).

More than the research on vocabularies or codes, studies of social dramas put shared representations in movement. They investigate performance. Dramaturgical perspectives vary widely in sociology, from Erving Goffman's (1961) insights on the mundane interaction rituals of everyday life to Joseph Gusfield's (1981) account of the public drama of drunk driving, with its heroes, villains, frontstage and backstage audiences, and moral messages. For studies of civic culture, the larger-scale viewpoint of Gusfield, Victor Turner (1974), or Alexander (2005, 2006) can be especially useful. In this view, dramatic scripts and conventions organize the space for civic action. Social dramas played out by institutional actors shape a public's perception of social problems as well as actors' own perceptions, even apart from the "objective" facts of risk or harm. Performance not only organizes the story but also invites and privileges particular emotional responses in the civic space, as when Falung Gong activists dramatize their suffering in China in ways that invite American publics to feel sympathy for oppressed religious practitioners and disgust for their governmental adversaries (Junker 2008).

Rich as these analyses are, they tell us the language, code, or script without telling us how these cultural forms take shape when people speak them, or the responses they generate in different everyday settings. Joining a growing body of other studies,[7] this essay conveys a practical, cultural sociology. Social space for problem solving depends on not only shared, moral representations but also shared ideas about how to coordinate action, especially when the actors share little or do not know what they share. A pragmatic cultural perspective sensitizes us to the ways people enact, or try to enact, shared representations that sociologists abstract from everyday settings and identify as discourses or scripts. The pragmatic perspective puts them back in interaction, sees how they mutate, and on occasion even become their opposite. In everyday *interaction*, the familiar American moral language of expressive individualism—frequently criticized as an apolitical and atomizing focus on self-gratification—sometimes helps timid citizens say very political things and work together with other citizens on public projects. For suburban environmental activists, the language of "express yourself" or "personal empowerment" does not mean "do your own thing regardless of anyone else"; it sometimes means, "it is ok to express yourself as a citizen by challenging local authorities, for the public good" (see Eliasoph and Lichterman 2003; Lichterman 1996).

My pragmatic, cultural perspective does not deny the value of identifying narratives, codes, or scripts, especially for historical work that wants to encompass *la longue durée*. Rather, it illuminates how people speak and live those discourses or codes in specific situations. Quite often the "how," the way of coordinating action, has its own patterns—sometimes durable ones, which we cannot reduce to side-products of something "more cultural" or "more real."

Civic Customs

In different ways, Tocqueville and John Dewey both grasped something basic about associational life, and I have followed their insight: A group's shared customs have a reality of their own, a power apart from that of members' individual traits or shared representations. It is easy to think of individuals who seem different in a group from what they are like outside it. Groups' customs call forth abilities, perspectives, and even deeply held beliefs that individuals may not exercise outside the group. My own research continues this line of inquiry.

With an imagination for context, we see that vocabularies, codes, dramas, or narratives always are embedded in social settings. Civil society creates and recreates itself, as people continue enacting different customary forms of membership in those settings. The civic customs that concern me here are the ones that give groups routine ways of coordinating themselves and defining the meaning of membership in the group as the group is acting. They are what we have called "group style" elsewhere (Eliasoph and Lichterman 2003), and it is useful to discern three elements of group style: Customarily, groups draw *boundaries* around themselves on a wider social map; they sustain *bonds* that define a good member's obligations to the group; and they observe *speech norms* that define the meaning of speaking in the group.

These customs open room for some lines of conversation and action, and close or dampen others. Different sets of customs enable or disempower different kinds of working together and cultivate different kinds of goods. Different customs of citizenship are themselves meaningful and have their own histories (Schudson 1998); they are not simply derivatives of a group's formally stated purpose or beliefs.

In her study of American civic groups, for instance, Nina Eliasoph (1998, 1996) showed that being a member of a volunteer group meant being an upbeat, "can-do" person who carried out tasks efficiently instead of fretting about big social issues. I found (Lichterman 1995b, 1996) that being a member of an activist group could mean being someone willing to make a deeply personalized contribution, or someone who upholds a communal will and brackets individuality. Groups with different customary styles had difficulties working together, even when they all affirmed the same "environmental justice" discourse. Researchers have conceptualized customs of group membership within different theoretical traditions, calling them "cultures of commitment" (Lichterman 1996), "civic practices" (Eliasoph 1996, 1998), "cultural models" in the case of Becker's (1999) study of church congregations, or "constitutive rules" in Armstrong's study of lesbian and gay organizations (2002). Each is getting at something roughly like the "group style" (Eliasoph and Lichterman 2003) that a group sustains as it goes about ordinary business.

Are there patterns in the ways that particular sets of customs and particular discourses or narratives tend to go together? It was important to establish the reality and force of group style or customs before proceeding to this question, but some clues became available in my earlier primary and secondary research on social activists: The most culturally radical discourses seemed to be propounded most by groups with extremely personalized group styles. People who promoted fundamental change in the ways modern people live life—radical feminists, "deep ecologists," and the most spiritually oriented proponents of the Green movement—seemed especially likely to insist on decentralized authority and highly individualized participation. Ethnographic observation showed me that people with less fundamentally culture-challenging viewpoints on the environment and politics also seemed less invested in, and sometimes more impatient with, a very personalized group style. I proposed (Lichterman 1996) that culturally radical discourses complemented a personalized group style not because of the logic of the discourses but because discourses rarely heard in established institutions could not be spoken meaningfully in conventional, well-institutionalized group formats. When we take discourse as communication in settings rather than language on paper, it becomes easier to see why: People communicate, make meaning, in relation to each other as they perceive each other (see Eliasoph and Lichterman 2003). To communicate any particular discourse, we have to imagine ourselves and others as the *kind* of people who speak or hear that discourse. Discourses that have little or no association with institutionalized, conventional political forums will be disorienting to speaker and audience alike if spoken in a conventionally styled group. New research combining ethnographic and network analysis is investigating the relation between discourse and group style more systematically with a wide variety of cases.[8] In the case of cultural radicalism, observers have tended to argue that these activists choose untraditional organizational formats because they want their own practice to "prefigure" a future world that is more participatory and less sexist, (Epstein 1991, Breines 1982). Perhaps a reflection of activists' own thinking, this explanation relies on a simple model of how ideas cause action, and underestimates the variety of ways people coordinate action around shared ideas.

Group styles powerfully shape the meanings and uses of collective representations, what the neo-Durkheimian culture scholars conceive as vocabularies, dramas, or codes. Studying group style and representations together illuminates how civic groups measure up to the virtues imputed to them by many theorists of civil society. The volunteer group style shuts down open-ended conversation that ideally characterizes the public sphere. In groups, volunteers avoid discussing what they may worry about in private interviews—that skinheads at the local high school threaten race relations, for instance (Eliasoph 1998). The personalized style of some environmental and queer activist groups (Lichterman 1995a, 1996, 1999) encourages public-spirited deliberation—despite social scientists' claims that personal, self-expressive talk distracts people from truly political concerns and diminishes civic action (Bellah et al. 1985; see also Breines 1982). In theory, civic participation teaches citizens how to mobilize relationships and resources for a greater public good (Putnam 1993, 2000; Skocpol and Fiorina 1999). Yet different group styles promote different ways of shepherding resources and defining ties, and different ways of working with state institutions, apart from group members' religious or political beliefs or social backgrounds (Lichterman 2005). Tallying up "social capital" (Putnam 2000) misses the varied and powerful work of group style.

All of these studies assume that culture has strong enabling and constraining effects on what people can say or do. They assume too that "culture" is more than one thing and that we ought to specify the kind of culture we are investigating in particular settings and time periods, using a variety of culture concepts instead of the generic term—in the same way that network analysts and scholars of class hierarchies normally deploy their particular terms of analysis rather than saying "I am studying social structure." Here, I have discussed two elements of civic culture: representations and styles of action. We can find both working together in two large fields of sociological study that can benefit from a civic-cultural lens.

CIVIC CULTURE IN THE STUDY OF RELIGION

Historic changes in the United States and around the globe have inspired exciting new social research on religion. A lot of that research begins with some version of the question that puzzles scholars and citizens alike: What is religion making people do in public? In the past fifteen years many people have asked if religion is creating warlike political divisions in the United States; if religion helps social service providers do their jobs more effectively or compassionately; if religion can reknit the social fabric of a frayed and fragmented civil society; or if resurgent religion around the world is pitting East against West. Often we assume that religion is interesting because it does things to people, or makes people do things they would not otherwise do.

The problem is that the same religion "on paper" can do very different things in different circumstances. People make different meanings from the same religious beliefs. Evangelical Protestants can use the same biblical passages to condone or condemn racism, for instance (see Lichterman, Carter, and Lamont 2009). And rarely if ever could we predict exactly how any single group of religious people would coordinate action around its shared beliefs. Using a group's religious affinities to explain how it chooses its goals or how it works together would produce at best a very inexact and broad-brushstroke account if not simply the wrong picture. Even if longstanding liberal Protestant teachings often call worshippers to act for the social good, we need to know something about contemporary customs of "networking" to understand why an urban church alliance would be so intent on responding compassionately to drastic cuts in welfare benefits, yet so unable to coordinate an effective response (Lichterman 2005). Similarly, the fact of a shared devotion to Muslim practice does not help us understand why some Parisian Muslims insist that Muslim women without the traditional headscarf give Islam a bad name, while others, equally devout, avoid presenting their Muslim identity publicly (Amiraux 2006). The difficulties in using "religion" in the abstract to predict group action only multiply when religiously identified groups do not use religious rationales to legitimate their goals at all, or when, in the case of an anti-racist coalition of Christian pastors, for example, they agree on the goals but argue passionately over the means (Lichterman 2008).

I have argued at length elsewhere[9] in contrast, that religion has a civic life. It makes more sense to ask what people do with religion than what religion does to people. A contextual approach to religion holds that when people act religiously, with religious identities, they are drawing on secular as well as religious culture. What counts as "religious culture" must be an interpretive and historical question (Asad 2003). The point is that religious groups—whether congregations, associations, or movements—exist in a social and cultural context, and they coordinate their action with the help of vocabularies and group styles some of which likely will not be absolutely unique to religious collectivities. When people go public as religious actors, in other words, they draw on *civic culture*, not just "purely" religious beliefs.

Secular vocabularies and symbolic orders regularly inhabit everyday religious settings. If a Methodist church's social action committee uses a personalized, emotional language to talk about whether or not to include lesbian and gay members in the congregation (Moon 2004), it may well be the same personalistic language we hear in a lot of grassroots progressive politics. The social action committee is making meanings with a civic culture that is not particular to Methodist church groups—and not simply a derivative, or rough or randomly varying approximation, of formal theologies or denominational statements. Just as there may be customary religious knowledge that has little to do with any "official" texts, secular culture also powerfully shapes religious organizations. This may be obvious, as when congregations adopt secular organizational models (i.e., committees or boards, rather than elders or deacons). Or it may happen in ways that members may take for granted, as when pastors or congregants rely on widely shared, often mass-mediated language to interpret current events in their sermons or social outreach committees. Narrowly and specifically religious belief, in short, is not the only kind of culture that matters in religious associations. If we want to understand the public power of religion, we benefit from asking what people do with religious and secular culture to create civic life. We need to see how religious people articulate themselves and form their groups in the medium of civic culture.

In contrast, social research still often essentializes and decontextualizes religion. We assimilate uncritically some religious people's own self-understandings that, as religious people, they act outside a cultural or secular context.[10] Both the celebrants of religion's virtues and detractors of religion often share a commonsense theological determinism. They assume that public religious groups are propelled *directly* by religious beliefs. If we want to explain these groups' action by this logic, we look for the biblical or denominational teaching that seems closest to the action in question and assume the actors acted with this teaching in mind.

The point is hardly that theological beliefs are irrelevant, but this beliefs-centered understanding of religious groups brackets cultural and organizational phenomena that shape religious action, *constituting* and not just "adding to" the practice of religion. Even the most otherworldly religious practice, sociologically speaking, is embedded in some shared understandings, preferred ways of speaking, and routine styles of acting that do not derive directly from sacred texts but that nevertheless set limits on what it is possible to say, do, think, or be as a religious person. Instead of assimilating the self-understandings of religious people who see their religious practice as fundamentally set apart from the cultural world, sociological analysis must keep the socially, culturally embedded character of religious groups in mind when investigating how they become civically engaged. The civic culture concept can help us do just that.

If we limit our questions about culture and communication in religious groups to questions about what those groups' religious beliefs make them say or do, we risk relying on an essentialism of religious beliefs. Religion research can do better, and of course sometimes it has. Sociologists of religion have long implied that religious collectivities take form in a broader cultural context. In the 1960s, for instance, Peter Berger (1967) and Thomas Luckmann (1967) argued that consumerism drove Americans to shop for a congregation the way they might shop for a new car. More recently, sociologists have observed that the widespread organizational forms of modern society suffuse the American religious world, making some aspects of congregational life very much like a bureaucracy, a family, or a therapy group.[11] The civic culture concept becomes increasingly crucial to religion research as more and more researchers investigate religious people's cultural milieus on the notion that these are not detachable aspects of lives already religious but rather *embody* religious lives and constitute religious collectivities.

CIVIC CULTURE IN THE STUDY
OF SOCIAL MOVEMENTS

Ironically, the sociology of social movements in the past twenty years has touted a cultural perspective more than the sociology of religion—a field more obviously tied to something cultural. A lot of scholarship has developed around a few specialized culture concepts that social movement scholars use, and major position statements in the field include some attention to the role of symbolic constructions in collective action (for instance, McAdam, McCarthy, and Zald 1996; Tarrow 1994; McAdam, Tarrow, and Tilly 2001). As with research on religion, a refurbished civic culture concept can contribute a contextualizing perspective to this lively field and a hedge against over-reifying the object of study.

Two well-known concepts in the social movements area are collective action frames and collective identity. The extremely popular "framing" approach turns on the assumption that definitions of public problems and solutions are never self-evident or natural and never a simple extrapolation from silent group interests. Deciding whether chemical effluents in a town's groundwater constitute "toxic waste" or a breach of "environmental justice" is a matter of framing, not nature or logic, as is deciding whether to respond with "not in my back yard" or "not in anybody's back yard." Movement scholars study how grievances and solutions are "framed" by activists, countermovements, media, state authorities, or business leaders for a variety of audiences.[12] They also study how organizations or informal groups articulate the collective identity of the aggrieved people: In the case of chemical pollution, are they town residents, people of color, or "low-to-moderate income Americans"?[13] The two concepts here turn scholars' attention to slogans, images, and story lines—all material for cultural analysis.

The civic culture concept can contribute a broader context to these investigations, and one informed by cultural sociologists' understandings of culture, which differ somewhat from those in some other fields (see Jacobs and Spillman 2005). First, where do frames or collective identities come from? With important exceptions, social movement scholarship has tended to emphasize emergent meanings—collective actors' ability to innovate new messages from existing texts. "Social movement culture" has tended to mean the individual subcultures of distinct groups or organizations, in line with the "second Chicago school" orientation of some of the most experienced investigators. There also has been a strong if not universal assumption that strategic interest is the motivating impetus for movement culture. Framing research has tended to assume that collective action frames reflect the interests of the groups doing the framing—their interest in spinning reality in ways convenient to them, inconvenient to foes, and resonant with potential audiences (for instance, Snow and Benford 1988). In this view, interests exist outside of cultural definition; actors size up their opportunities, bring their interests to the civic arena, and use them to shape frames and identities (Bernstein 1997). It is easy enough to assume, and as decades of social research confirm, that groups do indeed innovate new meanings and create new subcultures.

The civic culture lens developed in this essay would emphasize, though, that people do not create meanings from scratch, nor do they experience interests without meanings or communication. There are cultural as well as other constraints on what even the most creative activists say and do together. It is no surprise, then, that the Southern civil rights movement offered a "master frame" that oriented problem solving for women, youth, Latinos, and other collective identities for several decades

(Snow and Benford 1992). That master frame came out of a much older strand of American civic culture, as Rhys Williams would point out (1995), one that defines the public good in terms of individual rights and defines a good citizen as one who seeks to expand rights (Schudson 1998). This tradition of civic culture enabled a succession of U.S. movements at midcentury. With an historical imagination, researchers can see an enduring tradition of personalized, cultural radicalism (Lasch 1966) behind contemporary forms of environmentalism, feminism, and identity politics (Lichterman 1996, 1999). With the same perspective, we can say forms of civic culture also have constrained the imaginations of activists trying make their cause more popular, as when pro-choice activists stick to a "rights" understanding of abortion even when it alienates potential supporters (Condit 1994). Civic culture is a broader cultural form from which social movements draw their slogans, identities, and passions. It set limits on what activists can imagine their interests to be, and who they can imagine themselves to be as they fight for what they want.

Civic customs, as well as shared vocabularies or dramas, form the broader cultural context for specific social movements. For instance, when the Justice Task Force of a Midwestern U.S. city's urban religious coalition planned educational workshops to alert other churchgoers to the ills of the 1996 welfare policy reforms, they gravitated toward customs of social criticism (Lichterman 2005). They defined their group in stark opposition to corporate power and media complacency; they privileged righteous denunciation over calm deliberation; and they defined good members as radical sojourners who stick together, not explorers who learn from each others' differences. Their group customs, in other words, are recognizable from a long history of left oppositionalism. When an African American radio personality with a radical morning show suggested that this almost entirely white group of churchgoers draw some of their sustenance and identity from a shared Christian faith, the normally voluble group grew quiet, the topic went nowhere, and the radio announcer did not come to another meeting. Though he agreed with the thrust of their critique, he had in effect proposed different civic customs.

The tenacity of this group's customs illustrates the point that civic culture constrains the framing people do and even their sense of what is possible to frame. The Justice Task Force framed welfare reform as a strategy to boost corporate profits, aided and abetted by an ideology-spewing media that made middle-class people blame poor people for their own insecurities. Even in their politically liberal city, the task force's framing of welfare reform did not resonate strongly with many attendees at its educational workshops. It was not very *strategic* even in a quite liberal city, but task force members continued to frame the new welfare policies in this way because their boundary-drawing and speech customs promoted an us-versus-them, denunciatory view of the world. A more nuanced or carefully reasoned frame would have threatened the task force's customs—its continued existence as a group. The "choir" it ended up preaching to was very small.

Previous research also has linked social movements to broader cultural trends and traditions. One example is the Bellah team's study mentioned earlier, which suggested that some youth and middle-class radicalism of the 1960s and 1970s bore the mark of a therapeutic individualism, rooted in the romanticism of Walt Whitman, that had become a major feature of American culture by that time. Less critical interpretations made the same analytic move, linking 1960s and 70s activism to broad cultural trends (Clecak 1981, Roszak 1969). While some would criticize these accounts as normative, armchair commentary more than rigorous sociology, other ways of linking social movements to broader cultural forces have replayed the mistakes of the classic civic culture approach. They link a surge of "lifestyle movements" such as environmentalism, youth, or peace activism with a growth of "post-materialist" values (Inglehart 1981), as inferred from aggregated survey research responses. They reduce culture to a sum of individual attitudes and then generalize loosely about "the culture" of an entire society.

A strong civic culture concept gives us other ways of linking social movements to a broad cultural context, without smudging differences inside and between movements, and without normative blinders. In earlier ethnographic work, for instance, I argued we should view the expressive individualism in contemporary social movements dispassionately, not as an "anti-civic" culture that curdles politics but as a cultural form with its own virtues as well as drawbacks for civic action, and one that people like the Green activists I studied used to create political communities. Viewing a string of grassroots social change efforts between the mid-1960s and early 1990s, I proposed we could see strong family resemblances that would escape researchers intent on studying only the specific frames or collective identities of different, discrete movements. The frames and identities of Greens, anti-nuclear activists, radical feminists, and animal liberation activists differed but the ways in which people affirmed them, linked them to publics, and organized collective action around them looked very similar.

If we see culture as an enabling and constraining set of symbolic processes that we can study with sociological rigor, we should be able to study how culture shapes a variety of social movements. We should be able to make careful cross-national comparisons that at least begin to parse the different contributions of culture, state structure and other factors to the development of social movements in different societies and eras. To do those things we need a concept that sets the more limited notions of social movement culture in a broader context, and the civic culture concept can do that work.

CONCLUSION

Probably the most controversial aspect of the case for a revamped civic culture concept is the descriptive rather than normative meaning I am promoting. Conventional usage as well as a lot of social science writing, implicitly if not explicitly, uses civic and civic culture as synonyms for things that are good for democracy, society in general, and the human spirit. Noble traditions of political theory use "civic" in these ways also. I am arguing for a concept that does not depend on referents particular to the "golden era" of American civic participation between World War II and 1970. In order to understand how people create civic life in different contexts or eras, we need a concept that allows us to compare different kinds of associations or acts—including ones we may consider undemocratic or distasteful though people in other places or times may not. The concept I propose does not depend on researcher and reader sharing the same moral evaluations.

Of course, there are alternatives to this essay's action-centered and pragmatist approach. This is not the place to indulge in extensive theoretical comparison, but two alternative approaches to civic culture stand out. Each is valuable for other kinds of questions about public life or other dimensions of the public activity that my civic culture concept also addresses. Alexander's focus on the socially and culturally integrative work of institutions in the "civil sphere" (Alexander 2006), mentioned before, is one approach that has different questions to ask: The choice of approaches is one of intellectual mission more than differing empirical values. This work on the civil sphere advances historical accounts of modernity and social differentiation that have long driven sociological inquiry. My pragmatic cultural approach, in turn, invites a somewhat different history of cultural styles and everyday practices for which we are still finding the best conceptual tools. There is a lot of good work to be done.[14]

Others, in the tradition of Jürgen Habermas and later critical theory, treat "civic" in terms of "civil society," as a sphere of social self-direction, where people maintain traditions, develop new cultural meanings reflexively, and sometimes resist colonization by the market or state (Cohen 1982, Cohen and Arato 1992). My pragmatic approach has affinities with it especially by way of a shared intellectual debt to John Dewey, with his focus on problem-solving, communicating publics. Many already know the criticisms that the Habermasian approach carries normative biases and blind-spots that would obscure particular kinds of actors, speech styles, or sites that other scholars would want to consider civic. Less often remarked are the problems with conceiving "civil society" as a separate sector or sphere. My pragmatic, cultural approach intentionally narrows the realm of things civic to a more empirically defensible focus that preserves the core concerns of a variety of civil society theorists inside and outside the Habermasian circle.

It may be controversial too to define civic culture in a way that leaves out collectivities that exist mainly for socializing as an end in itself. I mean the soccer clubs, bird-watching societies, and yes—bowling leagues—which figure prominently in studies of civic engagement (Putnam 1993, 2000). Sociability continues to be an underappreciated topic of sociological inquiry despite a renaissance of interest in Simmel (see Citroni 2010). The current, close association of sociability with "civic," though, is not natural or logical but at least partly an artifact of the civic engagement scholars' embrace of a social capital concept that supposes almost all social relationships generate social interdependence. In this view, any group or relationship is a unit of generalized value that brings "civic" effects. Groups are functionally equal units of "capital," in this point of view, so the more social ties someone or some group has, the more society increases its store of civic-minded capacities. I propose in contrast that we honor an older, still valuable understanding of "civic" that would distinguish different kinds of public collectivities, and find a sporting club to be civic actor only when it decides to define a public problem and pursue a cause, the cause of more funding for after-school sports, perhaps. The outpouring of research on social capital over the past two decades has benefited sociology by putting civic action back on many scholars' research agendas. Yet these studies have traded on a loose, overly broad definition of civic engagement that avoids questions of meaning and action which mattered to a variety of civil society theorists and should matter to cultural sociologists of any theoretical persuasion (see Lichterman 2006).

The approach here invites scholars to a more precise, more contextually sensitive concept. Many studies continue to recirculate the methodological and implicitly normative assumptions of *The Civic Culture* and its contemporary descendents. Often they employ "social capital" as a conceptual box for the group memberships or social ties that they are counting. Much as the social capital concept is useful for some questions, it flattens cross-national comparisons and obscures dimensions of difference (or similarity) that could matter greatly in both institutional and everyday life. For these questions, we need a nonnormative concept that allows us to make sense of potentially inconvenient discoveries. The Ku Klux Klan (KKK) may represent "the dark side of social capital" (Putnam 2000), and we may be loath to count its memberships in an index of social capital, but at its height in the 1920s, local KKK groups held community barbecues and created a kind of togetherness (McVeigh 2009) that might be the envy of some progressive groups far more congenial to the vast majority of social researchers. A practical, cultural sociology allows us to follow elements of civic culture as they travel to curious places and as people enact them in perhaps surprising ways, for better and worse.

NOTES

1. Tocqueville (1969 [1835]), p. 513.
2. Tocqueville (1969 [1835]), pp. 506, 513, 521–524.
3. Tocqueville (1969 [1835]), p. 513.
4. For a few statements on these points from varied perspectives, see Alexander and Seidman (1990); Alexander and Smith (1993); Sewell (1992); Swidler (2001); Eliasoph and Lichterman (2003); Wuthnow (1987, 1992).
5. We could include here studies of narratives in social history and cultural sociology, which hold that events in the social world become meaningful, and people become able to act toward them, only when they get articulated in words; the words often take the form of a story. For a representative sample of theory and research, see Somers (1994), Kane (1997), Wuthnow (1991).
6. For a few examples, see, for instance, Bellah et al. (1996); Hart (1992); Teske (1997); Tipton (1982); Witten (1993); Wood (1999, 1994); Wuthnow (1992, 1991).

7. See my recent argument for a "practical cultural sociology" and the studies I refer to there, in Lichterman (2007a).

8. I share this multi-method research project with Chris Weare, Nina Eliasoph, and Nicole Esparza, all at the University of Southern California. We are exploring how group styles and ways of articulating public issues come together in different kinds of organizations that address housing and environmental issues.

9. See Lichterman and Potts (2009). This section follows closely our argument about the cultural context of religion and the dangers of essentialism. See also the demonstration of a "contextual" approach to religion in Lichterman (2007b).

10. For a valuable, extended argument on this point, see Ammerman (2003).

11. On organizational formats, see Demerath et al. (1998), Becker (1999), and Lichterman (2005).

12. For some germinal statements, see Snow et al. (1986), Snow and Benford (1988), McAdam, McCarthy and Tarrow (1995), Gamson (1992), Ferree et al. (2002). For a recent review, see Polletta and Ho (2006). The use of the frame concept in social movement research differs in important ways from Erving Goffman's use of the concept, as Snow and colleagues (Snow et al. 1986) themselves noted; see also Lichterman and Cefaï (2006) on this point.

13. For a review of research on collective identity in social movements, see Snow (2001) or Polletta and Jasper (2001). For germinal statements and research on the topic, see Melucci (1989) or Taylor and Whittier (1992). Regarding the specific example here, in the 1980s, local citizens fighting pollution often called themselves "anti-toxics" activists who considered their struggles local if loosely related to those of other locales. Later, the problem broadened from one of pollution to that of "environmental racism," implying that the aggrieved are people of color. Meanwhile, a well-known, nationwide community organizing outfit, ACORN (Associated Communities Organized for Reform Now), continued to refer to the constituents of its various campaigns as people of low to moderate income.

14. For some solid ideas on integrating ethnographic and historical inquiry, see Trom 2002; see also Cerutti 2004; Diehl and McFarland 2010).

REFERENCES

Addams, Jane. 2002 [1902]. *Democracy and Social Ethics*. With an introduction by Charlene H. Siegfried. Urbana: University of Illinois Press.

Alexander, Jeffrey. 1988. *Durkheimian Sociology: Cultural Studies*. Berkeley: University of California Press.

——. 2006. *The Civil Sphere*. New York: Oxford University Press.

Alexander, Jeffrey, and Steven Seidman, eds. 1990. *Culture and Society: Contemporary Debates*. Cambridge, UK, and New York: Cambridge University Press.

Alexander, Jeffrey, and Philip Smith. 1993. "The Discourse of American Civil Society: A New Proposal for Cultural Studies." *Theory and Society* 22: 151–207.

Almond, Gabriel, and Sidney Verba. 1963. *The Civic Culture*. Princeton, NJ: Princeton University Press.

Amiraux, Valérie. 2006. "Speaking as a Muslim: Avoiding Religion in French Public Space." Pp. 21–52 in *Politics of Visibility: Young Muslims in European Public Spaces*, edited by G. Jonker and V. Amiraux. New Brunswick, NJ: Transaction Publishers.

Ammerman, Nancy. 2003. "Religious Identities and Religious Institutions." Pp. 207–24 in *Handbook for the Sociology of Religion*, edited by M. Dillon. Cambridge, UK: Cambridge University Press.

Armstrong, Elizabeth. 2002. *Forging Gay Identities*. Chicago: University of Chicago Press.

Asad, Talal. 2003. *Formations of the Secular: Christianity, Islam, Modernity*. Stanford, CA: Stanford University Press, 2003.

Baiocchi, Gianpaolo. 2006. "The Civilizing Force of Social Movements: Corporate and Liberal Codes in Brazil's Public Sphere." *Sociological Theory* 24: 285–311.

Banfield, Edward. 1958. *The Moral Basis of a Backward Society*. New York: Free Press.

Becker, Penny Edgell. 1999. *Congregations in Conflict: Cultural Models of Local Religious Life*. New York: Cambridge University Press.

Bellah, Robert, Richard Madsen, William Sullivan, Ann Swidler, and Steven Tipton. 1996. *Habits of the Heart: Individualism and Commitment in American Life*. 2nd ed. with a new introduction. Berkeley: University of California Press.

Berger, Peter. 1967. *The Sacred Canopy*. Garden City, NY: Doubleday.

Berger, Peter, and Richard John Neuhaus. 1977. *To Empower People: From State to Civil Society*. Washington, DC: AEI Press.

Bernstein, Mary. 1997. "Celebration and Suppression: The Strategic Uses of Identity by the Lesbian and Gay Movement." *American Journal of Sociology* 103(3): 531–565.

Boltanksi, Luc, and Laurent Thévenot. 1991. *De la Justification*. Paris: Gallimard.

Breines, Wini. 1982. *Community and Organization in the New Left, 1962–1968*. New York: Praeger.

Cerutti Simone. 2004. "Microhistory: Social Relations versus Cultural Models?" Pp. 17–40 in A.M. Castrén, M. Lonkila and M. Peltonen, eds. *Between Sociology and History. Essays in Microhistory, Collective Action, and Nation-Building*. Helsinki: SKS.

Citroni, Sebastiano. 2010. "Inclusive Togetherness. A Comparative Ethnography of Cultural Associations Making Milan Sociable." PhD diss., Department of Sociology, Universitá degli Studi di Milano-Bicocca.

Clecak, Peter. 1981. *America's Search for the Ideal Self*. New York: Oxford University Press.

Cohen, Jean. 1982. *Class and Civil Society: The Limits of Marxian Critical Theory*. Amherst: University of Massachusetts Press.

Cohen, Jean, and Andrew Arato. 1992. *Civil Society and Political Theory*. Cambridge, MA: MIT Press.

Condit, Celeste. 1994. *Decoding Abortion Rhetoric*. Urbana: University of Illinois Press.

Demerath, Jay, Peter Hall, Terry Schmitt, and Rhys Williams. 1998. *Sacred Companies: Organizational Aspects of Religion and Religious Aspects of Organizations*. New York: Oxford University Press.

Dewey, John. 1927. *The Public and Its Problems*. Denver: Allan Swallow.

Diehl, David, and Daniel McFarland. 2010. "Toward a Historical Sociology of Social Situations." *American Journal of Sociology* 115(6): 1713–1752,

DiMaggio, Paul and Walter Powell, eds. 1991. *The New Institutionalism in Organizational Analysis*. Chicago: University of Chicago Press.

Durkheim, Émile. 1957. *Professional Ethics and Civic Morals*. Translated by Cornelia Brookfield. London: Routledge and Paul.

Eliasoph, Nina. 1996. "Making a Fragile Public: A Talk-Centered Study of Citizenship and Power." *Sociological Theory* 14(3): 262–289.

———. 1998. *Avoiding Politics. How Americans Produce Apathy in Everyday Life*. New York: Cambridge University Press.

Eliasoph, Nina, and Paul Lichterman. 2003. "Culture in Interaction." *American Journal of Sociology* 108(4): 735–794.

Epstein, Barbara. 1991. *Political Protest and Cultural Revolution*. Berkeley: University of California Press.

Etzioni, Amitai. 1968. *The Active Society*. New York: Free Press.

Faucher-King, Florence. 2005. *Changing Parties: An Anthropology of British Political Party Conferences*. New York: Palgrave Macmillan.

Ferree, Myra, William Gamson and Jürgen Gerhards. 2002. *Shaping Abortion Discourse*. Cambridge, UK: Cambridge University Press.

Gamson, William. 1992. *Talking Politics*. Cambridge, UK: Cambridge University Press.

Goffman, Erving. 1961. *Encounters: Two Studies in the Sociology of Interaction*. Indianapolis, IN: Bobbs-Merrill.

Gramsci, Antonio. 1971. *Selections from the Prison Notebooks*. Translated by Q. Hoare and G. Smith. New York: International Publishers.

Gusfield, Joseph. 1981. *The Culture of Public Problems*. Chicago: University of Chicago Press.

Hall, Stuart. 1977. "Culture, the Media and the Ideological Effect," Pp. 215–248 in *Mass Communication and Society*, edited by J. Curran, M. Gurevitch, and J. Woolacott. London: Edward Arnold.

Hart, Stephen. 1992. *What Does the Lord Require?* New York: Oxford University Press.

Hartz, Louis. 1955. *The Liberal Tradition in America: An Interpretation of American Political Thought since the Revolution*. 1st ed. New York: Harcourt.

Inglehart, Ronald. 1977. *The Silent Revolution*. Princeton, NJ: Princeton University Press.

———. 1981. "Post-Materialism in an Environment of Insecurity." *American Political Science Review* 75: 880–900.

———. 1990. *Culture Shift in Advanced Industrial Society*. Princeton, NJ: Princeton University Press.

Jacobs, M. D., and L. Spillman. 2005. "Cultural Sociology at the Crossroads of the Discipline." *Poetics* 33: 1–14.

Jacobs, Ronald. 2000. *Race, Media, and the Crisis of Civil Society*. New York: Cambridge University Press.

Janowitz, Morris. 1975. "Sociological Theory and Social Control." *American Journal of Sociology* 81: 82–108.

Junker, Andrew. 2008. "Inner Revolutions and Other True Stories: Culture, Narrative and Belief." Paper presented at the Annual Meeting of the American Sociological Association, Boston, August.

Kane, Anne. 1997. "Theorizing Meaning Construction in Social Movements: Symbolic Structures and Interpretation during the Irish Land War,1879–1882." *Sociological Theory* 15(3): 249–276.

Kaufman, Jason. 2002. *For the Common Good?* New York: Oxford University Press.

Kertzer, David. 1990. *Comrades and Christians: Religion and Political Struggle in Communist Italy*. Prospect Heights, IL: Waveland Press.

Lancaster, Roger. 1988. *Thanks to God and the Revolution*. New York: Columbia University Press.

Lasch, Christopher. 1966. *The New Radicalism in America: 1889–1963*. New York: Knopf.

Lichterman, Paul. 1995a. "Piecing Together Multicultural Community: Cultural Differences in Community Building Among Grass-Roots Environmentalists." *Social Problems* 42(4): 513–534.

———. 1995b. "Beyond the Seesaw Model: Public Commitment in a Culture of Self-Fulfillment." *Sociological Theory* 13(3): 275–300.

———. 1996. *The Search for Political Community: American Activists Reinventing Commitment*. New York: Cambridge University Press.

————. 1999. "Talking Identity in the Public Sphere: Broad Visions and Small Spaces in Sexual Identity Politics." *Theory and Society* 28(1): 101–141.

————. 2005. *Elusive Togetherness: Church Groups Trying to Bridge America's Divisions.* Princeton, NJ: Princeton University Press.

————. 2006. "Social Capital or Group Style? Rescuing Tocqueville's Insights on Civic Engagement." *Theory and Society* 35(5/6): 529–563.

————. 2007a. "Invitation to a Practical Cultural Sociology." Pp. 19–54 in *Culture, Society and Democracy: The Interpretive Approach*, edited by Isaac Reed and Jeffrey Alexander. Boulder, CO: Paradigm Publishers.

————. 2007b. "Beyond Dogmas: Religion, Social Service, and Social Life in the United States." *American Journal of Sociology* 113(1): 243–257.

————. 2008. "Religion and the Construction of Civic Identity." *American Sociological Review* 73: 83–104.

Lichterman, Paul, and C. Brady Potts. 2009. *The Civic Life of American Religion.* Stanford, CA: Stanford University Press.

Lichterman, Paul, and Daniel Cefaï. 2006. "The Idea of Political Culture." Pp. 392–414 in *The Oxford Handbook of Contextual Political Studies*, edited by Robert Goodin and Charles Tilly. New York: Oxford University Press.

Lichterman, Paul, Prudence Carter, and Michèle Lamont. 2009. "Race-Bridging for Christ? Conservative Christians and Black-White Relations in Community Life." Pp. 187–220 in *Conservative Christians and American Democracy*, edited by S. Brint and J. Schroedel. New York: Russell Sage.

Luckmann, Thomas. 1967. *The Invisible Religion: The Problem of Religion in Modern Society.* New York: Macmillan.

MacIntyre, Alasdair. 1972. "Is a Science of Comparative Politics Possible?" Pp. 8–26 in *Philosophy, Politics and Society*, 4th series, edited by P. Laslett, W. G. Runciman, and Q. Skinner. Oxford: Blackwell.

McAdam, Doug, John McCarthy, and Mayer Zald. 1996. *Comparative Perspectives on Social Movements.* Cambridge, UK: Cambridge University Press.

McAdam, Doug, Sidney Tarrow, and Charles Tilly. 2001. *Dynamics of Contention.* Cambridge, UK: Cambridge University Press.

McVeigh, Rory. 2009. *The Rise of the Ku Klux Klan: Right-Wing Movements and National Politics.* Minneapolis: University of Minnesota Press.

Melucci, Alberto. 1989. *Nomads of the Present.* Philadelphia: Temple University Press.

Moon, Dawne. 2004. *God, Sex and Politics.* Berkeley: University of California Press.

Parsons, Talcott, and Edward Shils, eds. 1951. *Toward a General Theory of Action.* Cambridge, MA: Harvard University Press.

Pateman, Carole. 1980. "The Civic Culture: A Philosophic Critique." Pp. 57–102 in *The Civic Culture Revisited*, edited by G. Almond and S. Verba. Boston: Little Brown.

Polletta, Francesca, and James M. Jasper. 2001. "Collective Identity and Social Movements." *Annual Review of Sociology* 27: 283–305.

Polletta, Francesca, and M. Kai Ho. 2006. "Frames and Their Consequences." Pp. 187–209 *The Oxford Handbook of Contextual Political Analysis*, edited by Robert Goodin and Charles Tilly. Oxford: Oxford University Press.

Putnam, Robert. 1993. *Making Democracy Work.* Princeton, NJ: Princeton University Press.

————. 1996. "The Strange Disappearance of Civic America." *The American Prospect* 24 (Winter): 34–48.

————. 2000. *Bowling Alone.* New York: Simon and Schuster.

Putnam, Robert, and Katherine Goss, eds. 2002. *Democracies in Flux: The Evolution of Social Capital in Contemporary Society.* New York: Oxford University Press.

Roszak, Theodore. 1969. *The Making of a Counter Culture*. Garden City, NY: Doubleday.

Schudson, Michael. 1998. *The Good Citizen*. New York: Free Press.

Sewell, William, Jr. 1980. *Work and Revolution in France*. Cambridge, UK: Cambridge University Press.

———. 1992. "A Theory of Structure: Duality, Agency, and Transformation." *American Journal of Sociology* 98(1): 1–29.

Skocpol, T., and M. P. Fiorina. 1999. *Civic Engagement in American Democracy*. Washington, DC: Brookings Institution Press.

Snow, David. 2001. "Collective Identity and Expressive Forms." Pp. 2212–2219 in *The International Encyclopedia of the Social and Behavioral Sciences*, Vol. 4, edited by Neil Smelser and Paul Baltes. Oxford: Elsevier.

Snow, David, and Robert Benford. 1988. "Ideology, Frame Resonance, and Participant Mobilization." *International Social Movement Research* 1: 97–217.

———. 1992. "Master Frames and Cycles of Protest." Pp. 133–155 in *Frontiers in Social Movement Theory*, edited by Aldon Morris and Carol Mueller. New Haven, CT: Yale University Press.

Snow, David, E. B. Rochford, Jr., et al. 1986. "Frame Alignment Processes, Micromobilization, and Movement Participation." *American Sociological Review* 51(4): 464–481.

Somers, Margaret. 1994. "The Narrative Constitution of Identity: A Relational and Network Approach." *Theory and Society* 23: 605–649.

———. 1995. "What's So Political and Cultural about Political Culture and the Public Sphere?" *Sociological Theory* 13: 229–274.

Swidler, Ann. 2001. *Talk of Love*. Chicago: University of Chicago Press.

Taylor, V., and Whittier, N. 1992. "Collective Identity in Social Movement Communities: Lesbian Feminist Mobilization." Pp. 104–130 in *Frontiers of Social Movement Theory*, edited by A. Morris and C. Mueller. New Haven, CT: Yale University Press.

Teske, Nathan. 1997. *Political Activists in America*. Cambridge, UK: Cambridge University Press.

Tipton, Steven. 1982. *Getting Saved from the Sixties*. Berkeley: University of California Press.

Tocqueville, Alexis. 1969 [1835]. *Democracy in America*. Edited by J. P. Mayer. Garden City, NY: Doubleday.

Trom, Danny. 2002. "Ethnographic Inquiry and the Historicity of Action." In *Social Science Methodology in the New Millennium: Proceedings of the Fifth International Conference on Logic and Methodology*, 2nd ed., edited by J. Blasius, J. How, E. de Leeuw, and P. Schmidt. Cologne, Germany: Leske + Budrich. CD-ROM.

Turner, Victor. 1974. *Dramas, Fields and Metaphors*. Ithaca, NY: Cornell University Press.

Verba, Sidney, Kay Schlozman, and Henry Brady. 1995. *Voice and Equality: Civic Voluntarism in American Politics*. Cambridge, MA: Harvard University Press.

Warren, Mark R. 2001. *Dry Bones Rattling*. Princeton, NJ: Princeton University Press.

Williams, Rhys. 1995 "Constructing the Public Good: Social Movements and Cultural Resources." *Social Problems* 42: 124–144.

Witten, Marsha. 1993. *All Is Forgiven: The Secular Message in American Protestantism*. Princeton, NJ: Princeton University Press.

Wood, Richard. 1994. "Faith in Action: Religious Resources for Political Success in Three Congregations." *Sociology of Religion* 55(4): 397–417.

———. 1999. "Religious Culture and Political Action." *Sociological Theory* 17: 307–332.

———. 2002. *Faith in Action*. Chicago: University of Chicago Press.

Wuthnow, Robert. 1987. *Meaning and Moral Order*. Berkeley: University of California Press.

———. 1991. *Acts of Compassion*. Princeton, NJ: Princeton University

———, ed. 1992. *Vocabularies of Public Life*. New York: Routledge.

CHAPTER 9

CULTURAL SOCIOLOGY AND CIVIL SOCIETY IN A WORLD OF FLOWS: RECAPTURING AMBIGUITY, HYBRIDITY, AND THE POLITICAL*

GIANPAOLO BAIOCCHI

How well does cultural sociology travel? Specifically, how well do our frameworks of politics and culture hold up "in most of the world," to use Partha Chatterjee's provocative phrase for the Global South (Chatterjee 2004)? It makes sense that cultural sociologists often avoid comparisons, or at least shy away from what Steinmetz (2008) has termed "experimentalist" sorts of comparisons that hold such a privileged place elsewhere in our discipline. The excesses of a prior generation prior whose efforts at defining national character, national values, or *the* culture of poverty have been doubly influential: once in defining an agenda for modernizationist social science, and again, in discouraging more recent scholarship from engaging in comparisons by making it seem that theoretical ambition and cross-national work are bound to end up in simplistic caricature. Current exercises in civilizational diatribe—attempts to define "the" Islamic character, for example—do not help the cause either. Whatever the cause, cultural sociology seems impoverished for it; despite some recent notable exceptions, cultural sociologists have often focused on

* With thanks to Ron Jacobs, Nathaniel Berman, Agustin Lao-Montes, Keith Brown, and Vasuki Nesiah for their comments and suggestions on this chapter.

North America and, to a lesser extent, Europe. But more to the point, we have too seldom put our comparative imaginations to work, and not extended our horizons nearly enough.

This chapter is an effort at "provincializing" cultural sociology, and to be more precise, the cultural sociology of politics and civil society. The analytic exercise I engage in here is to call into question its purported universalism (Chakrabartty 2000; Burawoy 2007) and engage in theoretical stretching. It is not my intention to revive old corpses, and much less to call for comparative methods per se. Much of the richness and subtlety of what we do might be lost in tidy comparisons and the search for failed and successful cases, as comparative scholars sometimes do. It is also not my intent to evoke charges of "Eeurocentrism" for its own sake, and engage in a reverse Orientalist exercise that, in the end, simply states that "things are different" in other places. Instead, I propose here that cultural sociology might be enriched by a wider consideration of the horizon of the possible meanings that concepts might assume once our frame of reference is more global in scope. The contemporary scholarship has by now noted plural and hybrid forms of discourse in civil societies of the postcolonial world, and levied a host of critiques against attempts at using democratic theory originating in the Global North in the South (see, e.g., Mamdani 1996). More generally, it has become fashionable to criticize the concept and theory of civil society, especially when linked to its pervasive deployment in development prescriptions or democracy promotion.[1] By and large, the cultural sociology of politics and civil society has so far remained untouched by much of this discussion.

In this chapter, I develop a slightly different, but parallel, critique about the democratic theory that informs cultural sociology as a way to suggest that it might be useful for scholarship in and about the Global North to keep this broader frame of reference in mind. Loosening assumptions might lead to theoretical stretching, interesting engagement with colleagues elsewhere, and perhaps even unexpected insights into cultural processes in the changing United States.

This chapter moves in parts. After a brief sketch of the origins of what is distinctive about the cultural sociology of civil society, I then consider its three unspoken assumptions. While Alexander's recent *Civil Sphere* is the central text that serves as my reference for the discussion below, the assumptions I raise are widely used. First, I address the assumption of *minimal stateness* in the lives and worlds of social movements and civil society. Scholars have questioned the assumption of the separateness of state and civil society that informs liberal theory. But cultural sociologists have less often addressed what might be called the *stateness* of political culture itself, the ways that images of states can come to loom large in the practices and representations of civil society. Second, I look at the *nexus of civil and civilized*. I raise the issue that liberal democracy in the postcolonial world has as often been part of imperial statecraft as of the political rationality of projects of liberation, and that the very idea of civil society itself has often been part of a "civilizing mission" imposed from outside. This makes the idea of a civil sphere much more ambiguous, and the idea of movements as agents of social repair more contradictory. And third,

I consider that the *social location of the political* in nonliberal societies might be different than in established liberal societies. Acceptable domains of conflict, and what might actually be at stake in those conflicts, could be much wider in societies where the routinization of conflict and the institutionalization of civil society are seemingly so complete, as is the case in the United States.

As a demonstration of the usefulness of this exercise, I also consider ways in which loosening these assumptions might make cultural sociology travel "better." Throughout the chapter, I consider examples referring to civil society in places in the Global South before considering some implications of these arguments for looking at settings in the Global North. This essay escapes some of the traditional genres for similar essays—it is neither fully a literature review nor a theoretical intervention, nor is it a completely developed analytical exercise in which cases are fully developed. Rather, it is a response to the challenge laid by the editors of this volume for the authors to think out loud about what shapes our perspectives as cultural sociologists and in what ways we see the field moving forward. What I discuss below, as its assumptions, certainly does not apply to every cultural sociological study, and is written in the spirit of Tilly's (1994) *Pernicious Postulates*—part provocation and part call to reform—but nonetheless addressing real undercurrents of our scholarship. It is also, more specifically, a response to the implicit challenge of Alexander's *The Civil Sphere* to identify a specifically sociological terrain from which to engage pressing normative issues. While it argues for shifting the terrain, the argument here implies broad agreement with the project itself.

From Norms and Values to Practices and Meanings: Cultural Sociology Looks at Civil Society

Civil society is definitely back on the intellectual agenda of sociologists. The concept has experienced a revival in recent years, after a first revival in the late 1980s driven by the waves of democratization in Eastern Europe and Latin America (Berezin 1997; Calhoun 1992; Somers 1995). Political scientists developed a whole framework of transition studies that examined democratization processes, first in Southern Europe (in the 1970s), then in Latin America in the 1980s, and then in East Asia and Eastern Europe (in the 1980s and 1990s). The most famous of these was the "Third Wave" thesis of Samuel Huntington's (Huntington 1986). Sociologists joined the conversation slightly later and with a greater emphasis on "society-side" factors. The translation of *The Public Sphere*, in 1989, was particularly influential (Calhoun 1992). With the resurgent interest in the "cluster of citizenship concepts" (Somers 1998), sociologists of culture once again have started to pay serious attention to questions of political culture, turning to cultural explanations for outcomes in terms of citizenship, participation, and even economic development (Berezin 1997). Concepts like the "public sphere" and "citizenship" have been operationalized in ways that highlight that political practices are culturally specific to peoples, places, and issues.

But civil society was always a central preoccupation of sociologists, even if not always assuming the language. In sociology, under the guise of community studies, since the 1930s scholars have engaged in direct observation of neighborhood activists, political networks, and the day-to-day life of politics. Many of the most famous such studies, such as Robert and Helen Lynd's *Middletown* studies (1929; 1937), Floyd Hunter's study of Atlanta (1953), or Viditch and Bensman's study of Candor, New York (1956), were studies very much concerned with what we might think of today as civil society: voluntary activities, local politics, democratic engagement.

Up until the 1960s, much of the work was at this point largely influenced by versions of Parsonian modernization theory and functionalism. As is well known, Parsons was centrally preoccupied with the role of civil society in preserving democracy. For instance, such themes are found in the work of scholars like Banfield (1956), who purported to have found in the culture of Southern Italy the "moral bases" of that "backward society" in the insistence on honor, the favor, and asymmetrical relationships. How could democracy ever flourish, Banfield wondered (1956, 8), in places where a peasant can "satisfy his aspirations by reaching out his hand to the nearest coconut?"

Civil society throughout this period was understood as the terrain of the construction of democratic or anti-democratic values. Much of the theoretical work went into defining schemes that that differentiated the ideal characteristics of traditional and modern societies, and these tended to inform the way that social scientists in general, and sociologists in particular, approached civil society. Modern societies were differentiated, democratic, universalistic, and meritocratic. Traditional societies were undifferentiated, authoritarian, particularistic, and based rewards on ascriptive characteristics. Studies asked about the conditions under which societies achieved these characteristics. Almond and Verba's 1963 study of political culture in five nations asked of the attitudes and beliefs of citizens of various nations as either impediments or preconditions to democratic development. Reinhard Bendix developed similar arguments in *Nation-Building and Citizenship* (1964). Lipset's work throughout the 1960s sought to understand the preconditions for democracy. In *The First New Nation* (1963), he offered a comparison of the history of the United States with that of European countries and argued that American history had fostered a set of values of achievement and equalitarianism that made for a stable democracy. He found remnants of elitism in both France and Germany, which made them, in this view, unstable democracies.

Enter Cultural Sociology

New sociologists of culture argued that an older generation of culture scholars had succumbed to a number of bad, modernist biases—subtextually linked to the conservatism of the 1950s—that now had to be transcended if the field was to move forward. The worst of these was an alleged tendency toward "essentialism," which manifested itself in different ways: a marked preference for analysis of cultural wholes, whose boundaries were assumed to be coextensive with those of the nation-state; the view that the maintenance of social equilibria requires a high degree of value consensus, anchored in the integration of the social and cultural systems through processes of socialization and mechanisms of social control; and the assumption that—the Parsonian insistence on voluntarism not withstanding—cultural values and beliefs are, in those instances where other processes of social determination are not at play, largely determinative of social action. These tendencies were deemed essentialist because they all assumed that the culture of a society represented a more or less stable essence on the order of a Platonic form, whose consequences for social life could be assessed through the incorporation of straightforward readings of the cultural ethos into structural-functionalist models of the social system, with little attention paid to the nature of agency.[2]

Nonetheless, civil society reentered the conceptual vocabulary of sociologists in a significant way in the 1990s, when they turned to the symbols and meanings attached to political life, political practice, and in particular democracy and civic life. This move had been prefaced by a number of other studies dealing with politics in the 1980s that had increasingly cultural dimensions. Social movement scholars, for example, had become attentive to individual actors as well as meaning-making, especially under the guise of frames analysis (Gamson, Fireman, and Rytina 1982; Snow and Benford 1988). McAdam's study of Freedom Summer (1988), for example, explored the biographical roots of activism in depth, and relies in large part on the understanding of participants to make sense of events. Gamson's study (1992) of how "average working people" talk politics relies on the observation of "peer groups"—a variant of the focus group, in which a small group of peers talks in a nonbureaucratic setting and the facilitator plays a minor role in keeping the conversation going. Concerned with distorted views of the mass public that portray the average person as a passive consumer of media information, and well as with understanding the sort of political consciousness that can lead to collective action, Gamson presented his participants with topics and observed how talk naturally occurred, coding it for frames.

Another influential cultural strand in the study of democracy comes from the team of researchers headed by Robert Bellah that published *Habits of the Heart* in 1985. Bellah and his co-authors asked about the "state of democracy" in the United States, and concluded that an individually oriented culture was eroding the bases for collective life and civic engagement. Bellah et al.'s investigation of the nature of the relationship between public and private life in the contemporary United States is concerned with understanding action in the public sphere, and "the resources Americans have for making sense of their lives, how they think about themselves and their society, and how their ideas relate to action" (Bellah et al. 1985, ix).

But it was the 1989 English translation of Habermas' *The Structural Transformation of the Public Sphere* that changed the tenor of the discussion. Its attention to democratic deliberation as a potentially emancipatory activity gave sociologists greater leeway to examine political culture as something other than ideology or the expression of class interests. Another extremely influential work, related to the issues raised by Bellah et al. (1985), but also echoing the work of earlier scholars like Banfield (1956), was Robert Putnam's (1993) *Making Democracy Work*. It compared the South and North of Italy and concluded that the South lacks the proper cultural conditions for an active democratic life. Putnam's more recent *Bowling Alone* (2001) has argued that Americans are becoming more self-centered and community life has ceased to have the vitality it once did.

The twin influences of Habermas on one hand, and Bellah/Putnam on the other, have inspired a lively discussion on how to understand civic association in the United States (Perrin 2007; Wood 2002; Eliasoph 1998; Lichterman 1996, 1999). These add to a resurgence in studies based in the Global South, especially among the Latin American urban poor, also largely inspired by concepts of civil society and in dialogue with some version of the Habermassian image of deliberation and association (Mische 2006; Arias, 2006; Baiocchi, 2005; Sawyer 2004; Auyero 2000; Edelman 1999; Gay 1995).

But one of the central and distinctly cultural analysis of civil society is that based on the work of Jeffrey Alexander. Alexander's *The Civil Sphere* (2006) is the most articulated version of the framework that synthesizes and extends earlier writings on culture and civil society by him and his students. The project of *The Civil Sphere* is to understand the question of solidarity and its underpinnings. The civil sphere is an independent sphere of "values and institutions that generates the capacity for social criticism and democratic integration at the same time" (4). In democratic societies, the civil sphere expresses its influence through its regulative institutions—the law, the mass media, voluntary associations—which project communicative judgments. Actually existing civil spheres are contradictory and exist in tension with other spheres, such as "the family, religious groups, scientific associations, economic institutions, and geographically bounded regional communities still produced different kinds of goods and organized their social relations according to different ideals and constraints" (Alexander 2006, 404). Civil repair is the project of extending the values and judgments of civil society outward, and it is the work of civil repair that occupies social movements and other reformers who want to project the utopian ideals of the civil sphere onto uncivil institutions and spheres.

Civil society is understood as a primarily cultural phenomenon. The utopian vision that drives members of civil society to extend solidarity is maintained and held in a set of practices and rituals. As in his earlier work (1985; see also Alexander and Smith 1993), a central role is afforded to the "independent causal importance of symbolic classification, and the pivotal role of the symbolic division between sacred and profane" (Alexander 1989, 57). In the United States, the ideal type of civil society, the "discourse of American civil society" provides a cultural grid that maps the motivations of actors, relationships, and institutions as democratic or counter-democratic. Actors motivated by these codes then draw on them to create categories of inclusion/exclusion: those who are worthy of rights (citizen) and those who are not (enemy). The cultural work of civil repair is the symbolic struggle to liken characteristics of certain groups to the sacred elements.

SHIFTING THE FRAME

This "cultural turn" in the discussion of civil society certainly advances the discussion from its earlier guise of modernization-influenced theory. The move away from the idea of democratic values (as in Almond and Verba 1963) to the concept of democratic practices or democratic symbols makes the idea of the culture of democracy much more social as well as contingent. Democratic practices take place in contexts that make them possible, and the connection to democratic symbols is ultimately contingent on rituals, narratives, or the symbolic work of civil repair. Cultural sociology also provides an important corrective to the social-scientific lens that too often sees only objective interests, institutional logics, and rationality instead of meanings, practices, and contingencies. Having moved away from an earlier values approach of modernization theory, cultural sociology now promises to offer us accounts that give flesh to the idea of association in different contexts. It is also now possible to speak of cultural difference without necessarily attributing cultural deficiency. *The Civil Sphere*, for example, is a text that advances normative positions aware of their own historicity. A distinctly cultural, and distinctly sociological, intervention has become possible in the terrain normally reserved for political philosophy (Jason, 2007).

The move from norms and values to practices and meanings opened possibilities for understanding a new range of relationships to the culture of citizenship, a view of "a multiplicity of public spheres, communities and associations nested within one another" (Jacobs 1996, 1239). Though these are all "organized by a shared cultural environment" of the national culture of citizenship (Jacobs 2000, 138). Yet, when we engage in the effort of seriously considering civil society as a set of practices and symbols "in the rest of the world," there is something that doesn't quite travel. Specifically, there is an element of ambiguity and hybridity at the core of that culture in much of the world that cultural sociology is ill-equipped to understand.

For almost two decades now, there has been vibrant discussion in other disciplines about the assumptions behind the concepts of civil society and the limits of its application outside of Europe and the United States.

Three Extreme Examples

Let us consider three extreme examples of the way that the cultural codes of democracy have been taken up outside of Europe and North America.

First, let us consider one example of the way in which the meanings of democracy have been embraced. At one end of the spectrum might be the discourses and practices of an organization like Al-Haq, a civil society organization in Palestine organized in the 1960s to "promote the rule of law" and "the respect of human rights and liberties" in Palestinian society. Like the actors of civil repair in Alexander's framework, the activists of Al-Haq exert communicative judgments to noncivil spheres—be they authoritarian elements within Palestinian society or the violation of the rights of Palestinians by Israeli institutions. The charter of Al-Haq reads like ideal typical examples of the values of civil society. It seeks to:

- Protect the rights and freedoms of the Palestinians in Palestinian society.
- Enhance human rights concepts in Palestinian society.
- Develop Palestinians' concepts and awareness of public rights and freedoms.
- Lay the foundation to, and epitomize, the international principles of human rights and freedoms throughout Palestinian society.

The values the charter promotes—rights, freedoms, and responsibility—are consistent with the code of liberty and with the democratic values described in *The Civil Sphere*. Implicit in the charter is a notion of an active public that takes responsibility for the awareness of its own rights, the notion of an active citizen. When it comes to the national question, Al-Haq's charter is unambiguous in its defense of the rule of law and its advocacy for legimate and lawful means of redress (Rabbani 1994). It pledges to:

> Strengthen governmental as well as nongovernmental international support for the Palestinian people's legitimate rights to self-determination and the creation of their independent state.
> Defend the rights of Palestinians through various legitimate means in accordance with national and international laws and treaties.[3]

The practices of Al-Haq—its reports of human rights violations, its legal cases on behalf of victims, its advocacy and public awareness campaigns—are premised on the vision, consistent with the cultural sociology of civil society, that even in the context of the Israeli/Palestinian conflict, it is by making appeals to dominant civil society (and global arenas) where "even the most dominated outgroup historically unprecedented levels of accessibility and respect" (Alexander, 2006, 416).

But consider another extreme example, in which the language and rhetoric of democracy and rights in the postcolonial world are used completely instrumentally. Robert Mugabe, rated the "worst dictator in the world" for 2009,[4] gave a speech at the United Nations in 2007 that displayed another relationship to the discourse of rights and democracy than Al-Haq's embrace. In power in Zimbabwe since 1980, Mugabe has run a blatant "kleptocracy" in which family and allies live lives of luxury funded by public coffers, while inflation and food shortages have caused human catastrophe for regular citizens, and political opponents have been beaten and killed by the scores. In 2006 and 2007, there were calls for sanctions against his government, to which he responded at the UN by criticizing the "hypocrisy" of Western nations and suggesting adherence to even *higher* standards of human rights, which he argues Western countries themselves have undermined in Africa:

> Zimbabwe won its independence on 18th April, 1980, after a protracted war against British colonial imperialism which denied us human rights and democracy. That colonial system which suppressed and oppressed us enjoyed the support of many countries of the West who were signatories to the UN Universal Declaration of Human Rights.
>
> ...For the West, vested economic interests, racial and ethnocentric considerations proved stronger than their adherence to principles of the Universal Declaration of Human Rights. The West still negates our sovereignties by way of control of our resources, in the process making us mere chattels in our own lands, mere minders of its transnational interests.
>
> ...I am termed dictator because I have rejected this supremacist view and frustrated the neo-colonialists.
>
> Let Mr. Bush read history correctly. Let him realise that both personally and in his representative capacity as the current President of the United States, he stands for this "civilisation" which occupied, which colonised, which incarcerated, which killed. He has much to atone for and very little to lecture us on the Universal Declaration of Human Rights....We say No to him and encourage him to get out of Iraq. Indeed he should mend his ways before he clambers up the pulpit to deliver pieties of democracy.
>
> In conclusion, let me stress once more that the strength of the United Nations lies in its universality and impartiality as it implements its mandate to promote peace and security, economic and social development, human rights and international law as outlined in the Charter. Zimbabwe stands ready to play its part in all efforts and programmes aimed at achieving these noble goals.[5]

This speech of Mugabe's is consistent with his other domestic pronouncements on the subject.[6] That is, in response to criticisms about human rights and the lack of democracy in his country, Mugabe often counters with calls for the protection of the sovereignty of Zimbabwe. He accuses Western powers of neocolonialism and paternalism when international human rights standards are applied to Zimbabwe. But what his speeches reveal, more than individual pathology or dishonesty, or even, the power of nationalist discourses, is a completely cynical use of the language of democracy to justify the use of arbitrary power and violence. And one could find similar examples throughout the world. That is, the language of democratic codes is known, but not embraced. It is understood, but something about its historic association with the powerful makes this kind of rhetoric possible to the extent that it is almost a trope by dictators to proclaim the hyprocrisy of Western powers when human rights are under discussion.

But consider a third, less extreme example. Rather than the embrace of liberal codes by Al-Haq, and quite different than the blatant cynical appropriation of such by Mugabe, there is the possibility of what might be called a critical distancing, or partial embrace of the language games of democracy. This is well exemplified by the discourses and attitudes of community activists I interviewed in the city of Salvador, in the northeast of Brazil.[7] There, these activists from the city's poorer neighborhoods found themselves caught between the blatant corruption of politicians linked to the powerful family that (at that time) essentially ran the whole state, and the universalism of social movement reformers, whom they found unconvincing. For them, the world of the community was experienced as virtuous and the worlds of the government and of political parties were experienced as opaque and dishonest, and inaccessible.

For them, engaging in clientelist exchanges with politicians was a sacrifice or exchange that must be made if the neighborhood wanted something from the government. By doing this, neighborhoods increased their chances of being acknowledged by governmental entities while city-council members and candidates pursued opportunities to increase their electoral base. Though the activists disliked such an approach, and disliked the feelings of dependency fostered as a result, they engaged in it. One neighborhood-based organizer described this process as "selling himself" to politicians by saying:

> Look, [we don't have a relationship with a party or politician] the neighborhood association president usually sells, sells himself to politicians. Whoever gives more to help my neighborhood, I'll support.

Salvador was not a city without social movements, or social movement reformers who would engage in the process of civil repair. But many community activists were skeptical of social movements and the issues they promoted, such as human rights. There was recurrent suspicion of the motives of movement activists and their alleged connections with politicians. A neighborhood organizer claimed that, despite the rhetoric of inclusion, movements reproduced the same patterns that she saw among the city's political elites:

> [Movement leaders] are the small-time powerful people. You see this pyramid inside the social movement, inside the political movement that attempts to create social inclusion, that says you are equal, that you have all the rights, that you can do anything. [But what you have] is the powerful way up high on top and the people down here at the bottom.

The respondent's comment demonstrates suspicion of social and political organizing in general, and much suspicion regarding any group that organizes and achieves some type of official influence. These groups are seen as too close to politicians who cannot be trusted in a system in which "whoever gives more" gets what is needed.

In as much as it is possible to make blanket statements about the "Global South," it can be said that these three very different relationships to democratic codes— the embrace, instrumental use, and critical skepticism—exist with frequency in the postcolonial world, often at the same time and in competition and clashing with one another. The embrace of democratic codes and practices by organizations like Al-Haq or by pro-democracy reformers in authoritarian contexts poses no problem for cultural sociology. The project of civil repair by such actors may be a difficult one, but it is one we understand without difficulty: Actors that identify with democratic codes work to extend it to other, nondemocratic spheres, though the overall context may be inauspicious. Scholarship by Ku, Lo, Baiocchi, Edles, among others, discusses the way that democratic cultural codes come up against other traditions in particular "democratizing" contexts.

But the cultural contexts that underpin the resolute cynicism of a dictator like Mugabe are less easy to grasp, as are contexts that make strategies, such as those of community activists. These are cultural contexts in which the invocation of democracy is, for many people, an empty and meaningless gesture. These are contexts in which symbols and practices of democracy might be divorced from their meaning. Wickramsighe has with some irony charged that:

> so ubiquitous is the phrase "civil society," however, that it is easy to believe that it has always been an existing entity, in the same way as the state or the market, in an ephemeral but nevertheless secure manner. This is because so many voices speak about it, name it, give it a shape and an aura of certainty, almost like Hannah Arendt's stray dog, whose chances of remaining alive increase once named. (Wickramasinghe 2005)

The central problem that critics identify is this: The theory of civil society idealizes the historical experiences of the West. In looking at actually existing practices of civil society and NGOs, scholars have charged that this idealized experience stands as a sort of "anti-politics." It is also argued that, as part of a new rationality of government that calls forward an entrepreneurial citizen, civil society emphasizes some of the most important characteristics of that citizen: self-regulation, responsibility for his or her own problems, and a nonconflictive partnerships with the state (Li 2005; Ong 2006). Finally, there is the problem that an idealized, Western notion of civil society misses a range of practices that fall outside of liberal notions of citizenship and democracy.

In practice, and with specific reference to cultural sociology, this means addressing three assumptions of the scholarship: its unproblematic relationship with "the civil," its assumption of a minimal state, and its bracketing of the political.

Problematizing the Civil and the Uncivil

A first assumption of the cultural sociology of politics is that it has an unproblematic relationship with "the civil." That is, for many cultural sociologists, the "civil" in civil society represents an unmediated notion of democraticness, voluntarism, and general virtue. As the argument goes, civil society exerts its civilizing pressure on the state, and on noncivil structures such as hierarchy, discrimination, and authoritarianism.

There are two problems with this. First, by not having a critical distance from the normative ideal of civil society, we are unable to have a critical distance from its power. Alexander, for example, is fully aware that the discourse of civil society always calls forth an *other*. "Because meaning is relative and relational," he writes, "the civility of the self always articulates itself in the language of the incivility of the other" (2006, 50). But he sees *in civil society itself* the utopian possibility of civil repair, even in conditions of internal colonialism, as "conditions for emancipation are sometimes fostered within the structure of domination itself" (2006, 416). The deployment of the regulative power of civil society is understood as normatively good, and undesirable only insofar as it is incomplete.

Cultural sociologists are generally not concerned with the double connotation of civility as both the rules by which the society of citizens in public space interacts, but also, the opposite of "the barbarity of those who have not been civilized" (Chartier 1999, 78; cited in Ikegami 2006, 22). That is, in the myriad studies of citizenship in which citizenship's others are summoned (whether it be the image of the apathetic, disengaged, or corrupt citizen), there is little reflection about the operation of power that constructs that other as undesirable, barbaric, or uncivilized. It is generally assumed that those undesirable characteristics ought to indeed be banished. Cultural sociologists do not, in other words, link the *civil* in civil society with the process of *civilizing* with its connotations of power, hierarchy, or conformity that has worried critics like Elias, Freud, or Foucault.[8]

Once we move our frame of reference, however, the meanings of civil society become potentially more ambiguous and it is difficult to avoid the association with civilization. One need not share Foucault's or Freud's pessimism to consider the issue: What if civil codes were to be *understood* as an imposition from the outside by more powerful countries? In reflecting about the possibility of a Fascist resurgence in Germany, Parsons wrote that

> in Germany on the other hand the political symbols of a liberal democratic regime could be treated as having been ruthlessly imposed on a defeated and humiliated Germany by the Alien enemy." (Parsons 1947, 145)

Scholars have noted the close connection between liberal thought and imperial ambitions in Africa and Asia (Mehta 1999; Metcalf 1997; Dirks 2006). Imperial ambition found justification in liberal thought, and liberal thought found a *project* in the deficiencies of colonized peoples:

> The rule of law was to replace arbitrary despotism; political institutions would be modeled on the political life of the metropole...; the extirpation of native practices which scandalized the morality and sensibility of Europeans, and indeed provided the clearest justification for intervention and reform. (Bhuta 2008)

Thus, when we turn to democracy and the civil sphere as a cultural project—layered with meanings and interpretations—the rejection of the civil because of its association with the powerful is something that needs to be taken into consideration when we contemplate less powerful nations. This was true even in Europe. In the 1930s, for example, Berezin (1997) argues that Fascist culture in Italy was a self-conscious and nationalist rejection of liberal culture. In Brazil, during the Vargas years (1930–1945), the "revolution against liberalism," as its leaders represented it, was a period in which regime leaders railed "against liberal fictions of formal legalities and free-birth, of equality and liberty" and the other liberal errors (Gomes 1982, 127). Whether there are truths in these claims or not, it is important to recognize that the association of democracy, or democratic codes, with powerful outsiders is central to the way that the cultural meanings of democracy are shaped in much of the Global South.

But even more complicated, from our perspective, is that civility stands in for the standards of the powerful in a society. For the powerless, perhaps, for whom the formal political system is closed and the standards of civility inaccessible, there are legitimate claims that might escape civility. Chatterjee invites us to consider the possibility of situations

> in which the imaginative power of a traditional structure of community, includ-ing its fuzziness and capacity to invent relations of kinship, has been wedded to the modern emancipatory rhetoric of autonomy and equal rights. These strate-gies, I am suggesting, are not available within the liberal space of the associations of civil society transacting business with a constitutional state. For the majority of people in post-colonial societies, the normative status of the virtuous citizen will remain infinitely deferred until such time as they can be provided with the basic material and cultural prerequisites of membership of civil society. (Chatterjee 1998, 282)

Sociological work belies many such possibilities. Macfarlane (2008), in the context of India, has argued that slum populations remain "populations outside the sphere of citizenship," and that "citizen associations" work hard to displace the poor from city spaces. Smilde, in his work on Venezuela, mentions the distance between *la sociedad civil*, which criticizes political parties and promotes solidarity and social reform, though "largely formed among the middle and upper-middle classes," and the poor, urban sectors more concerned with survival (2007, 26). Auyero's investi-gation of "political clientelism" among the urban poor in Villa Paraíso, a shanty-town on the outskirts of Buenos Aires is exemplary. Clientelism has long been understood as citizenship's other in the context of Latin America and has been a powerful symbol of the deficiency of the democracies in the region. But by observ-ing it closely and unpacking its meanings for poor participants, something else emerges—"agency and improvisation of the poor," strategies of survival, and prob-lem solving.

Fundamentally, then, cultural sociology needs to recapture a sense of ambiguity of the meaning of civil society. It needs to consider the possibility, that as a cultural project, civil society, "correctly" or not, has often been associated with powerful countries and with the powerful within societies.

The Minimal State and Other Liberal Fictions

In addition to recapturing a sense of ambiguity, cultural sociology also needs to more carefully consider the possibility of nonliberal political cultures and other hybrids. There are two interlocking assumptions about the political culture that animates civil society: first, that it is based on the notion of the freestanding individual, and second, that states play a very limited role in shaping it. These assumptions stand in contrast to the contemporary scholarship that has noted plural and hybrid forms of discourse in civil societies of the postcolonial world (Mamdani 1996).

The cultural notion of a freestanding, rights-bearing individual, born of liberal tradition is assumed to be the only possible framework for civil society. Habermas, for instance, intimates that the public sphere "can only emerge in the context of a liberal political culture and corresponding patterns of socialization." Other scholars have also generally assumed that the long tradition of civic virtue in North Atlantic nations is a precondition to democracy (Barber 1998; Crook and Manor 1994; Dahl 1989; Tocqueville 1945). Cultural sociologists today, while not as determinist as those of a generation ago, still emphasize the importance of a culture of individual rights. Alexander's attention to the "the symbolic dimension" of the civil sphere emphasizes the "independent causal importance of symbolic classification," which provides a cultural grid that maps the motivations of actors, relationships, and institutions as democratic or counterdemocratic. The centerpiece of that grid is the rights-bearing freestanding individual. Cultural sociologists often assume that such nonindividualist codes, by definition, imply the *absence* of civil society and the impossibility of democratic action in the public sphere, a position shared by theorists like Seligman, Habermas, and Gellner, who insist on the necessity of liberal values as a precondition for democratic engagement (Seligman 1992; Gellner 1997; Habermas 1989).

Also consider, for a moment, the kind of state and society that Alexander describes in *The Civil Sphere*, a "society of individuals before the state." The regulative institutions of the civil sphere—the media, the law and the courts, and civil society organizations—exert communicative judgments outward to other spheres, sometimes backed by the necessary force of the state. The state—either as holder of the monopoly of legitimate symbolic violence, or as representative and shaper of the common interest—for Alexander exists only in its minimal form. Missing from the framework are all of the state agencies that also regulate the social, like welfare agencies.

In this way, much cultural sociology also assumes a minimal state and a separateness of state and civil society. Alexander argues for the necessity of "the independence of the communicative institutions of civil society from consequential control by state power. Standing firmly inside the civil rather than the state sphere, communicative institutions become free to broadcast interpretations that are not only independent of the state, but can challenge its commands" (108). Cultural sociologists have neglected interstitial spaces between the state and civil society as potential sites for public sphere activities (Eliasoph 1998). Most studies of existing civil society have been squarely located within settings of voluntary associations: Sociologists have studied social movement and church settings, neighborhood associations, Internet discussion boards, volunteer meetings, among other similar settings.

On the other hand, scholarly accounts have challenged the assumptions of the minimal state and the individualist political culture. Scholars have documented the way that diverse sorts of nonindividualist political cultures serve as a basis for civic engagement. An earlier generation of scholars, such as Fortes and Evans-Pritchard (1940), Banfield (1956), and Dumont (1992), have highlighted the way that collectivist political cultures both stymied and enabled civic engagement. In the contemporary world, there are a number of important accounts of civil society where the state looms large, and where the language of individualism co-exists with other political cultural influences. Whether in Brazil (Banck, 1998), Turkey (White 1996), Syria and Jordan (Rabo 1996), Argentina (Auyero 2000), Mexico (Guttman 2002), or even Italy (Kertzer 1980), ethnographic accounts have clearly demonstrated that collectivist political cultural codes can serve as basis for activism and discourse in the public sphere, even if such collectivist codes have contradictory influences. Collectivist may exist in deep tension with individualist legal bases of citizenship (or even aborted or incomplete liberal political projects) in each of these societies, where the formation of the "as-yet-to-be-constituted private subject" threatens these collectivist cultural bases (Seligman 1992,155).

It is also possible to imagine political cultures where nonindividualist cultural grammars exist in deep tension with individualist legal bases of citizenship. I have described at length public discussions in Brazil during its transition to democracy (Baiocchi 2005), and similar examples exist for Hong Kong (Ku 2000) and Spain (Edles 1997), among others. In Turkey, for example, political culture is more "statist," and a combination of secular and Islamic cultural and political forces was at work. Symbols of both the secular and Islamist regimes have become a part of everyday life for people living in Turkey, are central to the nature of how the civil sphere functions in that country (Navarro-Yasheen 2002).

Relocating the Political

A third broad issue with the cultural sociology of civil society is its assumption of the separateness of political domains from civil society. As Mohan writes, by positing this separation, scholars inadvertently "focus only on the 'good' elements of civil society" (Mohan 2001). In terms of cultural sociology, the assumption is that there exists a differentiated sphere—the civil sphere, where "civil power rather than social or political power" reigns. Thus, it also then assumed that civil power is free from the instrumentality of political power. If shifting our frame of reference to a more global scale, as I have suggested, means we recapture the ambiguity of civil society (considering its association with civilizing projects of the powerful), as well as its potential hybridity (founded on the cultural bases of nonindividualist and statist cultures), then we have to also consider the possibility of its overlap with political realms.

The idea of the separation of the "civil" from the "political" that runs through much of cultural sociology has its roots in liberal political theory as well. The civil and the political represent distinct activities, motivations, and modes of association. This separation is clearest in the work of Putnam in his description of civic engagement in *Bowling Alone*, but is also present in *The Civil Sphere*, and runs through as an implicit assumption for many cultural sociologists. "Political" activities and "civic" ones are different.

First, there is ample empirical evidence that the spheres may not be so sharply delineated in many contexts outside the United States. Contexts of endemic inequality may render disinterested civic participation nonsensical or impossible;

or perhaps less functional differentiation may make these realms not separate. In the context of Brazil's transition to democracy, Mische (2006) discusses at length the ways that civic and partisan activities co-created each other in the context of Brazil's transition to democracy. Not only is partisanship unavoidable in democracy, it can "in some circumstances, be a creative, motivating, and institutionally generative source of civic involvement and reform" (23). At the heart of the argument is the productive tension between partisan and public motivations and styles of discourse, which rather than as portrayed in liberal democratic theory as always opposed, here find themselves to be mutually constitutive in unexpected ways. In a similar fashion, Smilde (2007), for example, argues that evangelicals in Venezuela participate in religion in ways that are far from the disinterested and moral, but rather, are both pragmatic and political.

The related dimension is that there is a possibility in the Global South or postcolonial societies that what is up for debate through the communicative pronouncements of the civil sphere might be broader than the imagined, such as the very cultural grammar of civil society itself. In these less-established civil societies, periods of crisis may not result in a ritual reassertion of a nation's values as Alexander imagines for the United States, but rather in the establishment of another set of codes altogether (Baiocchi 2006).

More generally, thinking about civil society in the Global South invites us to a kind of democratic theory that does not hope to "bracket" the effects of power in civil society, and does not disengage from the "the political," broadly speaking, that inescapable realm of human conflict, which in highly unequal societies means that issues of access to material resources and issues of partisan conflict are bound up with questions of the civil sphere itself.

Coda: The Civil Sphere in the United States Is More Ambiguous, More Hybrid, and More Political than You Think

So far I have discussed a kind of "Global South exceptionalism"—a fairly common trope in critical theory and one that fuels the analytics of many of the works cited throughout in this review. But the claim can be greater. As the Comaroffs have challenged us, "Until we address such historical and cultural specificities, until we leave behind stereotypic, idealized Euro-concepts, we foreclose the possibility of looking at *either* African or Western civil society" (Comaroff and Comaroff 1999, 23). The three issues in question—hybridity, ambiguity, and the political—can be useful lenses for an expanded cultural sociology of the civil sphere in the United States.

First is the possibility of hybridity. On one hand, in the United States, what I've referred to as the stateness of political culture might be more salient than presumed. Scholars like Skocpol and Fiorina have examined the ways "in which the institutions and activities of the US government have influenced the identities, organizational forms, and strategies of voluntary organizations." Throughout U.S. history, social welfare agencies have been notable targets of social movements and have themselves, for better or worse, exerted civil pressures on other spheres, like the family

(Skocpol 2003). And once we leave the United States for European, or Canadian, examples, the importance of the welfare state in shaping civic life is even more apparent. Scandinavian societies might be hard to understand without the web of state institutions that infiltrate and shape voluntary realms at every turn (Svedsen and Svedsen 2006). And in settings like France, the state's self-conscious civilizing project, imparting *laïcité* (secular societal values) to immigrants and working people alike, is central to understanding the nature of solidarity in that country (Akan 2009). And in Canada, there is direct support for multicultural organizations, in which the Canadian government provides direct support to ethnic organizations, promotes interethnic dialogue, and facilitates immigrant participation in Canadian society (Bloemraad 2006).

This also brings attention to the issue of nonindividualist elements in U.S. political culture. As is well known, there were periods in U.S. history when some of the origins of American political culture behind the code of liberty, such as *Herrenvolk* democracy and Jacksonian free labor ideology, were self-consciously advocated by actors in opposition to ideas from the slaveholding South (Roediger 1994; Almaguer 1994). Rabinovitch (2001) argues that, in addition to the code of liberty, a code of nurturing was also in operation in the debate on womanhood in the nineteenth-century United States. Similarly, Schudson (1999) has argued that trust and deference were actually more important than the "rational citizen" until the progressive era, while Fischer (1989) has argued that there was a great deal of regional political variation and contestation in the period of establishment of U.S. democracy.

And at the very least, we have to recognize the possibility that immigrant political cultures are shaping emergent civil discourses around combinations of symbols and practices from the United States and home countries. Fox (2005) has argued that, for example, Mexican "hometown associations"—migrant organizations that are engaged simultaneously in the United States and Mexico,

> have created a public sphere that is clearly Mexican, not only because of its participants' national origin, but also because of its culture, organizational style, symbolic references and principal counterparts. (2005,10)

And hometown associations are not an anomaly. Mexican organizations, according to some studies, mobilize between 250,000 and 500,000 in California alone. And they are a common phenomenon for immigrants from other Latin American countries as well, present wherever there are concentrations of immigrants (Villacres 2010). And if we consider the range of publications (the so called ethnic media) and associations for all immigrant groups in the United States, we would find a range of combinations of symbols and practices undergirding these civic cultures (Zhou and Cai 2002).

This opens up the issue of the nature of reception of civic virtue and citizenship by subaltern communities. That is, we have to recognize the ambiguity of the meaning of democracy for its less entitled citizens throught U.S. history, for whom the civilizing mission of the state may have been more salient than the emancipatory potential of civil society. For those who felt themselves "victims of Americanism," rather than "a patriot, or a flag-saluter, or a flag-waver," as Malcom X once described African Americans ("the twenty two million victims of democracy") (X and Breitman 1990, 26). And certainly, we have to recognize that violations of dignity done in the name of well-meaning citizenship, from "last arrow ceremonies" for Native Americans to become U.S. citizens (Bizzarro 2004), to forced public health campaigns to bathe arrivals from Mexico in the 1910s (Stern 1999). Some historians have come to argue for the centrality of the "imagined fraternity of White men" as the historic bases of U.S. citizenship (Nelson 1998). And in a related vein, how often challenges to that power by the excluded have animated the spaces where citizens have developed "group identity, public skills, and values of cooperation and civic virtue" (Evans and Boyte, 1992, 17).

CIVIL SOCIETY AND CULTURAL SOCIOLOGY IN A WORLD OF FLOWS

> It has now become something of a truism that we are functioning in a world fundamentally characterised by objects in motion. These objects include ideas and ideologies, people and goods, images and messages, technologies and techniques. This is a world of flows.
>
> —Appadurai 2000, 5

There is no doubt that civil society is a "millennial idea" and that cultural sociologists have been adding to the debate in interesting and useful ways. Having rejoined the fray, cultural sociology provides us with an important corrective to the social-scientific lens that too often sees only objective interests, institutional logics, and rationality instead of meanings, practices, and contingencies. Having moved away from an earlier values approach of modernization theory, cultural sociology promises to offer us accounts that give flesh to the idea of association in different contexts. However, despite notable exceptions, much of cultural sociology continues to be bound by the historical experiences of the "West," and seems to be informed by assumptions of liberal theory that idealizes the experiences of the "West." In this chapter, I've brought to light three different assumptions—born of the experience of the United States—that prevent cultural sociology from traveling better: its assumptions about the minimal state, the nature of the civilizing process, and the place of the political. The more cultural sociology can consider these caveats, the more global can our conversations become.

Part of the challenge is that democracy has always been a traveling culture, and much more so in recent years. And more than ever, it has been a "moving target, not a static structure. Democracy is a juxtaposition of institutions and practices with quite different histories" (Markoff 1999, 689). But democratic ideas travel in conjunction with ideas about the market, modernity, and other "allegedly cultural-neutral forms (science and technology, industrialization, secularization, bureaucratization, and so on)" (Gaonkar 2002, 5) in the context of an unequal world. The history of association of democracy (and notions of the civil sphere and individual rights) with colonial histories, and later, with powerful nations and local elites needs to be considered centrally in any cultural framework looking at the Global South, as does the way that local civil societies draw on different cultural vocabularies and operate in vastly different realms than we normally imagine.

To engage in such a project implies looking at the "criss-crossing family resemblances" that make up democratic discourses around the globe, where liberal-democratic values are only one possible set of shared beliefs among the "manifold of practices and pragmatic moves aiming at persuading people to broaden the range of their commitments to others" (Mouffe 2000, 66). Remembering that these are "inseparable from specific forms of life" (Wittgenstein, 1953, 201) suggests that we pay careful attention to the situated and specific publics where such communication takes place. But engaging in such a project also means being attentive to history and the "genetic and political sociology of the formation, selection, and imposition of systems of classification" that make up distinct political cultures (Bourdieu and Wacquant 1992, 14).

And in the current moment, where flows of people, ideas, resources, and institutions are more intense than at any other point in history, there is greater uncertainty and flux about what the boundaries of the civil sphere, as well as new contradictions between territory and forms of authority (Held 1999). As we map these flows and become attentive to "global effects, notoriously unintended and unanticipated" (Bauman 2001), questions of boundaries of the civil sphere become even more relevant: what groups of persons it extends to and what parts of the common good ought to extend to them, resulting in uncertainty in the structuring of *political spaces,* the political "inside" and "outside" (Mouffe 1993). Discourses that aim to extend or shorten the reach of citizenship cause the intense competition over ambiguous and unstable "frontier effects" over the boundary of this political space, and constant articulation with the *res publica* (Mouffe 1992, 134). On one hand, once we consider this, that solidarity exists at all is surprising. But on the other hand, this suggests greater attention to novel transnational publics and new utopian possiblities that imagine "a new way of combining the local, the national and the transnational" (Olesen, 2005, 420).

NOTES

....

1. There is a very extensive discussion that I do not cite in this paper for the sake of brevity. For some exemplars, see Harriss 2005; Chandoke 2003; Encarnación 2003; Li 2007; Cornwall 2003; Ferguson and Gupta 2002; Giles 2002; Leal 2007; Alvarez 2006; and Cooke and Kothari 2001. This selective list includes different sorts of critiques anchored in different intellectual traditions and having slightly different objects. But this abbreviated

list gives a sense of the suspicion the idea of civil society has come to evoke in some quarters.

2. See a critique of Parson's "weak" value theory of culture (Alexander 1998).

3. Al-Haq's Bylaws. Edited English version.doc26/12/2006.

4. A yearly ranking published by *Parade Magazine*, based on reports by Human Rights Watch, Freedom House, Reporters Without Borders, and Amnesty International. The 2009 rankings are available at http://www.parade.com/dictators/2009/the-worlds-10-worst-dictators.html.

5. Statement by His Excellency the President of the Republic of Zimbabwe Comrade R. G. Mugabe on the occasion of the 62nd Session of the United Nations General Assembly, New York, 26 September, 2007. Available at http://www.nathanielturner.com/robertmugabesunspeech.htm.

6. See any number of pronouncements in the *Zimbabwe Herald*: http://www1.herald.co.zw.

7. The results of this research project are partially reported in Baiocchi and Corrado (2010).

8. After Freud's visit to the United States, he wrote:

that most menacing where the social forces of cohesion consist predominantly of identifications of the individuals in the group with one another.... The state of civilization in America at the present day offers a good opportunity for studying this injurious effect of civilization which we have reason to dread.

REFERENCES

Akan, Murat. 2009. "Laicité and Multiculturalism: The Stasi Report in Context." *British Journal of Sociology* 60(2): 237–256.

Alexander, Jeffrey. 1985. "Three Models of Culture and Society Relations: Toward an Analysis Of Watergate," Sociological Theory 3: 290–314.

Alexander, Jeffrey. 1988. "Culture and Political Crisis: 'Watergate' and Durkheimian Sociology." Pp. 187–224 in *Durkheimian Sociology: Cultural Studies*, edited by J. Alexander. Cambridge, UK: Cambridge University Press.

Alexander. 1997. "The Paradoxes of Civil Society." *International Sociology* 12(2): 115–133.

Alexander. 2006. *The Civil Sphere*. Oxford, UK: Oxford University Press, 2006.

Alexander, Jeffrey, and Phillip Smith. 1993. "The Discourse of Civil Society: A New Proposal for Cultural Studies." *Theory and Society* 2: 151–207.

Almaguer, Tomás. 1994. *Racial Fault Lines: The Historical Origins of White Supremacy in California*. Berkeley and Los Angeles: University of California Press.

Almond, Gabriel Abraham, and Sidney Verba. 1963. *The Civic Culture: Political Attitudes and Democracy in Five Nations*. Princeton, NJ: Princeton University Press.

Alvarez, Sonia E. 2006. "*Governance*, Govenabilidade, e Governamentalidade: Interrogações sobre a 'Agenda Sociedade Civil' in o (Futuro do) Debate sobre a Construção Democrática no Século XXI, Seminário Internacional, at Universidade Estadual de Campinas, Campinas, São Paulo, Brazil, 7–8 June.

Appadurai, Arjun. 1990. "Disjuncture and Difference in the Global Cultural Economy." *Theory, Culture and Society* 7: 295–310.

————. 2000. *Modernity at Large: Cultural Dimensions of Globalization*. Minneapolis: University of Minnesota Press.

Arias, Desmond. 2006. *Drugs and Democracy in Rio de Janeiro*. Chapel Hill: University of North Carolina Press.

Auyero, Javier. 2001. *Poor People's Politics: Peronist Survival Networks and the Legacy of Evita*. Durham, NC: Duke University Press.

————. 2007. *Routine Politics and Collective Violence: The Gray Zone of State Power in Argentina*. Cambridge, UK: Cambridge University Press.

Baiocchi, Gianpaolo. 2005. *Militants and Citizens: The Politics of Participatory Democracy in Porto Alegre*. Stanford, CA: Stanford University Press.

————. 2006. "The Civilizing Force of Social Movements."

Banck, Geert Arent. 1998. *Dilemas e símbolos: estudos sobre a cultura política do Espírito Santo*. Vitório - ES, Brazil: Instituto Histórico e Geográfico do Espírito Santo.

Banfield, Edward C. 1958. *The Moral Basis of a Backward Society*. Glencoe, IL: Free Press.

Barber, Benjamin. 1998. "Three Challenges to Reinventing Democracy." In *Reinventing Democracy*, edited by Paul Hirst and Sunil Khilnani. Cambridge, MA: Blackwell, p 144–156.

Bauman, Zygmunt. 2001. *Globalization: The Human Consequences*. New York: Columbia University Press.

Bellah, Robert, RIchard Madsen, William Sullivan, Ann Swiddler, and Steven Tipton. 1985. *Habits of the Heart; Individualism and Commitment in American Life*. New York: Harper & Row.

Bendix, Reinhard. 1964. *National-Building and Citizenship*. New York: Free Press.

Berezin, Mabel. 1997. "Politics and Culture: Toward a Less Fissured Terrain." *Annual Review of Sociology* 23: 361–383.

Bhuta, Nehal. 2008. "Against State-Building." *Constellations* 15(4): 517–542.

Bizzaro, Resa Crane. 2004. "Shooting Our Last Arrow: Developing a Rhetoric of Identity for Unenrolled American Indians." *College English* 67(1): 61–74.

Bloemraad, Irene. 2006. *Becoming a Citizen: Incorporating Immigrants and Refugees in the United States and Canada*. Berkeley: University of California.

Bourdieu, Pierre, and Loïc J. D. Wacquant. 1992. *An Invitation to Reflexive Sociology*. Chicago: University of Chicago Press.

Burawoy, Michael. 2005. "Provincializing the Social Sciences." Pp. 508–525 in *The Politics of Method in the Human Sciences: Positivism and Its Epistemological Others*, edited by George Steinmetz. Durhman, NC: Duke University Press.

Calhoun, Craig. 1992. *Habermas and the Public Sphere*. Cambridge, MA: MIT Press.

————. 2002. "Constitutional Patriotism and the Public Sphere: Interests, Identity, and Solidarity in the Integration of Europe." Pp. 275–312 in *Provincializing Europe: Postcolonial Thought and Historical Difference*, edited by Pablo De Greiff and Dipesh Chakrabarty. Princeton, NJ: Princeton University Press.

Chandhoke, Neera. 2003. *The Conceits of Civil Society*. New Delhi: Oxford University Press.

Chartier, Roger. 1992. *The Cultural Origins of the French Revolution: Roger Chartier*. Durham, NC: Duke University Press.

Chatterjee, Partha. 2004. *The Politics of the Governed: Reflections on Popular Politics in Most of the World*. New York: Columbia University Press.

Cleaver, Francis. 2001. "Institutions, Agency, and the Limitations of Participatory Approaches to Development." P144–156 in In *Participation: The New Tyranny?* edited by Bill Cooke and Uma Kothari. New York: Zed Books.

Comaroff, Jean, and John L. Comaroff. 2001. *Millennial Capitalism and the Culture of Neoliberalism*. Durham, NC: Duke University Press.

Cooke, Bill, and Uma Kothari, eds. *Participation: The New Tyranny?* London: Zed Books, 2001.

Cornwall, Andrea. 2003. "Whose Voices? Whose Choices? Reflections on Gender and Participatory Development." *World Development* 31(8): 1325–1342.

Dahl, Robert. 1989. *Democracy and Its Critics*. New Haven, CT: Yale University Press.

Dirks, Nicholas B. 2006. *The Scandal of Empire: India and the Creation of Imperial Britain*. Cambridge, MA: Belknap of Harvard University Press.

Dumont, Louis. 1992. *Essays on Individualism: Modern Ideology in Anthropological Perspective*. Chicago: University of Chicago Press.

Edles, Laura Desfor. 1995. "Rethinking Democratic Transition: A Culturalist Critique and the Spanish Case." Theory and Society 24(3): 355–384.

Edwards, Bob, Michael W. Foley, and Mario Diani, eds. 2001. *Beyond Toqueville: Civil Society and the Social Capital Debate in Comparative Perspective*. Hanover, NH: University Press of New England.

Eliasoph, Nina. 1996. "Making a Fragile Public: A Talk-Centered Study of Citizenship and Power." *Sociological Theory* 14(3): 262–289.

Eliasoph, Nina. 1998. *Avoiding Politics: How Americans Produce Apathy in Everyday Life*. Cambridge, UK: Cambridge University Press.

Encarnacion, O. G. 2003. *The Myth of Civil Society: Social Capital and Democratic Consolidation in Spain and Brazil*. New York: Palgrave MacMillan.

Evans, Sarah, and Harry Boyte. 1992. *Free Spaces: The Sources of Democratic Change in America*. New York: Harper & Row.

Ferguson, James, and Akhil Gupta. 2002. "Spatializing States: Toward an EthnogWiraphy of Neoliberal Governmentality." *American Ethnologist* 29 (4): 981–1002.

Fortes, Meyer, and E. E. Evans-Pritchard. 1940. *African Political Systems*. London and New York: Oxford University Press.

Fox, Jonathan A. 2005. *Mapping Mexican Migrant Civil Society*. Santa Cruz, CA: Center for Global, International and Regional Studies.

Gamson, William A., and Andre Modigliani. 1989. "Media Discourse and Public Opinion on Nuclear Power: A Constructionist Approach." *American Journal of Sociology* 95: 1–37.

Gaonkar, Dilip. 2002. "Toward New Imaginaries: An Introduction." *Public Culture* 14(1): 1–19

Gay, Robert. 1995. *Popular Organization and Democracy in Rio De Janeiro*. Philadelphia: Temple University Press.

Gellner, Ernest. 1997. *Nationalism*. New York: New York University Press.

Gomes, Angela Maria de Castro. 1982. *Burguesia e Trabalho: Política e Legislação Social no Brasil, 1917–1937*. Rio de Janeiro: Editora Campus.

Gupta, Akhil. 1995. "Blurred Boundaries: The Discourse of Corruption, the Culture of Politics, and the Imagined State." *American Ethnologist* 22(2): 375–402.

Gutmann, Matthew C. 2002. *The Romance of Democracy: Compliant Defiance in Contemporary Mexico*. Berkeley: University of California Press.

Habermas, Jürgen. 1989. *The Structural Transformation of the Public Sphere: An Inquiry into a Category of Bourgeois Society*. Cambridge, MA: MIT Press.

Hansen, Thomas B. 1999. *The Saffron Wave: Democracy and Hindu Nationalism in Modern India*. Princeton, NJ: Princeton University Press.

Held, David. 1995. *Democracy and Global Order*. Cambridge, UK: Polity.

Henderson, S. 2003. *Building Democracy in Contemporary Russia: Western Support for Grassroots Organizations*. Ithaca, NY: Cornell University Press.

Hunter, Floyd. 1953. *Community Power Structure: A Study of Decision Markers*. Raleigh, NC: Chapel Hill.

Huntington, Samuel. 1991. *The Third Wave: Democratization in the Late Twentieth Century*. Norman: University of Oaklahoma Press

Ikegami, Eiko. 2005. *Bonds of Civility: Aesthetic Networks and the Political Origins of Japanese Culture*. Cambridge, UK: Cambridge University Press.

Inglehart, Ronald. 1997. *Modernization and Postmodernization: Cultural, Economic, and Political Change in 43 Societies*. Princeton, NJ: Princeton University Press.

Jacobs, Ronald N. 1996. "Civil Society and Crisis: Culture, Discourse, and the Rodney King Beating." *American Journal of Sociology* 101: 1238–1272.

———. 2000. "The Racial Discourse of Civil Society: The Rodney King Affair and the City of Los Angeles." Pp. 138–161 in *Real Civil Societies: Dilemmas of Institutionalization*, edited by J. C. Alexander. London: Sage.

Kaviraj, Sudipta. 1997. "Filth and the Public Sphere: Concepts and Practices about Space in Calcutta." *Public Culture* 10: 98.

Kerkvliet, Benedict J. 2005. *The Power of Everyday Politics: How Vietnamese Peasants Transformed National Policy*. Ithaca, NY: Cornell University Press.

Kertzer, David I. 1980. *Comrades and Christians: Religion and Political Struggle in Communist Italy*. Cambridge, UK: Cambridge University Press.

Kothari, Uma. 2001. "Power, Knowledge, and Social Control in Participatory Development." 144–156 In *Participation: The New Tyranny?* edited by Bill Cooke and Uma Kothari. New York: Zed Books.

Ku, Agnes S. 2001. "Hegemonic Construction, Negotiation and Displacement: The Struggle over Right of Abode in Hong Kong." *International Journal of Cultural Studies* 4(3): 259–278.

Leal, Pablo Alejandro. 2007. "Participation: The Ascendancy of a Buzzword in the Neo-Liberal Era." *Development in Practice* 17(4): 539–548.

Li, Tania. 2007. *The Will to Improve: Governmentality, Development, and the Practice of Politics*. Durham, NC: Duke University Press.

Lichterman, Paul. 1997. *The Search for Political Community: American Activists Reinventing Community*. Cambridge, UK: Cambridge University Press.

Lipset, Seymour Martin. 1963. *The First New Nation; the United States in Historical and Comparative Perspective*. New York: Basic Books.

Lynd, Robert S., and Helen Merrell. 1937. *Middletown in Transition: A Study in Cultural Conflicts*. New York: Harcourt, Brace and Company.

Mahmood, Saba. 2005. *Politics of Piety: The Islamic Revival and the Feminist Subject*. Princeton, NJ: Princeton University Press.

Malcom X, and George Breitman. 1990. *Malcom X Speaks: Selected Speeches and Statements*. New York: Grove Press.

Mamdani, Mahmood. 1996. *Citizen and Subject: Decentralized Despotism and the Legacy of Late Colonialism*. Princeton, NJ: Princeton University Press.

Matta, Roberto da. 1979. *Carnavais, Malandros E Heróis: Para Uma Sociologia Do Dilema Brasileiro*. Rio de Janeiro: Zahar Editores.

McAdam, Doug. 1988. *Freedom Summer*. New York: Oxford University Press.

Metcalf, Thomas R. 1997. *Ideologies of the Raj*. Cambridge, UK: Cambridge University Press.

Mohan, Giles. 2001. "Beyond Participation: Strategies for Deeper Empowerment." In *Participation: The New Tyranny?* edited by Bill Cooke and Uma Kothari. New York: Zed Books.

———. 2002. "The Disappointments of Civil Society: The Politics of NGO Intervention in Northern Ghana." *Political Geography* 21(1): 125–154.

Mouffe, Chantal, ed. 1992. *Dimensions of Radical Democracy: Pluralism, Citizenship, Community*. London: Verso.

———. 1993. *The Return of the Political*. London: Verso.

———. 2000. *The Democratic Paradox*. London and New York: Verso.

Navaro-Yashin, Yael. 2002. *Faces of the State: Secularism and Public Life in Turkey*. Princeton, NJ: Princeton University Press.

Nelson, Dana. 1998. *National Manhood: Capitalist Citizenship and the Imagined Fraternity of White Men*. Durham, NC: Duke University Press.

Nilufer, Gola. 2002. "Islam in Public: New Visibilites and New Imaginaries." *Public Culture* 14(1): 173–190.

Ong, Aihwa. 2003. *Buddha Is Hiding: Refugees, Citizenship, the New America*. Berkeley: University of California Press.

Paley, Julia. 2001. *Marketing Democracy: Power and Social Movements in Post-Dictatorship Chile*. Berkeley: University of California Press.

———. 2009. *Democracy: Anthropological Approaches*. Santa Fe, NM: School of American Research.

Perrin, Andrew J. 2006. *Citizen Speak: The Democratic Imagination in American Life*. Chicago: University of Chicago.

Pollock, Sheldon, Homi Bhabha, Carol Breckenridge, and Dipesh Chakrabharty. 2000. "Cosmopolitanisms." *Public Culture* 12(3): 1–28.

Putnam, Robert. 2000.*Bowling Alone: The Collapse and Revival of American Community*. New York: Simon & Schuster.

Putnam, Robert, Robert Leonardi, and Raffaella Y. Nannetti. 1993. *Making Democracy Work: Civic Traditions in Modern Italy*. Princeton, NJ: Princeton University Press.

Rabbani, M. 1994. "Palestinian Human Rights Activism under Israeli Occupation: The Case of Al-Haq." *Arab Studies Quarterly* 16(2): 24–36

Rabo, Annika. 1996. "Gender, State and Civil Society in Jordan and Syria." Pp. 155–178 in *Civil Society Challenging Western Models*, edited by Chris Hann and Elizabeth Dunn. New York and London: Routledge.

Roediger, David R. 1991. *The Wages of Whiteness: Race and the Making of the American Working Class*. New York: Verso.

Schatz, Edward. 2004. *Modern Clan Politics: The Power of "Blood" in Kazakhstan and Beyond*. Seattle: University of Washington Press.

Schudson, Michael. 1998. *The Good Citizen: A History of American Civic Life*. New York: Martin Kessler Books.

Seligman, A. 1992. *The Idea of Civil Society*. New York and Toronto: Free Press.

Skocpol, Theda. 2003. *Diminished Democracy: From Membership to Management in American Civic Life*. Norman: University of Oklahoma.

Smilde, David. 2007. *Reason to Believe Cultural Agency in Latin American Evangelicalism*. Berkeley: University of California.

Somers, Margaret. 1993. "Citizenship and the Place of the Public Sphere: Law, Community, and Political Culture in the Transition to Democracy." *American Sociological Review* 58(5): 229–273.

———. 1995. "Narrating and Naturalizing Civil Society and Citizenship Theory: The Place of Political Culture and the Public Sphere." *Sociological Theory* 13(3): 229–273.

———. 1998. "Fear and Loathing of Citizenship: How (and Why) to Deconstruct a Knowledge Culture." Paper presented to International Sociological Association.

Steinmetz, George. 2007. *The Devil's Handwriting: Precoloniality and the German Colonial State in Qingdao, Samoa, and Southwest Africa*. Chicago: University of Chicago.

Svendsen, Gunner Lind Hasse, and Gert Tinggaard Svendsen. 2006. *The Creation and Destruction of Social Capital, Entrepreneurship, Co-Operative Movements and Institutions*. Northampon, MA: Edwar Elgar Publishers.

Tilly, Charles. 1984. *Big Structures, Large Processes, Huge Comparisons*. New York: Russell Sage Foundation.

Tocqueville, Alexis de. 1945. *Democracy in America*. New York: Alfred A. Knopf.

Tsing, Anna Lowenhaupt. 1993. *In the Realm of the Diamond Queen: Marginality in an Out-of-the-Way Place*. Princeton, NJ: Princeton University Press.

Verba, Sidney, and Norman H. Nie. 1972. *Participation in America: Political Democracy and Social Equality*. New York: Harper & Row.

Vidich, Arthur J., and Joseph Bensman. 1958. *Small Town in Mass Society: Class, Power Amd Religion in a Rural Community*. Garden City, NY: Doubleday.

Wedeen, Lisa. 1999. *Ambiguities of Domination: Politics, Rhetoric, and Symbols in Contemporary Syria*. Chicago: University of Chicago Press.

White, Jenny B. 1996. "Culture and Islam in Urban Turkey." Pp. 143–154 in *Civil Society: Challenging Western Models*, edited by Chris Hann and Elizabeth Dunn. New York and London: Routledge.

White, Sarah C. 1996. "Depoliticizing Development: The Uses and Abuses of Participation." *Development in Practice* 6(1): 6–15.

Wickramasinghe, Nira. 2005. "The Idea of Civil Society in the South: Imaginings, Transplants, Designs." *Science & Society* 69 (3): 458–486.

Wittgenstein, Ludwig, and G. E. M. Anscombe. 1953. *Philosophical Investigations*. Oxford: Oxford University Press.

Wood, Richard Lawrence. 1995. *Faith in Action: Religion, Race, and the Future of Democracy*. Chicago: University of Chicago Press.

Zhou, Min, and Guoxuan Cai. 2002. "Chinese Language Media in the United States: Immigration and Assimilation in American Life." *Qualitative Sociology* 25(3): 419–441.

PART IV

THE MEDIA AS CULTURE

CHAPTER 10

MEDIATIZED DISASTERS IN THE GLOBAL AGE: ON THE RITUALIZATION OF CATASTROPHE

SIMON COTTLE

When reporting disasters, a terrible "calculus of death" has seemingly become institutionalized and normalized in the professional judgments, practices, and news values of the Western news media. Based on crude body counts and news thresholds as well as proximities of geography, culture, and economic interests, this journalistic calculus recognizes some deaths, some disasters as more newsworthy than others (Galtung and Ruge 1981; Benthall 1993; Allen and Seaton 1999; Moeller 1999; Seaton 2005; Cottle 2009a). This also no doubt feeds into the Western "emergency imaginary," a discerned cultural outlook that naturalizes distant human emergencies by seeing them as sudden and unpredictable and by dissimulating our Western standpoint of observation (Calhoun 2004, p. 376; 2008). But this professional calculus of death and Western imaginary do not exhaust the story of disaster reporting.[1]

The news media sometimes perform a more elaborate part in visualizing and even humanizing the suffering of distant others, positioning victims and survivors within a mediated ethics of care and variously alerting publics and power-holders to their plight (Cottle 2006a, 2009a; Chouliararki 2006; Pantti, Wahl-Jorgensen and Cottle *forthcoming*).[2] Some disasters, as we shall discuss, are reported extensively and intensively, dramatically reliving moments of danger and loss and publicly channelling discourses of tragedy and trauma into appeals to imagined national community and international solidarity. When based on the perceived ineptitude of authorities and/or the failures of governments to act, some disasters can also be narrated in ways that highlight public anger and propel the possibility of political scandal. And yet others may even become full-blown moments of moral censure and international condemnation, as moral opprobrium is directed by the news media at political regimes with poor democratic credentials and human rights records now spotlighted in the world's media. When dramatized and visualized on the global news stage, then, some disasters seemingly have the potential to become "cosmopolitan events" (Beck 2006), globalizing emotions and encouraging a sense of a global collectivity and responsibility. But *how* exactly this is conducted in and through the news media warrants further thought and closer empirical engagement.

In such cases, the news media are doing more than simply reporting and representing disasters; they are *performatively enacting* them, *constituting* them on the public stage, and visualizing and narrating them in ways that can demand recognition and response. In such cases, the news media publicly *enter into* disasters and may even shape their subsequent course and conduct. They *mediatize* them. Sometimes, then, there is more cultural complexity (and political contingency) in mediatized disaster reporting than the pessimistic and generalizing accounts of the journalistic calculus of death and Western emergency imaginary seemingly permit. And, as we shall also see, culturally there is often more to disaster communications than the "communication of information" that disaster specialists hope will counter the mass mediated images of "passive victims" and assist "active survivors" to become self-help communities (Rodriquez, Quarantelli, and Dynes 2007, p. xviii).

From a sociological perspective, disasters represent the failures to deal with threats and hazards and are therefore contingent on the social structures, collective vulnerabilities, and power relations that both precede and mediate them, as well as the available resources allocated to their prevention, mitigation, and response (Rodriquez, Quarantelli, and Dynes 2007). As John Holmes, United Nations Under-Secretary-General for Humanitarian Affairs and Emergency Relief Coordinator, and Markku Niskala, Secretary-General of the International Federation of the Red Cross and Red Crescent Societies, maintain: "There is no such thing as a natural disaster. Floods, hurricanes, cyclones, typhoons, heat waves, droughts, even non-climate-related events like earthquakes, are natural hazards. They become disasters only when they exceed a community's ability to cope" (Holmes and Niskala 2007, p. 2). Approached thus, disasters can be seen as profoundly social phenomena (Perry and Quarantelli 2007) and the news media are often singled out as centrally involved in their social construction. As Jonathan Benthall observed many years ago, "(T)he coverage of disasters by the press and media is so selective and arbitrary that, in an important sense, they 'create' a disaster when they decide to recognize it," and he also noted how "such endorsement is a prerequisite for the marshalling of external relief and reconstructive effort" (Benthall 1993, pp. 11–12).

This chapter takes these social premises of disasters as given, but also argues for their *cultural constitution* in respect of *how* some disasters become extensively and intensively *enacted* and *performed* within the news media. When infused with *symbols* and *meanings* that emanate from both media and civil society, mediated disasters can command not only our attention but also, on occasion, our collective empathy and critical engagement. Here, ideas of cultural performance and media ritualization prove essential if we are to better fathom how disasters are culturally made to mean and, importantly, politically matter. In a world where humanitarian impulses and the institutionalization of human rights find wide normative if not universal assent, and in a globalizing world where disasters and crises are now becoming increasingly deterritorialized in terms of global origins and scope (Beck 2006, 2009), *how* the news media infuse disasters with cultural meanings can reverberate nationally, internationally, and transnationally (Cottle 2009a, 2009b). Through their performative enactment of some disasters, the news media both interact with and serve to instantiate the "civil sphere" (Alexander 2006a).[3]

The discussion that follows develops these claims across two sections. The first considers contemporary forms of media ritualization evident across a range of "exceptional" media phenomena, from moral panics and media events, to mediated scandals and mediatized public crises. When approaching disasters in terms of news performance and ritualization, there are already established and productive theoretical grounds on which to do so. The second part of the chapter then moves more empirically to illuminate how some of these different forms of media ritualization enter into and shape the public elaboration of major disasters, including the South Asian tsunami (2004), Hurricane Katrina (2005), and Cyclone Nargis in Burma and the Sichuan earthquake in China (2008). The performative nature of these media treatments reveals how disasters today can become *variously* inscribed with appeals to imagined community and/or international solidarity, discourses of criticism and dissent, and moral infusions rooted in the deep binaries of civil society. In such ways, mediatized disasters not only become communicated across extensive geographical distances but are also culturally intensified and rendered available for wider appropriation by diverse discourses and political projects—nationally, internationally, and globally.

MEDIATIZED RITUALS

When mediatized, disasters can be profoundly shaped in the communicative encounter with the news media and in ways that shape subsequent reactions and responses. There are however many possible roles or stances *performed* by the news media when mediatizing events whether that of "narrator," "conductor," "mediator," "watchdog," "advocate," "campaigner," or "champion" (Cottle 2004; Cottle and Rai 2006), just as there are diverse roles adopted by the news media in situations of conflict more generally (Wolfsfeld 1997). These moreover can modulate through time and in relation to the changing dynamics of the political center and/or surrounding movements for change (Hallin 1986; Bennett 1990; Butler 1995; Bennett, Lawrence, and Livingston 2007). They can also be enacted differently across different mediums, forms, and outlets (Elliott et al. 1986; Cottle 2004, 2011) and the media can sometimes demonstrate reflexivity in respect of the media's own performative "doing" (Cottle 2004).

How news media adopt and perform these differing stances has yet to find detailed comparative analysis. We know from the field of conflict studies, however, that both structural and cultural dimensions are likely to be at work (Wolfsfeld 1997; Cottle 2006a, pp. 13–32). The news media today occupy a pivotal site in the power plays of contending interests and identities that seek to mobilize discourses and harness frames to their goals (Cottle 2003). But the news media can also sometimes refashion cultural templates, narratives, and frames and grant news stories shape, form, and meaning (Cottle and Rai 2006). And, exceptionally, as already suggested, the news media can sometimes assume a steering role in the public definition and elaboration of events. It is in and through this institutionally mediated, strategically pursued, and normatively informed encounter between news media, state, and the discourses and projects of civil society, therefore, that meanings come to infuse and frame events. Though it is not possible to explore these complex fields of initiation and interaction here,[4] the discussion can pursue *how* the news media place their cultural stamp on disasters, variously making them mean and politically matter. Ideas of media performance and media ritualization prove critical.

For heuristic purposes, I define mediatized rituals as "*those exceptional and performative media enactments that serve to sustain and/or mobilize collective sentiments and solidarities on the basis of symbolization and a subjunctive orientation to what should or ought to be*" (Cottle 2006b, 2008). Approached in these deliberately encompassing terms, mediatized rituals may make use of institutionalized ceremonies or formal rituals staged by authorities or others elsewhere, or they may be staged and enacted entirely within/by the media themselves. When reporting on institutional ceremonies conducted elsewhere however, to become a "mediatized ritual," the media will be "doing" something more than simply reporting (Austin 1975); they will be performatively eliciting/encouraging collective solidarities based on ideas and feelings (collective sentiments) about how society should or ought to be.

Mediatized rituals today are far more differentiated, unpredictable, and politically contested or even disruptive than either functionalist or structured in dominance views of either media or ritual permit (Cottle 2004, 2005a). This flows, in part, from the news media's occupation of cultural space in the contours and contests of civil society, its professionalized obligations to the institutions and processes of governance, as well as its own logics and pursuit of corporate and competitive goals. In this context, James Carey's often quoted view of media rituals as "sacred ceremonies drawing people together in fellowship and commonality by the creation, representation, and celebration of shared even if illusory beliefs" (Carey 1989, p. 43) reads as a little too indebted to Durkheim's original "binding" and integrative formulation of ritual (Durkheim 1865 (1915), pp. 466–467; Giddens 1971; Lukes 1973; Thompson 1998). In today's complexly structured, culturally diverse, and politically contested societies, we need to situate our analysis of processes of ritualization in respect of a particular constellation of social relations at a particular moment in time and, importantly, to see these as often conflicted (Lukes 1975; Kertzer 1988), culturally informed, and, importantly, mediatized.

It follows that the organizing force of rituals need not always be consensual or uniformly inflected (Chaney 1986; Shils and Young 1956; Alexander 1988; Mihelj 2008), much less co-extensive with a singular collectivity resident behind national borders. A neo-Durkheimian reading of ritual as "society in action," but one that sees "society" as itself an internally contested project and that therefore also antici-pates the capacity to build particularized solidarities or "publics" (Jacobs 2000; Cottle 2004) through the discursive appropriation of sacred symbols and purposeful alignment of collective sentiments, provides the foundation for a more temporally dynamic and politically contested view of ritual—one that may even permit on occasion transformative possibilities (Cottle 2004; Alexander 2006a, 2009). Today, "society in action" is often enacted in and through the media sphere.

The broad definition of mediatized rituals above, then, makes no prescriptions about whether they are essentially hegemonic or contested, spontaneous or pre-planned, or consensual or disruptive in terms of the prevailing social order. These are essentially empirical questions that are not usefully theoretically predetermined in advance. It is also important to recognize that though news performativity often exhibits considerable rhetorical force and expressive appeals, such crafted invita-tions only come alive—experientially, emotionally, subjunctively—when actively read by audiences/readerships who are prepared to commit to them as symbolically meaningful to them and who can accept the "solidarity" offered (Ryfe 2001). Deep-seated presuppositions about "justice," "democracy," and "fraternity" and ideas of the "good society" rooted in the civil sphere (Alexander 2006a) can all, for example, form the basis for such solidaristic appeals. Established ideas and concep-tualizations of "moral panics," "media events," "media spectacles," "mediated scan-dals," and "mediatized public crises" all serve to underline the media's role(s) in the performative enactment and ritualization of different events, ideas that have rele-vance for understanding mediatized disasters and the ritualization of catastrophes. Let us briefly take each in turn.

Though Stanley Cohen didn't frame his celebrated analysis of moral panics (Cohen 1972) in terms of mediatized ritual, his account resonates with Durkheimian ideas of ritual as "society in action." The mobilization of collective fears and anxiet-ies amplified and sensationalized by the media and focused in relation to a symbolic other—a folk devil—ultimately serves processes of societal control by policing col-lective moral boundaries. Moral panic theory, notwithstanding the extensive criti-cisms and refinements over the forty years or so since Cohen's seminal publication (e.g., Goode and Ben-Yehuda 1994; McRobbie 1994; Media International Australia 1997; Thompson 1998; Critcher 2003; Altheide 2009), continues to secure analytical purchase on an exceptional class of performative media reporting.

The conceptualization of "media events" (Dayan and Katz 1994) also builds on Durkheimian themes of ritual, with its account of how ceremonial and celebratory occasions of state can build hegemony through ritualized affirmation and integra-tive appeals to collectivity. Daniel Dayan and Elihu Katz characterized media events as *interruptions* of broadcasting routines that are *monopolistic, live, organized outside the media,* preplanned and presented with *reverence* and *ceremony* that can *electrify very large* (TV-viewing) *audiences.* In these ways, media events are taken to *integrate* societies and evoke a *renewal of loyalty* to the society and its legitimate authority (pp. 4–9, italics in original). Different genres of media events, whether *contests* (the epic contests of politics and sports), *conquests* (charismatic missions), or *coronations* (the rites of passage of the great), are all essentially taken as serving to reconcile, rather than challenge or transform, the political status quo and thereby buttress hegemonic interests and *the establishment.* Nonetheless, we also know that some media events prove to be more conflictual than consensual, more challenging than hegemonic, more disruptive than integrative, and of longer duration and more media-propelled than Dayan and Katz's special case of "media events" seems to allow (see also Kertzer 1988; Chaney 1986, 1993; Emirbayer 2003). As Elihu Katz has presciently observed since: "Media events of the ceremonial kind seem to be receding in importance, maybe even in frequency, while the live broadcasting of disruptive events such as Disaster, Terror and War are taking centre stage" (Katz and Liebes 2007, p. 158).

Conflicted "media events," according to John Fiske, are "sites of maximum visibility and maximum turbulence" (Fiske 1994, p. 7) and threaten, as in the O.J. Simpson case, the televised beating of Rodney King, and the Los Angeles "riots," to bring to the surface normally subterranean conflicts within wider society (Fiske 1994; see also Hunt 1999). This focus on the conflicted nature of some major media events is productive. But the role of culture in such discursive contests is arguably short-circuited when directly related to the play of contending interests and ideologies, rather than as seen as exerting its own autonomy and conditioning impacts on the field of politics and play of power. These approaches to "media events" can also be questioned in that they generally fail to address the longer-term dynamics that propel some events and happenings, both scripted and unscripted, into becoming exceptional "media events" (Scannell 2001)—criticisms that can also be leveled at recent approaches to "media spectacle."

Douglas Kellner (2003), building on Guy Debord's (1983) "society as spectacle" thesis, argues that media spectacle is becoming one of the organizing principles of the economy, polity, society, and everyday life. But notwithstanding criticisms of Debord's work for providing a "rather generalized and abstract notion of spectacle," theorists of "media spectacles" too often offer a similar, totalizing theorization and one seemingly divorced from either considerations of political economy or the political play of strategic interests (Cottle 2006b, pp. 25–29; Compton and Comor 2007).

Whether approached in consensual (Dayan and Katz), conflicted (Hunt, Fiske), or spectacular (Kellner) terms, therefore, the discussion of "media events" has seemingly become a victim of its own success, suffering conceptual inflation and reduced analytical utility when generalized to such very different forms of media events. They each recognize nonetheless the exceptional and intensive nature of their respective media phenomena, including the subjunctive news orientation that embeds or elicits collective sentiments and appeals to imagined community. For a better grasp of the temporal, narrative, and cultural dynamics found within ritualized media events, however, we need to look elsewhere.

Studies of "mediated scandals" and "mediatized public crises" offer a more dynamic understanding of media performativity moving through time and, often, a sequential structure akin to Victor Turner's "social dramas" (Turner 1974, 1982). This frequently makes it difficult to predict final outcomes (Thompson 2002, pp. 72–73). Media scandals, for example, typically depend on revelations and claims that are followed up by further mediated disclosures and/or counterclaims that build to a climax and demand some form of socially or morally approved sanction. According to James Lull and Stephen Hinerman, "*A media scandal occurs when private acts that disgrace or offend the idealized, dominant morality of a social community are made public and narrativized by the media, producing a range of effects from ideological and cultural retrenchment to disruption and change*" (emphasis in original) (Lull and Hinerman 1997, p. 3).

As with the theorization of moral panics, media scandals are seen as invoking collective boundaries that serve to police perceived transgressions. They are also seen as highly symbolic "affairs" (figuratively or literally) that involve public performances designed to salvage institutional and/or personal reputations, trust, and legitimacy (see Carey 1998). As such, media scandals are essentially struggles of symbolic power. In their media enactment, collective solidarities are summoned and the media stage hosts public performances that variously make calls on imagined moral community. Interestingly, Lull and Hinerman make no prescriptive statement about the exact effects of media scandal because these can be variously integrative or disruptive, hegemonic, or transformative. Media scandals, however, also exhibit highly ritualized characteristics, invoking and/or reaffirming moral boundaries and idealized collective norms of behavior, and incorporating performative (evaluative) response to perceived transgressions.

Jeffrey Alexander and Ronald Jacobs' conceptualization of "mediatized public crises" also provides a more dynamic approach to disruptive media enactments, and does so by theoretically distinguishing its understanding of cultural power from celebratory "media events":

> Celebratory media events of the type discussed by Dayan and Katz tend to narrow the distance between the indicative and the subjunctive, thereby legitimating the powers and authorities outside the civil sphere. Mediatized public crises...tend to increase the distance between the indicative and the subjunctive, thereby giving to civil society its greatest power for social change. In these situations, the media create public narratives that emphasize not only the tragic distance between is and ought but the possibility of historically overcoming it. Such narratives prescribe struggles to make "real" institutional relationships more consistent with the normative standards of the utopian civil society discourse. (Alexander and Jacobs 1998, p. 28)

This is a sophisticated approach that both revises traditional Durkheimian views of ritual as necessarily binding collectivity and distances itself from neo-Marxist outlooks predisposed to view all public rituals as deterministically, instrumentally, and materialistically working in the service of hegemonic interests. As we can detect above, the analytical focus shifts to the performative, processual, and contingent nature of mediatized public crises and how the latent power of civil societies, rooted in widely held cultural presuppositions and normative horizons, can become mobilized within and through them (Alexander 2006a). Once the mediatized wheel of a public crisis begins to turn, public performances it seems are obligated, cultural scripts become resurrected, symbols are deployed, and "performing the binaries" gives shape, form, and cultural meaning to the myths and discourses of civil society (see below). Approached thus, mediatized public crises, from Watergate to the political fall-out from September 11, are theorized and conceptually explicated in terms of "cultural pragmatics," "symbolic action," and "ritual" (Alexander 1988, 2009; Alexander and Smith 2003; Alexander, Giesen, and Mast 2006).

Alexander is aware of the deep suspicions held by contemporary social theory toward the concept and efficacy of ritual in today's segmented and fragmented societies. *Ritual fusion* between social performance and group, he concedes, was more readily accomplished in earlier, less complex societies (Alexander 2006b) and historical processes of *de-fusion* have contributed to a more complex environment in which "the context for performative success has changed" (Alexander 2006b, p. 42).[5] But *ritual-like* performances nonetheless continue to characterize social action in contemporary societies, including those staged in mediatized public crises—and they do so notwithstanding today's enhanced reflexivity toward the artifice of staged public performances.

For Alexander and colleagues working within this "strong programme in cultural sociology" (Alexander 2009; Alexander and Smith 2003; Alexander, Giesen, and Mast 2006), the possibility of *re-fusion* remains not only possible but also critical because "only if performances achieve fusion can they reinvigorate collective codes" (Alexander 2006b, p. 80). It is in such moments that the civil sphere comes alive, publicly instantiated in and through the communication of utopian discourses, and appeals to solidarity and the elaboration of wider "structures of feeling." Cultural pragmatics, theorized as strategic or instrumental action that is necessarily conducted in and through wider cultural codes, symbolism, and meanings, is both conditioned by but also serves to instantiate something of the civil sphere when operating, as it must, "between ritual and strategy" (Alexander 2006a, 2006b, 2009). Here, then, the civil sphere is not conceived in Habermasian (1989) terms as a rational "public sphere" of deliberation that is allergic to the cultural, symbolic, and performative, but rather as the widely diffused and in-depth cultural values and myths that coalesce under the normative horizons of civil society. These periodically become mobilized in mediatized public crises and advanced on the basis of normative ideas and values of "justice," "fairness," "democracy," or the "good society" or, indeed, their binary opposites when ascribed to the "enemies" of civil society.

As this brief review has sought to make clear, ideas of media performance and ritualization continue to register powerfully in the theorization and conceptualization of diverse "exceptional" events and their enactments in the news media. James

Ettema, developing on Victor Turner's model of social dramas, put it eloquently when he said mass-mediated rituals are "more conceptually complex and politically volatile than the transmission of mythic tales to mass audiences" because they are "an important cultural resource both for waging and for narrating politics" (Ettema 1990, pp. 477–478; see also Elliott 1980; Wagner-Pacifici 1986; Alexander 1988; Jacobs 2000; Cottle 2004, 2005). Turner himself, of course, powerfully invited just such a politically dynamic view of ritual when elaborating how "social dramas" can produce moments of liminality and communitas outside of normal space and time. "I like to think of ritual essentially as *performance,* as *enactment* and not primarily as rules or rubrics," he said, "The rules frame the ritual process, but the ritual process transcends its frame" (Turner, cited in Mitchell 1981, pp. 155–156; see also St. John 2008). The relevance of these ideas for better understanding how mediatized disasters are variously made to mean and politically matter can now be explored further.

MEDIATIZED DISASTERS

This second part of the discussion moves to explore more empirically some of the ritualized forms and political dynamics that characterize mediatized disasters. We consider first the reporting deployed in the South Asian tsunami (2004) and how this embedded emotions of grief and empathy, invited public performances from elites and survivors, and variously invoked notions of imagined national community and international moral solidarity. We then consider how some mediatized disasters, exemplified here by Hurricane Katrina (2005), can unfold very differently across time and space, providing opportunities for elite framing as well as discursive contention and political dissent—whether on the national or international news stages or transnationally. And, finally, we briefly consider how Cyclone Nargis in Burma and the Sichuan earthquake in China (2008), both in the same month, became an opportunity for the news media to performatively compare and evaluate these two disasters and how they did so by invoking deep cultural binaries and infusing moral approbation and opprobrium into their public accounts of government actions and inactions. Though each of the above disasters was subject to extensive and intensive forms of media ritualization, each in fact became culturally constituted differently—with different political ramifications.

The South Asian Tsunami: Rituals of Solidarity

The South Asian tsunami of December 2004 was caused by an underground earthquake in the India Ocean off the coast of Aceh on the northern Indonesian island of Sumatra. The devastating waves led to massive destruction and an estimated loss of over 220,000 lives across coastal regions of Indonesia, Thailand, Burma, India, Sri Lanka, Maldives, Somalia, and Seychelles. The sheer scale of the loss of life, devastation, and multiple countries and regions affected positioned it as an unprecedented international disaster. At first, predictably perhaps, it became reported through geopolitical outlooks and the journalistic "calculus of death," fixating on the ever-rising death toll, as these typical frontpage headlines illustrate:

> "Deathwave. Death Toll 9,500 and counting. India 3,200" (*The Indian Express*, 27.12.04)
> "Wave of Destruction. World's Biggest Earthquake for Forty Years Devastates Asia. Wall of Water 10 Meters High Inundates Popular Tourist Resort. Toll passes 7,500 with Sri Lanka, India and Indonesia the Worst Hit" (*South China Morning Post*, 27.12.04)
> "Toll Tops 24,000 as Disease Fears Grow" (*The Age*, 28.12.04)
> "Toll in Undersea Earthquake Passes 26,000. A Third of the Dead are said to be Children" (*New York Times*, 28.12.07)
> "After the Destruction, The Grief. Tsunami Death Toll Climbs to 25,000, 30,000 Missing on Remote Indian Islands, Disease Fears as Huge Relief Effort Launched" (*The Guardian*, 28.12.04)

Among the calculations of death, however, newspapers also sought to provide background and analysis of what exactly had happened, many providing elaborate maps charting the course of the destructive waves and their devastating impact on different islands and coastal communities. Also prominent among this early coverage was a concerted effort to relay first-person accounts, bearing witness, and providing graphic testimonies of the death and destruction caused by the tsunami. News articles under first-person headlines such as the following were common: "How Paradise Turned to Hell" (*The Age* 27.12.04), "Suddenly We Heard This Loud Rumbling Noise" (*The Guardian* 27.12.07), and "I Was Being Swept Out to Sea, I Felt Afraid, Powerless" (*The Indian Express*, 27.12.04). In such prominently displayed, graphic testimonies, readers were invited to contemplate the destruction, fear and carnage of the event as experienced by survivors, and relived in the news media.

As time moved on, national newspapers reported on government relief responses. *The Age*, in Australia, for example, produced headlines such as: "Federal Aid Up by $35m 'With More to Come'" (*The Age* 30.12.05) and "Canberra Steps Up Help for Indonesia" (*The Age*, 31.12.07). But it was the involvement of their own nationals, predominantly tourists killed and missing, that preoccupied the press in many countries such as Australia. "Fears Rise for Thousands of Missing Tourists" (*The Age*, 28.12.07), "A Jet Ski in the Lobby, A Shark in the Pool…"(*The Age* 28.12.07), "For a Ruptured Family, the Net Recovers a Toddler Believed Lost in the Waves", "Holiday Trip Turns into Horror Ride" (*The Age*, 30.12.07), "Waiting and Hoping For a Phone Call That Never Comes" (*The Age*, 31.12.07). In such headlines, we hear not simply news interest in involved nationals, *en masse*, but the deliberate attempt to provide personalized stories and emotive accounts encouraging identification and empathy with the plight and suffering of *their* national victims. Everyday, taken-for-granted objects and technologies—mobile phones, computers, the Net, and even a jet ski incongruously found in a swimming pool (alongside a shark)—all help to relay added poignancy and gravitas in the aftermath of disaster, the visible signs of ordinary lives shattered, routine expectations turned upside down, and the desperate attempts to reconstitute normality and relocate lost loved ones.

Such news reporting certainly exhibits geopolitical outlooks and reveals the professional calculus of death at work but, as we can detect in such headlines, the press is also making a concerted effort to invoke something of the perceived human reality of these same events and their aftermath. It does so through the deliberate embedding of personal experiences and emotive accounts of the tragedy of lives cut short and families wrenched apart by the destructive force of nature. This performative enactment of "cultural trauma" was not *naturalistically* determined by the grievous social dislocation and rupture wrought by the tsunami itself, but rather by the performative interventions of the news media (see Alexander 2004). By crafted, journalistic means, the disaster became signified as a moment outside of normal time and space, a liminal period, constituted in the media through its intensive and extensive forms of news reportage and asserting both "communitas" and the reassertion of social "structure" (Turner 1982).

After the initial disaster and aftermath reports, reporters soon began to emphasize the bonds of community and solidarity born of adversity as well as sympathetic responses from distant countries and communities. In such ways, newspapers provided a moral infusion into the wasted human landscape, seeking out and celebrating the selfless and heroic acts of survivors and rescuers as well as publicizing collective forms of solidarity embodied in institutional relief efforts, charity donations, and the symbolic actions of elites. Collectively, such stories re-colonized space and place momentarily lost to the amoral (immoral) forces of nature anthropomorphized in the media in terms of "The Cruel Sea" (*International Express*, 4–10.1.05), "Deadly Sea, Brutal and Indiscriminate" (28.12.04), and "Nature's Fury" (*The Courier Mail*, 7.1.05).

This public valorization of moral community found expression through a succession of newspaper articles and features with headlines and captions such as: "Britain Unites to Help Victims," "£1 Million Raised in One Hour After Tidal Wave Disaster," "Generous Britons Pledge To Help Victims" (*International Express*, 4–10.1.05); "Friendship Blossoms in the Rubble, Indonesia, Australia Closer" (*The Sydney Morning Herald*, 5.1.05); "Aid Forges Closer Links," "Generosity Worldwide Amazes UN," and "We're in For the Long Haul, Howard Tells Indonesians" (*The Courier Mail*, 7.1.05).

In the aftermath of catastrophic disasters, politicians and other elites are obliged to go on "media parade," symbolically positioning themselves among the carnage and devastation, conducting walkabouts and meeting survivors, and commending emergency services and relief workers on their professionalism and heroic efforts— all in front of news cameras. The cultural pragmatics of disaster performances obligate that their public deportment must conform to the known cultural scripts of how to behave in times of grief and human loss, though their exact execution remains a possible source of public opprobrium (*de-fusion*) if perceived by the viewing public to be disingenuous or simply too "staged." In such moments, then, elites are obliged to publicly demonstrate their personal concern as well as active agency in "taking charge" and restoring normality. These symbolic images encode relations of social hierarchy and power at the same time as they proclaim to represent collective solidarity and community compassion. Ordinary people, as we have heard, are also afforded enhanced news presence in the preferred *personae dramatis* of mediatized disasters and allocated moral roles and established cultural scripts. An article headlined "Reluctant Angel of Patong Dives into Hell" (*The Courier-Mail*, 7.1.05), for example, commends and discursively constructs the selfless actions of a young Australian woman who returned to the scenes of devastation to help. She becomes publicly sacralized as a "reluctant angel," a signification reinforced through her voluntary entry into "hell." As Pantti and Wahl-Jorgensen observe in their study of disaster emotions, "The shift of focus from the sufferers to the heroes allows the rhetorical shift from despair to hope and national pride" (Pantti and Wahl-Jorgensen 2007, p. 14).

As time passed, further opportunities presented themselves for the ritualization of catastrophe through public ceremonies of remembrance—both religious and secular. For many people, such religious and civic rituals are principally enacted within and through the news sphere: "Let Us Pray: A Nation Stops to Remember" (*Sunday Telegraph*, 16.1.05); "They Are Not Alone: Australia Stops in Sorrow, In Fraternity" (*Sydney Morning Herald*, 15–16.1.05). Here, the news media did not hold back in its efforts to craft powerful visual frontpages in international solidarity, and ones encoded with suitable reverence and emotions for such ritual occasions. Images of bereaved children, mothers, and wives served to symbolize the victims of the tragedy and became positioned as the focal image around which an imagined nation was summoned and seemingly united as a moral community in sympathy and grief. For example, a particularly memorable image comprised an unusually aestheticized, not to say angelic, portrait of a mother and child *survivor*—evidently a carefully choreographed image and in stark contrast to earlier "raw" newspaper photographs of mangled bodies and people in distress (*Sydney Morning Herald* 15–16.1.05). In comparison to these earlier "victim" scenes, the depicted image provides by far a more dignified, even reverential, view of the "survivor" as subject, and one more fitting to the projected ritual occasion.

In such aesthetic, affective, and emotionally laden ways, then, the tsunami became heavily ritualized by the press and was subject to the discourses and sentiments, performances and symbols, rhetoric and ideals of national collectivity and moral community. A more in-depth examination of the tsunami and its news reportage around the world would also no doubt detect important differences between national and regional contexts, reflecting differences of geopolitical outlooks and national cultures (see Robertson 2010). Such an analysis would also find evidence for less than fully harmonious or integrative forms of media coverage. Some points of narrative disruption would include, for example, the British press criticisms leveled at British Prime Minister Tony Blair for remaining on vacation when his leadership was seemingly demanded at home; the controversy surrounding some relief agencies that requested the public desist from making donations given the unprecedented funds already collected for emergency relief; media scares about trafficking and the prostitution of orphaned children; as well as the failure of countries in the tsunami region to install early warning systems.

Dissent and disagreement, then, certainly surfaced in the media's treatments of the tsunami, but this at most assumed a muted aspect when set against the generally integrative tenor of the reporting of the tsunami and its ritualization of collective grief and inscriptions of moral community described above. Here, the media powerfully and performatively resurrected "known" cultural scripts of disaster and populated their images and discourses with roles and responsibilities deemed appropriate to the moral drama and its sequencing through discernible stages of disruption, crisis, response, and the reconstitution of social and moral order. Not all mediatized disasters, however, occasion such consensual and integrative forms of news ritualization.

Hurricane Katrina: Disaster Myths and the Ritualization of Dissent

Some disasters, evidently, do not always lend themselves to rituals of national integration and solidarity based on the public elaboration of emotions and consensual values, but become the site for discursive contention and even political dissent. News reporting of Hurricane Katrina illustrates a powerful case in point. In their analysis of *The New York Times, The Washington Post,* and *New Orleans Times-Picayune* coverage, Kathleen Tierney and colleagues (2006) document how media reporting perpetuated the "disaster myth," the idea that under such circumstances survivors panic, social order breaks down, and a state of chaos and lawlessness ensues that requires a law-and-order or even a military response. In fact, argue Tierney, Bevc, and Kugligowski, disaster situations in the United States and elsewhere are known to generate altruistic social behaviors and group bonding as people try to organize and help each other under abnormal and adverse conditions—a point generally borne out in the expert literature on disasters (see Rodriguez, Quarantelli, and Dynes 2007). This, however, was most definitely not the image portrayed by the U.S. press:

> Chaos gripped New Orleans on Wednesday as looters ran wild....Looters brazenly ripped open gates and ransacked stores for food, clothing, television sets, computers, jewelry, and guns. (*The New York Times,* 1.9.05)
>
> Things have spiraled so out of control (in New Orleans) that the city's mayor ordered police officers to focus on looters and give up the search and rescue efforts. (*The Washington Post* 1.9.05)

These and many other examples provided by the authors demonstrate the general news framing of the aftermath situation in terms similar to riot reporting. As the authors say, "The distinction between disasters and urban unrest is an important one" but this did not hinder the news media's sensationalizing rumors, innuendo, and unsubstantiated claims including, for example, the widely reported claims of multiple murders, child rape, and people dying of gunshot wounds in the Superdome where survivors had taken refuge. Though later found to be groundless, these news reports had accepted such claims, say the authors, because they were consistent with the media frame that had characterized New Orleans, to use a press headline of the time, as "the snakepit of anarchy" (Tierney, Bevc, and Kugligowski 2006, p. 68).

Over time this "civil unrest" frame gave way to an "urban war zone" frame that inevitably supported a militarized response. Curfews and a suspicious view of survivors' movements around the city inhibited neighborhood residents helping one another and also led officials to ignore the possibility of working with survivors to deliver assistance. Emergency responses became diverted to law enforcement, jeopardizing the lives of the hurricane survivors. News media images of looting and lawlessness may also have caused organizations outside the region to hesitate before committing resources and help. And the racial divides of U.S. society are also likely to have become further entrenched on the basis of the news media's stereotypical portrayal, a finding supported by pubic attitude surveys after the worst of the disaster. On the basis of this detailed analysis, Tierney and her colleagues propose that "Hurricane Katrina may well prove to be the focusing event that moves the nation to place more faith in military solutions for a wider range of social problems than ever before" (Tierney, Bevc, and Kugligowski 2006, p. 78; see also Klein 2007).

However, both the mainstream media in the United States and international media also gave vent to a wider array of discourses and emotions surrounding Hurricane Katrina, not all of which supported elite interests and the disaster frames described above. Criticisms of city officials, failed evacuation plans, inadequate relief efforts, and the seeming abandonment of some of the poorest people in American society to their fate as well as the militarized response to the aftermath also became voiced in the news media. Then U.S. President George Bush was targeted by some as the source of blame; others suggested that Hurricane Katrina exposed the normally invisible inequalities of "race" and poverty in American society. Hurricane Katrina, then, became an opportunity for political appropriation by different projects and discourses.

Unlike the principle of broadcast ceremonies that, according to Tamar Leibes, "highlights emotions and solidarity and brackets analysis," the "shared collective space created by disaster time-out, zooming in on victims and their families, is the basis not for dignity and restraint but for the chaotic exploitation of the pain of participants" and "the opportunistic fanning of establishment mismanagement, neglect, corruption, and so on" (Liebes 1998, pp. 75–76; see also Kyriakidou 2008). In the aftermath of Katrina, the U.S. president was forced to publicly try and offset the mounting criticism of his lackluster response, inadequate disaster planning, and lack of resources made available by his political administration. Other federal officials such as Michael Brown, head of the Federal Emergency Management Agency (FEMA), also became singled out for public criticism as claims of incompetence, fanned by the media, circulated and effectively undermined George Bush's initial commendation of government officials for "doing a great job."

Hurricane Katrina not only played out in the U.S. press however, but also in the world's press and other media. The BBC online news website, for example, positioned itself as a portal for world opinion, exhibiting opinion pieces from America and around the world and providing hyperlinks to some of the world's press. It is instructive to examine just a few of these different voices found in the world's press and reproduced on the BBC's webpage:

> Bush is completely out of his depth in this disaster. Katrina has revealed America's weaknesses: its racial divisions, the poverty of those left behind by its society, and especially its president's lack of leadership.
>
> —Phillipe Grangereau in France's *Liberation*

> The biggest power of the world is rising over poor black corpses. We are witnessing the collapse of the American myth. In terms of the USA's relationship with itself and the world, Hurricane Katrina seems to leave its mark on our century as an extraordinary turning point.
>
> —Yildrim Turker in Turkey's *Radikal*

> Hurricane Katrina has proved that America cannot solve its internal problems and is incapable of facing these kinds of natural disasters, so it cannot bring peace and democracy to other parts of the world. Americans now understand that their rulers are only seeking to fulfill their own hegemonic goals.
>
> —Editorial in Iran's *Siyasat-e Ruz*

> Co-operation to reduce greenhouse gas emissions can no longer be delayed, but there are still countries—including the US—which still do not take the issue seriously. However, faced with global disasters, all countries are in the same boat. The US hurricane disaster is a "modern revelation," and all countries of the world including the US should be aware of this.
>
> —Xing Shu Li in Malaysia's *Sun Chew Jit Poh*

> This tragic incident reminds us that the United States has refused to ratify the Kyoto accords. Let's hope the US can from now on stop ignoring the rest of the world. If you want to run things, you must first lead by example. Arrogance is never a good advisor.
>
> —Jean-Pierre Aussant in France's *Figaro*

> Hurricane Katrina will bury itself into the American consciousness in the same way 9/11 or the fall of Saigon did. The storm did not just destroy America's image of itself, but also has the power to bring an end to the Republican era sooner than expected. America is ashamed.
>
> —Michael Streck in Germany's *Die Welt*

> Katrina is testing the US. Katrina is also creating an opportunity for world unity. Cuba and North Korea's offer of sympathy and aid to the US could also result in some profound thinking in the US, and the author hopes that it will not miss the opportunity.
>
> —Shen Dingli in China's *Dongfang Zaobao*

As we can see, differences of geopolitical interests and cultural outlooks clearly register in these very different national views from around the world and here relayed on the global media stage—but all normatively informed by and appealing to the moral horizons of an expanded transnational civil sphere. The exposure of America's continuing racial divides and depth of poverty for some sullied its projected international image as a "free democracy." Countries normally regarded as political pariahs or as economic supplicants by the U.S. government turned the tables and offered their support to the world's mightiest power in its evident failure to respond to its home-grown humanitarian disaster. And yet others took the opportunity to make the connection to climate change and the irony of the U.S. position of not having signed on to the Kyoto treaty. Indeed, such was the mounting criticism played out in the news media that commentators even began to speak of George Bush's "Katrinagate." But, as we have also heard, the part played by some sections of the U.S. media in circulating myths of urban warfare both nationally and internationally undermines a generalized argument about the U.S. media regaining its critical independence and acting as a collective political watchdog. Still, the world press's reporting on Hurricane Katrina undoubtedly provided a diverse range of nationally inflected responses circulated and available via webpages and the so-called blogosphere that infused information on, criticisms about, and much-needed insider accounts into the chaos and confusion of Hurricane Katrina (Allan 2006, pp. 156–165; Robinson 2009).

In such ways, Hurricane Katrina was extensively and intensively mediated around the globe, reverberating across the wider geopolitical field and becoming infused with diverse discourses and political projects. Contrived, satirical images of George H. W. Bush and his son fishing from a rowing boat in the flooded streets of New Orleans or singing to the distraught residents seeking sanctuary in the Super Bowl stadium also circulated on the Internet (http://www.bushbusiness.com and http://www.q-dog.co.uk) and gave expression to the mounting political skepticism toward the presidency of George Bush and his administration's inept handling of the Katrina disaster and, possibly more so, the transparency of his cultural performances designed to regain the political initiative and moral high ground.

Cyclone Nargis and the Sichuan Earthquake: Performing Moral Opprobrium and Approbation

Cyclone Nargis hit the Burmese coast on May 2, 2008, with winds in excess of 120 mph. The resulting tidal waves and flooding caused devastation across much of the Irrawaddy delta and killed an estimated 138,000 people, leaving 2.4 million people destitute. The Burmese junta refused permission for overseas aid workers to gain access to some of the worst affected areas and communities, prompting widespread international condemnation. Ten days later on May 12, a devastating earthquake shook Sichuan province of China. An estimated 87,000 people died, including many schoolchildren killed beneath collapsing school buildings, with up to 5 million people made homeless. The Chinese authorities' response was also subject to explicit commentary (possibly encouraged by China's hosting of the Olympic Games later that year), but unlike the Burmese junta, the Chinese regime and its disaster response were often praised in the media.[6]

Both the temporal proximity of these two disasters, as well as the different responses by the Burmese and Chinese authorities to the plight of their people, led to explicit comparative evaluations. This was given cultural shape and form, and added political charge, by the news media's performative invocation of deep cultural binaries rooted in normative views and moral precepts about how governments "are meant to behave" or "should respond" to the humanitarian needs of their populations. As we have heard, the civil sphere can be conceived of not only as an arena for information conveyance and deliberation but also as a cultural space "where actors and events become typified into more general codes (e.g. sacred/profane, pure/impure, democratic/antidemocratic, citizen/enemy)" (Alexander and Jacobs 1998, pp. 29–30). The following BBC news report, first broadcast on BBC television news and then transcribed and made available at the BBC website, was representative of many such news reports at the time. Here, it serves to demonstrate perfectly this journalistic moralization of events, encoded in and through its "thick descriptions" (Cottle 2005b) and purposeful "performing of the binaries" (Alexander 2006a). Consider first the opening sequence with its crafted, visceral bodily "descriptions" of these two disasters:

Burma and China: Tale of Two Disasters

The BBC's Paul Danahar reported on the aftermath of the cyclone in Burma before flying to China to cover the Sichuan earthquake. Here he compares the two disasters, and the response from both governments.

It is the stench of death that distinguishes these two disasters. It still blows across the vast flooded plains of the Irrawaddy delta. It is not a faint smell that slowly creeps up on you. It just suddenly hits you in the face, filling your mouth and nose, smothering your senses.

And it assaults those in the delta even now, more than two weeks after the cyclone smashed into the coastline.

But in Sichuan province, in neighbouring China, the air is still breathable. Death is being swept away. Corpses are being collected and buried. Families, where possible, are receiving the grim comfort of a body to grieve over; a ritual to mark the passing of a loved one; a point from which to try to rebuild what remains of their lives.

In Burma the bodies of many of those lost in the cyclone receive attention only from the birds. Five days into the earthquake in China, the trucks of aid and relief supplies were too many to count. At the same stage in Burma I counted only two. That was during a whole day of traveling along the main highway into the delta from the former capital Rangoon.

Building on these bodily/sensory accounts and perceptions, the report next both contextualizes and historicizes the different approaches of the two regimes to offers of international assistance, and thereby further moralizes their different actions and inactions toward the humanitarian plight of their citizens.

Aid Void

In Burma people sat in the wreckage of their homes. Bloated, rotting corpses floated around the rivers and inlets. Often help was not on the way. The generals in Burma chose not to save lives. It was their decision to make. They could not control the cyclone, and they could not cope with the disaster. But they still controlled borders and, as they have for decades, they thumbed their noses at influence from the outside world. Even when, in this case, that influence was undisputedly for the good of their people.

> China was once like this. Thirty-two years ago the government of
> Chairman Mao reacted in the same way after the Tangshan earthquake, close
> to the capital Beijing. At least 250,000 people died. Under-resourced and
> overwhelmed by the natural calamity, the government of China literally
> buried the evidence of their incompetence. In a phrase echoed recently by
> Burma's military junta, they announced the beginning of reconstruction
> before the relief effort had really begun. Bulldozers consigned the true scale
> of the disaster to the speculation of future historians.

Finally, the report explicitly declares its informing political evaluation and moral verdicts on the two regimes—persuading, perhaps compelling its audience to do likewise.

> Inhuman?
> The Chinese reaction this time could not be more different. It has been a
> model of disaster relief. There have been recriminations about why so many
> buildings, particularly schools, collapsed so easily. There are accusations that
> corrupt local officials conspired with unscrupulous builders to construct
> structures that turned into death traps. But there is a distinction that must be
> made in modern China between the local administrations and the central
> government. For while some local officials may prove to have blood on their
> hands, the Chinese government has done all that could be expected of it.
>   The generals in Burma find themselves accused of an "inhuman"
> response to their disaster, bordering on a "crime against humanity".
>   In contrast China has found itself in the unusual position of being
> showered with international praise, both for its reaction to the disaster and
> the openness with which it has allowed the details to be reported. The
> government of modern China has thrown in every resource at its disposal
> and it has been prepared to have its efforts judged openly. And, unlike the
> generals across the border, they have nothing to be ashamed of.[7]

As we can clearly see, read, and possibly feel across this BBC news report crafted at the height of the news coverage of the Burmese cyclone, the comparison of these two disasters is structured around powerful binary contrasts. These are at work, ascribing cultural meanings and moral evaluations and effectively purifying and polluting the public standing of the two political regimes and their respective actions. Binary oppositions are often most powerfully at work, say Alexander and Jacobs, when "contrasts between purifying and polluting motives, relations, and institutions permeate news accounts linking the presuppositions of civil society to the ongoing rush of social events" (Alexander and Jacobs 1998, pp. 29–30). In this case, the venal, uncaring, corrupt, and essentially inward-looking and inhuman regime of Burma is simultaneously denounced as it is described, and in terms that are the mirror image of the reportedly administratively competent, publicly oriented, well-organized, and, increasingly, internationally responsive and socialized Chinese state. As the BBC report concludes: "Unlike the generals across the border," the government of modern China "has nothing to be ashamed of."

   In such morally infused terms, the deep cultural binaries of the "civil sphere" are not simply at work as unspoken or taken-for-granted cultural assumptions that inform the journalist's story. They are, in fact, actively narrated, enacted, and performed, granting structure, sense, and meaning to these twinned disasters and enabling moral judgments—opprobrium and approbation—to publicly pollute and purify the key protagonists involved. When mediatized in such morally infused "thick descriptions," in such crafted forms of journalism, "civil society becomes organized around a bifurcating discourse of citizen and enemy" and this contributes a powerful classificatory and evaluative dimension to public discourse (Alexander and Jacobs 1998, p. 30). This can powerfully condition the context and opportunities for political action.

Conclusion

The scale of death and destruction or the potentially catastrophic consequences of major threats and disasters, we know, are no guarantee that they will necessarily register prominently in the world's news media. So-called forgotten disasters, hidden wars, and permanent emergencies still abound in the world today and, because of their media invisibility, often command neither wider recognition nor political response. But we have also seen how the news media are capable on occasion of staging and narrating crises in ways that serve to invest them with emotional and cultural resonance, forcing them into the public eye and appealing to identities of moral community and ideas of the public good.

When mediatized, some disasters, as we have seen, become performatively enacted and ritualized in the world's news media, reverberating powerfully outward beyond the immediate scenes of death and destruction. Some are represented with awe and symbolism, and embedded with emotion and appeals to community. Others become opportunities for dissent and criticism with authorities and institutions rendered politically vulnerable by the tragedy, trauma, and emotions that are publicly played out on the media stage. And some mediatized disasters may even serve to expand moral horizons and boundaries of the "civil sphere" (Alexander 2006a) when deep cultural meanings (binaries) rooted in the presuppositions of civil societies are attached to events and institutions, agents, and their motives in faraway places. On these occasions, a universe of moral as much as political evaluation comes into public view.

This discussion, then, has pointed to a more variegated and expressive range of mediatized responses to disaster than is often countenanced by established social science approaches, whether framed through generalizing accounts of the professional calculus of death or Western hegemonic power, or indeed by disaster communication specialists preoccupied with processes of disaster cognition and information flows. Drawing on ideas of cultural performance, symbolic action, and ritual under an encompassing heuristic of mediatized rituals, the discussion has sought to illuminate some of the culturally expressive forms of mediatized disasters and how these can support differing political responses. Clearly, more detailed analysis of these and other mediatized disasters is now needed if we are to better understand the differentiated, performative and ritualizing responses of the news media to select disasters around the world. And we also must attend more closely to processes of mews mediatization in interaction with the field of surrounding institutional interests and discourses of civil society. But even this limited empirical engagement has begun to discern how news media can performatively enact and ritualize disasters quite differently, thereby making them culturally mean and politically matter.

Major disasters are now on the increase (Oxfam 2009) and in a globalizing world they are destined to become ever more deterritorializing in nature, scope, and outcomes. Inevitably, this will grant increased centrality and importance to global media systems and communication networks (Cottle 2009b). Situated in global context, mediatized disasters speak to our global age and the extent to which disasters and misfortunes in one part of the globe are recognized and responded to in another. Disasters are no longer confined within or behind national borders; they have become a litmus test for the wider, transnational field of humanitarian and political responses. Mediatized disasters offer perhaps one of the ways in which "spaces of our emotional imagination have expanded in a transnational sense" (Beck 2006, pp. 5–6) but, as we have begun to see, their different forms of cultural expression challenge easy claims that they will necessarily produce "cosmopolitan pity which forces us to act" (Beck 2006, p. 6). (See also Höijer 2004; Kyriakidou 2008.) To better understand the complexities of empathy and engagement, politics and pity that are variously summoned through mediatized disasters, we need to better understand how some disasters become performatively enacted in the world's news media. We need to understand how they are culturally made to mean and how, potentially, this makes them politically matter.

NOTES

1. This chapter draws on the author's previous publications on mediatized rituals and disaster reporting, including Cottle 2004, 2005a, 2006a, 2008, 2009a, 2009b.

2. For an in-depth and theoretically acute account of how different types of television news items variously encode different "regimes of pity" or appeals to compassion, see Chouliaraki 2006, and for more in-depth study and discussion of processes of audience reception with respect to "compassion" and "disasters," respectively, see Höijer (2004) and Kyriakidou (2008). This discussion deliberately pitches its sights more widely on mediatized disasters approached as an exceptional class of performative media enactments that are narrativized over time and that can variously construct disasters as national events, cosmopolitan moments, or political opportunities for dissent and change.

3. Ideas of performance and performativity, whether those developed in the fields of linguistics and language studies (Austin 1956/1975), symbolic interactionist sociology (Goffman 1959), anthropology and ethnography (Turner 1969, 1974, 1982; Geertz 1992; Hughes-Freeland 1998; Schieffelin 1998), or gender and identity studies (Butler 1990), invite us to move beyond the referential or "constantive" (Austin 1975) level of communication and consider how, respectively, words, social encounters, culture, and identity are

performed and are thereby "doing" something, and invariably doing so with an awareness of an audience (Bakhtin 1986; Carlson 1996).

4. A good place to start such an exploration would be the theorization of source fields and news access (Cottle 2003). The field of journalism occupies a pivotal site in the communication of culture and conflicts and in relation to the surrounding views and voices that contend for media influence, representation, and participation. Who secures media access, and how, inevitably raises fundamental questions about the nature of media participation and performance and the play of power transacted between the news media, government, corporations, and wider civil society. To date, researchers working within the *sociological paradigm* have tended to forefront media-source interactions in terms of *strategic framing and definitional power*, examining *patterns of news access, routines of news production*, and *processes of source intervention*, and how each conditions the production of *public knowledge*. Researchers working within a *culturalist paradigm*, on the other hand, have tended to theorize news access in terms of *cultural representation*, and are sensitized to the *symbolic role* of news actors and how these are positioned according to the conventions of news—*story, narrative, form*—and thereby help contribute to and sustain wider *cultural myths* that resonate within *popular culture*. While the sociological paradigm encourages us to look at the role of *strategic power* in the *public representation of politics* (broadly conceived), the culturalist paradigm invites us to see how *cultural forms* and *symbols* are implicated within the *politics of representation* (more textually conceived). However, a third approach both incorporates and, in part, departs from the previous two, and this examines *communicative power* by attending to the dynamics and contingencies of *source-media interactions, cultural performances*, and *engaged media encounters* sensitized to the *communicative architecture* of journalism and its communicative modes of "display and deliberation" (Cottle and Rai 2006). In such ways, the study of source fields and contention promises to overcome traditional paradigmatic approaches and may yet serve to better ground a more holistic *cultural sociology* of news media-source interactions, and one that is of use for the comparative exploration and explanation of mediatized disasters (Cottle 2003, 2006b; see also Alexander 2006a, pp. 293–391, 2006b).

5. Major processes of de-fusion identified by Alexander include: (1) the separation of written foreground texts from background collective representations, (2) the estrangement of the means of symbolic production from the mass of social actors, and (3) the separation of the elites who carried out central symbolic actions (Alexander 2006b, p. 45).

6. In fact, the potential for critical media framing and even media-propelled scandal was also obtained in the Sichuan earthquake, where the parents of children killed in collapsed school buildings blamed local officials and corruption for the construction of deficient school buildings. But this did not fit comfortably with the preferred overarching frame guiding the Western news media's comparative moral evaluation of the Chinese and Burmese authorities.

7. BBC article published 19/05/2008. http://news.bbc.co.uk/go/pr/fr/-/1/hi/world/asia-pacific/7407927.stm.

REFERENCES

Allan, Stuart. 2006. *Online News: Journalism and the Internet*. Maidenhead, UK: Open University Press.

Allen, Tim, and Seaton, Jean, eds. 1999. *The Media of Conflict: War Reporting and Representations of Ethnic Violence*. London and New York: Zed Books.

Alexander, Jeffrey. 1988. "Culture and Political Crisis: 'Watergate' and Durkheimian
    Sociology." In *Durkheimian Sociology: Cultural Studies*, edited by Jeffrey Alexander,
    pp. 187–224. New York: Cambridge University Press.
———. 2004. "Toward a Theory of Cultural Trauma." In *Cultural Trauma and Collective
    Identity*, edited by Jeffrey Alexander, Ron Eyerman, Bernhard Giesen, Neil Smelser,
    and Piotr Sztompka, pp.1–30. Berkeley: University of California Press.
———. 2005. "Globalization as Collective Representation: The New Dream of a
    Cosmopolitan Civil Sphere." http://research.yale.edu/ccs/research.
———. 2006a. *The Civil Sphere*. Oxford: Oxford University Press.
———. 2006b. "Cultural Pragmatics: Social Performance between Ritual and Strategy." In
    Social Performance: Symbolic Action, Cultural Pragmatics, and Ritual, edited by Jeffrey
    Alexander, Bernhard Giesen, and Jason Mast, pp. 29–90. Cambridge, UK: Cambridge
    University Press.
———. 2009. "The Democratic Struggle for Power: The 2008 Presidential Campaign in
    the USA." *Journal of Power* 2(1): 65–88.
Alexander, Jeffrey, and Ronald Jacobs. 1998. "Mass Communication, Ritual and Civil
    Society." In *Media, Ritual and Identity*, edited by Tamar Liebes and James Curran,
    pp. 23–41. London: Routledge.
Alexander, Jeffrey, and Phillip Smith. 2003. "The Strong Program in Cultural Sociology:
    Elements of a Structural Hermeneutics." In *The Meanings of Social Life: A Cultural
    Sociology*, edited by Jeffrey Alexander. pp. 11–26. Oxford: Oxford University Press.
Alexander, Jeffrey, Bernhard Giesen, and Jason Mast, eds. 2006. *Social Performance:
    Symbolic Action, Cultural Pragmatics, and Ritual*. Cambridge, UK: Cambridge
    University Press.
Altheide, David. 2009. "Moral Panic: From the Sociological Concept to Public Discourse."
    Crime, Media, Culture 5(1): 79–100.
Austin, John. 1975 (1956). *How to Do Things with Words*. Cambridge, MA: Harvard
    University Press.
Bakhtin, Mikhail. 1986. *Speech Genres and Other Late Essays*. Austin: University of Texas
    Press.
Beck, Ulrich. 2006. *Cosmopolitan Vision*. Cambridge, UK: Polity Press.
———. 2009. *World at Risk*. Cambridge, UK: Polity Press.
Bennett, Lance. 1990. "Towards a Theory of Press-State Relations in the United States."
    Journal of Communication 40(2): 103–125.
Bennett, Lance, Regina Lawrence, and Steven Livingston. 2007. *When the Press Fails:
    Political Power and the News Media from Iraq to Katrina*. Chicago: Chicago University
    Press.
Benthall, Jonathan. 1993. *Disasters, Relief and the Media*. London: I.B. Tauris.
Butler, David. 1995. *The Trouble with Reporting Northern Ireland*. Aldershot, UK: Avebury.
Butler, Judith. 1990. *Gender Trouble: Feminism and the Subversion of Identity*. London:
    Routledge.
Calhoun, Craig. 2004. "A World of Emergencies: Fear, Intervention, and the Limits of
    Cosmopolitan Order." *The Canadian Review of Sociology and Anthropology* 41(4):
    373–395.
———. 2008. "The Imperative to Reduce Suffering: Charity, Progress, and Emergencies in
    the Field of Humanitarian Action." In *Humanitarianism in Question: Politics, Power,
    Ethics*, edited by Michael Barnett and Thomas Weiss, pp. 73–97. Ithaca, NY, and
    London: Cornell University Press.
Carey, James. 1989. *Communication as Culture*. London: Unwin Hyman.

———. 1998. "Political Ritual on Television: Episodes in the History of Shame, Degradation and Excommunication." In *Media, Ritual and Identity*, edited by Tamar Leibes and James Curran. pp. 42–70. London: Routledge.

Carlson, Marvin. 1996. *Performance: A Critical Introduction*. London: Routledge.

Chaney, David. 1986. "The Symbolic Form of Ritual in Mass Communication." In *Communicating Politics: Mass Communication and Political Process*, edited by Peter Golding, Graham Murdock, and Philip Schlesinger, pp. 115–132. Leicester, UK: Leicester University Press.

———. 1993. *Fictions of Collective Life: Public Drama in Late Modern Culture*. London: Routledge.

Chouliaraki, Lilie. 2006. *The Spectatorship of Suffering*. London: Sage.

Cohen, Stanley. 1972. *Folk Devils and Moral Panics: The Creation of the Mods and Rockers*. London: MacKibbon and Kee.

Compton James, and Edward Comor. 2007. "The Integrated News Spectacle, Live 8, and the Annihilation of Time." *Canadian Journal of Communication* 32(1): 29–53.

Cottle, Simon. 2003. "News, Public Relations and Power: Mapping the Field." In *News, Public Relations and Power*, edited by Simon Cottle. pp. 3–24. London: Sage.

———. 2004. *The Racist Murder of Stephen Lawrence: Media Performance and Public Transformation*. Westport, CT, and London: Praeger.

———. 2005a. "Mediatized Public Crisis and Civil Society Renewal: The Racist Murder of Stephen Lawrence." *Crime, Media, Culture* 1(1): 49–71.

———. 2005b. "In Defence of 'Thick' Journalism; Or How Television Journalism Can be Good for Us." In *Journalism: Critical Issues*, edited by Stuart Allan, pp. 109–124. Maidenhead, UK: Open University Press.

———. 2006a. "Mediatized Rituals: Beyond Manufacturing Consent." *Media, Culture & Society* 28(3): 411–432.

———. 2006b. *Mediatized Conflict: Developments in Media and Conflict Studies*. Maidenhead, UK: Open University Press.

———. 2008. "Mediatized Rituals: A Reply to Couldry and Rothenbuhler." *Media, Culture & Society* 30(1): 135–140.

———. 2009a. *Global Crisis Reporting: Journalism in the Global Age*. Maidenhead, UK: Open University Press.

———. 2009b. "Global Crises in the News: Staging New Wars, Disasters and Climate Change." *International Journal of Communication* 3: 494–516. http://ijoc.org/ojs/index.php/ijoc/article/view/473.

———. 2011. "Television Agora and Agoraphobia Post September 11." In *Journalism Post September 11*, Second Edition, edited by Stuart Allan and Barbie Zelizer, pp. 232–251. London: Routledge.

Cottle, Simon, and Mugdha Rai. 2006. "Between Display and Deliberation: Analyzing TV News as Communicative Architecture." *Media, Culture & Society* 28(2): 163–189.

Critcher, Chas. 2003. *Moral Panics*. London: Routledge.

Dayan, Daniel, and Elihu Katz. 1994. *Media Events: The Live Broadcasting of History*. Cambridge, MA: Harvard University Press.

Debord, Guy. 1983. *Society of the Spectacle*. Detroit, MI: Black and Red.

Durkheim, Emile. 1965 (1915). *The Elementary Forms of Religious Life*. New York: Free Press.

Elliott, Philip. 1980. "Press Performance as Political Ritual." In *The Sociology of Journalism and the* Press, edited by Harry Christian, pp. 141–177. Sociological Review Monograph No. 29. Staffordshire, UK: University of Keele.

Elliott, Philip, Graham Murdock, and Philip Schlesinger. 1986. "'Terrorism and the State: A Case Study of the Discourses of Television." In *Media, Culture and Society—A Critical*

Reader, edited by Richard Collins, James Curran, Nicholas Garnham, Paddy Scannell, Philip Schlesinger, and Colin Sparks. pp. 264–286. London: Sage.

Emirbayer, Mustafa, ed. 2003. *Emile Durkheim: Sociologist of Modernity*. Oxford: Blackwell.

Ettema, James. 1990. "Press Rites and Race Relations: A Study of Mass Mediated Ritual." *Critical Studies in Mass Communication* 7: 309–331.

Fiske, John. 1994. *Media Matters: Everyday Culture and Political Change*. Minneapolis: University of Minnesota Press.

Galtung, Johan, and Marie Ruge. 1965. "The Structure of Foreign News: The Presentation of the Congo, Cuba and Cyprus Crises in Four Newspapers." *Journal of International Peace Research* 1: 64–90.

Geertz, Clifford. 1992. "The Balinese Cockfight as Play." In *Culture and Society: Contemporary Debates* edited by Jeffrey Alexander and Steven Seidman, pp. 113–121. Cambridge, UK: Cambridge University Press.

Giddens, Anthony. 1971. *Capitalism and Modern Social Theory—An Analysis of the Writings of Marx, Durkheim and Max Weber*. Cambridge, UK: Cambridge University Press.

Goffman, Ervin. 1959. *The Presentation of Self in Everyday Life*. New York: Double Day.

Goode, Erich, and Nachman Ben-Yehuda. 1994. *Moral Panics: The Social Construction of Deviance*. Oxford: Blackwell.

Habermas, Jurgen. 1989. *The Structural Transformation of the Public Sphere*. Cambridge, UK: Polity Press.

Hallin, Daniel. 1986. *The "Uncensored" War: The Media and Vietnam*. Oxford: Oxford University Press.

Höijer, Birgitta. 2004. "The Discourse of Global Compassion: The Audience and MediaReporting of Human Suffering." *Media, Culture and Society* 26(4): 513–531.

Holmes, John, and Markku Niskala. 2007. "Reducing the Humanitarian Consequences of Climate Change." International Federation of Red Cross and Red Crescent Societies. http://www.ifrc.org/Docs/News/opinion07/07101001/index.asp.

Hughes-Freeland, Felicia, ed. 1998. *Ritual, Performance, Media*. London: Routledge.

Hunt, David. 1999. *O.J.Simpson: Fact and Fictions*. Cambridge, UK: Cambridge University Press.

Jacobs, Ronald. 2000. *Race, Media and the Crisis of Civil Society: From Watts to Rodney King*. Cambridge, UK: Cambridge University Press.

Katz Elihu, and Tamar Liebes. 2007. "'No More Peace!' How Disasters, Terror and War have Upstaged Media Events." *International Journal of Communication* 1(1): 157–166.

Kellner, Douglas. 2003. *Media Spectacle*. London: Routledge.

Kertzer, David. 1988. *Ritual, Politics and Power*. New Haven, CT: Yale University Press.

Klein, Noami. 2007. *The Shock Doctrine: The Rise of Disaster Capitalism*. London: Allen Lane.

Kyriakidou, Maria. 2008. "Rethinking Media Events in the Context of a Global Public Sphere: Exploring the Audience of Global Disasters in Greece." *Communications* 33: 273–291.

Liebes, Tamar. 1998. "Television's Disaster Marathons: A Danger for Democratic Processes?" In *Media, Ritual and Identity*, edited by Tamar Liebes and James Curran, pp. 71–84. London: Routledge.

Lukes, Steven. 1973. *Emile Durkheim: His Life and Work*. London: Allen Lane.

———. 1975. "Political Ritual and Social Integration." *Sociology* 9(2): 289–308.

Lull, James, and Steven Hinerman, eds. 1997. *Media Scandals: Morality and Desire in the Popular Market Place*. Cambridge, UK: Polity Press.

McRobbie, Angela. 1994. "The Moral Panic in the Age of the Postmodern Mass Media." In *Postmodernism and Popular Culture*, edited by Angela McRobbie, pp. 198–219. London: Routledge.

Media International Australia. 1997. "Panic: Morality, Media, Culture." Special Edition. *Media International Australia* Volume 85 (November): 4–90.

Mihelj, Sabina. 2008. "National Media Events: From Displays of Unity to Enactments of Division." *European Journal of Cultural Studies* 11(4): 471–488.

Moeller, Susan. 1999. *Compassion Fatigue: How the Media Sell Disease, Famine, War and Death*. London: Routledge.

Oxfam. 2009. *The Right to Survive: The Humanitarian Challenge for the Twenty-First Century*. Oxford: Oxfam International.

Pantti, Mervi, and Karin Wahl-Jorgensen. 2007. "On the Political Possibilities of Therapy News: Media Responsibility and the Limits of Objectivity in Disaster Coverage." *Estudos em Communição* 1: 3–25.

Pantti, Mervi, and Karin Wahl-Jorgensen and Simon Cottle. (forthcoming) *Disasters and the Media*. New York: Peter Lang.

Perry, Ronald, and Enrico Quarantelli, eds. 2007. *What Is a Disaster? New Answers to Old Questions*. Xlibris.

Robertson, Alexa. 2010. *Mediated Cosmopolitanism: The World of Television News*. Cambridge: Polity.

Robinson, Susan. 2009. "A Chronicle of Chaos: Tracking the News Story of Hurricane Katrina from *The Times-Picayune* to Its Website." *Journalism* 10(4): 431–450.

Rodriguez, Havidan, Enrico Quarantelli, and Russell Dynes, eds. 2007. *Handbook of Disaster Research*. New York: Spinger.

Ryfe, David. 2001. "From Media Audience to Media Public: A Study of Letters Written in Reaction to FDR's Fireside Chats." *Media, Culture and Society* 23(6): 767–781.

Scannell, Paddy. 2001. "Media Events." Review Essay. *Media Culture and Society* 17(1): 151–157.

Schieffelin, Edward. 1998. "Problematizing Performance." In *Ritual, Performance, Media*, edited by Felicia Hughes-Freeland, pp. 194–207. London: Routledge.

Seaton, Jean. 2005. *Carnage and the Media: The Making and Breaking of News about Violence*. London: Penguin.

Shils, Edwards, and Michael Young. 1956. "The Meaning of the Coronation." *Sociological Review* 1(2): 63–82.

St. John, Graham, ed. 2008. *Victor Turner and Contemporary Cultural Performance*. New York: Berghahn Books.

Thompson, John. 2000. *Political Scandal: Power and Visibility in the Media Age*. Cambridge, UK: Polity Press.

Thompson, Kennith. 1988. *Emile Durkheim*. London: Tavistock Publications.

———. 1998. *Moral Panics*. London: Routledge.

Tierney, Kathleen, Christine Bevc, and Erica Kugligowski. 2006. "Metaphors Matter: Disaster Myths, Media Frames and Their Consequences in Hurricane Katrina." *The Annals of the American Academy* 604: 57–81.

Turner, Victor. 1969. *The Ritual Process: Structure and Antistructure*. Ithaca, NY: Cornell University Press.

———. 1974. *Dramas, Fields, and Metaphors: Symbolic Action in Human Society*. Ithaca, NY: Cornell University Press.

———. 1981. "Social Dramas and Stories about Them." In *On Narrative*, edited by William Mitchell, pp. 137–164. Chicago: University of Chicago Press.

———. 1982. *From Ritual to Theatre: The Human Seriousness of Play*. New York: Performing Arts Journal Publication.

Wagner-Pacifici, Roberta. 1986. *The Moro Morality Play: Terrorism as Social Drama*. Chicago: University of Chicago Press.

Watney, Simon. 1997. "Moral Panics." In *Policing Desire*, pp. 38–57. London: Comedia.

Wolfsfeld, Gadi. 1997. *Media and Political Conflict*. Cambridge, UK: Cambridge University Press.

CHAPTER 11

....

MEDIA, INTELLECTUALS, THE PUBLIC SPHERE, AND THE STORY OF BARACK OBAMA IN 2008

....

ELEANOR TOWNSLEY

IT is not an overstatement to say that in the United States in 2008, the belief in the efficacy of democratic processes to bring about meaningful social change was given wings by Barack Obama's historic win of the U.S. presidency. This was evident in massive voter turnout, including elevated turnout among sectors of the public traditionally alienated from the electoral process. It was also revealed by the millions of citizens who made the trip to Washington, D.C., in January 2009 to witness President Obama's inauguration. Indeed, celebrations were held all over the planet when it was announced that Obama had won the election. For these reasons, too, Obama's win was widely troped as "historic." Among citizens, there was hope that the perceived irrationality of the inherited economic and military crises might be correctable.

There are many moments that capture this renewed democratic sensibility in the United States, but surely one of the most compelling was when President-elect Obama stepped onto a stage to greet the enormous crowd who had assembled to witness his victory in Chicago's Grant Park on November 4, 2008. The overwhelming sense was that the process of democratic deliberation, crystallized in the vote, had been hugely successful. It felt like the public had redeemed itself. The Grant Park speech was also a moment of high cultural drama, one shared by millions of people in the complex civil societies we inhabit. Unlike the heavily scripted events that were to follow with the transfer of power—the oath of office, the parades, and the first White House press conference—that November election night was for many especially stirring. It broke the almost unbearable electoral tension with the news that Obama had indeed finally won the presidency, and the world would be new. One did not have to have bought into the Obama mythos to have been moved by the moment; even cynics acknowledged the massive social solidarity it created.

Thinking through Obama's victory from a public sphere perspective, I ask: What accounts for this epoch-making sense of the election and the heightened solidarity it produced? How were the mass media involved in creating these meanings? Was Barack Obama's victory the culmination of a rational democratic process of opinion-and-will formation, in the sense that classical theories of the public sphere imagine them? How autonomous were the political and cultural actors who participated in the election—as candidates, commentators, and citizens? How important was the rational-critical discourse of the candidate in creating the victory? And, is it true that a black president means that formerly excluded constituencies are now included in the solidarity of the national community?

I address these questions through a close analysis of the night Barack Obama was elected to serve as the 44th President of the United States. Before turning to my case study, however, I elaborate a sociological model of the public sphere by combining insights from field analysis and the Strong Program in cultural sociology. I argue that while Habermasian, Bourdieuian, and Alexandrine approaches all contribute to an understanding of how the actually existing public sphere operates, combining insights from all three perspectives yields a richer sociological analysis.

Habermas and the Promise
of Democratic Rationality

In his influential *Structural Transformation of the Public Sphere* (1989 [1962]), Habermas locates the origins of the bourgeois public sphere in the rational-critical discourses of the salons, coffeehouses, and table societies of seventeenth- and eighteenth-century Europe. In these nascent spaces of public opinion, private people came together as a political public for the first time and engaged in critical, democratic discussions about matters of common concern. Habermas argues that these discussions established a rational basis for democratic deliberation because they institutionalized the publicity of reason—of logic and the force of the better argument—as more important than the status of the speaker in deciding debates. In time, these rational-critical publics came to engage elites, requiring authorities to articulate the reasons for their policies in public.

Habermas' historical analysis has been influential for several reasons, but surely one is that it is normatively appealing. His account emphasizes the universality, rationality, civility, and inclusiveness of the public sphere. While these principles were never fully realized historically, he argued that they were always "more than ideology" (1989 [1962], p. 88). The reason is that rational-critical democratic discourses are self-correcting and, thus, are always open to rational respecification (1992, pp. 478–479, also see Cohen and Arato 1992). So, for example, in the face of political or cultural censorship, critics can use rational democratic discourses to challenge the rules of the game and insist that formerly excluded topics be included. Or, excluded groups may assume the mantle of the universal human subject to claim formal equality and social inclusion. Indeed, in the face of the many distortions of public reason, Habermas has steadfastly asserted the positive possibility of this kind of substantive democratic rationality for nearly fifty years. It is the goal of his life's work and especially of his theory of communicative action.

While it is normatively appealing, however, Habermas' model does not fully account for the communicative organization, the cultural diversity, or the institutional complexity of actually existing public spheres. As many critics have argued— and as Habermas has since acknowledged—the historical analysis in *Structural Transformation* is constricted by the logic of class analysis (Calhoun 1992; Habermas 1992; Benson 2004, 2009; Benson and Neveu 2005; Jacobs 1996). The resulting model of the public sphere is more singular, abstract, and rational than any empirical public sphere probably ever can be. Habermas does not reengage empirical questions of institutional diversity or the nonrational dimensions of public communication in his later work either. Instead, he shifts his focus to consider the communicative conditions for the kind of rational-critical democratic discourse which he identified in the early bourgeois public sphere and to which he continues to aspire.

What a sociology of the public sphere offers in this context is the possibility of a more grounded, empirically faithful model of public communication. Philosophers and democratic political theorists have developed extremely useful specifications of the normative issues of the public sphere that are so powerfully asserted in the Habermasian tradition (Fraser 1992; Young 2000; Benhabib 2002; Baker 2002), and I take them up in analyses elsewhere.[1] Less central to these theoretical and philosophical inquiries, however, have been questions about institutional dynamics, the organization of intellectual life, and the diversity of cultural forms. These are the issues that animate this essay. Along with other critics and media sociologists (Alexander 2006; Calhoun 1992; Benson 2004, 2009; Benson and Neveu 2005; Jacobs 1996, 2000), I argue for a more sociological approach to the public sphere that balances empirical with normative elements to develop a sociologically "thick" substantive understanding of the public sphere.

Specifically, I propose a model of the public sphere that is densely mediated, highly intellectualized, and culturally differentiated. I follow Habermas' fundamental insight by focusing on the political public sphere as a social space where major issues are framed and debated and where the major lines of social conversation are aggregated and represented for abstract (typically national) publics; but I critically reconstruct Habermas' account through a selective reading of Bourdieu's analysis of cultural fields and Alexander's cultural theory of the civil sphere. From Bourdieu, I borrow the idea of the autonomy of cultural fields as a way to understand the major institutional relationships of the public sphere, including how we understand the media. Here, I am interested in the ubiquity of intellectuals, intellectualizing practices, and intellectual traditions in social communication (Eyerman 1994), and I seek to tease apart ideas about cultural fields and power to think about communication in terms of fields. In this effort, I rely on Alexander's (2006, 2009) insight that social communication is always shaped by cultural processes; that is, the public sphere is always subject to the dynamic of cultural struggles through which divisions between the civil and uncivil, democratic and undemocratic, and sacred and profane are made. Indeed, social solidarity is central to communication in the public sphere; a crucial precondition for both the political autonomy of intellectuals and the democratic rationality so central to deliberative politics as it has been imagined in the Habermasian tradition.

My model shares some of the concerns of new institutional thinking about the media (see Benson 2009 for an excellent review), but it also points in several new directions. First, an empirical understanding of the public sphere should describe and analyze the dynamics of solidarity-generating communicative connection as well as exclusionary or exploitative power dynamics. Second, any model of the public sphere should pay particular attention to the crucial role of intellectuals and intellectual traditions in defining and expanding democratic media. Third, a cultural sociological perspective on communication in the public sphere should engage the great diversity of cultural forms that circulate there, many of which fail to meet the ideal of rational communication as it has been developed in democratic theory or as it has been understood on the ground in contemporary democracies.[2] Arguably, these forms of communication have long informed democratic life in the large, bureaucratic mass-mediated societies we inhabit and, as such, deserve close empirical scrutiny.

MEDIA, INTELLECTUALS, AND THE PUBLIC SPHERE

As the environment in which public discourse circulates, media institutions have played a central role in actually existing public spheres from the very beginning. Indeed, cultural actors are only able to invoke, represent, and connect the many publics of civil society if they use the media; that is, if they create or use the institutional channels, follow the communicative forms, and enter into the intellectual cultures of the media. As a matter of historical fact, it has been novelists, artists, journalists, jurists, and a wide variety of social movement intellectuals who have acted through media institutions to define and expand actually existing public spheres.

This was true from the earliest development of civil society in the constitutional monarchies and revolutionary democratic republics of Western Europe (Bendix 1980). In eighteenth-century Britain, for example, which Habermas presents as the public sphere's "model case" of development (Baker 1992, p.189), politicians relied heavily on media intellectuals such as Defoe, Swift, Pope, and Bolingbroke to establish a new form of political journalism. The effect was to institutionalize a permanent presence in the political public sphere for the parliamentary opposition (Habermas 1989, pp. 59–64). Similarly, in France one can point to Voltaire and Condorcet, Remusat, Cousin, and the other young men of *Le Globe*, Comte and other Saint-Simonians writing in *Le Producteur*, as well as later political journals such as *Le National, La Presse, Journal des Debats*, and many others (Furet 1995). By the end of the nineteenth century, when intellectuals such as Zola, Gide, and Mauss entered the political public sphere to defend Dreyfus, the effect was to reshape the definition of the intellectual as someone who was engaged in political debate in the media (Bourdieu 1992; Jennings and Kemp-Welch 1997; Eyerman 1994; also see Bauman 1989). In the United States, the nineteenth century saw the challenge of slavery and the goal of fashioning a distinctly American voice formulated by intellectuals like Emerson, Longfellow, and Lowell, who wrote for magazines such as *The Nation* and the *Atlantic Monthly*. Examples could be found for other national and colonial contexts, as well as for extra-national publics. The point here is simple: The mode of political intervention of intellectuals has often been the act of writing in print media in a way that draws on the autonomous authority derived from their positions in the cultural field, broadly construed. In the process, intellectuals have been crucial agents in summoning and building modern publics, and, in this sense, I would observe that modern intellectuals have always been media intellectuals who purport to speak on behalf of autonomous publics.

Both the mediated organization and intellectual character of public discourse are described in Habermas' classic account of the public sphere, but they are not central to it. Rather, the focus is on the way the public sphere expresses the social rationality of the newly ascendant bourgeois class. Habermas' account gives pride of place to the eighteenth-century periodicals and journals in England through which coffeehouse discussions were disseminated in wider circles of debate and argument. The newsletters and periodicals typically produced letters of response that were discussed and then published in the journals the following week (Habermas 1989, p. 42). It was in this circulation of arguments that public opinion was formed. But although Habermas' refers to the important role played by media institutions in this process of rational opinion formation, he views the media more as a resource that either enabled or constrained rational-critical discourse, rather than the institutional field that actually made expanded rational-critical discourse conceivable in the first place. It is therefore unsurprising that Habermas neither develops a wider analysis of print technologies nor considers the varieties of discourses and publics they mediated—except insofar as they affected the development of a distinctly bourgeois sensibility.

Scholars of early modern Europe, however, have described this context, and they suggest that the public sphere was considerably more complex than Habermas described it, even in its earliest forms (Zaret 1992; Eley 1992). They emphasize that by the early eighteenth century, when the newsletters and coffeehouse journals that

Habermas identified as crucial to the bourgeois public sphere were being published, media institutions and the political and literary discourses they disseminated were already well developed (Zaret 1992, Keane 1991), and publics of "enlightened persons" who used rational arguments to criticize prevailing artistic and literary norms were already well established (Habermas 1989; Baker 1992; Zaret 1992). Media existed in a variety of forms, too. Advertising, novels, plays, poetry, scientific treatises, and pamphlets, all circulated from the 1600s onward in reading societies, lending libraries, social clubs, scientific societies, theatrical institutions, performances, meeting halls, and lectures (Eley 1992). To be sure, these products were part of growing cultural markets, increasingly organized by capitalist firms, but they were also organically connected to a range of concrete social groups in civil society and expressed more than simple class position. As part of the burgeoning associational life of civil society, this diversity of media created the wider cultural context in which public opinion was formed. The extent of this associational life varied between countries (Eley 1992), but it was differentiated from the state and the market and, as such, provided spaces for public conversations oriented to religious, educational, popular, and literary concerns as well as economic and political ones.

This double identity of media institutions as economic enterprises as well as cultural and intellectual ones continues to characterize media institutions in the public spheres of contemporary societies. For Habermas, this is a problem: First, because commercial mass media have a history of distorting open, rational democratic processes of social communication; and second, because intellectual elitism and tendencies toward professional closure effectively preempt authentic social communication. In this sense, Habermas' central concern is normative, since he thinks the media should serve as a more or less neutral vehicle for "the spontaneous flow of communication" (1992, p. 451), and that intellectuals should participate in the public conversation as citizens rather than intellectuals or experts. Indeed, it is this very pure idea of social communication which premises the tragic narrative in the second half of *Structural Transformation*, where Habermas shows how an increasingly commercial and bureaucratic media systematically impoverishes public discourse. Echoing his Frankfurt school teachers, he emphasizes the ways that the public conversation becomes distracted by entertainment, manipulated by advertising and propaganda, and censored by expert cultures.

It is true that Habermas' later work moves away from this overwhelmingly negative reading of how media institutions and intellectual cultures distort authentic social communication. Thus, in *Between Facts and Norms* (1996, pp. 373–379), Habermas offers a slightly more optimistic prognosis, describing a public sphere that is far more institutionally varied and plural, and he poses the question of the *relative degree* of distortion in public processes of communication.[3] But in the end, he is not very hopeful. Habermas concludes that most of the time in highly complex societies, the public sphere is "infiltrated by administrative and social power and dominated by the mass media" (p. 379). It is only at times of crisis that the informal publics of civil society can be effectively mobilized against the dehumanizing logic of the system world. In contemporary societies, then, the possibility of authentic social communication among a truly autonomous public seems extremely tenuous.

It is my contention, however, that by evaluating actually existing media institutions against a very high normative standard, and by requiring the conditions of social communication to always take the radically egalitarian form of a relationship between citizens, Habermas leaves us with an overly pessimistic understanding of the possibilities for democratic rationality in the highly mediated public spheres of contemporary life. In place of this pessimistic analysis of the public sphere, I want to suggest a more empirically grounded, sociological perspective that relaxes the normative expectation of rational-critical discourse to ask; how are actually existing public spheres organized? Specifically, how do media institutions work to organize social communication? Who communicates in and through media institutions and on what basis? What is the nature of their communication? Habermas (1996, pp. 377–378) recognizes that his model does not provide this kind of empirical analysis saying: "It is by no means clear how the mass media intervene in the diffuse circuits of communication in the political public sphere." I think, however, that any account of the public sphere needs to engage such an analysis, and thus it must identify and analyze the institutional organization of public discourse.[4]

To do this, I draw on Bourdieu's analysis of cultural fields as a way to map the institutional geography of the contemporary public sphere (Calhoun 1992; Benson and Neveu 2005). I adopt the analytical idea that social space is structured by a relational logic in which cultural actors strive to distinguish themselves in terms of historically evolved understandings of value, and I use this insight to think about the internal organization of the social space of opinion and news commentary that is the communicative core of the political public sphere.[5] This reading aims to connect Bourdieu's comparatively narrow conception of the relative autonomy of cultural fields to a more expanded idea of political and cultural autonomy as it has been imagined in democratic theories of the public sphere.[6]

AUTONOMY, RATIONALITY, AND DEMOCRACY

The idea of autonomy is central to the public sphere tradition. From the perspective of democratic theory, autonomy means that individuals can speak in their own voices and act in society without undue constraint or censorship (Habermas 1989, 1985; Cohen and Arato 1992). Autonomy thus includes the idea that the import and quality of speech be judged independently from considerations of the speakers' status (Habermas 1989); that speech be free from state censorship or interference from other powerful actors in the economy or media (Keane 1991, Habermas 1989, 1996); and that communicative structures—including formats, resources, and conditions of access—should enable autonomous speech among nominal social equals rather than constrain it (Habermas 1996, 1985).

Prominent among the examples of cultural projects that rely on this understanding of autonomy are the intellectual and social movements for a free press that have characterized the Anglo-American context during the last four hundred years (Tonnies 1922; Bendix 1980; Keane 1991). In this sense, as I argued earlier, media institutions—and the movements for expanded intellectual autonomy they have publicized—have been crucial to the establishment and expansion of actually existing public spheres (Starr 2004; Keane 1991; Schudson 1978). John Keane's *Media and Democracy* narrates a concise history of the development of the legal and political ideas in this tradition. He documents, for example, how struggles around the liberty of the press in England in the seventeenth and eighteenth centuries were tied up with the expansion of liberal ideas of personhood and the emergence of democratic public institutions, very much like those Habermas describes in *Structural Transformation*. Keane's gripping account of the famous defense of Thomas Paine in 1792 made by Thomas Erskine, the Attorney General to the Prince of Wales, is illustrative. Under conditions of a free press, Erskine contended, citizens could read Paine's seditious pamphlet and make their own judgments about his arguments: "Every man," Erskine emphasized, "may analyze the principles of its constitution, point out its errors and defects, examine and publish its corruptions, warn his fellow citizens against their ruinous consequences" (Keane 1991, p. 4). Here, Habermas' idea that citizens can make rational political judgments about texts circulating in the public sphere is clearly in evidence; indeed, it is a critical component of Erskine's attempt to win legal recognition for liberty of the press and the idea of a rational-critical public the press championed. Similar arguments were made for the importance of newspapers and journals in political communication among the American colonies, with the result that these were eventually protected by the First Amendment to the U.S. Constitution in 1791 (Starr 2004; Alterman 1999; Schudson 1978; Keane 1991). Undoubtedly then, the idea of a free press has been influential in the constitution of autonomous publics in Habermas' sense. This is a rich idea of autonomy in which social communication is seen as an authentic expression of the lifeworld, created through the rational-critical dialogue of democratic citizens, and able to act back against the system logics of the economy and bureaucratic administration.[7] And this rich idea of autonomy does not only exist in academic theory. Ideas of democratic citizenship, freedom, personhood, and rationality have clearly been central in real social struggles over the rights of citizens as they were represented in and through media institutions in different times and places.

It is important to note, however, that an autonomous media or even an autonomous public does not inevitably lead to rational democratic dialogue—the mere absence of constraint does not mean that the authentic energy of the lifeworld will well up and wash away the evils of the system world. Thus, although the idea of intellectual autonomy associated with objective journalism or a free press is sometimes conflated with the idea of rationality, it is not identical with it. Conditions of political autonomy, including autonomous cultural production, do not guarantee that public discourse will be civil, inclusive, or democratic. In fact, it is probably more useful to see autonomy as a necessary but not sufficient condition for achieving democratic rationality; that is, cultural and intellectual autonomy is probably necessary if journalists and the media are to pursue their role as the "mandatary of an enlightened public" and organize an objective, rational, and inclusive public conversation (Habermas 1996, p. 378).

Once we distinguish the autonomy of speech from the rationality of speech in this way, it becomes easier to see how the value of rational-critical discourse in the public sphere is, in fact, the product of historically specific claims for a particular kind of cultural autonomy typically made by intellectuals, within a particular kind of political system—democracy.[8] Once we do this, it then becomes easy to see why, when journalism began to professionalize in the nineteenth and twentieth centuries, formal codes of journalistic ethics invariably made a connection between the autonomy of journalism, the objectivity of the news, and the wider rationality that is central to a democratic public conversation (Schudson 1978). It makes sense, too, that this is also the type of media ethics on which Habermas relies to make a case about how the media *should* function in modern democratic societies (1996, p. 378; Gurevitch and Blumler 1990). It also explains why intellectual actors like social theorists, scientists, teachers, and other kinds of intellectuals also find these claims so normatively appealing; it fuses with our philosophical predispositions and occupational vocations. Finally, it also suggests why thinkers like Habermas are so quick to identify abridgements of journalistic autonomy as reductions of democratic rationality.

But with a more historically delimited understanding of rationality and autonomy in hand, surely the central question about media and the public sphere is different than the one Habermas asks. That is, the central question about media institutions cannot only be whether or not they are commercial or independent, as if the autonomy of the media can be simply read off the facts of ownership and the autonomy of the public judged on that basis. Rather, the central empirical question about autonomy in the public sphere must be: To what degree and in what ways are media institutions and the intellectual practices which organize social communication autonomous from political and economic power? More specifically, how is that autonomy organized and expressed and with what consequences?

FIELD LOGICS AND SOCIAL COMMUNICATION IN THE POLITICAL PUBLIC SPHERE

In an effort to answer these questions and map the institutional geography of the public sphere, it is useful to think about journalism as a particular historical constellation that makes a claim to cultural autonomy based on objective methods of reporting and unbiased news commentary. As Bourdieu has emphasized (2005), the question is not whether or not an individual journalist is more or less objective or more or less critical. Rather, the question is the extent to which the entire field of social relations that defines journalism is autonomous from wider economic and political forces. Following this logic, we can think of the relationships expressed in struggles over the autonomy of cultural fields like journalism as the embodiment of the institutional logic of the public sphere.

It is a key insight of the field perspective that claims to autonomy in cultural fields are *always* asserted against a range of alternative positions and are therefore the object of struggle within them.[9] Thus, it is a central fact of the journalistic field that extremely powerful alternative positions compete with high-end professional understandings of journalistic autonomy to shape the environment of journalistic action. Such alternative positions rely on external sources of distinction such as circulation size, audience ratings, and advertising revenue.[10] In addition, because the journalistic field is part of the field of power, there is an important alternative position that comes from a journalist's proximity to political elites or to official representatives of the state (Bourdieu 2005; Darras 2005).[11] These forces shape the internal structure of the journalistic field, positioning those individuals, publications, and cultural styles that are more able to uphold the canons of professional journalistic autonomy against those individuals, publications, and cultural styles which are less able to do so. In fact, Bourdieu argues that journalism is a "weakly autonomous" field, precisely because it is more easily steered by external sources of distinction than are other cultural fields like the academy or literature (Bourdieu 2005, p. 33).

What this means is that journalism, at least in its dominant tendency (i.e., general-interest media), is more susceptible to the influence of money and power than are many other fields of cultural production (Bourdieu 2005; Benson and Neveu 2005, p. 5). Bourdieu's argument here shares Habermas' normative disdain for commercial media. But it is important to remember that Bourdieu's analysis is a historical one. He chronicles the privatization of French television in the mid-1980s, showing how this undermined journalistic autonomy and the quality of public discourse, and he makes a scathing critique of commercial television (Bourdieu 1999; Benson and Neveu 2005). Importantly, however, Bourdieu does not argue that the decreasing autonomy of the French media was inevitable. The logic of fields means that internalist principles of distinction continue to be important, and projects for expanded journalistic autonomy remain possible. Those principles associated with the exercise of autonomy in the form of quality in-depth reporting and incisive commentaries on the op-ed page continue to operate as the principles of high distinction within the journalistic field—even when they come under challenge.

Indeed, even in the highly corporately concentrated journalistic field of the United States, the exercise of journalistic autonomy is sanctified through prestigious awards such as the Pulitzer Prize and the Peabody Award.[12] Thus, while media mogul Rupert Murdoch has always been highly critical of the pursuit of Pulitzers (Bowden 2008; Murdoch, *Wall Street Journal*, March 11, 2010), many journalists continue to orient their professional practice to these prestigious symbols that mark both the cultural autonomy of the journalistic field and its intellectual and political aspirations for a rational, democratic public sphere.[13] The point is that the autonomy of cultural fields is always a matter of contention.

So this is the first way that the relational logic of the journalistic field shapes the institutional geography of the public sphere; namely, as it distinguishes the values, practices, and personnel of high-end journalism from those associated with the competing principles of profit and political expediency, and as it arrays particular individuals, formats, and events in terms of these distinctions. This is the sense in which professional columnists writing in the *New York Times* can be considered to be more autonomous than those who write opinion columns responding to editorial prompts in the *USA Today* or those who appear as guests on the primetime Fox News show *Hannity & Colmes*. But the conceptualization of the public sphere in terms of cultural fields is relational in a second sense as well; that is, that fields are related to each other. Thus, the journalistic field is shaped not only by the structure of its internal relationships but also by its proximity to adjacent fields and the boundaries between them.

The most significant fields adjacent to the journalistic field in contemporary industrial societies are the political field and the social science field because actors in these three fields compete to define the legitimate vision of the social world (Bourdieu 2005, p. 40). For the United States, which we study, we would add to Bourdieu's description the increasing number of think tanks that are situated in a field (or field-like space) somewhere between politics and social science and that present new challengers in the competition to define the social world (Medvetz 2007).[14] In fact, Bourdieu himself founded such an institution in an attempt to influence public conversation in France in the later years of his career (Swartz 2003). In other times and places, the religious field, the literary field, or the field of cinematic production may be more important to the political public sphere. But in most contemporary Western societies, it is the overlap between the journalistic, academic (social science), and political fields that provides the immediate institutional context of the political public sphere.

As relatively autonomous cultural fields, however, it is equally true that the social relations of the political field and the academic field also exist outside the political public sphere proper, and anchor it in a broader social context. What this means is that while a great many institutions are proximate to the political public sphere—including the disciplinary constellations of the academic and scientific fields, publishing, film production, social movements, religious institutions, and para-political organizations like think tanks, advocacy groups, and professional organizations—these relationships are not fully contained within the political public sphere. This is an important point, because it suggests the ways that wider social dynamics shape the political public sphere.

It is true that Bourdieu has very little theory of the public sphere per se, despite the fact that toward the end of his career, he became more interested in pursuing a public intellectual role (Swartz 2003). Some have even argued that Bourdieu's understandings of habitus and symbolic domination make it impossible for him to conceptualize the cultural nature of social communication (Alexander 1995; 2006). But even if this is the case, it does not prevent the synthetic theoretical act of joining a broad idea of cultural communication to the understanding of a cultural field.

Once we do this, it becomes possible to see that each of the fields that lie adjacent to the journalistic field and that intersect in the political public sphere possesses its own communicative capacity; thus, each field possesses its own internal conversation, forms of discourse, and media institutions; and therefore, each field possesses resources to influence the conditions and norms of the political public sphere. It follows from this that the autonomy of cultural production in other parts of society can have the effect of enhancing or reducing the autonomy of the journalistic field and, therefore, the autonomy of the political public sphere.[15]

What the public sphere tradition offers to field theory, then, is the idea that fields have a communicative logic—interpretive traditions, cultural rhetorics, and media forms.[16] Thus while the political public sphere is organized by the media and the relations of the journalistic field, it is not wholly contained by them. Public discourse is also affected by the complex institutional and communicative logics of adjacent and overlapping cultural fields. These shape what Habermas (1996) has called the "partial publics" of actually existing public spheres as well as the relationships between them. Thus, an understanding of the media must be developed that moves past an analysis of the relative cultural autonomy of cultural fields and also considers the cultural and communicative dimensions of fields and the connections between them.

Bourdieu does not develop the idea that cultural fields have communicative logics that link them to the opinion circuits of the public sphere. Indeed, to the extent that he conceptualizes the connection between the media and other sectors of social communication at all, Bourdieu worries that the increasing influence of the journalistic field structures the distinctions of these other cultural fields, primarily by establishing a connection among media publicity, the principles of distinction, and success in those other fields (Bourdieu 2005, pp. 41–45; also see Bourdieu 1998, especially pp. 68–78).[17] He concludes on this basis that the weak autonomy of the journalistic field is adversely affecting the autonomy of other cultural fields.

But these are open empirical questions. If journalism is influencing other cultural fields, it is also likely that these other cultural fields impact the journalistic field. This is especially true for the elite spaces of media opinion and commentary that define the political public sphere. Indeed, in my collaborative research with Ron Jacobs, which analyzes large samples of published opinion from U.S. newspapers and television from the early years of the Clinton and Bush administrations (1993–1994, 2001–2002), there is evidence that the political public sphere of the United States is not only expanding in size but also becoming considerably more diverse. In the first instance, there is diversification of modes and media platforms built on the rising tide of technology and social relations organized through the Internet. More importantly, however, this change is accompanied by a second trend, which is a greater diversity of opinion speakers from cultural fields adjacent to, but not contained by, the journalistic field.[18] In fact, the proportion of opinion authors from the journalistic field, represented by professional columnists, journalists, and media professionals, declined significantly in all media between 1993–1994 and

Table 11.1 Occupation of Opinion Authors by Sample Period

	Sample period		Total
	1993–1994	2001–2002	
Television hosts	15.9	15.6	15.7
Columnists	31.0	21.3	25.0
Journalists	8.9	5.3	6.7
Media strategists	6.3	5.9	6.0
Elected politician	13.5	11.5	12.3
Executive branch officials	5.3	6.8	6.2
Civil society organizations	7.5	12.5	10.6
Academics	4.4	10.1	7.9
Lawyers	2.7	1.9	2.2
Writers	1.7	5.0	3.7
Others	2.7	4.2	3.6
	100.0%	100.0%	100.0%
	(697)	(1122)	(1819)

Source: Jacobs and Townsley. *The Space of Opinion: Media Intellectuals and the Public Sphere*

2001–2002, as Table 11.1 shows, while the representation of academics, writers, and authors from civil society organizations like professional organizations, think tanks, and advocacy groups increased markedly.

The balance of our research goes on to show that when academics, lawyers, novelists, or other cultural producers participate in the opinion space, they offer the possibility of alternative definitions of truth, competing claims of authority, different topics of discussion, and different rhetorical styles of argument. These alternative styles enter into a symbolic competition with the styles put forth by journalists and columnists, and can challenge the dominant definitions of what constitutes good commentary, good public discourse, and acceptable democratic deliberation. To the extent that such challenges are successful, there will be important consequences for the kinds of arguments that get made in the political public sphere.

Thinking about the internal structure of the public sphere in terms of cultural fields, then, is productive in several ways. First, it prompts us to consider how various intellectual and cultural projects for democratic rationality took the form of struggles to institutionalize relatively autonomous cultural fields, quite often expressed in the form of relatively durable media institutions. Second, seeing journalism as a type of cultural field is useful because it reminds us that while media are central to the public sphere, they are more than just the public sphere. Media are shaped by social, cultural, political, and economic factors that do not involve the normative ideals of civil society and deliberative democracy. Importantly, it allows us to realize this without reducing the analysis to a political economy of the media industry (Benson and Neveu 2005). Third, a focus on cultural fields allows us to see the possibility that autonomy is a more complex phenomenon than the political economy approach allows and that it requires much closer empirical investigation. Our research on the space of political opinion in the United States asks, for example, how spaces of media commentary are characterized by varying levels of autonomy, differing commitments to the value of autonomy, and different understandings of what an effective and autonomous voice looks like. Finally, if we connect Bourdieu's field concept to the public sphere tradition to consider more explicitly how each cultural field operates as a communicative space—that is, as a space that is more or less connected to social communication in other cultural fields—we can see how various projects for intellectual autonomy, democratic access, or political authority are linked together by media institutions, intellectual networks, and discursive traditions that span cultural fields.[19]

To take just one example of these kinds of links between fields, consider an essay from the *New York Times*, "Elevating Science, Elevating Democracy" (2009). Written by Dennis Overbye, a science writer for the *Times,* the article opens with the image of "a dark cloud lifting like a sigh from the shoulders of the scientific community" when Barack Obama proclaimed in his inaugural speech that he would "'restore science to its rightful place.'" The essay goes on to explicitly link scientific autonomy to political autonomy and democratic rationality, quipping "[s]cience and democracy have always been twins....If we are not practicing good science, we probably aren't practicing good democracy. And vice versa." The centerpiece of the argument is that scientific values and democratic values depend on each other. "Those values," Overbye asserts, "are honesty, doubt, respect for evidence, openness, accountability, and tolerance, and indeed hunger for opposing points of view." It is not an accident that this list could also serve as the list of values for good professional journalism. The point is, that the essay, published in the prestigious science supplement of the *New York Times,* is used to explicitly articulate links between scientific and political autonomy across several cultural fields and their institutional domains.[20]

To be sure, these kinds of claims to cultural autonomy, especially those associated with democratic rationality, are central to the public sphere tradition that we have inherited. But it is important to observe that they are not the only forms of social communication in the public sphere. As I argued earlier, rational-critical discourses are best understood as historically specific phenomena, typically associated with the projects of particular groups of intellectuals pursuing specific goals. What this means is that we should not assess all social communication against the very high standards of rationality or even in terms of the political logic of the relative autonomy of cultural fields. To do so is to fall into an analytical trap. Ironically, it limits our ability to see the full range of social forms of communication in the public sphere and how they might work to enhance or constrain social possibilities—including the possibility of critical rationality itself. Thus, once we have an institutionally specific understanding of the public sphere in terms of the autonomy of cultural fields and the specificity of particular intellectual projects that are connected together through media institutions and shared intellectual networks and cultures, the next task of a more empirically grounded analysis must be to ask: What is the range of different kinds of projects in the public sphere? What are their communicative forms and social logics? What are their goals and consequences?

MEDIA, SOLIDARITY, AND THE CULTURAL DYNAMICS OF THE PUBLIC SPHERE

When we consider the diversity of communicative forms in the public sphere, we very quickly find a number that go beyond the dispassionate, rational debate so lauded by Habermas and that are quite different from claims to cultural autonomy from political and economic forces on which Bourdieu focuses. These include cultural and psychological processes of communication, such as symbolism, aesthetic expression, psychological extension, and emotional identification. These processes affect virtually all social communication in the public sphere, and they are much more than simply distortions of rationality or ideological veils for class interest.

Among contemporary theorists of civil society, Alexander makes this argument the most forcefully. He points out that neither Habermas nor Bourdieu's theories are likely to be able to capture the cultural, aesthetic, and performative aspects that produce the solidarity required for public life. Habermas' problem is that he translates the philosophical vocabulary of the Enlightenment into a theory of rational speech acts (Alexander 2006, pp. 44–45). The result is that he unnecessarily limits the empirical analysis of public discourse to a consideration of how reasonable, reciprocal, and transparent that discourse is. In this view, nonrational forms of communication are seen as antithetical to democratic rationality, by definition. Bourdieu is even more problematic. Because his analysis of the symbolic world is always defined in terms of vertical relations of domination, it has no place for the possibilities of solidarity which are premised on expansive ideas of the universal. As Alexander asserts, "Democracy, and the kind of systematic possibilities for civil repair that it generates cannot be conceptualized if the possibilities of moral universalism and trans-sectional solidarity are denied in principle" (2006, pp. 561–562). Bourdieu is unable to comprehend the public sphere, Alexander concludes, because he understands all human action as inevitably strategic and therefore all cultural meaning as inevitably ideological.

Against both of these views, Alexander asserts a model of the civil sphere in which authentic social communication is deeply embedded in shared cultural structures. The signal feature of the public sphere is that it is organized into cultural codes and dramatic narratives that divide the world into good and bad, pure and impure, trustworthy and suspect, sacred and profane. In fact, the operation of civil society, and its public sphere institutions more specifically, is to produce solidarity by making distinctions between civil and uncivil things. Thus, public discourse is characterized by how it distinguishes those objects, institutions, and persons that are included and given full rights and respect in the solidary community from those objects, institutions, and persons who are to be excluded. This is fundamentally a cultural process of separating the sacred from the profane.

It follows from this that the first goal of democratic deliberation or of any claim to political or cultural autonomy must be an attempt to develop a shared understanding of the issues of the day. Such shared understandings are developed through both cooperative and competitive processes, and they always include debates about a variety of cultural issues, such as:

- What is the central dramatic conflict that defines the issue?
- Who are the central protagonists and antagonists in the battle to resolve the issue?
- What are the character attributes of these protagonists and antagonists?
- Who is to be trusted to act in the public interest?
- What kind of attitude or subject position should members of the public adopt as the audience to the deliberation?
- To what extent do new events, new evidence, new voices, and new arguments work to realign these types of symbolic orderings?

It is in this sense then, that social solidarity is a major, if not the primary goal of communication in the public sphere, since solidarity is the condition on which all other cultural or political projects are premised. In short, if there is no rationality without autonomy, there can be neither rationality nor autonomy in the absence of solidarity.

Bourdieu and Habermas both discuss issues related to solidarity at some point in their respective oeuvres, but both tend to see solidarity as a feature of groups that tend (inevitably?) to act in their own particular interests. Bourdieu's contribution to the analysis of solidarity is very thin, since he typically sees claims to universalism or shared identity as strategic and inevitably ideological. Nonetheless, if we step back from Alexander's vitriolic critique of Bourdieu and consider what the tradition of field analysis might tell us about solidarity, one useful idea is that groups must be imagined and represented through processes of social communication in the public sphere before they can become conscious of themselves as groups. Thus, individuals engage in "group-making practices" to persuade others to view themselves as group members and to act accordingly (Bourdieu 1985). This is a useful insight because it underlines the fact that many of the practices that produce solidarity are intellectualizing practices; that is, those who engage in group-making practices are typically intellectuals of some kind since these are agents who specialize in those practices of representation that divide group members from nonmembers.

Habermas' historical account also points to the importance of solidarity in the formation of early publics and describes the intellectual practices that created the cultural space for the expression of bourgeois identity. Central to this solidarity were the literary and legal discourses that defined the individual personhood of each bourgeois. It was novelists, political philosophers, jurists, and journal editors who created the resources for imagining the private bourgeois individual abstractly and who represented the bourgeois back to himself as a member of an enlightened public. And it was this bourgeois understanding of the human being, Habermas argues, that enabled these private persons to come together and imagine themselves as a public for the first time—which allowed them to debate the nature of freedom, to declare the rights of man and citizen, to deploy critical argument, and to call the authorities to account on the basis of reason. But although he makes these observations about the intellectual and cultural preconditions of the public sphere, Habermas never develops a systematic analysis of the cultural dynamics of the public sphere; indeed, he cannot, since he views ideas like those associated with bourgeois personhood as inevitably ideological—the false universalism of a new dominant class.[21]

This is where Alexander's cultural sociology contributes to a more complex and empirically sensitive model of the public sphere, namely, by offering a nuanced understanding of the cultural processes through which social solidarity is narrated and performed. To be sure, there is a growing literature on aesthetic publics and aesthetic public spheres (e.g., Tucker 2010, ch 4. for a review). The idea of a separate aesthetic public sphere has a long history in sociology (Weber 1946; Habermas 1985 Vol. 1, pp. 230), but cultural sociology makes a somewhat different observation. By identifying the cultural codes of civil society, the pragmatics of cultural performance, and the importance of narrative elements like genre, plot, and character, cultural sociology shows how all social communication—including rational-critical discourse—is fundamentally embedded in cultural and aesthetic structures (Alexander 2006, 2010; Jacobs, Chapter 12, of this volume). From this perspective, intellectual traditions of democratic rationality, journalistic objectivity, or scientific skepticism are all part of the historically developed rhetorical heritage of contemporary public spheres. Of course, so are traditions of sacralizing major political figures like U.S. presidents, narrating melodramas of natural disasters, wars, and sporting victories, not to mention the grand traditions of vilifying enemies and former allies. What particular performances or cultural traditions will affect public discourse around a particular issue is, of course, an empirical question. What Alexander's perspective tells us is that some cultural performances are more likely than others, as people use an inherited repertoire of cultural codes and narrative forms to make sense of their worlds.

This more cultural understanding of the public sphere is also very useful for thinking about the mediated and intellectualized nature of social communication in the public sphere. With this more cultural understanding, it becomes clear very quickly that the media are not simply the technical vehicles through which public opinion is formed or through which different partial publics or cultural fields are connected together. Rather, media are central to the public sphere because they provide the common cultural rhetorics—and therefore the intersubjectivity and solidarity—that make both group identities and deliberation possible (and even desirable) in the first place. In this connection, too, the media are also primary institutional sites of the intellectual activity (and intellectual networks) that make social communication possible at all.[22]

This broader cultural idea of social communication is not only more faithful to the way social communication occurs in actually existing contemporary public spheres, but it also offers an alternative account of why people participate in social communication in the public sphere in the first place. Rather than duty or a will to power, the sociocultural model of the public sphere emphasizes that people respond to the media emotionally and affectively because they enjoy the feelings of social solidarity such engagement can produce. In Habermas' theory, citizens are compelled to participate in the public sphere out of a sense of duty. As a member of the public, one has a responsibility to demand that the state justify its legitimacy in a transparent way. Even Bourdieu, who was initially aloof from the media and the French tradition of the total/public intellectual, eventually decided that participation in the public sphere through the media and in political activity was an important way to pursue social change and fight for social equality (Swartz 2003). What both of these approaches miss, however, is any account of the psychological dimension of public sphere participation and especially of emotions like pleasure. As Bauman (2003, p. 151) argues, any moral dialogue requires that interlocutors enjoy the other person's company and take pleasure in what each other has to say. In the absence of this kind of pleasure, we are likely to invest most of our energy trying to disqualify our adversaries from participating in the dialogue (Jacobs 2004) or in some other way trying to ignore them.

This kind of pleasure in the connection to the public sphere is premised upon an acceptance of a variety of aesthetic and performative structures. The playfulness of argument, the clever use of dramatic techniques to place moral conflict into bold (and usually overstated) relief, the use of recognizable genres, and the identification of present public figures with mythic archetypes—all of these increase the level of involvement in the public sphere, in official as well as informal publics. The fact that an individual "hates" Sean Hannity, Paul Krugman, or David Brooks makes it more likely that that individual will participate in the political conversation. Indeed, without an attachment to some of the regular "characters" of the official publics of the mass media, it is unlikely that most individuals will sustain a regular level of participation (and enjoyment) in the wider publics of civil society.

Such a view departs from the normative commitments of either Habermas or Bourdieu, since it sees the goal of the public sphere as solidarity rather than rationality or autonomy. In this view, the role of the mass media is not to preserve the conditions for rational-critical discourse above all else but rather to keep the conversation going—to connect citizens to the public conversation, to provide avenues and feedback loops so public opinion can shape the official conversation, and to generate broad interest within civil society about these official conversations. The ways that speakers in the public sphere achieve this are varied. Certainly, people engage in rational dialogue, argument, and criticism. But they also typically engage in dialogue by rendering compelling narratives of the central characters in political and cultural life: by unfolding dramas of intrigue and honor; articulating and defending central social values; and presenting themselves and others as more or less heroic characters in the struggle for the good—be it freedom, democracy, equality, or the United States itself. These cultural projects find their way into the types of authority claims that people make, the kinds of arguments they put forth, and the way that they engage critically with competing arguments. In this context, then, the ideal of rational dialogue and dispassionate deliberation is only one of several performative modes available to cultural actors in the public sphere.

Below, I draw on Habermasian, Bourdieuian, and Alexandrine perspectives to analyze the election of Barack Obama to the U.S. presidency in 2008.

The Election of Barack Obama and Rational Processes of Democratic Opinion-and-Will Formation

From a Habermasian perspective, Barack Obama's historic win of the U.S. presidency in November 2008 might be understood as a rational correction of the excesses of the system world, a correction carried through by a social movement born in civil society during a crisis that pursued change using the democratic process. To be sure, Barack Obama is a privileged social actor—a Harvard Law School graduate and a high elected official—but his race, relative youth, and unusual biography made him an outsider in a way that enabled him to convincingly represent a great many other outsiders. In fact, he became the consecrated representative of wide sectors of civil society as the huge electoral turnout and the eventual electoral victory proved. Importantly, too, the Obama campaign mobilized forces in civil society in new ways, accomplishing massive fundraising through the Internet and creating widespread engagement among traditionally alienated and detached voters. For all these reasons, the Obama victory has been widely heralded as a triumph for democratic rationality over the exclusions caused by a long history of racial inequality in the United States, since the son of an African immigrant has now won the highest office in the land.

Certainly, this interpretation of the victory that emphasizes the rational, expansive processes of democratic deliberation among citizens in the public sphere makes some sense. This interpretation is widely shared in society and reflects the narrative as it has been told by President Obama and his campaign, and as it has been repeated in a multitude of media.[23] As the president-elect stated on election night:

> I will never forget who this victory truly belongs to—it belongs to you.... It was built by working men and women who dug into what little savings they had to give five dollars and ten dollars and twenty dollars to this cause. It grew strength from the young people who rejected the myth of their generation's apathy; who left their homes and their families for jobs that offered little pay and less sleep; from the not-so-young people who braved the bitter cold and scorching heat to knock on the doors of perfect strangers; from the millions of Americans who volunteered, and organized, and proved that more than two centuries later, a government of the people, by the people and for the people has not perished from this Earth. This is your victory.

The focus given by President Obama and his administration to civility in engaged political dialogue also underlines the commitment to democratic processes that are understood as rational and socially transformative. So, for example, in his acceptance speech President-elect Obama explicitly reached out to those who opposed him in the election and asked for their support:

> And to those Americans whose support I have yet to earn—I may not have won your vote, but I hear your voices, I need your help, and I will be your president too.

In this connection, Obama has been called a "deliberative democrat" and a "deliberative conversationalist," and debates continue to unfold on blogs and discussion boards about whether or not he follows Jurgen Habermas or John Rawls in his democratic philosophy.[24] Whatever the answer to this scholastic question, there are clearly major themes from contemporary democratic philosophy in President Obama's rhetoric.[25] Thus, as an interpretation of the Obama victory, a Habermasian reading that emphasizes the rational self-correcting nature of democratic discourses in the U.S. public sphere is informative. It suggests the way that civil society can act back on the system to bring about positive social change, and it gives credence to Habermas' normative model of the communicative rationality of the public sphere.

At the same time, however, the Habermasian analysis does not provide an account of the institutional and cultural dimensions of Obama's win. There are questions, for example, about the institutional dynamics through which the social mobilization of the Obama campaign was organized. What was the nature of the public that the candidate mobilized, and what was the institutional character of the social movement he led? In this connection, what was the role of the media in creating the victory? Second, the Habermasian emphasis on the centrality of rational-critical discourse to processes of democratic deliberation tends to under-emphasize the emotional and solidary aspects of President Obama's win. These nonrational elements were clearly important to the social movement, the presidential campaign, and to the kind of heightened social solidarity that marked the Grant Park speech in November 2008.[26] Third, while the emphasis on rational deliberation is profoundly appealing to anyone interested in open democratic societies, it is also the case that President Obama's *performance* of rationality and considered judgment must be considered a key to the large public trust he earned. In this connection, the media have been central in representing the democratic process. Finally, there are several competing frames for interpreting the degree to which President Obama represents the democratic expansion of the U.S. public sphere to minorities formerly excluded by racial alienation and inequality. Some have pointed to the exhaustion of old elites, while others question the President's racial status. In either case, they attempt to reinvoke the wounds of racial inequality and exclusion, with as yet unknown consequences.[27] In this connection, a more empirical approach than Habermas' might ask questions about the levels of democratic engagement of formerly excluded people and publics over time and ask what this means for the solidarity of the national community in the United States. In short, as I have argued throughout, we need a more empirically faithful model of the public sphere that can capture these broader institutional and cultural dynamics.

OBAMA AND THE AUTONOMY OF CULTURAL FIELDS

Looking at the Obama campaign from the perspective of cultural fields helps us to discern the institutional dynamics of his campaign more clearly. It also helps to pose questions about whether or not and to what extent the rules of the game in the political field will change under an Obama administration. From a field perspective in particular, there are questions about whether or not shifts in cultural autonomy, and especially journalistic and scientific autonomy, will attend the new regime.

From Bourdieu's perspective, any analysis of Obama's victory presupposes locating the new president in the field of social relations in which he acts—thus in the political field. As a relatively autonomous field of cultural production, the political field is differentiated from the field of power in the social field as a whole.[28] Since the journalistic field intersects the political field in the social space of opinion, it is also important to consider President Obama's position in relation to the journalistic field, as it operated relatively autonomously from the capitalist logic of the economic field, and the administrative forces of the state during the election. On this basis, one could argue that as a political candidate for the presidency, and therefore as an important political figure in the media, Obama used the democratic political process to accumulate symbolic capital and win the political game.

Importantly too, Obama was the focus of group-making practices—his candidacy and presidency have called new groups into being and redefined old groups in new ways. For each of the positions he has held during the electoral process, field analysis would identify Obama as an agent consecrated by a variety of social groups—social movements, political institutions, and other social forces—to represent the "legitimate mode of perception" of the social world (Bourdieu 1985, p. 730). Indeed, this is precisely the object of the symbolic struggle in elections. As an inextricable part of the control of political office and the material resources that that entails, Obama's overwhelming electoral victory also carried with it the right to assert the official vision of U.S. society. This is precisely what President-elect Obama did in his Grant Park speech in November 2008. This mandate to articulate the legitimate mode of perception is a fundamental social power as Bourdieu has emphasized:

> The capacity to make entities exist in the explicit state, to publish, make public (i.e., render objectified, visible, even official) what had not previously attained objective and collective existence and had therefore remained in the state of individual or serial existence—people's malaise, anxiety, disquiet, expectations— represents a formidable social power, the power to make groups by making *common sense*, the explicit consensus, of the whole group. (Bourdieu 1985, p. 729)

Indeed, to the extent that President Obama's victory seemed so "right," or even foreordained, this testifies to the achievement of precisely this "common sense."

From a field perspective, it is also important to see the election of President Obama as one produced by the political field as a whole. This includes the important role played by the journalistic field as it mediated the discourse of the political public sphere and also a range of political institutions, such as the Democratic Party, the campaign organization down to the local level, the occasional publics of campaign rallies and whistle-stop speeches, and the abstract publics of the mainstream mass media like television as well as the newer publics of the Internet and online communities. To be sure, Obama was the charismatic representative of this wider mobilization, but he did not make a new vision of the social world out of whole cloth. As a candidate and then president-elect, he played and won by the existing "rules of the political game."[29] In this connection, the cultural autonomy of the political field was a crucial condition for his success.

Thinking about Obama's victory from a field perspective also allows us to refine questions about autonomy as they might bear on social communication in the public sphere more generally. We can ask first, to what degree is the political field more or less autonomous from the economic field following Obama's victory? This question goes to the enduring issue of whether or not in large democracies, characterized by the competition between elites, if an electoral victory like Obama's is anything other than a changing of the guard in the same establishment. The answer from the public sphere tradition is certainly that democratic competition matters. If it is a meaningful, deliberative process, then it is a path to a substantive social rationality. In this view, Obama is the representative of civil society forces pursuing social change. To a lesser degree, this is true for Bourdieu too, despite his understanding of the primacy of power and capitalist exploitation in structuring society. That is, there is an understanding in field theory that cultural autonomy creates social space for actors to mobilize against the forces of political-economy in the interests of social change. Thus, there are better and worse versions of capitalism, and better and worse political administrations (Eyal et al. 2003). It is for this reason that democratic social struggle is a reasonable course for actors seeking social change (Bourdieu 1999; Swartz 2003).

A second question asks to what degree change in the political field will have consequences for the cultural autonomy of other fields, such as science, literature, and journalism. Certainly, President Obama has made clear his commitment to "restore science to its rightful place" and thus the initial answers to these questions appear to be affirmative. The Obama administration has not only indicated that it seeks to regulate and oversee the operation of the economic field more systematically than has been the case in recent years, but in their stated commitments to open scientific inquiry, their preference for deliberative political processes, and in their conduct with regard to the news media, the Obama administration has signaled that official state policies will support broader conditions of cultural autonomy more generally.

With regard to the journalistic field in particular, it seems clear that journalists who had experienced conditions of greatly reduced autonomy during the eight years of the Bush administration had, and continue to have, great hopes for the Obama presidency. Journalists and columnists hate feeling like they are being managed, and they hate it even more when their access is restricted. This is one of the main reasons that so many journalists were critical of former President George W. Bush. I suspect it is also part of the reason why so many journalists who had liked John McCain turned against him during the election. Although historically, McCain had been very friendly with journalists, during the campaign he restricted journalistic access to a greater degree than ever before, and he was perceived to speak more frequently in the language of Republican sound bites than he had previously. In contrast, the Obama team signaled a commitment to much greater openness and transparency in political communication, and these are central values for professional journalism. Whether or not this early promise will be fulfilled is a historical matter.

This raises the connected issue of the degree to which different cultural fields—the academy, think tanks, policy institutes, and the journalistic field—will be communicatively connected. That is, do conditions of increased autonomy tend to lead to communicative density or detachment between different fields? Or are these dimensions unconnected? By joining the public sphere tradition with an analysis of cultural fields, this question can be posed for the first time.

Finally, there is the question of whether or not President Obama represents a wider social unity in his "vision of the social world." On some measures, he undoubtedly does. Electoral turnout was the highest in forty years for a U.S. presidential election, and turnout was particularly high among minority and young voters, both of which are groups with typically lower turnout rates. In his Grant Park speech in November 2008, President-elect Obama also claimed to represent a wider social unity, and he specifically enumerated important civic identities in contemporary U.S. society. In this rhetoric, race was assimilated to a wide array of cultural and economic differences, all of which were incorporated in the greater national community:

> …Young and old, rich and poor, Democrat and Republican, black, white, Latino, Asian, Native American, gay, straight, disabled and not disabled—Americans who sent a message to the world that we have never been a collection of Red States and Blue States: we are, and always will be, the United States of America.

As an intellectual project to define the "legitimate mode of perception of the social world" then, this wider unity was certainly represented and crystallized in the Grant Park speech.[30] President-elect Obama mentioned many groups who had never before been claimed by official representatives of the state, importantly, gay and disabled groups, and his invocation of race as a difference that could be transcended was ratified by his own biography and the complexity of his racial identity.

What is less well-emphasized in a field analysis of President Obama as a consecrated representative of the political field, however, is the role played by other institutions and social forces in the victory. These include agents like high-end fundraisers and donors and political operatives inside and outside the traditional political party structures. Although he did thank his campaign staff in his Grant Park speech on election night, these more traditional political and economic players are not described as representatives of civil society in his speech. Representatives of civil society who were highlighted were community organizers, college students, and other "ordinary" citizens. Yet these are all part of the complex and heterogeneous social movement that the Obama campaign mobilized and that, to some degree, they organized.

Particularly glaring from the point of view of the public sphere are the actors in the media who were not mentioned at all in Obama's official narrative of democratic redemption. Indeed, it is ironic that while the widespread power of this democratic narrative has been achieved largely through its circulation in the mass media, the media are largely absent from official narratives of the political process. Important media figures including television hosts like Jon Stewart and Stephen Colbert on the Comedy Channel's satirical political shows, and a wide range of other political pundits, opinion columnists, and news commentators in the mainstream and alternative new media, were crucial actors in mobilizing the groundswell of sentiment for candidate, President-elect, and then President Obama. These media intellectuals and institutions of media opinion were not merely conduits for channeling the opinions of individual citizens as Habermas might have it— although, arguably they did play this role. Media intellectuals like Jon Stewart and David Brooks also guided and shaped public sentiment in a particular direction.

OBAMA, CULTURAL SOCIOLOGY, SOCIAL SOLIDARITY

Of particular interest in this connection were conservative columnists like David Brooks who withdrew their support from Obama's Republican opponents as the general election drew near in October 2008.[31] Brooks is a major conservative figure in the opinion space with a regularly syndicated column in the top U.S. and international newspapers, regular appearances on the major television political talk shows, and a significant online presence. For this reason, Brooks' positive descriptions of Barack Obama were an enormous symbolic win for the Democratic candidate. While both the Habermasian and Bourdieuian description of democratic processes fails to capture these important dynamics, Alexander's focus on the code of civil society provides a key to analyzing the last crucial weeks before the election.

For example, the way David Brooks positioned Obama in terms of liberal democratic theory as a thoughtful, inner-directed person with great political judgment relied heavily on the democratic code of civil society (Alexander and Smith 1993). In a series of widely read and circulated op-ed columns leading up to the election in November, Brooks emphasized repeatedly that Obama's rationality, calmness, even-handedness, intelligence, and powers of observation could make him a great

president in the mold of FDR and Ronald Reagan. The contrast Brooks drew with
Republican challenger John McCain was powerful:

> When Bob Schieffer asked him [Obama] tough questions during the debate
> Wednesday night, he would step back and describe the broader situation. When
> John McCain would hit him with some critique—even about fetuses being left to
> die on a table—he would smile in amusement at the political game they were
> playing. At every challenging moment, his instinct was to self-remove and
> establish an observer's perspective. Through the debate, he was reassuring and
> self-composed. McCain, an experienced old hand, would blink furiously over the
> tension of the moment, but Obama didn't reveal even unconscious signs of
> nervousness. There was no hint of an unwanted feeling. (Brooks 2008, p. 7)

Thus, while Obama is portrayed as rational, reasonable, calm, and controlled,
McCain is pictured as excitable, passionate, and tense. In this way, Brooks, who is a
highly respected conservative intellectual, uses the democratic code of civil society
to pollute John McCain (and Sarah Palin) and to throw his weight behind Barack
Obama as the best candidate for the presidency. This is not to say that David Brooks'
support was crucial to the electoral outcome, or that Obama could not have won
without Brooks' support. Rather, it is to observe that Brooks' opinion is important
in the opinion space as it both reflected and invoked wider intellectual and public
sentiment in the weeks leading up to the election. It is also important that Brooks
might have lost social capital, in the end, if Obama had won while Brooks had continued to support the failed Republican candidate. In this context, what Brooks'
opinion columns did was to further pollute the Republican candidates, already
weighed down heavily by their perceived responsibility for the economic and military crises produced by U.S. policy in the preceding Republican administrations. In
this sense, professional opinion columnists like David Brooks can be seen to use the
cultural codes of civil society to distinguish between civil (democratic) and uncivil
things—be they candidates, policies, nations, or events.

Similarly, it is difficult to comprehend the massive public outpouring of affection for Barack Obama without some analysis of the social solidarity created in the
social communication during the democratic process of his election. From this perspective, it was not simply a matter of canvassing door-to-door, fundraising at the
individual level, or even holding mass rallies that mobilized people and led to a
heightened sense of social connection. Importantly, the social solidarity created by
Obama was a product of cultural processes of mediated solidarity.

The mass media were crucial in creating the social solidarity around Obama,
especially that high moment of solidarity in Grant Park when President-elect
Obama strode down the long stage to the podium to accept the U.S. presidency—
on TV. Arguably, this was a more important moment than Obama's official taking
of the presidential oath in January of the following year. As with other major media
events, television not only made it possible for the new president-elect's speech to
be shared with hundreds of millions of viewers on that November night (Dayan and
Katz 1994), but pundits and a wide range of other commentators also provided the
scripts for narrating events as they unfolded. Special attention was paid to describing

the main characters and parsing the emotional response of "the public" both in the United States and around the world. A fundamental trope in this narration was that the Obama victory was also a triumph for democratic rationality over the exclusion caused by a long history of racial inequality in the United States. To be sure, behind the main story were tales of other individuals associated with the campaign, analyses of the logistics of fundraising and getting out the vote, and details of political infighting. And this is not to mention the actions of media institutions and opinion leaders in constructing the details of the political process for wide and varied audiences in the long two-year electoral cycle that preceded the final vote. But still, watching the speech in Grant Park that November night, there was a transcendent quality to the story of the new President Barack Obama. As he walked out onto that stage, it was as though the happy conclusion had always been pre-destined rather than the unlikely long-shot it had seemed at the beginning. It is this very effect, produced in and through the story-telling of media intellectuals, that contributed to the great historic sense of Obama's victory.

The emotional connections achieved through the election coverage also contributed to a heightened sense of social solidarity—a solidarity that was conspicuously absent in the much closer and contested presidential elections of 2000 and 2004. Coverage of the 2008 election included footage of huge celebratory crowds in major U.S. cities, not least of all Chicago. There was footage shown of similar celebrations all around the world. Coverage also included the moment when the pundits and commentators on television simply watched the victory along with other members of the public. Oprah's position in the crowd of citizens in Grant Park as she watched Obama accept the presidency was poignantly democratic, as was the reaction of veteran black journalist Roland Martin, on whom CNN's camera lingered to observe his tearful reaction to Obama's acceptance of the presidency.[32] This was only the beginning of the race-framed narrative of victory as in quick succession, reporters asked every black citizen and television figure to which they had access—"How does Obama's election make you feel?" It was very clear that the vast majority of commentators and journalists felt very good indeed. This was the palpable sense in which the public seemed to have redeemed itself, as jubilant statement followed jubilant statement, that "see, really, anyone can grow up to become President of the United States." All of these features of the media coverage contributed to the sense of heightened social solidarity on election night 2008.

In the end, a sociocultural model of the public sphere must acknowledge that the Obama victory was certainly as much about social solidarity as it was about rationality or autonomy. The great wave of social solidarity and sense of shared purpose that Barack Obama has ridden as the consecrated representative of society is simply not fully comprehensible in terms of rationality or autonomy. Habermas' focus on rationality cannot capture the emotion—the hope and desire—that the Obama campaign ignited, and Bourdieu's concern with autonomy from economic and political forces simply misses the horizontal ties that bind people regardless of their other differences and the inequalities between them. As I have argued, an empirically faithful model of the public sphere that captures these dynamics must identify the symbolic and cultural character of public discourse as a necessary condition of autonomous and rational democratic publics.

NOTES

1. I take up questions of democratic deliberation more centrally in Chapter 3 of my book co-authored with Ron Jacobs *The Space of Opinion: Media Intellectuals and the Public Sphere*(Oxford 2011). In that work, the empirical focus is the space of opinion in the elite political public sphere of the United States. This essay relies heavily on that work to draw out a more detailed conceptual model of the public sphere. See also note 18.

2. In this way, I hope to provide resources to solve the paradox at the heart of Habermas' legacy. Namely, at the same time that Habermas offers a profound, optimistic affirmation of communicative rationality, his standards are so pure that very little actual human communication can ever meet them. Ironically then, the romantic utopian vision inevitably leads to a negative, gloomy diagnosis of actually existing public spheres.

3. Importantly, Habermas suggests that the power of the mass media might be reduced, *in principle*—that through journalistic codes of ethics and political provisions for a free press, the power of the media can be "neutralized and the tacit conversion of administrative or social power into political influence blocked" (1996, p. 379).

4. Thus, I follow Calhoun's recommendation to think about the public sphere as "a socially organized field, with characteristic lines of division, relationships of force, and other constitutive features" (Calhoun 1992, p. 38). Here, Calhoun is recommending a Bourdieuian approach, a recommendation that is widely made. See also Bourdieu 2005 [1989] and Vandenberghe 1999, note 2. See also importantly Benson and Neveu (2005, p. 18) and their discussion of other models for developing this kind of mid-range level of analysis, such as Hallin and Mancini's (2004) and Hilgartner and Bosk's (1988).

5. Habermas (1996, p. 374) describes the contemporary public sphere as differentiated by substantive foci as well as "communicative density, level of organizational complexity and range—from the *episodic* publics found in taverns, coffeehouses or on the streets; through the *occasional* publics or 'arranged' publics of particular presentations and events, such as theater performances, rock concerts, party assemblies, or church congresses; up to the *abstract* public sphere of isolated readers, listeners, and viewers scattered across large geographic areas, or even round the globe, and brought together only through the mass media." Habermas argues that despite its differentiation, various parts of the public sphere are always able to be connected together. Various partial publics are always "porous" to each other, and one "can always build hermeneutical bridges from one text to the next."

6. This includes the notion of individual autonomy, as I will argue below, as well as the autonomy of culture to act back on other domains. It also allows for the idea that the socio-cultural logic of different fields as autonomous sets of relations can be disjunctive and contradictory in Daniel Bell's (1978 [1976]) sense, or more recently in Appadurai's (2003) conceptualization of disjunctive "scapes."

7. Habermas (1996, p. 375) poses the question of autonomy—what he calls the "cardinal question"—in the following way: "…the question arises of how autonomous the public is when it takes a position on an issue, whether its affirmative or negative stand

reflects a process of becoming informed or in fact only a more or less concealed game of power. Despite the wealth of empirical investigations, we still do not have an answer to this cardinal question. But one can at least pose the question more precisely by assuming that public processes of communication can take place with less distortion the more they are left to the internal dynamic of a civil society that emerges from the lifeworld."

8. Or, to borrow from Crossley's (2004, p. 97) discussion of similar issues: "Journalists (and artists and scientists) are only rational and critical…to the extent that they are constrained and have incentives to be so."

9. This discussion of the internal distinction within fields is drawn from Jacobs and Townsley 2011, ch. 4.

10. The interplay of internal and external principles of distinction is typically expressed in struggles to define who is a part of the cultural field and who is not, who is making a "real" journalistic or scientific or artistic contribution, and who is a hack or a sell-out. In this sense then, a field is more than a profession, and it involves more than the desire to restrict entry by new members. Rather, a field "functions somewhat like a prism which refracts every external determination: demographic, economic, or political events are always retranslated according to the specific logic of the field" (Bourdieu 1993, p. 164). What this means is that while the logic of each field tends to be defined by a few basic distinctions, the kinds of symbolic strategies that specific individuals use within the field tend to be related to the kinds of resources they bring with them into their struggles.

11. We can see this in the preference for "official sources" drawn from the state and political parties, as well as the way that politicians tend to dominate the guest-list of many of the political talk shows on television (Darras 2005; Jacobs and Townsley 2011)

12. In fact, the relative paucity of journalism awards versus literary awards in France tells part of the story of the historical development of the intellectual fields that shaped the public sphere in France compared to the United States.

13. Indeed, Murdoch himself is arguably playing in that game with his acquisition of prestige papers in the United States. See discussions in Dover 2008 and Wolff 2008.

14. Compare this model with the one offered in Benson (2005, 2009). While different, they share the idea that the public sphere is a chaotic intersection of different fields, each with its own logics, institutional specificities, and cultural traditions. See Benson and Neveu (2005) for a particularly useful review of alterative concepts for conceptualizing the public sphere such as comparative media systems and arenas.

15. And thus of the "universal public sphere"—that abstract public defined by its relationship to the political system as a whole (Habermas 1996, p. 374).

16. This is a different point than one that asks under what conditions is communicative rationality "strategically viable" (Crossley 2004; Benson 2009, p. 184).

17. This is one way to interpret the public intellectual movement, including, for example, the public sociology movement (e.g., Burawoy 2005)—as reflecting renewed struggles over the role of media publicity in defining what is valued/important in the academy as well as think tanks and the foundation sector (Townsley 2006).

18. The analysis which follows draw from the discussion in our book which analyzes large representative samples of opinion columns in national newspapers (the *New York Times* and *USA Today*) and political speech from national talk shows on network, public and cable television (*The NewsHour with Jim Lehrer, Face the Nation, Crossfire, Hannity & Colmes*). These institutions are major players in the political public sphere—places where the communicative forces of society are the most likely to be able to engage the forces of administrative rationality. They are fundamental to that broader conversation, centralizing connections across an increasingly wide range of media through relationships of

cross-citation, cross-platform connection, reporting, and intertextuality. The space of elite political opinion provides crucial research materials for a more empirically grounded understanding of the public sphere because it illuminates questions of access to the public conversation in the mass media, the way media organizations structure the public conversation, and the form, content, and style of opinionated speech (Jacobs and Townsley 2011).

19. For example, there is marked variation in the way different parts of the academic field are connected to the public sphere, with some topics and speakers more likely to gain access to the public conversation than others, and some topics and speakers simply unconcerned with or almost entirely detached from the political public sphere. Thus, elite institutions and individuals are much more likely to appear in the political public sphere than less prestigious academics and academic institutions (Jacobs and Townsley 2011). The disciplinary order also shapes the relationship of different academic formations to the public sphere (Jacobs and Townsley 2011; Townsley 2000). Finally, consider that the journalistic field also overlaps the academic field in schools of journalism and non-profit media projects with high levels of autonomy exercised outside the social space of opinion proper and outside the political field. These spaces are clearly connected to the journalistic field and the space of opinion and public discourse more generally, but they enjoy a certain academic distance from the capitalist organization of publishing and the daily newsroom routines of television and print journalism (Townsley 2006). Thus, the case of academic journalism schools illustrates how field analysis offers analytical purchase on both the internal complexity and external contexts of public discourse in the public sphere.

20. Sociologists have long noted that scientific claims to autonomy and social legitimacy tend to be made in the public sphere (Merton 1979, 1996; Gieryn 1999).

21. Habermas' discussion of the discursive melding of the idea of the *bourgeois* with the idea of the *homme* that created the idea of the modern individual is particularly fascinating in this connection:

> In general, the two forms of the public sphere blended with each other in a peculiar fashion. In both, there formed a public consisting of private persons whose autonomy based on ownership of private property wanted to see itself represented as such in the sphere of the bourgeois family and actualized inside the person as love, freedom and cultivation—in a word, humanity.

This conclusion—that the bourgeois public sphere was based on the "fictitious identity of the two roles" of "property owners and the role of human beings pure and simple" (1989, p. 56)—is critical to Habermas' later understanding of the self-correcting nature of democratic rationality. And while Habermas concludes with the Frankfurt school that this fiction was an ideological mask which held up bourgeois political emancipation as universal human emancipation, it is also the case that in the historical and a sociological analysis which precedes this conclusion, Habermas shows that the intellectual products of literary and scientific intellectuals were entirely bound up with and constitutive of the political discourses of the public. Despite this, he tends to paint these intellectual figures as bit players rather than as the central actors in the drama of the public sphere. See also an excellent critique of this move in *Structural Transformation* by Neil Saccamano (1991).

22. Alexander understands this point in a passive way, and he also observes that the role of the intellectual in modernity is to make distinctions between civil and uncivil things (2009). But intellectuals and their connection to communicative media and learning institutions are not a central theoretical focus of his work. A good example of this from Alexander's corpus comes from his analysis of the Holocaust as a sacred evil, in which he

describes how various intellectuals—including social theorists, publishers, and teachers—worked to publicize and institutionalize the teaching of *The Diary of Anne Frank* in schools all over the world. As Alexander presents the analysis, Anne's story is pivotal in universalizing the story of the Holocaust as a sacred evil. But there is no further attention to specific groups of intellectuals, their particular intellectualizing practices, their institutional locations and constraints, or cultural traditions. In this, Alexander is similar to Habermas insofar as he *relies* on an analysis of intellectuals and their roles but he does not take them to be central to a theory of the public sphere. As I suggest here, however, a fuller analysis of the geography of the public sphere would take into account both the particular historical conditions of intellectual practice as well as the media and social learning institutions through which intellectuals pursue their projects.

23. The problem, as the Obama campaign so frequently repeated, was not only that their opponents pursued wrong-headed and failing policies, but problematically, that they continued to pursue those policies long after it was clear that they had failed. The Obama campaign implied further that their opponents engaged in nondeliberative, autocratic styles of government. It was precisely against this form of administrative power in the form of the old boys network, special interest money in politics, million dollar attack ads and the like that the Obama campaign asserted a deliberative style of political argument, calling repeatedly for opponents to engage the issues, and pursued on the basis of a large-scale social movement that raised money and other resources through the Internet. Whether or not the differences between the campaigns were as marked as has been claimed, the idea that Obama represented a deliberative democratic correction in U.S politics is widespread.

24. One major place where this has occurred is on legal blogs concerned with political and legal philosophy, for example, http://www.uslaw.com/law_blogs/?item=129822, and political blogs, for example, http://www.gonepublic.wordpress.com/2008/01/30/what-kind-of-democrats-are-obama-and-clinton/ and http://www.sgrp.typepad.com/sgrp/2008/01/politicsmetapol.html.

25. There have been repeated assertions that the Obama administration will listen to anyone with good ideas. They emphasize conversation, dialogue, and civility as essential parts of the political process. This is evident in the following excerpt from a February 15, 2009 interview on *Meet the Press* with top Obama advisor David Axelrod. Axelrod argues that even though Republicans did not vote for the stimulus package, they had been part of the democratic dialogue that produced it.

> MR. GREGORY: You wanted this to be a bipartisan package. It is not. Out of 219 total Republicans in the House and the Senate, you got three Republican votes....The opposition by Republicans; do you think this was principled opposition, or do you think this was a calculated effort on the part of the party to rebrand itself?
>
> MR. AXELROD: I don't know. I think they have a point a view. The point of view was expressed in the economic policies of the last eight years. Those economic policies have not worked, and that's one of the reasons we're in the mess we're in. So we had good conversations back and forth with the Republicans. I think their influence was felt in this legislation. It may—but, but what we weren't going to do was repeat the same economic theory that...
>
> MR. GREGORY: All right, so how was their influence felt?
>
> MR. AXELROD: Well, I think in tax—in terms of tax cuts. I think the tax cuts reflect some of their, their thinking. I mean, we agreed with them in terms of tax cuts to help small businesses get through this. They—their—the AMT is now added. The AMT fix is now added to this. The, the, the Web site recovery.gov was suggested by Representative Cantor, the leader of the opposition in the House.

26. These are outlined in detail in Jeffrey Alexander's book *The Performance of Politics* 2010.

27. A somewhat more ironic position was expressed on Comedy Central's *News Hour with Jon Stewart* when a guest, speaking as a politician of color, suggested that Obama won because now the mess was so bad, you "let us have it."

28. The status of the political field is somewhat confusing in Bourdieu's oeuvre (Swartz 2003). For the purposes of the current analysis, I follow an earlier description of the political field (Bourdieu 1985) because it suits my reading and connects better with the idea of the autonomy of the public more generally.

29. With regard to the racial question in particular, Bourdieu seems to see racial and ethnic difference and segregation as a mask for underlying class difference (Bourdieu 1985). This does not mean, however that his ideas cannot be used for incisive analyses of racial dynamics (e.g., Carter 2007, Banks 2010).

30. It is also key to Obama's liberal version of nationalism and American empire, which has drawn criticism in some quarters.

31. There were many conservatives who publicly endorsed Obama in politics, including Colin Powell and Susan Eisenhower. There were also prominent neoconservative intellectuals like Francis Fukuyama, legal scholar David Kmiel, and representatives from media and journalism, including Christopher Buckley who resigned the editorship of *National Review* and talk show host Michael Smerconish. A fuller accounting of conservatives for Obama can be found in *The Economist* in an October 23, 2008, article entitled "The Rise of the Obamacons." The article also reported that "[a]t least 27 newspapers that backed Mr. Bush in 2004 have endorsed Mr. Obama."

32. Interestingly, when asked by Anderson Cooper whether or not he wished he could be in Grant Park for this historic win, Martin responded that he was exactly where he should be—a black journalist in the tradition of Ida B. Wells chronicling and commenting on events.

REFERENCES

Alterman, Eric. 1999. *Sound and Fury: The Making of the American Punditocracy*. Ithaca, NY: Cornell University Press.

Alexander, Jeffrey, and Philip Smith. 1993. "The Discourse of American Civil Society: A New Proposal for Cultural Studies." *Theory and Society* 22: 151–207.

Alexander, Jeffrey C. 1985. "Habermas' New Critical Theory: Its Promise and Problems." *American Journal of Sociology* 91(2): 400–424.

———. 1995. "The Reality of Reduction: The Failed Synthesis of Pierre Bourdieu." In *Fin de Siecle Social Theory: Relativism, Reduction and the Problem of Reason*. London: Verso, pp. 128–217.

———. 2004. "Cultural Pragmatics: Social Performance Between Ritual and Strategy." *Sociological Theory* 22: 527–573.

———. 2005. *The Meanings of Social Life*. Oxford: Oxford University Press.

———. 2006. *The Civil Sphere*. Oxford: Oxford University Press.

———. 2009. "Public Intellectuals and Civil Society." Pp. 19–28 in *Intellectuals and Their Publics*, edited by Andreas Hess, Christian Fleck, and E. Stina Lyon. Surrey, UK, and Burlington VT: Ashgate Books.

————. 2010. *The Performance of Politics: Obama's Victory and the Democratic Struggle for Power.* New York: Oxford University Press.

Alexander, Jeffrey C., Bernhard Giesen, and Jason L. Mast, eds. 2006. *Social Performance: Symbolic Action, Cultural Pragmatics, and Ritual.* Cambridge, UK: Cambridge University Press.

Appadurai, Arjun. 2003 [1996]. *Modernity at Large.* Minneapolis, MN: University of Minnesota Press.

Baker, C. Edwin. 2002. *Media, Markets, and Democracy.* Cambridge, UK: Cambridge University Press.

Baker, Keith Michael. 1992. "Defining the Public Sphere in Eighteenth Century France: Variations on a Theme by Habermas." Pp. 181–211 in *Habermas and the Public Sphere*, edited by Craig Calhoun. Cambridge, MA: MIT Press.

Banks, Patricia. 2010. *Represent: Art and Identity Among the Black Upper-Middle Class.* New York: Routledge.

Bauman, Zygmunt. 1989. *Legislators and Interpreters: On Modernity, Post-modernity and Intellectuals.* Cambridge, UK: Polity Press.

————. 2003. *Liquid Love: On the Frailty of Human Bonds.* Cambridge, UK: Polity Press.

Bell, Daniel. 1978 [1976]. *The Cultural Contradictions of Capitalism.* New York: Basic Books.

Bendix, Reinhard. 1980. *Kings or People: Power and the Mandate to Rule.* Berkeley and Los Angeles, CA: University of California Press.

Benhabib, Seyla. 2002. *The Claims of Culture.* Princeton, NJ: Princeton University Press.

Benson, Rodney. 2004. "Bringing the Sociology of Media Back In." *Political Communication* 21(3): 275–292.

————. 2009. "Shaping the Public Sphere: Habermas and Beyond." *American Sociologist* 40(3): 175–197.

Benson, Rodney, and Erik Neveu, eds. 2005. *Bourdieu and the Journalistic Field.* Cambridge, UK: Polity.

Bourdieu, Pierre. 1984a. *Homo Academicus.* Translated by Peter Collier. Stanford, CA: Stanford University Press.

————. 1984b. *Distinction.* Cambridge, MA: Harvard University Press.

————. 1985. "The Social Space and the Genesis of Groups." *Theory and Society* 14(6): 723–725, 727–729.

————. 1998. *On Television.* New York: New Press.

————. 1990. *In Other Words: Essays Towards a Reflexive Sociology.* Stanford, CA: Stanford University Press.

————. 1992. *The Logic of Practice.* Stanford, CA: Stanford University Press.

————. 1993. *The Field of Cultural Production.* New York: Columbia University Press.

————. 1999. *The Weight of the World.* Cambridge, UK: Polity.

————. 2005. "Political, Social Science, and Journalistic Fields." Pp. 29–47 in *Bourdieu and the Journalistic Field*, edited by Rodney Benson and Erik Neveu. Cambridge, UK: Polity.

Bowden, Mark. 2008. "Mr. Murdoch Goes to War." *The Atlantic* 301(1): 106–114.

Brooks, David. 2008. October 18. "Thinking About Obama". *New York Times*

Burawoy, Michael. 2005. "For Public Sociology." *American Sociological Review* 70(1): 4–28.

Calhoun, Craig. 1992. "Introduction." In *Habermas and the Public Sphere.* Cambridge, MA: MIT Press, pp. 1–50.

Carter, Prudence. 2007. *Keepin' It Real: School Success Beyond Black and White.* New York: Oxford University Press.

Cohen, Jean, and Andrew Arato. 1992. *Civil Society and Political Theory*. Cambridge, MA: MIT Press.

Crossley, Nick. 2004. "On Systematically Distorted Communication: Bourdieu and the Socio-Analysis of Publics. In *After Habermas: New Perspectives on the Public Sphere*. Oxford, UK, and Malden, MA: Blackwell, pp. 88–112.

Darras, Eric, 2005. "Media Consecration of the Political Order." Pp. 156–173 in *Bourdieu and the Journalistic Field*, edited by R. Benson and E. Neveu. Cambridge, UK: Polity Press.

Dayan, Daniel, and Elihu Katz. 1994. *Media Events: The Live Broadcasting of History*. Cambridge, MA: Harvard University Press.

Dover, Bruce. 2008. *Rupert Murdoch's China Adventures: How the World's Most Powerful Media Mogul Lost a Fortune and Found a Wife*. Clarendon, VT: Tuttle Publishing.

Eley, Geoff. 1992. "Nations, Publics, and Political Cultures: Placing Habermas in the Nineteenth Century." Pp. 289–339 in *Habermas and the Public Sphere*, edited by Craig Calhoun. Cambridge, MA: MIT Press.

Eyal, Gil, Iván Szelényi, and Eleanor Townsley. 2003. "On Irony: An Invitation to Neoclassical Sociology." *Thesis Eleven* 73(1): 5–41.

Eyerman, Ron. 1994. *Between Culture and Politics: Intellectuals in Modern Society*. Cambridge, UK: Polity.

Fraser, Nancy. 1992. "Rethinking the Public Sphere: A Contribution to the Critique of Actually Existing Democracy." Pp. 109–142 in *Habermas and the Public Sphere*, edited by Craig Calhoun. Cambridge, MA: MIT Press.

Furet, Francois. 1995. *Revolutionary France 1770–1880*. Oxford, UK, and Cambridge, MA: Blackwell.

Gieryn, Thomas F. 1999. *Cultural Boundaries of Science: Credibility on the Line*. Chicago: University of Chicago Press.

Gurevitch, M., and J. Blumler 1990. "Political Communication Systems and Democratic Values." Pp. 269–289 in *Democracy and the Mass Media*, edited by Judith Lichtenberg. Cambridge, UK: Cambridge University Press.

Habermas, Jurgen. 1985. *The Theory of Communicative Action, Volume 1: Reason and the Rationalization of Society*. Translated by Thomas McCarthy. Boston: Beacon Press.

———. 1989 [1962]. *The Structural Transformation of the Public Sphere*. Translated by Thomas Burger. Cambridge, MA: MIT Press.

———. 1992. "Further Reflections on the Public Sphere" and "Concluding Remarks." Pp. 421–480 in *Habermas and the Public Sphere*, edited by Craig Calhoun. Cambridge, MA: MIT Press.

———. 1996. *Between Facts and Norms: Contributions to a Discourse Theory of Law and Democracy*. Cambridge, MA: MIT Press.

Hallin, Daniel C., and Paolo Mancini. 2004. *Comparing Media Systems: Three Models of Media and Politics*. Cambridge, UK: Cambridge University Press.

Hilgartner, Stephen, and Charles L. Bosk. 1988. "The Rise and Fall of Social Problems: A Public Arenas Model." *American Journal of Sociology* 94(1): 53–78.

Jacobs, Ronald N. 1996. "Civil Society and Crisis: Culture, Discourse and the Rodney King Beating." *American Journal of Sociology* 101(5): 1238–1272.

———. 2000. Race, Media, and the Crisis of Civil Society: From Watts to Rodney King. Cambridge University Press.

———. 2003. "Toward a Political Sociology of Civil Society." *Research in Political Sociology* 12: 19–47.

———. 2004. "Bauman's New World Order." *Thesis Eleven* 79: 128–137.

————. 2005. "Media Cultures(s) and Public Life." In *The Blackwell Companion to the Sociology of Culture*. Malden, MA: Blackwell, pp. 80–96.

Jacobs, Ronald N., and Eleanor Townsley. 2011. *Media Intellectuals and the Social Space of Opinion*. New York: Oxford University Press.

Jennings, Jeremy, and Anthony Kemp-Welch, eds. 1997. *Intellectuals in Politics: From the Dreyfus Affair to Salman Rushdie*. London and New York: Routledge.

Keane, John. 1991. *The Media and Democracy*. Cambridge, UK: Polity.

Lichtenberg, Judith, ed. 1990. *Democracy and the Mass Media*. New York: Cambridge University Press.

Medvetz, Thomas. 2007. "Think Tanks and Production of Policy-Knowledge in America." PhD diss. University of California, Berkeley.

Merton, Robert K. 1979. *The Sociology of Science: Theoretical and Empirical Investigations*. Chicago: University of Chicago Press.

————. 1996. *On Social Structure and Science*. Edited by Piotr Sztompka. Chicago: University of Chicago Press.

Overbye, Dennis. 2009, January 27. "Elevating Science, Elevating Democracy." *New York Times*. Science Supplement, Section D, p. 1

Saccamanno, Neil. 1991. "The Consolations of Ambivalence: Habermas and the Public Sphere." *Modern Language Notes* 106(3): 685–698.

Schudson, Michael. 1978. *Discovering the News*. New York: Basic Books.

————. 1998. *The Good Citizen*. New York: Free Press.

————. 2002. *The Sociology of News*. New York: W.W. Norton.

Starr, Paul. 2004. *The Creation of the Media: The Political Origins of Mass Comunications*. New York: Basic Books.

Swartz, David L. 2003. "From Critical Sociology to Public Intellectual: Pierre Bourdieu and Politics." *Theory and Society* 32: 791–823.

Tonnies, Ferdinand. 1922. *Kritik der Offentlichen Meinung*. Berlin. Cited in Keane, John. 1991. *The Media and Democracy*. Cambridge, UK: Polity, p. 6.

Townsley, Eleanor. 2000. "A History of Intellectuals and the Demise of the New Class." *Theory and Society* 29(6): 739–784.

————. 2006. "The Public Intellectual Trope in the United States." *American Sociologist* 37(3): 39–66.

Tucker, Kenneth. 2010. *Workers of the World Enjoy!Aesthetic Politics from Revolutionary Syndicalism to the Global Justice Movement*. Philadelphia: Temple University Press.

Vandenberghe, Frederic. 1999. "The Real Is Relational": An Epistemological Analysis of Pierre Bourdieu's Generative Structuralism." *Sociological Theory* 17(1): 32–67.

Weber, Max. 1946. "Religious Rejections of the World." Pp. 323–359 in *From Max Weber*, edited by Hans Gerth and C. Wright Mills. New York: Oxford University Press.

Whipple, Mark. 2005. "The Dewey-Lippman Debate Today: Communication Distortions, Reflective Agency and Participatory Democracy." *Sociological Theory* 23(2): 156–178.

Wolff, Michael. 2008. *The Man Who Owns the News: Inside the Secret World of Rupert Murdoch*. New York: Random House.

Young, Iris Marion. 2000. *Inclusion and Democracy*. Oxford: Oxford University Press.

Zaret, David. 1992. "Religion, Science, and Printing in the Public Spheres in Seventeenth-Century England." Pp. 212–235 in *Habermas and the Public Sphere*, edited by Craig Calhoun. Cambridge, MA: MIT Press.

CHAPTER 12

....

ENTERTAINMENT MEDIA AND THE AESTHETIC PUBLIC SPHERE

....

RONALD N. JACOBS

ONE of cultural sociology's central contributions is its development of a more meaning-centered theory of civil society and the public sphere. Most other approaches to the question of civil society and public discourse tend to emphasize the normative importance of critical rationality (Habermas 1989, 1996), autonomy (Fraser 1992; Bourdieu 2005), inclusion (Barber 1984; Young 2000), deliberation (Benhabib 2002; Gutmann and Thompson 1996), and generalized trust (Putnam 2000). To be sure, all of these are important principles, and they inform the idealized images that most civil societies paint for themselves. But this is an incomplete representation of how "real civil societies" actually operate in practice. By treating these principles only as normative ideals, we miss the way that they are part of a larger "discourse of civil society," based on binary principles of purity and pollution.[1]

Rather than evaluating how well real, civil societies match up to idealized principles, then, cultural sociology has chosen to study the discourses of civil societies themselves. In studies of war (Smith 2005), race (Eyerman 2001; Jacobs 2000; Alexander 2006), religion (Alexander 2006; Lichterman 2005), sexuality (Seidman 2002; Meeks 2001), and democratization (Ku 1999; Baiocchi 2006), cultural sociologists have demonstrated that civic virtues are only made meaningful through the symbolic identification of civic vices. Furthermore, because civil ideals are always part of a larger semiotic system, they can be used either to open or to close the public sphere. Rationality can be deployed as an ideal to be strived for, or it can be used as a symbolic weapon to exclude from the public sphere those who are considered to lack sufficiently rational qualities. Trust can be used to create solidarity and intersubjectivity, or it can be used to symbolically pollute and exclude those who are seen as cynical, self-interested, and distrustful.

The point is that the public sphere is not an arena of rational deliberation, but rather it is a site of symbolic creation and contestation. In other words, there is an aesthetic dimension to all public discourse. Actors in civil society do not simply make arguments in the public sphere and then wait to see whether their arguments are the most rational or the most convincing. If they have any civic skills at all, they will have developed their arguments by relying on existing cultural styles, traditional narrative forms, and well-known character types to express and authorize their arguments. And these arguments will include specific types of cultural performances, where civic actors try to convince a (typically mediated) public audience that they are authentically committed to the greater public good. There is still a kind of public deliberation here, but it involves much more than a critical debate about the propositional content of competing arguments. It also involves the attempt to develop a shared understanding—developed through cooperative as well as competitive processes—of the dramatic and aesthetic dimensions that surround the issues of the day.

What does this cultural revision of the public sphere mean for a theory of media and opinion formation? First, it is necessary to understand how the cultural codes and rhetorical structures of media discourse are connected to the conversations that individuals have about matters of common concern. People do not only get facts and information from the media. Arguments and opinions, discourses and narratives, scripts and performances—all of these can be found in the media, and all of them find their way into the conversations individuals have with others about matters of common concern. In this view, citizens are cultural actors who rely on the forms, genres, and values of the mass media to achieve the intersubjectivity required to deliberate about matters of common concern. In other words, participation in the public sphere is premised upon an acceptance of a variety of aesthetic and performative structures. These include rational argument and the presentation of evidence, as traditional models of media and the public sphere would expect. But they also include more playful forms of argument, such as the clever use of dramatic techniques to place moral conflict into bold (and usually overstated) relief, the careful cuing of recognizable genres, and the elaborate identification of contemporary public figures with mythic archetypes.

FROM AN AESTHETIC VIEW OF THE PUBLIC SPHERE TO A VIEW OF THE AESTHETIC PUBLIC SPHERE

While cultural sociology has made important contributions in identifying the aesthetic dimensions of the public sphere, it has tended to do so by emphasizing public debates that concern putatively "serious" topics, such as politics, public policy, secular commemorative rituals, crises, cultural traumas, etc. Correspondingly, these theories tend to focus on the more "fact based" media that organize these debates, such as political forums, the representational practices of social movements, and, most importantly, news media. To be sure, these emphases are shared by most other theories of civil society. Indeed, many political theories of the public sphere view entertainment as a degenerative intrusion into a potentially rational civil society (e.g., Habmermas 1989; Putnam 2000; Adorno and Horkheimer 2001; Bourdieu 1998). And there are important exceptions in cultural sociology, where attempts have been made to think about the relationship between factual and fictional media (e.g., Alexander and Jacobs 1998; Alexander 2006; Jacobs 2007). Nevertheless, there is still much work to be done before we can have a more complete understanding of how fiction and entertainment media influence civil society. This is the central goal of the present chapter.

I want to introduce the concept of the "aesthetic public sphere" as the best way for cultural sociologists to understand the civic impact of entertainment media.[2] The idea of the aesthetic public sphere builds from Habermas' discussion of the literary public sphere but pushes it in a more cultural and historically even-handed direction. In the first half of his *Structural Transformation of the Public Sphere*, Habermas noted the important connection between entertainment media and the development of democratic communication norms. His specific focus was on the novel and the set of communicative institutions that developed around it. At the level of the social imaginary, the novels that bourgeois families were reading in the eighteenth and nineteenth centuries worked to sentimentalize the intimate sphere of the family, communicating to the reading public the values of empathy and understanding (Habermas 1989: 50). The bourgeois novel was also linked to the creation of a literary public sphere, which "was established as a sphere of criticism of public authority...already equipped with institutions of the public and with forums for discussion" (Habermas 1989: 51). The creation of these public, impersonal mass forums was centrally important for separating the content of an argument from the status of the speaker. And, eventually, the infrastructure and the logic of the literary public sphere were extended to the political realm, leading to the democratic principles of publicity and critical rationality. All this took place despite the fact that the novel, as Williams (1983: 306) points out, was for a long time derided as a "vulgar phenomenon."

Unfortunately, Habermas' public sphere theory developed in a way that undercut his earlier sensitivity to entertainment media and prevented a usable theory of an aesthetic public sphere from gaining any intellectual influence. The first problem is that Habermas was never able to imagine how entertainment media might serve any useful purpose other than to form a sort of proto-public sphere. The orientation to intersubjectivity, the development of critical literary forums, the separation of speaker and argument—all of these created the conditions for the principles of publicity and critical rationality, and nothing more. Furthermore, once these principles had been institutionalized within a relatively autonomous political public sphere, then the civic contributions of entertainment media were no longer needed.

In other words, even in the best-case scenario, Habermas never imagined that entertainment media would have a civic value that was more than fleeting, temporary, and subsidiary.

In fact, though, Habermas' historical narrative places entertainment media in a much more polluted position than this best-case scenario suggests. In effect, his critique of advertising, public relations, and consumption brought his argument more closely in line with the Frankfurt school theory of mass society, including derision directed at the culture industries most responsible for the rise of these manipulative communication techniques. In fact, Habermas' analysis magnified the problems of the Frankfurt school critiques. Adding a technological determinism to his mass culture critique, Habermas insisted that the technologies of radio, film, and television naturally reduced the capacity for rational-critical orientation because of their putative greater, "natural" intimacy (Habermas 1989: 172). In the end, it was difficult to use these arguments to develop, in a fruitful way, an empirically concretized theory of entertainment media and civil society. All that was possible was the standard, cultural politics of denunciation, which substitutes sweeping generalizations for close empirical analysis or nuanced analytical reflection.

In order to recover a useful theory of the aesthetic public sphere, we need to marshal three central insights from the Strong Program in Cultural Sociology.[3] First, we need to recognize that civic ideals do not only exist at the subjunctive, aspirational level, that is, as disembodied standards against which to judge "reality." In addition, civic ideals operate in a concrete way in empirical civil societies, as part of a semiotic system of purity and pollution. Most of the civic ideals that are enshrined in normative political theory—deliberation, trust, rationality, inclusion, seriousness, and so forth—also act as privileged cultural styles that are used to include some and exclude others as legitimate participants in the public sphere. These kinds of cultural hierarchies inform the public legitimacy associated with fiction and entertainment media.

For entertainment media and the aesthetic public sphere, this means that we must remain attentive to the ways in which the political culture of modernity has tended to draw a sharp distinction between the serious world of public affairs and the diversionary realms of play and leisure—privileging the former and casting a suspicious eye on the corrupting influence of the latter. In other words, entertainment media are always already inserted into a discourse of civil society, but in a semi-polluted symbolic position that demands justification according to the dominant tests of worth.[4] It is surely wrong to simply dismiss entertainment media as some kind of anti-civil distraction that is corrosive to civil society, as some scholars continue to do (e.g., Postman 1985; Gitlin 2001; Putnam 2000). This kind of visceral rejection ignores how the civic ideals these critics are defending—rationality, seriousness, engagement, critical reflection—are only made meaningful through the identification of a polluted symbolic term, which entertainment media so often provide within the elite public sphere.[5] It also misses a good deal more about the civic capacities of entertainment media, as I will try to demonstrate later. But it is equally wrong to take the celebratory approach that we so often see in cultural studies, which treats the consumers of entertainment media and popular culture as heroic agents resisting hegemony (e.g., Fiske 1989; Jenkins 1992). This approach also fails to see how entertainment media are symbolically positioned in a larger discourse of civil society, in a way that continually calls out for justification and which puts limits on their emancipatory potentials by placing them within clearly institutionalized cultural hierarchies.

The second insight we can borrow from the Strong Program is its commitment to intertextuality, in which any text is part of a larger cultural environment composed of multiple and overlapping texts and where meaning-making involves complicated processes of signification between these different texts. Rather than imagining a world of "serious" texts and a world of "popular" texts, in which each world is an island unto itself, an emphasis on intertextuality comes with the recognition that these two worlds are continually self-referencing. For example, as Robert Park noted in a series of early essays, the modern newspaper did not invent its distinctive cultural forms *ex nihilo*, but rather borrowed from fiction and other dramatic forms in a way that made the cultural structure of the news story and the fiction story very similar (see Park 1923, 1938, 1940). In fact, Park (1938: 204) argued that a good deal of what was printed in the newspaper—most notably, the human-interest story—was read by its audience as if it was literature, in the sense that it was read to stir the imagination rather than to focus public discussion or public action. The same was true of many breaking news stories, which tended to be written and read as if they were "realistic literature like the 'true stories' of the popular magazines and of the earlier ballads that preceded them in the history of the newspaper" (Park 1941: 374–375). Park was also attentive to the ways that literature was being shaped by the existence of the newspaper, in its choice of subject matter as well as in its use of specific poetic techniques. Thus, as Park (1940: 686) commented, "Emile Zola's novels were essentially reports upon contemporary manners in France just as Steinbeck's *The Grapes of Wrath* has been described as an epoch-making report on the share-cropper in the United States."

The point is that readers and viewers do not join a serious, civic, interpretive community when dealing with factual news media, or a trivializing, escapist one when they are interacting with fictional entertainment. Rather, each textual environment reacts on the other in the interpretive practices of individual minds as well as the larger social environments of public discussion and commentary. To the extent that mass media feed the public imagination and organize the public sphere, they do so largely through the interaction of their factual and fictional forms.

This brings us to the third central insight of the Strong Program, which is that meaning-making is a public enterprise that involves more than the interaction between text and reader. A variety of public processes and institutions are inserted between the text and the reader, particularly in modern and postmodern societies. These include communities of critics and other expert interpreters whose interpretations and evaluations are published in high-profile media that shape the public understanding and reception of a given text; communities of creative personnel whose interactions and commentaries play a role in the way that texts are "encoded" as well as the strategies used to respond to critics; and communities of consumer-citizens who participate in internet forums, blogs, and other communicative spaces in order to participate in a collective discussion of what the texts and the official commentaries swirling around them all mean. These institutions of public commentary and interpretation have existed for a long time in the world of fictional media. If anything, what is new and interesting about the present period is the way that the same kinds of interpretive and critical practices have been proliferating in the world of factual media.

From these insights, it is possible to identify three analytically separable components of the aesthetic public sphere. First, aesthetic publics work at the level of the social imaginary, providing important meaning structures and cultural scripts that individuals use in order to make sense of themselves and the world around them. Second, aesthetic publics provide a space for commentary about important matters of common concern. In other words, spaces of cultural criticism link a discussion of entertainment media to a broader discussion about society, politics, and public life, and they do so within the same organizational spaces—the media—that organize the more privileged and "serious" public debates. Third and finally, aesthetic publics encourage debates about cultural policy in a way that increases the importance of cultural citizenship within civil society. I provide a more elaborated discussion of each of these below, trying to be attentive to the existing cultural hierarchies that privilege the "serious" over the "entertaining" and thinking about how these hierarchies influence the attributions of civic purity and pollution that are available within aesthetic publics. I conclude with a tentative cultural mapping of how the aesthetic public sphere is connected (in terms of its communicative infrastructure as well as its deeper cultural structures) to the political public sphere.

Aesthetic Publics and the Social Imaginary

One way that entertainment media engage aesthetic publics is by introducing elements of the subjunctive and the imaginary into the lifeworlds of their audience and into the publics in which those audiences circulate. To be sure, the introduction of the subjunctive into the public sphere is not limited to entertainment media; as Cottle (2006) has argued for the case of news media, one of the most important cultural outcomes of a mediatized crisis is the introduction of the subjunctive into public debate. Where entertainment media are concerned, however, there is an entire history of justifications (going back to the eighteenth and nineteenth centuries) that attaches "the arts" to an alternative "imaginative" truth that was purported to offer a superior, transcendent reality to its audience (Williams 1983) Rather than trying to reflect actual worlds that were constrained by "mere facts," those in the arts instead created compelling, cathartic, and emancipatory worlds that could mobilize people to change themselves and the world around them (Alexander 2006). And yet, while entertainment media developed their cathartic impact from the fact that they operated at a temporal remove from the events of the day, they were nevertheless organized around the binary moral categories that organized the civil discourses of their times:

> Expressive media stipulate events and figures that are relevant to members of civil society. Drawing on the repertoire of dichotomous categories, their plots make these events and characters "typical", placing them into revealing and easily interpretable situations that represent civil and uncivil motives and relations.…
> In so doing, the novels [and other entertainment media] mobilized public opinion against polluting threats to the ideals of civil society. (Alexander 2006: 76)

The moral and civic power that Balzac's, Dickens', or Austen's novels had for their time are clear enough to see with the benefit of historical hindsight. What is different about the current era, of course, is that the elements of social imagination are more likely to be drawn from the cultural industries of film and television. There are obvious and important differences between the kinds of aesthetic publics that are likely to emerge out of these very different cultural fields. After all, the cultural industries have a much different organization of production, where the autonomy of creative personnel is more of a struggle, but where the material rewards for success are far greater than what a Balzac or Austen could ever have imagined (Hesmonhalgh 2007). There is a different institutional complex of expert criticism, with the expert critics in the culture industry being more closely tied to the journalistic field than they are in the arts (see Baumann 2007). There is a different audience, with the consumers of the culture industry's products having a much more diverse and transnational composition than the novel, whose audience still remains surprisingly contained within a national setting (see Corse 1997). Finally, despite the fact that the cultural industry's products reach such a large and diverse audience (or, perhaps, because of it), they generally occupy a more compromised position within the cultural hierarchies of aesthetic and public worth. Surely, all of these factors will influence the ways in which today's fictional media are able to engage the subjunctive powers of the aesthetic public sphere.

It is probably worth beginning this discussion by pointing out that in television, film, and the rest of the cultural industries, outstanding achievements are mostly surrounded by mediocre products. This is no different from the rest of the arts. In the world of high culture, though, this uncomfortable fact is finessed by the claim that it is the outstanding products that attract the most critical attention and most powerfully engage the imaginative moral faculties of their audience, resulting in an influence that is far greater than their direct consumption (Williams 1983). In contrast, where cultural industries are concerned, most critics have tended to adopt a somewhat different perspective, arguing that the mediocrity that defines most products overwhelms the ability of any of the quality products to attract attention or inspire imagination (see, e.g., Postman 1985; Adorno 1990). Surely, this interpretation is the result of the different symbolic position that the cultural industries occupy as compared to the more autonomous regions within the cultural fields (Bourdieu 1993; Hesmonhalgh 2006). Before accepting such an uneven analytical strategy, however, it probably makes more sense to examine the subjunctive and moral properties of the "quality" texts within the cultural industries.

In order to maintain analytical consistency, I will restrict my focus primarily to television. There are several reasons for this choice. First, television continues to be the dominant technology for entertainment media with the largest audience and the greatest revenues. In other words, if we want to study the impact that entertainment media have on the general public sphere, then we have to include television as a central focus of our study. Second, television operates within a much more compressed temporality than film, allowing it to provide ongoing commentary on current events that is simply not possible in film (or in novels, for that matter). This enables television entertainment to operate more effectively than film as a "counterfactual public sphere"—a topic I will return to shortly. Third, because television is more closely connected than film to national broadcasting policies, it is more likely to be the subject of cultural policy debates (Lewis and Miller 2003: 83).[6] Finally, television is lower than film in the symbolic hierarchy of the cultural field, despite the fact that the two share many of the same creative and management personnel (Hesmondhalgh 2007) and despite the fact that television drama was initially heralded as a greatly superior aesthetic product (Barnouw 1990: 154–167). This fact means that television faces more frequent challenges for justification and tests of its worth.

So, what are the subjunctive and moral properties of television's "quality texts"? At first glance, such a question seems perplexing. Already by the early 1950s, writers' hopes of producing serious drama and live theater quickly gave way to the recognition that television would consist primarily of situation comedies (e.g., *I Love Lucy*, *The Beverly Hillbillies*), variety shows (*The Ed Sullivan Show*), police dramas (*Dragnet*), light Westerns (*Gunsmoke*), and game shows—all of which relied on simplistic formulas that demanded little sustained concentration from their audience. Indeed, when William Froug, the producer of the critically acclaimed *Twilight Zone* series, was hired in 1964 as the executive producer in charge of drama at CBS, he was instructed quite clearly and bluntly that "your job is to produce shit" (Barnouw 1990: 347). But these developments obscure a much more complicated history. In the initial years of the U.S. television networks, there was a significant amount of quality live theater. Programs such as *Philco Television Playhouse*, *Goodyear Television Playhouse*, and *Kraft Television Theater* were big attractions to writers from the New York theater, including such luminaries as Rod Serling, Reginald Rose, Tad Mosel, and Paddy Chayefsky (Barnouw 1990: 154–165). Ultimately, this "golden age of television" was done in by a number of factors, including the switch from live video to film (Gould 2002: 41–43), the rising popularity of formula series (e.g., comedies, Westerns, etc.), and the growing influence of blacklist pressures (Barnouw 1990: 166–167). In its early years, though, television was seen as an excellent medium for screening quality drama.

What were the aesthetic, moral, and subjunctive qualities of these early programs? Among the most promising possibilities of the early medium were its intimacy and immediacy, particularly in the live theater productions that populate the early years of the industry. As *New York Times* television critic Jack Gould wrote in a 1948 column:

The camera lifts the television viewer out of the usual orchestra or balcony seat and takes him directly into the group upon the stage. Unlike the "canned" Hollywood film, however, this is done without sacrificing the qualities of spontaneity and sustained performance, which are the heart of true theatre. (Gould 2002: 37)

Gould also appreciated the ability of live television drama to provide a "disciplined appreciation of reality in everyday life" (Gould 2002: 44). In other words, television dramas provided compelling portraits of the lifeworld as individuals struggled to find meaning and dignity in the modern world. Paddy Chayefsky's 1953 production of *Marty*, for example, offered a poignant portrayal of a shy and plain-looking working-class man and his struggles with loneliness (Gould 2002: 43–44; Barnouw 1990: 157–159). Reginald Rose's *Thunder on Sycamore Street* provided a portrait of neighborhood intolerance in a teleplay that was inspired by a racial incident that had taken place in suburban Illinois. Rod Serling's *Requiem for a Heavyweight* told the story of an aging boxer and his unscrupulous manager, while J. P. Miller's *The Days of Wine and Roses* offered a tragic portrait of alcoholism (Gould 2002: 49–51).

What these programs had in common was the desire to dramatize a social issue through an intimate psycho-social portrait of individuals in pain, all trying to salvage some degree of moral dignity in a cold and heartless world. These dramas did not simply entertain through easy formulas or ideological messages about happiness-through-consumption. Instead, they challenged their viewers to empathize with the damaged, the weak, and the compromised. At the same time, these dramas expanded the collective understanding of what counted as a matter of common concern. Breaking down the barrier between public and private, these psychological portraits were deeply sociological in the way they suggested a link between biographical problems and socio-historical structures.

While these golden-age dramas gave way during the 1960s to formula series, the "vast wasteland" described by FCC chair Newton Minow turned out to be relatively short-lived. Indeed, television scholars such as Thompson (1997) have argued that the 1970s and 1980s ushered in a "second golden age" of American television defined by aesthetic quality, public relevance, and self-reflexivity. The idea that entertainment programs could deal successfully and popularly with "serious" issues of the day had been demonstrated with the runaway success of *All in the Family*, which was the most popular show on television from 1971 to 1976. The real turning point, Thompson argues, was the appearance of two new shows that appeared in the 1980s: *Hill Street Blues*, a police drama that ran from 1981 to 1987; and *St. Elsewhere*, a medical drama that ran from 1982 to 1988. These shows received extensive critical praise and established new formulas for a host of other quality dramas that emerged during the 1980s and 1990s.

The quality programs of the 1980s all relied on a number of devices that allowed them to produce a particular kind of moral discourse. First, they relied on large ensemble casts, which allowed them to develop multiple storylines, some of which were resolved in a single episode and others that developed over a longer period of time. Second, most of the programs included an examination of the conflict between work life and private life, showing how the two were connected in complex and often contradictory ways. Third, and perhaps most importantly, these programs dealt to a greater extent than ever before with "real-life" issues of the time, such as urban decay, hospital administration, anti-abortion violence, racial conflict, and baby-boomer angst. And they did all this while maintaining the sense of intimacy and empathy that has always characterized quality television.

The engagement with current social issues allowed the quality programs of this "second golden age" to create something like a counterfactual public sphere, in which fictional individuals gathered together to discuss matters of politics and common concern. Rather than limiting their presentation to the standard techniques of mainstream journalism, political speeches, or press conferences, these counterfactual public discussions increased their power by maintaining a connection to ongoing character development and overlapping storylines that characterized the programs. Indeed, because the writers for these programs could assume that their viewers had an ongoing relationship with (and attachment to) the programs, they were able to present their fictional public discussions in a way that was consistently thematic, in contrast to the disconnected and episodic nature of news coverage of public problems.[7]

As the engagement with current issues became the staple of many programs, the counterfactual publics of quality television have increasingly found themselves penetrating discussions taking place in "real" public spheres. For example, medical dramas such as *ER* and *Chicago Hope* have portrayed health-maintenance organizations (HMOs) as the villain in their dramatic plots, crystallizing a growing dissatisfaction that put HMOs on the defensive and forced them to justify their actions.[8] In 1992, the political debate about family values and single mothers was carried out in large part as a debate between Vice President Dan Quayle and the fictional television character Murphy Brown. More recently, episodes of the critically acclaimed *Mad Men* have provoked a good deal of public reflection about changing gender roles in the workplace, while various episodes of *The Wire* have produced public discussion about urban crime, politics, and the media.[9] These programs clearly engage the moral sensibilities and critical capacities of their viewers, and they do so at the individual, small-group, and public levels.

Aesthetic Publics in the "Official" Public Sphere

As I have suggested above, fictional entertainment media do not only enter the social imaginary through internal dialogues within the self (though these are certainly important); they also help to organize and motivate collective public dialogues about matters of common concern. In other words, entertainment media are part of an *aesthetic public sphere*. By combining cultural criticism with social commentary, aesthetic publics infuse popular media with a sense of public relevance, engaging the civic identities of their audiences at the same time as they provide the communicative infrastructure for constituting a critical public sphere. Today, entertainment media have all the infrastructure that is necessary to form a critical public sphere: texts that challenge public authority, a space of criticism (in the academic and journalistic fields) that serves to define the criteria for making evaluative judgments;

and a set of overlapping communicative spaces where individuals participate in collective television criticism.

The spaces of expert criticism are of particular importance because they allow television's civic influence to extend beyond the discussions taking place in the life-world, or in "enclave publics" that are subordinated to (and largely invisible from) the dominant publics. Indeed, the fact that television criticism is a regular part of the journalistic field means that it is connected to the "official" or "dominant" public sphere, which, after all, is organized primarily by mainstream news media. What I am suggesting is that we can think about the "arts" section of the newspaper—and television journalism, in particular—as an important part of the public sphere whose significance tends to be overlooked by researchers as well as by privileged political actors.

In an analysis of data from American television journalism in the 1990s, I have found repeated instances where articles engage in sophisticated media criticism that doubles as social criticism. One article discusses changing images of adultery on television, arguing that television programs since the 1990s have moved away from an unrealistic depiction of "unblemished monogamy" and toward a more nuanced development of unfaithful characters who remain sympathetic and likeable, reflecting a new cynical realism about the state of contemporary marriage.[10] Another article uses a comparison of the fictional television characters Ralph Kramden (*The Honeymooners*), Archie Bunker (*All in the Family*), and Jerry Seinfeld (*Seinfeld*) as a framework for developing a critical demography of New York City from 1950 to the present.[11] Other articles discuss increasing gay visibility on television, as a springboard for thinking about the advantages and disadvantages of normalization.[12] Still other articles discuss the visibility and representation of African Americans, women, and other minority groups on television, engaging in critical (and historical) commentary about the extent to which television has been able to portray these groups in a multidimensional, non-stereotyped manner, as well as additional commentary about the social forces that explain this progress (or lack of progress). This television journalism, which is a regular and widely read part of the newspaper, provides some of the most sociological commentary on race, class, gender, and sexuality that one can find in the mainstream public sphere.[13]

Even more interesting, perhaps, is the way that American entertainment media operate as a common focal point of criticism and dialogue in other national media. One way that this works is to use a popular American political drama as a metonymic frame of reference for comparing domestic and American political culture. For example, a 2001 *West Wing* episode about Indonesia received extensive news coverage in the *Jakarta Post*, which used the show as a device for commenting on American stereotypes about Indonesian politics, while also praising the show for allowing a fictional Indonesian diplomat to point to American hypocrisy in its commitment to human rights.[14] A recent editorial in *The Times* of London asked why British political dramas were so cynical and considered why the British were incapable of producing a more uplifting political drama such as *The West Wing*.[15] These are interesting cases because the focus on the American programs serves to denaturalize the domestic political culture at the same time that it highlights American hegemony and the political ideologies portrayed in American programming.[16]

In a systematic study of how American television serves as an object of commentary in other countries, Brian McKernan and I have found three different ways in which American television gets mobilized in order to make an argument in the "official" public sphere about a particular public issue. The first of these is *ideological critique* in which American television is criticized for its biases, stereotypes, and political messages. The article in the *Jakarta Post* mentioned above is an example of this kind of commentary. Other common ideological critiques include the charge that American television spreads commercialism and mindless trash; destroys national identity; and is inherently biased toward the geopolitical interests of the U.S. military and government.

A different way that American television serves as an object of commentary in the official publics of other countries is as a way of providing insight into the United States. In these commentaries, American television is assumed to provide an accurate portrayal and glimpse into the real character of American life. A good example of this style of commentary can be found in the British paper *The Guardian*, which discussed The Simpsons program as "a double-edged celebration of blue collar U.S. culture."[17] Similarly, we can find many articles about U.S. programs such as *Lost*, *24*, and *Battlestar Galactica*, which are taken as reflections of a more fearful and anxious post-9/11 America. Still other articles rely on American television programs as evidence of a schizophrenic and confused American attitude about sexuality. These types of articles are often quite analytical and critical in orientation, but they are different from the simple dismissals of American television as political ideology. Instead, critical readings of American programs are taken as accurate clues into the true character of American culture.

A third way that American television programs inform aesthetic publics worldwide is to act as a point of reference for more local concerns and debates. In fact, this is the most common type of commentary about American television programming worldwide, a fact that points to the important role that entertainment media play in shaping civic discourse and public debate. The article in *The Times* asking why the British could not produce a show like *The West Wing* is a good example of this type of commentary. The same is true of a series of articles in *China Daily* and *South China Morning Post,* which used the ratings failures of the television show *Desperate Housewives* to consider cultural differences between American and Chinese family life. Other articles used American television programs as a platform to discuss issues of gender, race, and sexuality—not in the United States, but rather in the national context of the newspaper's readers.

What is happening in all of these news articles is that a focus on entertainment programming is being used as a platform for more general social and cultural commentary and where the dialogue with American cultural products serves to reveal insights about the domestic civil society. In fact, the image of America as the "other" to domestic cultural policy often works simultaneously to encourage social reflexivity about the domestic political culture and about American global power.

This extends to the discussion of programming strategies in the home country, the organization of creative personnel, and to the relative merits of different market and nonmarket approaches to funding cultural production. In other words, the discussion of American television worldwide is often connected to the debate about cultural policy.

Aesthetic Publics, Cultural Policy, and Cultural Citizenship

The massive participation in entertainment media, and the corresponding discussions that swirl around them, have done more than simply draw people into the public sphere in a way that leaves it unchanged. Entertainment media have also helped to redefine the *subject position* of the contemporary citizen. While most theories of citizenship emphasize a subject who is engaged in debates about political and social policies, Miller (1998) has suggested that the subject of cultural citizenship is more likely to think about the public good in terms of *cultural* policy. In many instances, these debates are organized through a market discourse that emphasizes the freedom to consume whatever culture one likes, with the market determining what will be available. In other instances, discussions center on the kinds of culture that ought to be available in order to make a "better" society: This usually involves advocating for the protection of children, local cultures, minority cultures, heritage cultures, elite "high culture," or something else. Regardless of which kind of debate is taking place, the point is that cultural citizens have a significant *moral* investment in the culture industry. For many individuals, their participation in entertainment media, as well as their arguments about it, constitutes their most significant civic practices.

In the United States, these debates tend to assume the model of American commercial media and thus tend to be organized through a market discourse that emphasizes the freedom to consume whatever culture one likes, with the market determining what will be available. From this cultural framework, it comes as no surprise that the most active debates about television policy tend to be connected to social movements, which usually focus on specific programs that are viewed as unfair, uncivil, or dangerous to children. Furthermore, because these social movements also assume a market model for mass media, their critique usually takes the form of pressuring advertisers and viewers to boycott a specific program. Aside from these episodic outbursts of protest, there is little sustained attention in the United States to the kind of programming policy that is best suited to the cultivation of citizens.

Again, the situation outside of the United States is more complex. In many nations, there is a long tradition of debate about television policy and specifically about how to counter the threat of American hegemony. These debates actually began in the 1920s as the U.S. film industry achieved a position of global dominance. Shifting to the issue of television policy in the 1950s, the debates have intensified since the 1980s with the decline of the public service broadcasting model and the strengthening position of American television products (Gorman and McLean 2003).

As a result of these debates, many countries have specific legislation in place to limit foreign (i.e., American) media content. In France, current laws require that 40 percent of all television content be produced in France, with 60 percent being of European origin. Laws in Australia and Canada are similar, mandating that between 50–60 percent of media content be produced domestically. The Sri Lankan government has tried a different approach, recently introducing a tax on all imported film and television content. Despite the specific policy differences between countries, what is common among all of them is the regular debate about the need to protect national popular culture against American media. These debates came together in a 2005 UNESCO Convention on the Protection and Promotion of Diversity of Cultural Expressions where participating nations overwhelmingly approved a document affirming the rights of nations to enact legislation protecting cultural expression from foreign competition.

From the perspective of the aesthetic public sphere, what is important about all of this legislation is the public discussion that surrounds it and the way that American television serves as an object that continually reintroduces the topic of the popular as a legitimate point of common concern. If anything, the global hegemony of American television produces, for most national debates about cultural policy, a sense of urgency that is lacking in the United States. The following article, written during a 2002 British debate about communication policy and foreign ownership laws, expresses the stakes in clear and stark terms:

> What is at stake is identity....What defines "Britain"? Its democracy, of course, and its mix of peoples; but also its news programmes, documentaries and social concerns, its soap operas, its crime shows, its dramas, its sport. That's what we talk about. That's what keeps us us. The American media corporations which flood our imaginations through the cinema, the internet, music and much of television are not yet all-powerful, and that matters.[18]

Debates about broadcast policy proceed through two types of arguments. The first, which we see above, contrasts the American free-market view of culture with an alternative (French) model, which views culture as a central component of national heritage. In this argument, restrictions on foreign content are necessary to preserve national identity. In the second argument, American television is defined by sexuality and violence, and cultural policies limiting American content are seen as necessary to protect children from a morally degraded culture. These concerns about media violence exist in the United States as well, but they tend to be episodic and are easily sidetracked. In other countries, however, debates about television violence are also debates about Americanization, in which the violence of American television is linked to the violence of American society more generally. The following arguments illustrate how concerns about media violence are linked to concerns about Americanization:

> The crucial thing is to see that the violence aspect of U.S. television culture is not brought in cheaply to British television. That is why I want the preview right....[19]
> It has been proved in research that children who watch violent programs become

more aggressive in their behavior....It is quite disturbing to see Australia following American television trends.[20]

In these debates, the comparative context helps to legitimate the cultural policy
debates because most of the violent content comes from foreign programming
which reflects an exogenous culture that can be held up as a threat to the autonomy
of the domestic national culture. Again, the role of American television is to produce dialogue and social reflexivity.

Aesthetic Publics and the Symbolic Hierarchies of Civil Society

While it is clear that aesthetic publics have an impact on civic discourse, it is important not to overstate their significance and, by doing so, lapse into an uncritical
celebration of them as promoting some kind of unbridled participatory culture. At
the very least, we need to recognize the ways that entertainment media and aesthetic
publics are shaped by existing symbolic hierarchies, which privilege serious talk
about politics and policy and which call into question the importance of entertainment and other putative diversions. Because these hierarchies are deeply institutionalized, they establish readily available dismissals of entertainment. The result is
a tendency toward a certain defensiveness on the part of those who participate in
aesthetic publics, based on the always-present possibility that they will be called on
to justify the seriousness of their pursuits and the importance of their discussions.

We can see this symbolic hierarchy at work in the public persona of Jon Stewart
and the public commentary that swirls around his award-winning political-media
satire, *The Daily Show*. When Stewart and his program are the object of discussion
in the aesthetic public sphere, he receives overwhelmingly positive attention. And
yet Stewart himself is always quick to dismiss the show's relevance, emphasizing
that it is about "fake news" and that its only motivation is to be funny.[21] Critics of
Stewart rely on the same argument, dismissing him for being a "mere comedian"
who does not understand the complexity of the public issues that he is using as
fodder for his routines. Christopher Hitchens pushes the dismissal even further,
suggesting that people like Stewart are not very good entertainers either:

> Not long ago, I was teaching a class on Mark Twain at the New School in
> New York and someone asked me who, if anybody, would be the equivalent figure
> for today. I was replying that I didn't think there was one, though the younger
> Gore Vidal might once have conceivably been in contention, when someone
> broke in to say: "What about Jon Stewart?" I was thunderstuck at how many
> heads nodded...[a response] which has its vaguely alarming side. "Al Franken for
> Senator" is one thing (especially when the alternative is or was "Norm Coleman
> for Senator"). But Jon Stewart for Samuel Langhorne Clemens is quite another.
> What next? Stephen Colbert for Zola? Al Franken for Swift? (Hitchens 2009: 102)

In these criticisms of Stewart and his fellow entertainers, we can see two binary
distinctions at work. In the first, the entertainer is seen as someone who refuses to

engage in public issues in a serious or nuanced way. In the second, the entertainer is criticized as someone who is debasing comedy, by failing to engage seriously with the techniques of great satire (indeed, Hitchens goes on to criticize Franken and Stewart for confusing glib irony with more sophisticated satire, suggesting that both would do well to spend some time studying Swift and Baudelaire). Both criticisms place the entertainer on the polluted side of the serious/nonserious binary, a positioning that demands justification and that explains the wariness that many entertainers have about venturing into the political public sphere.

This suggestion that many entertainers' pursuits are insufficiently serious exerts a cultural pressure of potential pollution onto aesthetic publics. The fact that these aesthetic publics are increasingly organized around popular culture only magnifies this pressure. These discourses of symbolic pollution operate differently at the level of the social imaginary than they do for cultural policy debates or other public discussions that take place within the aesthetic public sphere. There is also a difference between those conversations that center around "native" and "foreign" culture. I briefly outline these different pressures below.

At the level of the social imaginary, the moral discourses of popular culture's "quality genres" are diluted by their cultural positioning as "only entertainment." To the extent that the audience accepts such a positioning, there is a correspondingly lower likelihood that they will recognize the programs they are watching as serious commentaries about important public issues. Instead, they will tend to consume the texts of popular culture in a more passive and distracted way, failing to develop an elaborated discourse about their cultural consumption and its place in their social worldview. In this sense, it is possible to see the passive and distracted consumer of popular culture as being not so much a product of the cultural industry, but rather the product of the discourse of civil society, which privileges seriousness over entertainment and which establishes these as binary and mutually exclusive categories. This, of course, was the point that Raymond Williams (1983: 289) was trying to make when he argued that there were no masses, but only discourses about masses.

It is because of this symbolic pollution of entertainment, and the way it is deeply institutionalized within the discourse of civil society, that aesthetic publics are so important. When Jack Gould wrote his television columns in the *New York Times* during the 1950s and 1960s, he was signaling to his readers that talk about television was indeed a serious matter of common concern. In more recent times, when critics have written about the deep sociological insight of critically acclaimed television programs such as *The Wire* or *Mad Men*, they remind the reader that there are important things to be learned from the texts of popular culture, particularly if the reader is careful to sample from the quality genres. The same kinds of signals are produced within Internet forums and blogs about popular culture, even if these publics lack the imprimatur of authority that we might find on the culture pages of more elite media.

But even for those aesthetic publics that are organized within the "official publics" of mainstream media, the potential impact of the aesthetic public sphere is limited by those culture structures that encourage a separation of entertainment from more serious issues. The arts pages of the newspaper may offer penetrating sociological insight, but they do so in a space that is segregated from the more serious news of the day, with the corresponding symbolic suggestion that they be read as such. And when entertainment programs are included as part of the conversation about an important public issue within the more "serious" parts of the official public sphere, there is always a risk of ridicule for the individual who introduces the entertainment program into the debate. We can see this clearly with the case of Vice President Dan Quayle, who famously used a quarrel with the fictional television character Murphy Brown in order to successfully get the conservative "family values" issue onto the national agenda. But Quayle accomplished this at great personal cost, as he saw his approval ratings plummet, and as he (once again) became the object of public critique. As *New York Times* columnist A. M. Rosenthal commented:

> [Quayle's] aides were well aware that they were straying into dangerous political territory, but no one expected the firestorm Quayle set off. Once again, the barbs were brutal: "Quayle also says there should be more honesty on television," Johnny Carson said. "He said there's no way a coyote could live after swallowing all that dynamite."[22]

The point is that it is risky to take entertainment programming as a serious object of commentary in the political public sphere unless the motivation is to criticize the programming as an obstacle to more serious pursuits. This is unfortunate because of the many different ways that aesthetic publics manage to provide penetrating social and cultural commentary about matters of common concern. It is equally unfortunate in the way that the seriousness/entertaining binary works to position the committed fan for entertainment as being somehow outside of civil society.

The Effects of Cultural Globalization

As the earlier discussion about the global reception of American television suggested, there is an irony to this binary relationship between the entertaining and the serious, which is that foreign programming is much more likely to be taken seriously as a legitimate object of public concern. When foreign entertainment holds an influential position in a given nation, then that nation's public discussions will be filled with debates about the threats to national identity, the ideological dangers of the foreign product, and the need to protect the national culture with clearly defined cultural policies. These concerns will often be countered by other discussions that consider the quality features of the foreign programming or that use the foreign programming as a window into a foreign culture, where both discussions take place as part of a dialogue between the foreign and the national. In other words, the presence of powerful foreign entertainment programming promotes reflexive and critical discussion—about cultural hegemony; different systems of cultural production; and the similarities between national and global cultural systems. The defensiveness that often surrounds aesthetic public debate is offset by the presence of foreign culture and the perceived need to preserve national identity through the creation and protection of an autonomous national cultural industry. In other words, cultural globalization works to break down the entertainment/seriousness binary and to reinforce the importance of the aesthetic public sphere. The conversations that take place within the aesthetic public sphere are more easily able to penetrate the "official" (and typically political) public sphere when there is a position of relative weakness in the larger global system of cultural industries.

On the other hand, when we consider the state of development of the aesthetic public sphere itself, we find more complexity and growth where there is a position of relative strength in the global system of cultural industries. In the United States and France, which are at the center of the cultural world system (Casanova 2005), there is a long history of aesthetic commentary about the arts and entertainment, which combines an established set of cultural critics with an equally established and autonomous set of critical journals and a regular place for sophisticated aesthetic commentaries within the mainstream press. The same is true in Japan, which occupies the central position of influence and prestige among the cultural industries in Asia (Iwabuchi 2002).[23] In these nations, where the cultural industry is powerful and where aesthetic commentary is serious business, there is a more elaborate and autonomous discourse about matters of aesthetic concern.

As a result of cultural globalization, then, we see two different forces impacting the relative development and position of the aesthetic public sphere. Centrality in the global cultural industries gives more autonomy and prestige to cultural critics, resulting in a more complex and confident discourse of aesthetic commentary. At the same time, though, because this cultural centrality pushes foreign programming to the margins of attention and distribution, it leaves the aesthetic public sphere more vulnerable to criticism from the binary of seriousness vs. entertainment. In other words, while the more hegemonic cultural nations are likely to have more elaborated aesthetic discourses, those discourses are also more likely to be segregated from the official political public sphere. In more peripheral nations, by contrast, we are likely to see much greater interaction between the aesthetic and political public spheres, but this interaction tends to take place in an environment where the aesthetic sphere itself has less autonomy from other social spaces. As a result, commentaries about the aesthetic properties of the texts under consideration tend to be underdeveloped, with an over-reliance on a discourse of realism to do the work of an aesthetic critique.

Conclusion

My goal in this chapter has been to map out a research agenda for studying entertainment media as part of an aesthetic public sphere. I have identified several different ways that aesthetic discussions and commentaries are connected to civil society and the public sphere.

- At the level of the social imaginary, entertainment media offer moral discourses that dramatize the relationship between social issues and the lifeworld. Relying on a greater intimacy with the characters in the stories, these texts and the "counterfactual publics" they create offer real advantages over the cool, distant, and episodic discussions that often occur in the political public sphere.

• Within the spaces of expert aesthetic commentary, discussions of entertainment programs often get connected to more wide-ranging social and political discussions. This is particularly important for discussions of foreign programs, where the aesthetic public sphere produces a kind of transnational critical reflexivity.

• Through cultural policy discussions talk about entertainment media is invested with moral significance in a way that widens the scope of what counts as a "matter of common concern" in the official public sphere. These discussions take on an added significance when there is a heavy presence of foreign programming, as the discussions about cultural policy are infused with a strong concern for protecting national identity, or avoiding cultural imperialism, or both.

While the aesthetic public sphere has a clear presence in the official mediated public sphere, there are other dynamics that act to limit its influence. Most of these dynamics are connected to the powerful cultural code of "serious vs. entertaining," which acts to place entertainment media (and the discussions that surround them) within a lower place in the cultural hierarchy. This cultural process means that the aesthetic public sphere often has a semi-polluted symbolic position, in which it is quite easy to demand that those involved in aesthetic commentaries justify the worth of their discussions.

This symbolic hierarchy has real consequences. At the level of the social imaginary, a lower position in the symbolic hierarchy increases the likelihood that the audience for entertainment will fall into a distracted style of consumption, falling instead into a distracted style of viewing that weakens the force of the moral discourses and counterfactual publics that are circulating within entertainment texts. The segregation of the "arts" pages from the more "serious" parts of the newspaper hardens the border between serious political matters and putatively trivial aesthetic ones, in a way that makes border crossings quite risky for actors in the political public sphere. At the global or transnational level, there is a complex relationship that links aesthetic sophistication with influence in the "cultural world system," meaning that a fully autonomous discursive infrastructure of aesthetic commentary is much more likely in those places that have cultural power. At the same time, though, this very cultural power is likely to drive out quite a lot of foreign programming, having the paradoxical result that aesthetic commentaries are most vulnerable to challenging "tests of worth" precisely in those places that have the most fully developed aesthetic public spheres. All of these dynamics place limits on the power that the aesthetic public sphere can have over the political public sphere.

Many of the arguments I have made in this chapter are based on empirical claims that call out for further research. Indeed, my central hope is that I have mapped out a clear research agenda for cultural sociologists who are interested in media and civil society. Such a research agenda would further the continued focus on the aesthetic, at the same time that it reinvigorated media sociology by pointing to previously unexplored cultural processes. Finally, it would open up new avenues for thinking about the development of a global or transnational public sphere in a way that highlights the media practices and meaning-making activities of real cultural citizens in real civil societies.

NOTES

1. See Alexander (2006) for the most developed expression of this argument.

2. The concept of the "aesthetic public sphere" has also been discussed in an interesting article by Jones (2007).

3. For a programmatic statement about the Strong Program in Cultural Sociology, a discussion of its achievements, and its differences from other paradigms in cultural sociology, see Alexander and Smith (2001, 2010).

4. In proposing this understanding of entertainment media, as being relationally situated alongside other cultural fields, I am drawing on the well-known work of Bourdieu (1993) and Boltanksi and Thevenot (2006).

5. For an interesting empirical study that explores this phenomenon through an examination of public debates about the meaning of celebrity, see McKernan (2010).

6. This is not to suggest that cultural policy debates about film are completely absent. For an interesting discussion of the British case, see Miller (2003).

7. On the episodic framing that tends to dominate most news coverage, particularly on television, see Iyengar (1994).

8. Caryn James, "On the Doctor Shows, Public Health Enemy No. 1" *New York Times*, November 8, 1998, p. B30.

9. See, for example, Frank Rich, "Mad Men Crashes Woodstock's Birthday", *New York Times*, August 16, 2009, p. K8; Sudhir Venkatesh, "What do Real Thugs Think of The Wire?" *New York Times*, January 8, 2008, p. B1.

10. Caryn James, "Straying into Temptation in Prime Time" *New York Times*, August 10, 1997, p. B1.

11. Blaine Harden, "Ralph Had Dreams, Archie Had Opinions, Jerry Had Neuroses. But They All Told a Story About Life and Times in the Big Apple", *Washington Post*, May 14, 1998, p. C1.

12. See, for example, Lisa de Moraes, "Gay TV Characters Break New Ground, Old Taboos", *Washington Post*, March 3, 1999, p. C1.

13. Viewed from this perspective, it is perhaps more understandable how Frank Rich was able to transition from a film and television critic (first at *Time* magazine, later for the *New York Times*) to a key op-ed columnist featured centrally in the *New York Times'* expanded weekend opinion pages.

14. *Antariksawan Jusuf, "The West Wing Looks at Puzzle of Indonesia", Jakarta Post,* July 28, 2001, p. 8.

15. Joe Joseph, "Why Can't we do a British West Wing?" *The Times*, May 29, 2002.

16. Joe Joseph, "Why Can't we do a British West Wing?" *The Times*, May 29, 2002.

17. Stuart Jeffries, "Welcome to Planet Simpson." *The Guardian* 11/23/1996 Features, p. 6.

18. Jackie Ashley, "Comment and Analysis: Puttnam is right to want broadcasting to stay British." *The Guardian* 07/31/2002 Guardian Leader Pages, p. 16.

19. Richard Evans, ""Watchdog head wins battle for preview power." *The Times* 05/17/1988 Issue 63083.

20. Andrew Conway, "Kids hit by TV violence; screen killings multiply—and children spend longer watching." *The Sydney Morning Herald* 09/20/1987 News and Features, p. 34.

21. See, for example,Michiko Kakutani, "Is Jon Stewart the Most Trusted Man in America?" *New York Times*, August 17, 2008, p. E1.

22. A. M. Rosenthal, "Quayle's Moment", *New York Times*, July 5, 1992, p. F11.

23. Iwabuchi emphasizes the central role that Japan plays in developing innovative cultural formats that get adopted throughout the Asian region. Preliminary research by Anne Lin suggests that Japan's position of cultural centrality is in fact connected to a more well-developed discourse of aesthetic commentary within the cultural industries, as compared to other Asian nations.

REFERENCES

Adorno, Theodor, 1990. "Culture Industry Reconsidered," in *Culture and Society: Contemporary Debates*, ed. J. Alexander and S. Seidman. Cambridge, UK: Cambridge University Press, pp. 275–282.

Adorno, Theodor, and Max Horkheimer, 2001. "The Culture Industry: Enlightenment as Mass Deception," in *Media and Cultural Studies: Key Works*, ed. M. Durham and D. Kellner. Malden, MA: Blackwell, pp. 71–101.

Alexander, Jeffrey C., 2006. *The Civil Sphere*. Oxford: Oxford University Press.

Alexander, Jeffrey C., and Ronald N. Jacobs, 1998. "Mass Communication, Ritual, and Civil Society," in *Media, Ritual, and Identity*, ed. T. Liebes and J. Curran. London: Routledge, pp. 23–41.

Alexander, Jeffrey C., and Philip Smith 2001. "The Strong Program in Cultural Theory: Elements of a Structural Hermeneutics," in *Handbook of Social Theory*, ed. J. Turner. New York: Kluwer, pp. 135–150.

———. 2011. "The Strong Program: Origins, Achievements and Challenges," in *Routledge Handbook of Cultural Sociology*, ed. J. Hall, L. Grindstaff, and M. Lo. New York: Routledge pp. 13–24.

Baiocchi, Gianpaolo, 2006. "The Civilizing Force of Social Movements: Corporate and Liberal Codes in Brazil's Public Sphere," *Sociological Theory* 24(4): 285–311

Barber, Benjamin, 1984. *Strong Democracy*. Berkeley: University of California Press.

Barnouw, Erik, 1990. *Tube of Plenty: The Evolution of American Television*, 2nd ed. New York: Oxford University Press.

Baumann, Shyon, 2007. *Hollywood Highbrow: From Entertainment to Art*. Princeton, NJ: Princeton University Press.

Benhabib, Seyla, 2002. *The Claims of Culture*. Princeton, NJ: Princeton University Press.

Boltanksi, Luc, and Laurent Thevenot, 2006. *On Justification: Economies of Worth*. Princeton, NJ: Princeton University Press.

Bourdieu, Pierre, 1993. *The Field of Cultural Production*. New York: Columbia University Press.

———. 1998. *On Television*. New York: New Press.

———. 2005. "The Political Field, the Social Science Field, and the Journalistic Field," in *Bourdieu and the Journalistic Field*, ed. R. Benson and E. Neveu. Cambridge, UK: Polity Press, pp. 29–47.

Casanova, Pascale, 2005. *The World Republic of Letters*. Cambridge, MA: Harvard University Press.

Corse, Sarah, 1997. *Nationalism and Literature*. Cambridge, UK: Cambridge University Press.

Cottle, Simon, 2006. "Mediatized Rituals: Beyond Manufacturing Consent," *Media, Culture & Society* 28(3): 411–432.

Eyerman, Ron, 2001. *Cultural Trauma: Slavery and the Formation of African-American Identity*. Cambridge, UK: Cambridge University Press.

Fiske, John, 1989. *Understanding Popular Culture*. New York: Routledge.

Fraser, Nancy, 1992. "Rethinking the Public Sphere: A Contribution to the Critique of Actually Existing Democracy," in *Habermas and the Public Sphere*, ed. C. Calhoun. Cambridge: The MIT Press pp. 109–142.

Gitlin, Todd. 2001. *Media Unlimited: How the Torrent of Images and Sounds Overwhelms Our Lives*. New York: Metropolitan Books.

Gorman, Lyn, and David McLean, 2003. *Media and Society in the Twentieth Century*. Malden, MA: Blackwell.

Gould, Lewis, ed., 2002. *Watching Television Come of Age: New York Times Reviews by Jack Gould*. Austin: University of Texas Press.

Gutmann, Amy, and Dennis Thompson, 1996. *Democracy and Disagreement*. Cambridge, MA: Harvard University Press.

Habermas, Jurgen, 1989[1962]. *The Structural Transformation of the Public Sphere*. Translated by Thomas Burger. Cambridge, MA: MIT Press.

———, 1996. *Between Facts and Norms: Contributions to a Discourse Theory of Law and Democracy*. Cambridge, MA: MIT Press.

Hesmondhalgh, David, 2006. "Bourdieu, the Media and Cultural Production," *Media, Culture and Society* 28: 211–231.

———, 2007. *The Cultural Industries*, 2nd ed. Thousand Oaks, CA: SAGE.

Hitchens, Christopher, 2009. "Cheap Laughs," *Atlantic Monthly* 396, 9: 101–106.

Iwabuchi, Koichi, 2002. *Recentering Globalization: Popular Culture and Japanese Transnationalism*. Chapel Hill, NC: Duke University Press.

Iyengar, Shanto, 1994. *Is Anyone Responsible? How Television Frames Political Issues*. Chicago: University of Chicago Press.

Jacobs, Ronald N., 2000. *Race, Media, and the Crisis of Civil Society: From Watts to Rodney King*. Cambridge, UK: Cambridge University Press.

———, 2007. "From Mass to Public: Rethinking the Value of the Culture Industry," in *Culture in the World, Vol. 1: Cultural Sociology and the Democratic Imperative*, ed. J. Alexander and I. Reed. Boulder, CO: Paradigm Press, pp. 101–128.

Jenkins, Henry, 1992. *Textual Poachers: Television Fans & Participatory Culture*. New York: Routledge.

Jones, Paul, 2007. "Beyond the Semantic 'Big Bang': Cultural Sociology and an Aesthetic Public Sphere," *Cultural Sociology* 1: 73–95.

Ku, Agnes, 1999. *Narratives, Politics, and the Public Sphere: Struggles over Political Reform in the Final Transitional Years in Hong Kong*. Aldershot, UK: Ashgate.

Lewis, Justin, and Toby Miller, eds., 2003. *Critical Cultural Policy Studies*. Malden, MA: Blackwell.

Lichterman, Paul, 2005. *Elusive Togetherness: Church Groups Trying to Bridge America's Divisions*. Princeton, NJ: Princeton University Press.

McKernan, Brian, 2010. "Celebrity as a Symbol: The Use of Celebrity in American Intellectual Magazines." Unpublished manuscript.

Meeks, Chet, 2001. "Civil Society and the Sexual Politics of Difference," *Sociological Theory* 19: 325–343.

Miller, Toby, 1993. "The Film Industry and the Government: 'Endless Mr. Beans and Mr. Bonds'?" in *Critical Cultural Policy Studies*, ed. J. Lewis and T. Miller. Malden, MA: Blackwell, pp. 134–141.

———, 1998. *Technologies of Truth: Cultural Citizenship and the Popular Media*. ?: University of Minnesota Press.

Park, Robert, 1923. "Natural History of the Newspaper." *American Journal of Sociology* 29: 273–289.

———, 1938. "Reflections on Communication and Culture." *American Journal of Sociology* 44: 187–205.

———, 1940. "News as a Form of Knowledge: A Chapter in the Sociology of Knowledge." *American Journal of Sociology* 45: 669–686.

———, 1941. "Morale and the News." *American Journal of Sociology* 47: 360–377.

Postman, Neil, 1985. *Amusing Ourselves to Death: Public Discourse in the Age of Show Business*. New York: Penguin.

Putnam, Robert, 2000. *Bowling Alone*. New York: Simon and Schuster.

Seidman, Steven, 2002. *Beyond the Closet: The Transformation of Gay and Lesbian Life*. New York: Routledge.

Smith, Philip, 2005. *Why War? The Cultural Logic of Iraq, the Gulf War, and Suez*. Chicago: Chicago University Press.

Thompson, Robert, 1997. *Television's Second Golden Age*. Syracuse, NY: Syracuse University Press.

Williams, Raymond, 1983. *Culture and Society, 1780–1950*. New York: Columbia University Press.

Young, Iris Marion, 2000. *Inclusion and Democracy*. New York: Oxford University Press.

PART V

RACE AND
IMMIGRATION
AS CULTURE

RETHINKING THE RELATIONSHIP OF AFRICAN AMERICAN MEN TO THE STREET

ALFORD A. YOUNG, JR.

INTRODUCTION

Over the past three decades, the public behavior of urban-based, low-income, African American men has been at the center of the cultural analysis of this population (Anderson 1990; Duneier 2001; Mincy 2006; Venkatesh 2000, 2006; Young 2004, 2006). This topic has been a matter of considerable public attention as well (Staff of the Washington Post, 2007). This attention has been driven by extreme curiosity about why these men seem to behave in ways that appear to be both antithetical to their long-term well-being and deeply threatening to other people. Essentially, at the very time in which urban-based, low-income African American men have become highly marginal to many of the so-called mainstream institutional spheres and social spaces in America (i.e., formal employment, formal schooling), interest in and curiosities about them remain fixed on the one sphere regarded as a predominant site for their behavior—the open, accessible, and highly visible sphere more colloquially known as the street.

Throughout much of the history of American sociology, the urban street corner was a mere structural backdrop for cultural sociological assessments of the behavior of these men (Drake and Cayton 1945; Du Bois 1899; Hannerz 1969, 1972; Liebow 1967). Over the past three decades, however, the street has taken on a virtual life of its own as a point of reference in discussions of the public behavior of African American men and the cultural analysis of that population. The socioeconomic transformations transpiring in the urban community throughout the second half of the twentieth century were central contributors to the changing status of the street in public assessments of these men, as well as the sociological research conducted on them. Furthermore, the immediacy in which more recent public assessments were made was facilitated by the fact that people who do not access the streets of low-income, urban America were enabled, via media portraits, and advances in communicative technology, to virtually venture into that space in order to explore their curiosities. Most importantly, they were able to do so in ways that posed no risk to personal safety and security.

Consequently, the street now serves as a unique structural artifact that, in a literal sense, grounds an ensemble of cultural readings and projections of African American men. It has been repositioned in academic considerations, as well as in the general public sentiment, from serving as a structural backdrop to a more active arena in the construction of images and understandings about the public behavior of these men. The form of publicity now attributed to that domain is rooted in the public and scholarly attention given to the urban sphere as a site for extreme violence, decadence, and social unease.

This essay examines how the street has been implicated in scholarly and public interpretations of urban-based, low-income African American men. I aim to demonstrate that too much attention has been given to the street as a backdrop for observing, making interpretations, and forming judgments about the behavior of African American men, such that a richer and broader plane for the cultural analysis and understanding of this population has been denied. In pursuing these aims, the essay first considers how the street has attained such an overriding centrality in the cultural analyses of low-income, urban-based African American men (especially in the formation of images and understandings about them). It then explores how and why these men have become viewed as a frighteningly disturbing presence on the street because of the social power they are assumed to have in affecting the actions and lives of others who make use of the streets (or avoid doing so precisely because they attribute such power to these men). The heart of the essay explores some critical vacancies in the pursuit of cultural inquiry on African American men that emerge precisely because the street corner holds such a prominent place in studies of this population. In posing a critique of this vision, the essay concludes by illustrating how the street is just one of multiple spheres relevant to their lives; but it is one that also has been both over-determined and incompletely theorized in terms of its significance for cultural analysis.

Giving the Streets Credibility: The Circumstances Facilitating the Cultural Analysis of African American Men in Public Space

The centrality of the street in cultural analyses of African American men derives from historically resource-deprived African American urban communities. The modern city emerged as a site for socioeconomic deprivation precisely because it housed a proximate reserve labor force for a rapidly developing industrial arena. Throughout the twentieth century, African Americans became a core component of that force (Drake and Cayton 1945; Du Bois 1899; Grossman 1989; Spear 1967; Trotter 1991). The association of threat and social instability within the urban sphere emerged not only because of the socioeconomic deprivation that became highly visible in that sphere, but also because vice activity (and much later, an elaborate narcotics industry) was situated in it, so people could easily access these opportunities and products without introducing the kind of social toxicity that came with them into their own residential communities.

The extension of the malaise in urban America continued throughout the century. More specifically, the period between 1960 and 1980 served as a particularly decisive time for transformations in the public reaction to the use of public space by African American men. In the 1960s, the notion first came to surface that the quality of life in low-income, urban communities was not only problematic for its inhabitants, but the root cause of circumstances that could result in problems for those who did not reside in such places. The turbulence and social unrest that came to American cities—as a result of African American frustration with the pace of the civil rights movement and the assassination of Rev. Dr. Martin Luther King, Jr. in 1968—pushed forth an era when the city began to be conceptualized as an unsafe space increasingly populated by the very African Americans (as white Americans began moving out of it) that represented threats to personal safety. These events portrayed a brand of African American agency that had not surfaced in the past, and it was one that frightened much of middle- and upper-class America (Chafe 1986; Flamm 2005; Gitlin 1993; Hodgson 1976; Lytle 2006; Sitkoff 1981; Sugrue 1996).

As historians of twentieth-century America argued, by the 1970s, the new sociopolitical mandate for the urban terrain would be the preservation of law and order (Hodgson 1976; Flamm 2005). This meant governmental surveillance, if not regulation, of the racialized poor who continued to reside in that arena. African American men served as the model constituency reflecting images of hostility, aggression, and threat as the urban sphere lost its status as idealized space for those who could access the suburbs following the end of the civil rights era. What occurred in the decades following the urban riots and intense activism was the forwarding of a lucid portrait of the urban terrain as an especially dangerous, hostile, and uninviting space, best encapsulated by claims of the existence of an entrenched underclass in urban America. The image emerging about African American men was rooted in sweeping public acceptance by the 1980s of the concept of the underclass as a meaningful way of defining and depicting the African American urban poor.

The term underclass implied that a criminally inclined, violent prone, despair-ridden, and culturally deficient group of individuals locked in an inescapable web of economic deprivation and pathology formed part of the African American urban poor.[1] Essentially, the underclass was made up of the most immobile and socially isolated of these urban dwellers. They had the fewest prospects for upward mobility, and they experienced little sustained interaction with those in more mobile positions (Wilson 1987). Most importantly, the concept became an identifier of behavior and public demeanor (Auletta 1982). Violence, aggression, and idleness emerged as the personal characteristics and images most often associated with the term.

A key condition resulting from the sociodemographic circumstances that led to the rise of the so-called underclass was that, in virtually every sense of the term, there seemingly was little safe public space remaining for African American men in the inner cities of America (Anderson 1990, 1999; Venkatesh 2000; Young 2004). By safe space, I refer to public arenas whereby men can easily or consistently express emotional or physical vulnerabilities. Thus, the conundrum confronting these men and others who inhabit these communities is that while the streets have become less safe throughout the latter half of the twentieth century, there has been no alternative site for such men to engage in everyday social life. Consequently, the quality and patterns of the social relations experienced by these men—and the public identities that have emerged in regard to them—have been sedimented in a vision of the street as a highly determinant construct of urban life.

The twentieth-century story of public urban space and low income African American men, then, was one of a gradual shift over time from the streets as a place of accessibility for them amidst limitations in accessing other social spaces to a site of social- and self-destruction. During that time, the streets became spaces that were no longer the province of white Americans. Rather, by the end of the twentieth century the streets were highly and particularly racialized spaces. That transformation took place as the quality of life in urban communities began to decline. Hence, the streets went from sites of crowded engagement, sociability, and some purposively placed pockets of vice activity, to sites of extreme violence, destitution, and despair. Along with that shift came a transition in public sentiment from the streets as a domain that was an always intriguing, and often exoticized, site for people with little access to private spaces to one that was inordinately hostile and insidious. The imaginations of those who felt threatened by the more contemporary reading of the streets were crystallized by the images constructed about it in the media and on television. Ultimately, this meant that distant observers could maintain a vivid picture of the streets without having to actually access them. The changing public reaction to the streets, and especially to the African American males who inhabited them, mirrored the patterns of change in the vision that sociologists held throughout the twentieth century of African American men in the urban community, and especially on the streets.

BUILDING THEORY FROM THE STREETS: FRAMEWORKS FOR THE CULTURAL ANALYSIS OF AFRICAN AMERICAN MEN

The social and political developments in urban America throughout the twentieth century allowed sociology to become the intellectual site for an emerging tradition of analyzing the public aspects of the lives of low-income, urban-based African American men. This tradition was focused quite specifically on the notion that there was something peculiar about the cultural dynamics promoted and embraced by these individuals. Over the course of that century, the emphasis concerning that particularity shifted from studies of why these men seemingly took to the streets with such immediacy to intrigue and attentiveness to the highly profligate activities in which they engaged.

The pioneer sociologist W. E. B. Du Bois (1899) argued that lack of access to private space meant that lower-income African Americans had only the street to allow them opportunities for social engagement and recreation. Never in the course of *The Philadelphia Negro's* over five hundred pages does its author, Du Bois, offer a thoroughly systematic analysis of why and how African American men engage public space as they do. However, he does suggest that the confinement and congestion of Philadelphia's Seventh Ward (where this study is situated) lent to public space being the most available arena for social interaction and expression. That is because most of the African Americans who inhabited that city in order to seek economic opportunity did not have the economic means to acquire abundant private space.

In what, a century later, can be viewed as a proto-cultural analysis of lower-income African Americans, Du Bois argued that being present on the street meant that its inhabitants were susceptible to various interpretations and assessments because street-centered behavior was immediately visible to observing parties. The inherent flaw in such assessments, argued Du Bois, is that they did not capture the full complexity of people, as the public was only one arena in which people lived their lives. Unfortunately, Du Bois did not explore precisely what was missed by such analyses. Yet in raising that point, he acknowledged the problem that this essay is confronting.

In adding greater specificity to Du Bois' the proto-cultural perspective, St. Clair Drake and Horace Cayton (1945) endeavored to document more concretely how much African American male cultural expression takes the form of public displays of social engagement and impression management. While never going as far as to say that African American males are the only social group that engages public space in meaningful and eventful ways, they did demonstrate that these men made use of that space in particular and unique ways. Furthermore, they argued that the lack of access to, and control of, copious private spaces results in their reliance on an arena that is both highly visible and accessible to other people. Therefore, a situation resulted in which these men maintained significant agency in forwarding impressions and images of themselves to other people.

By the mid-twentieth century, ethnographic sociology housed the cultural analysis of low-income, urban-based African American men. It did so by offering extensive examinations of how they engaged each other and other people, and what stakes these behaviors had in determining the social status and public imagery of such men. Ultimately, the vision of these men as a uniquely public people was crystallized in the ethnographic literature of the 1960s. It was then that a plethora of studies was produced that put the street corner as the locale for the expression of African American men's public identities in the foreground (Hannerz 1969, 1972; Liebow 1967; Rainwater 1970). The scholars who produced this work elucidated how these men used the streets as a stage for publicly acting out various identities and social roles that pertain to efforts to reconcile the despair and disadvantage that come with being residents of low-income, urban communities. For instance, Elliot Liebow's work was one of the first highly regarded urban ethnography to render images of the public persona of low-income African American men coping with defeat and deficiencies. He showed how men engaged in practices that elevated their public image among their peers (e.g., animated interaction with their children, for whom they otherwise could not provide much material support) and in the public venue more generally. In reading Liebow, one may gather that such men engage in other practices for the purpose of creating a positive impression for the generalized other. This concept implicates Charles Horton Cooley's (1922) depiction of an audience that is not actually there, but is imagined to be by people as they enact behaviors and attempt to make some kind of inner sense of themselves as social beings. Hence, Liebow argued that much of what these men did on the street corner helped them to present a positive public persona as compensation for the personal and family-based problems they encountered.

A later extension of the early approach taken toward African American men and public space was offered by Mitchell Duneier (2001) who examined how economically marginalized men (and some women) make use of the streets in a white-collar, professional, urban neighborhood to demonstrate their entrepreneurial capacities and social utility (doing so, e.g., by selling used books and other material on the sidewalk).

As the century progressed, ethnography began to explore how African American men portrayed a public persona consisting of highly expressive styles of public engagement that reflected their effort to cope with the bleaker aspects of their lives. This persona included displays of bravado and overtly sensational forms of conduct which were promoted in order to mask their weaknesses and vulnerabilities. For instance, in another of the 1960s-era publications, *Soulside*, author Ulf Hannerz illustrated how intensely preoccupied he was with the manner and style of public expression elucidated by African American men that he devoted a portion of his book to a discussion of "soul," a common term used in the 1960s and 1970s to refer to general attitudes and styles of expression by African Americans (pp. 144–158). Accordingly, Hannerz's emphasis on soul and other expressive dimensions of low-income life make his work, like other classic urban ethnographies of the 1960s, a strong statement about the public aspects of the lives of urban-based African Americans. Essentially, then, the work of this group of scholars demonstrated how significant the streets were as material resources for social engagement, impression, and identity management. This kind of emphasis was one of a series of cultural analytical frameworks that evolved concerning African American men and the streets

Another framework began to emerge in the 1960s that was an extension of these developments. This one was firmly rooted in an intellectual orientation on culture not simply as a by-product of social relations and the structural arrangements that undergirded them, but as a generative force in its own right for producing outcomes such as inequality, marginalization, and disadvantage. Associated with this type of focus was the urge of some sociologists to critically explore the potential relevance of the concept of subculture as a tool for extrapolating the differences and similarities between those who were socioeconomically disadvantaged and those who were defined as constituting mainstream America.[2] Implicated in this unfolding were scholarly efforts to ascertain whether African Americans were creators of their own distinct cultural repertoire, reflected in their manner of speaking, styles of bodily expression, and basic attitudes toward life (Keil 1966). Pursuit of this query sometimes veered toward celebrating the exotic in that in the 1960s, some scholars began to regard the general patterns of African American expressiveness as "cool." When the work on lower-class subculture was brought together with this brand of thinking, the existence of an African American lower-class subculture came to be taken as a given.

The turn toward a vision of African American men as producers of racially specific cultural traits was a decisive move away from the earlier vision of these men as little more than social actors who functioned in highly public spaces. In the 1960s, a range of ideas surfaced in sociology and other social sciences about class-based subcultures, the culture of poverty thesis, and the potential for articulating a distinct, urban-centered African American culture. This was the bedrock for the argument of some sociologists that there existed an *anomic* street culture in low-income communities that caused its inhabitants to function in unique and sometimes aggressive ways in order to survive their social environment (Rainwater 1970; Schultz 1969).[3]

Introducing that concept allowed studies to make more culturally specific (if ultimately highly questionable) arguments about why low-income communities differed so much from more affluent ones in terms of the potential for violence and the absence of social and institutional buffers from physical, economic, and emotional threat. The concept of an anomic street culture foreshadowed the ways in which the street corner would surface as a site of central concern and consternation about how the vision of low-income, urban-based African American men would unfold in the latter third of the twentieth century. It was during that latter period that urban ethnography in the age of the underclass came into being. In doing so, a formidable scholarly lens was placed on what became a uniquely stultifying cultural framing of African American men in the urban sphere.

Indeed, much of the urban ethnography of the latter third part of the twentieth century framed African American and other men of color as exemplars of so-called underclass behavior (Anderson 1978, 1990, 1999; Billson 1996; Hunter and Davis 1994; Williams and Kornblum 1985; Laseter 1997; Liebow 1967; MacLeod 1995; Majors and Billson 1992; Rainwater 1970; Sullivan 1989; Tolleson 1997; Venkatesh 2000, 2006). These studies revealed how poor African American men came to grips with living in poverty by assessing why they engage violent behaviors; how they manage turbulence and insecurity in family life; and how they behave in light of possessing goals and dreams that seem far from their current stations in life. Peer groups and formal institutions have been common focal points for these inquiries, and a core question that was explored is how both relate to, help determine, or are affected by the contemporary existence of an underclass in the modern urban sphere. A leading claim in ethnographic studies of that period was that African American men were psychologically wounded by both a labor market that did not provide them with what they need for sufficient living and by a community ripe with threats and uncertainty. Many such men began behaving in manners that reflected confidence, security, and mental and physical toughness in order to survive neighborhood streets that were, by now, commonly understood to be the domain of the underclass.

Ultimately, urban ethnography during the age of the underclass brought forth a highly captivating turn on the idea of an anomic street culture: Elijah Anderson's (1999) concept of the code of the street. This construct was his lexicon for the panoply of rules and sanctions associated with public space in urban, low-income communities. As Anderson has argued, the code is a "set of informal rules governing interpersonal public behavior, including violence (p. 33)." These rules, Anderson went on to say, "prescribe both a proper comportment and the proper way to respond if challenged... allows(ing) those who are inclined to aggression to precipitate violent encounters in an approved way" (p. 33). This concept was used to explain the unwritten rules of observation, personal comportment, and social negotiation that allowed people to maintain, to the best extent possible, emotional and physical security while engaging public space in economically deprived urban communities. This nomenclature delivered an idea, with clarity and precision, that had been surfacing since the rise of the underclass in the late 1970s; that the public space of urban communities was not simply a backdrop for behavior but, itself, was an arena designed by perniciousness and toxicity.

Although these and other studies offer images of poor African American men managing the paucity of resources available to them and maneuvering around the threats, dangers, and insecurities that constitute much of their everyday lives; the preeminent focus of the most recent work in urban ethnography has been the framing of poor African American men as prone to violence and decadence, or at least to attitudinal dispositions that lead to such behavior (Anderson 1999; Glasgow 1980; Majors and Billson 1992). These and other efforts have fostered a paradigm of cultural analysis of urban-based, low-income African American men that inescapably situates the street corner as the principal domain for such inquiry. Indeed, the rendering of that space in such a manner has virtually over-dertermined how

African American men who inhabit it are read as social beings. The emergence of the lexicon of underclass, then, resulted not only in the idea that these very men were menaces to society, but, as their behavior often took place in public space, that space was also began to be regarded as insidious (Auletta 1982; Venkatesh 2000; Wilson 1987; Young 2004). In essence, the streets became a part of the problem because public space in low-income communities was seen as an insecure and unpredictable terrain on which to conducts one's business and goals.

What was easily ignored in emphases of low-income, urban-based African American men as representatives of the underclass is that such men construct senses of self and maintain identities that extend beyond what can be associated with the streets. Ultimately, the emphasis on the street in recent literature has overshadowed the search for other cultural manifestations, such as the formation of worldviews and beliefs about daily life circumstances, especially those not directly connected to everyday life in poverty. One of the reasons as to why the street-centered depiction was problematic is that it became a public image associated with more urban-based men than to whom it could be appropriately applied. That image also prevented a more thorough and complex cultural portrait of these men from emerging such that the broader public often read them as wholly focused on hostility, threat, and anxiety. What this meant for low-income African American men who inhabited such urban spaces was that even if they did not fully embrace this kind of depiction, they often adapted styles of interaction and public engagement that provided measures of security and stability in communities that between the 1970s and 1990s were ravaged by the proliferation of crack and increasing rates of crime. Hence, a more aggressive pursuit of how these men articulate meanings about the various features of their lives is in order.

Turning the Corner in the Cultural Analysis of African American Men and the Street

The high visibility that the street corner allows should not encourage observers to accept that they have access to all that is relevant for making sense of the culture of the African American men who regularly occupy that space. Accordingly, cultural analysis must be pushed to aggressively unpack additional attributes of the existential condition of low-income, urban-based African American men that are not immediately brought to mind given the intense preoccupation with the street. This effort necessarily involves bringing the sociological study of these men into more direct conversation with contemporary theory in cultural sociology.

More specifically, this effort involves moving beyond Elijah Anderson's (1999) provocative cultural analysis of the street. Certainly, what is implicit in Anderson's articulation of the code is the relevance of cultural properties, such as interpretation and meaning-making. That is, rather than envisioning the occupants of urban, low-income communities as mere reactants to their environments, Anderson illustrates how people form understandings of the various people and social contexts that are associated with different kinds of public spaces and then take purposeful action in those environments that reflect their understanding, if not full embracement of, the code. Thus, the cultural properties of meaning-making are active elements in Anderson's analysis. Yet, this dimension of cultural analysis must be extended further in the quest to construct a richer cultural sociology of urban-based, low-income African American men.

Unfortunately, belief systems and meaning-making processes have remained the least developed of the conceptual terms that comprise the cultural vocabulary employed in modern urban ethnography. Instead, concepts such as values, norms, and behavior predominate in the modern cultural analysis of African American men because these terms have provided more license to dissect behavior and action on the street.

To be fair to the tradition, urban ethnography has at least a partial history of exploring beliefs and meaning-making as crucial cultural properties. Nearly forty years ago, urban anthropologist Ulf Hannerz provided a road map for undertaking more nuanced work with the vastly under-utilized terms of belief systems and meaning-making. In talking about what men do with each other on the urban street corner (which, at the time of his writing, was a space that was not yet derided in the way that it has become contemporarily), Hannerz argued that such men form shared understandings of how social forces like employment, family circumstances, and social institutions, such as the police force, affect the lives of African American men. The street corner banter is the social process by which ideas about these and other phenomenon are transmitted by these men.

However, Hannerz did not elaborate on how much farther a cultural analysis of meaning-making could proceed. Hence, he could not make a case for the capacity for cultural sociologists to explore the means by which such men may contemplate extensive moral quandaries about being black and male in America; how they may understand mobility, stratification schemes in their country, or the state of affairs of local economies; or how they may evaluate themselves in comparison to other social actors in modern life.

It is these and similar questions that are now in the grasp of cultural sociologists (whether they are committed to formal ethnography or to ethnographic interviewing) who aim to understand more fully the situation of such men. If these kinds of opportunity are pursued, then the cultural analysis of low-income, urban-based African American men will garner the insight that has currently been delivered by cultural analyses of working class men (as exemplified by the work of Michele Lamont [2000]) or how people gauge the shifts in mobility prospects over time for themselves and other Americans (as exemplified by the work of Jennifer Hochschild 1995). Thus, the fruits of a broader platform for cultural inquiry on disadvantaged African American men are found in having them talk at length about their sense of themselves, which the former approach favors, and about the issues raised in the latter approach. The potential for a renewed cultural sociology of African American men in poverty, then, is contingent upon allowing them greater voice on issues and concerns that may pertain to their lives on the street but are not necessarily fully absorbed by it.

The attention given to meaning-making must extend beyond—without fully neglecting—how men may consider the dangers and insecurities associated with being in public spaces, as well as how they construct a public self within them. This is so because both points of consideration do not offer much to challenge the notion that such men are greatly encapsulated by the imagery of the underclass. The more extensive work to be done involves bringing in how such men produce and act on understandings that have to do with more than the pernicious qualities of the public spaces they make use of in their lives. It is this dimension of meaning-making that can liberate African American men from the suffocating confines of underclass imagery.

As cultural sociology became a robust, formal, and identifiable subfield of sociology only within the past two decades, the tradition of cultural inquiry on African American men is considerably older than the formal subfield, itself. Hence, rather than this being a case where the rise of a subfield has given space for an emergent form of scholarly inquiry, the cultural analysis of African American men instead has become an interesting site by which to examine how theories and concepts in the subfield can be altered or enriched by a legacy of cultural analysis that has operated largely outside of the formal subfield's epistemological and empirical boundaries. It is also becomes possible, and indeed essential, to explore the extent to which the empirical tradition of studying the public dimension of the lives of African American men itself can be enriched as well as transformed given the intellectual and theoretical tools devised and employed in the subfield of cultural sociology.

The tools of cultural sociology, especially now that the subfield has emerged as a formalized arena of sociological inquiry, are well situated to inform richer and more thorough portraits of low-income, urban-based African American men. Much of this effort rests in broadening the cultural terminology applied to these men so that their public demeanor and dispositions in regard to the streets no longer maintains such primary place in cultural analyses of this population. A first step toward advancing this new vision is for sociologists to abandon explaining the culture of low-income, urban-based African American men as a coherent, consistent, and all-encompassing property (which has too often been the residual effect of the street-centered approach) and commit to using cultural inquiry as a resource for analyzing selected aspects of these men's orientation to their social worlds.

The mandate for pursuing this more particularistic, cultural analysis has been presented by others who bridge the fields of cultural sociology, race, and poverty research (Lamont and Small 2008).[4] My own effort in responding to this call has been to explore how framing and narrative function as tools for a more particularistic approach to assessing how low-income, urban-based African American men construct understandings and interpretations of the social world (Young 1997, 1999, 2004, 2006).

Essentially, my pursuits have involved pursuing understandings of how meaning-making about varied aspects of social reality unfolds for these men. I am interested in aspects that do not always directly pertain to the public spaces that they occupy in socioeconomically disadvantaged communities, but also to aspects of the social world such as the white-collar, professional employment sector, or other spheres that reflect common American orientations to opportunity or mobility but may not be easily accessible or understandable to these men. My commitment to these kinds of explorations rests in the belief that these men are theorists of their social lives in ways that do not surface given how their presence in low-income communities—and on the street—has served to deny them recognition as meaning-makers for matters other than those pertaining to that domain.

A key emphasis in my work is that belief systems and worldviews operate as cultural properties that shape action. In attempting to sustain this claim, I argue that these cultural properties are not simply reflections of the structural conditions circumscribing the lives of African American men. Nor are they freestanding, ideational elements that men select or endorse because doing so satiates their desire to view the social world and themselves in certain ways. Instead, my effort has been is to demonstrate the consistent interplay between life experiences and the construction of meanings and interpretations of the social world that facilitate subsequent action and also foreclose on imagining certain options and possibilities. Hence, these men, and people more generally, are highly affected, but not wholly restricted, by the structural conditions implicated in their lives. Furthermore, they also have access to various kinds of cultural properties. However, that access, itself, is not unrestricted.

I dedicate a major portion of my research to exploring how these dynamics operate in the lives of low-income African American men. For instance, in my book *The Minds of Marginalized Black Men* (2004), I discuss the life experiences and views of a man I refer to as Devin. A twenty-four-year-old ex-convict when I first met him, Devin was a notorious gang leader on the Near West Side community area of Chicago. Thus, at first site, he appeared as a prototypical product of the streets. Although his mother would lock the door and padlock the window gates of their public housing apartment on the West Side of Chicago to keep him from accessing the streets while she went to work, he eventually found his way into that space by picking the locks and climbing out of his second-story apartment window. Over the course of Devin's adolescence, his encounters with the streets led him down a path of gang membership and an enduring pattern of self-destructive behavior, which eventually included incarceration and an attempt on his life by rival gang members. During that time, Devin got himself expelled or else withdrew from all four of the public high schools that served the Near West Side area of Chicago.

Devin was keenly aware of his public identity as a menace. He believed that his options for finding secure employment and a healthier quality of life in Chicago were foreclosed by his past activities and reputation. Indeed, any casual observance of Devin as he operated in his neighborhood would create in the minds of observers an image of him as a prototypical street figure. Yet, there was much more to Devin than his life in the streets, and he revealed this to me over the course of a series of conversations about his goals and interests on life, and how they connected to his past experiences and encounters.

When I first encountered him in the spring of 1994, he was living with his girlfriend in a public housing apartment not far from the one in which he grew up. He was caring for their four-year-old son along with her three children from other involvements (a seven-year-old boy, a one-year-old boy, and a four-year-old girl). Although he had biological ties to only one child in the household, he called this assembly of people his family. In doing so, his entire point of emphasis on what he needed to improve his life prospects—which, for him, meant leaving Chicago and trying to begin again in a place like Mississippi, where his mother was born and that seemed to him to be the opposite of the urban, densely concentrated, and turbulent environment that was Chicago—was rooted in his desire to be a good husband and father. In fact, his preoccupation in talking about his future was not in what he wanted for himself, but what he hoped he could achieve for his children and family. When I asked him why he was so dedicated to raising children that he did not sire, he explained that his partner had supported him while he was incarcerated and had worked hard to be a good mother. Devin felt indebted to her.

Devin's cognizance of the effects of his past did not move him to be apologetic about it. As he explained to me, the choices he made were the appropriate options at the time in which he was confronted with them. Yet, he also was quite consumed with how those choices affected his present circumstances. Thus, while he was a gang leader who often struck fear in the hearts of his neighbors, he also was a family man who sought better opportunities for his spouse and children. He took serious stock of his past and was not proud of where it led him. He firmly believed that access to various avenues for mobility would be denied him, and, therefore, he was prepared to rethink what he needed to do to improve life prospects, not so much for himself, but for his family. Most intriguingly, he aspired to be a father to children of other men because he fully accepted that this was the family context that he encountered. His readings of these complexities constitute some of the missing elements in the contemporary street-entered focus that is ubiquitous in the cultural analysis of urban-based, low-income African American men.

As evident in my engagement with Devin, throughout the course of my work on African American men, I explore two related areas of their meaning-making activity. The first is the pattern of beliefs and worldviews about each man's own immediate life situation. This includes his sense of the specific probable, possible, and desirable outcomes that may come his way, as well as the barriers and obstacles that one may perceive to be associated with these outcomes. The second attends to his beliefs and worldviews about how others in the social world manage their mobility prospects and options. This two-fold approach allows for investigations of how the perceived plights and possibilities of others (especially those in similar life situations) may shape a man's understanding of himself, especially if he rejects the notion that the dilemmas befalling members of a social category that he shares with them—racial, gendered, or class-based—also will affect him. Moreover, this two-fold approach allows me to explore the extent to which what such men think about themselves and others in the social world helps in their efforts to define capacities for future action. Finally, explorations of their thoughts on these matters also illuminates why they behave in the ways that they do and how they think their behavior may effect their future prospects.

A more enriched understanding of how these men's worldviews are formed begins by taking seriously the fact that they often create provocative and intriguing, but also sometimes confusing, patterns of meaning about their social worlds. Even those patterns that appear provincial at the surface emerge out of a profound set of experiential circumstances and conditions. Such patterns are not adequately captured by analytical frameworks that highlight the capacity of poor people to focus only on their immediate situations, thus rendering them incapable of apprehending or planning for their lives in the long term. In challenging such flawed approaches, this work compliments recent analyses that have called for more complex and provocative investigations of the culture of the African American urban poor, and poor African American men in particular. It also represents a new approach for overturning a long legacy of urban ethnographic and related modes of research that have served to construct the standard and overly simplistic image of the underclass in general and of low-income African American men in particular.

A major implication of this kind of inquiry is that grasping the structured relationships between the different meanings created by such men is much more tenable. That is, rather than viewing patterns of belief simply as selections that people make from a repertoire of ideational options, it becomes possible to explore how beliefs emerge from particular life experiences and social contexts while also shaping and structuring forthcoming experiences and contexts.[5] Consequently, the kind of pursuit encouraged here also helps demonstrate that beliefs are not deducible from merely observing behavior, but rather that an intense consideration of beliefs helps to construct culturally informed understandings of why behavior emerges. In other words, the content of one's beliefs about the processes of social and personal mobility inform about how people choose to act with respect to future prospects and possibilities. With this analytical framework in mind, the importance of bringing to light the actual worldviews and beliefs of low-income African American men becomes evident.

The discussion, then, becomes one of not whether low-income African American men have the right values or not, if those values differ or are similar to those of who comprise "mainstream" America, or what degree of incentive may produce a particular outcome; but rather how certain social conditions or circumstances suppress certain kinds of agency for some poor people (like holding on to a job in a given week), while facilitating others (like deciding to take someone else's children into one's home even during a week when that individual has, for whatever reason, lost a job). Analyses that explore such phenomena advance comprehension of how people make, and adhere to, choices in ways that others might never consider doing.

CONCLUSION

A century-long period of cultural exploration of African American men, especially those from low-income and urban-based backgrounds, has involved preoccupation with one central question: Why do they commit to behaviors and to social outlooks that are so seemingly destructive? Responses to that question have been at the core of the one-hundred-year sociological inquiry into this seemingly troubled constituency. In its simplest form, the answer is that low-income, urban based African American men suffer from economic marginalization, family instability, insecure and turbulent social relations, and myriad challenges to their physical and emotional well-being such that, even if well-meaning, the choices that they make and the societal views that they hold contribute to their crippled capacity to advance themselves in an increasingly complex, modern American society.

Yet, the central goal of a renewed cultural analysis is to explore a wider range of low-income African American men's thoughts about the future, including how they think mobility unfolds for Americans in general. This new approach to cultural analysis must include consideration of social experiential bases as to why the men say what they do about all of these matters. Ultimately, this renewed approach to cultural analysis should render portraits of low-income, urban-based African American men as more than hyperpsychologically induced reactants to a turbulent world, but rather as people like the rest of us—meaning-makers who have different degrees of insight and understanding about ourselves and the world we live in.

In achieving this end, researchers must commit to the idea that the street must be rethought as a site for cultural expression. The critical challenge at hand, then, is to first think more seriously about these men's engagement of the street in terms of their behavior as analytically distinct from how they engage it cognitively and ideologically. When more attention is given to that latter domain of engagement, a different, broader, more penetrating, and more essential plane for the cultural analysis of these men comes into being. In making this step one certainly must take seriously that African American men, themselves, often think about the contemporary street corner as a threatening site. Their own reaction to that space involves acknowledging the risks that are involved in spending significant time there (Anderson 1999; Venkatesh 2000; Young 2004). Thus, the reaction of outside observers, as well as many African American men, is that the modern urban street corner is no longer a safe site for the reconstitution of identities, but rather the cementing of devalued identities and images of these men (Oliver 2006; Payne 2006; Payne 2008).

Consequently, the call here is for increased attention to space, which will inform considerations of how the street has been made to operate in a problematic fashion in the cultural sociological analysis of African American men. The lens must shift from the street as a backdrop for the social behavior and social relations of African American men to a more penetrating assessment of what it means for the street to become a device for steering perceptions of these men as much as it has in the past century.[6] This new foregrounding of space, especially the ways that urban space has been employed to substantiate social inequalities and power relations, has provided an opportunity to rethink the ways in which the street as been associated with public perceptions of low-income, urban-based African American men.

In committing to such re-thinking, it is important to note that although they are often applied too broadly and aggressively in efforts to explicate the cultural dynamics pertaining to urban-based, low-income African American men, the portraits of African American men as street figures are not wholly necessarily incorrect. Instead, their over-utilization has rendered an incomplete cultural portrait of these men, particularly in light of the vastly expanded array of tools, concepts, and ideas employed in contemporary cultural inquiry. Hence, what is in is order is a lens directed toward how the street places limits on understanding the cultural parameters of African American men's lives. The construction of that lens will assist in uncovering and answering a set of questions which have to do with precisely why the agenda in the cultural analysis of these men took the form that it did over the past century. These questions include: (1) why discussions of culture in regard to this group have consistently emphasized the public or social dimensions of their lives, and (2) does the orientation taken toward the public and social dimensions effectively lead to a coherent and consistent argument about the existence of a low-income, urban-based African American male culture? Finally, more critical observers also might ask what else may be going on in the lives of these men that pertains to the cultural analysis of them that is not illustrated by directly attending to their engagement of the public spaces (re: the streets), and how might that other activity be grasped and assessed through a cultural lens?

At the center of this new perspective lies the assumption that the behavior of these men emerges not simply from the adaptation of stretched values or alternative norms, but more fundamentally from the stocks of knowledge that they accumulate about how the world works and how they might work within it. Rather than appearing to be little more than dejected, demoralized, dehumanized, angry, or hostile, a careful and critical assessment of what these men have to say attunes the observer to the rationality inherent to their assessments of personal life experiences. It is this very rationality that is suppressed or denied when behaviors are assessed only at a surface-level, thereby leading to assumptions about poor African American men's capacity to function in ways that middle-class America regards as proper and appropriate. By challenging this suppression and denial, then, the tools of cultural sociology can serve to depathologize a population that thus far has been overly pathologized in prior scholarly portraits and traditions.

Cultural analysis in urban ethnography has been and should continue to be a site of lively debates. In short, one side of the current debate asks whether African American men adopt or promote distinct cultural patterns that contribute to, if not cause altogether, their demise. The other side asks whether these are men—who are taken to be cultural actors in the ways that other groups of Americans are—might simply experience unique life circumstances and conditions that over-determine the social outcomes comprising their everyday lives. It is not surprising that what African American men do in the course of their lives is sometimes harmful to themselves and others. This can be the case irrespective of whether the blame is placed on these men for adopting profligate behavior or on external factors, such as the declining employment opportunities or the lack of social support mechanisms in their communities. Wherever urban ethnographers fall along this continuum of perspectives, this tradition, despite its crucial role in framing a complex image of disadvantaged black men, has nonetheless helped advance an incomplete framework for their cultural interpretation.

A cultural analysis that more thoroughly foregrounds beliefs and meaning-making allows for a different positioning of the street, in part by allowing for a vision of these men as more than occupants of that space. Additionally, the kind of analyses that unfold under a new vision of cultural inquiry will provide better insight into how these men may contextualize the street as one of many relevant spheres in their lives and as one that is too often used to create a rigid and pestilent lens on these individuals. Undoubtedly, assessments of their public behavior, socialization practices, and interactions are important elements of everyday life and, therefore, must continue to be pursued. However, rather than disavowing this mode of research, the goal is to help to form a new analytical lens on a population that often has been a source of intrigue, bewilderment, and consternation in the scholarly and public imagination. If this can be achieved, then both urban-based, low-income African American men and their observers will benefit greatly from what will become a renewed approach to cultural analysis.

NOTES

1. This term "underclass" was first introduced in social science literature by the Swedish economist Gunnar Myrdal in a short book entitled *Challenge to Affluence* (1963). Myrdal used it as a descriptive device to discuss who he believed would be the greatest victims of deindustrialization in modern societies. His use of the term was meant to be a means of talking solely about an economically derived social category. However, the more recent behavioral and racial implications for the term came about in the 1970s and were established by the mid-1980s. The contemporary proliferation of this term was due in no small part to the publication of journalist Ken Auletta's book *The Underclass* (1982), which was written for a popular audience and widely distributed. Furthermore, sociologists Herbert Gans (1995) and Robert Aponte (1990) and historian Michael B. Katz (1989a, 1989b) provide detailed accounts of how the term was introduced and eventually applied to low-income, urban-based racial groups by researchers and in the media, especially in regard to African Americans.

2. Although anticipated by the research of earlier years, the idea of a lower-class subculture initially was created and sustained in large part by ethnographic studies of European-American ethnic enclaves in urban areas (Gans 1962; Suttles 1968; Whyte 1943) and studies and commentaries about lower-income Americans of various racial and ethnic backgrounds (Bordua 1961; Cloward and Ohlin 1960; Cohen and Hodges 1963; Coser 1965; Gans 1969; Miller 1958; Rodman 1963). A wave of ethnographic studies of low-income

African Americans provided additional intellectual ammunition to the notion of subculture by introducing a vision of a lower-class subculture in American life (Abrahams 1964; Hannerz 1969; Liebow 1967; Rainwater 1970; Reisman 1962; Schulz 1969). While research in the pre-1960s era asserted that African Americans generally believed in the possibilities for a better life, the 1960s research agenda assumed that the poorest African Americans increasingly saw little or no possibility at all for improvement of their social condition. Accordingly, the research agenda, whether produced by liberal or conservative thinkers, turned to detailed considerations of the norms, values, and behaviors exhibited by people who held fatalistic visions of their future (Banfield 1970; Harrington 1962; Moynihan 1965; Reissman 1962). Thus, the culture of poverty thesis greatly influenced the public mindset about the relationship of culture, poverty, and urban life in and since the 1960s. However, the thesis was not without its critics (Valentine 1966).

3. While the portraits of urban life for low-income and working-class Americans in the early and middle part of the twentieth certainly depicted disadvantage and despair (see Whyte 1943 and Gans 1962), they did not reflect the lucid sense of the danger and perniciousness that is reflected in the contemporary studies and commentaries about the urban landscape. Even those studies that appeared in the mid-twentieth century, as the city changed from the site where people of color invested in the city as the ticket to upward mobility, to that which began housing those who were socioeconomically marginalized and increasingly immobile, the image of these urban dwellers first took the form of a dispirited and despondent group of people rather than a coterie of belligerent and threatening type of people (Hannerz 1969; Liebow 1967; Rainwater 1970).

4. More specifically, sociologists Michele Lamont and Mario Small make the case for investing in analyses of how low-income individuals frame as aspects of the social reality, which then provides some purchase on the extent to which they perceive constraints or possibilities for action. This is only one of a series of particular kinds of cultural inquiry that they suggest (the others include studying culture as a repertoire of practices, beliefs, and attitudes, culture as narratives, culture as symbolic boundaries, culture as a form of capital, and culture as represented by formal institutions).

5. I thank Ronald Jacobs for encouraging me to reflect on how the mandate I present here extends beyond the culture-as-repertoires-of-options logic. Indeed, the extension beyond that vision toward one that considers how cultural properties can forcefully structure social outcomes is a cornerstone of the strong cultural sociology program promoted by Jeffrey C. Alexander (2003).

6. The opportunity to rethink that site is well grounded in a field of scholarly inquiry, commonly known as spatial analysis, that has informed cultural sociology from a distance. That is because this field, which has been advanced by the work of Michele Foucault (1984), Henri Lefebvre (1991), and Edward Soja (2000), did not emerge within sociology, but rather via an interdisciplinary spectrum of scholarship on urban societies and social relationships in modernity. In essence, spatial analysis has offered the idea that social relations, history, and space are indelibly intertwined, such that a thorough analysis of any one of these domains must include substantial attention to the other two. In making this case, the focus on space has been heightened as that was the domain given less analytical attention in the history of social research since the end of the dominance of the Chicago School of Sociology in urban studies.

Of course, space was central in the Chicago School of Sociology (Bulmer 1984; Fine 1995). However, its centrality was often regulated to viewing urban space as a physically constructed backdrop for relations between members of social groups. Like the size, shape, and composition of baseball fields in the major leagues in comparison to the performance of the athletes, space in Chicago School sociology was critical, but secondary, to attending to the actual behavior of people. It was the scholars who comprised the contemporary field of spatial analysis who argued that space does more than reflect, but also is made in varied and provocative ways to reinforce social inequalities.

REFERENCES

Abrahams, Roger D. 1964. *Deep Down in the Jungle*. Revised ed. Chicago: Aldine.

Alexander, Jeffrey C. 2003. *The Meanings of Social Life: A Cultural Sociology*. Oxford: Oxford University Press.

Anderson, Elijah. 1978. *A Place on the Corner*. Chicago: University of Chicago Press.

———. 1990. *Streetwise: Race, Class, and Change in an Urban Community*. Chicago: University of Chicago Press.

———. 1999. *Code of the Streets*. New York: W.W. Norton.

Aponte, Robert. 1990. "Definitions of the Underclass: A Critical Analysis." *In Sociology in America*, edited by Herbert Gans. Newbury Park, CA: Sage.

Auletta, Ken. 1982. *The Underclass*. New York: Random House.

Banfield, Edward. 1970. *The Unheavenly City*. 2nd ed. Boston: Little, Brown.

Billson, Janet Mancini. 1996. *Pathways to Manhood: Young Black Males' Struggle for Identity*. New Brunswick, NJ: Transaction.

Bordua, David J. 1961. "Delinquent Subcultures: Sociological Interpretations of Gang Delinquency." *Annals of the American Academy of Political and Social Sciences* 228: 120–136.

Bourgois, Philippe. 1995. *In Search of Respect: Selling Crack in El Barrio*. New York: Cambridge University Press.

Bulmer, Martin. 1984. *The Chicago School of Sociology: Institutionalization, Diversity, and the Rise of Sociological Research*. Chicago: University of Chicago Press.

Chafe, William Henry. 1986. *The Unfinished Journey: America since World War II*. New York: Oxford University Press.

Cloward, Richard A., and Lloyd E. Ohlin. 1960. *Delinquency and Opportunity: A Theory of Delinquent Gangs*. New York: Free Press.

Cohen, Albert K., and Harold M. Hodges. 1963. "Characteristics of the Lower Blue-Collars Class." *Social Problems* 10(4): 303–334.

Cooley, Charles Horton. 1922. *Human Nature and the Social Order*. New York: Charles Scribner's Sons.

Coser, Lewis. 1965. "The Sociology of Poverty." *Social Problems* 13(2): 140–148.

Drake, St. Claire, and Horace Cayton. 1993 [1945]. *Black Metropolis*. Chicago: University of Chicago Press.

Du Bois, W. E. B. 1996 [1899]. *The Philadelphia Negro: A Social Study*. Philadelphia: University of Pennsylvania Press.

Duneier, Mitchell. 2001. *Sidewalk*. New York: Farrar Straus, and Giroux.

Fine, Gary Alan, ed. 1995. *A Second Chicago School?: The Development of a Postwar American Sociology*. Chicago: University of Chicago Press.

Flamm, Michael W. 2005. *Law and Order: Street Crime, Civil Unrest, and the Crisis of Liberalism in the 1960s*. New York: Columbia University Press.

Foucault, Michel. 1984. "Space, Knowledge, and Power." *In The Foucault Reader*, edited by
     Paul Rabinow, pp. 239–256. New York: Pantheon Books.
Gans, Herbert. 1962. *Urban Villagers*. New York: Free Press.
———. 1969. "Culture and Class in the Study of Poverty: An Approach to Anti-Poverty
     Research." In *On Understanding Poverty: Perspective from the Social Sciences*, edited by
     Daniel P. Moynihan. New York: Basic Books.
———. 1995. *The War Against the Poor: The Underclass and Anti-Poverty Policy*. New York:
     Basic Books.
Gitlin, Todd. 1993. *The Sixties: Years of Hope, Days of Rage*. New York: Bantam Books.
Glasgow, Douglas G. 1980. *The Black Underclass: Poverty, Unemployment and Entrapment of
     Ghetto Youth*. New York: Random House.
Grossman, James. 1989. *Land of Hope: Chicago, Black Southerners, and the Great Migration*.
     Chicago: University of Chicago Press.
Hannerz, Ulf. 1969. *Soulside*. New York: Columbia University Press.
———. 1972. "What Ghetto Males are Like: Another Look." In *Black Psyche*, edited by
     Stanley Guterman, pp. 139–161. Berkeley, CA: Glendessay Press.
Harrington, Michael. 1962. *The Other America: Poverty in the United States*.
Hochschild, Jennifer L. 1995. *Facing Up to the American Dream: Race, Class, and the Soul of
     the Nation*. Princeton, NJ: Princeton University Press.
Hodgson, Godfrey. 1976. *America in Our Time: From World War II to Nixon, What
     Happened and Why*. Garden City, NJ: Doubleday.
Hunter, Andrea G., and James Earl Davis. 1994. "Hidden Voices of Black Men: The
     Meaning, Structure, and Complexity of Black Manhood." *Journal of Black Studies*
     25: 20–40.
Katz, Michael B., ed. 1989a. *The Underclass Debate: Views from History*. Princeton, NJ:
     Princeton University Press.
———. 1989b. *The Underserving Poor: From the War on Poverty to the War on Welfare*.
     New York: Pantheon.
Keil. Charles 1966. *Urban Blues*. Chicago: University of Chicago Press.
Lamont, Michele. 2000. *The Dignity of Working Men: Morality and the Boundaries of Race,
     Class, and Immigration*. New York and Cambridge, MA: Russell Sage Foundation and
     Harvard University Press.
Lamont, Michele, and Mario Small. 2008. "How Culture Matters for the Understanding of
     Poverty: Enriching our Understanding." In *The Color of Poverty: Why Racial and
     Ethnic Disparities Exist*, edited by David Harris and Ann Lin. New York: Russell Sage
     Foundation.
Laseter, Robert L. 1997. "The Labor Force Participation of Young Black Men: A Qualitative
     Examination." *Social Service Review* 71: 72–88.
Lefebvre, Henri. 1991. *The Production of Space*. Translated by Donald Nicholson-Smith,
     Malden, MA: Blackwell.
Lewis, Oscar. 1959. *Five Families: Mexican Case Studies in the Culture of Poverty*. New York:
     Basic Books.
———. 1961. *The Children of Sanchez*. New York: Random House.
———. 1966. *La Vida: A Puerto Rican Family in the Culture of Poverty, San Juan and
     New York*. New York: Random House.
Liebow, Elliot. 1967. *Tally's Corner: A Study of Negro Streetcorner Men*. Boston: Little,
     Brown.
Lytle, Mark H. 2006. *America's Uncivil Wars: The Sixties Era from Elvis to the Fall of Richard
     Nixon*. New York: Oxford University Press.

MacLeod, Jay. 1995. *Ain't No Making It: Aspirations and Attainment in a Low-Income Neighborhood*. 2nd ed. Boulder, CO: Westview Press.

Majors, Richard G., and Janet Billson. 1992. *Cool Pose*. New York: Lexington Books.

Miller, Walter B. 1958. "Lower Class Culture as a Generating Milieu of Gang Delinquency." *Journal of Social Issues* 14(3): 5–19.

Mincy, Ronald B., ed. 2006. *Black Males Left Behind*. Washington, DC: Urban Institute Press.

Moynihan, Daniel Patrick. 1965. *The Negro Family: The Case for National Action*. Washington, DC: U.S. Department of Labor.

Myrdal, Gunnar. 1963. *Challenge to Affluence*. New York: Pantheon Books.

O'Connor, Alice. 2001. *Poverty Knowledge: Social Science, Social Policy, and the Poor in Twentieth-Century U.S. History*. Princeton, NJ: Princeton University Press.

Oliver, William. 2006. "'The Streets': An Alternative Black Male Socialization Institution." *Journal of Black Studies* 36(6): 918–937.

Payne, Yasser A. 2006. "A Gangster and a Gentleman: How Street Life-Oriented U.S. Born African American Men Negotiate Issues of Survival in Relation to Their Masculinity." *Men and Masculinities* 8(3): 288–297.

———. 2008. "'Street Life' as a Site of Resiliency: How Street Life Oriented Black Men Frame Opportunity in the United States." *Journal of Black Psychology* 34(1): 3–31.

Rainwater, Lee. 1970. *Behind Ghetto Walls: Black Families in a Federal Slum*. Chicago: Aldine.

Rainwater, Lee, and William Yancey. 1967. *The Moynihan Report and the Politics of Controversy*. Cambridge, MA: MIT Press.

Reissman, Frank. 1962. *The Culturally Deprived Child*. New York: Harper.

Rodman, Hyman. 1963. "The Lower-Class Value Stretch." *Social Forces* 42: 205–215.

Schultz, David A. 1969. *Coming Up Black: Patterns of Ghetto Socialization*. Englewood Cliffs, NJ: Prentice Hall.

Sitkoff, Harvard. 1981. *The Struggle for Black Equality, 1954–1980*. New York: Hill and Wang.

Soja, Edward. 2000. *Postmetropolis: Critical Studies of Cities and Regions*. Oxford: Blackwell.

Spear, Allan H. 1967. *Black Chicago: The Making of a Negro Ghetto, 1890–1920*. Chicago: University of Chicago Press.

Staff of the *Washington Post*. 2007. *Being a Black Man: At the Corner of Progress and Peril*. New York: Public Affairs.

Sugrue, Thomas J. 1996. *The Origins of the Urban Crisis: Race and Inequality in Postwar Detroit*. Princeton, NJ: Princeton University Press.

Sullivan, Mercer L. 1989. *Getting Paid: Youth Crime and Work in the Inner City*. Ithaca, NY: Cornell University Press.

Suttles, Gerald. 1968. *The Social Order of the Slum*. Chicago: University of Chicago Press.

Tolleson, Jennifer. 1997. "Death and Transformation: The Reparative Power of Violence in the Lives of Young Black Inner-City Gang Members." *Smith College Studies in Social Work* 67(3): 415–431.

Trotter, Joe W. 1991. *The Great Migration in Historical Perspective: New Dimensions of Race, Class, and Gender*. Bloomington: Indiana University Press.

Valentine, Charles A. 1968. *Culture and Poverty*. Chicago: University of Chicago Press.

Venkatesh, Sudhir Alladi. 2000. *American Project: The Rise and Fall of a Modern Ghetto*. Cambridge, MA: Harvard University Press.

———. 2006. *Off the Books: The Underground Economy of the Urban Poor*. Cambridge, MA: Harvard University Press.

Whyte, William Foote. 1943. *Street Corner Society: The Social Structure of an Italian Slum*. Chicago: University of Chicago Press.

Williams, Terry, and William Kornblum. 1985. *Growing Up Poor*. Lexington, MA: Lexington Books.

Wilson, William Julius. 1987. *The Truly Disadvantaged: The Inner City, the Underclass, and Public Policy*. Chicago: University of Chicago Press.

Young, Alford A. Jr. 1997. "Rationalizing Race in Thinking About the Future: The Case of Low-Income Black Men." *Smith College Studies in Social Work* 67(3): 432–455.

———. 1999. "The (Non) Accumulation of Capital: Explicating the Relationship of Structure and Agency in the Lives of Poor Black Men." *Sociological Theory* 17(2): 201–227.

———. 2004. *The Minds of Marginalized Black Men: Making Sense of Mobility, Opportunity, and Future Life Chances*. Princeton, NJ: Princeton University Press.

———. 2006. "Low-Income Black Men on Work Opportunity, Work Resources, and Job Training Programs." In *Black Males Left Behind*. edited by Ronald Mincy, pp. 147–184. Washington, DC: Urban Institute Press.

CHAPTER 14

ETHNICITY, RACE, NATIONHOOD, FOREIGNNESS, AND MANY OTHER THINGS: PROLEGOMENA TO A CULTURAL SOCIOLOGY OF DIFFERENCE-BASED INTERACTIONS*

GIUSEPPE SCIORTINO

NEW kids appear on the block. Sometimes, they melt into preexisting social networks, classified according to preexisting criteria. Other times, they become part of a special category that lumps them all together.

Decent people, although deeply committed to freedom of religion, vote against the building of mosques and discriminate against "foreign" religions. Reacting to what they perceive as a new and unexpected threat, they make use of a language and

* This paper has benefited from the activities of the Eurosphere project, supported by the European Commission (*http://www.eurosphere.uib.no/*).

a set of symbolic distinctions that has been used for centuries across a variety of contexts, sometimes against people of their very own faith.

Scores of hotel managers welcome and behave amicably toward "Oriental" customers. Filling out a questionnaire a few weeks later, the very same managers—save two—answer that no "Oriental" would ever be welcome in their establishments (LaPiere 1935).

Countries whose publics are highly suspicious of, if not openly against, immigrant flows, may nonetheless register high levels of immigration. Other countries may sustain remarkably high inflows of migrants, placing strain on a variety of resources, without classifying—or even perceiving—them as "immigrants," but rather as "returning co-nationals."

Political actors wishing to advance claims based on the distinctive nature of their group do so through very standardized, symbolic templates, which have a long history and a global reach.

Emigrants to various countries from the same homeland areas (and with roughly similar socioeconomic backgrounds) participate in the public life of the receiving societies through the adoption of remarkably different forms of "primordial" identities.

Citizens advocate a tough stance on "illegal" immigration but, at the same time, petition against the deportation of members of their congregation.

A variety of fine-grained ethnic, racial, and nationalistic representations are used in everyday life for managing social interactions—sometimes to establish a superior status, sometimes to challenge it, and in still other cases to trigger what is essentially an aloof, ironic, egalitarian sociability.

These are only some of the curious phenomena social scientists encounter in their attempts to make sense of the social world. What they have in common is the presentation of identities, claims, and social forms that reference a classification based on discrete cultural differences—a distinction understood as *us-them* or *them$_1$-them$_2$*—operationalized on the basis of the social consequences of "descent."[1]

The implications of such classifications range from the celebratory to the trivial to the downright dangerous. Although modernity has radically changed the meaning of ascriptive differences, it has surely not eliminated them. Contemporary social worlds are ordered by differential distributions of economic resources, power, and prestige. But they are also organized through multiple horizontal segmentations, distinguished by codes of similarity and difference. Sometimes the placement of an individual in such horizontal categories allows us to predict the amount of economic resources, power, and prestige he or she may enjoy or aspire to. Sometimes the two dimensions appear largely unrelated.

To explain such complexities, we definitely need a good theory. The development of a coherent theoretical framework has been impeded, however, by the fragmentation of research and researchers according to issues rather than problems. Races, ethnicities, nationalistic mobilizations, and the various social consequences of spatial mobility, have all been considered as empirically different forms of social organization, inhabited by different kinds of empirical actors. Within each field, moreover, there exist pressures to stress the peculiarities of a single country, category, or "group" (Brubaker 2004; Wimmer and Schiller 2003). The times, however, are changing. One of the most positive trends in social scientific research in recent decades has been the emergence of an integrated field devoted to the study of ethnicity, race, and nationality (and thus, arguably, foreignness) as a "single integrated family of forms of cultural understanding, social organization and political contestation" (Brubaker 2009:22).

Participation in, and development of, this emerging field should be of particular interest to cultural sociologists. This field is replete with wonderful "strategic research materials," in Merton's (1987) sense, for those interested in the cultural dimension of social life. It is a field where the claim that meaning matters seems particularly easy to make. It is a field where, in Max Weber's straightforward definition, the key variables are subjective beliefs and socially constructed cultural similarities and differences (Weber 1978). It is a field where research has revealed that the relationship between symbolic coding and empirical referents is historically contingent and analytically arbitrary (and yet powerfully constraining and full of structural consequences). It is a field in which the fear of pollution and the promise of salvation; the patterned struggle over collective representations; and the role of collective rituals, symbols, and narratives are widespread and immediately visible—even to the untrained eye.

It is consequently puzzling that the cultural turn seems still to have made little headway in these fields (Levitt 2005). For many scholars interested in difference-based phenomena, culture is still a problematic issue. Mainstream sociological scholarship is still largely split between those who see cultural difference as mere decoy for power inequalities and those willing to take, at face value, the description of reality performed by the involved actors. The former end up thinking of cultural coding as epiphenomenal, thus reproducing the century-old problems associated with any structure-superstructure model. The latter mistake, as Brubaker (2004) has convincingly argued—accepting "categories of practice" as "categories of analysis"—involves taking performative actions for descriptive statements. In fact, most of the historical and sociological work in these fields seems trapped in a "debunking" mode. Consequently, attention to the contingency of difference-based discourses does not generate fascination with their meaning-structures or an interest in explaining the semantic structures that sustain (and constrain) their classificatory and persuasive power.

Meanwhile, some researchers associated with the Strong Program in cultural sociology have produced works that may be of interest for the analysis of difference-based phenomena.[2] But theoretical developments in cultural sociology have not yet contributed adequately to the research on difference-based interactions, nor have they triggered a sustained dialogue with its practitioners. The lack of such an encounter is unfortunate, and it constitutes a serious obstacle for understanding the social consequences of spatial mobility and ethnic and racial diversity. The disdain for cultural analysis and the lack of an adequate approach to the cultural dimension of difference-based interactions are also worrisome because this leaves the door open to recurring attempts—of which Samuel Huntington's (2004) recent work is just one example—to define cultural difference as an unproblematic empirical fact, ready to be sown into a ground for exclusion.

In this chapter, I argue that an adequate—and consequently possibly crucial—understanding of the cultural dimension of these types of interactions requires understanding deep meanings in a way that is consonant with the Strong Program. The tools of cultural sociology may contribute to, and further enrich, contemporary efforts to understand difference-based dynamics in a non-reductionist way. More specifically, the main claim here is that a systematic understanding of symbolic structures—paying their analytic autonomy its due—may be particularly useful in fostering the recent emphasis on boundary-making, rather than collective groups, as the focus of analysis (see also Brubaker 2009; Wimmer 2009). An adequate explanation of difference-based phenomena would profit considerably from taking seriously the idea that the structures of classification and the narratives—along with the semiotic processes that regulate them—are to be accounted for analytically as a specific dimension of social life, which may empirically converge but never coincide with the social processes of allocation of rewards and sanctions. The lack of automatic alignment between these boundaries, particularly if seen in the context of a shared public sphere defined by the overlap of many layers of social and symbolic memberships, may shed light on the intrinsic dynamism of exclusionary and inclusionary processes.

The primary aim of this essay is to provide the groundwork for such an encounter. First, I review briefly two major traditions in the study of difference-based phenomena: urban ecology and structural anthropology. Albeit very different, these classical approaches share several key features: first among them an unproblematic definition of ethnicity/race/nationality/foreignness as consisting of distinct groups with shared cultural traits and substantial intergroup differences. It is against the shortcomings of these traditions that it is possible to appreciate the importance and theoretical novelty of the generation of researchers that, since the 1960s, have pursued research programs oriented toward shifting the emphasis from collective actors to boundary-making processes (Section 2). As I argue in Section 3, although such programs sometimes distinguish between social and cultural boundaries, the latter have often been seen as following the dynamics of material interests and, thus, bound to align accordingly. Building on the achievements of this generation, however, it is possible to conceive a conceptual framework that allows culture an analytically autonomous status. Difference-based idioms and narratives would be considered as existing within a much larger set of symbolic resources available to participants in the civil sphere, where, in order to be heard, specific claims must be formulated in reference to a set of crosscutting memberships and semantics. This implies that boundary-making processes require creative interpretation of the cultural codes, classifications, and narratives that constitute a major resource for their creation and maintenance (Section 4). A second, and related, implication is that it is precisely the absence of any neat alignment between social and cultural boundaries that energizes difference-based claims in the public sphere—in inclusionary as well as exclusionary directions (Section 5).

1. CULTURAL DIFFERENCES
AND COLLECTIVE ACTORS

When taking a course on migration or ethnicity, students usually encounter a stark contrast between essentialists (ethnic groups are "natural" forms of sociality) and constructionists (ethnic groups are socially and historically constituted). Essentialists supposedly assume that one's ethnicity is ascribed at birth, whereas constructionists believe it is produced socially, varying across contexts. Essentialists supposedly see specific cultural attitudes and behaviors as consequences of membership in a certain category, while constructionists see such commonalities, when existing, as contingent outcomes of historical legacies and structural circumstances. Essentialists supposedly see ethnicity as a universal phenomenon with specific qualities, in contrast to constructionists, who define ethnicity as just one among many ways in which specific societies classify individuals and groups.

No matter how popular, these alleged distinctions present a major inconvenience: Nobody is able to find a living essentialist in the academic world (Rex and Mason 1986; Wade 2002). There are good reasons to question if, in fact, one ever existed—no major theorist, classical or contemporary, has ever assumed ethnic identities to be unchangeable and permanent. No major sociological theorist has ever assumed such identities to derive from a wholly nonsocial factor; all have assumed they are historical and social products. Not by chance, when asked to identify in detail an adversary, constructionists usually end up asserting that some other constructionist is "actually" a closet essentialist.

However, the main problem with the distinction between essentialists and constructionists is not its lack of historical accuracy or its functionality as an ordering principle for a review of the literature. It is the fact that by positing constructionism as the debunker of essentialism, we hinder the task of defining accurately the processes through which ascriptive classifications are constructed, maintained, and forced upon (or dissolved), the psychological, structural, and symbolic resources and constraints in these processes, and the ways in which actors produce categorical distinctions with different degrees of social organization and salience in specific contexts.

The primary difference between classical and contemporary research has nothing to do with the alleged essentialism of the former. It is rather that for quite a long time, social scientific understandings of ethnicity—as well as of national membership and largely of race—have conceived of such distinctions as self-evident collectivities, characterized by specific shared behavioral and motivational features as well as by a certain degree of collective mobilization (Brubaker 2002). The same applies to the social heterogeneity derived from processes of spatial mobility. Migrants have been defined as culturally distinctive groups of individuals endowed with a shared identity, which had to confront in the receiving society other groups of individuals, equally bounded by their membership, albeit more privileged (Wimmer 2009). To understand the pervasive nature of such a vision, I briefly review two influential and very different traditions, one more concerned with social boundaries (the Chicago school) and the second with symbolic boundaries (Lévi-Strauss's structural anthropology).

The "ethnic hierarchy" approach developed by the Chicago school, with its many variants, was concerned not with the differential distribution of resources among individuals, but rather with the collective outcome of the processes of competition, conflict, and accommodation (and eventually assimilation) among different groups, whose nature and identity, albeit historical in nature, was a given—at least for analytical purposes. The approach assumed in fact that all groups, although actively trying to alter the distribution of material resources in their favor, shared a preference for a stable system of collective social distances among groups and were thus able to make sense of their placement within the hierarchy. Prejudice, and particularly racial prejudice, were defined precisely as a reaction to a change in patterns of accommodation that alters the balance of social distances (Park 1950). Such groups were conceived as having a common "purpose and action," to use Robert Park's famous definition, and sharing an anthropological preference for cultural homogeneity with a certain degree of consistency. It was only in contexts where such structures of expectation were undermined, such as in a modernizing city, that the ethnic hierarchy was challenged and that individuals of disadvantaged groups underwent the trials, and sometimes the rewards, of their "marginal man" status (Park 1928). Even if the dynamics of their placement within the ethnic hierarchy was largely left to demographic and historical factors, the key element of this view, for my purposes, is that these groups were defined in the ideal anyway, by a specific ("traditional") cultural content and by unproblematic boundaries (see also Kivisto 2004). Over time, and because of structural trends, social boundaries may blur and even dissolve, but this occurs *against* the logic of existing cultural boundaries—and through their eventual disappearance. Such groups were considered to have evolved their cultural distinctiveness in previous (and rural) epochs, making their migration and their participation in urban life basically a story of loss, isolation, and trauma (Park 1928; Thomas and Znaniecki 1918). Changes and shifts in social boundaries are explained only as a consequence of collective adaptation to a changing social environment and the opportunities available (or not) in the host country. The existence of significant symbolic boundaries between the groups was acknowledged but largely treated as a function of spatial social relations, social proximity, and the degree of access to common resources: In other words, the changes in social boundaries determined the shape of the symbolic ones.[3] Finally, another fateful and often overlooked feature of the ethnic hierarchy framework is its reliance on a purely intergroup framework, with no notion of a wider solidarity in which these interactions are embedded and regulated. This is particularly evident in the identification of assimilation with the adoption of the mainstream culture, defined simply as the culture of the dominant group.

To see the widespread and crosscutting effect of some of these ideas about ethnicity and race, I compare and contrast the ethnic hierarchy model with one developed in a different discipline, space, and decade. At face value, the model elaborated by Lévi-Strauss for structural anthropology appears radically different and grounded in a much stronger understanding of culture. At a closer look, however, he provides an inverted, but ultimately equally one-sided, understanding.

By his own account, Lévi-Strauss' two influential papers on race were openly designed—after Nazism and in the context of worldwide decolonization—to provide a strong understanding of cultural differences that could (and should) be sharply distinguished from any biological or civilizational understanding (Henaff 1998). Like Park, Lévi-Strauss writes interchangeably about races, ethnic groups, or cultures (as well as about strata or subcultures), taking for granted that what defines all these units is the existence of a specific, unified culture and lifestyle, marked by a symbolic boundary that separates insiders from outsiders (Lévi-Strauss 1952). Consistent with his general theoretical framework, he defines such "cultures" as peculiar combinations of a universalized set of symbolic distinctions, rooted in the very same functioning of the human mind. Cultural differences are seen as specific combinations of a finite number of universal elements that cannot be ranked qualitatively without adopting (by now, in bad faith) the particularistic criteria of any given culture. At the core of each group, there is a cultural structure that codifies the differences from other groups as a difference between "meaning" and (lesser or greater forms of) chaos. The survival of any distinctive group is made possible only by the existence of a symbolic boundary that marks the culture of each group—not only as different, but also as "somewhat impermeable" to the others (Lévi-Strauss 1985 [1983]). Such a scheme does not preclude (limited) interaction or circulation of information between different groups/cultures, assuming as it does that any effective social grouping, to function effectively, must consist of a "coalition" of cultures. But it assumes that such interactions do not create a shared space of interpretation—but only a reciprocal, mutual, selective distortion according to one another's core principles. Socially, the natural tendency of each group is to operate under conditions of closure, up to the point that special cultural interdictions "force" the establishment of a system of alliances and interchanges. At the same time, however, Lévi-Strauss makes clear that the maintenance of any distinctive cultural identity requires a sharp minimization of contact across boundaries. Alternatives to social closure along the lines established by symbolic boundaries produce, in his view, either the disorganization and collapse of one of the two groups or a new combination irreducible to the previous ones (Lévi-Strauss 1971). Unsurprisingly, Lévi-Strauss defines modernity precisely in terms of the spread of an all-encompassing civilization that produces monotony and uniformity.

Lévi-Strauss' work may appear—and is in many respects—radically different from that of the Chicago School. But for the purposes of this chapter, it is worth stressing some subtle but important commonalities. First, both define ethnicity and race in terms of actual groups, characterized by definitive commonalities among their members and equally sharp differences with outsiders. They take for granted that the study of cultural difference is the study of a plurality of discrete, clearly demarcated groups whose changes imply cultural threat and psychological stress. Second, both approaches assume that the "normal" case is one in which social and symbolic boundaries are homologous and that cultural distinctions encode, to a large degree, actual social distinctions. Finally, both see the relationships between categories and groups as largely dependent on a shared material environment characterized by differential access to economic and political resources. The possibility of their functioning as aspects of processes of inclusion, exclusion, and domination within a social system characterized by wider solidary categorizations is largely absent. Short of full assimilation into the dominant group, there is at most space for temporary truces and coalitional alliances.

As I elaborate in the following section, an important and innovative challenge to these classical perspectives has emerged in the last thirty years. A variety of research programs—coalescing around the notion of boundary work as a key concept for the study of these phenomena, as well as a more general concept for social science research—has radically transformed theorizing about "cultural" differences (see, e.g., Abbott 1995; Alba 2009; Bauböck 1998; Brubaker 2004; Lamont 2001; Lamont and Molnar 2002; Pachucki, Pendergrass, and Lamont 2007; Sanders 2002; Tilly 2004; Tilly 2005; Wimmer 2008a; Wimmer 2008b; Wimmer 2009). These research programs have successfully challenged the assumption that difference-based phenomena represent actual cultural differences, self-evident communities, and group-mediated interactions. They have also demonstrated the fruitfulness of more dynamic and contingent frameworks that take social identities as problematic outcomes rather than as empirical givens (Brubaker and Cooper 2000). And they have provided a consistent alternative to Marxism and utilitarianism, the only traditions within the social sciences that, historically, have consistently refused to reify ethnicity, race, and nationality as social actors (Becker 1957; Daynes and Lee 2008; Rex 1970). I will argue, however, that this body of work has overemphasized criticism of the first assumption outlined above (ethnicity as a matter of actual cultural differences among concrete groups), unfortunately allowing the other two crucial lacunae—the analytical independence of symbolic boundaries and existence of a wider system of solidary symbolism—to remain solidly intact.

2. FROM THINGS TO BOUNDARIES

The roots of contemporary research on ethnicity date back to 1969 with the publication of Fredrik Barth's introduction to a short edited volume. His twenty-nine pages are surely among the most influential in contemporary social science, with more than five thousand references in Google Scholar at the beginning of 2010. Barth developed an implicit, but systematic and sustained, criticism of all previous anthropological understandings of ethnicity, particularly of the Lévi-Straussian variety. He began by denying that the creation and maintenance of ethnicity requires isolation, stressing instead its relational nature, contingent upon frequent interchanges with members of other categories. Barth also flatly denied that ethnicity could, or should, be conceived in terms of stable patterns of shared cultural traits. The significance of ethnicity is not rooted in actual cultural differences, but rather in specific patterns of social interaction. He did not deny that, of course, ethnic categories are available and that actors are able to identify themselves and others in these terms and to describe the world according to them. Such distinctions, however, did not originate in the fact that actors had different cultural patterns—what he called derogatorily "the cultural stuff." The origins lie, rather, in processes of boundary-making and boundary-maintenance, which involve sets of differential expectations concerning who may interact with whom and in which ways. Barth claimed that it was this system of differential expectations—not the cultural traits that may or may not be used to identify members of each category—that represented the key dimension of ethnic phenomena. Boundaries are not a consequence of the existence of different groups; they are the means through which groups and categories are created and maintained. Actors may produce and maintain such boundaries irrespective of any cultural commonalities or differences noticed by external observers. And, Barth argued, this is not surprising, because social actors use cultural resources to build and sustain boundaries, not the other way around. This is why ethnic differences may persist regardless of mobility across categories, high cultural commonality across different ethnic groups, or, on the contrary, high cultural variance within a group. In short, Barth claimed, the meaning of difference-based interaction is homologous only to the degree to which social interaction and exchange can be aligned according to such distinctions.

Barth's criticism has been highly influential and has contributed to a radically new way of understanding difference-based interactions in terms of boundary work rather than in terms of collective actors. In his attempt to shift the attention to the *social* organization of cultural differences, Barth's disdain for the "cultural stuff" and his emphasis on a sharp, processual, and ecological understanding of ethnic differences may be easily understandable.[4] His choice has proven successful, inspiring a radically different view of ethnicity. But it has also been a fateful choice, overshadowing the crucial relationship between social and symbolic boundaries for decades.[5]

Subsequent research has amply documented the utility of the concept of social boundaries and the importance of going beyond any understanding of difference-based interaction in terms of taken-for-granted differences in behavioral traits and concrete cultural preferences. Barth's work triggered a vast and innovative wave of research, of increasing theoretical sophistication and empirical scope (Lamont and Molnar 2002; Pachucki, Pendergrass, and Lamont 2007; Wimmer 2008b). Precisely because a body of literature is so important and promising, however, the best way to contribute to it is to look for ways in which it can be critically revised, improved, and strengthened. From the perspective of cultural sociology, two issues appear particularly relevant: the nature of the social organization of boundary-making and the relationships between social and symbolic boundaries.

As for the nature of boundary-making activities, most research seems to have adopted an increasingly strategic view of both social and symbolic boundary-making.

Consistent with his previous and subsequent ethnographic experience, Barth's original model has mainly been applied to pluralist societies—with "adjacent and familiar others," involving "co-residents in encompassing social systems"—leading more often to "questions of how 'we' are distinct from 'them', rather than to a hegemonic and unilateral view of the 'other'" (Barth 1994:13). Correspondingly, the examples in such texts have provided an ample variety of interactions, only some of which were oriented by economic exploitation or power domination. For Barth, the processes of boundary-making are compatible with the strategic reproduction of structural inequalities, but the latter does not necessarily explain the former. He later stressed that not all categorization implied, or was used for, the formation of boundaries (Barth 2000). Particularly under the growing influence of Pierre Bourdieu (Bentley 1987; Lamont 2001), research on boundary work has increasingly interpreted this process as the strategic outcome of actions targeted at social closure, which explains all of its aspects accordingly. Indeed, the description of boundary-making as an activity that employs symbolic resources mobilized *in order to* establish a difference from other groups, to defend specific positions, and to devalue the meaning of the practices of outsiders, seems so evident to many authors that no argument is required to justify it. Charles Tilly (1998), for example, defines boundary-making flatly in terms of strategies of social closure, operated by networks and groups in order to marginalize other potential competitors and to hoard any set of opportunities they may succeed in controlling. In his model of boundary shifts, he demonstrates that structural processes may lead to changes in the configuration of symbolic boundaries, while the inverse case is hardly ever mentioned (Tilly 2004).

Michele Lamont (see, among others, Lamont 1992; Lamont 2000; Lamont and Molnar 2002) has pioneered a rich research program on boundary-making activities, showing how actors may draw on multiple symbolic repertoires to categorize and separate different segments of the social world. She has also highlighted how ethnic and racial boundaries may be actually maintained or challenged—not through "ethnic" repertoires, but rather by drawing on a variety of wider functional, moral, and religious discourses. While her description of these actors is sophisticated and nuanced—and she is very careful in stressing the ambiguities of their boundary work—the synthetic framework employed to interpret them is basically restricted to a vision of actors pursuing a strategy of status group closure and resource monopolization (Lamont and Fournier 1992).

Something similar is evident in the work of Andreas Wimmer. In his empirical research on Swiss neighborhoods, Wimmer (2004) has shown that significant cleavages did not necessarily follow a prescribed or official ethnic lexicon, but embodied a variety of criteria, including differences in lifestyle and normative codes adopted to draw (cross-ethnically) a boundary around "decent"—as distinguished (again, cross-ethnically) from "indecent"—neighbors. In his path-breaking reformulation of boundary analysis in migration and ethnic studies, Wimmer (2008a) offers a sophisticated argument about the variety of ways in which actors draw symbolic boundaries, insisting that they cannot be derived automatically from the actual contents of social and cultural differences. He has also noted how strategies of boundary-making activities require the availability of convincing discourses, capable of redefining the meanings of ascriptive categories and that, in their absence, actors may resist and refuse boundary-making activities that would improve their social status (Wimmer, 2008a:1038). In his more programmatic work, however, such elements are marginalized in favor of a view of boundary-making as a strategic action heavily shaped by social structures alone (Wimmer 2008b). For example, in his framework for studying the outcomes of immigrant incorporation, the relevant elements of boundary change are institutional rules, power distribution, and networks of political alliances. The nature of the symbolic boundaries and the discourses supporting them receive little attention (Wimmer 2009). The ways in which boundaries are codified and cultural diacritica are selected are consequently seen as a strategic elaboration, oriented to extra-symbolic means.

Contemporary research on social boundaries has also further radicalized Barth in terms of the relationship between symbolic and social boundaries. With all his skepticism of culture, Barth's model could have easily contained a sharp, *analytical* differentiation of social and cultural boundaries, and an elaboration of their roles in establishing categories and groups. For instance, Barth himself argued that the ways members of an ethnic category employ a shared cultural standard in evaluating the action of co-members could have specific, but various, boundary-constructing properties. Later, Barth (2000) also argued that studying when and how a distinction is converted into a boundary requires attention to cognitive processes in their social context. Sociological boundary research, however, has hardly exploited such possibilities, leaving the study of symbolic boundaries largely under-theorized. They have been treated either as elements of a preexisting repertoire of categorical distinctions or as the outcome of a struggle over the categorical divisions of society. In the first case, symbolism becomes relevant only when useful in ratifying a social distinction (Lamont 2000). In the second, the conflict over meaning is considered homologous to—and largely dependent on—the ones that take place within the social field (Bourdieu 1991; Wacquant 1997).

In the first case, the point is not the acknowledgment of a rich and sophisticated repertoire of cultural scripts and moral narratives per se. For example, Lamont has convincingly shown the existence of a plurality of symbolic motifs—cultural, moral, and religious—that members of different categories use to establish both general notions of personal worth as well as specific interpretations of racial boundaries (Lamont 1999; Lamont 2000; Lamont and Fleming 2005; Lamont, Morning, and Mooney 2002). The structure of these motifs, however, and the ways in which they relate to deeper semiotic structures are never explored in depth. It is enough that such repertoires are available as repertoires—enough for the sociologist to focus on the social, as opposed to cultural, conditions that increase the likelihood of their use by specific categories of actors. In Lamont's catchy phrase, the symbolic is a "necessary but insufficient" condition for the establishment of a social boundary (Lamont 1992; Lamont and Fournier 1992; Lamont and Molnar 2002). The other direction, namely, that social boundaries—as differential patterns of association, connubiality, and commensality—are a necessary but insufficient condition for the establishment of a symbolic boundary, is not really stressed in her work.[6] A similar position is taken by Charles Tilly (1998; 2004), in his work on international migration. Although Tilly moves from a framework admittedly inspired by the CAT-NET model, where categories and networks are analytically independent, for Tilly, boundary-making is not simply any operation that aligns a specific network with a specific category to create a group. It is rather a network that draws a boundary, using the appropriate categorical distinction, in order to hoard certain sources of opportunities and to exclude others (Tilly 1998; 2005).

A second way of conceiving the relationship between symbolic and social boundaries, inspired largely by Pierre Bourdieu, is to posit a fundamental homology between the two dimensions. In this approach, social and symbolic boundaries are not only highly interrelated, but also follow the same logic of instrumental conflict: The creation of symbolic boundaries is a performative action that, using the language of revelation and construction, produces what it claims to have found in reality (Bourdieu 1991). Such a perspective could foster a rich cultural analysis, by focusing on the basic semiotic structures required to perform such claims and to be validated by an audience (see Section 3 below). In Bourdieu's (1992) framework, however, such analysis is largely unnecessary: Both the drives behind boundary-making as well as its eventual success are basically explained in terms of an instrumental power struggle. Conflict about legitimate ways of dividing the social world reflects an essentially homologous distribution of social power. From this stance, it is not surprising that in many such research programs, the significant symbolic boundaries are the ones that overlap with, and are functional to, specific social configurations.[7] The "interesting case" is the one in which symbolic and behavioral boundaries largely coincide, and the categorical differentiation made possible by the former is used to justify specific distancing acts. As Wimmer writes, it is possible to speak of a social boundary only when "the two schemes coincide, when ways of seeing the world correspond to ways of acting in the world" (2008b:975). The theoretical consequences of the discrepancies between the two become a residual category.

The use of a strong notion of boundary-making as a strategic activity, linked to a weak notion of the symbolic dimension of the same boundaries, is a widespread but analytically unnecessary aspect of contemporary research on this topic. It produces consequences that are, in much of the literature, highly undesirable. In particular, Bourdieu's emphasis on the social as a generalized and dematerialized political economy reduces dramatically the capacity to pay the autonomy of meaning its due. Although many researchers working in the social boundary tradition love to trace their origins to a Weberian definition of ethnicity and social closure, these conceptual constraints end up placing them in the footsteps of Pareto—more interested in symbols as resources for short-term, *post facto* rationalizations, than as a genuine concern for meaning. Further, such an analytically limited lens distracts researchers from the many interesting things that happen when symbolic categories and social clusters do *not* coincide. Boundary-making is a process supported by interactions configuring uneven and motley networks and asymmetric power relations. But it is also a cultural activity linked to a vision of the world, triggered and regulated by overarching semiotic structures that classify events and possibilities in structured patterns of codes and narratives. And it is here that a more systematic debate with cultural sociology may result in a better understanding of these phenomena.

3. The Stuff from Which Symbolic Boundaries Are Made

A more satisfactory theory of difference-based interactions requires taking symbolic boundaries and their construction as seriously as scholars currently consider social boundaries. The construction of symbolic boundaries is actually as "social" (and as complex) as building political alliances and mobilizing economic resources.

Stressing the importance of symbolic boundaries and their analytical autonomy does not imply going back to a vision of boundaries as reflective of actual empirical differences. Nor is it a return to the vision of boundaries only as a matter of subjective attribution. To claim that symbolic boundary-making is rooted in deeper cultural structures actually strengthens the view that social categories, social groups, identities, and subcultures do not exist in isolation. Their actual meaning is given by their position in the structural and symbolic orders that regulate social life. Such categories are a consequence of the specific form of the social and moral order in its historical developments, not its elementary, preexisting constituents.

In order to highlight the analytical independence of distinctions and the narration that may be employed to draw symbolic boundaries—and to highlight that boundary-making activities are not only socially, but also semantically constrained—it is important to stress that while national, ethnic, and racial semantic traditions are highly complex, redundant, and ambiguous, they are never completely malleable. A constructionist stance is hardly an "anything goes" attitude. Rather, distinctions are collective representations, linked not only to experiences and institutional rules but also to wider symbolic systems (Daynes and Lee 2008; Hanrahan 2005; Prager 1987). They are modes of perceiving, conceiving, and thinking in a Durkheimian sense.[8] In fact, the use of categorical distinctions, and the moral and symbolic orders generated through them, always involve both enabling and constraining functions. They are resources that account for actions, make sense of interactional anomalies, and invoke membership status or deny it. But they are also symbolic constraints, which induce potential structures of expectation, determine the appropriate rhetorical tropes, select the stage props used in the presentation of the self, and influence which kinds of membership claims will be heard by an audience and which will be ignored. As categories, they are patterned, and the adoption of a specific categorization always implies the potential activation of a complex set of binary oppositions. Any marking of an outside produces an inside; any commonality produces a difference (Luhmann 2002). Once a distinction—*us/them* or

$them_1/them_2$—is introduced, it may survive only through locating itself within a system of other distinctions (both ethnic and nonethnic), establishing relationships of opposition or complementarity with the other distinctions, both ascribed and achieved. The drawing of such distinctions is only a starting point, however, which would hardly be relevant for any social purpose if not linked to other distinctions through analogies and metaphors. Differences must be located in time and space. They must align semantically with other distinctions in a way that presents the latter as an implication of the former. They must generate enough rhetorical tropes to account for discrepancies and inconsistencies. They must generate interactional meanings that link such distinctions to interactionally observable traits. Difference does not operate alone, but only through narration. Narrations, not the distinctions themselves, establish meaningful links between cultural and social norms, and between normative and cognitive expectations.[9] Such narrations must not only be "realistic" but also pleasurable descriptions of reality as a morally and aesthetically ordered world (Daynes and Lee 2008; Friedland 2005). They must appear as "good to think with." Once established, such categorizations do not represent a self-evident foundation for some genre of action or claim, but rather a semantic resource, able to generate a never-ending set of understandings and claims.

Ethnicity, race, nationality, and foreignness manifest as forms of the rich family of semantic constructions dealing with social membership. What these sets of distinctions have in common is the existence of a diachronically operating genealogical dimension, implying the attribution of meaning to ancestral origin and descent. Not surprisingly, the codes that orient the distinctions of these genealogical dimensions are usually embedded in forms of narration regulated by some form of kinship or family metaphors (Roosens 1994). This explains the problematic significance of these discourses for defining the modern polity, as well as their contiguity to religious discourses on the constitution of society as such (Friedland 2001). While the fit between these semantic relationships may be historically highly interlocked— as when a specific racial phenotype is ascribed with the personal and cultural preconditions for civic participation or for serious sociability—it is important to remember that such distinctions are arbitrary in relation to the signifieds they evoke. As LaPiere's (1935) wonderfully ingenious research design showed long ago, the very same restaurant and hotel managers that declared in good faith they would never accept an "Oriental" in their business may, when faced with individuals rather than categories, behave exactly in the opposite way. This helps explain why face-to-face contact per se changes collective categorizations only in Hollywood movies.

Thus, Brubaker (2004) is more than right to argue that the oft-cited distinction between "civic" and "ethnic" nationalisms amounts to mistaking a category of practice, employed by actors in the social world, for a category of analysis. And it is also right to argue that the distinction between ethnicity and race obfuscates much more than it clarifies (Brubaker 2009; Loveman 1999). Acknowledging how pervasive such distinctions as categories of practices are, however, makes it clear that both civic/ethnic and race/ethnicity are powerful binary codes, able to structure and sustain wide-ranging narratives that support and make a variety of social and political actions meaningful. Studies of nationalist campaigns show how the distinction between ethnic and civic is not a description of concrete political projects, but rather a way to locate claims in reference to an established and deeply emotional symbolic template, which determines who is to be polluted as "ethnic" and who is bound to be purified as "civic" (Sciortino 1999). In the same way, the distinction between ethnicity and race is a poor descriptor of social reality, but it is a powerful set of polarized distinctions able to distinguish between legitimate (i.e., compatible with the modern cult of the individual) and illegitimate forms of difference-related attribution. Both in scholarly debates and in common parlance, race is involuntary, external, based on physical differences, rigid, hierarchical, and exclusionary; whereas ethnicity is voluntary, rooted in self-identification, based on diverse cultural preferences, flexible, horizontal, and the result of a process of inclusion. As categories of analysis, they are weak and misleading. As semiotic distinctions, they are remarkably stable signifiers, applied variously to a shifting set of signifieds.

They are templates for signification and invention, which explains the ease with which they can travel across contexts and adapt to a variety of conditions. At the same time, it implies that their application is a practical accomplishment, attained through performative action. Codes are stable, but their relationships with the signified are not.[10]

This strong notion of the symbolic is fully compatible with contemporary theories of ethnicity and, more generally, boundary-making, and, in my view, only enhances opportunities for further discovery. It requires moving beyond the assumption of culture as a repertoire (or a "toolkit")—with the inevitable implication of instrumentality and malleability—to see it analytically as a specific kind of structure, enabling and constraining, and regulated by specific semiotic mechanisms. If such symbolic structures are redundant toolboxes, this does not imply that they do not have some precise normative layout, with consequences for which tools will be more easily found and by whom.

In this context, the existence of a collective representation that defines the social world according to a set of discrete ascriptive categories—and attributes to membership in them a varying set of meaningful qualities—is, as such, largely independent from individual values and location. It is to take into account both anticipation of other peoples' actions and other peoples' reactions to such actions. As with all other collective representations, difference-based categorizations are largely independent from individual belief and social interaction. They can be, as indeed they often are, established, revised, and reproduced as typifying characters in mass-media narratives, defined by the specific roles they play in the development of a story—in a way, wholly independent from personal experience. The features that Anderson (1983) has identified as part of modern nationalism apply to the very nature of any modern difference-based configuration. Even taking the comparatively rare case of a difference-based "group" with a high level of self-identification and deeply entrenched subculture—or even a reasonably effective organizational infrastructure—those who claim rightful membership in the category do so as members of an imagined community rather than on the basis of actual membership in personal networks. The group is sustained by deeply symbolic encoded mental images of affinity and difference that obscure much more than they highlight. And, exactly as with Anderson's nationalism, all these collective representations are linked to utopian elements of deep horizontal comradeship, at least as much as to the desire to exclude others. These imagined communities, moreover, may expand and proliferate in the absence of direct intercategorical contacts (Anderson 1998).

The ways in which symbolic boundaries are drawn, the "style" in Anderson's terms (1983), are thus full of consequences for the ways in which the mundane activities of boundary-making occur and for the appeal they will have on their potential constituencies both inside and outside the membership the boundary is meant to cluster. There are many ways in which imagined communities may be historically imagined, and the manner of boundary work produces specific imaginaries, specific solidarities and specific enemies, specific dangers and specific promises of salvation. The assumption that a certain configuration of power and resources, as well as historical legacies, heavily constrains the kind of community that can be imagined is surely correct. But, as a generation of Marxists learned with their failures, the ways in which categorical distinctions define whose interests are to be taken into account as similar and whose positions must be considered as standing in a solidary relationship with one's own, are no less binding in social life.

4. Discourse of Differences in Their Contexts

A main limitation of the classical scholarship on ethnicity, migration, and race has been its overreliance on groups and group contact. It also implies an ecological, rather than systemic, vision of society. And subsequent research, though breaking radically with the assumption of taken-for-granted "groupness," seems to have maintained the assumption that whatever shared symbolic membership can be found or assumed is (at best) the culture of the dominant group.[11] A reductionist view of the cultural dimension, moreover, has contributed to seeing symbolic and social boundaries— thanks to the use of the former to create social closure—as largely homologous.

To grant analytical autonomy to symbolic boundaries reveals how, in complex societies, collective representations are rarely homologous with social structures. Bourdieu's current popularity within sociology has driven a significant stream of current research toward a remote past—a pre-Axial age where social stratifications and legitimization orders are not yet differentiated (Bellah 1964; Weber 1946). In complex societies, social and symbolic boundaries hardly ever coincide (Alexander 2007). Boundary-making processes are dynamic precisely because actors may pursue claims to social inclusion grounded in previous membership in symbolic categories, as well generate explanations of the actions of those members that pollute them and make them worthy of symbolic exclusion. Rather than reflecting *sic et simpliciter* the balance of powers among members of various categories, the dynamism of boundary-making is oriented to, and acting upon, the gaps and discrepancies between social and symbolic orders.

The sophisticated typology of boundary-making activities elaborated by Wimmer (2008a) defines precisely the range of possible actions that may be taken by actors to make sense of these discrepancies as well as to align one with the other. Their success depends upon the strength of their coalitions and their available resources. It also depends on the quality of the narrative they invoke and its capacity to mobilize members of the category for which they speak. But it also requires the ability to persuade significant sectors of the external audience not only of the practical necessity, but also of the moral worth of the proposed new boundary. To do so, the degree of generalization available in the symbolic environment is no less important than other structural factors in determining the success or failure of claims for inclusion or exclusion (Alexander 2006; Parsons 1965, 1966). And the forms of the master narratives available in each context are likely to be significant for how meaning may be created and narrated (Arnason 2010).

There are, of course, cases where social patterns and categorical distinctions are highly conflated. Such substantial homologies may have a strong reinforcing effect, contributing to naturalizing such differences. Moreover, such associations may be so strong that even the excluded participate in respecting them and policing the boundaries. Even in these cases, however, the gaps and discrepancies between social and symbolic orders matter. In complex societies, each categorical membership is a membership among others, and there are often larger symbolic categories that include both sides of each boundary. Barth's fateful decision to omit Leach's emphasis on the importance of a shared ritual space has marginalized the observation that even dominant categories incorporate symbolic elements that cannot be appropriated in full. In their empirical analyses, of course, social boundary theorists acknowledge the existence of a rich set of universalizing religions, large-scale political ideologies, and political orders based on highly abstract definitions of membership. But they do not really integrate this realization into their analytic frameworks, relegating it either as ideological decoy or as a set of symbolic resources appropriated by downtrodden groups in their search for dignity and inclusion. Categories and groups are consequently seen as using such elements ideologically, but in Marx's rather than in Geertz's sense.

The problem here is that the existence of widespread ramifications from the symbolic categorization of membership in terms of descent—especially differential access to resources—is only one piece of the puzzle. For modern societies, ascriptive differences have a specific meaning, provided by the symbolic relations such categories have with distinctly modern, post-traditional frames. It is simply not possible to adequately analyze difference-based interactions in modern societies without taking into account, among other elements:

(1) The lack of a taken-for-granted, institutionally explicit, and consistently sanctioned hierarchy of ethnic, cultural, and religious groups
(2) The existence of institutionally embedded individual rights

(3) The weakening of systematic regulation of individual lives according to inherited status

(4) The political legitimacy of rulers in terms of representing the citizenry

(5) The existence of a set of horizontal ties among abstractly defined citizens whose existence and functioning is not regulated by tradition but rather by personal choice (and often, sheer chance)

(6) The existence of significant processes of resource and identity acquisition managed through achievement-regulated social processes

All these elements are rooted in a definition of a highly abstract membership that transcends a large number of, though by no means all, categorizations based on origins and descent. For explicitly structural reasons, modern societies are intrinsically pluralistic (Parsons 1975; 2007). These universalistic elements are inadequately institutionalized, unevenly practiced, and often challenged. Many of its interpretations are ideologically self-serving and empirically inaccurate. They are surely far away from the prescription of liberal political theory and cosmically remote from the wholly asocial requirements set, precisely in order to condemn them, by critical theory. As in any abstract order, they are often embedded in a long series of particularistic self-understandings rooted in the history of the dominant carrier groups (Alexander 1990). As with any generalized symbolic code, their definition of membership implies inclusions as well as exclusions (Alexander 2006). But they are definitely different from the mere accumulation of symbolic power geared toward the conflict between elites over the dominant principle of domination (Bourdieu 1996). Nor do they embody the "culture" of the "dominant group." Rather, they represent a symbolic center, one among several, with its own wide-ranging periphery (Shils 1974). In a differentiated society, even the most powerful elites may claim, with varying degrees of success, closeness or contiguity to such a center, but not complete alignment or ownership of it. The gap between social and symbolic boundaries, as well as the necessity to relate one's identity discourses to such a universalistic order, is consequently a matter of degree—not of presence or absence.

5. CONCLUSION

Ethnicity, race, nationality, and foreignness are important social phenomena in contemporary societies. As I have underscored in this chapter, in recent decades, social scientific research has produced in these fields some of its most innovative and challenging research programs that have deeply changed the ways in which scholars understand and study such phenomena. They have effectively challenged any simplistic vision of these phenomena in terms of bounded groups defined by "natural" cultural differences. They have highlighted the importance of studying them through conceptual frameworks that do not assume beforehand the analytical distinctiveness of these phenomena. They have provided a new and more adequate perspective—centered on the notion of boundary-making and on the distinction between "categories" and "groups"—to study them. When compared with the classical, mainstream perspective—here summarized briefly with reference to the Chicago School and to structural anthropology—the conceptual and empirical advantages of these developments are tremendous. In these pages, I have argued that further positive developments will emerge through a more sustained critical collaboration between scholars in these fields and cultural sociologists. The debates I have presented bring to light the importance of taking symbolic boundaries seriously and, rather than analyzing descent-based symbolic classifications as mere ideological decoys, treating them as meaningful semiotic operations embedded in narratives that both enable and constrain social actors. Finally, the type of productive dialogue I suggest also helps researchers and theorists pay adequate attention to the modern democratic symbolic order and the role it plays in defining difference-based categorization and interaction.

NOTES

1. For obvious reasons of space, as well as a wish to stress the commonalities between the *problemstellung* of the fields of "race," "ethnicity," "migration," and "nationality," I will use "difference" as a synthetic label. This is, however, a mere signifier. It does not imply the empirical existence of a distinct realm of interaction or an empirical differentiation between difference-based and interest-based interactions.

2. For example, the cultural dimension of social solidarity has been explored in the context of transitions to democracy (Edles 1998), the inclusionary and exclusionary tendencies embedded in the coding of the civil sphere (Alexander 1990; 2006), the study of collective identities (Smith 2010), the processes through which a variety of processes of spatial mobility are coded as part of a single new phenomenon of immigration (Sciortino and Colombo 2004), the analysis of political events in the context of widespread alarm over the consequences of migration (Eyerman 2008), the use of different narratives by ethnically defined news media in accounting for racial crisis (Jacobs 2000), the study of legal and moral boundaries in a new immigrant destination (Jaworsky 2010), or the sociological interpretation of multicultural claims (Sciortino 2003).

3. Subsequent attempts by Herbert Blumer (1958) to add to the model a more culturally open process of reciprocal "collective definition," based on interpretation and imagination, were ultimately unsuccessful—highlighting the existence of a problem without dealing with it effectively (see also Lal 1983).

4. However, this was not a necessary consequence. The same argument could be, and actually had already been, formulated in a way that does not reduce boundary-making activities to merely a set of interethnic relations. For instance, a few years prior, Edmund Leach (1954) argued that cultures and social structures did not coincide and that ethnic formations in highland Burma were actually flexible, dynamic, and relational. He also stressed that many ethnic boundaries crisscrossed cultural differences, rather than aligning with them. Like Barth, he also argued that such elements were embedded in a system of

social relationships, where such identities could be both established and modified. At the same time, however, Leach highlighted the importance—for the very functioning of such social systems—of a shared grammar of ritual action, a shared symbolic language articulating categories and making room for performing them. In short, this relational view of difference-based phenomena and an emphasis on social boundary-making is actually more than compatible with a thick understanding of culture as distinct from catalogues of discrete concrete traits.

5. As often happens, Barth's initial choice has been further radicalized. His initial framework has even been criticized for not being processual enough (Sacchi 1990; Vermeulen and Govers 1994) and many of his successive reflections on the issue have failed to receive adequate scholarly attention (Barth 1994; 2000).

6. It is indicative of this stance that in her reviews of the literature, Lamont sometimes operationalizes the distinction between symbolic and social boundaries empirically rather than analytically, using the "symbolic" mostly for those identities more independent from face-to-face contacts and/or location in the socioeconomic stratification (Lamont and Molnar 2002:182). In the same vein, Mary Waters (1990) defines as "symbolic" those expressions of ethnic identities largely devoid of strategic consequences for social stratification.

7. There are however some important exceptions. Todd (2005) offers an interesting attempt to revise Bourdieu's framework, making it able to account for the autonomy of the categorical order in social transformation and not only reproduction. Bail (2008), in his analysis of symbolic boundaries against immigrants in Europe, argues that the materials employed to trace such boundaries have consequences on the integration processes.

8. Among the scholars working on ethnicity issues, Rogers Brubaker and his associates have argued—and studied in empirical settings—the cognitive dimension of ethnicity and nationalism as embodied and expressed in "everyday encounters, practical categories, commonsense knowledge, cultural idioms, cognitive schemas, mental maps, interactional cues, discursive frames, organizational routines, social networks and institutional forms" (2007:7). Their superb study has come remarkably close to the Durkheimian notion of collective representation, distinguishing sharply between "everyday ethnicity" and nationalist or ethnic political strategies, as well as portraying the former as a way of seeing, of talking, and of acting (Ibid:207). With regard to their view of ethnicity as a form of cognition (Brubaker, Loveman, and Stamatov 2004), I would add that differences and categories should be seen also as having normative and emotional dimensions.

9. The failure of many theorists to distinguish between cultural and social norms and between normative and cognitive expectations is crucial to Mark Gould's (1997; 1999) critique of the current scholarship on inner-city blacks in the United States. Moreover, Gould's criticism is highly consistent with some of the best ethnographic evidence available on the topic (Anderson 1976; 1999).

10. In his polemic with Roger Bastide, Talcott Parsons was the first to argue that no matter how stigmatizing skin color could be as a symbol of indignity and how entrenched the semantic complementarity with key forms of Protestant religious symbolism, the introduction of a more generalized definition of membership would have radically and rapidly altered the structure of such semantic complexes (see Bastide 1968; Parsons 1968). On Parsons and racial and ethnic differences, see Sciortino (2005).

11. The popularity of multicultural political philosophy, with its emphasis on societal cultures and group-differentiated rights, is only the most evident example of this conflation of "majority culture" and "shared culture" (Joppke 2001; Laden and Owen 2007).

REFERENCES

Abbott, Andrew. 1995. "Things of Boundaries." *Social Research* 62:857–882.

Alba, Richard. 2009. "Bright vs. Blurred Boundaries: Second Generation Assimilation and Exclusion in France, Germany and the United States." *Ethnic and Racial Studies* 28:20–49.

Alexander, Jeffrey C. 1990. "Core Solidarity, Ethnic Outgroups and Structural Differentiation: Toward a Multidimensional Model of Inclusion in Modern Societies." Pp. 267–293 in *Differentiation Theory and Social Change*. Los Angeles: Sage.

———. 2006. *The Civil Sphere*. Oxford: Oxford University Press.

———. 2007. "The Meaningful Construction of Inequality and the Struggles Against It: A 'Strong Program' Approach to How Social Boundaries Change." *Cultural Sociology* 1:23.

Anderson, Benedict. 1983. *Imagined Communities: Reflections on the Origins and Spread of Nationalism*. London: Verso.

———. 1998. *The Spectre of Comparisons: Nationalism, South-East Asia and the World*. London: Verso.

Anderson, Elijah. 1976. *A Place on the Corner*. Chicago: University of Chicago Press.

———. 1999. *Code of the Street: Decency, Violence and the Moral Life of the Inner City*. New York: Norton.

Arnason, Johann P. 2010. "The Cultural Turn and the Civilizational Approach." *European Journal of Social Theory* 13:67–82.

Bail, Christopher A. 2008. "The Configuration of Symbolic Boundaries against Immigrants in Europe." *American Sociological Review* 73:37–59.

Barth, Fredrik. 1969. "Introduction." Pp. 9–38 in *Ethnic Groups and Boundaries: The Social Organization of Culture Difference*, edited by Fredrik Barth. Oslo, Norway: Universitetsforlaget.

———. 1994. "Enduring and Emerging Issues in the Analysis of Ethnicity." Pp. 11–32 in *The Anthropology of Ethnicity: Beyond 'Ethnic Group and Boundaries*,' edited by Hans Vermeulen and Cora Govers. Amsterdam: Het Spinhuis.

———. 2000. "Boundaries and Connection." Pp. 17–36 in *Signifying Identities*, edited by Anthony P. Cohen. London: Routledge.

Bastide, Roger. 1968. "Color, Racism and Christianity." Pp. 34–49 in *Color and Race*, edited by John H. Franklin. Boston: Houghton Mifflin.

Bauböck, Rainer. 1998. "The Crossing and Blurring of Boundaries in International Migration." Pp. 17–52 in *Blurred Boundaries: Migration, Ethnicity, Citizenship*. Aldershot, UK: Ashgate.

Becker, Gary 1957. *The Economics of Discrimination*. Chicago: Chicago University Press.

Bellah, Robert N. 1964. "Religious Evolution." *American Sociological Review* 29:358–374.

Bentley, G. 1987. "Ethnicity and Practice." *Comparative Studies in Society and History* 29:24–55.

Blumer, Herbert. 1958. "Race Prejudice as a Sense of Group Position." *Pacific Sociological Review* 1:3–7.

Bourdieu, Pierre. 1991. *Language and Symbolic Power*. Cambridge, MA: Harvard University Press.

———. 1996. *The State Nobility*. Stanford, CA: Stanford University Press.

Bourdieu, Pierre, and Loïc J. D. Wacquant. 1992. *An Invitation to Reflexive Sociology*. Chicago: University of Chicago Press.

Brubaker, Rogers. 2002. "Ethnicity Without Groups." *Archives Europeenes de Sociologie* XLIII:163–189.

———. 2004. *Ethnicity without Groups*. Cambridge, MA: Harvard University Press.

———. 2009. "Ethnicity, Race and Nationalism." *Annual Review of Sociology* 35:21–42.

Brubaker, Rogers, and Frederick Cooper. 2000. "Beyond 'Identity.'" *Theory and Society* 29:1–47.

Brubaker, Rogers, Mara Loveman, and Peter Stamatov. 2004. "Ethnicity as Cognition." *Theory and Society* 33:31–64.

Brubaker, Rogers, Margit Feinschmidt, John Fox, and Liana Grancea. 2007. *Nationalist Politics and Everyday Ethnicity in a Transylvanian Town*. Princeton, NJ: Princeton University Press.

Daynes, Sarah, and Orville Lee. 2008. *Desire for Race*. Cambridge, UK: Cambridge University Press.

Edles, Laura D. 1998. *Symbol and Ritual in the New Spain*. Cambridge, UK: Cambridge University Press.

Eyerman, Ron. 2008. *The Assassination of Theo Van Gogh: From Social Drama to Cultural Trauma*. Durham, NC: Duke University Press.

Friedland, Roger. 2001. "Religious Nationalism and the Problem of Collective Representation." *Annual Review of Sociology* 27:125–152.

———. 2005. "Drag Kings at the Totem Ball: The Erotics of Collective Representation in Emile Durkheim and Sigmund Freud." In *The Cambridge Companion to Durkheim*, edited by Jeffrey C. Alexander and Philip Smith. Cambridge, UK: Cambridge University Press.

Gould, Mark. 1997. "Race and Politics: Normative Orders and the Explanation of Political Differences: The Simpson Verdict, the Million Man March and Colin Powell." *Social Identities* 3:33–46.

———. 1999. "Race and Theory: Culture, Poverty, and Adaptation to Discrimination in Wilson and Ogbu." *Sociological Theory* 17:171–200.

Hanrahan, Nancy W. 2005. "Difference and Cultural Systems: Dissonance in Three Parts." Pp. 48–62 in *The Blackwell Companion to the Sociology of Culture*, edited by Mark D. Jacobs and Nancy W. Hanrahan. London: Blackwell.

Henaff, Marcel. 1998. *Claude Levi-Strauss and the Making of Structural Anthropology*. Minneapolis: University of Minnesota Press.

Huntington, Samuel. 2004. *Who Are We? The Challenges to America's National Identity*. New York: Simon & Schuster.

Jacobs, Ronald N. 2000. *Race, Media and the Crisis of Civil Society: From Watts to Rodney King*. Cambridge, UK: Cambridge University Press.

Jaworsky, B. Nadya. 2010. "Immigrants, Aliens, and Americans: Mapping Out the Boundaries of Belonging in a New Immigrant Gateway." Working paper. New Haven, CT: Center for Cultural Sociology at Yale University.

Joppke, Christian. 2001. "Multicultural Citizenship: A Critique." *Archives Européennes de Sociologie* 42:431–447.

Kivisto, Peter. 2004. "What Is the Canonical Theory of Assimilation? Robert E. Park and His Predecessors." *Journal of History of the Behavioral Sciences* 40:149–163.

Laden, Anthony S., and David Owen eds. 2007. *Multiculturalism and Political Theory*. Cambridge, UK: Cambridge University Press.

Lal, Barbara Ballis. 1983. "Perspectives on Ethnicity: Old Wine in New Bottles." *Ethnic and Racial Studies* 6:154–173.

Lamont, Michèle. 1992. *Money, Morals, and Manners: The Culture of the French and American Upper-Middle Class*. Chicago: University of Chicago Press.

————, ed. 1999. *The Cultural Territories of Race: Black and White Boundaries*. New York: Russell Sage.

————. 2000. *The Dignity of Working Men: Morality and the Boundaries of Race, Class, and Immigration*. New York: Russell Sage Foundation.

————. 2001. "Symbolic Boundaries." Pp. 15341–15347 in *International Encyclopedia of the Social and Behavioral Sciences*, edited by Neil J. Smelser and Paul B. Baltes. London: Pergamon Press.

Lamont, Michèle, and Crystal Marie Fleming. 2005. "Everyday Antiracism. Competence and Religion in the Cultural Repertoire of the African American Elite." *Du Bois Review* 2:29–43.

Lamont, Michèle, and Marcel Fournier. 1992. *Cultivating Differences: Symbolic Boundaries and the Making of Inequality*. Chicago: University of Chicago Press.

Lamont, Michèle, and Virag Molnar. 2002. "The Study of Boundaries in the Social Sciences." *Annual Review of Sociology* 28:167–195.

Lamont, Michèle, Ann Morning, and Margarita Mooney. 2002. "North African Immigrants Respond to French Racism: Demonstrating Equivalence Through Universalism." *Ethnic and Racial Studies* 25:390–414.

LaPiere, Richard T. 1935. "Attitudes vs. Action." *Social Forces* 13:230–237.

Leach, Edmund R. 1954. *Political Systems of Highland Burma*. London: Berg.

Lévi-Strauss, Claude. 1952. "Race and History." Pp. 95–135 in *The Race Question in Modern Science*, edited by Leo Kuper. Paris: UNESCO.

————. 1971. "Race et Culture." *Revue internationale des sciences sociales* 33.

————. 1983. *Le Regard éloigné*. Paris: Plon.

Levitt, Peggy. 2005. "Building Bridges: What Migration Scholarship and Cultural Sociology Have to Say to Each Other." *Poetics* 33:49–62.

Loveman, Mara. 1999. "Is "Race" Essential?" *American Sociological Review* 64:891–898.

Luhmann, Niklas. 2002. *Theories of Distinction: Redescribing the Descriptions of Modernity*. Stanford, CA: Stanford University Press.

Merton, Robert K. 1987. "Three Fragments From a Sociologist's Notebooks: Establishing the Phenomenon, Specified Ignorance, and Strategic Research Materials." *Annual Review of Sociology* 13:1–28.

Pachucki, Mark A., Sabrina Pendergrass, and Michele Lamont. 2007. "Boundary Processes: Recent Theoretical Development and New Contributions." *Poetics* 35:331–351.

Park, Robert E. 1928. "Human Migration and the Marginal Man." *American Journal of Sociology* 33:881–893.

————. 1950. *Race and Culture*. Glencoe, IL: Free Press.

Parsons, Talcott. 1965. "Full Citizenship for the Negro American? A Sociological Problem." *Daedalus* 94:1009–1054.

————. 1966. "Why "Freedom Now," Not Yesterday?" Pp. xix–xxviii in *The Negro American*. Boston: Beacon Press.

————. 1968. "The Problem of Polarization on the Axis of Color." Pp. 349–372 in *Color and Race*. Boston: Houghton Mifflin.

————. 1975. "Some Theoretical Considerations on the Nature and Trends of Change of Ethnicity." Pp. 53–83 in *Ethnicity: Theory and Experience*, edited by Nathan Glazer and Daniel P. Moynihan. Cambridge, MA: Harvard University Press.

————. 2007. *American Society: A Theory of the Societal Community*. Boulder, CO: Paradigm.

Prager, Jeffrey. 1987. "American Political Culture and the Shifting Meaning of Race." *Ethnic and Racial Studies* 10:62–81.

Rex, John. 1970. *Race Relations and Sociological Theory*. London: Weidenfeld and Nicolson.

Rex, John, and David Mason, eds. 1986. *Theories of Race and Ethnic Relations*. Cambridge, UK: Cambridge University Press.

Roosens, Eugeen. 1994. "The Primordial Nature of Origins in Migrant Ethnicity." Pp. 81–104 in *The Anthropology of Ethnicity*, edited by Hans Vermeulen and Cora Govers. Amsterdam: Het Spinhouis.

Sacchi, Paola. 1990. "Fredrik Barth e l'analisi 'generativa' dei gruppi etnici." *Rassegna Italiana di Sociologia* XXXI:389–404.

Sanders, Jimy M. 2002. "Ethnic Boundaries and Identity in Plural Societies." *Annual Review of Sociology* 28:327–357.

Sciortino, Giuseppe. 1999. "'Just Before the Fall': The Northern League and the Cultural Construction of a Secessionist Claim." *International Sociology* 14:321–336.

———. 2003. "From Homogeneity to Difference? Comparing Multiculturalism as a Description and as a Field for Claim-Making." *Comparative Social Research* 22:263–285.

———. 2005. "How Different Can We Be? Parsons' Societal Community, Pluralism and the Multicultural Debate." Pp. 111–136 in *After Parsons*, edited by Renéè C. Fox, Victor M. Lidz, and Harold J. Bershady. New York: Russell Sage.

Sciortino, Giuseppe, and Asher Colombo. 2004. "The Flows and the Flood: The Public Discourse on Immigration in Italy, 1969–2001." *Journal of Modern Italian Studies* 9:94–113.

Shils, Edward. 1974. *Center and Periphery: Essays in Macrosociology*. Chicago: University of Chicago Press.

Smith, Philip. 2010. "Identities: Indigenous, National, Ethnic and Racial." Pp. 67–84 in *Sociology*, edited by R. van Krieken, et al. Sydney: Pearson.

Thomas, William Isaac, and Florian Znaniecki. 1918. *The Polish Peasant: Monograph of an Ethnic Group*. Chicago: University of Chicago Press.

Tilly, Charles. 1998. *Durable Inequality*. Berkeley: University of California Press.

———. 2004. "Social Boundary Mechanisms." *Philosophy of the Social Sciences* 34:211–236.

———. 2005. *Identities, Boundaries and Social Ties*. Boulder, CO: Paradigm.

Todd, Jennifer. 2005. "Social Transformation, Collective Categories, and Identity Change." *Theory and Society* 34:429–463.

Vermeulen, Hans, and Cora Govers, eds. 1994. *The Anthropology of Ethnicity: Beyond 'Ethnic Groups and Boundaries.'* Amsterdam: Het Spinhuis.

Wacquant, Loic. 1997. "For an Analytic of Racial Domination." *Political Power and Social Theory* 11:221–234.

Wade, Peter. 2002. *Race, Nature and Culture: An Anthropological Perspective*. London: Pluto.

Waters, Mary C. 1990. *Ethnic Options: Choosing Identities in America*. Berkeley: University of California Press.

Weber, Max. 1946. "Religious Rejections of the World and Their Directions." Pp. 323–362 in *From Max Weber: Essays in Sociology*, edited by H. H. Gerth and C. Wright Mills. New York: Oxford University Press.

———. 1978. *Economy and Society: An Outline of Interpretative Sociology*. Berkeley: University of California Press.

Wimmer, Andreas. 2004. "Does Ethnicity Matter? Everyday Group Formation in Three Swiss Immigrant Neighbourhoods." *Ethnic and Racial Studies* 27:1–36.

———. 2008a. "Elementary Strategies of Ethnic Boundary Making." *Ethnic and Racial Studies* 31:1025–1055.

————. 2008b. "The Making and Unmaking of Ethnic Boundaries: A Multilevel Process Theory." *American Journal of Sociology* 113:970–1022.

————. 2009. "Herder's Heritage and the Boundary-Making Approach: Studying Ethnicity in Immigrant Societies." *Sociological Theory* 27:244–270.

Wimmer, Wimmer, and Nina Glick Schiller. 2003. "Methodological Nationalism, the Social Sciences, and the Study of Migration: An Essay in Historical Epistemology." *International Migration Review* 37:576–610.

CHAPTER 15

BURNING SCHOOLS/ BUILDING BRIDGES: ETHNOGRAPHICAL TOUCHDOWNS IN THE CIVIL SPHERE

MATS TRONDMAN

Man, do you feel me, you have given me everything, but I am nothing.

—Mohammad, 17-year-old resident of the
Lockdale district, Malmö, Sweden

I find it of great importance to hold on to what the right thing is. We wanted to increase integration. Our local school wanted to contribute to new possibilities in this very segregated city in which we live our lives. This is something we believe in and must hold on to.

—Bengt, headmaster at the Old Harbor School,
Malmö, Sweden

We need a new concept of civil society as a civil *sphere*, a world of values and institutions that generates the capacity for social and democratic integration at the same time. Such a sphere relies on solidarity, on feelings for others whom we do not know but whom we respect out of principle, not experience, because of our putative commitment to common secular faith.

Multiculturalism frames a new kind of civil society.... It represents not the diminishing but the strengthening of the civil sphere, a sphere in which collective obligations and individual autonomy have always been precariously but fundamentally intertwined. Multiculturalism is a project of hope, not despair. It can be launched only amid widespread feelings of common humanity, of solidary sympathies....

—Jeffrey C. Alexander, professor in cultural
sociology, Yale University, New Haven, CT

Introduction

You have given me eyes to see.
What can I do for you?

—Bob Dylan

In *The New York Trilogy*, the novelist Paul Auster describes the "detective" as "one who looks, who listens, who moves through this morass of objects and events in search of the thought, the idea that will pull all these things together and make sense of them" (2006, p. 8). If the outcome of such a work is presented through a written account, "the writer" and "the detective," of course, "are interchangeable" (2006, p. 8). "The reader," Auster continues, "sees the world through the detective's eyes, experiencing the proliferation of its details as if for the first time" (2006, p. 8). I will conceive the ethnographer as the writing detective of cultural sociology. If the true marker of ethnography is "being there"[1]—to look, listen and move—I am in search of a cultural sociology that can pull ethnographical data together and make sense of them. Such a presupposition—that data can speak to us, even "surprise" us (Willis and Trondman, 2000, p. 12),[2] due to the theoretical attentiveness the ethnographer can bring to them—makes it possible for the reader to see that all possible aspects of encounters in everyday life "carry," as Auster puts it, "a meaning other than the simple fact of their existence" (2006, p. 8). Accordingly, "all scientific data are," as Jeffrey C. Alexander proclaims in *Theoretical Logic in Sociology*, "theoretically informed" (1982, p. 30).[3] "We can't get to the thing in itself, ever," Hustvedt writes in *The Sorrows of an American*, "but it doesn't mean there isn't a world out there" (2008, p. 130).

We cannot be but, again quoting Hustvedt, "all dependent on preordained representations" (2008, p. 130). Better, then, to know theoretically what will inform our ways of seeing the world we inhabit. If cultural sociology can give ethnography, in Bob Dylan's choice of words, "eyes to see," ethnography, in turn, must ask itself what it can do for cultural sociology. To determine the worthwhile quality of such "eyes to see" and to demonstrate what ethnography informed by such "eyes" can do for cultural sociology are the *aims* of this chapter.

I started out by giving voice to a young Arabian immigrant, a Swedish headmaster, and an American cultural sociologist. Muhammad, a Swede too, of course, told us that he had been given "everything," but feels he is "nothing." Living his life in the district of Lockdale—a segregated area in disrepute in postindustrial and multicultural Malmö, Sweden—he longs for recognition from the outside world. Bengt spoke devotedly about how he wants his local school in the Old Harbor—a junior high school located in one of the most privileged districts in Malmö—to "contribute" to "new possibilities" of social and multicultural "integration." He also stated the importance to "hold on to" what "we believe in." The image of the Old Harbor is to a very great extent the opposite of a district like Lockdale. In a too orderly version, the Old Harbor is considered middle-class, rich, educated, and, maybe, a haven for racists, who would do their best to avoid having immigrants as neighbors. Lockdale, in contrast, is thought of as an immigrant area, indicating dependency on social welfare, social disorder, educational failure, and, maybe, a place where people, some of them probably religious fundamentalists, do their best to escape integration into Swedish society. The voices of Muhammad and Bengt were followed by Alexander's statement on the civil sphere as "a world of values and institutions that generates capacity for social and democratic integration" (2006b, p. 4). I also exhibited with Alexander's understanding of multiculturalism—a mode of incorporation that "sits between integration and difference" (2006b, p. 4) and in which "collective obligations" and "individual autonomy" are "fundamentally intertwined" (2006b, p. 457). This is a multiculturalism in which Muhammad and Bengt at once can celebrate their right to be different—due to the way they have been shaped by their use of a concept from the political theorist Michael Walzer, "involuntary associations" (2004, p. 17)[4]—*and* share common ground with and belongingness to a "central civility" (Alexander, 2007, p. 29). In other words, as an ethnographer, I need "eyes to see" if people like Muhammed and Bengt *also* share, as Alexander puts it, "feelings of a common humanity, of solidary sympathies" (2006b, p. 457). Undoubtedly, which will be laid out, Muhammad and Bengt want to belong to a society in which individual autonomy, cultural belonging, and collective obligations are interdependent qualities of life as well as resources for societal and democratic development. They both thus share with Alexander the insight that "multiculturalism is a project of hope, not despair" (2006b, p. 457)—and they are not alone in having these beliefs.

A great majority of the Swedish population have positive experiences of encounters with immigrants. They believe immigrants should have the same social rights as citizens born in Sweden, and strongly support a multicultural society built on shared concerns for democratic values (Melia, and Palm, 2007, p. 3–5).[5] Accordingly, Muhammad's longing, Bengt's strife, and Alexander's civil sphere theory are where the majority of minds in favor of multicultural incorporation meet in search of social hope. They are all in their different walks of life—in Muhammad's heartfelt and streetwise commentary, in Bengt's institutional integration policy and practices, and in Alexander's academic theory—decisive contributors to a civil sphere that, as Alexander puts it, "relies on solidarity, on feelings for others whom we do not know but whom we respect out of principle, not experience, because of our putative commitment to secular faith" (2006, p. 4). It is with these "eyes to see"—where different minds and qualities meet due to what they also have in common that we need to look in order to know what ethnography can do for cultural sociology. The answer is that we need to seek out the possibilities of social integration and multicultural incorporation in the nitty-gritty of real life. Looking and listening, we need to move through its lived forms and record them. In lives such as Muhammad's and Bengt's, and in places such as Lockdale and the Old Harbor, we will find expressions of the civil centrality—the thought—we are in search of.

Trying to fulfill my aim by being informed through Alexander's understanding of the civil sphere and multicultural incorporation, I am in search of ethnographical answers to my *research question*: How is it and what can it look like when people in their everyday lives—despite unequal distribution of material, social, and symbolic resources—reconnect with strong commitments to values of solidarity and feelings for others whom they do not know in support of social integration and multicultural incorporation? In trying to answer this question, "cultural autonomy" becomes—as Alexander and Philip Smith claim in their strong program in cultural sociology—"the single most important quality" (2003, p. 13). Accordingly, I have to agree with the detective in Auster's *The New York Trilogy*: "In order to know, you must understand" (2006, p. 19).

No one, I think, can serve us better in this cause than the anthropologist Clifford Geertz. He took it as his task, in his own words, "to cut the idea of culture down in size" (1999, p. 8). This reframing of culture, or rather, cultural analysis, he writes, "boils down to one question: how to frame an analysis of meaning," that is, "the conceptual structures" humans "use to construe experience" (1999, p. 13). It means that the study of meaning, or people's cultures, involves "discovering who they think they are, what they think they are doing, and to what end they think they are doing it" (1999, p. 10). And to really learn from other people and cultures, it is "necessary to gain a working familiarity with the frames of meaning within which they enact their lives" (1999, p. 11). In my search for such symbolic structures of meaning—through which beliefs in social integration and multicultural incorporation can be enacted—I am very well aware that, as Alexander puts it, "the struggle for better placement inside the symbolic boundaries of civil society is constant, not episodic" (2007, p. 29). This is exactly why it is of such great importance to try to highlight those everyday life moments in which common themes of "civil centrality"—the things we need to share and celebrate in the name of solidarity and sympathy—come to life. To look, listen, and move in pursuit of lived answers to my research question is to make, what Alexander calls, "the invisible structuration of civil life" (2007, p. 29) visible. In a more specific way, it is also the fulfillment of my overall aim: to illuminate what ethnography can do for a cultural sociology that is deeply concerned with determining the democratic meaning and societal importance of the civil sphere. To do that, "we must," Alexander states, "make civil society into a major focus of empirical and theoretical thought and thus to everyday social life" (2006b, p. 551). Accordingly, "the normative stipulations of civil society"—yes, "we need to divide the scared from the profane if we are to pursue the good and protect ourselves from evil" (2006b, p. 4) not only concerns issues such as "politics" and "office": They also turn out to be "the language of the street," "the television," and "novels," and even "scandals" (2006b, p. 4).[6] The meaning of "the good" has, of course, an inevitably *normative ground*.

I am in full agreement with the political philosopher Leo Strauss when he states that most social scientific analysis involves "some thought of better and worse," and, hence, "implies thought of the good" (1988, p. 10). Normative thinking on what it is that constitutes "the good" is thus a value statement concerning how things ought to be. And such "values," Strauss argues, concern both "things preferred" and "principles of preference" (1988, p. 21).[7]

In *The Civil Sphere*, a landmark publication in cultural sociology, Alexander provides us with a distinctive way of doing cultural sociology that presents a new theory of society that is at once theoretically, empirically, and normatively informed. It understands the civil sphere as a "cultural structure at the heart of democratic life" (Alexander, 2006b, p. ix). Such a structure "lies beneath every particular demand for institutional reform" and "cultural reformation" Alexander, 2006b, p. 550). This is how Alexander formulates such a demand for justice and solidarity:

> Justice depends on solidarity, on the feeling of being connected to others, of being part of something larger than ourselves, a whole that imposes obligations and allows us to share convictions, feelings, and cognitions, gives us a chance for meaningful participation, and respects our individual personalities even while giving us the feeling that we are all in the same boat. (2006b, p. 13)

Cultural sociology, then, in this case, is about how a civil society, understood as the cultural structure of a civil sphere, "makes itself felt" as a "moral force" (2006b, p. 18).[8] It means that "individual desires and actions must defer to prevailing standards of justice or be stigmatized as a result" (2006b, p. 18). It also means that societies are not determined by "power alone" (2006b, p. 3). Nor are they "fueled by the pursuit of self-interest" (2006b, p. 3). "Feelings for others matter" (2006b, p. 3), and since these feelings are "structured by the boundaries of solidarity" (2006b, p. 3), they can be "broadened" (2006b, p. 3). "That solidarity can be broadened," Alexander states, "is the project of civil repair" (2006b, p. 7). In terms of multicultural incorporation it requires that "out-group qualities can be purified—that they can, in fact, become objects not only of tolerance but also of respect and even desire" (2006b, p. 8). "But," Alexander adds, "the siren song of difference can attract only if it represents a variation on the chords of civil society" (2006b, p. 8).

This reminds me of how the double-bass player and composer Dave Holland characterizes his big jazz band. "For me," he writes, "the essence of a big band is the celebration of the collective spirit by a group of highly individual personalities" (2002).[9] Accordingly, jazz musicians have, Holland writes, "their own distinctive styles and concepts, but each one also experiences the joy of sharing the musical journey with each other" (2002).[10] It is also of importance to add that outsiders, in order to be incorporated, might need to change "by interweaving their particular struggles with universal themes" (Alexander, 2006b, p. 7). Consequently, civil society is, as just stated, an ongoing project. But it is a project that cannot be "fully achieved, even in the fullest flush of success," nor can it ever, "despite tragedy and defeat," be "completely suppressed" (Alexander, 2006b, p. 9). It is with this restless but aspiring project, and these theoretical and normative "eyes to see," that I will try to fulfill my aim and give empirical answers to my guiding research question.

My empirical data rest on, what I would like to call, two *ethnographical touchdowns*. The first one concerns Lockdale and the encounter with, among others, Muhammad. It is a street conversation about a local school that was burned down to the ground. It also concerns experiences of local life in segregated Lockdale and young men's longing for recognition and multicultural incorporation. The second one regards Bengt's struggle to make his beliefs come through. He wants to open up the Old Harbor School to pupils with immigrant backgrounds from an area like that of Lockdale, so that they can mix with the "Swedish" middle-class pupils at his school.

If the first issue, *burning schools*, is a big, real, and mediatized social issue in contemporary Sweden,[11] the other, *building bridges* between seemingly worlds apart, is much less so. Hence, I would like to avoid—and this is my *additional aim*—yet another contribution to the discourse of discontent—not because I want to claim that "all is well and right" in Malmö, but because beneath the shrill public facts of burning schools and segregation, there are deeper symbolic meaning processes alive in favor of social integration and multicultural incorporation.[12] Yes, and I will keep on pointing it out, there is a civil sphere understood as a "world of values and institutions" that "generates the capacity for social and democratic integration," and this sphere "relies on solidarity, on feelings for others whom we do not know but whom we respect out of principle, not experience, because of our putative commitment to common secular faith" (Alexander, 2006b, p. 4).

What, then, do I mean by describing my ethnography in terms of "touchdowns"? According to *The New Oxford American Dictionary*, a touchdown is "the moment at which an aircraft's wheels or part of a spacecraft make contact with the ground during landing" (2005, p. 1781). In American football, again from the same dictionary, it means "scoring" by "carrying or passing the ball into the end zone of the opposing side, or by recovering it there following a fumble or blocked kick" (p. 1781). In accordance with these meanings, I want to point out three things. First, the ethnography being used here concerns my very first encounter with people in Lockdale and Old Harbor. For this reason, I am not relying on any long-term ethnography. Rather, the ethnography to be presented is what was happening on the ground while I was landing. In other words, my touchdowns are where my research on multicultural incorporation in Malmö—to be continued—started. Second, my two touchdowns are, as in American football, "in the end zones of the opposing sides" of Malmö, that is, in Lockdale and Old Harbor, respectively, whose too orderly but not completely biased representations have been outlined above. Third, and finally, my touchdowns are also about recovering. They are quite "thick descriptions"[13] and serious cumulative endeavors concerning tales of social hope in the name of solidarity and feelings for others coming out of the end zone of the two seemingly opposing sides. It is about blocking kicks that hurt and hide away existing, in Alexander's words, "feelings for others whom we do not know but whom we respect out of principle" (2006b, p. 4). I will thus look, listen, and move, in search of repair and reconciliation.

The two touchdowns displayed here are parts of my ongoing research project *A Malmö Dilemma*. This title is, of course, paraphrasing the Swedish economist Gunnar Myrdal's landmark study *An American Dilemma*. This is how he starts out:

> There is a "Negro problem" in the United States and most Americans are aware of it, although it assumes varying forms and intensity in different regions of the country and among diverse groups of the American people. Americans have to react to it, politically as citizens and, where there are Negroes present in the community, privately as neighbors. (1996, p. lxxvii)

If "Negro problem," "United States," and "Americans" are replaced by the words "immigrant problem," "Malmö," and "Malmö inhabitants," these lines, published in the United States in 1944, are still ringing true in Malmö, Sweden, in 2010 (1996, p. lxxvii). Myrdal claimed "the American Negro problem" to be "a problem at the heart of the American" (1996, p. lxxix). I would then like to claim that "the immigrant problem" is at the heart of the inhabitants of Malmö. At the "bottom" of the "Negro problem"—which was, of course, also problems of "economic, social, and political race relations"—Myrdal found "the moral dilemma of the American" (1996, p. lxxix). The same goes, I will argue, for Malmö. Myrdal understood this dilemma as "the conflict" between the American's "moral valuations on various levels of consciousness and generality" (1996, p. lxxix). This is how he puts it with rhetorical splendor in public:

> The "American Dilemma"…, the ever-raging conflict between, on the one hand, the valuations preserved on the general plane which we shall call the "American Creed," where the American thinks, talks, and acts under the influence of high national and Christian precepts, and, on the other hand, the valuations on specific plains of individual and group living, where personal and local interests; economic, social, and sexual jealousies; considerations of community prestige and conformity; group prejudice against particular persons or types of people; and all sorts of miscellaneous wants, impulses, and habits dominate his outlook. (1996, p. lxxix)

In other words, Myrdal, like Alexander, focuses on, as the former puts it, "the cultural unity" that "consists in the fact that all valuations are mutually shared in some degree" (1996, p. lxxx). And this "unity," he goes on, "is the indispensible basis for discussion between persons and groups" (1996, p. lxxx). It is "the floor upon which the democratic process goes on" (1996, p. lxxx). However, at the same time as "people will twist and mutilate their beliefs of how social reality actually is" (1996, p. lxxxi), most of them will also tend to agree "that the more general valuations"—those that refer to human beings as such and not to any particular group or temporary situation—"are morally higher" (1996, p. lxxx). It is this "floor" and "the more general valuation"—that is, the Alexandrian civil sphere supporting beliefs in social integration and multicultural incorporation—that concerns my project on Malmö's dilemma, and, accordingly, also this essay.

Muhammad and Bengt do not know each other. But deep in their hearts, they both know that people in their everyday lives, even they themselves, "twist" and "mutilate" their "beliefs." Still, in a more general sense, they are, as most other people are, informed by high moral precepts. They believe in and seek cultural unity. They, too, stand on the floor upon which differences in quality and shared beliefs are asked for and celebrated. It is with these "eyes to see" that my touchdowns are specific moments to remember and stories to tell. I wish them to be "exemplars" of counter tales to twisted and mutilated beliefs. I wish them to be counterpoints to the critical cynicisms of our time. In them, the nitty-gritty of real life is one with the creed where we think, talk, and act under the influence of high precepts of "the good" cultural structure of the civil sphere. Therefore, when I as the ethnographer look, listen, and move through the morass of objects and events, I am not collecting more or less neutral and fragmented facts from the field. Rather, I am borrowing a formulation from Siri Hustvedt's novel *The Sorrows of an American*, "listening for patterns, strains of feeling, and associations that may move us out of painful repetitions and into an articulated understanding" (2008. p. 96). Hence, with my "eyes to see," I try to make connections between meaningful moments that would, as Auster puts it in *The Invention of Solitude*, "otherwise be lost" (2005, p. 29). Doing so, we will learn, as I have done from Michael Dirda's understanding of Auster's novels, that when people "talk about what truly matters, they start and end by telling stories."[14]

This is exactly what Muhammad and Bengt do. They tell stories from opposite sides of a city that despite all the differences, twists, and mutilations reverberate the same beliefs in and social hope for social integration and multicultural incorporation. As an ethnographer, I cannot but do the same. I, too, will tell stories. And stories being told "can't," as Hustvedt formulates it, "be separated from the culture in which we live" (2008, p. 86). Or, as Alexander explains it in relation to Geertz' anthropology: "When he writes it is upon the capacity of theoretical ideas to set up the effective analogies that their values depends, Geertz reveals his own understanding: theory is culture too" (Alexander 2008, p. 166). It is within this hope that I end my introduction. If the reader is still with me, we have quite a journey ahead. When my chapter ends, I will have explored the meaning of Alexander's civil sphere theory by remembering and retelling stories from my two touchdowns. I will also have made some concluding remarks.

THE BURNING GROUND: TOUCHDOWN
IN LOCKDALE

> And I take you down to the burning ground
> And you change me up and you turned it around
>
> —Van Morrison

It was Saturday and around midnight. Freezing cold but no snow. Maybe Mamillius in William Shakespeare's *The Winter's Tale* is right in his response to his mother who wants him to tell a tale. "What wisdom stirs amongst you?" she asks him. As a presage of what is to come, he answers: "A sad tale's best for winter" (2007, p. 715). Laid and I stood before the burned down school building. The schoolyard was dark and deserted. "Here's the burned down school I wanted you to see," Laid said, and added: "No ideal picnic spot, is it?" I could not but smile. Laid was smiling, too. However, our mood was rapidly changing. Moods, Geertz writes metaphorically, are "like fogs, they just settle and lift" (1993, p. 97). However, they "go nowhere" (Geertz, 1993, p. 97). Neither did Laid and I as Laid started to explain.

"This is where I once was a teacher. This is where I got to know the children in this area. As you know I got to know the parents, too. I've been listening a lot to them. If they see me, they want to talk to me. They want to tell me their worries. It is like I am carrying them around. Inside here [pointing at his temple with his forefinger], they are talking to me all the time. They need to talk to someone who can understand, not judge, them. Do you feel me?"

Yes, I did know. I was once one of Laid Bouakaz' supervisors when he wrote his dissertation on Arabic-speaking parents' lack of involvement in this now burned down school.[15] "Well, at least you can see it for yourself now, can't you?" he stated, and then paused, took a deep breath, paused again, to, as I perceived it, let the words sink in and to rehearse in his mind what he just was about to say: "There's nothing left of it, is there, but this burning ground."

Just before arriving to Lockdale in my car, Laid, an ethnographer in Sweden but also a son of the Berber people inhabiting northern Algeria, had told me a very moving story from his childhood days in Kabyle: How the women, all clothed in beautiful dresses of different colors, gathered at the common well at the heart of the village. Not only to bring water home to their families, but to talk, to share experiences, and to make the everyday life of women meaningful. "Why these colorful dresses?" I had asked, and Laid had answered: "That's how the women of the village would know, by seeing, that now is the time for us to meet at the well." In his memory, he could still see the women coming down to the well on small pathways from all corners of his childhood village. "To me," I had remarked, "your memory is like an account of a beautiful oil on canvas." "Yes," Laid had replied, "that's really true, but I do recall their moves and voices too." To him, this specific memory of intertwined visuals, motions, and sounds is an expression of what I would like to call *the bitter-sweetness of belonging revisited.*

Standing before the burning ground with a vision of the beautifully dressed Kabyle women gathering at the well in my mind, I had gotten the message that Laid wanted to transmit to me. As the Algerian sociologist Abdelmalek Sayad puts it: "One cannot write on the sociology of immigration without, at the same time and by the very fact, outlining a sociology of emigration" (2004, p. 1) and, accordingly, "one cannot be explained without reference to the other (2004, p. 1).[16] A "*nostalgic reaction,*" Sayad argues, comes from someone "who is *attached to an order* that has been definitely and irremediably broken" (2004, p. 141). But "for *disorder* to appear," to be "the immigrant" defined as "a whole series of problems," a "second rupture must occur" (2004, p. 178), that which we tend to call "*the social problem of immigrants*" (2004, p. 178), that is, to be one with a spiral of significations of issues such as social housing, school failure, unemployment, health problems, missed social opportunities, and criminality.

My belief in reason as carrying, quoting the American philosopher Martha C. Nussbaum, a "special dignity that lifts it above the play of forces" (1997, p. 38) was now, thanks to Laid, submerged with concerns of loss and longing at the very heart of the human condition. A yearning from something lost "there," in Kabyle, and never gained again "here," in Malmö. As if everything was neither here nor there but yonder: "How places," to quote Hustvedt in her essay titled "Yonder," "live in the mind once you have left them, how they are imagined before you arrive, or how they are seemingly called out of nothing to illustrate a thought" (1998, p. 4). Yes, undoubtedly so, at this very moment, I did "feel" Laid. Sense and sentiment were connected with an insight I have learned from Nussbaum's reading of Aristotle: "That what is good also may be, to some extent, a function of the reader's own particular needs, background, and context" (1990, p. 233). We can try, fragile as we often are, as best as we can, to stand against, as the novelist Henry James formulated it, "the rule of the cheap and easy" (quoted from Nussbaum, 1990, p. 233), and, to add Nussbaum's remark on James' statement, "against, then, sloppiness, vulgarity, and the trivialization of important things" (1990, p. 233).

Laid's understanding of the burning ground was the opposite of the recalled memory of the Kabyle women gathering at the well. Standing, as we were, in front of a burned down school building, Laid's memory of belonging in a childhood village was a powerful re-awakener and an informer of lost opportunities of belonging here and now at a new place called Lockdale. It also generated a deep insight into lost childhood days in a village in Kabyle. It was, again, the "bitter-sweetness of belonging revisited": a hard-hitting "double play" of existential nostalgia "there" and social disorder "here." "Memory offers up its gifts only when jogged by something in the present," Hustvedt writes in her novel *The Sorrows of an American*, and continues: 'It isn't a storehouse of fixed images and words, but a dynamic associative network in the brain that is never quite and is subject to revision each time we retrieve an old picture or old words" (2008, p. 80–81).

"It doesn't need to be like this," Laid said. It is at this very moment that the line from Quinn, the man who becomes a sort of detective in Paul Auster's *The New York Trilogy*, rings true in my head: "In order to know, you must understand' (2006, p. 19)

Yes, again, I did "feel" what Laid felt the need to transmit to me. I had been taken to the crossroad where biography of "the marginal man"[17] was dealt with due to people suffering structural rupture, social sliding, and cultural disjunction. However, I could not know that all of what was happening was a potent instrument—not only for doing a cultural sociology of meaning but for self-knowledge. To me, Laid represents a living mediating character of crossroad possibilities. I had become a receiver that felt the urgency to become a sender: a cultural sociologically informed storyteller in the midst of my own professional and personal drama. Laid was my pathfinder. Not on Mars, but here in Lockdale.

We left the burning ground and headed toward the local shopping center. As we passed the badly reputed 202 building, a run-down and overcrowded block of apartments, we saw the lights from the local falafel kiosk.[18] Despite the late hour, it was still open. In front of the kiosk, we saw the four young men whom we were about to encounter. An extraordinary artist raised in Lockdale with a vision inspired by Edward Hopper's paintings of the "American Scene"[19] could easily have understood the meaning-fullness of painting the "Lockdale scene." Had such an artist existed, we would have seen evocative canvases of Lockdale rooftops, buildings, and interiors. The people painted would be, to quote Wieland Schmied's remark on Hopper, "restlessly on the move and tired of being restless" (2005, p. 11). They would be "despairing at their loneliness" (2005, p. 11). I imagine myself a Hopper-like painting named *Falafel Kiosk*—an exaggerated perspective on a lonely outpost. It would draw for the viewer, quoting one of Schmied's remarks on *Gas*, Hopper's famous painting of a gas station on the outskirts of town, "irresistibly into the narrow aperture, into a gloom from which there would seem to be no escape" (2005, p. 31). And inside the kiosk, as in *Nighthawks*, another famous painting by Hopper, the viewer would get a hint of the owner, possibly his name is Ahmed, who is soon about to turn off the lights and lock up for the night.

The presence of "the proprietor" outside the gas station, quoting the art critic Mark Strand, "who is still working, does nothing to dispel our uneasy sense of what lies ahead. Even he is working against time, staving off the night, extending the day" (1994, p. 15). In Hopper's paintings, as Schmied remarks, "there is rarely a denouncement or resolution" (2005, p. 57). However, I have to remind the reader that we are, inspired by Alexander's cultural sociology, in search of the cultural structures that generate a civil sphere characterized by the "capacity" of "feelings for others that we do not know" and "social and democratic integration" (2006b, p. 4). Yes, we are in search of social hope!

The young men standing in front of the falafel kiosk would easily fit into a Hopperesque painted touchdown in Lockdale. According to Strand's poetic entrance to the world of Hopper, "There is a lot of waiting going on. Hopper's people seem to have nothing to do. They are like characters whose parts have deserted them" (1994, p. 23). However, an artist raised in Lockdale would not have painted only the light of silence, loneliness, despair, and waiting. Such an artist in residence would *also* have captured, and thereby avoided the risk of being considered a Hopper epigone, the aesthetic flavor of a specific form of liveliness, laughter, and humor that is such a strong part of the lived culture of male subordination and segregation of the supposedly dangerous Arab male from a district of disrepute such as Lockdale. However, we have to remind ourselves that, to quote the American literary critic Kenneth Burke, "a poem about having children is not the same thing as having children" (1973, p. 8). The same, of course, goes for an encounter with young men in front of a falafel kiosk at midnight in Lockdale. An imagined painting of that *mise en scène* is not the same thing as a real encounter. But, as Geertz was to insist, borrowing an insightful formulation made by the cultural sociologist Fred Inglis, "all practices symbolize and that is the only way we can understand them" (2000, p. 10). The supposition is, then, in Burke's own words, that "nothing could be what it is but must always be something else" (1973, p. 31), or, as Geertz himself puts it, "the real is as imagined as the imaginary" (1980, p. 136). It means, Inglis concludes, "that public action, symbolic of ourselves, is all there is to go on' (2000, p. 10). Accordingly, the young men we were about to encounter—performing themselves, as if a capillary attraction, due to us being there informed by our cultural sociological imagination—"were in the end," paraphrasing Geertz' conclusion from his analysis of *Negara: The Theatre State in Nineteenth-Century Bali*, "neither illusions nor lies, neither sleight of hand nor make-believe. They were what there was" (1980, p. 136). Sociologist and ethnographer Mitchell Duneier is also perfectly right in his beautifully laid out *Slim's Table*: "Human beings desire to participate in a world that validates their own images of self-worth" (1992, p. 109).

One of the young men immediately recognized Laid and saluted him in Swedish, probably due to me immediately being recognized as a Swede. "Hi, Laid, the man, I know you!" he said. I learned that the name of the young man saluting Laid was Muhammad, and, hence named after the prophet who in early c. 610 in Mecca received the first of series of revelations that, as the Qur'an, became the basis of Islam. After the first revelation, according to the Qur'an translator Thomas Cleary, Muhammad, "fearful and demurred" (1998, p. xi), rushed home to his wife and "anxiously revealed what had happened to him" (1998, p xi). She reminded him of his "well-known virtues," "assured him that he was not mad," and "took him to a cousin, a Christian, who listened to the beginnings of the Recital and declared it to be the same Truth as brought by Moses and Jesus" (1998, p. xi). "All praise belongs to God, Lord of all worlds, the Compassionate, the Merciful":[20] These are the opening words of the Qur'an. Obviously, at the very roots of the Qur'an, there seems to be a shared common ground for, at least, Muslims, Christians, and Jews. As the Algerian philosopher and professor of Islamic studies Mustapha Chérif describes the core meaning of his conversation with philosopher Jacques Derrida in *Islam and the West*: "To reopen the horizon, to go beyond the divisions, to seek new form of alliance between individuals and peoples in love with justice" (Derrida and Chérif, 2008, p. 11). It was Derrida's deep belief that "one's relationship to the other, addressing the other, presupposes faith" (pp. 57–58). "I cannot address the other," he states, "regardless of his or her religion, language, culture, without asking that other to believe me and trust me" (pp. 57–58). Derrida. a Jew raised in Algeria and, thus, with an "affection for Algeria 'nostalgeria'" (p. xiv), and a Frenchman who lost and regained his citizenship,[21] also taught Chérif "that meaning can only be shared, that meaning goes beyond individuals, beyond all factions, beyond all factions, that there is a separate meaning, that its value is worthy in and of itself, independent of interventions, appropriations, demands" (p. 7). Accordingly, not even the founder of the method of deconstruction—"the process of identification and displacement of the oppressive structure" (p. xi), "concrete" or "conceptual" (p. xi)—then stands against the search of the common, or even "the universal."[22] "There is," as Chérif puts it, "a noble dimension in Derrida's thinking: he is concerned with the future of human dignity" (Derrida and Chérif, 2008, p. 7). This is good news for a cultural sociology that is interested in finding common ground within a civil sphere in a multicultural society. Accordingly, there are no clashes between civilizations—only within. This is how Nussbaum states it in *The Clash Within: Democracy, Religious Violence, and India's Future*:

> I argue that the real clash is not a civilizational one between "Islam" and "the West", but instead a clash *within* virtually all modern nations—between people who are prepared to live with others who are different, on terms of equal respect, and those that seek the protection of homogeneity, achieved through the domination of a single religious and ethnic tradition. (2007, p. ix–x)[23]

Muhammad from Lockdale knew Laid as one of the former teachers at the now burned down school. As soon as we all had said "hello" to each other by formally shaking hands, the youths switched to their native Arabian language.[24] I being "the Swede" or, in their lingo, *Svenne* (meaning "from Svensson," the son of Sven, a "real" Swede for generations, and, in places like Lockdale, easily recognized as "the other") understood nothing. The only thing I could pick up was that Muhammad and Laid were the talkative ones. The others, whose names I did not get, took a smaller part in the initial conversation. Now and then, as sidekicks, they filled the air with, as I interpreted it, clever comments and supportive laughter. It was like witnessing a lively group of joint Arabian stand-up comedians with no option of choosing a Swedish subtitle. Jokes, of course, as Mary Beard, professor of classics, has pointed out, could not be treated "as if there was no humorous intention behind them" (2008, p. 32).[25] I cannot now but think of professor of religion Cornell West's wonderful depiction of the painter Horace Pippin (1888–1946), whose pictures just came to his mind and, hence, "told his head to go own" (quoted from West, 2009, p. 54). "Pippin's art suggests," West writes in *Keeping Faith*,

> that black people within the normative gaze wear a certain kind of masks and enact particular postures, and outside the white normative gaze wear other kind of masks and enact different sorts of postures. In short, black people tend to behave differently when they are "outside the white world"—though how they behave within black spaces is shaped by their battles with self-hatred and white contempt. (1999, p. 55)

The purpose of Muhammad and his sidekicks, I thought, was probably not to confuse me. However, I strongly felt the presence of certain questions: "Who is this strange man that Laid drags around in Lockdale at this hour?" "Why is he doing that?"

and "What are they really up to?" To be honest, it was hard for me to really know whether they were occupied by each other and, hence, just lost me for a moment, or if their behavior was more or less conscious, a strategy for symbolic displacement. To give them an opportunity to talk and settle things, I told them that I was "really hungry" and thus "immediately craved an extra-large falafel." It would, after all, seem natural, I thought, to head for the falafel kiosk to purchase a falafel, not to socialize with people whom, at least, I could not know. As streetwise as I could possibly look—to consciously act naturally, I suppose, is an oxymoron—I escaped into the glassed-in front area of the kiosk. As I slipped away, I heard Muhammad, in a quite loud voice, as I perceived it, sending a message to the man in the kiosk. I understood two things. The young men and Laid found it very funny—they burst out in shared laughter. The name of the man in the kiosk was Ahmed. Before sending his message, Muhammad had been calling for his attention by repeating the eventual proprietor's name three times, each time louder and louder: "Ahmed! Ahmed!! Ahmed!!!" I did not have a clue what Muhammad was driving at. Ahmed, on the contrary, did not laugh when I entered the glassed-in spot. To me, he looked a bit unsettled but compensated for his unease with a strong dose of seriousness. "What on earth are they laughing at?" I wondered. Ahmed, very formally so, said he did not know. Maybe, I thought, he looked a bit wavering. However, he did make me a falafel. Two dollars is a nice price for a big and tasty meal.

Returning to Laid, Muhammad, and their sidekicks with an extra-large falafel in my hand, telling them, both because I thought so and inasmuch as I wanted to please them, that it was "a really nice one." "Great falafel kiosk, this is!" I added. However, despite my attempt to reconnect with the group, I seemed unable to break the spell under which I had been put. Looking at me eating and spilling falafel sauce all over my neckwear and winter coat in a fumbling way, these young men were all smiles up to their ears. Maybe there was a plot against me? Did I not, after all, experience a sort of team collusion here? "What is it that is so funny?" I asked them thick as a brick. The answer was a collective one; again, they were laughing out loud. Laid was laughing, too. In great need of reassurance, I tried to reach out to Laid. "Please, Laid," I beseeched, "I really want to know what this is all about." Laid then, as the charitable person he always is, turned to me and explained, still laughing, that they were all fully convinced that he was "hanging around" with an "undercover policeman." "What did they say?" I asked curiously. Laid answered by mimicking the young men in a teasing way, using the high-pitched voice of an eager little child: "Oh Laid, please tell us, is he an undercover, is he an undercover, Laid, tell us, please, we won't tell anybody, you know that, is he an undercover?" When I asked them why they were so convinced that I was an undercover policeman, one of Laid's sidekicks said—partly, I thought, as a way of displacing Laid's effective teasing—"Man, sorry to tell you, but you're a bit fat." Again, they all exploded in loud laughter. Laid, of course, could not help but laugh, too. I tried to cope with the situation by clutching my stomach. "Yeah, you're right," I heard myself saying, and adding: "Undoubtedly," and this statement was not an ingratiating lie, "I am a bit fat." If I were Shakespeare's fat, jolly, and debauched Falstaff character with an ethnographical gusto for life, they would be the rascals—those wretched, mischievous, and cheeky persons you could not effortlessly control but still easily have affections for. However, I wanted to move on and get into a deeper dialogue with these young men. And now, at last, having a possible entrée to a dialogue I asked how "my a-bit-fatness proved me to be an undercover policeman." Muhammad, obviously the main character and featured performer of the group, gave me the following analysis of how fatness symbolized not only undercover policemen but also their bosses.

"Well, you know, undercovers, I tell you, they all sit on their asses in their cars, and try to figure out what we are doing, you know, like, 'what are *blattarna* [immigrants signifying social disorder and problems] doing now, what are *blattarna* doing now?'[26] That's their job, do you get it. And they are getting like bored and hungry, so they eat hot dogs and mashed potatoes. Cops like to eat stuff like that. If they are *svennar*, that is. They never get out of their cars, except when they buy their hot dogs. So, they just sit in their cars and get fat. Man, I tell you, this is true, everybody knows, they are just so lazy. They like to sit in their cars…like…'Hey, I am the real cop. I'm in my patrol car. You better beware little *blatte* there.' Like that. And their bosses would know, wouldn't they, because before they became bosses, they were undercovers eating hot dogs and mashed potatoes, too. That's how you become a boss for undercovers? And they will sit on their asses in their offices and they will tell the younger undercovers: 'Well today you going to watch some *blattar* in Lockdale, you know, see how they are, so we better go undercover to investigate them, hey, if you want to be a boss like me.' Like that."

We could not but be amused by the late show that Muhammad was putting on. I not only saw paintings but also contemporary comedy. Being there at the center of attention, in this lit up world in front of the falafel kiosk at midnight, was like recalling Jaques' famous lines from Shakespeare's comedy *As You Like It*: "All the world's a stage / And all the men and women merely players." And these players, as if Shakespeare was making a methodological point on how to carefully represent postindustrial ethnographical settings, "They have their exits and entrances / and one man in his time may play many parts."[27] Enjoying being the now fully established crowd pleaser, Muhammad just kept on telling tales of profane, but still humanly sacred, revelation. Next, he targeted the social and cultural change in the Lockdale district, which before becoming known as an, to use a common Swedish label, "immigrant area," was a "Swedish" working-class and lower-middle-class area.

"But when they, you know, the bosses, were undercover, they couldn't investigate *blattar* because there weren't a lot of *blattar* then, so they were doing undercover investigations on real *svennar* who were on drugs and stealing like necklaces from their crazy mothers. Just like Ragnar. Now listen! How do you know that Ragnar is at home? I tell you. His mother is chasing him through the neighborhood like in her bathrobe. 'Ragnar, give me my necklace back, give me my necklace back,' and he just says, 'Oh, better be off, now, oh, better be off now,' you know. But nowadays the cops don't do undercover investigations on people like him, they're more like 'Hey, where are *blattarna*, hey, what are *blattarna* doing now?'"

Muhammad obviously knew about the Swedish "folk-home-exodus" out of districts like Lockdale that started decades beforehand. The well-off working-class and lower middle-class people moved to the suburbs, buying their own homes, or moved to apartments in more privileged parts of the city. At the same time, labor migrants and, more and more so, refugees from different parts of the world came to Sweden to take residence in left behind and hence available blocks of apartments. This is how districts like Lockdale became so-called segregated areas with "immigrants." In Muhammad's analysis of present-day Lockdale, the story of Ragnar and his mother is the story of how the least privileged Swedish working class were left behind and still, to some extent, live there.[28]

"I tell you another thing," Muhammed said, and yet again he took off. This is what I wrote down in my notebook later that night. Of course, to quote Auster from *The Invention of Solitude*, "memory" is "the space in which things happens for the second time" (2005, p. 87). And, as Hustvedt puts it in *The Sorrows of an American*, "memory fragments don't have any coherence until they're re-imagined in words" (2008, p. 47). We thus need to, she adds, "organize perceptions into stories with beginnings, middles, and ends" (2008, p. 47).

"Today, man, most of the policemen, and women, too, all police, undercover, *blatte* police too, of course, because they are 'immigrants'—do you feel me, I say nearly everyone—they eat falafel and sometimes kebab too. They go like, 'No I don't want a hotdog with mashed potatoes today. I want a falafel. I would really like a falafel.' You know, like that—everyone. Yes, I tell you, and this is really true. It's the truth, man, because it is mathematics. And you are from the university. You're like smart. Listen. In this town, I mean the whole of Malmö, in Sweden, man, if you count all the kiosks in this city, like you travel around and you go, well, there's a falafel kiosk, okay one, and there's another, okay two, and then, three, four, and so on, and then, okay, there is a hot dog kiosk, one, and so on.... I tell you, man, if you counted all the kiosks in Malmö like that, the falafel kiosks would win, easily. Man, listen, *blattarna* are taking over this city. Beware, man, beware. See, you just ate a falafel yourself. You'll know soon, think about it now, do you follow me, everyone is like, hey.... In the end, I don't say now, but in the end, when *blattarna* have taken over this city, you will have ... everyone saying like ... 'Hey, which way is Mecca?'"

Again, Muhammad got big smiles and laughter from the little crowd gathered in front of the falafel kiosk. "So you mean," I said, "that Malmö is going to be a Muslim city." "No man," Muhammad replied immediately. His mood was changing. He became very serious, saying something that would make Alexander very satisfied—both theoretically and normatively. Suddenly, Muhammad is the incarnation of social hope in the civil sphere: a streetwise Martin Luther King-like Muslim voicing social longings. He is the citizen who has "feelings for others" whom he wants to "respect out of principles, not experience" because of his "putative commitment to common secular faith" (see Alexander, 2006b, p. 4). Obviously, Muhammad has got a dream.

"I think we shall live together. People like you and me and Laid and everyone. I don't like racist. I don't like fundamentalist. They're like down in a basement and doing completely stupid things. And they walk around in the areas and say to kids, 'Come to us if you will have fun,' things like that. I hate it. And they knock on people's doors, too. Like, come with us, you know, things like that. It's happening, man. You have to admit one thing. There're idiots in all places. They're not many, but they do exist in all countries of the world. Here in Lockdale, too. I tell you, I don't like them. They're just stupid jerks. They should be sent to a school and learn the Qur'an. So, do you feel me, I am a Muslim, and you're not. I don't think you should be a Muslim if you're not, because you don't want to. Do I have a problem with that? No, do you understand me? I don't have a problem with that. How can I have a problem with that? Man, it doesn't work that way. Probably you're like, 'I don't believe in anything like God because I'm a Swede.' Do you follow me? Swedes are a bit like that, aren't they? And I am what I am. I'm a Muslim, but not like a stupid one, see, and we live here in Malmö—together. Okay, let's be serious. You and I and everyone here, we're serious now, okay? This is our city. We can talk. I can talk to you, you know. We can live here. I am not dangerous. You're not dangerous. Do you follow me, man? I say, drop all the shit, man, drop it!"

"Do you think he is right?" I asked Muhammad's sidekicks. They all nodded. "Yes, of course, he is right," one of them said, adding: "He was just playing around cause a lot of people are like so afraid of the Muslims." "Some people in Malmö, like in this neighborhood," one of the other two sidekicks commented, "are so fed up with the segregation and being like the problem, that they say like, 'Let's hoist our own flag,' you know, like if they had their own 'immigrant country' with their own 'immigrant flag' here." "They can say it like that, but for most people it's meant like a joke," the third sidekick remarked. "But it's in some ways somehow true," the second sidekick added, concluding: "Yes, I have to admit. Sometimes it feels like this is our own territory."

"So who am I then," I asked, "besides being a Swede and not being an undercover policemen?" "Relax, man," Muhammad answered, clapping my shoulder with the palm of his hand, and again his mood was changing. "We know," he said, "because Laid told us, you're from the university, you're a researcher. Laid told us that you write books about people like us." "So you sneak around like an undercover, too," one of the sidekicks commented. "But do you write," Muhammad asked, "like hey, they're not that dangerous? I've met them. They're kind of funny, they're like good people, that is, like if you really know them. Do you write stuff like that? Like…Swedish people, don't be afraid, things like that." I said that such was partly true. Thinking about Alexander's new theory of the civil sphere, I tried to say that I certainly did not want to write that all "Swedes" are in a certain way and that all "immigrants" are in another way—"good" or "bad." I was, I told them, looking for things that made us very much alike in our dreams and hopes rather than different, and this despite the fact that we might also be different due to things like culture, religion, money, upbringing, education, experience of war, and coming to a new country. "How much do you earn then?" Muhammad asked. I told him that a professor in Sweden earned around $8000 a month. "Man, do you feel me, you have to send me some money, man," he replied. "If you've had money now, what would you have done then?" I asked.

"I tell you, we would be downtown bowling. But we don't have any money, so what shall we do but stand here in front of a falafel kiosk, so we can see the 202 building—beautiful view, don't you think?—and behind 202 we've got a burned down school. Oh, yeah, yet another beautiful spot. Welcome to our neighborhood. So, hey, man, what can we do besides standing here talking to you?"

"How, then, do you feel about the burned down school?" I asked. "I tell you," Muhammad said, "When the school burned down—this is the truth—it was sick, man, I say it was really sick.... Like everyone who was there with their cell phones, you know, everyone was just calling everyone they knew. Like, 'Hey, you need to come down here, the school is burning, like hurry up, come on, the school is burning.' You know like 'some idiot has set the school on fire.' Like that. My friends called me, and I myself, I went at lightning speed. And I was calling everyone. So, within like minutes, everyone—I don't mean everyone—but a lot of people were there. And, then, you know, the firemen, they were working real hard, but they couldn't save the building. It was just too late. They could only save the other buildings around the burning building. The school building could not be saved, and this is true—you can ask anybody, I tell you, anybody who was there, or close to everyone who was there—they were like laughing, clapping their hands, big applause. They were like, though they hated it, having a good time."

"Adults too?" I asked. "Yes," Muhammad said, "adults too." "But why did they, at least it sounds like that to me, celebrate their own school burning down to the ground? Why celebrate disaster?" I was really eager to know. Muhammad was not without an answer.

"I tell you, you know, at the same time as you think it's wrong. I really mean it. It's like crazy. You know, all the people who were there, maybe besides some idiots who did it, they think like this is really altogether wrong. Remember, it was our school. It was our small children's school. This is the school of our neighborhood, you know. I told you it was like really, I say really, really sick."

"But how then," I went on, "could you explain that people were amused, laughing and applauding? Didn't they like the school?" The answers from Muhammad and his sidekicks were that most people in the neighborhood liked the school. "There were some really good teachers there," Muhammad said. "The building was fine," one of the sidekicks added, "nothing wrong with the building." "But, hey, admit it, it was a real *blatte* school," one of the other sidekicks remarked. "What does that that mean?" I asked. "Well, there were some really disorderly types there, but not many. You know, most people there were okay," he answered. "Yeah, we liked them," the third sidekick added. "Yeah, the school was good," Muhammad concluded, "but it had like a bad reputation. A lot of people thought it was like the worst place of all, but if you went to school there, you would know it was good." "But, then, again," I went on, "why this celebration in front of one's own well-respected school building burning down to the ground?" And then it came. The answer that, as I understand it, could sum up the existential experience of living one's life in places like Lockdale: *Man, I tell you, we are all mixed up—do you feel me?—I'm telling you now, we are all mixed up.* The mood had changed again. For a moment, I went into silence. I did not really know what to say, but after a short while, I came up with something like, "But to be, as you say, 'mixed up,' what does that mean?" "You know," Muhammad said, "you hate those damned idiots who did it, but you go there to the burning school, and you call everybody you know, and you like laugh, applaud, and you feel, though I hate it, like good too." To change the mood, I guess, one of Muhammad's sidekicks went back to practicing what might be called the young men's "dark" humor. "At least something real is happening in Lockdale," he said, and all of our faces gave way to small-sized smiles. "Moods," as Geertz pointed out, really are "like fogs, they just settle and lift" but they "go nowhere" (1993, p. 97). "But how," I insisted, "is it possible to somehow feel good when the school that you say you really liked is burning down to the ground?" Muhammad never seemed to be without an answer.

"You see, all the Swedish firemen, they were really trying to rescue the school. They worked like hell, running around. 'Hey, we have to put the fire out, hey, we have to put the fire out,' you know, like that. But they couldn't do it. You hate it, with the school and everything, but it's kind of funny. You just stand there. And you can see that they can't do it. You heard it yourself, didn't you, at least something was happening here in Lockdale."

"But what, then, about the firemen, don't you like them? Do you feel like they are against you?" Again, Muhammad came up with a story-like answer. He said something like the following.

"I tell you, you Swedes, you're trying like, 'Oh, that is interesting, how can we help this guy? How can we help the immigrants?' you know, like that. I tell you, in my country, where I come from, if you, like you are a Swede, if you come to our place, and you needed help, like 'help me,' there is just shit in my country, you know. I'm not sure that my country would help you out like you help people out here in Sweden, especially not if there were like Swedes burning down schools and shit like that, man. I mean if you were standing there applauding, man, they send the army in, and bang, you couldn't stand there clapping your hands. You know. I tell you, you in Sweden, you are—I really mean it—you really help people out, but when it doesn't work, you like, well, now, how can we help them out, you're really nice people, but then...."

"But then what...?" I asked, trying to push Muhammad for yet another answer. "But then," Muhammad said, "who am I here in Lockdale? *Am I not the idiot who could have burned my own school down to the ground? That is why we are mixed up. Man—do you feel me? —you have given me everything but I am nothing. I am telling you. I am nothing but a 'blatte.' I am allowed to live here, being the 'blatte,' and you try to help me here in Lockdale, but you, man, you live in Sweden. Do you feel me? I also want to fight for your good society.* "Yes, I do feel you," I said, "I do feel you." We all went into silence. The mood settled and could not really lift. No more jokes. This is how Hustvedt formulates my structure of feeling in *The Sorrows of the American*: "And it's all very close to me, as if these stories of breakthrough belong to me, too. Real meaning, true insight is rarely dry" (2008, p. 55).

When the silence broke, we talked about how freezing cold it was after midnight in Lockdale, and that one ought to be home sleeping now. "Yeah, we better be going,"

I said, and Laid agreed. We were all shaking hands. *Säg hallå till din familj och till hela ditt folk!* ["Remember me to your family and to your people"]. These were Muhammad's last words to me.

Leaving Lockdale in my car, Laid and I saw no one. I could not but slow my car down and turn around to take in the Lockdale scene for a last time. One of the side-kicks had left, but Muhammad and two of his sidekicks were still there. Ahmed was closing down now. *Dawn in Pennsylvania*, yet another painting by Hopper, came to my mind. "The feeling is," Strand remarks on the painting, "that we will be waiting a long time" (1994, p. 27). "Instead of walking somewhere," he adds, "we are waiting to go somewhere" (1994, p. 27). I spent the rest of the night trying to get everything down in my notebook. "Memory," Auster reminds me, is "the space in which things happen for the second time" (2005, p. 87). With my "eyes to see," I was in search of, again in Auster's words, "the thought, the idea" (2008, p. 8), "founded on," borrowing the words from Derrida's conversation with Chérif, "meditative thought and hope" (2008, p. 25). I wanted my ethnographical memory to become, again referring to the actual conversation, "an appeal for a way of thinking, a culture, a reflection on the universal to come. Through peaceful words, it aimed to build bridges, to meet the other, in the goal of finding a way to face the unforseeability of the future together" (2008, p. 25).

Building Bridges: Touchdown at Old Harbor

> The civil sphere is a promise, and this promise can be redeemed. Outsiders demand the expansion of the discourse of liberty. Stigmatized individuals and groups, polluted by the discourse of repression, can be purified and redeemed. If leaders are skillful, followers brave, and the stars are right, movements for civil repair can succeed.
>
> —Jeffrey C. Alexander (2006b, pp. 551–552)

Ingrid Robertson, the leading civil servant from the local authorities, started the evening meeting at the Old Harbor School by emphasizing the importance of "shared responsibility." "We all need to help each other out and contribute to the development of our city," she said and added: "Our city is not only this neighborhood but the city as a whole." Robertson's pleading words did not go over well. This was not the message the gathered parents of nearly two hundred had come to hear. They would not, it seemed, be persuaded to accept the actual proposal—that some fifty or more immigrant children from the Creek, yet another local district in Malmö with the same reputation as Lockdale, would become pupils at the Old Harbor

School. The auditorium oozed frustration. Robertson did not hesitate when she asked Bengt Christianson, the head of the Old Harbor School, to take the stand. It was now up to him to make plain to the angry crowd why it would be such a good idea to accept the children from the Creek as pupils at the school. Bengt started out by arguing that Old Harbor now had "a real opportunity to be at the very forefront of integration." "Our school," he continued, "would represent all citizens in this city." This would be, "something," he claimed, "to be proud of." Such an action—this was his second argument—would help to bring about a change in the way in which Old Harbor was perceived by the public: a district rejecting the social and cultural integration of children from other less privileged areas. Despite the present frustration and anger, he hoped the idea would fit in well with the educated, middle-class parents' understanding of themselves as open-minded, unprejudiced, and self-reflexive citizens. That did not seem to be the case. No demands on appeasement were set forth. Bengt, then, launched his third argument. He told the parents that the Old Harbor School had every capability to handle the new situation. The school, he pointed out, was known for its "experienced teaching staff," and, "there will be," he added, "extra resources available." Therefore, it would be possible to transform the Old Harbor School into a successful multicultural meeting-ground that would not thwart school achievement. But no matter how Bengt tried to put it, no one in the auditorium expressed a willingness to accept the arguments he tried to launch. He was continuously interrupted by critical questions from angry parents. It was as if an antagonistic genie was out of the bottle, and could not be put back in again. The parents, at least some of them, clamored for the right to speak. They had their questions. An indignant man announced that he represented a group of parents "who actually have come to an agreement," and "we," he added, "have chosen a spokesman for this meeting." An impatient and very upset woman stood up, with her right arm raised in the air. When she did not get the immediate attention she craved, she took the floor and declared herself to be "the chosen spokesman for," as she put it, "a number of the gathered parents." "I have to raise *our* questions," she said in a loud, highly strung voice. She expressed deep worries about a decline in the pupils' general level of knowledge. She also pointed out the obvious risk of increased conflicts between children from Old Harbor and the Creek. Small applause was heard in support of her point of view. A very upset man asked if the Old Harbor School was supposed to "accept" the children from the Creek just because "we feel sorry for them." When Bengt tried to answer the hail of questions, he was repeatedly interrupted. A man in a very foul temper, who had been noisily banging his hands on the tabletop where he was seated in hope of getting attention, declared in a clamorous voice that he demanded to know "why" Bengt "wanted to go through with this social experiment with the poor little kids from the Creek." Outright racism was also expressed. General statements were made on issues such as the relation between children's cognitive capacities and their ethnic background. Explicit pronouncements like these, even if they were few in number, and the strong rejection of integration of children from nonprivileged and multicultural areas scared Bengt stiff. "They do not go along with," he stated in a conversation with me, "the idea that permeates the school curriculum in Sweden; that all human beings have equal worth, and should be given equal opportunities." "If this group of parents had had tomatoes at hand," he said, looking back on the occasion, "they would have thrown them at me." In a final attempt to deal with the situation, Bengt asked the parents if all of them shared the opinions that had been expressed. In hopes of some diversity of opinion, a microphone was passed around among the parents, but no one took the chance to express alternative views. Still Bengt felt, strongly so, there probably were parents out there in the auditorium, possibly silenced by the angry minority, in favor of integration. The applause endorsing the critical few had after all not been joined in by the many.

The meeting came to an end. Before leaving, the group of critical parents announced that they would probably move their children to another school if the children from the Creek were accepted at the Old Harbor School. A strong and convenient rumor had already started to circulate. A new independent school might be opened in the Old Harbor district. No one knew what the parents from the Creek thought about their children being sent to a school in the Old Harbor district. They had not been asked. It was decided that a new meeting with the parents from Old Harbor would be held within a month.

About a month before the first meeting, Bengt had paid a visit to the Civic Center in the Old Harbor district. His presence had been detected by the head of education, who immediately invited him into his office. "If you would be given the possibility of getting more pupils from another area, not that far away," the head had asked, "would you be interested?" Bengt was, he asserted, "basically positive to the idea." It had to do with demographics. To avoid budget cuts, he needed more sixth- and seventh-graders to fill his classrooms, or else some of his teachers would lose their jobs. Bengt, of course, wanted to be briefed about which district and school the inquiry concerned. The name of the actual school, he was informed, could not be revealed. A formal decision had yet to be made. At that moment, he was quite convinced that it concerned pupils from the closed down school in Lockdale. Thinking back to the occasion, Bengt remembers how he conjured up in his own mind a prejudiced picture of the actual school and its pupils. Were the teachers at the Old Harbor School, he asked himself, capable of handling children from Lockdale? Yes, he thought so. His experienced staff could by all means manage the twenty pupils or so that were needed to fill all the classrooms at the Old Harbor School. But having pupils from Lockdale would also, after all, be a positive commitment to the principle of integration. This idea grew on him. Contributions to social integration and multicultural incorporation were definitely very much needed in Malmö. Would it not be great, then, Bengt thought if a local school in the privileged Old Harbor district became a meeting place for children from a variety of different backgrounds and from very different parts of Malmö? He could not but think that the idea was, indeed, very good.

A few weeks later, Bengt was summoned to a meeting with the head of education in the Old Harbor district. The new pupils, he was informed, would come from the Creek, yet another of many badly reputed and segregated areas in Malmö.

Presently, one out of every three pupils at the actual school, compared to 4 percent at the Old Harbor School, did not reach the expected levels of knowledge. Bengt understood the decision to be a starting point for further discussion and collaboration. If the integration project was to be carried through in a feasible way, he thought, it needed to be anchored through the support of staff, parents, and pupils—and at both ends. Unfortunately, such did not happen. Instead, all concerned could read about it in the local paper on a Saturday morning. Not even Bengt was informed about the decision being publicly announced. The article informed the reader, wrongly so, that 120 pupils from the Creek were to be transferred to the Old Harbor School due to building renovations. Monday morning, Bengt received around eighty emails and a never-ending procession of phone calls from indignant Old Harbor parents. Most of them expressed concerns about a decline in social order and correspondingly in school achievement. There were no emails or calls from the Creek. It was at this very moment that Bengt's superiors at the Civic Center had suggested an evening meeting with the parents at Old Harbor. Things needed, they thought, to be cleared up. The outcome of this suggestion was the first meeting described above. The teachers too, of course, were upset. Most of them knew nothing of what had been going on behind the scenes, and, hence, they felt, to say the least, misled. However, despite the unacceptable way in which the decision had proceeded, they were, with some few exceptions, in favor of a changed sociocultural composition of pupils. It was decided that they would not join the first meeting. The teachers themselves found this decision sensible.

Confronting the parent's indignation and legitimate censure from the staff, Bengt at first felt that his own beliefs in social integration and multicultural incorporation were placed under scrutiny. What was he up to? Could he really go through with this? At the same time, he argued with himself what he—and, with rare exception, his staff and probably most of the parents—really believed in and must be held onto: "to contribute to new possibilities in this very segregated city in which we live our lives." In Alexander's words, Bengt was about to "build symbolic bridges to the discourse of civil society, providing a cultural vernacular that makes proximity to civil sacrality seem merely a matter of everybody's normal and rightful place" (2007, p. 29). It was decided that some fifty pupils from the Creek were to become pupils at the Old Harbor School. It was now up to Bengt to try to make it come off in the best possible way. Repair work and reconciliation were definitely needed.

Bengt decided to spend a lot of time just talking to staff and parents about their fears and hopes. He seized every opportunity that presented itself and discovered that many rumors were making the rounds. When people talk about what truly matters to them, as in Auster's novels, they start telling all sorts of stories. Teachers exchanged worries. Parents talked when they encountered each other in the neighborhood. Staff ran into parents they knew while shopping in local stores. They were all in search of information—often so, it would appear, in support of their own beliefs and statements. Anxiety consumed the place and was the climate in every Old Harbor encounter. Undoubtedly so, the Creek pupils' imminent transfer to the Old Harbor School was the talk of the town. Bengt's aim, hence, was to increase information and participation. He wanted to be as inclusive as he possibly could. He was, using Myrdal's formulations, trying to find "the floor upon which the democratic processes could go on" (1996, p. lxxx). He was in search of, using Alexander's concept, the "civil centrality" (2006b, p. 4) we need to share in the name of solidarity and sympathy, or, again in Myrdal's choice of words, "the more general valuations" that are "morally higher" (1996, p. lxxx). He planned for staff training concerning democratic values, social integration, multiculturalism, models for learning, and language. Lecturers with different expertise were invited. He started the process of recruiting the new bilingual staff that was needed. Some teachers, who did not want to be part of the project or the "social experiment," as it was often called among the discontented, left for other schools.

Bengt also needed to develop a thorough understanding of the pupils. What kind of discussions did he need to have with them? What did the pupils think about sharing the Old Harbor School with the pupils from the Creek? And the pupils from the Creek: What were they saying? What did they know? Had their experiences and opinions been sought? Bengt understood the importance of letting the children from the Creek and the Harbor meet. Empathic thought and strategic activities like these came out of an action plan that he formulated in cooperation with a resource team specialized in multicultural issues, ethnic relations, and integration. He also held several meetings with people from the business world. Bengt had been advised to hold onto what he believed in, and to try to be as explicit as he possibly could concerning what he thought and wanted to bring about. Processes of change, the business representatives had told him, take time. Bengt understood the need to be open, patient, and consistent. In all his endeavors, he tried to treat all people with respect. "I cannot change another person's way of thinking," he stated in a conversation with me, continuing, "but I can change my own perception of that person, and by doing that, a change might come." There was no other way than with and through other people. "You can't," he said, "do integration alone." And also, to do integration with others whom you, quoting Alexander, "respect out of principle," you also need to "reform yourself" (2006b, p. 4). You need to recognize, face, and take the necessary actions regarding your own fears and hopes. It does not matter if you are a headmaster, a teacher, a parent, or a pupil of whatever primordial belonging and coloring; you need to develop and demonstrate your own civil beliefs and capacities, too.[29]

Bengt felt to an increasing degree that the wind was blowing his way. His actions appeared to serve his cause well. There was also the strong support he had received from local media. Bengt had invited a locally well-known columnist and debater of social and multicultural matters to the first meeting. The journalist was familiar with the Old Harbor School and its environment. He lived in the area and his own children had once attended the school. The day after the first meeting, his story on the school issue appeared in the local newspaper. In all possible ways—its description, argument, and judgment—Bengt found it very sound. The article's main point was that Old Harbor was not only the most segregated district in Malmö, but also a place where strong resistance to immigrants was explicitly expressed in public. The atmosphere of the meeting was depicted as rancorous. It was Bengt's experience that many parents were really touched to the core by the article. It created a lot of uncomfortable feelings among them. They did not like to read about themselves as aggressive and prejudiced citizens rejecting the integration of less privileged children. It did not really sit well with the self-image that most of the middle-class parents had about themselves, and how they wanted to be represented in public. According to Bengt, the journalist's chronicle stilled the loud debate and opened up the floor for a democratic process in search of public civility. The most outspoken, angry, and oppositional parents became silent. However, rumor had it that several school classes were about to leave the Old Harbor School for an independent school that would eventually open in the area. But no one really knew how many Old Harbor parents there were who had prepared to avoid integration by exodus.

The second meeting was considerably smoother than the first one. Bengt felt more confident that he was doing the right thing. Looking back on the occasion, he told me that "this was the time for me to be a good spokesman for the Harbor School; to show the parents powerfully that we [at the Old Harbor School] believed in integration and that we were determined to hold on to that belief." Bengt started out by informing the parents about new resources, the further education of staff, and new recruitments. He talked impressively about how integration would be developed. To reinforce his assurances, he asked some teacher representatives to join him on the podium. On behalf of their colleagues, they declared to the gathered parents that they considered themselves to have the professional skills and support that was needed. Together, Bengt and the Old Harbor staff also asserted their belief that every pupil, despite who he or she might be and where that student came from, should be treated equally and given the same opportunities. And "we" they emphasized "should and can do so." The parents seemed to be quite satisfied with all the well-performed messages and declarations. At least, no one spoke against them. The Old Harbor School thus seemed solidly united. However, there was one issue that still roused some worries and resistance. The parents who made their voices heard preferred to have the pupils from the Old Harbor and the Creek in separate school classes. Bengt and his staff believed, on the contrary, that it was necessary that the pupils from the two districts be mixed. Pupils from the Old Harbor and the Creek would constitute integrated school classes and, hence, should belong to and interact in shared classrooms. There could be no segregation, they thought, within a truly integrated school. Bengt's main argument was informed by linguistic and social research. The children's language skills and learning would be better developed if the classes were mixed. It would also be a much better strategy for social integration and multicultural incorporation. Mixed classes, he also argued, would minimize the risk of any stirred-up antagonism between "us" and "them" within the school. However, this was not an answer that satisfied the most critical and talkative parents. They wanted their children in Old Harbor classes and the other, "new children" in separate Creek classes. On this issue, Bent and the teachers could not persuade them. Instead, the bogged down discussion yet again focused on the questions of how the Old Harbor School would be influenced by the new independent school that was eventually to open in the district. What would happen if that school attracted more pupils than the Old Harbor School had expected? The independent school continually came up as a possible escape route from social integration and multiculturalism. Bengt expressed a positive attitude toward competition from an independent school. "It forces us," he told the gathered parents, "to sharpen our argument on what kind of school we want to have."

Even if the second meeting did not end in harmony, Bengt did feel the wind at his back. Most parents out there in the auditorium, he thought, were probably in favor of integration and multiculturalism—also in each and every classroom. Again, they had probably gone into silence due to the outspokenness of the critical minority. Before the gathered parents dispersed, it was decided that a third meeting would be held.

In-between the meetings, two important things happened. Bengt arranged a very successful meeting between children (and staff) from the Old Harbor School and the Creek. It was also confirmed that an independent school was about to be open in the Old Harbor district and decided that the most critical parents had probably already decided to move their children there. Be that as it may, Bengt's beliefs could not fail him now. He stood more firmly than ever. He had a dream and could not be moved. He took to the floor, more and more supported by the growing social fact of a symbolic structure—a central vitality—resting on the support of the majority of the parents. Yes, to reconnect with Alexander, "if the leaders are skillful, followers are brave, and the stars are right, movements for civil repair can succeed" (2006b, p. 552). However, to make a cultural sociological point, Bengt had only awoken the solidarity and sympathy within the majority of parents that were already compelled by a shared and embodied meanings system. In other words, his performances had mainly made possible what was to a great extent already, even if silenced, present.[30] Hence, we need to remember that cultural, or symbolic, structures are "not only external to actors but internal to them" (Alexander 2006b, p. 552). They are not only "out there" as social facts, but also "in there" as feelings and thoughts in social actors. Symbolic structures thus work through subjective processes of shared meaning-making. Let me turn to Falstaff—the at once "great deceiver" and "truth-teller" (Bate and Rasmussen, 2007, p. 893) in Shakespeare's historical two-part drama *Henry IV*—who provides us with a wonderful illustration of the intersection of "out-there-symbolic-structures" and "in-there-subjective-responsiveness." This is how Falstaff explains the possibility of wit and laughter: "I am not only witty in myself, but the cause of that wit is in other men" (Shakespeare, 2007, p. 969). In other words, Falstaff can only awaken a wittiness within human beings that is already compelled by a shared and embodied meaning system. The experience of meaningfulness within Falstaff is also by necessity belongingness to, or at least an acquaintance with, the meaningfulness within and among those who share the laughter. That this is so does not in any sense deny Falstaff's extreme wittiness or his character. Falstaff "*is*," as the literary critic Harold Bloom puts it, "Shakespeare's wit at its very limit" (1999, p. 273). Shakespeare, of course, knew how to be witty and create laughter among his audiences. Bengt, too, had character and was, undoubtedly so, skillful in his project, but not only within himself. The cause that made social integration and multicultural incorporation possible at the Old Harbor School was also in other human beings that, after all, belonged to a vital core of central civility. Again, they had only experienced a clash within. At this very successful moment in time and place, Bengt's beliefs and practices coincided with the task of cultural sociology: "To bring the unconscious cultural structures that regulate society and human beings into the light of mind" (Alexander, 2003, p. 3–4). Thus, we need to tell about yet another evening meeting at the Old Harbor School.

Parents from both the Old Harbor and the Creek were invited to the third meeting. For the first time during this ongoing process of incorporation, the adults from the different districts met. Bengt started out by launching a new fifteen-minute video. It was a recording of the encounter between pupils from the Old Harbor School and the pupils from the Creek. It displayed wonderful scenes where the children found common ground, and expressed their views on integration. They did not experience their encounters as a problem. "Adult prejudices," one of them told the camera, "don't matter when young people meet." "It doesn't matter if you are from Afghanistan or Malmö," another declared, "as long as you are kind and respect each other." The message from the children in the video was clear. They did not have any problem with children of different backgrounds attending the same school, or even occupying the same classroom. A girl representing the pupil's council at the Old Harbor School made the following statement before the camera and, hence, to the gathered parents from the Old Harbor and the Creek:

> If we do not make the pupils from the Creek feel welcome, they will not feel welcome. Think about what would have happened if it had been our school that was to be closed down and that we were the ones to be forced to move. If that was the case, I would have liked to be welcomed and be taken care of at the new school. If not, there will, of course, be trouble.

"With these words," as Bengt puts it, "the parents [from the Old Harbor] found it very hard to argue against the opinions of their own children." It is not an audacious remark to state that they, looking back on the experiences from the two earlier meetings in the light of their own children's statement, felt ashamed about their own, or, more so, the most critical parents' xenophobic expressions and rejection of the integration of children. The foul-tempered man who two months earlier at the first malignant meeting had been banging his hands on the tabletop where he was seated to get Bengt's attention now very seriously asked politely to be allowed to speak. He was full of remorse:

> I belonged to those parents who were very skeptical to the idea of moving the pupils from the Creek to the Old Harbor. I even have to admit that I expressed my views in a way that I now feel a bit ashamed over. I am now listening to reason, and I want to apologize for my previous statements. Let us now help each other out as parents and give the school our support so that it can succeed in what it rightfully so needs to do. This is *not* what I called a "social experiment." However, there are still problems we need to solve, and we need to do it together. My son will stay at the Harbor school.

All the gathered parents accentuated in one common spirit the need to work together. The parents from the Harbor, who had now accepted the idea of mixed school classes, focused on the size of the school classes. The parents from the Creek did not have any doubts about mixed classes, but raised concerns about transportation.

How would it be arranged so that their children might feel safe on their daily jour-
neys to the Old Harbor School and back home again?

The majority of the critical parents had decided not to attend the third meeting.
They did not share Bengt's and the other parents' hopes regarding social integration
and multicultural incorporation. They had decided, as had been previously surmised,
to drop out of the integration process and move their children to the new independent
school. They had carried out the threat they used during the whole negotiating process. These parents did not agree with Ingrid Robertsson's pleading words on how "we
all need to help each other out and to contribute to our city." They did not identify with
the normative hope of Alexander's new concept of the civil sphere, that is, "a world of
values and institutions that generates the capacity for social and democratic integration at the same time" (2006b, p. 4). They did not rely on "solidarity" and "feelings for
others whom we do not know but whom we respect out of principle, not experience,
because of our putative commitment to common secular faith" (2006b, p. 4). They did
not understand multiculturalism as a project of hope, but as a project of despair.

About fifty children became former Old Harbor School attendees. However, for
the majority of parents at the Old Harbor and the Creek, widespread feelings of
common humanity were launched, as well as solidarity and sympathies. Bengt was,
rightfully so, proud to state that he had succeeded in holding onto his beliefs, which
were, as it turned out, also the beliefs of a great majority of teachers, parents, and
pupils. Accordingly, there was no clash between the Creek and the Old Harbor
"civilizations"—only within the latter. Indeed, schools were burning, but from that
day forth, bridges were being built, too. I wish Muhammad and his rascals had been
from the Creek. I wish that they had been young enough to attend the Old Harbor
School. But, after all, "it is," as I have learned from Alexander, "the relative autonomy
of the civil sphere's meaning structures that makes every form of domination fundamentally unstable and every unequal distribution contestable" (2007, pp. 25–26).

This is how Alexander ends my "eyes to see," that is, *The Civil Sphere*:

> What we can know for certain is that the discourse and structure of the civil sphere
> will remain. It will still be restless, and its dynamism will be dangerous and contra-
> dictory. But the discourse of liberty will continue, and the hopes for civil repair will
> remain. Civil society is a project. It inspires hope for democratic life. (2006b, p. 553)

Some Concluding Remarks

> How can we not be attached?
> After all we're only human
>
> —Van Morrison

I started out by describing "the detective" as, quoting the novelist Paul Auster, "one
who looks, who listens, who moves through this morass of objects and events in
search of the thought, the idea that will pull all these things together and make sense

of them" (2006, p. 8). I also told the reader that I conceived of the ethnographer as "the writing detective of cultural sociology." Now that I have demonstrated what ethnography can do for cultural sociology I would like to leave the reader with the idea that this thought—these eyes to see, these touchdowns, and these stories—at once are, to borrow two formulations from the Swedish author and literary critic Kjell Espmark, "its own autonomous reality" and "a miniature world that also send words of the big world" (2008, p. 33). But what have I done? I think that I have demonstrated, again in the words of Alexander, the "need" of "a new concept of civil society as a civil *sphere*, a world of values and institutions that generates the capacity for social criticism and democratic integration at the same time" (2006b, p. 4). I also think I have caught "such a sphere" when it in its lived forms, as with Muhammad, Bengt, and others, "relies on solidarity, on feelings for others whom we do not know but whom we respect out of principle, not experience, because of our putative commitment to a common secular faith" (2006b, p. 4). Accordingly, social integration and multicultural incorporation are not only to be understood as a "moral preference"—they are also, as Alexander formulates it, "very much an empirical process" (2006b, p. 451). In the best of worlds, this "thought" and "empirical process" is not only about "us" and "now." In our minds and deep in the habits of our hearts, we also want it to represent, again quoting Espmark, "a wider and more conditioning validity" (2008, p. 34). In that sense, to yet again quote Hustvedt, "We don't experience the world. We experience our expectation of the world" (2008, p. 131). However, as Alexander puts it, "real societies are contradictory and fragmented" (2006b, p. 7), and it is their "dynamics" that "create the conditions for suppressing the very existence of the civil sphere" (2006b, p. 7). Nevertheless, "the ideals of civil society are never completely negated" (2006b, p. 7): They hold before us, as Alexander points out, "alternative possibilities, and from these general principles there emerge counterproposals for reform" (2006b, p. 7). Yes, Alexander again, "It is the idea of civil solidarity that allows divisions to be reconstructed" (2006b, p. 7). Or, to return to the conversation between Derrida and Chérif: "If God wanted it, he would have made you a single community, but he wanted, the Koran tells us, to test you through the gift of difference" (2008, p. 93). Thus, "that solidarity can be broadened is the project of civil repair (Alexander, 2006b, p. 7). Just as Duneier when writing *Slim's Table*, I have sought critically to "examine those ways in which city life promotes conflict between groups that responds to one another as categories, while promoting solidarity between those who share a consciousness of kind" (1992, p. 160). I too, metaphorically speaking, have been sitting at Slim's table in the cafeteria where, as Duneier studied, "the highest form of respectability resulted not from contrasts between one's group and others in the setting, but from positive relations with other categories of persons," that is, "with human beings who are different from oneself" (1992, p. 160). In other words, I have been informed by "the need" the visitors at the Valois cafeteria felt "to enter into a relationship with their society" (Duneier, 1992, p. 160). With my "eyes to see," in my two touchdowns and in my eagerness to tell stories and make all sorts of connections, I have been in search of the lived possibilities of intertwined and deeply shared meanings of solidarity, and sympathy that so easily seem to escape our critical minds. I have tried hard to be part of that broadening. In doing so, I would argue, by Dirda's comment on Austers's writing, that "each of us looks at existence through story-colored lenses" (2008, p. 38). Remembering and imagining, there is no clear border between them. And, yes, when "artists, or ordinary people, talk about what truly matters, they start and end by telling stories, wonderful, amazing stories" (Dirda, 2008, p. 38)—like those of Laid, Muhammad, Bengt, Jeffrey, Mustapha, Jacques, Shakespeare, Paul, and Siri. This is what ethnography can do *for* cultural sociology. As Joyce Carol Oates puts it in her diary on a writer's writing life: "There is nothing inherently better about writing *against* than *for*...*, and it is even more sophisticated to be for since that is difficult and will not seem, to shallow people, sophisticated at all" (2008, p. 62). I am living now in the grip of this spin.

This chapter is written in memory of my mother, Ann-Marie Trondman (1927–2008), a good and beautiful but very lonely person in life, who passed away while this essay was being written. Sitting beside her bed three days before her death, she told me to concentrate on my writing while she slept. There is also, of course, the sleep that Shakespeare described as "the death of each day's life." However, being the man in the dark and thinking back on the content of this chapter, the following lines from Siri Hustvedt come to my mind: "It's as if my sadness soaked the architecture. I can tell you a story about it, and I wouldn't be lying, but would that reconstruction of events be real or true?" I find it deeply true. Even worth living for.

NOTES

1. See Atkinson in which "being there" concerns "a commitment to the first hand experience and exploration of a particular social and cultural setting on the basis of (though not exclusively by) participant observation" (2004, p. 4). See also Van Maanen who argues that "fieldwork usually means living with...those who are studied" (1988, p. 2). Or, Wolcott: "There is no substitute for 'being there' and 'doing it'" (1999, p. 16). Basically, ethnographers will ask themselves and others, "What is going on here"? (Wolcott, 1999, p. 297) Thus, "'Being there'...is always being there in a particular and strategically chosen setting in which ethnographers try to move with what moves them" (Trondman, 2008, p. 118).

2. This is how Willis and Trondman put it: "Engagement with the 'real' world can bring 'sursprise' to theoretical formulation" and "theoretical resources can bring 'surprise' to how empirical data is understood" (2000, p. 12). Hence, Willis and Trondman recognize and promote a "dialectic of surprise" (2000, p.12). Such a "surprise" is a two-way stretch, a continuous process shifting forth and back, if you like, between induction and deduction.

3. Alexander is here following the neo-Popperian Imre Lakatos, who writes that "the problem is not...when we should stick to a 'theory' in the face of the 'known facts' and when the other way around" nor "what to do when theories 'clash with facts.'" "Theory and fact are, rather," Alexander adds, "terms of convenience, decided by the focus of scientific

attention at a particular time." "Weather a proposition is a fact or theory," Lakatos himself states, "depends on our methodological decision.... The problem is which theory to consider as the interpretative one which provides the 'hard' facts and which the explanatory one which 'tentatively' explains them." According to Lakatos, "Calling... statements 'observational'" is "a manner of speech." (All quotes from Alexander, 1982, p. 30.)

4. This is how Walzer states it: "There couldn't be a society of free individuals without a socialization process, a culture of individuality, and a supportive political regime whose citizens were prepared to be supportive in their turn. In other words, the society of free individuals would be, for most of its members, an involuntary association (2004, p. 17). From this follows that "we are not born free, we are not born equal. Involuntary association is the most immediate cause of inequality, for it consigns each person to a particular place or set of places in the social system. If we think of the hierarchies of property and status as the basic structures of an in egalitarian society, the involuntary association is the way men and women are locked into ranks and orders. The promise of liberal autonomy has always been that it will break the locks, enabling individuals to choose or at least to aim at the places they desire—and so create a society of free and mobile men and women who are also (more nearly) equal. This is a false or, better, a wildly exaggerated promise. We will succeed in challenging the social hierarchy only if we recognize and work on the realities of involuntary association. Denial is foolish, and abolition is impossible. Involuntary association is a permanent feature of social existence, and the people who fight for equality, like those who struggle to be free, are inevitably its creatures" (Walzer, 2004, pp. 2–3). And also: "Morality" is an important "feature of socialization, or written into the cultural code, or legally enforced by state officials..." (Walzer, 2004, p. 9). This "morality" is "a constraint that individuals confront not only as creatures of society, culture, and politics but also as individuals trying to do the right thing. They hear an internal voice of constraint, telling them that they should do this or that, which they have not (so far) chosen to do and would rather not do. Most important of my purposes here, the voice tells them (they tell themselves) that they ought to join this association or participate in that social and political struggle—or they ought not to abandon this association or withdraw from that struggle" (Walzer, 2004, p. 9). To me, in this chapter, Muhammad is an individual trying to find his freedom and recognition, despite the influences of all thinkable aspects of "involuntary association." Bengt is, of course, under the influences of his "involuntary association." At the same time, he is also hearing an internal voice, telling him what to do to increase the possibilities and life chances for people like Muhammad. Walzer and Alexander, provide "eyes to see" this ongoing struggle for social integration and multicultural incorporation, despite the unavoidable influences of involuntary association, and not to forget, thanks to a "morality" in the civil sphere for a more egalitarian liberalism. This is, I think, how we can understand, and even accept, differences *and* share the common beliefs that keep the social hope for multicultural incorporation alive.

5. It reminds me of John Adams, the second president of the United States, who stated that "facts are stubborn things, and whatever maybe our wishes, our inclinations, or the dictums of our passions, they cannot alter the state of facts and evidence" (quoted from McCullough, 2008, p. 68). However, in this case, the "facts" are on "our" side.

6. See also Mast, 2006, pp. 115–138.

7. I do agree with Strauss who argues that "it is impossible to study social phenomena, i.e., all important social phenomena, without making value judgements" (1988, p. 21). This is how Strauss puts it: "A man who refuses to distinguish between great statesmen, mediocrities, and insane impostors may be a good bibliographer; he cannot say anything relevant about politics and history.... Generally speaking, it is impossible to understand thought or action

or work without evaluating it. If we are unable to evaluate adequately, as we very frequently are, we have not yet succeeded in understanding adequately. The value judgements which are forbidden to enter through the front door of political science, sociology or economics, enter these disciplines through the backdoor..." (1988, p. 21). Thus, "we must not overlook the invisible value judgements which are concealed from undiscerning eyes but nevertheless most powerfully present in allegedly purely descriptive concerns" (1988, p. 21).

8. This statement, of course, reveals a strong relation between cultural sociology and the sociology of Emile Durkheim. Alexander writes: "Durkheim knew all this, but he did not very well conceptualize how it actually happened, or even what 'society' itself is" (2006b, p. 18). See also Alexander, 1989, pp. 123–155.

9. Dave Holland is quoted from the sleeve of Dave Holland Big Band's record *What Goes Around*, EMC, 2002.

10. See note 9 above.

11. According to the *National Rescue Services Agency* (Räddningsverket, Sweden), the number of schools burning in Sweden has doubled during the last ten years. The official statistical record shows that 500 schools burned in Sweden during 2006. Two hundred were considered the work of an incendiary. The yearly cost of schools burning in Sweden is, as of 2010, about 500 million crowns.

12. The idea of this "additional aim" comes from Alexander and Smelser (1999, pp. 3–17) who argue against, with strong social scientific proofs (facts are stubborn things!), what they call "the ideological discourse of cultural discontent," that is, both "the conservative and the radical versions of the discourse of discontent" (p. 17). "Beneath the shrill rhetoric of many intellectuals and opinion leaders," they state, "we have found a deep process of institutionalizing at work." They continue: "Despite the dire warnings of the right and the utopian claims of the left, the reformist projects of the movements of the 1960s have been realized to a great degree. Faced with the pressures of growing institutional complexity and cultural diversity, new forms of democratic integration have developed" (p. 17). And in conclusion: "In identifying the misdiagnoses of both the left and the right we are far from claiming that 'all is right with the world'. But we are convinced that the assertions about the death of common values are premature at best" (p. 17).

13. I am here, of course, referring to Clifford Geertz. I think that the concept of "thick description" is best understood as it is laid out in the following quote from Robert Darnton informing the reader how Geertz himself formerly taught hermeneutics and "thick description" to his students: "For example, in expounding the esoteric notion of the hermeneutic circle—the conception of interpretive understanding favoured by the philosopher Hans-Georg Gadamer—Cliff did not begin an exposition of Gadamer's general principles and a theoretical account of descriptive as opposed to causal explanations in the human sciences. Instead, he asked the students to imagine themselves explaining baseball to a visitor from Outer Mongolia whom they had taken to a game. You would point out the three bases, he said, and the need to hit the ball in such a way as to run around the bases and reach home plate before being tagged out by the defence. But in doing so, you might note the different shape of the first baseman's glove or the tendency of the infield to realign itself in the hope of making a double play. You would tack back and forth between general rules—three strikes, you're out—and fine details on the nature of the hanging curve. The mutual reinforcement of generalizations and details would build up an increasingly rich account of the game being played under the observer's eyes. Your description could circle around the subject indefinitely, getting thicker with each telling. 'Thick descriptions' would vary; some would be more effective than others; and some might be wrong: to have a runner advance from third base to second would be a clear

mistake. But the description, if sufficiently artful and accurate, would cumulatively convey an interpretation of the thing itself, baseball" (2007, p. 37). Accordingly, I see the attempts at "thick descriptions" that come out of my two ethnographical "touchdowns" as "cumulative endeavours" in search of an answer to my research question that also, at the same time, fulfill my overall respective additional aim.

14. This is how Dirda puts it: "The world we inhabit is literary shaped by Story. We all have our 'life stories', and these govern how we see ourselves and others. How we interpret events and memories and expectations. When our saviours and teachers speak to us about the greatest truth, whether of religion or philosophy, they always speak to us in parables. When artists, or ordinary people, talk about what truly matters, they start and end by telling stories, wonderful, amazing stories—like those in the works of Paul Auster" (2008, p. 38).

15. The title of Laid Bouakac's dissertation is "Parental Involvement in School: What Hinders and What Promotes Parental Involvement in an Urban School." It was published at Malmö University Press in 2007.

16. See also Trondman's writing on Sayad (2001).

17. See Stonequist, *The Marginal Man*, 1937. See also Trondman, 1994.

18. A falafel is, quoting *The New Oxford American Dictionary*, "a Middle Eastern dish of spiced chickpeas or other pulses formed into balls or fritters and deep-fried, usually eaten with or in a pita bread" (2005, p. 605).

19. In *Whitney Museum of American Art*, Hopper was placed under the heading "The American Scene." See Schmied, 2005, p. 7.

20. The first lines from the Qur'an are cited from Cleary, 2008, p. 1.

21. This is how Derrida himself puts it: "The community to which I belonged was cut off in three ways: it was cut off first from the Arabs and the Berber, actually the Maghrebin language and culture; it was also cut off from the French, indeed European, language and culture, which were viewed as distant poles, unrelated to its history; and finally, or to begin with, it was cut off from Jewish memory, from that history and that language that one must assume to be one's own, but which at a given moment no longer were—at least in a special way, for most of its members in a sufficiently living and internal way" (Derrida and Chérif, 2008, pp. 34–35).

22. This is how Derrida states it in *Islam and the West*: "To commit to a universal democratic ideal and want at the same time to be inspired by Islam is our right; justice and meaning are our demands, knowing that we must accept the idea that nothing is given in advance and that there is no pre-established path to follow" (2008, p. 9). At the same time, such "a civilization must be plural; it must ensure a respect for the multiplicity of languages, cultures, beliefs, ways of life. And it is in this plurality, in this alterity, that a chance—I won't speak of a solution—for the future is possible, namely, in multiplicity and plurality" (2008, p. 81).

23. Nussbaum also writes: "At a deeper level, the thesis of this book is the Gandhian claim that the real struggle that democracy must wage is a struggle within the self, between the urge to dominate and defile the other and a willingness to live respectfully on terms of compassion and equality, with all the vulnerability that such lives entails" (2007, pp. ix–x).

24. The Arabian language is considered to be the third most common language in Sweden. A rough estimate is that some 200,000 to 300,000 thousand people in Sweden probably speak Arabic on a daily basis. See Ingemansson, 2008, p. 30.

25. Beard makes this statement in relation to John R. Clarke's *Looking at Laughter: Humor, Power, and Progress in Roman Visual Culture, 100 BC–AD 250*. One of Clarke's points is that humor and laughter can be read as a social survival mechanism. In other words, laughter can save the day where social relations threaten the status of the members in a group.

26. Being a *blatte* (plural, *blattar*) is the opposite of being a *svenne*. *Blatten*, the singular form, would, seen from the outside among *svennar*, be "the immigrant" discussed as the problem. From the inside, among the young immigrants themselves, especially so in social housing projects, it will be the word that rascals use to counter their own subordination by using a word that would be impossible for *svennar* to use in public. However, if a "Swede" and an "immigrant" are the best of friends, they can playfully and in full comfort talk to and about themselves as being a *svenne* and a *blatte*. It is also common to say, when talking about which school to choose, "I will not go to a "*blatte* school," which often, both among "Swedish" and "immigrant" school achievers, means a school with a reputation of being, in Swedish, *socialt stökig*, that is, "socially disordered" and thus an improper environment in terms of prestige and school achievement. See also Trondman, 2006, pp. 431–451.

27. Quoted from the Royal Shakespeare Company's *William Shakespeare: The Complete Works*, 2007, p. 496.

28. However, it should also be said, that there are also some "Swedes" who could have moved but have preferred to stay because they like the area and its people.

29. This is how Alexander puts it: "The challenge for any progressive social movement, or for any more incremental gesture, is to convince core group members of one's civil capacities, to dispute polluting constructions, to demonstrate the qualities of fellowship, of civil depth and reliability, and, sometimes, of democratic heroism itself....Every immigrant and subordinated person knows this truth. Civil capacities must be demonstrated in the primordial colourings established by core groups" (2007, pp. 28–29). See also Trondman 2006, pp. 431–451.

30. The analytic strength of Alexander's "performance theory"—as presented in the "Cultural Pragmatics: Social Performance Between Ritual and Strategy" in the anthology *Social Performance: Symbolic Action, Cultural Pragmatics, and Ritual* edited by Alexander, et al.—could easily have been illustrated in all its aspects by Bengt's successful performance. See Alexander, 2006a, pp. 29–90.

REFERENCES

Alexander, Jeffrey C. 1982. *Theoretical Logic in Sociology. Vol. 1: Positivism, Presupposition, and Current Controversies*. London: Routledge & Keegan Paul.

———. 1989. "Rethinking Durkheim's Intellectual Development: On the Complex Origins of a Cultural Sociology." Pp. 123–155 in *Structure and Meaning: Rethinking Classical Sociology* by Jeffrey C. Alexander. New York: Columbia University Press.

———. 2006a. "Cultural Pragmatics: Social Performance Between Ritual and Strategy." Pp. 29–90 in *Social Performance. Symbolic Action, Cultural Pragmatics, and Ritual*, edited by Jeffrey C. Alexander, Bernard Giesen, and Jason L. Mast. Cambridge, UK: Cambridge University Press.

———. 2006b. *The Civil Sphere*. Oxford: Oxford University Press.

———. 2007. "The Meaningful Construction of Inequality and the Struggle Against It: A 'Strong Program' Approach to How Social Boundaries Change." *Cultural Sociology*1:23–30.

———. 2008. "Clifford Geertz and the 'Strong Program': The Human Sciences and Cultural Sociology." *Cultural Sociology* 2:157–168.

Alexander, Jeffrey C., and Smelser, Neil J. 1999. "Introduction: The Ideological Discourse of Cultural Discontent: Paradoxes, Realities, and Alternative Ways of Seeing." Pp. 3–18 in

Diversity and Its Discontents: Cultural Conflict and Common Ground in Contemporary Society, edited by Neil J. Smelser and Jeffrey C. Alexander. Princeton, NJ: Princeton University Press.

Alexander, Jeffrey C., and Smith, Philip. 2003. "The Strong Program in Cultural Sociology: Elements of a Structural Hermeneutics." Pp. 11–26 in *The Meanings of Social Life: A Cultural Sociology* by Jeffrey C. Alexander. Oxford: Oxford University Press.

Atkinson, Peter. 2004. "Editorial Introduction." Pp. 1–8 in *Handbook of Ethnography*, edited by Paul Atkinson, Amanda Coffey, Sara Delamonte, John Lofland, and Lyn Lofland. London: Sage.

Auster, Paul. 2005. *The Invention of Solitude*. London: Farber & Farber.

————. 2006. *The New York Trilogy*. New York: Penguin Classic.

Bate, Jonathan, and Rasmussen, Eric. 2007. "Introduction: The Two Parts of Henry the Fourth." Pp. 892–900 in *William Shakespeare's Completed Work*. London: MacMillan.

Beard, Mary. 2008. "Isn't It Funny?" *New York Review of Books* (12).

Bloom, Harold. 1998. *Shakespeare. The Invention of the Human*. London: Fourth Estate.

Bouakac, Laid. 2007. *Parental Involvement in School: What Hinders and What Promotes Parental Involvement in an Urban School*. Malmö, Sweden: Malmö University Press.

Burke, Kenneth. 1973. *The Philosophy of Literary Forms*. Berkeley: University of California Press.

Clarke, John R. 2008. *Looking at Laughter: Humor, Power, and Transgression in Roman Visual Culture, 100 BC–AD 250*. Berkeley: University of California Press.

Cleary, Thomas. 1998. *The Essential Koran. The Heart of Islam: An Introductory Selection of Reading from the Qur'an*. Edison, NJ: Castle Books.

Darnton, Robert. 2007. "On Clifford Geertz: Field Notes from the Classroom." *New York Review of Books*: Volume 54, Number 1: 32–33.

David Holland Big Band, *What Goes Around* [CD]. ECM Records GmbH, 2002.

Derrida, Jacques, and Chérif, Mustapha. 2008. *Islam & the West: A Conversation with Jacques Derrida*. Chicago: University of Chicago Press.

Dirda, Michael. 2008. "Spellbound." *New York Review of Books* 19:4–17.

Duneier, Mitchel. 1992. *Slim's Table: Race, Respectability, and Masculinity*. Chicago: University of Chicago Press.

Espmark, Kjell. 2008. *Albatrossen på däcket*.Stockholm: Norstedts.

Geertz, Clifford. 1980. *Negara: The Theatre State in Nineteenth-Century Bali*. Princeton, NJ: Princeton University Press.

————. 1993. "Religion as a Cultural System." Pp. 87–125 in *Interpretation of Cultures*. London: Fontana Press.

————. 1999. "A Life of Learning: Charles Homer Haskins Lecture for 1999." Paper No. 45, New York: American Council of Learned Societies.

Hustvedt, Siri. 1998. *Yonder. Essays*. New York: Henry Holt.

————. 2008. *The Sorrows of an American*. London: Hodder & Stoughton.

Ingemansson, Bitti. 2008."Ljusning för Sveriges tredje största språk." *Språktidningen* 6:11–27.

Inglis, Fred. 2000. *Clifford Geertz: Culture, Custom and Ethics*. Cambridge, UK: Cambridge University Press.

Mast, Jason L. 2006. "The Cultural Pragmatics of Event-ness: The Clinton/Levinsky Affair." Pp. 115–145 in *Social Performance: Symbolic Action, Cultural Pragmatics, and Ritual*, edited by Jeffrey C. Alexander, Bernard Giesen, and Jason L. Mast. Cambridge, UK: Cambridge University Press.

McCullough, David. 2008. *John Adams*. New York: Simon & Schuster.

Mella, Orlando, and Palm, Irving. 2007. *Mångfaldsbarometern*. Uppsala, Sweden: Uppsala University.

Myrdal, Gunnar. 1996. *An American Dilemma. Vol. 1: The Negro Problem and Modern Democracy.* New Brunswick, NJ: Transaction.

The New Oxford American Dictionary. 2005. Oxford: Oxford University Press.

Nussbaum, Martha C. 1990. "Reading for Life." Pp. 230–244 in *Love's Knowledge: Essays on Philosophy and Literature* by Martha C. Nussbaum. Oxford: Oxford University Press.

———. 1997. *Cultivating Humanity.* Cambridge, MA: Harvard University Press.

———. 2007. *The Clash Within: Democracy, Religious Violence, and India's Future.* Cambridge, MA: Belknap Press of Harvard University.

Oates, Joyce Carol. 2008. *The Journal of Joyce Carol Oates,* edited by Greg Johnson. New York: Harper Perennial.

Sayad, Abdelmalek. 2004. *The Suffering of the Immigrant.* Cambridge, UK: Cambridge University Press.

Schmied, Wieland. 2005. *Edward Hopper: Portraits of America.* New York: Prestel.

Shakespeare, William. 2007. *William Shakespeare: Complete Work,* edited by Jonathan Bate and Eric Rasmussen. London: MacMillan.

Stonequist, Everett V. 1937. *The Marginal Man: A Study in Personality and Culture Conflict.* New York: Charles Scribner's Sons.

Strand, Mark. 1994. *Hopper.* Hopewell, NJ: Ecco Press.

Strauss, Leo. 1959. *What Is Political Philosophy? And Other Studies.* Chicago: University of Chicago Press.

Trondman, Mats. 1994. *Bilden av en klassresa.* Stockholm: Carlssons Förlag.

———. 2001. "Utvandrade invandrare: Abdelmalek Sayads migrationssociologi." *Tvärsnitt: Humanistisk- och samhällsvetenskaplig forskning* 3:48–59.

———. 2006. "Disowning Knowledge: To Be or Not to Be 'the Immigrant' in Sweden." *Ethnic and Racial Studies* 3:431–451.

———. 2008a. "To Locate in the Tenor of Their Settings the Sources of Their Spell: Clifford Geertz and the 'Strong Program' in Cultural Sociology." *Cultural Sociology* 2:201–221.

———. 2008b. "Bypass Surgery: Rerouting Theory to Ethnographic Study." Pp. 115–139 in *How to Do Educational Ethnography,* edited by Geoffrey Waldorf. London: Tufnell Press.

———. 2009. "Review of Jeffrey C. Alexander's *The Civil Sphere.*" *Acta Sociologica* 2:190–191.

Walzer, Michael. 2004. *Politics and Passion: Toward a More Egalitarian Liberalism.* New Haven, CT: Yale University Press.

Van Maanen, John. 1988. *Tales of the Field: On Writing Ethnography.* Chicago: University of Chicago Press.

Willis, Paul, and Trondman, Mats. 2000. "Manifesto for Ethnography." *Ethnography* 1: 5–16.

Wolcott, Harry F. 1999. *Ethnography: A Way of Seeing.* Walnut Creek, CA: Altamira Press.

PART VI

RELIGION AS CULTURE

CHAPTER 16

THE CONSTITUTION OF RELIGIOUS POLITICAL VIOLENCE: INSTITUTION, CULTURE, AND POWER

ROGER FRIEDLAND

ONCE again, God walks in history.[1] Religion has become a political force and politics a religious obligation. Religion's reentry onto the public stage has been punctuated by deadly episodes of organized violence, sometimes executed by a few men, and often by masses of them—the Hindu nationalists at Ayodhya and Gujarat, India; Buddhist nationalists in Kandy, Sri Lanka; Shi'ite revolutionaries in Qom and Teheran, Iran; Sunni Islamists in Algeria and Egypt; Jewish nationalists and Palestinian Islamists in Hebron, Jerusalem and Gaza; Protestants in Londonderry, Northern Ireland; and, of course, by al-Qaeda in New York City and Washington, D.C. Half of the world's civil wars now involve religionists, the overwhelming majority of whom seek to impose religious law and suppress other faiths (Philpott 2007). The violence executed in the name of Islam has been particularly unnerving. These attacks, particularly suicidal ones that kill large numbers of civilians, seem beyond reason—on the one, the hand, nihilistic and irrational, and on the other, desperate or cynical—a pathology or a tactic, a defect in Islamic political culture or the new anti-imperial contradiction. To some it looks as though the city of God is becoming a political porn show.

How are we to understand the violence? Violence often appears to be the calling card for those who wish to harness religion as the animating principle of the nation-state, not to mention for those who wish to resist them. Some consider this violence, like the politicization of religion itself, as an instrument used by political elites and political organizations, having nothing to do with religion, indeed as an abrogation of religion's essential other or inner-worldly nature. Others consider this violence an expression of collective religious identities, a symptom of group boundaries threatened by an alien culture imposed from another time, another place. In this case the violence registers a religious affect, not a political effect. It expresses religious sensibilities of groups under siege; it does not follow a viable political logic.

Unexpected and unheralded by theorists of modernity, for those who guard the intellectual gates, the violence of politicized religion is the work of a monstrous hybrid they wish to purify. Politicized religion is variously judged to be neither truly religion, nor—in what appears to be its most violent and apparently antinomian forms—politics. One refuses politicized religion its religious ends; the other its political means. I wish to consider the rationality—or more precisely, the rationalities—of politicized religion's violence. What are its reasons? To understand its causes, we must also understand what it means.

To comprehend the violence of politicized religion, we must grapple with politicized religion on its own terms—not seek to purify one side or the other—and, then, give one primacy as the "real" ground of the phenomenon. Rather than a distributive or expressive struggle between groups, I propose that we understand politicized religion on institutional grounds. Its causes are, in part, located in the very shift in institutional architecture, which analysts seek to decouple or deconstruct, that is, the politicization of religion and the investment of the national state with religious significance. The violence of politicized religion, I shall argue, is both a corollary of attempted institutional transformation and, more specifically, of the institutional logic of religion itself. Religions, like states, organize and invest the making and unmaking of bodies with their own significance. That politicized religious movements tend toward violence and are preoccupied with the regulation of sexuality can be derived from the institutional logic of religion; its parallel and conflicting claims to the ontological ground of state authority; and the fraught relation among birth, death, and state authority that politicized religions expose and activate.

The institutionalism I forward is a cultural sociological project; it seeks to encompass, not displace, prior institutional constitutions. Institutions cannot be derived just from the limits of rational individual exchange as mechanisms to reduce transaction costs, forestall opportunism, or socialize externalities as in the economic institutionalism of Oliver Williamson (1983). Nor are they, as in the philosopher of language John Searle's approach, simply conversions of collective intentionality into nested networks of deontic powers that have a logic because the intentionality that produces them also does (Searle 2006: 15). Nor are they just "fields" homologously organized as dynamic structures of group domination (Bourdieu 1977, 1990; Friedland 2009c). Nor are they, as in sociologist Philip Selznick's original statements of institutional theory, forms of social organization invested with value beyond their practical effects—beyond the "technical requirements of the task at hand" (Selznick 1957: 17)—or, as later work showed, invested with practical effects because they are legitimate net of their practicality (DiMaggio and Powell 1983).

Institutions are themselves practical regimes of valuation, in the sense that they constitute institutional objects of value and particular kinds of subjects who value them. Institutions are constituted by orderings of means-ends couplets, regimes of practice, what I have called "institutional logics," that is, stable constellations of practice, and the objects and subjects that are coupled to them (Friedland 2009b, 2002; Friedland and Alford 1991). To understand the violence of politicized religion, one should look for the institutional logic of their practices, the ways in which these practices enact a religious ontology of the nation-state.

Religious Violence as Political Strategy

There are those who cast the politicization of religion and the use of violence in its name as strategic instruments by which political organizations and their elites reach for power in the pursuit of group interests, material benefits, and political power—interests having nothing to do with religion. The violence of politicized religion becomes an explicable tactic following from the theoretical normalization of protest and rule-breaking, a corollary of Foucault's rendition of politics as an extension of war (Foucault 1980: 93).

Religious violence doesn't just happen. It is both politically organized and efficacious. A growing body of work has documented the fabrication of religious nationalist violence. In the case of the Hindu nationalist riots in India, the site par excellence of perennialist readings, analysts have shown how political elites orchestrate collective religious violence as an instrument in their struggle for electoral advantage and the attainment of material and political benefits for their constituents (Brass 1997, 2002; Tambiah 1996; Wilkinson 2006). Political elites politicize local religious differences: globally narrate idiosyncratic local conflicts; employ trained activists, criminals, and the poor to engage in the violence; fail to deploy the coercive powers of the state to stop the violence; and then publicly interpret the violence as a primordial fact of nature (Mander 2002; Tambiah 1996). And they do so when there are likely to be electoral returns from such violence (Wilkinson 2006).

This religious violence often works. In the South Asian cases, it has produced population transfers that helped consolidate the hegemony of each group in their respective territories. In India, for example, violent acts not only increased the electoral strength of the Hindu nationalist party, but also the share of land, business, and jobs for the community whose members were the aggressors (Brass 1997; Wilkinson 2006). In Gujarat, the site of widespread Hindu nationalist violence against Muslims and their holy places, it is estimated that as many as 600,000 Muslims left the state (Kamdar 2002). Tambiah points to the material advantages of displacement of existing populations from urban areas, particularly poor areas, allowing for profitable urban redevelopment in its wake. This played an important role in many Indian religious riots, such as that in Delhi in 1984, the

1992–1993 riots in Bombay, and also in the Colombo, Sri Lanka riots of 1983 (Tambiah 1996: 331).

Politically efficacious consequences also followed in the cases of religious Zionist/political Islamic violence in Israel/Palestine, such as religious Zionist Dr. Baruch Goldstein's 1994 murder of Palestinians praying at Ibrahim mosque in Hebron; the 1995 Jewish nationalist assassination of Prime Minister Rabin as a *rodef*—a man about to murder and an apostate, as well as the launching of the more violent second Palestinian intifada in the aftermath of Ariel Sharon's official 2000 visit to the *haram al-sharif*; and the conduct of a series of Palestinian martyr-suicide operations by Hamas and the al-Aqsa Brigades of al-Fatah. These acts of politicized religious violence proved effective in undercutting rival political forces and preventing a mutually agreed partition of a contested territory (Friedland and Hecht 2000; Kepel 2002).

The dominant political approach understands this politicized religion and its violence as efficacious means, particularly for vulnerable groups, to reach for power and material resources within the nation-state. Suicide terrorism, for example, began as a secular tactic and has since, particularly post 2001, globally morphed into an Islamic phenomena (Argo 2006). Religious or not, proponents of this position argue that it follows an instrumental, geopolitical logic. Pape's survey of suicide terrorism campaigns in the last two decades of the twentieth century showed that this coercive strategy has been exclusively waged to coerce occupiers to withdraw from national homelands (Pape 2003). Aimed only at democratic states whose publics it sought to influence, it has been relatively successful in securing moderate territorial concessions, indeed more so than conventional forms of military and economic coercion. Others have questioned the efficacy of terrorist violence, particularly where it targetted civilians (Abrahms 2006).

For weak groups in repressive states, religion is often the only available medium for organization; violence is cheap and effective. The implication is that politics are likely to become both religious and violent under repressive conditions. Religious terrorists do tend to target more repressive states, particularly those that regulate religion, both of which are common in the Islamic world (Philpott 2007).[2] In this reading, the association between politicized religion and violence is, in consequence, largely spurious. This view tends to cast politicized religion and its violence as political means without religious meaning. Young Palestinian martyrs, including those who strike as members of religious units, typically do not come to their engagements through religio-political training, but through networks of friends and kin after having witnessed their deaths, torture, or humiliation (Ahmed 2005; Argo 2006). The same is the case for recruits to the global Salafi *jihadi* network (Sageman 2004). "Islam," declares an analyst of Islamic Palestinian fighters, "is no more than a mobilizing ideology to indoctrinate believers into not accepting oppression and subjugation" (Ahmed 2005: 100). Pape likewise understands the Islamic martyrology of its agents as a way to sacralize and moralize the tactic, thereby garnering popular support within the community and signaling more attacks to come for the target population (Pape 2003: 347).[3]

In this perspective, religion is a medium for the pursuit of secular ends. The eminent historian of religions Bruce Lincoln argues in his *Holy Terrors* that religious conflicts in postcolonial states should be understood in terms of "rival claims to scarce resources" and that politicized religion in opposition to the governing regime is a response to the failure of the secular state to deliver "on its promise to provide material well-being for its citizens" (Lincoln 2003:74–75). Lincoln reads politicized religious opposition as a power struggle by those elites displaced or marginalized by the "dominant fraction," and armed with its own legitimating discourse, whether it be secular or religious (Lincoln 2003: 79, 84). He writes:

> When objective conditions are good—peace prevails, prosperity in general, and
> all segments of society are generally healthy and well fed—the task of the religion
> of the status quo is easily accomplished, and there is little opportunity for
> religions of resistance to mount a serious threat. (Lincoln 2003: 86)

Political sociologist John Foran similarly understands the role of Shi'ite Islam in the Iranian revolution as a political medium to oppose material and political domination (Foran 1993). In Foran's view, Shi'ite Islam mediated between economic structure and oppositional, and particularly revolutionary, political action. In this account, the distinctive inequities and hardships—like displacement of the artisans and the bazaar merchants—generated by dependent development required a repressive personalistic state, the experience of whose exclusion generated a series of "political cultures of opposition"—Islam, republicanism, nationalism, Marxism, as well as their various syntheses. Foran understands Islam as a constituent of these oppositional cultures on the basis of which urban multiclass coalitions developed during the Constitutional Revolution of 1905–1911, Mussadiq's nationalization of oil in the early 1950s, and the Islamic revolution of 1979. In Foran's approach, religious political culture is a medium through which objective economic conditions are lived and interpreted, by which "structural determinants of grievances" achieve political form (Foran 1997).[4]

This instrumental view, in which religion is a medium for the pursuit of power and wealth, not only bolsters those commentators who intone that violence by religious militants has nothing to do with religion—a reading which would then apply equally to the Crusades, the Protestant Reformation, and Europe's wars of religion—it reduces politicized religion and its violence to political means,— whether effective or not—without any religious meaning.[5]

RELIGIOUS VIOLENCE AS RELIGIOUS SENTIMENT

The dominant cultural approach to politicized religion, and politicized Islam in particular, understands the politicization of religion and its violence as symptomatic expressions of sentiments and solidarities in defense of distinctive religious group identities and ways of life. The politicization of religion and its attendant violence is a defensive religious reaction of a group, not a political project for a society. This view reduces politicized religion to a defense of a religiously consti- tuted ethnic group or civilization, a religious refusal of modernity, or a kind of public pietism, *jihad* as an anti-Western and, hence, an anti-democratic, illiberal redemptive rite, not geopolitical strategy. Politics is either a medium of religious reaction, an anti-modern symptom, or a religious act lacking instrumental political significance.

Perennialism, which understands this violence as a reactive symptom in defense of one, among many, long-standing, pre-modern group attributes to both intra- national ethno-religious conflicts and international civilizational understandings of violent geopolitics, is one form of this approach.[6] Samuel Huntington has made much of Islamic opposition to Western efforts to "promote its values of democracy and lib- eralism to universal values." In his apparently prescient 1993 *Foreign Affairs* essay "The Clash of Civilizations," Huntington argued that after the Cold War, the new axes of geopolitical conflict were no longer economic or ideological, but civilizational, ordered according to religion (Huntington 1993). Civilizations, Huntington argues, are grounded in identity, not in what we want, but in who we are. Huntington claims:

> At a more basic level, however, Western concepts differ fundamentally from those
> prevalent in other civilizations. Western ideas of individualism, liberalism, constitu-
> tionalism, human rights, equality, liberty, the rule of law, democracy, free markets,
> the separation of church and state, often have little resonance in Islamic, Confucian,
> Japanese, Hindu, Buddhist, or Orthodox cultures (Huntington, 1993: 40).

Radical Islam, and al-Qaeda's terrorism against the West in particular, is often inter- preted as a religious refusal of democratic universalism. Huntington argues that Western efforts to "propagate" democratic ideals "produce instead a reaction against 'human rights imperialism' and a reaffirmation of indigenous values, as can be seen in the support of religious fundamentalism by the younger generation in non- Western cultures." There is some warrant for this view. Islamist radicals do deride the West's promotion of democracy. Bin Laden, shortly after the 9/11 attack, spoke of the Twin Towers as "those awesome symbolic towers that speak of liberty, human rights, and humanity" (Wright 2006: 176). This same taunting language goes back to modernity's first Islamic revolution—the Iranian. "Yes, we are reactionaries," the Ayatollah Khomeini declared, "and you are enlightened intellectuals....You, who want freedom, freedom for everything, the freedom of parties, you who want all the freedoms, you intellectuals: freedom that will corrupt our youth, freedom that will pave the way for the oppressor, freedom that will drag our nation to the bottom."[7]

For others, politicized religion does not mark a civilization, but a stage of soci- etal evolution, rendering their violence symptomatic, not strategic. Anti-modernist interpretations follow in this vein. Juergen Habermas, critical theorist of the public sphere, understands the politicization of religion as a religious anti-modernity, a refusal of group pluralism, a desperate, and ultimately futile, abrogation of the insti- tutional requirements of the immanent logic of the lifeworld. The communicative rationality of the lifeworld, he argues, requires a symmetrical openness to each other, a tacit agreement about the nature of truth, the possibility of its telling, and an adjudication of its content by taking the perspective of the other and engaging in rational contests over validity claims. Radical Islamists, indeed fundamentalists of all sorts, refuse to accept the "epistemic situation of a pluralistic society and insist—even to the point of violence—on the universally binding character and political acceptance of their doctrine" (Borradori 2003: 31).

Habermas understands these *jihadi* movements as a "return to the exclusivity of pre-modern belief attitudes," involving an "innocence of the epistemological situation"—both religiously plural and scientific—which is only compatible with universalism, and, hence, constitutional democracy (Borradori 2003: 32). While Habermas believes that radical Islamists promote their truth claims in an authoritarian manner because of the absence of democratic mechanisms for "mutual perspective-taking" by which relativization and the "fusion of horizons" might take place, he regards religion as an attribute of a group and a question of multicultural truth claims, as opposed to a question of institution and its boundary relations (Borradori 2003: 31, 37). Habermas thus refuses to grant the terrorism of radical Islam any political rationality. Speaking of the authors of 9/11, he writes, "They do not pursue a program that goes beyond the engineering of destruction and insecurity" (Borradori 2003: 29). Islamic terrorism, Habermas contends, "bears the anarchistic traits of an impotent revolt directed against an enemy that cannot be defeated in any pragmatic sense." Habermas, in fact, cannot imagine Islamic terrorism as a meaningful "political act."[8]

If Huntington sees radical Islam as a reaction not to the powers and policies of the West, but to its civilization—and Habermas espies in it an impotent anti-modernism—the great comparativist Islamicist Olivier Roy sees some of its most violent strains as an anti-Western, but nevertheless modernizing, pietism without political meaning in terms of the reformation of existent nation-states. Roy argues that, unlike the Islamists, al-Qaeda—like the Wahhabis, the Algerian GIA, Taliban, and Tablighi Jama'at—is an instance of what he calls neo-fundamentalism: de-territorialized and nonnational modernizing movements that sacralize daily life, focusing on salvation and the purification of self rather than political program, seeking to reconstitute a pure, but egalitarian, *umma* rather than a particular Islamic nation-state (Roy 2004: 243–254). Uninterested in the formation of an Islamic political party, in capturing or reconstituting the state, unconcerned with "socioeconomic issues," unidentified with and even hostile to a particular national culture, Roy claims we must understand their *jihad* as a redemptive rite, not as geopolitical strategy. Insistent on returning to a literalist, and deracinated, reading of the Qur'an, counting on the sufficiency of the application of Shari'a law alone, the neo-fundamentalists:

> …condemn the very concepts of democracy, human rights, and freedom, whereas Islamists try to show how Islam represents the best form of democracy (through the concept of *shura*, or consultation).…Neo-fundamentalists refuse to express their views in modern terms borrowed from the West. They consider that indulging in politics, even for a good cause, will by definition lead to *bid'a*

[innovation] and *shirk* [the giving of priority to worldly considerations over worldly values]. (Roy 2004: 247)

Neo-fundamentalists give primary to the reform of the soul, not the state; they seek a transportable individual purity, not state power. "For neo-fundamentalists, the aim of action is salvation, not revolution. Their objective is the individual, not society" (Roy 2004: 248).

Neo-fundamentalists, Roy contends, are not state-makers. Notwithstanding that many neo-fundamentalists originated in repressed Islamist movements or in response to the failures of existent Islamic polities, it is the temporal sequence and inner relation of *jihad* and *dawah,* or call to piety that is at issue. Neo-fundamentalists believe that territorial power will flow from faith, give primacy to the enforcement of Shari'a, and often seek to create self-governing territorial communities. Roy contends the *jihadi* violence of the neo-fundamentalists—while not theologically driven—has religious, not political meaning. Its aim is to please God, not to achieve state power and to recreate an imagined community of true believers, not to defend the existent territorial *umma.* The act, he contends, is more important than the result—a staging of faith, a form of worship. "Fighting," Roy concludes "is above all a spiritual journey. It is the ultimate proof of the reform of the self" (Roy 2004: 289, 246).

The first political approach claims that politicized religion and its violence are not religious, and the second cultural approach that they are not really political. I would suggest that they are both and that the two are related.[9] The dominant approaches understand politicized religion and its violence as a struggle between groups over power or resources—in which religion is a political means without religious meaning—or over group religious cultural values in which politics is a religious means without political meaning. The elemental thing to notice about politicized religion is that it seeks to change institutional boundaries, make the state religious and to politicize religion, and install religion as the basis of state authority and national identity. It is this threshold between politics and religion that these movements force us to reexamine.

THE INSTITUTIONAL FORM OF RELIGIOUS NATIONALISM

What is this nation-state to which religion claims a relation, indeed often a right? Nation-states join two symbolic orders, a nation and a state, a collective subject composed of people and an organizational apparatus claiming control over a territorially bounded population, a joining that grounds the state's sovereignty. Nationalisms are political movements that speak in the name of a nation. Nationalists derive their purpose and their legitimacy from that collective subject whom they claim to represent.

Nations do not exist on the ground; they must be constructed in the mind through categories of groupness and feelings of identification. The existence of nations depends on our thinking of them as if they were groups that are really real. Nations are not things; they are ontologically subjective. Their reality inheres in a shared subjective understanding, indeed a solidarity of feeling, that a people with particular attributes—common residence, language, ethnicity, culture, religion, or history—constitute a collectivity, indeed a collective subject capable of action, in other words an imagined agent to which an identity and interests are ascribed, both by themselves, as well as by their allies, competitors, and enemies. That collective agency implies—whether actually or potentially—a polity as its visible locus and medium.

Nations are political achievements. A nation, as anthropologist Benedict Anderson has famously remarked, is "an imagined political community," composed of people who will never know each other, but "in the minds of each, lives the image of their communion" (Anderson 1991). Carl Schmitt likewise pointed to the political formation of a people. He located the political not in the laws of the state, but in the sovereign decision on the enemy who is perceived to pose an existential threat to a "way of life." For Schmitt, it is the recognition of an enemy that is the "essence" of a people's "political existence," an enmity, however, preceded by a solidarity—the "intensity of human groupings, grounded in that 'way of life'" (Schmitt 1996: 49; see also Norris 1998). The groupness of a nation, in the felicitous words of Rogers Brubaker, is an "event" (Brubaker 2002: 168). Both the fact and the criteria of nationhood are stakes in "classification struggles" (Gorski forthcoming). These criteria vary so dramatically, Philip Gorski concludes, "a substantive definition of nationalism must always fail." The historical record suggests that nationalism, the political processes organized through or against the state in the name of nation, creates the nation, not the reverse (Tilly 1975; Giddens 1985; Mann 1986; but see Gorski 2006). "Nationhood," writes Craig Calhoun, "cannot be defined objectively, prior to political processes, on either cultural or social structural grounds. This is so, crucially, because nations are in part made by nationalism" (Calhoun 1998: 99; see also Smith 1991).

Nationalists seek to form nations as collective subjects through collective representation, through processes of political mobilization and ordination that aim at or work through or against sovereign states, either by struggling to take over an existent state or by establishing a new one. Nationalists may seek to nationalize an existent state, what Brubaker has termed, "nationalizing nationalism," in which claims are made in the "name of a 'core nation' or nationalism,…understood as the legitimate 'owner' of the state, which is conceived as the state *of* and *for* the core nation" (Brubaker, 1998). Or nationalisms may counter existing states, seeking some form of recognition within the state, or to break away from the state and form their own. A nation is always a potentially sovereign subject. Sovereignty is immanent in nationhood; nations without sovereignty are states-in-waiting, even if that wait may be forever, as the Armenians, Palestinians, Kurds, Tibetans, and Quebecois can all attest.

Nationalism is the collective movement that forms, and is in turn formed by, the making of the nation-state.[10] It is a program for the co-constitution of the state and the territorially bounded population in whose name it speaks, fashioning a collective subject as it seeks to create a nation-state. That territoriality is both the nation's site and its collective representation, critical to the imagination of this collective subject as a bounded, singular, and integral body to which one belongs and of which one partakes (Anderson 1991; Ramaswami 2002). The territory is the mirrored, unitary, bounded body of the collective subject.

Nationalism offers a form of representation—the joining of state, territoriality, and culture. It does not determine the content of representation, the identity of the represented collective subject, nor the sources of state law and legitimacy. Max Weber believed that nationalism involved a pathos, a "pathetic pride in the power of one's own community" (Weber 1978: 398). While Weber understood that the prestige of state power and of cultural values fused in the invocation, elicitation, and production of national group solidarity, he was acutely aware that the nation was "empirically…ambiguous" and that a "sociological typology would have to analyze all the individual kinds of sentiments of group membership and solidarity in their genetic conditions and in their consequences for the social action of the participants" (Weber 1978: 925). Weber did not develop such a sentimental typology. He did, however, enumerate four media by which that nationalist pathos might be accomplished: language, common custom, political memory, and religion (Weber 1978: 398).

Religion offers more than the grounding for sentiments of solidarity: It provides an institutionally specific way to organize this modern form of collective representation—how a collectivity represents itself to itself, the symbols, signs, and practices through which it is and knows itself to be. Religion need not change the national form of collective representation, only its content, privileging a basis of identity and a criterion of judgment that cannot not be collectively chosen by the people or the state. For religious nationalists—and here I include those Islamists who may deride nationalism, yet seek to Islamicize the nation-state—the religious criterion of judgment, like human rights, racial purity, or technical rationality, is beyond the reach of popular voice or the compelling interests of the state.

Some have argued that religious nationalists are not nationalists at all because the nation is not, as Brubaker contends, "the cardinal point of reference and justification for their political program" (Brubaker 2006: 18). Brubaker argues, "These programs claim to reorganize public life not 'in the name of the nation' but in the name of God. They work *through* the state, but this does not make them nationalists; as Said Amir Arjomand observed, it makes them statists" (Brubaker 2006: 18). The primacy of God, it is argued, reduces the nation-state to an instrument and an arena, thereby rendering their nationalism inert.

Religious nationalism is an amalgam of religion, nation, and state. Brubaker and others argue that using the state to serve God as one's ultimate ground is to be statist, not nationalist. Even on its own terms, thinking through what it means to be a religious statist, as opposed to a religious nationalist, requires that we think of the state's role in the institution of religion itself. Capitalism offers a parallel case. Capitalists use the state to form and legalize capitalist property relations, indeed, to thereby legally restrict the ability of that state to intervene in markets and production.

Does that make them statists? By securing state authority for capitalism, they promote a capitalist state, in part because they use the state to secure the legitimacy of capitalism, to constitute what it is, and because they delimit capitalist domains of activity where the state cannot intrude. But reciprocally the authority of the state is tied to the institution of capitalism, in that its viability depends on the capitalism whose institutional solidity it guarantees. By using the state to constitute and guarantee capitalism, they construct a capitalist state.

Religion, too, is statist, in its formation, reproduction, and differentiation. Just as the creation of capitalism depended on the state, so, too, did the creation of that institution we know today as "religion." The Christianities of the West secured their institutional status through the exercise of—or decision not to exercise—state power. Against the backdrop of Europe's early modern confessional struggles, Thomas Hobbes' state of nature was not a pre-political, creaturely condition, but a struggle over the political status of divergent forms of Christianity. The *Leviathan*'s sovereign decision on the enemy was a decision on divinity (Hobbes, 1985). The struggle over which God represented the absolute contributed to the absolutization of the sovereign state (Blumenberg1983: 89–91). The formation of the sovereign Western state, with its monopoly on legitimate violence, was achieved by compact— the 1648 Peace of Westphalia—denying the right to violence to religious communities and the transnational church, arrogating the right to make war to sovereign states alone. The state's legitimate monopoly of violence was built on the enforced delegitimation of religious violence, not simply of the transnational church, but the right to go war to secure a faith at all. On the one side, the violence of enemies was practically tied to sovereign states, not to religious communities or institutions. Only geopolitical enemies had a right to kill each other collectively. And on the other side, religion became an interior faith, a spiritual domain, one of the first freedoms.

Religionists who seek state authority to bolster their religion to constitute and stabilize it as an institution, have promoted a religious state, at least in the minimal sense that the state's authority is bound up with the definition of what constitutes a legitimate religion—not only which religion is legitimate, but whether religion is legitimate, and in what sense this domain of activity is outside the state's domain.[11] Even if the state is not itself religious, it remainders itself religiously. But more, as in capitalism, the state, in part, stakes its authority on the constitution, defense, and regulation of religion that shapes the social world it must ordinate. Depending as it does on the state that in turn depends on it, religion contains an inherent, political potential. Religious nationalists often seek to reverse the differentiation of nation-state and religion. But this can only be labeled statist from a differentiated condition; the charge is itself statist.

Modern religion is itself a political formation, shaped by the emergence of a "this-worldly" secular space, outside of and underneath the religious, upon which the nation-state and religion are now both assumed to rest (Asad 2003). But that space, which we today understand as secular, was itself religiously conditioned. It is not just that the Christianities of the West variously provided alternative models and media for the disciplining of the population and the organization of the state apparatus, from bureaucratic form to military discipline and welfare (Gorski 2003). The secular, democratic nation-state historically derives from a Protestant formation of the secular subject. It was the Protestants' very abjection, vis-à-vis their absolute God, that made Protestantism such a great a machine for democratic subjectification. For the Protestants both made God's distribution of grace unknowable and, thus, beyond human reason and good works, and yet made the individual's freedom into his most divine and religiously necessary attribute.

Just as late medieval nominalism provided the early modern model of the sovereign, it also provided the schematic ground for Protestantism and, through Protestantism, the modern subject (Taylor 2007: 43–83; Dupré 1993). Unlike the orthodoxy of Thomas Aquinas in which the universe is founded on God's reason, the nominalist universe is founded on God's unknowable productive will. Rather than God as Logos, knowledge of whom was the ultimate aim of every believer, nominalism sets up God as omnipotent free will, belief in whom must depend on faith beyond reason. Moreover nominalism, as the name implies, suggests that universal essences or ideas—of which individuals are but instances—are, in fact, just names. Only individuals and their sense experiences have ontological status as the real.

Martin Luther would insist on God's free, unknowable, and un-manipulable bestowal of grace as the medium through which one's sins were forgiven unmediated by any ecclesiastical structure. "Salvation," Taylor writes, "is a function of the absolute will of God, which is grounded in nothing other than itself" (Taylor 2007: 62). Protestantism created a new kind of religious subject whose salvation is justified by his own faith, a faith indicated by his certainty. (Dupré 1993). Nominalism's free, omnipotent God established the theological and ontological ground for the correlatively, free human subject.

It was the Protestant transcendent God's absolute, inscrutable power to elect that also helped make human election into a model of political organization. Luther proclaimed the priesthood of all believers, leveling access to God and stripping ecclesiastical authority of its sacrality. God no longer permeates the cosmos or the community of believers. Protestantism made religion into faith, a matter of choice, a direct relationship between the individual and his or her God. This transformed religion into fissiparous nodes of voluntary association. Indeed, the *anti-philosophes*, the Catholic opponents of the French Revolution, understood it as a Protestantism without God (McMahon 2001).

The individual becomes a sacred person, whose ultimate truth is located in his subjectivity, both his faith and his senses. Modernity's sacralization of the common man—of which Emile Durkheim made so much—and the valorization of his choices, derives, at least in part, from this religious understanding about his faith, his ability to choose God, and to read the founding texts which He revealed. One approaches God through the revealed text, through the word which all were required to read and interpret in the vernacular. It was this ground that made constitutional democracy possible, a polity comprised of and deriving its authority from the aggregation of monadic individual choices and individual readings of the text.

With Protestantism, God became transcendent, unavailable in the natural world or in the organization of a delegated church, but incarnated within the soul of the individual believer. There is a sense, then, in which the democratic nation-state becomes a secularized religious state.

Although Protestantism prepared the way for the reduction of all the Abrahamic, monotheistic religions to an interior, individual, other-worldly form of piety—to "relegate *aqida*," one's relationship to God, as Sayyid Qutb put it, "to the heart"—it also historically depended on the state's progressive shearing away religion's world-making capacities of its enforced differentiation as "religion" (Asad 2001; Elfenbein 2008). Religion was steadily reduced to a marker of collective identity, or more commonly, a private belief that barely rustled the waters of social exchange and was relegated to unobservable experiences of faith located in the chambers of one's heart. As the history of the Western nation-state itself makes clear, the contemporary religious reconstitution of the space of the social—not as a question of identity but what kind of subjects we are, the qualities of our sociality, and the attributes of the good—is a political act that can recast the ground, and, hence, the nature of the nation-state. The extent and content of religious regulation of social life always have political potential.

Of what does religious nationalism then consist? "The ultimate datum of nationalist politics," Brubaker writes, "—the ultimate point of reference and justification—is the claimed existence of a 'nation,' not the commandments of God. Does this not make nationalist politics fundamentally secular, or at least fundamentally distinct from forms of religious politics that seek to transform public life not in the name of the nation, but in the name of God" (Brubaker 2006: 22). This is, in my opinion, an instance of secular nationalist discourse, not an analytically viable distinction. It is the relation of God and nation-state that is at issue. God's proclaimed primacy does not negate the potentially religious nature of the nationalism. Nationalist politics cannot be religious only if there is a necessary contradiction between nation and God, or if we accept that making the state religious means rendering those means without religious meaning.

Religious nationalism fuses two ontologies, two kinds of imagined agents, two logics of action—that of divinity and of the nation-state. Religious nationalism exists where the nation-state itself becomes invested with religious meaning. This can, but need not, involve three elements. First, there is the religious identity of the nation, such that the nation-state as a collective subject is understood to represent an aggregation of its citizens' religious subjectivity, its religiously moral and legal concerns, and its metaphysical and ontological understandings.[12] The nation is a religious subject because its members are; the coherence of the collective subject is grounded in its common religiosity. In early modern Europe, translocal, cross-class religious mobilization was critical to the formation of the nation (Gorksi 2000, 2003). Islamists understand the population of an Islamic nation-state is bound together not by participation in a national culture, but by their common submission to *din,* to the way of life as revealed and modeled by the Prophet. *Din* is not without political meaning.[13]

Second, the nation itself can have religious meaning in that the nation—its constitution, its survival, and its actions—is understood to have redemptive or soteriological significance and its historical trajectory is invested with cosmological significance. In this case, the nation is "chosen" or "elect," a critical element, for example, in Christian, Hindu, and Jewish nationalisms (Friedland and Hecht 1996; Gorski 2000, 2003, 2007). A particular nation-state is understood to serve a divine purpose. Asad has argued that the liberal Western nation-state builds on the Christian crucifixion narrative which allows citizens of countries like the United States to understand themselves as a "progressive redemptive force, waging war in ranks of Christ's army" (Asad 2007: 87; see also Lincoln 2003). Given the Islamist hostility to the nation as a divisive source comparable to pre-Islamic tribalism, a Western-imposed impious medium for abrogating the unitary sovereignty of Allah and for secularizing the state by grounding it in human choice, this election is the element that typically is—but not always—missing from Sunni Islamist politics (Euben 1999; Piscatori 1986; Qutb 1990).

Third, there is the explicit religious derivation of the state's authority and laws from divine sources and revealed law. Here, the content of state law and the source of sovereignty are derived from divine sources, not from the historical decisions of a particular people. This can be written into law or into the organizational structure of the state such that religious authorities actually control law-making, such as the theocracy in Iran. All three elements invoke God as "the cardinal point of reference." All three invest the nation-state with religious significance.[14] Within the logic of religious nationalism, there is no necessary contradiction between nation-state and God.

Institutional Logic and Social Movement

To understand religious nationalism, including its violence, I begin not with power relations between groups, but with the institutional architecture of the social. I have been exploring the modalities of politicized religion, and particularly religious nationalism, which theologically invests the nation-state—the identity of its members, its redemptive role, and the sources of its authority—as a vehicle by which to develop an institutional understanding of the social (Friedland 2001, 2002, 2009b).

Modern societies are composed of a plurality of distinct, yet interdependent, institutions. Institutions are transrational ways of organizing persons and objects in space and time (Friedland 2009b, 2002; Friedland and Alford 1991). And they are themselves spaces and times—locations in which those persons and objects carry particular meanings. Institutions are constituted by orderings of means-ends couplets, regimes of practice—what I have called "institutional logics," that is, stable constellations of practice—and the subjects and objects coupled to them. Institutional objects are not ontologically objective, not things present-at-hand. The central objects of institutional life only exist as collective representations,

representations collectively accepted as real. Institutional practices are both media for subjectification, in that they enable and possess practitioners, and of objectification, in that those practices, and hence the subjects, hinge on their symbolic and performative production of the objects. It is through the institutional logic of practice that the two are co-constituted.

This institutionalism differs from the logic of practice in Pierre Bourdieu's field theory, dominated as it is by an agonistic, instrumental, distributional struggle over transinstitutional means and not a common striving to produce institutionally specific, substantive ends. Institutional logics are not first ordered by the distributive struggle over capital that sustains the stake as an *illusio* in which categorical oppositions are arbitrary transpositions of positional oppositions (Bourdieu 1990; Friedland 2009c). Institutions rather have a logic because practices and substances are internally co-constitutive. Every institutional resource allocation—of votes, money, property, force, knowledge, meals, love, territory, blessings, and sacraments— is a material semiosis in which the categories, instruments, and agents, through which that object is produced or distributed, are brought to life and made real. The central objects of institutional life are dually constituted, both conceptually and practically, as categories that point to objects of action and actors who engage in material practices that enact them. An institution's central objects, as such, do not exist. They are known only through their conjoint conceptual and practical specificity (Mohr and Duquenne 1997; Breiger 2000). Institutions are ideological formations, not just in the sense that they are organized around languages that legitimate power as control over persons and things, but in that they produce powers by authorizing practices that constitute subjects and objects through which the authority relation is organized. Institutional theory thus points beyond distribution, the classical ground of ideology—measured either as control over objective means or in trans-institutional operators like power, capital or utility—to the hegemonic construction of incommensurable, self-referential domains of activity and the extent of their scope as the systemic, as opposed to structural, ground of ideology.

Institutions are not primarily structures of power whose purposes are analytically external to their constitution. Institutional fields are structures of symbolically constituted, iterated powers whose exercise through interlocked congeries of practices—voting and legislating, buying and selling, officiating and participating in religious rite, marrying, cohabitation, sexuality and child-rearing, the fighting of wars and signing of treaties, or controlled experiment and observation, carried out by collectively recognized subjects—citizens, owners, members, families, officials, or scientists—presume and performatively produce non-objective "objects" or values: democracy, property, divinity, love, sovereignty, and knowledge. I call these "objects" or values institutional substances the central object of an institutional field and the principle of its unity.

The category derives from Aristotelian metaphysics where substance, or substantial form, is the foundation, or essence, of a thing which cannot be reduced to its accidental properties which attach to it, nor to the materiality of its instances (Aristotle 1998). For Aristotle, substance is not matter, but the form that makes matter a "this," "that by virtue of which the matter is in the state it is in" (Aristotle 1998: 167, 229). A substance exceeds its attributes, cannot be reduced to a thing's materiality, and thus cannot be described, only pointed to and named. While the category of substance is epistemologically problematic, it captures institutional reality rather well. Like Aristotle's soul as the substance of the human, an institutional substance does not exist; it is rather an absent presence necessary to institutional life. Institutional substances are unfounded, not because they are arbitrary and misrecognized media for empowerment—they are that too—but because they depend on practices of good faith. Nation, sovereignty, and God are each institutional substances. Religious nationalism seeks to meld these substances into a single institutional formation.

There are those who would parse the social through a matrix of domination, understanding society as variably structured power relations among social groups or between authorities and challengers (Tilly 1978; McAdam, Tarrow and Tilly 2001). Groupness, I would argue, depends not just on an interest given by distributional position, but on identification with a value, grounded in a set of practices organized by the logic of the institutions from which group projects are fashioned.[15] Religion is not just a doctrine, a set of myths, or a congeries of rite; it is an institutional space according to whose logic religious nationalists would remake the world. Religion offers not only a social space from which to mobilize, an alternative set of resources by which to counter other groups, but also a practical cosmos within which an alternative world can be imagined and prefigured. Institutional logic and collective representation are linked phenomena because groups form through particular institutional configurations and because institutions are defended and extended through group conflicts. Groups know themselves through their institutional projects, and by politicizing these projects, they reshape the logic of collective representation—not just who is represented in the public sphere but the nature of the representation, the political project, and, here potentially, the very ontology of the nation-state.

Social movements are not just about inclusion and exclusion, domination and subordination, of social groups. Group political power can also involve questions of institutional hegemony. There is an analytic difference between shifts in the institutional architecture of society as opposed to the social architecture of institutions, that is, between extending an institutional logic to a new domain of activity, such as the commodification of health care or the religionization of state authority, and the social extension or contraction of access to practices that follow existent institutional logic to different groups of people, such as the civil rights movement, feminist incorporations of women, or micro-lending. These distributional shifts, however, may involve institutional shifts elsewhere, as, for example, in the case of the promotion of civil and political equality for women. The movement of African captives and the prerogatives of rule out of the category of property—that is, the end of slavery and the rise of state bureaucracy—were distributional struggles because they were conflicts over institutional boundaries. Giving primacy to the former occludes the determining importance of the latter. Likewise although all social movements may be involved in "targeting system of authority in institutional structures"

(Taylor and Van Dyke 2004: 268), it is important to distinguish movements that contest authority in order to shift distributions from those that contest ontological orders constituting authority, which themselves have huge distributional consequences. For these latter social movements—of which politicized religion is exemplary— reality, not just distribution or power, is at stake. They must remake the world according to their own codes and must make their ideas matter.

Religious nationalism is not just about the representation of religious citizens within the state; it is about the religious ordering of collective representation. Religious nationalists seek to reground the nation-state in divinity and to transform its institutional logic. Religious nationalism seeks to extend the institutional logic of religion into the domain of the democratic nation-state. It seeks to derive authority from an absolute divine writ—not the subjective aggregations of the demos. It locates the nation's history in a cosmic drama that pushes toward redemption, not progress. It sustains agency through a disciplined self, bound by faith to God—not a sacralized, self-interested, pleasure-seeking monad. It constitutes society through the sexual flesh of the faith-bound family, not through the abstract, disembodied individual of the market. Religious nationalism is a double project of subjectifica- tion, seeking to create at once a new collective and an individual subject. It is not, as Habermas contends regarding political Islam, just "a new and subjectively more convincing language for old political orientations," namely Arab nationalism (Borradori 2003: 33).

This is not to say that understanding the organizational, social group and polit- ical contingencies involved in shaping the capacity for, and interest in, politicized religion and its violent forms—the coincidence of class, ethnic, and religious divi- sion, for example, the degree of religious geographic segregation and density, the level of cross-religious economic or political organization, foreign occupation, and the inclusiveness and capacity of the state—are not relevant as causes of the politi- cization of religion and its violence (Olzak 2004). However, they are not sufficient. They can explain how religion becomes politicized and/or becomes violent, but not why it does so. They do not address the cause for which religious nationalists kill and die, a cause—or more precisely a belief in the reality of a particular kind of object, God—that may have a relationship to the use of violence and the other political practices with which this violence is associated, not to mention a bearing on the sociological force of other situational and structural causes.

Although it may—indeed, must—simultaneously serve instrumental purposes, the core logic of an institution is a domain of *praxis* in the Aristotelian sense. Aristotle distinguished between *poeisis* and *praxis,* which he also termed as the distinction between production and action (Aristotle 2004). In the former, an act is derived instrumentally from an end external to the act, as in the case of a craftsman who uses his skill, or *techné,* to execute a preexisting plan for a chair. Word and act are related as a "making." In *praxis,* in contrast, the standards of action are internal to the action, and the goal of the action is the action itself. Word and act are related as a doing, or a performance.[16] Whereas *poeisis* is governed by a means-ends logic; *praxis* is not. In *praxis,* subject and object are both immanent in the act; A prudent man practices prudence. *Praxis*, unlike production, is a self-contained order of action. In production, Aristotle says, the actuality of the making is in the thing being made; in action, the actuality of action is located in the actor himself (Aristotle 1998).

Praxis is organized around ontologically subjective objects, objects that can only approximate appearance through practice, through the acts of subjects whose actions and subjectivities depend on them. In *praxis*, subjectification and objectification are co-constitutive. The objects of *praxis* are not objects at all, but rather substances, nonobservable reasons that cannot be reduced to rationality or sense, that can only be phenomenalized through practice. One can never arrive at them, only repeat the approach through practice. By comparison to the presence of things, an institutional substance is an absent presence toward and around which practice incessantly moves, known only through this movement. Institutional logics are ontological enactments—a"what" done through a "how": popular sovereignty through democratic election; justice through juridical practices that classify actions according to the binary of legal and illegal; divinity through pilgrimage and prayer; and romantic love through intimate exchange of body and word. Institutional logics depend on making the invisible substance visible. Institutional practices are the visible face and the condition of possibility of institutional substances, and, hence, the source of their identity across time. In the case of religious nationalism, one looks for the ways in which its practices seek to enact divinity within and through the nation-state.

THE POLITICAL CONSTITUTION
OF RELIGIOUS VIOLENCE

Institutional boundaries are potentially violent frontiers, particularly those of religion and state. There is a violence to institution. At the most elemental level, the institutional extension of religion cannot not be political. Institutions cannot guarantee their own boundaries, the scope of their reference. Institutions create the conditions of possibility of a specific practical regime of valuation but cannot assure the value will in fact be valued. Neither rationality nor justice, for example, can account for their own application. As the failure of theories of market failure and secularization both attest, we, in fact, still do not have an adequate theory about how the boundaries of institutions shift, the ways in which different activities, persons, and objects are appropriated, claimed, and/or captured by one field or another. Institutional boundary shifts involve questions of contingent material reference, control over the material world, and the adjudication of incommensurable valuations; control over ends-making.

Every institution rests on transcendent claims—on a foundation that cannot be reduced to the phenomenal world. Institutional practices render immanent the central institutional substance, an institution's "God" term, a term necessarily invoked by name while it evoked by practice. In that institutional powers are organized around these substances, or values—indexed and evinced through institutional practice, values that are themselves unobservable—they depend on faith and on submission to the institutional logic of practice, an institutional enchantment. Based on values that are incommensurable and that cannot be rationally adjudicated, whose valuation is always contingent, institutional boundaries are vulnerable to political contest, to extension and constrictions of material reference, to the promotion of new practices to index existent values, and even to the development of historically new institutional logics (Clemens 1997; Meyerson 2003; Meyerson and Tompkins 2007; Scott et al. 2000).

The referential scope of an institutional logic—to which objects, persons, and activities it refers—is potentially explosive because institutions depend on the unthinkability of their conventions, on the taking of institutional(ized) ontologies as inhering in the nature of things. Institutional boundary shifts thus involve both questions of contingent material reference, control over the material world, and the adjudication of incommensurable valuations, control over ends-making. It is this conjunction of the material and the moral that makes institutional boundary movements so fractious and contested. Extending alternative metaphorical orders is the trans-institutional core of profanation, the breaching of the ontologically other, or in quasi-Durkheimian terms, an intrusion of a domain defined not by absence but by an alternative, heterologous presence. Institutional boundary shifts involve the prospect of incommensuration, of a kind of placelessness, and the indeterminate subjectification that these open up, making institutional boundary movements explosive, energized, a generator of enemies, and the playground and the battlefield of the gods. These are conditions for the exercise of raw power, indeed for violence.

Power is both institutionally constitutive and constituted. Power is constitutive because institutions depend on faith, on unsecured credit and ungrounded knowledge. Instituting—the movement of institutional boundaries—involves incommensurabilities that cannot be adjudicated by argument or experience. Social movements often aim at, and are founded on, the production of these institutional heterologies and on the revelation of arbitrary regional ontologies of which the displays—often spectacular displays—of power, and hence violence, are indicative. The deployment of bodily pain (and pleasure) is here made to substantiate values immanent in, but transcendent to, practice. And through such social movements power—and hence the arbitrary faith on which existent institutions ultimately depend—is forced to reveal itself as mere force; denaturalized culture exposed as ideology.

Power is constitutive because this deployment of resources—and particularly human bodies their presentation and their risk—is an elemental mechanism through which an institutional substance is substantiated in the sense that that for which one is willing to stand—to risk bodily pain and even death—must consequently be real. Violence, terror; and unspeakable, unpredictable bodily pain, are an empowering language, and not just through corporeal constraint. Bodily suffering, as Elaine Scarry has argued, is deployed by states when substantiation is uncertain, where symbolic orders are contested, where language has reached its social limits. Through her studies of torture and war, she shows how the state apparatus seeks to appropriate human bodily pain—that which is really real to its sufferer, but resists ready representation—and make it work in the signification of power. Injuring, Scarry argues, "not only provides a means of choosing between disputants but also provides, by its massive opening of human bodies, a way of reconnecting the derealized and disembodied beliefs with the force and power of the material world" (Scarry 1985: 128). For the state—and by implication its challengers—human pain, injuring, and death are not just techniques, useful deterrents; they are a foundational display of its substance, a way to substantiate the unobservable ontological basis of its authority.

The implication is that the ability to deploy violence—to organize pain, suffering and death—is something that can never be domesticated. This calls into question Mark Juergensmeyer's argument that the cosmic warfare in which religious nationalists understand themselves to be participating ultimately in "battles against the most chaotic aspect of reality: death." Juergensmeyer struggles to align sacrifice as a domestication of a disordering violence, on the one side, and cosmic war, as the ultimate moral structuring, on the other. "[R]eligion," he writes, "has employed symbols of violence not only to deny death but to control all that is intimately related to death: disorder, destruction, and decay. By evoking and then bridling images of warfare, religion has been symbolically controlling not only violence but also all of the messiness of life" (Juergensmeyer 2000: 158). The surety of cosmic war is not order versus disorder, but good versus evil. Death is not the enemy of order; it is its guarantor. To both express and create a crisis of substantiation is just what religious violence in general, and terrorism in particular, is about. Religion sanctifies destruction, I would argue, because, just as for the state, to destroy is the necessary other side of God's power to create, constitutive of structure. Religious terrorism performs an alternative order, not the defeat of disorder.

The ground of religious nationalism is a meld of substances: nation, sovereignty, God. That the fashioning of this institutional precipitant often involves violence should not surprise us. Instituting tends toward violence because institutions depend on substances, transcendent and inviolable, absent presences beyond reason and experience, which are practically enacted. Most major institutional emplacements—the establishment of law, capitalism and wage labor, the nation-state, democracy, and, of course, established and disestablished religions—have occurred only through the sustained exercise of violence. It was the unprecedented barbarity of the wars of religion that prompted efforts to attenuate or sever the link between sovereignty and God (Lincoln 2003: 56–58).[17]

Theology is potentially political because politics is a kind of religious operation. Max Weber turned to the grace of Pauline Christianity, *charis,* to compose his term of extraordinary authority necessary to value formation, to the elicitation of loyalty when the benefits of compliance could not be counted on, and to chart a path when existent laws did not suffice. The state is a "religious" institution, one that depends on a God-like capacity to create a collective order, a capacity and an order grounded in a metaphysical vision evidenced by, but not reducible to, perceptible nature. And like a god, the founding of a nation-state, its authority, its law, its extent—like any institution—is without foundation.

Religious violence, *une terreur réligieuse,* counters and, thus, parallels the violence inherent in the founding of the state's law, the performative power that has no precedent—nothing before or outside of it—what Jacques Derrida has called authority's mystical origin.[18] "Here," he writes, "a silence is walled up in the violent structure of the founding act" (Derrida 1990: 943):

> Its very moment of foundation or institution...the operation that consists of founding, inaugurating, justifying law (*droit*), making law, would consist of a coup de force, of a performative and therefore an interpretative violence that in itself is neither just nor 'unjust and that no justice and no previous law with its founding anterior moment could guarantee or contradict or invalidate. No justificatory discourse could or should insure the role of metalanguage in relation to the performativity of institutive language or to its dominant interpretation. (Derrida 1990: 943)

In other words, the law has origins that cannot be derived from that law. Violence, like faith, is originary and integral to all political authority, a violence tamed, converted into metaphor and regulation, made crescive, invisible, and administrative, but there all the while.

Religious violence calls out and repeats that originary violence that can never be subordinated to, or derived from, the law, the violence of institution. Religious violence by nonstate actors operates in—locates and is aimed at creating—that zone beyond language that founds the state's truth, that is, its legitimate discourse and its legal authority (Borradori 2003). The violence thereby seeks to reveal how the state's truth is arbitrary and depends on state violence. Indeed, the terror of religious violence lies in its ability to exceed interpretation by the dominant discourse, a discourse that is accorded a certain general credit, a credit that hinges on the state's domination. The violence calls into question the worldhood of our world; it targets, as Derrida noted, our "hermeneutic apparatus" (Borradori 2003: 93). Terrorism operates by baring our faith and by bringing our discourse to the edge of meaninglessness.

THE RELIGIOUS CONSTITUTION
OF POLITICAL VIOLENCE

If transformations in institutional scope depend on power, often including violence, it is also the case that strategies of empowerment are conditioned by the institutional projects for which they are deployed. That there are nonreligious causes and consequences associated with politicized religious violence does not mean that the religious reason of these actions is inconsequential, not only to its ability to recruit actors, but to the forms of action in which they engage (see also Euben 1999). Social movements reach for resources as a condition of their reality-making, but they do so in ways that are conditioned by the reality they are seeking to make. There is, I would argue, a religiosity to religious violence, to its meaning, a meaning expressed in the patterning of its practices. The sources of politicized religion's violence are located not just in the often violent nature of instituting, but in the institutional logic of religion itself.[19]

Contemporary politicized religions are characterized by a particular conjunction. On the one hand, they tend towards bodily violence—the killing of officials, nonbelieving opponents and enemies inside and out. That violence is either enacted in the present or anticipated in an apocalyptic future. In the former case, its violence is typically executed by their own hands, not a distant technical killing, but one in which their own lives are close at hand, if not consumed, in the acts themselves. On the other hand, they are preoccupied with the regulation of sexuality—homosexuality, abortion, marriage, divorce, pre- and extra-marital sexuality, and evolution. This coupling of political practices has an institutional logic.

Although the formation of the world's religions was violent, legions of commentators—notably Western Islamicists—declare political violence an extraneous use and thus abuse of religion, an exploitation of God-talk for profane ends. Religious terrorism, however, is overwhelmingly grounded in political theology (Euben 2002; Philpott 2007). Religious political violence repudiates the state's monopoly on legitimate violence, pointing to and grounding itself in a divine source of authority outside the law. In this, it recapitulates the original "religious" foundation of state authority, the divine quality of the original exception on which sovereignty rests. Modern concepts of the state, Carl Schmitt, the fascist German political theorist, has argued, are "secularized theological concepts," models of a transcendent ordering power. Schmitt identified the sovereign as the locus of order, or, as he puts it, the "point of ascription" of legal norms that cannot itself be derived from those norms (Schmitt 1985: 32). The Western sovereign of the seventeenth and eighteenth centuries was built on this late medieval, nominalist model of the singular, transcendent God, a theology that supposed God as an agent whose sovereignty over creation, his absolute powers or *potentia absoluta*, are neither exhausted, nor bound, by his ordained laws or *potentia ordinata*. God, whose actions are not constrained by, nor amenable to human reason, is thus free to make the sovereign decision, the miracle, and the violent suspension of law. God is the law-giver not bound by the law. In nominalism, as we have seen, the authority of the law hinges on divine will, not right reason.

Schmitt saw the emergence of constitutional democracy in the nineteenth century, with its identity of ruler and ruled, as a secularized Deism. In Deism, which grew out of radical Protestantism, God no longer intervenes in the natural world, but has rather left man's destiny to man. Many of the framers of America's Constitution were Deists, as was Jean Jacques Rousseau, the fabricator of the "general will." For Deists, God is immanent in the world's lawfulness, in which the laws made by man are identified as analogues to natural laws, laws that can be applied without exception, a God whose book of nature operates as second scripture, such that a state can ground its authority and its laws in the nature of things, including man.

When Schmitt published *Political Theology* in 1922, it was the loss of the transcendent God's violence, a violence beyond and before the law, and his capacity to intervene at will in the course of human affairs in order to defend the order of things, a mode of life, which Schmitt found to be this political theology's most debilitating consequence (Schmitt 1996). Constitutional democracy's sovereign model destroyed the political, which he understood as the decision on the exception, an authority that cannot be derived from law, to locate an enemy—either inside or outside—and determine the situation where the law must be suspended, in short, the exercise of extraordinary violence, martial law or war. Unlike for Weber, it is not the legitimacy of violence, but the violence necessary to legitimate constitution that is key.

It is this absolute sovereign—this God who has and can move in extraordinary and unexpected ways in human history—whose revelation of law was one such extraordinary intervention, from which today's religious nationalists wish to derive the sovereignty of their states. The indeterminate historicity of God, and the collectivity's return to him, are of a piece. So, too, is the violence of their respective law-makings. God's entry into history was and is an awesome, often violent, intrusion. The collective return to God, like the original turn, is a miracle, both memorial and prefiguration. The movement of religious men and women into the public sphere, the politicization of religion, and the religious violence accompanying it, likewise express the extraordinariness of that divine force—God's historicity—in which the adherents of politicized religion not only believe, but participate. Politicized religions understand themselves as participating in a history in which the divine is an active force, not simply as a source of past revelation, but as human actors in the fulfillment of a divine plan for history, whose actions are made possible by God and which even play a role in a larger redemptive or eschatological historical process.

The politicization of the America's Christian right has not itself been violent: They reserve their violence for their government in the present and for God in an imminent apocalyptic future. In America, the Christian right has been dominated by an activist strain of dispensationalist Christianity which believes that Christ will return before the millennium, that history will end with the rapture of all Christians to heaven, and that the violent biblical prophecies concerning Israel and the Jews will be fulfilled during the time of tribulation (Harding 2000). The evangelical and fundamentalist Christians, who united behind figures such as the Reverend Jerry Falwell, did so based on the notion that God is active in history, that events such as the AIDS epidemic were God's judgment against America's sexual immorality, and that America's chosenness as a Christian nation—and indeed its survival as a powerful nation-state—depended on Christian political activism in this pre-tribulational period. Christians such as these understand history as a struggle between Christ and the anti-Christ, through which the latter seeks the erosion of American sovereignty particularly through international financial regimes, leading to a violent struggle in which they will be called upon to bear witness and from whose horrible devastation they will be delivered (LaHaye and Jenkins 1995). America's power, they contend, depends on the Christianization of the nation-state.

Islamists understand Allah to have both revealed a singular source and template for human governance and a telos of human history—its extension to all humanity in a global Islamic community—which Muslims are enjoined to realize in history as their enactment of God's will. Islamists believe that Allah continues to be active in the human realization of His ends. The radical Islamist, Sayyid Qutb, intellectual scion of the Muslim Brotherhood executed by Egyptian President Nasser in the 1950s, is a prime source and pertinent example (Qutb 2000: 188, 191, 202). His writings have been essential to the rise of radical Islam; indeed, they had a major influence on Osama bin Laden who was mentored by Qutb's brother. Islamists inspired by Qutb understand themselves to be living once again in a period of *jahiliyyah*, or ignorance of God, recalling the pre-Islamic polytheism and tribalism, this time more pernicious because it involves a "conscious ignorance" of the revealed oneness of God's sovereignty that "takes the form of claiming that the right to create values, to legislate rules of collective behavior, and to choose any way of life rests with men, without regard to what God has prescribed" (Bergesen 2008: 21). For Qutb, the impetus for this Islamist movement which would reestablish Islamic law as the ultimate arbiter of all human activity and restore God's sovereignty, lies not in human agency, but "outside the human sphere and beyond this world" (Qutb 1990: 86). Qutb writes:

> [Allah's wisdom] guarantees that believers will see the signposts along the road clearly and starkly, for [God's wisdom] establishes the course for those who wish to traverse this road to its end....If God intends to actualize His mission and His religion, only He will do so, but not as a recompense for human suffering and sacrifices. (Euben 1999: 73)

Islamists have restored the tradition of *jihad* of the sword to "bring religion into practice" as a realization of God's will, not only against occupying unbelievers, but against nominally Islamic rulers who seek to adumbrate Islam to conform to secular modernity (Euben 2002). Sunni militants now celebrate the suffering of their enemies which they take to be indicators of Allah's intercession (Israeli 2003, 1997). "God punishes those who do evil," declared al-Zarqawi's brother-in-law about the Sunni Islamist attacks on American troops in Iraq (*L'Espresso* 2004).

Some Islamists impute eschatological significance to their own political actions. In its 1988 Covenant, the Palestinian Hamas asserts, citing Hassan al-Banna in its preamble: "Israel will exist and will continue to exist until Islam will obliterate it, just as it obliterated others before it" (Hamas 1988). Hamas casts its violent *jihad* against Zionism as a fulfillment of the Prophet's proclamation, according to *hadith*, about the advent of the Day of Judgment. According to Article 7:

> The Islamic Resistance Movement aspires to the realisation of Allah's promise, no matter how long that should take. The Prophet, Allah, bless him and grant him salvation, has said: The Day of Judgment will not come about until Moslems fight the Jews (killing the Jews), when the Jew will hide behind stones and trees. The stones and trees will say, "O Moslems, O Abdulla, there is a Jew behind me, come and kill him."

Where Shi'ites traditionally endured—waiting for the return of Muhammad al-Mahdi, a descendent of Ali and the twelfth imam who disappeared in 874, as the Messiah who will install a reign of justice—the Shiite revolutionaries in Iran developed an activist model that a devout Muslim was to emulate the foundational Islamic martyrs, to struggle to the death, as Ali Shariati proclaimed, in "the name of God of the disinherited" (Kepel 2002: 39). Khomeini's doctrine was that one was to actively emulate the model of Hussein in Karbalah, cut down by the Ummayads, to struggle against injustice and to consciously seek martyrdom. Khomeini constructed the role of *faqih,* as a clerical guardian who would stand in for the Mahdi, and subsequent leaders understood the actions of their nation-state as, in the words of Iranian President Ahmadinejad, "hastening of the coming of Imam Mahdi."

Religious Zionists likewise understand themselves to be preparing the "footsteps of the Messiah" by their settlement of the covenanted lands, helping to speed the Messiah on his way (Friedland and Hecht 1996). When he assassinated Prime Minister Rabin in 1994, Yigal Amir found inspiration in Pinchas' extra-legal killing of an Israelite man who had been seduced by a foreign woman into worship of Ba'al just before the Israelites were to enter the land, a murder rewarded by God with perpetual priesthood (Friedland 2005). And Hindu nationalists historicize the coming of their gods, seeking the modern-day restoration of Ram's mythic kingdom. The violence of politicized religion expresses their belief that human and the divinity are conjointly active in history, that the sovereignty of the state must derive from divine sources, and that submission to a state not so derived is a form of idolatry, heresy, a profanation.

Schmitt located the political, and hence derived state violence from, the sovereign decision to defend not life itself, but a mode of life, a secularization of a divinely given order. The violence of politicized religion, seeking to impose, not to defend, a mode of life, points to the state as that organ which seeks a monopoly on symbolic violence—not on the legitimate use of force, but on the force of legitimation, and hence to the violence that occurs when that monopoly is contested. It also points to the political as a religious function, a necessarily extraordinary, extra-legal constitution of a collectivity, of the formation of a mode of life, of legitimate ends making, and of the enactment of divine agency in history. Their violence is not a violence of constitutional exception, it is an exceptional violence of constitution.

THE OTHER EXCEPTION: SEX, VIOLENCE, AND DIVINITY

More than divine historical agency is at stake in the practices of politicized religion. Political approaches can perhaps explain their violence, but not its conjunction with sexual projects. The religious communities, out of which politicized movements emerge, are all preoccupied with sexual regulation; what is distinctive here is its politicization as part of an often violent drive for political power. The most simple—and revealing—aspect of religious investments of love and death is their corporeality and their involvement in the making and unmaking of human bodies. These political practices have a politico-theological significance. Sex and violence are at religion's core, corollaries to the divine capacity to create and destroy human life. Aristotle, who made substance the ground of his theory of knowledge as an uncovering, as a revealability, sought its template in the human body. The practices of politicized religion likewise point to something uncovered, a relation to a naked, sacred, sensuous, and interior truth, an immanent transcendent. It is the truth of this life in which they would ground their state.

Politicized religions seize on life's exception to the law, to what the Italian political philosopher, Giorgio Agamben, calls "bare life," which he identifies as the referent of sovereignty (Agamben 1998: 112). In contrast to Schmitt, who understood sovereignty as a political-theological category, sovereign power, Agamben asserts, derives from an originary exclusion of this bare life from both law and religion. Contrary to Michel Foucault's periodized movement from classical sovereignty to the bio-power of governmentality, bare life is, and always has been, the content of sovereign power. It is this life, caught in the sovereign ban, declared outside the law and thus vulnerable to death, that is, he argues, the original sacred life, "the earthly foundation of the state's legitimacy and sovereignty" (Agamben 1998: 127).

In the nation-state, bare life becomes both the bearer of human rights and national sovereignty (Agamben 1998: 128–129). The modern nation-state, Agamben argues, grounds sovereignty as it seizes hold of *zoe* in a culturally unmediated biological people—not the people of the polis. It thus joins the status of citizenship to the biological fact of birth, if not of race, as well as of bodily pleasure, the pursuit of happiness. "Declarations of rights must therefore be viewed as the place in which the passage from divinely authorized royal sovereignty to national sovereignty is accomplished. This passage…means that birth—which is to say, bare natural life, as such—here for the first time becomes…the immediate bearer of sovereignty" (Agamben 1998: 128). The modern nation-state grounds its sovereignty not in free, political subjects, but in human life, *tout court*.

It is Agamben's bare life that politicized religious movements refuse, rejecting the modern state's foundation in biological life, the sufficiency of birth, the primacy of bodily existence, and the valorization of corporeal pleasure, utility, and biological need—precisely what Hannah Arendt disparaged as "the social"—as the basis of state authority and political action (Arendt 1958). For the followers of politicized religion, it is neither the abstract individual nor the physiological person, but human life understood as divine creation that must be the ontological ground of political authority. Politicized religions contest the secular state's capacity to take life because, they insist, it is not grounded in its divine making. They, too, seize on life's exception to the law; but it is not the same exception, not the same life. Both their violence and their sex point to a different substance, an alternative basis of sovereignty. Politicized religions center not on Arendt's natality as the nonrelational phenomenological ground, but on its creation as the loving relational ground of political action (Arendt 1958).

Agamben identifies bare life as the state of nature that Thomas Hobbes located both outside the sovereign order as its brutishly violent source and at its very inside in the sovereign's own, legally unmasterable, savage powers (Agamben 1998). But for the politicized religionists, God's capacity to make life is part and parcel of His capacity to take it; a power excessive to the law, a fecundating power that is pervasive, for example, in Moses' relation to God—a relation which Hobbes himself used as his model for the sovereign and was the template for numerous early modern European nationalisms (Gorksi 2000; Hobbes 1985). The sovereign God in whom religious nationalists would ground the sovereignty of their states is not only a law-giver who can deliver spectacular pains in defense of that sovereignty, but one who guarantees sometimes extraordinary birth, who rewards his followers with fertility, including collective birth, who not only takes, but also makes life, and the one who loves his people fiercely and jealously (Friedland 2009a). Not just death, but erotic love and the birth in which it results provides an originary template for institution and for making place for the law and the collective subject who adopts it as their own. The politicized religious model of state sovereignty is also a model of human procreation. Law and life both derive from an exceptional divine source. God's violence is but one side of His boundless love, His possessive desires, and exclusive demands.

The effort of these politicized religions to subordinate sexuality to divine law is of a piece with their desire to derive sovereignty from divinity and with their struggle to create a pious civil society as the ground for the national community over which the state claims sovereignty. Their sex, like their violence, partakes of, and must be ordered by, this divinity. Like the political communities fashioned in the seventeenth century by Calvinist reformists in Europe, those who seek to create a divinely ordered collective body likewise divinize the creation of the individual body and sustain the sacramental quality of sex. *Milestones*, Qutb's most influential political text, links sovereignties without God to natural, materialist understandings of procreation, which together reduce citizen men to their animal needs, precisely to what Agamben called modernity's beast, the wolf-man (Qutb 1990). The negation of the transcendent God and the consequent grounding of political order in nature, has led, Qutb argues, to Communist ideologies where "the basic needs of human beings are considered identical with those of animals, that is, food and drink, clothing, shelter, and sex," and to capitalist societies where "physical desires" reign supreme (Qutb 1990: 66). Without God, citizens are animals. For Qutb, man is not only more than animal, he is more than man. Man's "creation," Qutb writes, "is the result of the Will of Allah rather than of his father and mother. The father and mother may come together; but they cannot transform a sperm into a human being" (Qutb 1990: 74). Only by recognizing the divinity involved in conception, in birth, and in the making of life can a Muslim live a life worth living.

It is the procreative God whom religious nationalists deploy to counter modernity's investments of eros. Religions become politicized not only because nation-states are integrally involved in the delimitation of what religions can do, and hence what they are, but because of the state's regulation, and nonregulation, of this sexual domain, the remaining core of religion's competence. Foucault pointed to the rise of what he called bio-politics, "the taking charge of life, more than the threat of death" (Foucault 1980: 143). Sex is central here.

> We...are in a society of "sex," or rather a society "with sexuality": the mechanisms of power are addressed to the body, to life, to what causes it to proliferate, to what reinforces the species, its stamina, its ability to dominate, or its capacity for being used....Power delineated it, aroused it, and employed it as the proliferating meaning that had always to be taken control of again lest it escape. (Foucault 1980: 148)

Legitimate sexual behavior, child birth and abortion, the very right to bear children, sexual education, marriage and divorce, the sexual division of labor, the respective rights of husbands, wives and children, not to mention the right to die—all have become contested objects of legislation and administration by the modern state. This changing state of sex has brought religions around the world back into the public sphere. The secular repoliticization of sex is a spur to its redivinization.

It is the proliferation of a secularized sexuality—one subjected to state regulation, commodified incitement, and cultural sacralization—on which religious nationalists seize. Religious nationalists seek to reinscribe God in response to modernity's sexualization of social life, a sexualization deriving from the making of sex into an object of government intervention on the one side and its elevation into a substitute transcendence on the other. Politicized religions emerge against a backdrop of market liberalization that feeds on the expansion of desire, floods the labor market with newly employed women, and undercuts the welfare functions of the state. In a newly commodified world, energized by an expansive sensuous desire, in particular by woman's desired and desiring bodies, they seek to set their bodies apart, to construct a purity and a piety held in common in response to the increasingly unequal pleasures of a commodified world and to discipline the unnatural excesses of monetary and erotic exchange (Cooper 2008; Friedland 2002).[20] In a world that has transformed sex into pleasure and physical reproduction, they would recast it as divine creation. The secularity of the modern unregulated market is to them an immodest world of selfish bodily pleasures (Afary 2009; Mahmood 2005).

Supporters of Islamism, the surveys show, want our democracy; they, however, refuse our liberal, secular sex. Even Bin Laden's supporters do not see democracy as a Western imposition.[21] But they do refuse homosexuality, gender equality, divorce, and abortion. Ronald Inglehart and Pippa Norris, astute survey researchers, conclude: "These issues are part of a broader syndrome of tolerance, trust, political activism, and emphasis on individual autonomy that constitutes 'self expression values.' The extent to which a society emphasizes these self-expression values has a surprisingly strong bearing on the emergence and survival of democratic institutions" (2003: 67). It is not, I would argue, tolerance and trust, but the ontological construction of sexuality and an inability to cede sex to civil rights that are at issue.

Religious nationalism and political Islam have the organization of sexuality, indeed bodily desire, at their center. For the Islamists, the propriety of one's sex, the ability to properly order it, is constitutive of one's relationship to God, of the strength and political coherence of the community, and the kind of subject that predominates. For Qutb, for whom every external struggle is also an internal one in consciousness and community, the founding of relationships between men and women based on "lust, passion and impulse" is a defining trait of a *jahili*—backward or ignorant—society (Qutb 1990: 83; 2000: 189). Qutb reminded his followers that those societies whose members are unable to control their "unruly desires," who follow the counsel of those "given to excesses," Allah will eventually reduce to "stubble." In contrast, quoting Noah in the Qur'an (71: 10–12), those who ask God for forgiveness, will be made "powerful through wealth and children" (Qutb 1990: 85–86). This follows Islam's foundational narratives in which the initial conquests, the *futuh*, were understood to be consequences of the internal individual transformations resulting from the embrace of the Prophet's message, encouraging a pious asceticism so that they would be warriors by day and "monks by night" (Sizgorich 2009: 909; 2007). "Every community has its monasticism," Mohammed reportedly told his companions, "and the monasticism of my community is *jihad* on the path of God" (Sizgorich 2009: 911).

In Islamic thought, there is both an etymological and causal link between *fitna*, identified as sedition or deviation that divides the community in Islam's foundational civil wars, and sexual temptation (Ayubi 1991; Mahmood 2005). *Fitna*, as trial or temptation, has its template, as in an Augustinian Christian reading, in man's inability to control his sexuality, to contain his sex inside of marital bonds, a template for lawlessness associated with sedition, wrong belief, and secession (Pandolfo 1997; Swanson 1984; Roy 2004: 277).[22] This is associated with the *hadith* in which troops returning from battle were told by the Prophet: "You have come for the best, from the smaller *jihad* (*al-jihad al-asghar*) to the greater *jihad* (*al-jihad al-akbar*)." His followers did not understand so Mohammed clarified to what he was referring: "The servant's struggle against his lust" (*mujahadat al-'abdi hawah*) (Euben 2002). For Islamists like Qutb, the struggle against erotic desire within prepares one for the struggle against the enemy without (Euben 1999: 73–74). Islamic jurists link seduction to sedition (Mahmood 2005: 110–111).

The centrality of sex, of course, is tied to that of the family in which these movements seek to contain it. Religious nationalists give primacy to the family, not to democracy or the market, as the social space through which society should be conceived and composed. Familial discourse, with its particularistic and sexual logic of love and loyalty, is pervasive in religious nationalism. "The family," the Ayatollah Khomeini declared, "is the fundamental unit of society and the main center of growth and transcendence for humanity...." (Riesebrodt, 1993: 145). For Qutb, too, the family's production of moral beings "is the only measure by which true human progress can really be gauged" (1990: 83). In the United States, the unifying core of Protestant fundamentalism is likewise its defense of the heterosexual and male-dominated family. Pat Robertson, the founder of the Christian Broadcasting Network, writes,

"The basic unit of social, local, national, and international organization in God's world order is the family" (Robertson 1991: 237). Looking at the political programs of Islamic movements, there is no consistent economic policy or form of government. The two pillars of contemporary Islamic politics involve a restrictive regulation of sexuality, eliminating it as a public presence and containing it within the family, and the promotion of a welfare state—or a religiously organized civil society—that not only enables families to survive physically, and particularly to care for those—orphans and widows in particular as enjoined in the Qur'an—who cannot rely on families for support (Humphreys 1999).[23] Islamic politics are a politics of love.

Politicized religions seek to promote the materiality of the family, not only its sexual and gendered codes, but its capacity to cohere across time—from the logic of the capitalist market, which has commodified sexuality and transformed love into a consumption good, and from the state, which steadily intrudes upon its erotic life, extending the logic of rights and regulation into this intimate sphere. It is partly for this reason that so many women support these patriarchal movements, seeking to shore up the loyalty of their husbands and the value of their mothering. Against the gender-equalizing force of the market and the demos, they reassert a divinely ordered patriarchalism (Riesebrodt 1993). These movements—whether the evangelical Christians of America or Islamist movements in Egypt and Iran—do authorize female religious agency, including their moralization of men (Mahmood 2005; Afary 2009). Nonetheless the patriarchal family is for them a template for political order, the ground of a revitalized and moralized male agency.

Because the family is an order of creation, not merely an order of production or governance, religions all seek to stitch its transitions, its relations, into rite through which their transrational order is given concrete form. Religion emplaces the order of human creation within the cosmos, joining the life cycle to cosmogony, rites that point before life and after death. As Talal Asad has shown us, institutional differentiation is an open game (Asad 1993, 2003). Asad has written of our understanding of religion as reflecting the Western differentiation, in which religion came to be defined, as the regulation of the ethical self, the interiority of the soul, and the marking and meaning of the life course, in which the rites of the life-cycle—of birth, marriage, and death—are all that remain to the religious domain. This differentiation separates two spaces, the secular and the sacred. It is within the former that humans self-consciously make history and exact the truth of both nature and society, through the freedoms authorized by the nation-state (Asad 2003: 192–193). It also divides two temporalities, two times—that of collective history and individual biological life—from each other. The political-religious imaginary rejoins the meaning of one's life to the origin and telos of a redemption set in historical time, to a history that points beyond both birth and death, a joining of a collective and an individual afterlife.

Qutb, the Egyptian Islamist, wrote that as a result of modernity the "clouds that weigh over creation are thicker and denser than before." Qutb also refused modernity's progressive historical transcript, rather organizing time into successive periods of *jahilya,* or pre-Islamic and post-Enlightenment ignorance. Secular societies, he argued, have forgotten that their wealth, their children, their political power are all "gifts of Allah." The "organic body" of Islamic society must therefore again be "born" from the Islamic movement whose origins are "not the result of any human effort or thinking," but come from "the will of Allah." "This Divine element sows the seed of the Islamic movement in human hearts and simultaneously prepares them for action and practical life" (Qutb 1990: 86–88). In contrast to modernist Egyptian nationalist history, locating the well-springs of history either in a national culture traceable back to Pharaonic Egypt or a nationalized—and largely spiritualized—Islam, Qutb underscored true history as man's giving being to God's will (Elfenbein 2008). God is, as Abraham said, "He who gives life and death" (Qur'an 2:258). For Qutb, nonmaterialist creation and the resacralization of history are linked. One finds the same linkage in the Palestinian Hamas whose covenant declares its nationalism "part of the religious creed": "If other nationalist movements are connected with materialistic, human or regional causes, [the] nationalism of the Islamic Resistance Movement...is connected to the source of spirit and the granter of life, hoisting in the sky of the homeland the heavenly banner that joins earth and heaven with a strong bond" (Hamas, 1988).

Jerry Falwell, who headed the Moral Majority, drew a straight line between the moral making of a divinely given life and the making of pre-millennial history. Falwell declared:

> I believe as we trust in God and pray, as we Christians lead the battle to outlaw abortion, which is murder on demand, as we take our stand against pornography, against the drug traffic, as we take our stand against the breakdown of the traditional family in America, the promotion of homosexual marriages....As we pray and preach and lead, Christian friends, I think there is hope that God may one more time bless America....I believe that between now and the rapture of the Church, America can have a reprieve. God can bless the country and before the rapture, I believe we can stay a free nation. (Harding 2000: 244)

The preoccupation of politicized religions with sexuality and their violence point to an alternate temporality, a rejection of the regime of infinite progress, of methodical accumulation of uncertain knowledge, and of history that can be read off and in parallel with the predictability of nature. It is a modern rejection of our modernity, a modernity that itself derives, as the great German thinker Hans Blumenberg has pointed out, from the playing out of the theological contradictions of Christianity, not of progress as a secularized, Christian salvation narrative. Our modern, he argued, emerged as a self-assertive outgrowth of late medieval nominalism in which the *potentia absoluta* of God, freedom from His ordained laws, ultimately stripped the world's order not only of a certain knowledge, but of its providential meaning, such that it fell to man to subject its unfinished materiality to ends he sets himself rather than those set by nature (Blumenberg 1983: 214–215). Hypothetical knowledge and the assertion of human purposes were historically connected. Modern man's self-assertion was a reaction, over the long durée, to the very absoluteness of God's power that exculpated man. Against this backdrop, one can read politicized religion's preoccupation with sexuality as an effort to restore the link between human creation and human history, individual and collective bodies—their sexuality being potentially part and parcel of the redemptive meaning of history issuing from their participation in God's will.

A religiously ordered sexuality is integral to reestablishing the divine telos of human history. It seeks to reground political foundation in creation, collective birth in human birth, and the making of a new collective body in the formation of individual bodies. To forge a nation, the state depends on an abstract space, upon physiological birth, and the bland fact of residence—mere location—to build a universal citizen transcending other group loyalties. This anybody depends on any place. Modern citizenship depends on the empty space of the state. Religious nationalism fills that space—the joining of God to the territorial nation, the fusion of two collective representations, a couplet of spirit and matter, and a male collective subject joined to a female territorial body.[24] "The nation," as Richard Koenigberg puts it, "is the fantasy of an omnipotent ego, projected into the world" (Koenigberg 2006). Religious nationalism involves an outraged reaction to the effeminization of the collective public body as a result of military, economic, and cultural penetration of its boundaries. Individual and collective bodily egos are religiously reformed in concert (Friedland 2002). One turns to God, the Superman, for the individual agency to protect, inform, and activate the nation's collective body; and for the power to sacrifice, engage in purifying violence, perform masculinity, and to be—in the end—more than man, that is, to have more than human value and power. In this mating of two sacrificial orders, religious nationalism is a way to mark the land and defend or redefine a nation's boundaries. Religious nationalism's obsessive control of women's bodies is a parallel figuration, the policing of a bodily frontier. By clothing, controlling, and sequestering the female body—taking it out of the sites of collective representation—religious nationalists reassert the maleness of the public body and the femaleness of the territory as a loved body that must be maintained inviolate, a perpetual possession.

CONCLUSION

Institutional theory points to the institutional logic of practice, not to the attributes of those who adopt it or the conditions under which it occurs. Religious violence is not only an instrument for the pursuit of political power; it marks the boundaries of an institution and expresses divine sovereignty. Violence is an attribute of politicized religion because politicized religion contests the foundations of state authority, seeking to ground it in religion—not the demos or the law—in a logic of collective representation that points to authors beyond the collectivity; authors who intervene in history, who take place, and who make and unmake bodies, both individual and collective bodies, bodies that have boundaries, bodies that are alive, that have a sex. Their sacrificial violence repudiates bare life.

Politicized religions are involved in a contest over the very meaning of death, over the "for which" one is willing to die or to kill. Max Weber instructed that the meaning of death is the fundament out of which the authority of state is composed. "This location of death within a series of meaningful and consecrated events," he wrote, "ultimately lies at the base of all endeavors to support the autonomous dignity of the polity resting on force" (Weber 1978: 335). It is the political constitution of that death, and of life, that politicized religions contest.

The religious nationalist political practices of sexual regulation and physical violence are ontological enactments, comportments that index God's absent presence, the divine as sovereign, whose sovereignty is manifest in its relation to life, a life which must be excessive to the law and whose excess is precisely what grounds the sovereign's authority (Friedland 2009a). Although it is hardly the solution they would imagine, politicized religion thus aims precisely at what Hannah Arendt and Giorgio Agamben discern as the crippled core—life—of modern politics (Arendt 1958; Agamben 1998).

There is a sex to sovereignty that we need to rethink if we wish to understand politicized religion. At a time when the state's hold inside our underpants threatens to become intolerable, and our pleasures lose their social meaning, political erotics reveals itself as a territory that calls us back to where we already are: sensuous citizenship, living members of a body politic. The sovereign relation is sexual: between the sovereign and his God, between the subject and the law, and between the subject and himself. The nation-state is also a formation of desire. For the adherents of politicized religion, the dialectic of our time is not capital and labor; rather it is organized as God and body, in rival ontological claims to life, in the meaning of death upon which the authority of any state must feed.

NOTES

1. I am particularly grateful for the incisive editorial judgments of my friend Jeff Alexander, to Rogers Brubaker for his generous critical engagement, and to Ahmad Ahmad, Tom Carlson, Caleb Elfenbein, Nathan French, Ron Hassner, Heather Haveman. Patricia Kubala, Racha al Omari, Jamel Velji as well as the participants in Lisa Hajar's Law and Society graduate seminar at UCSB, Ron Hassner's Religion, Politics and Globalization program at UC Berkeley, and Christine Thomas's Mediterranean Borderlands seminar at UCSB for their advice and comment.

2. Although the association between repression and religious violence derives from Philpott, he explicitly emphasizes the causal role of political theology (Philpott 2007, 2009). Philpott also points to the way that Arab statist regimes seek to control Islam, co-opt Islamic groups, and thereby radicalize conservative clerics (2007: 516).

3. Although trenchantly pointing to the inefficacy of terrorism, Abrahms likewise explains their persistence despite, and indeed because of, their tactics, by the way these organizations serve members' needs for social solidarity. He writes: "The preponderance of evidence is that people participate in terrorist organizations for social solidarity, not for their political return" (Abrahms 2008: 94). This, of course, raises the question as to why one would choose terrorist organizations for a buddy-boy joy ride, as opposed to crime

families or ethnic gangs that are equally dangerous and solidaristic. In any event, the cosmological meaning of the movement is rendered irrelevant in his analysis.

4. Foran and Reed also develop a parallel analysis of the role of politicized Catholicism in the formation of revolutionary subjectivity in the Nicaraguan revolution of 1979 (Reed and Foran 2002; Reed 2002).

5. In his analytic meditation on Islamic "suicide bombing," Talal Asad refuses the analytic utility of imputing religious "motive" to Islamist warriors: "The motivations of suicide bombers in particular are inevitably fictions that justify our responses that we cannot verify" (Asad,2007: 3). We invoke "motives," he argues, only when causal explanation are deemed insufficient, and we therefore demand to know its "reasons," or "what the action means" (2007: 63). Asad dismisses the religious motives attributed because they impose Christian categories of sacrifice and don't accord with members' Islamic categories, making them into a "perverse form of national politics" (2007: 50), thereby reproducing the liberal West's ability to use to "terrorism" as a vehicle for defining and defending their civilization against the barbarians. Asad rather renders the suicide bombers as belonging "in an important sense to a modern Western tradition of armed conflict for the defense of a free political community" (Asad 2007: 63). The religious element in the conflict is located not on the Islamic side, but uniquely on the Western Christian side that has secularized Christ's "suicide" story as a redemptive story which simultaneously enshrines sacrificial death and infinite compassion for human suffering, thereby rendering Western armies as killers with good consciences. If the Christian West fights religious wars, so do the Islamic warriors.

6. See Smith 1998 for a discussion of the perennialist debate in national historiography.

7. Likewise in Egypt during the 1970s, the *takfiris*, those declared apostates by their fellow Muslims, for a while included those who voted in elections as living under a death warrant (Wright 2006: 47, 124, 176).

8. That al-Qaeda seeks to expel infidel forces from the sacred lands of the *umma* and that it seeks to topple regimes that fail to follow the Shari'a, regimes, which they understand to be sustained by their strategic alliance with the United States, seem to be actionable, realistic goals, goals no less realistic than the United States' mission of expanding "liberty," as former Secretary of State Rice put it, throughout the Islamic world. Indeed, one of the consequences of al-Qaeda's relentless attacks was the withdrawal of American forces from Saudi Arabia in the lead-up to the second Gulf War.

9. The first political approach also centers on causes and consequences of violent, politicized religion: how people join and the consequences of the acts. The second cultural approach centers on religion as a reason: religion's substantive rationality, its transcendent and absolute order, for example. Causes and reasons are not mutually exclusive. That people who suffer injustice, for example, join religious movements does not exclude the possibility that they understand their acts as religious and indeed, as I will argue here, that religion accounts for the kinds of political practices in which they engage.

10. Brubaker has criticized my understanding of nationalism as a state-centered form of collective subject formation (Brubaker 2006). "Where," Brubaker asks "is 'the nation' in this definition?" "Not all state-centered collective subject formation," he writes, "centrally involves 'the nation'; and not all projects involving 'the nation' are state-centered." The first is undoubtedly correct: States are integral to the formation of many kinds of corporate groups and authorized collective subjects, whether armies, status groups, professions, or associations of all sorts. It is the second claim that I find problematic. Brubaker says my definition is "underinclusive," because it neglects nationalist projects that are not state-centric, but rather "centered on an imagined *national* community that does not correspond with the boundaries of a state." However, as is clear in Brubaker's own typology of nationalisms, nations are

always subjects and objects of state action, both seeking and sought by states (Brubaker 1998). But, as he shows, they need not be both. However, as Brubaker points out, states may promote the formation and protection of nations or nationals without those nations becoming subjects, as in the case of Soviet Union that institutionalized national identities as ascribed administrative and political categories while suppressing actual nationalisms, or states like the Nazis or Russians today who promote the interests and identities of their nonresident nationals (Brubaker 1998: 277, 286–287). While Brubaker is correct to chide me for conjuring an image of nation-formation that is too state-centric, I would still maintain that there is no national project that does not imply a state, as target, objective, protector, guarantee, or expression. This appears to be Brubaker's own understanding: Nationalist politics, he argues, emerge based on a "perceived lack of congruence between" the "imagined community of the nation and the territorial organization of the state" (Brubaker 2006: 19).

11. Rival religious groups—traditional Southern Protestants versus liberals in America, liberal German Protestants versus Catholics in Germany—may also promote a religious nationalism in their interreligious struggles (Gorski 2007).

12. If religious communities use the state to serve their private needs, indeed to represent the nonreligious interests of their communities, this is certainly not religious nationalism even if the collectivities mobilized are "diacritically" marked by religious attributes.

13. Talal Asad refers to the Islamic *umma* as a "theologically defined space enabling Muslims to practice the disciplines of *din* in the world" (Asad 2003:197). The *umma* is not a purely theological space. Ibn Taymiyyah, a critical source for today's Islamists, writing in the late thirteenth and early fourteenth centuries, wrote that in a just community, "exercise of a public office is one of the most important duties of religion [*din*]; we would add that public office is essential to the very existence of religion [*din*]." Ibn Taymiyyah cited in Gardet, L. "Dīn." *Encyclopaedia of Islam*, 2nd ed., edited by P. Bearman, Th. Bianquis, C. E. Bosworth, E. van Donzel, and W. P. Heinrichs. Amsterdam: Brill, 2009. Brill Online. University of California Santa Barbara CDL. Available at http://www.brillonline.nl/subscriber/entry?entry=islam_COM-0168. I am indebted to Nathan French for providing me with this source and the pre-modern political senses of both *umma* and *din*.

14. I am, of course, mindful that Islam does not give theological significance to the nation, that Islam has a transnational tradition of the caliphate on which to draw and that radical Islamists have historically derided Arab nationalisms. Islamist nationalism tends to draw on membership and divine derivation of authority, not on the redemptive significance of a national collectivity. It seeks to Islamicize the nation, not to nationalize Islam. Just like Marxism, radical Islam has its Trotskys and Lenins. It is the Lenins, the religious nationalists, who tend to predominate. We see this in the Iraqi nationalism of the Shi'ite Moqtada al-Sadr, who faced off the American forces or the Grand Ayatollah Ali Sistani, who brokered his truce, the Palestinian nationalism of Sheik Ahmad Yassin of Hamas, or the Iranian nationalism of Ayatollah Khomeini. Indeed at the end of his life, Khomeini issued a fatwa, or theological decision, declaring that even the seven pillars of Islam could be superseded in the interests of the Islamic republic of Iran (Wright 2000: 181–182). Even where the nation-state is not itself invested with theological value, as in the case of the mainstream of radical Islam, including al-Qaeda, it is the Islamicization of existent nation-states that is their immediate or eventual objective. Al-Qaeda was formed by exiled Islamists, like the Egyptian doctor, Zawahiri, who sought to transform the basis of their own national states. Indeed, the doctor declared that his violent actions were aimed at the government of his home state as were bin Laden's aimed at toppling the regime in Saudi Arabia. The Taliban, with which al-Qaeda was aligned, sought to create a federation of Islamic republics, not a unitary Islamic state (Ali 2002: 212).

15. Conflicts between groups over their respective powers within an institutional field are important to inter-institutional transformation. Groups, as in the case of the working class, may deploy the logic of outside institutions in their distributional struggles within a given institution. And because institutions themselves are interdependent, dependencies with distributional consequences, group conflicts within a given institutional field may involve efforts to transform the inter-institutional configuration and vice versa. In the case of religious nationalism, marginalized clerics seeking to transform the relation between religion and state increased both their position within the religious field and the hegemony of the field itself (Riesebrodt 1993). However, one can neither adequately explain nor interpret the project from the fact of marginality. The same can be said of the class location of "the dominated fraction of the intellectual strata—schoolteachers, village pastors, lower-level civil servants" who were critical in the racialization of German nationalism (Gorski, forthcoming).

16. Aristotle understood virtue, exercised by free men in the public sphere, as the privileged domain of action. Speaking of prudence, Aristotle noted, is not like science or production. "For production aims at an end other than itself; but this is impossible in the case of action, because the end is merely doing *well*" (Aristotle 2004: 150).

17. The violence accompanying religion's recent entry into the public sphere was matched by an even greater incidence and intensity of violence accompanying its displacement as the original ground of the nation-state, not to mention the violence over which religion would be the religion of state.

18. From this point of view, the labeling of political violence as terrorism is part and parcel of the state's claim of a monopoly on legitimate violence. Terrorism comprises violent politics by nonstate actors that states and their citizens hold to be unconscionable, as opposed to wars, open and secret, that likewise terrorize civilians as part of the state's war-making strategy, or successful revolutions that seize state power and fabricate newly legitimate regimes. Terrorism is war by the weak; war is the terrorism of the strong. Terror is part of the republican tradition: We inherit the very category of terror from the fourth year of the French Revolution, the executions and suspension of civil liberties of *la Terreur* understood as necessary to purge the new French republic of its internal and external enemies.

19. I have centered this text on the argument that politicized religion is not just a religious medium for political purposes. Reciprocally, it is also true that politicized religion can never be just a political medium for solely religious or pietistic purposes, which is how Roy understands "neo-fundamentalism" (Roy 2004). This is so because religiously organized modes of living have to defend themselves against the state, which is typically understood as an irreligious threat that intrudes on patterns of socialization and the organization of religiously mandated forms of social and cultural life. Defending a mode of life is a political task, if only to keep the state at bay. Mobilization of religious groups typically leads to political capacities within civil society—particularly for neo-fundamentalist Islamic groups who seek to apply Shari'a—if not within the electoral arena as well. Apparently pietistic and religious movements that do not seek state power or to recast the state often derive from political religious movements that were repressed, if not decimated, by the state, as in the case of the Muslim Brotherhood in Egypt, for example. Building an alternative civil society always contains political potential and the regimes—and the neo-fundamentalists—know it. The division between neo-fundamentalists, jihadists, and Islamists is likely a temporal one, an attribute of phase or strategic choice, not immanent and essential. Otherwise, it would be difficult to understand the trajectory of the Muslim Brotherhood, the Shi'ite revolutionaries, the Christian fundamentalists or even the religious Zionists who successively moved into and out of political contestation.

20. Cooper rather, emphasizes woman's sexual body as a template for absolute value in a de-territorialized Islam adapting to a de-territorializing economy (Cooper 2008). Although I applaud Cooper's erotic economics, I suspect usurious interest and women's bodies semiotically align primarily through illegitimate reproduction, limitless desire, and territorial incorporation more than absolute value.

21. According to the Pew Center surveys in 2003, Muslim respondents do not see democracy as a colonizing Western form. The same countries where majorities support the proposition that Islam should play a large or larger role in their societies are also major supporters of democratic government in their home countries (Pew Research Center 2003). Commitment to the public relevance of Islamic values is not inconsistent with support for democracy. Bin Laden, of course, represents the quintessential neo-fundamentalist. Those who support bin Laden should hate the West's universalizing of political freedom. Pew asked respondents if they had confidence in bin Laden to "do the right thing." Those Islamic countries in which a sizable proportion had "a lot" or "some" confidence in bin Laden also had sizable majorities who believed that democracy was not simply a Western way of doing things and could work in their countries. But what about those Muslims who themselves support bin Laden's variant of radical Islam? The Pew Center kindly ran cross-tabulations for me with the question about support for bin Laden, and only for Muslim respondents. Reanalyzing 2003 survey date on Muslim support for democracy and support for al-Qaeda's jihadism, precisely a form of radical Islam with restrictive views of gender relations, majorities—often overwhelmingly ones—of respondents in Jordan, Kuwait, Lebanon, Morocco, Lebanon, Pakistan, Palestine, and Turkey who supported bin Laden's actions, also believed that their country could and should have a democratic future. When I got the printouts and reported my interpretation, the Pew project director's first response was that I must have misread the data. Cross-tabulations provided to the author by Nicole Speulda, Project Director, Pew Research Center for the People and the Press, September 20, 2004.

22. One of Pandolfo's Moroccan informants informs her that just as seduction by a woman sets a man on fire, so, too, "the society itself is on fire! *Fitna* of riches, *fitna* of children, *fitna* of invasion, razing, and war, *fitna* of blood, *fitna* of women…It is all *fitna*, one *fitna*, and it has no cure! *Fitna*s comes in different forms, but the sovereign *fitna*, the Sultan of *fitna*s, is the *fitna* of love!" (Pandolfo 1997: 98).

23. The Islamic regulation of family life has, in fact, been the core of Islamic law during this century. "[T]hroughout this century," writes Humphreys, "the sections on women, the family, and personal morality have been the most vital and living elements of the Shari'a, and in the courts of most countries they are the only parts of it still enforced" (Humphreys 1999: 212).

24. Freud writes: "…[T]he almighty and just God, and kindly Nature, appear to us as grand sublimations of father and mother, or rather as revivals and restorations of the young child's ideas of them" (Freud 1989: 83).

REFERENCES

2004. "In Afghanistan con Osma e Abu." *L'Espresso*, pp. 84–85.

Abrahms, Max. 2006. "Why Terrorism Does Not Work." *International Security* 31:42–78.

———. 2008. "What Terrorists Really Want: Terrorist Motives and Counterterrorism Strategy." *International Security* 32:78–105.

Afary, Janet. 2009. *Sexual Politics in Modern Iran*. New York: Cambridge University Press.

Agamben, Giorgio. 1998. *Homo Sacer: Sovereign Power and Bare Life*. Stanford, CA: Stanford University Press.

———. 2005. *State of Exception*. Chicago: University of Chicago Press.

Ahmed, Hisham H. 2005. "Palestinian Resistance and 'Suicide Bombing.'" Pp. 87–102 in *Root Causes of Terrorism: Myths, Reality and Ways Forward*, edited by Tore Bjorgo. New York: Routledge.

Ali, Tariq. 2002. *The Clash of Fundamentalisms: Crusades, Jihads and Modernity*. London: Verso.

Anderson, Benedict. 1991. *Imagined Communities: Reflections on the Origin and Spread of Nationalism*. London: Verso.

Arendt, Hannah. 1958. *The Human Condition*. Chicago: University of Chicago Press.

Argo, Nichole. 2006. "Human Bombs: Rethinking Religion and Terror." Pp. 1–6 in *Audit of the Conventional Wisdom*. Cambridge, MA: MIT Center for International Studies.

Aristotle. 1998. *The Metaphysics*. New York: Penguin Classics.

———. 2004. *The Nicomachean Ethics*. London: Penguin Classics.

Asad, Talal. 1993. *Genealogies of Religion: Discipline and Reasons of Power in Christianity and Islam*. Baltimore: Johns Hopkins University Press.

———. 2001. "Reading a Modern Classic: W. C. Smith's 'The Meaning and End of Religion.'" *History of Religions* 40:205–222.

———. 2003. *Formations of the Secular: Christianity, Islam, Modernity*. Palo Alto, CA: Stanford University Press.

———. 2007. *On Suicide Bombing*. New York: Columbia University Press.

Ayubi, Nazih N. M. 1991. *Political Islam: Religion and Politics in the Arab World*. London: Routledge.

Bergesen, Albert J. 2008. *The Sayyid Qutb Reader: Selected Writings on Politics, Religion, and Society*. New York: Routledge.

Blumenberg, Hans. 1983. *The Legitimacy of the Modern Age*. Trans. Robert M. Wallace. Cambridge: MIT Press.

Borradori, Giovanna. 2003. *Philosophy in a Time of Terror: Dialogues with Jurgen Habermas and Jacques Derrida*. Chicago: University of Chicago Press.

Bourdieu, Pierre. 1977. *Outline of a Theory of Practice*. Cambridge, UK: Cambridge University Press.

———. 1990. *The Logic of Practice*. Stanford, CA: Stanford University Press.

Brass, Paul R. 1997. *Theft of an Idol*. Princeton, New Jersey: Princeton University Press.

———. 2002. "The Gujarat Pogrom of 2002," *Items and Issues*, Social Science Research Council, Vol. 4., No. 1.

Breiger, Ron. L. 2000. "A Tool Kit for Practice Theory." Poetics, 27: 91–115

Brubaker, Rogers. 1998. "Myths and Misconceptions in the Study of Nationalism." Pp. 272–306 in *The State of the Nation*, edited by John Hall. Cambridge, UK: Cambridge University Press.

——— 2002. "Ethnicity without Groups." *Archives européennes de sociologie* XLIII, 2: 163–189

———. 2006. "Religion and Nationalism: Four Approaches." Conference on *Nation/Religion*. Konstanz, Germany: University of Konstanz.

Calhoun, Craig. 1998. *Nationalism*. Minneapolis: University of Minnesota Press.

Clemens, Elisabeth S. 1997. *The People's Lobby: Organizational Innovation and the Rise of Interest Group Politics in the United States, 1890–1925*. Chicago: University of Chicago Press.

Cooper, Melinda. 2008. "Orientalism in the Mirror: The Sexual Politics of Anti-Westernism." *Theory, Culture and Society*: 25 (6): 25–49.

Derrida, Jacques. 1990. "Force of Law: The 'Mystical Foundation of Authority.'" *Cardozo Law Review* 11:920–1039.

DiMaggio, Paul and Walter W. Powell. 1983. "The Iron Cage Revisited: Institutional Isomorphism and Collective Rationality in Organizational Fields." *American Sociological Review*, 48: 147–160.

Dupré, Louis. 1993. *Passage to Modernity: An Essay in the Hermeneutics of Nature and Culture*. New Haven, CT: Yale University Press.

Elfenbein, Caleb. 2008. "Differentiation and Islam: Colonialism, Sayyid Qutb, and Religious Transformation in Modern Egypt." Pp. 217 unpublished doctoral dissertation, Department of Religious Studies, . Santa Barbara: University of California Santa Barbara.

Euben, Roxanne. 1999. *Enemy in the Mirror: Islamic Fundamentalism and the Limits of Modern Rationalism*, Princeton University Press.

———. 2002. "Killing (for) Politics: Jihad, Martyrdom and Political Action," Political Theory 30 (1): 4–35.

Foran, John. 1993. *Fragile Resistance: Social Transformation in Iran from 1500 to the Revolution*. Boulder, CO: Westview Press.

———. 1997. "The Future of Revolutions at the Fin-de-Siècle." *Third World Quarterly*, Vol. 18, No. 5 (Dec., 1997), pp. 791–820.

Foucault, Michel. 1980. *The History of Sexuality: Volume I: An Introduction*. New York: Vintage.

Freud, Sigmund. 1989. *Leonardo da Vinci and a Memory of His Childhood*. New York: W.W. Norton.

Friedland, Roger. 2001. "Religious Nationalism and the Problem of Collective Representation." *Annual Review of Sociology* 27:125–52.

———. 2002. "Money, Sex and God: The Erotic Logic of Religious Nationalism." *Sociological Theory* 20:381–424.

———. 2005. "Religious Terror and the Erotics of Exceptional Violence." *Anthropological Yearbook of European Cultures* 14:39–71.

———. 2009a. "L'eros del Sovrano." *Reset* 111:63–68.

———. 2009b. "Institution, Practice and Ontology: Towards a Religious Sociology. " In *Ideology and Organizational Institutionalism, Research in the Sociology of Organizations*, edited by Renate Meyer, K. Sahlin-Andersson, Marc Ventresca, and Peter Walgenbach. vol. 27, Bingley: Emerald Publishing, pp. 45–83.

———. 2009c. "The Endless Fields of Pierre Bourdieu." *Organization* 16 (6): 887–917.

Friedland, Roger, and Robert R. Alford. 1991. "Bringing Society Back In: Symbols, Practices and Institutional Contradictions." Pp. 232–263 in *The New Institutionalism in Organizational Analysis*, edited by Walter W. and Paul DiMaggio Powell. Chicago: University of Chicago Press.

Friedland, Roger, and Richard Hecht. 2000. *To Rule Jerusalem*. Berkeley: University of California Press.

Giddens, Anthony. 1985. *The Nation-State and Violence*. Cambridge, UK: Polity Press.

Gorski, Philip S. 200. "The Mosaic Moment: An Early Modernist Critique of the Modernist Theory of Nationalism", *American Journal of Sociology* 105: 1428–68.

——— 2003. *The Disciplinary Revolution: Calvinism and the Rise of the State in Early Modern Europe*. Chicago: University of Chicago Press.

——— 2006. "Premodern Nationalism: An Oxymoron? The Evidence from England." Pp. 143–155 in *Sage Handbook of Nationalism*, edited by G. Delanty and K. Kumar. New York: Russell Sage.

———. 2007. "Religious Nationalism: A Neo-Weberian Approach." In *Religion and Nation*. Konstanz, Germany: University of Konstanz.

———unpublished ms. "Nation-ization Struggles: A Bourdieusian Theory of Nationalism." New Haven, CT: Department of Sociology, Yale University.

Hamas. 1988. *The Covenant of the Islamic Resistance Movement*. New Haven, CT: Avalon Project, Yale University Law School.

Harding, Susan Friend. 2000. *The Book of Jerry Falwell: Fundamentalist Language and Politics*. Princeton, NJ: Princeton University Press.

Heidegger, Martin. 1977. "The Age of the World Picture." Pp. 115–154 in *The Question Concerning Technology and Other Essays*. New York: Harper.

Hobbes, Thomas, 1985, ed. C.B. Macpherson. *Leviathan*. New York: Penguin.

Humphreys, R. Stephen. 1999. *Between Memory and Desire: The Middle East in a Troubled Age*. Berkeley: University of California Press.

Huntington, Samuel. 1993. " The Clash of Civilizations?" *Foreign Affairs*, Vol. 72, No. 3 (Summer, 1993), pp. 22–49.

Inglehart, Ronald F., and Pippa Norris. 2003. "Islam and the West: a 'Clash of Civilizations'?" *Foreign Policy*, March/April: 62–70.

Israeli, Raphael. 1997. "Islamikaze and Their Significance." *Journal of Terrorism and Political Violence* 9:96–121.

———. 2003. *Islamikaze: Manifestations of Islamic Martyrology*, Frank Cass, London, 2003

Juergensmeyer, Mark. 1994. *The New Cold War? Religious Nationalism Confronts the Secular State*. Berkeley: University of California Press.

———. 2000. *Terror in the Mind of God: The Global Rise of Religious Violence*. Berkeley: University of California Press.

Kamdar, Mira. 2002. "The Struggle for India's Soul," *World Policy Journal*, Fall: 11–27.

Kepel, Gilles. 2002. *Jihad: The Trail of Political Islam*. Cambridge, MA: Harvard University Press.

Koenigsberg, Richard. 2006. "The Human Body Becomes a Body Politic." Available at website on the Psychoanalysis of Culture, Ideology and History. http://www.psych-culture.com/docs/rk-humanbody.html

LaHaye, Tim, and Jerry B. Jenkins. 1995. *Left Behind: A Novel of the Earth's Last Days*. Wheaton, IL: Tyndale.

Landes, Joan B. 2001. *Visualizing the Nation: Gender, Representation, and Revolution in Eighteenth-Century France*. Ithaca, NY: Cornell University Press.

Lincoln, Bruce. 2003. *Holy Terrors: Thinking About Religion after September 11*. Chicago: University of Chicago.

McAdam, Doug, Sidney Tarrow and Charles Tilly. 2001. Dynamics of Contention (New York: Cambridge University Press.

Mahmood, Saba. 2005. *Politics of Piety: The Islamic Revival and the Feminist Subject*. Princeton: Princeton University Press.

Mander, Harsh. 2002. "Reflections on the Gujarat Massacre." Available at http://www.Boloji.com.

Mann, Michael. 1986. *The Sources of Social Power*. Cambridge, UK: Cambridge University Press.

McMahon, D. M. 2001. *Enemies of Enlightenment: The French Counter-Enlightenment and the Making of Modernity 1778–1830*. New York: Oxford University Press.

Meyerson, D. (2003). *Tempered Radicals: How Everyday Leaders Inspire Change at Work*, Harvard Business School Press.

Meyerson, D. and M. Tompkins. (2007). "Tempered radicals as institutional change agents: The case of advancing gender equity at the University of Michigan." *Harvard Journal of Law and Gender* 30(2): 303–322.

Mohr, John W. and Vincent Duquenne. 1997. "The Duality of Culture and Practice: Poverty Relief in New York City, 1888–1917." Theory and Society, Vol. 26/2–3: 305–356.

Norris, Andrew. 1998. "Carl Schmitt on Friends, Enemies, and the Political," Telos 112: 68–88.

Olzak, Susan. 2004. "Ethnic and Nationalist Social Movements." The Blackwell Companion to Social Movements. Pp. 666–693, edited by David A. Snow, Sarah Soule, and Hanspeter Kriesi. Malden, MA: Blackwell.

Pandolfo, Stefania. 1997. Impasse of the Angels: Scenes from a Morrocan Space of Memory. Chicago: University of Chicago Press.

Pape, Robert A. 2003. "The Strategic Logic of Suicide Terrorism." The American Political Science Review 97:343–361.

Philpott, Daniel. 2007. "Explaining the Political Ambivalence of Religion." American Political Science Review 101:505–525.

———. 2009. "Has the Study of Global Politics Found Religion." Annual Review of Political Science 12:183–202.

Piscatori, James P. 1986. Islam in a World of Nation-States. Cambridge, UK: Cambridge University Press.

Plato. 2002. Phaedrus. New York: Oxford University Press.

Qutb, Sayyid. 1990. Milestones. Indianapolis, IN: American Trust Publications.

———. 2000. In the Shade of the Qur'an, Volume 2, Surah 3. Leicester, UK: Islamic Foundation.

Ramaswamy, Sumathi. 2002. "Visualising India's Geo-body: Globes, Maps, Bodyscapes." Contributions to Indian Sociology 36:151–189.

Rao, Hayagreeva, Philippe Monin, and Rodolphe Durand. 2003. "Institutional Change in Toque Ville: Nouvelle Cuisine as an Identity Movement in French Gastronomy." American Journal of Sociology 108:795–843.

Riesebrodt, Martin. 1993. Pious Passion: The Emergence of Modern Fundamentalism in the United States and Iran. Berkeley: University of California Press.

Robertson, Pat. 1991. The New World Order. Dallas: Word.

Roy, Ollivier. 2004. Globalized Islam: The Search for a New Ummah. New York: Columbia University Press.

Sageman, Marc. 2004. Understanding Terror Networks. Philadelphia: University of Pennsylvania Press.

Scarry, Elaine. 1985. The Body in Pain: The Making and Umaking of the World. Oxford: Oxford University Press.

Schmitt, Carl. 1985. Political Theology: Four Chapters on the Concept of Sovereignty. Cambridge, MA: MIT Press.

———. 1996. The Concept of the Political. Chicago: University of Chicago Press.

Scott, Richard, et al, 2000. Institutional Change and Healthcare Organizations: From Professional Dominance To Managed Care. Chicago: University of Chicago Press

Searle, John R. 1997. The Construction of Social Reality. New York: The Free Press.

———. 2006. "Social Ontology: Some Basic Principles." Anthropoligical Theory, 6: 12–29.

Selznick, Philip. 1957. Leadership in Administration: A Sociological Interpretation. New York: Harper and Row.

Sizgorich, Thomas. 2007. "'Do Prophets Come with a Sword?' Conquest, Empire, and Historical Narrative in the Early Islamic World." American Historical Review 112:993–1015.

———. 2009. "Sanctified Violence: Monotheist Militancy as the Tie That Bound Christian Rome and Islam." Journal of the American Academy of Religion 77:895–921.

Smith, Anthony D. 1998. *Nationalism and Modernism: A Critical Survey of Recent Theories of Nations and Nationalism*. Hanover, NH: University Press of New England.

Swanson, Mark N. 1984. "A Study of Twentieth-Century Commentary on Surat al-Nur (24):27–33." *The Muslim World* 74:187–203.

Tambiah, Stanley. 1996. *Leveling Crowds: Ethnonationalist Conflicts and Collective Violence in South Asia*, Berkeley: University of California Press.

Taylor, Mark C. 2007. *After God*. Chicago: University of Chicago.

Taylor, Verta and Nella Van Dyke. 2004. "Tactical Repertoires, Action, and Innovation," in David A. Snow, Sarah A. Soule, and Hanspeter Kriesi, eds., *The Blackwell Companion to Social Movements*.Oxford: Blackwell Publishers. Pp. 262–293.

Thornton, Patricia H. 2009. "The Value of the Classics." Pp. 20–38 in *The Oxford Handbook of Sociology and Organization Studies: Classical Foundations*, edited by Paul S Adler. New York: Oxford University Press.

Tilly, Charles. 1975. *The Formation of National States in Western Europe*. Princeton, NJ: Princeton University Press.

———. 1978. *From Mobilization To Revolution*. Reading: Addison-Wesley Publishing Co.

Weber, Max. 1958a. "Politics as a Vocation." Pp. 77–128. In *From Max Weber: Essay in Sociology*, edited by Hans Gerth and C. Wright Mills. New York: Oxford University Press.

———. 1958b. "Science as a Vocation." Pp. 129–156. In *From Max Weber*, edited by Hans Gerth and C. Wright Mills. New York: Oxford University Press.

———. 1958c. "The Social Psychology of the World Religions." Pp. 267–301 in *From Max Weber*, edited by Hans Gerth and C. Wright Mills. New York: Oxford University Press.

———. 1958d. "Religious Rejections of the World and Their Directions." Pp. 323–362 in *From Max Weber*, edited by Hans Gerth and C. Wright Mills. New York: Oxford University Press.

———. 1958e. *The Protestant Ethic and the Spirit of Capitalism*. New York: Scribners.

———. 1978. *Economy and Society: An Outline of Interpretive Sociology*. Berkeley: University of California Press.

Wilkinson, Steven I. 2006. *Votes and Violence: Electoral Competition and Ethnic Riots in India*. New York: Cambridge University Press.

Williamson, Oliver E. 1983. *Markets and Hierarchies: Analysis and Antitrust Implications*. New York: Free Press.

Wright, Lawrence. 2006. *The Looming Tower: Al-Qaeda and the Road to 9/11*. New York: Knopf.

Wright, Robin. 2000. *The Last Great Revolution: Turmoil and Transformation in Iran*. New York: Knopf.

CHAPTER 17

GLOBALIZATION AND RELIGION

KENNETH THOMPSON

INTRODUCTION

It was once an accepted belief among sociologists that structural developments associated with a unilinear modernization process would lead to a decline of religion and the spread of a global secularization. This belief was prevalent among the European founders of sociology and was continued in the powerful arguments advanced by later European sociologists of religion who found this theory apparently confirmed by their experience of the weakened state of churches and sects in their homelands. This was particularly the case for British sociologists of religion, such as those influenced by Bryan Wilson at Oxford University (see Thompson 1990a, 1990b), although doubts were raised by David Martin at the London School of Economics and by the very different experience of American scholars (Martin 1978, 1991, 1999; Stark and Bainbridge 1985; Berger 1999). In fact, we are witnessing a net growth of religion in the twenty-first century. Far from religion disappearing from the public sphere into a private ghetto, one of the public debates is about a developing "clash of civilizations" between Christianity and Islam and of competition between expanding Christian groups such as Pentecostalism and Catholicism.

A controversial analysis of global trends that paid serious attention to changing religious patterns and their possible effects in the public sphere was Samuel P. Huntington's *The Clash of Civilizations and the Remaking of the World Order* (1996). Huntington's fears derived from his belief that a militant form of Islam was gaining ground in the public sphere, coupled with a forecast that the relative Christian share of global population would fall steeply in the twenty -first century and be supplanted by Islam. But his claims were disputed by Philip Jenkins in *The Next Christendom: The Coming of Global Christianity* (2002, revised 2007), who highlighted the rapid growth of Christianity in the Global South, arguing that far from Islam being the world's largest religion by 2020 or so, looking at current trends, Christianity should still have a substantial lead and would maintain its position into the foreseeable future. "By 2050 there will still be about three Christians for every two Moslems worldwide. Some 34 percent of the world's people will then be Christian, roughly what the figure was at the height of European world hegemony in 1900" (Jenkins 2007: 6).

Whether or not one accepts the complete reliability of forecasts of future demographic trends, the important questions for sociology are no longer concerned with charting an inevitable decline of religion in the face of the structural forces of modernization, but in seeking to understand the burgeoning religious cultures and their relations to the forces of globalization.

In examining these questions, the first part of this paper will make a distinction between teleological-homogenizing approaches to religious developments in modernity, which assume that secularization is inevitable, and those that emphasize cross-national variability and historical contingency. As we will see, although the latter approach often appears to give more emphasis to cultural factors, this need not be the case. The second part of the paper will begin to develop a stronger cultural argument that recognizes not only variation and contingency, but also the effect of cross-circulating discourses, boundary exchanges, translations, hybridization, and other cultural processes. Finally, it will be argued that this stronger cultural approach is more sensitive to the ways in which the discourses of religion (particularly Islam) and globalization are connected in a binary relationship to one another.

SECULARIZATION AND RELIGIOUS PERSISTENCE

For much of the history of sociology, from the time of Auguste Comte onward, it was taken for granted that religious culture was destined to decline as part of an inevitable process of secularization that was intrinsic to modernization (Thompson 1975). In part, this was linked to the predominant sociological logic according to which cultural phenomena could be regarded as ultimately determined by structural factors, such as structural differentiation (Wilson 1966). A more nuanced framework treated secularization as a multidimensional process within which macro, meso, and micro levels of analysis could be distinguished, and more specifically, three major processes: the functional differentiation of societal subsystems, the emergence of competitive religious markets, and the individualization and privatization of religious practice and belief (Dobbelaere 1981, 1999). But this leaves open the question of the relationship between the three processes.

One approach is to treat each as a separate hypothesis. Jose Casanova argues that of the three—differentiation, privatization, and decline—only one, the differentiation hypothesis, is plausible (Casanova 1994, 2006). Furthermore, he argues, the macro-level secularization (differentiation) actually sets the stage for a sort of meso-level desecuralization: the emergence of public religions. Shorn of their role as grand legitimators, responsible for integrating and regulating society as a whole, religions can become movements and pressure groups that vie with rivals in the public sphere.

The problem with many of the analyses of secularization, as has been pointed out by Gorski and Altinordu (2008), is that they operate with the teleological and ahistorical language of modernization theory and therefore have difficulty dealing with the cross-national variability and historical contingency of most secularization processes. This has led to calls for a fuller historicization of the secularization debate (Gorski and Altinordu 2008: 59). As these scholars go on to admit, there is one sociologist of religion who, for several decades, has sought to do this—the British sociologist David Martin. However, Gorski and Altinordu point out that, despite the title, Martin's *A General Theory of Secularization* (Martin 1978) is not a nomological account of a teleological process, but rather a conjunctural account of a variable process, an effort to explain the various forms of secularism in terms of historical events (e.g., the Reformation settlement) and structural configurations (e.g., the degree of religious pluralism). While that may be true of this particular book, it could distract attention from the other major component of Martin's approach, which is not simply concerned with the historical structural processes, but also with the importance of autonomous cultural factors. Above all, the strength of Martin's approach, especially in his rich studies of Pentecostalist movements, lies in its penetrating cultural analyses.

Martin sees sociology as "a human science which seeks regularities within the specific densities and local character of culture as that unfolds over time in an understandable narrative. It is a mode of telling 'the story'... It also subjects the inwardness of human culture to a certain amount of external redescription" (Martin 1997: 2). Consequently, he does not see religion as merely an epiphenomenon of social, economic, or political forces, but rather as possessing—especially in the Pentecostal context—a cultural autonomy of its own. For him, "culture is not merely a derivative sphere that picks up impulses from the supposed 'motors' of change, but one that autonomously generates its own transformations" (Martin 1996: 2). Hence, he repeatedly affirms the primacy of culture over structure and sees Pentecostalism in the contemporary period, like Methodism in the eighteenth century, as a historical validation of "the latent capacity of cultural changes held in religious storage to emerge over time when circumstances are propitious to activate them" (Martin 1990: 44). When this happens, "the cultural margin (or rather the margin we call culture) can effect the so-called centre" (1996: 16).

The value of this cultural sociology approach will be seen at its best when accounting for the religious phenomenon that provides the most startling refutation of the secularization thesis—the various forms of Pentecostalism that have attracted 500 million adherents, particularly in the Global South, with some predictions that this number will double by 2050 (even though there will still be more Catholics) (Jenkins 2007:9).

RELIGION AND GLOBALIZATION

How have religious cultural systems been involved with globalization? In a presidential address to the Association for the Sociology of Religion at the time of the Millennium, Jose Casanova maintained that one of the most important effects of globalization on cultural systems is their "deterritorialization" (Casanova 2001: 428). According to Casanova, deterritorialisation refers to the disembeddedness of cultural systems from their accustomed, "imagined" territories. The process of modern territorialization began with the dissolution of Western Christendom and its pluralization into nation-states and national churches. One of the earliest examples was that of the expulsion of the Jews and Moors from Spain on the grounds that they could not become subjects of the new Catholic nation-state. Another example was the assertion of the English Church's independence from Rome in the sixteenth century. By the time sociology appeared on the scene, it was already taken for granted that any reference to society was intended as a reference to a nation-state. However, with the acceleration of processes of globalization in the twentieth century, the boundaries of the sovereign state began to appear more porous and to be overlapped by transnational networks. Another dimension of this deterritorialization is that of 'glocalization', in which local spaces, real or imagined communities, identities, subcultures, and ethnic groups contest for spatial autonomy from the nation-state territories in which they had been embedded and circumscribed (Casanova 2001: 429).

One possible outcome of these developments is that global humanity itself becomes a self-referential unit, the reflexive point of reference for all peoples (Robertson and Chirico 1985). But this possibility is severely limited, as humanity as a whole presents a rather weak, imagined community, even though the developing emphasis on "human rights," as well as the threat of human extinction, might seem to be conducive to it. More typically, individual and collective identities tend to be plural and based on difference over the other(s), which enables reflexive awareness of particularity. The dream of a religion of humanity by early sociologists, such as Auguste Comte and Henri Saint-Simon, seems no closer to becoming a reality. More obvious is the fact that globalization has stimulated a return to old civilizations and world religions as cultural systems and imagined communities. Christianity and Islam provide striking examples of these transnational—indeed, truly global—trends. In the case of Christianity, the major growth versions are Catholicism and Pentecostalism. The corresponding Islamic revival has not been confined to radical versions, but is manifested in a more widespread heightening of Islamic consciousness among the masses in response to the challenges and opportunities presented by globalization.

CATHOLICISM

The reconstitution of Catholicism as a globalized ideological regime, or imagined community, might justifiably be dated fairly accurately in the year 1870. It was in reaction to the global spread of secular liberalism and modernism that the First Vatican Council proclaimed the dogma of papal infallibility and reaffirmed the Pope's supremacy over the universal Catholic Church. This kind of assertion had been weakened with the dissolution of Christendom and the collapse of the Holy Roman Empire, following which the papacy lost control of the national Catholic churches to Caesaro-Papist monarchs through concordats. The concordat with Napoleon in 1801, and its subsequent failure, represented perhaps the most spectacular modern example of this process. The spread of liberal conceptions of universal human rights, as in the Declaration of the Rights of Man by the French National Assembly, was repeatedly opposed by the popes, including Pius IX in the *Syllabus of Errors* (1864). But whereas Vatican I was composed mainly of Europeans bishops, the 2500 Fathers at Vatican II in the early 1960s included 228 indigenous African and Asian bishops and over 200 U.S. prelates. Its Declaration on Religious Freedom recognized the right of every individual to freedom of conscience and the sacred dignity of the human person. Similarly, Pope John XXIII's encyclical *Pacem in Terris* (1963) incorporated the modern discourse of universal human rights and enlisted the Catholic Church in the global human rights revolution. In the papacy of John Paul II, this global role was emphasized not simply by his constant world travelling, but also by his embrace of the role of spokesman of humanity. As Casanova puts it:

> The Catholic church has embraced globalization, welcoming its liberation from the strait-jacket of the territorial sovereign nation-state which has restricted its catholic universal claims. But the embrace is not uncritical. The church has remained one of the public voices left still questioning capitalist globalization and demanding the humanization and moralization of market economies and a more just and fair international division of labour and distribution of world resources. (Casanova 2001: 433)

The newly reaffirmed global cultural reach of the Catholic Church is not without hazards and tensions. Where the Church has sought to align itself with the needs of the poor in the global south—choosing the "option for the poor"—the "liberation" theology has had to be reined in by the Vatican for fear of becoming politically entangled. Similarly, the "pro-life" teachings of the Church have seemed to run against the efforts at population control and the fight against HIV/AIDS in developing countries.

Alongside, or in competition with, the liberation theology are the cultural indigenization or charismatic tendencies within Catholicism in the Global South. The problems created by indigenization and the adoption of folk religious elements have been a problem not just in South America, but even more so in Africa. Once again, the problems are part and parcel of remarkable growth. The expansion in Africa is put in perspective by the Catholic journalist John Allen:

> Africa in the twentieth century went from a Catholic population of 1.9 million in 1900 to 130 million in 2000, a growth rate of 6,708 percent, the most rapid expansion of a single continent in two thousand years of church history. (quoted in Jenkins 2007: 67)

Although liberation theology and the famous base communities, relying on heavy lay involvement and community organizing, had some success, a more important movement has been that of charismatic Catholic groups. In their use of modern technologies, techniques for raising the emotions of mass audiences, and belief in God's direct intervention in everyday life to bring health and wealth to the individual believer, the Catholic charismatics resemble the Pentecostalists with whom they are often in competition. Where once the faith was brought by Western missionaries—conveyed in Western thought forms—today, we are just as likely to see a reverse flow from the Catholic charismatic movements of the Global South, as in the case of expatriate Filipino workers who attend charismatic congregations in over twenty-five countries, including the United States and Canada.

The comparison of Catholic and Pentecostal movements, and their respective success rates in Latin America, provide a useful test case of the different theories and methodologies of two rival forms of explanation in contemporary sociology of religion—rational choice theory versus the cultural sociology approach. At its most basic level, rational choice theory of religion has been applied toward explaining the different rates of secularization (or its relative absence) based on the existence or absence of a religious monopoly in a society. The theory argues that the prior existence of a religious monopoly, such as a state church, would be likely to hasten secularization, whereas a more pluralistic, free market situation would be likely to stimulate religious competition and efforts to satisfy people's spiritual needs. This quasi-economic theory of market supply, which assumes religious demand remains constant, can have the effect of defining secularization out of existence "in much the same way that neoclassical economics defines irrational action out of existence" (Gorski and Altinordu 2008: 58).

Another version of rational choice theory was used by Anthony Gill in *Rendering unto Caesar* (Gill 1998), illustrating a cross-national study of the distribution of Catholic political radicalism. Here, rational choice is based on the idea that aggregate behavior in large-scale organizations can be analyzed in terms of marketing strategies directed toward survival. Social actors, in this case Church and state, behave so as to maximize their advantages, according to the information at their disposal, and they seek increased power and legitimacy, which in the case of the Church includes increased (or retained) market share. When the Church operated as a monopoly, it strove to preserve a position of privilege, enabling it to concentrate on an alliance with the well-off and powerful. However, once confronted by competition, either from revolutionary political parties or alternative faiths, it has to look after its market share among the masses. Apathy has to give way to activity. Thus, Gill predicts a positive relationship between the emergence of competition among the masses, whether religious or political, and the adoption by the Church of a "preferential option for the poor." The finding is that of the twelve countries studied, the best predictor of the option for the poor is indeed the emergence of competition. However, it is instructive to note the struggle that Gill has in explaining the two exceptions—Guatemala and Ecuador. In the case of Guatemala, the episcopate's failure to pursue the preferential option, in spite of evangelical competition, is explained in terms of entrenched attitudes among the episcopate, derived from a century of battling with liberalism. In other words, as David Martin remarks ironically, the bishops took too long to grasp their rational choice—much as economists dismiss buyers' failures to make the most rational choice as being due to "irrational" factors, such as entrenched attitudes (culture) (Martin 2002: 184).

A cultural sociology approach may shed some light on the question of why Pentecostalism has been more successful than liberation Catholicism in some Latin American countries, such as Brazil. One explanation, along these lines, is that liberation theology was a typically modernist project, whereas Pentecostalism is more capable of surviving in the fluid conditions of postmodernity. Manuel Vasquez' *The Brazilian Popular Church and the Crisis of Modernity* (1998) claims that the liberation Catholicism was based on a typically modernist formulation, uniting secular with religious utopias through a dialogue among Catholic doctrine, humanist Marxism, and existentialism. Furthermore, like any modernist project of structural change based on a "unified collective emancipatory subject" such as "the poor," it had reached the end of its viability. Pentecostalism showed itself much more capable of dealing with the Third World conditions of a mix of premodern, modern, and postmodern elements. Having retained a separation between the enclave of faith and the corrupt world, Pentecostalism was better able to bear the nonappearance of the political kingdom.

GLOBAL PENTECOSTALISM

Pentecostalism's astonishing growth can be interpreted in a variety of ways, as David Martin has shown (Martin 2002: 169). In so far as it registers in the popular Western mind, Pentecostalism is often equated with similar movements in Islam and Hinduism, belonging to a wave of fundamentalism sweeping world religions in a last-ditch defense against modernity. Or, contrastingly, it may be seen "as an adaptable form of heart-work and spiritual self-exploration breaking free of the restrictive protocols of enlightened reason into a New Age of postmodernity" (Martin 2002: 169). Perhaps because it is essentially engaged in personal and cultural revolution, however, Pentecostalism has not attracted the attention of the Western media or even of sociologists until quite recently. It took a sociologist with a finely tuned "musical" ear for religious cultures, such as David Martin, to point out its significance and to suggest why it had been underestimated:

> Pentecostalism is the Christian equivalent of Islamic revivalism, and as such part of the awakening self-consciousness of the "rest" of our global society. But it operates in a completely different mode, following the logic of a fissiparous pluralism, not of a "fortress Islam" militantly entrenched in a unity of people and faith. That is another way of saying that it is not inherently political, even though it trails the political and economic implications which follow from a competitive pluralism. Pentecostalism is very specifically a cultural revolution, and one undertaken from below, with no political theory to guide it and no political ideology to promote. What motivates the rival religious entrepreneurs who guide the revolution is pursuit of a particular kind of personal transformation, and their language is couched in personal stories and imagery rather than in abstract propositions. Because Pentecostalism is personal and cultural it does not need to deal in the violence intrinsic to political action, which is why it is virtually unnoticed by the western media, and comes as a surprise to the western academy. (Martin 2002: 167)

The strength of Martin's cultural sociology approach lies in the fact that it takes theology seriously and seeks to elucidate the affinities between doctrine and the exigencies of social reality as they are fused together in symbol and image. It is a typically gentle rebuke to the reductionist efforts of many other sociologists that he should state that "to elucidate the social reality in a theological register, or to hint as to the resonances of that register, is only to do sociology in an unfamiliar key" (Martin 2002: 169). He is able to show, from many examples, how the advantage enjoyed by Pentecostalism lies in its various ambiguities, which means that it is endlessly adaptable to the exigencies of local cultures and different social formations, for example, Chinese rural workers, the Singapore business elite, West African transnational intelligentsia in Lagos or London or Amsterdam, and ex-drug addicts in Rio de Janeiro. It is precisely that capacity for indigenization and "acculturation" that allows Pentecostalism to exhibit the qualities of Thai schemes of merit in one location and then Brazilian clientage or Korean shamanism in others. Catholicism has also assimilated many cultural traits, but it has done so as an absorbent system, whereas Pentecostalism is a prolific set of burgeoning affinities that resist being canalized for very long by a bureaucracy. Where that does occur, it soon leads to schism and dynamic outbreaks in alternative directions.

The future of Pentecostalism is hard to predict, especially for sociologists who question the inevitability of secularization and who are inclined to wonder whether modernity is giving way to postmodernity. In some ways, Pentecostalism's capacity to generate endless schisms as well as self-help religiosity expressed in thousands of micro-enterprises, renders it well suited to postmodernity. More broadly, the future of Pentecostalism becomes assimilated to the question of the future of religion. As Martin concludes:

> That in turn has to do with the dominance in so-called postmodernity of the more restrictive protocols of rationality espoused by western elites, above all in the academy, and with the retrieval of alternative modes, analogous to the arts, in particular the logic of symbol, image, and icon. Clearly, Pentecostalism, in common with Christianity generally, offers a narrative of transformations and transfigurations rather than a logic of linear implication or a theoretical render-ing of tested empirical linkages. You can dismiss these modes as superstitions, illusions which mysteriously linger into what ought to be an austere and rigorous human adulthood (perhaps because compensations are still required), or you can suppose that there are other forms of encounter through testimony, gesture, song, and healing, which do not lie under the guillotine of progress but are intrinsic to the human condition. (Martin 2002: 176)

ISLAM

The relation of Islam to globalization has also been widely interpreted in determin-ist terms in keeping with the secularization theory. It is frequently seen in terms of a desperate and irrational resistance to modernization, the very futility of which leads to ever more violent terrorist acts borne of frustration. In a more intellectually nuanced form, this notion of resistance has been developed by Bernard Lewis in such a way as to explain the upsurge of Islamic militancy as a wave of angst due to a traumatic domination by the West, resulting in an opposition to Western civiliza-tion and its creations—capitalism, democracy, and liberalism. The title of Lewis's influential article in *The Atlantic Monthly*, "The Roots of Muslim Rage" (Lewis 1990), encapsulated this idea of violent reaction against the globalization of Western modernity, including its secularism. According to Samuel Huntington, the Islamic notion of global *ummah* (community of believers) that links Muslims across bor-ders and states by faith alone threatened the normative basis of the Western concept of state sovereignty. This endangers globalization, which he calls the result of "broad processes of modernization that have been going on since the eighteenth century" (Huntington, 1996: 68).

The problem with this sort of portrayal of Islam, and its relation to globaliza-tion, is that it lacks the theoretical and historical discrimination that a cultural soci-ology could provide. Moreover, it can lead to essentializing portrayals of Islam as static and monolithic. As one critic has charged:

> This process of self-reification, one that assigns fixed meaning to Islam by freezing its symbols and discourses in a single frame, operates as the referent for a modern social science discourse that has tended to create conceptions of an unalterable incompatibility between "Western" and "Islamic" civilizations, which

oversimplifies the trajectories and complexities of Muslim communities, states, and organizations. In remedying this, a wider understanding of Islam must be explicated, one that accounts for the presence of multiple interpretations of its beliefs. (Yom 2002: 91–92).

Any survey of societies with large Muslim populations will quickly conclude that there are wide variations in culture and practice. The radical Islamist movement is very much a minority phenomenon and does not encompass all the disparate groups, beliefs, and practices across the Muslim world. Even where Islamism does exist, it is usually just one part of a wider Islamic revival that should be interpreted in terms of the global religious reawakening. This global religious resurgence signifies a deep desire by considerable portions of the world population to establish meaning and order in a rapidly changing, fluid environment. All these religious movements, including the Muslim ones, share in common a return to the foundations of their faith, reemphasizing the primacy of divine sovereignty, a divine human covenant, the centrality of faith, human stewardship, and the equality of all within the community of believers. As such, they challenge the expectations of modernization theory concerning the progressive secularization and Westernization of developing societies (Esposito 1998: 21). Religion has once again become a major ideological force, requiring a reconsideration of the connection between globalization and secularism.

The secular character of the state was a European invention that developed in Western political imagination during the seventeenth century. Rooted "in the desirability of grounding knowledge and the governance of society on nonreligious foundations of scientific rationality," secularism closely relates to the founding modern states, the division of humanity into discrete, organized territories that denied the primacy of transcendent religious loyalties (Yom 2002: 98). Historically, the 1648 Treaty of Westphalia is usually taken to mark the starting point of the international system of states, and therefore also the rise of the secular state. This was then combined with the Enlightenment views on rationality and reason, cementing secular philosophy as a dominant discourse that ordered, signified, and produced structures and domains of human knowledge. Finally, the rise of the nation-state as the defining mode of existence—"imagined communities" (Anderson 1983)—operationalized secularism through the separation of church and state throughout the Christian world, and then the rest of the world through colonization and conquest. However, globalization has subsequently problematized and destabilized secularism through the realization that the boundaries of the state are becoming less relevant. In addition, the particular ideological character of Western-originated globalization, incorporating secularism, has also been brought into question. This form of globalization is a narrative that excludes religious experiences from consideration as either viable modes of relations or legitimate products from the realm of knowledge; secularism has essentially colonized and directed the ideational structure of globalization using nonreligious terms. The argument that Islam will inevitably contest globalization is based on the particular secular-religious dichotomy characteristic of the Western-originated narrative. Islamic revivalists, like other religious revival movements, are challenging the secularist character of globalization. But their rhetoric often feeds off the same dichotomy enshrined in that narrative, so that they seem to need to demonize the profane "Other" in order to establish their own difference and distance from it, just as secularism needs the existence of a religious "Other" to legitimize its practices. In this paradoxical consanguinity, "tradition must not only deny or suppress the historical and philosophical grounds of its foundational interdependence with the other, but must also constantly recreate the 'difference' between itself and the other by defining the other's mere existence as a threat to the universality of the practices, traditions, order of the self" (Hurd 2001: 21).

Too often, commentators have reproduced this dichotomy in which secularism represents reason and modernity, and religion the irrational and anti-modern. Secularism, represented by globalization, and religion, represented by Islam, are given fixed meanings that do not change over time and space. To a culturally discerning critic, such as Sean Yom, this binary view, however false, is precisely the fiction that girds global chaos theories of Islam and its impending battle with globalization. When, in fact, it should be made clear that "each representation is not a uniformly stable set of meanings, divided from the Other by insurmountable differences, but rather a kind of 'moral enclavism' that defines its traditions and goals in terms of what the Other is not. Hence, each mode of thought constitutes the Other; they transform one another in a mutually dependent relationship" (Yom 2002: 106).

An adequate analysis of the relations of Islam and globalization will only be achieved when both sets of discourses are deconstructed so as to reveal the operation of the inherent binaries at play in the narratives that result in them being fatally bound together. A cultural sociology analysis along these lines would not only deconstruct the working of binaries in the narratives, but might also take a more performative view of agency. The consequence would be that Islam, in all its forms and expressions, could not be characterized as a "self-contained collective agent" with a life of its own (Hurd 2001: 3). It would be viewed as "a performative, discursive tradition, understood as an organized, socially significant, historical narrative that interacts with globalization" (Yom 2002: 109). As Yom concludes, "Islam does not operate as some nebulous, abstract variable; rather, actors that perform behaviors under its mantle reconstitute, redirect, and reify it through adherence to their own peculiar geographic, strategic, political, and economic needs, ultimately contributing to their syncretic identities" (Yom 2002: 109).

Conclusion

It would be wrong to see globalization as a concern purely of the late twentieth and early twenty-first centuries. Durkheim, early on in the twentieth century wrote:

> There is no people and no state which is not a part of another society, more or
> less unlimited, which embraces all the peoples and all the States with which the

first comes in contact, either directly or indirectly; there is no national life which is not dominated by a collective life of an international nature. In proportion, as we advance in history, these international groups acquire a greater importance and extent. (Durkheim 1961: 474)

However, as in many of his works, Durkheim's *The Elementary Forms of the Religious Life* contained seemingly contradictory elements. On the one hand, it reveals a societal-specific moral relativism, and on the other hand, there is a humanity-orientated moral universalism. Durkheim shared with other early contributors to sociology the belief that a new religion of humanity would replace the old theocentric religions. As Casanova noted, "What none of the Enlightenment prophets and positivist sociologists could have anticipated was that, paradoxically, the old gods and the old religions were going to gain new life by becoming the carriers of the process of sacralization of humanity" (Casanova 2001: 430).

The problems confronted by the sociology of religion have often been due to a perceived need to reconcile an interpretive understanding of the adaptive capacities of religion, in different movements and localities, with a more structurally determinist theory of globalization and secularization. The early sociologists, such as Comte and Durkheim, thought they had reconciled the two via a notion of an emerging global religion of humanity, based on scientific knowledge and morality. This has proved unconvincing. At the same time, at least in the case of Durkheim, the foundations were being laid for a cultural sociology that promises to give a more adequate understanding of the adaptive capacities of religious beliefs and practices. This has resulted in more culturally informed critiques of the unsatisfactory generalizations and predictions stemming from structural-determinist theories of modernization, secularization, and globalization.

REFERENCES

Anderson B. 1983. *Imagined Communities*. London: Verso.

Berger P. L. 1999. The desecularization of the world: A global overview. In *The Desecularization of the World: Resurgent Religion and World Politics*, ed. G. Weigel, D. Martin, J. Sacks, G. Davie, T. Weiming, and A. A. An-Na'im, pp. 1–18. Grand Rapids, MI: Eerdmans.

Casanova J. 1994. *Public Religions in the Modern World*. Chicago: University of Chicago Press.

———. 2006. Rethinking secularization: A global comparative perspective. *Hedgehog Review* 8: 7–22.

Dobbelaere K. 1981. Theories of secularization. *Current Sociology* 29: 15–30.

———. 1999. Towards an integrated perspective of the process related to the descriptive concept of secularization. *Sociology of Religion* 60: 229–247.

Durkheim E. 1961. *The Elementary Forms of the Religious Life*, translated by S. W. Swain (French original 1915). New York: Collier Books.

Esposito J. 1998. Religion and global affairs: Political challenges. *SAIS Review* 18(2): 19.

Gill A. 1998. *Rendering unto Caesar: The Catholic Church and the State in Latin America.* Chicago: University of Chicago Press.

Gorski P. S., and Altinordu A. 2008. After secularization? *Annual Review of Sociology* 34: 55–85.

Huntington S. 1996. *The Clash of Civilizations and the Remaking of World Order.* New York: Simon & Schuster.

Hurd E. 2001. Toward a comparative analysis of two theopolitical orders: Secularism and political Islam in historical context. Paper presented at APSA Annual Meeting (30 August–2 September).

Jenkins P. 2007. *The Next Christendom: The Coming of Global Christianity.* New York: Oxford University Press.

Lewis B. 1990. The roots of Muslim rage. *The Atlantic Monthly* 266(3): 47–60.

Martin D. 1978. *A General Theory of Secularization.* Oxford: Blackwell.

———. 1990. *Tongues of Fire: The Explosion of Pentecostalism in Latin America.* Oxford: Blackwell.

———. 1991. The secularization issue: Prospect and retrospect. *British Journal of Sociology* 42(3): 465–473.

———. 1996. *Forbidden Revolutions: Pentecostals in Latin America, Catholicism in Eastern Europe.* London: SPCK.

———. 1997. *Reflections on Sociology and Theology.* Oxford: Clarendon Press.

———. 1999. The Evangelical Protestant upsurge and its political implications. In *The Desecularization of the World*, ed. P. Berger. Washington, DC: Ethics and Public Policy Center.

Robertson R., and Chirico J. 1985. Humanity, globalization, and worldwide religion resurgence: A theoretical explanation. *Sociological Analysis* 46: 219–242.

Stark R., and Bainbridge W. S. 1985. *The Future of Religion: Secularization, Revival and Cult Formation.* Berkeley: University of California Press.

Thompson K. 1975. *Auguste Comte: The Foundation of Sociology.* New York: Wiley.

———. 1990a. Religion: The British contribution. *British Journal of Sociology* 41(4): 531–535.

———. 1990b. Secularization and sacralization. In *Rethinking Progress: Movements, Forces and Ideas at the End of the Twentieth Century*, ed. J. C. Alexander and P. Sztompka, 161–178. London: Unwin Hyman.

Vasquez M. 1998. *The Brazilian Popular Church and the Crisis of Modernity.* Cambridge, UK: Cambridge University Press.

Wilson B. R. 1966. *Religion in Secular Society.* London: Watts.

Yom S. L. 2002. Islam and globalization: Secularism, religion, and radicalism. In *International Politics and Society* 4: 84–109.

PART VII

SOCIAL MOVEMENTS AS CULTURE

CHAPTER 18

NARRATIVE AND SOCIAL MOVEMENTS

FRANCESCA POLLETTA AND PANG CHING BOBBY CHEN

FOR social movement activists, the key question about narrative is this: Are groups challenging the status quo well-served by telling their stories? If you are a feminist charging sex discrimination in hiring, are you better off documenting statistical disparities in women's promotion rates or having a few women testify to their stifled aspirations? If you are an adult survivor of child abuse, does telling your story of pain and humiliation motivate others with the same experience to step forward? Or does it alienate people who are unwilling to see themselves as victims? If you are in a group protesting the war in Iraq and you are lucky enough to secure a spot on the evening news, should you tell poignant stories of mothers who lost their soldier sons? Or should you concentrate on enumerating the political and economic benefits of military withdrawal?

Our answer to these questions is mixed. Yes, stories are powerfully persuasive rhetorical devices. The research in communication that we will cite shows convincingly that stories are better able than other kinds of messages to change people's opinions. This is especially true when audiences are not already invested in the issue in question, a situation that social movement activists confront routinely. So telling stories can help movements elicit public interest and support.

But telling stories is also risky, for at least two reasons. One is that people understand stories in terms of stories they have heard before. Stories that stray too far from the familiar risk seeming unbelievable, idiosyncratic, or simply strange. Insofar as activists often have to challenge the ideological commonsense that underpins laws, policies, and practices, however, they *have* to tell new stories. We will show that activists have found themselves bedeviled by audiences' tendency to assimilate their stories to the familiar, no matter what they actually say.

This is one way in which activists struggle with the constraints levied by narrative. The other has less to do with narrative's form than with the conventions of its use and evaluation. Modern Americans view stories in diverse, indeed, contradictory ways: as authentic but also deceptive, universal but also idiosyncratic, and normatively powerful but also politically unserious. However, these views are patterned: Concerns about the credibility, generalizability, and value of storytelling are more likely to be triggered by some users and in some contexts rather than others. Narrative's power, in other words, is unevenly distributed. In this sense, culture may curb challenge less through the canonical limits on what kinds of stories can be imagined than through the social conventions regarding when and how stories should be told.

Neither set of constraints has been much explored by sociologists of social movements. We believe that both are crucial to understanding the trajectories and fates of movements. Moreover, each illuminates cultural dynamics that reach well beyond movements. This is, in part, because of movements' relationship with the cultural mainstream. Insofar as activists seek to change the status quo, they have a stake in hewing to dominant cultural codes where it serves them and challenging such codes where it does not. By paying attention to the trade-offs they face in doing both—conforming to and challenging cultural commonsense—as well as to the calculi by which they rule options in and out of consideration, we can see how culture sets the terms of strategic action, without simply locating those processes in people's heads.

Another reason for studying storytelling in movements is that it points to a broader approach to culture, one that treats culture less as texts than as rule-governed performances. Sociologists of culture have tended to analyze *meaning* more than *the social organization of the capacity to mean effectively.* Not everyone is equally able to convey the meaning they want, however. This is not only because of the way they speak, but also because of the way they are heard. Particular statements, but also particular discursive *forms,* such as storytelling, arguments, statistics, and interviews, are judged to be more or less authoritative depending on the setting, the topic, and the speaker. Paying attention to the norms of narrative's use and evaluation—and to the variable character of those norms—offers, thus, a second way to see how culture reproduces the status quo.

The rest of the essay proceeds as follows. We discuss briefly the main approach to culture in movements, that of collective action framing. Then we show how a study of storytelling can respond to gaps in framing theory and, in particular, can help to account for the cultural and institutional constraints activists face in trying to develop persuasive messages. We draw on examples from a range of movements, mainly American, including second wave feminism, the gay and lesbian movement, animal rights activism, campaigns to reform the criminal justice system, and the contemporary right. In each case, we show what activists have been up against in their efforts to use culture strategically. We treat activists as practical, instrumental actors, but also ones who, like the rest of us, rely on commonsensical criteria of instrumental rationality. These criteria both open up strategic possibilities and shut them down.

One can study stories as a way to understand other dimensions of social movements. For example, tracing the institutional processes by which old stories become contested or new ones available can shed light on the conditions in which new movements emerge (Polletta 2006; Luker 1984; Davis 2005; Alexander 2004). Scholars have turned to stories to account for movement endurance and dissolution (Benford 2002; Voss 1996; Jansen 2007; Owens 2009) and for movement success and failure (Meyer 2006). These are all fruitful lines of analysis. We choose to focus on activists' variable success in using stories as a persuasive tool because it may produce insights that are valuable to sociologists of culture more broadly.

Frames and Narratives

Scholars have drawn on an array of concepts to capture the role of culture in movements—among them, ideology, discourse, schema, identity, rhetoric, and belief. But the concept of collective action "framing" has held pride of place (for a good overview, see Snow 2004). Frames are sets of beliefs that "assign meaning to and interpret relevant events and conditions in ways that are intended to mobilize potential adherents and constituents, to garner bystander support and to demobilize antagonists" (Snow and Benford 1992: 198).

What makes a frame successful in doing those things? Frames that are clear (Stoecker 1995: 113), articulate, focused, and coherent (Cress and Snow 2000: 1072, 1078, 1079) are more likely to persuade people to join and support the cause. The diagnostic, prognostic, and motivational components of the frame should be richly developed and interconnected (Snow and Benford 1992: 199). There should be a clear "we"—those to whom the injustice is done—and an obvious "they" who are responsible for the injustice (Gamson 1992; Stoecker 1995). Effective frames are "empirically credible," that is, they are consonant with what their audiences know to be true (Benford and Snow 2000). Those who articulate the frame should be credible as well (Benford and Snow 2000).

Effective frames are, in addition, "salient" to their audiences. That is, they call on beliefs that are already strongly held. Frames also should be "experientially commensurable" (Snow and Benford 1992: 208; Benford and Snow 2000). They should resonate with people's everyday experiences. Finally, they should be characterized by "narrative fidelity" or "cultural resonance." They should accord with familiar "stories, myths, and folktales" (Snow and Benford 1992: 210; Gamson 1988).

Framing theorists talk about narrative in two ways. Effective frames accord with cultural narratives (Snow and Benford 1992; Gamson 1988). And frames often make use of stories as a powerful rhetorical device (Benford 1993; Gamson 1992). Both claims seem right. However, fuller attention to storytelling—drawing on the insights of a multidisciplinary body of scholarship—can respond to at least two problems in framing theory.

One problem centers on framing theorists' contention that effective frames are clear, coherent, and consistent. These claims have been more asserted than empirically tested. We simply do not know whether clear frames are more effective than ambiguous ones; whether frames with consistently related diagnostic, prognostic, and motivational components are more mobilizing than those without; and whether effective frames do rely on a sharp delineation of adversaries.

When it comes to stories, logical consistency is by no means a criterion for persuasiveness. Good stories rely on ellipses, allusion, and ambiguity (Polletta 2006, ch. 2). Of course, stories may persuade differently than do frames rendered through other discursive forms such as arguments or exhortations. Later we will suggest that that is the case. Another possibility, however, is that even frames rendered in those other discursive forms *also* make sense in terms of familiar narratives. Such narratives may constitute a backdrop of understanding against which logical arguments have meaning. We use the terms "story" and "narrative" interchangeably in this essay, but one might, alternatively, conceptualize "story" as a discursive form on a par with arguments, statistics, and explanations, and "narrative" as those background myths in terms of which all discursive forms have meaning.[1]

Of course, aside from the methodological difficulties of getting at narratives that are so familiar as to not need articulating (Gerteis 2002), the previous statement seems to suggest that only a limited number of stories are even thinkable. That seems implausible given our capacity to rework familiar stories, that is, to rearrange plotlines or recast characters so as to arrive at a completely different endpoint. In fact, we will argue in a moment that stories structure common sense less though their uniformity than through their variety. Our point for now, however, is that we need a better understanding of how persuasion works than framing theory has yet provided.

Such an understanding must encompass the commonsensical assumptions that exist alongside people's explicit beliefs. To give an example that we will take up again later, a judge may believe firmly in women's equality with men. And, yet, he may hand down rulings that systematically disadvantage women. This is not because his professed egalitarianism is a lie but rather because he understands gender equality in the context of a whole cluster of assumptions about men and women and difference and biology and preferences. Those assumptions may bias his decisions without his even realizing it. Activists often find themselves struggling to craft a frame capable of debunking symbolic associations that are difficult to even name. As analysts, we need tools to get at these processes.

The second problem in framing theory's calculus of frame effectiveness is a limited understanding of how frames are shaped by their audiences. Certainly, framing theorists have always acknowledged that there are multiple audiences for movements' framing efforts. Although early work concentrated on potential recruits, researchers since then have studied activists' framing to reporters, in court, and on television talk shows. They have drawn attention especially to the conflicts created by the generally moderate messages required by the public and the more radical ones that resonate with movement participants (Ferree 2003; Whittier 2001).

However, to talk about the different audiences to which activists must appeal risks suggesting that frame success is just a matter of resonating with the personal beliefs of the people who have power within a given institutional arena. It misses the specifically institutional requirements of claimsmaking. These requirements often center less on the substance of a group's claims than on the form in which claims are to be made. To return to the example above, a judge may require that women in court tell stories of the discrimination they have experienced because that is the standard way of testifying about discrimination, even though individual stories may be incapable of documenting the type of discrimination that is at issue. In short, to understand why particular frames succeed or fail, we need to know more about how institutional and popular norms of cultural expression shape what activists can say.

Why should an analysis of narrative help us to do these things? Thanks to substantial literature on narrative in diverse fields, we know a great deal about how narrative achieves its rhetorical effects. This should contribute to a fuller understanding of persuasion than framing theory currently provides. In addition, narrative is a folk concept. Unlike frames, ideologies, and discourses, all of whose referents are defined by analysts rather than the people who produce or act on them, most people know when they are telling a story. They know how to construct a story, when and why they should tell stories, and how to respond to a story. Some conventions of storytelling are formalized, as is the case in courtroom testimony. Other conventions are not formalized and can be gleaned, rather, from stories' distribution across settings and speakers and topics of discussion. People often reflect openly on what they see storytelling as good for and where they see its limitations. From there, we can begin to determine the work that popular theories and conventions of storytelling do in sustaining institutions and in shaping strategies for transforming them (Polletta et al. 2011).

In the following, we treat narrative as an object of analysis (rather than, as Ewick and Silbey [1995], put it, a means of analysis or a mode of presentation), but we do so in three ways. One, we treat narratives as identifiable chunks of discourse, comprised of standard features that can be isolated in texts. Two, we treat narratives as background accounts in terms of which messages, whether they are narrative in form or not, are understood. And three, we treat narrative as a practice that is guided by institutional norms.

How Stories Persuade

We define a narrative, fairly uncontroversially, as an account of a sequence of events in the order in which they occurred so as to make a point (Labov and Waletsky 1967). Formally, narratives are composed of (1) an orientation, which sets the scene;

(2) a series of complicating actions (implicit "and then…" clauses) ending with one that serves as dénouement; and (3) an evaluation that can appear at any point in the story, establishing the importance of the events related (Labov and Waletsky 1967).

Narratives have characters: protagonists, antagonists, allies, and witnesses. Events are recounted from a point of view. The point of view may be that of the protagonist (which is usually the case in first person stories); or it may be that of another character or an unnamed narrator or it may shift among characters. Events are usually recounted in order, with later events explaining earlier ones. What links events, however, is less empirical probability than the gradually revealed structure of the story. This structure or "plot" is familiar from other similarly emplotted stories. The dénouement of the story is both explanatory and evaluative. It projects a normative future; this is the moral of the story (Bal 1985; Brooks 1984; Jacobs 2004; Polletta 2006).

Finally, along with its reliance on characters, point of view, plot, and a normative point, narrative is distinctive in its allusiveness. Stories require our interpretive participation. They require that we work to resolve ambiguities as events unfold and to anticipate the normative conclusion to which the story is driving. Of course, analyses, arguments, descriptions, and formal mathematical proofs can also be interpreted to yield multiple meanings. But we *expect* to have to interpret stories, and, accordingly, we are more likely to do the work necessary to make sense of a confusing passage or what appear to be contradictory developments (Polletta 2006, ch. 1; Miller 1990).

As psychologists, folklorists, and sociologists have shown, we tell stories for many reasons: to entertain, instruct, envision alternatives, comfort, dramatize, live with the contradictions that are an unavoidable feature of existence, grasp temporality, and feel—the list goes on. We also tell stories to persuade, that is, to change people's opinions. It is narrative's persuasive capacity that is of most interest to those challenging the status quo.

Ask anyone if stories are persuasive and the answer will be affirmative. Stories "tug at our heartstrings," people often say. They "identify" with the characters; they are "gripped" by the plot, "sucked in," "transported," and "involved." Later, we will subject these popular beliefs to scrutiny. For now, we point out simply that people's intuitive grasp of the power of stories is in some ways right. Recent experimental work in communication has demonstrated the persuasive force of stories. Until recently, communication scholars argued that audiences processed messages in one of two ways: "centrally," where they scrutinize a message and evaluate its claims critically, or "peripherally," where they absorb a message casually, judging it less by its content than by the appeal of the speaker or by the mood they are in at the moment (Petty and Cacioppo 1986). Peripheral processing may lead to attitudinal change, but it does not last. To get people to change their opinions requires that they process information centrally. The hitch is that they are likely to do that only when they already have a personal stake in an issue (Slater and Rouner 2002). For activists, the challenge is to persuade people who do not already have a personal stake in the issue, since they represent the vast majority of the public.

This is where narrative comes in. Recent research suggests that audiences process stories neither centrally nor peripherally, but rather by a third route. They immerse themselves in the story, striving to experience vicariously the events and emotions that the protagonists experience. Green and Brock (2000) found that subjects who were highly absorbed in a story (indicated by statements like "activity going on in the room around me was not on my mind" while reading the story, and "I could picture myself in the scene of the events described in the narrative") were likely to report beliefs consistent with those implied in the story. To probe the dynamic involved, subjects were asked to circle every "false note" in the story. The more absorbed they were, the less likely they were to see such false notes (Green and Brock 2000). This suggests that when they hear or read stories, audiences suspend their proclivity to counterargue, that is, to raise doubts about the veracity or relevance of the information they are hearing. They truly suspend disbelief, and they do so in a way that has lasting effects. The attitudinal change brought about by stories tends to persist or even increase over time (Appel and Richter 2007). Tell an absorbing story, this research suggests, and you can win people to your cause.

However, narrative research has also identified an important condition for stories' persuasive power. Stories have no effect if their message is too explicit (Slater and Rouner 2002; Slater, Rouner, and Long 2006). This is not surprising. Readers resist being beaten over the head with the moral of the story. They want the events recounted in the story to yield their own meaning. But events in a story *never* yield their own meaning. We evaluate, even understand, what is happening in a story by reference to stories we have heard before. As we listen or read, we gradually recognize events as part of a David and Goliath story about the little guy triumphing over the big guy or a "Pride Before a Fall" story about the little guy biting off more than he can chew (Brooks 1984). The plotlines available are multiple and diverse, and the stories they undergird take innumerable versions. Still, stories that stray too far from the familiar risk seeming unbelievable, unintelligible, or just strange.

A story's dependence on previous stories offers activists valuable resources. Movement groups can gain moral authority and political capital by linking themselves to celebrated revolutionaries and freedom fighters (Jansen 2007; Nepstad 2001). Leaders secure followers by recounting their personal transformation from apathy to commitment and blindness to clarity in terms known from other stories (Hunt and Benford 1994; Wechsler 1982). They denaturalize the current state of things by substituting a familiar story of exploitation for one of legal entitlement (Kane 1997) and justify violence by incorporating it into a tale of heroic fortitude (Fine 1999). They withstand setbacks by interpreting them as narratively familiar tests of character on the way to victory (Voss 1996).

Insofar as stories constitute a kind of cultural backdrop, against which, not only stories, but also arguments and assertions make sense, they may make it possible for diverse beliefs to hang together in a way that defies logical consistency. For example, advocates for welfare reform in the 1990s argued that welfare was fostering in its recipients a pathological dependence on the state. The idea that government was responsible for people's poverty—logically, a surprising claim—made sense because it was heard against the backdrop of stories of women's, especially black women's, addictions. In those stories, dependence was psychological or chemical, a character flaw rather than a structural relation. And in line with those stories, Linda Gordon and Nancy Fraser (1994) have shown, economic dependency came to be more broadly understood not as something that everyone at some point experiences, but as a personal failing to be remedied by the denial of assistance. The arguments made by welfare reform advocates seemed logical only because of the stories behind them.

How Stories Constrain

Stories' canonicity also poses real problems for those wanting to effect social change. The storytelling that takes place in small groups may lead people to recognize their problems as more than personal—to see them as political and as demanding of collective action. But it may not do those things. In the group discussions about sexual assault that Joyce Hollander (2002) observed, women sometimes described themselves successfully resisting their assailants. But they characterized those episodes, just as much as ones where the victim was raped, as experiences of victimization. In other words, their stories of forestalling rape were assimilated to stories of victimization in a way that ended up reproducing a view of women as always vulnerable. Collective storytelling may discourage the emergence of a collective oppositional consciousness.

Even when activists have succeeded in creating a movement, and in gaining access to the venues where they can make their case, familiar stories pose a problem. Here, the problem lies less in the stories activists tell than the stories with which they are heard. Let us give an example of the problem and then try to clarify it. When women went to court in the 1980s to prove employers were discriminating by sex, they armed themselves with statistical evidence of longstanding disparities in men's and women's rates of hiring and promotions (Schultz 1990). That evidence should have countered employers' claim that women simply did not want jobs that had traditionally been held by men.

But in case after case, Vicki Schultz found, judges were not satisfied with that evidence. They wanted victims—individual women who could tell a story of having aspired to the higher-paying job and been denied it. As the judge in the famous *EEOC v. Sears* case put it, plaintiffs might have won had they produced "even a handful of witnesses to testify that Sears had frustrated their childhood dreams of becoming commission sellers" (Schultz 1990: 1809). To which the answer should have been: Who dreams of becoming a commission seller? The stories judges wanted to hear mistakenly assumed people's work preferences were forged only before they entered the work world, rather than also evolving in line with the possibilities they perceived once in the work world. Such stories left the real problem intact: the practices of sex-segregated advertising and word-of-mouth recruiting that effectively defined high-status jobs as male. Plaintiffs should have been able to say, "This is a story not about dreams, but about the obstacles to dreaming." But that story—not really a story at all—would have been much harder to tell.

Moreover, when plaintiffs did tell stories about aspiring to the higher-paying but traditionally masculine jobs, they often met with skepticism. Employers argued that most women did not want jobs that were stressful, "heavy," "dirty," and took time away from their families. That argument was convincing against the backdrop of the countless stories we have all heard of girls being different from boys—girls liking "clean" things, women sacrificing for their families, families being a haven in a heartless world, and so on. By contrast, when plaintiffs claimed that they wanted what men wanted, they seemed to be saying that women were identical to men. That claim flew in the face of common sense, as more than one judge put it.

Plaintiffs in these cases were encouraged to tell their stories. But the particular assumptions about women and work that those stories had to challenge were already part of more familiar stories. Importantly, those stories came in so many versions and forms that they seemed to capture a complex reality. This is the larger point. Stories' power comes less from the explicit moral instruction they provide than from the normative possibilities that are excluded from the pattern of their relationship. The argument, which goes back to Claude Lévi-Strauss's (1963) structuralist analysis of myth, is that culturally resonant stories chart, in similar fashion, the relations between the privileged and the denigrated poles of familiar cultural oppositions. For example, we grasp what reason is by telling stories that thematize not only reason's difference from passion, but its similarity to men's difference from women, and culture's difference from nature, and so on.

What poststructuralist theorists add is the insight that it takes active *work* to ensure that alternative relations are ruled out (Derrida 1978; Scott 1994). To continue with the example, our understanding of reason requires that people make emotional performances of reason; in other words, that they demonstrate in speech, tone, and gesture the seeming lack of affect that passes for reason, while at the same time maintaining that emotion and reason are opposed. The stability of legal, political, and other institutions, to extend the argument, depends on institutions' promotion of stories that thematize familiar oppositions. Such stories are powerful, not because they are told over and over again in identical form, but rather because they mesh with other familiar stories that navigate similarly between the poles of well-known oppositions (see Polletta 2006, ch. 1 for a fuller development of this argument; and see Smith 2005 and Jacobs 2004 for somewhat different arguments linking binary codes to politically powerful narratives).

What activists are up against is not one single, canonical story, but many stories, whose diversity and complexity give them the feel of the real. Against that backdrop, activists' stories are likely to seem thin and abstract. They may be easily assimilated to one of the other more familiar stories. Or they may be heard as simply idiosyncratic. When plaintiffs in the sex discrimination cases told stories of women having *wanted* stressful, dirty, masculine jobs, the stories were heard as atypical or implausible.

Let us give another example, this one from activists' efforts to secure legal equality for battered women. Battered women who strike back at their abusers should be able to plead innocence by reason of self-defense. After all, they acted to save their own lives. And yet in the early 1990s, only a quarter of the battered women who pleaded self-defense in homicide cases were acquitted (Trafford 1991). More significant, convictions of battered women who pled self-defense were overturned on appeal at a substantially higher rate than were convictions in other homicide cases (40 percent compared to 8.5 percent [Maguigan 1991]).

The problem was not the law itself. The legal standards for pleading self-defense were not inherently biased against battered women. Most jurisdictions did not impose a duty to retreat before using force, and those that did usually exempted a person attacked in her home. No jurisdiction prohibited the use of a weapon against an unarmed attacker. Standards for self-defense were just as capable of handling violence in which parties were intimates and where the imminence of danger extended over a substantial period.

The problem was not the legal standards but the fact that judges, juries, and even women's own defense lawyers were unwilling to see battered women's use of deadly force as reasonable under those standards (Schneider 2000; Maguigan 1991). Why not? Because it would have required seeing battered women both as victims and as rational agents. In our society, those categories are seen as unalterably opposed. As legal theorist Martha Mahoney puts it, "Agency does not mean acting for oneself under conditions of oppression; it means *being without oppression*, either having ended oppression or never having experienced it at all" (Mahoney 1994: 64). Victimization, for its part, means being without agency. We have heard countless stories of victims—real victims—as passive, pitiable, and pathetic. We have heard stories of people who are smart, savvy, and agentic, who avoid being victimized or escape victimization. And we have heard stories of people who *pose* as victims, people who disingenuously and sometimes cunningly feign victimization. These stories, which appeared in multiple versions, constituted the background of "reality" against which battered women defendants' stories were heard.

The woman who had killed or assaulted her abuser accordingly faced two equally unacceptable options. She could assert her agency, telling a story of her actions in which she appeared composed and in control of herself. But then she might not be seen as victimized at all. Or, she could emphasize her victimization. But then her actions risked being seen as unreasonable. They might be excused through an act of judicial solicitude but they would not be seen as justified by her experience of abuse. If she departed from the stock image of the victim, moreover, if she was angry, aggressive, or insufficiently remorseful, or if she was none of those things but was black (given images of black women as powerful), she might not be seen as a victim, no matter what she said (Stark 2007; Schneider 2000).

So, did telling stories work for battered women? Lawyers, judges, and juries heard the stories that battered women told. But they heard them through clusters of familiar plotlines. On one side were the familiar plotlines of legitimate self-defense: the soldier on the battlefield, the man defending his home against an unknown intruder, and the barroom brawler. On the other side were stories of mad women who were victims and bad women who were not. As a result, the legal plea of self-defense, which was ostensibly available to women, was effectively denied to them.

If whatever activists say is heard in terms of familiar stories, stories that, variously, naturalize gender differences and make victims irrational, what should activists do? Are their stories doomed to be heard either as supporting the conventional wisdom or as unintelligible? No. We want to suggest two possible answers to the problem. One is that audiences can be instructed to suspend their narrative expectations. For example, in her 1998 ruling on the status of expert testimony in cases of battering, Canadian Supreme Court Judge Claire L'Heureux Dubé wrote, "A judge and jury should be told that a battered woman's experiences are generally outside the common understanding of the average judge and juror, and that they should seek to understand the evidence being presented to them in order to overcome the myths and stereotypes which we all share" (quoted in Schneider 2000: 142). People can be encouraged to understand in ways that are not narrative (Tilly 2002). Presumably, Judge L'Heureux Dubé thought this was possible. Whether it is possible or not, or just how difficult it is, remain open questions.

The second answer is to tell stories, but noncanonical ones. This takes literary skill. Contrary to the commonplace view that powerful messages are simple ones, it is worth pointing out that great writers do not write simple stories. They write stories that tap into our expectations and defy them. They jigger familiar plotlines, characters, and situations. They use tropes like irony, ellipsis, and shifting points of view to make what is familiar strange. They let us think we're hearing one kind of story and then tell us another.

This suggests that, rather than trying to tell simple stories, activists should use all the literary tools at their disposal to tell stories that are canonical enough to make sense but different enough to expose the flaws in the familiar. For example, in a film made to try to reform the law around battered women's legal defense, advocates in Maryland did the usual things: They had four women who were serving sentences for homicide tell their stories of domestic abuse. At first glance, the film seemed to cater to views of battered women as passive and pathetic. When three of the four women admitted that they didn't even remember taking the action that killed their partners, they seemed the opposite of reasonable actors—so brutalized as to be unconscious of their own actions (Public Justice Center 1990).

Yet the film also worked powerfully to counter that impression (Polletta 2010). The women came off as victimized, but also as sharply insightful. They used irony not only to comment on their own naiveté but to draw attention to the social norms that led them to mistake a man's pathological possessiveness for caring and to believe that keeping the family together was more important than their own safety. Halfway through the film, they substituted a heroic storyline for a tragic one. Through a series of discordant images, the film became not about each woman's decision to kill but about her discovery that she wanted to live. The climax of the film was the moment when each woman discovered her wherewithal, her agency, when she *stopped* being a victim, when she won the battle with herself. Indeed, when each woman described attacking her partner, it was anticlimactic, simply an extension of her decision to live.

After the governor of Maryland saw the film, he not only became an ardent supporter of the cause but in his public statements repeatedly referred to battered women defendants as both victimized *and* rational (Lewin 1991). Such a combination surely would have seemed odd to those who had only heard standard stories of victimization. The lesson for activists might be: Use the familiar to draw audience into the story. When they are absorbed, use the most sophisticated literary tropes you can find to tell your audience something different than what they are expecting to hear.

WHAT STORIES ARE GOOD FOR

In her study of activism by adult survivors of child abuse, Nancy Whittier (2001; 2009) found that when survivors gathered in movement conferences and at marches, speakers told stories of personal fortitude and of fear ceding to pride. With titles like "Sing Loud, Sing Proud" and "Courageous, Always Courageous," movement magazine articles and workshops encouraged participants to emphasize their recovery rather than the details of their abuse. When survivors appeared in court to seek compensation as crime victims, however, the stories they told were different. Survivors described the fear, grief, shame, and hurt produced by their abuse but made no mention of their subsequent anger and pride. These kinds of emotional performances were required in order to prove that the survivor was a victim deserving of compensation. Articles in movement magazines warned that going to court was a demeaning experience and that survivors should find outlets to tell other parts of their stories— but that betraying their anger in court would hurt their case.

On television talk shows, another place in which child abuse activists appeared frequently in the 1980s, survivors told stories of abuse and enduring trauma. Guests often cried while clutching stuffed animals or speaking in childlike voices. They were usually joined by therapists who interpreted their stories to the audience, further reinforcing an image of them as childlike. Whittier (2001) points out that that image may well have repelled others suffering from abuse, who might have been mobilized by stories of focused anger and personal overcoming.

Certainly, one can challenge the conventions of narrative performance. Survivors could have told stories of anger on talk shows and could have recounted moving from shame to pride in courtroom hearings. But doing so would have been risky. Culture shapes strategy in the sense that abiding by the rules of cultural expression yields more calculable consequences than challenging them.

Moreover, there is no reason to expect that activists themselves are immune to popular beliefs about storytelling. The animal rights activists whom Julian Groves (2001) studied discouraged women from serving in leadership positions because they believed that women were seen by the public as prone to emotional storytelling. That would cost the movement credibility. However, activists spent little time debating whether women were in fact prone to emotionalism or whether emotional stories rather than rational arguments were in fact bad for the movement (see Jasper 1999). So their calculations were strategic but only in the context of a set of questionable assumptions about the relations between emotion, reason, stories, and gender.

What are those assumptions? If "story," like other cultural objects, has meaning in terms of the symbolic oppositions along which it is aligned, then it makes sense that beliefs about what stories are good for come from the structure of those oppositions. Of course, such beliefs are historical (Plummer 1995; Polletta 2006, ch. 5; Illouz 2008). Today, we argue, Americans tend to see stories as better able to capture particularity than universality, and concreteness rather than abstraction (Polletta 2006; Polletta et al 2011). They tend to associate stories with emotions rather than logic and see them as typical of informal and personal relations more than formal and public ones. As a result, they associate narrative with groups, settings, and ways of knowing that are also associated with the particular, the emotional, the personal, the concrete, and the informal. So they think of storytelling as characteristic of women and nonprofessionals, as common in private settings rather than public ones, as good for expressing moral concerns rather than strategic ones, and as the hallmark of folklore rather than science and custom rather than rules.

The foregoing is misleading, however, in suggesting that people have a single and consistent view of storytelling. That is not the case. Just as they evaluate the other terms we mentioned in mixed ways (the "public" is important but also impersonal; what is "moral" is right but also impractical; "custom" is comfortingly familiar but also constraining), most people are ambivalent about storytelling. Compared to other discursive forms, stories, and especially personal stories, are seen as normatively powerful but politically unserious, as authentic but also deceptive, and as universal in their implications but also dangerously idiosyncratic.

This ambivalence on its own poses challenges for activists. Even more challenging is the fact that people's mixed views of storytelling are contingent on the speaker and the setting. Concerns about stories' triviality, deceptiveness, and generalizability are more likely to be triggered by lower-status speakers than by higher ones. Indeed, higher-status speakers may be less likely to be heard as telling stories, rather than stating facts or advancing logical explanations.[2] Concerns about stories' worth are also likely to be triggered on occasions that are seen as technical, procedural, or expert. Since activists are often in a position of having to call attention to the political dimensions of ostensibly neutral categories and criteria, they may be tempted to tell stories to do so—and disserved in the process.

That said, activists have also been able to capitalize on Americans' complex views of storytelling. For example, storytelling is symbolically opposed to technical expertise. But Americans are often skeptical of technical expertise, seeing it as impersonal, sometimes impractical, and manipulative. Against these views, storytelling has the appeal of common sense. This may account for the surprising presence of ordinary people and grassroots groups in the mainstream American press (Ferree et al. 2002; Gamson 2001). Research has shown that when audiences hear or read news stories in which someone affected by an issue is profiled, they are likely to see that person's views both as widespread and persuasive. This is true even if audiences are presented factual evidence that contradicts the profiled person's views (Zillman and Brosius 2000). By supplying news producers with the "person on the street" who has been affected by an issue, movement groups can also communicate their perspective on the issue (see discussion in Polletta 2006, ch. 5).

In his study of a movement to institutionalize alternatives to criminal prosecution for drug offenders, James Nolan (2002) shows that activists made the case for drug courts by telling poignant stories of drug addicts diverted from a life of crime. Even in the absence of compelling statistical data on recidivism rates for drug court graduates, the testimony of judges who had been emotionally touched by particular graduates was apparently enough to secure continued financial support for the courts. Storytelling was successful, Nolan argues, because of the broadly therapeutic bent of contemporary American culture (see also Illouz 2008). But on a slightly different reading, personal storytelling was compelling because it was counterpoised—and seen as a corrective—to the abstract (ir)rationality of the criminal justice system.

Activists have also dealt with the conventions of storytelling by making them the target of explicit challenge. Indeed, one of the ways in which movements may have an impact is by gaining institutional purchase for new distributions of storytelling authority. For example, in the 1980s, AIDS activists succeeded in gaining formal representation on federal research review committees. But they also gained recognition for AIDS patients' personal accounts of their illnesses as authoritative knowledge in drug research (Epstein 1996). The 1980s movement against child abuse successfully reformed laws around the admissibility of children's stories of abuse: in many cases, relaxing the requirement that children testify in court or confront their abuser (McGough 1994). Children's stories were granted legal authority that they simply had not had before (and, according to experts concerned about children's suggestibility and capacity for recall, should not have had).

CONCLUSION

Paying attention to activists' strategic use of storytelling can shed light on the distinctly cultural obstacles that activists face in effecting change. Such obstacles are never insuperable, but like the distribution of financial resources or the structure of mainstream politics, they operate for the most part to support the status quo.

Culture does not constrain challenge only, or even mainly, by limiting what activists can aspire to. Just as much as the analysts who study them, activists are broadminded in the options they perceive and canny in devising ways to pursue them. They use culture generally, and stories in particular, practically and creatively. The problems they face are twofold. One is that the stories that they tell cannot but seem thin and abstract compared to the multiple, diverse, and overlapping stories that together make up a common sense about an issue. Against that backdrop, stories that challenge the conceptual oppositions underpinning the common sense about an issue are either disbelieved or assimilated to more familiar stories.

The other problem lies in the norms governing how stories are heard and evaluated: when they are considered appropriate, believable, serious, and so on. Such norms are historical, but also institutional. This is why activists telling stories of their victimization have fared better in the media than in court. In the media, activists' stories have been heard as those of "Everyperson." Activists have been able to connect their own experiences to a larger normative point. In court, by contrast, storytellers have been expected to hew to familiar images of victims—passive, pitiable, and like all other victims—and then penalized when they have done so.

The picture is not entirely grim, however. Activists have also been able to capitalize on the norms of narrative's form and evaluation. For example, they have pitched their stories to the media at the same time as they have struggled to tell them effectively in court and they have used canonical storylines in the service of their cause. Even more interesting, we believe, are the ways in which activists have been able to counter the challenges posed by the norms of narrative's form and evaluation. In one strategy, activists have used literary tropes, such as irony and shifting points of view, and have combined genres to craft appeals that resonate while still being heard as truly different from what people have heard before. In this respect, activists have leaned not on audiences' attraction to the familiar, but rather on audiences' assumption that a story will be allusive and their willingness to do interpretive work to make sense of it. In another strategy, rather than limiting storytelling to venues in which it is acceptable, activists have challenged head-on the hierarchies of credibility in terms of which rhetorical forms are heard. There may be strategic advantage to demanding authority for personal storytellers where science reigns supreme and, conversely, fighting for the admission of statistics where personal stories are deemed appropriate.

For cultural sociologists, an analysis of narratives in, by, and about movements points to dynamics that go well beyond movements. It suggests, first, that hegemony operates, not by way of a single canonical story repeated over and over again in identical form, but rather by way of many stories that are quite different from each other but navigate similarly between the culturally privileged and denigrated poles of familiar symbolic oppositions. Stories are not the only way we make sense of and reproduce those oppositions. But stories' resistance to critical evaluation, that is, the fact that we truly do suspend disbelief when we hear a story, may allow stories to "hang together" in a way that produces the complex, variegated feel of the real.

Our second conclusion—that activists' success in telling stories is shaped as much by beliefs *about* storytelling as it is by the actual stories they tell—suggests a broader approach to culture. Rather than focusing on meaning, this approach centers on the social organization of meaning, or better, the social organization of the capacity to mean effectively. Just as there is a prevailing common sense about what narrative is good for, when it is appropriate, and what relation it has to truth, so there is a common sense about other discursive forms. Speeches, confessions, interviews, statistics, and biographies are the subjects of popular beliefs about their epistemological status and conventions of their proper uses. Most people know what those conventions are. They know when it is inappropriate to give a speech, and why analysis is more trustworthy than storytelling. If they do not know personally, they can turn to any number of practical guides. The researcher, too, can draw on these materials to piece together a cultural common sense about the interview or storytelling and, in particular, an epistemology of the form: a set of assumptions about its relation to truth and knowing.

A sociology of any of these discursive forms would look to see how beliefs about them have evolved over time; how they vary across institutions; what stands behind them; what political and social work they do; and how they shape selves and social interactions. It would also investigate the possibility that such beliefs vary depending on the context and the speaker and would try to decide whether the contingency of such beliefs works to reproduce existing inequalities.

NOTES

1. We choose not to do that for two reasons. One is that theorists have distinguished story from narrative in a variety of ways; for example, treating story as the events as they occurred and narrative as the represention of events (Bal 1985); or reserving story for fictional events (Polkinghorne 1988); or treating story as a less analytic version of narrative (Mahoney 1999). To avoid confusion, we rely on conventional usage, which treats the two as the same thing. The other reason is that treating narrative as more general meta-stories risks assuming, rather than showing, that all background understandings are narrative in form. We do not believe that is the case; whether it is or not, we emphasize narrative's difference from other discursive forms as a way to elucidate the distinctive work narrative does.

2. This is similar to Bourdieu's (1984; 1991) argument that people have socially endowed levels of competence to use culture effectively. However, we argue that the authority and value of cultural *forms* are contingent on the status of their users and the occasion of their use.

REFERENCES

Alexander, Jeffrey C. 2004. "On the Social Construction of Moral Universals: The 'Holocaust' from War Crime to Trauma Drama." Pp. 196–263 in *Cultural Trauma and Collective Identity*, edited by Jeffrey C. Alexander, Ron Eyerman, Bernhard Giesen, Neil J. Smelser, and Piotr Sztompka. Berkeley: University of California Press.

Appel, Markus, and Tobias Richter. 2007. "Persuasive Effects of Fictional Narratives Increase Over Time." *Media Psychology* 10(1): 113–134.

Bal, Mieke. 1985. *Narratology: Introduction to the Theory of Narrative*. Translated by Christine van Boheemen. Toronto: University of Toronto Press.

Benford, Robert A. 1993. "'You Could Be the Hundredth Monkey': Collective Action Frames and Vocabularies of Motive within the Nuclear Disarmament Movement." *Sociological Quarterly* 34(2): 195–216.

————. 2002. "Controlling Narratives and Narratives as Control within Social Movements." Pp. 53–75 in *Stories of Change: Narrative and Social Movements*, edited by Joseph E. Davis. Albany: State University of New York Press.

Benford, Robert A., and David A. Snow. 2000. "Framing Processes and Social Movements: An Overview and Assessment." *Annual Review of Sociology* 26: 611–639.

Bourdieu, Pierre. 1984. *Distinction: A Social Critique of the Judgment of Taste*. Translated by Richard Nice. Cambridge, MA: Harvard University Press.

————. 1991. "Price Formation and the Anticipation of Profits." Pp. 66–89 in *Language and Symbolic Power*, edited by John B. Thompson, translated by Gino Raymond and Matthew Adamson. Cambridge, MA: Harvard University Press.

Brooks, Peter. 1984. *Reading for the Plot: Design and Intention in Narrative*. Cambridge, MA: Harvard University Press.

Cress, Daniel M., and David A. Snow. 2000. "The Outcomes of Homeless Mobilization: The Influence of Organization, Disruption, Political Mediation, and Framing." *American Journal of Sociology* 105(4): 1063–1104.

Davis, Joseph E. 2005. *Accounts of Innocence: Sexual Abuse, Trauma, and the Self*. Chicago: University of Chicago Press.

Derrida, Jacques. 1978. "Structure, Sign, and Play in the Discourse of the Human Sciences." pp. 278–294 in *Writing and Difference*, translated by Alan Bass. Chicago: University of Chicago Press.

Epstein, Steven. 1996. *Impure Science: AIDS, Activism, and the Politics of Knowledge*. Berkeley: University of California Press.

Ewick, Patricia, and Susan S. Silbey. 1995. "Subversive Stories and Hegemonic Tales: Toward a Sociology of Narrative." *Law and Society Review* 29(2): 197–226.

Ferree, Myra Marx. 2003. "Resonance and Radicalism: Feminist Framing in the Abortion Debates of the United States and Germany." *American Journal of Sociology* 109(2): 304–344.

Ferree, Myra Marx, William A. Gamson, Jurgen Gerhards, and Dieter Rucht. 2002. *Shaping Abortion Discourse: Democracy and the Public Sphere in Germany and the United States*. New York: Cambridge University Press.

Fine, Gary Alan. 1999. "John Brown's Body: Elites, Heroic Embodiment, and the Legitimation of Political Violence." *Social Problems* 46(2): 225–249.

Frank, Thomas. 2004. *What's the Matter with Kansas? How Conservatives Won the Heart of America*. New York: Henry Holt.

Fraser, Nancy, and Linda Gordon. 1994. "A Genealogy of Dependency: Tracing a Keyword of the U.S. Welfare State." *Signs* 19(2): 309–336.

Gamson, William A. 1988. "Political Discourse and Collective Action." Pp. 219–244 in *International Social Movement Research, Vol. 1*, edited by Bert Klandermans, Hanspeter Kriesi, and Sydney Tarrow. Greenwich, CT: JAI Press.

————. 1991. "Commitment and Agency in Social Movements." *Sociological Forum* 6(1): 27–50.

————. 1992. *Talking Politics*. New York: Cambridge University Press.

————. 2001. "How Storytelling Can Be Empowering." Pp. 187–198 in *Culture in Mind: Toward a Sociology of Culture and Cognition*, edited by Karen A. Cerulo. New York: Routledge.

Gerteis, Joseph. 2002. "The Possession of Civic Virtue: Movement Narratives of Race and Class in the Knights of Labor." *American Journal of Sociology* 108(3): 580–615.

Green, Melanie C., and Timothy C. Brock. 2000. "The Role of Transportation in the Persuasiveness of Public Narratives." *Journal of Personality and Social Psychology* 79(5): 701–721.

Groves, Julian McAllister. 2001. "Animal Rights and the Politics of Emotion: Folk Constructions of Emotion in the Animal Rights Movement." Pp. 212–229 in *Passionate Politics: Emotions and Social Movements*, edited by Jeff Goodwin, James M. Jasper, and Francesca Polletta. Chicago: University Chicago Press.

Hollander, Jocelyn A. 2002. "Resisting Vulnerability: The Social Reconstruction of Gender in Interaction." *Social Problems* 49(4): 474–496.

Hunt, Scott. A., and Robert D. Benford. 1994. "Identity Talk in the Peace and Justice Movements." *Journal of Contemporary Ethnography* 22(4): 488–517.

Illouz, Eva. 2008. *Saving the Modern Soul: Therapy, Emotions, and the Culture of Self-Help*. Berkeley: University of California Press.

Jacobs, Ronald C. 2004. "Narrative, Civil Society and Public Culture." Pp. 18–35 in *The Uses of Narrative: Explorations in Psychology, Sociology, and Cultural Studies*, edited by Molly Andrews, Shelly Day Sclater, Corinne Squire, and Amal Treacher. New Brunswick, NJ: Transaction Books.

Jansen, Robert S. 2007. "Resurrection and Appropriation: Reputational Trajectories, Memory Work, and the Political Use of Historical Figures." *American Journal of Sociology* 112(4): 953–1007.

Jasper, James. 1999. *The Art of Moral Protest*. Chicago: University of Chicago Press.

Kane, Anne E. 1997. "Theorizing Meaning Construction in Social Movements: Symbolic Structures and Interpretation during the Irish Land War, 1879–1882." *Sociological Theory* 15(3): 249–276.

Labov, William, and Joshua Waletsky. 1967. "Narrative Analysis: Oral Versions of Personal Experience." Pp. 12–44 in *Essays on the Verbal and Visual Arts: Proceedings of the 1966 Annual Spring Meeting of the American Ethnological Society*, edited by June Helm. Seattle: University of Washington Press.

Lévi-Strauss, Claude. 1963. "The Structural Analysis of Myth." In *Structural Anthropology*, translated by Claire Jacobson and Brook G. Schoepf. New York: Basic Books.

Lewin, Tamar. 1991. "More States Study Clemency for Women Who Killed Abusers." *New York Times*, Feburary 21, Section A.

Luker, Kristin. 1984. *Abortion and the Politics of Motherhood*. Berkeley: University of California Press.

Mahoney, James. 1999. "Nominal, Ordinal, and Narrative Appraisal in Macrocausal Analysis." *American Journal of Sociology* 104(4): 1154–1196.

Mahoney, Martha R. 1994. "Victimization or Oppression? Women's Lives, Violence, and Agency." pp. 59–92 in *The Public Nature of Private Violence: The Discovery of Domestic Abuse*, edited by Martha Albertson Fineman and Roxanne Mykitiuk. New York: Routledge.

Maguigan, Holly. 1991. "Battered Women and Self-Defense: Myths and Misconceptions in Current Reform Proposals." *University of Pennsylvania Law Review* 140(2): 379–486.

McGough, Lucy S. 1994. *Child Witnesses: Fragile Voices in the American Legal System*. New Haven, CT: Yale University Press.

Meyer, David. S. 2006. "Claiming Credit: Stories of Movement Influence as Outcomes." *Mobilization* 11(3): 281–298.

Miller, J. Hillis. 1990. "Narrative." Pp. 66–79 in *Critical Terms for Literary Study*, edited by Frank Lentricchia and Thomas McLaughlin. Chicago: University of Chicago Press.

Nepstad, Sharon Erickson. 2001. "Creating Transnational Solidarity: The Use of Narrative in the U.S.-Central America Peace Movement." *Mobilization* 6(1): 21–36.

Nolan, James L. 2002. "Drug Court Stories: Transforming American Jurisprudence." pp. 149–177 in *Stories of Change: Narrative and Social Movements*, edited by Joseph E. Davis. Albany: State University of New York Press.

Nunberg, Geoffrey. 2006. *Talking Right: How Conservatives Turned Liberalism into a Tax-Raising, Latte-Drinking, Sushi-Eating, Volvo-Driving, New York Times-Reading, Body-Piercing, Hollywood-Loving, Left-Wing Freak Show*. New York: Public Affairs.

Owens, Lynn. 2009. *Cracking Under Pressure: Narrating the Decline of the Amsterdam Squatters Movements*. University Park: Pennsylvania State University Press.

Petty, Richard E., and John T. Cacioppo. 1986. *Communication and Persuasion: Central and Peripheral Routes to Attitude Change*. New York: Springer-Verlag.

Plummer, Ken. 1995. *Telling Sexual Stories: Power, Change, and Social Worlds*. New York: Routledge.

Polkinghorne, Donald E. 1988. *Narrative Knowing and the Human Sciences*. Albany: State University of New York Press.

Polletta, Francesca. 2006. *It Was Like a Fever: Storytelling in Protest and Politics*. Chicago: University Chicago Press.

———. 2009. "How to Tell a New Story About Battering." *Journal of Violence Against Women* 15 (12): 1490—508.

Polletta, Francesca, Pang Ching Bobby Chen, Beth Gharrity Gardner, and Alice Motes. 2011. "The Sociology of Storytelling." *Annual Review of Sociology* 37: 109–130.

Public Justice Center. 1990. *A Plea for Justice* [Video]. Group Two Productions.

Schneider, Elizabeth M. 2000. *Battered Women and Feminist Lawmaking*. New Haven, CT: Yale University Press.

Scott, Joan W. 1994. "Deconstructing Equality-versus-Difference: Or, the Uses of Poststructuralist Theory for Feminism." Pp. 282–298 in *The Postmodern Turn: New Perspectives on Social Theory*, edited by Steven Seidman. New York: Cambridge University Press.

Shultz, Vicki. 1990. "Telling Stories about Women and Work: Judicial Interpretations of Sex Segregation in the Workplace in Title VII Cases Raising the Lack of Interest Argument." *Harvard Law Review* 103(8): 1749–1843.

Slater, Michael D., and Donna Rouner. 2002. "Entertainment-Education and Elaboration Likelihood: Understanding the Processing of Narrative Persuasion." *Communication Theory* 12(2): 173–191.

Slater, Michael D., Donna Rouner, and Marilee Long. 2006. "Television Dramas and Support for Controversial Public Policies: Effects and Mechanisms." *Journal of Communication* 56(2): 235–252.

Snow, David A. 2004. "Framing Processes, Ideology, and Discursive Fields." Pp. 380–412 in *The Blackwell Companion to Social Movements*, edited by David A. Snow, Sarah A. Soule, and Hanspeter Kriesi. Malden, MA: Blackwell.

Snow, David A., and Robert D. Benford. 1992. "Master Frames and Cycles of Protest." pp. 133–155 in *Frontiers in Social Movement Theory*, edited by Aldon D. Morris and Carol McClurg Mueller. New Haven, CT: Yale University Press.

Smith, Phillip. 2005. *Why War? The Cultural Logic of Iraq, the Gulf War, and Suez*. Chicago: University of Chicago Press.

Stark, Evan. 2007. *Coercive Control: How Men Entrap Women in Personal Life*. New York: Oxford University Press.

Stoecker, Randy. 1995. "Community, Movement, Organization: The Problem of Identity Convergence in Collective Action." *The Sociological Quarterly* 36(1): 111–130.

Tilly, Charles. 2002. *Stories, Identities, and Social Change*. New York: Rowman & Littlefield

Trafford, Abigail. 1991. "Why Battered Women Kill: Self-Defense, Not Revenge, Is Often the Motive." *Washington Post*, February 26, Magazine, p. 6.

Voss, Kim. 1996. "The Collapse of a Social Movement: The Interplay of Mobilizing Structures, Framing, and Political Opportunities in the Knights of Labor." Pp. 227–258 in *Comparative Perspectives on Social Movements*, edited by Doug McAdam, John D. McCarthy, and Mayer N. Zald. New York: Cambridge University Press.

Weschler, Lawrence. 1982. *The Passion of Poland: From Solidarity through the State of War*. New York: Pantheon Books.

Whittier, Nancy. 2001. "Emotional Strategies: The Collective Reconstruction and Display of Oppositional Emotions in the Movement against Child Sexual Abuse." Pp. 233–250 in *Passionate Politics: Emotions and Social Movements*, edited by Jeff Goodwin, James M. Jasper, and Francesca Polletta. Chicago: University of Chicago Press.

———. 2009. *The Politics of Child Sexual Abuse: Emotion, Social Movements, and the State*. New York: Oxford Univ. Press.

Zillmann, Dolf, and Hans-Bernd Brosius. 2000. *Exemplification in Communication: The Influence of Case Reports on the Perception of Issues*. Mahwah, NJ: Erlbaum.

CHAPTER 19

....

THE POLITICS OF AUTHENTICITY: CIVIC INDIVIDUALISM AND THE CULTURAL ROOTS OF GAY NORMALIZATION

....

STEVEN SEIDMAN, CHET MEEKS, AND JAMES JOSEPH DEAN

ASIDE from brief periods of social upheaval between 1969–1973 and the early years of the AIDS crisis, when ACT UP and Queer Nation seemed to promise a renewed political militancy, a liberationist politic has been the exception in postwar American gay and lesbian movements. In the 1950s, homosexual activists and organizations rallied around a politics of assimilation. They longed for a time when "the homosexual" as a distinct personage would disappear from the social landscape. Such individuals would simply be recognized as "human" and "American." And, from roughly the mid-1970s, when gay liberationism and lesbian-feminism were consigned to the social margins, gay and lesbian politics have been about identity normalization, rights, authenticity, and social integration. In the early twenty-first century, nearly every influential U.S. national lesbian and gay organization—the Human Rights Campaign, Lambda Legal Defense and Education Fund, and even the left-leaning National Lesbian and Gay Task Force—has adopted the political vocabulary and agenda of normalization.[1]

There was nothing inevitable about the triumph of a politics of normalization. Liberationists and their successors (e.g., ACT UP, Queer Nation, Lavender Menace) were simply unable to sustain popular support or organizational traction. Still, for the last thirty years, an agenda of normalization and mainstreaming has gone almost unchallenged. Why?

For the most part, scholars have ignored what in our view should be a central problematic in the literature on the formation of the American gay and lesbian movement. Researchers often seem preoccupied by the failure of liberationism or lesbian-feminism to achieve organizational and political sustainability. For example, D'Emilio (1983, 1992), surely one of the premier interpreters of the American gay and lesbian movement, highlights, in an overview of this movement, the waning of liberationism by the mid-1970s and the movement's "retreat to respectability." But, this "retreat" has lasted some three decades and D'Emilio offers no serious account of how or why this occurred. Instead, perhaps reflecting his normative standpoint, he makes a point of underscoring the continuing cultural legacy of liberationism (visibility, challenge to the closet, a culture of pride and affirmation). Furthermore, D'Emilio outlines an event-based account of the political decline of the Gay Liberation Front (GLF) and liberationism in general, concluding that the "GLF was not well suited for the long march through institutions that a sustained movement would have to undertake" (1992, p. 245). But, exactly why the GLF wasn't "well suited" to sustain its social activism, and what it was about post-liberationist normalizing politics that made its politics of respectability and rights "well suited" to sustain a movement, are not addressed.

Similarly, in his historical account of the politics of gay marriage, Chauncey underscores the important point that the marriage agenda was "a distinctly minority position" among liberationists (2004, p. 93) and was hardly discussed through the 1980s. But, by the mid-1990s, it had become perhaps the defining issue of the lesbian and gay movement. As an historical study, we would expect an accounting, and one that at least in part appealed to the internal development of the movement. In fact, Chauncey does allude to the historical parallel between the marriage agenda and the ascendancy of a gay rights focus in the lesbian and gay movement of the 1990s. Yet, his explanation focuses almost exclusively on contextual events such as a shift in gender relations, the waning of a conservative family values politic, the lesbian baby boom, and, most importantly, AIDS. "The gay quest for equal rights in marriage…gained impetus because of the profound changes wrought in lesbian and gay life in the 1980s and 1990s by the AIDS crisis and the boom in lesbian and gay parenting" (2004, p. 3). No doubt, AIDS and gay parenting infused a new salience into issues such as partner rights or inheritance. But, many of these developments and concerns extend back to the 1980s and, more to the point, this contextual account is nowhere supplemented by a sustained analysis of the internal development of the gay and lesbian movement; nor is there any explanation for why the marriage agenda has been articulated almost completely in the cultural idiom of rights and normalization (see Meeks and Stein 2006).

Until recently, social scientists have only been marginally engaged in research-ing the formation of the gay and lesbian movement in the United States (exceptions include Adams 1987; Taylor 1989). However, over the last few years, social scientists have begun to apply movement theory to the gay and lesbian movement. Important contributions have addressed the role of organizational dynamics (Armstrong 2002), political elites (Rimmerman 2007), social class (Valocchi 1999), or economic factors (Chasin 2000) in the formation of lesbian and gay movements. Much of this research, though valuable and innovative, has been, at best, indirect in addressing the three-decade ascendance of a normalizing politics. Moreover, a good deal of this research has displayed a decidedly structuralist disposition.

Engel's (2001) exceptionally well-researched *The Unfinished Revolution* offers a particularly good illustration, especially since he also addresses the triumph of a rights-oriented politic by way, once again, of explaining the failure of liberationism. Engel underscores the failure of the lesbian and gay movement in the United States to achieve lasting institutional change of the sort that would parallel its apparent successes in the realm of pop-culture. As he puts it, "Political reality lags far behind the televisual fantasy" (p. xix). While Americans are now exposed to affirmative TV images of gay and lesbian people, and while political elites like Barack Obama or Andrew Cuomo actively court the gay vote, the movement has not achieved the kinds of transformative institutional changes that would yield greater legal protec-tion and actual social equality.

Engel explains this contradiction through the lens of the "political process model" (cf. McAdam 1997). Ultimately, the stalled social revolution is, for Engel, a result of the Federalist configuration of political institutions in America, where decision-making processes devolve to the states. "[M]ovement organizations have a multitude of venues in which to achieve their aims," yet "most American gay-themed legislation has been passed at the state level, and, due to the nature of Federalism, such legislation has varied from state to state" (pp. 161–162). The Federalist system obstructs a national-level politic of institutional transformation. The "unfinished revolution" is explained by the unique political structure of American politics.

Engel fails, however, to recognize that the sort of transformative challenge to the institution of heterosexuality that he (normatively) takes to be the abiding core of the gay and lesbian movement has not been a serious, sustained political focus since the mid-1970s. As with many other sociological accounts, Engel's analysis is overdetermined by a perspective that evaluates the successes and failures of social movements in light of their organizational structure, movement elites, or political opportunities. Moreover, to the extent that "culture" has been introduced into this literature, it often occurs by appealing narrowly to the notion of a collective identity (Armstrong 2002; Taylor and Whittier 1995; Bernstein 1997; Gamson 1996). Reducing the cultural field to identity strategies surrenders the core of the field to nonculturalist accounts.

All too often, the field of social movements seems caught up in a futile episte-mological game of "factoral" additions and revisions—fueled by the fiction of a complete model or theory of social movements. If this fiction is abandoned, the issue at stake is not which factor or combination yields the right account; rather, revision is useful only to the extent that it can offer a fresh interpretation or a novel rethinking, thereby opening up new avenues of research and/or politics. With this caveat in mind, we wish to sketch a robust culturalist account of the sustained dominance of a rights-oriented politics of normalization in the United States. Following recent work in the area of social movements (Flam and King 2005; Zald 2000; Jasper 1999; Melucci 1996; Polleta 2006) and cultural sociology (Alexander 2005, 2007), we argue that political agendas, strategies, solidarities, and ideologies are always embedded in a thick cultural realm of collective beliefs, affective and cognitive attachments, and narrative framings.

Symbolic contestation over the meaning and regulation of the body and desire, over personal and social identity, narrative struggles over the sequencing and main plot lines of history and contemporary trends are the stuff of movements. This is not to say that movements are *not* political—only that under the surface of agenda-setting, political maneuvering, and ideology-building and identity strategies is a "lifeworld" only partly ever recognized by movement actors. And, what is political is itself a site of symbolic contestation. Comprehending this field of cultural depth is crucial for understanding how one particular political agenda and cluster of strategies, tactics, interventions, and mobilizations come to define a social movement's politics.

From this perspective, the dominance of a politics of normalization also signals the triumph of a culture—one that, as we will show, champions a grammar of individual agency, moral virtue, authenticity, and personal responsibility. Indeed, we believe that the dominance of a politics of normalization is, in part, explained by the sustaining force of this cultural matrix.

We introduce the notion of a "cultural code" to understand something of the cultural grounds of postwar gay and lesbian politics. A code structures the practice of representation, narration, and discourse (Alexander 2007; Barthes 1974; Douglas 1966; Sahlins 1978; Silverman 1983). Codes create an intelligible and coherent sense of order by classifying, arranging, and assigning moral value. A code has at least three dimensions. First, a code creates order through binaries, such as rational/irrational, normal/abnormal, West/East, homosexual/heterosexual, public/private, speech/writing, sacred/profane, or purity/pollution. Second, codes are abstract and generalizing. They have structuring force across varied types of discourses (scientific, therapeutic, political, and administrative). Third, codes are sustaining over long periods of time. Once a code is formed and socially embedded, it is not easily dislodged or undermined. However, dominant codes may be elaborated in various ways and, at times, challenged by countercodes.

Cultural codes are part of the lifeworld and invested with considerable emotional and normative force. Cultural codes derive their social power then not only from structuring representations but they also resonate in deep affective, evaluative, and often unconscious ways with social actors. Whether a political agenda is received as reasonable or compelling will depend, in part, on whether it articulates the codes that organize the lifeworld in a language that feels "right" or "appropriate."

We argue that "civic individualism" has been a dominant cultural code in contemporary America. This code formed the cultural context that structured the development of American sexual politics. Specifically, civic individualism has shaped a friendly cultural environment for a politics of normalization, while forming an inhospitable cultural context for a liberationist or transformative politic.

Civic individualism relies on three binaries: individual/society, self-responsibility/social accountability, and personal/public. Civic individualism stipulates that the individual be real, whereas society is an "artifice." The former is constant, while the latter is transient and changes. The individual is assumed to be the only social agent. The individual is history-making, whereas society is its effect or a passive medium of individual action. However, "the social" can become a constraint or even a source of evil if individuals think it is real, if some individuals enforce their interests as the interests of society, and if some individuals use society to suppress the individual. In essence, though, social dramas are coherent as individual struggles. If there is social inequality, the source is individual behavior and the remedy is individual struggle. Accordingly, this code assigns moral responsibility to the individual for his or her social status. Individual choice, not social forces, accounts for the shape of a life. Furthermore, if the individual is "real" and morally responsible for his or her decisions and social fate, the "personal" is also said to be the site of "authenticity." It is in the experience and expression of our personal world of feelings, desires, thinking, and actions that we manifest the deepest, truest core of who we are. By contrast, the "public" is a realm of roles, pretense, performance, and insincerity. Additionally, the personal is understood as a fulcrum of social change. By representing human truths in an exemplary way, the individual can edify or educate the public, thereby changing beliefs and behaviors.

At the center of civic individualism is an abiding, almost unshakeable belief in the essential goodness of America. From its founding moment through the turmoil of a civil war, labor and suffrage battles, the Cold War, and the cultural wars of the postwar period, America's civil religion has hardly wavered in imagining this nation as the chosen people whose "'manifest destiny" is to serve as a beacon of freedom for all of humankind. The "graced" status of America rests ultimately on this claim of national exceptionalism. In this regard, civic individualism implies a final binary: America/world. Whereas America has preserved the preeminence of individual freedom, in Europe and the rest of the world the individual has "fallen" into a state of dependence on society.

The culture of civic individualism may not always be expressed in such a clear and consistent manner. Moreover, a code may be articulated in different vocabularies. As we will show, despite the varied political vocabularies of assimilation, rights, or multicultural integration that characterize postwar reform-oriented lesbian and gay politics, each expresses the core principles of civic individualism—assumes the agency of the individual (voluntarism) and champions personal virtue, authenticity, and a politics of edification as the most effective way to bring about social change.[2]

HOMOPHILE POLITICS: THE FOUNDING MOMENT

The notion that gay liberationism was the founding moment in the gay and lesbian movement, if not literally then symbolically, is still widely held. Liberationism is imagined as symbolizing the moment when gay men and lesbians refused a life in the shadows. Accordingly, the "Stonewall rebellion" has become iconic in American gay and lesbian culture. From this perspective, the marginalization of liberationism and the triumph of a rights and integrationist politics are at times interpreted as a betrayal of the true spirit of the movement.

In fact, liberationist politics was a brief episode in lesbian and gay politics. The founding moment was the appearance of the first national political organizations in the 1950s. They established the conceptual grammar of a gay and lesbian politics. They articulated civic individualism into a political ideology and agenda, which has been more or less sustained across five decades.

We begin then with a curious historical fact. Scholars today agree that a wave of social repression and homophobia swept across America in the 1950s and 1960s, creating the social conditions of the closet (Corber 1997; D'Emilio 1983; Epstein 1994; Eskridge 1999; Johnson 2004). McCarthyist America compelled nonhetero-sexuals to live a shadowy or "double" life, a life of enforced silence and invisibility. However, nowhere in homophile discourses and politics is there a concept of insti-tutionalized heterosexual domination or homosexual oppression.

In response to a state-driven antihomosexual politics, three homosexual orga-nizations formed: the Mattachine Society, the Daughters of Bilitis (DOB), and the One Institute. Initially, the politics of these organizations were unsettled. Harry Hay, the founder of the Mattachine Society, who had activist roots in the Communist Party and labor activism (Hay 1996), sketched an "institutional" theory and politics of homosexuality. Hay argued that American society oppresses homosexuals. "Our people...are victimized daily..." (1996, p. 132). Institutional persecution produced a reality of homosexuals as an "oppressed minority" (1996, p. 132). Hay reasoned that if homosexuality is a social problem in America, it is because this nation is an "antihomosexual society." While Hay acknowledged the key role of education in changing prejudices and behavior, he advocated that homosexuals develop their own unique collective identity and culture as they struggle to be recognized as first-class citizens (1996, pp. 81, 114, 131–132). Tellingly, Hay's institutional social theory and politics were repudiated by the members of the Mattachine Society. Hay soon left the organization he helped found.

The activists in the Mattachine Society and DOB rejected the view that American society is organized to persecute and oppress homosexuals. Homosexuals are not compelled by social forces to be outsiders or to live in a disreputable underworld. Homosexuals can *choose* to live as ordinary productive Americans.

The chief problem facing homosexuals is not institutional persecution or vic-timization but individual prejudice based on ignorance (Norman 1959, p. 17; see also Anonymous 1955a, p. 7; Harding 1956; Logan 1956; Benjamin 1958; Leroy 1958).

Moreover, *all* Americans, homosexual and heterosexual, are said to experience sexual prejudice, which reflects this nations' Puritan heritage (Osborne 1957, p. 7). Individual homosexuals, just like heterosexuals, must learn to accept and manage their sexuality. If homosexuals feel rejected or uncomfortable about their sexuality, it is a personal problem. "The problem is really one of the homosexual rejecting himself. This is the problem of anyone who rejects himself for any reason. The unhappy, unfulfilled heterosexual's problem is not different" (Osborne 1957, p. 7). Or, as an editorial in the Daughters of Bilitis put it, "Much of the rejection [the homosexual] feels is self-imposed" (quoted in Blasius and Phelan 1997, p. 333).

Unfortunately, argued homophile activists, many homosexuals do not assume personal responsibility for their own problems. They blame society for their problems while they embrace a psychology of victimization or retreat into a shadowy underworld or, worse, celebrate their exoticism instead of assuming responsibility for their own lives. For example, some homosexuals complain about discrimination at work, but homosexuality is an issue of the workplace only if it is introduced by the individual. "No employment questionnaire asks...if you are a homosexual. This problem comes into being only if you yourself bring it to the job" (Anonymous 1957, p. 17). Similarly, many homosexuals feel that they are victimized by the burden of role-playing (passing). "But how often has the homosexual considered the many roles the heterosexual is also forced to play....Is not the heterosexual also beleaguered by family, teacher, boss—yes, even the police?" (cited in Blasius and Phelan 1997, p. 333).

The homosexual's political struggle is, at bottom, a personal struggle. Self-acceptance is understood as a precondition of social acceptance. And self-acceptance means understanding that being homosexual is just another way to be a man or a woman, and an American. "Before change can be effected in others who know him, the homosexual must accept himself first as a man or woman more alike than different from other men and woman—accept himself as a person, as a doctor, a truck-driver, or an artist, and then, secondarily as having a sexual adjustment that is different than the majority....[He] will discover that he can be accepted by others" (Baker 1957, pp. 15–16; Zeff 1958; see also Anonymous 1962b, p. 20).

Furthermore, in order for self-acceptance to translate into social acceptance, the public has to be exposed to "normal" self-respecting homosexuals. Only homosexuals who exemplify the personal and social traits of the ideal American citizen should publicly represent the homosexual community. In this regard, homophile activists advocated what we call a "politics of edification." Prejudice and ignorance are to be confronted with the rockbottom truth of the shared humanity of homosexuals and heterosexuals. "Our avowed task," states an editorial in the *Mattachine Review*, "is to ameliorate inter-relationships between homosexuals and the general public through education and favorable social contact....If we are aspiring for recognition from the public we must earn it by dispelling egregious and lopsided conceptions of the homosexual....*We must place ourselves before the eyes of the public in a positive and constructive way*" (Los Angeles Mattachine 1957; Burns 1977, p. 289). Social change transpires by means of a process of public education.

There is considerable historical and sociological research supporting the view that the institutions and public culture of America in the 1950s and 1960s compelled homosexuals to accommodate by passing, living a double life, or being closeted. But, as we've seen, homophile activists did not conceptualize homosexuality as an institutional problem—and therefore could not theorize the notion of homosexual oppression. To do so would have forced these activists to question a core belief in the goodness of America. In a sense, Hay was marginalized because his institutional critique of American homophobia challenged this belief. These activists also did not waver in their belief that at bottom, politics was about the moral courage to confront public ignorance with the truth of the homosexual—as just human and as just an ordinary American.

Liberationists: Challenging Civic Individualism

Gay liberationism in the late 1960s and early 1970s marked a dramatic shift in gay and lesbian politics. As much as this change was about strategy and agenda, it was also a challenge to the American culture of civic individualism. Liberationists articulated an "antivoluntarist" or institutional social theory and politics. The grammar of individual agency, moral integrity, and responsibility was marginalized in favor of a vocabulary of compulsory heterosexuality, homosexual oppression, the closet, and collective identity. A politic of edification gave way to a politic of "coming out," collective mobilization, and far-reaching institutional change.

Drawing from the institutional politics of black power and women's liberation, liberationists argued that homosexuals are oppressed by an institutional social order. American government, the church, public schools, scientific-medical institutions, families, and popular culture enforce heterosexuality as the only acceptable way to organize personal and social life. Against the voluntaristic politics of the homophiles, liberationists maintained that under conditions of the institutional enforcement of normative heterosexuality, homosexual forms of personal and social expression are disrespected, disenfranchised, and socially disadvantaged. The problem of homosexuality in America *is* America.

Liberationists viewed American society as fundamentally antihomosexual, and its basis was not ignorance but the compulsory institutional status of heterosexuality.[3] As one of the editors of the liberationist anthology *Out of the Closets*, stated, "hostility [toward homosexuality] is institutionalized—in the legal system, in the canons of religion and psychiatry, in the educational system and the mass media, and in the very structure of the nuclear family" (Young in Jay and Young 1975, p. 85; cf. Grahn 1970, p. 36; Radicalesbians Health Collective in Jay and Young 1972, p. 123; Wittman 1975). Under conditions of compulsory heterosexuality, the only "choice" homosexuals have is either to live openly and risk daily threats of dishonor, violence, arrest, and loss of family and job, or conduct lives involving dissimulation and deception. It was liberationists who invented the concept of the closet as the other side to the notion of compulsory heterosexuality (e.g., Anonymous 1969; Pinney 1970, p. 13; Woodhul 1972, pp. 2–3; Canceris 1973, p. 7; Gilbert 1976; Young 1976, p. 25). The closet referred to the way individuals feel forced to accommodate to an America whose core institutions persecute and pollute homosexuals. The conditions of the closet were said to signal a social condition of homosexual oppression. "One is oppressed as a homosexual every minute of every day, inasmuch as one is restrained from acting in ways that would seem normal to a heterosexual. Every time one refrains from an act of public affection with a lover where a straight couple would not—in a park, on the movie line—one dies a little. And gay people, of course, die a little every day, causing nervous breakdowns, suicide, self-hate" (Byron 1992, p. 59; see also Third World Gay Revolution 1969, p. 16; The Red Butterfly in Jay and Young 1972, pp. 164–165).

If America's core social institutions oppress homosexuals, a politics of edification might make integration possible but would leave in place a society that enforces heterosexuality as normative. Only by challenging the compulsory status of heterosexuality would homosexual freedom be possible. Moreover, liberationists maintained that true homosexual freedom would mean freedom from sexual and gender roles, which would not be possible without the sexual liberation of all Americans. In other words, liberationists criticized America for being sexually and socially repressive for all Americans. Accordingly, as the Gay Liberation Front declared, "Complete sexual liberation for all people cannot come about unless existing social institutions are abolished" (cited in D'Emilio 1983, p. 234).

Liberationists introduced the idea of a *politics of coming out.* "The liberation of homosexuals…would involve destroying the closet. What was needed…was a 'coming out,' a denying of all false security, a rejecting of the self-hatred and guilt of the closet.…Coming out…was a coming together of the oppressed.…Coming out was a means for denying all the normative values of heterosexual society—on imperialism, racism, sexism, class bias, etc." (Dotton 1977, p. 3; Denneny, 1983, p. 409). Liberationists interpreted coming out as a collective political act involving the mobilization of a gay/lesbian community and its alignment with other political movements to battle sexual and social injustice (Anonymous 1969, p. 5). Against a culture of civic individualism, the liberationist notion of coming out suggests that the *public realm* of collective identity and politics is the principal site of identity, authenticity, and citizenship.

Liberationists did not however entirely break from the culture of civic individualism. Coming out also referred to a process of personal change. Coming out involved a struggle for personal authenticity. For example, the Radicalesbians declared that "together, we must find, reinforce and validate our *authentic* selves.… We feel a *realness,* feel at last we are coinciding with ourselves" (quoted in Blasius and Phelan 1997, p. 399; Wittman in Blasius and Phelan 1997, p. 383). Self-liberation required, above all, that the individual abandon a straight life: "If we attempt to copy straight life styles we will only perpetuate the subterfuge, self-hatred and loneliness in which we've wallowed for too long" (Alinder 1969, p. 10).

Personal conduct and lifestyle choices took on considerable moral significance in liberationist politics. Decisions about whether to be closeted, about sexual and gender identity, and about intimate and social behavior were interpreted as signs of self-liberation and authenticity. It was but a short step from the linkage of coming out with a struggle for personal authenticity to framing coming out as about being true to oneself, being virtuous, courageous, and, self-empowering; while being in the closet was dishonest, inauthentic, and cowardly. In one of the signature statements of liberationism, Carl Wittman condemns the "closet queen," as if being closeted was an immoral choice and a betrayal of the community. "To pretend to be straight sexually or…socially is probably the most harmful pattern of behavior. Closet queenery must end. Come out" (Wittman 1972, p. 334). Despite its antivoluntarist social theory, many liberationists surrendered to civic individualism in its view that coming out is a moral choice. It was not though until a normalizing politic was nationally consolidated in the 1980s and 1990s that a political culture stamped by the grammar of individual agency, moral integrity, personal responsibility, and authenticity became truly triumphant.

Rights and Reform: Mainstreaming in the 1970s and 1980s

Between the late 1960s and mid-1970s, the shape of the movement was unsettled. Various organizations with sometimes rival political agendas competed to represent a population on the verge of national mobilization. Although homophile politics was at odds with the new activist spirit of the late 1960s, in the long run it was liberationist politics that proved at odds with American civic individualism. By at least the mid-1970s, liberationism was pushed to the social and cultural margins of the gay and lesbian movement. Liberationists were dismissed as out of sync with the real lives of gay and lesbian Americans. In the pages of the *Advocate*, we can trace the marginalization of liberationists and the renegotiation of a politics of the closet in the moralistic grammar of voluntarism.

Launched in 1967 as the first gay and lesbian national news magazine, the editors of the *Advocate* staked out a politics of rights and normalization in opposition to liberationism. Against the core liberationist claim that the institutional order of America is oppressive to homosexuals, the editors aggressively defended the voluntaristic sexual theory of the homophiles. "We can't help but be amused by some of the gay militants who try to equate repressive, anti-homosexual laws and attitudes with some sort of capitalist plot. What rot! Like any other prejudice, prejudice against homosexuals stems from a variety of interrelated factors—chiefly ignorance, fear, insecurity, and religious dogmas" (Michaels 1970, p. 22). Reasserting the language of civic individualism, the editors declared that the gay and lesbian movement should be a "battle for our [individual] rights" (Michaels 1970, p. 22).

In 1975, David Goodstein became the publisher and editor of the *Advocate*. Goodstein argued that the liberationist image of a "fascist" and "imperialist" America was "unrealistic and destructive," and its revolutionary agenda at odds with the mainstreaming aspirations of most gay and lesbian Americans (1976 p. 5). Goodstein introduced an historical rationale that would be repeatedly invoked in order to dismiss liberationism. He interpreted liberationism as an understandable protest against excessive government and police discrimination in the early postwar period. However, the defining national trend, he argues, has been toward the social incorporation and normalization of gays and lesbians. Goodstein argued that in the course of the 1970s, gay and lesbian rights were recognized in a number of cities and states, discriminatory laws and policies successfully challenged, and activists steadily gained access to public officials and the mass media. Despite a backlash in the late 1970s, Goodstein insisted that America had become a tolerant society. The most dramatic marker of this change is the mass exiting from the shelter of the closet. "Gay parties were (once) private and secretive, public events only sparsely attended. Gay pride celebrations, athletic events…theater offerings and other social alternatives have opened the closet doors and brought our fun-loving spirit into the open—the long journey from the secretive 'homosexual' haunts of yesteryear is, hopefully, behind us once and for all" (Goodstein 1978, p. 15).

Goodstein reasoned that the chief challenge facing gay men and lesbians in America of the late 1970s and 1980s was not institutional but personal: a psychology of shame or "low self-esteem" (1984, p. 6). Sounding a prominent homophile theme, Goodstein declared: "As a practical matter, I am more convinced then ever that we create our experience of oppression" (1983, p. 6). Goodstein rearticulates the liberationist grammar of the closet in the language of civic individualism. Instead of conceiving of the closet as a forced accommodation to the institutionally compulsory status of heterosexuality, Goodstein believed that, unlike in the previous decade or two, individuals today *choose* to be in the closet out of a sense of shame and fear that is no longer warranted. He condemned individuals who made this choice for lacking the moral integrity and responsibility to be who they are. "I take a dim view of staying in the closet.…What brings up my irritation at this time…is…the price we un-closeted gay people pay for the *cowardice and stupidity of our [closeted] brothers and sisters*" (our emphasis; 1981, p. 6).

If the choice to be closeted was undermining an agenda of enfranchisement and integration, a central focus of politics must be the personal act of coming out. Goodstein understood coming out as an act of personal integrity and authenticity. "Coming out…involves being who you are wherever you are, not hiding a fundamental piece of yourself" (1981, p. 6). Goodstein expected individuals to come out as an act of personal and political responsibility. Coming out is political in the homophile sense of being an act of public edification that can change peoples' attitudes and behavior. In this regard, Goodstein relates how his father initially rebuffed him after he came out. But, soon after, "he called to tell me how he admired my courage.…Now we are clear that we love each other.…My experience is that coming out…has given me a truly enriched life" (1981, p. 6). The burden of social change rests on the courage and moral integrity of the individual to educate and enlighten a public by exemplifying his or her common humanity in the act of coming out.

The architects of a politics of mainstreaming, such as Goodstein, dismissed liberationists as romantics unable or unwilling to seriously consider the changing realities of ordinary gay men and lesbians. Interestingly, reformers such as Goodstein never felt obligated or pressured to do more than invoke anecdotal evidence or "changing social conditions" to dismiss liberationist arguments about compulsory heterosexuality. In a sense, they didn't have to do more because they were expressing the widely held ideas and sentiments of a culture of civic individualism. Against liberationists, reformers had only to affirm America as a good society and reassert their deep faith in the reformative powers of personal courage and truth-telling. Faced with the all too human reality of ordinary homosexuals, prejudicial stereotypes would lose credibility and eventually disappear. The 1970s and 1980s were not, however, the 1950s. The new reformers abandoned the narrow homophile goal of assimilation (with its anticipation of the disappearance of "the homosexual") in favor of the social integration of the "normal" or quasi-ethnic "gay/lesbian-American."

1990S: THE TRIUMPH OF THE POLITICS OF VIRTUE

By the time Goodstein stepped down as editor of the *Advocate*, it seemed that the ideological foundations of the lesbian and gay movement were settled. Indeed, as well-funded bureaucratic national organizations such as Lambda Legal Defense or the Human Rights Campaign gained considerable power, liberationist theory and politics were sustained by those on the social margins, such as sex radicals, artists, and academics. Yet, in the early 1990s, there was a renewal of the spirit of liberationism in the politics of ACT UP and Queer Nation. This provoked a renewed ideological clash over the politics of the movement.

Bruce Bawer's *A Place at the Table* (1993) was an influential defense of the politics of normalization that forcefully articulated the language of civic individualism. Bawer's ideas position him as part of a tradition stretching back to the homophile activists. He dismissed critics who claimed that America is organized to oppress its gay and lesbian citizens: "They think that their enemy is conscious oppression, when in fact their enemy is ignorance and their salvation lies in increased understanding" (1993, p. 47).

Against the new liberationists, Bawer invoked the motif of "America [as] basically a tolerant nation" (1993, p. 47). Like Goodstein, he concedes that homophobia and discrimination were widespread in the early postwar period. Understandably, individuals at that time retreated into the closet or gay and lesbian enclaves for protection and support. Angry and embittered, some of these individuals unfortunately championed their "otherness" and advocated social revolution. Worse, still, these liberationist critics became the public face of gay and lesbian America. Liberationists in the past, and neoliberationists in the present, have misled Americans into believing that gay men and lesbians are different from their straight counterparts and want a new America. This embrace of exoticism and radicalism has made it "harder for many heterosexuals to see gays as [ordinary] individuals, and in particular to make distinctions between the largely invisible millions of gays who lead more or less conventional lives and the conspicuous few who don't" (1993, p. 32).

However, the America of the 1990s is not the America of the 1960s, and nowhere is this difference more evident than in the changing status of gays and lesbians. Tolerance and the social integration of gay men and lesbians, not institutional persecution and victimization, best describe the reality today. "Tolerance is greater than it was a generation or two ago. Things have improved. People are more enlightened....A gay man...has the option of living either alone or with a companion, as a more or less openly gay man" (1993, p. 33). Discrimination and prejudice have not disappeared but they are less institutionally driven than sustained by individual ignorance and prejudice. And, contrary to the liberationist romance with "otherness" and rebellion, the hearts and minds of the no longer "silent majority" of gays want "integration into mainstream society" (1993, p. 35). The vast majority of gay Americans have rejected liberationists as "out of touch with...the trend in the U.S...toward normalization" (1993, pp. 54–56).

As America accommodates, however incompletely, lesbian and gay citizens need to choose to join the social mainstream. Aligning himself with a voluntarist politics of edification, Bawer counsels individuals to confront prejudice with the truth of who they are. "The ultimate enemy of anti-gay prejudice, then, is truth...*as more gays have become honest about their homosexuality, more heterosexual friends, relatives, and coworkers have rethought ill-informed prejudices*" (our emphasis; 1993, pp. 30, 88–89, 121, 184). The personal act of coming out acquires considerable moral and political weight. If coming out has the power to discredit stereotypes and dissolve prejudice, individuals shoulder a moral duty to enlighten the public by displaying their ordinariness and normality. The political fate of gay and lesbian people depends then on the courage and moral integrity of the individual to choose to live an open life. In Bawer's political vision, the language of institutional politics surrenders to a moral vocabulary of personal integrity and responsibility.

Despite the dominance of a politics of normalization and integration, the AIDS crisis and the anti-gay backlash it provoked were troubling to a reform narrative of progress. In this somewhat unsettled time, efforts to renew a liberationist politic gained some credibility once again. In *Virtual Equality* (1995), Urvashi Vaid offered a spirited defense of a liberationist theory and politics but, as we will show, her perspective was ultimately compromised by a disposition to collapse politics into an ethic of personal virtue.

Vaid acknowledged that there have been significant social and legal reforms benefiting many gay and lesbian Americans between the 1970s and 1990s. Still, the normative status of heterosexuality continues to be institutionally enforced "by silence or hostility in the media, in schools, churches, local government, civic associations and the business world" (1995, p. 363). The reality "for most of our people…[remains] dominated by fear, permeated by discrimination, violence, and shame" (1995, p. 5). Accordingly, Vaid defends the continued political relevance of the antivoluntarist theory and politics of liberationism.

Vaid's institutional theory of normative heterosexuality is, however, at odds with her view of the politics of coming out. In the face of institutional pressures to silence or censor lesbians and gay men, Vaid still maintains that claiming a public voice and presence is a central—indeed, obligatory—political act. Instead of coupling coming out to a process of collective political mobilization against institutionalized heterosexual domination, Vaid describes coming out as a voluntary act of moral integrity and truth-telling. "Until each gay and lesbian person tells the truth about his or her life—coming out every day, everywhere, and in every situation—the heterosexual world will be able to deny the existence of homosexuality" (1995, p. 30)

By framing the individual act of coming out as a fundamentally political act, Vaid also suggests that being closeted is an individual choice. In a stunning departure from a liberationist theory, she condemns the closet, or more correctly, the choice to be closeted, on moralistic grounds: "Being in the closet ought to be viewed *as immoral behavior…as intrinsically evil*" (our emphasis; 1995, p. 31). If being in the closet is evil, rather than the institutions that enforce it, coming out becomes a sign of personal virtue. "Coming out is an act of goodness, integrity, and is a precondition for any gay person wishing to live a moral life. I suggest that *being out of the closet may best be defined as a moral act because it moves us closer towards truth…towards virtue*" (our emphasis; 1995, p. 31).

Vaid risks collapsing politics into a morality tale of individual virtue or good and evil. She condemns the individual decision to be closeted as immoral instead of criticizing the institutional and social forces that enforce the closet. And, then, she describes coming out as a virtuous act of moral integrity and responsibility, which contradicts the liberationist idea of coming out as a collective political act that challenges compulsory heterosexuality. Without recognizing the lineage of this narrative, Vaid has surrendered to the politics of edification—to the view that social change occurs through individual acts of speaking truth to power. As more and more gay men and lesbians come out, Vaid seems to reason, misrepresentation, prejudice, and discrimination would be contested everyday, repeatedly and relentlessly. And so, like Bawer, her antagonist, Vaid has perhaps unintentionally placed the moral courage and integrity of the individual and the choice to come out at the center of sexual politics.

CONCLUSION

The 1960s in America were a period of heightened political and cultural turmoil. Black power and women's liberation didn't only challenge a rights and reform agenda but articulated an alternative civic code. Against a language of voluntarism, moral individualism, and personal authenticity that underpinned civil rights movements, liberationists argued that black Americans and women are subject to structural conditions of inequality. Blacks and women were said to be oppressed by the institutional order of America—by its government, laws, schools, cultural representations, and discourses. The critical concepts of "the ghetto" and a "women's sphere" underscored a structural condition of racism and sexism. Moreover, black power and women's liberation challenged an apparent postwar consensus that the individualism and tolerance of America are the antithesis of Soviet state tyranny and European class-based societies. Black power and women's liberation dared to portray America as exhibiting its own distinctive patterns of social tyranny—of white and male supremacy, and the tyranny of capital over labor.

Gay liberationists participated in the making of this "counterculture." Against the civic individualism of homophile politics, liberationists theorized homosexuality as a "problem" only because heterosexuality has been institutionally enforced as a requirement of personal and social life. As a result, the core institutions and culture of America disrespect, disenfranchise, and degrade its nonheterosexual citizens. America was said to be illiberal and unjust; homosexuals were oppressed by a "heterosexual dictatorship."

From the perspective of liberationist social theory, a politics of edification would leave the structural supports of compulsory heterosexuality, such as a binary gender order, government policies and laws, and a culture of heterosexual romance and marriage, intact. Liberationists invented a new politics of coming out: Coming out meant becoming part of a community, developing a collective identity that rested on a condition of gay/lesbian oppression, challenging institutionalized heterosexual domination, and forming coalitions with other oppressed groups.

Liberationists introduced a "thick" politics in contrast to the "thin" politics of the homophiles and their heirs. The liberationist idea of compulsory heterosexuality meant that institutions, culture, gender, and everyday life were political. By contrast, as we've seen, reformers abandon this notion and the link between sexuality and nonsexual social dynamics, such as gender and political economy. And in place of the liberationist politicizing of the personal realm of the body, gender, eroticism, and intimacy, reformers substitute a morality of personal authenticity and virtue.

Liberationists were not entirely untouched, though, by the culture of civic individualism. They insisted that social change required a personal transformation. Coming out was also a process in which the individual adopted "liberated" social values (nonconsumerist, nonsexist, noncolonialist) and a "liberated" sexual-intimate lifestyle (nongendered, not premised on ownership or monogamy). As a sign of self-liberation, coming out acquired considerable moral significance for liberationists as well.

It was then easy for reformers to claim liberationism as part of their heritage and thereby enhance their legitimacy. As we've seen, reformers appropriated but rearticulated the language of the closet and coming out in the grammar of civic individualism. They renegotiated the meaning of the closet as an individual choice (rather than a social structural condition) and as an indicator of moral weakness (rather than as a sign of social oppression). Similarly, coming out was understood as a moral act of courage, virtue, and personal responsibility (rather than a collective public act challenging institutional injustice). In the political culture of the 1980s and 1990s, the line between morality and politics was blurred as politics was centered on public acts of truth-telling, with the "respectable" homosexual serving as an exemplar of a common humanity and a normal American citizen.

A liberationist political culture has survived on the edges of lesbian and gay life. As a critique of the institutionalization of normative heterosexuality and gender binarism, liberationism lives on in critical sex theory, local grassroots activism, and a culture of sexual, gender, social, and cultural experimentation. It may, yet again, give expression to movements of collective protest.

However, a politics of normalization—with its political vocabulary of rights, identity pride, visibility, and multicultural integration—has dominated gay and lesbian movement organizations. As a *partial* explanation of this development, we have introduced the notion of a culture of American civic individualism: a culture that assumes that the individual is the real agent of social life, assumes a notion of personal responsibility for the individual's social fate, assumes that personal life is the site of authenticity and moral integrity, assumes that change occurs through public acts of exemplifying homosexual normality and humanity, and assumes that America is "good" precisely because it promotes a world of individual freedom, virtue, and authenticity.

NOTES

1. The politics of normalization refers to a movement that aims at bringing the figures of the "gay man" and the "lesbian" into the mainstream of America. This means, in the first instance, that homosexuals are treated with respect and, in the eyes of the law, are first-class citizens. Normalization assumes that homosexuals share a common humanity with heterosexuals; that they share similar motivations, needs, aspirations; and so on. Normalization *also* means that homosexuals aspire to "normality" in the historically specific sense of exhibiting those traits and aspirations imagined or stipulated as normative in America, for example, gender conventionality, a couple-centered, love-based, monogamous intimacy, patriotism, and so on. The politics of normalization can take various forms from "assimilation" (and the end of a distinct sexual identity) to multicultural incorporation (the recognition of lesbians and gays as an ethnic group).

2. In order to trace civic individualism in postwar lesbian/gay politics in the United States, we focused on political discourses. Such discourses refer to elaborated accounts of the unequal social status of lesbians and gay men and proposals to bring about social change. We further circumscribed the realm of political ideas by trying, wherever possible, to attend to those discourses that have a clear connection to movement organizations. For example, our interpretation of homophile political ideas is based on an analysis of the publications of the Mattachine Society and the Daughters of Bilitis, two of the central political organizations of the 1950s and 1960s. Similarly, our view of gay liberationism relies on publications such as

Fag Rag, Gay Sunshine, or *The Furies*, which were closely linked to liberationist organizations such as the Gay Liberation Front or the Furies Collective. This strategy proved more difficult as we turned to the politics of normalization. National organizations such as the National Lesbian and Gay Task Force and Lambda Legal Defense were less connected to newspapers or magazines, which would serve as sites of ideological discussion. We take this relative absence or thinness of organizationally based discourses defending normalization as a sign that ideological debate over this politic was by and large settled by the mid- to late 1970s or at least that dissent had been effectively marginalized. For an analysis of a rights-oriented integrationist politics, we relied on an examination of the *Advocate*, especially the editorials of David Goodstein in the 1970s, since we believe he was a key bridge figure between liberationism and a normalizing politics. It was in the early to mid-1970s that the ideological clash between liberationism and its normalizing successor took place, and this clash occurred prominently in the *Advocate*. The 1990s were a period of renewed ideological contestation, in large part because of AIDS, ACT UP, and the emergence of a queer intelligentsia. We think the juxtaposition of Bawer and Vaid offers a particularly vivid illustration of that clash. Arguably, they offered the most forceful defense of each political agenda. Finally, a word on our schematic history that differentiates four phases: the homophile movement (1950s to mid-1960s), gay liberationism and lesbian-feminism (late 1960s to mid-1970s), normalizing politics (mid-1970s to 2000). We present these movement phases in a linear fashion, although they have often been parallel currents. For example, during the period of homophile politics in which individual assimilation was the goal, an ethnic minority model emphasizing group difference surfaced as an alternative political position.

3. Our research suggests that the term "compulsory heterosexuality" was first used in an editorial, "An Unmanifesto," in *Fag Rag* (1974).

REFERENCES

Adams, Barry. 1987. *The Rise of a Gay and Lesbian Movement*. New York: Twayne.

Alexander, Jeffrey. 2005. *The Meanings of Social Life*. Oxford: Oxford University Press.

————. 2007. *The Civil Sphere*. Oxford: Oxford University Press.

Alinder, Gary. 1969. "Alternative Culture." *San Francisco Free Press* (November 15–30): 10.

Anonymous. 1955a. "Editorial: An Open Letter to Mr. and Mrs. America." *Mattachine Review* 5 (July): 7.

————. 1955b. "Editorial: Answers to Questions You May Be Asking." *Mattachine Review* 1 (January–February): 2.

————. 1957. "Editorial." *Mattachine Review* 3 (July): 2.

————. 1962a. "Purpose of the Daughters of Bilitis." *The Ladder* 6 (September): 1.

————. 1962b. "Editorial." *Mattachine Review* 8 (January): 20.

————. 1969. "An Interview with New York City Liberationists." *San Francisco Free Press* (December 7–21): 5.

Armstrong, Elizabeth A. 2002. *Forging Gay identities: Organizing Sexuality in San Francisco, 1950–1994*. Chicago: University of Chicago Press.

Baker, William. 1957. "A Step towards Acceptance." *Mattachine Review* 3 (December): 14–17.

Barthes, Roland. [1970] 1974. *S/Z: An Essay*. New York: Farrar, Straus, and Giroux. Translated by Richard Miller. Paris: Editions du Seuil.

Bawer, Bruce. 1993. *A Place at the Table*. New York: Simon & Schuster.

Beam, Joseph. 1986. "Leaving the Shadow Behind." Pp. 13–18 in *In the Life*, edited by Joseph Beam. Boston: Alyson.

Benjamin, Harry. 1958. "In Time We Must Accept." *Mattachine Review* 4 (April): 4–7.

Bernstein, Mary. 1997. "Celebration and Suppression: The Strategic Uses of Identity by the Lesbian and Gay Movement." *American Journal of Sociology* 103: 531–565.

Berson, Ginny. 1972. "Editorial." *The Furies* 1 (January): 2.

Blasius, Mark, and S. Phelan, eds. 1997. *We Are Everywhere: A Historical Sourcebook of Gay and Lesbian Politics*. New York: Routledge.

Brown, Rita Mae. 1971. "Living With Other Women." *Women* 2(2): 33–34.

Bunch, Charlotte. 1972. "Lesbians in Revolt." *The Furies* 1 (January): 8–9.

Byron, Stuart. [1972] 1992. "The Closet Syndrome." Pp. 58–65 in *Out of the Closets*, edited by K. Jay and A. Young. New York: New York University Press.

Canceris, Signo. 1973. "From the Closet." *Fag Rag* 4 (January): 7.

Chasin, Alexandra. 2000. *Selling Out*. New York: Palgrave.

Chauncey, George. 2004. *Why Marriage? The History Shaping Today's Debate Over Gay Equality*. Cambridge, MA: Basic Books.

Come Out! Collective. 1969. "Editorial: Come Out!" *Come Out!* (November 14): 2.

Corber, Robert. 1997. *Homosexuality in Cold War America*. Durham, NC: Duke University Press.

Cory, Donald Webster. 1951. *The Homosexual in America*. New York: Greenberg Press.

Dansky, Steve. 1970. "Hey Man." *Come Out!* 1 (June/July): 3–4.

D'Emilio, John. 1983. *Sexual Politics, Sexual Communities*. Chicago: University of Chicago.

———. 1992. *Making Trouble: Essays on Gay History, Politics, and the University*. New York: Routledge.

Denneny, Michael. 1983. "Gay Politics: 16 Propositions." Pp. 409–424 in *The Christopher Street Reader*, edited by Michael Denneny, C. Ortleb, and T. Steele, pp. 409–424. New York: Putnam.

Dotton, Thomas. 1977. "Gay Is Straight." *Fag Rag* (Summer): 3–5.

Douglas, Mary. 1966. *Purity and Danger: An Analysis of the Concepts of Pollution and Taboo*. London: Routledge and Kegan Paul.

Duberman, Martin. 1993. *Stonewall*. New York: Penguin.

Engel, Stephen M. 2001. *The Unfinished Revolution: Social Movement Theory and the Gay and Lesbian Movement*. New York: Cambridge University Press.

Epstein, Barbara. 1994. "Anti-Communism, Homophobia, and the Construction of Masculinity in the Postwar U.S." *Critical Sociology* 20: 21–44.

Eskridge, William. 1999. *Gaylaw*. Cambridge, MA: Harvard University Press.

Fag Rag Collective. 1974. "An Unmanifesto." *Fag Rag* 6 (Fall–Winter): 14–15.

Flam, Helena, and Debra King. 2005. *Emotions and Social Movements*. New York: Routledge.

Gamson, Joshua. 1996. "Must Identity Movements Self-Destruct?: A Queer Dilemma." Pp. 395–420 in *Queer Theory/Sociology*, edited by Steven Seidman. Cambridge, MA: Blackwell.

Gilbert, Bruce M. 1976. "Coming Out 'S' In Print." *Fag Rag* (23/24): 7.

Goodstein, David. 1976. "Editorial: Opening Spaces." *The Advocate* (January 14): 5.

———. 1978. "Editorial: Opening Spaces." *The Advocate* (July 12): 15.

———. 1981. "Editorial: Opening Spaces." *The Advocate* (April 16): 6.

———. 1983. "Editorial: Opening Spaces." *The Advocate* (August 6): 6.

———. 1984. "Editorial: Opening Spaces." *The Advocate* (July 24): 6.

Grahn, Judy. 1970. "Lesbians as Bogeywomen." *Women* 1 (Summer): 36–38.

Guidry, John A., Michael D. Kennedy, and Mayer N. Zald. 2000. *Globalizations and Social Movements: Culture, Power, and the Transnational Public Sphere*. Ann Arbor: University of Michigan Press.

Harding, Carl. 1956. "Whom Should We Tell." *Mattachine Review* 2 (August): 8–12.

Hay, Harry. 1996. In *Radically Gay*, edited by Will Roscoe. Boston: Beacon Press.

Jasper, James. 1999. *The Art of Moral Protest: Culture, Biography, and Creativity in Social Movements*. Chicago: University of Chicago Press.

Jay, Karla, and A. Young, eds. 1970. *Out of the Closets*. New York: Douglas Books.

Johnson, David. 2004. *The Lavender Menace*. Chicago: University of Chicago Press.

Leroy, John. 1958. "Defeating Fear." *Mattachine Review* 4 (September): 22.

Logan, John. 1956. "You're Fired!" *Mattachine Review* 2 (June): 29.

McAdam, Doug. 1982. *Political Process and the Development of Black Insurgency, 1930–1970*. Chicago: University of Chicago Press.

Meeks, Chet, and Arlene Stein. 2006. "Refiguring the Family: Towards a Post-Queer Politics of Gay and Lesbian Marriage." Pp. 136–155 in *Intersections Between Feminist and Queer Theory*, edited by Diane Richardson, Janice McLaughlin, and Mark E. Casey. New York: Palgrave MacMillan.

Melucci, Alberto. 1996. *Challenging Codes: Collective Action in the Information Age*. Cambridge, UK: Cambridge University Press.

Michaels, Dick. 1970. "Editorial." *The Advocate* (January): 22.

Murdoch, Joyce, and D. Price. 2001. *Courting Justice: Gay Men and Lesbians v. the Supreme Court*. New York: Basic Books.

Norman, Stanley. 1959. "Whom Should We Not Tell." *Mattachine Review* 3 (May): 15–17.

Osborne, Nancy. 1957. "One Facet of Fear." *The Ladder* 1 (June): 6–7.

Penelope, Julia, and Susan Wolfe, eds. 1989. *The Original Coming Out Stories*. 2nd ed. Berkeley, CA: Crossing Press.

Pinney, Morgan. 1970. "Out of Your Closets." *Gay Sunshine* 1 (October): 13.

Polletta, Francesca. 2006. *It Was Like a Fever: Storytelling in Protest and Politics*. Chicago: University of Chicago Press.

Rimmerman, Craig. 2007. *The Lesbian and Gay Movements: Assimilation or Liberation?* Boulder, CO: Westview.

Sahlins, Marshall. 1978. *Culture and Practical Reason*. Chicago: University of Chicago Press.

Shively, Charles. 1991. "Indiscriminate Promiscuity as an Act of Revolution." Pp. 257–263 in *Gay Roots: 20 Years of Gay Sunshine*, edited by Winston Leyland. San Francisco: Gay Sunshine Press.

Silverman, Kaja. 1983. *The Subject of Semiotics*. New York: Oxford University Press.

Taylor, Verta. 1989. "Social Movement Continuity: The Women's Movement in Abeyance." *American Sociological Review* 54: 761–775.

Taylor, Verta, and Nancy Whittier. 1995. "Analytical Approaches to Social Movement Culture: The Culture of the Women's Movement." Pp. 163–187 in *Social Movements and Culture*, edited by Hank Johnston and Bert Klandermans. Minneapolis: University of Minnesota Press.

Third World Gay Revolution. 1969. "Untitled." *Come Out!* 1 (November): 16.

Vaid, Urvashi. 1995. *Virtual Equality*. New York: Doubleday.

Valocchi, Steve. 1999. "The Class-Inflected Nature of Gay Identity." *Social Problems* 46: 207–224.

Whittier, Nancy. 2002. "Persistence and Transformation: Gloria Steinem, the Women's Action Alliance, and the Feminist Movement, 1971–1997." *Journal of Women's History* 14: 148–150.

Woodhull, Jennifer. 1972. "Darers Go First." *The Furies* 1 (June/July): 2–3.

Young, Ian. 1976. "Closet Wrecking." *Gay Sunshine* 28 (Spring): 25.

Zeff, Leo. 1958. "Self Acceptance v. Rejection." *Mattachine Review* 5 (May): 4–9.

PART VIII

TRAUMA AS CULTURE

RETHINKING CONFLICT AND COLLECTIVE MEMORY: THE CASE OF NANKING

BARRY SCHWARTZ

Collective memory is reputed to be an ambiguous and complex concept (Olick and Robbins 1998; Olick 2008; Roediger and Wertsch 2008); in fact, no concept is clearer or simpler. Memory is a fundamental property of the human mind, an indispensable component of culture, and an essential aspect of tradition. Mind, culture, and tradition are, indeed, inconceivable without memory. Although individuals alone possess the capacity to contemplate the past, they never do so singly (Schwartz and Schuman 2005); they do so with and against others situated in different groups and through the knowledge and symbols that predecessors and contemporaries transmit to them (Schwartz 2001, 2007). Collective memory therefore refers to the *distribution* throughout society of what individuals believe, feel, and know about the past, how they judge the past morally, and how closely they identify with it. That every distribution has a central tendency means that a total dissensual memory is impossible; but the very existence of a distribution means there can be no total consensus. Also, when these distributions reappear in samples composed of individuals unknown to one another, they must be treated as "social facts" (Durkheim [1895]1982) that are independent of the persons they comprise.

Understandings of the past, moreover, are not randomly distributed through society; different groupings, organizations, and institutions have elective affinities for different remembrances. Max Weber refers to these as "carrier strata" whose social role is to propagate their ideas and to disparage those of others.

Two perspectives, each based on unique premises about power, distortion, and objectivity, have guided the study of conflict and collective memory. The most widely held is "the politics of memory," which assumes that power legitimates itself by determining what we remember and forget. A second perspective proceeds from the assumption that conflict is a process involving attributions of credit and blame. These two perspectives—the first structural; the second, psychological—lead to two very different views of how history and memory interact.

This case study explores the politics of memory and attribution theory through expert and popular beliefs in Japan about the 1937–1938 Nanking Massacre. Japanese debate over Nanking is a useful case because it is highly politicized, transparent, and involves participants ideologically committed to competing historical narratives.

The first part of this chapter examines the assumptions of the politics of memory and attribution theory; in the second part, the two theories are reviewed in light of Japan's Nanking debates. The final section generalizes what has been learned, specifying what new understandings of Nanking add to the existing body of collective memory scholarship.

Politics of Memory

Conceived as a product of political conflict, memory assumes pluralistic and centralized forms. The fate of artistic and presidential reputations, Holocaust commemoration, place-naming, monument-making, and the organization of museums show how multiple memories emerge out of a context of cross-cutting interests, coalitions, power networks, and enterprises (Tuchman and Fortin 1989; Wagner-Pacifici and Schwartz 1991; Barthel 1996; Fine 2001). Memory works differently in its centralized form: Historians and commemorative elites create hegemonic narratives and symbols to manipulate the loyalty of the masses (Abercrombie, Hill, and Turner 1980; Gillis 1994).

Beliefs that serve a group interest and also happen to be *true* are anomalies, given the politics of memory's premises. Conservative agents supposedly fabricate a past that sustains existing power distributions; liberal agents challenge fixed views of the past. Counterhistory and countermemory, based on new moods rather than new data, took root in the ideologically sensitive 1980s. In an age of ideologies, according to Arnoldo Momigliano (1984), "an increasing proportion of historical research is made in the form of rhetorical and ideological analysis...while the interpretation of old facts is more frequent than the discovery of new facts" (pp. 495–496). In this context, established ideas about what *constitutes* a past are challenged. New ideas, based on the egalitarian principle of multiple perspectives and power in the service of diversity, are transparent ways of claiming that good history centers on discoveries of suffering and excluded minorities (Schlesinger 1992) and is represented in general museum display and specialized sites like the National Museum of the American Indian, the National Museum of African American History and Culture, the United States Holocaust Memorial, and the proposed national women's and Latino history museums. The problem with such minority platforms is not that they tell painful truths about history; the problem is that, given liberal premises, what is not painful is often not worth remembering, often not worth investigating—and often not true.

That good history means the acknowledgment of past crimes and recognition of diversity is a manifesto set forth in bad faith. No museum or university is interested in teaching the perspectives of race supremacists, although they do not hesitate to include in their cultural diversity programs the ideology of radical Islam or even justifications of jihadism.[1] The internment of Japanese American citizens, a Smithsonian Museum favorite, is not contextualized by information on the size of the intelligence network that Japan had established during the 1930s on the West coast; it is unaccompanied by exhibits of Japanese massacres of American and allied prisoners of war, or information about the relatively small proportion of prisoners surviving Japanese captivity (Chambers 1999:560–561).

Museums embody cultural power, and power, according to Michel Foucault (1975), determines memory; further, "if one controls people's memory, one controls their dynamism" (p. 25). Four prominent works exemplify this point. For Eric Hobsbawm (1983), the void left by the late-nineteenth-century decline of authoritarian regimes led to invented traditions to sustain order in the face of democratic reforms. Likewise, John Bodnar (1992) explains that commemorative resources have always been controlled by a dominant stratum (Protestant middle-class businessmen in the nineteenth century; professionals, editors, and government officials in the twentieth) whose official "programmers" seek to promote loyalty to the state and its leaders.

Official programmers have their work cut out for them. Richard Handler (in Gillis' [1994] *Commemorations*) explains the dilemma. Collective identities are consecrated by hegemonizing myths, but what of oppressed minorities that have profitably created their own myths and new identities? Handler is remarkably candid. He wants to "make sure our critiques of identity focus on those mainstream claims that too often go unchallenged. Rather than writing exclusively of the 'invention' of minority identities, traditions, and cultures, we can turn our attention to the ways in which the majority or mainstream is itself continually reconstructed" (p. 38). To reveal "oppressors'" fictions while ignoring the fictions of their "victims" is Handler's project.

Handler openly converts social science into political advocacy. Maria Sturken is subtler. "Cultural memory is a field of cultural negotiation through which different stories vie for a place in history" (p. 1). In her effort to build on Foucault, she turns to the 1991 Gulf War, explaining that the United States attacked Iraq in order to test new weapons and assert its post-Cold War dominance (p. 124). That Iraq conquered and raped Kuwait, had poised troops to attack Saudi Arabia, and threatened the oil supply of poor countries, as well as rich ones, are unmentioned.

Deep similarity exists among the liberal "thought styles" (Fleck [1935] 1979) of Eric Hobsbawm, John Bodnar, Richard Handler, and Marita Sturken. All show that the victims of state power are the weak and vulnerable—double-losers because their oppression (never their wrongdoings or gains) is factual and because earlier historians and media have ignored their plight. Roy Rosenzweig and David Thelen's *The Presence of the Past* (1998) reproduces this logic. Their telephone surveys show that family history is more relevant to most people than national history, but many family members discuss national events and individual experiences in terms of one another. Parents, when asked what their children should learn about the past, are twice as likely to name American history as family history. Rosenzweig and Thelen dismiss this answer as "blandness" and "prepackaged civic ideology," reflecting "obligation rather than conviction" (pp. 128–129). What is not prepackaged, or how to tell the prepackaged from the unprepackaged, is left to the reader's imagination. Neither African American nor Native American historical understanding is dismissed as "prepackaged" or "bland." Mexican American citizens are much less likely to define themselves as victims and more inclined to embrace the "pious," "nation-centered accounts" of American history. Why so? Fear of deportation is the only reason Rosenzweig and Thelen can fathom. Because such a fear can apply only to *illegal* immigrants, the authors exaggerate their presence in the survey in order to explain the embarrassing presence of a patriotic minority.

These recent exercises in collective memory—and many more could be cited (including Handler and Linnekin 1984 and Alonso 1988)—reflect powerfully the Gramscian and "dominant ideology" (Abercrombie, Hill, and Turner 1980) conceptions of culture, and they are energized by a multicultural, victim-centered bent of mind. But if multiculturalism grants to every community the past it wants, the result is never tranquility, for there is always a community to dispute what others claim.

Focusing on and giving "voice" to "petit narratives" (Lyotard 1984), especially those of minorities who would be otherwise written out of history, politics of memory theories set up a competitive system between admirers and critics of national legacies. These theories, inspired by multiculturalism, are beset by contradiction. They imply the elite can only exploit, never assist, the masses, exaggerate the difficulty of knowing the past, and press too far the claim that perception of the past is rooted in present interests and experience. Overestimating dissensus, they assume that conflict is the natural state of society. Strong ideological leanings make the liberal elite theoretically schizoid: They are positivist when addressing mainstream society's sins (facts about atrocities committed against African Americans are taken for granted) and constructionist when addressing mainstream society's virtues (facts about Henry Ford's accomplishments are "constructions" designed to make us love capitalism).

The politics of memory provides a rich view of the symbolic objects (books, films, monuments, etc.) that subordinate memory to political power, but it fails to clarify how these objects perform their function, which includes self-serving distortion of reality, and why some representations of the past are accepted while others are rejected. The merit of the attribution theory of memory conflict turns on precisely these issues.

CONFLICTING ATTRIBUTIONS

Conflicting historical understandings are based on conflicting attributions. Attribution theory, as Fiske and Taylor (1991) describe it, "deals with how the social perceiver uses information to arrive at causal explanations for events. It examines what information is gathered and how it is combined to form a causal judgment" (p. 23). Many versions of attribution theory exist, each addressed, in its own way, to a particular domain of activity.[2] In the domain of collective memory, attributions are pivotal because so many historians and commemorative agents sympathize with or despise the very groups they contemplate. The concept of "political correctness" manifests this tendency, which includes causal attributions that exaggerate minority group virtue, suffering, and achievement and/or obfuscate responsibility for wrongdoing. Political correctness is the opposite of ethnocentric distortion, which stereotypes out-group members negatively; in-group members, positively.

At the national level, most conflict involves the exertions of the ideological left and right. Throughout the first three-quarters of the twentieth century, leftist resistance to injustice and indignity manifested itself in great acts of courage, but left-thinking people not only champion the cause of the weak and oppressed; they need the weak and oppressed to realize their own sense of who they are. Defending the oppressed, then, is not a means but an end in itself, the raison d'être of leftist existence. To this end, cases of real minority oppression are very often exaggerated.[3]

Maintaining unconditional compassion for victims requires nimble thinking: Some information must be exaggerated; some ignored; certain conventions for determining causation and responsibility must be suspended; new ways of attributing motives must be found; innovative approaches to understanding aggression and defense must be concocted. So far as left-leaning observers treat minorities as "protected groups," they cannot formulate explanations implying blame. Left observers require "external" or "structural" explanations of minority groups' wrongdoing (e.g., oppression, deprivation of opportunity, humiliation, injustice) and avoid "internal" or "dispositional" explanations that relate the conduct of the protected to personality and the internalized values of their culture (Rotter 1966; Felson 1991).

Right-leaning observers, in contrast, are more likely than the left to defend the conventions, representatives, and projects of the "dominant" majority. To realize their interests, the right applies structural (external) reasons for majority vices and psychological (internal) reasons for their virtues. That the attitude of the right is the "traditional" or what may seem the "natural attitude" is suggested by experiments demonstrating that people tend to account for in-group vices and virtues by external and internal explanation, respectively; out-group vices and virtues by the opposite rule (see, e.g., McArthur and McDougall 1995; Klein and Licatta 2001; Khan and Liu 2008). In recent years, psychologists sensitive to differences in cultural values have accumulated evidence showing, at the individual level, that East Asia's collectivist values, concern for interdependence, and harmony within society incline individuals to withhold self-serving attributions, but self-serving bias against out-groups and foreign nations is the rule (Muramoto and Yamaguchi 1997; Ma and Karasawa 2006).

Conceiving conflict in collective memory as a process of competing *attributions* allows us to drop the misleading *power* assertion.[4] If collective memory reflects conflict and power, it does so only by way of the attribution of credit and blame.[5]

In credit and blame analysis (Felson 1991), a theory is judged in terms of its implications for the group that the analyst wishes to protect. The Japanese left rejects theories that attribute their forebears' atrocities to external sources of motivation—provocation, fatigue, casualties, inadequate supplies, poor leadership. Conservatives emphasize precisely these factors and reject theories that attribute Japanese atrocities to an internalized culture of violence, love of aggression, contempt for Chinese inferiority, and disposition toward cruelty. Successful blame analysis, then, represents itself as a value-neutral causal theory; in fact, it does not identify the cause of an event but rather accepts or rejects causes depending on their implications for the esteem and identity of a protected group.[6]

Because liberal-conservative tension is grounded in irreconcilable attribution principles, memory wars, although variable in intensity, are long-lasting. During the late twentieth and early twenty-first centuries, Western memory wars, an aspect of Western "culture wars" (Hunter 1991; Himmelfarb 1999), intensified as minorities' spokespersons, in many important arenas, successfully challenged official (allegedly hegemonic) narratives—some true; some false. In these times, the theory of the politics of memory, already matured, became the dominant branch of collective memory scholarship. Politics of memory studies are typically binary: They distinguish between the memories of center and periphery, dominant and subordinate, authority and revisionist, us and them, elite and public—with the former member of each pair determining the latter's content. The tone of this scholarship ascribes disproportionate credence to minority memories, which are construed to be a form of resistance to tyranny of the majority. Conservatives, for their part, champion the majorities (to whom liberals refer disdainfully as society's "dominant" stratum), exaggerating their accomplishments and minimizing their wrongdoing.

The politics of memory is a special case of attribution theory. Many cases exist in which power fails to shape memory's content; no cases exist in which attribution fails to play a part. The politics of memory derives from attribution process because its key concepts—hegemony, construction, legitimation—result from the way credit and blame are applied. Thus, liberals and conservatives alike apportion credit and blame, reward and punishment, admiration and censure according to the same attribution principles. Power can make attributions credible, but it cannot explain why or how they are devised

Unless power is absolute, credit and blame cannot be attributed any way one pleases. Neither political nor cultural elites can say what they want about the past because others, including reliable eyewitnesses, will challenge them. Michael Schudson (1992:208–211) believes this competitive process works best within liberal democracies; yet, the claims of a given authoritarian state, although not successfully opposed from within, are challenged by other states making competing claims.

Whether claim-makers are individuals or states, conflict inevitably adds the issue of objectivity to the issue of credit and blame. If we cannot know the past as it was, we cannot know how, or whether, a given attribution distorts or affirms it. Conflicting narratives are the principal means for this determination.

Everyone makes sense of experience by translating it into narratives (MacIntyre 1989:138–157). Narrative genres—including *tragic* and *mimetic* (of which more will be said later)—provide templates that define the significance of evidence (Smith 2005). However, James Gustafson insists that narratives, whatever their genre or function, "need to be checked against facts and figures and political analysis" (cited in Hauerwas and Jones 1989). Alasdair MacIntyre (1989), too, considers "degenerate" any research tradition that has "contrived a set of epistemological defences which enable it to avoid...recognizing that it is being put in question by rival traditions" (p. 147). MacIntyre concedes, however, that without omissions of truth and inclusions of falsehood, many narratives would not work. To determine whether narratives are autonomous myths or the products of real events is thus a longstanding problem.

Two theoretical approaches to conflict and collective memory are now distinguishable. The first relates history and memory to power struggles; the second subsumes these struggles under conflicting causal attributions. The question is what this relation adds to the understanding of real events. Can the study of such events lead to a synthetic theory that integrates the claims of power and attribution, or does a single, unifying element exist beneath both? Conflict over what happened in Nanking, China's capital, in late 1937 will be the case in point. The Nanking Massacre is a good specimen because the conflict over its volume and nature is intense, data-driven, and relevant to the national identities of both the Chinese and Japanese people.

Nanking Debate

The Japanese are widely believed to be reluctant to discuss their country's role in World War II. Charles Maier's (2000) thoughtful comparison of postwar Japan and Germany makes this belief plausible, but his qualification of Germany's repentance is more informed than his qualification of Japan's nonrepentance. In fact, the Japanese now discuss the war openly. Unlike some European countries, where denial of Holocaust atrocities is a crime, Japanese conservatives assert their point of view within a legal environment of free speech, without fear of imprisonment. Informed challenges to beliefs about atrocity sharpen debate and lead to a truer appraisal than if they were prohibited and punished. Such has not always been the case.

Between 1945 and 1972, the Japanese people felt *themselves* victims of the devastating war their government had started. Beginning in 1972, when Japan and China normalized diplomatic relations, left politicians tried but failed to catch up with new opinion by convincing their government to recognize the suffering Japan had caused.[7]

Not until the 1982 textbook controversy did the Nanking Massacre become an object of official concern (Penney 2008). In the 1990s, debate began. The number of books on Nanking published in Japanese roughly indexes the excitement. Between 1940 and 1979, a forty-year period, the Worldcat archive indicates a total of 8 books published—an average of two per decade. During the 1980s, 30 books appeared: 26 during or after 1982, the year of the "Textbook Incident." In the 1990s, 55 books appeared: 39 during or after 1995, the fiftieth anniversary of the end of World War II. The total for 2000–2009, based on annual means for the first seven years, is 67 books.[8] In addition to the Nanking book explosion, new topics—including comfort women; prime ministers visiting the notorious Yasukuni Shrine, which honors war criminals among ordinary soldiers, and the wartime role of Hirohito—became controversial. Iris Chang's (1998) book, detailing Nanking victims' accounts, became an American best-seller and stirred international indignation.

In Japan, the Nanking case divides liberal and conservative thought collectives (Fleck [1935] 1979), each gathering and analyzing large quantities of information. Out of the process emerged a centrist collective producing a third body of knowledge. From this triadic structure, which is based largely on *primary data*, arise my conclusions.[9]

Context

No discussion of the Nanking Massacre makes sense apart from the total wartime devastation. Japanese atrocities defy description, far transcending Nanking; they include biological experimentation on human beings, chemical weapons, torture, slave labor, rape, forced prostitution, looting. Above all were mass killings, including the bayoneting and beheading of civilians and prisoners of war. In one single killing factory, the Unit 731 biological experiment station, where human subjects were injected with lethal bacterial and other agents, 300,000 died. Biological weapons killed more than 200,000 (Chang and Barker 2003).

The war's casualty counts signify the misery caused by Japan's military. China, with its 20 million dead, suffered the greatest loss. In Indonesia, the war caused the death of 4 million; in India, 1.6 million; in French Indochina, 1 million. When violence against the Burmese, Koreans, Malayans, Filipinos, Micronesians, Timorese, Singaporese, and Thai are included, the total death count reaches almost 28 million.[10]

In light of the massive suffering caused by the Japanese, it seems trivial to focus on a single event, and many observers have said as much—largely because one event diverts attention from the larger atrocity. But Nanking is "good to think with"; conflict over what happened in that one city reflects efforts to comprehend the very meaning of being Japanese, to define ultimate human rights and responsibilities, and to know the world that Japanese power had destroyed. What is a nation to do with the fact that its forebears caused so much destruction, so much grief?

Memories of misconduct influence most when carried by influential groups. This chapter's opening section drew attention to the existence of such "carrier" groups, namely, institutions, organizations, communities, and other groupings whose function is to interpret, preserve, and propagate memory of a given event—in this case, the Nanking Massacre. Such groups (for a typology, see Schluchter 1989:96–99) are versions of the moral and reputational entrepreneurs (Becker [1963] 1997:147–64; Lang and Lang 1991; Fine 2001:60–94) who have a stake in cultivating or discrediting the reputation of favored or disdained individuals. Three carrier groups participate in the Nanking memory war: (1) the maximalists, composed of moderate and radical liberals who attribute causes that emphasize their forebears' wrongdoing; (2) revisionists—strong and extreme conservatives who attribute causes that emphasize their forebears' virtue and minimize blame for atrocities; and (3) centrists, including moderate liberals and conservatives who, unlike their maximalist and revisionist colleagues, are unattached to organizations of like-minded analysts and deliberately detach implications of blame from their conclusions. Thus, memory wars involve not only causal and blame attribution but also casualty estimates, narrative genres, connection to or independence of organized intellectual and political communities. Assessment of each group's premises, analysis, and conclusions clarifies the relation among power, attribution, and memory.

Maximalists

Katsuichi Honda's *Travels in China* (1971), a series for the *Asahi Shimbun* newspaper, published later as a book (1999), was the first hint of an impending public debate. Honda, a well-known journalist of the left and longtime critic of Japan's moral shortcomings, interviewed one hundred Chinese survivors of World War II and reported their accounts of Japanese cruelty. Shichihei Yamamoto attacked the *Asahi Shimbun* newspaper's serialized version of Honda's book, which included a fictional account of the "One-Hundred Man Killing Contest."[11] Honda's repetition of this myth made him vulnerable to criticism, as did his belief that Hirohito was a war criminal who should have been tried by the Tokyo Tribunal.[12] The essence of his exposé, however, was valid and won supporters.

Honda introduced his witnesses, one by one, describing their stories of the killing of innocent civilians by gunshot and bayonet. He documented the disappearance of entire families, the terror of arbitrary bloodlust. He showed a defeated army abandoned by its own leaders and a conquering army allowed by its leaders to murder and rape at will. He revealed commanders ordering soldiers to execute prisoners of war in open fields and along river banks. He recorded Westerners' efforts to protect civilians by pleading with generals and diplomats at Japan's embassy.

Honda's narrative is *tragic*. The basics of tragedy, according to Philip Smith, comprise

> the futility of human striving, including the striving for self-preservation, the horror of suffering, the disintegration of society, and the movement from social integration to social isolation and atomization. In effect, things go horribly wrong.... The object of struggle is often an innocent and largely passive victim who has been sadly let down by the poor decisions, bad luck and evil doing of others. (p. 23)

To say that Honda gave his countrymen a tragic vision of Nanking is to say he gave them a narrative of what atrocities were committed in Nanking, who caused them, and how. Doing so, he challenged his countrymen by contrasting Nanking's fate with their own ideals.

However, if Nanking was "the forgotten Holocaust," as Iris Chang declared, few countries forgot more completely than China. Between 1946 and 1982, a thirty-six-year period, Jeffrey Alexander and Rui Gao (2007) found only fifteen articles in which the key words "Nanking Massacre" appeared in the Chinese *People's Daily*.[13] Not until 1979, as Xiaohong Xu and Lyn Spillman (2009) demonstrate, did Chinese middle school textbooks, for political reasons, begin briefly to mention Nanking.

Extreme Japanese claims accelerated the rise of Nanking in Chinese consciousness during the 1970s. Many maximalists accepted the Nationalist government's (1945) estimate of 430,000 Nanking deaths.[14] Akira Fujiwara, a leftist Japanese historian, believed his forebears murdered 300,000. Tomio Hora, a moderate maximalist, calculated 150,000 to 300,000 deaths; Kasahara Tokushi, author of *One Hundred Days in the Nanking Safety Zone* and one of the original members of the Research Committee on the Nanking Incident, an organization formed to fight the massacre deniers, estimated between 100,000 and 200,000 killed in Nanking and its six counties between December 4, 1937, and March 28, 1938—a four-month period (Yamamoto 2000:254; Yoshida 2006:138).

Maximalists work with data ranging from the International Military Tribunal for the Far East (IMFTE), which estimated 200,000 illegal deaths, to the *Ch'ung shan-t'ang*, a charitable organization whose estimate of buried bodies ranged from 30,000 to 100,000. The IMFTE and *Ch'ung shan-t'ang* figures are inconsistent, probably because the former are exaggerated; the latter, forged. The more dependable records of the Red Swastika Society, a Chinese charitable organization using the Buddhist/Hindu swastika symbol, indicate 38,000–42,000 burials.

The main issue separating maximalists from their right-wing challengers, however, is the execution of civilians, which Askew (2007) estimates at approximately 3,266 (p. 102), and the execution of prisoners of war and "plain clothes soldiers" (many of whom were armed). Liberals consider prisoner of war executions illegal; moderate conservative revisionists rarely question their legality. Extreme conservatives openly declare that Japan's limited force made these executions necessary (Yamamoto 2000:254).

Although maximalists undertake no systematic analyses of what caused the Japanese army to act as brutally as it did, their beliefs are clear. They see Nanking as one phase of a continual campaign of atrocity, and they believe conditions unique to the city cannot explain the brutality that occurred within it. Japan's culture of racism and aggressiveness were the strong links of the causal chain (Honda 1993:47–126). Fujiwara is certain that early denials of the Nanking Incident were connected to both the central command's ordering the murder of prisoners of war and the postwar yearning of Japan's right wing to restore early-twentieth-century militarism. Maximalist analysis, thus, focuses on the atrocity's internal, not structural, causes, locating, by implication, Japanese blame in Japanese ruthlessness (Honda 1993, 1999). Fujiwara (1997), in particular, names five internal causes leading to the massacre: (1) officers' faith in an irrational "fighting spirit"; (2) military training that made officers contemptuous of international laws governing war; (3) inadequate training, including failure to suppress recruits' personal motives; (4) a resulting decline of discipline and soldiers' ignorance of the broader purpose for which they were fighting (cited in Takuji 2007). Among Chinese historians, however—and almost without exception—the Nanking Massacre was "a major display and act of Japanese militarist *bushido* spirit" (Yang 2001:73).

In the late 1990s, a fresh analysis of qualitative data appeared in English. Iris Chang, a Chinese American educated in journalism, was inspired to write about Nanking because her own grandparents had escaped from the city and told her stories about what they had seen. Her book is based largely on survivor interviews and secondary sources chosen to suit her beliefs.

Chang's logic is as problematic as her sampling. Extrapolating the number of deaths in a six-week period to four years, the approximate duration of the Jewish Holocaust, she concludes that Nanking, on a per diem basis, was comparable in severity." She was also less than meticulous. The Japanese publisher, distinguished for its careful editing and translation, presented Chang with a long list of factual errors, which she refused to correct. A long controversy led to the cancellation of her book contract. Many neutral and highly informed American historians[15] found the book to be wanting, but Chang wrote it to inform the public, not to advance Asian studies. *The Rape of Nanking: The Forgotten Holocaust of World War II* (1997) was an immediate sensation.

Despite its bias and abundant errors, including the uncritical acceptance of the People's Republic's death estimate and serious inflation of the number of civilian casualties, Chang reinforces Honda's tragic narrative by elaborating its fundamentals. Her book does not center on fatality counts but on the life of ordinary people during six weeks of Japanese barbarism. Her respondents, like Honda's twenty-five years earlier, recounted the aerial bombardments; mass killings of prisoners of war, alternately by machine gun, sword, and pistol. Some of Chang's other reports are controversial: live burials; mutilation (the excision of body parts by sword and knife); the setting of human beings on fire; turning loose of hungry dogs on helpless crowds; rapes followed by shooting and mutilation, including the insertion of bamboo poles into victims' vaginas. One need not tarry over the validity of this or that testimony; the magnitude of the accumulated cruelty, however great Chang's exaggerations, is convincing and unforgettable.

John Rabe (1998) was no historian, but his diary, which Chang discovered, provided the single most compelling eyewitness account of the Nanking Incident. A German representative of the Siemens Company, Nazi party member, and director of the International Committee of the Nanking Safety Zone (ICNSZ), Rabe had been in close and regular contact with the Japanese military and in a position to describe its atrocities in detail. The ICNSZ was located in the area containing most of Nanking's embassies and large institutions—local and foreign-supported hospitals, foreign businesses, universities, and municipal service units. The zone was considered neutral by its residents and most of Nanking's population, a large proportion of which took refuge there. The Chinese and Japanese military, however, routinely violated its neutrality. Rabe's diary accounts of soldiers running amok could not be more harrowing, and nothing in it suggests that unique circumstances forced the Japanese to do what they did. Mid-level officers' failure to command and control their troops enabled the latter to follow their own inclinations, which included looting and rape. Rabe's analysis is less gripping than Chang's, but its scope is wider; its documentation, more certain.

Chang and Rabe prompted a backlash on the Japanese right. "In recent years," observed Tokushi (2001), "more books questioning the massacre have been published [in Japan] than those confirming the facts of the incident" (cited in Askew 2002:12). Iris Chang, despite her raising consciousness of the Nanking massacre in the United States, had a devastating effect on the maximalist project in Japan. Her exaggerations, open contempt for the Japanese people, attribution of the massacre's causes to their inner character, refusal to correct errors, and, of equal if not greater importance, her statue, which stands prominently in Nanking, China outside the Nanking Memorial, led Japan's maximalists into the peculiar position of arguing against their most influential Western spokesperson.

Maximalism, however, transcends the activity of any one of its members. Institutionalized through special-purpose organizations, their views are *sui generis*. In the post-World War II years emerged the Japan Teachers Union; Association for History Educators (1949); Association for Japan-China Friendship (1950); Association for Preserving Peace (1950), and Returnees from China (1957)—former prisoners of war, unharmed by the Chinese, who condemned Japan's atrocities out of a debt of gratitude to their former captors. After 1990, the very period in which Japanese surveys showed a dramatic increase in both critical attitudes toward the war and friendly attitudes toward Japan's neighbors, at least ten maximalist groups formed, including the Society to Support the Demands of Chinese War Victims (1995). These groups were supported by sister organizations outside Japan, such as the Global Alliance for Preserving the History of World War II in Asia. As these and other maximalist bodies disseminated their findings, they hosted numerous international conferences on Nanking. If such efforts had not been effectively opposed, however, we would have a weaker grasp of the truth.

Revisionists

The revisionist school consists largely of conservative academics, politicians, and ideologues publishing in popular magazines, conservative newspapers, and books. The most extreme revisionists believe the Nanking Massacre to be a left-wing fantasy, and among these, Shudo Higashinakano is most representative (Tokushi 2007:304–329). A former student of social thought, he established the Japan Nanking Studies Association at Asia University, a center of conservative and reactionary activity. Asia University was founded in 1955 by a prewar ultranationalist and wartime minister of education arrested for war crimes but released and denied future government positions. Its board of directors in the late 1990s was chaired by a former general in charge of tactical military planning in China. Higashinakano denies that any illegal killings occurred, and his vision is dramatized in a (2008) film titled *The Truth about Nanking*.

Higashinakano's fatality estimates are totally wrong, but the structure of his argument exemplifies the revisionist case. Where maximalists present their case in the form of a tragic narrative, extreme revisionists find no tragedy to report, little or no blame to be attributed. Japanese forces committed blameworthy actions because of circumstances beyond their control, including the illegal tactics of Chinese officers and soldiers, which is why Higashinakano and other revisionists tend to present their narrative in an impersonal and passive voice. Furthermore, Higashinakano proceeds not with case studies of suffering but methodological principles. First, one must begin with an assumption of innocence, not guilt. Because the Nanking Massacre never happened, the burden of proof is on those who claim it did. Second, validity can only be established by interconnected proofs: If one part of a claim is disproven, the entire claim must be rejected.

Higashinakano confronts the maximalists one point at a time. He asks how many Chinese died during and after the battle of Nanking. If 300,000 died, where are their corpses? Rabe's diary indicates 5000 burials in the month of February 1938; the Red Swastika Society, a total of 30,000. Without explaining why, Higashinakano (2002) declares the Red Swastika's comprehensive number to be "inflated" and endorses Rabe's partial figure (p. 99). Both figures omit the thousands executed and deposited into the Yangtze River.

How many prisoners of war were executed? International law, set down in the Le Hague Regulations of 1907, defines a belligerent to be a fighter under the command of a superior. He must be in uniform, carrying weapons openly and conducting combat operations legally. Because Chinese commanders fled to escape the Japanese army's advance, soldiers got into civilian dress and concealed their weapons, rendering themselves illegal combatants. Unprotected by Le Hague, they were fair game. Recognizing that only legal combatants could be "executed," even foreign journalists reported that Chinese prisoners were "slain" or "killed." By implication, they acknowledged Japan's right to eliminate illegal uniformed and plainclothes soldiers (Higashinakano 2002:102).

Higashinakano (2002) goes further. He believes no mass murder of civilians occurred in Nanking, and he indicates that a principal source of statistics, the Documents of the Nanking Safety Zone, provides no information on the total number of civilians illegally killed; "Therefore, I think that there were two or three cases of murder in Nanking" (p. 107). He draws on the same non-sequitur, and the same premises, in his account of rape.

In cases where data are available, imperfections render them useless. For example, Miner Bates, an American professor at Nanking University, reports from burial statistics that "close to forty thousand unarmed persons were killed within and near the walls of Nanking, of whom some 30 percent had never been soldiers." How could Bates partition his data so finely when the Red Swastika Society made no military-civilian distinction in its records? Any honest observer is forced to the conclusion that only soldiers were buried (Higashinakano 2002:110).

The Chinese themselves confirm Higashinakano's argument. Chiang-Kai shek's propaganda machine said nothing about Nanking; it emphasized Japan's poison gas and air attacks on civilians. The Communists, likewise, said nothing about Nanking in their wartime newspapers (Alexander and Gao 2007). They ignored Nanking because nothing unusual happened there.

If the maximalist narrative evokes Northrop Frye's conception of tragedy, the revisionist template is *low mimetic*, the term "mimetic" being based on Greek for "copy" or "realist representation." In the low mimetic mode, all characters, Japanese and Chinese alike, are morally similar; each side acts rationally, if not successfully. Low mimesis is a mundane narrative based on bureaucratic criteria of efficiency. Its discourse is low-key, void of moral passion. But the adjective in *low* mimesis suggests a vertical continuum of mimetic templates. Smith's (2007) adaptation of Frye's low mimesis is most applicable to Higashinakano's writing because no particular moral informs his story; no one theme ties everything together. Low mimesis, as Smith defines it, "sits very uncomfortably with military action because it does not provide a convincing and legitimate justification for blood sacrifice" (p. 25). Low mimesis resonates weakly with slaughter because it evokes none of the ideals, feelings, or moral sentiments that would motivate it. Higashinakano's low-mimetic account does not even condemn the Chinese "enemy"; he only attacks critics whom he believes dwell on a situation that never existed. Higashinakano, like other Nanking deniers, claims that Nanking stories are not even hyperbole; they are illusions.

Revisionists who recognize that a massacre occurred in Nanking are represented by the works of Tadao Takimoto and Yasuo Ohara (*Japan's Rebuttal to China's Forged Claims,* 2000) and Masaaki Tanaka (*What Really Happened in Nanking: Refutation of a Common Myth,* 2000). Tanaka had attended the funeral of Central China commander General Matsui Iwane, hanged in 1948 by the Tokyo Tribunal. He condemns his forebears for surrendering after Nagasaki and regularly expresses his hatred of the West. He believes in the legality of executing prisoners of war, but he counters inflated death statistics with Lewis Smythe's household survey, which listed 2136 dead, 2745 injured, and 4200 (probably war prisoners) "taken away" (Yoshida 2006:51–52). Cartoonist Yoshinori Kobayashi, for his part, believes that much of the evidence on which the maximalists depend is hearsay. He concludes that the number of massacre victims was about 10,000. Tadao Takemoto, a professor of French literature, and Yasuo Ohara, a Shinto scholar, concede that atrocities happened, but they believe China inflated the number of Nanking deaths in order to drive a wedge between Japan and the United States. They estimate 10,000 deaths, which is in line with other revisionist counts, including textbook revisionist Nobukatsu Fujioka's 10,000.

All revisionist estimates exclude prisoners of war. The Chinese surrendered in massive numbers, and by allowing them to live, Fujioka and others believe, the Japanese would have put themselves in danger (Yoshida 2006:145). The prisoner of war narrative is low mimetic because it describes rational conflict. Rational? Ten thousand executions in one city? *C'est la guerre.*

Revisionist deniers and minimizers of the Nanking atrocity have two further things in common: Not only do both exclude prisoners of war from their atrocity estimates; both denounce Japan's "masochistic" history textbooks and resent Japan-bashing by other nations. A kind of paranoid streak runs through their discourse. Given the universal hatred of Japan, opposition to maximalism is imperative: "If we remain silent," television executive Satoru Mizushima declares, "anti-Japanese propaganda will speed across the world" (Yoshida 2006).

Shortcomings in the maximalists' argument strengthen the revisionists'. The initial population of Nanking was one million, but 80 percent abandoned the city after Japanese bombing began, leaving 200,000 behind. The number of illegal killings, therefore, could have been nowhere near the typical maximalist count of 300,000. The 200,000 who remained could not afford to leave the city, and after it fell to the Japanese army, almost all took up residence in the Nanking Safety Zone (12.5 percent of the city's area, which afforded considerable if not total protection. (For detail, see Askew 2007.)

Japan's brutality must not prevent us from asking whether its wrongdoing has been exaggerated by the left. Nationalist China's massacre claim appeared long after the war ended, and international discussion began only after China complained about it for political reasons in 1982. Victim counts presented at the various war crimes trials were notoriously padded by prosecutors, while many photos exhibited in Chinese museums and Iris Chang's book are famous forgeries.

Maximalists also ignored the context of the battle for Nanking, and by doing so, they produce what Clifford Geertz (1974) would call a "thin description." The result: excessive blame on the Japanese. Ill-conceived logistics forced the Japanese to live off the land and to pillage. The assault on Nanking itself was long and difficult, and history shows that atrocities are common after costly sieges. Although Nanking was indefensible and constituted a natural trap for the Chinese army, Chiang-Kai shek refused to surrender peacefully; in fact, he decided to use an already worn-out army in a fight to the death in house-to-house warfare. His special "battle encouragement" forces not only killed soldiers unwilling to throw themselves against the Japanese; they brought wounded soldiers into the city to die In the chaos of retreat, surviving Chinese soldiers committed rape and pillage. The Chinese army even insisted on building defenses within the International Safety Zone, which rendered its inhabitants military targets. After Nanking fell to a relatively small and tired Japanese force, tens of thousands of Chinese soldiers discarded their uniforms (which the Japanese counted) and then merged with the general population. They were impossible to distinguish from the guerrillas who had caused havoc during the Japanese advance from Shanghai. Were it not for these circumstances, more than one revisionist explained, the Japanese military would have occupied the city without violence. Attributing blame for Japanese atrocities to Chinese soldiers merging with civilians may be a case of blaming the victim, but it is a reasonable, if fallible, case.[16] In this connection, Ian Buruma (2002), a man never known for conservative views, has observed: "The revisionists may be onto something, for the wrong motives, perhaps, and drawing the wrong conclusions, but onto a legitimate problem nonetheless. The history of the Nanking Massacre has indeed...been encrusted with a mythology of one kind or another. If the revisionists encourage us to act as proper historians and start sifting facts from myths, they will have done us all a service" (p. 5).

The presence of deniers and minimizers suggests two levels of revisionist discourse. If the narrative of Higashinakano and his associates is *low mimetic*, that of Kobayashi, Takemoto, Ohara, Tanaka, Itakura, and Fujioka may be described, in the absence of a better term, as *high mimetic*. It is clearly the minimizers, not the deniers, the high rather than low mimeticists, that "may be onto something"—and for good (scholarly) rather than wrong (ideological) motives. Both sets of revisions, however, are reinforced by the Chinese state, which, in order to propagate its progressive narrative, with its emphasis on optimism and strength, let thirty years pass before recognizing the story of Nanking (Xu and Spillman 2010).

At the very end of the twentieth century, revisionists, like their maximalist rivals, organized themselves into a web of organizations. The list is long and even a small segment of it would be tedious to readers if it did not convey the character of opposition to the maximalist agenda: the Nippon Council (formerly National Council to Defend Nippon), the Society for Japanese History Textbook Reform, the Association for the Advancement of the Liberalist [conservative] View of History, National People's Council to Defend Japan, the League of the Diet (which also advocates returning the emperor as the head of state), Association of Bereaved Families, Diet Members' League for the Fiftieth Anniversary of the End of World War II (1994), Diet Members for the Transmission of a Correct History (1995), Diet Committee to Examine History (1993). The Japan Association for Nanking Studies (2000) also supported the revisionist account. Revisionist commemorations include "The Celebration of Asian Nations' Symbiosis," which recognizes Japan's contribution to the end of Western colonialism.[17] These organizations institutionalize and so reinforce revisionism's content.

The mood driving revisionists reveals itself within these organizations, dramatized by the Diet debate (1994) over attribution of blame during the tenure of Morihiro Hosokawa, the first nonconservative prime minister since 1955. In his inaugural address, he admitted Japan's war guilt and urged Diet members to declare their remorse for the suffering Japan had caused. The conservative Liberal Democratic

Party condemned Hosokawa's view of the war. When he appeared before the budget committee, one of its members asked him whether the Russian army, which had invaded northern Manchuria and Japan's northern islands, committed atrocities against civilians. Hosokawa answered in the affirmative, whereupon his interrogator asked whether he intended to demand an official apology. Another committee member declared that the prime minister had been brainwashed by American and Japan Teachers Union propaganda (Yoshida 2006:133). There was no need to apologize to anyone, the two LDP men claimed, for other nations had conducted the war with equal ferocity.

The revisionist movement gathered steam in 1995, the fiftieth anniversary of the end of World War II, when Socialist Prime Minister Tomiichi Murayama proposed to his cabinet a resolution promising to reflect publicly on Japan's aggression. Angry Liberal Democratic opponents agreed only to a revised, meaningless resolution. Japan's conservatives not only opposed government admission of war guilt; they were also bent on revisiging the Japanese textbooks that implied such guilt. The 1997 statement of purpose of the Society to Create a New Japanese History Textbook, whose vice chair was Tokyo University's Nobukastsu Fujioka, raised a serious issue: whether Japan is suffereing from a surfeit rather than deficit of memory:

> Postwar education in history has not just ignored culture and tradition that must
> be passed on to the Japanese people; it has stripped them of all pride in being
> Japanese. The history of modern and contemporary Japan, in particular, is
> portrayed in ways that force children to view themselves as convicted felons
> bound by fate to apologize for past sins until they die. Even their children,
> grandchildren, and great-grandchildren, too, must continue to beg for forgive-
> ness. Such masochistic trends in education intensified after the Cold War ended,
> so that textbooks now in use present wartime enemy propaganda as historical
> facts (cited in Tokushi 2007:305).

Fujioka's statement seems to favor the substitution of blame analysis for causal analysis in history texts. His version of history, indeed, makes the entire Japanese nation a "protected group" and immunizes it against blame. The statement could have been rephrased: Even if all the atrocities of the war were affirmed and accepted, do they define the essence of Japanese history? Can Japan's national identity be reduced to its darkest historical moments? Is there no end to what left-oriented textbooks demand, no limit of liability that severs national identity from past wrongs?

CENTRISTS

Between the accusations of maximalism and defenses of revisionism stand the claims of the centrists. The centrist school consists of both liberal and conservative investigators, but its estimates, and the narratives that go along with them, typically conform more closely to the revisionists'. Unlike the revisionists, however, centrists insist that Japan committed great atrocities in Nanking, and they have a story to tell about them. It is not the kind of story told by Honda, Chang, and other maximalists, one filled with dramatic accounts of murder and rape. It is more like a documentary history punctuated with case studies. From the outset, it is clear that the authors of this story are writing from a distance and see themselves as outsiders; they give the impression of "understanding" the offenders whom they criticize and sympathizing with victims with whom they cannot identify.

According to Nanking scholar Bob Wakabayashi (2001), Masahiro Yamamoto's *Nanking: Anatomy of an Atrocity* is the best-documented, most thoughtful and objective account of the Massacre (pp. 531–537.) In the first segment of his book, Yamamoto takes up the matter of "What Causes War Atrocities." His is a highly contextualized story sandwiched between a detailed account of the battle of Shanghai, the march to Nanking, the Nanking Massacre's aftermath up to 1945, the War Crimes trials, and present controversies, wherein he critically examines the existing maximalist and revisionist literature. Yamamoto's narrative falls between the *tragic* and *low mimetic* dimensions we have taken from Smith (2005), but to name its mimesis as high (rather than low) would underestimate its recognition of the Massacre's seriousness. The centrist narrative would be more accurately defined as *low tragedy*, for one reads centrist accounts with a definite sense of something hideous having occurred. Centrism embodies deflated tragedy rather than inflated mimesis.

In the centrist case, too, numerical data frame narrative understanding. Kazuya Fukuda, a self-professed nationalist, estimates 50,000 illegally killed at Nanking; David Askew (2002), a Nanking Massacre scholar, expressly identifies himself as a centrist and sets his estimate a little below Fukuda's. John Rabe,[18] who helped to save tens of thousands of Chinese, was present and active during the December–January massacre period, and he estimated 50,000 unlawful deaths—a figure close to that of Fukuda, Askew, and the high end of Yamamoto's 15,000–50,000 estimate. Businessman and amateur historian Yoshiaki Itakura leans strongly toward the revisionists, even co-authored works with well-known revisionists writers like Tanaka, but he broke with the school by asserting openly that the killing of prisoners of war was illegal. He estimated the number killed between 10,000 and 20,000. Historian Ikuhiko Hata is sympathetic to the Chinese people and recognizes, in a sense, their belief that 300,000 had been killed. Hata defines the high count as a "symbolic figure"—a sign, as it were, of the inhuman carnage beginning December 1937. The exaggeration, he adds, was unintentional, "ascribable to the victim's psychology" (Yamamoto 2000:253). At the same time, he condemns the "intellectual masochism" of the left, their uncritical acceptance of the IMFTE figure, and concludes on the basis of his own research that 38,000–42,000 had been killed. What binds Hata and Itakura (moderate and conservative centrists) together is their denial that civilians were murdered en masse[19] and their belief that prisoners of war, including many soldiers believed to be out of uniform, comprised the bulk of the illegally executed (Yamamoto 2000:251–258).

Masahiro Yamamoto (2000) mentions the many mitigating circumstances that form the backbone of the revisionist argument but emphasizes their uniqueness to the Nanking battle. Hangchou, after all, fell about the same time as Nanking but suffered no wholesale massacres, lootings, rapes, or burnings. Yamamoto places particular emphasis on the Shanghai to Nanking offensive in which the Japanese incurred many casualties, mainly from guerrilla fighters. This campaign, including the siege of Nanking, sensitized soldiers to the danger of all Chinese men, whether in or out of uniform. But unlike the revisionists, and this point cannot be overemphasized, Yamamoto defines external factors as causes, not mitigating circumstances reducing blame. His list of "internal" factors—derision of Chinese culture; revenge killings to offset the dishonor of casualties; and, above all, deeply-rooted contempt for soldiers who surrender, and there were tens of thousands of them—is as long as his list of "external" factors that would diminish blame. Yamamoto's is a causal analysis, not a blame analysis, of the Nanking Massacre.

Of all the atrocity estimates, Yamamoto's is assembled most carefully, which does not mean it is the most valid, but that it is the most transparent and open for inspection by other scholars. He divides casualties into four categories: deaths caused by the Chinese army; by Japanese in normal combat; execution of prisoners of war and plainclothes soldiers, and murder of civilians of military age. His analysis begins with burial statistics, including corpses thrown into the Yangtze River and those killed outside the city in one particular suburb.[20] Assuming two ratios for illegal to military-related deaths, he estimates a total fatality count of 45,000–65,000; among these, 15,000–50,000 were killed illegally, including 5000–22,000 civilians (pp. 109–115).

Yamamoto's range, 15,000–50,000, will dissatisfy those who wish more precise information on the number of innocents slaughtered in Nanking, but its significance is threefold: First, it reflects the barriers that the most careful and honest researcher faces in trying to make an accurate estimate; second, he presents strong evidence of an upper limit: no more than 50,000 innocents were murdered. The maximalist estimates, as noted, range from 150,000–300,000. Finally, many of his documents indicate that local Japanese commanders were responsible for allowing their soldiers to rampage and to murder prisoners of war.

Maximalists criticize Yamamoto both for limiting his analysis to the city and one of its counties, and for limiting the time frame of the massacre to four weeks. Yet, the six "counties" surrounding the city equal the size of the state of Delaware. The one county that Yamamoto does include is Kiangning Hsien, in which Nanking itself is located. Given the topic of his book, the Nanking Massacre, Yamamoto believes the addition of this entire county is inappropriate, but he includes it in order to make his analysis "as flexible as possible" (p. 114). As for the four-week duration of the massacre, Yamamoto's critics are right. His analysis missed a seven-day orgy of violence that took place in late January and early February. When Chinese officials at the time urged the Safety Zone refugees to return home, no one expected another wave of Japanese murder, theft, rape, and mayhem (Brook 1999:8, 215).[21] Equally reasonable are criticisms of Yamamoto's sources, which include a larger than average number of battle reports and military administrative reports. Such documents were never meant to identify atrocities (Wakabayashi 2001:533–537). Yamamoto's omissions, then, suggest that his estimate of 15,000–50,000 illegal killings is low, but even if we set his upper limit at 75,000 rather than 50,000, it would fall far short of the maximalists' estimates. On the other hand, Yamamoto claims that because Japanese committed no atrocities in Hangchou, which fell shortly after Nanking, the latter carnage must have been unique. This statement is dubious. Notwithstanding Hangchou, the Japanese army committed atrocities throughout China.

One striking feature of centrism is that so few of its members are associated with organizations devoted to study of the Nanking atrocities.[22] Centrists approximate Karl Mannheim's "relatively unattached intelligentsia," which is supposedly trained and disciplined to envisage problems from multiple perspectives. The term *relative* is important because none of the parties to the Nanking debate is absolutely unattached. There is no purely neutral position; there is a centrist group whose members lean acutely toward neither the right nor the left. Centrism's carriers are therefore relatively *sozialfreischwebende* (socially free-floating): their views, unlike those of the maximalists and revisionists, evolve outside tightly knit organizational networks.

Maximalist and revisionist investigators form organizations to cultivate data, support research, and inform the public; these same organizations energize their like-minded members, multiply relations among them, accelerate the exchange of ideas, and put their members into closer agreement.[23] This is perhaps why maximalists and revisionists, each carrying important truths about the Nanking Massacre, nevertheless ignore one another's value.

Ideology is the chain binding liberal and conservative extremists to their respective organizations. For these men and women, the quest for historical truth is not only a search for fact but also for a definition of the national community, its enemies, and the nature of Japaneseness. Each side, therefore, needs the other. Many years ago, Georg Simmel declared in his ([1908] 1955) essay "Conflict" that contestants who believed they represented a cause transcending their personal interests struggled most intensely against their opponents (pp. 38–43). Because centrism is relatively unpoliticized, however, its members play neither the *divide et impera* nor *tertius gaudens* role that Simmel (1964) attributes to third members of triads (pp. 145–169). That truth, not domination, is at stake is evident in the value-neutral tone of centrist rhetoric: The language is decidedly less angry, less accusatory, less self-righteous, less self-confident. Centrism, however, performs no *mediator* function, as Simmel defines it. Centrism does not strip maximalist-revisionist debates of their passion and reformulate the factual residue. Its goal is not to refine and synthesize extreme positions. Centrists distinguish themselves by expressly refusing to infer *blame* from the establishment of *cause*.

Differences among maximalists, revisionists, and centrists are summarized in Table 20.1, which aligns each of the three schools with their characteristic fatality estimates, narrative genre, justification for Japan's operations, target of attribution, and affinity with public opinion.

Table 20.1 Three Conceptions of the Nanking Massacre

	Fatality Estimates	Narrative Genre	Justification of Japanese Action	Target of Causal Attribution	Affinity with Public Beliefs	Relative Ideological Bias	Supporting Organizational Structure
Maximalists	200,000–300,000	Tragedy	None	Internal	Closest	Liberal	Very strong
Centrists	15,000–50,000	Low Tragedy	Weak	Internal/External	Close	Neutral	Very weak
Revisionists	0–10,000	Low Mimesis	Strong–Very strong	External	Least close	Conservative	Very strong

Although this table describes attributions of cause, it makes no causal claims of its own. It merely summarizes the configuration of attitudes, story genres, and correspondences that compose the Nanking memory war.

DEATH COUNTS, RESPONSIBILITY, AND PUBLIC BELIEF

It is only a matter of time until more adequate statistical analyses are performed, with geographical and temporal breakdowns of illegal deaths. But how critical will they be? Here we come to a key distinction. For maximalists and liberal centrists, Japan's moral responsibility for crimes committed in Nanking and elsewhere is independent of body counts. This is not to say that maximalists are indifferent to numbers; on the contrary, they have assembled considerable bodies of evidence and gone to great lengths to establish their validity. Rather, maximalists believe that the magnitude of Japan's crime is irrelevant to Japan's moral responsibility. Japan is unconditionally responsible for all suffering, whatever its magnitude, for the simple reason that Japan started the war. Conservative centrists, on the other hand, believe that Japan's responsibility must be aligned to the damage done in specific incidents. As we move from maximalism to centrism, the cause of the war loses relevance and its consequences gain relevance. In Yamamoto's (2000) words, the centrist position is the strongest because it is the most clear-cut: "It tries to determine the scale and nature of the atrocities by critically analyzing documentary and numerical data for the purpose of establishing how and to what extent the Japanese were responsible for the atrocities" (p. 258). If, by this reasoning, 50,000 rather than 300,000 illegal deaths occurred in Nanking, then Japan is five-sixths less responsible than the maximalists believe.

The obfuscatory implications of Yamamoto's comment are unmistakable. Notwithstanding its low tragic content, Yamamoto's narrative not only minimizes the state's responsibility for causing a devastating war; it also relativizes moral consequence by calibrating it with degrees and types of harm caused. Memory war, however, presses facts about degree and type of harm caused to the service of morality—the opposite direction of Yamamoto's calibration. This is why Japanese history textbooks, despite compelling centrist evidence, shifted toward the maximalist position in the 1990s. By 1997, six out of the seven major texts informed students that 100,000–200,000 Chinese were killed during and after the battle of Nanking, and that the Japanese military made no effort to protect innocent civilian victims. Four of the texts mentioned, but did not endorse, the Chinese claim of 300,000 deaths (Yoshida 2006:139–141). Nevertheless, these texts triggered strong conservative reactions. By 2005, in fact, history books generally omitted fatality estimates, the word "massacre" appeared less often, as did mention of the word "rape" (Schneider 2008:116). The 2005 revisions in one of the textbooks were so striking to the Chinese government that, despite useful relations with Japan, it tolerated, if not encouraged, anti-Japanese street protests.

All disputes over moral responsibility are disputes about the attribution of blame, but the details of the Nanking dispute, however politically laden, are empirical, and in this it differs from the typical conflicts reported in the Western memory literature. Instead of "narratives" that marginalize or elevate minority groups, we see fact-finding, analysis, and contested conclusions. Askew (2002:10) observes, presenting only partial detail, that the maximalists have revised their estimates "dramatically downward." This means that maximalists, although still committed ideologically (pp. 16–17) to the left, recognize and respond to evidence. Maximalist compromise, however, is not limitless. Askew (2002) believes the differences between maximalist and centrist death tolls would diminish greatly if comparisons were made within the same units of geographical and temporal analysis (pp. 9–10;17); but neither of the contending parties has an interest in doing so. Centrists stay within Nanking's municipal limits for analytic reasons: to assess "the rape of Nanking," not "the rape of China." In contrast, maximalists include all contiguous counties, despite their independence of the Nanking metropolitan area, in order to maximize the death count. They extend the length of the Nanking Massacre far beyond the point of the last spate of killings. Methodology remains ideology-laden.[24]

Maximalists have revised their argument in a way that reinforces the status of the Chinese as a "protected group" and underscores their suffering. Reluctance to offend China, according to Yamamoto (2000), is one of the reasons maximalists avoid debating the death count issue publicly (pp. 250–251). Tokushi, to take one example, removed himself from any scientific debate when he declared, for the sake of protecting Chinese feelings, that "over 100,000, perhaps nearly 200,000 or even more" were killed in Nanking. The undefined upper limit exemplifies a hesitation to limit the *volume* of harm to be analyzed.

Memory Problem

Conflict reduction and consensus about Nanking do not presuppose one another, for they are both part of a broader, Northeast Asian memory war. Despite rapid modernization, memory runs deeply and vitally through Asia, and nowhere is this more evident than in the fact that elites have developed a concept—"the history problem," to describe it—and that ordinary citizens recognize and feel this problem themselves. No comparable "history problem" exists in the West, where relations among former enemies are relatively free of recrimination and international business proceeds without reference to the sins of earlier generations.[25] Over transactions among Asian businessmen, however, looms the cloud of World War II (Schwartz and Kim 2010).

Japan's history problem refers to the question of blame for World War II and how the Japanese people conceive responsibility for their ancestors' wrongdoing.

In 2000, the *Asahi Shimbun Survey* asked respondents whether they should "reflect on Japan's past wrongs." Eighty-five percent said "yes." The same year, the *Asahi Survey* asked, "Do you think that Japan has apologized and compensated those victim countries and people in those countries enough for Japan's invasion and colonial rule?" Fifty-one percent answered, "not enough"; 36 percent, "enough." In 2001 and 2005, national surveys commissioned by the *Asahi Shimbun* and *Yomiuri Shimbun* newspapers asked, "Do you think the history issues are important for Japan's relations with China and South Korea?" Sixty-seven and 75 percent, respectively, replied "important." In 2005, a comparable sample was asked, "What should Japan do to better relations with China?" Two-thirds responded, "Respect Chinese culture and history." Three years later, Japanese were asked, "What do you think both China and Japan should do in order to improve the relationship between the two countries?" The modal response (36.7 percent) was "Solve history issues between Japan and China." A full 60 percent answered negatively when asked, "Do you think that the history issue of Japan's compensation to the former victims in the era of colonization has been solved?" The same percentage (60 percent) answered "no" to the question of whether "the issue of Japan's history issue with neighboring countries such as China and South Korea has been solved."[26] The content of these history issues involves material compensation, but it is also premised on assumptions about causation. A significant minority of the Japanese population believe their country was forced by external circumstances to go to war. In 1994 and 2000, surveys conducted by NHK (a television company) showed that 27 and 30 percent of respondents believed the war to have been inevitable (Takuji 2007:350). The *history* problem, then, includes the conflicting emotions and moral judgments of memory (Schwartz and Kim 2010:1–27).

These findings suggest that the public leans toward a tragic rather than mimetic narrative of the Japanese war in China. But what does this mean on the level of personal responsibility, and does it include the Nanking Massacre? When students at two Japanese universities were asked to name the greatest source of "dishonor, disgrace, and shame" in Japanese history, the most frequently named was Japan's war in Asia (54.4 percent); the second most frequent response was the Pacific War (against the United States and its allies [24.6 percent]). Also, a substantial percentage of students felt a personal connection with the events about which they were questioned. Forty-two percent of the respondents agreed with the statement, "As a Japanese national, I consider myself [or my generation] responsible for the 1937 'Nanking incident.'" Regarding the annexation of Korea and the comfort women issue, the responses were almost identical. These figures, compared to those in the United States, indicate that Japanese are four times more willing to accept responsibility for their country's wrongdoing (Schwartz, Fukuoka, and Takita-Ishi 2005:258–262. See also Fukuoka and Schwartz 2010). The *NHK Survey* (September 2000) on "responsibility for the national past wrongs," based on a nationwide sample of Japanese adults, shows similar results: Fifty percent believed the Japanese must, personally, bear responsibility for historical offenses. The figures for the wartime, postwar, and current generations, however, are 37 percent, 52 percent, and 60 percent, respectively.[27] Those who attribute the cause of war to their own country are thus drawn disproportionately from the younger sectors of the population.

These surveys were conducted at the turn of the twenty-first century when media and academic attention to World War II peaked and Japanese attitudes toward their neighbors assumed unprecedented sympathy and friendliness. During this time, respondents not only expressed willingness to assume responsibility for their forebears' wrongdoing; they also identified *themselves* as Asians, thus forging a civilizational connection that had not existed since Japan's rush to modernity. Student interviews, however, show decidedly more ambivalence about Nanking than national surveys suggest (Fukuoka and Schwartz 2010). Also, students rarely refer to their high school textbooks when asked to explain their answers to atrocity questions, but they do seem to know that Japan started the war and caused immense hardship and bloodshed.[28]

This gap between expert opinion and popular opinion leads to an important point about ideology and the academy. Although social scientists resent being told that their research conclusions are ideologically driven, liberals complain routinely that certain theorists are too conservative (uncritical lovers of the system), while conservatives insist that most theorists are too liberal (unloving critics of the system). These charges hang at the edge of blame analysis. Commenting on Masahiro Yamamoto's "thick (highly contextualized) description" of the mop-up of plain-clothes soldiers and his observation that no large-scale massacres occurred after Nanking, Bob Wakabayashi (2001) declares that Yamamoto "risks being mistaken for advancing the very denial thesis that he disputes" (p. 537). To identify dispassionately the conditions promoting atrocity without taking this risk is difficult—unless one is prepared to substitute blame analysis for causal analysis. Likewise, David Agnew (2004) approaches the boundary of blame analysis when he explains that the discussion of Nanking is a threat to Chinese identity. "It is sometimes difficult to distinguish between legitimate revisionism and illegitimate apologetics" (p. 63). "I am not arguing that the Chinese orthodoxy needs to be accepted without question.... However, once aware of the fact, all who participate in the debate need to show some sensitivity to it" (Askew 2002:20–21). Askew's caution cannot increase confidence in his objectivity. Whether or not a particular investigator is "sensitive" or "insensitive," his or her problem is to know how problems are framed, causes inferred, and conclusions validated. Clearly, blame is inferable from every causal analysis, whether the investigator resides on the left or the right, but the investigator has no *professional* warrant to exploit this inference.

CONCLUSION

This essay is concerned with two approaches to the analysis of conflict and collective memory: the politics of memory, which traces the substance of beliefs about the past to those possessing the power to impose them, and memory as an attribution process that assigns causes, credit, responsibility, and blame—at once a scientific and moral exercise. The present analysis of the Nanking debate demonstrates why conflicting memories cannot be understood if viewed solely as a political contest. When memory is partitioned into attributions of credit and blame, we learn at once that blame activates sharper moral distinctions than does credit (Tilly 2008). Blame creates firmer boundaries, greater distance between in-groups and out-groups; accentuates antithesis, binary relations, and the resentments accompanying social distance. The Nanking memory war is a war about cause and blame alike, and our major problem is to distinguish between them.

The conversion of cause to blame is practiced with equal skill on the Japanese left and right. Because right-leaning revisionists are sympathetic to Japan's 1937 Japanese military situation, they cannot formulate causal explanations implying fault. Right observers depend not only on structural explanations of their protected group's atrocities but also condemn cultural and psychological explanations as "masochistic." Not Japanese cultural values or character but shortages of supplies, heavy battle losses along the trek to Nanking, fear of invisible enemies in civilian dress, the universality of post-siege rage, inadequate discipline, and poor tactical leadership—these conditions, over which ordinary soldiers lacked control, make terror at least understandable.

These and other attribution patterns become morally meaningful when translated into narratives—maximalists' high tragedy, revisionists' low mimetic, and centrists' low tragedy. For most men and women, these genres affect the way the past is contemplated, felt, and judged. Among experts, casual evidence, not blame, informs theoretical conclusions. In other words, and here I wish to specify Philip Smith's conclusions in *Why War?* (2005), Japanese attribution of blame is conveyed, not produced, by means of tragic and mimetic genres.

Narratives, according to Milton Rokeach (1960), express cognitive patterns that satisfy two needs: to accumulate information in order to know and manage the world, and to defend against knowledge that undermines existing worldviews. Liberals have an interest in knowing about Japanese lust for vengeance, socialization within a culture of violence, eagerness to do the will of a bloodthirsty emperor. Their interest is *not* to know that *Manchester Guardian* correspondent Harold Timperley, who first reported on Japanese atrocities, was a paid propagandist for the Nationalist Chinese government, or that a collaborationist army of 2 million Chinese soldiers fought for Japan, or that Japanese officers entering the Safety Zone to recruit Chinese girls for brothels found that "a considerable number of young refugee girls stepped forward" (Brook 2007:204), or that Chinese municipal officials collaborated with the Japanese military in governing Nanking after the massacre. Nanking's local government included the Nanking Self-Government Committee, an anti-Western body that helped to round up Chinese men and boys for execution. Conservatives, for their part, have an interest in knowing how the Chinese army's riotous withdrawal from Nanking, including thousands of soldiers transforming themselves into civilians, precipitated indiscriminate Japanese violence, and in *not* knowing about direct orders from Japanese general officers to kill prisoners of war.

That most professional scholars are aware of one another's biases takes us to the inner working of narrative forms. Japanese liberals are more critical of their country, more likely than their conservative counterparts to believe Japan has dealt unwisely with "the history problem," that the government is a force for harm, that conservatives cherish the old days of militarism and seek to reinstate the vestiges of an oppressive imperial regime. Conservatives, on all counts, believe the opposite, seeing in their country a lamp of virtue for all the world. In the matter of ascribing credit and blame, liberals and conservatives differ only in what they consider commendable and blameworthy. Both protect their favored groups by attributing their wrongdoing to external circumstances; both attribute the righteous conduct of their protected groups to internal traits: virtuous character, beneficent values, moral sentiments, and personal dispositions.

Whatever the merit of their exculpatory accounts, revisionists force maximalists to reexamine old documents, search for new ones, and lower their victim count. Maximalist-revisionist conflict thus differs from Western memory wars. In the Western view, whoever controls the memory factories—producers of research monographs, textbooks, and commemorative symbols—controls the past. Power makes more of a difference than it should; reality, less of a difference. This argument cannot be generalized very far, for journalists and academicians are influential, not hegemonic. Changing textbook and research monograph content cannot explain Japanese public opinion, which, on the Nanking Incident, leans to the left.

Much has been left unsaid. One of the biggest issues is the Nanking Massacre's parameters. Death count differences between the maximalists and centrists would narrow if temporal and spatial units were uniform, but this does not mean that centrists deliberately limited the Nanking campaign to four weeks in order to minimize atrocity estimates. If they did make their choice on such grounds, it would mean they had constructed rather than discovered their evidence. In contrast, maximalists insist on including in their data massive areas that are functionally independent, economically and politically, from the capital city. They also insist on stretching out to twelve weeks an operation whose last surge of violence ended in late January/early February 1938—slightly more than six weeks after the city was conquered. Expanding the Nanking Massacre's temporal and spatial limits is not needed to prove that Japan's war against China was a war of continuous cruelty and atrocity. Insisting on definitions that possess little geographic or temporal significance, the maximalists undermine their own argument and become vulnerable to the charge of fabrication.

Space limits prevent exploration of *the politics of regret* (Olick 2007) that, in the Northeast Asian case, with its controversial rituals and culture of apology, would require a separate essay.[29] The same limits prevent us from explaining why leftist scholars elsewhere distort trauma in such characteristic ways. The American left, which sympathizes with Japanese suffering, fixates on the number of Hiroshima and Nagasaki casualties, while vastly underestimating the casualties America would have suffered in an invasion of the Japanese homeland. Left scholars not only underestimate Japanese power opposing a 1945 American invasion of Kyushu and Honshu

(Allen and Polmar 1995); they ignore the 1000 Americans killed and wounded daily during the week *before* the bombing of Hiroshima (Fussell 1988).[30]

Eventually, conflict provides the force that gets objects at rest to move and change; it prompts the formation of new organizations and energizes new biographical and historiographic projects. Conflict generates knowledge. One side's discovery of facts eventually forces opponents to revise their conceptions. This point is clearest when the objects of dispute are not *perspectives* but documented *actions*. Reality is the essential object of memory wars—at once the object of dispute and the criterion for dispute resolution. Therefore, no one can observe the Nanking debate without concluding that the politics of memory, at least in its vulgar form, requires revision.

The question raised in this chapter's introduction is how the politics of memory and attribution theories of memory are related to one another. The theory of the politics of memory is a special case of the attribution theory of memory, while power enhances one's ability to make attributions stick. All attributions, however sticky, are biased, but we can identify them as such only if we *know* the historical truth, and we can *theorize* that truth only if we include it, as an attribution benchmark (Gingras and Schweber 1986), in empirical accounts of the world's memory wars.

To insist that we should parenthesize historical reality, that we only know its narratives and texts, not the past itself (White 1978), leads to a theoretical dead-end. Without a *best estimate* of the past, including the Nanking Massacre as it actually was, we (1) cannot know whether accounts of a historical event have been accurately represented or distorted; (2) cannot tell what kind of distortion is occurring: Exaggeration or muting? Fabrication of external or internal, structural or dispositional, factors? Selective remembering and forgetting? Removing an event from its context? Deliberate misrepresentation? Unwitting error? Without a best estimate of the past as it was, we (3) cannot adjudicate among competing interpretations and attributions; (4) cannot know what symbolic structures would be most appropriate to commemorate it, and (5) cannot know its consequences.[31]

Memory analysis is weakest when investigators commit themselves to a theoretical program before they attend to the facts to which the theory refers; as a result, facts become theory-laden without theory becoming fact-laden.[32] As Michael Schudson declares in his groundbreaking essay "The Resistance of the Past," "there are limits to the past that can be reconstructed, and there is an integrity to the past that deserves respect" (p. 221). Conflict promotes this resistance and this integrity. The merit of the Nanking debate is to demonstrate conflict's *primary* function: not to accumulate power by reinterpreting the past but to make known its reality.

NOTES

1. The politicization of Middle East programs has been a topic of intense debate, within and outside the academy, for many years, as has been the Middle East Studies Association (MESA), long regarded as a bastion of anti-Western rhetoric and activism.

If one work represents the mind-set of such programs, it is *Orientalism*, written by a comparative literature scholar who knows nothing of classical Arabic and is innocent of the great issues of Islamic research. For a detailed critique of Edward Said's Islamic "scholarship," see Bernard Lewis, 1993, *Islam and the West*, New York: Oxford University Press (pp. 99–118).

2. See Fiske and Taylor 1991 on the distinction between general "attribution theory" and "attributional theories" restricted to specific content domains (p. 23).

3. Correspondingly, the representatives of such minorities are assigned virtues they never possessed. Prominent examples include the far left's canonization of Fidel Castro, Mao Zedong, Ho-Chi Minh, and Yasser Arafat. The term "canonization" refers to the total ignoring of the millions of innocents murdered by these anticapitalist and anticolonial champions. Falsehoods embodied in film also exemplify the new canonization motif. In one popular film, boxer Rubin "Hurricane" Carter is portrayed as the clear winner of his 1964 middleweight fight against champion Joey Giardello. The judges, as portrayed in the film, are racist and give Giardello the most rounds and declare him the winner. Sportswriters on the scene, however, all attest to the beating Giardello gave to Carter. Giardello sued the film producer for libel and won an out-of-court settlement. No such redress is possible for the victims of trendy dictators.

4. For a related interpretation, see Tilly 2008:120–151.

5. Fritz Heider (1944, 1958) demonstrated that people perceive a finite amount of causal force: For any spate of credit or blame attributed to one source, the less is attributable to another. Causal *theories*, however, are judged in terms of their capacity to explain variation in conduct, not to their capacity to attribute credit and blame.

6. The consequences include legal claims for compensation and remedial action. For details on the functions of blame analysis, see Felson 1991.

7. Lack of recognition, as Xu and Spillman (2010) have shown, does not imply lack of knowledge. For detail, see Penney 2008.

8. At a given time, a small number of books on Nanking might be unrelated to the massacre, but their percentage of the total remains constant across the years.

9. These conclusions do not lend themselves to Karl Mannheim's "synthetic method" based on competing perspectives (see especially Mannheim 1936:147–153). "All points of view," Mannheim observed, are partial because "historical totality is always too comprehensive to be grasped by any one of the individual points of view which emerge out of it. Since, however, all these points of view emerge out of the same social and historical current, and since their partiality exists in the matrix of an emerging whole, and it is possible to see them in juxtaposition, their synthesis becomes a problem which must be continually reformulated and resolved" (p. 151). The things to be synthesized, for Mannheim, however, are "points of view," not the facts to which they refer.

10. Decisions of the war crime tribunals established throughout victim countries after the war have been widely criticized. The Tokyo trials lasted almost three years and resulted in more than 5300 indictments, 920 executions, 475 life sentences, 2944 prison terms, and 1018 acquittals. Although legally imperfect, the correspondence between crimes committed and penalties imposed was not entirely arbitrary. For evidence on Korean, Philippine, Singaporese, and Chinese war fatalities, see Rudolph J. Rummel,1998, *Statistics on Democide: Genocide and Mass Murder since 1900*, New Brunswick, NJ: Transaction; Rummel, 1991, *China's Bloody Century*, New Brunswick, NJ: Transaction (pp. 32–38). For evidence on Burma, see Michael Clodfelter, 2002,*Warfare and Armed Conflicts: A Statistical Reference to Casualties and Other Figures, 1500–2000*, 2nd ed., Jefferson, NC: McFarland (p. 556). For evidence on French Indo-China, Indonesia, and

Malaya, see John W. Dower, 1986, *War Without Mercy: Race and Power in the Pacific War*, New York: Pantheon (pp. 296–297); for India, see Commonwealth War Graves Commission, *Annual Report*, 2007–2008, Statistics and Service (p.10; available at http://www.cwgc.org); for Timor, Australian Department of Defence, 2002, *A Short History of East Timor*.

11. For a full discussion, see Wakabayashi 2000.

12. One supporter, Suzuki Akira, who identified himself as a non-fiction writer, had no interest in the Nanking Massacre until he read Honda's account. So struck was he by the high victim estimate that he conducted his own investigation and deemed the left-wing accounts of mass murder to be an "illusion." But Suzuki never denied the reality of the massacre itself, and he allied himself with the centrists (Yoshida 2006:85–87), who will be discussed later.

13. To say that China "forgot" the Nanking Massacre is to underestimate the significance of oral communication, including many instances in which its content differs from or conflicts with the interests of the state. Yet, the consequences of state interests are patent. Between 1937 and 1945, Communists and Nationalists regarded one another as enemies, despite their temporary coalition against Japan. Between 1945 and 1949, the civil war accelerated, with each side condemning the other rather than Japan. After the 1949 Communist takeover of China, new fears of the United States and Japanese remilitarization preoccupied the People's Republic. The act that brought the Nanking atrocities to the center of official Chinese attention was the 1982 "Textbook Incident," which openly and dramatically challenged China's understanding of the war. For detail, see Xu and Spillman 2009.

14. This and all subsequent information about the nature and consequences of the Nanking Massacre is taken from English translations of the major Japanese publications. For an English-language survey of primary Nanking data, see Timothy Brook, 1999, *Documents on the Rape of Nanking*, Ann Arbor: University of Michigan Press.

15. Prominent reviewers include David M. Kennedy (1998) and Joshua A. Fogel (1998).

16. Maximalists' tendency to overlook the shortcomings of their protected group transcends local issues. Honda Katsuichi, for example, covered the Vietnam War before he wrote his groundbreaking book on Nanking. He believed American forces were the main reason for the suffering of the Vietnamese people, but he never asked why these forces were in Vietnam to begin with. Embracing the North Vietnamese as his protected group, he was silent about the 200,000 "bourgeois" landholders executed and millions who fled south after the 1954 Geneva Accords, the countless thousands imprisoned, and the millions who fled the country after the fall of Saigon. Honda never even attributes these atrocities to external (extenuating) circumstances; he simply ignores them.

17. Takashi Yoshida (2006) presents the most comprehensive listing and description of maximalist and revisionist organizations.

18. Rabe was a devoted Nazi and anti-Semite, but when he returned to Germany to tell his story about its ally, he was arrested and warned not to say or publish anything about his experience. He died impoverished.

19. The Red Swastika Society reveals only 129 women and children among more than 40,000 corpses buried. The overwhelming predominance of men does not mean that most of the dead were soldiers, but that they died in war-related situations, that is, combat or execution as prisoners of war.

20. These figures are based on Ginling College [Nanking] Professor Lewis Smythe's household survey entitled *War Damage in Nanking Area:* December 1937–March 1938).

21. Brook (1999) mentions this peak, but he gives no victim count.

22. The most prominent of these few organizations is the Center for Research and Documentation on Japan's War Responsibility.

23. See also Durkheim's ([1911] 1974) comment on "the movement of collective enthusiasm which, in the twelfth and thirteenth centuries, bringing together in Paris the scholars of Europe, gave birth to Scholasticism. Such were the Reformation and the Renaissance, the revolutionary epoch and the Socialist upheavals of the nineteenth century....At such times the ideal tends to become one with the real...." (p.92).

24. Revisionist and centrist definitions of Nanking's boundaries are accepted by the Chinese because they concentrate and thus increase the hideousness of the now official 300,000 fatality count.

25. The tone and texture of this history problem are evident in Japan's "Textbook Incidents." When, in 1982, the Japanese Ministry of Education suggested that an author revise his textbook to show that Japan "advanced" into rather than "invaded" Chinese cities, the Chinese government reacted explosively: It withdrew its ambassador, condemned the Ministry's action, and declared that bilateral relations would never be the same. In the streets, angry Chinese students demonstrated their indignation. Later, in November 1982, Japan's Ministry adopted a "Neighboring Country Clause" to make history textbooks consistent with international harmony. Because this clause was only a symptom of the still unresolved history problem, however, future textbook crises were inevitable.

26. These survey materials were brought to my attention by Kazuya Fukuoka, Department of Political Science, St. Joseph's University, Philadelphia, PA.

27. For detail on generation differences in factual and moral judgments of World War II among Germans and Japanese, see Schuman, Akiyama, and Knauper 1998.

28. Public beliefs about important issues and events are typically based on fragments of knowledge rather than detailed mastery of the facts. Nevertheless, different fragment clusters are uniform across different groups and consistent with their interests and values (Page and Shapiro 1992).

29. See, for example, Wagatsuma and Rosett 1986 and Lee 2006.

30. This high death rate is a measure of the *cost* of giving the Japanese government more time to decide whether to surrender.

31. Consequences define the significance of historical events. For example, 25 percent of the Confederacy's military-age males died during the Civil War. The resulting postwar sex ratio determined the fate of women, marriage choices, and family structures. The same effect is evident in massacres that target or affect one sector of the population more than another. The present status of European Jewry would be different if the Holocaust had not occurred, regardless of whether, how, or when information about it was transmitted. The *consequences* of events are, thus, independent of their representation.

32. Jeffrey Alexander's (2004) effort to understand the nature of trauma and its relation to collective memory illustrates this problem. "Only if the patterned meanings of the collectivity are abruptly dislodged," he declares, "is traumatic status attributed to an event. It is the meanings that provide the sense of shock and fear, not the events in themselves. Whether or not the structures of meaning are destabilized and shocked is not the result of an event but the effect of a sociocultural process" (p.10). Trauma-work, as Alexander conceives it, involves claim-making, carrier groups, unfolding of the event into a new master narrative, depictions of victims and their pain, the relation of a victimized group to an audience, attribution of responsibility. His point is reasonable: If one is investigating the construction of trauma, one cannot invoke the trauma itself as a determinant without engaging in circular argument. Because the measurable consequences of the trauma can be separated from the way people react to it, however, the event cannot be solely defined by its subjective meaning.

REFERENCES

Abercrombie, N. S. Hill, and B. Turner. 1980. *The Dominant Ideology Thesis*. London: Allen & Unwin.

American Council of Trustees and Alumni. 2002. *Defending Civilization: How Our Universities Are Failing America*. Washington, DC.

Alexander, Jeffrey C., and Rui Gao. 2007. "Remembrance of Things Past: Cultural Trauma, the Nanking Massacre, and Chinese Identity." Pp. 266–294 in *Tradition and Modernity in Comparative Perspectives*. Peking-Yale University University Conference. Beijing: Peking University Press.

Alexander, Jeffrey C. 2004. "Toward a Theory of Cultural Trauma." Pp. 1–30 in Jeffery C. Alexander, Ron Eyerman, Bernhard Giesen, Neil J. Smelser, and Piotr Sztompka. *Cultural Trauma and Collective Identity*. Berkeley: University of California Press.

Allen, Thomas, and Norman Polmar. 1995. *Code-Name Downfall: The Secret Plan to Invade Japan—and Why Truman Dropped the Bomb*. New York: Simon and Schuster.

Alonso, Ana Maria. 1988. "The Effects of Truth: Re-Presentations of the Past and the Imagining of the Community." *Journal of Historical Sociology* 1: 33–57.

Askew, David. 2002. "The Nanking Incident: Recent Research Trends." *Electronic Journal of Contemporary Studies*. April 4. http://www.japanesestudies.org.uk/articles/Askew.html.

———. 2004. "The Contested Past: History and Semantics in the Nanking Debate." *Ritsumeikan International Affairs* 2: 63–78.

———. 2005. "Part of the Numbers Issue: Demography and Civilian Victims." Pp. 86–114 in *The Nanking Atrocity 1937–38: Complicating the Picture*. Bob Tadishi Wakabayashi, ed. New York: Berghahn Books.

Barthel, Diane. 1996. *Historic Preservation: Collective Memory and Historical Identity*. New Brunswick, NJ: Rutgers University Press.

Becker, Howard S. [1963] 1997. *Outsiders: Studies in the Sociology of Deviance*. New York: Free Press.

Bodnar, John. 1992. *Remaking America: Public Memory, Commemoration, and Patriotism in the Twentieth Century*. Princeton, NJ: Princeton University Press.

Brook, Timothy, ed. 1999. *Documents on the Rape of Nanking*. Ann Arbor: University of Michigan Press.

———. 2007. "Chinese Collaboration in Nanking." Pp. 196–226 in *The Nanking Atrocity, 1937–38: Complicating the Picture*. Bob Tadashi Wakabayashi, ed. New York: Berghahn Books.

Buruma, Ian. 2002. "The Nanking Massacre as a Historical Symbol." Pp. 3–9 in *Nanking 1937: Memory and Healing*. Fei Fei Li, Robert Sabella, and David Liu, eds. Armonk, NY: M.E. Sharpe.

Chambers, John Whiteclay, II. 1999. *Oxford Companion to American Military History*. New York: Oxford University Press.

Chang, Iris. 1997. *The Rape of Nanking: The Forgotten Holocaust of World War II*. New York: Penguin.

Chang, Maria Hsia, and Robert P. Barker. 2000. "Victor's Justice and Japan's Amnesia: The Tokyo War Crimes Tribunal Reconsidered." *East Asia: An International Quarterly* 19: 55–86.

Durkheim, Emile. [1911] 1974. "Value Judgments and Judgments of Reality." Pp. 80–97 in *Sociology and Philosophy*. New York: The Free Press.

———. [1895] 1982. *Rules of the Sociological Method*, Stephen Lukes, ed. New York: The Free Press.

Felson, Richard B. 1991. "Blame Analysis: Accounting for the Behavior of Protected Groups." *American Sociologist* 22: 5–23.

Fine, Gary A. 2001. *Difficult Reputations: Collective Memories of the Evil, Inept, and Controversial.* Chicago: University of Chicago Press.

Fiske, Susan T., and Shelley E. Taylor. 1991. *Social Cognition.* New York: McGraw-Hill.

Fleck, Ludwig. [1935] 1979. *Genesis and Development of a Scientific Fact.* Fred Bradley and Thaddeus J. Trenn, trans. Thaddeus J. Trenn and Robert K. Merton, eds. Chicago: University of Chicago Press.

Fogel, Joshua A. 1998. "The Rape of Nanking." *Journal of Asian Studies* 57: 818–820.

Foucault, Michel. 1975. "Film and Popular Memory: An Interview with Michel Foucault." *Radical Philosophy* 11: 24–29.

Fujiwara, Akira. 2007. "The Nanking Atrocity: An Interpretive Overview." Pp. 29–54 in *The Nanking Atrocity, 1937–1938: Complicating the Picture.* Bob Tadashi Wakabayashi, ed. New York: Berghahn Books.

Fukuoka, Kazuya, and Barry Schwartz. 2010. "Responsibility, Regret, and Nationalism in Japanese Memory." Pp. 71–97 in *Northeast Asia's Difficult Past.* Mikyoung Kim and Barry Schwartz, eds. Basingstoke, UK, and New York: Palgrave Macmillan.

Fussell, Paul. 1988. "Thank God for the Atom Bomb." Pp. 13–44 in *Thank God for the Atom Bomb and Other Essays.* New York: Summit Books.

Gillis, John R., ed. 1994. *Commemorations: The Politics of National Identity.* Princeton, NJ: Princeton University Press.

Gingras, Yves, and Silvan S. Schweber. 1986. "Constraints on Constructionism" (Review of Andrew Pickering, *Constructing Quarks: A Sociological History of Particle Physics*). *Social Studies of Science* 16: 372–383.

Handler, Richard, and Jocelyn Linnekin. 1984. "Tradition, Genuine or Spurious?" *Journal of American Folklore* 97: 273–290.

Hauerwas, Stanley, and L. Gregory Jones. 1989. *Why Narrative? Readings in Narrative Theology.* Grand Rapids, MI: Eerdmans.

Heider, Fritz. 1944. "Social Perception and Phenomenal Causality." *Psychological Review* 51: 358–374.

———. 1958. *The Psychology of Interpersonal Relations.* New York: Wiley.

Higashinakano, Shudo (Osamichi). 2002. "The Overall Picture of the 'Nanking Massacre.'" Pp. 95–120 in *Nanking 1937: Memory and Healing.* Fei Fei Li, Robert Sabella, and David Liu, eds. Armonk, NY: M.E. Sharpe.

Himmelfarb, Gertrude. 1999. *One Nation, Two Cultures: A Searching Examination of American Society in the Aftermath of Our Cultural Revolution.* New York: Alfred A. Knopf.

Hobsbawm, Eric. 1983. "Mass-Producing Traditions: Europe, 1870–1914." Pp. 263–307 in *The Invention of Tradition.* Eric Hobsbawm and Terence Ranger, eds. Cambridge, UK: Cambridge University Press.

Honda, Katsuichi. [1971] 1999. *The Nanking Massacre: A Japanese Journalist Confronts Japan's National Shame.* Karen Sandness, trans. Armonk, NY: M.E. Sharpe.

———. 1993. *The Impoverished Spirit in Contemporary Japan: Selected Essays of Honda Katuichi.* John Lie, Eri Fujieda, and Masayuki Hamazaki, trans. New York: Monthly Review Press.

Hunter, James D. 1991. *Culture Wars: The Struggle to Define America.* New York: Basic Books.

Johnson, Walter. 1991. *Modern Times: The World from the Twenties to the Nineties.* New York: HarperCollins.

Kahn, Sammy S., and James H. Liu. 2008. "Intergroup Attributions and Ethnocentrism in the Indian Subcontinent: The Ultimate Attribution Error Revisited." *Journal of Cross-Cultural Psychology* 39: 16–36.

Kennedy, David M. 1998. "The Horror." *Atlantic Monthly* 281 (April): 110–116.

Klein, Olivier, and Laurent Licata. 2001. "Explaining Differences between Social Groups: The Impact of Group Identification on Attribution." *Swiss Journal of Psychology* 60: 244–252.

Lang, Gladys, and Kurt Lang. 1991. *Etched in Memory: The Building and Survival of Artistic Reputation.* Chapel Hill, NC: University of North Carolina Press.

Lee, Ilhyung. 2006. "The Law and Culture of the Apology in Korean Dispute Settlement (with Japan and the United States in Mind)." *Michigan Journal of International Law* 7: 1–53.

Lyotard, Jean-Francois. 1984. *The Postmodern Condition.* Minneapolis: University of Minnesota Press.

Ma, Weijum, and Minoru Karasawa. 2006. "Group Inclusiveness, Group Identification, and Intergroup Attributional Bias." *Psychologia* 49: 278–290.

MacIntyre, Alasdair. 1989. "Epistemological Crises, Dramatic Narrative, and the Philosophy of Science." Pp. 138–157 in *Why Narrative? Readings in Narrative Theology.* Stanley Hauerwas and L. Gregory Jones, eds. Grand Rapids, MI: Eerdmans.

Maier, Charles S. 2000. "Foreword." Pp. vii–xvi in *The Nanking Massacre in History and Historiography.* Joshua Fogel, ed. Berkeley: University of California Press.

Mannheim, Karl. 1936. "The Prospects of Scientific Politics." Pp. 109–191 in *Ideology and Utopia.* Louis Wirth and Edward Shils, trans. New York: Harcourt, Brace & World.

McArthur, G. Bruce, and Daniel McDougall. 1995. "Effects of Confirmatory and Contradictory Stimuli and Development on Children's Intergroup Attribution." *Journal of Genetic Psychology* 156: 333–343.

Momigliano, Arnoldo. 1982. "History in an Age of Ideologies." *American Scholar* 51: 495–507.

Muramoto, Yukiko, and Susumu Yamaguchi. 1997. "Another Type of Self-Serving Bias: Coexistence of Self-Effacing and Group-Serving Tendencies in Attribution among Japanese." *Japanese Journal of Experimental Social Psychology* 31: 65–75.

Olick, Jeffrey K. 2007. *The Politics of Regret: On Collective Memory and Historical Responsibility.* New York: Routledge.

Page, Benjamin I., and Robert Y. Shapiro. 1992. *The Rational Public.* Chicago: University of Chicago Press.

Penney, Matthew. 2008. "Far from Oblivion: The Nanking Massacre in Japanese Historical Writing for Children and Young Adults." *Holocaust and Genocide Studies* 22: 25–48.

Rokeach, Milton. 1960. *The Open and Closed Mind.* New York: Basic Books.

Rosenzweig, Roy, and David Thelen. 1998. *The Presence of the Past: Popular Uses of History in American Life.* New York: Columbia University Press.

Rotter, Julian. B. 1966. "Generalized Expectancies for Internal vs. External Control." *Psychological Monographs* 80: 1–28.

Schlesinger, Arthur M., Jr. 1992. *The Disuniting of America.* New York: W.W. Norton.

Schluchter, Wolfgang. 1989. *Rationalism, Religion and Domination: A Weberian Perspective.* Neil Solomon, trans. Berkeley, CA: University of California Press.

Schneider, Claudia. 2008. "The Japanese History Textbook Controversy in East Asian Perspective." *Annals of the American Academy of Political and Social Science* 617: 107–122.

Schudson, Michael. 1992. *Watergate in American Memory: How We Remember, Forget, and Reconstruct the Past.* New York: Basic Books.

Schuman, Howard, H. Akiyama, and B. Knauper. 1998. "Collective Memories of Germans and Japanese about the Past Half-Century." *Memory* 6: 427–454.

Schwartz, Barry. 2001. "Commemorative Objects." Pp. 2267–2272 in *Encyclopedia of Social and Behavioral Sciences.* Neil Smelser and P. B. Baltes, eds. Amsterdam: Elsevier.

————. 2007 . "Collective Memory." Pp. 588–590 in *Blackwell Encyclopedia of Sociology*. George Ritzer, ed. New York: Wiley-Blackwell.

Schwartz, Barry, and Mikyoung Kim. 2010. "Introduction: Northeast Asia's Memory Problem." Pp. 1–27 in *Northeast Asia's Difficult Past: Studies in Collective Memory*. Mikyounng Kim and Barry Schwartz, eds. Basingstoke, UK, and New York: Palgrave Macmillan.

Schwartz, Barry, and Howard Schuman. 2005. "History, Commemoration, and Belief: Abraham Lincoln in American Memory, 1945–2001." *American Sociological Review* 70: 183–203.

Schwartz, Barry, Kazuya Fukuoka, and Sachiko Takita-Ishi. 2005. "Collective Memory: Why Culture Matters." Pp. 253–271 in *The Blackwell Companion to the Sociology of Culture*. Mark D. Jacobs and Nancy Weiss Hanrahan, eds. Oxford: Blackwell.

Simmel, Georg. [1908] 1955. "The Sociological Nature of Conflict." Pp. 13–123 in *Conflict*. Kurt H. Wolff, trans. New York: Free Press.

————. 1964. "The Triad." Pp. 145–169 in *The Sociology of Georg Simmel*. Kurt H. Wolff, ed. and trans. New York: Free Press.

Smith, Philip. 2005. *Why War? The Cultural Logic of Iraq, the Gulf War, and Suez*. Chicago: University of Chicago Press.

Sturken, Marita. 1997. *Tangled Memories: The Vietnam War, the AIDS Epidemic, and the Politics of Remembering*. Berkeley: University of California Press.

Takuji, Kimura. 2007. "Nanking: Denial and Atonement in Contemporary Japan." Pp. 330–354 in *The Nanking Atrocity, 1937–38: Complicating the Picture*. Bob Tadashi Wakabayashi, ed. New York: Berghahn Books.

Tilly, Charles. 2008. *Credit and Blame*. Princeton, NJ: Princeton University Press.

Tokushi, Kasahara. 2007. "Higashinakano Osamichi: The Last Word in Denial." Pp. 304–329 in *The Nanking Atrocity 1937–38*. Bob Tadashi Wakabayashi, ed. New York: Berghan Books.

Tuchman, Gaye, and Nina Fortin. 1989. *Edging Women Out: Victorian Novelists, Publishers, and Social Change*. New Haven, CT: Yale University Press.

Wagatsuma, Hiroshi, and Arthur Rosett. 1986. "The Implications of Apology: Law and Culture in Japan and the United States." *Law and Society Review* 20: 46–98.

Wagner-Pacifici, Robin, and Barry Schwartz. 1991. "The Vietnam Veterans Memorial: Commemorating a Difficult Past." *American Journal of Sociology* 97: 376–420.

Wakabayashi, Bob Tadashi. 2000. "The Nanking 100-Man Killing Contest Debate: War Guilt amid Fabricated Illusions, 1971–75." *Journal of Japanese Studies* 26: 307–340.

————. 2001. "Review: The Nanking Massacre: Now You See It…." *Monumenta Nipponica* 56: 521–544.

————, ed. 2007. *The Nanking Atrocity, 1937–38: Complicating the Picture*. New York: Berghahn Books.

White, Hayden. 1973. *Metahistory: The Historical Imagination in Nineteenth-Century Europe*. Baltimore: Johns Hopkins University Press.

Wickert, Erwin, ed. 1998. *The Good Man of Nanking: The Diaries of John Rabe*. New York: Alfred A. Knopf.

Xu, Xiaohong, and Lyn Spillman. 2010. "Political Centers, Progressive Narratives, and Cultural Trauma: Coming to Terms with the Nanking Massacre in China, 1937–1979." Pp. 101–128 in *Northeast Asia's Difficult Past: Studies in Collective Memory*. Mikyoung Kim and Barry Schwartz, eds. Basingstoke, UK, and New York: Palgrave Macmillan.

Yamamoto, Masahiro. 2000. *Nanking: Anatomy of an Atrocity*. Westport, CT: Praeger.

Yoshida, Takashi. 2006. *The Making of the "Rape of Nanking": History and Memory in Japan, China, and the United States*. New York: Oxford University Press.

CHAPTER 21

CULTURAL TRAUMA: EMOTION AND NARRATION

RON EYERMAN

THIS chapter will elaborate the theory of cultural trauma by contrasting it to the classical notion of trauma and illustrating the similarities and differences of these terms in a discussion of political assassination. The latter is based on research I'm currently doing concerning the assassinations of Martin Luther King, Jr. (1968), Robert Kennedy (1968), and Harvey Milk (1978) in the United States; Olof Palme (1986) and Anna Lindh (2003) in Sweden; and Pim Fortuyn (2002) and Theo van Gogh (2004) in the Netherlands. The idea of cultural trauma was first developed during a year-long sojourn at Stanford University's Center for Advanced Study in the Behavioral Sciences. The results of these seminars and discussions were compiled as distinctive, research-based essays in the volume *Cultural Trauma and Collective Identity* (California 2004) collectively edited by Jeffrey Alexander, Ron Eyerman, Bernhard Giesen, Neil Smelser, and Piotr Sztompka, all of whom had worked together for that year. The theory of cultural trauma has evolved into a core research interest and framework under the rubric of cultural sociology, and several works have been published, including Giesen 2004; Eyerman 2001, 2008 and 2011; Goodman 2009; and Eyerman, Alexander, and Breese 2011.

CLASSICAL TRAUMA THEORY

The word "trauma" stems from the ancient Greek, meaning "wound," and came to be applied to surgical wounds, "conceived on the model of a rupture of the skin or protective envelope of the body resulting in a catastrophic global reaction in the entire organism" (Leys 2000:19). In the late nineteenth century, the term was reinvented for use in the treatment of the aftereffects of railway accidents (see Leys 2000 for one genealogy of the term's meaning and usage, and Fassin and Rechtman 2009 for another). However, in contemporary medical, psychiatric, and literary usage, "The term *trauma* is understood as a wound inflicted not upon the body but upon the mind." The wound is inflicted by a shock so powerful that it breaches "the mind's experience of time, self and the world," eventually manifesting itself in dreams and flashbacks (Caruth 1996:3–4).[1] In the same tradition, Geoffrey Hartman (1996:159) defines trauma as "events or states of feeling that threaten" the limits of experience and that "puncture lived time and exist only as phantasms." For Dominick LaCapra (2004:61), "Trauma is a shattering experience that distorts memory…and may render it particularly vulnerable and fallible in the reporting of events." In this conception, an occurrence is traumatic not simply because it is forceful, but because it is unthinkable, in that it "resists simple comprehension"(Caruth 1996:6) and cannot be easily assimilated into already established frameworks of understanding. Trauma is an experience so powerful that it cannot be understood as it occurs, but must be recalled and reconstructed from the deep recesses of memory (Freud 1990; Breuer and Freud 1957). When describing their real-time experience of the murder of Swedish Foreign Minister Anna Lindh, both the country's prime minister and the chief investigating police officer said it felt "unreal" (*overklig*). Sirhan Sirhan, a perpetrator not a victim, claimed to have a memory blackout during the shooting of Robert Kennedy (apparently not unusual in violent crimes), and witnesses to that occurrence reported that things seemed to move in slow motion and be out of time.

The perceived unreality of an occurrence is part of what is meant by shock, a numbing of the senses and an inability to accept or take in what has, in fact, happened. There is also a probable mixing of "this has not happened" and "this cannot happen," as well as "this cannot happen here." The latter was part of the collective shock experienced in both Sweden and the Netherlands, where political murder and violence were rare. Such experience is usually relatively short-lived, as the possibility of denial fades and "reality" forces itself onto individual and collective consciousness. However, for some victims of shocking experience, the aftereffects never fade and continue to haunt the memory and behavior of those affected. Newspaper accounts following the murders of John Kennedy and Olof Palme report a "stunned" nation, and the banner headline of the *San Francisco Chronicle* following the murder of the city's mayor and Harvey Milk, a member of the governing board, proclaimed, "The City Weeps." Such collective attributions may be difficult to scientifically maintain, but they are easy to understand and accept. Public opinion surveys taken after such occurrences confirm this. A survey of contemporary reactions to the assassination of American president John Kennedy (1963) showed that: 79 percent of those interviewed felt they had lost a dear and close friend; 73 percent said they were angry that such a thing could happen; 83 percent felt ashamed that such a thing could happen in the United States; 53 percent acknowledged they had cried upon hearing the news; and 97 percent reported they thought about the hurt inflicted on the victim's family (data provided by R.S. Sigel in Sigel, ed. *Learning about Politics 1970*, cited in Åsard 2006:103–104; see also Bonjean et al. 1965). Public reaction to the Palme murder was comparable: 90 percent reported feeling upset that such a thing could happen in Sweden; 84 percent could not believe it; 82 percent felt angry that such a thing could happen in Sweden; 80 percent contemplated the hurt inflicted on the family, and as many felt sad. Forty-two percent felt as if they had lost a close friend (Bonjean et al. 1965:170). While these reactions and statistics might not represent "the nation," they do reflect a shared sense of shock. Erikson (1978) reports similar collective shock in his study of the aftermath of the flood at Buffalo Creek for which he uses the term "collective trauma" and proposes that "trauma can create community," just as a shocking occurrence can destroy it (Erikson 1995:185). Those who experienced and survived the flood felt only those with similar experience could truly understand them.

Such natural disasters can provide an occasion for affected collectivities to reflect on themselves in another sense. Along with its devastation, Hurricane Katrina in 2005 revealed aspects of the United States that were well hidden from many of its citizens. That poor people existed, and that many of them were black, were probably well known, but the powerful winds that battered New Orleans and pierced its levees, causing millions to flee their homes, exposed this reality in an unprecedented way. Who will forget the images of families stranded on roof tops and on highway overpasses waiting for days for help to arrive? Not only did this mediatized event bring the issue of race and poverty forcefully to collective awareness, the victims— who they were, how they should be labeled (were they refugees?), and how they were treated—became cause for national debate. This public discourse raised not only the issue of responsibility but also the broader one of "what type of society we are," in which such a tragedy could happen. This is one indicator of cultural trauma: An emerging broad public discourse in which collective foundations are opened for reflection.

Political assassinations are similar in that they can bring to the surface aspects of a society that normally lie deeply hidden and that they can be a catalyst for broad public debate. One major difference between assassinations and natural disaster equates to a difference between a so-called force of nature and the human hand (see White 2008 for a related discussion concerning event and fact). The issue of human responsibility was raised in regard to Hurricane Katrina, both in relation to the construction of the levee system that was meant to protect the city of New Orleans and in the response of political authorities to the disaster. But the main cause, the forceful winds, were largely seen as lying outside human control. I say "largely" because an argument can be made that some of the blame for that extraordinarily powerful hurricane may lie in what has been called global warming, the causes of which lie in human actions and decisions.

In the shock they evoke, natural disasters and political assassinations raise the question "why has this happened to us?" They have the capacity to awaken a sense of collective belonging, to create a "we," while at the same time raising questions about the grounds on which that collectivity rests. Such occurrences not only raise the issue of "why has this happened to us?" but also "who or what was responsible?"

The religious might see an act of God, a sign, or a punishment in such an occurrence. For the secular, natural disasters are just that, natural, something inflicted by forces outside human control. From this perspective, while we might be able to track their path or even make predictions about their likely occurrence, natural phenomena, like hurricanes and earthquakes, are not interpreted as the direct result of human action. Political assassinations on the other hand *are* the result of human actions: There is no one and nothing else to blame. The question "why has this happened to us?" which implies a collectivity—an "us"—also involves the search for those responsible. It is here that what I will call traumatic occurrences align with cultural trauma, as will be described and discussed in the following section. Attributing blame, settling on who is responsible, is a central part of the process of cultural trauma; and in political assassination, as opposed to natural disasters, the responsible party is a human agent. The process of reforming a collectivity, of bringing it to consciousness, and of naming the outside other that is responsible is a political process. What would more likely turn such a traumatic occurrence into a cultural trauma would be if the responsible party was someone inside the collective. The point I wish to make here is that for the analyst, political assassinations provide a unique opportunity to study the foundations of collective identity, as well as those of collective memory that are intimately intertwined. This has been a central issue in sociological thought since its origins in the nineteenth century.

According to Fassin and Rechtman (2009:30), it was London doctors treating the effects of railroad accidents in the late 1860s who "opened the path to trauma psychiatry." While Freud and Breuer first associated trauma with sexual fantasy and to what they labeled hysteric response, restricting its application to women (Leys 2000). Freud later expanded this notion to the affects of industrial and transportation accidents and elaborated these reflections in connection with the treatment of the victims of trench warfare during the First World War, even appearing as an expert witness in a famous court case against an eminent psychiatrist (Eissler 1986; see also Fassin and Rechtman 2009:52). This expanded the sources of trauma and the affected group to include men, though it still limited the term to the effects on combatants that were then primarily men. This conception of wartime trauma has now been expanded to include noncombatants, such as nurses and relatives of victims, most especially mothers (see Higonnet 2002). Trauma as applied here makes reference to a real occurrence, a physical blow that overwhelms the senses and against which the mind and body must defend itself. In addition to numbness—a condition where the capacity to feel pain is temporarily suspended—amnesia is another defense mechanism of the mind. The victim simply forgets or denies that anything has occurred. In developing a dynamic model, Freud called this the period of latency, where in this state of denial or protective forgetting, the trauma victim can appear quite normal in carrying out everyday routines. In this model, there is no exact time frame for this period. Iit could last for days or years, but the experience will at some point reemerge and manifest itself either in nightmares or some otherwise inexplicable, abnormal behavior. Freud's notion of trauma, while leaving open the question of direct experience and clearly identifiable victims, is firmly rooted at the individual level. For later theorists in this tradition, however, Auschwitz and Hiroshima fully disclosed the catastrophic potential of modernity, including not only bureaucratic rationality, but also faith in science and technology: Trauma and modernity were thus intimately linked in a much more general and abstract way (Horkheimer and Adorno 2002; Bauman 1989; Kaplan 2005; Caruth (1996); and LaCapra 2001.[2] From this perspective, one of the manifestations of a catastrophic age is taken to be the insufficiency of word and narrative to capture the affect of traumatic experience. Insufficient or even illegitimate as it may be, there has been an array of theoretical reflections around the idea of traumatic experience and traumatic memory (LaCapra (2001; White 2004 e.g.).

Contemporary revisions of the classical notion of trauma focus on two aspects: first, the traumatic affects on the victim, the recurrent unwanted intrusion of memory and its effect on behavior; and second, the call of attention to the limits of representation or rather as Caruth (1995) expresses it, the "impossibility" of memory and the specific kind of repressed experience that becomes available not only to the therapist but also to the theorist. Trauma, in other words, opens up a hidden world to the observer and, in this tragic sense, creates an opportunity to see what would otherwise remain deeply buried. In this sense, trauma at the individual level resembles crisis at the societal level. A crisis, such as a severe economic depression or a natural disaster, is a shocking occurrence that can cause a breakdown in daily routines and expose, at the same time, the largely taken-for-granted values that guide them: Crises, in this sense, reveal to a collective, the grounds of its collective identity (Habermas 1975).[3] Like individual trauma, a societal crisis is both a shock and an opportunity, revealing and making available for reflection what otherwise remains deeply hidden. At the collective level, such trauma can be inclusive as well as exclusive, and old collectivities can be reaffirmed, as well as new ones created.

TRAUMATIC OCCURRENCE

What is a traumatic occurrence? A traumatic occurrence is one that leaves those who experience it, directly or indirectly, with long-standing memory traces which affect not only emotional life, but also behavior in unexpected and uncontrollable ways. More importantly, in our context, however, a traumatic occurrence creates a biographical and historical watershed—as sense of before and after—that can shape individual memory and create a group consciousness, as Erikson has shown and as Karl Mannheim (1967) suggested with his notion of generational consciousness. One can distinguish individual and collective trauma, as well as gradations and levels with respect to traumatic occurrences, according to nearness to the actual situation, for example, being in the pantry room at the Ambassador Hotel during the shooting of Robert F. Kennedy (RFK) left a very deep, emotional impression on those there, but also effected great collective emotion as well. A sense of intimacy with the victim would also affect the force of the trauma, even if one was not actually present. Göran Persson, the Swedish prime minister, was a close friend of Anna Lindh, so close, that five years later he reported still having her phone number pre-recorded in his cell phone. Although not actually present at the scene of her murder, he remains deeply affected by her death. Similarly, one of the state prosecutors involved in the Lindh investigation reported feelings of great uneasiness when meeting the press, feelings she traced back to her work on the Palme investigation; the memory of that failure had set itself in her body. A third category could be identification with the person or with what the person represented. Upon hearing the announcement of Lindh's death, members of the working press and police corps openly wept. Photographer Bill Eppridge (2008) reports snapping photos as tears ran over his face, as he took pictures of mourners as the funeral train carrying the body of RFK moved from New York to Washington, DC. He and a colleague were so struck by Kennedy's murder that they refused to take a photograph of his casket being lowered into the ground, as if they could not, and would not, accept what had happened. There is another category that could be added: those occurrences that are remembered as traumatic, but not necessarily experienced. We will touch on this issue later on.

The reactions of these professionals to political assassination point to different types of shock and trauma—for individuals and for collectivities. The murders of RFK and Anna Lindh were similar in the sense that both were representative political figures, but not heads of their respective nations. Both were perhaps on their way to this position, and their deaths were similarly shocking in that respect. Reactions to their deaths evoked great collective sadness, as well as shock, a sense of loss, and thoughts about what could have been had they lived. These strong emotions left long-standing memory traces for their respective nations. We can say this with surety with reference to RFK, as forty years have passed, and the affects are still present and discussed. However, direct collective emotional reaction to these deaths varied. Though some feared that violence would erupt in the wake of Kennedy's death, none did. No one expected violence in the aftermath of Lindh's death. Great waves of violence erupted after the announcement of Martin Luther King's death and, on a much lesser scale, that of Theo van Gogh. Though neither was an elected official, both King and van Gogh were representative public figures, nonetheless, and both identified partisan constituencies who felt they were affected by this death. The death of Pim Fortuyn evoked strong displays of collective emotion, as his supporters blamed both the opposing political parties and the mass media for his murder. Immediately following Fortuyn's death, there were massive demonstrations, but few incidents of violence. Fortuyn was the leader of an opposition party and an anti-establishment movement; and even though he might very well have been elected prime minister in the coming election, he did not represent the nation, neither in the sence of some fundamental values nor as a formally elected political authority, in the same way as Lindh or Robert Kennedy. Nonetheless, Fortuyn's death set the stage for the violent reaction that would follow the assassination of his friend, Theo van Gogh thirty months later (Eyerman 2008).

CULTURAL TRAUMA

In an insightful discussion of the difference between psychological and cultural trauma, Neil Smelser (2004) finds one essential difference in the fact that cultural traumas are made, not born. He goes on to define cultural trauma as "an invasive and overwhelming event that is believed to undermine or overwhelm one or several essential ingredients of a culture or the culture as a whole" (Smelser in Alexander et al. 2004:38). Though acknowledging the discursive aspect of cultural trauma, Smelser grounds the process in an event. I think, however, that the key phrase here is "believed to undermine," a notion which undercuts any idea that an event could be traumatic in itself. This opens two vital questions: (1) Can any occurrence or event be made traumatic? (i.e., so that it is "believed to undermine" an established collective identity); and (2) if not, what is it that permits some occurrences to become traumatic in this sense and not other seemingly equally powerful or shocking occurrences to become traumatic? The first question points to the power to create belief. A radical social constructivist might argue that given the ultimate power to persuade could turn any occurrence into a "trauma."[4] This would be to push the idea that "traumas are made not born" to its limits. At the other extreme, a strong naturalist or lay trauma account (Alexander 2004) would make the claim that certain events are traumatic in themselves, that is, be the direct cause of traumatic affect. Elsewhere (Eyerman 2001, 2008), I have made the case for a middle position that argues certain occurrences—in our current example, political assassinations—may create conditions conducive to setting in motion a process of cultural trauma, without being traumatic in themselves. This will not happen without the aid of meaning-making forces, such as mass media and certain carrier groups (Alexander 2004) like intellectuals, who influence the formation and direction of a process of cultural trauma.[5] However, not all or any interpretative frame will "fit" or make sense. There must be some relation, real or perceived, to some referent, an occurrence, experience or event, which itself appears "always there."

Cultural traumas are not things, but processes of meaning-making and attribution, a contentious contest in which various individuals and groups struggle to define a situation and to manage and control it. I would add that these forces are unlikely to create a trauma out of nothing; there is likely to be some powerful, shocking occurrence that creates the possibility, providing the opportunity to mobilize opinions and emotions.[6] There are thus two sides to a cultural trauma—an emotional experience and an interpretative reaction. Shocks arouse emotion by breaking everyday routines (behaviors as well as cognitive frameworks) and, as such, demand interpretation, opening a discursive field where well-placed individuals can play a determinate role. In modern societies, access to mass media is significant in this interpretative and representational process. The usually asymmetrical polarity between perpetrator and victim is what distinguishes cultural trauma as discourse. In this sense, cultural trauma is a contentious, discursive process, framed by a dichotomy between perpetrator and victim, that is spurred by a powerful, unforgettable occurrence, even one occurring in the distant past. Neil Smelser (2004:44) formalizes cultural trauma in this way: "A memory accepted and publically given credence by a relevant membership group and evoking an event or situation which is a) laden with negative affect, b) represented as indelible, and c) regarded as threatening a society's existence or violating one or more of its fundamental cultural presuppositions." This implies that an established collective identity is shaken and its foundations called into question. Cultural trauma is a discursive process where the emotions that are triggered by a traumatic occurrence are worked through, and an attempt is made to heal a collective wound (Erikson 1995). There is no guarantee, however, that healing or repair will be successful.

Cultural traumas are thus more than discursive struggles between competing individual and collective actors to define a situation, distinguish perpetrator and victim, and identify the nature of the pain. That would limit the process to instrumental or strategic interaction that could be analyzed through a discourse analysis, similar to that employed in frame analysis. Cultural traumas reflect deeply felt emotions and identities that are publicly expressed and represented in this discursive process, implying an expressive and communicative dimension that makes claims to authenticity and sincerity. The veracity of such claims must be addressed; something which points beyond traditional discourse analysis. More than that, as discursive process, resulting from extreme violence and exposing the deep emotional base that grounds individual and collective, cultural trauma is both an articulation/representation of this emotional grounding and at the same time a working-through, a searching attempt at collective repair. Such a process is certainly open to strategic attempts to "define the situation" and to manipulation by agents and entrepreneurs, but it cannot be reduced to them or to this. Anything connected to identity falls within the realm of the sacred (Giesen 2004) and as such is bound up with powerful emotions, such as dignity, envy, shame, self-confidence, and assurance. There are deeply rooted emotions and scripted identities drawn upon in cultural trauma—ethnic or national identities, for example—that may lie under the surface of everyday interactions but also may be mobilized in the face of a shocking occurrence, such as a political assassination. This was the case with the assassination of Archduke Ferdinand in 1914 that spiraled into a war which fundamentally altered the political geography of Europe. In this sense, a cultural trauma is a meaning-struggle emerging out of current or recalled shocking occurrences where collective identities, as well as collective memories, are at stake (Eyerman 2001).

Smelser (2004:37–38) makes another distinction—usefully illustrated through political assassination—between social and cultural trauma. While a cultural trauma invokes public discourse on the fundaments of an established collective identity, social trauma refers to "strains on institutions" and "disruptions of social life." Smelser's example of cultural trauma is the Protestant Reformation, which posed a successful "fundamental threat to the dominant Catholic world view" (2004:38). Social trauma refers to a process similar in form to cultural trauma, but delimited to particular institutions or groups in a society rather than to the social whole. Smelser's example of social trauma is the Great Depression, which impacted the lives of most Americans but never appeared to threaten their fundamental values or beliefs, though there were of course organizations and movements that sought to make that happen. There is, thus, an element of mediation, success, and failure in the relation between social and cultural trauma in Smelser's account. Shocking events like political assassinations may appear to shake an entire nation, but the long term effects may be more strongly felt and lasting within specific institutions or by particular groups. Two examples should illustrate this. The murder of Olof Palme in Sweden shocked the nation in a powerful way, but its long-term effects appear to be most strongly felt in the Social Democratic Party and in the police corps—institutions that were most directly affected. The murder, and its representation, also affected journalism and the mass media; and Swedish journalism—that includes radio as a central feature—was fundamentally altered after the Palme murder. This event remains a prime reference point in the education of journalists.[7] Similarly, the murder of Martin Luther King, Jr. (MLK) in the United States was shocking. It was called a national tragedy. Though felt most powerfully among African Americans, MLK has since become an icon of the "American experience," and a national holiday, celebrating his birth not his death, is commemorated annually.

We can now return to the question of how it is that a collective comes to believe that an occurrence "overwhelms" their already established collective identity. Collective identities are rooted in beliefs that are maintained in everyday life through routine practices. Routines provide confirmation and security in that they allow beliefs to be taken for granted and to be, in a sense, forgotten. An example may help illustrate what I mean. One of the first public statements made by the Swedish Prime Minister after the death of Anna Lindh was, "This is an attack on our democratic society." That Sweden is a democratic society is a fundamental belief and a value grounding modern Swedish collective identity. This belief is not only taught in schools but is also bound up in routine practices, like voting every three years to elect the government. The fact that Sweden is a "democracy" is normally taken for granted. The murder of Anna Lindh was shocking, not only because she was a well-known member of the collective, but also because she was a political figure, a representative of that democratic process. At least for the prime minister, another representative figure, her murder presented a threat to that fundamental value/ identity, as well as to the political process that underpins it. It was thus important for the security and the stability of that identity, not only that the murderer be caught—which was a police matter—but also that the rules and procedures of the political system that would guarantee stability were immediately put on display. This was even clearer in the murder of Prime Minister Olof Palme, where the same radio bulletin which announced the murder to the public also confirmed that the government was already meeting to ensure the succession of his replacement. Since shocking events like political assassinations break everyday routines and can call into question fundamental taken-for-granted beliefs, it is, thus, important that those in positions of authority act quickly to reaffirm those basic identities.

To act in this manner is one way of assuring, or attempting to ensure, that the shock caused by political assassination will be contained and limited to an institution or set of institutions—in this case, that of politics and law enforcement—and not involve the society at large. Not to do so, or if such performances of authority fail, extends the risk that a social trauma will become a cultural trauma.

This allows us to make use of one more idea in Smelser's discussion of cultural trauma, that of shocking occurrences as being "potentially" traumatic which must be successfully "endowed with negative affect" in order to be fully realized. Central in the meaning-struggle—and, thus, to the making of a cultural trauma—is the successful attribution of terms like "national tragedy," "national shame," and "national catastrophe" and their acceptance by a significant part of the collective. This is what is meant by the phrase, come to "believe to undermine," where a signifi-cant number—who can say how many—members of a collective come to believe that the shock is a "national tragedy" that undermines the fundamental values which have defined the collective. This is what turns or transforms a shock into a cultural trauma and leads to Smelser's more formal definition: "A cultural trauma is a mem-ory accepted or given credence by a relevant membership group and evoking an event or situation which is a) laden with negative affect, b) represented as indelible, and 3) regarded as threatening a society's existence or violating one or more of its fundamental cultural pre-suppositions" (Smelser 2004:44).

Even when speaking of a collective, one must ask, "trauma for whom?" (Giesen 2004, Eyerman 2008). Imaginary collectivities, like nations or ethnic groups, are rarely unified or univocal. One effect of a traumatic occurrence can be to provide a sense of coherence and collectivity, even if this is also imaginary and temporary, as Erikson suggested. The attack on New York's World Trade Center in 2001 appeared to unify the American nation into an emotional collective, producing ritual prac-tices that helped sustain it, just as the phrase "9/11" is meant to evoke and signify shared experience and collective understanding. But digging beneath that ephem-eral surface, in large part facilitated through mass-mediated representations, one would undoubtedly find individuals, and even groups, who would dissent in that feeling. In this sense, a traumatic occurrence has the potential to both unify and divide, to create insiders and outsiders. This potential must however be realized, and it is here that what Alexander (2004:11)—following Max Weber—called "carrier groups" play an important role. Such groups articulate and represent trauma, making it available for communication and shared understanding. They help transform emotional response into words and images that can be dispersed and remembered. Artists, writers, journalists, and political and religious leaders are important social categories in this articulation and play an important role in the trauma process, but the idea of carrier groups is broader than these professional categories. Carrier groups can be preexisting or form in response to a particular traumatic occurrence, while professional categories, such as those mentioned, may be significant agents within them. For example, the murder of Pim Fortuyn was clearly traumatic for his followers, and this group played an important role in turning that occurrence into a national event. However, the media in general, and journalists in particular, also played an indispensible role in that process, whatever their feelings toward Fortuyn. Many have noted that both the rise and fall of Fortuyn were strongly influenced by the mass media. In fact, at the mass demonstrations that followed his death, one of the slogans repeated over and over by his supporters was that he was, in fact, murdered by the mass media, even if the actual killer was a lone individual already in custody (Faber 2008).

Carrier groups not only are central to the making of cultural trauma, they are important in its continued affect. Carrier groups are bearers of memory. As mentioned, the groups most affected in the long term by the murder of Olof Palme were the Swedish Social Democratic Party and the Swedish police corps. The murder of Anna Lindh seventeen years later brought the memory of Palme's murder directly to life for both groups. The reactions of the police to Lindh's murder was determined to a great extent by their sense of failure regarding Palme's murder, and the Social Democratic Party was viscerally reminded of the loss of their exulted leader when Foreign Minister Anna Lindh, also a party member, died. Cultural trauma in this sense refers to a process through which collectivities are articulated, formed, and reformed in the light of traumatic occurrences like political assassinations. Shocking occurrences and traumatic events need not only have negative outcomes for all concerned. The failed assassination attempt on American President Ronald Reagan on March 30, 1981, just sixty-nine days into his presidency, actually served to strengthen his public image and gave him more political capital. He was able to push through his political platform with greater ease.

Carrier groups include collective actors placed under broad-umbrella concepts, such as the "mass media." In a remarkable passage written soon after the assassination of John F. Kennedy (JFK), Theodore White, an American journalist responsible for a series of firsthand accounts of "the making of the president," described the power of television in helping to create a sense of collective belonging that would become part of the myth and legend of collective memory:

> The spectacle of the next three days is so new to memory that to retell it falls impossibly short of still-fresh emotions. What will be difficult for historians to grasp, however, was that the ceremonies that followed were more than spectacle— they were a political and psychological event of measureless dimension. And in this event the chief servant was American television, performing duties of journalism with supreme excellence. Within minutes of the shot, American television was already mobilizing. In half an hour all commercial programs had been wiped from the air, and thereafter, abandoning all cost accounting, television proceeded to unify the nation....The political result of this participation, of this national lament, was a psychological event which no practical politician will ever be able to ignore....The drama gave all people a sense of identification, and translated the majesty of leadership into an intimate simplicity of Biblical nature. There was in the drama of the four days all things to bind men—a hero, slain; a sorrowing wife; a stricken mother and family; and two enchanting children. So broad was the emotional span, embracing every member of every family from schoolchild to grandparent, that it made the grief of the Kennedys a common grief. (White 1965:13–14)

What then is the relation between shocking occurrences and cultural trauma? An attempt at a schematic diagram would look like this: shocking occurrence; traumatic event (mass media); attempts at management and repair (performing authorities); cultural trauma (carrier groups); and collective memory. This could be called a weak social constructivist viewpoint, something that I have more fully developed in two books (Eyerman 2001, 2008). As previously mentioned, cultural trauma is a historically bound and produced narrative in which the positions of the perpetrator and victim are central. It emerges in the context of shocking occurrences and carries the notion that "we are not the same" after such an occurrence. In this sense, periodization—as sense of before and after—is as central to the trauma narrative as perpetrators and victims. In political assassinations, there are at least two victims, the murdered individual and the collective that associates itself with that individual. Carrier groups articulate the significance of this occurrence for the collective, and to the extent they are successful, the occurrence becomes a vital part of that group's collective memory. Wider than this however, the polarity between perpetrator and victim is encased within a culturally specific, normative framework wherein, for example, but not necessarily, perpetrators are represented as evil and tainted, where victims are good and innocent. In some cases, such as that of Anna Lindh, perpetrators can also be represented as victims. The framing of victim and perpetrator is part of the meaning-struggle in the trauma process. The specific content of this normative framework varies according to the historical narratives which define the parameters of national identity. In the Netherlands, for example, the Second World War marked a significant turning point in defining what it meant to be Dutch (Eyerman 2008). The surprisingly quick defeat of the Dutch army, and the occupation of the country by the Germans, provided a newly refined moral framework for what was good and evil, with good being associated with a rather ambiguous loyalty to the exiled House of Orange and evil with ideology of the occupier, Nazism, in particular, and fascism, more generally. This framework helped shape public discourse both before and after the murders of Pim Fortuyn and Theo van Gogh., and it provided, to an extent at least, the framework through which the murders were interpreted. For those on the political left, as the charismatic leader of a social movement, Fortuyn represented a revitalized fascism; while Theo van Gogh heard the thumping of black boots when he looked at Muslims. Both these victims of assassination claimed to be defending the innocent Dutch from impending evil. The portrayal of the perpetrator in each case varied significantly. While it was not difficult to paint the killer of Theo van Gogh as the epitome of evil, it was more difficult in the case of the solidly Dutchman who murdered Fortuyn.

Another "root narrative" (Wagner-Pacifici (1986), through which these occurrences were filtered, was that of the right to free speech and expression, a discourse which took new form in the 1960s. As representative figures of that expressive and self-centered generation, Van Gogh and Fortuyn both claimed the right to publically say what they felt and to live their lives accordingly, no matter what others might think or do. The right to free expression and to choose one's "life style" provided a principled standpoint around which many diverse individuals could collectively rally in the aftermath of these murders.

Their respective killers also interpreted their actions through a normative, moral framework. Volkert van der Graaf viewed his victim as representing an evil that threatened the foundations of a just and caring Dutch society, just as Mohammed Bouyeri saw in Theo van Gogh all the evil that was Western civilization. From the point of view of the established order, one dimension of the cultural trauma process is the potential rupture and the attempts to maintain and repair such a moral framework. If the killer of Pim Fortuyn had turned out to be the Muslim extremist as many anticipated, this would have confirmed and reinforced some established notions of good and evil. When it turned out that the killer was a rather ordinary Dutchman, the affect was confusion and the search for explanation. That he could be labeled an "animal-rights activist" provided some consolation. This labeling of the perpetrator as an extremist also reaffirmed the claim that this was a political assassination, something which became a centerpiece at the perpetrator's trial.

It is possible to construct a schematic like the following where the crossing of two lines define a field of traumatic and nontraumatic political assassinations:

Victims
Good/Evil
Perpetrators

As defined by an assumed consensus, the persons killed in my examples all fall within the space where victims were represented as good and the perpetrators as evil. One can think of other cases where the opposite is true, where the the victim was portrayed as evil and the perpetrators portrayed as good, such as that of the Black Panther leader Bobby Hutton killed by the police two days after Martin Luther King, a killing viewed by some as an assassination. This labeling would presumably play a role in any trauma process and shape the possibility of an emergent cultural trauma.

Pointing to the moral framework highlights the cultural aspects that condition the emergence of cultural trauma. Asking the question "under what conditions does a traumatic occurrence like political assassination evolve into cultural trauma"; to use concepts like "carrier groups"; and to scrutinize how well legitimate authority manages this occurrence, is to follow a well-established explanatory path best laid out by Max Weber in his comparative studies of the emergence of modern capitalism. Adding a moral framework adds a specifically cultural dimension to this explanation. A factor, or to use traditional language, variables determining what does or does not become a cultural trauma are the specific cultural structures, the moral framework defining good and evil, and the grounding myths of the nation present in any society at a given time. These help define what are understood as threats to the collective and give political assassinations some of their force. This is another way of saying that our emotional reactions, even those to shocking occurrences, are necessarily filtered through an already existing and readily available cultural framework. This includes reactions to assassinations. One of the central cultural discourses grounding the self-understanding of modern democracies is that of being civilized, not primitive—a notion which encompasses reactions to acts of violence, even those which may threaten national stability. Assassinations and assassins must thus be treated in way that conforms to this notion, which explains why one of the acts of established authority is the call for calm and "reasoned" response. Political assassinations are almost by definition potentially traumatic far beyond the experience of those present, but if a perpetrator can be defined as a mentally unstable, lone individual, some of the force of that potential is mitigated. The event can then be more easily stabilized and contained as shocking and traumatic for a time and even included in the collective memory, but will not have the long-term negative impact of a cultural trauma.

Cultural traumas can only be known and studied retrospectively. It is only after the passing of time—how much exactly is uncertain—that we can know if the affect of a traumatic occurrence is still felt, still alive. In this sense, cultural trauma resembles the trauma experienced by individuals, and its effects remain under the surface and become visible, are revealed, sometimes long after the fact. As it is currently reinterpreted, trauma disrupts narrative (LaCapra 2001; Caruth 1996) in the sense that it ruptures the flow of everyday experience. Here, trauma lies outside existing narrative, awaiting its formal representation. More broadly, trauma has also been linked to modernity (Kaplan 2005) and to the modern experience of time. The modern experience of time is that of a constant and continual flow moving irrevocably forward, as in the expressions, "time moves on" and "time heals all wounds." Trauma in this view is out of time, a break in this flow, and is at once symptom and cause. Trauma presupposes this view of time in order for it to be experienced as interrupted, broken, and shattered. Trauma is experienced through symptoms, the involuntary reactions to a past event, and an acting out that requires working-through. In this sense, trauma is always already there, awaiting representation.

Cultural trauma implies something different. For cultural trauma theory, trauma emerges through narration, through argumentation and counter argumentation, which gives form to its emotional content. This discursive process, a trauma drama, makes visible, articulates, and gives meaning and words to what is strongly felt but not grasped. Trauma is named and given voice through the ongoing public dialogue or meaning-struggle. It does not exist as a thing-in-itself, but only comes to be through dialogue and narration. This process or trauma drama is at one and the same time an acting out (in both a psychological and social sense) and a working-through. It is also a process in which the mass media play a leading role, both in terms of articulating and representing and in the healing and working-through. The media can orchestrate—being a prime and self-interested agent—as well as a forceful agent in the process of social repair.

Finally, the theory of cultural trauma provides a framework of analysis, a heuristic device constructed by the social theorist as a tool to retrospectively map a discursive process. Here, the theory becomes a model through which one can organize historical and empirical material in a structured and coherent way, allowing one to make sense of seemingly disparate occurrences through a coherent narrative.

As a framework of analysis, cultural trauma allows one to study the struggle to come to grips with traumatic occurrences, to locate the central actors in this meaning-struggle, and to trace the process over long periods of time. In my study, the role of the memory of slavery in the formation of African American identity (Eyerman 2001), for example, I was able to trace this process over several generations, and Rui Gao and Ivana Spasic (both in Eyerman et al 2011.) were able to map the "trauma narratives" in Mao's China and in Serbia, respectively. In such accounts, the relation to the actual experience of "traumatic occurrences" or even their existence may be contested. In fact, the phrase "chosen trauma" has been coined in reference to the transgenerational transmission of national or large-group identities of this sort (Volkan 2001). Still the issue of the veracity of these narratives and their relation to actual events and experience can be addressed. Foundational narratives of collective identity, such as that described by Eyerman, Gao, and Spasic mentioned above, are often rooted in a traumatic occurrence that forms the primal scene of the group's identity where there is an affinity to myth. But even foundational narratives— whether we view them as myths, ideologies, or narrated collective memory—must "fit" the changing world in which a collective finds itself. In this sense, they open themselves for reflection and for criticism. In addition to this, traumatic occurrences, like political assassinations, can open such foundational narratives to critical reflection, creating a crisis of identity as well as opening a meaning-struggle to define the situation. In such a situation, as happened in the United States after a series of assassinations in the 1960s, the older, established narrative is called into question and claimed to be "mistaken," if not "false," on the basis of now problematized taken-for-granted truth claims. In this sense, "the sixties" can be described as a cultural trauma, where the foundations of the collective, the meaning of being an American, were exposed and fought over in a trauma drama which may still be ongoing.

Let me conclude on a methodological note. Cultural trauma is a theoretical construct, a heuristic that permits us to set borders around an occurrence that reaches back into the past and forward into the future. The aim is to make deeply buried, culture structures available to the analyst. Like the frame around a painting, the theory of cultural trauma allows us to mark off a historical process, to distinguish foreground and background, and to highlight specific features. Unlike the construction of a theoretical model, the aim is not to construct hypotheses but to uncover layers of meaning that help us gain a deeper understanding of significance and consequence. The theory of cultural trauma permits one to analyze the mediatized process from occurrence to event (Mast 2006). Occurrences, even relatively rare ones like political assassinations, become events through mediated representations, whereby they are reconstructed as broadly significant and meaningful. This process of event-making necessarily involves conflicting interpretations and the attempt by various agents and agencies to define the situation in a particular way and from a particular perspective. Not all occurrences become an event, but traumatic occurrences, like political assassinations, clearly have that potential. Turning an occurrence into an event involves a struggle to affix meaning. As a meta-theoretical framework of interpretation, and as a middle-range framework of analysis, cultural trauma allows one to highlight these meaning-struggles, while at the same time making possible a multilayered analysis of the entire process, including the "meaning" of the event-making process itself. In this analysis, individual responses to, and mediated representations of, powerful, event-generating occurrences are interpreted in the light of scripted frameworks and internalized as collective representations, sediments of individual and collective memory. This permits not only the identification of key agents in the struggle to affix and stabilize meaning but also allows the identification of significant collective processes. Analyzing the process of event-making helps make visible deeply rooted collective representations that in turn may aid in explaining why the occurrence is powerful or contains the traumatizing potential that it does. The aim of such analysis is at one and the same time to identify the agents and the scripted representaitons and to articulate the deep structure of collective representation.

NOTES

The author would like to thank Jeffrey Alexander, Nicolas Demertzis, Marc de Leeuw, and Jensen Sass, as well as all the participants at the Workshop at the Center for Cultural Sociology, Yale University, for their comments on earlier drafts of this essay. Many of the ideas presented here are further elaborated in Eyerman 2011.

1. The views expressed by Caruth are strongly criticized by Leys in her account of the geneology of trauma. For a defense of Caruth against Leys, see Felman 2002.

2. It is possible, I think, to say that certain books by Adorno, Bauman, and Freud were written in connection to working-through personal trauma.

3. Jurgen Habermas opens *Legitimation Crisis* (1975) with a discussion of the concept crisis, making clear the difference between the term's medical, aesthetic, and social scientific uses. In its medical usage, he associates crisis with the "idea of an objective force that deprives a subject of some part of his normal sovereignty...in classical aesthetics... crisis signifies the turning point in a fateful process that, despite all objectivity, does not simply impose itself from outside and does not remain external to the identity of the persons caught up in it" (Habermas 1975:1–2). Habermas then goes on to develop a social scientific notion of crisis which takes its starting point in systems theory, where "crisis states assume the form of a disintegration of social institutions" and threatens collective identity. He makes the claim that "social systems too have identities and can lose them" (Habermas 1975:3), creating conditions in which a complex process of unfolding can spiral and threaten a social system to its core. Looked at in this sophisticated sense, and of course as common sense, crisis may well be a term which could be applied to the aftermath of political assassinations. Indeed, there are similarities in Habermas' use of crisis and my use of cultural trauma. Against an objective notion of crisis used in the medical sciences, which are similar to the medical use of trauma, Habermas argues that crises must be interpreted and understood as such. They must in other words be narrated to be understood as crises. This is also characteristic of cultural trauma, which, in one of its applications, can be defined as a public discourse in which the foundations upon which a collective identity rests are opened for reflection and debate. Both concepts make reference to a shattering of everyday routine and the taken-for-granted assumptions that guide them. Cultural trauma

is a form of collective identity crisis, in which an established collectivity loses the secure sense of itself and seems to be adrift, existing in that liminal space Durkheim called anomie. Cultural trauma differs from crisis not only in that the foundations of a collective identity are threatened, thus engaging the social whole, and not only one or several institutions (see Smelser on the difference between a social and cultural trauma), but also with regard to longevity and long-term affect. Cultural traumas can be passed across generations, with their affect preserved in individual and collective memory, only to emerge in later generations in what could be called post-crisis symptoms. The deeply felt sense of crisis analyzed by Habermas might also evoke strong emotional response. Such emotional content is absent, however, or rarely mentioned in his account. The economic crises of the 1930s left deep scars and had long-term affects on the generation that experienced it, such as the mistrust in banks and in the credit system. Narrated as the "Great Depression," an economic crisis became a cultural trauma, affecting the way individual citizens and national leaders would react to seemingly similar crises, where deeply hidden anxieties could trigger seemingly irrational or impulse responses, as well as rational reflection and contextual comparison. Think, for example, of the world financial crisis of 2008, where immediate comparison to the Great Depression was drawn or denied. Crises can develop into cultural traumas through a meaning-struggle in which perpetrators and victims are named and asymmetrically positioned. Trauma requires narration of a specific kind, one in which neither irony nor humor is possible: the shock to the system is experienced as too great. Like crises, trauma produces a loss of confidence, in the world, in the individual, and for the nation. The assassinations of King and Kennedy helped produced such a loss in the United States, which came to final fruition in the loss of the Vietnam War. The reaction of 9/11 can perhaps be understood with reference to that, an acting out of repressed traumatic memory. Cultural traumas are as much about acting out as working-through, two key notions in the classical notion of trauma.

4. This is a different way of speaking about "radical constructivism" than LaCapra (2001:8) who uses it in the context of the line between history writing and fiction. In his sense, those—like Hayden White who argue that on the formal level there is no fundamental difference between writing history and writing fiction because both necessarily make use of narration—are radical constructivists.

5. A parallel might well be the Marxian idea of class consciousness and the distinction between class-in-itself and class-for-itself.

6. There is a growing literature on imagined and invented trauma. The former is rooted in the classical notion of trauma and concerns victims of trauma, such as childhood abuse where the child may misremember or block out information (see, e.g., Freyd 1997). At the opposite end, this category might also include those false memories and memoires of the Holocaust which have been written. Invented or mythical trauma can be found in the attempts by various individuals or social movements to ground a collective identity, such as in Serbian nationalism (Ivana Spasic, in Eyerman et al 2011.). Varnik Volkan (2001) prefers to speak of "chosen trauma" when discussing the collective identity of large groups, like ethnic, national, and religious groups. In his usage "a chosen trauma refers to the shared mental representation of a massive trauma that the group's ancestors suffered at the hand of an enemy" (2001:79). Since this "trauma" is most likely to have occurred long in the past, presumably no one recalling it was its direct victim, but rather a trauma narrative is constructed which defines the self-understanding of the group. In this sense, the trauma is chosen or imagined, but it is no less real for that.

7. Zelizer (1992:4) writes similarly of American journalism after the assassination of John Kennedy: "It was a turning point in the evolution of American journalistic practice

not only because it called for the rapid relay of information during a time of crisis, but also because it legitimated televised journalism as a mediator of national public experience."

REFERENCES

Alexander, Jeffrey, Ron Eyerman, Bernard Giesen, Neil Smelser, and Piotr Sztompka (eds.) (2004). *Cultural Trauma and Collective Identity*. Berkeley: University of California Press.

Alexander, Jeffrey, Bernhard Giesen, and Jason Mast (eds.) (2006). *Social Performance.* Cambridge, UK: Cambridge University Press.

Åsard, Erik (2006). *Det Dunkelt Tänkta* (Dark Thoughts). Stockholm: Ordfront

Bauman, Zygmunt (1989). *Modernity and the Holocaust.* Ithaca, NY: Cornell University Press.

Bonjean, Charles, Richard Hill, and Harry Martin (1965). "Reactions to the Assassination in Dallas" in Bradley Greenberg and Edwin Parker (eds.), *The Kennedy Assassination and the American Public.* Stanford, CA: Stanford University Press, pp. 178–198.

Breuer, Josef, and Sigmund Freud (1957). *Studies on Hysteria.* New York: Basic Books.

Caruth, Cathy (ed.) (1995). *Trauma: Explorations in Memory.* Baltimore: Johns Hopkins University Press.

———. (1996). *Unclaimed Experience.* Baltimore: Johns Hopkins University Press.

Demertzis, Nicolas (2009). "Mediatizing Traumas in the Risk Society. A Sociology of Emotions Approach" in D. Hopkins, J. Kleres, H. Flam, and H. Kuzmia (eds.), *Theorizing Emotions.* Frankfurt, Germany: Campus.

Eissler, K. R. (1986). *Freud as Expert Witness.* Madison, CT: International Universities Press.

Erikson, Kai (1978). *Everything in Its Path.* New York: Simon and Schuster.

———. (1995). "Notes on Trauma and Community" in K. Caruth (ed.), *Trauma: Explorations in Memory.* Baltimore: Johns Hopkins

Eyerman, Ron (2001). *Cultural Trauma Slavery and the Formation of African American Identity.* Cambridge, UK: Cambridge University Press.

———. (2008). *The Assassination of Theo van Gogh.* Durham, NC: Duke University Press.

———. (2011). *The Cultural Sociology of Political Assassination* New York: Palgrave Macmillan.

Eyerman, Ron, Jeffrey Alexander, and Elizabeth Breese (2011). *Narrating Trauma: On the Impact of Collective Suffering.* Boulder, CO: Paradigm.

Faber, Johan (2008). *Wat Bezielde Volkert Van Der G.* (What Possessed Volkert Van Der G.). Amsterdam: Nijgh & Van Ditmar.

Fassin, Didier, and Richard Rechtman (2009). *The Empire of Trauma.* Princeton, NJ: Princeton University Press.

Felman, Shoshana (2002). *The Juridical Unconscious.* Cambridge, MA: Harvard University Press.

Ford, Franklin (1985). *Political Murder.* Cambridge, MA: Harvard University Press.

Frank, Gerold (1972). *An American Death.* New York: Doubleday.

Freud, Sigmund (1990). *Beyond the Pleasure Principle.* New York: Norton.

Freyd, Jennifer (1997). *Betrayal Trauma: The Logic of Forgetting Childhood Abuse.* Cambridge, MA: Harvard University Press.

Giesen, Bernhard (2004). "The Trauma of the Perpetrators: The Holocaust as the Traumatic Reference of German National Identity" in Alexander et al.2004, pp. 112–154.

Goodman, Tanya (2009). *Staging Solidarity*. Boulder, CO: Paradigm.

Habermas, Jurgen (1975). *Legitimation Crisis*. Boston: Beacon Press.

Hartman, Geoffrey (1996). *The Longest Shadow* Bloomington: Indiana University Press.

Higgonnet, Margaret (2002). "Authenticity and Art in Trauma Narratives of World War 1." *Modernism/Modernity* 9(1): 91–107.

Horkheimer, Max, and Theodor Adorno (2002). *Dialectic of Enlightenment*. Stanford, CA: Stanford University Press.

Kansteiner, Wulf (2004). "Genealogy of a Category Mistake: A Critical Intellectual History of the Cultural Trauma Metaphor." *Rethinking History* 8(2): 193–221.

Kaplan, E. Ann (2005). *Trauma Culture*. New Brunswick, NJ: Rutgers University Press.

Kaplan, E. Ann, and Ben Wang (2004). *Trauma and Cinema*. Hong Kong: Hong Kong University Press.

LaCapra, Dominick (2001). *Writing History, Writing Trauma*. Baltimore: Johns Hopkins University Press.

Leys, Ruth (2000). *Trauma: A Geneology* Chicago: University of Chicago Press.

Mannheim, Karl (1967). *Essays in the Sociology of Culture* London: Routledge and Kegan Paul.

Mast, Jason (2006). "The Cultural Pragmatics of Event-ness: The Clinton-Lewinsky Affair" in Alexander et al. 2006, pp. 115–145.

Smelser, Neil (2004). "Psychological and Cultural Trauma" in Alexander et al 2004.

Volkan, Vamik (2001). "Transgenerational Transmissions and Chosen Traumas: An Aspect of Large-Group Identity." *Group Analysis* 34: 79–97.

Wagner-Pacifici, Robin (1986). *The Moro Morality Play*. Chicago: University of Chicago Press.

White, Hayden (2004). "The Historical Event." *Journal of Feminist Cultural Studies* 19(2): 9–34.

White, Theodore (1965). *The Making of The President 1964* New York: Harper Collins.

Zelizer, Barbie (1992). *Covering the Body*. Chicago: University of Chicago Press.

CHAPTER 22

REMEMBRANCE OF THINGS PAST: CULTURAL TRAUMA, THE "NANKING MASSACRE," AND CHINESE IDENTITY

JEFFREY C. ALEXANDER AND RUI GAO

TRADITIONALLY, the "science of society" has been associated with a resolutely objective and external point of view. The object of this view has been to locate the invisible, social structures that determine actors' lives from outside of their consciousness, via political and economic coercion or reward. Karl Marx and Max Weber have each been responsible for creating parts of this modern, social science legacy.

Cultural sociology provides an alternative perspective on the social and how to study it. Inspired particularly by an interpretation of the later ideas of Emile Durkheim, but also by the more cultural strand of Weber's work, cultural sociology connects this legacy from social science with humanistic scholarship and theory, drawing from such thinkers as Wilhelm Dilthey, Ferdinand Saussure, Ludwig Wittgenstein, Claude Lévi-Strauss, Roland Barthes, Northrup Frye, Victor Turner, and Clifford Geertz. The cultural-sociological perspective suggests that socially structured consciousness is, in itself, a highly significant cause of action. Individual actors are trying not only to avoid punishment or gain reward, but also to be faithful to their beliefs, emotionally engaged, and coherent in a moral sense.

From the cultural-sociological perspective, consciousness is not only individual. Social organizations from couples in love to peer groups, from gangs to political parties, and from organizations to nations—each of these collectivities has a consciousness of its own. Every group has a collective consciousness, whether fragmented or integrated, which exerts as much power as social structure in the more traditional, external sense. But collective consciousness exerts its force differently. Composed of symbols rather than instrumental resources, it draws boundaries between inside and outside and protects the space in between. The symbols that compose collective consciousness are organized by binary codes that compose variations on "us" versus "them," and by narratives that convert this religious-like division between the sacred and profane into stories about struggles between good protagonists and threatening or deviant antagonists, in which the life of the collectivity—its very collective identity—is at stake.

Cultural sociology has been applied to a range of empirical areas, from the impact of computers on society and environmental movements to musical performances and painting; from social movements for civil rights to movements for men's rights; and from studies of the transition from authoritarianism in Spain to studies of truth and reconciliation in the new South Africa. In these and other studies, *cultural* sociology has emerged as a distinctively "strong" program in contrast with the "weak" sociology *of* culture approach. The latter takes cultural phenomena as an object, understanding such objects as reflections of social structure rather than as meaningful forces in themselves. It employs methods and models drawn from the more mechanistic social and natural sciences, rather than placing itself squarely inside what Dilthey called the *Geisteswissenschaften*, or the human studies.

Cultural sociology directs itself not only to the effects of external and material objects, but also—and most distinctively—to representations of these objects, for in the empirical practices of social life, objects and their representations are woven inextricably together. In this sense, cultural sociology addresses the textual dimension of social life; its object is to ferret out meanings, not mechanisms. Cultural structures are causal; but they are, in the first place, semiotic, not mechanical, in their causal force. Cultural sociology employs rational methods, but these are primarily interpretive rather than experimental and statistical. When one studies meaning, it is impossible to achieve objectivity in the same manner as natural science, for it is one's own experience and consciousness that make it possible for one to understand the meaning of social action. This experiential boundary limits the possibilities of cultural sociology, but it enables it at the same time.

THE THEORY OF CULTURAL TRAUMA

One new area of research and theorizing that has been constituted by cultural sociology is collective trauma (see Alexander et al. 2004; Eyerman et al. 2011). In the course of the twentieth century, the notion that individuals and groups can suffer harm became an enduring social and political trope in Western social thought. The idea of "trauma" first emerged in Western thinking in the aftermath of World War I, with notions of shell shock, and the psychoanalytic movement later drew attention to deep emotional injuries whose effects could linger for years but whose origins and etiology remained unknown in the victims' conscious life. The type case for contemporary thinking about trauma is the Nazi Holocaust against the Jewish people in Europe, in which 6 million Jews were murdered between 1940 and 1945. It was the postwar reaction against this horrendous event that introduced the concept of genocide into collective consciousness, a term that in the 1990s generated the associated idea of ethnic cleansing.

From a cultural sociological perspective, collective trauma should not be considered as natural or automatic. Painful experiences can happen to individuals, but they are not necessarily transferred to the level of the group. For example, individuals in an urban area can be victims of painful crimes, from theft to violence, but the collective consciousness of the city itself may not be affected; it may see itself as safe, progressive, or exciting. It took decades for non-Jewish people to feel that they, too, were somehow affected by the Nazi genocide. Eventually, the event came to be central to the collective existence of non-Jewish people in the West. It helped define them as a collectivity; they felt that the Nazis' mass murder of millions of innocent people had somehow, in a symbolic manner, happened to them, in the sense that it damaged their sense of themselves as a moral collectivity. It was from this sense of collective trauma that such notions as international human rights arose, a collective, supra-national responsibility to prevent genocide and racial and ethnic cleansing in the present day. Of course, this responsibility is only very partially institutionalized and only fitfully carried out.

In order to understand the contingency of the movement from actual event to collective trauma, we need to accept a fundamental, if seemingly paradoxical, theoretical fact. A social event does not have any particular, determinate, or natural representation. In semiotic terms, there is a gap between the signifier (the symbol) and the signified (the social fact), and this gap can be bridged in a number of different ways. We see protestors gathering in a central city street, marching, and waving signs. Is this a progressive protest or a reactionary betrayal of hope? Is this a well-organized and planned movement, or a riot of irrational, intimidated persons? Are they inspired by a thoughtful charismatic leader or are they dupes, manipulated by conspiring demagogues? The symbolic media of representation can, and usually do, produce accounts of both kinds, and such competing signifiers are often attached to the same set of social signifieds.

Events are one thing; their interpretation another. We know this in our individual lives: How, after we experience something, we often need to think further about what it meant. On the collective level, it is the same, only more so. Things happen, but their representation is up in the air. What determines the collective representation of a social event? One important element is the established understandings that precede it. These set a kind of base line, a broad language that supplies basic intuitions about what things mean. But preexisting understandings are general; they must be interpreted vis-à-vis any specific event. There are always new and specific interpretations offered for every social event. They are proposed by individuals, but most often by institutions and carrier groups; parties, ethnic, class, gender, and racial groups; national representatives; and states. Via the symbolic media of communication, "claims" are proposed about what has just happened and what it means. If an event becomes significant, there is a struggle over representation, and in the course of this struggle, meanings can be changed, sometimes in drastic ways.

What affects this outcome? One factor is how effectively such symbolic claims are made. In 1847, two relatively unknown social philosophers, Karl Marx and Fredrich Engels, were engaged by a small group of German émigré workers in London to make a claim on their behalf. Against the background of early industrial capitalism, Marx and Engels cast a complaint so broad and so big—and they wrote it so skillfully—that their claim resounded for more than a century and eventually changed the world. *The Communist Manifesto* defined a trauma (capitalist exploitation), identified victims (the industrial proletariat) and perpetrators (the bourgeoisie), and set forth a solution (Communist revolution) that became fateful for Western and Eastern peoples alike.

These challenges are faced by every trauma claim, if it is to be generalized as a wound to the broader collectivity. Claims may be made on behalf of this or that group, but they must then be convincingly projected to a broader collectivity. This cultural work is a complex process. It begins with defining, symbolizing, and dramatizing what "happened." In the course of this narration, the identity of the victims must be established, and so must the identity of the perpetrators, tasks which are related to defining the trauma but have independence from it as well. Finally, a solution appropriate to these three "facts" must be proposed. The stakes are obviously high, and cultural struggle ensues over each phase of this trauma-creating process. Social resources such as power, status, and money vitally affect, but do not by themselves determine, the outcome. If a trauma-interpretation succeeds, it can put the carrier group into power, and its members have the chance to institutionalize their interpretation of past events in powerful ways.[1]

THE NANKING MASSACRE AND ITS INITIAL CONSTRUCTIONS

In Nanking, China, in December 1937, an event transpired that, sixty years later, a young Chinese American author would characterize as "the forgotten Holocaust" (Chang 1997).[2] After a six month struggle against Chiang Kai-shek's armies in the Yangtze Valley, Japanese military forces invaded the bustling coastal city of Nanking and engaged in a premeditated, systematic campaign of mass murder. Using such primitive techniques as cannons, pistols, fire, and swords, the soldiers created a horrendous massacre in which blood literally flowed through the streets. Seven weeks later, more than one-quarter million Chinese lay dead.[3]

Certainly, what came to be known, in the West, as the "Rape of Nanking" was immensely traumatic for the individuals who lived in that tragically desiccated city.

The cultural sociological question is why this event did not become traumatic on a more collective level as well. Why did it not became a major point of reference for China as a nation, searing itself into the collective memory, defining institutions, and demanding reform—as the nuclear bombings of Hiroshima and Nagasaki did for the Japanese people, the Jewish genocide for the Germans, and the enslavement of Africans for many groups in the West?[4]

The Japanese massacre in Nanking did not escape notice. For many contemporaries, inside China and outside, it was the subject of great consternation, despair, and dispute. Western observers were in and around Nanking, as diplomats, missionaries, and journalists. They broadcast alarmed and urgent representations of the event, and reports appeared in large black letters in newspapers and newsreels around the world. The horror was clear, the victims observed, and the perpetrators clearly seen as Japanese.

This initial construction of the mass murder does not, at first glance, seem cultural at all. The contemporary accounts, and retrospective histories such as Chang's, are angry descriptions that present themselves in an entirely naturalistic manner, as simply narrating a series of actually existing facts. If we step back from these accounts, however, we can see that the initial reports of alarm and outrage were deeply informed by the existing cultural structures of their time. We do not have to deny the brutal facts of the massacre, for example, to see that the reports were made in the context of the binary coding of "West" versus "East." The Second World War had not yet been declared, so that even representatives of the German Nazi government could criticize the massacre from within this centuries-long symbolic binary, and they did.[5] The barbarians from the East were at it again, acting in an unchristian way. For these Western observers, then, the massacre was seen against the backdrop of Japan's polluted rising sun; the shocking birth of an industrial Japan; its early victories over China and Russia; its occupation of Manchuria and Korea; and its militarization from the 1920s onward—all of which were constructed as an unprecedented, and unjustified, Eastern challenge to the West.

This "cultural stuff" mediated the feeling and perception of the mass murder at Nanking for the Western audience; it was not only empathy for the Chinese victims or ethical outrage as such. As the cultural-historical framework changed, the Nanking Massacre faded from view. When Americans themselves became the object of "Japanese perfidy," at Pearl Harbor on December 7, 1941, it became, in the words of President Franklin Roosevelt, "a day of infamy" that would live "forever," and the trauma was consecrated by the American people for the next fifty years. Yet, while the death of many hundreds of Americans on that sunny and peaceful morning in Hawaii truly was a human tragedy, it represented a mere asterisk in the history of human perfidy, a blip compared to the truly horrendous massacres in Nanking that had occurred only slightly more than four years before.

It is collective identity that matters in the construction of trauma, and the scope of this identity depends on identifying with a putative trauma's victims. It was Americans who had died at Japanese hands in Hawaii, and their deaths had been claimed as a national wound by no less than the president of the United States.

Constructed as further evidence of the barbaric "East," the event immediately became a national American trauma. Its solution was the Pacific War and the achievement of Japan's unconditional surrender, and it "required" inflicting revenge on hundreds of thousands of Japanese.

This shift from Western concern to Western silence about the massacre in Nanking makes cultural sense, then, even if it was unjustifiable from an ethical point of view and inexplicable from a purely rational, naturalistic perspective. What seems more difficult to perceive is why this trauma also disappeared from the consciousness of the Chinese.

The Disappearance of the Nanking Massacre

Contemporary awareness of the massacre, and extraordinary concern about it, had also initially extended to the Chinese. On December 20, 1937, on the front page of *Jiu Guo Shi Bao* (Saving the Country Times), a newspaper produced by Chinese Communist Party (CCP) members in Paris, there is a brief report on the retreat of the Kuomintang (Nationalist) army from Nanking, the capital city. While most of this article reports on the action and strategy of the army, a short paragraph records eyewitness testimony that three hundred Kuomintang POWs had been shot by the Japanese invaders and that their mutilated bodies had been piled high in the city's streets. Fuller reports on the atrocity appeared in a later issue. In an article entitled "The Killing and Raping by the Japanese Enemy Are Inhuman Atrocities" (*Jiu Guo Shi Bao*, 1/31/1938, p. 1),[6] a writer listed dozens of horrendous atrocities, including the "killing competitions," drawing mainly from published reports of foreign witnesses. At the end of the article, the writer cried out that such outrageous brutality must be revenged—that "those who do not want their own people to be wantonly murdered, who do not want their own sisters to be raped" must take action. To fight "until the last trench" would "be not only to defeat the enemy of China but also to wipe out evils against all of humanity!" (*Jiu Guo Shi Bao*, 1/31/1938, p. 1). Similarly heightened rhetoric can be found in a short commentary in *Qun Zhong* (The Masses), a CCP weekly journal published in Hankou city, on January 1, 1938. Under the title "Enemy Atrocities Despised by Humanity" (*Qun Zhong*, Vol. 1, 1938, p. 56),[7] the massacre in Nanking is depicted as the most "unprecedented bloody brutality that human history ever recorded," as a declaration of war against not only the Chinese nation but also the human race. The last short piece on the massacre appears in the January 29, 1938, issue of *Qun Zhong* and briefly mentions the infamous "killing competition."

These representations of the massacre were crowded into the time immediately following the incident, the short period of active attention that usually characterizes the span of media coverage for important news happenings. After this brief window, the record goes virtually silent. Indeed, with the scant exceptions we will note below, there is virtually no reference to the Nanking Massacre, in the literature produced by the CCP, either before or after the 1949 revolution, for almost half a century. It can fairly be said that the infamous incident, widely publicized and remembered at the time, vanished from the Chinese nation's tightly controlled mediascape after its intense, but very brief, initial coverage.

In what follows, we are primarily concerned with the Communist reaction to the Nanking Massacre, for it was on this left side of China's twentieth-century civil war that control of the national collective identity came to rest. The CCP's "nationalist" opponents did, in fact, give to the massacre more significant attention. In the International Military Tribunal of the Far East, in 1945, legal claims about the Nanking events were made by the anti-Communist Kuomintang (KMT) that had fought the CCP for decades and had represented the government of China both during the War of Resistance and afterward until 1949. KMT media also offered fervent representations of the massacre on its tenth anniversary, in 1947. The first of these claims, however, were confined largely to the international legal-institutional sphere, and they were quickly dropped from Kuomintang's priority as the government shifted its postwar energies back to the fight against the CCP. As for the second group of the KMT representations—those that emerged around the massacre's tenth anniversary—they were contextualized in a manner that relativized their significance, as we shall later see.[8]

When the Communists took power in 1949, the silence about Nanking continued. For at least two decades after the revolution, the massacre went thoroughly unmentioned in the new China's elementary and junior middle school history texts.[9] For instance, in the 1950 edition of the history textbook for the final year of elementary school, when the text came to the temporal point of the incident, there is simply this plain, brief, and passive voice sentence: "Nanking was lost on December 13."[10] Similarly, in the 1956 edition of a junior middle school history manual, the Nanking tragedy did not make it into the narrative devoted to historical occurrences in 1937; instead, the text seemed keen on exposing the hopeless and breathless retreats of Kuomintang forces in the face of the invading Japanese army: "At the end of 1937, Kuomintang forces that were originally stationed in north central China had retreated to regions close to the banks of Yellow River. In central and south central China, Shanghai was lost in November 1937, and then Nanking in December. By October the next year, the Japanese forces had occupied Guangzhou and then Wuhan. Thus, Kuomintang had thrown away half of China and fled all the way to Chongqing, Sichuan."[11] The silence on Nanking even applied to some of the reference books that were made available to teachers.[12] It was not until 1979, forty years after the event, that a brief documentation of the massacre first appeared, in a history text for junior middle schools, and not until 1992 that the massacre entered into the required reading for elementary schools in post-Maoist China.[13]

This absence of representation in the identity-forming texts of young Chinese was matched by silence about the massacre in the public rhetoric broadcast to their parents. An examination of *People's Daily* articles between 1946 and 1982 finds only fifteen articles in which the key words "Nanking Massacre" ever appeared. Even these articles were mostly not *about* the massacre, but, rather, arose in response to international conflicts, with reference to the massacre being made in the course of reporting about them. These articles do not refer to the massacre in their titles, and they take neither the event of the massacre nor its memorization as a main theme.[14]

In the years after the massacre, there may have been carrier groups inside Nanking making claims about the terrible events of 1937, and perhaps elsewhere in China as well. There can be no doubt that hundreds of thousands of persons had to make individual sense of their calamitous losses. Whether some more collective efforts did emerge during these times is a topic for future research. We would have some reason to doubt, however, even if such efforts did occur, that they were able to push the trauma construction process very far. When Nanking was controlled by the Japanese occupier, the trauma creation process was subject to control by the very groups who had perpetrated the crime. Evidence of the massacre was destroyed, observers silenced, and counternarratives disseminated throughout the occupied territories. Certainly, foreigners were not allowed to visit, and dissemblance was the order of the day.[15] All this recalls German Nazis and the Holocaust. The concentration and death camps were located on Nazi-occupied soil. It was impossible for these events to be consecrated and convincingly represented as evil as long as the perpetrators controlled the means of symbolic communication and the sites where the representation of genocide would have to be made.

This did not mean, however, that representations about trauma could not have been made from Chinese groups and areas outside Japanese control during the war period, and it certainly does not explain why the trauma process did not emerge after China's liberation from the Japanese in 1945, much less after the creation of a stable and more powerful Chinese state in 1949. What fascinates our historical and sociological imagination is that it did not. The reason is that the Chinese had other fish to fry. The potential carrier groups did not carry.

The Nationalists (KMT) and the Communists each had significant control over the means of symbolic production.[16] They not only had mass followings but also local, national, and worldwide audiences. If either had decided to make the Nanking Massacre an issue—if either leadership had chosen to represent the Nanking murders as a central trauma, projecting trauma narratives aimed at generating sympathy and interest—they would surely have been able to do so. What the effects of such representation might have been belong to the world of counterfactuals, but they are still worthy of speculation. If either of these carrier groups had been successful in projecting the Nanking trauma experience, the massacre might well have become inscribed in the collective memories of "China," in one or another of its national guises, and, as a result, the massacre would be much more widely known in the world today. What might the results of such familiarity have been? The dissemination of a "Nanking Massacre" trauma drama might have compelled Japan's postwar leadership to confront not only its own war-related traumas, but its neighbors' as well, triggering an expansion of Japanese empathy and solidarity that would have had far-reaching consequences in contemporary Asia. A more widespread understanding of this trauma drama also might also have provided another, importantly different lesson about ethnic cleansing and genocide from which the putative "world community" would have searched for lessons.

But these are counterfactuals. The historical reality was different. The mass murder in Nanking was not narrated as a collective trauma, and the opportunities to extend psychological identification and moral universalism were not taken up.[17] Again, the sociological question is why.

CONCENTRATING ON OTHER TRAUMAS: THE PARADOXES OF SOLIDARITY

The answer has to do with the paradoxes of solidarity, boundary-making, and collective identity. Traumas are constructed not only as threats to already existing collective identity, but also as symbolic vehicles that allow future collective identities to be formed. Neither for the Kuomintang nor for the Communists did the Nanking Massacre fit with who they thought they were, and even less with who they wanted to become. Before, during, and after the Nanking events, these two groups were engaged primarily with one another, in a massive, continent-wide civil war. Despite the Japanese invasion, and the eight long years of what came to be known as the "War of Resistance against Japan," neither side felt it was able to offer primary symbolic space to a powerful, massacring antagonist from the Japanese side. The KMT had nominally controlled Southern China in 1937, during the time and in the place the massacre had occurred. If they were to consecrate the massacre, they would have had to portray themselves as weak and ineffective victims; such imagery would not have sustained their all out war with the CCP. For the Communists, it would have been different; but collectivizing and commemorating the trauma would have symbolically unified the Chinese nation and defined as evil another nation, the Japanese. This would have contradicted the culture structures that motivated the revolutionary movement and that were already in place.

The system of cultural representations, against which the CCP perceived the events of those days, was sharply bifurcated. The CCP could not be itself without imagining a frightening and polluted antagonist on the other side. Mao Tse-tung (1967, 7) famously made this a cardinal principle: "Who are our friends, and who are our enemies? This is a question of the first importance for the revolution." Marxist philosophy gave Mao a format for concretizing this cultural necessity in terms of the social contradictions—the signifieds—of that day. In his theoretical essay "On Contradictions," Mao (1962) was flexible about how this binary logic could be applied. There were, he suggested, major and minor contradictions, and the relationship between them changed continuously over historical time.[18] The sacred was always the proletariat, represented by the identity and behavior of the Party. But alliances could be made with other parties, too, and the profane other could shift and change. Generally, the CCP's enemies included all those who opposed

Communism and revolution; during the Japanese occupation, however, the Party formed a pragmatic alliance with the Kuomintang, allowing Japanese imperialists to become the main antagonist for the nation as a whole. But this marked only a temporary reconfiguring of the major contradiction. The main story line was different—publicly for many years before the occupation, privately inside the Party during the years of occupation, and publicly after the occupation and for decades after that.

REVOLUTION AS A RESPONSE
TO TRAUMA CONSTRUCTION

China had indeed suffered great traumas, but these were represented as injuries to the Communist collectivity itself and to the Chinese people insofar as they were signified symbolically through the Party's texts. According to official CCP histories, there had been a series of systematic persecutions and mass murders for more than twenty years, from 1927 to 1949. These had been perpetrated by the Kuomintang regime. In each and every single edition of required history textbooks, an independent section was devoted to vivid depictions of "the Anti-Revolutionary Incident of April 12th," widely known as the "April 12th Massacre,"[19] that portrayed, in gruesome and emotional language, how bodies of revolutionary people were piled up into huge mounds and "the entire streets were turned into ocean of blood!"[20] According to these school history texts, this "massacre" was perpetrated by the arch-traitor of revolution, Chiang Kai-shek, and together with the "July 15th Anti-Revolutionary Incident,"[21] it commenced a series of dark historical moments known as "White Terror," during which vast numbers of CCP members and some enormous part of the revolutionary masses—"the most distinguished daughters and sons of the Chinese nation"[22]—were arrested, tortured, and "brutally massacred by Kuomintang regime."[23] Indeed, according to one text, during the period "from 1928 to 1930" alone, "the revolutionary martyrs that died under the butcher knife of Kuomintang amounted to 730,000."[24] Such merciless mass killing, moreover, was not halted when the KMT and the CCP were officially allied in the Second United Front during the War of Resistance. Lamented in all editions of required history texts[25] is the fact that, in 1941, just when the nation was in dire need of resistance forces, elite CCP fighters were subjected to a shameless ambush launched by a Kuomintang force, during which in a "bloody massacre," approximately 8000 of the CCP's "heroic revolutionary fighters" were "slaughtered" and "disastrous losses" incurred to CCP's fighting units (Lin 1965, 17).[26]

To have focused on the 1937 massacre of Nanking's Chinese population—that included members of all classes, and a large dose of Kuomintang militia as well—would have defined the victims in the wrong way. Such a definition of victim groups was culturally prohibited.[27] For narrative purposes, the oppressed and traumatized had to be not just national compatriots but forces of progress. To have made the Japanese the principal perpetrators of this trauma would, from the perspective of the CCP, been equally wrongheaded in a symbolic sense. The perpetrators, like the victims, had to be part of the major contradiction, the core binary that identified pollution in terms of Marxian class analysis. Only if this binary and narrative were in place would the trauma story demand a resolution in the form of social revolution. In the alternative construction of massacre-induced trauma, by contrast, the story could have resolved itself in the defeat of the Imperial Japanese army and international peace.

These underlying cultural forces were made visible immediately after the War of Resistance ended. The rapid return and powerful illumination of the chief enemy were made strikingly conspicuous by the contents of the *People's Daily* on August 15 and September 3, 1946, the dates, respectively, of the memorial day for the defeat of Japan and victory in World War II. One might have imagined that on these early anniversaries of such a devastating, almost decade-long war, the CCP would have paid homage to the memory of those who died in the struggle, denouncing the Japanese as perpetrators of unspeakable war crimes. It is striking that this was not the case. Forty-two articles appeared in the *Daily* on those two days. Thirteen were devoted to fierce condemnation of the Kuomintang Party and its U.S. master for their evil-doings against the Chinese people. One article, for example, was headlined "Kuomintang Army Committed Looting, Raping and Killing Everywhere They Went!"[28] Another was entitled "The Kuomintang Government Insisted on Waging Civil War and the Economy Pushed to the Verge of Collapse."[29] Trauma-making and trauma-defining were clear themes, but the perpetrators were the Kuomintang civil enemy, not the foreigners, the Japanese. It was not the "rape of Nanking" that was targeted, but the "raping" and "killing" that were "everywhere," which had been committed by other Chinese. The trauma was also economic; it involved poverty and exploitation, not only death and physical destruction. The antidote for these traumas was clear. Only the Communist Party could save the Chinese people. Indeed, the majority of the forty-two stories appearing in these anniversary issues were devoted to extolling how the Party had been saving "the people" from their misery.

To "liberate" the nation from trauma and to mobilize as many people and resources as possible for the revolution, there could only be one big devil, one single target toward which hatred and bitterness could be aimed. So attention shifted quickly away from bitterness against Japan to the urgent struggle against international and domestic class enemies. In this battle to overcome the great trauma, even the old devil could be recruited for help. Mao's Marxist narrative suggested that the Japanese "people" could be split off from Japan's ruling oligarchy and aligned with the progressive forces on the Chinese side. Two articles from the war-ending memorial issues did, in fact, deal with Japan. One suggested that "under the manipulation of the U.S. Army, the Yoshida Government of Japan became more reactionary and there was a demonstration [against it] by more than 12,000 Japanese people in Tokyo." The second recorded that, "refusing to be utilized by the Kuomintang reactionaries, seven Japanese soldiers escaped to our army." Faced with the true trauma of capitalist domination, the Japanese masses were joining the "world people" in their struggle for socialism and democracy. Such culturally induced splitting of "Japanese" into polluted ruling class and purified proletariat had already been visible in the immediate aftermath of the Nanking Massacre itself. On February 12, 1938, a long essay in *Qun Zhong* was entitled "Unite with the Anti-War People in the Enemy Country."[30] Two weeks later, in the same journal, another article was headlined "7500 Anti-War Youths Were Arrested in the Enemy Country." Indeed, on the second anniversary of the massacre, December 18, 1939, while not a single word about the earlier mass murder appeared in *New China News*, a lengthy article entitled "The Anti-War Voice of the Japanese People"[31] occupied a conspicuous position on page 2.

Under the sign of this Marxist binary, moreover, it made cultural sense that, as the Japanese perpetrators were demoted as antagonists, the weighting of evil would increasingly fall on the American side. In the civil war, the Americans had given tacit and often explicit support to the Kuomintang. In cultural if not historical terms, it made sense to align the Americans with the KMT as perpetrators of China's national trauma and to allow any reference to the former Japanese enemies to fall away. Throughout the post-1945 Civil War period, and extending well into the Korean War, CCP mass media highlighted how "U.S. fascists" conspired with the Kuomintang Party in exploiting and killing the Chinese people, suppressing progressive causes all over the world, including the righteous struggle of the Japanese proletariat.[32]

CCP representations of the Kuomintang evolved in a parallel manner, from "robbers," "thieves," "bandits," and "pirates" to "traitors," "tyrants," and "fascists," and a series of heinous atrocities were attributed to them. Between 1946 and 1949, the *People's Daily* reported that it was Kuomintang airplanes that "bombarded Yanan and murdered innocent civilians" (8/15/1946, p. 1); that it was their "spiteful" spies who "came to sabotage the liberated areas" (9/3/1946, p. 2); that it was their corruption that "causes the masses of people to languish in the despair of starvation and poverty"(12/13/1946, p. 1; 9/13/1947, p. 1); that their callous apathy had "risked millions of people's lives by digging out the bank of the Daqing river" (9/3/1947, p. 1); that their stupidity had "harmed the interests of the nation in their negotiation with Japan" (8/15/1947, p. 1); and that their government had "corrupted the country and sold the country out to please its U.S. master" (8/15/1946, p. 1; 9/31947, p. 1).

As our discussion suggests, the trauma-history constructed by the postwar CCP was generated less by "true events" of the time than by their emplacement inside a freestanding, already existing binary code and revolutionary narrative.[33]

This interpretation is supported by the fact that this postwar construction fit neatly inside two broader, more general, and preexisting trauma stories, whose cultural structure it continued and helped complete. The first was the story the CCP told about itself from its founding in 1921 to the 1949 revolution, almost thirty years later. This history provided a familiar narration of traumatic collective experiences, with the Party and the people represented as victims and the Kuomintang Party as perpetrator. A series of famous phrases—speech genres, in Bakhtin's sense

(1986)—condensed this cultural message. For example, *xue yu xing feng*, which translates as "bloody rain and gory wind," was coined by the CCP to evoke the incessant and heartless hounding and slaughter of revolutionaries by the KMT. The years immediately following this first chapter of CCP history, the "Great Revolution Period" of 1924– 1927, was concluded by a bloody massacre of CCP members by the Kuomintang "traitors" in 1927. This was followed by another "Great Revolution Period," from 1927 to 1937, known also as the Land Reform War time, memorialized by the epic Long March, the horrendously difficult thousand-mile march during which more than half the CCP army perished. During the ensuing period of Japanese occupation, when the Communist army "inspired the people to join the national united front to resist Japanese aggression" and to "battle courageously against the savage onslaughts of the Japanese invaders," the Kuomintang regime was represented not only as having failed to resist the invading army, but also as having repeatedly turned its guns toward its own people and the patriotic CCP members, sabotaging resistance, and "blockading the liberated areas in attempts to starve and exhaust us [i.e., the CCP]."[34] Perhaps nothing could be more concise and illustrative of the grisly picture of trauma as constructed by CCP narratives than the following quotation from the *The East Is Red*, a song and dance epic of the Chinese revolution. It reads: "From the beachhead of the Huangpu River, to the levees of the Pearl River, from the banks of Xiang River, to the head and tail of the Yellow River, from the inner plain of the Great Wall to the wildness out there, the entire nation was reddened by the blood of CCP members and revolutionaries."[35]

This second trauma story, which recounted the CCP's tragedy and triumph, was itself adumbrated inside the authorized history of the entire century-long period of China's encounter with Western modernity. *Sang quan ru guo*—literally, "losing the sovereignty and mortifying the nation"—communicates the collective trauma induced by the series of unequal treaties that China was forced to sign under the threat of more violent aggression. *Shui shen huo re* and *min bu liao sheng*—respectively, "in deep water and burning fire" and "there was no way for people to make a living"—figuratively evoked the inexpressible pain suffered by ordinary people under the stifling oppression of the "Three Big Mountains"— imperialism, feudalism, and bureaucratic capitalism— suggesting the people were "constantly drowned in the depth of the water, and burned in heat of fire." Describing how the nation had sunk into a spiral of a dark abyss of despair, the CCP narration spoke about *duo zai duo nan*, which translates as "being plagued with manifold disasters," and *qian chuang bai kong*, "thousands of ulcers and hundreds of holes," which describes the traumatic effects in a metaphorically wrenching physical way. Performances of *The East Is Red* were inaugurated with an opening explication that reconstructs, in dramatic and expressive language, the abyss into which China had fallen since the mid-nineteenth century: "Gloom and darkness shrouded the earth and sky. The people groaned in misery.... The night was unending and the journey seemed endless. Dawn came slow [sic] to the Crimson Land!"[36]

MEMORIALIZING THE REVOLUTION:
COMMUNISM AS THE TRAUMA DRAMA'S RESOLUTION

From definitions of trauma—the reconstruction of injury, victims, and perpetrators—visions of ameliorating and transcending action arise. In 1949, the triumphant new national anthem proclaimed that "from each one" of China's earlier traumas "the urgent call for action comes forth." By asserting the dreadfulness of its enemies and the awfulness of its wounds, the Party could highlight the heroic sacrifices it endured and the Herculean feats it had achieved, strengthening its savior status among the Chinese people. It was the Party and Chairman Mao who had come to the rescue of the dying nation and salvaged the masses from their miserable fate. The days of the "old society" were tragic and dark. The revolution brought light into this gloomy China sky. As one of the most widely circulating songs of that era proclaimed, "The East is red and the sun has risen; there came a Mao Tse-tung from China who is the great savior of the people."

After the revolution, the trauma stories of these tragic but eventually triumphant struggles were disseminated via the media of mass communication in newspapers, magazines, radio, movies, plays, and novels, all of which promoted the vicarious experience of suffering and symbolic identification with the victims.[37] Memorial Day rituals and museums allowed these sentiments of trauma to be crystallized in more concrete, long-lasting ways. The most frequently visited and conspicuous was the sculpture standing in the center of *Tian'an men* Square that was inscribed in this way: "Long live the people's heroes who have died in the various struggles since 1840 for the cause of resisting enemies inside and outside China and the independence of the nation and the freedom and happiness of the people!" Memorial museums were erected to preserve and display the torture chambers and prisons where Communist traumas had taken place. They became popular sites of pilgrimage. One of the most widely known, in Sichuan province, came to be regarded as a sacred shrine that every Party member felt compelled to visit.[38]

Hong Ri (The Red Sun) was one of the most famous of the "revolutionary novels" to appear in the 1950s.[39] Widely read and beloved by young people of that time, it remains today part of the CCP's officially endorsed "Red Canon Series" recommended for people of all walks and ages. The story is about the civil war and is based, with small alterations, on a true story. Its major antagonist is Zhang Lingfu, a general in the Kuomintang "reactionary army," an archetypically evil figure who is depicted as cruel, rash, and stupid, and who has stubbornly persisted on the road to self-destruction in the fight against his own people. The Kuomintang army was predictably defeated, and Zhang Lingfu was killed in battle by the heroic protagonists of the People's Liberation Army. In the last pages of the novel, Lingfu's well-deserved sinful ending is portrayed without the slightest sense of mercy: "Lying on the ground was a huge body…of a purplish skin[,] the fat head was immersed in a pool of blood.…Zhang Lingfu, this sly, barbaric, and vile brute who used to lord it over the people, was killed by the bullets of PLA soldiers! In this tiny cave on the back of Men Liang Gu Mountain, he found his own grave" (Wu [1957] 2004, 534).

The evil figure of Zhang was so vividly delineated that he became one of the most widely known historical figures for generations of Chinese after 1949. Recently, however, there has circulated a "rumor" on the Chinese Internet that this polluted historical figure, Zhang Lingfu, actually was a great hero in the War of Resistance, who led the Kuomintang army in some of its toughest victories against Japan's invading army. According to historical accounts on the Kuomintang side, this "rumor" is historical fact. In the biography of Zhang published in Taiwan, Zhang was depicted as a distinguished military talent who had indeed achieved significant military feats in some major battles launched by Kuomintang forces against Japan that include the Changsha world-renowned and Changde battles. It is also recorded in these biographies that, before Nanking fell in 1937, Zhang had been fighting bravely in its vicinity, refusing to leave the battlefield even when his arm was severely wounded (see Huo 2008, 111–114, 126–131). The photograph of Zhang on the cover of one of these books shows a good-looking young man in uniform, a picture that makes the ugly "fat" body depicted at the end of *Hong Ri* barely imaginable. Whether this alternative historical account is historical fact or not, it serves to illustrate the distance between cultural representations of trauma and their "history." In terms of cultural logic, if not in historical fact, it is possible for brave soldiers who fought against the perpetrators of the "Rape of Nanking" to become known by the victims of this atrocity as perpetrators themselves.[40] It is no wonder that a memorial museum for the massacre at Nanking was not built until 1985, and that this dark day of human history has remained relatively unmarked up to the present day.

After Communism: *Writing "Nanking" into China's Trauma Drama*

This does not mean, however, that CCP representations, vis-à-vis the Nanking Massacre, have not changed. As we mentioned briefly earlier in this paper, in 1982 there was a sudden eruption of articles about the massacre in *People's Daily*, and articles and reports concerning the incident have increasingly appeared. They have reported on such activities as the building of the 1985 memorial, the publication in 1987 of an historical book on the massacre, and on subsequent conferences and discussion panels about its history.

These articles have continued to operate within the binary Japanese people/ Japanese elite. The former putatively share the innocent and righteous status of victims of the war with the Chinese people, while the latter are constructed as remnants who have somehow inherited the prewar imperialist ideology and who are responsible for all its evil-doings. According to this binary logic, for every article accusing the Japanese government of irresponsible behavior, there must be a counteracting article demonstrating how the ordinary Japanese people have shown sincere repentance and are now the true friends of the Chinese people.[41] Such symbolic opposition between the majority "people," who must be sacred according to Communist ideology, and the minority "rulers," who remain the source of all evils, continues one strand of the cultural logic that has regulated the representation of the massacre ever since 1937. It also reminds us that in China such mass media representations continue to be controlled by the Party state.

Yet, while the construction of this new attention remains entwined with earlier frames, the return to "Nanking" marks a response to deeper concerns about collective identity.[42] The debacle of the Cultural Revolution, the death of Mao, the repudiation of revolutionary activism, and the clear, if resigned, acceptance of capitalist relations in production—these intertwined events have severely, if gradually, eroded the Chinese nation's cultural foundations. The response has been the current, highly fraught process of negotiating and constructing a new collective Chinese identity. It was at such an intersection of history that the massacre began to draw attention.

The old narrative of collective trauma has gradually lost its persuasiveness. Perhaps the story of the massacre harbors the potential for constructing a new traumatic history for the Chinese nation, whereby a post-Communist and more nationalist collective identity is coming into being?

APPENDIX I

THE YASUKUNI SHRINE IN TOKYO

EXHIBITION HALL 10: THE "CHINA INCIDENT"

The Tokyo Shinto Memorial Shrine is dedicated to the souls of the Japanese who have died in national wars. In the 1980s, a private veterans' association funded an ambitious reconstruction project there. The result is an elaborate multiroom museum that narrates Japan's foreign policy from a conservative perspective thoroughly justifying Japan's military campaigns from the Meiji Restoration onward, campaigns directed against Russia, Korea, China, Europe, and the United States. In the Exhibition Hall 10, entitled the "China Incident," half the display is devoted to chronological description of the "China Incident 1937–1938." This display includes seven different illustrative panels, each of which is accompanied by both Japanese and English descriptions. The fourth of these seven concerns the Nanking "Incident." It is preceded by panels concerning the "China Incident" and the

"Nanking Operation." The narrative depicts the Chinese as the aggressors, and Japan as reluctantly responding on the grounds of self-defense. The Japanese invaders of Nanking are constructed as civil and concerned with limiting violence. Rather than innocent victims of mass murder, the dead are constructed as "heavy casualties" that resulted from a two-sided military contest in which Chinese soldiers were vulnerable because their generals had either deserted or surrendered, even while ordering them to fight to the death. According to the narrative denouement, "the Chinese were soundly defeated" and "inside the city, the residents were once again able to live their lives in peace."

Below is a transcription of the relevant displays. We are grateful to Ms. Haruna Yamakawa, an undergraduate student at Sophia University, for fact-checking this account and providing us with these transcriptions. (See also http://www.yasukuni.or.jp.)

支那事変

日中関係は、10年〔昭和――1935年〕8月の中国共産党の八・一宣言以来テロが続発し再び悪化した。翌11年12月の西安事件で、反共の蒋介石が共産党との提携に踏み切ると反日行動は一層激しくなった。盧溝橋の小さな事件が、中国正規軍による日本軍への不法攻撃、そして日本軍の反撃で、北支那全域を戦場とする北支事変となった。背景には、日中和平を拒否する中国側の意志があった。戦場を上海・南京へと拡大し、広大な国土全体を戦場として、日本軍を疲弊させる道を選んだ蒋介石は、大東亜戦争終戦までの8年間を戦い、戦勝国側の一員となった。

CHINA INCIDENT

Sino-Japanese relations improved with the conclusion of the Tangau Agreement in 1933, but worsened again when Chinese terrorist acts followed the CCP Declaration of August 1935. The Xian Incident (December 1936) convinced Chiang to join the Communists in a united front against Japan, and hostilities escalated thereafter. In extending the hostilities to Shanghai and Nanking, Chiang hoped to sap the strength of Japanese troops by turning all of China into a battlefield. Chiang fought fiercely for eight years, until the end of World War II, when he joined the ranks of the victors.

南京攻略作戦

中国の戦争意思を挫折させる目的で首都南京を包囲攻略した作戦。日本軍の開城勧告を拒否した防衛司令官唐生智が部隊に固守を命じて自らは逃走したため、戦闘が始まると指揮官を失った将兵は潰走または投降して壊滅。南京城は12月13日に陥落した。

NANKING OPERATION

The purpose of the Nanking Operation was to surround the capital, thus discouraging the Chinese from waging war against the Japanese. Tang Shengzhi, commander-in-chief of the Nanking Defense Corps, ignored the Japanese warning to open the gates of the city. He ordered his troops to defend Nanking to the death and then escaped. Therefore, when the leaderless Chinese troops either deserted or surrendered, Nanking fell on December 13.

南京事件
昭和12年12月、南京を包囲した松井司令官は、隷下部隊に外国権益や難民区を朱
書した要図を配布して「厳正な軍規、不法行為の絶無」を示達した。敗れた中国軍将兵
は退路の下関に殺到して殱滅された。市内では私服に着替えて便衣服となった敗残兵
の摘発が行われたが、南京城市内では、一般市民の生活に平和がよみがえった。

NANKING INCIDENT

After the Japanese surrounded Nanking in December 1937, General Matsui Iwane distributed maps to his men with foreign settlements with the safety zone marked in red ink. Matsui told them that they were to observe military rules to the letter and that anyone committing unlawful acts would be severely punished. He also warned Chinese troops to surrender, but Commander-in-Chief Tang Shengzhi ignored the warning. Instead, he ordered his men to defend Nanking to the death and abandoned them. The Chinese were soundly defeated, suffering heavy casualties. Inside the city, residents were once again able to live their lives in peace.

NOTES

1. Communist and fascist revolutions can be thought of in this manner, allowing the aggrieved collectivity, whether the proletariat or the folk, or more specifically its political and intellectual representatives, to take power and fashion a new social system that supposedly will prevent such traumas from occurring in the future. We will develop this theme in the latter part of this essay in regard to the Chinese revolution of 1949.

2. Chang's book has inevitably become a lightning rod for controversy, and this is apparently true, for reasons that should be evident, in some quarters of Japanese politics and scholarship. In terms of its reception in the Anglophone world, we are not aware of serious challenges to the general empirical claims advanced in Chang's work. In his foreword to the book, William C. Kirby, Professor of Modern Chinese History at Harvard University (Kirby 1997, x) attests that "Ms. Chang shows more clearly than any previous account" the "bestial behavior" committed by "Japanese commanders and troops" during the seven weeks of confrontation at Nanking. Other expert analysts agree. Peter Li (2000, 57) later called the Nanking Massacre the "best kept secret about World War II." Referring to such events as the Nanking Massacre, Eugene Sledge (1998) claims that "the best secret of World War II is the truth about Japanese atrocities." See also James Yin and Shi Young (1996) and Siyun Lin, *Nan Jing Bao Wei Zhan yu Nan Jing Da Tu Sha* [*The Battle in Defense of Nanking and the Massacre in Nanking*] (2011), available at http://www.china-week.com/html/548.htm. While Lin Siyun's motives are more political and ideological than scientific—he is a right-wing amateur historian who has, on many occasions, attempted to defend the Jingoistic Japanese war policy—this does not necessarily invalidate his findings. In this case, Rui Gao's subsequent research in her 2011 Yale Ph.D. dissertation, *Eclipse and Memory: Public Representation of the War of Resistance in Maoist China and its Official Revision in Post-Mao Era*, has confirmed that what Lin has claimed about the contents of history books in CCP China is generally correct. See also note 3 below.

3. After the conclusion of the Pacific War, the International Military Tribunal of the Far East estimated that there were more than 260,000 noncombatants murdered. Some experts place the total at over 350,000 (Chang 1997, 4). When presenting the paper on which this chapter is based at Sophia University in Tokyo Japan, we were informed that some respected Japanese scholars have challenged these estimates, placing the number of victims at "only" 200,000. There is, inevitably, some controversy about such factual assertions in regard to long past historical events, and it is not the intention of this essay to offer definitive empirical estimates in quantitative terms. We believe, nonetheless, that the available historical evidence does not challenge our basic presupposition here—that mass murder on a "world-historical" scale did occur during these weeks in Nanking. Assuming these historical events to have taken place, our aim in this essay is to offer new interpretations of the reaction to them.

4. The reference to the atomic bombings as traumas that helped define postwar Japanese identity raises the obvious question of where, in this process of Japanese identity construction, a sense of responsibility for the Nanking Massacre might lie. The answer, many observers have suggested, is close to "no where at all." Chang provides a bitingly critical overview of Japanese denials, not only of their responsibility for the massacre, but of its very empirical existence, characterizing this process as Japan's "second rape" of Nanking (Chang 1997, 199–214). To speak of the Japanese nation as a collectivity in this manner clearly runs the risk, however, of effacing the controversies that divide the country in the struggles over how to remember its militarist past, as Akiko Hashimoto has made clear in "The Cultural Trauma of a Fallen Nation: Japan, 1945" (Eyerman et al. 2011). That said, the relative insensitivity of the Japanese government to such issues as the Nanking Massacre has indeed played a powerful role in textbook, scholarly, and media trauma construction for the Chinese people and plays some role in Japan's interstate relations in Asia today. Yet, while the case of Japan's relation to the massacre is increasingly debated (see Schwartz in this volume), China's relation to the massacre has rarely been thematized, despite the fact that China's own attitude to the massacre in the decades after 1937 had enormous repercussions, even for the Japanese. See note 17 below and Appendix I for further discussion of the contemporary Japanese relation to the massacre.

5. Chang treats this German involvement as evidence of the factual transparency of the massacre, but it can also, at the same time, be taken as evidence of the widespread appeal of the Orientalist frame, such that it could even provide a framework for bridging the gulf between Nazis and anti-Nazis. For the concept of Orientalism, see Edward Said's classic, *Orientalism* (New York: Vintage, 1979).

6. The original Chinese title is *Ri Kou de Can Sha Jian Yin Mie Jue Ren Xing!*

7. The original Chinese title is *Ren Lei Suo Gong Qi de Bao Xing.*

8. see note 33 below. We must acknowledge, however, that our investigation of KMT representations of the massacre is far from complete. We were able to look only at *Zhong Yang Ri Bao* (the Central Daily), the major news daily published by the KMT government, and for this source only for the dates before 1937 and after 1945. While we did closely examine this newspaper on the three memorial day periods of the massacre—on December 13 from 1945 to 1948—it is certainly possible that, in the period preceding, significant representations of the trauma at Nanking were made. We would expect, however, that such representations would reveal how, and why, the Nanking Massacre did *not* enter centrally into the KMT's version of Chinese identity. Because it estimated the CCP enemy to be as insidious as the Japanese, and ultimately, indeed, a much greater danger, this Kuomintang carrier group could not weigh perpetrator evil in the manner required by trauma construction. Our reasoning on this question is further elaborated below, in note 33.

9. In earlier drafts of this essay, we primarily depended on secondary data for the case of school textbooks. For the current draft, we have had access to original data as made available by the Library of the People's Education Press in PRC, the central publishing institution that was exclusively in charge of compiling, editing, and distributing school textbooks in the PRC. According to the librarian of the Press, for at least two decades after the building of PRC began in 1949, the press monopolized control over textbook publishing. This means that the textbooks edited and published by the press were widely adopted in elementary and middle schools throughout the China of Mao's era; in fact, they provide very likely the only versions of events that were made available for students during that time. For the purpose of this research, we checked all the history textbooks for elementary, junior, and senior middle schools and their respective teacher's reference books. Except for one "new" edition of 1961—which did not, it turned out, ever enter into circulation—our data pool represents all the history textbooks circulating in PRC during the two decades after 1949. While history texts for elementary and junior middle school displayed deep silence about the massacre, we did find exceptions in the 1958 edition of history texts for senior middle school and some of the teacher reference books. Mitigating these exceptions are three considerations. First, extra materials offered in to teachers were in principle only supplementary to history texts; they were not required to be taught to students or memorized by them. Second, in the sole history text where the incident was mentioned, the 1958 edition of a senior middle school text, the enormous horror of Nanking was confined to a one-sentence narrative: "In Nanking, the Japanese invading forces conducted an inhuman killing, raping and looting, and in more than one month, the number of civilians being murdered amounted to no less than 300,000" (*Senior Middle School Textbook for Chinese History,* Book 4, Beijing: People's Education Press, 1958, p. 40). While the incident is identified here with "horror," it is not symbolically heightened by such metaphors as "massacre," "mass killing," or "mass murder," terms that were applied to murderous events in which the Kuomintang were involved during the period of "White Terror" (see note 26 below for such semiotic hierarchy). Third, the number of readers who would ever be able to read the sentence, namely, the students receiving senior middle education in China in the 1950s and 1960s, remained small in comparison with elementary or junior middle school. During the ten years known as the era of the "Cultural Revolution," the People's Education Press declined, and stopped publishing textbooks. Schools were mostly closed during the first three years, and, when they resumed, the use of textbooks was chaotic. Without a standardized system, each province or region had its own edition of textbooks published. While we do not have access to most of the dozens of editions of history textbook published during this period, we expect that they gave intense class struggle supreme social significance, with the result that there would not have been symbolic space for the incident in Nanking to assume historical significance. As in the case of the articles in *People's Daily* that we discuss shortly, there was throughout this period an effort to focus on the impotence and negligence of the Kuomintang, which featured as a general representation of class enemies.

10. *New Edition of History Textbook for Senior Elementary School,* Book 4, edited by Compiling and Editing Committee for Textbooks of Ministry of Education, People's Government of North Central China, Xin Hua Bookstore, 1950, p. 24. The history textbooks for elementary and junior middle school that were published by the People's Education Press during the two decades of Mao's China, which were also examined in our research, include: *New Edition of History Textbook for Senior Elementary School,* Book 4, edited by Compiling and Editing Committee for Textbooks of Ministry of Education, People's Government of North Central China, Xin Hua Bookstore, 1950; *Senior Elementary*

School Textbook History, Book 4, People's Education Press, 1956; *Senior Elementary School Textbook History,* Book 2, People's Education Press, 1961; *Junior Middle School Textbook Chinese History,* Book 4, People's Education Press, 1956; *Senior Middle School Textbook for Chinese History,* Book 4, People's Education Press, 1958; *Teacher's Reference Guide for Senior Middle School Textbook for Chinese History,* Book 4, People's Education Press, 1958; *Full-Time Ten Year School Junior Middle Textbook (Experimental Edition) Chinese History,* Book 4, edited by History Edition Team for General Textbooks for Elementary and Middle School, People's Education Press, 1979; and *Elementary Textbook History,* Book 2, edited by Division of History of People's Education Press, People's Education Press, 1992.

11. *Junior Middle School Textbook for Chinese History,* Book 4, edited and published by People's Education Press, 1956, p. 74.

12. In the 1959 edition of the teachers' reference guide for junior middle school, for example, the section devoted to the Kuomintang's struggle with Japanese forces in 1937 was limited to one short paragraph, and, again, it seemed to be intended more as evidence for the cowardice and impotence of the Kuomintang regime. This reference to Nanking consisted of five words: "In December, Nanking was lost." *See Teacher's Reference Guide for Junior Middle School Textbook for Chinese History,* Book 4, edited by People's Education Press, People's Education Press, 1959, p. 83.

13. See *Full-Time Ten Year School Junior Middle Textbook (Experimental Edition) Chinese History,* Book 4, edited by History Edition Team for General Textbooks for Elementary and Middle School, People's Education Press, 1979, and *Elementary Textbook History,* Book 2, edited by Division of History of People's Education Press, People's Education Press, 1992.

14. These findings are the result of a computer search through the archives of *People's Daily* for references to "Nanking Massacre" in the thirty-six years between 1946 and 1982. There were two mentions in the *People's Daily* in 1950: March 14 (p. 1) and December 8 (p. 2); six mentions in 1951: February 24 (p. 3), February 27 (p. 1), March 4 (p. 4), April 21 (p. 4), May 1 (p. 5); two mentions in 1952: April 9 (p. 1), September 7 (p. 1); and six mentions in 1960: May 16 (p. 1, 2), May 23 (p. 4), May 26 (p. 3), May 30 (p. 6). In note 32 below, in the context of our explanation of why the Nanking Massacre did not enter centrally into Chinese collective identity, we will discuss the content of this handful of references and offer an interpretation of why they occurred when they did. In 1982, this long silence was broken with a surge of new articles and references, which continued over the course of the decade, for reasons which will become clear.

15. See Chang's (1997) discussions of "Japanese Damage Control" (p. 147), "Japanese Propaganda" (pp. 149–153), and "The Occupation of Nanking" (pp. 159–167).

16. For this concept, "the means of symbolic production," and a systematic discussion of broad range of elements required for successful symbolic performances vis-à-vis social audiences, see Alexander (2004) and, more broadly, Alexander, Giesen, and Mast (2006).

17. In April 2005, large-scale anti-Japanese demonstrations broke out in major cities throughout China. Among the major rhetorical protests of these demonstrations was the accusation that Japanese elementary and high school textbooks narrated Japan's military history against China in a distorted manner, one that neglects or denies Japan's wartime atrocities against Asian nations, including the Nanking Massacre. While these actions were, of course, stimulated and controlled by the Communist state, they also responded to mass sentiment. Whatever the source of the protests, that official Japanese accounts have avoided responsibility for the massacre cannot be denied. See Appendix I.

18. "Among the big and small contradictions determined or influenced by the basic contradiction," Mao writes, "some become intensified, some are temporarily or partially

solved or mitigated, and some emerge anew; consequently the process reveals itself as consisting of different stages" (Mao 1962, 225).

19. See *New Edition of History Textbook for Senior Elementary School,* Book 4, edited by Compiling and Editing Committee for Textbooks of Ministry of Education, People's Government of North Central China, Xin Hua Bookstore, 1950, p. 14; *Junior Middle School Textbook for Chinese History,* Book 4, People's Education Press, 1956, pp. 31–32; *Senior Middle School Textbook for Chinese History,* Book 4, People's Education Press, 1958, p. 21; *Teacher's Reference Guide for Senior Middle School Textbook for Chinese History,* Book 4, People's Education Press, 1958, p. 52.

20. *Junior Middle School Textbook for Chinese History,* Book 4, People's Education Press, 1956, p. 32.

21. The major figure that initiated the incident was known to be Wang Jingwei, a political figure of Kuomintang who later collaborated with Japan and became the head of the puppet government in Nanking. His famous anti-Communist slogan as proposed during the incident—"better to kill one thousand non-Communists by mistake than allow a true Communist to slip through the net"—later became a monumental piece of evidence for CCP in its narrative construction of the suffering of its members at the hands of Kuomintang reactionaries.

22. *Junior Middle School Textbook for Chinese History,* Book 4, People's Education Press, 1956, p. 32.

23. *Senior Middle School Textbook for Chinese History,* Book 4, People's Education Press, 1958, p. 21.

24. Ibid., p. 23.

25. One could refer to *Junior Middle School Textbook for Chinese History,* Book 4, People's Education Press, 1956, pp. 79–80 for the original text. One could also find such text sections in all the other editions listed in note 10.

26. Because Lin was a military and political guru whose rank and prestige was second only to chairman Mao's, his commemoration monograph from which these quotations were drawn can be regarded as an authoritative version that sets the overall tone for the narration of the War of Resistance as well as shaping the interpretation and collective memoires among the public. In her article on memorization of the war and the Communist trauma, Gao (2011) has reconstructed the narrative elements of Lin's article. Among its other salient features, she has discovered a semiotic hierarchy between the conspicuous enemy of the war, the Japanese invading forces, and the true evil of all time, the Kuomintang regime as the general representative of class enemies. In this semiotic ranking, the Japanese were not only portrayed as a much lesser evil than the Kuomintang regime but are generously endowed with the likelihood of symbolic redemption, access to which the latter is completely denied. See Gao (2011).

27. In "Revolutionary Trauma and Representation of the War," Gao (2011) traces the narrative construction of the Communist trauma as established in Mao's China (1949–1976), which defined the class enemy as the ultimate evil and the proletarian masses as the traumatized and trampled victims. Gao suggests that the overwhelming success of this narrative construction, along with the sacred new collectivity of revolutionary China, was based on the universal class victimhood that prevented the War of Resistance from emerging as a collective trauma. The vertical nature of the Chinese resistance conflict, Gao finds, posed an inconvenient contradiction of the horizontal symbolic demarcation of the world of the oppressed, as entailed by class trauma.

28. The original Chinese title is *Jiang Jun Dao Chu An Wu Tian Ri, Jian Sha Jie Lue Tu Tan Ren Min.*

29. The original Chinese title is *Jiang Zheng Fu Jian Chi Du Cai Nei Zhan, Jing Ji Mian Lin Quan Mian Beng Kui.*

30. The original Chinese title is *Tuan Jie Di Guo Fan Zhan Ren Min.*

31. The original Chinese title is *Ri Ben Ren Min de Fan Zhan Hu Sheng.*

32. It was, in fact, under the camouflaging cover of such references to the polluted American enemy that the brief references noted earlier (note 14 above) to the Nanking Massacre in postrevolutionary China appeared. Both mentions of the massacre in 1950 in *People's Daily*, for example, appeared in news reports decrying the evil-doings of the "American imperialists" who had not only robbed the "world's people" of postwar victory but now threatened the hard-won world peace. One article *(People's Daily, 3/14/1950, p. 1)*, entitled "The Monstrous Crimes of MacArthur" (*Mai Ke A Se de Tao Tian Zui Xing*) accuses the American general of abusing power in the proceedings of the International Military Tribunal of the Far East by shielding the Japanese war criminals—including those who were perpetrators in Nanking, which is where the massacre was mentioned. In 1951, the massacre was briefly mentioned in an article *(People's Daily, 5/1/1951, p. 5)* entitled "Oppose Invasion by the U.S. and Defend World Peace" (*Fan Dui Mei Guo Qin Lue, Bao Wei Shi Jie He Ping*). The point was that such a tragedy would be repeated if the Americans got their way and were able to rearm the Japanese imperialists. Both these stories tellingly demonstrate how the postrevolutionary focus of attention had effectively shifted to the new enemy of the nation, the American imperialists. The Nanking Massacre was relevant only as a piece of indirect evidence for the evilness of this new target.

Just as the massacre was recruited as part of the war propaganda in the Korean War in the early 1950s, it was incorporated, and subordinated into, the larger framework of class struggle in news coverage about the Japanese student movement against the U.S.-Japan Security Treaty in 1960. In each of the six articles that mentioned the massacre during this year, the dominant motif was the student movement and, more broadly, the Chinese people's positive responses to it. The point, in other words, was not to make the massacre a trauma drama for the Chinese people, but to make use of its memory to recall the trauma of the anti-Japanese struggle and to transform the memories of that trauma into a struggle against the Japanese alliance with the United States. The war crimes were constructed as having been committed by the Japanese imperialists, so that the proletariat, the Japanese "people," remained innocent victims. The more evil the Japanese imperialists, as powerfully illustrated by their unforgivable crimes in the massacre, the more justified the current struggle of the Japanese people against them. Therefore, to fight against the current Japanese imperialists, who were supported by the most dangerous enemy of all, the American imperialists, the Chinese people must ally themselves with the righteous struggle of the Japanese people—as one of the articles suggested, "Let's unite and fight together!" (*Hu Xiang Tuan Jie, Hu Xiang Zhi Chi, Gong Tong Dou Zheng*) (*People's Daily, 5/16/1960, p. 2*).

33. The same can probably be said, more conditionally, for trauma construction by the KMT. We have not, as we mentioned earlier, had sufficient access to Kuomintang media to make a secure judgment on this matter. Certainly, we have reason to believe that the conservative side paid more attention to the mass murder. They were, after all, in control of Nanking, then the Chinese capital, when the massacre took place. Nonetheless, it does not appear that the Kuomintang widely publicized the massacre; they did not make it central to their collective identity, to the identity of (one national variant of) modern "Chinese." On the tenth anniversary of the massacre, on December 13, 1947, on the second page of *Central Daily,* we found a feature story titled "This Day of Nanking Ten Years Ago: Massacre! Massacre!" With the help of accompanying photos, this article communicated a traumatic event replete with vivid and gruesome details of atrocities, and was filled with

phrases such as "tragic beyond compare in this human world," "atrocities of unparalleled savage," and "unprecedented in the human history."

At the same time, however, and we believe this marks a telling parallel with the cultural logic of the CCP, this Kuomintang construction of "atrocities" linked them to enemies whose evil was weighted just as heavily as the Japanese perpetrators. These were the civil enemies inside China. Only one week after the anniversary issue, on the third page of the *Central Daily* of December 19, 1947, there appeared an essay that depicted the means of killing and torturing in as gruesome detail as the descriptions employed in the story about the massacre. This time, however, the antagonists in the plot were the "Communist bandits," not the Japanese. This parallel version of the Kuomintang narrative was just as powerfully bifurcated into good and evil; it employed the image of hell on earth and even evoked the language of class struggle: "The North-Western Part of Shangxi Province Has been Transformed into Hell: People were Moaning under the Class Struggle." There was even a sensational news report that these "Communist bandits" in Shangxi province had forced their Kuomintang POWs to eat the bodies of their fellow prisoners (*Central Daily*, 12/21/1947, p. 4). The displacing effect of such a construction seems clear. The construction of trauma drama depends on weighting evil; the perpetrator must be constructed as having committed a unique and unparalleled crime that it becomes engorged with evil, a sacred monster set apart from everything human. This cannot happen if a traumatic event is relativized by placing it side-by-side with another, committed by an entirely different party, but which is constructed in very similar terms. When one asks, which protagonist is truly evil—the one who tortures, kills, and commits cannibalism against individuals and small groups, or the one who commits mass massacre?—the answer is not so clear.

34. *The East Is Red* was a song and dance epic of the Chinese revolution, a gigantic performance project proposed and coordinated by no less than Zhou Enlai, the premier of the PRC in Mao's era. The words introduce Act Four, which is devoted to the depiction of the War of Resistance. The performance debuted in Beijing in October 1964. In celebration of the fifteenth anniversary of the founding of the new republic, the epic performance presents a vivid depiction of Chinese revolution in the form of songs, dance, opera, and ballet and thus offers an ideal text for interpreting how the nation represents its own past and defines its collective identity to the public, including the representation of the War of Resistance in public arena. To a certain extent, the textual part of this theatrical performance, including both its verse and its song lyrics, composes a highly condensed version of modern Chinese history as seen from the perspective of CCP. The entire script of the performance and its English translation may be found at the following website: http://www.wyzxsx.com/Article/Class12/201007/165476.html (last accessed on September 30, 2010). We modified the English translation found on this website.

35. Ibid. While these words are meant to introduce Act Two, which is devoted to the first Great Revolution Period and the anti-Communist massacres committed by Kuomintang regime that brought this time to a tragic end, its figurative language and emotional expression vividly illustrate the thematic "goriness" with which the CCP constructed its trauma of revolution.

36. Ibid.

37. CCP's Ministry of Propaganda obviously played a critical role in this crystallization and memorialization process, initiating a series of large-scale artistic and literary projects since 1949 to strengthen "propaganda" work. According to Cheng (2002), one of the most influential of these projects was to publicize and advocate for *San Hong* (the Three Reds) among younger generations. These refer to three revolutionary novels that were singled out as the most important materials for ideological inculcation. Each was

devoted to depicting the heroic feats of Chinese Communists during their long-time struggle before 1949, and all had in their titles a Chinese character that means "red," the color regarded as representing Communism: *Hong Qi Pu* (Keep the Red Flags Flying), *Hong Ri* (The Red Sun), and *Hong Yan* (The Red Crag). These novels were not only published and distributed exclusively by the Youth Press of China, under direct supervision of the Central Committee of the Chinese Communist Youth League, but also formed an essential component of the required reading collections for tens of millions of school kids and young people for generations. Among the three, the most influential, *The Red Crag*, was based on the experience of Communist martyrs who were jailed and eventually killed in a prison conglomerate controlled by Kuomintang in the suburb of Chongqing. The novel was republished more than twenty times between 1961 and 1980s, with a total distribution of 8 million (Cheng 2002). It was also adapted into the movie *Lie Huo Zhong Yong Sheng* (To Acquire Eternal Life in the Raging Fire), and an opera titled "Sister Jiang," the name of a major female CCP figure. The characters in the novel have become such an important component of the social imagination in contemporary China that the name of a CCP traitor portrayed in it, Pu Zhigao, has become an alternative expression for traitor in the Chinese language, and one of its major female CCP martyr figures, Jiang Jie (Sister Jiang), has become a consecrated heroine whose name is often used as a metonymy for the entire Communist martyr group. As a now deified embodiment of Communist virtue and loyalty, her holiness might be compared with that of France's Joan of Arc. The prison conglomerate where these CCP figures were portrayed as having been incarcerated and murdered became a revolutionary museum, as we mention in the notes following. See Guangbin Luo and Yiyan Yang, *Hong Yan* (The Red Crag) (Beijing: Youth Press of China, 1961), and Bin Liang, *Hong Qi Pu* (Keep the Red Flag Flying) (Beijing: Youth Press of China, 1957).

38. This refers to the Geleshan Cemetery of Revolutionary Martyrs in Chongqing, later known as the Revolutionary Museum of Geleshan, built on the base of the prison conglomerate where the story in *The Red Crag* happened. The museum not only exhibits the "original" torture chamber but also offers a vivid reenactment of the primal torture scene for visitors. According to a pamphlet dedicated to the museum (Li et al. 1998), it remains one of the important heritage sites under state protection, and also one of the One Hundred Model Patriotic Education Bases under the direct supervision of CCP's Ministry of Propaganda. It claims to be "one of the most visited museums in the country," the number of visitors in 1997 amounting to more than 2 million (ibid., pp. 126–144).

39. See Qiang Wu, *Hong Ri* (The Red Sun) (Beijing: Youth Press of China, [1957] 2004). The novel was published first in 1957, and has been frequently republished for subsequent generations of Chinese, right up until today. While there are no official statistics on the number and distribution of readers of this novel, that it belongs to "The Three Reds" should put the broadness of circulation beyond doubt. See note 37.

40. Tragically and ironically, Zhang's polluted figure as a perpetrator in Communist trauma seems to have been perpetuated by the building of a "memorial"—more accurately, a line of carving on the wall in celebration of the victory of PLA—at the site of his death in the cave of the Meng Liang Gu mountain. It coldly reads: "This is the Site Where Zhang Lingfu Was Shot to Death."

41. Examples abound. Consider an issue of the *People's Daily* published in 1985. This year marked the 40th anniversary of the victory in the war and there had been large-scale commemoration activities in the public sphere of the PRC, including the building and opening of the memorial for the Nanking Massacre. In the commemoration discourse, the Japanese ruling party was condemned as being guilty of undermining world peace, while

Japanese people were portrayed as brothers and sisters of the sacred camp of peace-lovers. In an article titled "Japanese Public Figures Talk on the 40th Anniversary of Victory in the War of Resistance; People from Japan and China Unite to Defend Peace in Asia as well as in the World," it was asserted that the Japanese ruling party and politicians "kept on behaving in opposition to the will of Japanese people, hurting the feelings of the people in countries that had been occupied by Japanese Jingoists" (*People's Daily*, 9/2/1985, p. 7). On page 6 of the same paper, an article with the title "Treasure the Present while Remember the Past" appeared. In this article, the reporter interviewed some famous "Japanese friendly person-nel" and veterans who were formerly stationed in China. These representatives of the Japanese people all enthusiastically pledged to continue promoting Sino-Japanese friend-ship. It is particularly illuminating that at the end of the article, a statistic is presented as evidence for the reassuring conclusion that "the absolute majority of Japanese people had drawn profound historic lessons from the distressful war experience":

> According to the survey conducted by Asahi News on Japanese people's attitude towards the issue of Yasukuni Shrine: among all the 624 letwters from the readers, 544 showed disapproval to visits to the shrine, which compose 87% of the sample, and only 49 letters showed approval. This demonstrates the strong wish of Japanese people to learn from history. (p. 6)

Two weeks from the day after news reports covering the building of the memorial for the Nanking Massacre were published, an article appeared, on August. 27th (p. 6), with the title "Not to Let the Tragedy Repeat Itself!" It was reported in detail how the "Japanese mass people" made efforts to avoid "making the same mistake"; "would gather each year on August 15th, to commemorate the day, to oppose war and to advocate for world peace"; how they would put on anti-war exhibitions and build memorials for Chinese slave labors who had died in Japan; and avow that they would "never go into war again."

   42. Besides the media coverage, increasing internet space has been dedicated to the massacre and its memorization. Such websites include www.nj1937.org, www.njmassacre. org, www.china918.org, and www.china918.net. Though not singularly devoted to the massacre, all specialize in the War of Resistance. Many are radically nationalistic, and they seem to represent a spontaneous collective attempt to build a new sacred national identity that is negatively rooted in the profaned memory of the war.

REFERENCES

Alexander, Jeffrey C. 2003. *The Meanings of Social Life: A Cultural Sociology*. New York: Oxford University Press.
———. 2004. "Cultural Pragmatics: Social Performance between Ritual and Strategy." *Sociological Theory* 22 (4): 527–573.
Alexander, Jeffrey C., Bernhard Giesen, and Jason L. Mast, eds. 2006. *Social Performance: Symbolic Action, Cultural Pragmatics, and Ritual*. Cambridge, UK: Cambridge University Press.
Alexander, Jeffrey C., Ron Eyerman, Bernhard Giesen, Neil Smelser, and Piotr Sztompka. 2004. *Cultural Trauma and Collective Identity*. Berkeley: University of California Press.

Bakhtin, Mikhail M. 1986. *Speech Genres and Other Late Essays*. Austin: University of Texas Press.

Chang, Iris. 1997. *The Rape of Nanking: The Forgotten Holocaust of World War II*. New York: Basic Books.

Cheng, Guangwei. 2002. "Reconstructing Narratives of China: the Artistic Creation in *Keep the Red Flag Flying, the Red Sun and the Red Crag*." *Southern Cultural Forum (Nan Fang Wen Tan)* 2002 (3): 22–26.

Eyerman, Ronald, Jeffrey C. Alexander, and Elizabeth Breese, eds. 2011. *Narrating Trauma: On the Social Construction of Human Suffering*. Boulder, CO: Paradigm.

Gao, Rui. 2011. "Revolutionary Trauma and Representation of the War: the Case of China in Mao's Era," pp. 53–80 in *Narrating Trauma*, edited by R. Eyerman, J. C. Alexander, and E. Breese. Boulder, CO: Paradigm.

Hashimoto, Akiko. 2011. "The Cultural Trauma of a Fallen Nation: Japan, 1945," pp. 29–52 in *Narrating Trauma*, edited by R. Eyerman, J. C. Alexander, and E. Breese. Boulder, CO: Paradigm.

Huo, Anzhi. 2008. *The Military Commander Zhang Lingfu: Early Career and the War of Resistance*. Taipei, China: Lao Zhan You Press.

Kirby, William C. 1997. "Foreword," in pp. ix–xi in *The Rape of Nanking: The Forgotten Holocaust of World War II*, by Iris Chang. New York: Basic Books.

Li, Hua, et al. 1998. *Hong Yan Hun: Chongqing Geleshan Geming Jinianguan* (The Soul of the Red Crag: Geleshan Revolutionary Museum). Beijing: Encyclopedia Press.

Li, Peter. 2000. "The Nanking Holocaust Tragedy, Trauma and Reconciliation." *Society* 37: 56–66.

Liang, Bin. 1957. *Hong Qi Pu* (Keep the Red Flag Flying). Beijing: Youth Press of China.

Lin, Piao. 1965. *Long Live the Victory of People's War! In Commemoration of the 20th Anniversary of Victory in the Chinese People's War of Resistance Against Japan*. Beijing: Foreign Language Press.

Luo, Guangbin, and Yiyan Yang. 1961. *Hong Yan* (The Red Crag). Beijing: Youth Press of China.

Mao, Tse-tung. 1962. "On Contradiction," pp. 214–241 in *Mao Tse-Tung: An Anthology of His Writings*, edited by Anne Fremantle. New York: New American Library.

———. 1967. *Quotations from Chairman Mao Tse-tung*. New York: Bantam Books.

Said, Edward. 1979. *Orientalism*. New York: Vintage.

Sledge, Eugene B. 1998. "The Old Breed and the Costs of War," Chapter 13 in *The Costs of War: America's Pyrrhic Victories*, edited by J. V. Denson. New Brunswick, NJ: Transaction.

Wu, Qiang. [1957] 2004. *Hong Ri* (The Red Sun). Beijing: Youth Press of China.

Yin, James, and Shi Young. 1996. *Rape of Nanking: An Undeniable History in Photographs*. Chicago: Triumph Books.

PART IX

EVENTS AS CULTURE

EVENTS AS TEMPLATES OF POSSIBILITY: AN ANALYTIC TYPOLOGY OF POLITICAL FACTS[1]

MABEL BEREZIN

EVENTS, WALLS, AND METAPHORS

On June 12, 1987, Ronald Reagan stood at the Brandenberg Gate and famously told Mikhail Gorbachev: "Tear down this wall." Reagan was referring to a metaphorical wall, the Iron Curtain, as well as the material wall that divided East and West Berlin. Indeed, two years after Reagan's famous speech, ordinary citizens tore down the Berlin Wall brick by brick and revealed a divide riddled with ideological fissures. Reagan's admirers often cite his speech and give him credit for the fall of the wall. A material piece of the wall exists about 20 feet from Reagan's grave at his presidential library in Simi Valley, California. Most specialists on the Soviet Union and Eastern Europe would agree that Ronald Reagan and his administration's foreign policy were not determining factors in its fall. Yet, Reagan's speech at the Brandenberg Gate was politically important even if it was not causal with respect to the collapse of the Soviet Union and Eastern bloc.

Reagan's speech was an *event*—a *caesura* in the flow of public time—a moment with, to borrow from Aristotle's conception of plot, a beginning, middle, and end that produced an enduring and multivalent metaphor of political transformation.[2] The multiple narratives of Reagan's speech intertwined with the collective memory of it represent the intersection of *events* and political meaning. The speech and its afterlife underscore how difficult it is to extract explanations of political consequences from public political spectacle. This chapter confronts this challenge head-on. It takes politics as its object and asks what cultural analysis can bring to bear on the study of politics.

In a series of review articles (Berezin 1994a; 1997a) written when the linking of politics and culture was novel among political sociologists, I identified nodal works and mapped the contours and possible trajectory of the field. Politics and culture are no longer a novel coupling. Wide-ranging empirical studies populate the field. My own work on Fascist Italy (Berezin 1997b) and European populism (Berezin 2009) serves as one example. It represents the tip of a huge iceberg that includes work on family capitalism (Adams 2005), nationalism (Brubaker 1992; Kumar 2003; Calhoun 1994; Wagner-Pacifici 2005), colonialism (Steinmetz 2007), religion (Gorski 2003; Zubrzycki 2006; Lichterman 2005), social movements (McAdam and Sewell 2001; Tarrow 2008), memory and identity (Glaeser 2000; Olick 2005; Spillman 1997), as well as ethnographic accounts of American politics (Perrin 2006; Lichterman 1996; Eliasoph 1998). Yet, even the important and influential collection of Adams, Clemens, and Orloff (2005) contains no essay written explicitly on the intersection of the political and the cultural.[3]

Beginning where my earlier iterations left off, this chapter engages recent methodological moves in historical and institutional analysis.[4] It extends the concept of events to bring cultural analysis to bear on political explanation and privileges "thick description" (Geertz 1973) and narrative as methodological tools. Borrowing from sociologist Emile Durkheim ([1895]1964), this article argues that events constitute "social facts"—phenomena with sufficient identity and coherence that the social collectivity recognizes them as discrete and important. Events incorporate space and temporality, culture and history, agents and structure. Recognition or collective perception is integral to the constitution of a "social fact" and by extension the identification of a significant political event.

In order to locate social practices in a broader sphere of collective meanings and to approximate scientific rigor, social scientists have invoked "toolkits" (Swidler 1986), influenced by various iterations of French sociology, "boundaries" (Lamont and Molnar 2002), structure (Sewell 1992), and "frames" (Benford and Snow 2000). For the most part, these analytic approaches are metaphors that attempt to concretize social processes that analysts either explicitly or implicitly ascribe to culture.

In *Keywords*, British cultural critic Raymond Williams (1976) interrogated the social history of concepts.[5] He notes that culture in its original form was an agricultural term that described an action. It was a verb, not a noun. Culture, as Williams points out, became a noun, that is, the medium in which things grow, as well as a verb in the nineteenth century. Williams' insights are worth revisiting as they underscore the dynamic as well as the sustaining or nurturing dimensions of culture. It is the tension between change and sustenance (positively referred to as modernity and tradition; negatively as progress versus reaction) that lies at the core of political as well as cultural analysis. It is relatively easy to describe political institutions and behavior and map their variations over time. The intersection between the political and the cultural is more resistant and requires a new metaphor and an appropriate analytic frame to capture the relation between dynamism and sustenance.

To adjudicate this tension, I turn to a metaphor from sports and biology that unites agency and nature. When athletes, even star athletes, reach a point where they can push their bodies no further, they call that point "hitting the wall." Of course, this is not literal. There is no real wall involved. But walls, due to their noted durability, are impossible to walk through in the ordinary sense. To walk through a wall, one needs to literally blast it away. Walls make limits manifest. Culture as it intersects the political is akin to an invisible brick wall. At certain historical moments, societies or individuals reach their cultural limits just as athletes reach their physical limits. When one, individually or collectively, hits the invisible brick wall of culture, one can go no further unless one finds a way to either blast the wall away or somehow develop a path through it. The metaphor of the invisible brick wall differs from the metaphor of a "boundary" that can be negotiated, or redrawn, or a "toolkit" that is unchanging, always available for use. Invisible walls have more plasticity than "frames" or "structures." An invisible brick wall does not imply that culture is unchangeable, but simply that it is extremely durable and durability has merits. We would not want our walls falling down on a daily basis. Walls also crumble if they are not repaired and may collapse seemingly of their own accord.

How then does the metaphor of the "invisible brick wall" translate to the study of politics? Reagan's wall speech is a Durkheimian "social fact" and therein resides its political importance. The intersection between collective perception and event that Reagan's speech embodied lies at the core of the relation of the political to the cultural. Events and the collective perception of them make manifest the "invisible brick wall" and reveal when that wall serves as a barrier, when it is crumbling, and when it is in danger of being blasted away. To listen to Reagan's speech is to hear cheering crowds. His speech was politically important because it revealed a political and cultural fault line—the meaning of which became manifest two years later in November 1989.

Political and cultural analysis demands more than a new metaphor—no matter how clever. It demands a framework that is analytically rigorous and empirically serviceable. This chapter is a modest move in that direction. First, it addresses the intersection of events and experience as an analytic category that incorporates the "counterfactual" turn in historical analysis. This section includes William Sewell's engagement with it as background to a political culture of events. Second, it relates the Durkheimian concept of "social fact" to political and cultural perception and argues for the existence of "political facts." Third, the last section lays out a typology of political facts based on the classification of events along a temporal or spatial axis. The typology develops a logic of political explanation that incorporates cultural analysis.

EVENTS AND THE COUNTERFACTUAL TURN

Cultural sociology and the field of historical institutionalism and political analysis have grown in tandem over the last fifteen years. There is no necessary overlap between cultural sociology and historical institutionalism, yet there is intellectual kinship between them. A subset of interdisciplinary scholars who are interested in culture, politics, and history provide the family ties.[6]

Historical institutionalism embraces the counterfactual as it carries the aura of hard science. Path dependence is the core concept of political institutionalism. Identifying the paths that polities took in the development of core institutions permits analysts to speculate about the paths not taken and to address the role of causality in the development of institutions. The union of path analysis and counterfactual thinking in a historical sense permits the development of hypotheses subject to empirical testing. It also unites temporality and choice. Not all historical institutionalists are rational choice theorists. Yet, the emphasis on the timing of events and the choices made or not made are attractive to choice analytic theorists. Path dependence is at the core of the concept of analytic narrative developed by economic historians (Bates, et al. 1998).[7]

Cultural sociology and the historical study of political institutions often share terminology—although terms tend to have vastly different meanings depending on which subfield is invoking them. Narratives are a core component of counterfactual historical institutional analysis because it relies heavily on being able to tell alternative stories so as to eliminate them in a propositional and hypothesis-testing manner. Narratives are also a core of cultural analysis (for a classic account, see Polletta 2006). In contrast to the counterfactual use of narrative that aims at explanation, the cultural narrative aims at interpretation. The former is hypothesis-confirming or -disconfirming; the latter is hypothesis-generating—left for others to prove or disprove.[8] Narratives are also descriptions, and description lurks in the interstices of even the most resolutely scientific analyses. Description is fundamental to human experience. Cross-culturally, the first questions that a child asks are, "What is it?" "What does it look like?" As Susanne Langer (1957) elegantly argues in *Philosophy in a New Key*, denotation comes before connotation. What it *is* precedes what it *means*.

Institutionalists often view history as enacting a causal process and events are seen as crucial conjunctures on a causal trajectory. Path dependence is the term that encapsulates the intersection of events and trajectory (Mahoney 2000; Pierson 2004). Borrowed from economic theory and economic history, path dependence assumes that at crucial moments collective decisions or events push collective actors down particular routes of "paths." Once a path is taken, it precludes others; makes course corrections difficult, if not impossible; and sets the course of future choices. Thus, the path taken, the choices made, are of critical importance for historical outcomes. The path and the choice are, in effect, causal with regard to the next set of choices.

Path analysis is attractive to some historical institutionalists because it has the aura of causality attached to it. Path analysis is amenable to counterfactual analysis because it permits formulations such as these: If this choice had been made or not made, what might the outcome have been? Path dependence does a good enough job of explaining why something does not happen and why some actions are blocked. It does a considerably less effective job of explaining the *meaning of what actually happens.* Capoccia and Kelemen (2007) point to the limits of "critical junctures" and argue that an analytic emphasis on critical choices actually blocks the ability to identify significant events that may not be immediately causal. In addition, path dependence is subject to the criticism of first, being overly deterministic and second, being difficult to operationalize. Rigorous causal reasoning demands a focus on extremely discrete events if one is to be able to specify all the steps in a path with confidence.[9]

Within the field of political science, a strict version of path analysis has had its critics and important modifications (Mahoney and Thelen 2010). Yet, historical and political sociologists who share a concern with culture and history have recognized central insights of path analysis and institutionalism and built on them in important ways. Historical sociologists have focused on events to counter some of the more problematic claims of path analysis. Historical sociologists (Sewell 2005; Abbott 2001) have recently argued that events as units of analysis may yield robust forms of political cultural explanation. For example, Sewell's (1996b) thick description of the storming of the Bastille as a unitary event permits him to develop a nuanced account of a larger phenomenon, the French Revolution, than traditional analyses that limit themselves to causes and consequences.

Sewell (1996a, 1996b) has become the leading exponent of a sociological theory of *events.*[10] He (1996a) argues that classic path analysis is not capable of dealing with change because it assumes that "causal structures are uniform through time" (p. 263). Sewell posits an "eventful temporality" that recognizes that the "radical contingency" of some events allows for social change and transformation. Sewell's (1996b, p. 844) refinement of his argument defines a historical event as "(1) a ramified sequence of occurrences that (2) is recognized as notable by contemporaries, and that (3) results in a durable transformation of structures." The event that Sewell discusses is the storming of the Bastille in Paris in 1789—an event that historians agree was pivotal to the series of events that constituted the French Revolution. Sewell's theory of *events* has several characteristics. Events are the subject of narrative and are recognized as significant when they occur. Events reveal "heightened emotion" and collective creativity, take ritual form, and—most importantly—generate more events.

Sewell's elegant elaboration of events is subject to critique on multiple levels. He is, for one thing, interested in events that change the course of history. But arguably, there are many events that occur and recur in political life that are not as iconic as the storming of the Bastille, however constituted, and that still have importance within a nationally constituted political space. Patterson (2007) has critiqued precisely this part of Sewell's argument as well as its neglect of causality. Steinmetz (2008) has challenged Sewell's insistence on recognition. Whether or not the course of history is altered in the short or the long run, Sewell elaborates salient features of events (particularly his emphasis on collective recognition, emotion, and narrative) that transpose well to political cultural analysis.

Sewell enriches the concept of event as a unit of analysis, and extends the field of historical sociology beyond institutions and path dependence. Sewell does not offer a fully integrated model of politics and culture, yet his engagement with these issues advances our thinking because it suggests a way to move forward. First, his critique of path dependence underscores its principle *lacuna* and its principle strength. Counterfactual analysis cannot incorporate all possible paths. Yet, it does take issues of temporality and sequencing seriously. Sewell's (1996b) story of the Bastille depends heavily on sequencing, but he also uses "thick description" to embed his analysis in its cultural particularity. His richly contextualized narrative underscores the importance of collective perception, performance, and emotion.

Sewell leaves us with two questions from which to begin a more codified approach to the intersection of the political and the cultural. First, how do we identify what matters? Or to put it another way, what constitutes political importance? Do we know that in July 1789 the group that stormed the Bastille, or French citizens in general, understood the importance of the event when it occurred? Second, Sewell (1996b) astutely notes that "events generate more events" (pp. 871–874). How do we categorize and order events so that they have explanatory as well as interpretive power. The next section of this chapter takes up the issue of importance; the following two sections turn to the issue of categorization and explanation.

WHAT MATTERS? EVENTS AND IMPLICIT CULTURAL KNOWLEDGE

In the realm of politics, what matters is crucial for analysis. Why does meaning suffuse some events more than others? How do we distinguish an event, a moment with political and cultural significance, from an occurrence—a normal blip in the flow of time?[11] Implicit cultural knowledge assigns importance to some events and not others. Political scientists and sociologists by training and disposition give short shrift to implicit meaning. In contrast to their colleagues in the "hard" social sciences, anthropologists have developed a sophisticated theoretical apparatus around the concept of collective understanding and shared cultural knowledge that is useful for political analysis.

In his essay on "thick description," anthropologist Clifford Geertz's (1973, pp. 6–7) elucidation of the difference between a "twitch" and a "wink" permits us to segue into this question. A twitch and a wink are basically the same neurological phenomena. The eyelid shutters and flashes open and shut almost involuntarily. The description of the physical phenomenon, the denotation, is the same whether one is twitching or winking—but the connotation, the meaning, is vastly different. In Western cultures, the twitch is usually a sign of nervousness or neurological disease—a body part out of control. A wink is also a playful or flirtatious gesture. There are some circumstances in which a wink would be vastly inappropriate. For example, professors who wish to avoid sexual harassment charges should not wink at students given the structures of authority at the university. A brain surgeon twitching away as he operated would not generate confidence. What is critical as Geertz argues is to know the context, and if you know the context, you share the meaning. In other words, a winking professor might really be a twitching professor—an extremely nervous or shy person before a lecture hall filled with undergraduates.

But what if you do not share the meaning? How might one excavate the meaning and particularly in ways that are relevant for the study of politics? Collectivity is the core of politics; culture is the invisible brick wall that encloses collectivity. The task of any cultural analysis is to understand the collective perceptions that bind a community and to aggregate upward to the macro-level constructs such as the polity. Since Freud's ([1905] 1999) classic essay on wit and the unconscious, social analysts of various stripes have recognized that jokes are instructive when attempting to theorize the relation between macro-level structures and micro-level perceptions.

Anthropologist Mary Douglas (1975) argues that "a joke cannot be perceived unless it corresponds to the form of the social experience: but I [MD] would go a step further and even suggest that the experience of a joke form in the social structure calls imperatively for the joke form to express it" (pp. 153–54). Douglas continues: "Jokes being themselves a play upon forms can well serve to express something about social forms…. [The] joke connects and disorganizes. It attacks sense and hierarchy" (p. 156). Macro-level structures that we experience as part of daily life such as political institutions are analogous to "social forms." In order to "get" the meaning of a joke, Douglas argues that the individual or the group has to understand its subversive elements. They must belong to a community of shared culture where meaning is implicit and thus unspoken—until challenged in the form of a joke.

Events re-calibrated as "social facts" serve as conduits to implicit political and cultural meaning. We may think of political events, such as Reagan at the Brandenberg Gate, much in the same way that Emile Durkheim ([1894]1964) described "social facts," that is as "ways of acting, thinking, and feeling that present the noteworthy property of existing outside the individual consciousness" (p. 2). Social facts are "every way of acting, fixed or not, capable of exercising on the individual an external constraint; or again, every way of acting which is general throughout a given society, while at the same time existing in its own right independent of its individual manifestations" (p. 13).

Social facts include collective phenomena—the law, the economy, the unemployment rate—as well as the individual and collective perception of them. Thus, Durkheim argues that a "social fact" is a structural and a psychological fact that goes beyond structure. He labels this combination of material and mental phenomena as "social currents" and describes them as

> the great movements of enthusiasm, indignation, and pity in a crowd [that] do not originate in any one of the particular individual consciousnesses. They come to each one of us from without and can carry us away in spite of ourselves.

Of course, it may happen that, in abandoning myself to them unreservedly, I do not feel the pressure they exert upon me. But it is revealed as soon as I try to resist them. Let an individual attempt to oppose one of these collective manifestations, and the emotions that he denies will turn against him. (pp. 4–5)

It is a short analytic leap from a *social* to a *political fact*. Within the realm of cultural analysis, political facts, rather than politics or the polity per se, are social facts that combine emotional valence, collective perception, institutional arrangements—and implicit cultural knowledge. We must now turn our attention to how collectivities experience events as political facts and how events can be ordered and codified in ways that are culturally sensitive and analytically rigorous.

EVENTS AS TEMPLATES OF POSSIBILITY: EXPERIENCING *POLITICAL FACTS*

Building on the insights of institutional scholarship and Durkheimian sociology, we can argue that *events* are *templates of possibility that collectivities experience as political facts*. In contrast to historical institutionalism, we argue that events are important for *what* they force us to imagine—and these imaginings may generate hope as well as fear, comfort as well as threat—rather than *how* they determine choice. *Events* are sociologically and politically important because they permit us to see relations and interconnections that speak to broader macro- and micro-level social processes. *Events* speak to collective resonance, present possibilities, and offer visions of possible paths—even if those paths are *not* pursued. *Events* make manifest what *might* happen, rather than predict what *will* happen. Public political events, such as Reagan's speech at the Brandenberg Gate, engage the collective imagination and have the capacity to alter public perceptions that *may* in the future alter political actions. Because they make manifest the possible, they have the power to engage collective emotions from fear to collective euphoria and the range of emotions that lie in between these polarities.

Experience is central to how collectivities understand the meaning of events—large and small. *Experience* implies a thick conception of temporality that can be marshaled to theorize the collective significance of political events. *Experience* works well as an analytic category because it interrogates the past and imagines the future. It is emotional and cognitive; conservative and transformative. *Experience, individual and collective*, is a temporal and spatial phenomenon that consciously or unconsciously draws on the past to assess the future.[12] *Experience* creates a tension between imagined possibilities and perceptions of constraint. Without experience, individual or collective, there would be no social or political facts because as individuals or a society, we would not have the grounds of collective recognition. *Experience*, individual and collective, does not simply float unanchored in social and political space.

As Parsons ([1942] 1954, p. 147)) observed in his discussion of propaganda, institutions anchor experience since they define expectations. Thus, institutions are, in the argument of this essay, a necessary but not sufficient dimension of political cultural analysis.

Smail (2008) in a recent exegesis on "neurohistory" argues that the past, the collective past, is hard-wired in the brain. This suggests that experience, the social manifestation of this biological phenomenon, is both determinant and conservative. Smail's argument has a lineage. For example, William James ([1879] 1956) in his essay "The Sentiment of Rationality" defines this phenomenon as the "comfort of the familiar." The "familiar" would only be "comforting" if assessments of the past were always positive. Here, Koselleck's (2004) distinction between "experience and expectation" proves useful. In a conservative environment, the gap between experience and expectation, past and future, is narrow. Modernity expands this gap and introduces complexity in the form of collective judgment and imagination.

Events take on their collective meaning and significance in the *moment*—the brief temporal space between judgment and imagination, the cognitive and the creative. *Moments* bear a kinship relation to experience but they are analytically and ontologically opposite. *Moments* are events that generate experiences. *Moments* represent an intense present-ness. They are sensate rather than cognate phenomena. Braudel ([1969] 1980) underscores this point when he observes: "Take the word *event*: for myself [*FB*] I would limit it, and imprison it within the short time span: an event is explosive, a "*nouvelle sonnante*" ("a matter of moment") as they said in the sixteenth century" (p. 27). *Moments* are often invoked but rarely theorized. Where moments are discussed, they are conceptualized as "critical junctures" or "turning points." But, not all turning points are tipping points.

Moments are more often moments of recognition—subtle changes in collective perceptions. The overlooked paradox is that often subtle course corrections precede turning points and most turning points are locations of recognition and not changes in direction. Actions, changes in direction, come later and they can be negative or positive. The Prince's lament in Giuseppe di Lampedusa's *The Leopard*, "For things to remain the same, everything must change," is an affirmation that course corrections are required to avoid social cataclysms, but the words also betray a recognition that a turning point in collective perception has already occurred. In his address to the 2008 Democratic National Convention, former President Bill Clinton argued that a reason to vote for Barack Obama was that Obama was "on the right side of history." What Clinton meant was that Obama was in the moment—and the moment was a complete break with the collective perception of what an American president was. But, those perceptions did not change overnight. Those perceptions were the result of fifty years of collective national experience in which the meaning of difference changed. We have only to recall that in 1960, Americans perceived John F. Kennedy as "different" because he was Roman Catholic.

Experience lies in those moments when biography and history intersect. Past and present, experience and moments are embedded within events and imbue them with their aura of futurity and possibility. Obama did not have to win the 2008

American presidential election. The moment was propitious. His campaign and election were imaginable and they became an event. Reagan did not tear down the Berlin Wall, but his speech clearly tapped into the moment of popular imaginings and discontent that later became a political reality. *Events* are *templates of possibility*, but their analytic power and political salience are not simply ad hoc. In the last section of this chapter, we turn to how we can focus on events in a systematic way so as to form the basis of a cogent political analysis that incorporates culture.

FROM MEANINGS TO EXPLANATIONS: AN ANALYTIC TYPOLOGY OF EVENTS AS *POLITICAL FACTS*

This essay is a pragmatic as well as theoretical discussion. Events worthy of study force changes in collective perception. They fracture or affirm community. For example, it would be difficult to argue that the event of 9/11 did not alter the collective perception of security in the United States. Since 9/11, the trope of safety has been a large part of American political campaigns.

As argued earlier, not all turning points are tipping points. It is rare that a single event has the impact of a 9/11. So which events matter and how do they advance a rigorous cultural understanding of the political? Comparison is crucial to the claim of cultural and political significance. Spatial or temporal variation provides the comparative dimension that supports analytic leverage. For analytic purposes, we can organize events as *contiguous, sequential,* and *spectacular.* Depending on context, events may have properties of all three categories—the *contiguous,* the *sequential,* and the *spectacular.*

Contiguous events refer to one event or class of events that has similar or different meanings, depending on the physical space in which the event occurs. Space might be as restricted as a neighborhood or as expansive as a nation-state or geographical region. Spatial context is a demarcator of cultural specificity. What is salient for political cultural analysis is how an event is collectively processed or perceived in a different milieu and the effects of that process on political action or nonaction. Difference depending on spatial location becomes a key to political analysis. For example, Ronald Reagan's trip to Berlin in 1987 was viewed with cynicism in the United States where some factions saw him as encouraging a militaristic stance toward the Soviet bloc, whereas in Berlin, his words were words of hope and possibility.

Clifford Geertz' slim book *Islam Observed* (1968) represents an early iteration of the focus on *contiguous events.* Morocco and Indonesia are Muslim countries, but the practice of Islam in each country is remarkably different. Laitin's (1986) study of the Yoruba in Nigeria reverses Geertz' strategy. He examines the political and cultural factors that enable part of Nigeria to be Christian and the other part to be Muslim.

The strategy of *contiguous events*, even if not labeled as such, has been a mainstay of much comparative cultural political analysis since the early 1990s. While not strictly political sociology, Lamont's (2000a, 2000b) studies of the comparative perception of social boundaries as well as her concept of "repertoires of evaluation" (Lamont and Thevenot 2000) are seminal exemplars of this method.

Within the more restricted area of political sociology, the category of event has been somewhat elastic in practice. In his study of nationalism, Brubaker (1996) argues that nationhood should be studied as a "contingent event." This is an articulation of a methodological orientation that he deploys implicitly in an earlier work (Brubaker 1992) on citizenship law and nationhood in France and Germany. Brubaker (1992) asked why, when confronted with the same increase in immigrant populations, France and Germany chose completely different methods of incorporation. He argues that France and Germany developed different "political idioms" about membership in the nation based on longstanding practices grounded in geopolitical necessities. Once embedded in the collective consciousness, the "political idiom," in my terminology, became a *political fact*, durable and resistant to revision—an "invisible brick wall" of meaning around who could and could not be a citizen. Brubaker's book is now nineteen years old. Yet, in the ensuing years, French and German citizenship laws have only changed marginally.

Somers (1993) studies the development of citizenship law in eighteenth-century England using the method of contiguous events. Challenging the classic writings of T. H. Marshall, Somers argues that citizenship is an "instituted process" rather than a status bestowed upon individuals. She then proceeds to demonstrate how within England, a single nation-state, region and geography determined political development. By contrasting the cultural practices of "arable" and "pastoral" regions, Somers was able to show how political and economic organization contributed to different versions of citizenship and democracy. Elites governed the "arable" lands. These lands were poor learning grounds for democracy. In contrast, small landowners and farmers cooperated among themselves in the "pastoral" lands, creating cultures of solidarity. Democracy flourished in the pastoral lands and a "local public sphere and political culture of rights" (Somers 1993, p. 593) developed.

The analysis of *contiguous events* has grown increasingly sophisticated. Somers and Block (2005) deploy it creatively in their analysis of market fundamentalism and social welfare regimes. They take two unrelated events—welfare reform in England in 1834 and welfare reform in the United States in 1996—and find ideological parallels across time and space. Spillman (1997) has analyzed bicentennial commemorations in the United States and Australia as adjudicators of national identity. Steinmetz's (2007) study of German colonial practices reveals different strategies on different continents. He points to a concept of colonialisms rather than colonialism even within a single national state. Smith (2005) takes on the phenomenon of war and examines its "cultural logic" in three diverse iterations in different time periods—in Iraq, the Gulf, and Suez.

My own research on political violence employs a variation of *contiguous events* to analyze the policy consequences of different moral evaluations of terrorist activity. My empirical focus is the 1985 hijacking of the *Achille Lauro*. I examine the different collective perceptions of the event in the three countries that were involved in adjudicating the hijacking—the United States, Italy, and Egypt. The *Achille Lauro* was an Italian cruise ship that was hijacked in international waters by a splinter group from the Palestinian Liberation Organization. The Italians and the Egyptians successfully negotiated the release of the ship. When the hijacking was over, it was determined that an American passenger, an elderly man in a wheelchair, had been shot and thrown overboard. From that moment, the hijacking became an international event with vastly different meanings for those involved. The Italians saw it as a problem of Middle Eastern politics and they congratulated themselves at first with keeping peace in the Mediterranean; the Americans viewed it as a direct attack on an American citizen and the United States.

President Ronald Reagan ordered the interception of an Egyptian civilian passenger plane that was carrying the hijackers back to Italy in order to stand trial. Italy saw the attack on the Egyptian airliner as an insult and a violation of international law. The Americans viewed it as a triumph in the cause of justice. In the end, the legal interpretation held. But for Americans, the event hinged on the fact that terrorism was perceived as a moral issue, a crime against persons and under the jurisdiction of criminal law. The United States was particularly unhappy that the hijackers would be brought to trial in Italy—a country without the death penalty. In contast, the Italians (and virtually everyone else) viewed it as a political event that demanded adherence to the rule of extant international law. The event pointed to a moral evaluation of terrorism that has had political consequences as the United States has had to deal with the broader issues of international terrorism that 9/11 generated.

Sequential events focus on analogous events that move forward in time and in aggregate build new experiences. Whereas spatial context was constitutive of *contiguous event* analysis, temporal context or history is constitutive of *sequential event* analysis. *Sequential events* are future-oriented and lead to the imaginings of new possibilities. The contours of those imaginings and possibilities provide the basis of political analysis. The analysis of sequential events is aligned with, but not the same as, traditional path analysis. Turning points figure in the sequence, but they are viewed as contingent and their consequences less deterministic. *Sequential* analysis of events differs from path dependence or "analytic narratives" in two important respects. First, *sequential events* emphasize the *flow qua flow* of analogous events rather than the linkage of events in a monocausal chain. Second, analogues are sequential events because they occur within a similar spatial context but with a variable time frame. For this reason, periodization is an important dimension of *sequential event* analysis. *Sequential events* highlight the fissures in the cultural wall and foreground where the possibilities of political and cultural change might lie.

My analysis of "illiberal politics" (Berezin 2009) in contemporary Europe relies on the *sequential* analysis of events. The analytic core of the book is the French

National Front. The theoretical analysis focuses on the durability of national identities and practices, and the vulnerabilities of various national states to right-wing
politics. The broader theoretical point that incorporated a political and cultural
analysis sets the work apart from more standard approaches to the European right
that limit themselves to electoral analysis. I examine the French National Front's
political trajectory in the years between 1997 and 2002. This is a relatively compressed time period. For this period, I identify a series of key events: the 1997
Strasbourg Party convention; the 1998 success in the regional elections and the rupture of the National Front as a political party; and the 1999 "failure" in the European
parliamentary elections. The culmination of the National Front's story was the first
round of the 2002 presidential election when Jean Marie Le Pen, the party leader,
netted second place.

The events in the National Front's story were "political facts." French citizens
recognized them as important and for the most part they generated national anxiety and fear. But, they were not the only "political facts" in France, or in Europe
during this period. I mapped the salient events within the National Front's trajectory against a series of events in French civil society, the French state and European
politics more broadly. I was able to identify three narratives that moved in parallel
sequences. The story of Europe, or more appropriately the European Union, was a
story of geographical expansion and political integration. The central point of
this story was the 2004 draft constitution. The European story had an effect on
every nation-state on the continent—albeit in different ways. As Europe was expanding, Europeanization was becoming associated with globalization and market fundamentalism across the continent. In 1998, social movements within French civil
society that had mobilized against Le Pen turned their attention to issues of globalization. ATTAC, the anti-globalization group, that has since become transnational
was founded in France in 1998. The French state was espousing multiculturalism
and Europe during this period, while at the same time reasserting French national
identity.

In 1998, France won the World Cup and the French political establishment
hailed the victory as a triumph of multiculturalism and toleration in France. Its star
players were second-generation Algerians. At the same time, the French state was
restricting immigration and refusing to ratify the European Union's "Regional
Language" initiative. The culmination of the reassertion of nation-ness came with
two events in 2005. The first was the French state's decision to uphold the law affirming *laicite* by banning the wearing of religious symbols in public places. In practice,
this meant that young Muslim women could not wear headscarves to school. The
second event was the French rejection of the European constitution after a popular
referendum in May 2005. It was not only French citizens that rejected Europe.
French political parties of diverse ideological persuasions, from the National Front
to some segments of the Socialist Party, were vehemently opposed to the draft
constitution.

By pursuing a sequence of analogous events in different spheres from the
National Front to civil society, to the state to the European Union, and by looking at

the points in which events intersected, a new story of illiberal politics both in France and in Europe emerges. First, if we restrict the analysis to the National Front, we see that from 1997 on, the National Front shifted its public discourse from immigrants and immigration to Europe and globalization. If we look across spheres at the same point, we find that the language of national identity and anti-globalization was gaining momentum among members of the French political class as well as in civil society. The exogenous force that was threatening France at the moment was not immigration but Europeanization, and it was a force that not only applied to France. Most analysts viewed 1999 as the end of the National Front and Le Pen. Le Pen's second place in the first round of the 2002 presidential election proved them wrong. I argue that 1999 was the end of the beginning for Le Pen—not the beginning of the end. The end did come—but it came much later—in 2007 with the election of Nicholas Sarkozy. In 2007, the National Front and Le Pen's fortunes suffered a reversal for the first time in ten years. Sarkozy shrewdly detached Le Pen's message from the messenger. Sarkozy used those portions of Le Pen's messages that suited his strategy of strong nation-ness and an ambivalent commitment to Europeanization and globalization.

A *sequential* analysis of analogous events allowed me to locate a turning point in 1999—where few would have located it—but it was a turning point that applied not only to the National Front. French civil society and the French state were having second thoughts about Europe. The sequential analysis enabled me to make a broader theoretical point about the relation between "illiberalism" and European-ization. This is a story that extends beyond France and beyond Europe. My analysis speaks to a core relation between security and democratic sentiment in a world beset by crises from the political to the financial that feels increasingly insecure to many people.

Sequential analysis may also focus on a single event that changes its meaning over an extended period of time. Alexander's (2003) study of how the Nazi genocide of the Jews became the Holocaust provides an illustration. He demonstrates how a variety of political and cultural actors came to identify the mass murders in German concentration camps as a Holocaust. This identification did not happen overnight. Political facts in the international and national public sphere defined periods in postwar history, during which time the collective conception of genocide evolved. The events that occurred in Nazi Germany have come to denote one among many events that the term Holocaust demarcates. Alexander's careful historical analysis demonstrates that today the term "Holocaust" stands as a "bridging metaphor" that connotes moral failure and evil in a variety of global contexts and describes a variety of events.

Spectacular events are the last category of events to consider. They are public performances of various types (Alexander 2004; Berezin 1994b). *Spectacular events* are central to anthropological, and some historical, accounts of politics. Geertz' (1980) "theater state" is a classic example. *Spectacular events* are the class of events to which cultural sociologists often refer when they speak of culture and politics. *Spectacular events* are visible and require an audience. In contrast to *contiguous* events that draw on *past* experience and *sequential* events that deal with *developing* experiences, *spectacular* events aim to *create* experiences that can be reabsorbed into collective experience. Spectacular events exist in an *eternal present* and give narrative form to political facts.

Social analysts often take *spectacular events* at face value. Elsewhere (Berezin 1997b), I have argued that *representations of power do not equal realities of power.* *Spectacular events* are dense cultural forms that derive their political significance in relation to other events. Spectacle is a form of public sociability. German social theorist Georg Simmel ([1910] 1971) argues that sociability is based on an implicit knowledge of rules of behavior that inhabitants of particular cultural and social contexts share. Simmel juxtaposes sociability, or form, against values, or content. He argues: "Where a connection, begun on the sociable level...finally comes to center about personal values, it loses the essential quality of sociability and becomes an association determined by a content—not unlike a business or religious relation, for which contact, exchange, and speech are but instruments for ulterior ends, while for sociability they are the whole meaning and content of the social processes" (p. 131). Sociability is an end in itself—it is "*the play-form of association* [emphasis in original]" (p. 130). Moving from Simmel's insights on social forms to political spectacle is a short step. Political spectacle is the "*play-form*" of politics. Spectacle as a political form articulates what is legitimate and what is not. Spectacle as the "play-form" of politics uses theatricality to communicate the boundaries of political legitimacy. *Spectacle events* aim to engage the political public—but we cannot assume that they do. They may create a "community of feeling" (Berezin 1997b) or they may fall on deaf collective ears.

Spectacular events are either *ritualistic* or *mediated*. Ritual events repeat. National commemorations and celebrations focus on a single event of national history, such as endings or beginnings of wars, constitutions, or prominent leaders. National holidays as a strategy of commemoration always raise a question as to what extent they tap into the memory they wish to commemorate. Citizens may also view them as simply a day off from work.[13] In recent years, memory studies have developed as a specialized subfield within cultural and historical sociology (see, e.g., Olick and Robbins 1998). Before modern technology, ritual events occurred in real time. Medieval lords, kings, and political leaders up to the advent of film were restricted to the live political ceremony. Modern politicians still use live events but technology has greatly expanded their repertoire of possibilities. Modern mass media permit the theatricalization of events that might otherwise be left to restricted and local commemoration. The annual ceremonies at the site of the World Trade Center in New York permit grieving relatives to air their private sorrows on national television, but also keep the events and the dangers of terrorism ever-present in the American collective psyche.

Spectacular events may be spontaneous and then captured by national media and aired over and over. The World Trade Center Towers have fallen thousands of times. Less dramatic examples include: the crowds that lined the streets when Diana Princess of Wales died; the masses of people that regularly showed up during the

2008 presidential campaign when Barack Obama spoke; the riots in Iran after the June 2009 presidential election.

The moment of silence observed around the 2006 bombing of a London subway train provides an illustration of how the media may facilitate creating an event that makes a political statement. On July 7, 2006, a cell group of Middle Eastern terrorists set off a bomb in a London subway station during rush hour. Many persons were killed. The British government declared that a ritual moment of silence in solidarity with the victims be observed on July 14, 2006—a week after the event. While the public ritual occurred in London, with both the queen and the prime minster participating, the event became a European event denouncing terrorist activity.

Ever since Europe began expanding as an integrated union in the early 1990s, collective solidarity has been at issue. Despite a common monetary system, flag, and various ad hoc holidays, national identities have been as resilient as ever. The London bombing that occurred just a few months after the terrorist bombing of a Madrid commuter train presented European bureaucrats with an opportunity to promote a collective European identity. A European moment of silence in solidarity with the victims was declared to occur at the same time as the commemoration in London. Television programming and public radio were halted in all European Union countries at the moment in which the bomb hit. The only programming available was coverage of the queen and Tony Blair in England. After the moment of silence ended, normal broadcasting resumed, but not before a national political figure made a comment on the presence of terrorism in Europe and the need to stand together in its wake. Thus, a terrorist event was turned into a media event that was used not only to underscore the importance of fighting terrorism, but also to underscore the necessity of a collective European solidarity. Timing is crucial here. The summer of 2006 was one year after French and Dutch citizens had rejected in national referenda a European constitution. Europe as a solidarity project was frayed in the summer of 2006, and the terrorist attacks and their commemoration in European media became an event in the *sequence* of events surrounding Europeanization.

Spectacular events rarely stand alone. They provide an important adjunct to *contiguous* and *sequential* events and often serve as component parts of *contiguous* or *sequential* events. In *Making the Fascist Self* (Berezin 1997b), I analyzed *spectacular* events in both a *contiguous* and *sequential* manner to make broader points about political development in Fascist Italy and fascism as a political ideology more generally. In one set of chapters, I analyzed the annual commemoration of the March on Rome—the "founding" event of Italian Fascism. The ceremonies that I describe took place in the capital. In another chapter, I analyzed (thanks to a Fascist Party calendar) all Fascist spectacle events that occurred in Verona—a small city far away from the center—over a twenty-year period. The calendar permitted me to compare in contiguous fashion Fascist celebration in the center and periphery. Histories that describe Fascist ritual without taking this comparative approach often tell a story of Fascist ideology being transmitted through these public events. But my comparative eventful analysis yielded a far more nuanced account. The Fascist ideological project was a struggle from the beginning. The years of standing together in the piazza in the end were a training ground for the civil war that ensued in Italy between 1943 and 1945. It also provided ritual form for the execution of Mussolini, whose body was hung by its heels in a central piazza in Milan where the citizenry gathered to defile it.

As if: The Meaning of what Actually Happens

Events focus our analytic attention. Events as objects of study offer methodological as well as theoretical advantages. Events as theorized in the preceding sections allow for historical and cultural analysis of the political. A cultural analysis of politics shifts the unit of analysis from political actors, whether voters or party operatives, to events that marked salient moments in collective national perceptions. Events are embedded in social and political relations. Events incorporate structure and culture, institutions and actors. Events permit us to hear the voices of multiple subjects at the same time.[14]

Past experience defines the meaning of *contiguous events*. Past perceptions and practices affect present interpretations and shape the repertoire of imaginings of collective social actors. Analyzing *contiguous* events in different spatial milieus underscores the durability of culture—the brick wall—and particularity of different cultures. The emphasis on past experience points in the direction of conservative rather than transformative political behavior. *Sequential events* interrogate the past and imagine the future. They are building events. Restricted to one spatial milieu, *sequential events* reveal the fissures in the brick wall of cultural—the points for repair and renewal—the malleability of culture. In the political sphere, they point us in the direction of transformation—they do not guarantee the nature of that transformation. Learning may take a reactionary as well as revolutionary form. Spectacular events derive their analytic power from their capacity to be inserted among analogous *contiguous* or *sequential events*.

Events as political facts lend analytic rigor to the cultural analysis of politics. The methods proposed in this chapter depart from both institutional and cultural analysis in important ways. In contrast to institutional analysis, events are not simply links in a causal chain. Events are templates of possibility only for agents. Political analysts must treat events *as if* they were fixed—with the full understanding that different agents might assign different possibilities to them.[15] Mikhail Gorbachev did not tear down the Berlin Wall because Ronald Reagan asked him to do so. In fact, neither Gorbachev, nor Reagan tore down the Berlin Wall—although they both may have felt as though they did. The citizens of East Berlin tore down the material wall that divided the city.

Many events led to the collapse of Communism in 1989. The wall was fissured long before it fell. But without the fixity of the "fall of the wall in 1989," it would be analytically difficult to locate the events that led to the collapse of Communism in a series of events. It would be difficult to talk about the different propensities for democracy and authoritarianism in the post-socialist East. It would be difficult to analyze authoritarian regimes in other parts of the globe. Without cultural analysis, we underestimate the importance of emotion and meaning, the invisible brick walls that surround politics. But without acting as if events are fixed and real, that events actually happen, our political analyses are attenuated; our critical capacities are impoverished; and a wall of incomprehension remains.

Table 23.1 Typology of Political Facts

			Spectacular	
	Contiguous	*Sequential*	*Ritual*	*Media*
Event	Single	Multiple	Multiple	Single
Spatial Dimension	Multiple	Single	Single	Multiple
Temporal Dimension	Single	Multiple	Multiple	Multiple
Experience	Past	Future	Present	Present
	Tradition	Building	Creating	Creating
Political Potential	Conservative	Transformative	Conservative or Transformative	

NOTES

1. I drafted the first version of this chapter when I was a Fernand Braudel Senior Fellow in the Department of Social and Political Sciences at the European University Institute in Fiesole, Italy. I thank Peter Mair, the chair, as well as the staff and faculty of the department, for their generosity and collegiality. I am appreciative of Phil Smith for his critique of the first version of this chapter. Jared Peifer and Laura Ford helped with manuscript preparation and provided important substantive comments. Chris Cameron designed the table. I presented an earlier version of my arguments at the Cornell-Giessen Workshop: Transnational Approaches to the Study of Culture (April 3, 2009). I thank Leslie Adelson of the Department of German Studies for asking me to participate. My paper benefited from the questions and insights of the workshop participants.

2. As a concept, *event* engages the current concern with narrative theory in comparative historical sociology (Sewell 1996a, 1996b; Somers 1994, 1995; Büthe 2002). Polletta (2006) and Tilly (2002), from divergent perspectives, have analyzed how narratives or "stories" influence politics. As an analytic category, the "event" captured the imagination of literary theorists (Deleuze 1969) and historians, "l'histoire événementielle" (Braudel [1969] 1980, p. 27), before attaining its current salience in political science and sociology.

3. The intersection of political and cultural analysis has a luminous, if problematic, history in social science. Modernization studies defined political culture in the 1950s and 1960s. Almond and Verba's ([1963] 1989) study of "civic culture" and Banfield's (1958)

account of a southern Italian village are classic examples. These studies measured the diffusion of Western values as an index of democratic dispositions. They seem quaint in the face of the massive political upheavals and cultural complexity of the late twentieth and early twenty-first century. Yet, Almond and Verba as well as Banfield have contemporary counterparts as the essays in Harrison and Huntington's (2000) anthology, *Culture Matters*, illustrate. Samuel Huntington's *Clash of Civilizations* (1996) locates culture in civilizations that are based on shared religions. Though politically conservative, these studies have value in that they point in the direction of a thick conception of culture that owes more to anthropology than to political science. Political anthropology focuses on shared practices and social actions as revelatory of meaning spheres, ranging from the political to the economic. See Paley (2002) for a review of this literature as well as Ortner (2006).

4. See essays in Adams, Clemens, and Orloff (2005) and Steinmetz (2005) for discussions of theory and method in comparative historical sociology.

5. See Somers (1995) for a discussion of a "historical sociology of concept formation."

6. The number of important review essays in both fields coupled with the interdisciplinarity of their citations support this assertion (see, e.g., Immergut 1998; Hall and Taylor 1996; Thelen 1999; Clemens 2007; Lamont 2000; and Alexander 2003, pp. 3–26).

7. For a critique, see Adams (1999, pp. 98–122) and Somers (1998).

8. Although by no means a cultural analyst, political scientist Arend Lijphart (1971) outlines how case studies may serve as valid analytic tools.

9. The comparison of Griffin (1993) versus Mahoney (2003) illustrates this dilemma.

10. Sewell, who acknowledges a debt to Marshall Sahlins (1991), reformulated these theories in *Logics of History* (2005).

11. Mast (2006) draws a distinction between event and occurrence.

12. Historians (e.g., Scott 1996; LaCapra 2004, ch. 1; Jay 2005) that privilege experience as an analytic category tend to focus on individual subjects. Their approach is inductive and is in contrast to the deductive and collective conceptualization of experience that this chapter proposes. See Throop (2003) for a critique from the perspective of anthropology.

13. See Schwartz (2008) for a study of the American holiday Presidents' Day.

14. See Table 23.1.

15. For a different approach to this point, see Wagner-Pacifici (2010).

REFERENCES

Abbott, Andrew. 2001. *Time Matters: On Theory and Method*. Chicago: University of Chicago Press.

Adams, Julia. 1999. "Culture in Rational-Choice Theories of State-Formation." Pp. 98–122 in *State/Culture: State Formation after the Cultural Turn*, George Steinmetz, ed. Ithaca, NY: Cornell University Press.

———. 2005. *The Familial State: Ruling Families and Merchant Capitalism in Early Modern Europe*. Ithaca, NY: Cornell University Press.

Adams, Julia, Elizabeth Clemens, and Ann Orloff, eds. 2005. *Remaking Modernity: Politics, History, and Sociology*. Durham, NC: Duke University Press.

Alexander, Jeffrey C. 2003. "On the Social Construction of Moral Universals: The Holocaust from War Crime to Trauma Drama." Pp. 27–84 in *The Meanings of Social Life: A Cultural Sociology*. New York: Oxford University Press.

————. 2004. "Cultural Pragmatics: Social Performance between Ritual and Strategy." *Sociological Theory* 22: 527–573.

Almond, Gabriel A., and Sidney Verba. 1963. *The Civic Culture: Political Attitudes and Democracy in Five Nations*. Princeton, NJ: Princeton University Press.

Anderson, Benedict. 2006. *Imagined Communities: Reflections on the Origin and Spread of Nationalism*. London: Verso.

Banfield, Edward C. 1958. *The Moral Basis of a Backward Society*. Glencoe, IL: Free Press.

Bates, Robert H., Avner Grief, Margaret Levi, Jean-Laurent Rosenthal, and Barry R. Weingast, eds. 1998. *Analytic Narratives*. Princeton, NJ: Princeton University Press.

Benford, Robert D., and David A. Snow. 2000. "Framing Processes and Social Movements: An Overview and Assessment." *Annual Review of Sociology* 26: 611–639.

Berezin, Mabel. 1994a. "Fissured Terrain: Methodological Approaches and Research Styles in Culture and Politics." In *Sociology of Culture: Emerging Theoretical Perspectives*, ed. Diana Crane. London: Basil Blackwell, pp. 91–116.

————. 1994b. "Cultural Form and Political Meaning: State-Subsidized Theater, Ideology, and the Language of Style in Fascist Italy." *The American Journal of Sociology* 99: 1237–1286.

————. 1997a. "Politics and Culture: A Less Fissured Terrain." *Annual Review of Sociology* 23: 361–383.

————. 1997b. *Making the Fascist Self: The Political Culture of Interwar Italy*. Ithaca, NY: Cornell University Press.

————. 2009. *Illiberal Politics in Neoliberal Times: Culture, Security and Populism in the New Europe*. New York: Cambridge University Press.

Braudel, Fernand. [1969] 1980. *On History*, Sarah Matthews, trans. Chicago: University of Chicago Press.

Brubaker, Rogers. 1992. *Citizenship and Nationhood in France and Germany*. Cambridge, MA: Harvard University Press.

Büthe, Tim. 2002. "Taking Temporality Seriously: Modeling History and the Use of Narratives as Evidence." *The American Political Science Review* 96: 481–493.

Calhoun, Craig. 1994. *Neither Gods nor Emperors: Students and the Struggle for Democracy in China*. Berkeley: University of California Press.

Capoccia, Giovanni, and R. D. Kelemen. 2007. "The Study of Critical Junctures: Theory, Narrative and Counterfactuals in Historical Institutionalism." *World Politics* 59: 341–369.

Clemens, Elisabeth S. 2007. "Toward a Historicized Sociology: Theorizing Events, Processes, and Emergence." *Annual Review of Sociology* 33: 527–549.

Deleuze, Gilles. 1969. *Logique du Sens*. Paris: Éditions de Minuit.

Douglas, Mary. 1975. *Implicit Meanings: Essays in Anthropology*. London: Routledge & Kegan Paul.

Durkheim, Emile. [1885] 1964. *The Rules of Sociological Method*, translated by Sarah A. Solovay and John H. Mueller. New York: Free Press of Glencoe.

Eliasoph, Nina. 1998. *Avoiding Politics: How Americans Produce Apathy in Everyday Life*. Cambridge, UK: Cambridge University Press.

Freud, Sigmund. [1905] 1999. *Wit and Its Relation to the Unconscious*, edited by A. A. Brill. London: Routledge.

Geertz, Clifford. 1968. *Islam Observed; Religious Development in Morocco and Indonesia*. New Haven, CT: Yale University Press.

————. 1973. "Thick Description." Pp. 3–30 in *The Interpretation of Cultures: Selected Essays*. New York: Basic Books.

————. 1980. *Negara: The Theatre State in Nineteenth-Century Bali*. Princeton, NJ: Princeton University Press.

Glaeser, Andreas. 2000. *Divided in Unity: Identity, Germany, and the Berlin Police*. Chicago: University of Chicago Press.

Gorski, Philip S. 2003. *The Disciplinary Revolution: Calvinism and the Rise of the State in Early Modern State*. Chicago: University of Chicago Press.

Griffin, Larry J. 1993. "Narrative, Event-Structure Analysis, and Causal Interpretation in Historical Sociology." *The American Journal of Sociology* 98: 1094–1133

Hall, Peter A., and Rosemary C. R. Taylor. 1996. "Political Science and the Three New Institutionalisms." *Political Studies* 44: 936–957

Harrison, Lawrence E., and Samuel P. Huntington, eds. 2000. *Culture Matters*. New York: Basic Books.

Hunt, Lynn A. 1984. *Politics, Culture, and Class in the French Revolution*. Berkeley: University of California Press.

Huntington, Samuel P. 1996. *The Clash of Civilizations and the Remaking of World Order*. New York: Simon & Schuster.

Immergut, Ellen M. 1998. "The Theoretical Core of the New Institutionalism." *Politics & Society* 26: 5–34.

James, William. [1879] 1956. "The Sentiment of Rationality." Pp. 63–110 in *The Will to Believe and Other Essays in Popular Philosophy*. New York: Dover.

Jay, Martin. 2005. *Songs of Experience: Modern American and European Variations on a Universal Theme*. Berkeley: University of California Press.

Koselleck, Reinhart. 2004. *Futures Past: On the Semantics of Historical Time*. New York: Columbia University Press.

Kumar, Krishan. 2003. *The Making of English National Identity*. Cambridge, UK: Cambridge University Press.

LaCapra, Dominick. 2004. *History in Transit: Experience, Identity, Critical Theory*. Ithaca, NY: Cornell University Press.

Laitin, David. 1986. *Hegemony and Culture*. Chicago: University of Chicago Press.

Lamont, Michele. 2000a. "Meaning-Making in Cultural Sociology: Broadening Our Agenda." *Contemporary Sociology* 29: 602–607.

———. 2000b. *The Dignity of Working Men: Morality and the Boundaries of Race, Class, and Immigration*. New York: Russell Sage Foundation.

Lamont, Michèle, and Laurent Thévenot. 2000. *Rethinking Comparative Cultural Sociology: Repertoires of Evaluation in France and the United States*. New York: Cambridge University Press.

Langer, Susanne K. 1957. *Philosophy in a New Key; a Study in the Symbolism of Reason, Rite, and Art*. Cambridge, MA: Harvard University Press.

Lichterman, Paul. 1996. *The Search for Political Community: American Activists Reinventing Commitment*. Cambridge, UK: Cambridge University Press.

———. 2005. *Elusive Togetherness: Church Groups Trying to Bridge America's Divisions*. Princeton, NJ: Princeton University Press.

Lijphart, Arend. 1971. "Comparative Politics and Comparative Method." *American Political Science Review* 65: 682–693.

Mahoney, James. 2000. "Path Dependence in Historical Sociology." *Theory and Society* 29: 507–548.

———. 2003. "Long Run Development and the Legacy of Colonialism in Spanish America." *American Journal of Sociology* 109: 50–106.

Mahoney, James, and Kathleen Thelen, eds. 2010. *Explaining Institutional Change: Ambiguity, Agency and Power*. Cambridge, UK: Cambridge University Press.

Mast, Jason L. 2006. "The Cultural Pragmatics of Event-ness: The Clinton/Lewinsky Affair." Pp. 115–145 in *Social Performance: Symbolic Action, Cultural Pragmatics, and Ritual,*

Jeffrey C. Alexander, Bernhard Giesen, and Jason L. Mast, eds. Cambridge, UK: Cambridge University Press.

McAdam, Doug, and William H. Sewell, Jr. 2001. "It's About Time: Temporality in the Study of Social Movements and Revolutions." Pp. 89–125 in *Silence and Voice in the Study of Contentious Politics*, Ronald R. Aminzade, et al., eds. New York: Cambridge University Press.

Olick, Jeffrey K. 2005. *In the House of the Hangman: The Agonies of German Defeat, 1943–1949*. Chicago: University of Chicago Press.

Olick, Jeffrey K., and Joyce Robbins. 1998. "Social Memory Studies: From 'Collective Memory' to the Historical Sociology of Mnemonic Practices." *Annual Review of Sociology* 24: 105–140.

Ortner, Sherry B. 2006. *Anthropology and Social Theory*. Durham, NC: Duke University Prerss.

Paley, Julia. 2002. "Towards an Anthropology of Democracy." *Annual Review of Anthropology* 31: 469–496.

Parsons, Talcott. [1942] 1954. "Propaganda and Social Control." Pp. 142–176 in *Essays in Sociological Theory*, 2nd ed. Glencoe, IL; Free Press.

Patterson, Orlando. 2007. "Review of William H. Sewell, Jr., Logics of History." *American Journal of Sociology* 112(4): 1287–1290.

Perrin, Andrew J. 2006. *Citizen Speak: The Democratic Imagination in American Life*. Chicago: University of Chicago Press.

Pierson, Paul. 2004. *Politics in Time: History, Institutions, and Social Analysis*. Princeton, NJ: Princeton University Press.

Polletta, Francesca. 2006. *It Was Like a Fever: Storytelling in Protest and Politics*. Chicago: University of Chicago Press.

Sahlins, Marshall. 1991. "The Return of the Event, Again: With Reflections on the Beginnings of the Great Fijian War of 1843 to 1855 between the Kingdoms of Bau and Rewa." Pp. 37–99 in *Clio in Oceania: Toward a Historical Anthropology*, Aletta Biersack, ed. Washington, DC: Smithsonian Institution Press.

Schwartz, Barry. 2008. "Collective Memory and Abortive Commemoration: Presidents' Day and the American Holiday Calendar." *Social Research* 75(1): 75–110.

Scott, Joan W. 1996. "The Evidence of Experience." Pp. 379–406 in *The Historic Turn in the Human Sciences*, Terence J. McDonald, ed. Ann Arbor: University of Michigan Press.

Seigel, Jerrold E. 2005. *The Idea of the Self: Thought and Experience in Western Europe since the Seventeenth Century*. Cambridge, UK: Cambridge University Press.

Sewell, William H. 1996a. "Three Temporalities: Towards an Eventful Sociology." Pp. 245–280 in *The Historic Turn in the Human Sciences*, Terrence J. McDonald, ed. Ann Arbor: University of Michigan Press.

———. 1996b. "Historical Events as Transformations of Structures: Inventing Revolution at the Bastille." *Theory and Society* 25: 841–881.

———. 2005. *Logics of History: Social Theory and Social Transformation*. Chicago: University of Chicago Press.

Simmel, Georg. [1910] 1971. "Sociability." Pp. 127–40 in *On Individuality and Social Forms*, Donald N. Levine, ed. Chicago: University of Chicago Press.

Smail, Daniel Lord. 2008. *On Deep History and the Brain*. Berkeley: University of California Press.

Smith, Philip. 2005. *Why War?: The Cultural Logic of Iraq, the Gulf War, and Suez*. Chicago: University of Chicago Press.

Somers, Margaret R. 1993. "Citizenship and the Place of the Public Sphere: Law, Community, and Political Culture in the Transition to Democracy." *American Sociological Review* 58: 587–620.

———. 1995. "What's Political or Cultural about Political Culture and the Public Sphere? Towards an Historical Sociology of Concept Formation." *Sociological Theory* 13(2): 113–144.

———. 1998. "'We're No Angels': Realism, Rational Choice, and Relationality in Social Science." *American Journal of Sociology* 104: 722–784.

Somers, Margaret R., and Fred Block. 2005. "From Poverty to Pervisity: Ideas, Markets, and Institutions over 200 Years of Welfare Debate." *American Sociological Review* 70: 260–287.

Spillman, Lyn. 1997. *Nation and Commemoration: Creating National Identities in the United States and Australia.* Cambridge, UK: Cambridge University Press.

Steinmetz, George, ed. 2005. *The Politics of Method in the Human Sciences: Positivism and Its Epistemological Others.* Durham, NC: Duke University Press.

———. 2007. *The Devil's Handwriting: Precoloniality and the German Colonial State in Qingdao, Samoa, and Southwest Africa.* Chicago: University of Chicago Press.

———. 2008. "Sewell's Logics of History as a Framework for an Integrated Social Science." *Social Science History* 32(4): 535–553.

Swidler, Ann. 1986. "Culture in Action: Symbols and Strategies." *American Sociological Review* 51: 273–286.

Tarrow, Sidney. 2008. "Charles Tilly and the Practice of Contentious Politics." *Social Movement Studies* 7(3): 225–246.

Thelen, Kathleen. 1999. "Historical Institutionalism in Comparative Politics." *Annual Review of Political Science* 2: 369–404.

Throop, Jason. 2003. "Articulating Experience." *Anthropological Theory* 3(2): 219–241

Tilly, Charles. 2002. *Stories, Identities, and Political Change.* Lanham, MD: Rowman & Littlefield.

Wagner-Pacifici, Robin E. 2005. *The Art of Surrender: Decomposing Sovereignty at Conflict's End.* Chicago: University of Chicago Press.

———. 2010. "Theorizing the Restlessness of Events." *American Journal of Sociology* 115(5): 1351–1386.

Williams, Raymond. 1976. *Keywords.* New York: Oxford.

Zubrzycki, Geneviève. 2006. *The Crosses of Auschwitz: Nationalism and Religion in Post-Communist Poland.* Chicago: University of Chicago Press.

CHAPTER 24

....

CULTURAL PRAGMATICS AND THE STRUCTURE AND FLOW OF DEMOCRATIC POLITICS

....

JASON L. MAST

THE focus of this chapter is the public life of democratic politics in turn-of-the-century America: the performative dimensions, causes, and consequences of the struggle for political power in a fragmented and differentiated society committed to democracy and regulated by open and unabashed struggles for influence and public legitimation. Unfortunately, social scientific approaches to power and politics have had little to say about such processes, for they have been mired in instrumental approaches that emphasize calculation and domination, and by an understanding of power that is thoroughly inappropriate to the democratic struggle for power and governance in a civil society. Counter to these trends, I outline a cultural pragmatic approach (Alexander 2004b; Alexander and Mast 2006; Mast 2006) to analyzing political dynamics, one that places character and plot development, collective representations, and pragmatic embodiment through performance, at its center.

POLITICAL SOCIOLOGY, POLITICAL SCIENCE, AND PRESIDENTIAL STUDIES: A REVIEW

....

Weber set up the key problem, indeed the field of political sociology, by establishing the relative autonomy of politics (vis-à-vis Marxism and culturalist ideas) and also by introducing the critical problem of legitimation. But the field of political sociology has had a very uneven relation to the legitimation problem, and increasingly under the influence of various kinds of structuralism, the field has not followed up on it effectively. One reason goes back to Weber himself: He defined modern legitimacy primarily as rational-legal, which is way too broad and merely procedural to be much use in any concrete study. Weber meant it as an historical category for delineating modernity, and he did not distinguish democratic from nondemocratic societies.

Mid-twentieth-century sociologists and political scientists built on and extended Weber's insights by: (1) developing classificatory schemas of states, focusing largely on the key features that distinguish democratic from nondemocratic forms of governance (Almond 1956; Dahl 1956; Lipset [1960] 1981; Almond and Verba 1963); (2) examining the social origins of democracies and dictatorships (Lipset [1960] 1981; Moore 1966; Skocpol 1979); (3) characterizing the power structure within modern America (Mills 1956; Dahl [1961] 2005; Domhoff 1967); and (4) exploring the barriers to, incentives for, and effects of popular participation in politics (Lipset [1960] 1981; Verba and Nie 1972). The Marxist, Grascian, and even Weberian-oriented approaches tended to dismiss or reduce the significance of process and symbols in the problem of legitimation. Victory was often theorized as the result of prior power, of self-confirming hegemony, or else the contingent result of calculations that were thought to be material and interest-based only. The systemic and functional approaches were often mired in the vestiges of Parsons' AGIL system and his latent cultural determinism, rendering their findings static, and even Lipset ([1960] 1981: 64–80) struggled to fully distinguish legitimacy from the notion of a state's effectiveness.

In multiple works, Inglehart (1988, 2003; Inglehart and Baker 2000) has tried to overcome the static features of the political culture framework inspired by Almond and Verba (1963) by extending the comparative dimensions and adding a longitudinal dimension to the analysis of attitudes, beliefs, and values associated with support for democratic governance. The following pages demonstrate that the meanings of power, authority, legitimacy, and democracy are relational and processual. While their meanings are rooted in cultural structures, they are also dynamically negotiated through performative struggles. Value analysis does not capture these key dynamics. The extent to which the political culture approach has overcome the static issue is debatable, but what is obvious is the approach's paucity of conceptual tools afforded by the cultural turn, those inspired by Geertz's (1973) semiotic theory of culture, for instance, as well as those imported from cultural analytical fields like anthropology (Levi Strauss 1966; Sahlins 1981), literary theory (Frye 1957; Barthes 1972), linguistics and semiotics (Saussure [1959] 1966; Eco 1976), and the philosophical discussions about performativity (Austin 1962; Derrida [1977] 1988; Butler 1990). Studies in political culture remain focused on attitudes, beliefs, and values, while cultural sociologists examining the political realm have turned to rituals (Smith 1991; Edles 1998), narratives (Sherwood et al. 1994; Smith 1996; Jacobs 1996; Kane 2000), genres (Jacobs and Smith 1997; Schudson 1998), codes (Alexander and Smith 1993; Smith 1991; Jacobs 2000), and most recently, performances (Alexander 2004a, 2004b; Apter 2006; Eyerman 2006; Giesen 2006; Goodman 2006; Mast 2006; Rauer 2006).

Richard Neustadt's (1960) hallmark book *Presidential Power: The Politics of Leadership* drew widespread attention to how presidents conceive of and exercise their authority and legitimacy. "The power to persuade," Neustadt argued, "is the power to bargain. Status and authority yield bargaining advantages" (1990: 32). Neustadt was primarily concerned with the president's ability to encourage Congress and Washington elites to acquiesce to his authority, to agree to bargain with him and do his will. In later editions of *Presidential Power*, Neustadt drew more attention to the fact that public opinion of the president could boost the president's power in these bargaining situations. Neustadt's book became something of a modern version of Machiavelli's *The Prince*, offering a template or script for presidents to follow as they tried to enact their policy agendas in Washington's corridors of power. The book was influential among presidents and scholars, and contributed to an academic movement oriented toward analyzing how and when "going public" could enhance the president's ability to exercise his or her will. In effect, scholars of the presidency were like critics of presidential power, not in terms of criticizing the president's use of the public to enhance one's power, but in terms of studying how the technique could best be deployed and enacted.

Since Neustadt's pioneering study, political scientists have increasingly interpreted presidential power as an exercise in communicating with the public. John Mueller (1970, 1973) further institutionalized this movement in political science by treating public opinion poll indicators as a dependent variable. As social conditions changed, or dramatic events developed, public opinion indicators of the president's performance would vary accordingly. Mueller showed, for instance, that the public would rally around the flag and support the president during wartime, and that presidential approval would decrease during economic downturns. Over time, public opinion polls played an increasingly important role in both political science scholarship of the presidency (Gronke and Newman 2003) as well as in the actual practice of political leadership: Poll results, Neustadt argued, "are very widely read in Washington" and are "widely taken to approximate reality" (quoted in Gronke and Newman: 501).

In what might be called a modest "reflexive turn" in political science, Neustadt's seminal work eventually drew some criticism, and was accused of facilitating the rise of the "imperial presidency," the term used to characterize L. B. Johnson's and Richard Nixon's approaches to amassing and practicing presidential power. Neustadt's book, it turns out, proved a powerful script. Finally, improving on a practice initiated by John F. Kennedy, Ronald Reagan courted the public so effectively that he earned the laudatory nickname of "the Great Communicator." Reagan's success with the practice inspired political scientists and presidential scholars to examine the "new strategies of presidential leadership" associated with the method of "going public" (Kernell 1986), and to declare that the United States had entered the age of the "public relations president" (Brace and Hinckley 1993: 382).

Political science offers some explanations for these transformations, suggesting, for instance, that power has shifted away from "protocoalitions" of Washington elites due to the erosion of party and group loyalties and the desire for quicker results (Kernell 1986). What they decidedly lack, however, is a strong cultural sensibility, and the theoretical and conceptual insights that grew out of the cultural turn, and still more recently, the performative turn. It is no wonder that scholars of transformations in presidential leadership styles like Ryfe (2005), Kernell (1987), and Tulis (1987) cite Geertz's (1973) seminal work on the semiotic dimensions of culture. Nonetheless, culture remains in the broader discipline a severely undertheorized and underutilized dimension in the approach to power. In their penetrating critique of conventional political science approaches to Monicagate, Lawrence and Bennett (2001) conclude by calling for a more cultural intervention in the discipline's studies of such events.

CULTURAL PRAGMATICS: BETWEEN COLLECTIVE REPRESENTATIONS AND ACTION

As an alternative to the approaches outlined above, I introduce a cultural sociological understanding. This will be a new kind of cultural sociology, however, one that offers a clear break with both classical (Durkheim [1915] 1995; Van Gennep [1908] 1960) and modern approaches (Shils and Young 1953; Warner 1959; Bellah 1967; Douglas 1966; Turner [1969] 1977, 1974, 1982; Alexander 1988). At the core of cultural sociology is the insistence that social action is neither interest-based nor contingently calculated in an interest-based way, but that action is meaningful and that, to be meaningful, it is carried out in relation to structures of understanding that are social, collective, and extra-individual in nature (Alexander and Smith 1993, 2001).[1] In classical and modern forms of cultural sociology, however, the understanding of cultural structures and meaningful action focused on ritual behavior, highly stylized moments that created parallels with actions in primitive societies. The problems with this ritual focus are clear: (1) It imposes too rigid a structure on the event's processural flow, (2) it tends to assume a unidirectional relationship between ritual producers and their intended audiences, (3) it presupposes that rituals either succeed or fail to achieve their theorized social functions, (4) it does not allow for exploring ambiguous, complex, or multifaceted outcomes, and (5) it suggests that only big events have meaning.[2]

Recently, there has developed a radically new form of cultural sociology that promises to maintain the emphasis on meaning while avoiding the drawbacks of ritual theory. This is cultural pragmatics, which has initiated the performative turn in sociology (Alexander 2004b; Alexander, Giesen, and Mast 2006).

Performance theory pays attention to background structures of meaning, but takes a pragmatic understanding of whether actors can effectively embody them (e.g., Schechner 1985, [1988] 2003, 1990, 1993; Turner 1982, 1986; Roach 1996, 2000; Taylor 1995; Aston 1991; Carlson 1984, 2001). Scripts have to be forged out of these background representations, and this requires creativity, and in modern politics this occurs in teams. Even when scripts are developed, however, they must walk and talk—actors need a place to stand, a stage, and access to means of symbolic production. Actors must create a scene, compel media attention, and communicate their messages in real time. Put another way, teams must create an event's mise-en-scène. Finally, teams need a sense of audience, which in performative terms is filled with agency of its own.

Contemporary politics are the product of a constant interaction between teams of performers and audiences. Political actors experience, react to, and work to gain control over "micro-events" within a broader effort to project stable images of power and legitimacy. Politics flows in episodes, and actors work within and between episodes to control micro-events so that they are well positioned when large-scale events, which compel broad public attention, form and appear to take on a life of their own. Audiences are bombarded by these micro-events, or political "occurrences" (Molotch and Lester 1974), which, while meaningful, exist only temporarily and relatively discretely in people's awareness. Political occurrences do not transcend their originating contexts or take root in the larger public's consciousness; they do not become part of the narrative of history. Yet, political actors are always engaged in mediating them in an effort to control their potential future meanings in case they do, in fact, become plot points in an "event" writ large. For political actors, controlling "events," or narratively interconnected occurrences that achieve "generalization" (Alexander 1988; Smelser 1963), means securing one's own favorable interpretation over potent, historically influential, political symbols. The cultural pragmatic framework outlined here reconstructs the meaning-texture of these flows, showing how occurrences are transformed into culturally meaningful events, as characters emerge and plots are formed, and the meaning-texture of political life is continuously rewoven.

To analyze politics as a flow of occurrences and events, the performative approach attends to the internal structure of political sequences both diachronically, in terms of the overall flows of dramatic phases, and synchronically, by looking at variations within phases. Isolating each phase facilitates identifying unpredictable opportunities that arise in an event and analyzing how they may be seized on and narrated to influence the larger event's flow and outcome.

Within the flow of events, multiple forms of audience-to-production relations develop. Performance theory conceives of audiences as—to a greater but qualified degree—more interpretive, critical, and agentic than the ritual framework's theorized audiences. Audiences can actively participate in productions, or they can contemplatively absorb and reflect on them. They can cheer or hiss at productions, or they can simply ignore them or turn off their televised images. Political teams strive to draw in their audiences and to win over new audience members, and they affect changes during the event's flow to accomplish these ends.

Through accounting for alternative theatrical modes of presentation, performance theory allows for analyzing how various genres cultivate different audience-to-production relationships. A farcical production may succeed to the extent that the audience laughs at the production, or shrugs it off, thus compelling the audience members to return to their various individual routines. Alternatively, tragedies and melodramas can lead to highly ritualized processes, drawing their audiences in to the degree that the line between production and audience is erased—the audience comes to identify with the production, and thus liminality may develop, potentially affecting social- and culture-structural transformations.

In the following analysis, I will demonstrate how these ideas offer a new approach to a democratic politics, and specifically to our understanding of American presidential elections. I begin with the working hypothesis that any effort to gain power or sustain political power in American society must situate this effort in terms of a public, civil binary discourse that divides the world into the democratic sacred and the anti-democratic profane (Alexander and Smith 1993). The codes of civil society are empirically derived cultural codes that structure the ways social actors attempt to frame themselves and their foes to influence spectators' interpretations of them. The codes have an evaluative dimension that, when applied by motivated contestants in the political or public realms, plays a key role in the determination of public contestations. The codes have proven remarkably stable over time, and are evidenced in political contestations ranging from debates over Ulysses S. Grants' fitness for holding the presidency in the 1870s, to political battles during the Teapot Dome Scandal in the 1920s, to Watergate in the 1970s, and to the Iran Contra Affair in the 1980s (ibid).

The codes are present in Clinton's rise and in his presidency as well. But—and this is an all-important qualification—from the perspective of cultural pragmatics, this background code is only a place to begin, not end. The efforts and struggles of actual politics are entirely contingent: Each side must place the other in terms of the profane, and oneself in terms of the sacred. To do this is difficult, in itself. It is made even more difficult with the fragmentation of audiences and the multiplicity of actors, the differential and continuously shifting access to means of symbolic production, and the incessant mediation by journalists and critics, conditions that define turn-of-the-century American politics.

It is these concerns that will be our primary focus in the remaining pages of this chapter. The central empirical mystery this study explains is how Bill Clinton achieved a level of legitimacy sufficient enough to defeat the Republican incumbent, George H. W. Bush, and obtain the presidency in 1992. Explaining Clinton's assumption of power requires that we analyze how candidates' characters formed and performed: how they discursively constructed themselves and worked to define their adversaries in the political field. It is critical to understand that characters achieve their legitimacy in relation to the other characters in the drama. Due to length considerations, I will spend more time analyzing Clinton's performances than the other characters in the competition, such as the incumbent Bush, Democratic contender Paul Tsongas, and Independent candidate Ross Perot. The 1992 election is particularly interesting because it involved the defeat of an incumbent, a character already wrapped in the symbols and aura of legitimacy that only the office of the presidency can afford.

SYMBOLIC COMPETITIONS FOR POWER:
THE 1992 PRESIDENTIAL CAMPAIGNS

....

When Bill Clinton stepped onto the national stage to announce his candidacy for the presidency of the United States, the spotlight cast two distinct and restless shadows. Over the course of 1992, the American public witnessed the formation of two Bill Clintons. The Clinton that won in November appeared hopeful, empathetic, inclusive, and brilliant. The other seemed to treat the truth the way a grifter handles a deck of cards; he would play with it masterfully and deal you any hand he wanted. In the remaining pages, I will describe the formation of these two characters and explain how the positive, democratic side gained dominance and won the presidency.

The two Bill Clintons developed through a series of mini-scandals and campaign performances. "Slick Willie" dominated the stage during the first third of the year's election drama. Between January and April, the Clinton presidential campaign was threatened with destruction by *Star* magazine's stories of long-running adulterous affairs and episodes of sexual harassment, the *Wall Street Journal's* allegations of draft dodging, and Clinton's own ambiguous and clumsy confession of casual drug experimentation. A second Clinton, a previously faint but expressive character that seemed to spring naturally from a Horatio Alger story, forcefully emerged midyear during the Democratic National Convention and the bus tour that followed. This Clinton solidified during the presidential debates and effectively stole the spotlight from the candidate's less flattering persona.

Election results indicate that Bill Clinton won in November less because he was a beloved candidate to a majority of voting Americans or even because he was considered all that desirable as a national leader. Neither of his presidential victories was accompanied by a strong voter mandate, and neither time did he win a majority of the popular vote.[3] More so, incumbent George H. W. Bush lost the race by the summer of 1992, while Clinton and Ross Perot skillfully and masterfully ensured that President Bush could not redeem himself in voters' eyes. Bill Clinton's success stemmed from his and Perot's dramatizations of the slumping economy and from their principal competitor's unpopularity and apparent aloofness. Clinton's 1992 victory is in large part the story of Bush Sr.'s dramatic—in both senses of the term— failure. The explanation that follows is more than a simple list of scandals. It is a reconstruction of the processes by which characters and events were given form, and an analysis of how particular cultural structures galvanized to form a plot. Finally, it is an examination of how the lead characters brought the plot to life on the national stage and compelled voting publics to participate in the election drama.

Clinton entered 1992 on the verge of seizing control of the Democratic race and was poised to win the party's primaries outright. His chairmanship of the Democratic Leadership Council gave him a platform for reaching his party's leaders and organizers, and his Southern roots and experience as governor of Arkansas made him an attractive candidate to the party. The Democrats, of course, faced Republican President George H. W. Bush, a popular wartime incumbent who had experienced record high approval ratings little over a year prior. Despite his waning national popularity, Bush remained the contest's favorite and was expected to win reelection in November.

Over the course of the primaries, Clinton would weather a serious challenge for the nomination from centrist Democrat Paul Tsongas, the former senator of Massachusetts. He would also weather a series of damaging assaults on his character from Democratic challenger and former California Governor Jerry Brown. Bush Sr.'s nomination to lead the Republicans in a second term, on the other hand, was all but guaranteed. His popularity among the Republican base, and his party's ideological coherence, however, were severely unsettled by candidate Patrick Buchanan's attacks on the incumbent from the right. Rounding out the election's cast of characters was the third party candidate and Texas billionaire Ross Perot, who staged an awkward yet surprisingly powerful campaign fueled by grassroots populism and the narrative appeal of the promise of reform.

POLITICAL CAMPAIGNS AS PLOT DEVELOPMENT

Campaigns work through theatrical and narrative means to impose a particular dramatic structure on an electoral competition. They seek to define the event's protagonists, emplot them into a world characterized by the centrality of particular issues facing the voting community, and dramatize the consequences of audiences' potential voting actions. Put another way, campaigns are in the business of character development and plot construction. In an election cycle, campaigns work to dramatize the sociopolitical order as threatened by particular conditions or as in some crucial way deficient of the normative ideal. These conditions and social problems get reduced and subsumed under the sign of a "campaign issue." In its simplest form, a plot includes an action and a reason for why it took place. As elections are dramatic events in the making, campaigns use issues as plot devices to motivate potential voters to act in the election drama's crucial, final act: the Election Day vote. In addition to the issue-problem, election plots include both a hero figure capable of righting the discursively constructed sociopolitical wrong, and a particular plan by which the wrong will be righted. Seeking to attain heroic status, election candidates must continually perform for potential voters in a manner that makes the most of constructed issues and compels them to join the election drama by getting out to vote.

As with any election against an incumbent, the Democratic challengers could not just create their candidacies as competent alternatives. They also had to make a case for change. In their competitions against one another for their party's nomination, Democratic hopefuls Bill Clinton and Paul Tsongas established their cases for change by constructing the same issue, Bush Sr.'s responsibility for a lingering economic recession.

Early in 1992, the two leading Democratic contenders began to construct the election's plot using a particularly effective dramatic practice, turning Bush's expressive sound bites back on him. The much derided sound bite is actually an extraordinarily potent performance technique for introducing potential voters to an electoral narrative. The felicitous delivery of a well-scripted sound bite reduces an election's complexity to a pithy mouthful. It clarifies and facilitates understanding by dramatically emphasizing a campaign's plot point. Its performance also embeds the plot in a more fleshed-out narrative that touches on broader cultural themes. Sound bites tell voters why they must get out and perform the drama's final act by voting.

Paul Tsongas, the former Massachusetts senator and Clinton's closest competitor, for instance, blamed the nation's economic woes on Bush's "voodoo economics—continued,"[4] borrowing and extending the sarcastic phrase Bush leveled against Ronald Reagan during their 1980 bids for the Republican nomination. Tsongas differentiated himself from his Democratic competitor and symbolically associated Clinton with incumbent Bush Sr., by calling Clinton's economic proposals "voodoo economics with a kinder, gentler face."[5] Clinton, on the other hand, exploited one of Bush's most intimate of political relationships to develop the same dramatic plot structure as Tsongas, stating: "President Reagan set a simple standard as to whether you get your contract renewed....Are you better off today than you were four years ago"?[6]

This practice of turning a sound bite back on its initial issuer lends the present performance added narrative and historical depth. Just as classic dramatic roles are haunted by past actors that have inhabited them (Carlson 2001: 10; Roach 2000: 10), playing on past sound bites sparks recognition and draws the past's context and performance into the present. The citational technique encourages listeners to consider at some conscious level the ways the two situations resemble one another—in this case, to consider how the election context today is similar to that of the day Bush and Reagan first used them against one another and then against their competitors as running mates.[7]

Tsongas and Clinton's comments symbolically linked the current election cycle with the Reagan/Bush campaign that unseated Democratic incumbent Jimmy Carter in 1980. Tsongas's gibe parodied Bush's assertion that Reagan's campaign promises were based on "voodoo economics" because of their implausibility, promising more government services while taking in less revenue in taxes. Tsongas's mocking revival of Bush's sound bite was doubly potent—a rhetorical checkmate, of sorts—because Bush had been accused of not only passively accepting Reagan's economic strategies as his vice president, but also continuing them under his own tenure as president. Bush could have disputed this charge by emphasizing that he had raised taxes, but this of course would have raised the specter of how he had contradicted his powerful 1988 presidential campaign sound bite, "Read my lips: No new taxes."

Clinton's "are you better off now" line, on the other hand, was effective because Reagan, Bush's political father-figure, had unseated an incumbent partially due to the rhetorical strength of this criterion of judgment. In its invocation, Clinton played on Reagan's landslide victory over Carter, suggesting to contemporary audiences that if Reagan's folk wisdom was persuasive during the Carter recession, it should be persuasive now during Bush's. The invocation symbolically separated Bush from Reagan, and communicated that it was possible to remain loyal to one's prior support for Reagan without necessarily supporting Bush again. After all, Clinton's performance suggested, by Reagan's own rules, Bush's contract should not be renewed. With each invocation, Tsongas and Clinton performed the symbolic desacralization of the incumbent.

The net effect of the 1992 primary contenders' theatrics would be the constitution of one of the election's central issues. The primaries would tell us who the party's ultimate contender would be, and the issues that emerged from the competitors' individual efforts would establish a cause for action to take place in November. That is, their performances of this issue began to define why and how supporters should participate in the drama by voting. With the economic recession cast as one of the election's central themes,[8] over the course of 1992, the Clinton campaign worked to fashion its lead an intelligent, personable, and youthful self-made man capable of revitalizing the nation and its slumping economy. First, however, he had to win the Democratic nomination.

In social dramas, the particular means of symbolic production a party employs to stage its performances shape the meanings the production ultimately imparts to its audiences. Means such as clothing, handheld props, places to perform, decorative stage scenery, and other sorts of expressive equipment serve as iconic representations that help dramatize and make visible the invisible meanings the team is trying to represent (Alexander and Mast 2006; Carlson 2001: 10). Social dramatic production teams mobilize particular symbolic means to invoke certain latent, invisible collective representations; they work with symbolic objects to assemble a particular meaning structure about themselves, and through difference, to define their opponents as well.

The meaning of a particular election campaign derives from these physical manifestations of culture structures and from the discursive practices its characters articulate. However, a campaign production's meaning is also derived through its symbolic relationships—analogical and antipathetic—to its competitors' productions. In this sense, each campaign may be seen as a particular, discrete sign carrier working to embody and evoke a particular set of meanings. The particular meaning the campaign ultimately communicates is derived from the background cultural referents and signs it intentionally associates with itself through performance, on the one hand, and from differences between its pragmatically achieved sign structure and the sign structures of its competitors, on the other. Thus, a social dramatic production never fully controls its own meaning as its ultimate meaning structure is only partially the result of its own symbolic work. One production's meaning is also the product of simple juxtaposition to other productions, and in symbolic competition, of course, productions act strategically to demonize their competitors and to paint them in counterdemocratic shades.

FUSING NARRATIVE AND CANDIDATE, PART 1: THE RISE OF "SLICK WILLIE"

Rumors of marital indiscretions began to cloud Clinton's campaign once he formally announced his candidacy in October 1991. Despite this, Clinton appeared the clear favorite for capturing the Democratic nomination well into January 1992. His front-runner status changed dramatically when the tabloid magazine *Star* published a series of articles documenting allegations of Clinton's sexual improprieties while governor of Arkansas.[9]

The race toward the Democratic primaries had garnered typical if scant national attention up to this date. The tabloid's articles changed this and forced the quality of Clinton's character and integrity directly onto center stage, drawing immediate and wide public attention to the Democratic race. Perhaps most significantly, the tabloid's articles turned rumors about a candidate's private life into a durable, crystallized issue that would dominate the political stage throughout Clinton's tenure as president. After playing an important role in Gary Hart's dramatic departure from the 1988 presidential competition, the question of "character"—how one's private life shapes one's public service—returned and once again became a concrete, stable dimension of political discourse, a seemingly natural and important concern for citizens. Some critics decried character's increasing centrality in political discourse, and many more joined the chorus in 1998.[10] Despite these alternative voices, character began to appear almost as natural a political issue as the economy. More immediately, the articles almost turned rumors into the makings of a campaign-ending scandal.[11]

The contents of the *Star* stories spread immediately to other news and entertainment organizations, and through these organizations to the nation's intrigued publics. Any control the Clinton team had exercised over the symbolic framework of its main signifier—Clinton himself—promptly evaporated. While "character" was stabilizing as a seemingly legitimate issue, the content of Clinton's character was quickly transformed from a semi-stable signifier to a more fluid site of symbolic contestation. No party vied more actively for control over the meaning of this critical political object than Clinton's team itself. Taken by surprise, the Clinton team responded with immediate if ad hoc denials and deflections, calling the material "ridiculous" and the work of "the president's Republican operatives."[12] These constructions were reported but not robustly engaged by media critics, which is tantamount to being ignored. The deflections did, however, afford the Clinton team time to orchestrate a more complex, persuasive framing of Clinton's personal history.

Though the team felt deeply threatened by the stories, the campaign placed a tremendous amount of faith and confidence in their lead's ability to regain control over his character if they could arrange for him to perform on enough American television screens. "The calculation is that the issue has to be dealt with cleanly and as decisively as possible," one Clinton advisor commented. "It's necessary to focus the American people on who Bill and Hillary Clinton are, what they believe and what they think this election is about."[13] The Clinton team's dramatic strategy involved placing their strongest asset, Clinton's performative skills, on a stage voters would read as legitimate, professional, and dignified, and inserting this scene into the living rooms of as many American homes as possible.

The Gennifer Flowers scandal broke just prior to 1992's NFL Super Bowl, a television event that routinely garners extraordinarily high numbers of viewers. In a bold yet risky strategy to regain control of Clinton's symbolic framework, the Clinton team arranged for Bill and Hillary to appear directly after the game on the same network on which the game would be televised, CBS. The Clinton team and the network had to agree on the proper staging for the event. Originally, CBS planned to follow the Super Bowl with an episode of the entertainment-news magazine show *48 Hours*. While an interview directly following the Super Bowl would guarantee enormous exposure, to the Clinton camp, framing their lead within the *48 Hours* format would have been only an incremental semiotic step above and away from *Star* magazine's "sleazy"[14] pages dedicated to detailing celebrities' sex scandals and weight-gain travails. An interview on *60 Minutes*, on the other hand, a news show known for its hard-hitting, interrogation-like interview tactics and imagery, would lift Clinton out of the scandal sheet and place him back into legitimate news formats. "The only way to get Bill Clinton on CBS was to make it on *60 Minutes*. I don't believe Bill and Hillary Clinton would have gone on *48 Hours* because it's not their format," commented CBS *PrimeTime* Executive Producer Rick Kaplan, explaining why CBS agreed to broadcast the interview as a 17-minute-long version of *60 Minutes* cutting into the infotainment format of the scheduled *48 Hours*.[15] This shift in programming indicates a conscientious effort to affect staging that would convey a desired degree of legitimacy to the event and the interview subjects. Put another way, it represents controlling the means of symbolic production in order to communicate and emplot oneself within a particular semiotic domain. Despite *60 Minutes'* history of staging interrogation-like interviews, the Clintons would appear in a living room setting, one that conveyed domesticity and the private realm.

The step was a high-stakes gamble for the Clinton campaign: The *60 Minutes* episode promised uncomfortable discussions of sexual indiscretions and testaments regarding motives and ambitions for political power with both marriage partners present. Performative success would yield high rewards and allow Clinton to regain tenuous symbolic control of his character. A poor performance would likely drive him from the race. *60 Minutes* interviews affect interrogation-like imagery and dynamics. In this interview, a fire burned in the fireplace, the Clintons sat on a sofa, separated from Steve Kroft by a coffee table. Kroft asked penetrating questions the Clintons answered—and refused to answer—and critiqued and probed evasive responses.

Kroft opened the segment by introducing Clinton as the Democratic frontrunner whose campaign was facing "long-rumored allegations of marital infidelity" that had "finally surfaced in a supermarket tabloid." The allegations, Kroft continued, came from "a former television reporter and cabaret singer, Gennifer Flowers, in a tabloid interview for which she was paid."

Kroft's preface introduces two semiotic domains to the interview. One is the seamy world of Gennifer Flowers, a pretty face that chirps in the smoky atmosphere of a low-status cabaret and bar culture and sometimes surfaces to appear behind a local news camera or lands some cover space on a tabloid publication. This world is contrasted to the legitimate, analytical, and skeptically detached world of the news program itself, the objective news culture in which *60 Minutes* resides.

Kroft opens the interview by probing the connection between the two worlds: How are you, the Clintons, appearing on *60 Minutes* and sitting in a pleasant, suburban living room atmosphere, connected to this other world? Clinton answers by positing that money spread through dirty politics in a context of economic desperation bridges the worlds:

> BILL CLINTON: It was only when money came out,—when the tabloid went down there offering people money to say that they had been involved with me that she changed her story. There is a recession on. Times are tough, and—and I think you can expect more and more of these stories as long as they're down there handing out money.
>
> KROFT: I'm assuming from your answer that you're categorically denying that you ever had an affair with Gennifer [sic] Flowers.
>
> BILL CLINTON: I've said that before and so has she.
>
> KROFT: You've said that your marriage has had problems, that you've had difficulties. What do you mean by that? What does that mean? Is that some kind of—help us break the code. I mean, does that mean…
>
> BILL CLINTON: I don't me…
>
> KROFT: …You were separated?…
>
> KROFT: You've been saying all week that you've got to put this issue behind you. Are you prepared tonight to say that you've never had an extramarital affair?
>
> BILL CLINTON: I'm not prepared tonight to say that any married couple should ever discuss that with anyone but themselves. I'm not prepared to say that about anybody. I think that the issue…
>
> KROFT: Governor, that's what—excuse me. That's what you've been saying, essentially, for the last…
>
> BILL CLINTON: But that's what I believe.
>
> KROFT: …couple of months.
>
> BILL CLINTON: Look, Steve, you go back and listen to what I've said. You know, I have acknowledged wrongdoing, I have acknowledged causing pain in my marriage. I have said things to you tonight and to the American people from the beginning that no American politician ever has. I think most Americans who are watching this tonight, they'll know what we're saying, they'll get it, and they'll feel that we have been more candid. And I think what the press has to decide is: Are we going to engage in a game of gotcha?…

KROFT: I think most Americans would agree that it's very admirable that you had—have stayed together, that you've worked your problems out, that you seem to have reached some sort of an understanding and an arrangement.

BILL CLINTON: Wait a minute, wait a minute.

KROFT: But…

BILL CLINTON: Wait a minute. You're looking at two people who love each other. This is not an arrangement or an understanding. This is a marriage. That's a very different thing.[16]

Key dynamics in this interview would be repeated multiple times during the following eight years, dynamics such as Clinton's subtle evasions and redirections, his shifts in verb tenses and ambiguous use of pronouns, Hillary's defense of and support for her husband, and the interviewer's frustrated attempts at clarification. Subjects raised here would live on, too, such as the nature of the Clinton marriage, Bill Clinton's references to causing and feeling pain, and the relevance of the candidate's private life to his public service. All parties express discomfort with the issues that brought them together.[17] The journalist Kroft suggests that he is not happy pursuing lines of questioning into Clinton's personal life but insists that the questions are fair, that they are part of public and political discourse, and that it is incumbent on the candidate to defuse the issue honestly and convincingly. Kroft expresses his personal distaste for the subject but states that he is duty bound to push forward and that he is inquiring in terms that are well within journalistic norms.

The Clintons voice their distaste for the subject but argue that they are agreeing to the questioning to the fullest extent that reason, common decency, and polite society could expect. Yet, Kroft will not desist in his inquiries at Clinton's desired boundaries, moments in the interview when he feels his questions are being evaded, and Bill Clinton will not acquiesce to the terms of access or parameters of openness pursued by the journalist. This interview, as a frustrated and frustrating interaction, launches into the public domain a long-running drama focused on marital and sexual irregularities, the tension between the right of the press to inquire and the people to know versus the right to privacy, the terms of reasonable lies and evasions, and very critically, it crystallizes an adversarial relationship between the future president and segments of the press.

Though the airing secured high ratings,[18] the Clintons' performances were persuasive if insufficient against the rising tide of scandal and suspicion. Soon after the interview, in early February, the *Wall Street Journal* began reporting on the young Clinton's reactions to the Vietnam War draft, characterizing his interactions with his draft board as deceptive and his subsequent explanations of his actions as intentionally evasive and fallacious. This story also spread rapidly through news and entertainment organizations and the pace of the election drama hastened as the New Hampshire primaries approached.

As a disembodied sign, Clinton's character remained a site of contestation up to and through the Democratic primaries. During this time, use of the nickname "Slick

Willie" mushroomed. Heading into the New Hampshire primary, critics doubted the Clinton production's ability to redefine its lead and predicted that the rumors of infidelities and draft dodging would devastate the campaign: "The prevailing wisdom, or much of it, seems to be that they must drive him from the race, that they are burdens no candidate can bear,"[19] and Clinton's allure to Democratic leaders began to wane: "National party leaders fear the cumulative effects of these stories could erode Clinton's credibility with voters and cripple him for the fall campaign against Bush."[20]

The campaign stayed afloat by willing itself forward, leading with its strongest asset, Clinton's performative skills. "In the week before the New Hampshire primary," the campaign "embarked on a breakneck schedule of live half-hour television shows and public appearances."[21]

Clinton's closest competitors at this point were former Massachusetts Senator Paul Tsongas, and former California Governor Jerry Brown. Tsongas, described as a "comic Greek tortoise snapping at the heels of democratic hares" heading into New Hampshire, won the primary with 34 percent of the vote; Clinton finished second with 26 percent. The bookish former senator's lead was short-lived, though. The race became a competition of styles.[22] Clinton, the second place finisher, almost immediately began to perform and narrate his way into the role of lead contender for his party's nomination, as described by a reporter:

> A week ago, many political pundits declared Clinton's candidacy dead. But tonight he was alive, beaming, pushing his fist into the air and saying he could not wait to take his resurrected campaign across the country.
> "New Hampshire tonight has made Bill Clinton the Comeback Kid," [Clinton declared].
> Sticking out his chin almost in the fashion of a young and fearless Muhammad Ali in the ring, Clinton added: "This has been a tough campaign, but at least I've proven one thing—I can take a punch."[23]

Critics reacted to Clinton's triumphal performance with irony: "For democrats who didn't win, victory has many definitions."[24] Despite Tsongas's initial victory, he was forced from the race one month later. The reason for his departure lies in his performative style. Many were allured to Tsongas's ideologically hybrid message; however, primary voters read into the candidate's performances signs of insufficient strength to fill the presidential role as they expected it should be played. Tsongas, voters commented,

> "makes a lot of sense, and has some very interesting ideas, but he might not be strong enough to be president. If he gets a little more exciting on the podium, that would be good. He has to get a little bit sexier up there," and "The appearance of a lack of forcefulness 'is what is holding me back' from choosing [him] over Clinton."[25]

The race also became a competition of organizations, geography, and timing. Clinton's team ran the most clearly national campaign, was the best-funded, and was by far the best-positioned entering the Southern primaries, which dominated the race heading into Super Tuesday, March 10th. Clinton's victories in the South, particularly in Florida and Texas, eroded the race's contingency. Reinvigorated by their successes, "the Clinton organizers were able to throw a raucous, balloon-strewn victory party for the local television cameras [in Chicago]. The party was intended to throw voters a distinct message: Bill Clinton would inevitably be the democratic nominee."[26] Tsongas agreed and dropped out of the race after losses in Illinois and Michigan. The Clinton team redirected its dramatic purpose: "Now the job is to define George Bush."[27]

By this time, critics and Republican loyalists were beginning to define Bush's reelection campaign as drifting rudderless in an "ill wind" and languishing in "a wave of discontent." Clinton had performed his second place finish in New Hampshire by thrusting his fist in the air in a show of victory. Bush, by contrast, reacted to his 18-percentage-point victory over Patrick Buchanan by issuing a statement calling the primary results a "setback."[28] Critics were more forceful: "Bush takes a pasting," declared The *Washington Post* (2/19/92). Bush's weak victory was framed as a "jarring political message"[29] signifying a "protest vote"[30] against the incumbent's apparent detachment from, and inattentiveness to, people's everyday concerns.

Despite reportedly being "stunned" by their limited victory in New Hampshire, a month later, the Bush team still lacked an advertising team[31] and showed no signs of changing its tack: "The republican primary seems to be conforming to the expectations of dullness. Neither President Bush nor Vice President Quayle has any campaign appearances planned."[32]

By mid-March, Clinton's hold on the Democratic nomination looked secure. Tsongas's withdrawal had left Clinton the clear leader in the race's overall delegate count and the rest of the primaries began to look like formalities. Yet, the social dramatic process remains contingent, and the following campaign events left lasting scars on Clinton's political skin. Five days after Tsongas dropped out, Jerry Brown, former Democratic governor of California, won the March 24th Connecticut primary largely by hammering Clinton on character issues. Consequently, New York's April 7th primary assumed renewed gravity. The Clinton team could ill-afford to lose further control of their candidate's symbolic framework to Brown's "renegade"[33] efforts, particularly given the New York media organizations' ability to influence other regions' campaign coverage.

Following Tsongas's withdrawal, the Clinton team blinked and "lost control over the campaign's dynamic in the crucial days leading up to the New York primary."[34] In Connecticut, Brown had succeeded in questioning Clinton's character and tendency toward evasiveness, two issues the New York press corps and television news outlets eagerly embraced. In an attempt to evade the press's constitutive power, the Clinton team called for six debates with Brown during the week leading up to the primary date. The team hoped to "speak more directly to New York voters [to minimize] the press's role in the April 7th primary" because, as Clinton put it, all the voters heard was "bad stuff [being] dumped on" him. The team also hoped the debates would "break the flow of unflattering sound bites that [had] made up most of his television news coverage in New York."[35]

The strategy was risky because performative gaffes were the only content sure to garner wide media coverage. In his March 29th debate with Brown, Clinton committed just such a performative blunder. In a series of questions, Clinton was asked if he had ever used drugs and if he had ever broken any state or international laws. To the latter, Clinton responded:

> I've never broken any state laws, and when I was England, I experimented with marijuana a time or two. And I didn't like it, and I didn't inhale and I never tried it again.[36]

His response quickly became national news and entertainment.[37] On television and in print, Clinton's answer was juxtaposed to past responses to similar questions, to which he had made a practice of stating flatly, "I have never broken the laws of my country." His evasiveness, and the deftness with which he practiced the casuistry, were constructed as "the kind of verbal gymnastics"[38] that confirmed there were "two Bill Clintons."[39] On the one hand, pundits and critics examined and discussed Clinton's syntactic techniques and theorized about what this tendency to prevaricate suggested about his character. In columnist Richard Cohen's words:

> This is the behavior that has earned Clinton the nickname "Slick Willie." It's a behavior so at odds with the rest of the man that we are entitled to wonder about its cause.... Is this the really smart kid who thinks he can out-talk and out-think anyone? Is this, maybe, the small-town wiz, the anointed hope of his community, who thinks the rules were made for others? Whatever the cause, Clinton's behavior is childish and troubling. It dilutes his promise, mocks the seriousness of his purpose—comes up behind him at somber events and puts up two fingers above his head as the picture is snapped.[40]

Clinton's performance was also transformed into a national punch line. During the Oscar ceremony the following night, host Billy Crystal stopped the ceremonies suddenly, fixed his face intently on the camera, and joked disbelievingly, "*Didn't inhale?*" drawing boisterous laughter from the audience.

Nonetheless, Clinton won the New York primary handily and Brown, finishing third in a two-man race,[41] dropped out of the competition for the Democratic nomination. Thus, the political consequences of Clinton's overperformance would not be felt immediately. The dramatic consequences, however, became immediately apparent: The performance catalyzed the symbolic bifurcation of Clinton's symbolic framework. It confirmed his brilliance, but it also demonstrated that Clinton would use his skills to circumvent a question's normative thrust to deceive the questioner. He would tell a truth, but not about the exact subject normatively embedded in an inquirer's question. Consequently, the performance irreversibly fused "Slick Willie" to the symbolic patchwork that was beginning to constitute his character. Use of the epithet in print and television journalism, as well as in popular culture, rose dramatically, its usage peaking in March and April and experiencing a strong resurgence in the late summer.

FUSING NARRATIVE AND CANDIDATE, PART 2:
THE RISE OF A PRESIDENTIAL CLINTON

Jerry Brown's departure from the race ended the Democratic infighting and allowed the Clinton team to begin rebuilding their lead's character. His formal nomination at the Democratic National Convention in New York helped this process significantly. Party nominating conventions are the height of orchestrated political theater. They are staged in venues organized to create the greatest symbolic effect, and are moments in which contingency is virtually suffocated out of the social dramatic process, if temporarily. Clinton had failed miserably four years prior when delivering the keynote address at Dukakis's nominating convention, yet he departed from his own nominating convention with a twenty-four-point lead over the incumbent in the polls, a lead unseen in the past fifty years.

Moreover, Clinton sustained his lead during a six-day, postconvention bus tour "back to the heartland of America."[42] The Clinton team's bus tour was designed to encode a nostalgic, decidedly populist structure to the Democratic ticket. Through defining its own candidate as a traditional populist and preaching "plenty of old-time democratic religion,"[43] the Clinton team also defined Bush Sr.'s tenure in power by playing on and exaggerating differences between the two candidates. Instead of engaging Bush Sr. within the field of institutional presidential symbolism by wrapping their candidate in signs of power and bureaucratic mastery, the Clinton team increased their lead's symbolic distance from insider Washington images. For instance, instead of exiting the Democratic Convention in an executive-style jumbo jet and flying off above and beyond ordinary Americans' heads, the Clinton ticket immediately boarded a bus and headed through America's rust belt toward the breadbasket states. By reducing the physical distance between its candidate and the American people, by going out to meet voters on their local turf, the campaign strove to symbolically return government to "the people." At a deeper symbolic level, Clinton's willingness to engage the audience suggested a willingness to sacrifice himself for the community (Marvin and Ingle 1999: 253–257). The bus tour allowed Clinton to merge with the public body, which stood in stark contrast to Bush's apparent distaste for such contact. Discourse was scripted to lend narrative symmetry to the bus imagery, to explain it plainly to the audiences that were gathered at arranged "leg-stretching" stops along the route.[44] Clinton would explain to those gathered:

> You are here for yourselves, your children and your future because you want your country back. And Al and I are going to give it to you.[45]

The Clinton team strove to portray its lead as Kennedy-esque, recalling the sense of youthful revival of politics that followed Kennedy's defeat of Nixon in 1960 and the end of the Eisenhower era of politics. Busts of Kennedy loomed behind Clinton and Gore at their bus stops, the team stopped in John F. Kennedy Park in McKeesport, PA, and Clinton invoked Kennedy in ways that suggested this election was about another generational change in political power. "In 1960, John Kennedy came here and said it's time to change," the candidate would proclaim.

The bus tour received considerable national coverage and was lauded by critics, and further extended the bounce in the polls that the Democratic team received from their nomination convention. In addition to the bus tour, the Clinton team made use of an unprecedented number of diverse popular television shows and networks to construct their candidate as "closer" to average Americans than their opponent. To name but a few of his more publicity-generating appearances, Clinton played the saxophone on *The Arsenio Hall Show*, he defended himself and debated the relevance of the "character issue" on the *Phil Donahue* talk show, and made an appearance to field questions from young voters on *MTV*, a network Bush Sr. shunned dismissively, stating "I'm not going on any teenie-bopper network."

In terms of character formation, Clinton's national identity was young and formative but developing quickly. Bush's national identity, on the other hand, had been developing in public imaginations for over a decade. In 1992, Bush's character was a composite of actions vis-à-vis international relations and the global projection of American military power, his perceived lack of attention to civic and race relations, and most crucially, his degree of concern and mastery over contemporary domestic economic conditions.

The Bush team let the Clinton team define the election, that it was about the "economy, stupid." Bush had fastened his political identity to economic issues during his 1988 campaign. Trailing Bob Dole in his bid for the Republican nomination, Bush famously declared that he would not raise taxes if given the nomination and elected president. He reiterated his pledge forcefully when given the nomination at the Republican National Convention: "The Congress will push me to raise taxes, and I'll say no, and they'll push, and I'll say no, and they'll push again, and I'll say to them, 'Read my lips: No new taxes.'" It was a powerful message that resonated with Republicans and enough Reagan Democrats to help Bush defeat Dukakis. It was also so powerful, however, that when Bush contradicted himself by raising taxes in the summer of 1990,[46] he severely restricted his ability to present himself to his supporters as a principled man of his word that was "above politics." The contradiction also restricted his ability to project himself as a person knowledgeable of economic forces. If he understood economic trends and processes after all, then certainly he would have known that his no new taxes pledge was absurd and untenable. The contradiction seemed to force his character into something between a liar and a fool.

The national economy, as measured by the gross national product, slipped into negative growth between the third and fourth quarters of 1990 under the weight of the enormous national deficit that developed during the Reagan years. The negative growth continued through the first quarter of 1991. earning the trend the official title of "recession." Though the recession technically ended when the economy began to grow slowly in 1991's second quarter, its symbolic weight continued to stifle and sour the national atmosphere throughout the 1992 campaign. Throughout 1992, Bush acted as though he was so stung by the embarrassment and shame of having contradicted his "no new taxes" pledge that he was absolutely unwilling to engage in strong, declarative political theater again when the economy was the subject.

Bush appeared to be at the recession's mercy despite taking the potentially bold performative steps of raising taxes and lowering interest rates to turn the economy around. Bush could have performed coherence, certainty, and mastery by, for instance, insinuating that responsibility for the recession lay in the excesses of "Reaganomics." Alternatively, he could have placed blame on Congress's shoulders and insisted that his management had shortened a potentially lengthier recession. Instead, in March 1992, Bush called his decision to raise taxes in 1990 a "mistake" and agreed with former President Reagan's statement that the tax increase was the "worst mistake of his [Bush's] presidency."[47] After contradicting one of his most powerful performances in the 1988 campaign, Bush in 1992 appeared reluctant to engage in forceful, potentially constitutive performances that would distance him from Reagan and his economics, or to portray himself as in some way a positive force in the face of the economic doldrums. Bush instead projected incoherence, appeared out of touch, and persistently sounded apologetic when he would dwell publicly on his mistakes.

As the incumbent, Bush represented the Republican center. Yet, while his campaign meandered and limped along, Bush seemed reluctant to lead and hesitant to make a forceful ideological stand. This lack of strength and certainty at the center produced unease and dissension within the conservative core. Vexed by the candidate's disaffection and disinterest, conservative ideologue and Republican administrator William Bennett stated on a Sunday morning talk show in late July that Bush needed to ask himself, "Do I really want to do this?"[48] Conservative commentators Rowland Evans and Robert Novak labeled Bush's "the worst-conceived incumbent presidential campaign in memory," one that carried the "smell of defeat." "A sense of direction," they continued, "can only come from the Oval Office and there is no leadership shown there."[49] Also in late July, conservative commentator George Will wrote a column suggesting Bush reinvigorate the ticket by replacing Vice President Dan Quayle with Colin Powell. One week later, Will stated that perhaps Bush himself "should withdraw from the race," and that "a startling number of significant Republicans privately say they wish he would." Will continued, critiquing what Bush's communicative style indicated about his character:

> Bush's meandering rhetoric stopped being amusing long ago, when it became recognizably symptomatic of two things. One is the incoherence that afflicts a public person operating without a public philosophy. The other is Bush's belief that he need not bother to discipline his speech when talking to Americans because the business of seeking their consent is beneath him.[50]

While Bush's bid for reelection was cracking apart in the middle, it was being pulled apart at the edges by charismatic critics like H. Ross Perot and Patrick J. Buchanan. Centrists and "Reagan Democrats," who had either identified with Reagan or had some affinity for fiscal conservatism, remained only weakly committed to Bush or shifted their allegiance from his reelection bid altogether in favor of H. Ross Perot's

Reform Party campaign. On the other hand, far right social conservatives were finding a champion in Pat Buchanan's popular bid for the Republican ticket.

The Bush campaign vessel continued to drift rudderless through July and into August, its mast cracking and hull splintering under the pressure of the Clinton, Perot, and Buchanan campaigns. Trailing Clinton by an enormous nineteen-point deficit just days before the Republican National Convention would begin in mid-August, Bush tried to signal a step to the helm, a renewed and forceful command, by dramatically changing his cabinet and campaign leadership, most notably by moving his longtime friend and advisor James Baker from secretary of state to chief of staff.

Perot and Buchanan represented threats from opposing ends of the Republican ideological spectrum. Perot represented a threat from the center-right, a Republican alternative to the Clinton Democratic challenge. Preaching fiscal and social pragmatism and responsibility, Perot's personal wealth and success in the private sector conveyed a sense of fiscal knowledge and "real-world" expertise. His message was similar to Clinton's, yet his persona and biography differed markedly. Perot's folksy charisma, however, was tinged with an air of the erratic: He never officially announced his candidacy, he unofficially started and stopped his campaign three times during the year, and when he bowed out of the race for the first time, he announced that he was doing so because of the efforts of a Republican conspiracy that had taken aim at his daughter during her wedding. Buchanan's challenge, on the other hand, was more dangerous to Bush's reelection bid because he was stealing energy from the incumbent's base of support. Buchanan dropped out of the race, but was invited to give the keynote address at the Republican Convention, whereupon he delivered one of the most divisive and racially charged speeches in recent history, setting the symbolic context for what David Broder would later call the Republicans' "Meanness Problem."[51]

Vying for Legitimacy: The Debate

With his reelection bid continuing to struggle, Bush needed inspired performances in the fall's televised debates. Clinton, on the other hand, had been inspiring national audiences. The two leads' performances in the presidential debates cemented Clinton's symbolic dominance in the election social drama. One incident in particular captures Clinton performing a critical symbolic difference between himself and Bush Sr. Debates as performative forums have a moderate amount of contingency structured into them, and each production team lobbies extensively prior to the event to control the sources that do not play to their candidate's strengths. The second debate was structured around the candidates answering questions posed directly from audience members. This structure made the event more interactive from the voter's perspective by removing the celebrity news figures that typically ask the debate questions and thus mediate between candidates and citizens, making the forum more of a traditional television show than a town hall meeting.

> During the debate, audience member Marisa Hall asked the candidates:
> How has the national debt personally affected each of your lives? And if it hasn't, how can you honestly find a cure for the economic problems of the common people if you have no experience in what's ailing them?

Taking Hall's question literally, President Bush fumbled awkwardly, trying to relate the national debt to his personal life. The debate moderator, Carole Simpson of ABC News, tried to rearticulate the question with the national recession as its subject, but Bush was unable to adjust to the reformulation. His reply again meandered awkwardly, from wanting his grandchildren to be able to afford an education to reading about teenage pregnancies in a bulletin at a black church outside Washington, DC. Growing increasingly agitated, Bush asked Hall defensively, "Are you suggesting that if somebody has means, that the national debt doesn't affect them?"

The Clinton team's social dramatic strategy, portraying their candidate as one of the people and the incumbent as out of touch with ordinary Americans' lives, was forcefully brought to life in Bush's performance. The script the Clinton team had labored to wrap their opponent in walked and talked upon the stage at that moment. The debate forum brought Bush face to face with an ordinary American, and both the style and substance of his response dramatized a profound subjective distance—real or fictional—from ordinary Americans' lives. Bush grew increasingly agitated with the question and appeared resentful of what he perceived to be its subtext—that he as a man of means was incapable of understanding ordinary Americans' lives. In his editorial review of Bush's performance, *Washington Post* columnist Jim Hoagland claimed Bush appeared "dispirited, disjointed, and disengaged."[52]

Clinton's response to Hall performed his campaign theme; he walked and talked "feeling the typical American's pain" that, he had argued, was the result of the national recession and Bush's failed economic policies.

Clinton began his response by approaching Hall and asking her to repeat how she was affected by the recession again. His movement played with the notion of the forum's stage. It eroded the symbolic boundary separating candidates from audience members. His movement toward Hall effectively eradicated the stage and the symbolic boundaries separating them, and by asking her to repeat her personal narrative, Clinton brought her character into the debate's plot. The narrative of his response fused with his movements into a kind of symbolic symmetry in which he was a wandering sage who has personally witnessed those hurt by the recession. After symbolically removing the stage, Clinton's performance dominated the moment and the event:

> I see people in my state—middle-class people, their taxes have gone up in Washington and their services have gone down, while the wealthy have gotten tax cuts. I—I have seen what's happened in this last four years when—in my state, when people lose their jobs, there's a good chance I'll know them by their names. When the factory closes, I know the people who ran it. When the businesses go

bankrupt, I know them. And I've have been out here for 13 months meeting in meetings just like this ever since October with people like you all over America, people that have lost their jobs, lost their livelihood, lost their health insurance.[53]

In his response, Clinton narrated the social drama's culprit—Bush's economic policy—and identified the reason for action to take place in November:

> It is because we've had 12 years of trickle-down economics. We've gone from first to 12th in the world in wages. We've had four years where we've produced no private sector jobs. Most people are working harder for less money than they were making 12 years ago. It is because we are in the grip of a failed economic theory. And this decision you're about to make better be about what kind of economic theory you want, not just people saying, "I want to go fix it," but what are we going to do?[54]

In so doing, Clinton's performance articulated a script to the characters that would perform the social drama's final scene: "The decision you're about to make," he proclaimed, the vote you will cast, can change your economic and social conditions.

Clinton beat Bush in November to become the forty-second president of the United States. He entered office, however, with a split symbolic framework. His campaign left Americans with both hope and unease. PBS's *NewsHour* conducted focus groups with undecided voters after each of the presidential debates. Commenting on Clinton's performance in the second debate, graduate student Allen Ramsay, an independent, claimed that though Clinton "did a very good job explaining" his new programs, he also "seemed overly sensitive to the audience, and it gave him a fake feeling from me, and that didn't do much to help me believe him." Accountant Robin Ganzert, a Democrat, responded to Ramsay's critique by stating, "I disagree....I feel like he [Clinton] was much more sincere, especially in response to that one woman's question" about the recession. "Bush seemed very fake," she continued, "Clinton actually came across very sincere. He's been out talking with the people. He has been affected and seen."[55]

Whereas some saw authenticity and sincerity, others interpreted Clinton's mental and performative abilities with caution and concern, detecting insincerity and slickness. In a column closing the year 1992, Robert Samuelson reflected on Clinton's victory and his forthcoming presidency:

> There have been two Bill Clintons in the past year. The first is Bill the Bold. He's a guy who seems eager to break with past dogmas and face the daunting problems of government. The second is Bill the Pleaser. He's someone who will say almost anything (with a few exceptions) to satisfy the audience of the moment, and as a result, he's said a lot of contradictory things. We still don't know which Clinton will govern—or if both will try....
>
> Whatever Clinton does, it will be calculated. His economic summit told us more about his political character than about his economic policies. His vast knowledge of policy means that any inconsistencies in his positions almost surely reflect deliberate choices, not inadvertent confusion. He may try to skip deftly around all of his promises. But too much fancy footwork could spawn cynicism and resurrect another Clinton: Slick Willy.[56]

CONCLUSION

Clinton and Bush Sr. battled for political power and legitimacy through performative means. As social actors, they varied from poor to prescient, and embodied and spoke their symbolic intentions with varying degrees of deftness. They shaped their own meanings through their speeches and comportment, but they were never fully in control of their own semiotic domains. The meanings audiences attributed to them as characters in the election drama were formed through the candidates' symbolic relations to one another; each developed into a character not only through what he said about himself, but also through what each said about the other. Their meanings were also derived from how their characters fit into the competing plots that were crafted. Political plots diagnose the past, current, and future states of the nation. They identify broad discursive domains like the economy or the moral status of the collectivity, and within these domains they construct problems and solutions. Each character becomes subject to the plots' narrative demands, and each character tries to position oneself within these symbolic formations in the most advantageous way possible. In 1992, the plot of economic stasis gained purchase, and Clinton's character was interpreted as more capable of working through the plot's intricacies, of leading the nation toward a satisfying dramatic resolution, than Bush Sr.'s character.

The candidates' audiences decoded what the actors worked to encode. Clinton and Bush communicated culturally familiar content, messages that their audiences could interpret and understand. Audiences interpret performances in variable ways, depending on their social, cultural, and biographical familiarity or symbolic distance from the material being performed. Symbolic content communicates to audiences on both a cognitive and an emotional level. Audiences could agree or disagree with the factual content while having conflicting emotional reactions to other symbolic cues by, for instance, appreciating the message but not liking the messenger.

Clinton and Bush employed means of symbolic production to project particular meanings. The material objects they surrounded themselves with, from their stages and settings, to props and costumes, all contributed to the meanings their performances projected. As candidates for office, they also had to ensure that the means of symbolic *distribution* were in place in order to project their messages to distant audiences. The relative autonomy separating the state from the mass media means that the candidates had to be seen as compelling enough to warrant attention, and to be seen as interesting enough for a media organization to decide to devote its communicative spaces to distributing their performances, let alone reviewing or critiquing their events, and thereby devoting to them extra-communicative resources.

Making political texts walk and talk upon the stage requires spatial and temporal choreography; bringing actors, props, and cameras together; and putting them into motion in a predetermined way. Put another way, the bringing together of these dramatic components and putting them into action are the construction of the mise-en-scène, or the images that appear on the television screen at any particular time. All political performances are directed and produced to some degree, with commercials and conventions representing the height of choreographed control, and live debates and town hall meeting representing the other end of the controlled performance continuum.

Politics are the product of interactions between these elements of performance: actors, collective representations, audiences, means of symbolic production, and the mise-en-scène. Politics is about power, and political performances are shaped by power. Forms of power are distributed unequally, of course, and social performances are enabled and constrained accordingly. Access to the variety of forms of social power (Mann 1986) influences the size, scope, and reach of performances, but the quantity of power by no means determines a performance's effectiveness. Challengers beat incumbents, the latter of whom hold more institutional power and are already cloaked in the symbols of institutional legitimacy. Bush Sr. and Clinton battled over legitimacy, over who the audience would determine was more capable of inhabiting the normative expectations of the office of the presidency. In the political sphere, the office of the presidency affords a vast array of forms of power, yet the president's exercise of power is continuously interpreted and critiqued through the performative lens. Power—institutional, material, and social power—can be exercised in ways that allow or disallow performances, that enhance or detract from them. But, and this is a crucial point: The usage of power always contains a performative dimension, and its usage is interpreted by audiences in important and highly consequential ways. Political power, I have tried to demonstrate, operates through performative power. As such, power is always held in check and shaped by the other elements of social performance.

NOTES

1. Ann Swidler's (1986) "toolkit" theory of culture in action has become the reference of choice for studies seeking to highlight how culture is used in calculated, interest-based ways. Taking on Parsons's voluntaristic theory of action, Swidler argues that culture should be examined in terms of "means," or "strategies of action," as opposed to "ends," or ultimate values. Her argument contains two main points: (1) Culture should be conceived as representing a kind of "toolkit," and (2) culture functions differently during "settled" as opposed to "unsettled" times.

My examination of the Clinton presidency demonstrates the limitations of the "toolkit" approach. Culture is, in part, like a toolkit, or a reservoir of symbols and rituals that social actors develop through localized socialization, and draw on strategically to navigate their social environments. Yet, it is also far more than a toolkit. Social actors use words and symbols intentionally to try to communicate particular ideas for particular reasons. Nonetheless, culture's relevance to social life depends on its relative autonomy from the social structure, in its structural form or *langue* (language) (Saussure [1959] 1966;

see Kane 1991). While culture is made present through *parole* (speech), or through an actor's use of a particular "tool," it is made meaningful and comprehensible, and therefore socially influential, because of the "tool's" analogical and antipathetic relations to other tools in the "kit" that are not explicitly in play, but that nevertheless exercise power in the experienced social situation (Barthes [1968] 1977; Eco 1976; Saussure 1985). Derrida ([1977] 1988) demonstrated that action is always citational. Each instantiation of meaning draws forth unseen signs and symbols, rooted in the cultural fabric, into momentary if nonconscious presence. Finally, on this point, Swidler's notion of a social actor's cultural "kit" is exaggeratedly local and slim. Political discourse and broad opinion formations during the Clinton years demonstrate that deep, structuring cultural codes, narratives, and myths penetrate far and wide beyond any one social actor's localized social environment (e.g., Alexander and Smith 1993). While localized social formations may demonstrate cultural particularities (Fine 1987), they also share an enormous amount of cultural elements with the dominant cultures within which they are embedded.

My analysis of the Clinton presidency also suggests that Swidler's second assertion, that culture works differently during "settled" and "unsettled" periods, needs to be radically reformulated. Once culture is defined as a "toolkit," it is turned into something that is dispensable and absent in "settled" times, yet present, exercised, and investigated during "unsettled" times. My investigation of the Clinton presidency strongly supports a more Geertzian (1973) understanding of culture, an ever-present framework of meaning more akin to a web that structures and supports social life than a kit that can be picked up and dropped depending on one's sense of how "settled" one's life is. Culture is present and influential during periods of "scandal fatigue," such as when American publics feel tired and bored by politics, and it is equally present and influential during scandals and rituals.

2. See Alexander and Mast (2006) for a discussion of various theoretical responses to the ritual framework's limitations.

3. Clinton was the first two-term president since Woodrow Wilson (1912–1920) to fail to win a majority of the popular vote in either election (Schier 2000: 6).

4. *Washington Post*, 1/29/92.

5. *Washington Post*, 2/22/92.

6. *Washington Post*, 4/26/92.

7. For a discussion on parody's demands on the audience, see Hutcheon 2000.

8. "One wing of the floor is consultant James Carville's domain. It is where the marketing strategy for candidate Clinton is debated and devised. Carville has a chalkboard in the middle of the room, where he lists the basic rules of how to present the campaign. The key rule never changes. In Carville's blunt language, it is: 'The economy, stupid.' Another rule is to contrast Clinton's message of change with the Bush presidency's 'more of the same'" (*Washington Post*, 8/3/92).

9. The two articles detailed the allegations contained in the lawsuit and Gennifer Flowers assertion of a twelve-year affair with the governor.

10. See Klein, "The Politics of Promiscuity," *Newsweek*, 5/9/94, p. 16, and Klein (2002: 108).

11. Discussions of topics that reside at the boundary of legitimate news, like Clinton's private affairs, led the press to engage in self-critique and self-evaluation. Of course, being media outlets, it engages in self-critique publicly in print and on talk shows. Its expressions of discomfort and guilt at pursing boundary topics on the one hand are accompanied by rationales and self-justifications on the other.

12. *The Guardian*, 1/18/92. While calling the charges "ridiculous" framed them as the stuff of absurd comedy, suggesting that they were produced by Bush's political team served to inflate Clinton's importance. The framing portrays Clinton as such a threat to Bush that

the president has had to assign "operatives" to focus solely on controlling the threat. It also portrays Bush in a counterdemocratic light, as working secretly and in the shadows.

13. *Washington Post*, 1/25/92.

14. Reading from a prepared statement, DeeDee Meyers, Clinton's spokesperson, called the allegations "trash and untrue." "This is irresponsible, sleazy tabloid journalism" (*The Guardian*, 1/18/92). This approach silences mainstream journalists who want to distance themselves from "sleazy tabloid journalism" and forces the press to engage in self-critique and self-justification.

15. *USA Today*, 1/28/92.

16. CBS News transcripts, 1/26/92.

17. "The Bill and Hillary show is the latest, but surely not the last, step in the degradation of democracy by televised image-making, of substituting for political thought the audience catharsis of highly contrived dramas. It is the spiritual descendant of Richard Nixon's 1952 Checkers speech, of John Kennedy before the Houston Ministerial Association inquisitors, of Ronald Reagan declaiming, 'I paid for this microphone,' of Oliver North showing his chestful of medals to congressional investigators and Clarence Thomas accusing his critics of a public 'lynching'" (*Washington Post*, 1/28/92).

18. CBS News estimated that approximately 40 million viewers watched the *60 Minutes* interview (*Washington Post*, 1/28/92).

19. *Washington Post*, 2/14/92.

20. *Atlanta Journal-Constitution*, 2/7/92.

21. *New York Times*, 3/20/92.

22. Clinton's response to his New Hampshire defeat demonstrates the power of performance to constitute an event's meaning, and indicates the need for a robust semiotics of gesture.

23. *Washington Post*, 2/19/92.

24. *Washington Post*, 2/18/92.

25. *Boston Globe*, 1/17/92.

26. *New York Times*, 3/20/92.

27. *New York Times*, 3/20/92.

28. *Washington Post*, 2/19/92.

29. *New York Times*, 2/19/95.

30. *Washington Post*, 2/19/92.

31. *New York Times*, 3/20/92.

32. *New York Times*, 3/19/92.

33. *Washington Post*, 3/20/92; *New York Times*, 3/26/92.

34. *New York Times*, 4/1/92.

35. *New York Time*, 4/1/92.

36. *Washington Post*, 3/30/92.

37. Elizabeth Kolbert of the *New York Times* reacted to Clinton's verbal gymnastics thusly: "Watching the New York primary campaign unfold on television recently has been like watching one of those awkward movies in which the leading actor seems to be performing a part from the wrong film. Gov. Bill Clinton arrived in New York last week playing the role of an out-of-towner who comes to the big city, is treated like a hick, but still manages to charm the metropolis. The script that has actually been produced, however, goes more like this: Governor of small state comes to big city, is heckled, loses his cool and finally admits to having smoked marijuana" (*New York Times*, 3/30/92).

38. *New York Times*, 3/31/92.

39. *Washington Post*, 3/31/92.

40. *Washington Post*, 3/31/92.

41. Tsongas, who had already officially dropped out, finished second.

42. *Washington Post*, 7/18/92.

43. *New York Times*, 7/19/92.

44. Costumed in sweaters and khakis, Clinton and Gore would run around tossing a football back and forth in young Kennedy fashion at bus stops, and Bill Clinton would chew on a piece of straw while leisurely talking to locals.

45. *New York Times*, 7/19/92.

46. On June 26, 1990, President Bush signed a bipartisan bill that increased taxes in response to a ballooning budget deficit. A recession set in anyway.

47. In the interview in which he agreed with Reagan's characterization, Bush said he regretted the tax increase because of the "flack it's taking" and because of the "political grief" it caused him, not because of any negative consequences it spurred in the economy (*Atlantic Journal-Constitution*, 3/3/92). Ann Devroy of the *Washington Post* (3/4/92) quoted a Bush senior official as saying that campaign aides believed Bush "would never reestablish his credibility with the American people" if he did not admit he erred in entering the 1990 pact. Without such a confession, the official said, "All his pledges [will] ring hollow."

48. ABC News, *This Week* transcript, 7/26/92.

49. *Chicago Sun Times*, 7/29/92.

50. *Atlanta Journal-Constitution*, 7/30/92.

51. *Washington Post*, 11/30/94.

52. *Washington Post*, 10/17/92. There is ample evidence indicating that Bush failed poorly with many other viewers. John Harris, also a *Washington Post* columnist, reported on a study conducted at Virginia Commonwealth University, which used "debate meters" to gauge uncommitted voters' reactions to what the candidates said. "Bush scored one of his two most negative responses of the evening with his response to Hall," Harris reported. "His other low point was when he attacked democratic presidential nominee Bill Clinton's character. 'It spoke to the perception that here is someone who is out of touch,' said Robert Holsworth, a Virginia Commonwealth political scientist who helped conduct the debate-meter experiment" (10/16/92).

53. ABC News, The 92 Vote: The Second Presidential Debate transcript, 10/15/92.

54. ABC News, The 92 Vote: The Second Presidential Debate transcript, 10/15/92.

55. *The MacNeil/Lehrer NewsHour* transcript, 10/16/95.

56. *Washington Post*, 12/30/92.

REFERENCES

Alexander, Jeffrey C. 1988. "Culture and Political Crisis: 'Watergate' and Durkheimian Sociology," pp. 187–224 in *Durkheimian Sociology: Cultural Studies*. New York: Cambridge University Press.

———. 2004a. "From the Depths of Despair: Performance, Counterperformance, and 'September 11.'" *Sociological Theory* 22(1): 88–105.

———. 2004b. "Cultural Pragmatics: Social Performance Between Ritual and Strategy." *Sociological Theory* 22(4): 527–573.

Alexander, Jeff, and Phil Smith. 2001. "The Strong Program in Cultural Theory: Elements of a Structural Hermeneutics," pp. 135–150 in J. Turner (ed.). *Handbook of Social Theory*. New York: Kluwer Academic Publishers.

Alexander, Jeffrey C., and Phillip Smith. 1993. "The Discourse of American Civil Society: A New Proposal for Cultural Studies." *Theory and Society* 22: 151–207.

Almond, Gabriel A. 1956. "Comparative Political Systems." *The Journal of Politics* 18(3): 391–409.

Almond, Gabriel A., and Sidney Verba. 1963. *The Civic Culture, Political Attitudes and Democracy in Five Nations*. Princeton, NJ: Princeton University Press.

Apter, David. 2006. "Politics as Theatre: An Alternative View of the Rationalities of Power," pp. 218–256 in *Social Performance: Symbolic Action, Cultural Pragmatics, and Ritual*, Jeffrey Alexander, Bernhard Giesen, and Jason Mast (eds.). New York: Cambridge University Press.

Aston, Elaine. 1991. *Theatre as Sign System: A Semiotics of Text and Performance*. New York: Routledge.

Austin, John L. 1962. *How to Do Things with Words*. Cambridge, MA: Harvard University Press.

Barthes, Roland. 1972. *Mythologies*. New York: Hill and Wang.

———. [1968] 1977. *Elements of Semiology*. New York: Hill and Wang.

Bellah, Robert. 1967. "Civil Religion in America." *Journal of the American Academy of Arts and Sciences* 96(1): 1–21.

Brace, Paul, and Barbara Hinckley. 1993. "Presidential Activities From Truman Through Reagan: Timing and Impact." *The Journal of Politics* 55(2): 382–398.

Butler, Judith. 1990. *Gender Trouble: Feminism and the Subversion of Identity*. New York: Routledge.

Carlson, Marvin. 1984. *Theories of the Theatre: A Historical and Critical Survey, From the Greeks to the Present*. Ithaca, NY: Cornell University Press.

———. 2001. *Haunted Stage: The Theatre as Memory Machine*. Ann Arbor: University of Michigan Press.

Dahl, Robert. 1956. *Preface to Democratic Theory*. Chicago: University of Chicago Press.

———. [1961] 2005. *Who Governs? Democracy and Power in an American City*, 2nd ed. New Haven, CT: Yale University Press.

Derrida, Jacques. [1977] 1988. *Limited Inc. ABC*. Baltimore: Johns Hopkins University Press.

Domhoff, William G. 1967. *Who Rules America?* Englewood Cliffs, NJ: Prentice-Hall.

Douglas, Mary. 1966. *Purity and Danger: An Analysis of the Concepts of Pollution and Taboo*. New York: Routledge.

Durkheim, Emile. [1915] 1995. *The Elementary Forms of Religious Life*. New York: Free Press.

Eco, Umberto. 1976. *A Theory of Semiotics*. Bloomington: Indiana University Press.

Edles, Laura. 1998. *Symbol and Ritual in the New Spain: The Transition to Democracy After Franco*. New York: Cambridge University Press.

Eyerman, Ron. 2006. "Performing Opposition or, How Social Movements Move," pp. 193–217 in *Social Performance: Symbolic Action, Cultural Pragmatics, and Ritual*, Jeffrey Alexander, Bernhard Giesen, and Jason Mast (eds.). New York: Cambridge University Press.

Fine, Gary Alan. 1987. *With the Boys: Little League Baseball and Preadolescent Culture*. Chicago: University of Chicago Press.

Frye, Northrop. 1957. *Anatomy of Criticism: Four Essays*. Princeton, NJ: Princeton University Press.

Geertz, Clifford. 1973. "Thick Description: Toward an Interpretive Theory of Culture," pp. 3-30 in *The Interpretation of Cultures*. New York: Basic Books.

Giesen, Bernhard. 2006. "Performing the Sacred: A Durkheimian Perspective on the Performative Turn in the Social Sciences," pp. 325–367 in *Social Performance: Symbolic*

Action, Cultural Pragmatics, and Ritual, Jeffrey Alexander, Bernhard Giesen, and Jason Mast (eds.). New York: Cambridge University Press.

Goodman, Tanya. 2006. "Performing a 'New' Nation: The Role of the TRC in South Africa," pp. 169–192 in *Social Performance: Symbolic Action, Cultural Pragmatics, and Ritual,* Jeffrey Alexander, Bernhard Giesen, and Jason Mast (eds.). New York: Cambridge University Press.

Gronke, Paul, and Brian Newman. 2003. "FDR to Clinton, Mueller to ?: A Field Essay on Presidential Approval." *Political Research Quarterly* 56(4): 501–512.

Hutcheon, Linda. 2000. *A Theory of Parody: The Teachings of Twentieth-Century Art Forms.* Urbana: University of Illinois Press.

Inglehart, Ronald. 1988. "The Renaissance of Political Culture." *The American Political Science Review* 82(4): 1203–1230.

———. 2003. "How Solid Is Mass Support for Democracy: And How Can We Measure It? *Political Science and Politics* 36(1): 51–57.

Inglehart, Ronald, and Wayne E. Baker. 2000. "Modernization, Cultural Change, and the Persistence of Traditional Values. *American Sociological Review* 65(1): 19–51.

Jacobs, Ronald N. 1996. "Civil Society and Crisis: Culture, Discourse, and the Rodney King Beating." *American Journal of Sociology* 101(5): 1238–1272.

———. 2000. *Race, Media and the Crisis of Civil Society.* Cambridge, UK: Cambridge University Press.

Jacobs, Ronald N., and Philip Smith. 1997. "Romance, Irony, and Solidarity." *Sociological Theory* 15(1): 60–80.

Kane, Anne. 1991. "Cultural Analysis in Historical Sociology: The Analytic and Concrete Forms of the Autonomy of Culture." *Sociological Theory* 9: 53–69.

———. 2000. "Reconstructing Culture in Historical Explanation: Narratives as Cultural Structure and Practice." *History and Theory* 39(3): 311–330.

Kernell, Samuel. 1986. *Going Public: New Strategies of Presidential Leadership.* Washington DC: CQ Press.

Lawrence, Regina G., and W. Lance Bennett. 2001. "Rethinking Media Politics and Public Opinion: Reactions to the Clinton-Lewinsky Scandal." *Political Science Quarterly* 116(3): 425–446.

Lévi-Strauss, Claude. 1966. *The Savage Mind.* Chicago: Chicago University Press.

Lipset, Seymour. [1960] 1981. *Political Man: The Social Bases of Politics,* expanded ed.. Baltimore: Johns Hopkins University Press.

Mast, Jason L. 2006. "The Cultural Pragmatics of Event-ness: The Clinton/Lewinsky Affair," pp. 115–145 in *Social Performance: Symbolic Action, Cultural Pragmatics, and Ritual,* Jeffrey Alexander, Bernhard Giesen, and Jason Mast (eds.). New York: Cambridge University Press.

Mills, C. Wright. 1956. *The Power Elite.* New York: Oxford University Press.

Molotch, Harvey, and Marilyn Lester. 1974. "News as Purposive Behavior: On the Strategic Use of Routine Events, Accidents, and Scandals." *American Sociological Review* 39: 101–112.

Moore, Barrington. 1966. *Social Origins of Dictatorship and Democracy: Lord and Peasant in the Making of the Modern World.* Boston: Beacon Press.

Mueller, John E. 1970. "Presidential Popularity from Truman to Johnson." *The American Political Science Review* 64(1): 18–34.

———. 1973. *War, Presidents, and Public Opinion.* Lanham, MD: University Press of America.

Neustadt, Richard E. 1960. *Presidential Power: The Politics of Leadership.* New York: Wiley.

————. 1990. *Presidential Power and the Modern Presidents: The Politics of Leadership from Roosevelt to Reagan*. New York: Free Press.

Rauer, Valentin. 2006. "Symbols in Action: Willy Brandt's Kneefall at the Warsaw Memorial," pp. 257–282 in *Social Performance: Symbolic Action, Cultural Pragmatics, and Ritual*, Jeffrey Alexander, Bernhard Giesen, and Jason Mast (eds.). New York: Cambridge University Press.

Roach, Joseph. 1996. *Cities of the Dead: Circum-Atlantic Performance*. New York: Columbia University Press.

————. 2000. "Cutting Loose: Burying the 'First Man of Jazz,'" pp. 3–14 in *Joyous Wakes, Dignified Dying: Issues in Death and Dying*, Robert Harvey and E. Ann Kaplan (eds.). Stony Brook: Humanities Institute of the State University of New York at Stony Brook.

Ryfe, David Michael. 2005. *Presidents in Culture: The Meaning of Presidential Communication*. New York: Peter Lang.

Sahlins, Marshall David. 1981. *Historical Metaphors and Mythical Realities: Structure in the Early History of the Sandwich Islands Kingdom*. Ann Arbor: University of Michigan Press.

Saussure, Ferdinand de. [1959] 1966. *Course in General Linguistics*. New York: McGraw-Hill.

Schechner. Richard. 1985. *Between Theater & Anthropology*. Philadelphia: University of Pennsylvania Press.

————. [1988] 2003. *Performance Theory*. New York. Routledge.

————. 1990. *By Means of Performance: Intercultural Studies of Theatre and Ritual*. New York: Routledge.

————. 1993. *Future of Ritual. Writings on Culture and Performance*. New York: Routledge.

Schier, Steven E. 2000. "A Unique Presidency," pp. 1–16 in *The Postmodern Presidency: Bill Clinton's Legacy in U.S. Politics*, Steven E. Schier (ed.). Pittsburgh: University of Pittsburgh Press.

Schudson, Michael. 1989. "How Culture Works: Perspectives from Media Studies on the Efficacy of Symbols." *Theory and Society* 18(2): 153–180.

Sherwood, Steven Jay, Philip Smith, and Jeffrey Alexander. 1994. "Narrating the Social: Postmodernism and the Drama of Democracy." *Journal of Narrative and Life History*. 4(1/2): 69–88.

Shils, Edward, and Michael Young. 1953. "The Meaning of the Coronation." *Sociological Review* 1: 63–81.

Skocpol, Theda. 1979. *States and Social Revolutions: A Comparative Analysis of France, Russia, and China*. New York: Cambridge University Press.

Smelser, Neil J. 1963. *Theory of Collective Behavior*. New York: Free Press.

Smith, Philip. 1991. "Codes and Conflict: Toward a Theory of War as Ritual." *Theory and Society* 20(1): 103–138.

————. 1996. "Executing Executions: Aesthetics, Identity, and the Problematic Narrative of Capital Punishment Ritual." *Theory and Society* 25(2): 235–261.

Swidler, Ann. 1986. "Culture in Action: Symbols and Strategies." *American Sociological Review* 51: 273–286.

Taylor, Diana. 1995. "Performing Gender: Las Madres de la Plaza de Mayo," pp.275–305 in *Negotiating Performance: Gender, Sexuality, and Theatricality in Latin/o American*, Diana Taylor and Juan Villegas (eds.). Durham, NC: Duke University Press.

Tulis, Jeffrey K. 1987. *The Rhetorical Presidency*. Princeton, NJ: Princeton University Press.

Turner, Victor W. [1969] 1977. *Ritual Process: Structure and Anti-Structure*. Ithaca, NY: Cornell University Press.

————. 1974. *Dramas, Fields, and Metaphors: Symbolic Action in Human Society*. Ithaca, NY: Cornell University Press.

————. 1982. *From Ritual to Theatre: The Human Seriousness of Play*. New York: Performing Arts Journal Publications.

————. 1986. "Dewey, Dilthey, and Drama: An Essay in the Anthropology of Experience," pp. 33–44 in *Anthropology of Experience*, Victor W. Turner and Edward M. Bruner (eds.). Urbana: University of Illinois Press.

Van Gennep, Arnold. [1908] 1960. *The Rites of Passage*. Chicago: University of Chicago Press.

Verba, Sidney, and Norman Nie. 1972. *Participation in America: Political Democracy and Social Equality*. New York: Harper and Row.

Warner, W. Lloyd. 1959. *The Living and the Dead: A Study of the Symbolic Life of Americans*. New Haven, CT: Yale University Press.

PART X

MATERIALITY AS CULTURE

....

CONSUMPTION AS CULTURAL INTERPRETATION: TASTE, PERFORMATIVITY, AND NAVIGATING THE FOREST OF OBJECTS

....

IAN WOODWARD

THROUGH its varied theoretical and empirical contributions, cultural sociology shows that myth and narrative are elemental meaning-making structures that form the bases of social life. Collectively experienced and personally felt, they allow social structures to find an internal life, compelling and committing us to the diverse things we hold sacred. We interact with these meaning-structures in a variety of ways, but one of the most important is through the material and objectual forms with which we engage. We reside within a forest of objects (cf. Turner 1967). Most of these objects have not been directly made or produced by us, but through visual, corporeal, and imaginative engagements, we negotiate and construct their meanings, using them to make ourselves and, in turn, a larger universe of meaning. Rich with symbolism, demanding our attention, sparking our imaginations and bodies, rife with possibilities for pleasure, devotion, distinction, and play, we revel in and among this material forest (Bollas 2009). Material objects constitute much of what we as members of a society know and are also the means by which we come to know it. Materiality, the substance of consumer societies that needs to be analytically and morally disentangled from the trait of materialism, becomes a basic means for immersing ourselves within this forest of meaning.

Perhaps the most important contribution of consumption studies within the last few decades has been to bring these objects into the center of any analysis of sociality. Social actors are not just immersed in a material world where objects are mere scaffolds or props that have silently enlisted them—nor are they oppressed or alienated by them—but they actively seek out objectual engagements and put these objects to a variety of social uses. Through various scenarios of consumption—where people use goods or services not just as a practice in the world, but as a means to understand and construct the world and their place in it—social life is inescapably object-oriented. Engagements with consumption objects bridge physical, pragmatic, psychic, and cultural imperatives, connecting us to a world of meaning through everyday practices, such as shopping, eating, playing or watching sports, driving a motor vehicle, or listening to music. Put simply, consumption studies deals with the processes, practices, and outcomes of people's use of, and engagement with, objects. In focusing on processes of objectification—the way meaning is materially created and communicated and the way social action is materially mediated—consumption studies has allowed sociologists to explore questions of reception and use in the commodity world and the material world broadly. Beyond this, as the classical statements in economic anthropology have reminded us, the economic activities of exchange and consumption actually constitute the circulation of cultural ideals (Douglas and Isherwood 1979; Mauss 1954; Sahlins 1974). What is valued, exchanged, and used are not just "commodities", but material containers of cultural meaning. From a cultural point of view, what we call "the economy" is fundamentally a networked system of symbolic exchange, rather than a merely field of social action defined by models of instrumental rationality and commercial contract.

In the United States especially, sociologists have often ignored consumption and have come to appreciate its sociological significance later than their British and European counterparts (Zukin and Maguire 2004). Much of modern life and the type of sociology it required and encouraged was devoted to understanding the problems of production within industrial societies. Questions of labor, industry, production units, social, legal and economic institutions, technology, and social class were the core stuff of mainstream social inquiry through much of the twentieth century. In mainstream sociology, consumption was, for most of the discipline's history, simply not a relevant analytic category. Or, if it was contemplated, it was predominantly configured through discourses of triviality, excess, vulgarity or cultural superiority, and domination. For example, as much as sociologists are likely to profess enjoying Veblen's (1899) caustic dissection of the leisure class of nineteenth-century America, his work has in fact done much to segregate consumption to the arena of individualism, emulation, and competitive display. Rather than assigning consumption to limited realms of social action, in the last few decades, researchers have increasingly situated practices of consumption and a consumerist ethic as central for understanding broader social and cultural change. There is ample theoretical and empirical warrant for this, as consumption is identified as being increasingly central to diverse aspects of social life. This increased sensitivity to consumption patterns and processes has impacted on the way sociologists have conceptualized such diverse areas of social change as cultural and economic inequality, urban and spatial development, identity and selfhood, gender relations and performativity, media and advertising, and eating and dining practices. So, in significant ways, the move to bring in consumption has been a recent revolution in the cultural sciences and has led to the consideration of topics that were previously marginalized, and indeed not even conceived of, in mainstream sociological theory.

The profusion of consumption studies is evidenced by the fact that—after only a little more than a decade of intensive research and focus within the social and cultural sciences—Miller (1995) declared consumption to be "the vanguard of history." His proclamation celebrated the profusion of groundbreaking, predominantly theoretical work in that era, and the subsequent paradigmatic consolidation of the field in the decades of the 1980s and 1990s. Within the field of consumption studies—and also to a significant degree within the discipline of object studies more widely (see Knorr-Cetina 1997; Latour 2007; Pels, Hetherington, and Vandenberghe 2002)—it seems apt to observe that materiality, objects, and "stuff" are the new frontier, as sociologists position questions of materiality and object-based practices of consumption at the forefront of their studies (Appadurai 1986; Miller 1987; Dant 2005, 2008; Swedberg 2005).

In reflecting on the consequence of these changes, we can identify that the development of the field of consumption studies has been significant within the larger intellectual field of sociology in a couple of ways. First, it offered a correction to the entrenched productionist, materialist, and institutionalist tendencies inherent within mainstream sociological and cultural theory; and in this context can be considered more generally as part of the cultural turn in sociological theory. In addition, this new field has opened up fresh thinking on the lives and biographies of commodities, person-object relationships, and meaning-making processes with objects and materials. By emphasising the cultural bases of economic and commercial activity, consumption theory defines the world of goods in cultural terms. Furthermore, it has increasingly pointed out that it is not just what we consume which is cultural, but what is produced (du Gay and Pryke 2002; Jameson 1991). In addition to merely the consumption side of economic activity, forms of cultural expertise and planning begin to shape the production process and influence the form and content of economic activity, including consumption.

Towards a Cultural Approach to Consumption and Materiality: The Central Problems

In this chapter, the current state and future of consumption studies is considered through the lens of intersecting research vectors in the fields of consumption studies, taste, and materiality. These latter two concepts are fundamental dimensions of most consumption practices. To have a "taste" for certain objects, experiences, and goods is an elementary cultural trait, rather than a preserve of any particular social class. Cultural tastes reflect necessary, inevitable, and active orientations to the social world in the form of culturally structured, personally felt, and aestheticised preferences. As Bourdieu says: "Taste is the basis of all one has—people and things—and all one is for others" (1984: 56). Materiality, likewise, is a foundational mode of human experience. It is an element of all material-based consumption practices, though not a universal component of consumption, as people also consume services or engage cognitively with aspects of consumption via desire, daydreaming, or idealization.

The central contention of this chapter is that the potential of this new consumption studies to be fruitful has been obstructed by the manner in which the study of consumption has been theorized and carried out by some, though not all, of its leaders. In particular, in this chapter, I take up the following arguments about the state of research in the field. First, I argue that sociologists have typically not gotten to the core of consumption as a cultural phenomena because they have been overly concerned with customary sociological questions of class, status, and social inequality. As a relatively new field, consumption studies have tended to draw on traditional sociological approaches and concepts. Important advancements have been made, for example, within the oeuvre of postmodern studies of consumption in the 1980s (e.g., Featherstone 1987; Jameson 1991); in studies of the production and circulation of consumer objects (e.g., Molotch 2003; Foster 2006); in material culture studies (Appadurai 1986; Miller 1987, 2008) that emphasizes the cultural-anthropological dimensions of objects; and more recently in areas such as the practices and pragmatics of consumption (e.g., Dant 2008; Shove and Southerton 2000; Warde 2005; Watson and Shove 2008). Yet, the overall pattern is that studies of consumption have inherited less useful features of customary approaches that tend to comprehend consumption through particular frames and that encourage a less sensitive understanding of consumption practices. For example, despite a couple of decades of intensive research on consumption, the fundamental question of why people have continuously revitalized appetites for consumer objects remains relatively unaddressed in both theoretical and empirical terms. Historically, the sociological focus has been on questions of systemic alienation and consumer exploitation, on distinction and emulation, or on coordinating systems of consumer practices.

Second, I suggest that in largely neglecting the meanings actors attribute to their own consumption practices, sociologists have assumed an outsider stance and have never been able to bring themselves to fully account for the attractions and seductions of consumption experienced by most everyone else. This has been to the detriment of a culturally informed theory of consumption that is able to understand the deep relations between social actors and objects, and indeed the agentic capacity of the objects themselves. Moreover, much sociological research effort goes toward addressing the distributions and outcomes of consumption practices; essentially, what comes after consumption, or its distributed social effects. This is in contrast to actually understanding its basis and nature as a culturally and materially structured form of social action. As I will elaborate in this chapter, this pattern of intellectual inheritance is particularly evident in sociological studies of taste, where social patterns of tastes are frequently studied as distributions of variables representing preferences for cultural objects. Here, we can visualize the social distributions of certain taste preferences and surmise the role they might play in social reproduction, but we cannot get a sense of the cultural qualities, feelings, performances, and practices that inform, accomplish, or construct these tastes.

Third, in developing a program for a cultural sociological approach to consumption, I argue that sociologists would profit by reconceptualizing consumption as a universal practice of cultural interpretation where social actors seek ritualized, enchanting engagements with objects that originate across the economic and cultural spectrum and which are perceived to symbolize variegated ideals such as goodness, beauty, authenticity, or truth. To adopt this principle is not to deny that much consumption is about mundane utility or the transitioning of daily needs. But, even here in what we might think of as the most mundane field of provisioning, notions of care, love, and, truth are found to structure consumption activities and practices, linking everyday provisioning practices to the deepest human needs, motivations, and desires (Miller 1998). Likewise, even in the most aestheticized and identity-driven fields of consumption, such as new technologies (Belk and Tumbat 2005), motor vehicles (Cardenas and Gorman 2007), clothing, food, and drink brands (Holt 2004), research shows that consumers of these goods connect to deep, fundamental cultural narratives through their relationship with these objects. We cannot assume either category of consumption is "shallow" or "deep." Rather, all types of consumption, be they reflexive or banal, routinized or thrilling, are sought out by us for the purpose of experiencing and delineating that which is good, beautiful, or sacred. In fact, we might even say that our economic system is organized in such a way as to produce and distribute these elementary culture-structures in material form (Alexander 2008b). There is accordingly a dialogic process which connects cultural discourses of sacred and profane with the sometimes mundane—and sometimes rousing—engagements with objects, experiences, and places that we call "consumption." It might even be, as Callon, Meadel, and Rebaharisoa (2002) have argued, that consumers and producers are reflexively involved in a type of tryst which brings these good and services into being. In the final section of this chapter, I point to ideas about materiality, civility, and consumption etiquettes to seek potentially fruitful links with work in economics and economic sociology where researchers are trying to integrate culture into their accounts of consumptive economic behaviors.

Within sociological studies of consumption, three main subfields have been prominent over the last few decades. First, there have been the bodies of literature associated with theories of postmodern cultural change and associated literatures on the cultural turn. In countering the dominance of critical theory through the twentieth century, this work emphasized the relative freedoms of consumption through tropes of lifestyle, the flexible construction of self-identity, abundant commodity culture, and principles of variety, choice, and novelty (Featherstone 1990;

Jameson 1998 Lash and Urry 1994). The second oeuvre derives from the work of Bourdieu (1984), whose studies of the social structures that both form, and derive from, certain varieties of consumption emphasizes the role of consumption for reproducing social inequality. Bourdieu's work has inspired a large volume of research into the way cultural consumption relates to social difference and inequality. Recently, his legacy has coalesced in a large body of research on cultural omnivorousness and its relationship to changing status systems (Emmison 2003; Petersen and Kern 1996; Van Eijck 2000; Warde, Wright, and Gayo-Cal 2007). Finally, recent strands of research have emphasized the materialized nature of consumption and the way people use objects of consumption. In the section that follows, each of these major theoretical schools is critically investigated.

A FLAWED REVOLUTION: POSTMODERN THEORIES OF CONSUMPTION

To a significant degree, the theoretical innovations enabled in postmodern theory challenged hitherto productionist and materialist logics, showing the centrality of consumption to both the economic logics of "late capitalism" and affixing to identities and lifeworlds a consumerist and individualist core. In doing so, its impact on the field was alternately liberating and exciting, reductive and misguided. Baudrillard's (1996, 1981) early structural theories that posited consumer objects as the "scaffolding" of contemporary society were an important point of inspiration for the postmodern account of consumption. Fundamental to Baudrillard's progress toward a political economy of consumer objects is the realization that in contemporary society continual inroads are made by commodification processes to the extent that consumer objects are now primarily things acquired and used for symbolic value: "Signs (culture) are produced as commodities" (Baudrillard 1981: 147). Social actors are "symbol processors," a point of view vigorously taken to extreme positions by scholars, influenced by postmodernism, through the next few decades.

Featherstone's (1991, 1992) account of the contours of contemporary consumer culture is perhaps the most significant within this oeuvre, and is principally indebted to the theoretical work of Jameson (1991), Lash and Urry (1987), Harvey (1989), and the pioneering semiotic analyses of Barthes (1957) and Baudrillard (1996). Featherstone's analysis of the move to a postmodern consumer culture finds the concept of lifestyle to have particular salience in a postmodern regime of consumption. Featherstone (1990) emphasizes the role of pleasure and desire in framing current consumption practices, centralizing the notion of lifestyle that he argues should not necessarily be seen as a form of play outside of any social determinants, rather it "should be regarded merely as a new move within it" (1991: 84). The development of a postmodern consumer culture rests on an assumption about the widespread use of goods as communicators of lifestyle, rather than merely being utilities.

Featherstone (1992) sees this trend as one component of what he has labeled "the aestheticisation of everyday life," for in a society where the commodity sign dominates, by default, each person is a symbolic specialist.

Having outlined three senses in which the concept of aestheticization has been employed, there are two relevant applications of Featherstone's (1991) discussion of the concept that are applicable to consumers, or at least some social fractions of them. The first is where life is conceptualized as a project of style—where originality, taste, and aesthetic competence are measures of individuality (1991: 67)—and thus becomes important in shaping social action. This is a project that is not merely accomplished by the outlay of sheer sums of disposable income. While Featherstone assigns the avant-garde and intellectuals an important role in the dissemination of new consumption ideas—and he also endorses Bourdieu's (1984) emphasis on the new middle class as the fiscal backbone of the consumer economy—all classes are held to approach the project of lifestyle with an outlook that Featherstone labels as "calculating hedonism, a calculus of stylistic effect and an emotional economy" (1991: 86). The notion of "having a lifestyle" is particularly useful for Featherstone's formulation of consumer culture because it suggests how people across the social-cultural spectrum act as symbol processors through the coherent and meaningful deployment of "economies" of commodity objects that may not necessarily act as social communicators (though they could), but more centrally they afford people various capacities with which to navigate objects, people, and events:

> Rather than unreflexively adopting a lifestyle, through tradition or habit, the new heroes of consumer culture make lifestyle a life project and display their individuality and sense of style in the particularity of the assemblage of goods, clothes, practices, experiences, appearance and bodily dispositions they design together into a lifestyle. The modern individual within consumer culture is made conscious that he speaks not only with his clothes, but with his home, furnishings, decoration, car and other activities which are to be read in terms of the presence and absence of taste. (Featherstone 1991: 86)

The background to this body of work as it emerged in theoretical expositions of the 1990s is that consumption has been aestheticized and semioticized by economically configured processes of hyper-commodification (Featherstone 1991; Jameson 1991; Lash and Urry 1994; Lury 1996). The logic behind it is a flight from critical versions of consumption theory built on the substantial body of literature that has emerged in the 1980s and 1990s concerning social and economic processes of spatialization and semioticization associated with what have been labeled "late" (Jameson 1991) forms of capitalism (see also Beck 1992; Harvey 1989; Lash and Urry 1987, 1994; Soja 1989). The scene-setting for this approach rests on the identification of a variety of fundamental transformations in the circulation of global capital and on an array of associated cultural changes that include shifts in the way consumer objects are produced and consumed. A principal claim advanced in this literature is that the nature of consumption has changed as capitalism spatializes and semioticizes in unique ways at an accelerated pace; and as a corollary, consumption is commonly theorized as an important sphere for reflexively monitoring self-trajectories. The predominance of commodification processes and the cultural dominance of consumption are intrinsic counterparts to these processes emphasizing the "culturalizing" of the economy. Jameson (1988, 1991) was one of the first to highlight the incorporation of aesthetic production into commodity production, a trend that signifies postmodern tendencies regarding the breakdown of distinctions between high culture and mass culture. Thus, objects that circulate in consumer society, including the examples used by Jameson of clothes, furniture, and buildings (1983: 124), are aestheticized as new waves of consumption and are framed through design, style, and art. The quantitative change in this sphere has been an "immense dilation in the sphere of commodities, and a quantum leap in the aestheticisation of reality" (Jameson 1998: 124).

From the 1980s onward, the postmodern-inspired position became something of a mantra and thereafter extremely influential as a point of reference for studies of consumption and, to some degree, studies within the related field of material culture studies. At its basis is a broad historical contrast: If consumption could ever be characterized in historical perspective as predominantly utilitarian, then by contrast in the postmodern era, it is characteristically constructive—identity-forming, reflexive, expressive, and even playful. Taken at face value, such a position seems revolutionary, and it certainly performed an important paradigm challenging function at the time. As an historical proposition, however, it is undoubtedly a myth because the degree to which we can ever divorce meaning, reflexivity, and symbolism from consumption and object relationships—postmodern or premodern—is dubious. Furthermore, though it dresses itself up as a cultural account, this position is based on a type of old-fashioned economic determinism and offers only a partial insight into the nature of consumption practice. Jameson presents a clever twist on economic materialism, but one where the cultural realm remains overdetermined by shifts in economic structures. Granted, ideas on the incorporation of the aesthetic into economic production and questions of post-fordist regimes of production and consumption are observable and important macroeconomic shifts. However, we cannot read from them assumptions about the nature of consumption nor can we use the insight to develop a theoretical model of consumption, for we would always be looking to larger social and economic changes as explanatory models, rather than looking into the autonomous structures of consumption processes themselves. The positive theoretical shift enabled by the postmodern move was to suggest a radical separation of consumption from production and a certain freedom for consumers from the determinants and fixities of class, social location, and ascribed identities, offering an analytic scheme that empowered their creativity and flexibility. Though it may ultimately have overemphasized the degree of such freedoms, largely ignored questions of materiality and, in addition, framed consumption as dependent upon processes of economic flexibilization rather than conceiving it in culturally autonomous terms, in doing so it offered an extremely important historical corrective.

THE MEANINGS OF CONSUMPTION: HEDONISM, CIVILITY, AND THE COLLECTIVE ORIENTATIONS OF CONSUMPTION

One of the primary points of contention surrounding the discourses of consumption centers on questions of individualism and hedonism, and the extent to which consumerism is culturally and socially divisive or constructive. As we have seen, the postmodern turn in consumption studies has been essential in redirecting the course of contemporary consumption studies, though its focus on hedonistic, individualistic, and fundamentally differentiating dimensions ignores the collective, civil, and socially expressive bases of consumption. Bell's (1976) work—though influential amongst social scientists and general readers alike—constitutes a characteristically shortsighted reflection on hedonism in relation to consumption that rests on a narrow view of the socially corrosive consequences of consumption. In doing so, it reproduces some of the myths of critical theory and sits with a cache of well-known authors from Erich Fromm, John Kenneth Galbraith, Christopher Lasch, and E. F. Schumacher who have in various ways constructed consumer societies and consumption as against sociality and the principles of informed citizenship. Bell's master thesis concerns what he labels a "chiasmus in culture," the cultural contradiction of contemporary society, and "the deepest challenge to its survival" (Bell 1976: 480). Bell claims a fundamental disjuncture between the systemic social imperatives of rationality, productivity, and efficiency, and the rising cultural impulses of lifestyle, hedonism, and freedom. As a consequence, he fears the loss of a transcendent ethic in then emergent post-industrial society to guide a common framework for social values. At the heart of this anxiety is the apparently hedonistic regime of consumerism, which "fosters the attitude of carpe diem, prodigality and display, and the compulsive search for play" (Bell 1976: 478). Ironically—for these values are based most commonly within the middle class—such values undercut traditional bourgeois ways of life and thus represent a challenge to the most virtuous features of modernism. In Bell's view, they have tipped the social balance in favor of depthless, corrosive, and individualistic consumption habits.

Bell's thesis falls short of a full understanding of the nature of hedonism in relation to consumption. He sees it as essentially unproductive and potentially damaging, both socially and psychologically. Realistically, and in contrast to Bell's view, hedonism should be understood as one dimension—but not a singular one or necessarily of central dimension—of the ongoing generation of a robust ethic of consumption, meaning that to assign hedonism as a defining component of consumption is misplaced. Working from Miller's (1998) ethnographically based proposal of a theory of shopping—based on notions of love, sacrifice, and devotion—it is possible to see the aspects of material culture and questions of taste based on a logic quite different to that expected by the theory that gives priority to hedonism and individualization. In fact, it may be that while hedonism—understood generally as pleasure-seeking through consumption—is an important historical discourse in consumerism, such a discourse exists alongside a counterbalancing and complementary discourse. If left unchecked, the identification of hedonism is frequently perceived by consumers to be counterproductive and personally destructive. There is evidence of growing consumer reflexivity in this regard (e.g., Soper 2007; Wilska 2002; Woodward 2001, 2006). This accounts for the checks consumers impose on the expression of their individual taste narratives and consumption desires. Thus, the existence of a hedonistic attitude to consumption—that is unlikely if considered a general, universal feature of consumption, but believable as a style of consumption sometimes adopted by all people—has a complementary, disciplining discourse of restraint to keep it in check.

This discourse of restraint, self-discipline, and delayed gratification is, in part, provided for by the construct of taste that should be seen as a type of etiquette of consumption. This etiquette is identifiable in commonsense notions of "too little" or "too much," "appropriateness," "consideration," and a multitude of other concepts used to make judgments about consumption, taste, and material culture (see Woodward and Emmison 2001). Consumption and judgments of taste are not merely individualistic and hedonistic; and even if they sometimes are, they are bound by their own cultural rules and forms of personal and social discipline. These etiquettes of hedonism serve to morally discipline people's consumption choices within meaningful frameworks enabled by the contexts of their choices. By providing rationales, narratives, and texts, they frame individual choices as edifying, life-sustaining, and generally "good." This helps people define themselves not as desiring subjects, but as seekers of experiences, objects, and practices which improve and sustain the self (Woodward 2001, 2003). This etiquette of disciplined hedonism is a robust ethic of consumption because it serves to orient and position the individual to others through a collective sentiment. The notion of taste as an orientation to others is apparent in the way acting in good taste is commonly conceptualized as an attunement to others that, in turn, relies on a disciplining or "tempering" of the self (Miller 1993) to fit in and a general respect for other people, especially those who are alike. Centrally, it involves questions of individual conscience and prudence in relation to one's judgment about collective processes and interests (Miller 1995; Schudson 2007).

As a form of pleasure-seeking social behavior, consumption is in some ways and circumstances hedonistic. However, to characterize it as this solely is misleading. Hedonist desires might account for some of the drive to consumerist practice, though consumption is tempered by counterdiscourses of consumption that include the etiquette of taste and the goal of living the authentic, sacred or "good life," however that might be defined (Soper 2007). Consumption practices, understood through frames of taste via complexes of other related practices, thus offer a concrete point of connection for people to their cultural values through a variety of leisure, aesthetic, and material practices, whether they be woodworking, billiards, car driving, shopping, or fashion. Consumption thus cannot be strongly contrasted with notions of citizenship—the former coded with negative traits of individualism, materialism, and selfishness and the latter a positive modern political ideal separated from the realm of consumption. Such a reading fails to acknowledge the way consumption—in whatever seemingly insignificant way, or in ways some may perceive to be commodified, tasteless, or trivial depending on their own taste judgments—can be a political act, an act of refusal and individual empowerment, fueled by discourses associated with social participation, equality, or inclusivity (Schudson 2007). This is not to argue that consuming will always have positive effects on such matters, or that it is some type of panacea, but that participation is in itself a matter of importance in establishing part of the contour of civil affiliations and belonging. Bauman (1988), for example, has also pointed out that the ability to consume is implicated in social inclusion and exclusion, being an important dimension of contemporary citizenship and belonging.

Campbell's (1987) thesis on hedonism and modern consumption is a more promising attempt to account for the rise and endurance of a consumer ethic of hedonism. Campbell identifies the basic problem of modern consumerism to be that the gap between wanting and getting a consumer good never closes. In contrast to economic, utility-based theories of consumption, he finds the basis of modern consumption to be a form of pleasure-seeking based in emotions rather than in physical sensation. As such, his thesis is now likely perceived by some as outdated and out of fashion due to its "immateriality," but I maintain cultural sociologists need to look to his work to combine materiality-inspired approaches with the emotional and cognitive realms. In his model, the pleasurability of consumption is the manipulation of psychological desire and meaning inherent in goods, rather than in their actual, physical consumption—"wanting rather than having is the main focus of pleasure-seeking" (Campbell 1987: 86). The irony of contemporary consumerism is that hedonism isn't actually about consuming particular objects, but the pleasurable mental dramas associated with pondering how the consummation of desire might alter one's reality. Hedonism is thus predominantly autonomous and imaginative, involving fantasy, daydreaming, and imagination.

Much of the attention given to consumption in the last few decades has been directed toward theorizing it as zeitgeist—a defining gestalt of the era. Such a position has flagged consumption as a crucial domain of the contemporary lifeworld. However, the downside of this grand levering of consumption "as a more general trope for assertions about the so-called postmodern world" (Miller 1998: 164) is that theoretical adumbration has been more common than empirical investigation, especially as it has played out in the British social theory tradition. The established view of recent accounts is that consumerism is the most visible element of the historical trend toward individualization. Further, consumerism is readily identified as the most empty, shallow manifestation of the trend to individualization and is held to be indulgent, hedonistic, and socially divisive. While the social and environmental implications of some forms of Western consumerism are to be acknowledged and should not be ignored by scholars, close sociological attention to the meanings and motivations of consumers has shown that consumption and matters of taste are more complex than ideologically motivated accounts of "consumerism" have imagined and that to understand consumerism, we need better theories of consumption, including sensitive accounts of its attractions. As Schudson (2007: 248) comments: "We need to move from moralism and complaint to analysis and action where the necessary and often enjoyable acts of consuming are appreciated—but where the political structure that makes those acts possible is made visible." Tastes can be said to be consumption patterns enchanted and enveloped by narrative. It is by carrying out some reconceptualization in the field of taste studies that we can make some progress along the path suggested by Schudson.

Aestheticized, Intricate Reductionism: Bourdieu, Consumption, and the Social Correspondences of Tastes

Tastes refer to the range of sensual and cognitive techniques for evaluating the universe of people, objects, events, and experiences to which people are routinely exposed. When measured in the traditional sociological way—by preferences for, and knowledge of, particular cultural goods—tastes can be shown to be intricately structured and patterned according to particular social variables. This is the principle contribution made by sociological studies of culture in the field of aesthetic tastes. But, there is a different route to take. As Mary Douglas has perceptively expressed it, the contemporary problem of taste and aesthetic choice is not so much knowing that people have unique preferences that can be mapped according to certain theoretical principles to form social patterns; but it "is to get at some underlying principle of discrimination" (Douglas 1996: 62). As opposed to tastes understood in ways which privilege the will to develop models of structure, we should be focusing on tastes as ways of being in the world. Hennion (2007: 98) has argued that social actors immersed in the to-and-fro of the flow of objects, images, and people do not routinely think of people or things as having "tastes." This is because tastes are in fact a processual and experiential dimension of everyday life; they are performed and have a performative quality. Tastes are felt rather than thought in the first instance, and reflexively exercised via continually unfolding experiences that bring people and objects together and where principles of evaluation and satisfaction come into play as a matter of course. For cultural sociology then, the most relevant aspect of tastes are the ways in which they combine feelings for things and styles of interaction with objects and people—with the senses of taste, touch, hearing, and sight—to draw or repel people to various objects.

To tackle the standard models for addressing the question of taste, we must look principally to the work of Bourdieu. It is Bourdieu's cultural strand of critical materialism that is embodied in a number of his key empirical works but most notably in *Distinction* (1984), which has most effectively challenged the Kantian notion of a pure aesthetic judgment. Bourdieu's powerful thesis—which is strong on distributions and socioeconomic matrices, but rather weakly articulated in terms of cultural interpretation—is impelled by a complex theoretical armory and the particular idea that a pure, disinterested judgment of taste is erroneous. Moreover, Bourdieu maintains that because taste judgments are based on the unequal distribution of quotients of cultural capital that have been sanctioned by socially dominant classes, aesthetic distinctions are both generative and reproductive of substantial social cleavages. Tastes—again, at least in the way they can be measured and represented in social surveys and statistical analysis—are thus essentially differentiating containers of economic capital that have been converted into culture.

There are two critiques I wish to make of Bourdieu. The first relates to his methodology and the aspects of taste that such an approach reveals and, inevitably, obscures. The burden associated with the application of survey methodology to studying tastes is its focus on "objective," variable-friendly measures of taste as stated preferences in art, music, literature, and the arts of living. While numerous studies of the social distribution of these objective tastes in different domains can be found—and much empirical debate and specification continues in this field—there is a relative indifference to the actual logics that inform and, perhaps, even constitute these patterns. In their aggregate form and treated primarily as symbolic markers of a social position, as displays of status and distinction, these objective "judgments of taste" have become reified or objectified and severed from their underlying lay conceptual or discursive moorings (Woodward and Emmison 2001). Leaving aside the substantial question of whether cultural tastes, differences, and modes of evaluation are important generative resources for social differentiation—and it is reasonable to think they probably do matter in important ways—the attention to the notion of cultural dominance in Bourdieu's work is at the expense of uncovering in a systematic way the everyday, discursive cultural schemes of taste used by actors to accomplish a position on taste (see Woodward and Emmison 2001). In this sense, Hennion's (2007) reflection on the sociological study of tastes as a type of performative search is constructive. Not committed to a strong version of actor-network approaches, but nevertheless focusing on the performative elements of people-object engagements, he argues that "taste" refers to the way in which individuals deal with the diverse array of objects, events, and people that they face in everyday settings. Tastes discriminate; they also agitate cultural performance and classification.

There is another serious gap in Bourdieu's program for a sociology of taste. Bourdieu is so determined to demonstrate his point about tastes being resources for social differentiation and cleavage that he fails to engage with earlier classical conceptions of the social meaning of tastes that was developed in the work of Simmel and Blumer, and which were apparent—though in ways overlooked by Bourdieu—in Kant's Critique of Judgement. In Bourdieu's (1984) influential model of taste and aesthetic judgment, morality and ethics play an insignificant part in strategies of distinction. Bourdieu overlooks the collective and moral dimension of taste because his survey method predominantly affords an account of the social distribution of cultural preferences. There is little or no methodological opportunity for him to develop insights into the moral and collectively contoured dimensions of such preferences, a point which forms the basis of Lamont's (1992) important study of the moral basis of modes of interpersonal evaluation. Bourdieu's conceptual model is thus primarily based in the domain of private, individual preferences rather than public, civil expressions, where we could expect collective and moral dimensions to be exercised. In contrast, the studies of Halle (1993), Miller (2008), Riggins (1994), and Woodward (2001, 2003) begin to account for the diverse forms of "astructural" knowledge associated with tastes—the realm of emotion, identity, meaning, and narrative. This does not mean that this type of approach could not be consistent with the development of structural accounts, but that such methodologies and approaches afford insight into a more diverse range of aesthetic expressions and experiences and a consideration of their socially productive effects. The language of these studies is grounded in concepts—such as contemplation, meaning, intimacy, kinship, and emotion—as opposed to Bourdieu and his intellectual predecessors in this vein, Veblen and Simmel, who focus on dynamics of status, prestige and emulation.

While both of these bodies of work—postmodern studies of consumption and Bourdieu's cultural materialism—have been extremely important in energizing contemporary consumption studies, neither has been decisive in addressing central problems relevant to understanding contemporary consumer culture. The former has usefully emphasised freedom, play, and self-identity, and to a large degree is responsible for contemporary assumptions about consumption as an active process of symbolic interpretation and manipulation. But, it has largely ignored the anchoring culture-structures which animate and make sense of consumption. The latter of these influential oeuvres within consumption studies is inspired by the work of Bourdieu. Though this body of research is apparently empirically sophisticated, along the lines of methodological positivism, it can be criticized as reductivist and unidimensional because through its focus on the distributed patterns and effects of consumption, it has largely ignored questions of meaning, interpretation, and performance; the things that comprise and constitute the very social efficacy of tastes. Bourdieu's ouevre—and the subsequent work it has inspired—is largely a variable-centered approach; useful for establishing benchmark patterns and the socioeconomic correlates of consumption patterns; but it obscures as much about consumption and tastes as it reveals. For various reasons then, which are discussed further in this chapter, recent sociology has been unable to answer basic questions about the fundamental cultural characteristics and dimensions of consumerism as an aesthetic relationship to the world of commodity objects.

MATERIALITY AND MATERIAL CULTURE: OBJECTS RELATIONS AND CONSUMPTION

More recently, and happening somewhat in parallel to the development of these two fields, there has been a growing interest in materiality and material culture. Attention to objects as rudimentary elements of consumer culture has acquired renewed, and now rather central, status in sociocultural accounts of consumption processes in late-modern societies. While sociologists and social anthropologists have histori-cally had an enduring concern for the material constituents of culture (Goffman 1951; Mauss 1954; Simmel 1904; Veblen 1899), the recent interest in objects has developed in the context of prominent sociocultural accounts of modern consum-erism, and, in turn, the emphasis these have given to the material basis of consump-tion processes (Appadurai 1986; Douglas and Isherwood 1979; Miller 1987; Riggins 1994). This field of work began in recent cultural anthropology, especially in the work of Miller (1987), but also the earlier influential study combining anthropologi-cal and economic perspectives by Douglas and Isherwood (1979) and Sahlins (1974), both of whom, of course, looked in no small part to Lévi-Strauss and Durkheim for inspiration.

The dominant approach to theorizing consumption processes that was founda-tional in the sociology of consumption has arisen through theoretical frameworks generated by the core motifs of conventional sociological practice: Constraint and opportunity, and freedom and fixity. Broadly, questions of consumer conscious-ness, the political nature of consumerism, and the relative power of the consumer vis-à-vis the structural forces of capitalism have been the primary concern for this approach. The principal feature here is the positioning of consumption within a social-structural context, informed by an understanding of issues such as media, marketing, and social class. The organizing themes which frame consumer practice in this approach are centered on background models of political and economic power, choice and constraint. At a more abstract level, they are grounded broadly in questions of agency and structure. This reliance on dichotomous theoretical meta-phors is what led Miller (1995) to summarize this type of sociology of consumption as encouraging the reductionist myth that consumerism was either "good" or "bad," rather than a complex, multidimensional process. The lineage of these approaches can be traced from Marx, and through twentieth-century varieties of critical thought, such as Lukács, Marcuse, Horkheimer, and Adorno. In contrast, the "object turn" in studies of consumer culture transfers attention to the intrinsic materiality of many consumption processes. Particularly, it has suggested a role for objects in generating cultural meanings; in doing social and cultural work through processes of differentiation, objectiÞcation, and integration (Appadurai 1986; Baudrillard 1996; Douglas and Isherwood 1979). While the material culture approach to con-sumption retains a concern for consumer practice and ideation—as the founda-tional studies of consumption had previously emphasized—it devotes particular attention to the object of consumer interest as "the visible part of culture" (Douglas and Isherwood 1979: 44) that serves to animate practice and evoke feelings in con-sumers. The field of material culture studies has provided perhaps the most promis-ing and culturally sophisticated approach to consumption, emphasising symbolism, ritual, and meaning as the basis for defining consumption as a type of cultural interpretation. Yet, while this body of work coming under the rubric of material culture studies has been extremely valuable in a range of ways, again it has not been decisive in addressing basic questions about consumer culture. Often, it has led to methodologically reflexive, locally contextualised studies of the uses of objects within small cultural groups and by individuals who have demonstrated agency, emotionality, and complexity (Warde 2005), but done little to expose the cultural structures that are at the core of the cultural sociology approach.

A more recent and related development—that looks to move beyond material culture studies but still deals with materiality—comes largely from sociological studies of science and technology and has been expressed recently in the form of studies of consumption practices and pragmatics. In social theory, this focus on "assemblages of materials" has been associated with actor-network theory that deals with collapsing the distinction between people and material objects and the formation of material assemblages. In new studies of objects as "actants"—inspired by ideas of relationality and pragmatics and blended with new ethnography in the work of Latour and then also a cache of writers who have extended and applied his insights in very useful ways (e.g., Law 2002)—the "material" element has been the subject of much research and theoretical interest often at the expense of the "culture" aspects. What comes first are the material interlinkages of person and object, rather than questions of meaning, narrative, and interpretation. To some degree, this is compatible with the most exciting anthropological work in the tradition of Mauss, Durkheim, and Gell, but in sociology, it has been used most frequently in relation to technological systems, assemblages, and engagements, and indeed has eschewed questions of human motivations and meanings that would seem central when one wishes to understand consumption. It has also been represented in emerging studies of the "practices" of consumption (Dant 2008; Warde 2005; Watson 2008; Watson and Shove 2008). Here, too, though coordinated networks of people and things are given priority in organizing social life, questions reside with material pragmatics and networked relationality more than actual consumption practice, obviously leaving significant cultural elements relatively unaddressed. To some, this focus on practice seems productive because it does not presume or speculate about cultural categories, meaning, or symbolism but identifies how "consumption occurs within and for the sake of practices" (Warde 2005: 145). The appeal of attending to such consumption practices seems to be that they are universal, habitual, and continually unfolding within interrelated networks of other practices and hence have an apparent recursive material quality. But, this view also offers a rather restricted and truncated account of consumption, leaving out questions of cultural complexity, interpretation, and meaning. Such a view is in danger of radically selling short the cultural realm, despite Warde's suggestion that culture has received too much emphasis in studies of consumption (2005: 147). Warde even goes so far to state that "it is the fact of engagement in the practice, rather than any personal decision about a course of conduct, that seems to explain the nature and process of consumption" (Warde 2005: 138). A whole body of work within sociology and consumer behavior studies enables a more complex picture to be drawn (see, e.g., Belk 1988; Belk and Tumbat 2005; Holt 2004; Kleine and Kernan 1991; McCracken 1988; Richins 1994). Warde further states that most consumption is directed toward the "fulfilment of self-regarding purposive projects" (2005: 147), which itself suggests we need to look well beyond the realm of pragmatics of material interactions to understand consumption. In short, this is not to suggest that the physical, material, and sensual components of various modes of "doing"—driving a car, drinking wine, hitting a ball, preparing food—are not important, but that the risk with the "practices" approach is that we develop distinctly thin accounts that attend to systems of coordinated perceptions and physical manipulations and lose much of the cultural context that could afford us a stronger theory of consumption as an enduring cultural-economic activity. To do this must involve using ideas of taste to think more deeply about the nature of "self-regarding purposive projects" to which Warde (2005) refers.

Interest in the capacity of objects to afford movement between pragmatic, aesthetic engagements "at the surface," and the depth of meanings within things, is one fruitful way to overcome the deficiencies of the practices approach. Though not originating from a pragmatic basis, such an approach nevertheless deals with matters of materiality and surfaces, but seeks to connect them with the social discourses and narratives beneath. Alexander's (2008b) study of iconicity, for example, models the exchanges between social actors and objects. He shows how objects afford movement from surface to depth via a form of "immersion." Immersion involves a dual process: one called "subjectification" where people are able draw an object into themselves, transforming it from object to subject and allowing it to take on a life whereby one no longer sees the object itself, but "oneself, one's projections, one's convictions and beliefs" (Alexander 2008b: 7). Simultaneously, through a process called "materialization," a person is drawn into an object, effectively becoming it, or what it is seen to stand for. Via immersion, what exists is not an object, nor a person, but a oneness of material and human, united by a material-affective—rather than merely mechanical or pragmatic—connection. Such connections with consumed, material objects are the basis for the performance and learning of norms and ideals and—through the use of typifications and iconic representations—the foundation for our collective life. Though not all engaging with ideas of iconicity, Swedberg (2005), Benzecry (2008), and Miller (2008) work from similar assumptions and connect material culture to questions of narrative, belonging, myth, and discourse.

An Argument for a Morally Situated Performative Theory of Consumption: Taste and Consumption as a Search for the Sublime

At a literal and mundane level, taste is the evaluation of things, such as matching colors, appropriate skirt lengths, or shoe heel sizes; the optimal way to spend leisure time; one's choice (or nonchoice) in lounge covering, preferences for antique or new furniture, how one's kitchen renovation was planned; and the search for appropriate, beautiful, or functional things to fill one's house. But, is there a larger meaning to such minutiae of everyday aesthetics? The elementary place to start is with a bedrock ideas of good and bad. To judge something or someone as good or bad is a philosophical problem of substance, for it involves a series of thought processes that subsume notions of desirability, needs and wants, satisfaction, rightness, efficiency, pleasure, and obligation (Sparshott 1958). At the same time, from a sociological point of view, judgments of what is good and bad for us or others would seem to be routine, recurrent, and taken-for-granted elements of life. However philosophically foggy and misplaced vernacular evaluations of good and bad may be in orienting tastes, they seem an inescapable component of social existence and can be found in myriad mundane feelings, such as: "eating something would be good," "exercise would be good for me," "to buy a new shirt would be good." Sparshott (1958: 122) outlines the simple meaning of good to be that which "is such to satisfy the wants of the person or persons concerned." While Sparshott does not concern himself with notions of bad things, it is reasonable to assume that bad things fail to satisfy the wants, or at least people believe that they will fail to satisfy particular wants. It seems likely that everyday notions of what is perceived as likely to satisfy, and what is perceived as likely to fail to satisfy, are reflective of almost universal human habits and traits of judgment or evaluation. Such notions of satisfaction invariably carry references to a state of incompleteness, equivalent to Baudrillard's idea of lack, because there is an implied reference to a desirable "good" or undesirable "bad" object or person which has potential to satiate desire. Sparshott puts it this way in his inquiry into goodness, "desires and needs are alike deficiencies, and carry a reference to a perfected or completed somewhat" (1958: 133). Judging the ability of a thing or person to potentially complete or satisfy is an essential element of our culture—it is the basis of the act of consumption, and is a mandatory routine of our lives that involves navigating myriad options in order to weigh value, to find merits or deficiencies, and to decide in favor or against something (Sparshott 1958: 128). As Sparshott pointed out over half a century ago, we live in a culture of evaluation, and the notion of good—and by implication also the notion of bad—are universal binary operators in these everyday judgments: "Such arguments tend to present themselves in the form: good or bad?"(Sparshott 1958: 128).

Durkheim and Mauss's (1963) theory of classification is an elementary theoretical signpost in considering this aspect of consumption. The deduction to be drawn from their work is that notions of aesthetic taste are primarily systems of classification and that these complex and nuanced systems of practice are related to the fundamental moral organizing notions of "good" and "bad." Thus, considering consumption, certain practices of taste, and particular types or styles of material culture (e.g., fashion and clothing, domestic objects, motor vehicles), come to be evaluated as "beautiful," "timeless," "elegant," "vulgar," "garish," or "unsuitable"; but, in the end, are classified as in the realm of good or in the realm of bad. This is a simple, bipartite system of classification, and condensing the complexities of taste and aesthetic judgment to this binary scheme is a useful guiding principle of inquiry, rather than a strategy for directing empirical inquiry. However, it has the advantage of illustrating how such judgments come to acquire an ethical force and, hence, an explanatory advantage. Aesthetic judgments are embellished with a variety of concepts and words and located within a range of discursive rationales, however, in the end, they are judged as satisfying or not, good or bad. One of Durkheim and Mauss's other principal insights is that classification is a process of marking-off, of demarcating things which are related but have distinct points of difference to another. These systems of ideas of relation and difference serve to connect and unify knowledge about the world. They build up a hierarchical system where ideas form chains of meanings, and these meanings come to be concretized in material forms. In *The Elementary Forms of the Religious Life* (1915), Durkheim extends this theory of classification to two important areas that are relevant. The first is to show that systems of classification have moral qualities. Classifications are not merely technical accomplishments, but come to obtain their cultural weight by virtue of a moral quality attached to their deliberation (1915: 451). In weighing up the world of objects, a moral force comes to be activated, and this, in large part, explains their robustness and depth. Merely pretty or sparkling surface is not enough, but such aesthetic qualities are united with the strongest cultural powers when they draw participants into the moral and aesthetic meanings of an object (Alexander 2008b). The Durkheimian tradition also establishes these material-moral systems of classification as evidence of the socialness of systems of representation. Systems of classifying people, objects and things are thus linked to a collective consciousness—they obtain meaning by reference to other socially sanctioned classifications. The sentiments of taste contained in aesthetic judgments are not merely representative of emptied-out, ersatz forms of individualism, nor are they merely distributed variables representing social structures of inequality, but have acquired a moral force that gives them durability and strength as principles directing everyday social action.

Combined with this idea that consuming affords people entry to particular moral depths, ideas about social performance within cultural sociology offer a viable way to imagine consumption as an active and contextual process demonstrated through ongoing performances that fuse people with objects of consumption in particular social settings. Recent developments in performance theory within cultural sociology have emerged by fusing a range of theoretical traditions. Goffman (1959) used the concept of performance to explain the enactment of social roles according to the logic of status management. More recent developments in performance theory (Geertz 1973; Turner 1982; Schechner 1993; Butler 1997; Alexander 2004a, 2004b) seek to understand the performative character of identity by drawing on theoretical resources of symbolic action and ritual and social drama to show how social action is contingent on history and collective sentiments, but must be brought into existence by continuous performative acts that actualize and reproduce the identities of social actors (Butler 1997: 409). In his exposition of the elements of performance, Alexander (2004b: 529) defines cultural performance as

> the social process by which actors, individually or in concert, display for others
> the meaning of the social situation. This meaning may or may not be one to
> which they themselves consciously adhere; it is the meaning that they, as social
> actors, consciously or unconsciously wish to have others believe. In order for their

display to be effective, actors must offer a plausible performance, one that leads those to whom their actions and gestures are directed to accept their motives and explanations as a reasonable account.

Cultural performance models could be fruitfully applied within the field of consumption studies. They suggest that the way consumer objects acquire their cultural meaning is within local settings, where people confer consumption objects as social life through their use and by offering active, creative accounts, or narratives that link in some ways to autonomous cultural discourses. Such narratives are locally accomplished phenomena, existing within various social settings where individuals are called to offer a believable, convincing, or "fused" (Alexander 2004a) account of their relations with consumer objects. The performative model suggests there should be an aesthetic "fusion" between the material and discursive, articulation and reception: "A coming together of background meaning, actors, props, scripts, direction and audience" where performances are experienced as convincing or authentic by participants (Alexander 2004a: 92). Such a model suggests a useful way of thinking about consumption, integrating materiality with narrative, context, desire, meaning, and communication within contextualized settings.

CONCLUSION

Along with developing culturally sensitive empirical approaches that account for human-object interactions, cultural sociologies of consumption must begin to schematize the basic culture-structures that inform consumer practice. Here, an elemental structure needs reemphasis. The pursuit and evaluation of things that are perceived to satisfy or give pleasure is a basic human pursuit. Good things satisfy and give pleasure. Bad things generate anxiety, contaminate, and offend. Deciding what is poor, polluted, bad, or somehow inferior, and hence to be avoided, and alternately, what is safe, pleasurable, good, and enhancing is a fundamental cultural trait. Skills of discernment and evaluation operate in numerous domains of life and are cultural proficiencies that are at the very heart of practices of consumer behavior, tastes, and material engagements. In fact, it may be correct to see that one of the reasons people become attached to having consumer "freedoms" is that these seemingly minor, routine choices become occasions for feeling the empowerment of one's discriminatory faculties and for seeking potentially ecstatic, transformative engagements with objects.

It is in these engagements with the world of commodities—as we do such apparently mundane human things as nourish, entertain, decorate, play, and ponder—that we make culture. Norbert Elias pointed out in *The Civilising Process* that the character of human threats has undergone an historical change. For the most part, he pointed out, we no longer live in fear of physical threat or danger; but one threat we continually face is social embarrassment and shame that derives from a breach of rules of civility. Elias highlighted the sphere of manners as a domain of etiquette that had potential to generate individual anxiety. But his historical, processual theory suggests that the location of the source of threats will change, so that zones of experiencing shame continuously shift to new provinces of social life. The allied domains of consumption and aesthetic taste are contemporary fields for the negotiation of social acceptability, the exclusion, or minimization of contaminating material culture, and the striving for approval, individuality, and transcendence. In a society where commodities, styles, fashions, and taste proliferate to a degree beyond what could be considered general abundance, people's understandings of what constitutes good taste—and good more universally—become increasingly fixed on the navigation of a meaningful course through the forest of consumption choices. The activity of judgment and classification has a universal application to human culture. Assessment, evaluation, and discernment are routine elements of daily life—myriad choices confront people to which, in the interests of efficient, culturally acceptable social conduct, they must selectively acknowledge and make responses. The operation of judgment and the establishment of a choice is especially salient in an era where new consumption domains have emerged, being driven by the interplay of structural dynamics, such as aestheticization, commodification, and individualization.

Though clear and unmediated symbolic communication should not be assumed in any culture where symbols proliferate and change meaning with speed, we can say that material culture—the objects, things, or commodities people purchase and use—affords symbolic evidence of a person's taste, and more broadly, is generative of their social identity. Yet, they communicate as much about oneself to oneself as they do to others. Further, notions of what is civil and uncivil, meaningful and meaningless, valuable and trite, are founded in part on the decisions a person makes in relation to what is worthy or suitable for wearing, watching, possessing, listening to, and eating. The market for commodities has thus become a sphere for the establishment of norms of civility. These cultural values become visible and expressed via material means. Explaining how commodities are important for realizing feelings of collective and civil belonging should be one concern of cultural sociological inquiries into taste and aesthetics. Studies of taste should be seen to constitute investigations of etiquette, and studies of everyday aesthetic judgment are not just about what is considered beautiful (contra Kant), but what is considered good. Accounts of civility, social inclusion and exclusion, boundaries, social etiquette, and the human desire for pleasure can be illuminated by studying everyday understandings of taste and their accomplishment through processes of judgment, selection, and justification. Seen in this light, the exploration of a consumption field is actually an analysis of the social boundaries of goodness, worth, and value, as expressed by the participants' notions of taste and the deployment of material culture.

This line of argument is founded partly on the assumptions that decisions of taste and judgments of aesthetic value contain an implied commitment to a collective—but obviously socially variegated to some degree—notion of what is good and bad to consume. The deployment of the notions "good" and "bad" are not experienced as philosophical conundrums for actors, as they become natural or taken-for-granted modes of interaction with the world. Judgments about people, their behaviors, and material culture happen routinely and are frequently based on this binary opposition of good and bad, helpful or harmful, worthy or worthless. While a collectively shaped notion of "good" and "bad" becomes the basis or master scheme for a retrievable complex of resources or narratives used in everyday judgments; according to variables such as age, class, peer group, and education level, we embellish these oppositions with a variety of words and concepts that give "goodness" and "badness" unique hues across different contexts. In this way, it is possible to see how the idea of distinguishing between good and bad types has particular relevance to the practice of consumption, for at its core, consumption is a process of selection or discernment of things that are perceived to satisfy. It is not correct that judgments of good and bad are always about civility and never about power, authority, difference, and inequality. In fact, these things are part and parcel of the establishment of such civilities. Clearly, consumption becomes a process of making and marking boundaries by materializing cultural categories. Yet, by insisting that acts of consumption and judgments of taste are worthy of sociological consideration in their own right—and that domains of consumption can be analyzed as an autonomous sphere of cultural activity—an alternative to predominant strands in the sociology of taste that privilege structure and status in accounts of aesthetic judgment can be posited.

The etiquettes of aesthetic cultures constitute an important area for further research in the field of consumerism. If consumerism is identified as an enduring social, economic, or environmental problem or issue, then to understand why it is so robust, energetic, and appealing as a way of life, sociologists should direct attention to showing how it is internalized in the language, narratives, and dreams of people, objects, and events. Campbell's (1987) ambitious theoretical work on the possibility of an historically embedded romantic ethic of consumption seems to be one of the most promising explanations of why consumerism is such a robust ideology, yet his work remains largely at the level of historical interpretation and theory. There is a need for studies of consumption that attempt to integrate culture and cognition in order to assess the role of fantasy, daydreaming, and other a culturally relevant psychosocial factors in generating cultural responses. Bourdieu, despite the flaws in his approach identified in this chapter, has perceptively pointed out that sociological understandings of taste are akin to psychoanalysis because they dwell on the deep reasons why individuals are attracted to particular forms of culture (1984: 11, 77).

A cultural sociological account of consumption can also help to shape aspects of emerging theories within economic sociology. In the last few decades, cultural research, as well as work within the discipline of economics, has argued that idealized, abstracted models of the economic actor that dominate mainstream economic theory are too narrowly conceived to capture the complexity of economic behaviors. Questions of identity, social status, desire, group norms, and cultural categories are starting to become crucial for economists. For example, Akerlof and colleagues (Akerlof 1997; Akerlof 2007; Akerlof and Kranton 2000) have positioned cultural concepts such as identity and status perception at the core of these new theories, which seek generally to incorporate nonpecuniary motivations into accounts of economic behaviors. These groundbreaking efforts are closer to a socio-logical psychology than a cultural sociology, but better models of cultural-economic action can inform future modeling. Likewise, the field of economic sociology and cultural sociology have begun to address questions of price, value, preference, and utility from their own perspectives (e.g., Wherry 2008). The basic principle here is that economic action is culturally meaningful and culturally derived, rather than merely rational from an economic point of view. Here, literatures in the sociology of arts and cultural sociology that investigate the aesthetic surface of objects and their capacity not only to represent aspects of reality, but also to prompt reflexive, cognitive responses in actors and collectives are important (see Acord and Di Nora 2008; Alexander 2008b; Eyerman and Ring 1998; Eyerman and McCormick 2006; Swedberg 2005). Thus, economic actors orient their actions to goals that make sense not just in terms of price and utility, but in a range of other matters which are at the heart of cultural sociological investigation. The emergent cultural sociological approach suggests that we should think of the economic behaviors of individuals as guided by ideas, impressions, fantasies, irrationalities, asymmetries, perceptions of self and others, and impressions of "what is going on" with their own budget and the broadly configured "economy." All this is fueled by circulating texts within the economy including such things as product advertising, magazines, commodity branding, and the reporting of pronouncements from official economic bodies and economic commentators. As much as powerful economic modeling, the goal of generating a convincing theory of economic behavior requires a strong theory of culture and sensitive empirical approaches. As a starting principle, this research agenda requires a cultural sociological model that fuses performative understand-ings of the materiality and sensuality of consumption with consideration of the power of myth, narrative, and meaning generation.

REFERENCES

Acord, Sophia, and Tia DeNora. 2008. "Culture and the Arts: From Art Worlds to Arts-in-Action." *The ANNALS of the American Academy of Political and Social Science* 619: 223–237.

Akerlof, George A. 1997. "Social Distance and Social Decisions." *Econometrica* 65(5): 1005–1027.

———. 2007. "The Missing Motivation in Economics." *American Economic Review* 97(1): 5–36.

Akerlof, George A., and Rachel Kranton. 2000. "Economics and Identity." *Quarterly Journal of Economics* CXV(3): 715–753.

Alexander, Jeffrey C. 2004a. "From the Depths of Despair: Performance, Counterperformance, and 'September 11.'" *Sociological Theory* 22(1): 88–105.

————. 2004b. "Cultural Pragmatics: Social Performance Between Ritual and Strategy."
    Sociological Theory 22(4): 527–573.
————. 2008a. "Iconic Consciousness: The Material Feeling of Meaning." *Environment and
    Planning D: Society and Space* 26: 782–794.
————. 2008b. "Iconic Experience in Art and Life: Surface/Depth Beginning with
    Giacometti's 'Standing Woman.'" *Theory, Culture and Society* 25(5): 1–19.
Appadurai, Arjun. 1986. "Introduction: Commodities and the Politics of Value." Pp. 3–63 In
    The Social Life of Things: Commodities in Cultural Perspective, ed. Appadurai, Arjun.
    Melbourne: Cambridge University Press.
Bauman, Zygmunt. 1988. *Freedom*. Buckingham, UK: Open University Press.
Barthes, Roland. 1957. *Mythologies*. Trans. Lavers, Annette. London: Vintage.
Baudrillard, Jean. 1981. *For a Critique of the Political Economy of the Sign*. Trans. Levin, C. :
    New York: Telos Press.
————. 1996. *The System of Objects*. Trans. Benedict, J. London: Verso.
Beck, Ulrich. 1992. *Risk Society: Towards a New Modernity*. Trans. Ritter, Mark. London:
    Sage.
Becker, Howard. 1974. "Art as Collective Action." *American Sociological Review* 39(6):
    767–776.
Belk, Russell W. 1988 "Possessions and the Extended Self." *The Journal of Consumer Research*
    15: 139–165.
Belk, Russell W., and Gulnur Tumbat. 2005. "The Cult of Macintosh." *Consumption,
    Markets and Culture* 8(3): 205–217.
Bell, Daniel. 1976. *The Cultural Contradictions of Capitalism*. New York: Basic Books.
Benzecry, Claudio E. 2008. "Azul y Oro: The Many Social Lives of a Football Jersey." *Theory,
    Culture and Society* 25(1): 49–76.
Bollas, Christopher. 2009. *The Evocative Object World*. New York: Routledge.
Bourdieu, Pierre. 1984. *Distinction: A Social Critique of the Judgement of Taste*. London:
    Routledge.
Butler, Judith. 1997. "Performative Acts and Gender Constitution: An Essay in
    Phenomenology and Feminist Theory." Pp. 401–18 In *Writing on the Body: Female
    Embodiment and Feminist Theory*. Ed. Katie Conboy, Nadia Medina, and Sarah
    Stanbury. New York: Columbia University Press.
Callon, Michel, Cecile Meadel, and Vololona Rebaharisoa. 2002. "The Economy of
    Qualities." *Economy and Society* 31(2): 194–217.
Campbell, Colin. 1987. *The Romantic Ethic and the Spirit of Modern Consumerism*. New
    York: Blackwell.
————. 1995. "The Sociology of Consumption." Pp. 95–124 In *Acknowledging
    Consumption. A Review of New Studies*, ed. Miller, Daniel. London: Routledge.
Cardenas, Cardenas, and Ellen Gorman, eds. 2007. *The Hummer. Myths and Consumer
    Culture*. New York: Lexington Books.
Dant, Tim. 2005. *Materiality and Society*. Buckingham, UK: Open University Press.
————. 2008. "The Pragmatics of Material Interaction." *Journal of Consumer Culture* 8(1):
    11–33.
Douglas, Mary. 1996. *Thought Styles. Critical Essays on Good Taste*. London: Sage.
Douglas, Mary, and Baron Isherwood. 1979. *The World of Goods. Towards an Anthropology
    of Consumption*. New York: Basic Books.
du Gay, Paul, and Michael Pryke, eds. 2002. *Cultural Economy: Cultural Analysis and
    Commercial Life*. London: Sage.
Durkheim, Emile. 1915. *The Elementary Forms of the Religious Life*. London: Allen and
    Unwin.

Durkheim, Emile, and Marcel Mauss. 1963. *Primitive Classification*. London: Cohen and West.

Elias, Norbert. 1994. *The Civilising Process*. Oxford: Blackwell.

Emmison, Michael. 2003. "Social Class and Cultural Mobility: Reconfiguring the Cultural Omnivore Thesis." *Journal of Sociology* 39(3): 211–230.

Eyerman, Ron, and Lisa McCormick. 2006. *Myth, Meaning and Performance: Toward a New Cultural Sociology of the Arts*. Boulder, CO: Paradigm.

Eyerman, Ron, and Magnus Ring. 2006. "Towards a New Sociology of Art Worlds: Bringing Meaning Back In." *Acta Sociologica* 41(2–3): 277–283.

Featherstone, Mike. 1987. "Lifestyle and Consumer Culture." *Theory, Culture and Society* 4: 55–70.

———. 1990. "Perspectives on Consumer Culture." *Sociology* 24(1): 5–22.

———. 1991. *Consumer Culture and Postmodernism*. London: Sage.

———. 1992. "Postmodernism and the Aestheticisation of Everyday Life." Pp. 265–90 In *Modernity and Identity*, ed. Lash, S., and Friedman, J. Oxford: Blackwell.

Foster, Robert. 2006. "Tracking Globalization. Commodities and Value in Motion." Pp. 285–302 In *Handbook of Material Culture*, ed. Tilley, C., Keane, W., KŸchler, S., Rowlands, M., and Spyer, P. London: Sage.

Geertz, Clifford. 1973. *The Interpretation of Cultures*. New York: Basic Books.

Goffman, Erving. 1951. "Symbols of Class Status." *British Journal of Sociology* 2(4): 294–304.

———. 1959. *The Presentation of Self in Everyday Life*. New York: Doubleday.

Halle, David. 1993. *Inside Culture: Art and Class in the American Home*. Chicago: University of Chicago Press.

Harvey, David. 1989. *The Condition of Postmodernity*. Oxford: Blackwell.

Hennion, Antoine. 2007. "Those Things That Hold Us Together: Taste and Sociology." *Cultural Sociology* 1: 97.

Holt, Douglas. 2004. *How Brands Become Icons. The Principles of Cultural Branding*. Boston: Harvard Business School Press.

Horkheimer, Max, and Theodor W. Adorno. 1987 (1944). *Dialectic of Enlightenment*. Trans. John Cumming. New York: Continuum.

Jameson, Frederic. 1991. *Postmodernism, Or, The Cultural Logic of Late Capitalism*. London: Verso.

———. 1998. "Postmodernism and the Consumer Society." Pp. 1–20 In *The Cultural Turn: Selected Writings on the Postmodern, 1983–1998*, ed. Fredric Jameson. London: Verso.

Kant, Immanuel. 1952. *The Critique of Judgement*. Trans. Meredith, J. C. Oxford: Clarendon Press.

Kleine III, Robert E., and Jerome B. Kernan. 1991. "Contextual Influences on the Meanings Ascribed to Ordinary Consumption Objects." *Journal of Consumer Research* 18: 311–324.

Knorr Cetina, Karin. 1997. "Sociality with Objects: Social Relations in Postsocial Knowledge Societies." *Theory, Culture and Society* 14(4): 1–30.

Lamont, Michele. 1992. *Money, Morals and Manners: The Culture of the French and the American Upper-Middle Class*. Chicago: University of Chicago Press.

Lash, Scott, and John Urry. 1987. *The End of Organised Capitalism*. Cambridge, UK: Polity Press.

———. 1994. *Economies of Signs and Space*. London: Sage.

Latour, Bruno. 2007. *Reassembling the Social: An Introduction to Actor-Network Theory*. Oxford: Oxford University Press.

Law, John. 2002. *Aircraft Stories: Decentering the Object in Technoscience*. Durham, NC: Duke University Press.

Lury, Celia. 1996. *Consumer Culture*. Cambridge, UK: Polity.

Marcuse, Herbert. 1964. *One Dimensional Man*. London: Abacus.

Mauss, Marcel. 1954. *The Gift*. London: Cohen and West.

McCracken, Grant. 1988. *Culture and Consumption: New Approaches to the Symbolic Character of Consumer Goods and Activities*. Bloomington: Indiana University Press.

Miller, Daniel. 1987. *Material Culture and Mass Consumption*. Oxford: Blackwell.

———. 1995. "Consumption as the Vanguard of History." Pp. 1–52 In *Acknowledging Consumption: A Review of New Studies*, ed. Miller, Daniel. London: Routledge.

———. 1998. *A Theory of Shopping*. Cambridge, UK: Polity Press.

———. 2008. *The Comfort of Things*. Cambridge, UK: Polity Press.

Miller, Toby. 1993. *The Well-Tempered Self: Citizenship, Culture, and the Postmodern Subject*. Baltimore: Johns Hopkins University Press.

Molotch, Harvey. 2003. *Where Stuff Comes From*. New York: Routledge.

Pels, Dick, Hetherington, Kevin, and Frederic Vandenberghe. 2002. "The Status of the Object: Performances, Mediations, and Techniques." *Theory, Culture and Society* 19(5/6): 1–21.

Peterson, Richard A., and Roger M. Kern. 1996. "Changing Highbrow Taste: From Snob to Omnivore." *American Sociological Review* 61 (October): 900–907.

Richins, Marsha L. 1994. "Valuing Things: The Public and Private Meanings of Possessions." *Journal of Consumer Research* 21(3): 504–521.

Riggins, Stephen H. 1994. "Fieldwork in the Living Room: An Autoethnographic Essay." In *The Socialness of Things. Essays on the Socio-Semiotics of Objects*, ed. Riggins, Stephen Harold, pp. 101–147. Berlin: Mouton de Gruyter.

Sahlins, Marshall. 1974. *Stone-age Economics*. London: Tavistock.

Schechner, Richard. 1993. *The Future of Ritual: Writings on Culture and Performance*. London: Routledge.

Schudson, Michael. 2007. "Citizens, Consumers and the Good Society." *The ANNALS of the American Academy of Political and Social Science* 611: 236–249.

Shove, Elizabeth, and Dale Southerton. 2000. "Defrosting the Freezer: From Novelty to Convenience." *Journal of Material Culture* 5(3): 301–319.

Simmel, Georg. 1904. "Fashion." *The American Journal of Sociology* LXII(6): 541–558.

Soja, Edward. 1989. *Postmodern Geographies: The Reassertion of Space in Critical Social Theory*. London: Verso.

Soper, Kate. 2007. "Re-thinking the 'Good Life': The Citizenship Dimension of Consumer Disaffection with Consumerism." *Journal of Consumer Culture* 7(2): 205–229.

Sparshott, Francis. E. 1958. *An Enquiry into Goodness, and Related Concepts: With Some Remarks on the Nature and Scope of Such Enquiries*. Chicago: University of Chicago Press.

Swedberg, Richard. 2005. "August Rodin's The Burghers of Calais: The Career of a Sculpture and its Appeal to Civic Heroism." *Theory, Culture and Society* 22(2): 45–67.

Turner, Victor. 1967. *The Forest of Symbols. Aspects of Ndembu Ritual*. Ithaca, NY: Cornell University Press.

———. 1982. *From Ritual to Theatre: The Human Seriousness of Play*. New York: Performing Arts Journal Publications.

Van Eijck, Koen. 2000. "Richard A. Peterson and the Culture of Consumption." *Poetics* 28 (2/3): 207–224.

Veblen, Thorstein. 1899. *The Theory of the Leisure Class: An Economic Study of Institutions*. London: Unwin Books.

Warde, Alan. 2005. "Consumption and Theories of Practice." *Journal of Consumer Culture* 5(2): 131–153.

Warde, Alan, David Wright, and Modesto Gayo-Cal. 2007. "Understanding Cultural Omnivorousness: Or, the Myth of the Cultural Omnivore." *Cultural Sociology* 1(2): 143–164.

Watson, Matthew 2008. "The Materials of Consumption." *Journal of Consumer Culture* 8(1): 5–10.

Watson, Matthew, and Elizabeth Shove. 2008. "Product, Competence, Project and Practice: DIY and the Dynamics of Craft Consumption." *Journal of Consumer Culture* 8: 69–89.

Wherry, Fredrick. 2008. "The Social Characterizations of Price: The Fool, the Faithful, the Frivolous and the Frugal." *Sociological Theory* 26(4): 363–379.

Wilska, Terhi-Anna. 2002. "Me, a Consumer? Consumption, Identities and Lifestyles in Today's Finland." *Acta Sociologica* 45(3): 195–210.

Woodward, Ian. 2001. "Domestic Objects and the Taste Epiphany: A Resource for Consumption Methodology." *Journal of Material Culture* 6(2): 115–136.

———. 2003. "Divergent Narratives in the Imagining of the Home Amongst Middle-Class Consumers: Aesthetics, Comfort and the Symbolic Boundaries of Self and Home." *Journal of Sociology* 39(4): 391–412.

———. 2006. "Investigating the Consumption Anxiety Thesis: Aesthetic Choice, Narrativisation and Social Performance." *The Sociological Review* 54(2): 263–282.

Woodward, Ian, and Michael Emmison. 2001. "From Aesthetic Principles to Collective Sentiments: The Logics of Everyday Judgements of Taste." *Poetics* 29(6): 295–316.

Zukin, Sharon, and Jennifer Smith Maguire. 2004. "Consumers and Consumption." *Annual Review of Sociology* 30: 173–197.

CHAPTER 26

THE FORCE OF EMBODIMENT: VIOLENCE AND ALTRUISM IN CULTURES OF PRACTICE

ARTHUR W. FRANK

> The *habitus* is a metaphor of the world of objects, which is itself an endless circle of metaphors that mirror each other *ad infinitum*.
>
> —Pierre Bourdieu, The Logic of Practice[1]

INTRODUCTION: EMBODIMENT AS PRACTICE

As sociological studies of bodies have accumulated during the last twenty years, research emphasizes *practice*: what people *do* with bodies. Practice is the intersection of external demands and internal predisposition. In some practices, these reconcile, and in others, they grate against each other. Studies of embodied practice involve actors not only using their bodies, but more specifically, shaping those bodies: fixing, improving, disciplining, and training bodies. Bodies become what they practice to be, whether that practice is unintended or consciously undertaken to make a body seem naturally fitted to its practice. The relation of bodies to practice is analogous to what Randall Collins writes about ritual: "When the practices stop, the beliefs lose their emotional import, becoming mere memories, forms without substance" (2004, p. 37). Bodies are given substance and emotional import in practice; if the practices could ever stop, embodiment would lose its force.

Studies of embodied practice need theory, lest they become a mere accumulation of ethnographic fascinations—but what kind of theory is a debated issue (Crossley 2006). First-generation sociology of the body (Turner 1984; Frank 1990) organized dichotomies into neat typologies delimiting ideal types. Instead, this chapter proposes but what can be called an *irregularly bounded theoretical space of possibility*. This space is conceptually oriented, but at its core are typical stories about bodies, not typologies of bodies. The point is not to synthesize, but rather to bring different explorations into dialogue around common lines of inquiry. As a form of theorizing, an irregularly bounded space of theoretical possibility is generous, insofar as its interest is neither to delimit boundaries between theorists nor to argue the limitations of specific theories. The value of complementarity—suggesting linkages between what seems most useful—outweighs the risks of eclecticism.

This chapter is organized around two stories that foreground significant practices of embodiment: violence and altruism. The stories are interpreted through two theoretical interests that are central to studies of the body: habitus and networks. The idea of habitus, with roots in ancient and medieval philosophy, is utilized by multiple twentieth-century theorists—most significantly, Edmund Husserl, Marcel Mauss, Norbert Elias, Maurice Merleau-Ponty, and Pierre Bourdieu. Bourdieu (1990; Bourdieu and Wacquant 1992) most explicitly specifies the volition of habitus theories to overcome dualisms: interior and exterior, subject and object, subjective and objective, action and structure, motivation and control, individuality and membership, having a body and being a body. Habitus places equal emphasis on *both* the experience of living as a body and also the historical and cultural location of any body; each aspect is understood as making the other possible.

Habitus presupposes practices; it becomes engrained in the body through repeated actions. Actors carry this durable habitus with them—or more accurately, it carries them—even into fields where acting that way is not a route to acceptance.[2] But despite this durability, habitus imagines bodies as always *in process*, never finished, just as bodily locations are never constant. Bodies and their spaces are always changing in response to each other.

Complementary to the perspective of habitus, understanding bodies' participation in networks foregrounds the resources that make possible different forms of embodiment. The predominant metaphor is *companionship*. The theorists I associate with this perspective—Donna Haraway, John Law, and Annemarie Mol—emphasize how bodies are *enacted*, with practices understood as works of enactment. The network perspective opens up understandings of this chapter's second story about embodied altruism.

Bodily practices express culture, and bodies are expressed—they are given speech, they are directed toward practices, and practices are endowed with rationality—in stories that are both about cultures and products of cultures.[3] This chapter seeks to show the inextricability of bodies and culture; that is, the force of culture in shaping bodies, and the reciprocal force of bodies in enacting culture.

THE HABITUS OF VIOLENT BODIES

This chapter's first story is from Norbert Elias, whose long career has as its bookends two major works. *The Civilizing Process* (1984) was completed in 1939 and survived almost being lost during World War II, to be translated into English only in 1978. *The Germans* (1996) comprises writing done throughout Elias' career and published in German in 1989, just before Elias' death. Our story is from *The Germans*, but understanding it depends on Elias' earlier work.

The Civilizing Process presents two narratives that seem so different that the book's first English publication was in two volumes: the history of manners and the history of state formation. The history of manners describes the progressive raising of humans' "shame-repugnance threshold," which Elias demonstrates by presenting advice from etiquette books over several centuries. Elias infers that if the authors of these books felt they had to be specific about proscribing some practice—such as relieving oneself in corridors—then people at the time must have been doing that sort of thing, neither ashamed nor repulsed by it. Changes in manners exemplify how society develops through the reciprocity between what Elias calls *psychogenesis* and *sociogenesis* (Mennell and Goudsblom 1998).

Psychogenesis involves people acquiring the internal dispositions to use their bodies in ways that are acceptable to groups they belong to. Sociogenesis involves people shaping, structuring, and occasionally creating groups that legitimate and require uses of the body with which these same people feel comfortable. What Elias calls an historical *figuration* is a period of institutionalized human interdependence during which psychogenesis and sociogenesis are relatively stable. People feel it is right and natural to use their bodies as the collectivity prescribes, they feel repulsed by what it proscribes, and the collective is sustained by such uses of bodies.

Figurations develop and change, but the general direction of change is for the shame-repugnance threshold to rise in its sensitivities. How change occurs is the topic of Elias' second narrative in *The Civilizing Process*. State formation begins in material possibility: Better roads allowed more shipping of commodities, especially food. Shipping food allowed courts to be centralized, with the king now permanently in residence and nobles summoned to spend longer periods at court; hence, those who previously led their local armies now became courtiers. Distinction at court was gained not by feats of arms but by displays of manners. Being well mannered became the new mark of nobility, and because nobles were objects of generalized emulation at that time, the new courtly manners diffused throughout society. Thus, the two narratives—the history of manners and state formation—are inextricable as a single figuration, although this figuration is perpetually in process.

Elias brings together these two narratives in *The Germans*, writing about how Germans could become the sort of people, individually and collectively, who not only instigated World War II and the Holocaust, but who were capable of believing in these projects. Elias, a Jew, was forced to leave Germany early in his career, eventually settling in London where a Dutch refugee organization supported him while he wrote *The Civilizing Process*. Elias' parents died early in the Holocaust, and he lived his life in various degrees of displacement, however well honored he was during his last decades (Elias 1994). The problems of German militarism and anti-Semitism shaped him intellectually as well as personally.

This preface is necessary to understanding why Elias would include in *The Germans* a story told in a long quotation from a novel by Walter Bloem, lawyer, soldier, and novelist, describing with ethnographic realism the German dueling fraternities of the later nineteenth century, of which Bloem was probably a member. The scene involves a younger student, Achenbach, visiting an older fraternity member, Klauser, who is now an ex-member because he "had not satisfied the standards of his fraternity brothers in a fencing match" (Elias 1996, p. 109). Elias, who studied medicine for several years, underscores the calculated violence of these matches: "The rapiers ... were essentially designed to cut through the skin of the face and skull and the blood vessels lying below the surface. Only the eyes were protected. One could injure one's opponent with a single blow so that the skin of the head hung down in great shreds" (1996, p. 107). Elias describes the fraternity culture as "a pitiless human habitus" (1996, p. 107).[4]

In this simply plotted but disturbing story, Achenbach visits the disgraced and injured Klauser to ask what has happened, or in Bourdieu's terms, to learn the rules and stakes of the game in which he finds himself embarked. The plot is that Klauser hopes to be given a chance at another match, so that he can regain entry into his fraternity. Klauser's account of his willingness to use his body in this practice of dueling exemplifies habitus as a conjunction of embodiment and culture. He tells the younger student:

> "Well, look here, for us corps students, fencing is not a simple sport, a game with weapons, but a ... a means of upbringing. That is, the corps student is supposed to prove in fencing that bodily pain, disfigurement, even severe wounds and death ... that all that is a matter of indifference to him. ... When you have been in the corps longer, you will learn to understand all this better." (Elias 1996, pp. 109–110, ellipses in original)

The conversation continues, with the younger student protesting that the violence of the fraternity code is "crazy," to which the older student does not disagree, but replies that how he was judged is "just tough luck."

The key line for understanding bodies and habitus occurs when Achenbach says, with apparent irony: "You are truly feeling the blessings of this wonderful institution with your own flesh and blood…at this very moment!" (1996, p. 110). If Klauser hears the irony, he ignores it. He repeats the phrase, affirming it as a mantra for his action: "With my own flesh and my own blood! Yes, I am.…" The exchange ends with Klauser, his head in thick bandages, saying that he would make the same decisions over again: "That it is all just so, so that we shall become useful for what is to come later" (1996, p. 110). For Elias, telling this story with hindsight, "what is to come later" includes two world wars and the mass murders of the Holocaust.

The story poses a specific problem that crystallizes the relation between culture and bodies: What explains Klauser's willingness, his unqualified affirmation, to endure using his body in this way? Elias' explanation invokes his version of habitus, described as "second nature" (1996, p. 111):

> His entire habitus—his attitudes, ways of expressing himself, fundamental ideas about human beings, distinguish him as such. That is his reward. In this society, of which the top court-aristocratic groups owed the continuance of their supremacy to victory in war, military forms of behaviour and feeling played a leading role.…These conceptions were hardly ever expressed in thinking at a higher level of synthesis.…At most, they were articulated by them in current sayings like the one the author puts into the mouth of a young student [Klauser] in a perilous situation: "Grit our teeth. So that we become men." (1996, p. 111)

Three points deserve to be underscored. First, readers should sit for a while with the horror of the casualness with which Klauser speaks of "bodily pain, disfigurement, and even severe wounds and death" (1996, p. 110; quoted above). Second, Klauser assumes that his junior, Achenbach, will develop a similar attitude, "When you have been in the corps longer." Finally and most significant for the relation between bodies and culture, the story is not about Klauser's *beliefs*, much less his *ideas*. The story is about Klauser's trained capacity to feel, to think, and to choose "With my own flesh and my own blood!" (1996, p. 110).

That feeling, thinking, and choosing *with* flesh and blood—the willingness and even compulsion to risk flesh and blood—is the force of embodiment in the story Elias retells. Dueling is an embodied practice arising from and perpetuating a compulsion to use one's body against another body, and to display that body usage to peers for their approval. The story offers, in microcosm, an account of the pedagogic processes through which a particular disposition toward violence can become not simply normalized but literally *incorporated*—made of the flesh. This disposition or habitus becomes the individual's tacit rationality, experienced in the muscle fibers as a natural embodied orientation. Should this disposition be held up for scrutiny, as in the conversation with the younger student, Klauser's defense is that even if it is not natural to act as he has acted and will continue to act, it remains necessary to act that way. Bourdieu (1990, p. 25) cites as an epigraph Wittgenstein's famous line, "If I have exhausted the justifications I have reached bedrock, and my spade is turned." Klauser's spade is turned.[5]

For social scientific usage of *embodied* to be more than a pro forma nod acknowledging bodies, it requires an image like that of Klauser, his head in bandages, certain that his future depends on having another opportunity to duel.[6] *Embodied* needs images sufficiently powerful to convey the claustrophobic necessity with which subjects know themselves, flesh and blood, as answering the call of the culture in which they live, as their habitus conditions which call they hear, with what sense of necessity or possible alternatives. This necessity could equally be for pleasure as for risk, but as Elias says, it will "hardly ever [be] expressed at a higher level of synthesis" (1996, p. 111, quoted above). When analytic writing about bodies aspires to that higher level of synthesis, it risks losing the sense of necessity that grounds actors' embodied engagements.[7]

One final point on which Elias is clear: Society is neither one hegemonic habitus nor a unified collection of discrete habitus; all members do not fit neatly. Society is not a machine endlessly producing individuals whose actions reproduce society's dominant structures. Even in figurations in which some fields are dominant, as the military was in Germany around 1900, people respond to multiple aspects of cultures: "Personal traits of individual persons [may develop] in the interstices, so to speak, of the web or rules of such a society, but they are not incorporated into the code" (Elias 1996, p. 109). What distinguishes the habitus of the dominant field, *if* one habitus is dominant in that figuration, is its capacity to render other ways of being as either invisible or deprecated. "One of the oddities of this code is that a whole range of aspects of human social life are not comprehended in it," Elias writes (1996, p. 109). Dominance is constituted by its capacity to disregard, which is its entitlement.

In the gestalt of German culture from Bismarck to Hitler, the warrior habitus was the foreground. All manner of embodied thoughts, feelings, dispositions, and impulses were left untouched and unformed by this habitus, emerging in other social spaces, including those that Elias inhabited.[8] However, in the social spaces occupied by the dueling fraternities and linked to multiple other dominant institutions (the military, the law, the monarchy), the warrior habitus enjoyed unchallenged hegemony. The webs of interdependence supporting its norms and deployment exerted on those who were subject to it a compulsion felt not only, or even primarily, externally. The compulsion was felt from *within*, as a call of flesh and blood.

Crucial for Elias, figurations are constant processes of change.[9] Compared to the period Elias describes in Germany, the gestalt of the contemporary Western era seems to be far less rigidly divided between a dominant foreground habitus and other modes of being pressed into background interstices. Individuals like Klauser who live according to a singular, self-enclosed habitus may have become the exception. For most people, at least for much of their lives, life is lived at the interstices of *multiple* habitus.

This chapter now has a story, with leading and supporting characters, and it has Elias' opening of a theoretical space of bodies and *habitus*. To explore further the idea that people now tend to live at the interstices of multiple habitus, we move to theorists a generation younger than Elias.

Habitus in Its Field, Seeking Capital

Pierre Bourdieu expands and specifies Elias' conceptualization of habitus and embodiment. For Bourdieu, habitus can be a second nature of dispositions only within a *field*, which he understands as space structured around certain objective positions.[10] The hierarchy of positions depends significantly, if not exclusively, on the capital required to achieve and sustain that position. The potential to accrue more capital is one result of occupying that position. *Capital* is whatever the field defines as valued and as accruing value; Bourdieu elaborates multiple forms.[11] In Elias story, fraternity membership is a form of capital, leading to entry into the military field, which in turn leads elsewhere, as well as providing its own rewards. Achenbach and Klauser both occupy objective positions as candidate for fraternity membership and candidate for readmission, respectively. Those who judge Klauser's fencing to be inadequate occupy a position with more capital. In the military, as in many corporations, positions are clearly specified in hierarchical relation to each other; less so in universities or in leisure groups. Yet even in fields with less formally specified positions, membership involves knowing and acting in response to the relative values of forms of capital in that field, whether capital takes the form of income, publication rate, or bowling scores.

Capital is gained and lost through the use of bodies. Crucially for Bourdieu, while this gaining and losing are oriented toward consciously imagined ends, their strategies are more tacit than planned; the body, not the mind, is the locus of action. Bodies are *disposed*—habitus being defined as typical dispositional structures—first in their emotions and capacity for action, and then in their recognition of opportunities to acquire relevant capital. Or for some bodies, their nonrecognition and incapacity, which keeps the distribution of privilege within fields reasonably constant.

Klauser is being the best friend he knows how to be to Achenbach, the younger student, by tutoring him on what counts as capital. In the corps, capital accrues from the willingness to incur disfigurement and even death for the stake of membership in a fraternity, that membership in turn leading to what Elias calls "the top court-aristocratic groups" (1996, p. 111, quoted above). In this pitiless habitus, scars are a form of capital, as those scars mark the body's willingness to risk and endure. In Bourdieu's terms, what counts as capital are embodied markers of investment in the stakes of a game around which the field is structured, whether those markers are scars or cosmetic practices. Fields *require* of bodies. Success in a field depends on experiencing those requirements as natural obligations to fit the body, through practice, to display acceptance of those requirements.[12]

The dueling fraternity lies at one end of a continuum of fields in the singularity of its focus on one relevant form of capital. For example, important as skill in trigonometry might be for a future artillery officer, such skill apparently will not compensate for willingness to duel, at least not in Klauser's generation. But again, Elias understands change as constant, so relevant capitals will change within fields, just as field boundaries will shift. What seems to count at any time is displaying oneself as taking the privileged form of capital seriously—which generally requires *feeling* their seriousness.[13] Klauser is being a friend because he initiates the younger student into what Bourdieu calls the *illusio* of the field: Klauser not only tells Achenbach what the relevant *stakes of the game* are—the forms of capital worth attaining in that field—Klauser embodies those stakes for the younger student. Klauser says as much as he can articulate about taking these stakes *seriously* in the line he repeats: "With my own flesh and my own blood! Yes, I am ..." (Elias 1996, p. 110). Readers of *The Germans* are not told whether the ellipsis after "I am" is original or Elias's insertion. Whichever, the silence after "I am" gives the words the force of an existential statement of identity. Klauser is what he is disposed to do with his body. In his field, his body is both a means and medium of capital accumulation. His *illusio* is so complete that he can imagine no alternative. Should he be denied another match, or fail again, suicide might well seem his only option. An extreme habitus, certainly, but exactly how extreme?

In Bourdieu's (2008) *Sketch for a Self Analysis*, he describes doing fieldwork in Algeria during the warfare of the last years of French colonial rule. Bourdieu never calls himself courageous to have gone places where he could find some interview, observation, or archive, even if those were places where people were accustomed to using their guns and Bourdieu carried minimal credentials. What Bourdieu evokes is his thrill of research: how being caught up in that activity, he was not oblivious of the risks, but did not count them for much against what he hoped to see, photograph, or record. Bourdieu might well say that he sought this capital with his own flesh and his own blood, as that flesh and blood were disposed to act in the field in which he was engaged: the research game, to use his metaphor, played in Algeria under conditions of unusual physical risk.

Klauser in his field and Bourdieu in Algeria both make what Bourdieu would later call *unchosen choices*.[14] Each chooses in the sense of planning a course of action while having what an observer would regard as alternative choices. But, that observer exists outside the particular *illusio* of those in the field, like Achenbach who thinks what Klauser is doing is crazy. Achenbach believes that Klauser has a choice. From a perspective within habitus, there is no autonomous, cognitively rational choice. From the perspective of habitus, the flesh and blood choose, as the flesh and blood are risked in that choice.[15]

Bourdieu begins *The Logic of Practice* (1990) underscoring the falsity of dualisms between objectivity and subjectivity and rejecting any perspective that privileges one over the other. Humans choose subjectively and strategize, but their terms of choosing both objects of strategic action and modes of acting are disposed by lifetimes of participation in a field with its embodied practices, its relevant forms of capital, and its *illusio*. Klauser can imagine no way to be, existentially, other than to keep fighting, literally, to regain the fraternity membership without which he feels himself to be nothing. Again, the violence of Klauser's particular unchosen choices may be extreme (though hardly uncommon in the world as a whole), but is his logic of action that extreme?

A frequently expressed objection is that such a world seems deterministic, literally hopeless. Three responses can be offered. One returns to Elias' point quoted earlier (1996, p. 109)—that within any figuration, many people put together lives in the interstices. Or in Bourdieu's terms, people play the game required by a field while they are in that field, and many people play in multiple fields.

A different response observes that people's sense of determinism in their lives is one aspect of what Elias would call the psychogenesis of any figuration. An example is Lewis Hyde, writing here as a literary folklorist, commenting on ambivalences in the contemporary sense of determinism:

> If you see Michael Apted's film 35 *Up*, which follows a group of English men and women from age seven to age thirty-five, it is immediately clear the great degree to which the situation of birth determines the shape of a life. We talk of temperament, of genetic predispositions, of class and race and gender, of the family that raised us with its patterns of privilege and abuse going back generations—all of which were "there before birth" and all of which a person may try to uncover and understand when his or her path is mysteriously blocked. (Hyde 1998, p. 109)

Hyde presents Apted's film as documenting contemporary concerns about determinism; not as evidence that life is determined, but as showing how lives are interpreted. My point is that critiquing the determinism of a sociological theory requires a sociology of sensibilities toward determinism: People resist determinism in principle, but are quick to appeal to versions of it when their lives are "mysteriously blocked," as Hyde writes.

A third response is that life may actually be significantly determined, in the sense that people do make unchosen choices, especially when the stakes are high enough to require the most careful reflection. One of the saddest of any stories I know is Elias (1994) telling how his parents visited him in London in 1938 and then insisted on returning to Germany, where they would both die within a year. Elias tried to persuade them to remain in England, but his father argued that they who had "broken no laws" would be safe. Bourdieu (2000) associates habitus with what he calls "principles of vision and division," literally what we are able to see, and how we organize our perceptions according to what we value or devalue. Elias' parents' habitus offered no vision of how lawless the Nazis were, and it perpetrated an obsolete division between those who are lawless and thus vulnerable versus those who are lawful and thus safe. Their habitus was their fate.

Yet, Bourdieu might add that this blinkered vision is not odd but necessary, in order for a disposition to achieve embodied force, enacting the *illusio* of the field. Elias' father's earlier successes in business depended on the unquestioning faith in legal process that now dooms him; this is tragically ironic but neither illogical nor uncommon. A principal, practical value of habitus to the actor in a field is the liberation it provides from having to consider alternatives. Habitus enables immersion in the *illusio*: the unquestioned stakes of the game and the seriousness of winning those stakes. The complementary danger of habitus is that same lack of reflection, the danger being to both the person whose *illusio* is so narrowly focused and to those on whom that person will act.

Practices of Truth Games

Michel Foucault does not write about habitus, but he is probably the preeminent theorist of embodied practice, and his work can be read as a specification of Elias's psychogenesis: how culture produces bodies that are disposed to reproduce that culture. Foucault describes how engagement in practices—whether disciplinary practices described in his middle period of *Discipline and Punish* (1977), or the ethical disciplining practices of his final work (Foucault 2006)—forms subjects' bodies as means and medium of self-knowledge and knowledge by others. The effect of how people drill, labor, and engage in ethical practices is that they *know themselves*.[16] People hold particular knowledge as truth because, through repetitions of embodied practice, their flesh and blood have become the embodied affirmation of those truths. Institutions—hospitals, courts, factories, schools—routinize practices that imprint their knowledge schema onto bodies. Foucault's corollary to Bourdieu's unchosen choices is the effect that living, working, feeling, and often suffering in these institutions has on subjects' possible sense of themselves and their possibilities for action.

To return to the duelist Klauser, in what sense is he playing what Foucault (2006) would call a *truth game*? A truth game is a practice in which a judgment on one's body is also a judgment on one's self: that it is too fat or too thin, unsanctified or overly ascetic, productive or unproductive, healthy or ill, well governed and thus ethical or insufficiently governed, and in Klauser's case, courageous or lacking courage.[17] The stakes on the duel, in the military field of Germany in the decades around 1900, are not only the symbolic capital that enables future capital rewards of membership; equally at stake is the sense of self that derives from the solidarity imagined to exist only in that membership. Elias (1996) compares dueling to other societies' initiation ceremonies that require acceptance of pain and scarification. Submission to those rituals is a truth game, as surely as submission to competitive examinations is in rational-bureaucratic societies.

As to why people play truth games, Foucault seems in accord with other poststructuralists, especially psychoanalyst Jacques Lacan (2004) that selfhood is an empty shell. The development and maintenance of any sense of oneself require seeing and identifying with images of oneself. For Lacan, those images occur first in a mirror. For Foucault, images of a potential self occur in truth games that offer terms of judging fitness to be a self. The terms of the game might be educational, spiritual, economic, or ethical. Engagement is required, because the alternative is nothingness. Again, the emptiness in the ellipsis after Klauser's "I am…" marks the fear of losing the only terms in which a self can imagine affirming its own existence. That is one kind of response to this question of why people play truth games: to be or not to be.

A different response looks toward Bourdieu, following Elias: People play truth games because they seek the material and symbolic advantages that come with attaining certain positions in a field, and the truth game attests to fitness for those positions. Such action seems objectively strategic: Klauser seeks reentry into a fraternity because that is a career route. But strategies are the products of dispositions that have long since become second-nature. When Achenbach's incredulousness offers Klauser an opening to question whether he wants to continue with dueling, Klauser cannot perceive that as an opening. Within the dispositional structure that he has not simply acquired but that he has become—that is now the force of his embodiment—the one strategic line is inevitable.

A third answer to the question of why people play the truth games is that some people do not; they resist. Both Foucault and Bourdieu proclaim possibilities of resistance, yet resistance seems curiously residual to their conceptual schema and actual examples. Resistance is acknowledged and even romanticized in Foucault, but it is never accounted for and rarely given substantiation in examples.[18] Bourdieu's response would probably be his insistence that while habitus is durable, it is never determining. But neither Bourdieu nor Foucault seems interested in developing the possibility of what Elias called subjectivity in the interstices of truth games, a line of thought followed by Erving Goffman in his study of total institutions: "Our status is backed by the solid buildings of the world, while our sense of personal identity often resides in the cracks" (1961, p. 320).

My observation of contemporary Western societies follows Goffman. Unlike the hierarchical, top-down modeling of manners the Elias observed from early state formation through the Germany of the world wars, identities formed in various interstices may now predominate. Our theoretical space thus needs more capacity to handle multiplicity. Elias, Bourdieu, and Foucault may not presuppose the singularity of a body in their practices, but their examples predominantly treat bodies as singular. To enable our irregularly bounded theoretical space to conceptualize the multiplicity of practices in which bodies are enacted, this chapter needs different theorists, leading toward a different story.

Networks of Enacted Bodies

Emphasis on either habitus or truth games requires selves for whom participation in embodied practices makes sense, as those practices are molding the self and shaping its rationality. Other theorists shift the emphasis to how bodies are *enacted* within networks. The crucial practices to be observed are those of enactment, not body-selves reproducing external demands.

Annemarie Mol's major work is significantly titled *The Body Multiple* (2002), and the title's claim is well supported by the ethnographic materials she presents. Mol studies atherosclerosis as it is diagnosed and treated in a Dutch hospital. She describes the practices that take place in four sites: the pathology lab where arteries are examined to verify that surgical amputation was necessary; the clinic where patients describe symptoms, and their responses to template questions are used to determine their diagnosis; the angiography lab where the diagnostic gold standard is enacted by injecting dye and recording an x-ray image of how it disperses; and a Doppler imaging lab, where measuring the pressure of blood flow can produce different diagnoses from angiography, generating a contest over which actually is the gold standard.

Each of these sites *enacts*—the verb choice is crucial—its version of atherosclerosis. What a body *is* enacted, and enactments differ. A pathologist who invites Mol to look at a frozen section of an artery tells her:

> "Look. Now there's your atherosclerosis. That's it. A thickening of the intima.
> That's really what it is."
> And then he adds, after a little pause: "Under a microscope." (Mol 2002, p. 30)

That quotation could be the epigraph for each diagnostic site. Each site enacts atherosclerosis according to what its particular tools enable, relying on criteria that are materialized in these tools. Tools, clinicians, sometimes patients, and sometimes patients' amputated limbs all work together, and this combination of human and nonhuman actors (e.g., the microscope in the pathology lab) constitutes the actor-network.

The multiplicity of the body that Mol proposes is subtle and easily misunderstood, so it is worth quoting her frequent collaborator, John Law, for his careful gloss on exactly what the argument is. Law proposes a category of beings, in which bodies are prime candidates for inclusion, that he calls *material semiotic*: both material—fleshy—and signifying.[19] Culture is already material and semiotic in Elias' writing: material as the bandages on Klauser's head and semiotic as scars' capacity to signify within the interpretive scheme of that particular figuration. The stitches hold the flesh together; the scars require a form of reading.

Law describes Mol's contribution to understanding material-semiotic modes of being:

> It is tempting to say that these are different perspectives on a single disease. This, however, is precisely what Mol rejects. In material-semiotic mode, she argues that each practice generates its own material reality. This means that for atherosclerosis there are four actor-networks or realities rather than one. Then she says that how these relate together, if they do so at all, is a practical matter. Sometimes, and for a time, they may be coordinated into a single reality, but often this does not happen. So Mol's claim is counter-intuitive. In theory the body may be *single* but in practice it is *multiple* because there are many body practices and therefore many bodies. (Law 2007)

Law proceeds to discuss the problem of translation, which is such a core issue that some actor-network theorists propose *sociology of translation* as a preferred label for what they do (Callon 1986; Law 1999). In Mol's research, for the practical purpose of treating patients, the four sites in the same hospital have to coordinate their different enactments. There are different ways of accomplishing translations between sites, and those specifics are beyond this chapter's interest (Latour 1998; Law 2004). Suffice it to say that the politics of the hospital are enacted in translation practices—which site's version of atherosclerosis trumps who else's version, for what purposes. Those contests underlie Mol's significant phrase, *political ontology*: the recognition that multiple enactments of ontology become relatively stabilized, or not, in practices of translation, and these practices involve contests best described as political.

What matters most for this chapter's theoretical space is Law's and Mol's conceptualization of bodies as *perpetually being translated*. Law writes:

> Mol has…wash[ed] away a single crucial assumption: that successful translation generates a single co-ordinated network and a single coherent reality. Any such coherence, if it happens at all, is a momentary achievement. The logic is [Michel] Serres-like: most of the time and for most purposes practices produce chronic multiplicity. They *may* dovetail together, but equally they may be held apart, contradict, or include one another in complex ways.

> How do different realities relate together? How might we think of these
> partial connections? And then, a new question, how might this patchwork of
> realities be enacted in better ways? (Law 2007)[20]

Law's closing questions open new ways of understanding Elias' story about the unfortunate duelist, Klauser. What stories do, often too well, is engage readers with a character. Engagement with Klauser's plight or with Achenbach's future focuses on the single actor-network of the fraternity, because that network fills the central characters' horizon. Mol and Law recognize the presence of other actor-networks that are equally necessary for the action in the story to take place. These include at least the medical network, which bandages Klauser and restores his body to the fitness required for a second match, and the military network, which expects dueling as career preparation. In Elias' other stories of nonfraternity duels in which people are shot and killed, the legal network is crucial for its *work* of sustained inattention to what happens. Thinking of these as *networks* rather than as *fields* encourages recognition of the multiple actors and directs attention to relations between mutually supporting networks. Of course, thinking of them as fields also encourages other observations, including objective positions and contests over forms of capital accruing to these positions. A theoretical space has to be large enough for both ways of thinking and observing.

Mol and Law lead us to ask not what Klauser's habitus is—what embodied dispositions make dueling an unchosen choice for him—or what systems of discipline and self-knowledge prepare him to risk his body, or what truth games dueling satisfies, although each of these concerns remains; none is at all irrelevant. Mol and Law direct observation toward the duel as a practice of enacting. Just as atherosclerosis comes to be only under a microscope, so the student-soldier comes to be only in duels. Moreover, they open up the translation practices that determine which among the student's multiple body enactments will be the gold standard for evaluating the body; how all other practices (e.g., the student's academic work) are rendered secondary to the duel. Finally, the dueling body is understood as one of those rare moments when, to paraphrase Law's earlier quotation, a coordinated network (including universities that support the fraternities and forges that craft the rapiers) produces a reality that is remarkable in its coherence and singularity.

When the duel is understood as material-semiotic enactment within an actor-network, then German *culture* is not the explanatory principle of dueling but quite the opposite. Culture comprises a number of embodied practices that exhibit more or less coherence. What counts—to rephrase Elias' problem—is to study the interconnections between practices through which Germany sustained for so long a remarkably singular political ontology of the body. Regardless of which faction ruled, or who was killing whom, the singularity of a privileged body—both as habitus and as practices of enactment—was maintained from Bismarck through Hitler. Of course, in Germany during these decades there were, in reality, multiple bodies; as Elias writes, many embodied lives created in the interstices. But translation practices, as the enactment of what can be called German culture, were sufficiently stable for enough German bodies to be remarkably singular for decades, during which most other Germans regarded these warrior bodies as exemplary.

Mol self-consciously refrains from asking questions about how patients experience different sites of the hospital: what it means to be represented by enactments accomplished in one site and then translated to another.[21] She acknowledges those questions but places them beyond her scope. Mol's research, however, unavoidably poses the issue of the *lived experience* of being a body multiple. Not only must hospital actors do translation work in order to sustain its collegial order—the pathology lab must verify that the surgeons were correct to operate, the surgeons must produce a single diagnostic judgment from the sometimes conflicting reports of angiography and Doppler labs without impugning colleagues in either department, and so on. Patients also must do their translation work. One culmination of this work is signing a consent form for surgery; another is refusing surgery and seeking some therapeutic alternative, such as the walking therapy that Mol describes.

Walking therapy is remarkably effective at relieving the symptoms of atherosclerosis—the remarkability being that this therapy lacks any standard clinical rationale; it just works. The limitation of walking therapy seems to be its lack of coordination with the realities of bodies that are enacted in other clinical sites. Walking therapy does not translate, but it remains an option, more or less acknowledged. Elias might say that the walking body exists in an interstice. Patients have to decide whether they would rather try walking therapy or go to surgery. They must do their own translating. Understanding who chooses which way of living with atherosclerosis takes us back to questions of habitus.

To summarize our irregularly bounded theoretical space of possibilities: Elias provides an initial version of the body as a habitus that makes different ways of acting feel natural and compelling, including perpetrating violence on other bodies and accepting violence toward one's own body. Bourdieu places habitus within fields that include positions with access to different forms of capital. Contests over access to capital and what counts as capital are constant. Within these contests, bodies' different capacities for *illusio*—the ability to become caught up in pursuing the stakes of the game—predict success. Foucault emphasizes the internal contests of truth games, in which bodies evaluate their own fitness in an ethical sense. Bodies not only risk themselves, they also take care of themselves, yet self-care involves its own risks of failing to sustain a particular truth that is accepted as the measure of who the person ought to be.

Mol and Law open the theoretical space to the multiplicity of material-semiotic bodies that are enacted differently in different sites. These multiple bodies are translated with an ideal of producing single, coherent bodies, but translations at most reduce or manage multiplicity; they rarely produce total coherence and singularity. Because translations are generally partial, people live as bodies that are not incoherent, but might be called *sufficiently coherent*, with that sufficiency varying as bodies and their circumstances change.[22] Any coherence is always temporary, fragile, and contingent on what happens in multiple sites that, in Law's choice of verbs, sometimes dovetail and other times produce chronic multiplicity.

THE COMPANIONSHIP OF ALTRUISTIC BODIES

Elias' version of habitus foregrounds self-restraint stories. "The restraint exerted by social custom has largely turned into second nature and, thus, into self-restraint," he writes (Elias 1998, p. 187). Whether Elias is describing the brutality of Greek Olympic boxing, or German fraternity dueling, or warfare through the ages, using the body in acts of violence requires both overriding self-protective instincts and also exercising progressive restraints on the timing and degree of violence perpetrated on others. Bodies' adaptation to different perpetrations of violence is one way to tell the story of the civilizing process, but civilizing is also about enactments of *attractions* between bodies.[23] Shame and repugnance are movements *away from*; they mark avoidances and prohibitions. This dimension is one aspect of bodies' mutual relations, certainly. But shame and repugnance are counterbalanced by bodies' movement *toward*. Elias' shame/repugnance threshold needs to be complemented by an altruism/obligation threshold, for which this chapter needs a new story.

Many years ago a friend of mine proved to be the compatible donor for a family member who was dying of kidney failure and offered to donate her kidney. Some time later, she framed her story of the experience as a kind of joke. Her pre-surgical workup included being interviewed about her motives for donation, undoubtedly according to the hospital's ethics protocol. The key question, she said, was why she was consenting to donate a kidney.

"I don't really have much choice, do I?" she responded. In telling the story of this interview, she presented that tagline, "do I?" as a punch line. The humor was the "how could they be so silly" genre.

As I retell this story, now shaped by my memory, this tagline poses a rhetorical question, and laughter is only part of what this not-so-funny joke seems intended to elicit. The tagline expresses the force of the donor's embodiment: her moral will to undergo surgery and accept what surgery altered. The tagline placement acknowledges that this moral will, real as it is, is another of Bourdieu's unchosen choices, and the joke hinges on listeners recognizing that paradox.

This kidney-transplant story could be interpreted as a shame story in which the donor would have been ashamed to appear within her family if she had let her relative die. Most body stories can be told as shame stories, but the morally preferred telling foregrounds attraction. The body of the diseased relative *calls out* to the donor, and she responds to that call at considerable cost—not financial cost, at least in Canada, but the cost of taking a leave from work, costs of suffering the surgery, costs of long-term surgical effects—and risk to herself.

My interest is not to rehearse the altruism of donation (Diprose 2002; Titmuss 1997), but to consider this crucial aspect of bodies: how one body calls out to another, and how the imperative to respond can negate any rational, articulate accountability. This capacity and compulsion of bodies to respond to each other's call posit a body-in-relation, contrasting with the mistaken illusion that Elias (1998, p. 248) called *homo clausus*, the body as self-enclosed, existing independently. The body-in-relation is the final possibility that this chapter will bring into the irregularly bounded theoretical space that it has constructed, although by no means closing that space.

The process of bodies responding to the call of other bodies is a variation of Louis Althusser's (1971) *interpellation*. Althusser, using Lacanian psychoanalytic concepts to understand a persistent issue in Marxist thought, was concerned with how selves, or *subjects* in his usage, are "hailed" by "ideological state apparatuses" (ISAs). An ISA hails the *subject*, calling on it to acknowledge possessing the identity that the ISA requires. Ideological hailing typically involves some form of policing. The hail renders the subject's body vulnerable to others' claim upon it.[24]

Foucault may not use the language of interpellation, but his studies with Althusser are evident. Disciplinary knowledges—medical, economic, legal, and so forth—hail subjects through the medium of truth games, requiring them to know themselves as particular kinds of subjects. The genius of the truth game is that subjects develop a sense that they are hailing themselves, acting as the principles of their own ideological placement. But if my kidney-donation story is understood as being about interpellation, and if the foreground is altruism as a form of attraction between bodies, then we need Donna Haraway's version of interpellation with its potential for an ethics of bodies.

Haraway's project can be described as making life welcoming and habitable to the broadest multiplicity of entities and beings. Species differences reflect not only biological differences, but also different forms of life in Wittgenstein's sense. Technoscience, especially the biological and life sciences, creates an increasing density of contact among species: viruses, bacteria, cells, seeds, animals, and humans. The same can be said of globalization. That increasing density underscores what, for Haraway, has always been fundamental: Life depends on living together in relations of *companionship*. Companions shape each others' bodies, mutually (Haraway 2003, 2008).

Interaction is too thin a word for what is at stake in a world in which the quality of companionships is a matter of survival; *interaction* seems like an optional activity for beings that could be complete in themselves. Haraway emphasizes that the opposite of companionship is failure to survive. To be *together* or not to be, that is Haraway's question. Thus, the relation between someone with kidney failure and a potential donor is a good companionship story. What seems mistaken in the hospital's question about the kidney donor's motives is the presupposition of the donor as existing independently of the recipient, as *homo clausus*. The donor's response posits an inescapable companionship.

Companionships may rarely be symmetrical, but they need to be unfailingly respectful. One of Haraway's (2004, p. 144) teaching tales for companionships between differently embodied beings is a 1962 science fiction novel, *Memoirs of a Spacewoman*, about space exploration "told from the point of view of a woman xenobiologist and communications expert named Mary." Mary's adventures lead Haraway to reconceptualize interpellation:

> In Althusser's sense, in *Memoirs of a Spacewoman* subjects are interpellated, or hailed, into being in a world where the law is not the policeman's "Hey, you!" [Althusser's example] or the father's "Thou shalt not know," but a deceptively

gentler moralist's command, "Be fruitful and multiply; join in conversation, but know that you are not the only subjects. In knowing each other, your worlds will never be the same." (Haraway 2004, p. 145)

Haraway thus offers interpellation *without* ISAs, because there is neither ideology as ideas reflecting the interests of some and the exploitation of others, nor is there a state as a central locus of interpellations. Bodies are still hailed, and bodies become their full material-semiotic being in the process of hail and response. But the ethical importance of Haraway's revision of Althusser is that subjects have significant choice whether to be hailed by the policeman/father or by the "gentler moralist's command."

Haraway's starting point is the material-semiotic reality of bodies: "Organisms emerge from a discursive process" (2004, p. 67). Her more radical recognition is that "humans are not the only actors in the construction of the entities of any scientific discourse"; machines and "other partners" are also "active constructors" (2004, p. 67). "The whole point about discursive construction," Haraway writes (2004, p. 67), "has been that it is *not* about ideology. Always radically historically specific, always lively, bodies have a different kind of specificity and effectivity; and so they invite a different kind of engagement and intervention." Lest there be any doubt that this engagement and intervention are ethical, she says a bit later in the same essay, "Lives are built; so we had best become good craftspeople with the other worldly actants in the story" (2004, p. 68).

Haraway opens up a different understanding of my organ donation story that takes seriously the curiosity of the term, *compatible donor*. The donor was not the family member who was closest to her dying relative in either affective relation or degree of kinship. Rather, their closeness was enacted by a technology that rendered them *compatible* according to its strict practices of categorization and measurement. In Mol's terms, one of the donor's multiple bodies was enacted as the donation-compatible body; medical technology rendered two bodies *compatible* as a material-semiotic relation. The donor-recipient relationship, or companionship, is made possible and then enacted by what Haraway describes as "machines and other instruments that mediate exchanges at crucial interfaces and that function as delegates for other actors' functions and purposes" (2004, p. 68). The recognition of that delegation of functions and purposes can be heard in the donor's response that she really has no choice. At most, she allowed herself to be chosen. She recognized the legitimacy of the medical interpellation of her body as an ethical imperative. The habitus that is relevant to becoming a donor has as much to do with the *illusio* of medical science—taking its stakes seriously—as with the *illusio* of family obligation.

Prospective to donation, medicine tells a story about two bodies: a body that will die without the transplant, and a body that can offer the transplant with manageable risk. Only within a figuration in which technoscience counts as legitimate rationality would such a story make sufficient sense for it to be a basis of ethical interpellation. The relevant predisposition is not only family obligation. It is also medical credibility; that is, the capacity to understand one's embodied self as being what medicine enacts. Donation requires trusting not only the surgeons who will mediate the gift relation, but also the whole array of machinery and pharmaceuticals that, as Haraway says, "function as delegates for other actors' functions and purposes" (2004, p. 68, quoted earlier).[25]

Interpellation speaks not only in the voice of the policeman, but also in the voice of Haraway's "gentler moralist" (2004, p. 145, quoted earlier), intoning: "Know that you are not the only subjects." Haraway notes that *interpellation* derives from the past participle *interpellatus*, or "interrupted in speaking" (2004, p. 117). The donor body is interrupted in its everyday life by the need of a relative. The call of this need is enacted by an actor-network that diagnoses the disease, prognosticates a future without transplantation, and designates compatibility. The response to the call depends on an *illusio* of the network's capacity to construct a relationship that is material and semiotic; a relationship of blood, tissues, and operating rooms, and also of symbolic gift exchange. One moral of the story is that for organ donation to happen, a lot more of what Haraway calls "other worldly actants" (2004, p. 68, quoted earlier) have to be good companions than just the human actors.

The foundational theorist of this gentler-moralist interpellation story may not be Althusser but rather G. H. Mead (1967; see also Crossley 2001, 2006). As Mead theorizes the possibility of human communication, the body that speaks also hears itself speaking, and the speech signal calls out the same response in the speaker that is called out in the listener. The speech relation has the possibility of being intercorporeal because it is also *intra*corporeal: Speakers must be bodies that first hear and then respond to what they hear. Or, a body is called by the calls it directs toward others.

Bourdieu seems to echo Mead when he writes, "The body believes in what it plays at" (1990, p. 73). In communication, two bodies each believe in what they play at together; their joint activity elicits their belief. Mead's body is necessarily material-semiotic; the symbols with which it signals and communicates require, and then act upon, a material body that speaks, hears and sees others, and hears itself. As long as the body that calls out has this Meadian capacity to hear itself and to be affected by its own call, interpellation can never be linear. To interpellate the other is to experience that interpellation calling oneself. If interpellation lends itself to a repressive form of policing, it is also a practice that makes companionship inescapable.

The kidney donor recognized that she had no choice because although she could choose not to donate, she could not choose to be dis-interpellated. There really is no question of why people respond to interpellations. The interpellating call can never be called back; it cannot be unheard. But once the interpellation is understood as not necessarily policing, it becomes not a lack of choice, but rather a possibility of companionship.

CULTURE AS EMBODIED PRACTICE:
A SELF-ANALYSIS

One problem with irregularly bounded theoretical spaces of possibility is how to end discussion without the performative contradiction of closing the space. One solution may be found in Bourdieu's (2008) *Sketch for a Self-Analysis*, which creates a new genre of theorizing. Bourdieu declares it is emphatically "not an autobiography" (2008, p. v) and seeks—his success is not an issue here—to avoid the tropes of conventional memoir. Bourdieu intends to apply his conceptual apparatus to his own life, understanding his choices as products of the habitus he brought to the fields that he was cast into: the positions available and the hierarchy of subfields. That model invites similar self-analyses from each reader, and I will use it as a form of conclusion.

Each of the theorists in this chapter causes me to reconsider how I have lived during the particular historical moments that Weber would call the fate of my times. Elias, beyond his analytical contribution of showing that self and society require no reconciliation because each is the ground of possibility for the other, is a great theorist of violence. More of my life than I generally reflect on has been structured by the violences of my times. Coming of age during the Vietnam War meant necessarily being interpellated by that war: how one responded, and there were options, defined one's identity. Elias' shame/repugnance threshold seemed to open in both directions: To refuse service in the war carried a stigma, but as the war became more obviously pointless in its destruction, participation was shameful. Balancing on the threshold, I accepted an army commission through undergraduate reserve officer training, but then remained in the reserves and, with considerable luck of timing, stayed out of Vietnam. Decades later, my moral confidence about not fighting is that of a body no longer subject to the stakes of that game then. In the 1960s, I was anything but confident.

Bourdieu also helps me to understand situations of relative failure in my life. As an adolescent, I never had the feel for competitive sports. I performed the moves of games without the habitus of one who participates un-self-consciously in the *illusio*. The fault, Bourdieu would counsel, is not in ourselves but in our attempts to fit into fields in which the seriousness of the stakes is not second-nature to us. Bourdieu offers comfort to all those oppressed by assertions that the stakes of particular fields have universal value. Rather than people judging themselves on their achievement of those stakes, Bourdieu recommends understanding the stakes as the means by which the few for whom such stakes are second-nature claim their superiority. I thus reframe some of my supposed failures as moral refusals of stakes I was unreflectively wise not to take seriously. And, humbly, I reframe any successes as the contingent vacancy of positions that my habitus prepared me for.

Foucault (1977) helps me to understand those periods of my life spent within disciplinary institutions. The twin principles of military life are panopticism—there is no privacy; a soldier in basic training is always under surveillance—and drill. Drill finds its formal practice on parade fields, but as a generalized category means doing things repeatedly according to precisely prescribed routines of practice, drill comprises all the routines that make up the military day, from getting dressed and making beds to cleaning rifles and polishing boots (in the uniform of those days). Training consists of embodying these routines, making them second-nature. In my case, the practices never had the institutionally desired effect. Here, Bourdieu complements Foucault: I found the army less effectively authoritarian than the secondary school I had attended, and that facilitated my resistance to the military *illusio*.

Yet—and here is my own experiential truth of habitus—decades later those disciplinary practices remain with me as routines I recognize my body is impelled to follow, sometimes usefully and other times to my dismay. The routines enact me. Like Freud's *das Es, it* acts. And I realize that I am *it*, and *it* is part of who I am, durably and in whatever field I am transposed to. My body in early old age is the sedimentation of all the bodies it has practiced to be. Each of those bodies still acts, often unexpectedly and oddly in my present life, in a way I can describe only as kinetic: It moves with a volition that is undeniably of me but not strictly mine.

Mol and Law lead me to include in this socio-analysis observations of my affinity or nonaffinity with material objects, recollecting how objects enabled my enactments of my body. Those objects have not been mere tools that I used according to purposes already there before the object. The object shaped what became the purpose, and my use of the object became an aspect of my self. I was as content as I was in the military, in part, because I had grown up with guns, both rifles and pistols; one of my uncles was a great pistol collector. But habitus takes unpredictable forms: My interest was solely in target shooting; I never considered hunting. Thus, my feel for the military game extended only as far as the target range; I had no *illusio* for combat or for the military as a career—I was like Achenbach, finding all of it crazy. My superior officers would see me as having potential, only to be frustrated by what to them was my unpredictable disengagement. Others could have interpreted my actions as a sociologist's irrepressible tendency to stand back and analyze whatever is going on—Bourdieu's scholastic disposition, expressed in the wrong field.

Besides objects I have held, worked with, and to which I have shaped my embodiment, including rifles and typewriters, there are also objects that have enacted my being as an actionable reality for different institutional purposes: the 1960s computers that scored my SATs tests leading to university admission, medical imaging scanners that diagnosed my cancer in the 1980s, the airplanes that have made my body readily moveable in space and thus enabled my career since the early 1990s. These machines have each enacted one of my multiple bodies for different institutional purposes. They have been jealous machines, each claiming priority over who I am and what I should do.

Finally, Haraway leads me to ask which voice of interpellation I have chosen to hear at different moments in my life: that of the policeman or what she calls the "deceptively gentler moralist" (2004, p. 145, quoted earlier). What makes the moralist *deceptively* gentler? Perhaps, and I emphasize the interpretation is open, because while the moralist's interpellation exhorts gentler relations with companions, that voice is scarcely less directive in what it calls bodies to be. This chapter's two stories, the duelist and the kidney donor, mirror each other insofar as their respective protagonists each acts without the ability to give a reasoned account of his or her own action. For the kidney donor, no less than for Klauser, necessity will "hardly ever [be] expressed at a higher level of synthesis" (Elias, 1996, p. 111, quoted earlier). Those who study stories of embodied practice do well to heed Bourdieu's advice "to avoid asking of it more logic than it can give" (1990, p. 86).

The two mirroring stories seem to have clear ethical implications. Yet, when I seek any principle of an ethics of bodies in these stories, only the obvious emerges: Klauser acts against bodies, including his own as much as any opponent's; the kidney donor is being fruitful and multiplying. Why anyone chooses one form of life over another returns us to fields, habitus, and unchosen choices. Human fate is to be thrown into a field and either to acquire the *illusio* of that field, or to be lucky enough to find a different field, or to live a life of estrangement: Bourdieu's *hysteresis*. Habitus seems considerably a matter of moral luck (Nussbaum 2001)—the contingency of which fields interpellate bodies, when those bodies are most in need of identity. The ethics of bodies may never be determined by that luck, but some life courses are comparatively more difficult to change.

Culture is practices, at least in the theoretical space constructed in this chapter. Bodies practice forcefully, and in that, embodiment gains force. Getting on with life requires practices that fit bodies to fields in which those bodies feel comfortable. But to get on with life is not necessarily to live a good life. There are also practices of recognition: to recognize how bodily practices affect people who do not share the *illusio* of the field and feel victimized by the pursuit of that field's stakes, and to recognize how people like Klauser are victimized by the costs of their unquestioning participation in a field. These recognitions require an empathic embodiment that might be called communicative (Frank 1995), companionable (Haraway 2004), or maybe simply moral.

NOTES

1. Bourdieu 1990, p. 77.

2. Bourdieu's descriptive term for the disjunction between habitus as disposition to act in certain ways and the objective demands of a field is *hysteresis*. See Bourdieu 1990, p. 62.

3. "The body is not mute, but it is inarticulate; it does not use speech, yet begets it." Frank 1995, p. 27.

4. Elias' duelists could not contrast more dramatically with the boxers described by Wacquant (2004). In boxing, injury to the body is expected, but is regarded as a side effect of engaging in the sport. Boxers are taught to protect the physical capital of their bodies, and appropriate equipment and rules support protection. Dueling is organized to incur injury. But the most significant difference is that duelists need to prove themselves only a limited number of times, and then the symbolic capital gained in those engagements is readily convertible to enhance careers in which duels become undesired background possibilities. Boxers seek to have careers boxing, and at the end of those careers, their opportunities for converting capital are scarce to nonexistent (Wacquant 2004, p. 59).

5. Klauser's willingness to duel again could also be explained in terms of Collins' (2004) interaction ritual chains. The duel models the core elements that define an interaction ritual: group assembly, barriers to outsiders, mutual focus of attention, and shared mood (2004, p. 48). These conditions generate a strong sense of group solidarity, which increases the emotional energy of individuals, as well as their investment in membership

symbols—fraternity membership leading to military rank—and "a sense of rightness in adhering to the group" (2004, p. 49). For Klauser, dueling again is a moral matter. Collins provides the crucial element that both Elias and Bourdieu leave implicit: the *emotional energy* that animates practice, giving risky practice its particular rationality.

6. In Collins' (2004) terms, the emotional energy generated by prospective engagement in the ritual overrides the pain and fear.

7. These comments echo Bourdieu's frequent critiques of the inability to recognize or represent the imperative character of action that is caught up in practical engagement. I find it significant that Bourdieu begins his last major work, *Pascalian Meditations* (2000), discussing the "scholastic disposition." Bourdieu seems to have understood what distinguishes academic observation and analysis from practical engagement as the beginning point of his contributions.

8. For examples, see Isherwood 2008. Elias' own milieu was that of the culturally assimilated upper middle class, some distance from either dueling fraternities or Isherwood's world.

9. Thus, Elias changes the preferred designation of his sociological approach from figurational sociology to *process sociology*. See Mennell and Goudsblom 1998.

10. See Swartz 1998 for a selection of Bourdieu's changing definitions of habitus. For a systematic review of the concept of habitus, see Maton 2008.

11. Most notably *economic* capital, which is the most general form and the medium through which other forms of capital are converted; *cultural* capital as what a person knows; *social* capital as those whom a person can call upon; and *symbolic* capital, not restricted to honors and status but denoting a generalized capacity to recognize the relevant form of capital in a field—an ability that distinguishes actors. For a systematic overview of Bourdieu's shifting understanding of forms of capital, see Swartz 1998.

12. Atkinson (2003) uses Eliasian figurational theory to interpret tattooing as a contemporary practice of bodily markers of investment in the stakes of different games.

13. Again, Collins' (2004) concept of emotional energy explains how these feelings are ramped up. Collins usefully shifts the emphasis of disposition formation from early in life—family of origin—to ongoing practices and, especially, participation on rituals (see note 4).

14. Unchosen choice is a frequent refrain in Bourdieu (2000).

15. Like almost all the ideas in this chapter, this one has been developed in the contemporary literature on the sociology of bodies. Mellor and Shilling (1997) call these choices "carnal knowledge," which is their descriptive term for volitions of the body that are not wholly accessible to reflective thought.

16. On the centrality of question of how subjects come to know themselves through practices, see especially Rabinow and Rose 2003.

17. As Foucault (Rabinow and Rose 2006, pp. 2–3) wrote about himself: "Foucault has now undertaken...to study the constitution of the subject as an object for himself: the formation of procedures by which the subject is led to observe himself, analyze himself, interpret himself, recognize himself as a domain of possible knowledge. In short, this concerns the history of 'subjectivity,' if what is meant by the term is the way in which the subject experiences himself in a game of truth where he relates to himself."

18. Foucault's clearest example of resistance is the story of the vagrant Béasse, whose insolence to the court reads like a stand-up comedy routine; Foucault (1977, pp. 290–291). On my reading, Bourdieu's best examples of resistance occur in his discussions of women's recognition of male pretensions (Bourdieu 2002).

19. The idea of material semiotic entities is also developed by Donna Haraway (2004).

20. For an extended example, see Mol and Law 2004.

21. Patients do not enter the pathology lab, but they do read pathology reports about their amputated limbs.

22. Certainly, many patients report intense frustration at the inability of medical specialists to coordinate their respective enactments; that is, failing to provide a diagnosis and treatment plan that allows the patient to experience him- or herself as sufficiently coherent.

23. Elias does tell this story in his discussion of courtly love in *The Civilizing Process* (1984). But attraction as a principle seems secondary to shame/repugnance.

24. A useful example is how people waiting in a physician's office are hailed to become *patients* by the time they reach the examining room; see Waitzkin 1991.

25. The increasing prevalence of robotic surgery makes this delegation more dramatic. The surgeon may well be in another room, another city, another country. Machines mediate all exchanges between the bodies of surgeons and patients.

REFERENCES

Althusser, Louis. 1971. "Ideology and Ideological State Apparatuses" in *Lenin and Philosophy and Other Essays*. New York: Basic Books.

Atkinson, Michael. 2003. *Tattooed: The Sociogenesis of a Body Art*. Toronto: University of Toronto Press.

Bourdieu, Pierre. 1990 [1980]. *The Logic of Practice*. Cambridge, UK: Polity Press.

———. 2000. *Pascalian Meditations*. Stanford, CA: Stanford University Press.

———. 2002. *Masculine Domination*. Stanford, CA: Stanford University Press.

———. 2008. *Sketch for a Self-Analysis*. Chicago: University of Chicago Press.

Bourdieu, Pierre, and Lois Wacquant. 1992. *An Invitation to Reflexive Sociology*. Chicago: University of Chicago Press.

Callon, Michel. 1986. "Some Elements of a Sociology of Translation: Domestication of the Scallops and the Fishermen of Saint Brieuc Bay." Pp. 196–233 in *Power, Action and Belief: A New Sociology of Knowledge?* edited by John Law. Sociological Review Monograph. London: Routledge.

Collins, Randall. 2004. *Interaction Ritual Chains*. Princeton, NJ: Princeton University Press.

Crossley, Nick. 2001. *The Social Body*. London: Sage.

———. 2006. *Reflexive Embodiment and Social Change*. Maidenhead, UK, and New York: Open University Press.

Diprose, Rosalyn. 2002 *Corporeal Generosity: On Giving with Nietzsche, Merleau-Ponty, and Levinas*. Albany: State University of New York Press.

Elias, Norbert. 1984. *The Civilizing Process*. Rev. ed. Cambridge, UK: Blackwell.

———. *Reflections on a Life*. 1994. Oxford: Polity Press.

———. *The Germans*. 1996. New York: Columbia University Press, 1996.

———. 1998. *On Civilization, Power, and Knowledge: Selected Writings*. Chicago: University of Chicago Press.

Foucault, Michel. 1977. *Discipline and Punish*. New York: Vintage.

———. 2006. *Ethics: Subjectivity and Truth*. Edited by Paul Rabinow. New York: New Press.

Frank, Arthur W. 1990. "For a Sociology of the Body: An Analytical Review." Pp. 36–102 in *The Body: Social Process and Cultural Theory*, edited by Mike Featherstone, Mike Hepworth, and Bryan S. Turner. London: Sage.

———. 1995. *The Wounded Storyteller: Body, Illness, and Ethics*. Chicago: University of Chicago Press.

Goffman, Erving. 1961. *Asylums: Essays on the Situation of Mental Patients and Other Inmates*. New York: Anchor.

Haraway, Donna. 2003. *The Compaion Species Manifesto: Dogs, People, and Significant Otherness*. Chicago: Prickly Paradigm Press.

———. 2004. *The Haraway Reader*. London: Routledge.

———. 2008. *When Species Meet*. Minneapolis: University of Minnesota Press.

Hyde, Lewis. 1998. *Trickster Makes This World: Mischief, Myth, and Art*. New York: North Point Press.

Isherwood, Christopher. 2008 [1946]. *The Berlin Stories*. New York: New Directions.

Lacan, Jacques. 2004. *Ecrits: A Selection*. New York: Norton.

Latour, Bruno. 1988. *Science in Action: How to Follow Scientists and Engineers Through Society*. Cambridge, MA: Harvard University Press.

Law, John, ed. 1999. *Actor Network Theory and After*. Sociological Review Monograph. London: Wiley-Blackwell.

———. 2004. *After Method: Mess in Social Science Research*. London: Routledge.

———. 2007. "Actor Network Theory and Material Semiotics." http:www.heterogeneities. net/publications/Law-ANTandMaterialSemiotics.pdf

Maton, Karl. 2008. "Habitus." Pp. 49–65 in *Pierre Bourdieu: Key Concepts*, edited by Michael Grenfell. London: Acumen.

Mead, George Herbert. 1967. *Mind, Self, and Society*. Chicago: University of Chicago Press.

Mellor, Phillip A., and Chris Shilling. 1997. *Re-forming the Body: Religion, Community, and Modernity*. London: Sage.

Mennell, Stephen, and Johan Goudsblom. 1998. "Introduction." Pp. 1–45 in Norbert Elias, *On Civilization, Power, and Knowledge: Selected Writings*. Chicago: University of Chicago Press.

Mol, Annemarie. 2002. *The Body Multiple*. Durham NC: Duke University Press.

Mol, Annemarie, and John Law. 2004. "Embodied Action, Enacted Bodies: The Example of Hypoglycaemia." *Body & Society* 10 (2–3): 43–62.

Nussbaum, Martha. 2001. *The Fragility of Goodness: Luck and Ethics in Greek Tragedy and Philosophy*. Cambridge, UK: Cambridge University Press.

Rabinow, Paul, and Nikolas Rose. 2003. "Introduction: Foucault Today." Pp. vii–xxxv in *The Essential Foucault*, edited by Paul Rabinow and Nikolas Rose. New York: New Press.

Swartz, David. 1998. *Culture and Power: The Sociology of Pierre Bourdieu*. Chicago: University of Chicago Press.

Titmuss, Richard. 1997. *The Gift Relationship: From Human Blood to Social Policy*. New York: New Press.

Turner, Bryan S. 1984. *The Body and Society*. Oxford: Blackwell.

Wacquant, Loïc. 2004. *Body & Soul: Notes of an Apprentice Boxer*. New York: Oxford University Press.

Waitzkin, Howard. 1991. *The Politics of Medical Encounters: How Patients and Doctors Deal with Social Problems*. New Haven, CT: Yale University Press.

CHAPTER 27

··

MUSIC SOCIOLOGY
IN A NEW KEY

··

LISA MCCORMICK

MUSIC is often referred to as a "performing art" along with theatre and dance. This is because music is commonly defined as organized sound, real or imagined, that is perceived to unfold in time rather than in space (Boorman 1999:405). Some would go so far as to claim that music "does not exist until it is performed" (Britten 1999:177). And yet one seldom gets this impression from the literature in the sociology of music. The problem is not that performers have somehow been overlooked. Scholars have produced an abundance of empirical studies that analyze musicians in their social contexts across an impressive range of genres, historical periods, and geographical locations. The conspicuous absence I am pointing to is the issue of performance. This concept has been central to social theories of action from Parsons' role theory to Goffman's dramaturgical metaphor, as well as postmodern theories of gender. Yet it remains curiously underdeveloped in the study of cultural forms, even for performing arts such as music.

My contention is that this is not a mere oversight, but a symptom of a more fundamental theoretical problem. Since Adorno, scholarship in the sociology of music has been dominated by an economic framework which I call the "production/consumption paradigm." This orthodoxy has had its benefits. It triggered a growth spurt in sociomusical studies by affording insights into previously unexplored aspects of music-making. The economic vocabulary also helped legitimize research on music in the eyes of those more inclined to promote a positivist sociology at a distance from the humanities. But the paradigm has serious limitations that must be addressed, especially now that it has started to creep into other disciplines, even musicology. The major shortcoming, in my view, is that this analytic framework can only construe music as a static object, rather than as a dynamic and inherently social process. The more obvious targets for this accusation are Bourdieu and the production of culture perspective. But I will demonstrate that the same logic defines Becker's art worlds approach, despite its association with symbolic interactionism. While the production/consumption paradigm has generated important research, it is rarely about the music and is usually only cultural in a weak sense. Having relegated culture to merely a dependent variable or a residual category, its central role in musical life has yet to be fully explored.

In this chapter, I explain how we have arrived at the current state of affairs. I begin by tracing the history of the production/consumption paradigm through its appearance in key texts, showing how it changes as it passes from Adorno and Bourdieu to the American production of culture perspective. The next section is a thematic overview of the literature where—to offer an alternative to the production/consumption dichotomy—my survey is structured using common operational definitions of music, namely, as a *text*, as the *product* of a social world or industry, as a *resource* in social action, and as *performance*. Through a discussion of representative studies in each vein, I identify both the strengths of established research agendas and the blind spots that reveal the need for a more cultural approach. Among the most promising new developments in this direction is the growing interest in performance that presents an opportunity not only to advance the study of music, but also to engage with the core theoretical issues in sociology.

The Production/Consumption Paradigm

The sociology of music is hardly a new development. Since the beginning of the discipline, scholars have found music not just "good to think with," but good for thinking through some of their most celebrated theories. Georg Simmel ([1882] 1968), who wrote extensively about culture and aesthetics over the course of his life, published his first essay on the origin of music. Max Weber ([1924] 1958) frequently wove in musical examples into his essays on religion, and he devoted an entire treatise to a comparative historical study of rationalization in music. Maurice Halbwachs ([1939] 1980) included a piece on musicians in his seminal work on collective memory, which Alfred Schutz ([1951] 1964) later critiqued to develop the concept of the "mutual tuning-in relationship" that he believed was fundamental to all human communication (p. 161). And in his later years, Elias (1993) examined the life and personality of W. A. Mozart in the context of his work in court society and the civilizing process.

But it was only with T. W. Adorno that a "sociology of music" proper took shape. He was the first to promote music from the status of an off-beat "case study" to a primary research focus in its own right.[1] Adorno was a prolific writer, and of his sizeable published oeuvre, over half was about music. This includes studies of specific composers such as Mahler (Adorno [1960] 1992), Berg (Adorno [1968] 1991), and

Wagner (Adorno [1952] 2005), as well as the programmatic *Introduction to the Sociology of Music* (Adorno [1962] 1976) published later in his career. But his genre of choice was the polemic essay, and those that are best known among sociologists are those that do not cast him in the most favorable light. His criticism of jazz (Adorno [1933] 2002; [1936] 2002), popular music (Adorno [1938] 1991; [1941] 2002), and the culture industry (Adorno [1963] 1991; Horkheimer and Adorno [1944] 2000) are easily—and regularly—read as elitist and reactionary. The tendency to see him as an infuriating embarrassment, along with the musicological complexity of his writing, have compromised Adorno's sociological legacy. This is regrettable because it has prevented us from recognizing how much we have inherited from him. Not only did he outline many of the issues that continue to fascinate researchers in the field, but he also provided the framework scholars still use to investigate them.

In the very first essay he published with the Institute for Social Research, Adorno ([1932] 2002) invoked the language of production and consumption to analyze the social situation of modern music and understand how industrial capitalism had completely transformed musical culture. Not only had distinction between "serious" and "light" become less important than music's relation to the market; the tension between art and popular genres had also been ratcheted up to twist what had previously been a relationship of renewal and exchange into a radical antipathy. The first part of the essay concerns production, which refers mainly to composition, while the second part focuses on its complement, consumption, which occurs when music is heard by an audience. But equally important for understanding music's social role was "reproduction," a term he uses instead of "performance" to refer to the realization of the musical score:

> The alienation of music from society is reflected in the antinomies of musical production: it is tangible as an actual social fact in the relation of production to *consumption*. Musical *reproduction* mediates between these two realms. It serves production, which can become immediately present only through reproduction, otherwise it would exist only as a dead text or score; [reproduction] is further the form of all musical consumption, for society can participate only in the reproduced works and never only in the texts. (p. 411)

For Adorno, the capitalistic process had effectively ensnared both the composer and the performer, forcing each to side either with society (the market) or the music. For the composer, resisting commodification amounted to self-imposed exile; society simply had no use for noncommercial music. For the performer charged with realizing the reified work, commodification could only be resisted by stifling artistic licence and strictly executing the score. The "reproductive freedom" that had been integral to musical culture even through the nineteenth century had disintegrated into the "interpretive personality" who manipulated the audience through creating the illusion that music could still be an "expression of individual human dynamics and private animation" (p. 416).

By the end of the 1960s, Adorno had fallen out of favor in sociological circles. But the economic framework he had employed in his analysis was not abandoned with him. Instead, it soon found new life in the hands of Bourdieu. Although he would have described himself as more of a Weberian than a Marxist, Bourdieu's repertoire of wordplay regularly exploited "production" and "consumption," with "capital" added into the mix as well. Nowhere is this more masterfully displayed than in his work on the arts that he analyzes as "fields of cultural *production*" (Bourdieu 1993, 1996). As it was for Adorno, the artist's orientation to the market is of key importance. "Producers of cultural goods" (artists) can invest in strategies to gain the economic capital that comes from commercial success in large-scale markets. But the rewards are potentially greater where the market is restricted and economic logic is inverted or "disavowed." Here agents operate in a "market of symbolic goods" where they compete for the prestige and recognition that brings more authority (and better economic return in the long run).

Bourdieu extends the economic analogy to the audience, as is clear from the opening lines of his magnum opus on the social determinants of taste:

> There is an economy of cultural goods, but it has a specific logic. Sociology endeavours to establish the conditions in which the consumers of cultural goods, and their taste for them, are produced, and at the same time to describe the different ways of appropriating such of these objects as are regarded at a particular moment as works of art.... (Bourdieu 1984:1)

He goes on to say that the fields of production and consumption are intimately related; the hierarchy of the arts, from ennobling to stigmatized, corresponds to a social hierarchy of consumers with varying degrees of "cultural capital," or competence in the codes necessary to decipher high art works. To illustrate how taste is used to create distinction and legitimize social differences, Bourdieu uses survey data that covers a broad range of cultural activities from food to furniture to film. But of them all, he singles out music as the best marker of social position: "Nothing more clearly affirms one's 'class', nothing more infallibly classifies, than tastes in music" (p. 18).

Performance, however, is completely absent from Bourdieu's adaptation of the production/consumption paradigm. He speaks of "reproduction," but to describe the perpetuation of social inequality inadvertently accomplished through cultural consumption. What Adorno had tried to capture with the same term was lost. Had he been more interested in more "performative" fields of cultural production than literature and visual art, he might have at least confronted this as an empirical issue. But the main reason for this blind spot is rooted in his theory of social action and the concept of *habitus*. Cultural producers and consumers navigate their respective fields according to their *habitus,* the "systems of durable, transposable dispositions" acquired through family upbringing and formal education. Embodied and largely nonreflexive, the *habitus* is often described as the "feel for the game"; they are the cluster of deep-seated inclinations that drive the actor's methods of accumulating symbolic or cultural capital. In this way, all action for Bourdieu is "unconsciously strategic"; the normative order and rational action are collapsed (Alexander 1995). Consequently, modes of communication, such as performance, which require external affective-symbolic environments and normative standards of evaluation, can only be seen in terms of exchange.

The production/consumption paradigm lost all its critical traces when it was taken up by the American "production of culture" perspective (for an overview see Peterson 1994; Peterson and Anand 2004). This "neutral position" toward culture industries was deliberate; they were to be approached as social facts rather than social problems (Santoro 2008a, 2008b). The economic framework was also stripped of any grand theoretical pretensions and recalibrated for a solidly empiricist and unapologetically middle-range research agenda. "Production" here is taken quite literally. As the central proponent of this perspective, Richard Peterson (1994) explains, the focus is on how cultural objects like music are shaped by the way they are manufactured and marketed, that is, on "how the content of culture is influenced by the [institutional and organizational] milieux in which it is created, distributed, evaluated, taught, and preserved." Less concerned with the intended meanings of a cultural object, this approach employs methods from industrial sociology and the sociology of organizations that are designed to "facilitate the uncovering of the so-called 'unintended' consequences of purposive productive activity" (pp. 164–165). For the last thirty years, the production perspective has been the mainstream in American sociology of culture. It has also been gradually making headway in Europe (Santoro 2008a).

Many of the classic studies from this perspective are, unsurprisingly, about the *production* of popular music (Peterson 1978, 1990; Peterson and Berger 1975). But the consumption side of the dichotomy has not been ignored. After Bourdieu, Peterson set out to glean "patterns of choice" from survey data to find relationships between social stratification and musical preferences. This exercise produced the "cultural omnivore" thesis (Peterson 1997b) that has gained considerable traction, having been observed longitudinally in the United States (Peterson and Kern 1996) and in other national contexts (Chan and Goldthorpe 2007; Sintas and Alvarez 2002; Sullivan and Katz-Gerro 2007). What is striking about this approach to consumption is that interpretation is again sidetracked. Peterson prefers to think of the individual consumer, taste groups, and even subcultures as *producers*, actively selecting and radically recombining cultural elements to symbolize identity. "Autoproduction," as he came to call it, comprises an important phase of the production cycle, as what was created informally is eventually reappropriated and commodified by the culture industry (Peterson 2000). This, along with the anti-Parsonian stance, helps explain why the issue of performance fails to emerge even in his analysis of authenticity in country music (Peterson 1997a). Because "culture" is defined in terms of fabricated objects rather than shared value commitments, Peterson reaches for concepts like "invented tradition" (Hobsbawm and Ranger 1983) rather than "impression management" (Goffman 1959) to discuss how the image of the authentic country singer has changed over time.

In each of its manifestations, the production/consumption paradigm has been attractive because it offered the analyst a way to think and talk about music that could challenge the commonsense view. For a truly sociological study of art to emerge, it was believed imperative first to jettison the ideologically loaded vocabulary of "art" and its corollaries "artist" and "artwork" and replace them with more neutral terms like "cultural forms," "cultural producers," and "cultural consumers." By adopting this vocabulary, sociologists thought they had effectively rejected the ideology of art, liberated themselves from its terms of analysis, and made these the very object of study (Inglis 2005). What I am arguing is that the production/consumption paradigm is neither as different nor as effective as it is held to be. Music's ontology is as much an object as it was for the aestheticians; the only difference is that sociologists prefer to explain this object in terms of real social forces rather than read or interpret it. The economic framework might help sociologists avoid the issues of meaning and performance, but it does not make them go away.

How, then, should the sociology of music proceed? I agree with DeNora (2004) that it is time to start taking *music* seriously. This would entail thinking about how musical properties enter into social processes. It would also involve paying "attention to the role of musical sound and its performance in social ordering in general and, more specifically, to the role of organised sound as a dynamic medium in relation to historical process and to cultural and political change" (p. 213). A good place to start is by looking at current research in a way that makes *music* the analytic focus. With this in mind, I have divided the discussion of the literature into sections that emphasize how music is defined—as a text, as a product, as a resource, and as performance. A further benefit of this arrangement is that it is easy to see how methodological choices follow from this presupposition. My hope is that this reorientation to the burgeoning field of music sociology will initiate a modulation out of the production/consumption paradigm and toward the "new key" alluded to in the title.

Music as a Text

For scholarship in this first category, "music" is primarily understood as a text created by an author. Through the formal analysis of its structure, the analyst attempts to demonstrate how musical properties can carry social meaning. Adorno's shadow looms large in this category. As we can see most clearly in his analyses of Bach and Schoenberg, he sought to demonstrate how musical form did more than just reflect or represent society; it reformulated social contradictions through musical materials. For this reason, composition for Adorno was as much a moral category as intelligence; composers were under "obligation to illuminate the truth of the subject's condition" in their historical moment through musical means (Witkin 1998:3). Those who abdicated this responsibility were guilty in his eyes of serving the forces of totalitarianism.

It is not all that surprising that Adorno's textual approach faded from sociology, not just because it demanded considerable knowledge of music theory, but also because the field lost its taste for this kind "grand theorizing" about the music/society nexus. What is more surprising is that musicology, a text-based discipline by definition, did not see fit to pick up his dropped thread until the 1990s (Subotnik 1991, 1996). The rediscovery of Adorno helped provide some impetus for the research program that came to be known as the "new musicology" that aims to find patterned similarities between musical and social structures.[2] Also in keeping with Adorno is the critical edge that often flavors analyses, if not from a Marxist angle, then from a Foucauldian, queer theory, or feminist perspective (see, e.g., Brett, Wood, and Thomas 1994; Leppert and McClary 1987; McClary 1991).

Not content to stay within the comfort zone of high art genres like opera, new musicologists have also investigated popular music including the blues (McClary 2000), heavy metal (Walser 1993), and rap (McClary 1998). They have also expanded the methodological kit to include such sophisticated tools as narrative analysis (Maus 1997) and semiotics (Agawu 1991). While it is now an established wing of the discipline, the "turn to the social" was initially met with hostility from more traditionally minded scholars (e.g., Rosen 1994; van den Toorn 1995). One might have expected a more enthusiastic response from music sociologists, but the reception has been lukewarm at best. Among the most damaging criticisms are an ignorance of developments in sociological theory directly relevant to their concerns and a failure to articulate the mechanisms through which music has social effects (see DeNora 2003; Martin 2006a).

Music as a Product

In many respects, scholarship in this vein positioned itself in opposition to that described in the first category. Leaving the "decoding" of texts to the humanities, the task here was to bring sociological analysis to bear on the social relations through which cultural objects are produced. This entailed importing insights from nonmusical theories and applying them to the social contexts in which music is created (Dowd 2004b). Those who favored a meso-level analysis assembled under the banner of "the production of culture." Many took Peterson's lead and analyzed the popular music industry (e.g., Dowd 2004a; Dowd and Blyler 2002; Lena 2006). But others found this a fruitful approach to art music, especially in combination with Bourdieu's theory of cultural capital. One of the classic studies of this kind is DiMaggio's (1982) institutional analysis of the founding of the Boston Symphony Orchestra and the Museum of Fine Arts in the nineteenth century. Another is DeNora's (1995) first book on the social construction of Beethoven's genius.

A different but sympathetic approach rooted was articulated by Howard Becker. Building on Everett Hughes' sociology of work and occupations, more than Herbert Blumer's symbolic interactionism (Chapoulie 1996), the "art worlds perspective" (Becker 1982) proposes that art is a form of collective action (Becker 1974) and that the artwork should be seen as the result of a complex division of labor. Recently, Becker (2006) has taken this insight to its most radical conclusion to argue that the "work itself" does not actually exist. He prefers to see the artwork as an endless series of choices made by actors, each of them selected from a range of possibilities defined by the art world. He calls this "the Principle of the Fundamental Indeterminacy of the Artwork":

> [I]t is impossible, in principle, for sociologists or anyone else to speak of the "work itself" because there is no such thing. There are only the many occasions on which a work appears or is performed or read or viewed, each of which can be different from all the others. (p. 23)

Like the production perspective, the art worlds approach stresses the importance of the social context, especially the occupational structure, in shaping the aesthetic values, interactions, status hierarchies, and personal identities of musicians. Another quality it shares with the production perspective is the aversion to "grand theory," offering instead methodological and analytical resources for empirical qualitative research. These have been fruitfully applied to a diverse range of musical worlds, including concert music (Gilmore 1988), American country and British punk (Lewis 1988), amateur orchestras, choirs, and bands (Finnegan 1989), barbershop singing (Stebbins 1996), jazz (Becker 2002; Lopes 2002), and blues clubs (Grazian 2003). In addition to securing canonical status in the United States, the art worlds approach has also been a successful export to Europe, finding passionate advocates in the United Kingdom (Martin 2006a, 2006b) and in France (Becker, Blanc, and Pessin 2004; Pessin 2004).

In terms of its analytical resources, the central concept in the art worlds approach is "convention." As Becker (1982) explains:

> People who cooperate to produce a work of art usually do not decide things afresh. Instead they rely on earlier agreements now become customary, agreements that have become part of the conventional way of doing things in that art. (p. 29)

To participate in an art world, one must learn how things are done so that action can be oriented accordingly. That does not mean, however, that there is no room for innovation. Convention might limit the range of possibilities, but it does not dictate choices:

> Conventions make collective activity simpler and less costly in time, energy, and other resources; but they do not make unconventional work impossible, only more costly and difficult. (Becker 1982:34–35)

In other words, commonly shared principles and norms constrain *and* enable action in the art world. It is in reference to them that choices are made at every phase of the artwork's construction, even if it is to deviate from them. But when it comes right down to it, conventions are really just labor-saving devices. For Becker, these norms guide social action, but in a purely pragmatic, nonsymbolic sense; they have more to do with efficiency than with meaning. Martin (2006b) praises this as a virtue that follows from dislodging musicians' activities from the discourse of art and relocating them in the discourse of work, allowing Becker to see "musicians' culture as a *consequence* of their occupational contingencies and problems (rather than considering the supposed qualities of the musical works themselves)" (p. 98, emphasis added). But I see this as an odd position for a symbolic interactionist to take. Culture does not participate in the definition of the situation, but is determined by it.

The unmasking of the artist as an ideological mirage is a fruitful analytic move; it brings into view the part of music-making that is an everyday, mundane job rather than the purely transcendent creative endeavor it is often made out to be. But because he is motivated more by a "congenital anti-elitism" than value-neutrality, Becker goes too far. He diminishes the moral valence of the social conventions that govern aesthetic activity, reducing everything to instrumental action. Becker's musicians do not act on the basis of the meanings social objects have for them; to the extent that they "take the role of the other" to select unusual materials or depart from conventions, it is to anticipate whether their deviance will be greeted as welcome innovation or resisted for fear that it might destabilize the existing network and threaten established positions.[3]

But this is not the only reason why, much to his dismay, the art worlds approach is sometimes mistaken for a more optimistic version of Bourdieu's field theory (Becker and Pessin 2006). Echoes of the *habitus* concept can also be found in his description of how aesthetic practices become so deeply internalized that action is sometimes nonreflexive:

> Conventions become embodied in physical routines, so that artists literally feel
> what is right for them to do....They experience conventional knowledge as a
> resource at a very primitive level, so deeply ingrained that they can think and act
> in conventional terms without hesitation or forethought. (p. 203–204)

Becker might come at it from a different direction, but the art worlds perspective winds up so close to the production/consumption paradigm that it is easily absorbed into its ranks.

MUSIC AS A RESOURCE

In this category, music is seen as a resource for accomplishing a social action, a tool for achieving an end. For Martin (2006a), looking at music in this way is the defining quality of the "sociological gaze"; what sociology explains that other disciplines cannot is how "music is *used* in a whole range of social situations, and the consequences of this" (p. 1). A major figure in this category is Bourdieu, who saw both the production and consumption of art as instrumental in the project of status accumulation and the legitimization of social hierarchies. While some scholars have built on Bourdieu's field theory in their studies of working musicians (Moore 2007; Prior 2008; Toynbee 2000), others have extended his work on the social functions of taste (Lizardo 2006a, 2006b). One of the more intriguing findings is that dislikes for particular musical genres can be just as important as preferences in drawing symbolic boundaries and enforcing social divisions (Bryson 1996; Savage 2006).

British cultural studies has also defined music as a resource. But rather than reproduce the class hierarchy as Bourdieu did, here it is utilized in "rituals of resistance" through which working class youth subcultures enact their rejection of the dominant class and resolve the hidden contradictions in the parent culture (Hall and Jefferson 2006a). Subcultures are defined through their lifestyle that, according to Cohen (1980), has two components: "plastic forms" (dress and music) and "infrastructural forms" (argot and ritual). While both are symbolic structures used to articulate what members stand for, music is said to be "plastic" because it was not produced by members themselves; it is a commodity that is selected for its resonance with subcultural values. In his ethnographic study of post-war "profane cultures," Willis (1978) explained this resonance in terms of "homology," the degree to which the "structure and content" of cultural items "parallel and reflect the structure, style, typical concerns, attitudes, and feelings of the social group" (p. 191). He articulated this symbolic fit by supplementing traditional ethnographic analysis with a sophisticated musicological one, identifying specific musical properties that facilitated the appropriation of early rock n' roll by the motorbike boys and progressive rock by the hippies. Hebdige's (1979) classic study also stands out for the unusually detailed analysis of the musical traditions that combined to create the "punk" style.

The golden age of subculture research in the Birmingham tradition was short-lived. After a burst of activity in the mid-1970s, it came under attack, most aggressively from within, for overestimating the importance of class, overlooking the role of women, overstating the strength of subcultural boundaries and members' identification, and ignoring the range of meanings cultural items can carry.[4] The emergence of rave culture in the mid-1980s provoked scholars to revisit the concept of subculture. But its reconsideration only served to pull it away from its Birmingham roots. Subcultures were sometimes reconceptualized as "club cultures," whether it was through the introduction of Bourdieu's concept of cultural capital (Thornton 1996) or postmodern theory (Muggleton 2000; Redhead 1997). A case was also made for abandoning the term entirely in favour of concepts like "neo-tribe" (Bennett 1999), which better reflects the unstable affiliations and flexible boundaries of groups centered on musical taste, and "scene" (Bennett and Peterson 2004), which better describes the texture of contemporary urban life, connections between geographically defined music communities and patterns of fan activity online. The "subculture" concept still has its defenders, however, who insist that inequality must remain central in studies of youth culture, music, and identity (Shildrick and MacDonald 2006).

Music has also been a tool in political projects. Cerulo (1993) has investigated how national anthems "constitute a nation's identity, the image of the nation projected by national leaders both to their constituents and to the world at large" (p. 243). The Eurovision Song Contest was created by the European Broadcasting Union to promote a pan-European identity, although nationalism, ethnicity, and sexual identity have regularly surfaced during this annual media event (see, e.g., Raykoff and Tobin 2007). High art genres have also been appropriated to serve ideological ends. Stamatov (2002) has shown how interpretive activists imposed political meanings on

Verdi's operas in the 1840s, while Buch (2003) has traced the complex history of Beethoven's Ninth Symphony that includes being selected to celebrate Hitler's birthday and serve as the anthem for the European Union. Whether political by design or politicized through social processes, music is often used to mobilize social movements and promote social change. Eyerman and Jamison (1998) have explored how songs can act as a cultural resource for collective action, whether as a repository of collective memory, a device to learn the values and goals of a movement, or as an expression of protest. Similarly, Roy (2002) has examined how academic elites and political activists created the genre of American "folk music" in an attempt to overcome racial boundaries institutionalized in the commercial music industry and in the broader society. The flipside of solidarity, however, is antagonism. The use of music as a weapon of interrogation in the global war on terror (Cusick 2008) reminds us that the state sometimes harnesses its power to incite, arouse, and inflict violence (Johnson and Cloonan 2008).

On a micro-level, music is used as a technology of the self, helping actors to focus attention, shift energy levels, reconstitute past experiences, and channel emotion in everyday life (DeNora 2000). It is also a resource in cognition, an instrument of control, and a material for social ordering (DeNora 2003). Music provides temporal structures for the experience of aging (Kotarba 2002) and narratives for fashioning gender identity (Rafalovich 2006; Whiteley 1997). Urban dwellers and commuters turn to iPods and other sound technologies to transform the urban environment, infusing nonplaces like highways, subway platforms, and airport terminals with meaning (Bull 2005). As these studies demonstrate, music can serve a function in every facet of social life.

Music as Performance

An emerging category in music scholarship focuses on the performativity of music. Small's (1998) terminology is instructive here; to discourage the tendency in Western culture to think of music as a thing, he suggests that we speak instead of "musicking," that is, as an activity that can take many different forms. Approaching music as an object has afforded great insight, but it has its limitations. Adorno ([1932] 2002) himself warned that a composer's "text is merely a coded script which does not guarantee unequivocal meaning" (p. 412). The realization of this "script" is an embodied action that necessarily involves interpretation. Even in traditions that use precisely notated scores, there are always ambiguities, omissions, and contingencies to which the performer must adjust, in the moment, in every encounter with a piece. Defining music as a product, even in the "art worlds" variant, also comes short of the mark, despite the promise of the "Principle of the Fundamental Indeterminacy of the Art Work." The creative process is not adequately described in terms of the division of labor; just as DeNora (2003) found that that production is intricately tied up with reception, neither can composition be completely untangled from performance. When music is defined as a resource in social action, there is performance, but not *musical* performance. Music remains a thing, and it is considered important only to the extent that it has produced measurable effects in a realm considered relevant to sociology, such as political protest, the construction of self-identity, or social stratification.

In the lifeworld of music-making, performance is of central importance to practitioners not just on the practical level, but on a philosophical one as well. As Dunsby (1995) astutely remarked, "getting all the right notes in the right order at about the right time is a good start," but beyond those initial steps, any "entanglement with music" involves facing a series of "riddles" that require reflection, rumination, and risk (pp. 7–8). Musicians spend countless hours in the rehearsal studio not just to improve their odds on a particular performance occasion, but also because it is through their interpretive stances that the "sonic self" (Cumming 2000) is constructed, displayed, and judged by various audiences.

Studying performance empirically presents considerable challenges because of its ephemeral nature. In musicology, this problem is compounded in the study of historical performance practice, where evidence is both sparse and contradictory.[5] The few primary sources that survive are suggestive at best because they were only ever meant to supplement, not replace, practical instruction and the cultivation of taste gained through experience. Nonetheless, scholars have spilled rivers of ink arguing over what might appear to outsiders as the minutiae of execution, including issues of unwritten notes, sonority, tuning, and tempo. Often described as a "movement," performance practice research has institutionalized itself in academia and transformed the way baroque and classical repertoire is performed and recorded in spite of the controversy surrounding it (see Butt 2002; Taruskin 1995). Scholars of nineteenth-century music have studied the discourse of music criticism in an effort to understand the cult of the virtuoso (Gooley 2004; Kawabata 2004). With the advent of recording and digital computer technology, new quantitative measures have been developed to analyze performance styles systematically (Clarke 2004). But only Cook (2001) has recognized that a shift from a text-based to a performance-based approach would shake musicology to its core, which is why he turns to interdisciplinary performance studies and ethnomusicology for conceptual models.

In sociology, a few studies of performance have come from the micro-traditions of symbolic interactionism and ethnomethodology. In *Ways of the Hand*, Sudnow (1978) provided an account of learning jazz improvisation at the piano showing that music is best understood as an embodied "process of doing." But like Schutz before him, Sudnow denies the centrality of the text and ignores the macro-level cultural codes that structure musical occasions to focus exclusively on the phenomenological experience of playing an instrument. Faulkner (2006) also draws on his own experience to analyze jazz improvisation that he describes as the interplay between organization and imagination. The organization comes from "shedding," the disciplined work accomplished alone in the rehearsal studio, while the imagination comes in the moment of "playing," when musicians break free of routines and "shed" ingrained templates to spontaneously explore possibilities. Because he is examining the creative process, Faulkner cannot avoid confronting the false dichotomy imposed by the production/consumption paradigm:

> My own work as a jazz improviser suggests that the distinction between culture producer and receiver or consumer is an analytic division that needs empirical investigation. Each "agent" in the culture production process of improvised playing is capable of, indeed even constituted by, being both player and consumer. (p. 105)

But he still does not manage to break free of it. Instead, he switches to the discourse of music as a resource and makes a futile effort to stretch its conceptual reach:

> [S]hedding via imitation indicates the practical way recorded productions of "cultural objects" by other musicians are "used"—or appropriated—by a jazz musician. As these solos or productions are thought about, worked on, worked over, imitated and transformed, they become "new" cultural objects. (p. 105)

While jazz has been the most popular choice, it is not the only genre to have been considered. In his ethnography of karaoke bars, Drew (2001) describes how amateur singers gradually develop a "performing self" by taking many factors into account including: the culture of a particular bar; the gendered, classed, and racialized expectations that come with particular songs; one's self-image; and one's technical abilities as a vocalist. He points to the performative element that makes music such a powerful means for defining the self and articulating collective identity: "Songs do things in karaoke bars, they seduce and repulse, embolden and embarrass, connect and divide" (p. 25). Recently, DeNora (2006) returned to the topic of Beethoven, not just to identify cultural developments that participated in the construction of his genius, but also to investigate why his piano compositions played a central role in creating gender segregation at the keyboard. She argues that his music made new demands on the performer's body that were not compatible with notions of aristocratic femininity. Just as women started to avoid this repertoire, it became strongly associated with images of heroism and genius, further restricting the opportunities for women to enact the form of agency configured by this music.

Hennion (2001) has argued that musical taste should be understood in terms of performance. Like Small, who included all forms of musical activity in the term "musicking" from composing to dancing, Hennion does not distinguish between listeners and performers. Instead, he investigates how "music lovers" (amateurs in the positive sense) form attachments and cultivate passions. In contrast to Bourdieu, he does not see taste as determined by one's social background. Drawing from pragmatism, he conceives of taste as a reflexive activity, often accomplished through carefully staged ceremonies designed to increase the likelihood of being taken over by sound (see also Hennion 2005). It is also in returning to pragmatism that Vannini and Waskul (2006) have made a case for music as performance, but by making the argument in the reverse direction. They propose that symbolic interaction be understood as music. Dramaturgy has illuminated the moral dimensions of everyday life while narrative analysis has revealed the logical structure of events.

A music metaphor, however, can sensitize the analyst to what Pierce called the iconic dimensions of meaning, as well as the aesthetic quality that Dewey insisted was "the condition for unity of *all* experience" (p. 13).

In my own work, I have developed a multidimensional "performance perspective" (McCormick 2006). The advantage of understanding music as a mode of social performance is that the strengths of structural and pragmatic theories of meaning can be combined, bringing the analysis of text, context, and interaction into one framework. While the production/consumption paradigm has tended to dwell almost exclusively on social power, social performance theory expands the explanatory apparatus to include five additional elements: the layered system of collective representations, actors, the audience and other observers, the means of symbolic production, and mise-en-scène (Alexander 2004). A musical occasion can achieve a ritual effect when all the elements of performance are aligned and become "fused." But the fragmentation and differentiation of contemporary society, along with the contingencies of performance environments, have made "fusion" more unlikely and difficult to achieve.

To examine the problems of performance in the realm of classical music, I have studied the controversial institution of international music competitions (see McCormick 2009). On a superficial level, competitions resemble public recitals; highly skilled performers play similar repertoire in the same venues for an appreciative audience that follows standard concert etiquette. But in contrast to recitals, a distinguished jury declares a winner at the conclusion of a competition that has a profound effect on how musicians play and how audiences listen. To understand how this event is culturally constructed, I used discourse analysis to trace the interpretive frameworks invoked in media coverage and publicity materials. Among the most common metaphors is the "musical Olympics" that implies that the event is a democratic mechanism for identifying the best among the musical champions assembled. While this framework resonates with the general public, it does not sit as well with critics and other professional musicians who try to undermine it through ironic commentary and debased metaphor.

I have also investigated the forms of musical agency available to competitors in this public labelling ritual. The programming of repertoire can be understood as a technique of impression management; musical scripts and other symbolic equipment are chosen carefully by competitors not only to display musical values and technical mastery, but also to embody popular images of genius, such as the prodigy or the fire-breathing virtuoso. These performances can only achieve fusion, however, if they are embraced by an audience that is both stratified and fragmented. Judges, critics, music students, patrons, host families, and professional musicians are differently engaged and differently positioned for interpreting competitors' performances, which helps explain why they frequently disagree about who deserves to win. Ultimately, I argue that competitions are more than just mechanisms for distributing symbolic capital, as a conventional sociological analysis would contend; they provide a forum for a critical musical public to debate performance ideals and question aesthetic authority, thereby renewing their cultural commitments to beauty, justice, and their art.

Conclusion

That sociologists have generally failed to pick up on the centrality of performance exposes a troubling discontinuity between matters of importance to inhabitants of the music world and those matters that preoccupy analysts. This inconsistency stems from the choice of theoretical frameworks adopted, especially the production/consumption paradigm. But it is also because scholars tend to develop research agendas based on the most powerful conceptual tools in their arsenal such as networks, occupational structures, and institutions, leaving to one side the more thorny issues of performance and meaning.

There are signs that the tide is starting to turn. Those of an ethnomethodological persuasion have succeeded in bringing embodiment and emotion back in, and DeNora's work (2000, 2003), particularly her notion of musical affordance, has made a persuasive case for seeing music as an active force in social life. But for sociomusical studies to become cultural in the "strong" sense (Alexander and Smith 2003), it needs to progress beyond conceiving of music as a social practice, which tends to reduce meaning to concrete circumstances, material interests, or social needs. It must recognize nonrational motivations for action and develop virtuosity in interpreting musical and social texts, equal to that already demonstrated in analyzing social structures and institutional settings. To return to the musical metaphor in the chapter title, the "new key" to which the field could transpose need not be distant and unrelated. A cultural sociology of music does not so much refute the production/consumption paradigm as build on the solid empirical grounding it has provided. Neither is it necessary to deny that music is a resource in accomplishing various social actions. It would be more accurate to say that this logic is extended a step further: Music does not only facilitate, but itself constitutes, a social action. It would follow that musical performance must be acknowledged as sociologically significant and culturally meaningful in its own right. The time has come for the sociology of music to become literally, and culturally, musical.

NOTES

1. For critical discussions of Adorno's work from a sociological perspective, see Witkin, Robert W., 1998, *Adorno on Music*, London and New York: Routledge; and DeNora, Tia, 2003, *After Adorno: Rethinking Music Sociology*, Cambridge, UK, and New York: Cambridge University Press.

2. For commentary on this vexed term and the future of this research program by one of its leading figures, see Kramer, Lawrence, 2003, "Musicology and Meaning," *The Musical Times* 144(1883):6–12.

3. *Artworlds* focuses on artistic production more than its reception, but the listener is disenchanted by extension. I find it telling that in his recent analysis of the initiation process of opera fans, Benzecry (2009) draws on Becker's earlier work on becoming a

marijuana user and not the artworlds approach. Moreover, Benzecry's addition to the model is an affective element, the passion or "instant of revelation," that is absent from both. See Benzecry, Claudio, 2009, "Becoming a Fan: On the Seductions of Opera," *Qualitative Sociology* 32(2):131–151.

4. For a reply to these criticisms, see Hall, Stuart, and Tony Jefferson, 2006, "Once More around Resistance through Rituals," pp. vii–xxxii in *Resistance through Rituals: Youth Subcultures in Post-War Britain*, London and New York: Routledge.

5. For an overview, see Lawson, Colin, and Robin Stowell, 1999, *The Historical Performance of Music: An Introduction*, Cambridge, UK, and New York: Cambridge University Press.

REFERENCES

Adorno, Theodor W. [1932] 2002. "On the Social Situation of Music." Pp. 391–436 in *Essays on Music*, edited by Richard D. Leppert, translated by Susan D. Gillespie. Berkeley: University of California Press.

———. [1933] 2002. "Farewell to Jazz." Pp. 496–500 in *Essays on Music*, edited by Richard D. Leppert, translated by Susan D. Gillespie. Berkeley: University of California Press.

———. [1936] 2002. "On Jazz." Pp. 470–495 in *Essays on Music*, edited by Richard D. Leppert, translated by Susan D. Gillespie. Berkeley: University of California Press.

———. [1938] 1991. "On the Fetish Character in Music and the Regression of Listening." Pp. 26–52 in *The Culture Industry: Selected Essays on Mass Culture*, edited by J. M. Bernstein. London: Routledge.

———. [1941] 2002. "On Popular Music." Pp. 437–469 in *Essays on Music*, edited by Richard D. Leppert, translated by Susan D. Gillespie. Berkeley: University of California Press.

———. [1952] 2005. *In Search of Wagner*. London and New York: Verso.

———. [1960] 1992. *Mahler: A Musical Physiognomy*. Chicago: University of Chicago Press.

———. [1962] 1976. *Introduction to the Sociology of Music*. New York: Seabury Press.

———. [1963] 1991. "Culture Industry Reconsidered." Pp. 85–92 in *The Culture Industry: Selected Essays on Mass Culture*, edited by J. M. Bernstein. London: Routledge.

———. [1968] 1991. *Alban Berg: Master of the Smallest Link*. Cambridge, UK: Cambridge University Press.

Agawu, V. Kofi. 1991. *Playing with Signs: A Semiotic Interpretation of Classic Music*. Princeton, NJ: Princeton University Press.

Alexander, Jeffrey C. 1995. *Fin de siècle Social Theory: Relativism, Reduction, and the Problem of Reason*. London and New York: Verso.

———. 2004. "Cultural Pragmatics: Social Performance between Ritual and Strategy." *Sociological Theory* 22(4):527–573.

Alexander, Jeffrey C., and Philip Smith. 2003. "The Strong Program in Cultural Sociology: Elements of a Structural Hermeneutics." Pp. 11–26 in *The Meanings of Social Life: A Cultural Sociology*, edited by Jeffrey C. Alexander. Oxford and New York: Oxford University Press.

Becker, Howard, and Alain Pessin. 2006. "A Dialogue on the Ideas of 'World' and 'Field.'" *Sociological Forum* 21(2):275–286.

Becker, Howard S. 1974. "Art as Collective Action." *American Sociological Review* 39(6):767–776.

————. 1982. *Art Worlds*. Berkeley: University of California Press.

————. 2002. "Jazz Places." Pp. 17–27 in *Music Scenes: Local, Translocal, and Virtual*, edited by Andy Bennett and Richard A. Peterson. Nashville, TN: Vanderbilt Press.

————. 2006. "The Work Itself." Pp. 21–30 in *Art from Start to Finish: Jazz, Painting, Writing, and Other Improvisations*, edited by Howard S. Becker, Robert R. Faulkner, and Barbara Kirshenblatt-Gimblett. Chicago and London: University of Chicago Press.

Becker, Howard Saul, Alain Blanc, and Alain Pessin. 2004. *L'art du terrain: Mélanges offerts à Howard S. Becker*. Paris: Harmattan.

Bennett, Andy. 1999. "Subcultures or Neo-Tribes? Rethinking the Relationship between Youth, Style and Musical Taste." *Sociology* 33(3):599–617.

Bennett, Andy, and Richard A. Peterson. 2004. *Music Scenes: Local, Translocal and Virtual*. Nashville, TN: Vanderbilt University Press.

Benzecry, Claudio. 2009. "Becoming a Fan: On the Seductions of Opera." *Qualitative Sociology* 32(2):131–151.

Boorman, Stanley. 1999. "The Musical Text." Pp. 403–423 in *Rethinking Music*, edited by Eric Clarke and Nicholas Cook. Oxford: Oxford University Press

Bourdieu, Pierre. 1984. *Distinction: A Social Critique of the Judgement of Taste*. Cambridge, MA: Harvard University Press.

————. 1993. *The Field of Cultural Production: Essays on Art and Literature*. Cambridge, UK: Polity Press.

————. 1996. *The Rules of Art: Genesis and Structure of the Literary Field*. Cambridge, UK: Polity Press.

Brett, Philip, Elizabeth Wood, and Gary Thomas. 1994. *Queering the Pitch: The New Gay and Lesbian Musicology*. New York: Routledge.

Britten, Benjamin. 1999. "On Winning the First Aspen Award." Pp. 175–181 in *Composers on Modern Musical Culture: An Anthology of Readings on Twentieth-Century Music*, edited by Bryan Simms. Belmont, CA: Schirmer Books.

Bryson, Bethany. 1996. "'Anything But Heavy Metal': Symbolic Exclusion and Musical Dislikes." *American Sociological Review* 61(5):884–899.

Buch, Esteban. 2003. *Beethoven's Ninth: A Political History*. Chicago: University of Chicago Press.

Bull, Michael. 2005. "No Dead Air! The iPod and the Culture of Mobile Listening." *Leisure Studies* 24(4):343–355.

Butt, John. 2002. *Playing with History: The Historical Approach to Musical Performance*. Cambridge, UK, and New York: Cambridge University Press.

Cerulo, Karen A. 1993. "Symbols and the World System: National Anthems and Flags." *Sociological Forum* 8(2):243–271.

Chan, Tak Wing, and John H. Goldthorpe. 2007. "Social Stratification and Cultural Consumption: Music in England." *European Sociological Review* 23(1):1–19.

Chapoulie, Jean-Michel. 1996. "Everett Hughes and the Chicago Tradition." *Sociological Theory* 14(1):3–29.

Clarke, Eric F. 2004. "Empirical Methods in the Study of Performance." Pp. 77–102 in *Empirical Musicology: Aims, Methods, Prospects*, edited by Eric F. Clarke and Nicholas Cook. Oxford: Oxford University Press.

Cohen, Phil. 1980. "Subcultural Conflict and Working-Class Community." Pp. 78–87 in *Culture, Media, Language: Working Papers in Cultural Studies, 1972–79*, edited by Stuart Hall, Dorothy Hobson, Andrew Lowe, and Paul Willis. London: Hutchinson.

Cook, Nicholas. 2001. "Between Process and Product: Music and/as Performance." *Music Theory Online* 7(2).

Cumming, Naomi. 2000. *The Sonic Self: Musical Subjectivity and Signification.* Bloomington: Indiana University Press.

Cusick, Suzanne G. 2008. "'You are in a place that is out of the world…': Music in the Detention Camps of the 'Global War on Terror.'" *Journal of the Society for American Music* 2(1):1–26.

DeNora, Tia. 1995. *Beethoven and the Construction of Genius: Music Politics in Vienna, 1792–1803.* Berkeley: University of California Press.

———. 2000. *Music in Everyday Life.* Cambridge, UK, and New York: Cambridge University Press.

———. 2003. *After Adorno: Rethinking Music Sociology.* Cambridge, UK, and New York: Cambridge University Press.

———. 2004. "Historical Perspectives in Music Sociology." *Poetics* 32(3–4):211–221.

———. 2006. "Music as Agency in Beethoven's Vienna." Pp. 103–119 in *Myth, Meaning, and Performance: Toward a New Cultural Sociology of the Arts*, edited by Ron Eyerman and Lisa McCormick. Boulder, CO: Paradigm.

DiMaggio, Paul. 1982. "Cultural Entrepreneurship in Nineteenth-Century Boston: The Creation of an Organizational Base for High Culture in America." *Media, Culture and Society* 4(1):33–50.

Dowd, Timothy J. 2004a. "Concentration and Diversity Revisited: Production Logics and the U.S. Mainstream Recording Market, 1940–1990." *Social Forces* 82(4):1411–1455.

———. 2004b. "Production Perspectives in the Sociology of Music." *Poetics* 32(3–4):235–246.

Dowd, Timothy J., and Maureen Blyler. 2002. "Charting Race: The Success of Black Performers in the Mainstream Recording Market, 1940–1990." *Poetics* 30(1–2):87–110.

Drew, Rob. 2001. *Karaoke Nights: An Ethnographic Rhapsody.* Walnut Creek, CA: AltaMira Press.

Dunsby, Jonathan. 1995. *Performing Music: Shared Concerns.* Oxford: Clarendon Press.

Elias, Norbert. 1993. *Mozart: Portrait of a Genius.* Berkeley: University of California Press.

Eyerman, Ron, and Andrew Jamison. 1998. *Music and Social Movements: Mobilizing Traditions in the Twentieth Century.* New York: Cambridge University Press.

Faulkner, Robert R. 2006. "Shedding Culture." Pp. 91–117 in *Art from Start to Finish: Jazz, Painting, Writing, and Other Improvisations*, edited by Howard Saul Becker, Robert R. Faulkner, and Barbara Kirshenblatt-Gimblett. Chicago: University of Chicago Press.

Finnegan, Ruth. 1989. *The Hidden Musicians: Music-Making in an English Town.* Cambridge, UK, and New York: Cambridge University Press.

Gilmore, Samuel. 1988. "Schools of Activity and Innovation." *The Sociological Quarterly* 29(2):203–219.

Goffman, Erving. 1959. *The Presentation of Self in Everyday Life.* Garden City, NY: Doubleday.

Gooley, Dana. 2004. *The Virtuoso Liszt.* Cambridge, UK, and New York: Cambridge University Press.

Grazian, David. 2003. *Blue Chicago: The Search for Authenticity in Urban Blues Clubs.* Chicago: University of Chicago Press.

Halbwachs, Maurice. [1939] 1980. "The Collective Memory of Musicians." Pp. 158–186 in *The Collective Memory.* New York: Harper & Row.

Hall, Stuart, and Tony Jefferson. 2006a. *Resistance through Rituals: Youth Subcultures in Post-War Britain.* London and New York: Routledge.

Hebdige, Dick. 1979. *Subculture: The Meaning of Style.* London: Methuen.

Hennion, Antoine. 2001. "Music Lovers: Taste as Performance." *Theory, Culture & Society* 18(5):1–22.

————. 2005. "Pragmatics of Taste." Pp. 131–144 in *Blackwell Companions to Sociology*, edited by Mark D. Jacobs and Nancy Weiss Hanrahan. Malden, MA: Blackwell.

Hobsbawm, Eric, and Terrence Ranger. 1983. *The Invention of Tradition*. Cambridge, UK, and New York: Cambridge University Press.

Horkheimer, Max, and Theodor W. Adorno. [1944] 2000. *Dialectic of Enlightenment*. New York: Continuum.

Inglis, David. 2005. "Thinking 'Art' Sociologically." Pp. 11–29 in *The Sociology of Art: Ways of Seeing*, edited by David Inglis and John Hughson. New York: Palgrave Macmillan.

Johnson, Bruce, and Martin Cloonan. 2008. *Dark Side of the Tune: Popular Music and Violence*. Aldershot, UK, and Burlington, VT: Ashgate.

Kawabata, Maiko. 2004. "Virtuoso Codes of Violin Performance: Power, Military Heroism, and Gender (1789–1830)." *19th-Century Music* 28(2):89–107.

Kotarba, Joseph A. 2002. "Rock 'n' Roll Music as a Timepiece." *Symbolic Interaction* 25(3):397–404.

Kramer, Lawrence. 2003. "Musicology and Meaning." *The Musical Times* 144(1883):6–12.

Lawson, Colin, and Robin Stowell. 1999. *The Historical Performance of Music: An Introduction*. Cambridge, UK, and New York: Cambridge University Press.

Lena, Jennifer C. 2006. "Social Context and Musical Content of Rap Music, 1979–1995." *Social Forces* 85(1):479–95.

Leppert, Richard D., and Susan McClary. 1987. *Music and Society: The Politics of Composition, Performance, and Reception*. Cambridge, UK, and New York: Cambridge University Press.

Lewis, George H. 1988. "The Creation of Popular Music: A Comparison of the "Art Worlds" of American Country Music and British Punk." *International Review of the Aesthetics and Sociology of Music* 19(1):35–51.

Lizardo, Omar. 2006a. "How Cultural Tastes Shape Personal Networks." *American Sociological Review* 71(5):778–807.

————. 2006b. "The Puzzle of Women's 'Highbrow' Culture Consumption: Integrating Gender and Work into Bourdieu's Class Theory of Taste." *Poetics* 34(1):1–23.

Lopes, Paul D. 2002. *The Rise of a Jazz Art World*. Cambridge, UK, and New York: Cambridge University Press.

Martin, Peter J. 2006a. *Music and the Sociological Gaze: Art Worlds and Cultural Production*. Manchester, UK: Manchester University Press.

————. 2006b. "Musicians' Worlds: Music-Making as a Collaborative Activity." *Symbolic Interaction* 29(1):95–107.

Maus, Fred Everett. 1997. "Music as Drama." Pp. 105–130 in *Music and Meaning*, edited by Jenefer Robinson. Ithaca, NY: Cornell University Press.

McClary, Susan. 1991. *Feminine Endings: Music, Gender, and Sexuality*. Minneapolis: University of Minnesota Press.

————. 1998. *Rap, Minimalism, and Structures of Time in Late Twentieth-Century Culture*. Lincoln: University of Nebraska–Lincoln.

————. 2000. *Conventional Wisdom: The Content of Musical Form*. Berkeley: University of California Press.

McCormick, Lisa. 2006. "Music as Social Performance." Pp. 121–144 in *Myth, Meaning, and Performance: Toward a New Cultural Sociology of the Arts*, edited by Ron Eyerman and Lisa McCormick. Boulder, CO: Paradigm.

————. 2009. "Higher, Faster, Louder: Representations of the International Music Competition." *Cultural Sociology* 3(1):5–30.

Moore, Ryan. 2007. "Friends Don't Let Friends Listen to Corporate Rock: Punk as a Field of Cultural Production." *Journal of Contemporary Ethnography* 36(4):438–474.

Muggleton, David. 2000. *Inside Subculture: The Postmodern Meaning of Style*. Oxford and New York: Berg.

Pessin, Alain. 2004. *Un sociologue en liberté: Lecture de Howard S. Becker*. Saint-Nicolas, Québec: Presses de l'Université Laval.

Peterson, Richard, and N. Anand. 2004. "The Production of Culture Perspective." *Annual Review of Sociology* 30:311–34.

Peterson, Richard A. 1978. "The Production of Cultural Change: The Case of Contemporary Country Music." *Social Research* 45(2):292–314.

———. 1990. "Why 1955? Explaining the Advent of Rock Music." *Popular Music* 9(1):97–116.

———. 1994. "Culture Studies through the Production Perspective: Progress and Prospects." Pp. 163–189 in *The Sociology of Culture*, edited by Diana Crane. Malden, MA: Blackwell.

———. 1997a. *Creating Country Music: Fabricating Authenticity*. Chicago: University of Chicago Press.

———. 1997b. "The Rise and Fall of Highbrow Snobbery as a Status Marker." *Poetics* 25(2–3):75–92.

———. 2000. "Two Ways Culture Is Produced." *Poetics* 28(2–3):225–233.

Peterson, Richard A., and David G. Berger. 1975. "Cycles in Symbol Production: The Case of Popular Music." *American Sociological Review* 40(2):158–173.

Peterson, Richard A., and Roger M. Kern. 1996. "Changing Highbrow Taste: From Snob to Omnivore." *American Sociological Review* 61(5):900–907.

Prior, Nick. 2008. "Putting a Glitch in the Field: Bourdieu, Actor Network Theory and Contemporary Music." *Cultural Sociology* 2(3):301–319.

Rafalovich, Adam. 2006. "Broken and Becoming God-Sized: Contemporary Metal Music and Masculine Individualism." *Symbolic Interaction* 29(1):19–32.

Raykoff, Ivan, and Robert Deam Tobin. 2007. *A Song for Europe: Popular Music and Politics in the Eurovision Song Contest*. Aldershot, UK, and Burlington, VT: Ashgate.

Redhead, Steve. 1997. *Subculture to Clubcultures: An Introduction to Popular Cultural Studies*. Oxford and Malden, MA: Blackwell.

Rosen, Charles. 1994. "Music a la Mode." *New York Review of Books* 41(12):55–62.

Roy, William G. 2002. "Aesthetic Identity, Race, and American Folk Music." *Qualitative Sociology* 25(3):459–469.

Santoro, Marco. 2008a. "Culture as (and After) Production." *Cultural Sociology* 2(1):7–31.

———. 2008b. "Producing Cultural Sociology: An Interview with Richard A. Peterson." *Cultural Sociology* 2(1):33–55.

Savage, Mike. 2006. "The Musical Field." *Cultural Trends* 15(2–3):159–174.

Schutz, Alfred. [1951] 1964. "Making Music Together." Pp. 159–178 in *Collected Papers: Studies in Social Theory*, edited and introduced by Arvid Broderson. The Hague: Martinus Nijhoff.

Shildrick, Tracy, and Robert MacDonald. 2006. "In Defence of Subculture: Young People, Leisure and Social Divisions." *Journal of Youth Studies* 9(2):125–140.

Simmel, Georg. [1882] 1968. "Psychological and Ethnological Studies on Music." Pp. 98–140 in *Georg Simmel: The Conflict in Modern Culture, and Other Essays*, edited by K. P. Etzkorn. New York: Teachers College Press.

Sintas, Jordi Lopez, and Ercilia Garcia Alvarez. 2002. "Omnivores Show up Again: The Segmentation of Cultural Consumers in Spanish Social Space." *European Sociological Review* 18(3):353–368.

Small, Christopher. 1998. *Musicking: The Meanings of Performing and Listening*. Hanover, NH, and London: Wesleyan University Press.

Stamatov, Peter. 2002. "Interpretive Activism and the Political Uses of Verdi's Operas in the 1840s." *American Sociological Review* 67(3):345–366.

Stebbins, Robert A. 1996. *The Barbershop Singer: Inside the Social World of a Musical Hobby*. Ontario: University of Toronto Press.

Subotnik, Rose Rosengard. 1991. *Developing Variations: Style and Ideology in Western music*. Minneapolis: University of Minnesota Press.

———. 1996. *Deconstructive Variations: Music and Reason in Western Society*. Minneapolis: University of Minnesota Press.

Sudnow, David. 1978. *Ways of the Hand: The Organization of Improvised Conduct*. Cambridge, MA: Harvard University Press.

Sullivan, Oriel, and Tally Katz-Gerro. 2007. "The Omnivore Thesis Revisited: Voracious Cultural Consumers." *European Sociological Review* 23(2):123–137.

Taruskin, Richard. 1995. *Text and Act: Essays on Music and Performance*. New York: Oxford University Press.

Thornton, Sarah. 1996. *Club Cultures: Music, Media, and Subcultural Capital*. Hanover, NH: University Press of New England.

Toynbee, Jason. 2000. *Making Popular Music: Musicians, Creativity and Institutions*. London and New York: Arnold.

van den Toorn, Pieter C. 1995. *Music, Politics, and the Academy*. Berkeley: University of California Press.

Vannini, Phillip, and Dennis Waskul. 2006. "Symbolic Interaction as Music: The Esthetic Constitution of Meaning, Self, and Society." *Symbolic Interaction* 29(1):5–18.

Walser, Robert. 1993. *Running with the Devil: Power, Gender, and Madness in Heavy Metal Music*. Hanover, NH: University Press of New England.

Weber, Max. [1924] 1958. *The Rational and Social Foundations of Music*. Carbondale: Southern Illinois University Press.

Whiteley, Sheila. 1997. *Sexing the Groove: Popular Music and Gender*. London and New York: Routledge.

Willis, Paul E. 1978. *Profane Culture*. London and Boston: Routledge & Kegan Paul.

Witkin, Robert W. 1998. *Adorno on Music*. London and New York: Routledge.

PART XI

KNOWLEDGE AS
CULTURE

CHAPTER 28

NARRATING GLOBAL WARMING

PHILIP SMITH

WE usually think of global warming—or more accurately climate change—in technical and meteorological terms as a process that requires the tools of natural science if it is to be understood. With our thermometers, satellite censors, atmospheric gas equipment, and consequent computer modeling, we can come to terms with the chemical and physical process through which the planet heats up. We can measure and predict consequent shifts in rainfall, extreme weather, and glacial ice distributions. With the logic of political science and social policy analysis, we can then make sensible suggestions for heading off resource conflicts and cutting down on our harmful emissions. Here, I want to open up another way of coming to terms with climate change. This is to take it not so much as the product and producer of social outcomes, but rather as a meaningful social fact. Climate change is something more than a process involving molecules, energies, oceanic currents, solar radiation, and the human impacts upon these—it is also a new and interesting concept, signifier, and drama in a surprisingly complex cultural field.

Perhaps there is nothing new in this turn of thought. Indeed, we can trace a lineage now one century or more old. In their work from 1903 entitled *Primitive Classification*, the pioneering sociologists Emile Durkheim and Marcel Mauss (1963) noted that we, as a society, can come to know the world around us only through our "collective representations." These are the shared signs, symbols, classifications, and myths through which we humans have placed ourselves in an environment and developed cosmologies that fix social ties and give life purpose. Looking to Aboriginal peoples, they have shown that such representations are not simply adaptive, cognitive or functional—they are about more than just survival, food production, or shelter. In belief systems, such as totemism, the natural world is narrated, first as a deeply meaningful cosmos and only secondarily for its instrumental value. The classifications and myths arising from this cultural process, Durkheim and Mauss argued, can themselves be understood as social facts—as the nonmaterial product of the collectivity that is, in turn, as influential upon human thought and action as any material law of nature. Settlement patterns, marriages, and political alliances are shaped by these collective representations. A little over a half-century later the anthropologist Claude Lévi-Strauss (1966) built on these insights, noting the centrality of a signified nature for the myth-making activity and for the self-understandings developed by people of their place in a wider and enchanted universe. Everywhere, he said, humans used nature to think with.

Two decades on Mary Douglas (1978; Douglas and Wildavsky 1982) worked these visions into a more systematic comparative model, one that would tether cosmologies to social structures and move away from the idealism that had plagued Lévi-Strauss. Small-scale societies, cults and sects, she said, were characterized by intense sensitivity to pollutions and visions of nature as inherently unstable. Hierarchical and large-scale societies tended to be more complacent. They believed that administrative and technical solutions could be found for most problems. Her model is elegant, but it has been dogged by a problem of fit. Cosmological views seem to be far more flexible and contingent than her vision of entrenched "cultural bias" might admit. Issues and fears flash onto and off the radar screen of public concerns with surprising rapidity. More troubling, still, contemporary societies appear to be plagued by pre-modern doubts and anxieties. There are recurrent fears of plague-like contagion and global doom. One thinks of Ebola, swine fever, bird flu, and the once-feared Y2K virus. These had dominated front pages in their day, their representation and iconography seemingly little different from that produced by medieval apocalyptic cults. Far from bureaucratic and cool, our late-modern "cultural bias" is looking superstitious.

One might explain away these episodes as simply the outcome of new and improved scientific information. Worry rises and falls as new data and theory become available and distributed images simply reflect the reasonable beliefs of enlightened experts. Such a position can be destabilized quite easily. There is often no consensus in the scientific community. Expert theories can persist for a long time before they cause popular alarm or interest. This response, when it does arise, is often transient. Diverse nations and communities, and nongovernmental organizations show radically divergent levels of concern, yet have access to the same basic facts. The flow of cognitive information is only part of the story. To understand this process, we need a firmer understanding of the role of myth, narrative, and symbolism in filtering raw natural science into something socially, rather than just scientifically, meaningful.

A starting point is to see that before it becomes relevant to a wider public or to a broader civil sphere, scientific information is itself subject to reworking into other sets of codes, deeply grounded myths, parables, images, and even slogans. We might say it becomes storied. These stories simplify, amplify, or diminish dangers. They allocate roles and responsibilities to governments, citizens, and experts, and identify appropriate emotions and subject positions. They are part of a social drama—sometimes portentous, sometimes soap opera—in which legitimacy is contested, moral authority gained, and public opinion formed. In this context, we can treat "global warming" and "climate change" not simply as a set of environmental processes in need of investigation, but rather as collective representations in need of interpretation. They are nonmaterial social facts, loosely coupled to material facts, steering opinion and anxiety, and thereby determinate in their force.

Importantly, some tools already exist for a comparative sociology of this storying-process. We do not need to theorize the reception and recognition of climate change from the ground up. Nor do we need to see stories about this process as just idiographic, local, history-bound, and unique to each setting. Like other unknowns, climate change presents a tableau of uncertainty and risk. So we might therefore profitably look to treatments of similar situations containing this "uncertainty and risk" for guidance. First developed in the context of the study of military crisis, foreign policy dangers, and war (Smith 2005), what is termed the *narrative genre model of risk evaluation* offers a systematic and comparative way of looking at the form and structure of storytelling and its consequences for human action. There are several core claims:

(1) Uncertain events and real world facts are "clues." These have little significance in and of themselves. People generally agree on these. They require a "genre guess" in order to have significance. This guess is vital for the reduction of information complexity, yet it carries with it deep implications for communicative and opinion process.

(2) We can see things as low mimetic, romantic, tragic, or apocalyptic. Following the literary theory of Northrop Frye and others, we can understand each genre as having certain properties. These define the powers of action of players (large or small); likely social outcomes (solidaristic or divisive); appropriate yardsticks for motivation and policy evaluation (pragmatic, business as usual, or utopian and heroic); and the issues at stake (local and ordinary or global and epochal).

(3) Binary oppositions play a role as building blocks for wider storytelling activity. These are particularly important for marking out the good or bad characters within our story or drama.

(4) The chosen genre from this cultural repertoire provides a gestalt that retrospectively determines how the clues are put together into a more coherent picture. There is an element of path dependence at work here. The genre guess works to close off alternative interpretative possibilities even as it makes the world meaningful.

(5) Some frames escalate perceived risks, while others talk them down. Struggles eventuate in which interested parties try to have their story taken seriously and to falsify or eliminate the stories of others. The combat between frames and their sponsors for interpretative authority is a further important source of social drama. Meta-narratives eventuate discussing narrative strategies and speculating on who will prevail.

(6) The distribution of these frames over nations, over time, or over constituencies and interest groups in a civil discourse indirectly shapes political outcomes as well as their timing.

To make this concrete, we can think about war. In the case of the buildup to the 2003 Gulf War, for example, an apocalyptic frame took hold and was promoted in the United States and the United Kingdom. This described Saddam Hussein as an individual capable of changing world history, a person of evil motivations, and a new Hitler who had to be stopped immediately. By contrast, France and other European powers had a low mimetic narrative in place. This saw the situation in Iraq as containable by means of "business as usual" sanctions, inspections, and diplomacy coordinated by the United Nations (Smith 2005). Diplomats and intellectuals struggled for interpretative authority over genre within and between nations. Higher-order commentators reflected on these efforts at narrative control in turn. I argue we can see a similar pattern with global warming.

GLOBAL WARMING IN THE WILDERNESS

Over the past few years, the issues of global warming, climate change, and greenhouse gas emission have undergone a series of transformations. First, the concepts have become familiar. They have moved out of the scientific domain and become a commonplace of everyday conversation and even humor. Media sources no longer need to provide little diagrams illustrating the core process, offer summaries of key terms, or put these in quotation marks (e.g., "What scientists are calling the 'greenhouse effect' is caused by carbon dioxide levels…"). Put another way, they have entered the attention space and have become routinized. Second, there has been a narrative shift toward apocalypticism rather than low mimetic forms of narration that once saw the problem as containable with routine policy solutions, or as finger-click solvable by our more technologically advanced descendants. Third, there has been a process of sensitization in which more and more aspects of planetary ecology and social experience are tethered in one way or another to this issue cluster. Climate change becomes a sort of master trope for building a comprehendible universe. In the natural world, we might make connections so as to explain retreating glaciers, stronger hurricanes, or hotter summers all in one fell swoop. In the social world, we now have a new way to think about trading in large SUVs; buying home insulation and lightbulbs; and following up on new gardening and angling possibilities. As the discourse of climate change becomes as ubiquitous as the white whale that was seen simultaneously in different latitudes, so do new kinds of ethical subjectivity and behavior come into play as moral yardsticks.

At the time of writing, the discourse of man-made and dangerous climate change is generally well established in the scientific community, as well as among social and liberal elites. There are a few holding out against the tide—recalcitrant oil and coal public relations consultants, thick-skinned snow mobile enthusiasts and V8 lovers, survivalists in compounds in Idaho, and others who believe the talk to be a conspiracy, hoax, or delusion in some combination. It is easy to mock critics in this way. Yet there are also legitimate scientists, here or there, who think we are on the wrong track, as well as a substantial proportion of the general public who feel the issue has been overblown. Some say global temperature change in recent decades might be due to natural factors. It is worth noting that global temperatures seem to have flattened out since 1998, yet CO_2 emissions have increased and benchmark thermometers at airstrips and in cities are increasingly surrounded by concrete and asphalt, leading to heat radiation and heat island effects. Further, it now seems possible that natural variations in oceanic circulation may well hold back global warming for decades, making widely circulating models and predictions hopelessly pessimistic (Keenlyside et al. 2008, Michaels 2008). The complexity of the climate system makes certainty about global warming hard to prove. The earth has been hotter in recent centuries, say, the medieval warm period when the Vikings were farming in Greenland. Such ambivalence about the core science—or at least the possibility for reasonable doubt—amplifies the importance of a genre selection process. And even if the human origins of climate change are accepted 100 percent at some future date, this fact still does not tell us how urgent the problem is, or how much sacrifice we should make to deal with it. Representations filtering information will still play a role in shaping societal responses to ecological information.

It is hard now to remember a time when talk of global warming was not around. In truth, it was always around, only nobody was particularly interested. We might trace the idea back as far as 1824, when the mathematician Jean Baptiste Joseph Fourier wrote about the balance of energy coming into and leaving the planet and speculated on the role of the atmosphere in preventing the loss of heat through radiation. In the 1890s, the Swedish chemist Svante August Arrhenius put the topic on a more rigorous footing by calculating the relationship between carbon dioxide levels and temperature, arguing that carbon dioxide fluctuations had been responsible for the Ice Ages. He spoke of the potential role of industry and other human actions in warming the globe. Somewhat interestingly, Arrhenius saw this as a positive thing—an early indication that a scientific theory or fact does not determine its own broader narration.

Just three or four decades ago, the problem of CO_2 was very much on the agenda of a significant number of scientists, but there was still little concern. A search of "global warming" in the *New York Times* index indicates just six stories about the subject from before 1980. The items seem remarkably prescient, but they are presented for the most part as quick reports on the talk of scientists in their conventions and publications. The basic science being propounded seems consistent with the one we have today. Yet the items are typically buried somewhere back in the science section and were run with other ecological stories. This was not an issue worthy of attention in the civil sphere. On December 21, 1969, we find on page 46, column 4, the following compressed note:

Physical scientist J. O. Fletcher warns man has only a few decades to solve problem of global warming caused by pollution; American Geophysical Union notes warming could cause further melting of polar ice caps and affect earth's climate; oceanographic chemist E. D. Goldberg warns man runs risk of allowing pollution to destroy life in oceans. (*New York Times* 1969)

Toward the end of the 1970s, treatments became more extended and have a contemporary feel: An 1800-word item in *The Economist* from 1977 covers all the bases familiar today in, say, *The Economist's* regular features on global warming. There is the difficulty of prediction, "the simplest model has to include 30 variables"; the crucial role of the Arctic and Antarctic, "the polar ice caps are what inflation and money supply are to economists"; an estimate that a "doubling of carbon dioxide" would lead to "global warming of nearly three degrees centigrade"; the possibility of flooding as "the oceans would rise nearly six meters" (*The Economist* 1977, p. 88). *The Economist* remained neutral as to the truth of the matter, yet it was unable to see unbridled disaster as the end of the line even if the prognostications were true. It wrote a couple of years later:

> The results could be relatively attractive: a climate something like that of the warm medieval period from 900 to 1050. There would be winners and losers: e.g., more benign conditions in northern Europe and some of today's arid African regions, but severe winters and frequent drought in Eastern Europe. On balance, however, the earth would probably be more productive. (*The Economist* 1979, p. 96)

It is tempting to see this as simply capitalist ideology. To do so would be mistaken. Similar views were held by influential stakeholder institutions at the interface between the laboratory, the political process, and civil society, such as the National Academy of Sciences. In 1983, its Carbon Dioxide Assessment Committee wrote a 496-page report that brought up the usual litany of issues and dangers but concluded:

> We do not believe, however, that the evidence at hand about CO_2-induced climate change would support steps to change current fuel-use patterns away from fossil fuels. Such steps may be necessary or desirable at some time in the future, and we should certainly think carefully about costs and benefits of such steps; but the very near future would be better spent improving our knowledge (including knowledge of energy and other processes leading to creation of greenhouse gases) than in changing fuel mix or use. (quoted in *New York Times* 1983, p. B5)

This cheerful line of reasoning is consistent with the Romantic genre of risk assessment whereby problems end up resolving themselves. There was no need to panic or even to make a decision. Growing prosperity was not the problem; to the contrary, it would take care of the problem:

> Generally, the more well-to-do countries can take in stride what may prove to be a reduction by a few percent in living standards that will likely be greater per capita by more than 100 percent over today's. (quoted in Shabecoff 1983, p. 1)

Squeezed out by the Romantic minimization of risk, a more concerned Environmental Protection Agency report released just a few days before that of the

National Academy of Science struggled for attention. It was dubbed "unwarranted and unnecessarily alarmist" by President Reagan's scientific advisor, George A. Keyworth II (quoted in Shabecoff 1983, p. 1). Though off to a poor start, as the 1980s moved on, apocalypticism started to gain traction as a credible genre guess. To some extent, this reflects the growing influence of environmentalism in everyday thinking, as well as the emergence of a broader "risk society" in which sensitivity to human harms was amplified. There were also more middle-range institutional drivers. NASA was particularly important here, taking advantage of its global remote-sensing capabilities to find a new relevance in the post-Apollo age. It coordinated a 2000-page report by 150 scientists from around the globe that was released in 1986. This was a prototype for many subsequent reports. Its language is more alarmist, conjuring up images of unknown futures and chancy gambles: "We should recognize that we are conducting one giant experiment on a global scale by increasing the concentrations of trace gases in the atmosphere without knowing the environmental consequences" (quoted in *New York Times* 1986, p. A11).

THE RISE OF THE APOCALYPTIC GENRE

Around the end of the 1980s we see even stronger ethical injunctions emerge, these fueled by growing apocalypticism. The social drama of global warming was heating up. Global warming had now created new forms of civic responsibility and subjectivity, reworking existing environmentalist tropes and converting them into categorical imperatives. The socially constructed representation of a scientific finding was starting to build its normative force in the civil sphere. Thanks to the growing acceptance of this apocalyptic global warming discourse, the genre guess that could once be dismissed as a fantasy of the Bay Area's Birkenstock-wearing classes, was becoming legitimate on Main Street U.S.A. Now we can find a guest columnist even in the middle-to-low-brow *USA Today* writing that "carbon dioxide and other greenhouse gasses...threaten a disastrous warming of the earth." Hence, we needed to "change the whole way we live" with "100% recycling," "public transportation, solar powered cars, bicycles or simply walking" ("Radical Lifestyle Changes Needed" 1989, p. 10). As the "problem" of global warming was ratcheted up, the genre hierarchy over the next few years—decisions and outcomes—became increasingly epochal. Thus, we find in the mid-1990s an op-ed in the *Christian Science Monitor* setting the stage for a Kyoto environmental summit in terms similar to those we find in the book of Revelation. One can almost hear John of Patmos intoning his visions of a Day of Judgment. "A warming unprecedented since the dawn of civilization is likely to happen in the coming decades," the *Monitor* warns. This would bring with it "destruction of entire forest systems and watersheds, rising sea levels, flooding, drinking-water shortages and the northward spread of tropical diseases.... [There was a] looming threat to geopolitical and environmental stability" ("Stem the Global

Warming Trend" 1997, p. 10). From the standpoint of structuralist poetics, we can see here the hallmarks of apocalypticism. Greenhouse gases are given extreme powers of action, the consequences of action or inaction are immense, and the future of the planet is at stake.

This apocalyptic discourse of global doom set high popular expectations for the 1997 meetings in Kyoto that were to address the problem. There were vague hopes for a potlatch ceremony of selfless action in which national interests would be thrown over the cliff. This ritual validation of the apocalyptic worldview might, some hoped, provide the foundation point for a new romantic narrative, one involving sacrifice, sharing, and the pursuit of a common good. Perhaps humanity would prevail. Yet in the narrative representations that came to surround the event, we find the sense that an opportunity was missed. The meetings in Kyoto were historic, but they had also been characterized by horse trading. As the event continued and then ended, the word "bargaining" became used more and more frequently to describe what had happened. From the apocalyptic viewpoint, what might, and indeed should have become a moment of ritual transcendence, had become simply politics and bureaucracy. Possibilities for disillusioned irony presented themselves to onlooking meta-narrators. A contributor to the *South China Morning Post* noted that history could have been made, but instead:

> After 10 days of circular and esoteric arguments about gas trading and forest counting that few understood, and a final dawn-to-dawn session culminating in negotiators nodding off as clauses were passed, history was on few people's minds: all most cared about was when it would all end. ("Earth Robbed in Kyoto" 1997, p. 10).

Likewise, the *Jerusalem Post* contrasted the potential import of the event with its mundane incarnation:

> There are times when the conference itself seems lost in a fog of deceit and uncontrolled verbal emissions. Most parts of the conference are highly technical and conducted in a version of United Nations English few English-speakers, let alone anyone else, can understand. This in itself, rather than the inevitable disagreements, could yet be the meeting's failure.... This supposedly vital 10-day conference of more than 160 nations started off infected by the numbing amalgamation of environmental sciences and UN bureaucracy. ("Planet Health Warning" 1997, p. 8)

Technocracy and diplomacy, the stock in trade of low mimetic politics, had somehow fended off high ritual fusion, preventing an emotional climax from emerging. Perhaps this reflected not only the Beckett-like dynamics of intergovernmental discussions, but also the genre fragmentation of this era expressed in the scientific and technical documentation. For example, the United Nation's Intergovernmental Panel on Climate Change itself issued a report in 1995 on the Economic and Social Dimensions of Climate Change. Here, we find little sense of urgency. The report suggests the problem could be dealt with through "a portfolio of actions aimed at mitigation, adaptation and improvement of knowledge" (IGPCC 1995, p. 5), and it draws attention to the widespread availability of "no-regrets" measures to deal with much of the problem. These are defined as "measures worth doing anyway" (IGPCC 1995, p. 15) because they reduce energy costs or local pollution levels.

The triumph of bureaucratic rationality and low mimetic meta-narration at Kyoto did not prevent moral evaluations of action persisting in a forceful way. The low mimetic genre had ruled the roost at the event, but the wider drama could remain somewhat inflated in genre precisely by means of ritually polluting mundane motivations. Pariahs could be identified. Those who avoided signing the protocols (the United States, Canada, Australia, and New Zealand) were widely narrated as mean-spirited free riders. These were uncivil actors driven by selfish motivations, such as electoral appeal, saving jobs, and preserving entrenched and privileged ways of life. Australia, for example, secured permission for an 8 percent increase in its emissions and for continued land clearing in the bush. Its Prime Minister, John Howard, spoke proudly of the need to "protect jobs in the coal industry" and to not "sell out Australia's interests in international forums" (quoted in Canberra Times 2007, p. A6). The angry EU environmental spokesman, Peter Jørgensen, called Australia's Kyoto deal "wrong and immoral....a disgrace" (quoted in Sydney Morning Herald 1997, p. 10). Those who signed up, by contrast, such as the members of the European Union, could undergo a status upgrade. No longer simply polluters, these were now ethically aware, global citizens who respected the scientific knowledge base and who realized the time had come to go beyond free rider concerns. Further, the apocalypticists insisted that something concrete had been achieved: Global warming was recognized as a legitimate problem deserving of workable solutions at the international and transnational levels.

Fertile soils had been prepared for *An Inconvenient Truth* (Guggenheim 2006). This remarkably successful documentary film of the mid-OOs saw the failed politician Al Gore presenting his slide show on the need to take global warming seriously. Gore's genius was to capture the prevailing mood rather than to shape it and, further, to provide iconic images to anchor his story. Scientific and technical reports on global warming make for fairly tedious reading for the general, educated reader. They are full of caveats, data disputes, and politically correct diplomatic talk that avoids pointing the finger. There are precious few diagrams and no photographs. I have explained in detail elsewhere how Gore was able to sidestep this numbing format (Smith 2010). Warning of catastrophic hurricanes, global flooding that would swamp coastal cities, horrific drought and heat, and wars; backing these up with the scientific authority of charts and graphs; flashing photos of collapsing icebergs, wilting trees, and flooded cities; and tying this together with a sense of pragmatic possibility, Gore's film intensified the moral drama. Further, it allowed Gore—a long-time global warming campaigner—to be reinvented as a self-sacrificing martyr who had transcended politics and who was prepared to swim against tide. Caring little for public esteem, here was a pragmatic parrhesiast telling it like it was to people who didn't want to hear his message. As negotiations came into place for a follow up to Kyoto, pressure intensified for nonbelievers to get out of the church.

Scientific reports around this time became increasingly uniform in their genre-inflated storytelling. The 2006 Stern Review on the Economics of Climate Change was the most influential to that date (Office of Climate Change 2006). Commissioned by Tony Blair's British Government, this sought to price the costs of action and inaction. After reviewing the available evidence in tremendous detail, Stern opted for a more apocalyptic reading of the dangers. These included threats to the water supply of "one sixth of the world's population," "declining crop yields…[which] could leave hundreds of millions without the ability to produce or purchase food," and "200 million people…permanently displaced due to rising sea levels, heavier floods and more intense droughts" (Office of Climate Change 2006 Executive Summary, p. vi). Stern also conjured the image of mass economic collapse along the lines of the Great Depression. Around this time, governments and bureaucracies that were perceived to be lukewarm in their commitment to tackling the problem were more strongly and widely polluted as engaging in undemocratic behavior. This trope could be most easily contrasted against the image of the hardworking, unpartisan scientist. In 2006, James Hansen, a leading climate scientist from the National Aeoronautics and Space Administration (NASA), was concerned about pressure from the Bush administration on discussions of risks and solutions. He noted that speakers were often followed by "minders": "It seems more like Nazi Germany or the Soviet Union than the United States," he told an audience at the New School (in Eilperin 2006, p. 7). Likewise, the *New York Times* (2003, p. A22) accused the Bush White House of "censorship on global warming" when it edited out material on the risks of global warming from an Environmental Protection Agency Report, leaving only "some pablum about the complexities of the issue and the research that is needed to resolve the uncertainties." The drama was expanding to include a full cast of characters: those struggling for narrative supremacy were themselves caught up in a wider narration of character, motivation, and morality.

Returning to the genre model of risk perception, we can summarize this story. Broadly speaking, it is one in which apocalyptic readings of threat have become more strongly institutionalized, particularly among governmental policy elites. Backed by the authority of a growing scientific knowledgebase and institutional brokers, such as NASA and the United Nations, these have slowly edged out low mimetic readings that envisage a cheap technological fix or endlessly defer the problem-solution until more information is available. They insist on urgent action and establish new categories of deviance. By the mid-2000s, resistance to this shift was framed more and more negatively as something other than the product of ignorance or justifiable doubt.

To date, my primary intent has been to describe, rather than explain, this shift in risk evaluation cosmology. Now is perhaps the time to offer a candidate sociological explanation. To begin with, we can observe a congress of interests. Scientists need funding for research projects, conferences, and jobs. It is hard to get resources from governments or international organizations such as the United Nations without tapping into existing lines of priority. If money is earmarked for "climate change research," then research will follow. The results themselves will not be falsified, but pressures will exist to upgrade consequences and to perhaps emphasize any distant threats and dangers that are possibly signaled in the hard data. As the 2009 "Climategate" scandal revealed, climate science has its messy backstage. Whether or not the scientific process is fatally warped is a moot point. However, any sociologist with an understanding of the literature on organizations, institutions, or scientific activity would be remiss not to consider this very possibility. Second, mass communications process also leads to risk amplification. Scientists and worried individuals, such as Al Gore, wish to generate public concern. This concern, manifested in movie audiences or opinion poll data, can then be used in symbolic struggles with governments over policy or funding. The wider public is little interested in fuzzy data, caveats, multiple projections, or measurement disputes. What is required is a simple and startling narrative that can compete in the news and public affairs attention space with other risks and dangers. As Al Gore himself put it:

> In the United States of America, unfortunately we still live in a bubble of unreality. And category 5 denials are an enormous obstacle to any discussion of solutions. Nobody is interested in solutions if they don't think there is a problem. Given that starting point, I believe it is appropriate to have an over-representation of factual presentations of how dangerous it [global warming] is, as a predicate for opening up the audience to listen to what solutions are, and how hopeful it is that we are going to solve this crisis. (Gore 2006)

Likewise, the global warming science pioneer Stephen Schnieder stated his frustration at a sound-bite world that does not provide space for the discussion of complexity. He controversially suggested that in order to gain attention perhaps:

> We have to offer up scary scenarios, make simplified, dramatic statements, and make little mention of any doubts we may have. Each of us has to decide what the right balance is between being effective and honest. I hope that means being both (Schnieder 1989)

Complicit in this process has been the mass media. Once again, there is a preference for stories that are newsworthy in the context of intense competition for space. Science journalism has long been handicapped by lack of narrative drive and the incomprehensible or non-urgent nature of most science findings. Stories that offer lukewarm global warming scenarios are likely to be cut out—that is unless they can be inserted into the wider drama over which genre will prevail. For the most part, the filtering and storying of the news lead again to risk amplification. Iconicity and visuality play a part in this. It is no accident that global warming stories often cluster around material that can offer a visual anchor, such as satellite images showing a chunk of Antarctic sea ice floating away or the diminished north polar ice cap. Nor is it pure chance that the emaciated polar bear looking for an ice floe has become the charismatic emblem of global warming as a cause of innocent suffering. Such images simplify climate change to a catalogue of disorders and vulnerabilities.

It is important to realize, however, that all this claim-making takes place against a regime of sedimented background representations. Instrumental actions, whether dedicated to audience share or to truth-telling, need to connect with powerful myths, tropes, and iconicities if they are to have force for opinion and policy. For Christians, the book of the Apocalypse shows that what goes around comes around. Sinners are punished for their sins and the proud for their hubris. The connection with CO2 emissions is not too hard to draw. Apocalyptic scenarios of global doom are not simply religiously embedded. They are widely circulated in secular literature and film. Agents of death have included nuclear holocaust (*On the Beach*), alien attack (*Independence Day*), malevolent artificial intelligence (*Terminator*), and meteorites (*Deep Impact*). In the post-apocalyptic movie or book, there is often generalized economic and social reversion to a neotribal state of nature, frequently in a semi-desert landscape (*Planet of the Apes, Mad Max Road Warrior, Blood of Heroes*) of the kind that we also encounter when cracked-earth images are shown documenting global warming in sub-Saharan Africa. The world where humans have failed to make the right decisions is almost invariably imagined as a hot one. Further, the discourse of global warming stands on the shoulders of a more general triumph of environmentalism in the late twentieth century. This has made a strongly normative indictment of pollution and propagated the belief that humans really are capable of destroying their planet, not just by means of nuclear war but also slowly and incrementally. By the year 2000, just about every major corporation and politician had to tout green credentials. To oppose or doubt global warming was to appear ecologically insensitive. As for the polar bear, this can mobilize opinion and interest only because of shifts and ruptures in the human/animal symbolic boundary with accompanying redefinitions of animals as sentient. The more Darwinian understanding of the polar bear as a killing robot is nowhere to be seen, nor is the frontier person's vision of the polar bear as a dangerous predator in need of culling.

APOCALYPTICISM CONTESTED

In his landmark study of *Risk Society*, written somewhat before climate change was at the center of the attention space of ecological anxieties, Ulrich Beck (1992) suggests that environmental dangers and unknown risks will lead to critical reflexivity and a new and more democratic global order. Spurred on by ecological uncertainty, citizens will demand more control over production and consumption processes and push for equity. What Beck misses is the way that this contested terrain has generated increased critical reflexivity, not only over science, progress, and politics, but also over public sphere representations themselves. Further, seemingly subscribing to the ecological world view, he does not seem to be able to envisage that this could itself become the target of critical reflexive activity. For example, the very hegemony of the apocalyptic mode allows critical and reflexive possibilities for a counterdiscourse. We might think of this as a set of cultural affordances: There are opportunity structures in place for particular meaning-motifs and dramatic structures to be mobilized.

Where the authority of the science base is weak—and where predictions cannot be confirmed by stark personal experience in everyday life—the constructed and artificial qualities of claims-making seem to stand out. Narrative struggles are inevitable. Sometimes these can be about data and measures. For example, critics of the Stern report charged that Stern had "cherry picked" the more severe risks and downsided consequences, underestimated the costs of mitigation, or had imposed an incorrect discounting rate for future costs and benefits of current action; thus moving him away from more prudent and less costly lines of action. These would include spending relatively small amounts of money in Africa to improve adaptive capacity for the truly disadvantaged (Lomborg 2006). The argument could even be made on the basis of science that global warming is a good thing. The downside risks were really global cooling and mini-ice ages. The climate was unstable, and cool spells had wiped out civilizations in the past. In this context, the release of carbon dioxide was like insurance against a more serious potential disaster: "It protects us from the unpredictable big freeze that could be far, far worse" (Steel 2002). If we can never live risk-free with a locked-in climate, then our task is to decide which risks we wish to live with. Such arguments, in effect, push for low mimesis grounded in the languages of science and technocracy.

Yet efforts at genre shifting need not involve just scientists and their data. They can also be the work of practical, organic intellectuals speaking to the public sphere about the representations of others. Focusing on the qualities of the discourses themselves—rather than on lower-order "facts"—a considerable component of the global warming cultural complex consists of efforts to ironically recast intellectual positions as culturally or ideologically shaped delusions. Much of the drama of climate change is about the struggles of representations and their sponsors rather than the movements of thermometers and glaciers.

Apocalypticism, as a cosmological stance, is particularly vulnerable to genre deflation making use of realism and irony. Narrations in this mode can be made out to be alarmist and their sponsors as fanatics. A column in Ireland's *Sunday Independent* captures the extra-scientific possibilities for critique quite neatly for our purposes. After noting that much science was now attributing global warming to nonhuman factors, such as solar activity, the witty and cutting Eilis O'Hanlon (2007) explains the rush of church leaders to "leap on the environmental bandwagon" was because "apocalypse was always their business." Environmentalists for their part were professional "doom mongers" who were unable to imagine the future as anything other than famine, disease, war, ecological disaster. Human history has shown that our species has the ingenuity to triumph over all adversity, and yet "the green Cassandras have us all convinced that our descendants will be back in the caves munching on raw thigh bones before Al Gore can say, 'I told you so.'" We need to "lighten up and have more optimism about mankind's continued ability to solve problems and make life better." Here, environmentalism is cast as a fad or fashion ("bandwagon"), one promoted by irrational, narrow-minded individuals who ignore common sense. More accurate, O'Hanlon ventures, would be a Romantic genre guess—this is why we need to "lighten up" and be "optimistic." Observe that O'Hanlon does not dispute the facts. She does not speak of sea ice or average global temperatures. She does not even dispute the anthropogenic hypothesis. She simply speaks to the matter of representations, and then juxtaposes these against experience.

In his book *An Appeal to Reason: A Cool Look at Global Warming*, former British Chancellor Nigel Lawson (2008) illustrates a more strident and less waggish mode of critique than O'Hanlon. Symbolically polluting his opponents, Lawson detects a closed "eco-fundamentalism" that has eliminated critical thinking. Particularly scathing of the Stern report, he dubbed this as alarmist. Consistent with the implicit call for genre-deflation that was in his book's title, Lawson suggests we should deal with problems as they come along rather than trying to second guess what they might be. "Steady as she goes," one might say. Al Gore became another magnet for criticism. His portrayal of Hurricane Katrina as caused by global warming was denounced as simplistic, and his mention of huge sea level rises without a time-frame misleading. According to climate-skeptic Richard Lindzen, this was "shrill alarmism" ("From a Rapt Audience, a Call to Cool the Hype" 2007).

But there is a stronger critique still lurking, one hinting at a drama about knowledge and human interests. It is one that moves beyond allegations of bandwagonism and closed thinking and that mirrors the negative representation we saw earlier of climate change skeptics repressing science. Apocalypticism is not only a bad genre guess that can be mocked, but also a hegemonic and anti-democratic force. Allegations can be made that the climate change skeptics were not being given a fair hearing and that only the most negative scenarios were given air time. Lawson, for example, spoke of the truth monopoly of the United Nation's climate change panel. Professor Richard Lindzen of MIT alleged in a 2006 issue of *The Wall Street Journal* that scientists who failed to follow the creed were having their funding cut. Anthropologist Benny Peiser suggested that widespread representations of scientific consensus on the anthropogenic origins of climate change were misleading. Further, he argued that Wikipedia editors had incorrectly written that he had changed his mind on this point and were refusing to let him edit his entry to reflect his still skeptical views (Newman 2008). The Climategate scandal of 2009 proved to many that leading climate change scientists were doctoring their evidence with statistical trickery and censoring opponents through the peer review process. We have a drama involving nefarious human forces as much as climatic ones.

So where are we now? It would seem that the narration of global warming is taking place at two levels. One is the assembly of clues from science and everyday experience into a narrative that includes agents, causes and consequences, and future projections. This discourse is about the relationship of the human and natural worlds. Here, we find what Niklas Luhmann (1989) calls ecological communication being shaped and filtered by genres with their consequent narrations of natural process. Technical information becomes storied, and with this colorful storying it becomes relevant to a wider society. The second level of narration is a meta-discourse over that narration. It asks who is doing the narrating, whether we have the right genre, and whether there are costs and consequences to particular collective representations. At both levels, global warming is the theme at the center of a moral and social drama. This is a story where there are good and bad actors, tragic and unintended consequences to action and inaction, and foolish and wise choices to be made. Global warming, then, is a complex and layered social fact, both material and ideal, where the cultural translation of scientific information lives alongside reflexivity over those very representations. More than just a series of thermometer readings, it is also a reading of thermometers and then again a reading of those readings.

REFERENCES

"Censorship on Global Warming." 2003. *New York Times*, June 20, p. A22.

"Changing the Climate." 1977. *The Economist*, June 4, p. 88.

"Don't Panic on Warming Report, PM Says." 2007. *Canberra Times*, November 19, p. A6.

"Earth Robbed in Kyoto." 1997. *South China Morning Post*, December 14, p. 10

"Europe Attacks Australia's Deal." 1997. *Sydney Morning Herald*, December 19, p. 10.

"Excerpts from Climate Report." 1983. *New York Times*, October 21, p. B5.

"From a Rapt Audience: A Call to Cool the Hype." 2007. *New York Times*, March 13, p. F1

"From Icebox to Greenhouse." 1979. *The Economist*, March 17, p. 96.

"Physical Scientist..." 1969. *New York Times*, December 21, p. 46.

"Planet Health Warning." 1997. *Jerusalem Post*, December 7, Opinion p. 8.

"Radical Lifestyle Changes Needed." 1989. *USA Today*, June 13. p. 10.

"Scientists Warn of Effects of Human Activity in Atmosphere." 1986. *New York Times*, January 13, p. A11.

"Stem the Global Warming Trend." 1997 *Christian Science Monitor*, September 23, Opinion/ Essays p. 10.

Beck, Ulrich. 1992. *Risk Society*. London: Sage.

Douglas, Mary, and Aaron Wildavsky. 1982. *Risk and Culture*. Berkeley: University of California Press.

Douglas, Mary. 1978. *Cultural Bias*. London: Routledge and Kegan Paul.

Durkheim, Emile, and Marcel Mauss. 1963 [1903]. *Primitive Classification*. Chicago: University of Chicago Press.

Eilperin, Juliet. 2006. "Censorship is Alleged at NOAA." *Washington Post*, February 1, p. A7.

Gore, Al. 2006. "Al Revere: An Interview with Accidental Movie Star Al Gore." *Grist Magazine*, May 9. http://www.grist.org/cgi-bin/printthis.pl?uri=news/ maindish/2006/05/09/roberts/index.html.

Guggenheim, Davis (director). 2006. *An Inconvenient Truth*. Paramount Home Entertainment.

Intergovernmental Panel on Climate Change. 1995. *Summary for Policymakers: The Economic and Social Dimensions of Climate Change—IPCC Working Group III*. Edited by J. P. Bruce, H. Lee, and E. F. Haites. http://www.ipcc.ch/ipccreports/assessments-reports.htm.

Jacobs, Ronald. 2000. *Race, Media and the Crisis of Civil Society*. Cambridge, UK: Cambridge University Press.

Keenlyside, N. S., M. Latif, J. Jungclaus, L. Kornbleuh, and E. Roeckner. 2008. "Advancing Decadal-Scale Climate Prediction in the North Atlantic Sector." *Nature* Vol 453: 84–88.

Lawson, Nigel. 2008. *An Appeal to Reason: A Cool Look at Global Warming*. London. Duckworth Overlook.

Lévi-Strauss, Claude. 1966. *The Savage Mind*. London: Weidenfeld and Nicholson.

Lomborg, Bjorn. 2006. "Stern Review." *The Wall Street Journal*, November 2.

Luhmann, Niklas. 1989. Ecological Communication. Chicago. University of Chicago Press.

Michaels, Patrick. 2008. "Global Warming Myth." *Washington Times*, May 16.

Newman, Melanie. 2008. "Debate Is an Endangered Species Says Climate Critic." *Times Higher Education*, September 4, p. 22.

O'Hanlon, Eilis. 2007. "Don't Put Your Faith in the Evils of Global Warming." *The Sunday Independent (Ireland)*, December 30.

Office of Climate Change. 2006. *Stern Review on the Economics of Climate Change*. London: Office of Climate Change.

Schneider, Stephen. 1989. "Interview." *Discover Magazine*, October, pp. 45–48.

Shabecoff, Philip. 1983. "Haste of Global Warming Trend Opposed." *New York Times*, October 21, p. A1.

Smith, Philip. 2005. *Why War?* Chicago: University of Chicago Press.

———. 2010. *Image and Text in Al Gore's "An Inconvenient Truth."* Paper presented at the International Sociological Association World Congress, Gothenburg Sweden.

Steel, Duncan. 2002. "Global Warming Is Good for You." *The Guardian*, December 5.

PART XII

CLASSIFICATION AND AMBIGUITY AS CULTURE

BROADENING CULTURAL SOCIOLOGY'S SCOPE: MEANING-MAKING IN MUNDANE ORGANIZATIONAL LIFE

NINA ELIASOPH AND JADE LO

CULTURAL sociologists do not often focus on daily, unremarkable life in organizations. Instead, we usually spotlight more public, visible action: either moments of high drama, when symbols glow with high emotional intensity, making frontpage news, or in organizations' explicit public self-presentations in newsletters and mission statements. Organizational sociologists, for their part, need a usable theory of culture. Many already use and develop culture concepts. To both subfields, we want to contribute a sensitive method of seeing how culture shapes everyday activities within organizations, and how, in turn, everyday activity can build up, bit by bit, to large-scale cultural change. We argue that people's everyday methods of coordinating action in organizations are, themselves, meaningful. Recognizing and documenting this everyday meaningfulness clinch the connection between scholarship in culture and organizations. To understand how this back-and-forth works, we need to examine patterns of interaction, not just in dramatic public disputes, but in unremarkable boring moments, inside the everyday lives of organizations. Cultural sociology and organizational sociology need each other. The goal of this chapter is to marry them—or, at least, to propose a more serious engagement between the two.

In proselytizing for a broader program for cultural sociology, our purpose is to make cultural sociology more useful for understanding more varied kinds of activity. It ought to be useful, not just for analyzing moments of drama and crisis, and not just for examining organizations' declarations about themselves, but for understanding the daily working of civic associations, businesses, government offices, and nonprofit agencies—all sorts of ongoing organizations. It is in formal organizations that most of us spend most of our days, so broadening the agenda is an important task. Seeing how mundane activity produces meanings that might ripple out to the broader culture is an important task, that is, *unless* we want to say that throughout most of the day, most people do not generate meaning, but just respond to meanings that were already generated elsewhere.

Our argument is that people do generate new meanings that become socially binding and shared both "from above" and "from below." We need to be able to trace both movements, both up and down: to show how well-established cultural categories from outside (or "above," to continue the up-and-down metaphor) of the face-to-face situation infuse everyday interactions, and to show how everyday meaning-making in mundane situations feeds "up" and out, into more public, shared, collective meaning-making.

What is missing from one or the other schools of thought that makes the engagement seem difficult?

First, cultural sociologists and organizational sociologists both tend to rely on a *sociolinguistic theory that is not cultural enough,* when they say that actors always have to improvise in an "ad hoc" way to figure out how to use collective representations in everyday life. Rather, we argue that everyday language use depends on people's filling in cultural, institutional knowledge, to make sense of the words. Meaningful speech is impossible unless people share these built-in references to institutions and culture. Through these, meanings enter the situation, without simply being generated in it. But these meanings are not quite "collective representations" of the sort that cultural sociologists usually examine; they make sense because of how they resonate with the situation.

Second, the definitions have to make sense of, and in, ongoing activity. They stick when they can do a job within a relatively predictable organizational form; they must be pragmatically usable by people who need to coordinate action in organizations. Participants need fine methods of distinguishing between different kinds of organizations, so they can know which definitions to put into play where. To explain peoples' methods of drawing such distinctions, cultural sociologists often point to big, broad categories—*the differentiation of spheres* of market, state, family, religion, and civic association. Using these categories is indeed part of how participants distinguish between one kind of organization and another, but not enough. In practice, almost no activities neatly adhere to one single sphere's implicit "logic." To orient themselves, to figure out what their organization is "a case of" at the moment, participants gather up a range of unspoken cues as informal evidence, not just the organization's proclamations about itself and its own definitions.

Like our second point, our third is also an element of pragmatic knowledge that participants have to share in order to keep an organization going. Cultural sociologists since Durkheim have said that both stability and change require moments of *collective effervescence*, when people reaffirm their bonds by jumping out of their skins, in ecstasy, momentarily "fusing" (Alexander 2007). Exciting moments momentarily sweep people out of their mundane activities and bind them together in a powerful sacred-feeling ritual—a political drama such as Obama's election is a good example. The world held its collective breath. But in everyday organizational life, breathing has to work differently. The collective representations that emerge from these intense moments extend promises of bliss that never can be met in ordinary life, when the logistical work of implementing the promises begins. Here, again, actors have to coordinate action together, partly drawing on collective representations even though the exciting collective representations never fully or accurately describe their action. In ordinary organizations, people have to learn how not to be swept away by unmeetable promises. Not all successful organizations have dramatic moments that affirm members' shared missions; in fact, any organization short of a cult whose members were so tightly bound together would not be able to function.

As cultural sociology maintains, people never start generating meaning from scratch in interaction— meanings are never simply generated from the ground up, never just in the course of interaction. Our agenda here is to show how researchers can complete the circle, to show how the process is much more of a chicken-and-an-egg story: to see how meanings filter into everyday interaction and circulate back out to solidify into publicly shared cultural structures and filter into interaction, in a cycle. *For all three elements of everyday meaning-making in organizations, routine and repetition create meaning, over time, when people have to get things done together.*

To illustrate these arguments, we trace transformations of words' meanings in everyday language use. Our first set of examples comes from a study of changes in the publishing industry; we begin by building on this study's insights, which bridge the subfields of organizational and cultural sociology. Our second two examples derives from a larger study of youth civic engagement projects in the United States. The uses of the words "leadership" and "volunteer" in these "Empowerment Projects" (Eliasoph 2011) will show how words' definitions change when they keep being misused in the same way over and over in a typical organization: After a while, the misuse becomes the use. Whatever goes on at a higher level, in national rituals or public events, words' definitions-in-use materialize and possibly transform through these repeated formations and possible reformations and deformations. After giving our three examples, we feed them through the essay's three-point argument, about cultural sociology's approach to *sociolinguistics*, to the *differentiation of the spheres*, and to *collective representations*, to show how to see the tiny integuments that connect culture to everyday activity in organizations.

ORGANIZATIONAL SOCIOLOGY AND CULTURAL SOCIOLOGY'S SHARED PERSPECTIVES ON CHANGE

Example One: Changes in the Publishing Industry

Some organization scholars already draw on and seriously develop cultural sociology. Drawing on and refining Robert Alford and Roger Friedland's idea of "institutional logics," for example, Thornton and Ocasio say that these logics are "supra-organizational," and they "order reality, provide meaning to action and structure conflicts" (1999: 803). They are

> the socially constructed, historical pattern of material practices, assumptions, values, beliefs, and rules by which individuals produce and reproduce their social reality…both material and symbolic…a set of assumptions and values, usually implicit, about how to interpret organizational reality, what constitutes appropriate behavior, and how to succeed. (1999: 804)

In Thornton and Ocasio's case, a shift in the U.S. publishing industry from an "editorial" logic rooted in editors' sense of professional wisdom, to a market logic in the 1970s, began as a response to changes in the economy. The shift was not, however, just a reaction to those "material" conditions; for the shift to matter for the organizations' operations, it had to become meaningful. It had to be institutionalized, solidified into new equipment—such as, for example, trade journals that focused on market competition in the book industry; new words and phrases such as "acquiring parent," "target company," and "deal price"; and the development of a subset of the banking industry that was now devoted to book publishing. In other words, Thornton and Ocasio's article shows how culture is generative, not just a response to conditions, but a creator of conditions, a condition in its own right. This is the core insight of cultural sociology: that culture is generative.

Another inspiration shared by culture and organization scholars is this: Tension prevails at the "borders" between each of these "differentiated spheres," and there are fierce battles over where to place an activity—like publishing, or like current arguments about education or health care (Alexander 1998). The second section of this chapter will show how these border struggles transform when they materialize in everyday life conditions.

Another shared inspiration is this: Rituals affirm an organization's collective bonds (Kunda 1991, e.g.), and organizations need them to survive; participants need to feel unified with their organizations through the intense collective representations that the rituals generate. Our third section will show how important it is for people to generate less intense, possibly flexible, lightly held representations as well.

If we went inside the organizations to get a closer glimpse at the process of change, we would find, in all of these, that people's methods of coordinating action over time, so that it could be relatively predictable, would be at the center of the analysis. Thornton and Ocasio examine the effects of the changes that they describe, but do not look inside the firms to see how such happened. They suggest that the process was incremental rather than revolutionary (826). Getting a closer glimpse of change, then, would require slowing down the camera, with an ethnographic or a historical investigation that focused on sequencing (Pierson 2004; Abbott 2001). If we did this investigation, what might we find? Why do some new words become prevalent and others do not? How do the symbols and the words absorb meaning from the contexts in which they are routinely seen and spoken?

Before turning to our theoretical arguments, then, we need a view of the insides of organizations in the process of transubstantiating old meanings. Our second and third examples come from a larger ethnographic study that one of the co-authors conducted on youth civic engagement projects.

Example Two: "The Leader"

In the past decades, the words "leader" and "volunteer" have changed dramatically. Once, a leader was someone who had followers; now, a leader is someone who takes the initiative and is responsible. "Leadership" programs for youth have inadvertently propagated this new definition.

Programs for disadvantaged youth in the 1980s were then called "prevention programs." But policy-makers realized that this smacked of condescension, as if the policy-makers were treating the youth as "problems," rather than as responsible, self-propelled actors. Influenced by social research that described the "disempowering" effect of highlighting deficiencies, policy-makers funded programs that aimed to ferret out and develop potential "leadership," even before the potential leaders had actually led anything.

We can observe the initial puzzlement that this new use of the word could provoke by drawing on my study of youth empowerment projects: At a meeting, about twenty-five teen "volunteers" are asked to break up into small groups and discuss what the qualities of "a leader" are. Many small groups misinterpret the question, giving answers like "tall, athletic, does well in school, and handsome." Upon hearing these summaries of the small-group discussions, Roberta, the adult organizer who had posed the initial question, recognized the error, and said, thinking aloud, that many of the teenagers did not consider themselves to be "leaders." She had to rephrase the question, so at a later meeting, she asked them how they *themselves* had become leaders. Many said that they were not leaders. However, eventually, after participating in this leadership group for a while, the disadvantaged youth learned that even if they never led anything, they were leaders. Soon, the new definition backfired: Roberta said to a meeting of other program organizers that their new definition had succeeded *too well*; that now, teens associated "leadership" with "programs for disadvantaged youth."

Calling people who have never led anything "leaders" makes sense if the mission is to help those potential leaders—if the organization is a kind of social service agency as well as a volunteer group. Calling them "leaders" does not make sense if the organization exists to help the needy, or to help distant others, and is not also doing double-duty as a social service agency. In organizations that blend social service with volunteer work for the purpose of "empowering" average citizens—"Empowerment Projects" (Eliasoph 2011)—the word "leader" is in the course of changing meaning.

These changes in meaning come about not simply because organizers declared that henceforth a word will mean something new. There was no exciting moment of collective effervescence branding the new meanings into people's consciousness.

Rather, the change in meaning walked hand-in-hand with much larger changes in the provision of social services over the past three decades. In this neoliberal form of governance, states and nonprofits try to help the needy by "empowering" them to take responsibility themselves, transforming them into volunteers who will be able to help themselves. The policy-makers' vision is that a person who helps others and becomes a leader will learn and grow, and eventually, by becoming the kind of person who is strong enough to give help, he or she will no longer need help. Thus, a social service agency that gets government funding also has to make sure that the recipients of aid are being treated as potential leaders. To coordinate action, participants need to hold *both* meanings in play, to keep both suspended for possible use, depending on what the participants are doing together: whether they are talking to funders—who can assume, from a distance, that needy recipients of aid can easily and instantly become "leaders"—versus when they are talking to fellow members, who need to know who is "really" leading, in the old-fashioned sense of the word.

Example Three: "The Volunteer" in the Empowerment Project

Our third example further illustrates this point. In the same kinds of projects, the words "volunteer" and "volunteer group" are also in the course of changing meanings, for the same reasons. A voluntary association was formerly a band of unpaid people who met informally to improve something on behalf of a collectivity. They could change course midstream as, in the course of meeting, they discovered new problems to solve. They did not need to account to any external authority for their actions or expenditures. Now, more and more, these defining features of volunteering are changing: Volunteer work is often organized from the top down, by nonprofits, corporations, and governments. Some members are paid. Their organizations have to render transparent accounts to funders, and cannot simply change course midstream. Formulating these accounts takes a great deal of time and thought. The collective representation—"volunteer"—is nearly sacred in American culture (Wuthnow 1991a, 1991b), and here we can see it while it is changing. It changes when it keeps being used in new ways; after a while, it transubstantiates in these new conditions.

Organizations have to make the public representation of "the volunteer" very explicit and easily readable, to document large quantities of volunteer work, and large numbers of volunteers, in order to demonstrate to their nonprofit and corporate funders that they have real grassroots support. To take a personal example that echoes dozens of others portrayed in *Making Volunteers*: One of the co-authors went to a river clean-up day sponsored by the Friends of the Los Angeles River, but was embarrassed at how little trash she picked up, and offered to bring youth volunteers to pick up the trash next time. The coordinator nodded enthusiastically, saying, "The more volunteers, the better; it shows our corporate funders that we *really have community support!*" Indeed, corporate logos peppered the backs of the t-shirts that all volunteers received. Some volunteers already had their own sponsors: A phalanx of them were wearing t-shirts from the Disney Corporation's "showyourcharacter.com" volunteer program, for example. The river clean-up was good for something, but keeping the river clean was probably not the main good that came from it. Part of the reason that a volunteer who arrived after about ten o'clock picked up so little litter was that other volunteers had already picked up most of it that Sunday. By the next Sunday, the river once again looked like the breeding ground for muddy plastic bags, Taco Bell soda cups, and broken shopping carts. So, the number of volunteers was not, in fact, the problem; rather, timing was. To clean the river, weekly visits would have been necessary. But doing that would be difficult, and would somewhat miss the point, because all that sponsors needed to know was that this organization could really muster large numbers of volunteers.

This changed definition of "volunteer" responded to and made sense of everyday practices and organizational forms. Without these changed organizational forms, the changed definitions, by themselves, would not have become meaningful and would not have lasted. And they would not have stuck if there had been no practical way of using these words in action. They would have sounded like nonsense, and if participants had tried to use them, their action would not have made sense, would not have been possible.

"Typification": A Missing Concept in Both Cultural Sociology and Organizational Sociology

For both organizational theory and cultural sociology, one missing link is a culturally grounded theory of everyday interaction. On the one hand, their linguistic theories hold that codes, languages, and myths develop a life of their own, and the signs within them relate to each other somewhat or completely independently of the interrelations of the objects to which the signs refer. We will return to this later.

On the other hand, both subfields have an overly random view of language, and Harold Garfinkel's work is the culprit. This may sound impressively obscure and nitpicking, but it really matters if an analysis has a thin theory of interaction, and both subfields rely on his work for their understanding of "interaction."

Garfinkel treats interaction as "ad hoc," constantly improvised and not patterned. He asserts that everyone who enters a new situation gropes around until he or she finds patterns, de novo in each organization.

His and fellow ethnomethodologists' agenda is to show how people improvise meanings in their everyday workings in an infinite reality. Even workers in a seemingly rule-bound office have to sort through files, and the rules cannot take account of all the infinite details of each file. People have to "fill in," with background knowledge that comes from elsewhere and can never be fully specified. For example, welfare office workers have to know how to greet applicants, how to tell when someone is waiting in line, how to distinguish applicants from other people such as delivery people who may enter the office, how to tell when the applicant is done talking and has given the final answer to Question 17 on the form; they have to know basic manners and to suspect deeper problems if the applicant does not, for example. Rather than assuming that bureaucracies really work by following all the rules, for example, old insights coming from management studies (Blau 1963, e.g.) and the labor movement itself show that any bureaucracy that rigidly followed the rules would collapse instantly. "Working to rule" is a way of calling going on strike, calling a halt to all action without leaving the building. So, ethnomethodology says, people improvise as they go.

The problem with Garfinkel's theory is that it allows us to imagine that words and deeds can be decoupled; as if in the daily workings of an organization, actors can ignore the organization's public representations, self-descriptions, and projected images. It throws out the baby with the bathwater, making it seem as if once we learn that people in bureaucracies can never work only according to the rules, we should therefore drop *any attempt* at categorizing organizations. Yes, ethnomethodology is right to say that bureaucrats act in a way that is less rule-governed than the standard image of bureaucracy implies, and that religious leaders act in a way that is less inspired and devout than the standard image of an otherworld-oriented religious organization. But this does not make the process of adjustment "ad hoc." That cannot be how organizations work. Rather, a person who enters a new organization can guess, rather accurately, what will happen next, and what to expect to happen in the next hour, day, or month, so that the new member can make plans and coordinate actions with fellow members. The new member needs to gather up tidbits of evidence in order to "typify" the situation, as in "the case of" a traditional school, alternative school, volunteer group, activist group, business, nonprofit, or other typical kind of organization.

To take Harvey Sacks' example (1971, 1972), when we hear, "The baby cried. The mommy picked it up," we immediately conjure up a whole story and impute motives: The mommy picked the baby up for the purpose of soothing it; maybe the baby was hungry or tired; the observed "mommy" was indeed the baby's mother. In contrast, when we hear, "The baby cried. The shortstop picked it up," we do not know what to think: Will the shortstop throw the baby to second base? Was the baby underfoot on the Astroturf, in the dugout, in the way? To understand the baby/mommy sequence, we need, and *have*, a set of cultural, collective knowledge that comes from outside of the immediate interaction. "Mommy/baby" may be humanity's most long-lived, stable meaning unit, institutionalized in every society in some way or another, but even here, the words may change and are never simple neutral labels, more and more so every year, as divorce and adoption make it harder to take only one "mommy" for granted. In other words, just knowing the stable meaning will not suffice: We *also* have to do some work in interaction—only a little bit, in this case—to make sure that there are no obstacles to our normal interpretation, which would be that this woman is this baby's mommy, not someone else's, for example, and that she was picking up the infant for the culturally expected, predictable reasons.

Rather than drawing on Garfinkel, both cultural sociologists and organization scholars could benefit from instead drawing on the work of Aaron Cicourel or Harvey Sacks, who show us how to use the concept of "typification" (Cicourel 1981; Schutz 1967; Cefaï n.d.). Through the process of typification, people learn to adjust the symbols, to adapt them, wiggling them until they seem to make sense in every-day contexts. When, as in the cases of "volunteer" and "leadership," the symbols accrete new meanings, it is not only in a dramatic watershed moment, but more often, it is in a more geological way, like stalactites that take a hundred years to grow a millimeter and eventually fill up a cave. When meanings change in dramatic moments, they take a while to filter into everyday practices and vice versa: When meanings change in practice, they take a while to filter into formal settings and eventually solidify in dictionaries.

Researchers who stay rooted only on the level of interaction leave open the *possibility* that symbols or metaphors are important for channeling people's emotions and actions (Katz 2001), but they do not press on with the investigation of symbols; it is not what these researchers are doing. They leave them for someone else to investigate while they themselves focus on participants' step-by-step groping. Researchers in this vein do not ask if these improvisations follow patterns: from one welfare office to another, one school or political party to another. We argue that the improvisations do come in patterns, and that the patterns themselves are meaningful.

In leaving the question of stability *across local sites* aside, research that ignores culture implicitly suggests that organizations might arrive at novel, unique, local, idiosyncratic solutions. If it were usually the case, however, creating and maintaining organizations would be impossibly difficult. Moving from one job to another, or even learning how to be client or customer from one store to another, would require learning from scratch each time. Publicizing and translating one organization's activities to another would be impossible. Part of asking any "how" has to include asking how people calculate or choose, or intuitively grasp at or develop, *patterns* of coordination when they enter an organization, and how they *transfer* knowledge and practices gleaned in one place to another. The "how's" almost inevitably extend far beyond any one organization itself, because most organizations have to represent themselves to multiple, distant others, in a complex society, with multiple, diverse audiences, actors, scripts, and props.

The concept of typification helps us grasp these how's, but we still need something more. Any act of typification has to draw on some culturally shared meanings, and yet people who are attempting to coordinate action in an organization cannot rely on meanings that are as big and blunt as "market, state, religion, civic, family." Making finer distinctions is not simply a matter of random improvisation, and actors need to make these finer distinctions right away, the moment they enter the relationship. Each time the word "volunteer" is used to point to the person who goes on the half-day river clean-up, the word changes a little, because participants have to learn what to expect when they respond to a call to "volunteer," or when organizers ask a high school "volunteer" who is getting school credit to come to an event, and then have to check to make sure that the "volunteer" deserves the credit necessary to graduate from high school.

Pragmatically, people in the organization need this knowledge, even before it has become sedimented into any public discourse. They have to know to expect something like the river clean-up, not a band of unpaid, local, independent folks. This kind of everyday tinkering eludes both organizational sociology and cultural sociology.

Structuralism in Practice

This kind of tinkering is not as necessary in very public cases, when the new symbol does not need to be immediately ready for use, to coordinate action, this minute. Alexander brilliantly shows that constellations of meaning are internally referential in his historical study of the rise of American anti-anti-Semitism: Before World War II, Americans were just about as anti-Semitic as Germans at the time. Later, in an effort to distinguish America from Nazi Germany, Americans sounded—and eventually *became*—much less anti-Jewish than they had been before the war. The opposition German versus Jew confronted the opposition German versus American; the result spawned a new creature: German anti-Semite versus American non-anti-Semite. Here is a perfect illustration of the way that cultural structures build up their own steam, develop their own momentum, regardless of any "conditions" aside from the need to create binary oppositions to distinguish one thing from another, and especially, to distinguish one's own group from the enemy. The structural logic Alexander describes has little to do with anyone's feelings or any material pressures, or anyone's immediate need to continue to coordinate action immediately with other people.

This approach works well for a dramatic historic reversal, but not well enough for explaining the changes inside organizations. In the cases of the words "leader" and "volunteer," we can see, day by day, inside organizations that change is happening. When change happens so incrementally, the logic is different from that of dramatic change: While the cultural structures form their own constellations, they also immediately, simultaneously have to have a connection to activity. A new usage that starts in one place filters and transforms in another, in an endlessly changing cycle, when people start to use old words in new ways, to do new things together. Wuthnow (1993), and Ghaziani and Ventresca (2005) show precisely how words change over the course of a long stretch of time, and how the changes articulate organizational changes—"articulate," as Wuthnow says, in both senses of the term: to give voice to the changes, and to link the changes the way sinews link bones so that the cultural structures can be used.

The primary task of cultural analysis should be "to identify recurring features, distinctions, and underlying patterns which give form and substance to culture" (Wuthnow et al. 1984: 255; see also Ghaziani 2004). Meaning—or the sense people make of the world or some aspect of it—is established from the relationship among these patterns" (Ghaziani and Ventresca 2005: 533).

A structuralist account would focus on how distinctions multiply primarily as patterns of binary oppositions between signs, but for everyday practical activity, that is not enough. "Giving substance to" cultural change is key in the above quote; it means more than finding out how new relationships between symbols arise. It also requires figuring out how people attach the meanings to everyday practices and equipment (Thevenot 2006; Callon 1986). In other words, the new meaning of "leader" depends on more than a constellation of meanings. It also depends on the way the patterns articulate to new organizational forms (Clemens 2005) and give them voice. These new "leaders" or "volunteers" make sense of and in organizations that are simultaneously supposed to be therapeutic social service agencies for the leader/volunteers and also civic associations. They are both "state" and "civic"; for the study of organizations, cultural sociology would start by pointing us to a finite number of such self-definitions that organizations can project into the public arena—"family, market, religion, profession, state," for example. This is a good step but, again, not precise enough if we want to understand how these distinctions materialize in organizations, as the next section will argue.

Border Disputes: Tinkering But Never Triumphantly Repairing

A busy hive of institutions like "state" and "market" shape and reshape, interpret and reinterpret, activities such as "publishing," "volunteering," or "leading"—transforming any actions' meanings depending on which "logic" is in play. This has, of course, been a central idea in sociology since Weber.

Family, market, religion, and the like are some of our most common and visible signposts, but there is a problem: There are also, to take Thornton and Ocasio's example, publishers with an "editorial, professional" logic and there are publishers with a "market" logic, both of which have to make enough of a profit to stay afloat as businesses in the marketplace. There are churches, but then, some are mega-churches with big parking lots and electric guitars, some are storefront evangelical churches whose members touch each other's thighs and sob together (Stohlman 2007), some are white clapboard, steepled churches with organs and no physical touching. Luckily for the church-goer, these subdivisions are easy to recognize, without making too many mistakes. But the big signpost "church" does not help a person know how to act in any particular type of church. The same holds for all the big signposts—"state," "market," "family," or "civic association"— particularly now that these "spheres" appear more and more in "hybrid" formats, all at once (Hall 1992; Eliasoph 2009; Dekker 2009).

If we think that culture matters for people's everyday actions, then it ought to be useful for understanding how people distinguish between the mega-church and the evangelical storefront church. If we think that culture matters in this regard, we will notice that there is a move "from the bottom up," which complements cultural sociology's usual move from the top down. To grasp this movement, we will notice that people "typify" the organizations quite nicely and the *accumulation of small differences*—the storefront church's acoustic guitars versus the mega-church's electric ones, storefront on a busy street versus big building behind a parking lot, hugs and screams versus polite chitchat, big versus small, to take some items that people might employ when informally classifying the two. These differences become meaningful; meaning hangs on them, but they themselves are not empty hangers. They, in turn, contribute to the actors' meaning-making. For example, since acoustic guitars have different properties than electric ones, allowing for more singing along, for example, the initial small differences create subsequent ones. The objects have their own steam that is not entirely dependent on the cultural structure (Callon 1986, e.g.).

- We will notice that all these little distinguishing features add up to a meaningful whole that becomes greater than the sum of its parts.
- We will notice that once people have gathered up this accumulation of small differences, the distinction that they make between the two sorts of churches is meaningful and likely to become more so every year on the world stage.

If, in other words, we think that organizations require meaningful action, then we need to know more than we learn from cultural sociology or organizational sociology. We still need to know, with more precision, how to extend the "strong program in cultural sociology" all the way down to the level of everyday organizational life.

To see how this works, let us take the redefinitions of "volunteer" and of "leader," and of a "good publisher." They are, indeed, what Alexander would call border disputes. These boundaries between institutions are inevitably "moral" boundaries, not just in the sense in which we normally use the term, to mean overarching, placeless, timeless values, ideals, beliefs, judgments, attitudes, or symbols; they are about everyday judgments about situations, about what is appropriate to say or do where, when, with whom, with what equipment—what Kenneth Burke (1969) called "the pentad": the actors, the characters they impersonate, the mise-en-scène (props, scenery, lighting), the audience, and script.

Yes, part of our explanation of the changed definitions of the key symbols of "volunteer" and "leader" relies on this longstanding assumption that different spheres of market, bureaucracy, civil society, family, and the rest promise different moral goods. People cannot decide what is "good" or "bad" unless they know where they are. They also cannot even figure out what is possible to do unless they know where they are. What is decent to do or say in one context is rude, wrong, and out of place in other.[1] Misplaced typifications of situations make people angry; they are "wrong" in both senses of the word: not only because they are mistakes, but also because they undermine participants' ability to know what is reasonable, decent, or good to say or do in that situation.

The boundaries between institutions, which tell us which justifications to muster where, are always tense, and therefore, where the interesting action is (Alexander 1999, 2003; Boltanski and Thevenot 2005; Lamont 1991). They are tense because gaps between promises and action are inevitable; each sphere exists by making promises that cannot be met (Alexander 1999): Bureaucracies promise to administer justice impartially; families promise unending loyalty; civic organizations promise free and equal relationships; markets promise fair competition.[2] Before utopia (in other words, forever), it will be impossible to fulfill all these promises all at once. The moral goods that are promised in one "world" are incommensurable with those of the others: Each set of promises is good in its own way, and each maintains its own blind spots. For example, what is proclaimed good in a bureaucratically organized relationship—fairness according to measurable criteria, spelled out rules, personal neutrality—is considered bad and weird in a civic group, and even worse and even weirder in a family-like setting. For Boltanski and Thevenot, only certain ideals can become "justifications": They each promise a different kind of equality— equal chances to compete in the marketplace so that you can be *better* than everyone else; sacred equality to be respected as a unique human being who does *not need to compare* him- or herself to anyone; legal equality so that everyone is the *same* under the law (see also Stone 1988). None of these promises can be met completely, but that does not make the stories irrelevant. To know what people consider to be "the good" in any particular instance of public decision making, you would need to know how they implicitly answer the question, "'The good' in relation to *which moral world?*"

Organizations cannot make good on their promises, but the expectations and hopes are not, therefore, "mere" fictions. As Alexander, Boltanski, and Thevenot and others insist, these collective representations organize how and where people can realistically make *public* claims, what ideas they can express where, and even what they can feel justified in feeling in public situations. For example, even though we might take it as obvious that the police do not treat everyone equally, or the government does not maintain roads in poor neighborhoods as nicely as it maintains roads in wealthy ones, we are justified in being outraged when they do not. And we are justified in expressing our outrage publicly. Taking boundaries as real means being able to hold the bureaucrat accountable for being inefficient or not following rules, for example, or it means being able to scold the civic group for not being egalitarian.

Here is what we add to this important set of insights: Saying that people implicitly figure out which moral world they are in, and act accordingly, does not mean that the "bad and weird, out-of-place things" do not happen. This is a crucial point, because in everyday organizational life, people need to know how to do the "out-of-place" activities without destroying members' shared implicit expectations about the organization. That is, they have to know how to uphold the borders correctly, which means that they have to uphold them in certain places and not others.

One might feel a bit queasy the first few times one hears churches using the tools of businesses, acting like businesses, calling Jesus their first "Chief Executive Officer" (Fox 2004) and the flock "consumers," or the first time one hears how much paperwork the Vatican has to do to name someone a saint. The unsettled feeling comes from having to make explicit what everyone had *already known* intuitively— churches do not simply inhabit a world of cherubim and seraphim, but have already been paying rent and raising funds and doing paperwork and designing parking lots and access ramps the whole time. The difference is in whether and how, and where people are noticing and talking about such. After a while, the collision starts to feel easy and normal, and spectators cease to be startled when they see church commercials on TV.[3] Actors rely on, while also constantly adjusting, potent symbols, and over time, the adjustments become the meanings.

Here, again, time and repetition matter. Keeping the "out-of-place" elements at bay is easier to do for the duration of a public performance than it is to do in an ongoing organization. Alexander says that people are always creatively "repairing" boundaries, as one world invades another (1999, 2001). This is a good metaphor for public speechmaking, but works less well for descriptions of ongoing organizations, unless we have in mind a "tinkerer" who never really finishes the job, because the out-of-place things continue happening, and the participants keep having to repair, constantly, never finally sealing up the leak, because after sealing up one leak, two new ones spring up.

After constant "tinkering" (Lévi-Strauss, 1963; de Certeau 1988; Swidler 2006), patterns emerge. Old "logics" expand into new conditions, and then they, in turn, solidify into newly predictable organizations. For example, in San Francisco's gay rights movement of the 1980s, a hiking club could become a "gay hiking club," a sewing circle could become a "lesbian sewing circle," a donut shop became "Sticky Buns," and a hamburger joint "Hot and Hunky," thus expanding the movement to include "things" like trail-heads and donut-holes that had previously been used only for recreational or commercial purposes. Suddenly, they are all on the same table, thus redefining activism and eating and hiking and sewing. Just by eating dinner at "Hot and Hunky" and having dessert at "Sticky Buns," you could feel the collective effervescence of the larger movement and, in some concrete though diffuse way, contribute to it. Eventually, the joke—the Hot and Hunky or Sticky Buns— becomes predictable and then, eventually, unremarkable, a "dead metaphor." People come to expect that some hiking clubs will be lesbian hiking clubs. Organizations settle into "styles" that new members quickly recognize as typical—they've seen an organization *like this* before. Activists tinkered with old organizational forms to create new ones (Armstrong 2002).

Similarly, members of American groups that lobbied for the right to vote at the beginning of the 1900s wondered, "What kind of group are we?" Are we like a political party, whose members should address each other formally and elect their leaders? Or are we like a social club that holds fetes with lovely food and fine dress? Or perhaps we are like a neighborly mutual aid group, whose solicitous members should cook for each other and take care of each other's children in times of need? People recognize patterns of coordinating action, so that they know that if their model is the charitable ladies' aid society, they should act personal and caring, not loudly plot about gaining power. This does not mean that the women in the charitable ladies' aid society do not plot about gaining power; they just do it behind-the-scenes: They learn what to say and do where, with whom, and how. Eventually, this organizational style feels typical and predictable.

When imagining how people construct these new organizational forms, think of LEGO® constructions, or broken-down cars in the front yard of a rural shack, being picked apart for their working pieces—"cannibalized." People do not make up organizations from scratch, but tinker their organizations together, cannibalizing other organizations' parts and combining them in somewhat unforeseen ways, ending up with somewhat new vehicles.[4] "Ending up," though, is not quite the right metaphor: The tinkering has to be slow enough for participants to know how to coordinate action together even when they are coordinating action that has not yet happened.

When making plans, they have to share rough predictions of their future together. Here, culture *must* enter (Tavory and Eliasoph forthcoming); since, obviously, the future has not yet happened, participants have to rely on culturally shared hints about it. If the tinkering systematically transforms deeply and passionately held symbols, it has to make the changes slowly enough for participants to do this. But the tinkering can never stop, because no organization lives up to the claims it makes about itself.

Routine ways of drawing the boundaries often invoke ambivalence: At the end of the long line in the bureaucracy, we are *surprised* if our problem is actually solved—surprised, that is, if the bureaucracy worked the way it was supposed to work. But we are still *outraged* if the problem is *not* solved. The "reality of moral expectations" (Boltanski and Thevenot 2000) is that they are complexly nuanced, not simply on or off. This does not mean that we can end the discussion by saying that in everyday life, boundaries are simply fuzzier versions of the dramatic renditions of the boundaries, or that everyday life is just a pale, constantly degrading image that gets reinfused with light and color at the next euphoric moment of collective effervescence. If that were so, cultural sociology would be irrelevant for the study of everyday life, but it is not so. Rather, it means that moral meaning-making happens through this process of wiggling the elements of the performance until they feel predictable. Our point is that "predictable" *is* a kind of morality; it is not the same as fusion and does not glow with the intensity of a collectively breathtaking moment. For the pentad to make sense in everyday life, making the elements cohere has to stretch out over a long period of time, and sediment into predictable formats. The elements of Burke's pentad "sediment."[5] That sedimentation takes place over time, and through repetition, not just in moments of ecstasy.[6]

Border Disputes within Organizations

In a "typical" complex organization, there are inevitably different subunits that need to tell different stories, to different audiences, using different props—in the manufacturing wing, the legal department, the advertising department, the benefits office. "This way to understanding organizations asks the observer to capture the audience as it is making itself…and notices that there are multiple situations, in which a group's internal unity and external relations, coordination in time and space, all become problematic. [In such an analysis] 'space' shatters into multiple places, each clamoring for public attention, in an architecture of scenes; 'time' explodes into different ways of marking time, each with its own rhythms and qualities…" (Cefaï 2002: 67–69).[7]

In a typical organization's "architecture," members know more or less how to put different justifications in play in different places. For example, parents and medical staff have systematically different responsibilities to seriously ill babies (Heimer and Staffen 1998). The two internal audiences require different performances, but still have to cooperate. And as organization scholars say, when people coordinate action, according to repetitive, predictable patterns, the patterns accumulate, building up, over time, into "institutions" (Jepperson 1991, e.g.). Alexander and others who examine dramatic public justifications say that there is a "how" but they do not press on with the investigation of the step-by-step groping; it is just not what these researchers are doing. They leave it to someone else to investigate the groping, while they themselves focus on participants' more intensely symbolic, imaginative, or transcendent "storied" moments.

In stable organizations, "out-of-place" activity happens all the time. So out-of-place activity usually becomes hidden, or ignored, laughed at, or smoothed away, in seemingly effortless, predictable ways. People move it "backstage" (Goffman 1958), or joke about it (Lichterman 1996), or otherwise keep it separate in time and space from the main interaction. This is all difficult to accomplish, and there are always mistakes, jokes, and willful transgressions. But the work of making it all cohere comes to feel normal, as people intuitively develop shared ways of minimizing, arguing about, or displacing activities that do not fit.

Moments of collective effervescence immediately are given a lie the next morning, when the new meaning is supposed to take hold, because the new meaning is always more glorious than any everyday organization could uphold. Both are true, but in different ways. The Obama election is a good example: The moment was beautiful and told a transcendent truth[8] about Americans and people in general. But the moment could not last, no matter how good a president he became, because that level of beauty cannot be sustained. It is not how organizations work.

To understand this "how," we need the concept of "organizational style" (Lichterman 2005; Eliasoph and Lichterman 2003; Eliasoph 2010).[9] For example, in some university-based activist organizations in Brazil (Mische 2008), members assume that the way to be a good member of a good group is to argue and plot ways of gaining power for the group. In these groups, hesitation, agreement, and cautious deliberation occur, but only behind the scenes. In other Brazilian youth groups, expressing harmonious feelings is the glue that holds people together; in groups like these, in turn, participants have to push disagreement backstage. Still other Brazilian youth activist groups highlight cautious, rational discourse; in these groups, anger and passion hide backstage. There still *is* agreement and self-doubt in the cantankerous groups; there still *is* disagreement in the consensus-based groups; and members in the rational groups still have strong feelings: They are just harder to express. As Mische argues, newcomers can recognize an organization's style by observing how members push some feelings, ideas, and relationships off the horizon here, but spotlight them there; by talking about some issues only in small, late-night huddles, and others in plain view, frontstage; by shunning some members for asking the wrong questions in the wrong tone. Within each style, it is easier to do or say some things, and harder to do others. Organizational style is another word for the classical concept of "practical knowledge" sometimes translated as "prudence"—a word that we would like to resurrect for this purpose, but doubt will stick.

Participants' methods of distinguishing between one organization and another have to work, in everyday practice, when they are "put to the test" (Boltanski and Thevenot 1991), so investing all of their trust in the organization's explicit promises will not usually be good enough. Here, again, typification and pragmatic action are the keys; situations become easy to recognize, solid-seeming, "institutionalized" for most people in a society, *even though*, as organization scholars argue, no situations actually ever fit the rules, stories, moral narratives, myths.[10] Even though bureaucratic rules do not work the way rule-makers say they work, people can usually still recognize a bureaucracy and predict what is likely to happen next in one.

People routinely massage unruly situations until they seem to fall into patterns, so that there are not just infinite, bewildering, unique situations dazzling us every day.

Many organizations share an "organizational form," but do not share a "style." Perhaps a good analogy is Darwin's well-known distinction between "unity of type" and "conditions of existence." Fins, flippers, and arms share a unity of type, so, at least for a few million years, this preservation of the form makes them recognizably related. Eventually, the adaptations become too distant to be recognizable, as the forms transform in everyday conditions. There are many empowerment projects, many similar welfare offices, many similar small "alternative schools," many similar environmental activist groups. We propose that a finite number of "organizational styles" will be easily available to most people who have any familiarity with a range of organizations that share a "form." After having participated in two strident student groups or two rigid bureaucracies or two more familiar ones (Gouldner 1956), a person knows how to "do" the third. When millions of people have the same experience, a predictable kind of organization solidifies.

Performance: The Need to Fail

Finally, we extend Alexander's concept of "performance" to see how organizations represent themselves, to their members and their external audiences.

Echoing Durkheim, Alexander starts by saying that societies need strong collective representations, and that these collective representations, feelings, and ideas are forged in extreme moments and endure until the next meltdown and reforging. An intense ritual brings people out of their individual selves, rewakens their sense of belonging, and reforges their ability to make meaning together. Alexander wisely contends that this was easier to do in pre-Antiquity, when ritual involved a ruler performing his own role as ruler, before an audience that was, itself, part of the ritual action, to enact a situation that was supposed to represent the ruler as perfect and the society as perfect. Alexander says that it is difficult to stage a convincing public performance in a diverse, complex society. Unlike ancient or tribal societies, Western societies since ancient Greece have separated out the scripts, audiences, actors, the characters whom they impersonate, and the society that they are supposed to reflect. Because of this differentiation, the play often fails: The actors, the characters they impersonate, the mise-en-scène, the audience, and script—the elements of Burke's pentad—do not match, do not "fuse," and the ritual's power is thus "de-fused." Different audiences, for example, may interpret the same performance in quite opposite ways. Or there may be suspicion that the actors are puppets, or the props on stage may undermine the message. In those cases, Alexander says, the performance "fails." In a successful performance, the spectator, as well as the actor, "identifies with something with which he is not identical." In the gap, solidarity grows; people who take a metaphoric leap together momentarily merge en route (Auerbach 2003 [1953]).

A metaphoric flight like this transports us together when we have no baggage, but in most cases, we do. This approach to performance assumes that in an effective, meaning-generating ritual, "saying is doing." Language philosopher J. L. Austin (1965) described cases when "saying is doing"—when the public official breaks the champagne bottle on the side of the ship and says, "I christen thee the Queen Mary"; when the police say "You are under arrest"; or the minister pronounced you man and wife. In ongoing organizations, however, participants have to know how and when they can "do things with words"; if I christen you, or say you are under arrest, it probably will not have any affect. To know when the performance will work and when it will not, people have to develop methods of attaching the ritual to their everyday conditions, with the equipment that they can muster, and only certain people can make the words stick. No matter how many times a business claims to be a family, if it still fires loyal employees, the words will not stick. Participants have to know how and when to invoke the words, and how to protect themselves from getting fired. No matter how often a business claims not to be a hierarchy, participants have to know, again, how and when and with whom to invoke the claims (Kunda 1992).

In the everyday life of organizations, the failure to fuse and take the metaphoric leap together does not result in organizational failure. It is normal and typical, and *necessary* for the organization's ability to survive and to change. Organizations' public representations never adequately describe what goes on inside them; all organizations make implausible promises, but the organizations keep bumbling along anyway—muddling through, in Charles Lindblom's words (1980). This means that participants have to learn precisely how to expect the performances to fail. Thornton and Ocasio's article, for example, implies that looseness of definitions is not a mistake, but is necessary. As organization scholars have long recognized (Meyer and Rowan 1977, e.g.), people can never use their ritual knowledge in everyday life undiluted; doing so would be to collapse the boundaries between the real and the symbolic. Maintaining both kinds of meaning is necessary in organizations. Too much depth or excitement would be a problem, not a goal. If organizations lack dramatic celebrations and glue, they keep muddling through anyway, precisely *because* members lack serious psychic investment, and know how and when to take the big promises seriously.

Our point is that that connecting or decoupling them is never just an on/off switch, but requires pragmatic precision. We argue, further, that through repeated couplings and decouplings of ritual knowledge and pragmatic action, new meanings arise. When, for example, the words "volunteer" and "leader" change meaning, the change is happening in a less dramatic, less public way than the changes Alexander describes. It is happening in such a way that even after people have redefined the word, they can still use the expression "an hour later" in its older definition, depending on what they need to get done at the moment. If someone who was just called "a leader" has no experience in leading anything, and the task at the moment is not to inspire future potential leadership but to get a specific task done, participants have to know this. They have to know which definition to use, to get something done together. Nonetheless, this new, flexible set of definitions ultimately also becomes culturally binding.

Alexander's key insight can be extended even further than he himself does: Doing the kind of performance that Alexander calls a "failure" would, in this case, be the only way to succeed. Participants have to learn how to say different things in different places; how and when to be cynical, timid, or combative; how and when to be friendly, intimate, or formal; which definition to muster where. Multiple, vague meanings are themselves the meanings that all but the most sect-like organization must reaffirm. Rather than a performance of extraordinary luminosity and fusion, people need to learn to perform these varied degrees of finely calibrated but unintense, vague attachment.

Further extending cultural sociology's reach, we argue that even if participation in most organizations works best and feels best when people calibrate their distance and are not carried away, this distance is not culturally meaningless. Participants have to do it with nuanced precision; the meaning and the practice are not just "decoupled," as organization scholars had once said. The precise method of "decoupling" word and deed eventually, if repeated often enough across enough different organizations, becomes itself part of a shared repertoire of meanings. These everyday methods may never be ritualized, but they may be commonly recognized nonetheless.

USING CULTURAL SOCIOLOGY TO SEE HOW PEOPLE IN ORGANIZATIONS COORDINATE ACTION

So, does all of this mean that we have reached the outer threshold of cultural sociology's relevance? Does it mean that cultural sociology is good only for brief moments like the Aborigines' seasonal gatherings, or moments when the whole world is riveted to the TV screen in judgment? No, it means that cultural sociology needs to find a way of talking about people's everyday life methods of making definitions feel as if they cohere, in everyday life.

Just as the strong program objects to sociology's usual treatment of "culture" as the soft stuff that is left over after all the causal structures have been pinpointed (Alexander 1999: 13), so does this chapter argue that patterns of interaction are not the soft stuff that is left over after cultural structures have been pinpointed. This is not a call for softening structuralism's edges, blurring them so we can give room for people to make ad hoc adjustments to the structures. Rather, the argument is that the processes of adjustment follow, and create, meaningful, recurrent patterns, and the patterns "sediment" into enduring, shared expectations, even if a dramatic performance does not stamp it in solid cement. To grasp the very precise manners in which people methodically create and recreate these patterns of motion, we suggested the concept of "organizational style."

In adding this dimension—time and motion—we have added three ingredients to both cultural and organizational sociology.

First, better sociolinguistic theories are needed than the ones currently in circulation in both organizational sociology and cultural sociology. We must see how normal everyday language use inevitably invokes and reinforces background knowledge about social institutions—about "mommies" versus "shortstops" in relation to "babies," for example.

Second, we need a theory of how people implicitly negotiate the borders between institutions in everyday situations, where the borders are not only never clear, but often must be kept intentionally vague, and not just vague, but vague in very precise ways. Part of how participants distinguish between one kind of organization and another is by relying on abstractions like "the differentiation of spheres," but that is not enough: They need finer methods of distinguishing between different kinds of organizations, all of which, in practice, blend activities that adhere to many spheres' implicit "logics." We need to understand how actors draw borders between institutions pragmatically, so that people actually know *what to do together*, in the next few minutes, hours, or years. The borders between institutions can look solid for a few moments, in a public speech, but the instant a person enters a real organization, maintaining any shared sense of "what is this organization a 'case of?'" is much more difficult; the borders change minute-by-minute, and the upkeep that they require must be both more precise and more flexible than the kind that a public performance can suggest.

Third, new meanings can jell without any binding ritual that seizes participants. In a ritual, participants can recognize failure when they fail to become sufficiently engaged, ecstatically taken out of themselves, or convinced. In an organization, in contrast, participants can recognize failure when they cannot figure out how to do things together, when they cannot reach any agreement on how to judge their actions, or how to feel about them. Meaning-making in organizations works pragmatically; something is meaningless when action halts. Action might feel meaningless even before that, but the convincing "test" is the pragmatic one: If people can act effectively together, the action inevitably bears some kind of meaning, even if the meaning as participants see it is "trivial, meaningless action." This may look like a simple semantic argument, about whether to say that meaninglessness is a kind of meaning, apathy a kind of action, a quarter-note rest a kind of sound, and silence a kind of speech. But it is more than that: It is to say that if people can work together, shoulder-to-shoulder, over time, repetitively, they are also making meaning together. We see the cultural dimension of this meaning-making when participants can decipher each other's actions enough to predict the future, fairly well.

For the study of organizations, our question has to be how to imagine the relationship between everyday sedimentation and the moments of high drama on the other. Our point has been that the marriage can be quite happy and stable, as long as we recognize that collective feelings and meanings also form and transform in more mundane practices, over time, as the layers and layers of subtle transformations build on one another. In all three additions, we argue that the concept of "typification" shows how actors coordinate action in the next few minutes, hours, or years. This does not mean that cultural categories are irrelevant; in contrast, it means that people must master the categories' subtly different *uses*, in different situations, with different audiences. By taking this crucial pragmatic step, learning exactly how and where and when to couple or decouple, then cultural sociology and organizational sociology can marry.

NOTES

1. These seemingly bland and obvious insights inspire some of the most exciting recent social theory and research, and follow a long tradition in Western thought From Aristotle to Hegel, to contemporary theorists (Walzer 1983; Smiley 1988; Alford and Friedland 1985, 1990; Stone 1988), theorists have challenged political philosophies that assume a decontextual sense of the good. Smiley, like Boltanski and Thevenot, does not say that goodness is all relative, that "anything goes," but rather, that we can only start from the situations that we have, from the raw material we have. This is a materialized understanding

of moral judgment. Boltanski and Thévenot place more weight than Alexander does on the incessant difficulties of getting from the justification (or the code, the cultural category) to the pragmatic "test," as they put it.

2. Boltanski and Thévenot place more weight than Alexander does on the incessantness of the difficulties of connecting the justification (or the code, the cultural category) with the situation, through the pragmatic "test," as the French authors put it. They call these different categories "justifications," making it clear that they are not talking about empirical categories. Their definition is more precise than the idea of "institutional logics," which includes, in some work, taken-for-granted practices, equipment, and rhetoric. A "justification," in contrast, might clash with the "equipment" that is in place in a real organization, when, to take our example, the volunteers must be counted and their hours documented on grant application.

3. And, as in any organization, people creatively "repair" its boundaries, as one moral narrative—in this case, financial—inevitably invades another—in this case, religious (Alexander 1999, 2001).

4. Similarly, when the government pays "community-based organizations" to do things that were formerly done by the government—preschool care or health care, for example—the organizations creatively blend political activism, volunteer work, and social work (Minkoff 2002). Rather than crushing community life and squelching politics, the government funding can create a "political machine": The community-based organization supports local politicians and, in turn, the politicians dispense goods and services to the organizations that support them (Marwell 2004).

5. Schutz (1970) and Ricœur (1991) both use the word this way, to make the same point. As Ricœur puts it, "The rules change under pressure of innovation, but they change slowly and even resist change in virtue of the sedimentation process....The rules that together form a new kind of grammar direct the composition of new words—new before becoming typical" (Ricoeur 1991: 430). See Robin Wagner-Pacifici's insightful use of this insight about time, in her work on the back-and-forth of public conflicts (2001).

6. Some neo-institutionalist theory uses the term "schemata" to describe this process, but the same authors' empirical research shows a much more sensual process. Like typifications, schemata link cognition, emotion, and moral judgment (DiMaggio and Powell 1991. e.g.), and through them, members coordinate action to create organizations. We emphasize that this everyday practical work is inseparable from the "things" that surround it. Vygotsky (1978) calls this network of people and things "activity systems"; it includes members' ways of gluing their "schemata" onto everyday practices. As Vygotsky, Latour, and others emphasize, one thinks by means of a whole entourage of "things."

7. Similarly, an exhaustive and suggestive literature review of neo-institutionalism's varied stripes reveals

> a number of clear prescriptions for the analysis of institutional change: disaggregate institutions into schemas and resources; decompose institutional durability into processes of reproduction, disruption, and response to disruption; and above all, appreciate the multiplicity and heterogeneity of the institutions that make up the social world....(Clemens and Cook 1991)

8. This is Bellah's concept of "symbolic realism" (1970).

9. The concept "organizational style" is like "group style," but the difference is important: A "group" is one unit that may or may not be part of a larger "organization." In a small, face-to-face group, there may be only one "style" in play, but in a large organization, there will be multiple subgroups, and part of how participants learn the style is by

learning which "group style" is in play in the different parts of the larger "organization." The "organizational style," in other words, includes this distribution of group styles across a range of sites within an organization. In other words, organizational style includes the "architecture" to which we referred earlier (see also Eliasoph 2011).

10. The classic statement on decoupling comes from DiMaggio and Powell 1991.

REFERENCES

Abbott, Andrew. 2001. *Time Matters: On Theory and Method.* Chicago: University of Chicago Press.

Alexander, Jeffrey. 2006. *The Civil Sphere.* New York: Oxford University Press.

———. 2004. "Cultural Pragmatics: Social Performance between Ritual and Strategy." *Sociological Theory* 22(4): 527–573.

———. 2003. *The Meanings of Social Life: A Cultural Sociology.* New York: Oxford University Press.

———. 1998. "Introduction." In *Real Civil Society: Dilemmas of Institutionalization,* ed. Jeffrey Alexander. London: Sage: 1–20.

Alford, Robert, and Roger Friedland. 1985. *Powers of Theory: Capitalism, the State, and Democracy.* Cambridge, UK: Cambridge University Press.

Armstrong, Elizabeth. 2002. *Forging Gay Identities.* Chicago: University of Chicago Press.

Auerbach, Erich. 2003 [1953]. *Mimesis: The Representation of Reality in Western Literature.* Princeton, NJ: Princeton University Press.

Austin, J. L. 1965. *How to Do Things with Words.* Oxford: Oxford University Press.

Bellah, Robert N. 1970. "Christianity and Symbolic Realism." *Journal for the Scientific Study of Religion* 9(2): 89–96.

Blau, Peter M. 1963. *The Dynamics of Bureaucracy: A Study of Interpersonal Relations in Two Government Agencies.* Chicago: University of Chicago Press.

Boltanski, Luc, and Laurent Thévenot. 2005 [1991], *On Justification.* Princeton, NJ: Princeton University Press.

———. 2000. "The Reality of Moral Expectations: A Sociology of Situated Judgement." *Philosophical Explorations* 3(3): 208–231.

Callon, Michel. 1986. "Some Elements of a Sociology of Translation: Domestication of the Scallops and the Fishermen of St. Brieuc Bay." In *Power, Action and Belief: A New Sociology of Knowledge?* ed. J. Law, 196–223. London: Routledge.

Cicourel, Aaron. 1981. "Notes on the Integration of Micro-and Macro Levels of Analysis." In *Advances in Social Theory and Methodology,* ed. Karin Knorr-Cetina and Aaron Cicourel, 51–80. London: Routledge and Kegan Paul.

Cefaï, Daniel, no date: "Type, typicité, typification: Un essai de sociologie phénoménologique." Unpublished manuscript. Paris: Ecoles des hautes études en sciences sociales.

Cefaï, Daniel, and Dominique Pasquier. 2003. "Introduction." In *Les sens du public: publics politiques; publics médiatiques,* ed. Daniel Cefaï and Dominique Pasquier. Paris: Centre universitaire de recherches administratives et politiques de Picardie/PUF.

de Certeau, Michel. 1988. *The Practice of Everyday Life,* trans. Steven Rendell. Berkeley: University of California Press.

Clemens, Elisabeth. 2005. "Two Kinds of Stuff: The Current Encounter of Social Movements and Organizations." *Social Movements and Organization Theory*: 351–365.

Clemens, Elisabeth, and James M. Cook. 1999. "Politics and Institutionalism: Explaining Durability and Change." *Annual Review of Sociology* 25: 441–466.

Dekker, Paul. 2009. "Civicness: From Civil Society to Civic Services?" *Voluntas* 20: 220–238.

Eliasoph, Nina. 2011. *Making Volunteers: Civic Life After Welfare's End*. Princeton, NJ: Princeton University Press.

———. 2009. "Top-Down Civic Projects Are Not Grassroots Associations: How the Differences Matter in Everyday Life." *Voluntas* 20: 291–308.

Eliasoph, Nina, and Paul Lichterman. 2003. "Culture in Interaction." *American Journal of Sociology* 1008: 735–794.

Fox, Richard Wightman. 2004. *Jesus in America: Personal Savior, Cultural Hero, National Obsession*. San Francisco: Harper Collins/Harper One.

Friedland, Roger, and Robert R. Alford. 1991. "Bringing Society Back In: Symbols, Practices, and Institutional Contradictions." In *The New Institutionalism in Organizational Analysis*, edited by Walter W. Powell and Paul J. DiMaggio, 232–263. Chicago and London: Chicago.

Ghaziani, A. 2004. "Anticipatory and Actualized Identities: A Cultural Analysis of the Transition from Aids Disability to Work." *Sociological Quarterly* 45(2): 273–301.

Ghaziani, A., and M. J. Ventresca. 2005. "Keywords and Cultural Change: Frame Analysis of Business Model Public Talk, 1975–2000."

Goffman, Erving. 1959. *The Presentation of Self in Everyday Life*. Garden City, NY: Doubleday.

Gouldner, Alvin W. 1954. *Patterns of Industrial Bureaucracy*. Glencoe, IL: Free Press.

Hall, Peter Dobkin. 1992. *Inventing the Nonprofit Sector*. Baltimore: Johns Hopkins University Press.

Heimer, Carol, and Lisa Staffen. 1998. *For the Sake of the Children: The Social Organization of Responsibility in the Hospital and the Home*. Chicago: University of Chicago Press.

Jepperson, Ronald L. 1991. "Institutions, Institutional Effects, and Institutionalism." In *The New Institutionalism in Organizational Analysis*, edited by Walter W. Powell and Paul J. DiMaggio, 143–163. Chicago and London: Chicago.

Katz, Jack. 2001. "From How to Why: On Luminous Description and Causal Inference in Ethnography" (Part II). *Ethnography* 2(4): 443–473.

Kunda, Gideon. 1992. *Engineering Culture: Control and Commitment in a High-Tech Corporation*. Philadelphia: Temple University Press.

Lamont, Michele. 1992. *Money, Morals, and Manners*. Chicago: University of Chicago Press.

Lévi-Strauss, Claude. 1963. *Structural Anthropology*, trans. Clair Jacobson and Brooke Grundfest Schoepf. New York: Basic Books.

Lichterman, Paul. 2005. *Elusive Togetherness: Church Groups Trying to Bridge America's Divisions*. Princeton, NJ: Princeton University Press.

———. 1996. *The Search for Political Community: American Activists Reinventing Community*. Cambridge, UK: Cambridge University Press.

Lindblom, Charles E. 1980. *Politics and Markets*. NY: Basic Books.

Marwell, Nicole P. 2004. "Privatizing the Welfare State: Nonprofit Community-Based Organizations as Political Actors." *American Sociological Review* 69: 265–291.

Meyer, John W., and Brian Rowan. 1997. "Institutionalized Organizations: Formal Structure as Myth and Ceremony." *American Journal of Sociology* 83(2): 340–363.

Minkoff, Debra C. 2002. "The Emergence of Hybrid Organizational Forms: Combining Identity-based Service Provision and Political Activism." *Nonprofit and Voluntary Sector Quarterly* 31(3) (September): 377–401.

Mische, Ann. 2008. *Partisan Politics*. Princeton, NJ: Princeton University Press.

Pierson, Paul. 2004. *Politics in Time: History, Institutions, and Social Analysis*. Princeton, NJ. Princeton University Press.

Ricœur, Paul. 1991. "Life: A Story in Search of a Narrator." In *Reflection and Imagination: A Paul Ricœur Reader*, ed. Mario Valdés, 482–490. Toronto: University of Toronto Press.

Sacks, Harvey. 1972. "On the Analyzability of Stories by Children." In *Directions in Sociolinguistics: The Ethnography of Communication*, ed. John Gumperz and Dell Hymes, 324–345. New York: Blackwell.

Schutz, Alfred. 1967 [1932]. *The Phenomenology of the Social World*. Evanston, IL: Northwestern University Studies in Phenomenology and Existential Philosophy.

Stohlmann, Sarah. 2007. "At Yesenia's House: Central American Immigrant Pentecostalism, Congregational Homophily, and Religious Innovation in Los Angeles." *Qualitative Sociology* 30(1): 61–80.

Stone, Deborah, 1988. *Policy Paradox and Political Reason*. Glenview, IL: Scott, Foresman

Swidler, Ann. 2006. "Syncretism and Subversion in AIDS Governance: How Locals Cope with Global Demands." *International Affairs* 82(2) (March): 269–284.

Tavory, Iddo, and Nina Eliasoph. Forthcoming. "Ordinary Prediction in Everyday Interaction." Unpublished manuscript.

Thévenot, Laurent. 2007. "The Plurality of Cognitive Formats and Engagements Moving Between the Familiar and the Public." *European Journal of Social Theory* 10(3): 409–423.

———. 2006. *L'action au pluriel: Sociologie des régimes d'engagement*. Paris: La Découverte.

———. 2001. "Pragmatic Regimes Governing the Engagement with the World." In *The Practice Turn in Contemporary Theory*, ed. Karin Knorr-Cetina, T. Schatzki, and Eike Savigny, 56–73. London: Routledge.

Thornton, Patricia H., and William Ocasio. 1999. "Institutional Logics and the Historical Contingency of Power in Organizations: Executive Succession in the Higher Education Publishing Industry, 1958–1990." In *American Journal of Sociology* 105: 801–844.

Vygotsky, Lev. 1978. *Mind in Society: The Development of Higher Psychological Processes*. Cambridge, MA: Harvard University Press.

Wagner-Pacifici, Robin. 2001. *Theorizing the Standoff: Contingency in Action*. New York: Cambridge University Press.

Walzer, Michael, 1983. *Spheres of Justice: A Defense of Pluralism and Equality*. New York: Basic Books.

Wuthnow, Robert. 1998. *Loose Connections: Joining Together in America's Fragmented Communities*. Cambridge, MA: Harvard University Press.

———. 1993. *Communities of Discourse:Ideology and Social Structure in the Reformation, the Enlightenment, and European Socialism*. Cambridge, MA: Harvard University Press.

——— 1991a. "The Voluntary Sector: Legacy of the Past, Hope for the Future?" In *Between States and Markets: The Voluntary Sector in Comparative Perspective*, ed. Robert Wuthnow, 3–29. Princeton, NJ: Princeton University Press.

——— 1991b. "Tocqueville's Question Reconsidered: Voluntarism and Public Discourse in Advanced Industrial Societies." In *Between States and Markets: The Voluntary Sector in Comparative Perspective*, ed. Robert Wuthnow, 288–308. Princeton, NJ: Princeton University Press.

CHAPTER 30

INBETWEENNESS AND AMBIVALENCE

BERNHARD GIESEN

INTRODUCTION

Social action presupposes a cultural order that—in a structuralist tradition—is generated by applying distinctions and classifications. Both sides of a distinction refer to contrasting or opposional meanings that, by this oppostion, constitute each other: Thus, inside hints at outside, past at future, equality at inequality, salvation at condemnation, rationality at irrationality, justice at injustice, parents at children, masters at servants, etc. We do not know the meaning of a concept unless we can conceive of its opposite. In our regular thinking we tend, however, not to refer to this opposite: It is the excluded or silenced other possibility (Derrida 1967). Thus, reconstructing the excluded other becomes the royal path of poststructuralist reasoning. While this reconstruction of the excluded other of an opposition has been widely accepted, the space in between the opposites—the third possibility, the transition between inside and outside, the "neither...nor" or the "as well as...," the space of hybridity—has been only marginally theorized by mainstream cultural sociology but centered by nonsociologist authors, such as Homi Bhabha, Gilles Deleuze, Michel Serres, or Yuri Lotman.

The following essay deals with this extraordinary space in between the opposites. It focuses on something that transcends the sucessful ordering and splitting of the world into neat binaries, and it maintains that this inbetweenness is essential for the construction of culture. Reality itself provides no firm ground for neat classification. Therefore, in applying classifications to raw reality, there will always be an unclassifiable remainder; and in specifying meaning, there is no way to achieve absolute clarity and to avoid a rest of fuzziness. Understanding can always fail;

interpretation can be disrupted by surprises and resistance; distinctions can hit undecidedness; routines can be diluted; rules can be violated; boundaries between inside and outside can be crossed by nomads and strangers (Simmel 1908; Lotman 1990); questioned by folds (Deleuze 1992); and disregarded by parasites (Serres 2007). Even if we define and specify meanings extensively, there will be always some remainder of uncertainty in the relation between signifier and signified, and this uncertainty cannot be dissolved by linguistic operations alone. Instead, it can be overcome by a deictic gesture pointing to the situation at hand (following Schütz: "Me, here, now, this"). Traditional sociology has acknowledged the existence of these phenomena of fuzziness and undecidedness, but it has treated them mostly as pathologies, disturbances, and crises that require stabilizing repairs and counteracting restorations of order.

The sociology of ambivalence reverses this position. It claims that ambivalences, disturbances, paradoxies, misunderstandings, and exceptions are not critical risks for social order, but instead, that they are indispensable elements of this order. Stability of social order relies not only on neat oppositions but also on the acceptance of the unclassifiable, of surprises and coincidences, and of ambiguity and fuzziness.

These phenomena of ambivalence do not simply exist, but they drive the process of social communication. Without surprises and disturbances, communication would lack its focus that catches common attention. Without irritations of a given background, there would be no signal, image, or sign. Without fuzziness, there would be no need and motive for understanding and interpretation. Without deviances and breaches, there would be no awareness of rules. What before has been treated as a crisis of social order and what, indeed, is seen by acting persons mostly as such a crisis is, thus, discovered as the indispensable key to the communicative reproduction of cultural order. Before we address, in the following remarks, various phenomena of inbetweenness—such as garbage and monsters, victims and seduction—we will briefly outline some theoretical concepts that point to the essence of inbetweenness.

Classical Theoretical Concepts

The issue of ambivalence has been only marginally addressed by mainstream sociology. There are, however, two notable exceptions. In his book *Modernity and Ambivalence*, Zygmunt Bauman (Bauman 1991) has suggested a perspective that explicitly opposes clearcut oppositions and neat distinctions as demanded by modern scientific thinking, as well as by the modern nation-state. Kant's epistemology, the modern thrust for national homogeneity, the attempt to design an ideal society in accordance with nature, and the modern exclusion of heterogenous, deviant, and homeless persons are all equally accused of engendering racist exclusion and fostering genocidal inclinations. Referring to Simmel's essay on the "stranger" and Mannheim's idea of the "freefloating intellectual," Bauman points to the essential and irredeemable thirdness of the wandering spirit that provides an epistemological advantage in contrast to native perspectives entrenched and entangled in localities. For all its merits, Bauman's theory of modernity has some shortcomings: For example, it tends to "ontologize" the position of natives and strangers and it falls short of extending the concept of ambivalence to cover all social classification, modern or premodern. This restricted perspective is overcome by a programmatic account that Neil Smelser gave in his presidential address in 1997 (Smelser 1998). Smelser, inspired by Freud's psychoanalysis, blew "ambivalence" up to the status of an encompassing conceptual paradigm on a par with rationality as the core concept of a sociological perspective on modernity, and, hence, he could challenge the rational choice paradigm and point to its limitations. Ambivalence, he argues, results from situations of dependency from which we cannot easily escape; it allows switching between attraction and rejection; and, in rejecting, denying, and hating the inescapable, it allows one to adapt to and accommodate it. While Smelser's program accounts well for some seemingly irrational social phenomena, such as traumatic denials and love-hatred relationships, its explanatory structure remains basically on the psychological level. He fails to provide a genuinely sociological account that, instead, relates ambivalence to the processes of social communication and cultural interpretation.

In distinction to mainstream sociology, some philosophical accounts of culture deal with ambivalence, hybridity, and inbetweenness as their core concern (e.g., Bhabha, Serres, and Lotman). Philosophy and cultural theory have even addressed this fundamental salience of ambivalence and ambiguity "avant la lettre." Some central concepts among them—"primary consciousness" in Freud, "Lebenswelt" in Husserl, "family similarity" in Wittgenstein, "liminality" in Turner, and "trauma" in Freud—provide models of ambivalence and inbetweenness before the terms took center stage in cultural theory.

Freud's notion of "primary consciousness" mediates between unconscious and somatic processes on the one hand and the realm of signs and orderly distinctions on the other. It cannot be reduced to the unconscious or to the symbolic systems, and it is only marginally structured. There is a sequential order of contents, but these contents merge and supersede each other, change from clear to murky, take an unpredictable twist, imagine the absent, and remember the past. "Primary consciousness" is a paradigm case of ambiguity and fleeting transitions, but it is also one of immediacy and presence. Nothing is more present and more certain than our consciousness. Our perceptions of the external world can be mistaken, illusionary, and wrong. Primary consciousness cannot: It is identical to itself. The primary consciousness is governed by a mythical temporality: Changes of form and sudden intuitions can occur; everything can be related to everything; and differences and distinctions are not yet in command.

This salience of ambiguity can also be shown in the level of elementary social interaction in everyday reality (Schütz 2004). Everyday worlds are constructed by repetition and commonality, as hinted at in phrasings such as "you know…" and "and so on…." They consist of a continous and encompassing background consensus that risks collapse when it is focused, examined, and scrutinized. Events that surprisingly deviate from rules and expectations divert attention from this background consensus and prevent it from being scrutinized (Lacan's Tyche). In pointing to this construction of a background consensus in everyday interaction, Schütz refers to Husserl's notion of "lifeworld." Husserl has separated the "lifeworld" strictly from the world as generated by scientific knowledge. In contrast to scientific knowledge that insists on the distinction between true and false, the lifeworld is immediately given and insurmountably certain. Similar to the stream of conscious-ness, there are no deceptions or illusions in it. The world is seen as it appears to us; the difference between sign and reference vanishes. Contradictions or inconsis-tencies between the elements of lifeworld knowledge appear only if we take an external stance—from the inside of a lifeworld, everything is meaningfully related to each other. We share the immediacy and certainty of the knowledge in a life-world, and we trust that everybody else sees the world as we do. This presupposition of shared knowledge can be upheld as long as we allow for a certain fuzziness and disregard the possible differences of perspective. Quine has called this disregarding of possible differences in the forgiving attitude of mutal understanding the "prin-ciple of charity" (Quine 1969).

Wittgenstein coined the term *Familienähnlichkeit* (family likeness) in order to refer to the most elementary structural features of comparison. It refers to an aggre-gate in which every element shares one property with one or several other elements, but no single property can be identified in all elements. Wittgenstein illustrates family likeness by pointing to games that comprise sports, as well as theatrical plays or children's games. Family-like elements are connected to each other via several steps, but there is no single criterion that unambiguously separates inside and out-side by defining membership. Each element is located in a position between other elements that are similar to it in varying respects but would lack any connection without this mediating element. Inbetweenness is thus the regular case in aggregates of family likeness. Family likeness is the most elementary structure that we can observe in a comparative way. It presupposes only that comparisons are possible and that similarities can be noticed; but it does not require stating one property that can be found in all elements of comparison. The discovery of family likeness con-veys to all elements a status of being an exception: Every element is unlike at least one other element and, thus, is excepted from a general likeness.

Victor Turner has argued that every structural differentiation requires anti-structures that suspend social differences and social norms in order to give way to an undifferentiated communitas (Turner 1995). Individual and social distinctions fade away; communality, homogeneity, and equality take over; social order recedes and allows for performing events that cannot be framed as a continuation of order but only as its breach. Suspending order by liminality should not be mixed up with a decay of order. Instead of relapsing into the state of nature—into anarchy or into the collapse of communication—liminality establishes strong forms of communi-cation that reduce the risk of misunderstanding. All participants see each other as equals, as mirrored by others. Because there are these occasions—times and places of extraordinary understanding (Bataille's "sacred communication")—we can presuppose that misunderstandings in everyday communication will not risk falling into a total abyss. Liminal communication is tied to corporeal presence and the contagiousness of lived experience among those present in a location. Here, the communication among bodies outrules the exchange of information.

Turner's notion of liminality resembles Bataille's concepts of heterogeneity or of sovereignty. Bataille sets the normal reality of norms and reason, work and measurement, as the realm of homogeneity apart from a reality that escapes normal order by trespassing norms, transcending everyday reality, and replacing calculated reason and the logic of scarcity by exuberance and waste: Violence, sacrifice, laughter, sexuality, art, and drunkenness are examples of these transgressions that generate a sovereign inbetweeness between regular social order and the state of nature.

A special inbetweenness—that transcends any finite experiences, events, and memories—marks the concepts of identity and trauma (Giesen 2004). They, too, refer to something extraordinary that transcends the order of everyday life. "Identity" assumes a continuity of the individual or collective self as the origin of creative actions, intentions, and memories. This self cannot be reduced to particular properties or stories. It occurs to us as ultimately certain, but it resists any attempt to represent itself by particular narratives or images. Any particular representation of identity can be rejected as distorted or mistaken. Identity is an essentially fuzzy and therefore contested concept. Ambiguity is the fundamental property of identity, but this ambiguity does not disrupt or challenge the unity of the self; instead, it yields continuous and homogenous integration. Identity tends to conceive of itself as authentic, homogeneous, and autonomous, but it cannot decouple itself from the other from which it distinguishes itself, which, however indispensable, is the address to which identity is presented. Hence, any construction of identity has to refer to a conception of the other. Without this reference, any representation of identity remains empty.

In contrast to this integrative ambiguity that allows for the conception of an enduring self, the notion of trauma points to its opposite. It refers to ruptures in the web of memory that challenge and question the assumption of an emcompassing self. Traumata are traces of the past that can hardly be erased. They are a mode of memory. Traumatic memories are produced by sudden encounters with invasive forces that, for a moment, recall and present mortality, not just as an abstract possibilty but as an event from which we narrowly escaped (Caruth 1996). This shocking encounter cannot be fitted into the well-established narratives of our lives; it appears as a dark hole, as a rupture in the web of meaning, or as an intrusion of a weird counter into our everyday world. An abyss of a chaotic and absurd world opens up; demonic forces crush the crust of the ordinary routines and the commonplace routines collapse. Similar to identity, the trauma resists representation (Alexander et al. 2004). At the beginning, it is repressed and silenced. Only from a distance, after some time has passed, can it be spoken out and worked through. Trauma and identity converge in a transcendental extraordinariness that sets them apart from concepts of consciousness on the one hand and from anthropological notions, like liminality, on the other.

While the path for a cultural sociology of ambivalence has been broken by the above-mentioned classical notions, more recent attempts in cultural theory address inbetweenness directly; but they use mainly metaphorical phrasings. Among them are Homi Bhabha's model of hybridity as the fundamental condition of identity construction, his idea of third spaces inbetween presumably homogeneous cultures and his challenge to any assumption of authenticity; Michel Serres' theory of communication centering on the parasite or the joker, which is at the same time inside as well as outside of a system and, hence, can mediate between inside and outside; Gilles Deleuze's notion of rhizom that connects everything to everything in manifold ways (and repeats, thus, a pattern of Wittgensteinian family likeness) or his idea of baroque folds that bring the boundary into multifarious motion and challenge any simple and neat delineation of inside and outside; and Lotman's narratological notion of semiosis by boundary crossing as a field in which the unpredictable can occur—in contrast to translation on the basis of a bilingual list of vocabulary. Although very influential in literary studies and cultural studies, these concepts have, until now, not yet stimulated much research or reflection in the domain of sociology (Serres who had some impact on Luhmann's late work is possibly an exception). They converge in their emphasis on inbetweenness as a fundamental given of cultural fields instead of treating it as an exceptional, or even pathological, state.

Classifying the Unclassifiable

Garbage

The outlined notions refer to an elementary inbetweeness, a fundamental ambiguity, and an indissoluble remainder that resists any attempt at unambiguous classification. This inbetweeness is essential and unavoidable for the operation of classifying, ordering, and coding the world. But it is disregarded, invisibilized, and silenced in the order that is generated by classification. In the natural attitude of everyday life, the world presents itself as neatly ordered. Cultural classification is, however, somehow weirdly aware of this elementary but excluded inbetweeness. It responds to this weirdness by producing order even in the realm that seems to escape from it. It classifies the unclassifiable; describes different kinds of ambiguity; delineates inbetweenness by symbolic figures; and classifies garbage, imagines monsters; and tells the story of the uncanny behind the boundary.

A pertinent example for this attempt to cope with this elementary ambiguity is our treatment of garbage. Garbage is not a problem of public health but a scandal for the cultural order of things. It is neither sacred nor profane, and this inbetweenness threatens our cultural order. Garbage is uncanny like living deads. Its pure and absurd materiality presses us to keep a distance and to remove it in order not to be contaminated by its decay and formlessness. If garbage cannot be removed immediately, its undeniable existance has to be concealed from our eyes and sealed from our noses. As long as garbage can be perceived, it remains scandalous and dangerous.

But the removal into nothingness is not the only way of coping with garbage. It can also be retransformed into something that can be located in the realm of usable and classifiable things or in the realm of the sacred. The first transformation is achieved by recycling; and the second occurs by treating garbage as collectibles, as art, or as souvenirs (Thompson 1979).

The transformation of garbage into usable, profane things follows the logic of separation and elementarization. Disgusting garbage is removed into a space beyond our perception. In these enclosed spaces, the decay of garbage is accelerated until it is dissolved into its elementary components. This elementary stuff that rids itself of any memory of its previous form can be encountered again as useful raw material that no longer causes disgust. The realm of profane and consumable things is directed by an increased commandment of presence. Any hint at transitoriness, at unavoidable decay, and at inevitable death by consumption is here a scandal that can be concealed only by presenting ever new, fresh, and alluring consumables. Garbage represents the death of things, and this death has to be hidden from our eyes.

Changing garbage into something sacred does not require material transformation. By contrast, its decay, and obvious temporality, are counteracted by all conservation. Because the sacred is eternal, we have to exempt the objects that embody it and represent it from decay. The logic of conservation is supported by the auratic attraction of the sacred as embodied in useless things—art, souvenirs, ruins. Even in its sacralized form, garbage remains in a position of inbetweenness, since it embodies the invisible sacred that represents the whole. We cannot stand the unmediated presence of the sacred, and we cannot stand the odor and sight of garbage. The unveiled sight of the sacred would blind us, like Theiresias who watched the goddess Athena bathing. The blind Theiresias was no longer able to cope with his everyday life but could forsee the future. Whoever has seen the unveiled sacred is lost for everyday business.

Monsters

Another embodiment of inbetweenness and ambivalence is the monster. Sometimes we encounter anormal, enigmatic, and irregular phenomena, and our attempts to assimilate these weird phenomena to normality fail. When we are unable to ignore these phenomena, or to classify them, then we are facing a monster. This encounter is threatening and dangerous because it disrupts the fragile reality of our social order. We feel pressed to reconstruct the boundary behind which we could ban the monstrous phenomena, or if this endeavor fails, we try to escape.

In simple cultures, the demonic and monstrous is interpreted as an autonomous source of agency. In this respect, it is similar to the sacred, but, in contrast to the sacred, it has evil or unclear intentions. Its true identity and intentions are hidden behind a façade that cannot be trusted. Demons introduce the possibility of deception into the world. Things are not always what they appear to be. Behind the surface, there is a reality that is stronger than the treacherous appearance. The world is under suspicion. It is driven by vampires and body snatchers, seducers, and tricksters and we are well advised to distrust the surface (Douglas 1966).

The first mode of coping with the invisible demon is to render it visible and to name it. At first this is achieved by symbolic operations: by imaginations of double creatures like sphinxes and centaurs, by tales of sorcery and witchcraft, stories of demonic conspirations, and rituals of exorcism.

As soon as they are visible, demons and monsters can be kept at a distance. They can be expelled and ostracized, banned and stigmatized. This holds true also for bodies that, by their physical features, evidently deviate from the regular and normal scheme. In many ancient cultures, disabled or disfigured children were frequently killed immediately after birth, or they were banned and forced to stay out of sight. Physical distance between the irregular or disfigured persons and the community of normals was to prevent contagion and contamination. Later on, disfigured persons were interned into asylums that shielded their shocking sight from regular everyday life.

But annihilation and distance were only one way of coping with shocking and monstrous heterogeneity. Occasionally, heterogenous persons were framed as sacred, as deities who were to be venerated and adored. For example, hermaphrodites were considered to unite both genders in one person and thus to overcome fundamental schisms in society. Killing, however, was the more common response to heterogeneity. This killing of the monster was frequently performed as a sacrifice. The sacrificed person was reframed as an animal, the killing of which did not engender any revenge. Thus, the ambiguity of the monster was turned into a neat distinction between the sacrificing humans, the sacrificed animals, and the gods who were venerated by the sacrifice.

A new mode of coping with monstrous disfigurations emerged at the princely courts of early modern Europe. Here, monsters were increasingly treated as curiosities, as miracles of nature, as rare objects of the princely collection. The extraordinary monster loses its awful and shocking impact. It is turned into a harmless sensation presented in a frame devoid of all practical considerations: pure extraordinariness. The demonological gaze was replaced by the museological one. Dwarfs and giants, defigured persons, or monstrous animals were watched from a close distance, but the thrill of facing the monsters no longer engendered anxiety or fear, but just a pleasing frisson—there was no real danger and no risk of contagion. The bar, the cage, or the chains tame the monster; and we can watch it at close distance, but we should not touch it.

The logic of collecting and exhibiting curiosities was, of course, not confined to princely courts. Wandering circuses and ethnic shows, anatomical museums and zoological gardens continued this museological gaze at monsters on a more popular level. It is quite telling that, even in the nineteenth century, the museological gaze did not distinguish between defigured and handicapped persons and people with non-white skin: Both were considered as being different from regular people, and this difference stimulated curiosity and amazement.

Victims

While the museological gaze continued to exist in popular arenas, the twentieth century also generated a new way to frame monsters. The monster was again regarded in terms of inferiority, but this inferiority was framed by pity, condescending charity, and emphatic compassion. The monster was turned into an innocent victim, one who could claim our support and aid. Victims are embodiments of a special ambivalence between human beings and profane things. They partake in the sacred nature of humans; but they have been treated as cattle—the killing of which will not engender blood revenge or be seen as a sin by the perpetrators. The imagination of victimhood mirrors this special inbetweenness (Agamben 1998; Giesen 2004). According to this imagination, victims have no face and name. They are denied a proper place within the community; they are expelled and displaced in camps in the outlands at the fringe of human communities; their bodies are submitted to violence and killing; their story is silenced; their remainders are burnt to ashes; and nothing should remind us of their existence. This state of exception, from regular civil rights, clashes with our conviction that they are human beings like us. Consequently, we try to reverse this expulsion from the civil community by remembering their name and their story, by compensating their handicaps, and by supporting their lifeways. Thus, the former expulsion of demonic monsters is turned into an emphatic identification and approachment: The disabled are like us, and we are in a certain respect disabled, too.

The public compassion conceals, however, a paternalistic condescendence. The victims are not on equal footing with those who advocate and voice their cause. Today a new class of professionals mediates between the common citizens and their uncommon counterimages: Social workers, medical doctors, welfare officers, and nurses take the place that, in the demonological gaze, has been occupied by witchcraft doctors and prison guardians.

This seemingly inclusive turn does not stop at the boundaries of the human race. Today, not only disabled and disfigured humans but also wild animals are discovered as victims. What was a dangerous wild beast before is now an endangered species that should not be put behind bars but live in its natural habitat and have its natural diet: The dragon is transformed into a pet dinosaur.

Charity and compassion toward the needy were, of course, not invented in the twentieth century. They belong to the ethical core of many religions. Traditional charity referred, however, mainly to the misery of others present in a locality. Giving alms redistanced a misery that came too close and reconstructs a vertical distance between giver and taker. Here, the misery of others is not yet a scandal, but an opportunity for embellishing the self of the donor.

By contrast, compassion with distant and anonymous victims is a relatively recent phenomenon. It presupposes translocal inclusions and eccentric solidarities that required a pattern of this-worldly salvation. Today, the misery of others is seen as an accident that could also have hit us, as a scandalous challenge to the promise of innerworldly salvation, as an unfortunate backwardness that could be compensated by development, teaching, and welfare politics.

Thus, the demonological gaze is transformed into its opposite. The victimological perspective centers on a discrepancy between obvious appearance and hidden essence, but the evaluation is reversed: Whereas the demonological gaze suspected the hidden evil core behind a harmless façade, the victimological perspective sees a sacred core behind a seemingly abnormal façade. Here, too, the ambivalent inconsistency between surface and essence thrusts for overcoming, but the evil of the façade no longer frightens or shocks us. This attenuation of emotions is generated by media reports about distant victims that avoid too abhorrent images, showing the monstrous deformation of victims. Instead, we watch faces that do not differ from our own faces. We listen to the voices of reporters and see pictures showing the traces of the evil. Hence, we can, on our sofas, surrender to a mild concernedness: We do not face the horror of victims, and we cannot change the view.

The victimological gaze can be unfolded only from a far distance (Boltanski 1999). Only from a distance can we opt for compassion. Only from a distance can we compensate for the impossibility of intervening. Faced with the dying victims, we can respond by crying mutedness and desperate attempts to aid. Represented and civilized by the media, however, the victims stay at a distance that precludes shock. The horror is banned by the image.

Heroes

At the opposite end of the range of inbetweenness, we find the charismatic hero (Rank 1909; Weber 1978; Campbell 1953). Like the saint or the prophet, the charismatic hero mediates between the world of humans and the world of gods. As a human person, he or she partakes in divine superiority. The charismatic hero is exempted from the regular social order. He or she defies death and common reasoning, commands a divine violence, and crushes the existing order in order to construct a new one. He or she is the autonomous sovereign if there is any at all. Charisma is extraordinary and diffuse. It fuses political authority with sacredness, and it overwhelms the community of followers in an effortless way—nobody may apply for it or argue in favor of it. Therefore, it provides the most precious foundation of political authority. The construction of monarchic authority in ancient societies referred strongly to charismatic foundations. The king was imagined as the founder of the kingdom, as the triumphant conqueror of the land, and as the victorious defender of his people. He represented, as a person, the original unity of society that once resulted from the bond of kinship.

This charismatic core of monarchic authority is, however, elusive and volatile. Charisma is bound to the dialectic of failure and reconstruction. The personal embodiment of the sacred in the prince can hardly stand the test of time and routine—any attempt to turn this extraordinary moment in which the hero is created into an ordinary and stable routine will finally result in the decay of genuine charisma. No hero can continuously work miracles.

Failure and misfortune will result in a dwindling belief among the hero's followers; doubts may be raised, questions asked, and the extraordinary hero is finally revealed as a mortal and ordinary human being. In the real world, the hero can hardly avoid the decay of his or her charisma (Giesen 2004).

The most common attempt to prevent this decay of charisma consists of the spatial separation between the charismatic hero and the mundane world of ordinary beings. It relates back to the assumption that the sacred is unevenly distributed in space, and that spatial distance represents and reinforces social separation. Because no mortal person is able to present him- or herself constantly in a charismatic way, the preservation of charisma requires that the hero escape and retreat to the "arcanum," where only confidants, personal servants, and close family members notice the hero's human weaknesses, respond to his or her need for advice, and communicate with him or her on equal footing.

Both poles—the "arcanum" and the "publicum"—are necessarily connected, and the charisma of the king presupposes a delicate balance between them. If the king's rule remains permanently in the arcanum, rumors about his death can spread, and his charisma will fade away, a risk depicted in the classical drama of El Cid or Kurosawa's movie *Kagemusha, The Shadow Warrior*. If, on the other hand, the king never retreats backstage, he risks appearing as just another ordinary human being—mortal and weak, dependent and commonplace. This mortality and weakness have to be concealed from the public eye; those who witness it—his servants and advisors—are obliged to be mute with respect to outsiders.

But the ordinariness of the charismatic hero can also be disclosed by separating the mortal person from the immortal office and by presenting him or her as a perpetrator. As soon as the hero, as a mortal person, violated the law and pursued private interests, professional legalists could, by their very office, turn the law—that is, the invisible and eternal rule of the king—against the mortal body of the king, against his erroneous opinions and private interests. The king, who was a sovereign hero beforehand, was now turned into a potentially demonic perpetrator. The mortal prince could be put on trial. Killing the king became a definite possibility. Instead of being *Lèse majesté*, the ultimate crime, regicide, could also be considered a restoration of the *maiestas legis* ("majesty of the law")—an act that gives way to a new embodiment of the law.

In the French Revolution, however, the king was beheaded not primarily because he could be accused of illegal activities (which were, of course, the indispensable pretext). His very existence as the former incarnation of personal rule was a scandal to the sacred core of revolutionary republicanism. His "two bodies" (Kantorowicz 2001)—the immortal representation of the sacred center and the mortal body of the individual—were reduced to one. The French Republic triumphantly took over the sacred core, dissipated it to the individual citizens, and centered it in the *comité du salut publique* headed by Robbespierre, the "incorruptible." Left was the mortal body of the king, who, however, still had the signs of his previous sacredness, and who hence, in order to demonstrate his mortality, had to be killed in public.

Seduction

There are also forms of inbetweeness that, instead of being embodied in figures, are generated by interaction patterns. One of the most important is seduction. Seduction is the opposite of blunt violence and naked truth. It relies on ambivalence, equivocality, and inbetweenness. It hints at a risk and allures one into a realm beyond the principled world of truth and law, morality, and rationality. Seduction is based on multifarious ambiguities and possibilities. It is inspired by dreams and fantasies, and is unreasonable and undecided. It occurs in a transitory space in which extraordinary phenomena may occur, but from which we also may return to well-known, everyday life. Seduction crosses the boundary between profane sobriety and the imagination of future elation, between the permissible and the forbidden, between the safe and the dangerous.

Taking this perspective, the French theorist Baudrillard has centered seduction as the central mode of symbolic order that differs strictly from the natural order of law and rationality (Baudrillard 1990). While Baudrillard values seduction and ambivalence as the realm of freedom, the modern imagination commonly opts for its opposite: natural order, strict rationality, and naked truth. They are treated as the proper frame of reference for social reality, while seduction and disguise are seen as an almost pathological derailing of social interaction. Such derailing of social interaction is attributed to the hypocritical pretensions, fake passions, and deceptive promises of society.

This image of society as the source of deception is rooted in the Judeo-Christian tradition: We have lost our original paradise and exchanged it for a world of sin and violence, thus repeating, entangled in society, the sin of Adam that deprived the divine Creation of its innonence. The sin of Adam followed Eve's seduction. Hence, seduction marks the loss of paradise and the beginning of history. After this sin, Adam and Eve became aware that they were naked. Attempting to cover their nakedness, both embarked into a land beyond natural paradise: society. Society becomes the realm of a false and treacherous life, in which distrust reigns, truth is concealed, and lies and deceptions rule. Whoever wanted to escape from this world of deception had to return to natural nakedness. Originally, this nakedness represented chastity and liminality, a trespassing of this-worldly rules and a step toward salvation by entering the original unity of God and world. Today, the ideology of nudism still hints at this salvatory core.

This originally religious transcendence was turned into the early modern epistemology of discovery and disclosure. Instead of searching for divine revelations, the modern scientist thrusts for universally valid knowledge about nature beyond the deceptions and idolatries that veil the truth. In Francis Bacon's "Novum Organum," religious beliefs, everyday opinion, and social custom appear as distortions of this natural truth.

In contrast to this widespread image of seduction as the origin of falsity and evil, we will, in the following remarks, present seduction as a constitutive and constructive pattern of social interaction of values that outweigh its disadvantages. The special inbetweeness of seduction even allows for major breakthroughs in cultural evolution. It started with female seduction and the original sin: Eve's sin is the seduction of Adam. By seduction, the paradisaical merging of men and nature is replaced by a social relationsship. The female seduction marks the end of mythical pre-history and the beginning of history. The story of the expulsion from paradise reflects this as well as the story about seduction of Paris by Helena and the mythical war of Troy.

Female seduction was aimed originally at the savage might of the warrior, later on, at the chastity of the priest or the honor of the citizen. When the warrior gives up his resistance and surrenders to erotic pleasures, he becomes impotent as a warrior, as recalled by the mythical story of Samson and Dalilah. Successful seduction terminates not only the natural paradise but also the natural violence between the sexes.

But seduction does not always succeed. It presupposes contingency—in contrast to rape and violence. Ancient myths mention this risk of failure: The seduction of Ulysses by Kirke failed; Salome could not seduce John the Baptist; and Joseph resisted the seduction of Pothiphar's wife, etc.

The resistence of males against female seduction is, however, not only a matter of male superiority. It can also be interpreted in a different way. As Adorno and Horkheimer have pointed out, with respect to Ulysses' refusal to accommodate Kirkes' seduction, this resistance provides the basis of an autonomous personality: The closure of a person against external influences creates an inner space in which autonomy can unfold because it is driven by resolve and determination that are not caused by anything external.

Female seduction operates not only through glances and smiles, but also through intentionally or unintentionally revealing parts of the female body—partial nakedness invites one to continue and to expect more. Seductive unveiling differs, however, strongly from complete and frontally presented nakedness. The unveiling of parts of the body keeps an indispensable ambivalence since it can be understood not only as an erotic invitation, but also as an unintentional result of negilence, of habits, or of fashion. The seductive lady can always withdraw by maintaining that she did not mean to invite, and the resisting gentleman can always justify his refusal by claiming that he did not understand this to be an invitation. The unequivocality of total nudity, however, violates the ambivalence without which seduction cannot be performed. If men do not comply with the unequivocality of total nudity, they offend, in a most embarassing way, those who expose their naked bodies. Complete nudity mates well with voyeurism but impedes seduction. It dissolves the realm of allures and temptations, confusions and bewilderments—the situation is reduced to sheer and rude corporality. Instead of artful conversation and hints at possibilities, the unconditional and unequivocal presence is in command.

Men appear as seducers in grand manner not before the seventeenth century (Duc de Lanson, Casanova, etc.). If we disregard some extraordinary cases as Abelaerd or the medieval Minnesingers, we have to assume that, in medieval times, even noblemen mostly relied on speechless violence in sexual matters (Elias 1983). From the seventeenth century onward, however, direct sexual violence was increasingly replaced by seduction: Speechless corporality, while not vanishing entirely, gave way to courteous communication about possibilities and contingencies.

This transition that brought out male seduction was driven by a structural change that turned feudal warriors into courtiers and that, in the princely court, turned the close encounter between men and women, who were not married to each other, into a permanent experience. Violence or distance could no longer regulate gender relationships under these conditions; they had to be replaced by dances and ceremonies, letters and glances. This shift was fostered and supported by a change in the cultural framing of war. After a century of incessant warfare in Europe, war had lost its heroic aura and was changed into an issue of bodily drill of commoners. The aristocracy, after being castrated in military matters by the princely sovereign, had to turn to new fields of noble excellence. Thus, court intrigue substituted for the battle, and the exchange of erotic letters began to rival the duel.

From now on, language became the major medium of eroticism. By speech and dance, promises and confessions, flattery and praise, the courtier had to imagine a tempting and confusing space of erotic fulfillment and self-growth and thus convince the seduced one to give up her caution. In male seduction, too, ambivalence and unequivocality are of prime importance. Whoever presents his erotic desire directly and bluntly has lost immediately his cause. The desired lady cannot avoid rejecting him. Every move has to be performed so as to allow various interpretations, withdrawal and retreat must be possible, faces have to be saved, and honor has to be preserved. Seduction is the contrary of rape; but it is also the contrary to a "safe bet." It presupposes the courtly civilization of affects, as well as techniques of indirect communication in which the literal meaning of speech cannot be taken for its intended one. Here, seduction becomes a game of possibilities, promises, and staged authenticity, and the players know that they might be victims of deception and fakery (Choderlos de Laclos 1961).

Thus, the ambiguity and ambivalence of seduction generate a very modern mode of sociality: Seduction overcomes the unilaterality of the voyeur's as well as of the rapist's gaze, and desire remains certainly the driving motive, but reciprocity and recognition of the presence of others are indispensable. Seduction marks the exit from the violent state of nature in a similar way as, from another perspective, the social contract does. Both contract and seduction presuppose a mutual recognition of personal freedom, and both exclude violence and turn contingencies into binding. While contracting, however, explains society as a normative order resulting from the pursuit of individual utilities, seduction explains social reality as a collective surrendering to the vivid immediacy of a present lifeworld.

From this perspective, social integration is possible only insofar as we no longer insist on facing the naked truth, the great totality, the fundamental injustice, the core of things; but, instead, accommodate to the superficial phenomena of our lifeworld. By contrast, the immediate look at unveiled naked truth is dangerous. If we would know what drives us and what the core of the world is, we would be lost for everyday life—like the Greek soothsayer Teiresias, who was damned to blindness after he had watched Athena, the goddess of knowledge, bathing. Unmasked and unveiled knowledge may be unbearable and horrible like the head of Medusa. This horror of immediate and merciless confrontation with the unveiled truth has to be prevented by disguise and indirect communication. Disguise, irony, and seduction impede us from facing monstrous and destructive truths and allow us to traverse everyday life.

What holds true for the merciless truth about ourselves and the enigmatic core of the external world pertains also for the reckless attempts to realize perfect morality and ideal society—these attempts ended often in monstrous heaps of dead bodies. By contrast, remaining within the confines of everyday life and keeping on our habitual masks, we can claim to be human. It avoids epistemological, moral, and expressive ventures that are bound to result in failure and catastrophies.

Striving for perfect morality, for absolute truth, and for immediate and unveiled knowledge about ourselves is not only merciless and dangerous, but it is actually impossible: Our truth always presupposes a perspective and a language, reflecting on ourselves. It cannot dispense with masks and the background imagery, and our attempts at bettering the world are always doomed to failure. Even if we are able to perceive absolute truth, this absolute truth would be completely void and empty.

Far from being an embodiment of evil, seduction can claim to establish a communicative inbetweeness: opening a space of chances, widening the range of possible interpretations, allowing one to switch levels; and it does all of this on a symmetrical basis and without using force. In this respect, it excels in laughter that also allows one to outdistance the earnestness of regular life, but at the price of degrading the person who is laughed about.

CONCLUSION

Starting from a short account of its conceptual presuppositions and intellectual predecessors in phenomenology, psychoanalysis, and anthropology, we have outlined the contour of a paradigm in cultural sociology that conceives of ambivalence and inbetweenness as a fundamental and indissoluble given of classification and interpretation. There is no classification without a remainder; there is no interpretation without an essential fuzziness; and there is no distinction without a third possibility that sits astride the boundary. When constructing social order, we tend to ignore and disregard these third possibilities that, from an everyday perspective, seem to jeopardize order but, in fact, are driving the process of social communication and cultural interpretation. By debunking this essential thirdness, cultural sociology provides a new avenue for analyzing the pragmatics of culture. Although postmodern cultural theory, outside of sociology, has extensively dealt with inbetweeness and ambivalence by figures as parasites, diaspora, hybridity, and nomadism, sociological analysis of different phenomena of inbetweeness is only gradually converging to form a new genuinely sociological paradigm that clearly surpasses the limitations of a narrow focus on postmodern conditions. We have tried to outline such a new perspective of cultural sociology on phenomena as diverse as garbage and monsters, as heroes and seduction. These phenomena are mostly seen as a scandal, seemingly subverting the cultural order, but, in fact, they drive our efforts to make sense of the world.

REFERENCES

Adorno, Theodor W., and Max Horkheimer. 2002. *Dialectic of Enlightenment. Philosophical Fragments.* Stanford, CA: Stanford University Press.

Agamben, Giorgio. 1998. *Homo Sacer. Sovereign Power and Bare Life.* Stanford, CA: Stanford University Press.

Alexander, Jeffrey C. 2003. *The Meanings of Social Life. A Cultural Sociology.* New York: Oxford University Press.

Alexander, Jeffrey C., Ron Eyerman, Bernhard Giesen, Neil J. Smelser, and Piotr Sztompka. 2004. *Cultural Trauma and Collective Identity.* Berkeley: University of California Press.

Bataille, Georges. 1962. *Death and Sensuality. A Study of Eroticism and the Taboo.* New York: Ballantine Books.

Baudrillard, Jean. 1990. *Seduction.* New York: St. Martin's Press.

Bauman, Zygmunt. 1991. *Modernity and Ambivalence.* Ithaca, NY: Cornell University Press.

Bhabha, Homi K. 1994. *The Location of Culture.* London: Routledge.

Boltanski, Luc. 1999. *Distant Suffering. Morality, Media and Politics.* Cambridge, UK: Cambridge University Press.

Campbell, Joseph. 1953. *The Hero with a Thousand Faces.* New York: Pantheon Books.

Caruth, Cathy. 1996. *Unclaimend Experience. Trauma, Narrative, and History.* Baltimore: John Hopkins University Press.

Choderlos de Laclos, Pierre Ambroise François. 1961. *Les Liaisons dangereuses.* Paris: Garnier.

Deleuze, Gilles. 1992. *The Fold. Leibniz and the Baroque.* Minneapolis: University of Minnesota Press.

Derrida, Jacques. 1967. *L'écriture et la différence.* Paris: Editions du Seuil.

Douglas, Mary. 1966. *Purity and Danger. An Analysis of Concepts of Pollution and Taboo.* London: Routledge & Kegan Paul.

Elias, Norbert. 1983. *The Court Society.* Oxford: Blackwell.

Eisenstadt, Shmuel. 1982. "The Axial Age: The Emergence of Transcendental Visions and the Rise of Clerics." *European Journal of Sociology* 23(2): 294–314.

Endres, Johannes. 2005. *Ikonologie des Zwischenraums: der Schleier als Medium und Metapher.* Munich: Paderborn.

Freud, Sigmund, and Josef Breuer. 1981. *Studies on Hysteria.* London: Hogarth.

Giesen, Bernhard. 2004. *Triumph and Trauma.* Boulder, CO: Paradigm.

Girard, René. 1997. *Violence and the Sacred.* Baltimore: John Hopkins University Press.

Heidegger, Martin. 1993. *Sein und Zeit.* Tübingen Niemeyer.

Husserl, Edmund. 1996. *Die Krisis der europäischen Wissenschaften und die transzendentale Phänomenologie.* Hamburg: Meiner.

Kantorowicz, Ernst H. 2001. *The King's Two Bodies. A Study in Mediaeval Political Theology.* Princeton, NJ: Princeton University Press.

Levine, Donald N. 1985. *The Flight from Ambiguity. Essays in Social and Cultural Theory.* Chicago: University of Chicago Press.

Lotman, Jurij M. 1990. *Universe of the Mind: A Semiotic Theory of Culture.* London: Tauris.

Merton, Robert K. 1976. *Sociological Ambivalence and other Essays.* New York: Free Press.

Morris, Ivan. 1975. *The Nobility of Failure: Tragic Heroes in the History of Japan.* New York: Holt, Rinehart & Winston.

Quine, Willard van Orman. 1969. *Word and Object.* Cambridge, MA: MIT Press.

Rank, Otto. 1909. *Der Mythus von der Geburt des Helden: Versuch einer psychologischen Mythendeutung.* Vienna: Deuticke.

Ricoeur, Paul. 1986. *The Symbolism of Evil.* Boston: Beacon Press.

Schütz, Alfred. 1988. *Strukturen der Lebenswelt Bd.1.* Frankfurt am Main: Suhrkamp.

———. 2004. *Der sinnhafte Aufbau der sozialen Welt.* Konstanz: University of Konstanz.

Serres, Michel. 2007. *The Parasite.* Minnesota: University of Minnesota Press.

Simmel, Georg. 1908. *Soziologie.* Leipzig: Dunker & Humblot.

———. 1996. "Die Koketterie." Pp. 256–277 in *Hauptprobleme der Philosophie. Gesammelte Aufsätze 14.* Frankfurt am Main: Suhrkamp.

Smelser, Neil. 1998. "The Rational and the Ambivalent in the Social Sciences. 1997 Presidential Address." *American Sociological Review* 63(1): 1–16.

Thompson, Michael. 1979. *Rubbish Theory. The Creation and Destruction of Value.* Oxford: Oxford University Press.

Turner, Victor. 1995. *The Ritual Process: Structure and Anti-Structure.* Piscataway, New Jersey: Aldine Transaction.

Weber, Max. 1978. *Economy and Society: An Outline of Interpretative Sociology.* Berkeley: University of California Press.

Wittgenstein, Ludwig. 2001. *Philosophical Investigations.* Oxford: Wiley Blackwell.

INDEX

....

"9/11," 573, 622

Abbott, Andrew, 76, 103 n. 10, 104 nn. 19; 23,
    200–4
Abolafia, Mitchel, 123–27, 137, 144, 168
action
    body as locus for, 704–5, 707
    civic, 213–17, 219, 224, 225–26
    collective/group, 19–20, 207, 209, 211–12, 220–22,
        224, 236, 437, 488–89, 494, 689–90, 728, 736
    economic (as culturally embedded), 127–32, 145,
        157–77, 178 n. 3, 178–79 n. 4, 693
    and habitus, 52–53, 725–26
    music as social, 722–23, 729–30, 732–33, 736
    narrative/storytelling and, 747, 753–54
    vs. observation, 195–96, 198, 202, 204–5
    in organizations, 763–83, 784 n. 6
    social, 16–17, 22, 27–28, 36–42, 60, 74, 129, 218,
        236, 263, 298, 438, 445–46, 464 n. 16, 511,
        583–84
    as symbolic/meaningful, 22, 96–101, 120, 266,
        401, 639, 660–61 n. 1, 672–75, 677,
        746, 788
    See also agency
actor-network theory, 172, 638, 686–87,
    708–11, 715
ad hocing, 19, 53–54, 764, 770, 782
Adorno, Theodor, 685, 722–28, 732, 800
Advocate, The, 517–18, 522–23 n. 2
aesthetic public sphere, 17, 318–37
    and cultural citizenship, 323, 330–32
    and cultural criticism, 323, 327–30
    and cultural sociology, 321–24
    serious vs. entertainment binary within,
        332–35
    and the social imaginary, 323–27
    symbolic hierarchies within, 332–34, 336
    See also public sphere
African American men,
    cultural analysis of, 343–61
    and cultural sociological analysis of, 17–18,
        351–54, 357–59
Agamben, Giorgio, 454–55, 461
agency, 7, 15, 17–18, 78, 90, 100–1, 137, 166, 169, 236,
    269–70, 345, 347–48, 356, 437, 445, 452, 458,
    481, 496–98, 510–11, 514–16, 615, 640, 685, 686,
    734–35
AGIL model, 637

Alexander, Jeffrey, 3, 7, 19, 125, 128–30, 135, 196,
    211–12, 216, 225, 233–34, 237–38, 245, 265–66,
    285, 286–87, 298–302, 307, 312–13 n. 22, 360 n.
    5, 405–6, 412, 413, 415, 418, 419–20 nn. 3–4, 421
    nn. 8; 12, 423 nn. 29–30, 538, 559 n. 32, 564, 573,
    626, 687, 689–90, 772, 775–76, 778, 780–1,
    783–84 nn. 1–2
Alford, Robert, 766
Al-Haq, 238–41
Almond, Gabriel, 209–11, 235, 630 n. 3, 637
Althusser, Louis, 713–15
ambivalence, 203, 789–803
American Dilemma, An (Myrdal), 396
Anderson, Benedict, 379–80, 437
Anderson, Elijah, 350, 351–52
anomie, 121, 579–80 n. 3
    and street culture, 349–50
anthropology
    and culture, 79–87, 104 n. 25, 106 n. 45, 630
        n. 3, 637
Appadurai, Arjun, 249, 310 n. 6
Architecture of Markets: An Economic Sociology of
    Twenty-First-Century Capitalist Societies, The
    (Fligstein), 165–66
Arendt, Hannah, 205, 242, 454–55, 461
Aristotle, 42, 141, 399, 443–44, 445–46, 454, 464 n.
    16, 613, 783–84 n. 1
arts, the, 46, 202, 323–24, 328, 333–37, 479, 683, 693,
    725
art worlds, 723, 728–30, 732
Artworlds (Becker), 736–37 n. 3
Asad, Talal, 442, 458, 462 n. 5, 463 n. 13
Askew, David, 538, 546, 551, 553
attribution theory, 530, 532, 533–35, 549–50, 553–56,
    557 n. 2
audience(s), 16, 99, 107 n. 54, 134–35, 216, 218, 222,
    263–64, 319, 323–25, 333, 336, 348, 376–77,
    487–94, 497–502, 603 n. 16, 626–27, 639–41,
    643, 645, 659–660, 690, 735, 771, 774, 778, 780,
    783
audience reception, 278–79 nn. 2–3
Auster, Paul, 391, 393, 399, 405, 409, 412,
    417–18
Austin, John L., 780
authenticity, 289–90, 511, 515–16,
    520–22, 726

authority, 296–97, 442–45, 500–2, 573, 576, 637–38,
     747–48
  political, 797
  scientific, 753–54, 756
  state vs. religious, 430, 435–36, 439–40, 442, 445,
     448–51, 454, 460–61, 463 n. 14
autonomy
  of cultural fields, 290, 292–98, 304–7, 324
  of journalism, 292–98, 305–6, 312 n. 19
  of national culture industries, 334–36
  within the public sphere, 290–92, 298–302,
     309–10, 310–11 n. 7, 312 n. 20, 314 n. 28
  See also culture, autonomy of

Bakhtin, Mikhail, 41, 594–95
Banfield, Edward, 118, 209–10, 235, 237, 245,
     630 n. 3
Barth, Fredrik, 372–75, 381, 383–84 nn. 4–5
Barthes, Roland, 6, 7, 583, 676
Bataille, Georges, 791–92
Baudrillard, Jean, 676, 688, 799
Bauman, Zygmunt, 36, 301, 681, 789–90
Bawer, Bruce, 518, 520, 522–23 n. 2
Beck, Ulrich, 756
Becker, Howard S., 9, 723, 728–30, 732
Belk, Russell, 141–42
Bell, Daniel, 310 n. 6, 679
Bellah, Robert, 215–16, 223–24, 236–37,
     784 n. 8
Bendix, Reinhard, 235
Berezin, Mabel, 15, 243, 628–29
Berger, Peter, 76, 122, 221
Between Facts and Norms (Habermas), 289
Bhabha, Homi, 788, 790, 793
Bhaskar, Roy, 33–34
Biggart, Nicole, 123, 125–26, 144, 158, 167–68, 178–79
     n. 4
binaries/binary oppositions, 39–40, 77–78, 104
     n. 19, 174, 267, 377, 446, 472, 481, 554, 587,
     593–94, 597–98, 747, 772–73, 788
binary codes
  of civil society/civil sphere, 22, 130, 216, 261, 266,
     274–77, 318, 323–24, 332–35, 378–79, 495,
     510–11, 584, 641
Birmingham School. See cultural studies, British
Blumer, Herbert, 32, 383 n. 3, 683, 728
body, the, 698–720
  and culture, 700, 702–3, 718
  sociological studies of, 698–99
Body Multiple, The (Mol), 708–9
Boltanski, Luc, 158, 174–75, 197, 200–1, 204, 213, 216,
     337 n. 4, 775, 783–84 n. 12
boundaries, 3, 8, 13, 17, 120, 130–31, 217, 250, 263,
     265, 277, 360 n. 4, 393–94, 435–36, 444, 446–47,
     554, 584, 614–15, 657, 691–92, 730–32, 774–78,
     784 n. 3, 789, 793, 799
  social vs. symbolic, 370–77, 380–83, 384 n. 6
  study of, 372–77, 623

boundary-making, 13, 223, 368, 372–77, 380, 383,
     383–84 n. 4, 591
Bourdieu, Pierre, 16, 21, 46–48, 51–54, 88, 103
     n. 9; 11; 16, 174, 178–79 n. 4, 285, 286–87, 290,
     292–95, 298–302, 304–5, 307, 309, 310 n. 4,
     314 n. 29, 337 n. 4, 374, 376, 443, 502 n. 2,
     674, 676, 677, 682–84, 692, 698–99, 701,
     703–6, 707–8, 711, 715–19, 723, 725–27, 728,
     730, 734
Bowling Alone, 237, 246
Brooks, David, 301, 307–8
Brown, Jerry, 650–52, 653
Brubaker, Rogers, 367, 378, 384 n. 8, 437–38, 441,
     462–63 n. 10, 623
Buchanan, Patrick, 643, 651, 655–56
Burawoy, Michael, 195–98, 201, 204
bureaucracy, 221, 444, 478, 752, 770, 774–75,
     777, 779
bureaucratic rationality, 568, 707, 753
Burke, Kenneth, 401, 774, 778, 780
Bush, George H. W., 240, 274, 641, 642–45, 650–51,
     653–63
Bush, George W., 272–74, 314 n. 31
  administration of, 295, 305–6, 754

Calhoun, Craig, 100, 310 n. 4, 437
Callon, Michel, 137–38, 168, 174, 176, 675
capital
  Bourdieuian notion of, 703–6, 710–11, 719
     n. 11, 725
  cultural, 55, 88–89, 106 nn. 36; 41, 178–79 n. 4,
     360 n. 4, 683, 725, 728, 731
  political, 493, 574
  scientific, 103 n. 11,
  social, 16, 210, 219, 225–26, 308
  symbolic, 47, 50, 304, 707, 718 n. 4, 735
capitalism, 30–31, 37, 62, 125, 137, 159, 305, 438–39,
     532, 576, 586, 595, 614, 685, 724
  democracy and, 120–22, 131–32
  late, 676–78
carrier groups, 382, 529, 537, 559 n. 32, 570, 573–76,
     585–86, 590
Cartwright, Nancy, 42–43 n. 5
Casanova, Jose, 473–75, 482
Catholicism, 57–59, 215, 462 n. 4, 463 n. 11, 471,
     474–77, 478, 571, 621
causality, 22, 27–28, 30–31, 33–35, 37–42, 80, 83,
     88, 106 n. 41, 199, 200–1, 215–16, 237, 245,
     421–22 n. 13, 461 n. 3, 462 n. 5, 533–35, 545,
     547, 549–50, 552–54, 557 n. 5, 616–17, 624,
     629
Chang, Iris, 536, 538–40, 543, 546, 587, 600 n. 2, 601
     nn. 4–5
charisma, 125, 131, 133, 585, 797–98
Charismatic Capitalism (Biggart), 125
Chatterjee, Partha, 232, 244
Chicago School, 222, 360–61 n. 6, 369–72, 383
Chinese Communist Party, 588–98, 606–7 n. 37

Christianity, 143, 223, 439–42, 448, 462 n. 5, 471–72, 474, 478–79, 755–56
  American, 121, 396, 451, 457–60
churches, 58–59, 220–21, 471, 474, 773–76
Cicourel, Aaron V., 20, 65, 103 n. 9, 771
citizen-consumers, 176, 322–23
citizenship, 19–20, 142, 211–12, 214–19, 223, 234–35, 237–38, 242–44, 246, 248–50, 277, 291, 454, 460–61, 515, 623, 679–81
citizenship, cultural, 323, 330–32, 337
civic culture, 19, 207–226, 248, 630 n. 3
  definition of, 211–14, 224–26
  and religion, 219–21
  and social movements, 221–24
Civic Culture, The (Almond & Verba), 209–11, 226
civic individualism, 13, 511, 514–18, 521–22
  binaries of, 511
civil repair, 237–39, 241–43, 394, 409, 415, 417–18
civil society, 17, 40, 61, 196–97, 199, 211, 217, 219, 225–26, 233–51, 260–62, 265–66, 276–79, 302–3, 307–8, 318–20, 412, 636
  civil vs. civilized within, 242–44
  as a civil sphere, 390–91, 394–95, 412, 418
  discourse of, 17, 124, 130, 136, 237–38, 277, 300, 307, 318, 321–22, 333, 641
  French, 635–26
  and immigrants, 248–49
  issues of power within, 242–44
  and media, 287–89, 296–98, 321–22, 335–37
  and religion, 464 n. 19
  role of the state within, 244–46
  and the welfare state, 248
  as Western, 242, 249
civil sphere, the, 13, 17, 196, 211–12, 225, 233–34, 237–39, 243, 245–47, 250, 263, 266, 276–77, 298–99, 368, 390–98, 402, 406, 409, 417, 418, 746, 749, 751
  and media, 261, 265, 275
  morality within, 277, 420 n. 4
  as separate from the political, 246–47
Civil Sphere, The (Alexander), 196, 233–34, 237, 238, 239, 245, 246, 394, 417
Civilizing Process, The (Elias), 690–91, 700–1, 720 n. 23
"Clash of Civilizations, The" (Huntington), 434, 471, 630 n. 3
Clash of Civilizations and the Remaking of the World Order, The (Huntington), 471
Clash Within: Democracy, Religious Violence, and India's Future, The (Nussbaum), 402
class, 52–54, 61, 63–65, 213–14, 219, 286, 288–89, 298, 300, 314 n. 29, 464 n. 15, 593–94, 602 n. 9, 604 nn. 26–27, 605–06 nn. 32–33, 673–74, 725, 731
class consciousness, 580 n. 5
classification, 14, 38, 65, 93–94, 162–63, 237, 245, 277, 366–68, 369, 383, 437, 510, 615, 637, 683, 688–89, 691, 745–46, 788–90, 793–94, 802

climate change. *See* global warming
Clinton, William J., 15, 621, 641, 642–63
  1992 presidential campaign of, 642–45
  administration of, 295
  as "Slick Willie, 642, 646–52, 658
codes, 13, 17–19, 85, 94, 96, 127, 130, 134, 173, 245–47, 266, 275, 336, 374, 376–80, 382, 510–11, 746, 769
  cultural, 76, 125, 130, 136, 214, 298–300, 319, 368, 488, 510–11, 641, 733, 783–84 n. 1
  democratic, 14, 135–36, 139–40, 143, 216–17, 237–43, 248, 307–8, 641
code of the street, 350–52
cognition, 8, 47, 63, 73, 90, 105 n. 33, 106 nn. 38; 43, 161, 167–68, 173, 375, 378, 384 nn. 8–9, 554, 681, 692–93
Cohen, Stanley, 263
collective consciousness, 583–85, 689
collective effervescence, 765, 768, 776–78
collective identity, 122, 129, 131–32, 211–12, 474, 509, 512, 514–15, 531, 734
  and cultural trauma, 567–68, 570–73, 578, 579–80 n. 36, 587–88
  and Nanking Massacre, 591–92, 598, 603 n. 14, 605–6 nn. 33–34
  and social movements, 222–24, 227 n. 13
collective memory, 11,
  and cultural trauma, 559 n. 32, 567, 571, 574–75, 579–80 n. 3,
  and conflict, 530–35, 537
  and music, 723, 732
  and Nanking Massacre, 535–56, 558 n. 13, 587, 590, 604 n. 26
  theoretical perspectives on, 11, 529–30, 535, 553–56
  See also memory
collective representation(s), 38, 120, 125, 134, 173–76, 218–19, 367, 377, 379–80, 384 n. 8, 437–38, 444–45, 460, 579, 585, 645, 660, 735, 745–47, 758, 764–67, 775, 780
Collins, Randall, 21, 51, 54–56, 104 n. 23, 140, 718–19 nn. 5; 6; 13
commemoration, 623, 627–28
commodities/commodification, 48, 130, 165, 456, 458, 675–78, 684, 690–91, 724, 726
  See also consumption/consumers
Communist Manifesto, The, 586
"Conflict" (Simmel), 548
consumption/consumers, 52, 59, 121, 126, 130–31, 141, 158, 159, 162–63, 171, 174, 176–77, 178–79 n. 4, 180 n. 14, 221, 672–93
  cultural, 321–24, 326, 330, 333, 336
  and cultural sociology, 675, 689, 690–93
  and hedonism, 679–82
  material culture approaches to, 684–87
  moral dimension of, 687–90
  and performance, 689–90
  postmodern theories of, 676–78
  See also commodities/commodification
consumption studies, 672–76, 684

Cooley, Charles Horton, 348
cosmologies, 442, 461–62 n. 3, 745–46, 754, 757
counterfactuals, 615, 616–18
Crane, Diana, 7
Critique of Judgment (Kant), 683
cultural analysis
　definition of, 773
　domain of color as a paradigm for, 48–51, 64
　endogenous vs. exogenous factors in, 75–76, 80,
　　83, 86–87, 104 n. 25, 164
　hermeneutic vs. non-hermeneutic styles of,
　　78–95
　as interdisciplinary, 7
　pragmatic perspective in, 216–17
　role of meaning in, 6–7, 21, 63, 77, 90, 352,
　　393, 773
　theory vs. method of, 74
　See also cultural sociology; as well as individual
　　topics
"cultural history, new," 6–8
"Cultural Meanings and Cultural Structures in
　Historical Explanation" (Hall), 39–40
cultural omnivorousness, 676, 726
cultural policy, 17, 323, 325, 329–37
cultural pragmatics, 16, 20, 129, 134, 266, 269–70,
　636–60
cultural sociology
　broad program in, 4
　definitions of, 4, 9–10, 12, 35–37, 367, 583–84, 637,
　　639, 671
　and Durkheim, 421 n. 8, 481–82, 583
　and ethnography, 391–94, 418–19
　goals of, 4, 12, 37, 193–95, 416, 693, 763–65
　history of, 3–10, 639
　and humanities, 4, 11–12, 74, 583, 722, 728
　and idealism, 18, 746
　impact of, 10–11, 400
　and inbetweenness/ambivalence, 788, 793,
　　802–3
　and institutionalism, 430, 616–18, 765
　interdisciplinary nature of, 3, 5–6, 616, 631 n. 6
　materiality-inspired approaches to, 681–82,
　　684–87, 690–93
　narratives of, 226 n. 5
　pluralistic nature of, 40–41
　pragmatic perspective in, 216–17, 226, 401
　and race, 17–18, 351–54, 357–59
　vs. rational choice approaches, 476–77, 693
　rationalization processes inside, 46–65
　as a research program, 37–41
　within sociology, 4–5, 8–10, 28
　vs. sociology of culture, 5–6, 9–10, 584
　and spatial analysis, 360–61 n. 6
　Strong Program in, 12, 22, 266, 285, 321–23, 360
　　n. 5, 367–68, 393, 584, 774, 782
　and study of civil society, 17, 232–51, 318–19,
　　335–36, 394, 400, 402
　and study of everyday interaction, 763–67,
　　769–73, 774, 777–78, 781–83

tensions within, 11–22, 42 n. 4
as universal vs. Western, 232–34, 238, 249–50
See also cultural analysis; cultural/culture
　structures; cultural studies; cultural trauma;
　cultural turn; culture; economic sociology;
　models/modeling; parallel scaling;
　performance theory; spatial scaling; as well as
　individual topics
Cultural Sociology, 9
cultural/culture structures, 12, 14, 15–16, 19–21,
　37, 39–40, 41, 85, 119, 124, 128–30, 135–36,
　144–45, 158, 212, 298, 323, 333–34, 367, 371,
　377, 382–83, 393–94, 397, 400, 415–17, 559–60
　n. 32, 576, 578, 584, 587, 591, 594, 637, 639,
　641–42, 645, 671, 675, 684–86, 690, 765,
　772–74, 782
cultural studies, 321–22
　British, 731
cultural trauma, 11, 564, 566, 567, 570–79, 579–80
　n. 3, 584–86
　vs. crisis, 579–80 n. 3
　as a framework of analysis, 577–79
　meaning struggles in, 571, 573, 577–79
　role of mass media in, 573–74, 577
　role of moral frameworks in, 576–77
　role of victim and perpetrator in, 559 n. 32,
　　566–68, 570–71, 575–77, 579–80 n. 3, 584–97,
　　599, 604 n. 27, 605–6 nn. 32–33, 607 n. 40
　vs. social trauma, 571–73
　See also carrier groups; collective identity;
　　collective memory; narrative(s); nation-state;
　　trauma construction; trauma theory;
　　traumatic occurrences
cultural turn, 4–10, 70–101, 164, 177, 238, 367, 637,
　639, 673, 675–76
　post-, 9, 76–78, 79, 87–95, 105 n. 31, 106 n. 43
　pre-, 9, 77–78, 79–87, 104 n. 28, 106 n. 43
culture
　and agency, 7
　autonomy of, 6, 11, 14, 16–17, 20, 120, 125, 130, 213,
　　264, 286–87, 290, 310 n. 6, 320, 368, 376, 393,
　　417, 473, 660–61 n. 1, 678, 692
　definition of, 212–14
　as a dependent variable, 723
　formal models of, 71–74
　as an independent/causal variable, 88–90
　measuring, 70–108
　principles for research on, 60–65
　and structure, 19, 35, 41, 87, 126–27, 164–66,
　　212–13, 219, 290, 354, 360 n. 5, 367, 379–81, 415,
　　472–73, 533, 583–84, 614–15, 629, 660–61 n. 1,
　　766, 782
　as a "thing," 79, 84, 90
　as tool-kit, 7, 170, 379, 614–15, 660–61 n. 1
　See also cultural analysis; cultural/culture
　　structures; cultural studies; cultural trauma;
　　cultural turn; economic sociology; models/
　　modeling; parallel scaling; performance theory;
　　spatial scaling; as well as individual topics

culture industry/ies, 9, 321, 324, 330, 333, 334–35, 724, 726
culture of poverty thesis, 232, 349, 359–60 n. 2
Cyclone Nargis (Burma), 261, 267, 274–77

Daily Show, The, 332–33
data analysis, 71–73, 103 n. 9, 108 n. 59
Davidson, Donald, 37–39, 42 nn. 2–3
Dayan, Daniel, 263–64, 265
definitions of culture. *See* culture
Deleuze, Gilles, 788, 793
democracy
   and capitalism, 121–22, 132
   and civil society, 17, 135–36, 235, 238–42, 247–50
   and culture, 129–30, 135–36, 139–40, 224–25, 235–46
   as Western, 434–35, 456, 465 n. 21, 630 n. 3
Democracy in America (Tocqueville), 120–22, 208
democratic theory
   and cultural sociology, 233–34
democratization, 234–35, 247
DeNora, Tia, 727, 728, 732–34, 736
Derrida, Jacques, 7, 401–2, 409, 418, 422 n. 21–22, 449, 660–61 n. 1
desire, 27–28, 38, 121, 141–42, 394, 510–11, 674–76, 680–81, 688, 690–93, 801
   and religion, 455–57, 461, 465 n. 20
Dewey, John, 211, 217, 225, 735
diachronic, 40–41, 86, 98–99, 378, 640
Dialectic of Enlightenment (Horkheimer and Adorno)
difference-based interactions, 377–80, 383 n. 1
   cultural sociological study of, 365–68, 372, 372, 381–83
differentiated ties, 170–71
differentiation, social, 128–29, 131, 225, 235, 289, 380, 382, 439–41, 458, 472–73, 683, 735, 791
"differentiation of spheres," 764–67, 782
Dilthey, Wilhelm, 20–21, 43 n. 6, 584
DiMaggio, Paul, 7, 21, 60, 79, 88–90, 100, 106 nn. 39–42, 127, 178–79 n. 4, 728
disasters,
   as mediated, 267–77
   as performatively enacted, 260–61, 277–78
disciplinary power
Disciplinary Revolution: Calvinism and the Rise of the State in Early Modern Europe, The (Gorski), 57–60
Discipline and Punish (Foucault), 707, 713
discipline, social, 50, 51, 57–59, 439–40, 445, 680, 707, 716–17
discourse, 18, 73–74, 90–95, 99, 106 n. 43, 107 nn. 51–52; 54–55, 137, 158, 216–18, 250, 293, 295, 298–302, 312 n. 19, 330, 374–75, 380–82, 421 n. 12, 449, 510, 522–23 n. 2, 570–71, 576–77, 579–80 n. 3, 675, 679–81
   aesthetic dimension of, 319, 332–35

of climate change/global warming, 748–49, 751–52, 756–59
   economic, 171–77
   vs. language, 96–97
   rational-critical, 285–92, 297, 300, 301, 303, 318–19
   See also civil society, discourse of
discourse analysis, 175–76, 179 n. 11, 571, 735
disenchantment, rational, 117–18, 120, 125, 144
Discovery of Grounded Theory, The (Glaser & Strauss), 32
Distinction (Bourdieu), 51–54, 682–84
Division of Labor in Society, The (Durkheim), 120
Dobbin, Frank, 160, 167, 178–79 n. 4
Douglas, Mary, 6, 141, 158, 619, 682, 747
dramaturgical perspectives on society, 216, 722, 734
Du Bois, W.E.B., 347–48
Duneier, Mitchell, 348, 401, 418
Durkheim, Emile, 29, 79, 132, 211, 377, 384 n. 8, 421 n. 8, 559 n. 23, 579–80 n. 3, 614–15, 685, 686, 688–89, 745–46, 780
   late, 7, 119–20, 128, 131, 144, 214, 447, 481–82, 583, 619–20, 765
   and religious sociology, 128, 440
   and ritual, 18–19, 262, 263, 265
Durkheimians, neo-, 39, 128–31, 144, 218–19, 263

Earthquake, Sichuan, 19, 261, 267, 274–77
economic life and culture, 157–80
economic sociology, 10, 118–22, 126–27, 157–58
   cultural analysis in contemporary, 122–27, 166–77, 177–79 nn. 2–5
   cultural production perspective in, 159–66, 169
   and cultural sociology, 127–45, 171–72, 175, 177, 692–93
   new, 121, 122–23
   See also economy and culture
economics/economists
   legitimacy of, 138–40
   performativity of, 138–39
economy, the,
   and culture, 117–45, 157–80, 672, 692–93
   cultural sociology of, 119–22, 127–45, 171
Economy and Society (Parsons & Smelser), 120–21
Elementary Forms of Religious Life, The (Durkheim), 119–20, 129, 131, 144, 482, 689
Elias, Norbert, 243, 690–91, 699–712, 716, 719 nn. 8; 9; 12, 720 n. 23, 723
Eliasoph, Nina, 20, 217–18
embeddedness, 121, 122–25, 127–32, 138, 145, 158, 163, 178–79 n. 4, 217, 221, 298, 383–84 n. 4, 510, 621–22, 629
embodiment, 698–720
   and altruism, 699, 712–15
   and violence, 699, 700–3

emotional energy (EE), 54–55, 718–19 nn. 5–6; 13
emotions, 125, 137, 141–42, 174, 195–96, 204, 267–72,
      277–78, 301, 303, 309, 495, 498–500,
      510, 568–79, 579–80 n. 3, 617–18, 620,
      681, 699
encoding, 270, 278 n. 2, 322–23, 371–72
Engel, Stephen M., 509
Engels, Friedrich, 586
environmentalism, 213–14, 217–19, 227 n. 13. *See
      also* global warming
essentialism, 53, 86–87, 95, 221, 227 n. 9, 236, 369
ethnic hierarchy approach, 370–71
ethnicity, 365–84
ethnographers as "detectives" of cultural
      sociology, 391, 417–19
ethnography, 32–33, 84, 169, 199, 205, 218, 391–97,
      686, 767
   as "being there," 391, 419 n. 1
   as "touchdowns," 395–97, 421–22 n. 13
   See also urban ethnography
ethnomethodology, 8, 19–20, 733–35, 736, 770
events, 12–14, 437, 613–31, 640, 662 n. 22
   contiguous, 622–24, 628–29
   critique of Sewell's theory of, 617–18
   and cultural trauma, 559–60 n. 32, 570–71,
      578–79, 585–86, 605–6 n. 33
   as "moments," 621–22
   as political facts, 620–29
   as ritualized, 627–29
   role of experience in, 620–22, 631 n. 12
   role of mass media in, 627–28
   sequential, 622, 624–26, 628–29
   spectacular, 622, 626–29
   speech, 96–97
   study of, 629–30
exchange, 10, 159–66, 168, 170–72, 177–78 n. 2, 672,
      714–15
   market, 10, 121, 130–32, 170, 171
exchange relations, 121
exchange value, 48
explanation, 6–9, 20–22, 27–29, 31, 33–34, 36,
      37–42, 46–48, 56, 64–65, 74, 90, 98, 101,
      105 n. 33; 35, 106 n. 41, 118, 157, 164, 178–79
      n. 4, 193, 199, 419–20 n. 3, 421–22 n. 13,
      462 n. 5, 476, 490, 533–34, 576, 614–18,
      676, 688–90, 735, 790
   See also generalization
Eyerman, Ron, 11, 564, 578, 532

"Fabrication of Meaning, The" (Griswold), 61
Featherstone, Mike, 676–77
fields
   cultural, 290, 292–98, 304–6, 311 n. 10, 337
      n. 4, 725
   and *habitus*, 703–5
   institutional, 169
   literary, 51
   political, 304–7, 314 n. 28

figuration (Elias), 700–1
financial crisis, world, 118–20, 132–33, 140, 144–45
financial markets
   sociology of, 123–25, 132, 136–38
First New Nation, The (Lipset), 235
Fiske, John, 264, 533
Fligstein, Neil, 122, 165–66, 168, 169, 173
flow(s), 249–50
"foreignness," 365–84
formal models. *See* models/modeling
Foucault, Michel, 7, 35, 87, 92–93, 95, 105 n. 36, 196,
      243, 360–61 n. 6, 431, 454, 456, 531, 706–8, 711,
      713, 716, 719 nn. 17–18, 728
frames/framing, 35, 47, 122, 126, 137, 161, 199,
      222–24, 227 n. 12, 236, 262, 489–91, 571, 614–15,
      747–48
Frankfurt School, 289, 312 n. 19, 321
free-floating intellectual, 789
French National Front, 624–26
Freud, Sigmund, 195, 243, 251 n. 8, 465 n. 24,
      567–68, 579 n. 2, 619, 717, 790
Friedland, Roger, 4, 15, 16, 103 n. 12, 766
Frye, Northrop, 7, 542, 583, 747
functionalism, Parsonian, 39, 235
   decline of, 5, 6–7, 119, 637
fusion, 19, 266, 690, 735, 752, 777, 781
   de-, 266, 269, 279 n. 4
   re-, 19, 266

Gadamer, Hans-Georg, 75, 421–22 n. 13
Gao, Rui, 538, 578, 604 nn. 26–27
garbage, 793–94
Garfinkel, Harold, 19–20, 769–71
gay and lesbian movement, 507–9, 512–23
   liberationism within, 507–9, 512, 514–23
   research on, 508–9, 522–23 n. 2
   See also normalization
Geertz, Clifford, 6, 7, 12–13, 40, 41, 42 n. 4, 90, 106
      n. 43, 124, 177–78 n. 2, 381, 393, 397, 398, 401,
      408, 421–22 n. 13, 543, 583, 618–19, 622, 626,
      637, 639, 660–61 n. 1
generalization, 20–22, 31, 33, 39, 50, 63–64, 158,
      171–77, 205, 321, 421–22 n. 13, 482, 510, 640
   See also explanation
genre, 28–29, 40–41, 98, 137, 535, 548–550, 554,
      594–95, 640–41, 747–48, 757–58
   apocalyptic, 751–59
   choices among sociologists, 200–2
Germans, The (Elias), 700–3, 705
Giddens, Anthony, 101
Gill, Anthony, 476–77
Glaser, Barney G., 32
Global South, 17, 232–50
global warming
   discourse and representations of, 12, 745–59
globalization, 180 n. 14, 261, 278, 625–26, 713
   cultural, 334–35
   and religion, 14, 471–82

Goffman, Erving, 18–19, 199, 216, 227 n. 12, 689, 708, 722
Goodstein, David, 517–18, 522–23 n. 2
Gore, Al, 753, 755, 757–58
Gorski, Philip, 51, 57–60, 437, 463 n. 11, 464 n. 15, 473
governance theory, 159–61, 164, 175–77
Gramsci, Antonio, 7, 213, 532, 637
Granovetter, Mark, 122–23, 163, 173
Griswold, Wendy, 7, 61–63
grounded theory, 32
group style, 217–19, 784–85 n. 9

Habermas, Jürgen, 11, 16, 225, 236–37, 245, 285–93, 295, 298–302, 303, 307, 309, 310 nn. 2; 3; 5; 7, 312–13 nn. 21–22, 320–21, 434–35, 445, 579–80 n. 3
Habits of the Heart (Bellah et al.), 215, 236
habitus, 698–99, 701, 703–6, 710–11, 716–19, 725, 730
Halbwachs, Maurice, 723
Hall, John R., 4–5, 9–10, 39–40, 77, 104 n. 22
Handbook of Cultural Sociology, The, 4, 9–10
Handbook of Economic Sociology, The, 3, 158
Handbook of Qualitative Research, The, 3
Hannerz, Ulf, 348–49, 352
Hanrahan, Nancy Weiss, 4–5
Haraway, Donna, 699, 713–15, 717, 719 n. 19
Healy, Kieran, 165, 178
Hegel, Georg Wilhelm Friedrich, 55, 143, 783–84 n. 1
hegemony, 16, 321–22, 334–35, 431, 501, 530, 531, 534, 637, 703
  of American television, 328–31
  institutional, 443–44, 464 n. 15
  and mediatized rituals, 263–65
  See also power
Hennion, Antoine, 682–83, 734
hermeneutic circle, 215–16, 421–22 n. 13
hermeneutic turn, 74–75
hermeneutics, 28, 34, 36, 41, 70–71, 78–101, 106 nn. 41–43; 45
  definition of, 78
  structural, 90, 92
Higashinakano, Shudo, 541–42, 544
Hindu nationalism, 431–32, 442, 453
Hobbes, Thomas, 439, 455
Holocaust, the, 142, 312–13 n. 22, 535, 539, 559 n. 31, 580 n. 6, 585, 590, 626, 701–2
  "forgotten" (Nanking), 538–39, 586
Honda, Katsuichi, 537–39, 546
Hong Ri (The Red Sun), 596–97, 606–7 nn. 37–39
Hopper, Edward, 400–1, 409, 422 n. 19
Horkheimer, Max, 685, 800
Hume, David, 42, 56
Huntington, Samuel, 234, 368, 434–35, 471–72, 479, 630 n. 3
Husserl, Edmund, 790–91
Hustvedt, Siri, 391–92, 397, 399, 405, 408, 418–19
hybridity, 238, 244, 246–49, 788, 790, 793, 802–3

iconicity/iconic representations, 645, 687, 735, 746, 755–6
iconology, 203–4
ideal types, 64–65, 102 n. 6, 699
identity, 94–95, 107 n. 49, 179 n. 9, 278–79 n. 3, 369–71, 382, 434, 510, 571, 675–76, 678, 684, 689, 691–93, 705, 708, 713, 726, 731–32, 792–93
  See also collective identity
Identity and Control (White), 107 n. 47
ideological state apparatus (ISA), 713–14
ideology, 16, 29, 285–86, 443, 447, 548, 553
images, visual, 202–4, 270–71, 478–79, 755–56
imagined community/ies, 130–31, 137, 261, 265, 379–80, 436, 462–63 n. 10, 474–75, 480
immigrants/immigration, 13–14, 248, 366, 384 n. 7, 392–97, 399, 404–8, 423 nn. 26; 29, 623, 625–26
impression management, 134–35, 199, 202, 347, 726, 735
inbetweenness, 788–803
individualism and individuality, 122, 194–95, 208–9, 215–17, 223–24, 236, 244–46, 312 n. 21, 326–28, 378–79, 381–82, 420 n. 4, 434, 440–41, 472, 520–22, 529, 619–20, 676–77, 679–81, 691, 702–3
  See also civic individualism
Inglehart, Ronald, 210, 456, 637
institutional analysis, 90–95, 100–1, 103 n. 12, 107 nn. 49–50, 133–35, 176, 614–15, 620–21, 629, 673
institutional boundaries, 435–36, 446–47, 773–75, 782–83
institutional dynamics of the Obama campaign, 303–7
institutional dynamics of the public sphere, 285–87, 290, 292–302, 311 n. 14
institutional fields, 464 n. 15
institutional logics, 15, 164, 238, 249, 431, 442–46, 447, 450, 766, 784 n. 2
  of religion, 430–61
institutional oppression of homosexuals, 507–22
institutional theory, 460, 512, 514, 520
institutionalism, 76–77, 99, 118, 133–35, 168, 430–31
  historical, 15, 616–18, 620
  neo/new-, 8, 76, 106 n. 41, 118, 135–36, 158, 161, 164, 166–67, 169, 173–75, 177, 212, 287, 784 nn. 6–7
institutionalization, 15, 160, 193, 234, 421 n. 2, 464 n. 15, 779
institutions, 74, 86, 92–95, 103 n. 11, 107 n. 50, 108 n. 59, 159, 161, 165–66, 175, 442–46, 464 n. 15, 529, 571–73, 579–80 n. 3, 707, 764, 773–75, 778, 782
  of civil society/civil sphere, 211–12, 237, 245, 298–99, 392, 395, 417–18
  media, 287–92, 296–97, 300, 309, 311–12 n. 18, 312–13 n. 22, 322–23
  narrative and, 488–89, 491, 495, 500–2

integration (of society), 14, 128–29, 384 n. 7,
    392–97, 409–17, 418, 420 n. 4, 421 n. 12, 507,
    515, 517–19, 538, 801–2
intellectuals
  media, 307–9
  public, 294, 301, 311 n. 17
  and the public sphere, 287–89, 292, 294,
    297–300, 312–13 nn. 21–22, 757
interaction, 32–33, 124, 196, 202, 212–13, 713, 763–65,
    769–72, 790–91, 799
    See also difference-based interactions
interaction rituals, 216, 718–19 n. 5–6; 13
interactionism, 19, 122, 169. See also symbolic
    interactionism.
interests, 143, 175–76, 208–9, 222–23, 264, 299, 431,
    511, 559 n. 28, 639, 660 n. 1
Internet, the, 295, 302, 305, 313 n. 23, 322–23, 333
interpellation, 713–15, 717–18
interpretation, 20–22, 27–43, 57–65, 70, 72–76,
    78–79, 85–101, 105 n. 35, 106 n. 45, 107 n. 52,
    170, 172–74, 178 n. 3, 193–94, 205, 215–16,
    421–22 n. 13, 578–79, 584–86, 616–18, 802
  minimal and maximal, 28–42
intersubjectivity, 168, 300, 318–20
intertextuality, 311–12 n. 18, 322
Introduction to the Sociology of Music
    (Adorno), 724
Invention of Solitude, The (Auster), 397, 405
involuntary association, 420 n. 4
Islam, 220, 232, 246, 401–2, 422 n. 22, 429, 432–36,
    441–42, 450, 452–53, 456–59, 461
    n. 2, 462 nn. 5; 8, 463 n. 13, 464 nn. 19–21,
    465 n. 23, 471–72, 474–75, 477–78, 531,
    556–57 n. 1
  and democracy, 463 n. 14
  and globalization, 479–81
  and nationalism, 463 n. 14
Islam Observed (Geertz), 622
Islamism, 456, 480

Jacobs, Mark, 4–5
Jacobs, Ronald, 17, 216, 265, 295, 310 n. 1,
    360, 495
James, William, 202, 621
Jameson, Frederic, 196, 676, 678
Japan
  "history problem" in, 551–53, 559 n. 25
  and World War II, 535–56, 586–87, 601 n. 4
Jones, Gareth Stedman, 47, 61
journalism, 279 n. 4, 291–98, 304–6, 310 n. 3, 311
    nn. 8; 10; 12, 312 n. 19, 324, 327–28, 555, 572–74,
    641, 662 n. 14
  political, 288, 311–12 n. 18
  science, 755
  television, 328, 580–81 n. 7
  See also media, news
justifications, 775, 783–84 nn. 1–2

Kai-shek, Chiang, 536, 542–43, 586, 592, 599
Kant, Immanuel, 71, 682–83, 691, 789
Katrina, Hurricane, 19, 261, 267, 271–74,
    566, 758
Katz, Elihu, 263–64, 265
Kaufman, Jason, 75–76, 86, 211
Kennedy, John F., 565, 574, 580–81 n. 7, 621, 638,
    653–54, 662 n. 17, 663 n. 44
Keywords (Williams), 614–15
kinship, 40, 84, 94–95, 121, 125–26, 177, 244, 378,
    684, 714, 797
Knorr Cetina, Karin, 123–25, 144, 168
Kroeber, Alfred, 79–84, 86–87, 89, 100, 104–5 nn.
    25; 28; 30–33
Kuhn, Thomas, 31, 64, 75–76

Lacan, Jacques, 707, 713, 791
Lakatos, Imre, 419–20 n. 3
Lamont, Michèle, 8, 62, 352, 360 n. 4, 374, 376, 384
    n. 6, 623, 683–84
language, 6, 12, 40–41, 78, 85–86, 96–97, 101, 107 n.
    55, 108 n. 61, 220, 430, 448–49, 764–65, 769–72,
    780, 782, 801–2
  public, 214–17
  See also linguistics; sociolinguistics
language-games, 6, 76, 105 n. 35, 240
Languages of Class (Jones), 47, 61
Langue, 40–41, 660–61 n.1
Last Best Gifts: Altruism and the Market for Human
    Blood and Organs (Healy), 165
Latour, Bruno, 168, 686, 784 n. 6
Law, John, 699, 709–11, 717
Leach, Edmund, 381, 383–84 n. 4
leaders/leadership, 164, 493, 638–39, 767–68,
    772–75, 781
legitimacy, 93–94, 139–40, 143–44, 161, 436, 636–38,
    640–41
  state, 301, 438–39, 454
Legitimation Crisis, The (Habermas), 759–80 n. 3
Lévi–Strauss, Claude, 6, 12, 39–41, 79, 84–87, 90–91,
    94–95, 98, 100, 104 n. 25, 105 n. 35, 106 n. 43,
    370–72, 495, 583, 685, 746
Leviathan, The (Hobbes), 439
Lichterman, Paul, 20, 218, 227 nn. 7; 9; 11–12
lifeworld, 18–19, 74, 123–24, 326, 328, 434–35, 510,
    676, 681, 733, 801–2
  Habermas on, 291, 310–11 n. 7
  Husserl on, 791
liminality, 19, 203, 267, 269, 641, 790–92, 799
linguistics, 64, 84–86, 108 n. 61, 769. See also
    language; sociolinguistics
Lipset, Seymour Martin, 235, 637
Logic of Practice, The (Bourdieu), 698, 705
Long, Elizabeth, 3, 5
Lotman, Juri, 788, 790, 793
Luckmann, Thomas, 76, 122, 221
Luhmann, Niklas, 758, 793

Mackenzie, Donald, 136–37, 140, 168, 176
Making Democracy Work (Putnam), 237
Making the Fascist Self (Berezin), 628
Mannheim, Karl, 548, 557 n. 9, 568, 789
Mao Tse-Tung, 276, 557 n. 3, 591, 593, 596, 598,
    603–4 nn. 18; 27
Marcuse, Herbert, 685
"marginal man, the," 370, 400
*Markets from Culture: Institutional Logics and
    Organizational Decisions in Higher Education
    Publishing* (Thornton), 164
Martin, David, 471, 473, 477–79
Marx, Karl, 10, 48, 56, 64, 140–41, 381, 583,
    586, 685
Marxism, neo-, 8, 265–66
Marxist/Marxian theories, 19, 28, 213, 372, 380,
    433, 463 n. 14, 477, 591, 593–94, 636–37, 713,
    725, 728
mass media. *See* media
material-semiotic, 709–11, 714–15
materialism, 10, 21, 56, 455, 673, 676, 678, 680, 682,
    684
materiality, 18, 136, 443–44, 458–59, 671–93,
    793–94
    vs. materialism, 671
Mauss, Marcel, 137, 288, 686, 688–89, 699, 745–46
Maxwell, Grover, 33
McCain, John, 306, 308
Mead, George Herbert, 195, 715
meaning
    as central to social analysis, 4, 6–11, 22, 249
    changes in, 767–69, 771–73, 777–78
    and cultural trauma, 559–60 n. 32, 578–79
    and domination/exclusion, 16
    and economic sociology, 120, 122–26, 157–58, 693
    and events, 622–30
    and interpretation, 27–42, 105 n. 35
    and materiality, 671–76, 682–90
    and opposition, 788–89
    and storytelling, 488–90, 492–93, 499, 501–2
    structures of. *See* cultural/culture structures
    study of, 46–48, 60–65, 74–78, 90–101, 102 n. 6,
        106 nn. 38; 41, 318, 321–23, 393–94, 584, 618–19,
        639–40, 645, 659, 660–61 n. 1, 662 n. 22, 731–32,
        735–36, 764–65, 774
    and texts, 84–87, 101, 107 n. 52, 727
meaning-making
    cultural trauma as a process of, 570–71
    economic, 157–58, 166–77
    in groups, 217–23
    in interaction, 769–71
    in mundane situations, 763–65
    in organizations, 780–83
    role of agency in, 169–70
    Strong Program views on, 322–23
    study of, 351–56
meaning-structures. *See* cultural/culture
    structures

means of symbolic production, 16, 279 n. 5, 590,
    603 n. 16, 640–41, 645, 647, 659–60, 735
measurement, 70–72, 84–85, 87–88, 91, 102
    nn. 3–4, 103 n. 10, 106 n. 38
mechanisms, 34, 55, 63–64, 75–76, 105 n. 33, 179
    n. 11, 584
media
    and cultural sociology, 279 n. 4, 307–10, 319–20,
        335–37
    entertainment, 320–37
    factual vs. fictional, 320–22
    global, 260, 273, 278
    mass, 200, 220, 237, 260, 285, 287, 289–90, 301,
        305, 307–8, 310 nn. 3; 5, 311–12 n. 18, 319, 322,
        330, 514, 517, 569–70, 572–75, 577, 594, 598, 627,
        659, 755
    news, 259–79, 307, 661 n. 11
    performativity of, 261–67, 269, 274–75
    and the public sphere, 287–92, 300, 308–9
    sociology of mass, 11, 279 n. 4
    See also institutions, journalism; mediatization;
        television
media events, 263–65
media scandals, 265–66
media spectacles, 264
mediatization, 259–79
mediatized public crises, 265–66
Memoirs of a Spacewoman (Haraway), 713–14
memory, politics of, 530–32, 534, 556
method(s), 20–22, 63, 74–78, 105 n. 34, 107 n. 50,
    233, 557 n. 9, 584, 623, 629
    See also methodology; positivism
Method and Measurement in Sociology (Cicourel), 65
methodology, 36, 96–101, 199, 205, 419–20 n. 3,
    578–79, 614, 683–84
    qualitative vs. quantitative, 80–81, 87, 102 n. 4
    See also methods; positivism
Milestones (Qutb), 455
Miller, Daniel, 673, 679, 684, 685, 687
Millo, Yuval, 138, 140, 176
mimesis, 201, 535, 542–44, 546, 549, 552, 554, 747–48,
    752–54, 757
Mische, Ann, 92, 247, 778–79
"Modeling Foucault: Dualities of Power in
    Institutional Fields" (Neely), 92–93
models/modeling, 12, 21–22, 102 n. 4, 103 nn. 9–10;
    12; 15, 106 n. 45, 310 n. 4, 692–93
    block, 92–95
    covering law of, 34, 37
    formal, 70–108
    formal cultural, 78–95, 98–101, 105 n. 33, 106
        nn. 41–42; 39; 45, 179 n. 11
modernity/modernization, 321, 371, 435, 440,
    455–56, 458–60, 568, 577, 789–90
    and religion, 471–73, 477–79
Modernity and Ambivalence (Bauman), 789
modernization theory, 235, 238, 249, 473, 480,
    630 n. 3

Mohr, John, 4, 9, 21–22, 92–93, 106 nn. 38–39; 41, 172
Mol, Annemarie, 699, 708–11, 714, 717
money, sociology of, 119, 124, 126, 132, 139–44
monsters, 794–95
moral communities, 265, 269–71
moral goods, 774–76, 783–84 nn. 1–2
moral panics, 263
moral vocabularies, 214–16, 519
Mugabe, Robert, 239–42
multicultural incorporation, 391–97, 409–17, 418, 420 n. 4, 522 n.1
multiculturalism, 384 n. 11, 391–92
music, 46, 53
    cultural approaches to, 723, 736
    as performance, 722–23, 732–36
    as a product, 728–30
    as a resource, 730–32
    sociology of, 15, 87–88, 92, 162, 722–37
    as a text, 727–28
musicology, 727–28, 733
Myrdal, Gunnar, 359 n. 1, 396–97, 413
myth, 578, 671, 745–46, 755, 769
    disaster, 271–74
    hegemonic, 531
    rationality as a legitimizing, 271–74
    study of, 84–87, 105 n. 35, 495

Nanking Massacre, 530, 535–56, 558 n. 13, 557 n. 24, 586–91, 597–98, 600 n. 2, 601 nn. 3–4, 603 n. 14
    Chinese Communist Party representations of, 606–7 nn. 35; 37; 38; 40
    Kuomintang representations of, 601 n. 8, 605–6 n. 33
    media representations of, 605 n. 32, 607–8, nn. 41–42
    role of Chinese Communist Party in, 588–92, 606 n. 35, 606
    role of Kuomintang in, 588–92
    textbook representations of, 536, 538, 543–45, 550–51, 555, 558 n. 13, 559 n. 25, 589, 592, 602 n. 9, 603 n. 12, 603 n. 17
    See also cultural trauma; Yasukuni Shrine in Tokyo
narrative(s), 13, 18, 98, 145 n. 7, 200–2, 226 n. 5, 265, 300, 378–79, 381, 481, 502 n. 1, 510, 532, 534–35, 538, 542–44, 546, 549, 554–56, 584, 616–18, 624, 627, 630 n. 2, 640, 682, 690, 745–48, 793
    apocalyptic, 751–59
    and cultural trauma, 575–78, 579–80 nn. 3–4, 586–95, 604 nn. 26; 29
    inflation and deflation of. See mimesis
    and social movements, 487–89, 493–502
    See also stories/storytelling
narrative genre model of risk evaluation, 747–48
nation/nation-state, 179 n. 9, 431–42, 454, 474, 480, 625–26
    and cultural trauma, 566, 569, 572–74, 576, 580 n. 6, 587, 591, 601 n. 4

Nation-Building and Citizenship (Bendix), 235
nationalism, 379–80, 436–42, 462–63 n. 10
    religious, 438–39, 441–42, 445–46, 448, 455–60, 463 nn. 11–12; 14, 623, 731
nationhood, 365–84
Negara: The Theatre State in Nineteenth-Century Bali (Geertz), 401
Neely, Brooke, 92–93
networks, 51, 54–56, 699
    analysis of, 77, 90–92, 103 n. 9, 106 nn. 44–45, 203, 218–19, 376, 699
    See also actor-network analysis
Neustadt, Richard, 638
New York Trilogy (Auster), 391, 393, 399
News Hour with Jon Stewart, 314 n. 27
newspapers, 268–70, 291, 322, 328–29, 333–34, 336
Niethammer, Friedrich Immanuel, 55–56
Nietzsche, Friedrich, 105 n. 36
normalization, 13, 328, 431, 507–8, 518–20, 522–23 nn. 1–2
novels, 61–62, 320, 324, 397
    revolutionary, 596–97, 606–7 nn. 37; 39
Nussbaum, Martha, 399, 402, 422 n. 23

Obama, Barack, 16, 284–85, 297, 302–9, 313 nn. 23; 25, 314 nn. 30–31, 621–22, 627–28, 765, 778
objectification, 73, 97, 442–43, 446
objects, 32–33, 136, 162–63, 165, 169–70, 202, 442–43, 532, 584, 671–93, 717, 769, 774
    cultural, 725–26, 728, 734
Ocasio, William, 766–67, 773, 781
"Ontological Status of Theoretical Entities, The" (Maxwell), 33
organizational borders, 773–79, 782–83, 784 n. 3
organizational culture, 167–69
organizational legitimacy, 119, 133–36
organizational style, 778–79, 782, 784–85 n. 9
organizations
    and cultural sociology, 763–67, 769, 774, 782–83
    and culture, 172–75, 222, 726, 763, 771, 777
    and performance, 780–82
    sociology of, 20, 76, 106 n. 41, 125–26, 161–62, 164–66
Orientalism (Said), 556–57 n. 1, 601 n. 5
Other, the, 242, 401–2, 481, 792

parallel scaling, 47–48, 50–51, 51–59. See also spatial scaling
Park, Robert, 322, 370–71
parole, 40–41, 660–61 n.1
Parsonian functionalism, decline of, 5, 6–7, 39, 119, 235, 637
Parsons, Talcott, 41, 42 n. 4, 87, 119–21, 131, 133, 135, 144, 177–78 n. 2, 210, 243, 384 n. 9, 621, 637, 660–61 n. 1, 722

Pascalian Meditations (Bourdieu), 719 n. 7
path dependence, 616–18, 624, 747
Pentecostalism, 14, 473–74, 476–79
performance/performativity, 126, 216, 278–79 n. 3,
    423 n. 30, 644–45, 722–23, 732–35, 780–82
  cultural, 19, 127, 129, 134, 261, 300, 319
  media, 262, 265–67, 269–70, 277–78, 279 n. 4
  political, 659–60
performance theory, 16, 639–41, 689–90
performative turn in sociology, 15–16, 127, 638–39
Pernicious Postulates (Tilly), 234
Perot, Ross, 641–43, 655–56
Peterson, Richard, 7, 87–88, 106 n. 41, 162, 726, 728
Place at the Table, A (Bawer), 518
Plato, 55, 107 n. 51
plot, 324, 492–93, 496–97, 613, 643–45, 659
political assassinations, 564, 566–67, 569, 572–78
political culture, 165–66, 208, 235–37, 244–48, 321,
    328–29, 433, 630 n. 3
  analysis of, 617–18, 621–23, 637
political facts, 620–31
political sociology, 179 n. 9, 250, 614, 617, 623,
    636–39
politics
  cultural analysis of, 613–31
  of edification, 511, 513, 515, 519–21
  of pity, 200–1, 204
  of regret, 555
Polletta, Francesca, 18, 227 nn. 12–13, 495, 630 n. 2
pollution (symbolic), 321, 333
Polyani, Karl, 119–22, 123, 131, 144, 158
positivism, 37–38, 77, 684
  critiques of, 31–32, 34, 36
  post-, 28, 31–37, 40
postmodern/postmodernism, 7, 35–36, 40, 676–78,
    684, 802–3
postmodernity, 477–79
poststructuralism, 495, 707, 788
poeisis, 445–46
power
  and attributions of credit and blame, 534–35,
    537, 553–56
  of binary oppositions, 276–77, 583–84
  and boundary-making, 374–76, 380–82
  of civic culture, 214
  civil discourse and public opinion as
    autonomous source of, 16, 17, 136, 199, 285–86,
    301–2, 310–11 n. 7, 321–22, 327, 333–34
  within civil society/civil sphere, 242–44,
    246–47
  cultural, 88–89, 265–66, 336, 531
  cultural codes and, 510–11
  and data analysis, 73
  and definition of reality/the situation, 586,
    589–91, 591–98, 600 n. 1, 601 n. 4, 602 n. 9, 604
    nn. 26–27, 605–6 nn. 32–35; 606–7 n. 37
  difference-based claims, 13
  and economics, 126, 139–40, 141–42
  events and interpretive, 618–22, 627–30
  and field logics, 103 n. 11, 169, 292–98, 304–7
  Foucauldian views on, 92–93, 455, 706–8, 713
  Gramscian views on, 213
  of group styles, 217–19
  and *habitus*, 702–6, 710–11
  historical memory and, 529–32
  iconic, 10
  institutional, 15, 164, 442–46, 447–48,
    464 n. 15
  and interpellation, 713–15
  and materiality, 18, 685, 689, 693
  meaning as a tool for, 7, 11, 176
  media and, 262–67, 270–71, 277–78, 279 n. 4,
    290–92, 300–2, 307–10, 310 n. 3, 324, 574
  of narrative/storytelling, 18, 488, 489–90,
    492–93, 495–500, 747–48
  performance of, 15–16, 639–41, 659–60
  political, 197, 431–36, 453–60, 636–41,
    659–60
  in the public sphere, 287, 289–90
  of religion, 220–21, 449–51, 457–60, 466–67
  and reproduction of hierarchies, 17–18, 350–51,
    356–59, 366–67
  representations of use of, 537–51
  ritual, 126, 128, 780
  social, 32, 35, 134–35, 304, 310 n. 3, 344, 376, 510,
    660, 735
  sovereign, 454–55
  state, 15, 61, 245, 436, 438–39, 464 nn. 18–19, 732
  symbolic, 167, 265, 382
  technology as a species of, 103 n. 16
  and unchosen choices, 705–6
  Western, 240, 249–50, 277
  See also hegemony
pragmatism, 20, 42 n. 3, 145, 207, 211, 216–17, 225,
    686–87, 734–35
  neo-, 37
praxis, 445–46
presidential politics, 641, 642–45, 659–60
Presidential Power: The Politics of Leadership
    (Neustadt), 638
presidential studies, 636–39
Primitive Classification (Durkheim and Mauss),
    745–46
production/consumption paradigm, 162, 722–27,
    730, 734–36
production of culture perspective, 7, 9, 159–66,
    723, 726, 728
profane, the, 128–29, 135, 141, 237, 287, 298–99, 394,
    481, 510, 584, 641, 675, 731, 793–94
Professional Ethics and Civic Morals (Durkheim),
    120
Protestant ethic, the, 30–31, 125
Protestant Ethic and the Spirit of Capitalism, The
    (Weber), 30–31, 63, 121
Protestantism, 57–59, 120, 220, 384 n. 10,
    440–41

public sphere, 234–37, 284–314, 311 n. 14
  and the academic field, 312 n. 19
  counterfactual, 325, 327, 335–36
  and cultural sociology, 245–46, 285, 287, 300,
    307–10, 318–20
  Habermasian views on, 245, 266, 285–92, 295,
    298, 301, 302–4, 310 nn. 2; 5, 311 n. 15, 312 n. 21,
    320–21, 434–35
  literary, 320
  and religion, 451, 456, 464 n. 17, 471
  See also aesthetic public sphere; media
purity, 128, 318, 321, 323, 510
Putnam, Robert, 210, 215, 237, 246

Qutb, Sayyid, 441, 452, 455, 457–59

Rabinow, Paul, 74–75, 78, 719 n. 16
race, 17–18, 314 n 29, 365–84
  in the United States, 272–74, 302–3, 306, 309,
    359–60 nn. 1–2
  See also African American men
Rancière, Jacques, 53–54
Rape of Nanking: The Forgotten Holocaust of World
    War II, The (Chang), 539
rational choice theory, 6, 177–78 n. 2, 476–77, 616,
    790
rationality, 20, 34, 174, 479, 480, 621, 790, 799
  critical, 318–21
  democratic, 285–87, 290–92, 297, 298–302, 312 n.
    21
  as a legitimizing myth, 135–36
  of politicized religious violence, 430, 434–35, 462 n. 9
  technical, 117–18, 136, 438
  See also parallel scaling; spatial scaling
rationalization, 46, 65, 117–18, 165, 174, 723
  and cultural sociology, 46–65
Reagan, Ronald, 308, 574, 613–15, 619, 622, 624, 629,
    638, 644–45, 654–55, 751
  Berlin Wall speech of, 613–15, 620, 622
realism, 32–34, 37, 39–40, 50, 55
  critical, 36
reason, 399, 450, 477–78, 480–81, 495, 792
reenchantment, 120, 122, 127–29, 144
reflexivity, 4, 266, 329, 332
  critical, 336, 756
  consumer, 675, 677–78, 680, 682
  media, 261–62, 326
relative autonomy
religion, 64, 103 n. 12, 121–22, 126, 128–29, 139–40,
    227 n. 9, 270, 799
  and civic life, 215–16, 219–21
  cultural approaches to, 433–36, 462 n. 9
  and cultural sociology, 473–74, 476–79, 481–82
  and democracy, 434
  and globalization, 14, 471–82
  and politics, 429–36, 439–41, 451–53, 464 n. 19
  and the state, 439, 448–49

religious violence
  and politics, 429–36, 448–49, 449–53, 460–61,
    464 n. 17
  sexual aspects of, 453–60
Renaissance Revivals (Griswold), 63
Rendering unto Caesar (Gill), 476–77
"Resistance of the Past, The" (Schudson), 556
Ricoeur, Paul, 71, 73, 75, 78, 95, 96–101, 105 n. 35, 107
    nn. 54–55, 108 n. 61, 784 n. 5
risk society, 751, 756
Risk Society (Beck), 756
ritual(s), 15–16, 126, 128, 141, 265–66, 639–41, 699,
    752–53, 766, 780–81, 783
  events, 627–29, 631
  mediatized, 261–67, 270–71, 277–78
  public, 18–20
  of solidarity, 267–71
  See also fusion; interaction rituals
ritualization of dissent, 271–74
Rorty, Richard, 42 n. 3, 129
Roy, Oliver, 435–36, 464 n. 19

Sacks, Harvey, 770–71
sacred, the, 128–32, 141–42, 237–38, 287, 298–99,
    510, 571, 584, 641, 675, 680, 793–98
Sahlins, Marshall, 7, 139, 158, 179 n. 12 631 n. 10,
    685
Said, Edward, 556–57 n. 1, 601 n. 5
Salvador (Brazil), 240–41
salvation, 367, 380, 435–36, 440, 459, 788, 796
Saussure, Ferdinand de, 40–41, 43 n. 6, 583
Schmitt, Carl, 437, 450–53, 454
Schudson, Michael, 197, 248, 534, 556, 682
Schutz, Alfred, 723, 733, 784 n. 5, 789, 791
science, 297, 305, 746–47, 758–59
  social studies of, 102 n. 7, 686
secularism, 480–81
secularization, 139–40, 433, 439–42, 452–53, 456,
    458–59, 471, 472–74, 476, 478–79
seduction, 799–802
Seidman, Steven, 3, 5, 7, 13
self, the, 15, 198, 242, 312 n. 21, 327, 422 n. 23, 436,
    680, 708, 732, 734, 792
Selznick, Philip, 76, 430
semiotics, 6–7, 90, 92, 94, 173, 585, 676–78
Serres, Michael, 78, 790, 793
Sewell, William, Jr., 7, 214, 615, 617–18, 631 n. 10
sex and sexuality, 57–58, 124, 329, 331, 450
  and religion, 453–61, 465 n. 20
  See also gay/lesbian movement
Shils, Edward, 129, 131
Simmel, Georg, 140–41, 225, 548, 627, 683–84, 723,
    789
Sketch for a Self Analysis (Bourdieu), 705, 715–16
Skocpol, Theda, 247–48
Slim's Table (Duneier), 401, 418
Smelser, Neil, 120–21, 131, 177–78 n. 2, 421 n. 12, 564,
    570–73, 790

Smith, Adam, 194–99, 201, 203–4
Smith, Philip, 125, 128–30, 216, 393, 542, 554, 623
social construction/constructivism, 32–33, 76, 95, 164, 260, 369, 377
    radical vs. weak, 570, 575, 580 n. 4
social drama (Turner), 124, 216, 265, 267, 511, 645, 651, 653, 657–58, 747, 758
social facts (Durkheim), 22, 29, 176, 415, 529, 614–15, 619–20, 724, 726, 745–47, 758–59
social movements, 155–56, 215–16, 423 n. 29, 444–45, 447, 450, 732
    and culture, 488–89, 500–2, 509–10
    and narrative, 487–89, 493–501
    of the Obama campaign, 302–4, 307, 313 n. 23
    study of, 221–24, 510
    See also gay/lesbian movement
social scientists as "spectators," 193–205
socialization, 245, 420 n. 4, 464 n. 19
sociolinguistics, 764–65, 782. See also language; linguistics
sociology
    American, 8, 103 n. 10
    goals of, 195–201, 473
    role of morality in, 195
    public, 195–96, 204–5, 311 n. 17
    as spectatorship, 193–205
    See also cultural sociology
Sociology of Philosophies, The, 54–56
Socrates, 55
solidarity, 16–18, 197, 211–12, 237, 262–63, 265–72, 285–87, 298–302, 307–10, 383 n. 2, 393–97, 417, 418, 437–38, 461–62 n. 3, 628, 718–19 n. 5
Somers, Margaret, 210, 623, 631 n. 5
Sorrows of an American, The (Hustvedt), 391–92, 397, 399, 405, 408
Soulside (Hannerz), 348–49
spatial analysis, 360–61 n. 6
spatial scaling, 46–48. See also parallel scaling
Space of Opinion: Media Intellectuals and the Public Sphere, The (Jacobs and Townsley), 310 n. 1.
spectatorship
    as an element of sociological analysis, 193–205
speech acts, 97, 99, 298
Spillman, Lyn, 12, 18, 130–31, 176, 178–79 n. 4, 538, 557 n. 7, 623
state, the, 143–44, 242, 245–46, 435–42, 445, 448–50, 453–60, 463 n. 12, 464 n. 19, 480–81, 558 n. 13, 659
    See also nation-state
Stewart, Jon, 307, 332–33
stories/storytelling, 487–502
    and framing, 489–91
    vs. narratives, 502 n.1
    See also narrative
stranger, 789
Strauss, Anselm S., 32
Strauss, Leo, 394, 420–21 n. 7
"street, the," 343–51, 357–59

media depictions of, 346
    See also code of the street
Strong Program in cultural sociology. See cultural sociology, Strong Program in
Structural Transformation of the Public Sphere, The (Habermas), 234, 236–37, 285–86, 289, 291, 312 n. 21, 320
structuralism, 3, 6, 8, 84–87, 90–91, 495, 636–37, 772–73, 782, 788
structuralist poetics, 752
subcultural/subcultures, 167–69, 222, 349, 359–60 n. 2, 726, 731
subject positions, 193, 197–98, 201, 299, 330, 746
subtlety
    in the study of social life, 13, 193–205
Suicide (Durkheim), 120
Sullivan, William, 74–75, 78
survey methods/methodology, 88, 210, 683
Swedberg, Richard, 34, 119–21, 178–79 nn. 3–4, 687
Swidler, Ann, 125, 660–61 n. 1
symbolic interactionism, 8, 167–69, 723, 728, 730, 733–35
symbols/symbolism, 37, 39–41, 42, 59, 61, 96–99, 128–36, 139–43, 158–59, 170, 212, 220–22, 224, 237–38, 245–46, 248, 260–71, 277, 279 n. 4, 298–99, 318–19, 321–22, 332–34, 367–68, 380–83, 393, 401, 415, 478–80, 510, 532, 555–56, 584–86, 591, 642–60, 676–78, 691, 715, 731, 745–46, 771–73
system world, 289, 291, 302

taste, 53–54, 673–93, 725–26, 731, 734. See also consumption/consumers
Taylor, Charles, 41, 42 n. 3, 75
television, 17, 278 n. 2, 293, 295–96, 305, 307–9, 311–12 nn. 18–19, 321, 324–35, 337 n. 7, 498, 509, 574, 580 n. 7
    global effects of American, 328–32
    golden age of, 325–27
    and political campaigns, 640, 646–60, 662 n. 17
terrorism, 461–62 n. 3, 464 n. 18, 624, 627–28
    religious, 432, 434–35, 448–50
    suicide, 432, 462 n. 5
texts, 22, 70, 73, 74, 78, 84, 90, 94–95, 96–101, 238, 279 n. 5, 310 n. 5, 322–25, 327, 335–36, 440, 488, 491, 584, 693
    as datasets, 98–101
    formal models of, 98–101
    vs. images, 202–4
    music as a, 727–28
    vs. speech, 96–97
Theoretical Logic in Sociology, 391
Theory of Moral Sentiments (Smith, A.), 194
Thévenot, Laurent, 158, 172, 174–75, 213, 216, 337 n. 4, 775, 783–84 n. 12
thick description, 21, 158, 172–73, 175–76, 421–22 n. 13, 614, 617–20
Thompson, E. P., 7, 200

Thornton, Patricia H., 164–65, 766–67, 773, 781

Tilly, Charles, 234, 374, 376

Tocqueville, Alexis de, 119–22, 125, 132, 144, 208–11, 213, 217

Tognato, Carlo, 10, 130, 142–43

tragedy (genre of), 538, 542, 546, 549, 554

Transformation of the Public Sphere, The (Habermas), 236–37, 285–86, 289, 291, 312 n. 21, 320

transnational civil/public sphere, 273–74, 336–37

transnational publics, 250, 278

trauma construction
    and revolution (China), 592–97, 604 nn. 26–27
    See also cultural trauma

trauma and identity, 792. See also cultural trauma

trauma theory, classical, 564–68, 580 n. 6. See also cultural trauma

traumatic occurrences, 567, 568–69, 578–79. See also cultural trauma

Travels in China (Honda), 537

Treatise of Human Nature, The (Hume), 56

Truth about Nanking, The (Higashinakano), 541–42, 544

truth games, 706–8, 711, 713

Tsongas, Paul, 641, 643–44, 650–51

Tsunami (South Asian), 19, 261, 267–71

Turner, Victor, 6, 19, 124, 216, 265, 267, 583, 790–92

typification, 20, 275, 687, 769–72, 774–75, 779, 783

underclass, 345–46, 349–51, 353, 356, 359 n. 1

Unfinished Revolution, The (Engel), 509

universalism, 233, 298–300, 434–35, 465 n. 21, 482

urban ethnography, 32, 348–50, 352, 356, 358–59

urban spaces
    as dangerous, 345–46, 360 n. 3

Vaid, Urvashi, 519–20, 522–23 n. 2

values (Parsons on), 6, 131, 133, 135, 660 n. 1

Veblen, Thorstein, 672, 684

Verba, Sidney, 209–11, 235, 630 n. 3, 637

Verstehen, 98, 101, 105 n. 35

victim(s), 259–60, 270, 531–32, 533, 796–97. See also cultural trauma

victimization, 494–98, 501, 513

Virtual Equality (Vaid), 519

voluntary association/organization, 122, 208–9, 212, 225–26, 237, 245, 247–48, 392
    See also involuntary association

voluntaristic model of action, 660–61 n. 1

volunteers, 213, 219, 767–69, 772–75, 781

Wacquant, Loïc, 718 n. 4

Wagner-Pacifici, Robin, 7–8, 13, 784 n. 5

Wallendorf, Melanie, 141–42

Walzer, Michael, 36, 392, 420 n. 4

Weber, Max, 6, 7, 21, 28, 30–31, 37, 40, 42, 46–47, 63–65, 76, 97, 119–21, 131–32, 133, 140–41, 144, 157, 159–61, 178 n. 3, 367, 376, 438, 448, 451, 460–61, 529, 573, 576, 583, 636–37, 725, 774

Wealth of Nations, The (Smith, A.), 194

Wherry, Frederick, 10, 168, 174

White, Harrison, 21–22, 79, 90–95, 100, 106 n. 44, 122, 161, 172–74, 179 n. 11

White, Theodore, 574

Williams, Raymond, 320, 333, 614–15

Willis, Paul, 419 n. 2, 731

Wimmer, Andreas, 374–76, 381

Windelband, Wilhelm, 20–21

Wittgenstein, Ludwig, 6, 41, 76, 203, 583, 713, 790–91, 793

Wuthnow, Robert, 772–73

Yale Strong Program in cultural sociology. See cultural sociology, Strong Program in

Yamamoto, Masahiro, 547–48, 550, 553

Yasukuni Shrine (Tokyo), 598–600

"Yonder" (Hustvedt), 399

Zelizer, Viviana, 7, 10, 123, 126–27, 130, 132, 142, 144, 158, 170–71, 177–78 n. 2, 178–79 n. 4, 580–81 n. 7

Zerubavel, Eviatar, 8, 48

Printed in the USA/Agawam, MA
May 30, 2013